Lecture Notes in Computer Science　　10408

Commenced Publication in 1973
Founding and Former Series Editors:
Gerhard Goos, Juris Hartmanis, and Jan van Leeuwen

More information about this series at http://www.springer.com/series/7407

Osvaldo Gervasi · Beniamino Murgante
Sanjay Misra · Giuseppe Borruso
Carmelo M. Torre · Ana Maria A.C. Rocha
David Taniar · Bernady O. Apduhan
Elena Stankova · Alfredo Cuzzocrea (Eds.)

Computational Science and Its Applications – ICCSA 2017

17th International Conference
Trieste, Italy, July 3–6, 2017
Proceedings, Part V

 Springer

Editors
Osvaldo Gervasi ⓘ
University of Perugia
Perugia
Italy

Beniamino Murgante ⓘ
University of Basilicata
Potenza
Italy

Sanjay Misra ⓘ
Covenant University
Ota
Nigeria

Giuseppe Borruso ⓘ
University of Trieste
Trieste
Italy

Carmelo M. Torre ⓘ
Polytechnic University of Bari
Bari
Italy

Ana Maria A.C. Rocha ⓘ
University of Minho
Braga
Portugal

David Taniar ⓘ
Monash University
Clayton, VIC
Australia

Bernady O. Apduhan
Kyushu Sangyo University
Fukuoka
Japan

Elena Stankova ⓘ
Saint Petersburg State University
Saint Petersburg
Russia

Alfredo Cuzzocrea ⓘ
University of Trieste
Trieste
Italy

ISSN 0302-9743   ISSN 1611-3349 (electronic)
Lecture Notes in Computer Science
ISBN 978-3-319-62403-7   ISBN 978-3-319-62404-4 (eBook)
DOI 10.1007/978-3-319-62404-4

Library of Congress Control Number: 2017945283

LNCS Sublibrary: SL1 – Theoretical Computer Science and General Issues

Printed on acid-free paper

This Springer imprint is published by Springer Nature
The registered company is Springer International Publishing AG
The registered company address is: Gewerbestrasse 11, 6330 Cham, Switzerland

Preface

These multiple volumes (LNCS volumes 10404, 10405, 10406, 10407, 10408, and 10409) consist of the peer-reviewed papers from the 2017 International Conference on Computational Science and Its Applications (ICCSA 2017) held in Trieste, Italy, during July 3–6, 2017.

ICCSA 2017 was a successful event in the ICCSA conference series, previously held in Beijing, China (2016), Banff, Canada (2015), Guimarães, Portugal (2014), Ho Chi Minh City, Vietnam (2013), Salvador, Brazil (2012), Santander, Spain (2011), Fukuoka, Japan (2010), Suwon, South Korea (2009), Perugia, Italy (2008), Kuala Lumpur, Malaysia (2007), Glasgow, UK (2006), Singapore (2005), Assisi, Italy (2004), Montreal, Canada (2003), (as ICCS) Amsterdam, The Netherlands (2002), and San Francisco, USA (2001).

Computational science is a main pillar of most present research as well as industrial and commercial activities and plays a unique role in exploiting ICT innovative technologies. The ICCSA conference series have been providing a venue to researchers and industry practitioners to discuss new ideas, to share complex problems and their solutions, and to shape new trends in computational science.

Apart from the general tracks, ICCSA 2017 also include 43 international workshops, in various areas of computational sciences, ranging from computational science technologies to specific areas of computational sciences, such as computer graphics and virtual reality. Furthermore, this year ICCSA 2017 hosted the XIV International Workshop on Quantum Reactive Scattering. The program also features three keynote speeches and four tutorials.

The success of the ICCSA conference series in general, and ICCSA 2017 in particular, is due to the support of many people: authors, presenters, participants, keynote speakers, session chairs, Organizing Committee members, student volunteers, Program Committee members, international Advisory Committee members, international liaison chairs, and various people in other roles. We would like to thank them all.

We would also like to thank Springer for their continuous support in publishing the ICCSA conference proceedings.

July 2017

Giuseppe Borruso
Osvaldo Gervasi
Bernady O. Apduhan

Welcome to Trieste

We were honored and happy to have organized this extraordinary edition of the conference, with so many interesting contributions and participants coming from more than 46 countries around the world!

Trieste is a medium-size Italian city lying on the north-eastern border between Italy and Slovenia. It has a population of nearly 200,000 inhabitants and faces the Adriatic Sea, surrounded by the Karst plateau.

It is quite an atypical Italian city, with its history being very much influenced by belonging for several centuries to the Austro-Hungarian empire and having been through several foreign occupations in history: by French, Venetians, and the Allied Forces after the Second World War. Such events left several footprints on the structure of the city, on its buildings, as well as on culture and society!

During its history, Trieste hosted people coming from different countries and regions, making it a cosmopolitan and open city. This was also helped by the presence of a commercial port that made it an important trade center from the 18th century on. Trieste is known today as a 'City of Science' or, more proudly, presenting itself as the 'City of Knowledge', thanks to the presence of several universities and research centers, all of them working at an international level, as well as of cultural institutions and traditions. The city has a high presence of researchers, more than 35 per 1,000 employed people, much higher than the European average of 6 employed researchers per 1,000 people.

The University of Trieste, the origin of such a system of scientific institutions, dates back to 1924, although its roots go back to the end of the 19th century under the Austro-Hungarian Empire. The university today employs nearly 1,500 teaching, research, technical, and administrative staff with a population of more than 16,000 students.

The university currently has 10 departments: Economics, Business, Mathematical, and Statistical Sciences; Engineering and Architecture; Humanities; Legal, Language, Interpreting, and Translation Studies; Mathematics and Geosciences; Medicine, Surgery, and Health Sciences; Life Sciences; Pharmaceutical and Chemical Sciences; Physics; Political and Social Sciences.

We trust the participants enjoyed the cultural and scientific offerings of Trieste and will keep a special memory of the event.

Giuseppe Borruso

Organization

ICCSA 2017 was organized by the University of Trieste (Italy), University of Perugia (Italy), Monash University (Australia), Kyushu Sangyo University (Japan), University of Basilicata (Italy), and University of Minho, (Portugal).

Honorary General Chairs

Antonio Laganà	University of Perugia, Italy
Norio Shiratori	Tohoku University, Japan
Kenneth C.J. Tan	Sardina Systems, Estonia

General Chairs

Giuseppe Borruso	University of Trieste, Italy
Osvaldo Gervasi	University of Perugia, Italy
Bernady O. Apduhan	Kyushu Sangyo University, Japan

Program Committee Chairs

Alfredo Cuzzocrea	University of Trieste, Italy
Beniamino Murgante	University of Basilicata, Italy
Ana Maria A.C. Rocha	University of Minho, Portugal
David Taniar	Monash University, Australia

International Advisory Committee

Jemal Abawajy	Deakin University, Australia
Dharma P. Agrawal	University of Cincinnati, USA
Marina L. Gavrilova	University of Calgary, Canada
Claudia Bauzer Medeiros	University of Campinas, Brazil
Manfred M. Fisher	Vienna University of Economics and Business, Austria
Yee Leung	Chinese University of Hong Kong, SAR China

International Liaison Chairs

Ana Carla P. Bitencourt	Universidade Federal do Reconcavo da Bahia, Brazil
Maria Irene Falcão	University of Minho, Portugal
Robert C.H. Hsu	Chung Hua University, Taiwan
Tai-Hoon Kim	Hannam University, Korea
Sanjay Misra	University of Minna, Nigeria
Takashi Naka	Kyushu Sangyo University, Japan

| Rafael D.C. Santos | National Institute for Space Research, Brazil |
| Maribel Yasmina Santos | University of Minho, Portugal |

Workshop and Session Organizing Chairs

Beniamino Murgante	University of Basilicata, Italy
Sanjay Misra	Covenant University, Nigeria
Jorge Gustavo Rocha	University of Minho, Portugal

Award Chair

| Wenny Rahayu | La Trobe University, Australia |

Publicity Committee Chair

Stefano Cozzini	Democritos Center, National Research Council, Italy
Elmer Dadios	De La Salle University, Philippines
Hong Quang Nguyen	International University (VNU-HCM), Vietnam
Daisuke Takahashi	Tsukuba University, Japan
Shangwang Wang	Beijing University of Posts and Telecommunications, China

Workshop Organizers

Agricultural and Environmental Big Data Analytics (AEDBA 2017)

| Sandro Bimonte | IRSTEA, France |
| André Miralles | IRSTEA, France |

Advances in Data Mining for Applications (AMDMA 2017)

Carlo Cattani	University of Tuscia, Italy
Majaz Moonis	University of Massachusettes Medical School, USA
Yeliz Karaca	IEEE, Computer Society Association

Advances Smart Mobility and Transportation (ASMAT 2017)

| Mauro Mazzei | CNR, Italian National Research Council, Italy |

Advances in Information Systems and Technologies for Emergency Preparedness and Risk Assessment and Mitigation (ASTER 2017)

Maurizio Pollino	ENEA, Italy
Marco Vona	University of Basilicata, Italy
Beniamino Murgante	University of Basilicata, Italy

Advances in Web-Based Learning (AWBL 2017)

Mustafa Murat Inceoglu   Ege University, Turkey
Birol Ciloglugil   Ege University, Turkey

Big Data Warehousing and Analytics (BIGGS 2017)

Maribel Yasmina Santos   University of Minho, Portugal
Monica Wachowicz   University of New Brunswick, Canada
Joao Moura Pires   NOVA de Lisboa University, Portugal
Rafael Santos   National Institute for Space Research, Brazil

Bio-inspired Computing and Applications (BIONCA 2017)

Nadia Nedjah   State University of Rio de Janeiro, Brazil
Luiza de Macedo Mourell   State University of Rio de Janeiro, Brazil

Computational and Applied Mathematics (CAM 2017)

M. Irene Falcao   University of Minho, Portugal
Fernando Miranda   University of Minho, Portugal

Computer-Aided Modeling, Simulation, and Analysis (CAMSA 2017)

Jie Shen   University of Michigan, USA and Jilin University, China
Hao Chenina   Shanghai University of Engineering Science, China
Chaochun Yuan   Jiangsu University, China

Computational and Applied Statistics (CAS 2017)

Ana Cristina Braga   University of Minho, Portugal

Computational Geometry and Security Applications (CGSA 2017)

Marina L. Gavrilova   University of Calgary, Canada

Central Italy 2016 Earthquake: Computational Tools and Data Analysis for Emergency Response, Community Support, and Reconstruction Planning (CIEQ 2017)

Alessandro Rasulo   Università degli Studi di Cassino e del Lazio
                             Meridionale, Italy
Davide Lavorato   Università degli Studi di Roma Tre, Italy

Computational Methods for Business Analytics (CMBA 2017)

Telmo Pinto   University of Minho, Portugal
Claudio Alves   University of Minho, Portugal

Chemistry and Materials Sciences and Technologies (CMST 2017)

Antonio Laganà   University of Perugia, Italy
Noelia Faginas Lago   University of Perugia, Italy

Computational Optimization and Applications (COA 2017)

Ana Maria Rocha   University of Minho, Portugal
Humberto Rocha   University of Coimbra, Portugal

Cities, Technologies, and Planning (CTP 2017)

Giuseppe Borruso   University of Trieste, Italy
Beniamino Murgante   University of Basilicata, Italy

Data-Driven Modelling for Sustainability Assessment (DAMOST 2017)

Antonino Marvuglia   Luxembourg Institute of Science and Technology, LIST,
                       Luxembourg
Mikhail Kanevski   University of Lausanne, Switzerland
Beniamino Murgante   University of Basilicata, Italy
Janusz Starczewski   Częstochowa University of Technology, Poland

Databases and Computerized Information Retrieval Systems (DCIRS 2017)

Sultan Alamri   College of Computing and Informatics, SEU, Saudi
                       Arabia
Adil Fahad   Albaha University, Saudi Arabia
Abdullah Alamri   Jeddah University, Saudi Arabia

Data Science for Intelligent Decision Support (DS4IDS 2016)

Filipe Portela   University of Minho, Portugal
Manuel Filipe Santos   University of Minho, Portugal

Deep Cities: Intelligence and Interoperability (DEEP_CITY 2017)

Maurizio Pollino   ENEA, Italian National Agency for New Technologies,
                                Energy and Sustainable Economic Development, Italy
Grazia Fattoruso   ENEA, Italian National Agency for New Technologies,
                                Energy and Sustainable Economic Development, Italy

Emotion Recognition (EMORE 2017)

Valentina Franzoni   University of Rome La Sapienza, Italy
Alfredo Milani   University of Perugia, Italy

Future Computing Systems, Technologies, and Applications (FISTA 2017)

Bernady O. Apduhan   Kyushu Sangyo University, Japan
Rafael Santos   National Institute for Space Research, Brazil

Geographical Analysis, Urban Modeling, Spatial Statistics (Geo-and-Mod 2017)

Giuseppe Borruso   University of Trieste, Italy
Beniamino Murgante   University of Basilicata, Italy
Hartmut Asche   University of Potsdam, Germany

Geomatics and Remote Sensing Techniques for Resource Monitoring and Control (GRS-RMC 2017)

Eufemia Tarantino   Polytechnic of Bari, Italy
Rosa Lasaponara   Italian Research Council, IMAA-CNR, Italy
Antonio Novelli   Polytechnic of Bari, Italy

Interactively Presenting High-Quality Graphics in Cooperation with Various Computing Tools (IPHQG 2017)

Masataka Kaneko   Toho University, Japan
Setsuo Takato   Toho University, Japan
Satoshi Yamashita   Kisarazu National College of Technology, Italy

Web-Based Collective Evolutionary Systems: Models, Measures, Applications (IWCES 2017)

Alfredo Milani   University of Perugia, Italy
Rajdeep Nyogi   Institute of Technology, Roorkee, India
Valentina Franzoni   University of Rome La Sapienza, Italy

Computational Mathematics, and Statistics for Data Management and Software Engineering (IWCMSDMSE 2017)

M. Filomena Teodoro	Lisbon University and Portuguese Naval Academy, Portugal
Anacleto Correia	Portuguese Naval Academy, Portugal

Land Use Monitoring for Soil Consumption Reduction (LUMS 2017)

Carmelo M. Torre	Polytechnic of Bari, Italy
Beniamino Murgante	University of Basilicata, Italy
Alessandro Bonifazi	Polytechnic of Bari, Italy
Massimiliano Bencardino	University of Salerno, Italy

Mobile Communications (MC 2017)

Hyunseung Choo	Sungkyunkwan University, Korea

Mobile-Computing, Sensing, and Actuation - Fog Networking (MSA4FOG 2017)

Saad Qaisar	NUST School of Electrical Engineering and Computer Science, Pakistan
Moonseong Kim	Korean Intellectual Property Office, South Korea

Physiological and Affective Computing: Methods and Applications (PACMA 2017)

Robertas Damasevicius	Kaunas University of Technology, Lithuania
Christian Napoli	University of Catania, Italy
Marcin Wozniak	Silesian University of Technology, Poland

Quantum Mechanics: Computational Strategies and Applications (QMCSA 2017)

Mirco Ragni	Universidad Federal de Bahia, Brazil
Ana Carla Peixoto Bitencourt	Universidade Estadual de Feira de Santana, Brazil
Vincenzo Aquilanti	University of Perugia, Italy

Advances in Remote Sensing for Cultural Heritage (RS 2017)

Rosa Lasaponara   IRMMA, CNR, Italy
Nicola Masini   IBAM, CNR, Italy Zhengzhou Base, International
                      Center on Space Technologies for Natural and
                      Cultural Heritage, China

Scientific Computing Infrastructure (SCI 2017)

Elena Stankova   Saint Petersburg State University, Russia
Alexander Bodganov   Saint Petersburg State University, Russia
Vladimir Korkhov   Saint Petersburg State University, Russia

Software Engineering Processes and Applications (SEPA 2017)

Sanjay Misra   Covenant University, Nigeria

Sustainability Performance Assessment: Models, Approaches and Applications Toward Interdisciplinarity and Integrated Solutions (SPA 2017)

Francesco Scorza   University of Basilicata, Italy
Valentin Grecu   Lucia Blaga University on Sibiu, Romania
Jolanta Dvarioniene   Kaunas University, Lithuania
Sabrina Lai   Cagliari University, Italy

Software Quality (SQ 2017)

Sanjay Misra   Covenant University, Nigeria

Advances in Spatio-Temporal Analytics (ST-Analytics 2017)

Rafael Santos   Brazilian Space Research Agency, Brazil
Karine Reis Ferreira Brazilian Space Research Agency, Brazil
Maribel Yasmina Santos University of Minho, Portugal
Joao Moura Pires   New University of Lisbon, Portugal

Tools and Techniques in Software Development Processes (TTSDP 2017)

Sanjay Misra   Covenant University, Nigeria

Challenges, Trends, and Innovations in VGI (VGI 2017)

Claudia Ceppi	University of Basilicata, Italy
Beniamino Murgante	University of Basilicata, Italy
Lucia Tilio	University of Basilicata, Italy
Francesco Mancini	University of Modena and Reggio Emilia, Italy
Rodrigo Tapia-McClung	Centro de Investigación en Geografía y Geomática "Ing Jorge L. Tamayo", Mexico
Jorge Gustavo Rocha	University of Minho, Portugal

Virtual Reality and Applications (VRA 2017)

Osvaldo Gervasi	University of Perugia, Italy

Industrial Computational Applications (WICA 2017)

Eric Medvet	University of Trieste, Italy
Gianfranco Fenu	University of Trieste, Italy
Riccardo Ferrari	Delft University of Technology, The Netherlands

XIV International Workshop on Quantum Reactive Scattering (QRS 2017)

Niyazi Bulut	Fırat University, Turkey
Noelia Faginas Lago	University of Perugia, Italy
Andrea Lombardi	University of Perugia, Italy
Federico Palazzetti	University of Perugia, Italy

Program Committee

Jemal Abawajy	Deakin University, Australia
Kenny Adamson	University of Ulster, UK
Filipe Alvelos	University of Minho, Portugal
Paula Amaral	Universidade Nova de Lisboa, Portugal
Hartmut Asche	University of Potsdam, Germany
Md. Abul Kalam Azad	University of Minho, Portugal
Michela Bertolotto	University College Dublin, Ireland
Sandro Bimonte	CEMAGREF, TSCF, France
Rod Blais	University of Calgary, Canada
Ivan Blečić	University of Sassari, Italy
Giuseppe Borruso	University of Trieste, Italy
Yves Caniou	Lyon University, France
José A. Cardoso e Cunha	Universidade Nova de Lisboa, Portugal
Rui Cardoso	University of Beira Interior, Portugal
Leocadio G. Casado	University of Almeria, Spain
Carlo Cattani	University of Salerno, Italy

Mete Celik	Erciyes University, Turkey
Alexander Chemeris	National Technical University of Ukraine KPI, Ukraine
Min Young Chung	Sungkyunkwan University, Korea
Gilberto Corso Pereira	Federal University of Bahia, Brazil
M. Fernanda Costa	University of Minho, Portugal
Gaspar Cunha	University of Minho, Portugal
Alfredo Cuzzocrea	ICAR-CNR and University of Calabria, Italy
Carla Dal Sasso Freitas	Universidade Federal do Rio Grande do Sul, Brazil
Pradesh Debba	The Council for Scientific and Industrial Research (CSIR), South Africa
Hendrik Decker	Instituto Tecnológico de Informática, Spain
Frank Devai	London South Bank University, UK
Rodolphe Devillers	Memorial University of Newfoundland, Canada
Prabu Dorairaj	NetApp, India/USA
M. Irene Falcao	University of Minho, Portugal
Cherry Liu Fang	U.S. DOE Ames Laboratory, USA
Edite M.G.P. Fernandes	University of Minho, Portugal
Jose-Jesús Fernandez	National Centre for Biotechnology, CSIS, Spain
María Antonia Forjaz	University of Minho, Portugal
María Celia Furtado Rocha	PRODEB-Pós Cultura/UFBA, Brazil
Akemi Galvez	University of Cantabria, Spain
Paulino Jose Garcia Nieto	University of Oviedo, Spain
Marina Gavrilova	University of Calgary, Canada
Jerome Gensel	LSR-IMAG, France
María Giaoutzi	National Technical University, Athens, Greece
Andrzej M. Goscinski	Deakin University, Australia
Alex Hagen-Zanker	University of Cambridge, UK
Malgorzata Hanzl	Technical University of Lodz, Poland
Shanmugasundaram Hariharan	B.S. Abdur Rahman University, India
Eligius M.T. Hendrix	University of Malaga/Wageningen University, Spain/The Netherlands
Tutut Herawan	Universitas Teknologi Yogyakarta, Indonesia
Hisamoto Hiyoshi	Gunma University, Japan
Fermin Huarte	University of Barcelona, Spain
Andrés Iglesias	University of Cantabria, Spain
Mustafa Inceoglu	EGE University, Turkey
Peter Jimack	University of Leeds, UK
Qun Jin	Waseda University, Japan
Farid Karimipour	Vienna University of Technology, Austria
Baris Kazar	Oracle Corp., USA
Maulana Adhinugraha Kiki	Telkom University, Indonesia
DongSeong Kim	University of Canterbury, New Zealand
Taihoon Kim	Hannam University, Korea
Ivana Kolingerova	University of West Bohemia, Czech Republic

Alexey Rodionov	Institute of Computational Mathematics and Mathematical Geophysics, Russia
Cristina S. Rodrigues	University of Minho, Portugal
Jon Rokne	University of Calgary, Canada
Octavio Roncero	CSIC, Spain
Maytham Safar	Kuwait University, Kuwait
Chiara Saracino	A.O. Ospedale Niguarda Ca' Granda - Milano, Italy
Haiduke Sarafian	The Pennsylvania State University, USA
Jie Shen	University of Michigan, USA
Qi Shi	Liverpool John Moores University, UK
Dale Shires	U.S. Army Research Laboratory, USA
Takuo Suganuma	Tohoku University, Japan
Sergio Tasso	University of Perugia, Italy
Ana Paula Teixeira	University of Tras-os-Montes and Alto Douro, Portugal
Senhorinha Teixeira	University of Minho, Portugal
Parimala Thulasiraman	University of Manitoba, Canada
Carmelo Torre	Polytechnic of Bari, Italy
Javier Martinez Torres	Centro Universitario de la Defensa Zaragoza, Spain
Giuseppe A. Trunfio	University of Sassari, Italy
Unal Ufuktepe	Izmir University of Economics, Turkey
Toshihiro Uchibayashi	Kyushu Sangyo University, Japan
Mario Valle	Swiss National Supercomputing Centre, Switzerland
Pablo Vanegas	University of Cuenca, Ecuador
Piero Giorgio Verdini	INFN Pisa and CERN, Italy
Marco Vizzari	University of Perugia, Italy
Koichi Wada	University of Tsukuba, Japan
Krzysztof Walkowiak	Wroclaw University of Technology, Poland
Zequn Wang	Intelligent Automation Inc., USA
Robert Weibel	University of Zurich, Switzerland
Roland Wismüller	Universität Siegen, Germany
Mudasser Wyne	SOET National University, USA
Chung-Huang Yang	National Kaohsiung Normal University, Taiwan
Xin-She Yang	National Physical Laboratory, UK
Salim Zabir	France Telecom Japan Co., Japan
Haifeng Zhao	University of California, Davis, USA
Kewen Zhao	University of Qiongzhou, China
Albert Y. Zomaya	University of Sydney, Australia

Additional Reviewers

A. Alwan Al-Juboori Ali	School of Computer Science and Technology, China
Aceto Lidia	University of Pisa, Italy
Acharjee Shukla	Dibrugarh University, India
Afreixo Vera	University of Aveiro, Portugal
Agra Agostinho	University of Aveiro, Portugal
Aguilar Antonio	University of Barcelona, Spain
Aguilar José Alfonso	Universidad Autónoma de Sinaloa, Mexico
Aicardi Irene	Politecnico di Torino, Italy
Alberti Margarita	University of Barcelona, Spain
Alberto Rui	University of Lisbon, Portugal
Ali Salman	University of Magna Graecia, Italy
Alvanides Seraphim	University at Newcastle, UK
Alvelos Filipe	Universidade do Minho, Portugal
Amato Alba	Seconda Università degli Studi di Napoli, Italy
Amorim Paulo	Instituto de Matemática da UFRJ (IM-UFRJ), Brazil
Anderson Roger	University of California Santa Cruz, USA
Andrianov Serge	Saint Petersburg State University, Russia
Andrienko Gennady	Fraunhofer-Institut für Intelligente Analyse- und Informationssysteme, Germany
Apduhan Bernady	Kyushu Sangyo University, Japan
Aquilanti Vincenzo	University of Perugia, Italy
Asche Hartmut	Potsdam University, Germany
Azam Samiul	United International University, Bangladesh
Azevedo Ana	Athabasca University, USA
Bae Ihn-Han	Catholic University of Daegu, South Korea
Balacco Gabriella	Polytechnic of Bari, Italy
Balena Pasquale	Polytechnic of Bari, Italy
Barroca Filho Itamir	Universidade Federal do Rio Grande do Norte, Brazil
Behera Ranjan Kumar	Indian Institute of Technology Patna, India
Belpassi Leonardo	National Research Council, Italy
Bentayeb Fadila	Université Lyon, France
Bernardino Raquel	Universidade da Beira Interiore, Portugal
Bertolotto Michela	University Collegue Dublin, UK
Bhatta Bijaya	Utkal University, India
Bimonte Sandro	IRSTEA, France
Blecic Ivan	University of Cagliari, Italy
Bo Carles	ICIQ, Spain
Bogdanov Alexander	Saint Petersburg State University, Russia
Bollini Letizia	University of Milano-Bicocca, Italy
Bonifazi Alessandro	Polytechnic of Bari, Italy
Bonnet Claude-Laurent	Université de Bordeaux, France
Borgogno Mondino Enrico Corrado	University of Turin, Italy
Borruso Giuseppe	University of Trieste, Italy

Bostenaru Maria	Ion Mincu University of Architecture and Urbanism, Romania
Boussaid Omar	Université Lyon 2, France
Braga Ana Cristina	University of Minho, Portugal
Braga Nuno	University of Minho, Portugal
Brasil Luciana	Instituto Federal Sao Paolo, Brazil
Cabral Pedro	Universidade NOVA de Lisboa, Portugal
Cacao Isabel	University of Aveiro, Portugal
Caiaffa Emanuela	Enea, Italy
Campagna Michele	University of Cagliari, Italy
Caniato Renhe Marcelo	Universidade Federal de Juiz de Fora, Brazil
Canora Filomena	University of Basilicata, Italy
Caradonna Grazia	Polytechnic of Bari, Italy
Cardoso Rui	Beira Interior University, Portugal
Caroti Gabriella	University of Pisa, Italy
Carravilla Maria Antonia	Universidade do Porto, Portugal
Cattani Carlo	University of Salerno, Italy
Cefalo Raffaela	University of Trieste, Italy
Ceppi Claudia	Polytechnic of Bari, Italy
Cerreta Maria	University Federico II of Naples, Italy
Chanet Jean-Pierre	UR TSCF Irstea, France
Chaturvedi Krishna Kumar	University of Delhi, India
Chiancone Andrea	University of Perugia, Italy
Choo Hyunseung	Sungkyunkwan University, South Korea
Ciabo Serena	University of l'Aquila, Italy
Coletti Cecilia	University of Chieti, Italy
Correia Aldina	Porto Polytechnic, Portugal
Correia Anacleto	CINAV, Portugal
Correia Elisete	University of Trás-Os-Montes e Alto Douro, Portugal
Correia Florbela Maria da Cruz Domingues	Instituto Politécnico de Viana do Castelo, Portugal
Cosido Oscar	University of Cantabria, Spain
Costa e Silva Eliana	University of Minho, Portugal
Costa Graça	Instituto Politécnico de Setúbal, Portugal
Costantini Alessandro	INFN, Italy
Crispim José	University of Minho, Portugal
Cuzzocrea Alfredo	University of Trieste, Italy
Danese Maria	IBAM, CNR, Italy
Daneshpajouh Shervin	University of Western Ontario, USA
De Fazio Dario	IMIP-CNR, Italy
De Runz Cyril	University of Reims Champagne-Ardenne, France
Deffuant Guillaume	Institut national de recherche en sciences et technologies pour l'environnement et l'agriculture, France
Degtyarev Alexander	Saint Petersburg State University, Russia
Devai Frank	London South Bank University, UK
Di Leo Margherita	JRC, European Commission, Belgium

Dias Joana	University of Coimbra, Portugal
Dilo Arta	University of Twente, The Netherlands
Dvarioniene Jolanta	Kaunas University of Technology, Lithuania
El-Zawawy Mohamed A.	Cairo University, Egypt
Escalona Maria-Jose	University of Seville, Spain
Faginas-Lago, Noelia	University of Perugia, Italy
Falcinelli Stefano	University of Perugia, Italy
Falcão M. Irene	University of Minho, Portugal
Faria Susana	University of Minho, Portugal
Fattoruso Grazia	ENEA, Italy
Fenu Gianfranco	University of Trieste, Italy
Fernandes Edite	University of Minho, Portugal
Fernandes Florbela	Escola Superior de Tecnologia e Gest ão de Bragancca, Portugal
Fernandes Rosario	USP/ESALQ, Brazil
Ferrari Riccardo	Delft University of Technology, The Netherlands
Figueiredo Manuel Carlos	University of Minho, Portugal
Florence Le Ber	ENGEES, France
Flouvat Frederic	University of New Caledonia, France
Fontes Dalila	Universidade do Porto, Portugal
Franzoni Valentina	University of Perugia, Italy
Freitas Adelaide de Fátima Baptista Valente	University of Aveiro, Portugal
Fusco Giovanni	Università di Bari, Italy
Gabrani Goldie	Tecpro Syst. Ltd., India
Gaido Luciano	INFN, Italy
Gallo Crescenzio	University of Foggia, Italy
Garaba Shungu	University of Connecticut, USA
Garau Chiara	University of Cagliari, Italy
Garcia Ernesto	University of the Basque Country, Spain
Gargano Ricardo	Universidade Brasilia, Brazil
Gavrilova Marina	University of Calgary, Canada
Gensel Jerome	IMAG, France
Gervasi Osvaldo	University of Perugia, Italy
Gioia Andrea	Polytechnic University of Bari, Italy
Giovinazzi Sonia	University of Canterbury, New Zealand
Gizzi Fabrizio	National Research Council, Italy
Gomes dos Anjos Eudisley	Universidade Federal da Paraíba, Brazil
Gonzaga de Oliveira Sanderson Lincohn	Universidade Federal de Lavras, Brazil
Gonçalves Arminda Manuela	University of Minho, Braga, Portugal
Gorbachev Yuriy	Geolink Technologies, Russia
Grecu Valentin	University of Sibiu, Romania
Gupta Brij	Cancer Biology Research Center, USA
Hagen-Zanker Alex	University of Surrey, UK

Hamaguchi Naoki	Tokyo Kyoiku University, Japan
Hanazumi Simone	University of Sao Paulo, Brazil
Hanzl Malgorzata	University of Lodz, Poland
Hayashi Masaki	University of Calgary, Canada
Hendrix Eligius M.T.	Operations Research and Logistics Group, The Netherlands
Henriques Carla	Inst. Politécnico de Viseu, Portugal
Herawan Tutut	State Polytechnic of Malang, Indonesia
Hsu Hui-Huang	National Chiao Tung University, Taiwan
Ienco Dino	La Maison de la télédétection de Montpellier, France
Iglesias Andres	Universidad de Cantabria, Spain
Imran Rabeea	NUST Islamabad, Pakistan
Inoue Kentaro	National Technical University of Athens, Greece
Josselin Didier	Université d'Avignon et des Pays de Vaucluse, France
Kaneko Masataka	Kisarazu National College of Technology, Japan
Kang Myoung-Ah	Blaise Pascal University, France
Karampiperis Pythagoras	National Center of Scientific Research, Athens, Greece
Kavouras Marinos	University of Athens, Greece
Kolingerova Ivana	University of West Bohemia, Czech Republic
Korkhov Vladimir	Saint Petersburg State University, Russia
Kotzinos Dimitrios	University of Cergy Pontoise, France
Kulabukhova Nataliia	Saint Petersburg State University, Russia
Kumar Dileep	SR Engineering College, India
Kumar Lov	National Institute of Technology, Rourkela, India
Kumar Pawan	Institute for Advanced Study, Princeton, USA
Laganà Antonio	University of Perugia, Italy
Lai Sabrina	Università di Cagliari, Italy
Lanza Viviana	Lombardy Regional Institute for Research, Italy
Lasala Piermichele	Università di Foggia, Italy
Laurent Anne	Laboratoire d'Informatique, de Robotique et de Microélectronique de Montpellier, France
Lavorato Davide	University of Rome, Italy
Le Duc Tai	Sungkyunkwan University, South Korea
Legatiuk Dmitrii	Bauhaus University, Germany
Li Ming	University of Waterloo, Canada
Lima Ana	University of São Paulo (UNIFESP), Brazil
Liu Xin	École polytechnique fédérale de Lausanne, Switzerland
Lombardi Andrea	University of Perugia, Italy
Lopes Cristina	Instituto Superior de Contabilidade e Administracao do Porto, Portugal
Lopes Maria João	Instituto Universitário de Lisboa, Portugal
Lourenço Vanda Marisa	Universidade NOVA de Lisboa, Portugal
Machado Jose	University of Minho, Portugal
Maeda Yoichi	Tokai University, Japan
Majcen Nineta	Euchems, Belgium
Malonek Helmuth	Universidade de Aveiro, Portugal

Mancini Francesco	University of Modena and Reggio Emilia, Italy
Mandanici Emanuele	Università di Bologna, Italy
Manganelli Benedetto	Università degli studi della Basilicata, Italy
Manso Callejo Miguel Angel	Universidad Politécnica de Madrid, Spain
Margalef Tomas	Autonomous University of Barcelona, Spain
Marques Jorge	University of Coimbra, Portugal
Martins Bruno	Universidade de Lisboa, Portugal
Marvuglia Antonino	Public Research Centre Henri Tudor, Luxembourg
Mateos Cristian	Universidad Nacional del Centro, Argentina
Mauro Giovanni	University of Trieste, Italy
McGuire Michael	Towson University, USA
Medvet Eric	University of Trieste, Italy
Milani Alfredo	University of Perugia, Italy
Millham Richard	Durban University of Technoloy, South Africa
Minghini Marco	Polytechnic University of Milan, Italy
Minhas Umar	University of Waterloo, Ontario, Canada
Miralles André	La Maison de la télédétection de Montpellier, France
Miranda Fernando	Universidade do Minho, Portugal
Misra Sanjay	Covenant University, Nigeria
Modica Giuseppe	Università Mediterranea di Reggio Calabria, Italy
Molaei Qelichi Mohamad	University of Tehran, Iran
Monteiro Ana Margarida	University of Coimbra, Portugal
Morano Pierluigi	Polytechnic University of Bari, Italy
Moura Ana	Universidade de Aveiro, Portugal
Moura Pires João	Universidade NOVA de Lisboa, Portugal
Mourão Maria	ESTG-IPVC, Portugal
Murgante Beniamino	University of Basilicata, Italy
Nagy Csaba	University of Szeged, Hungary
Nakamura Yasuyuki	Nagoya University, Japan
Natário Isabel Cristina Maciel	University Nova de Lisboa, Portugal
Nemmaoui Abderrahim	Universidad de Almeria (UAL), Spain
Nguyen Tien Dzung	Sungkyunkwan University, South Korea
Niyogi Rajdeep	Indian Institute of Technology Roorkee, India
Novelli Antonio	University of Bari, Italy
Oliveira Irene	University of Trás-Os-Montes e Alto Douro, Portugal
Oliveira José A.	Universidade do Minho, Portugal
Ottomanelli Michele	University of Bari, Italy
Ouchi Shunji	Shimonoseki City University, Japan
Ozturk Savas	Scientific and Technological Research Council of Turkey, Turkey
P. Costa M. Fernanda	Universidade do Minho, Portugal
Painho Marco	NOVA Information Management School, Portugal
Panetta J.B.	Tecnologia Geofísica Petróleo Brasileiro SA, PETROBRAS, Brazil

Pantazis Dimos	Otenet, Greece
Papa Enrica	University of Amsterdam, The Netherlands
Pardede Eric	La Trobe University, Australia
Parente Claudio	Università degli Studi di Napoli Parthenope, Italy
Pathan Al-Sakib Khan	Islamic University of Technology, Bangladesh
Paul Prantosh K.	EIILM University, Jorethang, Sikkim, India
Pengő Edit	University of Szeged, Hungary
Pereira Ana	IPB, Portugal
Pereira José Luís	Universidade do Minho, Portugal
Peschechera Giuseppe	Università di Bologna, Italy
Pham Quoc Trung	HCMC University of Technology, Vietnam
Piemonte Andreaa	University of Pisa, Italy
Pimentel Carina	Universidade de Aveiro, Portugal
Pinet Francois	IRSTEA, France
Pinto Livio	Polytechnic University of Milan, Italy
Pinto Telmo	Universidade do Minho, Portugal
Pinet Francois	IRSTEA, France
Poli Giuliano	Université Pierre et Marie Curie, France
Pollino Maurizio	ENEA, Italy
Portela Carlos Filipe	Universidade do Minho, Portugal
Prata Paula	Universidade Federal de Sergipe, Brazil
Previl Carlo	University of Quebec in Abitibi-Témiscamingue (UQAT), Canada
Prezioso Giuseppina	Università degli Studi di Napoli Parthenope, Italy
Pusatli Tolga	Cankaya University, Turkey
Quan Tho	Ho Chi Minh, University of Technology, Vietnam
Ragni Mirco	Universidade Estadual de Feira de Santana, Brazil
Rahman Nazreena	Biotechnology Research Centre, Malaysia
Rahman Wasiur	Technical University Darmstadt, Germany
Rashid Sidra	National University of Sciences and Technology (NUST) Islamabad, Pakistan
Rasulo Alessandro	Università degli studi di Cassino e del Lazio Meridionale, Italy
Raza Syed Muhammad	Sungkyunkwan University, South Korea
Reis Ferreira Gomes Karine	Instituto Nacional de Pesquisas Espaciais, Brazil
Requejo Cristina	Universidade de Aveiro, Portugal
Rocha Ana Maria	University of Minho, Portugal
Rocha Humberto	University of Coimbra, Portugal
Rocha Jorge	University of Minho, Portugal
Rodriguez Daniel	University of Berkeley, USA
Saeki Koichi	Graduate University for Advanced Studies, Japan
Samela Caterina	University of Basilicata, Italy
Sannicandro Valentina	Polytechnic of Bari, Italy
Santiago Júnior Valdivino	Instituto Nacional de Pesquisas Espaciais, Brazil
Sarafian Haiduke	Pennsylvania State University, USA

Santos Daniel	Universidade Federal de Minas Gerais, Portugal
Santos Dorabella	Instituto de Telecomunicações, Portugal
Santos Eulália	SAPO, Portugal
Santos Maribel Yasmina	Universidade de Minho, Portugal
Santos Rafael	University of Toronto, Canada
Santucci Valentinoi	University of Perugia, Italy
Sautot Lucil	MR TETIS, AgroParisTech, France
Scaioni Marco	Polytechnic University of Milan, Italy
Schernthanner Harald	University of Potsdam, Germany
Schneider Michel	ISIMA, France
Schoier Gabriella	University of Trieste, Italy
Scorza Francesco	University of Basilicata, Italy
Sebillo Monica	University of Salerno, Italy
Severino Ricardo Jose	Universidade de Minho, Portugal
Shakhov Vladimir	Russian Academy of Sciences (Siberian Branch), Russia
Sheeren David	Toulouse Institute of Technology, France
Shen Jie	University of Michigan, USA
Silva Elsa	INESC Tec, Porto, Portugal
Sipos Gergely	MTA SZTAKI Computer and Automation Research Institute, Hungary
Skarga-Bandurova Inna	Technological Institute of East Ukrainian National University, Ukraine
Skoković Dražen	University of Valencia, Spain
Skouteris Dimitrios	SNS, Italy
Soares Inês Soares Maria Joana	Universidade de Minho, Portugal
Soares Michel	Federal University of Sergipe, Brazil
Sokolovski Dmitri	Ikerbasque, Basque Foundation for Science, Spain
Sousa Lisete	Research, FCUL, CEAUL, Lisboa, Portugal
Stener Mauro	Università di Trieste, Italy
Sumida Yasuaki	Center for Digestive and Liver Diseases, Nara City Hospital, Japan
Suri Bharti	Guru Gobind Singh Indraprastha University, India
Sørensen Claus Aage Grøn	University of Aarhus, Denmark
Tajani Francesco	University of Rome, Italy
Takato Setsuo	Kisarazu National College of Technology, Japan
Tanaka Kazuaki	Hasanuddin University, Indonesia
Taniar David	Monash University, Australia
Tapia-McClung Rodrigo	The Center for Research in Geography and Geomatics, Mexico
Tarantino Eufemia	Polytechnic of Bari, Italy
Teixeira Ana Paula	Federal University of Ceará, Fortaleza, Brazil
Teixeira Senhorinha	Universidade do Minho, Portugal
Teodoro M. Filomena	Instituto Politécnico de Setúbal, Portugal
Thill Jean-Claude	University at Buffalo, USA
Thorat Pankaj	Sungkyunkwan University, South Korea

Tilio Lucia	University of Basilicata, Italy
Tomaz Graça	Instituto Politécnico da Guarda, Portugal
Torre Carmelo Maria	Polytechnic of Bari, Italy
Totaro Vincenzo	Polytechnic University of Bari, Italy
Tran Manh Hung	University of Danang, Vietnam
Tripathi Ashish	MNNIT Allahabad, India
Tripp Barba Carolina	Universidad Autónoma de Sinaloa, Mexico
Tut Zohra Fatema	University of Calgary, Canada
Upadhyay Ashish	Indian Institute of Public Health-Gandhinagar, India
Vallverdu Jordi	Autonomous University of Barcelona, Spain
Valuev Ilya	Russian Academy of Sciences, Russia
Varela Leonilde	University of Minho, Portugal
Varela Tania	Universidade de Lisboa, Portugal
Vasconcelos Paulo	Queensland University, Brisbane, Australia
Vasyunin Dmitry	University of Amsterdam, The Netherlands
Vella Flavio	University of Rome, Italy
Vijaykumar Nandamudi	INPE, Brazil
Vidacs Laszlo	University of Szeged, Hungary
Viqueira José R.R.	Agricultural University of Athens, Greece
Vizzari Marco	University of Perugia, Italy
Vohra Varun	Japan Advanced Institute of Science and Technology (JAIST), Japan
Voit Nikolay	Ulyanovsk State Technical University Ulyanovsk, Russia
Walkowiak Krzysztof	Wroclaw University of Technology, Poland
Wallace Richard J.	University College Cork, Ireland
Waluyo Agustinus Borgy	Monash University, Melbourne, Australia
Wanderley Fernando	FCT/UNL, Portugal
Wei Hoo Chong	Motorola, USA
Yamashita Satoshi	National Research Institute for Child Health and Development, Tokyo, Japan
Yamauchi Toshihiro	Okayama University, Japan
Yao Fenghui	Tennessee State University, USA
Yeoum Sanggil	Sungkyunkwan University, South Korea
Zaza Claudio	University of Foggia, Italy
Zeile Peter	Technische Universität Kaiserslautern, Germany
Zenha-Rela Mario	University of Coimbra, Portugal
Zoppi Corrado	Università di Cagliari, Italy
Zullo Francesco	University of l'Aquila, Italy
Zunino Alejandro	Universidad Nacional del Centro, Argentina
Žemlička Michal	Univerzita Karlova, Czech Republic
Živković Ljiljana	University of Belgrade, Serbia

Sponsoring Organizations

ICCSA 2017 would not have been possible without the tremendous support of many organizations and institutions, for which all organizers and participants of ICCSA 2017 express their sincere gratitude:

University of Trieste, Trieste, Italy
(http://www.units.it/)

University of Perugia, Italy
(http://www.unipg.it)

University of Basilicata, Italy
(http://www.unibas.it)

Monash University, Australia
(http://monash.edu)

Kyushu Sangyo University, Japan
(www.kyusan-u.ac.jp)

Universidade do Minho
Escola de Engenharia

Universidade do Minho, Portugal
(http://www.uminho.pt)

Contents – Part V

Workshop on Mobile Communications (MC 2017)

Workshop on Mobile-Computing, Sensing, and Actuation - Fog Net-working (MSA4FOG 2017)

Workshop on Physiological and Affective Computing: Methods and Applications (PACMA 2017)

Workshop on Quantum Mechanics: Computational Strategies and Applications (QMCSA 2017)

Workshop on Scientific Computing Infrastructure (SCI 2017)

Workshop on Software Quality (SQ 2017)

Workshop on Advances in Remote Sensing for Cultural heritage (RS-CH 2017)

Workshop on Computational Mathematics, and Statistics for Data Management and Software Engineering (IWCMSDMSE 2017)

A Safe Depth Forecasting Model for Insuring Tubewell Installations Against Arsenic Risk in Bangladesh

Matilde Trevisani[1](✉) , Jie Shen[2], Alexander van Geen[3],
Andrew Gelman[4], Shuky Ehrenberg[5], and John Immel[6]

[1] University of Trieste, Via Tigor 22, 34123 Trieste, Italy
matildet@deams.units.it
[2] Capital One Auto Finance, Piano, USA
[3] Lamont-Doherty Earth Observatory of Columbia University,
Palisades, NY, USA
[4] Department of Statistics, Columbia University, New York, NY, USA
[5] JGB Management, Boston, USA
[6] Joyful Belly Ayurveda, Asheville, USA

Abstract. Nowadays large spatial databases are available to help analysts facing a variety of environmental risk problems. Statistically accurate and computationally efficient algorithms and models are then needed to extract knowledge from these, for inference and prediction of the studied phenomenon, and, ultimately for decision both at country-wide policy and local level. Arsenic concentrations are naturally elevated in groundwater pumped from millions of shallow tubewells distributed across rural Bangladesh. Deeper tubewells often make access to groundwater with lower arsenic levels. Thereby, also thanks to a relatively low installation cost, they have proven to be an effective method to reduce arsenic exposure. Relying on a large database of well tests conducted in thousands of villages, we propose a supervised learning technique to estimate the probability that a new well will be low in arsenic based on its location and depth. For villages lacking direct information to make a local prediction, our technique, that we call the Sister-Village method, combines data from villages with similar characteristics. To further promote safe well installations and to help disseminate the information resulting from our method, we also propose and price a simple insurance model.

Keywords: Arsenic-depth pattern similarity · Probability curve · Bayesian learning · Calibration plot · Stratified cross-validation · Probability score

1 Introduction

Bacterial contamination of streams and ponds – the main source of drinking water until a few decades ago – was a leading cause of very high rates of infant mortality in rural Bangladesh. Simple tubewell technology providing access to groundwater aquifers that are typically free of human pathogens was introduced by international and non-governmental organizations (NGOs) in the mid 1970s. Although tubewells were

© Springer International Publishing AG 2017
O. Gervasi et al. (Eds.): ICCSA 2017, Part V, LNCS 10408, pp. 3–19, 2017.
DOI: 10.1007/978-3-319-62404-4_1

effective in this regard, they introduced another deadly health hazard: widespread exposure to arsenic (*As*) levels exceeding the WHO guideline for *As* in drinking water of 10 μg As per liter (10 μg/L). A number of strategies have been suggested to help mitigate the harmful effects of groundwater *As*: water treatment, alternative water sources and tubewell based approaches. Tubewells are relatively cheap and robust, besides they may lead to positive interventions like well-switching and the digging of community wells [3, 4]. For these reasons, it is generally thought that a tubewell based approach will continue to play a major role in *As* mitigation for the near future [1].

The World Bank, UNICEF, and a number of NGOs contributed funding and data to the Bangladesh *As* Mitigation Program (BAMWSP) under which nearly five million wells were tested and identified for location, age, number of users, depth and *As* concentrations. Results of the program corroborated by other surveys indicate that there is a high degree of variability in the spatial distribution of groundwater *As*. The main reason is the spatial variability of the underlying geology. *As* is gradually flushed out of sandy aquifers over time resulting in lower concentrations in groundwater pumped from deeper (and therefore older) aquifers. However the transition to low-*As* aquifers may be quite abrupt, resulting in wells of similar depth reporting different levels of *As*, even in neighboring villages [7].

In our previous localized study of *As* in Araihazar upazilla (equivalent to a sub-district, of which there are about 500 in Bangladesh) we created a statistical model relying on village level *As* conditions – a spatial unit small enough to eliminate most of the previously mentioned variability [2, 7]. Our model was able to produce an individualized *safe depth* estimate for many villages: wells dug to a depth below the estimated threshold have a high probability of satisfying Bangladesh's standard for *As* in drinking water of 50 μg/L. Local decision analysis in Araihazar upazilla also led us to conclude that a strategy whereby individuals drinking from wells with high *As* concentrations would switch to a well low in *As* within walking distance could lead to a relevant exposure reduction.

Although previous information dissemination techniques were successful in inducing some well switching, preliminary survey information indicates that installation of wells to unsafe depths is still common, despite the occasional identification of a reliable safe depth by local drillers. Two of the most prominent reasons that have hampered the installation of safer wells are readily discernible. First, the *safe depth* identified by previous testing often requires a household to drill significantly deeper than they would otherwise, resulting in a marked increase in cost. Moreover, even at the pre-identified *safe depth* the probability of obtaining *As* free water is often well below 100%. Insurance could serve to significantly mitigate the risk component of drilling for the installation of a new well. Second, the statistical model underlying the *safe depth* method is incomplete, in the sense that there are instances where a *safe depth* is not discernible on the basis of data from existing wells. In the event that there are a very small number of *As* free wells in a village, it may not be possible to derive a *safe depth* (Fig. 1). Significantly, this occurs most frequently in areas exhibiting especially high concentrations of *As* and a dearth of safe wells – precisely the areas where new wells are most urgently needed.

In order to address the limitation of the *safe depth* method, we develop a new *Sister-Village* method for computing the probability of *As* contamination as a function of depth.

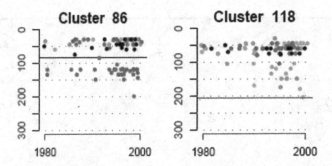

Fig. 1. Plots of *As* level as a function of depth and year of well installation in two village sized clusters. Cluster 86 allows for the computing of a *safe depth*, while cluster 118 does not (a lower bound – red line – below which the threshold cannot be derived is given instead).

The purpose of the *Sister-Village* method is two-fold: firstly it will allow us to arrive at a continuum of depth and safety probabilities. Secondly it is designed specifically to help overcome the *safe depth* method's informational failing. In order to magnify local information at the village level, we select, for each village, a number of sister villages on the ground of their similarity in terms of *As*-depth trend to the target village. Information available from these sister villages is then used to impute the probability of reaching *As* free water at different depths within the target village.

The paper proceeds as follows: part 2 presents exploratory data analysis; part 3 describes the *Sister-Village* model; part 4 examines its effectiveness by means of several cross-validation criteria; part 5 applies it to an insurance model and concludes.

2   Initial Analysis of Arsenic Distribution

We conduct our exploratory analysis in a subset of 16 of Bangladesh's 520 upazillas. Within these areas, 81% and 63% of sampled tubewells have *As* concentrations above the 10 μg/l WHO standard and, respectively, the 50 μg/l drinking water standard in Bangladesh. Figure 2 shows average *As* levels in each of the study area's 214 unions, the next administrative unit down from the upazilla, which are composed in turn of 3283 villages and represent a total of 355, 846 tubewells. The western region has the lowest levels of *As* contamination, while the area to the north-east suffers from the highest. But there is also significant patchiness at the union and even village level.

Depth profiles of *As* compiled for each of the 16 upazillas show a complex relationship between depth and *As* level (Fig. 4). In the study area, approximately 60% of the wells lie within a 60–120 ft depth interval, which unfortunately corresponds to the highest *As* concentrations, with shallower and deeper wells exhibiting lower average *As* levels (Table 1 and Fig. 3). Despite this general trend, there are certain upazillas where even shallow wells are extremely unsafe (e.g. Shahrasti) or even deeper wells have relatively high average *As* concentration (e.g. Banchharampur) or almost all the wells indicate low *As* levels throughout the depth range (e.g. Damurhada). Even if in general

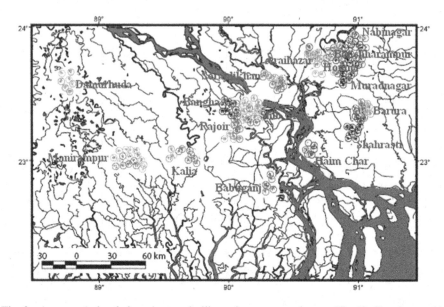

Fig. 2. Average *As* levels in unions and villages in our research area. The (0, 0) point on this graph corresponds to coordinates 23.36° North and 89.90° East. Colors indicate *As* levels: blue (less than 10 µg/l), green (10–50), orange (50–100), red (100–200), and black (>200). Each dot represents a village and each circle represents a union. (Color figure online)

Table 1. Number of wells and safe wells proportion for depth strata. The whole data (355, 846 wells) are considered.

Depth (ft)	Number of wells (%)	Safe wells proportion
D < 60	17.3	0.625
60 ≤ D < 75	18.1	0.333
75 ≤ D < 100	31.0	0.262
100 ≤ D < 125	15.6	0.318
125 ≤ D < 175	9.1	0.472
175 ≤ D < 225	5.2	0.535
225 ≤ D < 275	2.2	0.685
275 ≤ D < 325	0.5	0.711
325 ≤ D < 400	0.1	0.683
400 ≤ D < 500	0.1	0.703
D ≥ 500	0.8	0.906

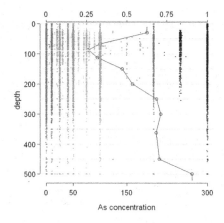

Fig. 3. Safe well proportion (top-axis) as function of well depth (*y*-axis) for the whole data. Dots are depicted as in Figs. 2 and 4. (Color figure online)

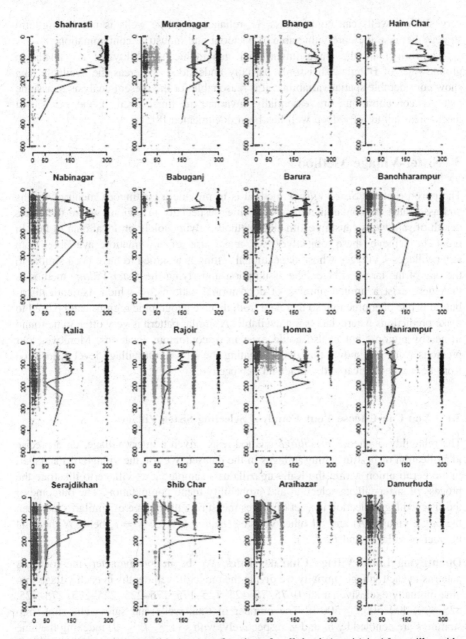

Fig. 4. *As* concentrations (*x*-axis) shown as function of well depth (*y*-axis) in 16 upazillas with each dot referring to one well and colors using a scale identical to the one of Fig. 2. The panels are arranged in decreasing order of average *As* concentration for each upazilla. The black line indicates average *As* concentration as a function of depth within each upazilla.

very shallow wells can contain less *As*, reliance on these wells is not a long-term strategy because they are vulnerable to bacterial and industrial contamination.

The origin of the three-dimensional geographic variability of *As* levels in groundwater of Bangladesh is only partially understood. Whereas the available data show considerable spatial variability, it is reasonable for the present analysis to assume that *As* concentrations are essentially invariant in time, even if the occasional mechanical failure of a deep well has been documented [8].

3   Sister-Village Method

The purpose of the *Sister-Village* method is to provide a continuous menu of depths and associated *As* contamination probabilities, especially in regions where there is a dearth of safe wells causing estimation methods relying solely on local data to fail. In order to achieve these objectives we make use of information available from sister-villages – villages whose depositional setting is assumed to have been similar to the one of the target village. The assumption underlying the *Sister-Village* method is that there exist a limited number of depositional patterns, of which *As*-depth distribution is one phenomenon, so that data from diverse geographic regions can be used to make predictions where data is not available. A similar pattern is very often to be found in nearby regions, but it also could exist in discontinuous locations. Moreover, our previous work has shown that disaggregating the data to the village level is justified from both a geological and a practical perspective.

3.1   You Can Choose Your Family – Selecting Sister Villages

The reliability of the *Sister-Village* method rests, given a query village, on a precise identification of best matching villages in the dataset. We use the village of Patershari in the Peruli union within the Kalia upazilla as a sample target village to illustrate the process of sister-village selection and probability menu computation. The outcome of the sister-village selection is a set of scores measuring the degree of similarity between the target village (*A*) and all other villages (B_i, $i = 1, 2, ..., N − 1$, being *N* the total number of villages and $B_i \neq A$).

Quantifying Local Village Characteristics. We begin by characterizing local *As* patterns in each village. Initially we divide the range of well depths in each village into nine mutually exclusive strata: 0–75, 75–125, 125–175, 175–225, 225–275, 275–325, 325–400, 400–500, ≥ 500 ft. The number of total wells and safe wells sunk into stratum k are denoted by n_k and y_k respectively, with k ($1 \leq k \leq 9$) indexing the nine different depth strata. In each stratum k, we obtain the estimated probabilities of safe depth in village *A* and B_i, $\widehat{\pi}_k^A$ and $\widehat{\pi}_k^B$ whose prior values are set to 0.5, as indicated by equations

$$\hat{\pi}_k^A = \frac{y_k^A + 1}{n_k^A + 2} \qquad \hat{\pi}_k^B = \frac{y_k^B + 1}{n_k^B + 2}. \tag{1}$$

The raw discrepancy between each village pair (A, B_i) in stratum k can be calculated as follows:

$$\hat{\theta}_k^{\text{raw}} = (\hat{\pi}_k^A - \hat{\pi}_k^B)^2 \quad \text{with } \widehat{\text{bias}} = \frac{\hat{\pi}_k^A(1 - \hat{\pi}_k^A)}{n_k^A + 2} + \frac{\hat{\pi}_k^B(1 - \hat{\pi}_k^B)}{n_k^B + 2}. \tag{2}$$

Combining the information from all k strata, we obtain:

$$\text{discrepancy}(A, B_i) = \sum_k (\hat{\theta}_k^{\text{raw}} - \widehat{\text{bias}}_k) \times \frac{n_k^A}{n_k^A + 5} \tag{3}$$

with an adjusting factor $n_k^A/(n_k^A + 5)$ assigning more weight to those strata of village A containing a higher concentration of wells. The smaller the value of the discrepancy – as described by Eq. (3) – the more similar villages A and B_i will be on average.

Categorizing Spatial Information. As mentioned previously, we assume that nearby geographical regions have similar geological properties. That being said, it is possible that similar geological properties can be observed in more distant geographic regions (i.e. in non-contiguous areas). We represent geographical variation amongst villages through a category difference function,

$$\text{Category difference } (A, B_i) = \begin{cases} 1, & \text{in the same union} \\ 2, & \text{in the same thana, but different unions} \\ 3, & \text{in the same division, but different thanas} \\ 4, & \text{in different divisions} \end{cases}$$

Two fundamental assumptions underlie our categorization method. Firstly, we assume that the administrative partition of villages reflects proximity. Secondly, we assume that proximity is related to some extent to the underlying geology that produced the observed patterns. Moreover, we assume that the distance score is a linear function of the administrative level. Figure 5 shows a scatter plot of discrepancy values as a function of category differences between each pair of villages (A, B_i).

Initially we make use of the geographic coordinates to measure the distance between any two villages. However, since only 10% of all sampled wells include this information, we are forced to make use of administrative partitions. Fortunately, a comparative analysis of the wells with geographic coordinates indicates that administrative partitions offer very good approximations for geographic distances. Furthermore, as Fig. 2 suggests, nearby villages are likely to have similar average As distributions.

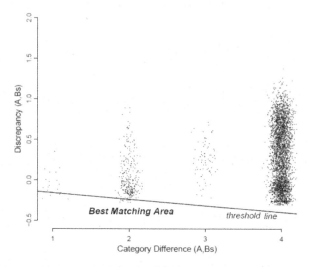

Fig. 5. Plot of discrepancy values as function of category differences for each village pair (A, B_i) with target village Patershari (A). Each dot represents a different village B_i (with a horizontal random jitter). Dots that fall below the threshold line are selected as the sister villages for A.

Selecting Sister Villages. We represent the total difference in As patterns within a village pair (A, B_i) as a weighted sum of local discrepancy and category difference score, to form a total score = discrepancy + $\alpha \cdot$ (category difference), with α indicating the relative weights given to non-spatial and spatial dissimilarity. This equation can be rewritten as

$$\text{discrepancy} \;=\; \text{total score} \;-\; \alpha \cdot (\text{category difference}) \tag{5}$$

Representing each village pair (A,B_i) as a dot on a two dimensional graph, we can use Eq. (5) to draw a threshold line defining the best matching area (Fig. 5).

Any two of the three parameters (α, total score, γ), with γ being the number of sister villages, are sufficient to determine a threshold line which in turn will determine village A's sister villages. The choice of γ depends on a tradeoff between two factors: on the one hand we need to have a sufficient γ for effective estimation; on the other, a high degree of similarity between the target village and its sisters must be maintained. The optimization of the floating parameters is discussed in Sect. 4.

Estimating the Probability that a Depth Interval is Safe. Next we estimate the probability that a well will be safe in a given depth stratum k for a village A, $\hat{p}_k^A$. First we pool the wells from village A' sister villages, with n_k^s and y_k^s indicating the total number of wells and number of safe wells in depth stratum k, respectively. Now, $\hat{p}_k^A$ is computed as a weighted sum of the information from village A's wells and from the wells in its sister villages,

$$\tilde{p}_k^A = \frac{y_k^A + \lambda/f(n_k^A \times y_k^s + 1)}{n_k^A + \lambda/f(n_k^A) \times n_k^s + (1/p_k^{\text{prior}})},$$ (6)

where λ is a constant and $f(n_k^A) = \sqrt{(n_k^A + 2)}$ Thus the weight $\lambda/f(n_k^A)$ associated with information from the sister villages is inversely proportionate to n_k^A, the total number of wells in the target village (consistent with the *borrowing strength* rule).

Let p_k^{prior} represent our prior information about the probability that a well in stratum k in village A is safe. We construct p_k^{prior} from As-depth distribution characterizing the upazilla of the target village, that is

$$p_k^{\text{prior}} = \frac{\text{number of safe wells in stratum } k \text{ in upazilla} + 1}{\text{number of wells in stratum } k \text{ in upazilla} + 2}$$

Besides, since the general geology of Bangladesh leads us to believe that deeper wells are on average safer, we adjust the probability curves for all villages to be monotone for deeper strata. For strata 5–9 (wells deeper than 250 ft) we draw an upper boundary curve requiring that the estimated probabilities of stratum k are equal to or greater than the probabilities of stratum $k - 1$. We also draw a lower boundary curve that works symmetrically to the upper curve, requiring that the estimated probabilities for stratum

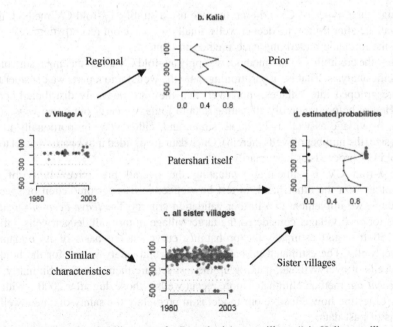

Fig. 6. Estimation of probability curve for Patershari (target village A) in Kalia upazilla. *As* level as function of depth and installation year for wells in A (plot a) and in the γ sister villages (c). Average safety probability curve for Kalia (b). Estimated probability curve for A (d).

k do not exceed those estimated for stratum $k + 1$. Thus, we produce an adjusted estimated probability curve as the average of the upper and lower bounds.

Figure 6 represents a scheme of the probability estimation process for a target village A starting from the well distribution (left plot) and ending with the estimated probability curve (right). The probability of a well being safe increases with depth, peaking at approximately 0.90 correspondent to a depth of 200 ft. Information derived from sister villages (bottom) and geographical trends (top) further supports tentative observations based on local information, indicating that 200 ft deep wells are very likely to be safe. Combining this information with monotonic adjustments then allows us to extend the probability curve below 200 ft, despite a lack of wells dug below this depth in village A.

4   Quantifying Uncertainty

Since predictive accuracy is important in the context of insurance, we use both calibration curves and probability-scores yielded by implementing three different cross validation (CV) criteria, to measure the level of uncertainty underlying our estimated probability curves. We also use probability scores as a criterion in the optimization of floating parameters when selecting sister villages.

4.1   Cross-Validation

We design three types of CV criteria: first we use a stratified k-fold CV method, then we reevaluate after truncating deeper wells, finally we leave out recently dug wells. We explain the rationale underlying each method in context.

To test the credibility of our method, we apply a k-fold CV albeit making it suitable to our specific analysis. That is, in partitioning data (the wells) into k parts we consider that wells are grouped into villages, moreover, that they are unevenly distributed across depth. Hence, before randomly allocating data to folds, we carry out a two-way stratification, by village as well as by depth strata, and, either way, proportionally to the stratum size (the number of wells therein). Once data are divided into k parts (k is set to 5), the k-fold CV proceeds as customarily.

The k-fold CV is aimed at evaluating the overall predictive ability of our methodology. On the other hand, to test how effective it is for prediction of specific data groups, we implement two further validation criteria. The *leave-deep-out* method removes for each village, considered the target village in turn, all deeper wells – those below 150 ft – and estimates the probability curve on the basis of its remaining shallower wells. The estimated probabilities and actual safety values for the holdout deeper wells of every village, making up the test set, are then recorded. Similarly, the *leave-recent-out* method eliminates more recent wells – those dug after 2000 – with the purpose of testing how effective our model is in predicting the safety of a new well on the basis of past data.

4.2   Calibration Plots and Probability Scores

CV results are summarized both graphically, by drawing calibration plots, and quantitatively, by means of probability scores.

The probability score (p–score) consists in the average log-likelihood of the set y_i, $i = 1,...,n$, constituting the test set of the undergoing CV method. More in detail, each well i of the test sample receives a score of either $\log(p_i)$ if it is safe ($y = 1$), or $\log(1 - p_i)$ if it is unsafe ($y = 0$) – with p_i indicating the estimated safety probability derived from fitting the model to the training sample as defined in the undergoing CV analysis – so that, by averaging, the p–score $= \sum_i \{y_i \log(p_i) + (1 - y_i) \log(1 - p_i)\}$ is obtained. The closer the score is to 0, the more reliable is our method.

Analyses of prediction performance are typically accompanied by calibration plots in which the relative frequencies of an event are plotted against the respective estimated probabilities. For example, Fig. 7 displays the calibration curves for the stratified *k*-fold, the *leave-deep-out* and *leave-recent-out* CVs (plot, respectively, at top, bottom left and right): the dots represent actual proportions of safe wells and corresponding estimated safety probabilities as averaged over a number – set to 20 – of equal probability intervals into which the range of estimated probabilities has been divided. All three calibration curves are very close to the 45 degree line, suggesting that the *Sister Village* method is highly reliable on aggregate. A more careful examination shows that there is

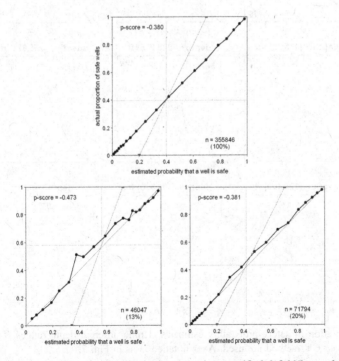

Fig. 7. Calibration of safety probability estimates using stratified *k*-fold/*leave-deep-out*/*leave-recent-out* CV (top, bottom left and right). p–score and number of tested wells (plus % over the total) are added to each plot. The 45° line shows the curve of perfect calibration.

a slight underestimation in the 0.3–0.8 probability range, both in predicting deeper wells and – less relevantly – recent wells safety. However, given the nature of the problem, it is at least reasonable if not prudent to err on the side of caution in our estimations. On the insurance side, it implies an overpricing, that is a lesser risk of under-coverage for the insurer.

In order to further corroborate the results for the overall data, we create additional calibration curves in which cross-validated data-after 2000 are disaggregated at both upazilla and depth-stratum levels. Our estimations hold up well at the upazilla level for the most part. Inspection by depth stratum (Fig. 8) indicates that the *Sister Village* method generally enjoys very high predictive accuracy at depth shallower than 275 ft, with some biases existing for deeper wells. However, these biases are not of especial concern since the vast majority of well installations occur above the 300 ft level.

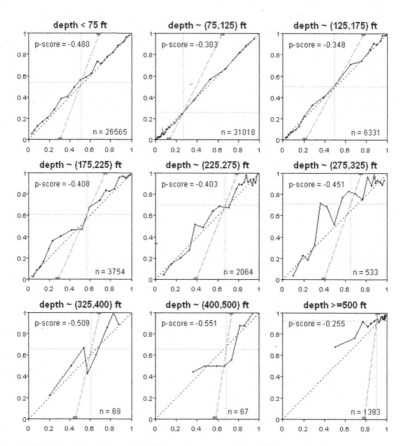

Fig. 8. Calibration of safety probability estimates at nine different depth ranges. Test data of *leave-recent-out* CV method are used. Axes notation is as in Fig. 7.

4.3   Optimal Determination of Floating Parameters

The *Sister-Village* model has three floating parameters: α and γ determine sisters villages' selection whereas λ controls the relative weight of sister and target villages. We select the parameter vector $\left(\widehat{\alpha}, \widehat{\gamma}, \widehat{\lambda}\right)$ which maximizes the p–score under the stratified k-fold CV.

Contours of p–score across a wide span of parameter values (Fig. 9) shows that information from sister villages (quantified by both γ and λ) is relevant to improve the method's predictive ability. Moreover, integration of geographic information

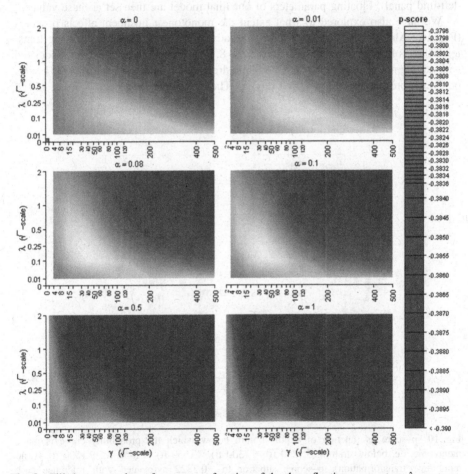

Fig. 9. Filled contour plots of p–score as function of the three floating parameters: λ versus γ (represented on y and x axes after being square-root transformed) conditional on α. p–score of case $\lambda = \gamma = 0$ (−0.3822) depicted as a point (red-colored) in the top-left panel ($\alpha = 0$) is the boundary level between parameter combinations in favor of the *Sister-Village* method (higher p–scores, increasingly lighter reds) and those against it (lower p–scores, increasingly darker violets). The maximum p–score (−0.3796) is achieved at $\lambda = 0.25$, $\gamma = 30$, $\alpha = 0.08$. (Color figure online)

(reflected by α) improves on performance as well. In fact, p–score obtained by using the sole local information (γ = λ = 0; see the left top panel, α = 0) is only −0.3822. Besides, note that sister villages are more efficiently selected when spatial similarity is taken into account: a relatively small number of sister villages (γ from 30 to 50 when α is around 0.1; see mid-panels) enables the method to achieve even better results than those produced by increasing γ solely (when α is about 0 the best scores correspond to γ from 100 up to 400). Lastly, as expected, there is a trade-off between γ and λ (contours are negatively oriented everywhere) so that an optimal balance between number of sister villages and weight of non-local information need to be found. Concluding, p–score reaches its maximum of −0.3796 at α = 0.08, γ = 30, λ = 0.25 (left-mid panel). Floating parameters of our final model are then set at these values.

We have also explored to what extent the monotone adjustment affects p–scores (Fig. 10). Almost everywhere p–score is relatively stable when the monotonic transformation is limited to deepest strata (k = 9, 8, 7) – practically at the level associated with having not transformed (k = 0) – while drops when is applied below 300 (k = 6), or, even more steeply, below 250 ft (k = 5). The maximum occurs at k = 7, i.e. 350 ft.

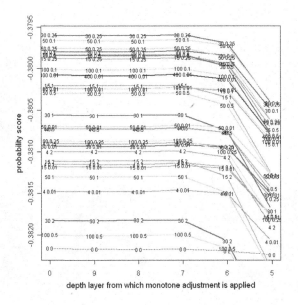

Fig. 10. p–score as function of depth stratum below which the probability curve is made monotonic, i.e. below stratum: 5 (250 ft), 6 (300 ft), 7 (350 ft), 8 (450 ft), 9 (500 ft), 0 (no monotonic transformation). p–scores superior to −0.3822 associated with reference case γ = λ = 0 (broken line) are only considered. The plot shows only a sample of parameter combinations, i.e. γ = 4, 15, 30, 50, 100, 400, coupled with λ = 0.01, 0.1, 0.25, 0, 5, 1, 2, all conditional on α = 0.08.

5 Insurance and Final Remarks

In order to mitigate the risks inherent in installing a new well with unknown ex post *As* properties, we devise an insurance plan. The insurance plan also serves as a useful tool for disseminating depth safety information, which is incorporated into the insurance model through the premium's pricing.

Individuals can choose to opt in to the insurance plan – essentially a money-back guarantee, by paying a premium. In the event that an insured well fails, the insurance plan will refund most of the costs associated with digging the well. We make use of the probability curves derived from the *Sister-Village* method in order to effectively price the insurance plan. Since the plan purpose is to reduce *As* exposure, and since our method provides somewhat conservative results, we assume a risk neutral insurer.

5.1 Rationale for Insurance: Risk Mitigation, Dissemination of Information

Classic economic theory suggests that the convexity of individual preferences results in risk aversion [5]. As a corollary, an individual exhibiting risk aversion will always choose to fully insure when faced with a fairly priced insurance contract. In the context of well digging, a newly dug well can be seen as a bet with expectation $E(V(w)) = C\Pr(As)$ where $V(w)$ is equal to the value of the well, C its cost, and $\Pr(As)$ indicating the probability of the well being contaminated. Assuming consumers are strictly risk-adverse will allow us to provide insurance at a fair price (plus transaction costs), while maintaining the long run solvency of the plan. Our hope is that the availability of insurance will result in individuals digging more and more expensive (deeper) wells, especially in high risk areas, since they are able to contract away their risk.

In addition to its risk mitigation properties, insurance can be used to disseminate information regarding safe depth. Firstly, we convey safety information through premium price menus – a safer depth will result in a cheaper insurance premium per foot. Secondly, we convey the information directly when possible by recommending that individuals dig to the optimal *safe depth*. As our previous analysis [2] has shown, a strategy based solely on information dissemination and well switching will reduce *As* exposure by 38%. Additional informed digging of a small number of wells based on the insurance model will serve to further reduce exposure significantly.

5.2 Pricing and Imperfect Credit Market

The basic price of an insurance contract for a risk neutral insurer is equal to the probability of the event being insured against occurring multiplied by the cost of restitution if it occurs. Transaction specific costs are then added to the basic price.

The cost of a well can be decomposed into two parts: the fixed costs of the head and filter, f, and the varying cost of a foot of depth, v. The total price of an uninsured well is therefore $p = f + dv$, with d indicating depth in feet. Likewise the price of an insurance contract can be decomposed into the fixed transaction costs (load, L) and the varying costs of providing insurance per foot of depth, $P = L + \text{Pr}(As)\ dv$.

There is no need to insure most of the fixed costs, since they are largely recoverable. In general it is our goal to insure all or nearly all unrecoverable costs.

The introduction of a load factor to the price of the insurance is likely to reduce its attractiveness. However, the fact that the load is fixed means that the optimal quantity of insurance purchased is not likely to change dramatically which involves that those who do choose to insure will choose to do so fully.

Due to the possibility of imperfect credit markets, we also make allowances for a price menu of partial insurance. An individual can choose how many feet to insure, while paying the per foot price of the deepest foot.

5.3   Adverse Selection, Moral Hazard and Contract Design

The structure of the *Sister Village* model may lend itself to inadvertent undesirable selection effects. If wells very close to a target well are better predictors than the model, and if individuals who have just had a well fail are more likely to want to insure than individuals digging a well for other reasons, they may select into our insurance plan heavily. These adversely selected wells would in fact be riskier than the model predicts, resulting in a higher frequency of claims. We are able to partially address these concerns by introducing more detailed geographic information. Moreover, we implement a "one shot" policy: a single individual can only insure one well.

A serious concern is that of collusion between the well owner and driller. They may contract to dig a shallower well that indicated to the insurance agent (at a lower cost), splitting the difference. In order to avoid this problem all wells will be measured before a claim is paid. Furthermore, all wells will be destroyed upon the payment of a claim so that people will not have an incentive to temporarily poison their well.

5.4   Conclusions

This work use spatial databases to help analyse a major environmental risk: soil As contaminating groundwater. In continuation of previous works, we develop a supervised learning technique for estimating a probability curve over depth of *As* water safety, also for villages lacking direct information by borrowing strength from sister villages. Our initial analysis is based on information about each well's depth, *As* level, year of installation and administrative location. There are a number of other variables which could potentially become available in the future, and so used to improve the reliability of our method. The first possibility is adding detailed geographic information about each well. This type of expansion may be relevant also to the insurance model as discussed above.

References

1. Ahmed, M.F., Ahuja, S., Alauddin, M., Hug, S.J., Lloyd, J.R., Pfaff, A., Pichler, T., Saltikov, C., Stute, M., van Geen, A.: Ensuring safe drinking water in Bangladesh. Science **314**, 1687–1688 (2006)
2. Gelman, A., Trevisani, M., Lu, H., van Geen, A.: Direct data manipulation for local decision analysis, as applied to the problem of arsenic drinking water from tube wells in Bangladesh. Risk Anal. **24**, 1597–1612 (2004)
3. Madajewicz, M., Pfaff, A., van Geen, A., Graziano, J., Hussein, I., Momotaj, H., Sylvi, R., Ahsan, H.: Can information alone both improve awareness and change behavior? Response to arsenic contamination of groundwater in Bangladesh. J. Dev. Econ. **84**, 731–754 (2007)
4. Opar, A., Pfaff, A., Seddique, A.A., Ahmed, K.M., Graziano, J.H., van Geen, A.: Responses of 6500 households to arsenic mitigation in Araihazar, Bangladesh. Health Place **13**, 164–172 (2007)
5. Rabin, M.: Risk aversion and expected-utility theory: a calibration theorem. Econometrica **68** (5), 1281–1292 (2000)
6. van Geen, A., Zheng, Y., Versteeg, R., Stute, M., Horneman, A., Dhar, R., Steckler, M., Gelman, A., Small, C., Ahsan, H., Graziano, J., Hussein, I., Ahmed, K.M.: Spatial variability of arsenic in 6000 tube wells in a 25 km^2 area of Bangladesh. Water Resour. Res. **39**(5), 1140 (2003). doi:10.1029/2002WR001617
7. van Geen, A., Trevisani, M., Immel, J., Jakariya, M., Osman, N., Cheng, Z., Gelman, A., Ahmed, K.M.: Targeting low-arsenic groundwater with mobile-phone technology in Araihazar. J. Health Popul. Nutr. **24**, 282–297 (2006)
8. van Geen, A., Cheng, Z., Jia, Q., Seddique, A.A., Rahman, M.W., Rahman, M.M., Ahmed, K.M.: Monitoring 51 deep community wells in Araihazar, Bangladesh, for up to 5 years: implications for arsenic mitigation. J. Environ. Sci. Health **42**, 1729–1740 (2007)

The Likelihood Ratio Test for Equality of Mean Vectors with Compound Symmetric Covariance Matrices

Carlos A. Coelho$^{(\boxtimes)}$

Centro de Matemática e Aplicações – CMA/FCT-UNL,
Departamento de Matemática, Faculdade de Ciências e Tecnologia,
Universidade Nova de Lisboa, Caparica, Portugal
cmac@fct.unl.pt

Abstract. The author derives the likelihood ratio test statistic for the equality of mean vectors when the covariance matrices are assumed to have a compound symmetric structure. Its exact distribution is then expressed in terms of a product of independent Beta random variables and it is shown that for some particular cases it is possible to obtain very manageable finite form expressions for the probability density and cumulative distribution functions for this distribution. For the other cases, given the intractability of the expressions for the exact distribution, very sharp near-exact distributions are developed. Numerical studies show the extreme good performance of these near-exact distributions.

Keywords: Beta distributions · Exact distribution · Likelihood ratio statistic · Near-exact distributions

1 Introduction

The likelihood ratio test for the equality of mean vectors, when the covariance matrices are assumed to be just positive-definite, but otherwise unstructured, is a well-known test in Multivariate Analysis, and the distribution of the associated test statistic has been extensively studied ([8, Chap. 9], [1, Chap. 8], [10, Chap. 10], [5,9]).

However, a similar test for cases where some common given structure is assumed for the covariance matrices is not available in the literature.

We say that a $p \times p$ positive-definite covariance matrix Σ_{CS} is compound symmetric if, for $-\frac{a}{p-1} < b < a$, it can be written as

$$
\Sigma_{CS} = \begin{bmatrix} a & b & b & \dots & b \\ b & a & b & \dots & b \\ b & b & a & \dots & b \\ \vdots & \vdots & \vdots & \ddots & \vdots \\ b & b & b & \dots & a \end{bmatrix} = (a-b)I_p + bE_{pp} = aI_p + b(E_{pp} - I_p),
$$

© Springer International Publishing AG 2017
O. Gervasi et al. (Eds.): ICCSA 2017, Part V, LNCS 10408, pp. 20–32, 2017.
DOI: 10.1007/978-3-319-62404-4_2

where I_p represents the identity matrix of order p and E_{pp} a $p \times p$ matrix of 1's.

Let us suppose that $\underline{X}_k \sim N_p(\underline{\mu}_k, \Sigma_k)$, $k = 1, \ldots, q$, where Σ_k are assumed to be equal and compound symmetric. Let us further suppose that we have a sample of size $n_k > p$ from $\underline{X}_k$ $(k = 1, \ldots, q)$ and that these q samples are independent, with $n = \sum_{k=1}^{q} n_k$. We will be interested in the test to the null hypothesis of equality of the q mean vectors $\underline{\mu}_k$ $(k = 1, \ldots, q)$, that is, the null hypothesis

$$
\begin{aligned}
H_0 : \underline{\mu}_1 &= \ldots \underline{\mu}_q \\
\text{assuming } \Sigma_1 &= \cdots = \Sigma_q (= \Sigma_{CS} \text{ non-specified}),
\end{aligned}
\tag{1}
$$

where Σ_{CS} represents a compound symmetric matrix of order p.

The interest in this test comes from the fact that such covariance structure is quite common or quite commonly assumed for covariance matrices in many situations and for many statistical models. See for example [6] for references. Moreover, in case the assumption of such structure for the covariance matrices is correct, then not accounting for it when carrying out the tests for the mean vectors will lead to losses in power. Therefore it is of interest to investigate the test for equality of mean vectors when assuming this structure for the covariance matrices.

2   The Likelihood Ratio Test Statistic

The $(2/n)$-th power of the likelihood ratio test (l.r.t.) statistic to test the null hypothesis in (1) is

$$
\Lambda = \frac{a_{11}^{**}(a^{**})^{p-1}}{c_{11}^{**}(c^{**})^{p-1}},
\tag{2}
$$

where

$$
a^{**} = \frac{1}{p-1} \sum_{j=2}^{p} a_{jj}^{**} \quad \text{and} \quad c^{**} = \frac{1}{p-1} \sum_{j=2}^{p} c_{jj}^{**},
\tag{3}
$$

with a_{jj}^{**} and c_{jj}^{**}, the diagonal elements of the matrices

$$
A^{**} = UAU' \quad \text{and} \quad C^{**} = U(A+B)U'
\tag{4}
$$

where U is a Helmert matrix of order p, which is a $p \times p$ orthogonal matrix with first row equal to $\frac{1}{\sqrt{p}}E_{1p}$ and i-th row $(i = 2, \ldots, p)$ equal to

$$
\frac{1}{\sqrt{(i-1)i}} \Big[\underbrace{1, \ldots, 1}_{i-1}, -(i-1), \underbrace{0, \ldots, 0}_{p-i} \Big] \quad (i = 2, \ldots, p).
$$

We may obtain the l.r.t. statistic in (2) by establishing a parallel with the l.r.t. statistic used when the covariance matrices Σ_k are assumed to be just positive-definite, which is the statistic

$$
\Lambda^* = \frac{|A|}{|A+B|}
\tag{5}
$$

where

$$A = \sum_{k=1}^{q}(n_k - 1)S_k \quad \text{and} \quad B = \sum_{k=1}^{q} n_k(\overline{X}_k - \overline{X})(\overline{X}_k - \overline{X})' \qquad (6)$$

where S_k and $\overline{X}_k$ are respectively the sample covariance matrix and mean vector of the k-th sample and

$$\overline{X} = \frac{1}{n}\sum_{k=1}^{q} n_k \overline{X}_k \,,$$

and by seeing that the l.r.t. statistic to test H_0 in (1) will be in its beginning similar to the l.r.t. statistic in (5), to which we have to add the fact that now the matrices Σ_k are assumed to be compound symmetric.

If we take into account that all the diagonal elements of Σ_{CS} are equal among themselves and that also all the off-diagonal elements of Σ_{CS} are also equal among themselves, the maximum likelihood estimator (m.l.e.) of Σ_{CS}, under the alternative hypothesis

$$H_1 : \exists j, j' \in \{1, \ldots, q\} : \underline{\mu}_j \neq \underline{\mu}_{j'},$$
$$\text{assuming } \Sigma_1 = \cdots = \Sigma_q (= \Sigma_{CS} \text{ non-specified}), \qquad (7)$$

where $\Sigma_{CS} = aI_p + b(E_{pp} - I_p)$, is $A^* = [a_{ij}^*]$, with

$$a_{ii}^* = \widehat{a}\,\big|_{H_1} = \frac{1}{p}\sum_{j=1}^{p} a_{jj} \quad \text{and} \quad a_{ij}^* = \widehat{b}\,\big|_{H_1} = \frac{1}{p(p-1)}\sum_{\substack{i=1 \\ }}^{p}\sum_{\substack{j=1 \\ i \neq j}}^{p} a_{ij} \quad (i \neq j),$$

while the m.l.e. of Σ_{CS} under the null hypothesis in (1) is $C^* = [c_{ij}^*]$, with

$$c_{ii}^* = \widehat{a}\,\big|_{H_0} = \frac{1}{p}\sum_{j=1}^{p}(a_{jj} + b_{jj}) \quad \text{and} \quad c_{ij}^* = \widehat{b}\,\big|_{H_0} = \frac{1}{p(p-1)}\sum_{\substack{i=1 \\ }}^{p}\sum_{\substack{j=1 \\ i \neq j}}^{p}(a_{ij} + b_{ij}) \quad (i \neq j),$$

where a_{ij} and b_{ij} represent the running elements of the matrices A and B in (5) and (6). Then, the l.r.t. statistic to test H_0 in (1) may be written as

$$\Lambda = \frac{|A^*|}{|C^*|} \qquad (8)$$

where

$$|A^*| = a_{11}^{**}\left(\frac{1}{p-1}\sum_{j=2}^{p} a_{jj}^{**}\right)^{p-1} \quad \text{and} \quad |C^*| = c_{11}^{**}\left(\frac{1}{p-1}\sum_{j=2}^{p} c_{jj}^{**}\right)^{p-1} \qquad (9)$$

where, as in (2) and (3), a_{jj}^{**} and c_{jj}^{**} represent respectively the j-th diagonal element of the matrices A^{**} and C^{**} in (4), so that Λ in (8) may be written as in (2).

We may note that, while a_{11}^{**} and c_{11}^{**} are the m.l.e.'s of $a + (p-1)b$, respectively under H_1 in (7) and under H_0 in (1), a^{**} and c^{**} in (2) and (3) are the m.l.e.'s of $a - b$, respectively under H_1 in (7) and under H_0 in (1).

3   Characterization of the Distribution of the L.R.T. Statistic

In order to obtain the distribution of the l.r.t. statistic Λ in (8) or (2), under the null hypothesis (1), now one only has to notice that, under this null hypothesis,

$$U \Sigma_{CS} U' = \Delta = diag\big(a + (p-1)b, \underbrace{a-b, \ldots, a-b}_{p-1}\big),$$

so that, since A and B are independent, with

$$A \sim W_p(n-q, \Sigma_{CS}) \quad \text{and} \quad B \sim W_p(q-1, \Sigma_{CS}),$$

A^{**} and $B^{**} = UBU'$ are independent, with

$$A^{**} \sim W_p(n-q, \Delta) \quad \text{and} \quad B^{**} \sim W_p(q-1, \Delta),$$

and as such,

$$C^{**} = A^{**} + B^{**} \sim W_p(n-1, \Delta).$$

The diagonal elements of A^{**} are thus independent, as well as the diagonal elements of B^{**} and C^{**}, with

$$\frac{a_{jj}^{**}}{\delta_j} \sim \chi_{n-q}^2, \qquad \frac{b_{jj}^{**}}{\delta_j} \sim \chi_{q-1}^2, \qquad \frac{c_{jj}^{**}}{\delta_j} = \frac{a_{jj}^{**}}{\delta_j} + \frac{b_{jj}^{**}}{\delta_j} \sim \chi_{n-1}^2; \qquad (j = 1, \ldots, p) \tag{10}$$

for $\delta_1 = a + (p-1)b$ and $\delta_2 = \cdots = \delta_p = a - b$.

Therefore, from (8), (9) and (10), we see that

$$\Lambda \overset{d}{\equiv} Y_1 \, (Y_2)^{p-1}$$

where Y_1 and Y_2 are independent, with

$$Y_1 \sim Beta\left(\frac{n-q}{2}, \frac{q-1}{2}\right) \quad \text{and} \quad Y_2 \sim Beta\left(\frac{(n-q)(p-1)}{2}, \frac{(q-1)(p-1)}{2}\right).$$

The h-th moment of Λ in (2) may thus be written as

$$E(\Lambda^h) = \frac{\Gamma\left(\frac{n-1}{2}\right) \Gamma\left(\frac{n-q}{2} + h\right)}{\Gamma\left(\frac{n-q}{2}\right) \Gamma\left(\frac{n-1}{2} + h\right)} \frac{\Gamma\left(\frac{(n-1)(p-1)}{2}\right) \Gamma\left(\frac{(n-q)(p-1)}{2} + (p-1)h\right)}{\Gamma\left(\frac{(n-q)(p-1)}{2}\right) \Gamma\left(\frac{(n-1)(p-1)}{2} + (p-1)h\right)}, \tag{11}$$

which will be used in deriving an exact finite form for the distribution of Λ for odd q and to obtain sharp near-exact approximations for its distribution in the other cases.

4   The Exact Distribution of Λ for Odd q

For odd q, by using the relation

$$\frac{\Gamma(a+n)}{\Gamma(a)} = \prod_{j=0}^{n-1}(a+k) \tag{12}$$

and given that the expression in (11) remains valid for any complex h, one may write the characteristic function (c.f.) of $W = -\log\Lambda$ as

$$
\begin{aligned}
\Phi_W(t) = E\left(e^{\mathrm{i}tW}\right) &= E(\Lambda^{-\mathrm{i}t}) \\
&= \frac{\Gamma\left(\frac{n-1}{2}\right)\Gamma\left(\frac{n-q}{2}-\mathrm{i}t\right)}{\Gamma\left(\frac{n-q}{2}\right)\Gamma\left(\frac{n-1}{2}-\mathrm{i}t\right)} \frac{\Gamma\left(\frac{(n-1)(p-1)}{2}\right)\Gamma\left(\frac{(n-q)(p-1)}{2}-(p-1)\mathrm{i}t\right)}{\Gamma\left(\frac{(n-q)(p-1)}{2}\right)\Gamma\left(\frac{(n-1)(p-1)}{2}-(p-1)\mathrm{i}t\right)} \\
&= \left\{\prod_{j=0}^{\frac{q-1}{2}-1}\left(\frac{n-q}{2}+j\right)\left(\frac{n-q}{2}+j-\mathrm{i}t\right)^{-1}\right\} \\
&\quad\times \left\{\prod_{j=0}^{\frac{(q-1)(p-1)}{2}-1}\left(\frac{(n-q)(p-1)}{2}+j\right)\left(\frac{(n-q)(p-1)}{2}+j-(p-1)\mathrm{i}t\right)^{-1}\right\} \\
&= \left\{\prod_{j=0}^{\frac{q-1}{2}-1}\left(\frac{n-q}{2}+j\right)\left(\frac{n-q}{2}+j-\mathrm{i}t\right)^{-1}\right\} \\
&\quad\times \left\{\prod_{j=0}^{\frac{(q-1)(p-1)}{2}-1}\left(\frac{n-q}{2}+\frac{j}{p-1}\right)\left(\frac{n-q}{2}+\frac{j}{p-1}-\mathrm{i}t\right)^{-1}\right\} \\
&= \prod_{j=1}^{(q-1)(p-1)/2}\left(\frac{n-q}{2}+\frac{j-1}{p-1}\right)^{r_j}\left(\frac{n-q}{2}+\frac{j-1}{p-1}-\mathrm{i}t\right)^{r_j}
\end{aligned}
$$

for

$$
r_j = \begin{cases}
1, & j=1,\ldots,(q-1)(p-1)/2 \\
& j \neq (j-1)(p-1)+1 \text{ for } \ell=1,\ldots,(q-1)/2 \\
2, & j=(\ell-1)(p-1)+1 \text{ for } \ell=1,\ldots,(q-1)/2,
\end{cases} \tag{13}
$$

which shows that for odd q the exact distribution of W is a GIG (Generalized Integer Gamma) distribution [3] and that of Λ an EGIG (Exponentiated Generalized Integer Gamma) distribution [2] of depth $(q-1)(p-1)/2$ with shape parameters r_j and rate parameters $\frac{n-q}{2}+\frac{j-1}{p-1}$ $(j=1,\ldots,(q-1)(p-1)/2)$.

The exact probability density function (p.d.f.) and cumulative distribution function (c.d.f.) of Λ are thus given by

$$
f_\Lambda(z) = f^{EGIG}\left(z\,\bigg|\,\{r_j\}_{j=1,\ldots,g}\,;\,\left\{\frac{(n-q)}{2}+\frac{j-1}{p-1}\right\}_{j=1,\ldots,g}\,;\,g\right)
$$

and

$$
F_\Lambda(z) = F^{EGIG}\left(z\,\bigg|\,\{r_j\}_{j=1,\ldots,g}\,;\,\left\{\frac{(n-q)}{2}+\frac{j-1}{p-1}\right\}_{j=1,\ldots,g}\,;\,g\right)
$$

for $g = (q-1)(p-1)/2$ and r_j given by (13). See [2] for the notation used for the p.d.f. and c.d.f. of the EGIG distribution.

5 Near-Exact Distributions of Λ for Even q

5.1 Near-Exact Distributions for Even q and Even p

When q is even, the exact p.d.f. and c.d.f. of Λ are not manageable. As such in this case we will develop near-exact distributions for Λ, which are asymptotic distributions that, opposite to common asymptotic distributions, will be asymptotic not only for increasing sample sizes but also for increasing values of p and q. The case where q and p are both even is somewhat more complicated and this is the one we will address in this subsection.

From (11), for even q and even p we may write the c.f. of $W = -\log \Lambda$ as

$$
\begin{aligned}
\Phi_W(t) = {} & \frac{\Gamma\left(\frac{n-2}{2}\right)\Gamma\left(\frac{n-q}{2} - it\right)}{\Gamma\left(\frac{n-q}{2}\right)\Gamma\left(\frac{n-2}{2} - it\right)} \frac{\Gamma\left(\frac{(n-1)(p-1)}{2} - \frac{1}{2}\right)\Gamma\left(\frac{(n-q)(p-1)}{2} - (p-1)it\right)}{\Gamma\left(\frac{(n-q)(p-1)}{2}\right)\Gamma\left(\frac{(n-1)(p-1)}{2} - \frac{1}{2} - (p-1)it\right)} \\
& \times \frac{\Gamma\left(\frac{n-1}{2}\right)\Gamma\left(\frac{n-2}{2} - it\right)}{\Gamma\left(\frac{n-2}{2}\right)\Gamma\left(\frac{n-1}{2} - it\right)} \frac{\Gamma\left(\frac{(n-1)(p-1)}{2}\right)\Gamma\left(\frac{(n-1)(p-1)}{2} - \frac{1}{2} - (p-1)it\right)}{\Gamma\left(\frac{(n-1)(p-1)}{2} - \frac{1}{2}\right)\Gamma\left(\frac{(n-1)(p-1)}{2} - (p-1)it\right)} \\
= {} & \left\{ \prod_{j=0}^{\frac{q-2}{2}-1} \left(\frac{n-q}{2} + j\right)\left(\frac{n-q}{2} + j - it\right)^{-1} \right\} \\
& \times \left\{ \prod_{j=0}^{\frac{q(p-1)-p}{2}-1} \left(\frac{(n-q)(p-1)}{2} + j\right)\left(\frac{(n-q)(p-1)}{2} + j - (p-1)it\right)^{-1} \right\} \\
& \times \frac{\Gamma\left(\frac{n-1}{2}\right)\Gamma\left(\frac{n-2}{2} - it\right)}{\Gamma\left(\frac{n-2}{2}\right)\Gamma\left(\frac{n-1}{2} - it\right)} \frac{\Gamma\left(\frac{(n-1)(p-1)}{2}\right)\Gamma\left(\frac{(n-1)(p-1)}{2} - \frac{1}{2} - (p-1)it\right)}{\Gamma\left(\frac{(n-1)(p-1)}{2} - \frac{1}{2}\right)\Gamma\left(\frac{(n-1)(p-1)}{2} - (p-1)it\right)} \\
= {} & \left\{ \prod_{j=0}^{\frac{q-2}{2}-1} \left(\frac{n-q}{2} + j\right)\left(\frac{n-q}{2} + j - it\right)^{-1} \right\} \\
& \times \left\{ \prod_{j=0}^{\frac{q(p-1)-p}{2}-1} \left(\frac{n-q}{2} + \frac{j}{p-1}\right)\left(\frac{n-q}{2} + \frac{j}{p-1} - it\right)^{-1} \right\} \\
& \times \frac{\Gamma\left(\frac{n-1}{2}\right)\Gamma\left(\frac{n-2}{2} - it\right)}{\Gamma\left(\frac{n-2}{2}\right)\Gamma\left(\frac{n-1}{2} - it\right)} \frac{\Gamma\left(\frac{(n-1)(p-1)}{2}\right)\Gamma\left(\frac{(n-1)(p-1)}{2} - \frac{1}{2} - (p-1)it\right)}{\Gamma\left(\frac{(n-1)(p-1)}{2} - \frac{1}{2}\right)\Gamma\left(\frac{(n-1)(p-1)}{2} - (p-1)it\right)}
\end{aligned}
$$

$$= \left\{ \underbrace{\prod_{j=1}^{((q-1)(p-1)-1)/2} \left(\frac{n-q}{2} + \frac{j-1}{p-1} \right)^{r_j^*} \left(\frac{n-q}{2} + \frac{j-1}{p-1} - \mathrm{it} \right)^{-r_j^*}}_{\Phi_{W,1}(t)} \right\}$$

$$\times \underbrace{\frac{\Gamma\left(\frac{n-1}{2}\right)\Gamma\left(\frac{n-2}{2} - \mathrm{it}\right)}{\Gamma\left(\frac{n-2}{2}\right)\Gamma\left(\frac{n-1}{2} - \mathrm{it}\right)} \frac{\Gamma\left(\frac{(n-1)(p-1)}{2}\right)\Gamma\left(\frac{(n-1)(p-1)}{2} - \frac{1}{2} - (p-1)\mathrm{it}\right)}{\Gamma\left(\frac{(n-1)(p-1)}{2} - \frac{1}{2}\right)\Gamma\left(\frac{(n-1)(p-1)}{2} - (p-1)\mathrm{it}\right)}}_{\Phi_{W,2}(t)}$$

$$\tag{14}$$

with

$$r_j^* = \begin{cases} 1, & j = 1, \ldots, ((q-1)(p-1)-1)/2 \\ & j \neq (\ell-1)(p-1)+1 \ \text{for} \ \ell = 1, \ldots, (q-2)/2 \\ 2, & j = (\ell-1)(p-1)+1 \ \text{for} \ \ell = 1, \ldots, (q-2)/2. \end{cases} \tag{15}$$

In (14) $\Phi_{W,1}(t)$ is the c.f. of a GIG distribution of depth $((q-1)(p-1)-1)/2$ with shape parameters r_j^* and rate parameters $\frac{n-q}{2} + \frac{j-1}{p-1}$ $(j = 1, \ldots, ((q-1)(p-1)-1)/2)$ and will be left untouched, while, based on the results in Sect. 5 of [11], which show that we can, for increasing values of a, approximate asymptotically a $Logbeta(a, b)$ distribution by an infinite mixture of $Gamma\,(b+k, a)$ $(k = 0, 1, \ldots)$ distributions, using a somewhat heuristic approach, we will asymptotically approximate $\Phi_{W,2}(t)$, which is the c.f. of a sum of two independent random variables whose exponential has a Beta distribution with a second parameter equal to $1/2$, by

$$\Phi_2^*(t) = \sum_{k=0}^{m^*} \pi_k \, (\lambda^*)^{1+k} (\lambda^* - \mathrm{it})^{-(1+k)}$$

which is the c.f. of a finite mixture of Gamma distributions, where λ^* is the rate parameter in

$$\Phi^*(t) = \theta (\lambda^*)^{r_1} (\lambda^* - \mathrm{it})^{-r_1} + (1 - \theta)(\lambda^*)^{r_2}(\lambda^* - \mathrm{it})^{-r_2}$$

which will be numerically computed together with θ, r_1 and r_2 in such a way that

$$\left. \frac{\partial^h}{\partial t^h} \Phi^*(t) \right|_{t=0} = \left. \frac{\partial^h}{\partial t^h} \Phi_{W,2}(t) \right|_{t=0}, \qquad h = 1, \ldots, 4.$$

The weights π_k, $k = 0, \ldots, m^* - 1$, will then be computed in such a way that

$$\left. \frac{\partial^h}{\partial t^h} \Phi_2^*(t) \right|_{t=0} = \left. \frac{\partial^h}{\partial t^h} \Phi_{W,2}(t) \right|_{t=0}, \qquad h = 1, \ldots, m^*,$$

with $\pi_{m^*} = 1 - \sum_{k=0}^{m^*-1} \pi_k$.

By doing this we obtain

$$\Phi_W^*(t) = \Phi_{W,1}(t)\, \Phi_2^*(t)$$

as a near-exact c.f. for W, which will yield as near-exact distributions for W mixtures with $m^* + 1$ components, each of which is a GIG distribution of depth $((q-$

$1)(p-1)-1)/2+1$, with shape parameters r_j^* $(j=1,\ldots,((q-1)(p-1)-1)/2)$ and a last one equal to $k+1$, and corresponding rate parameters $(n-q)/2+(j-1)/(p-1)$ and λ^*.

This gives near-exact distributions for Λ with p.d.f.

$$f_\Lambda(z) = \sum_{k=0}^{m^*} \pi_k \, f^{EGIG}\left(z \,\bigg|\, \{r_j^*\}_{j=1,\ldots,g}, k+1; \left\{\frac{n-q}{2}+\frac{j-1}{p-1}\right\}_{j=1,\ldots,g}, \lambda^*; g+1\right)$$

and c.d.f.

$$F_\Lambda(z) = \sum_{k=0}^{m^*} \pi_k \left(1 - F^{EGIG}\left(z \,\bigg|\, \{r_j^*\}_{j=1,\ldots,g}, k+1; \left\{\frac{n-q}{2}+\frac{j-1}{p-1}\right\}_{j=1,\ldots,g}, \lambda^*; g+1\right)\right),$$

for $g = ((q-1)(p-1)-1)/2$ and r_j^* given by (15).

This yields very manageable near-exact distributions for both W and Λ, which will match the first m^* exact moments of W and which, as it is shown in the next section, lie very close to the exact distribution and are asymptotic not only for increasing sample sizes but also for increasing values of p and q, that is, the number of variables in each vector $\underline{X}_k$ and the number of populations considered, opposite to the common asymptotic distributions which are asymptotic for increasing sample sizes, but which quickly degrade their performance for increasing values of p.

5.2   Near-Exact Distributions for Even q and Odd p

Indeed when q is even but p is odd, we may treat the c.f. of W still in a similar manner, but now taking advantage of the fact that in this case the c.f. of the negative logarithm of the r.v. Y_2 may be expressed as the c.f. of a GIG distribution. Since in this case $p-1$ is even, we may write

$$
\begin{aligned}
\Phi_W(t) = {} & \frac{\Gamma\left(\frac{n-2}{2}\right)\Gamma\left(\frac{n-q}{2}-it\right)}{\Gamma\left(\frac{n-q}{2}\right)\Gamma\left(\frac{n-2}{2}-it\right)} \, \frac{\Gamma\left(\frac{(n-1)(p-1)}{2}\right)\Gamma\left(\frac{(n-q)(p-1)}{2}-(p-1)it\right)}{\Gamma\left(\frac{(n-q)(p-1)}{2}\right)\Gamma\left(\frac{(n-1)(p-1)}{2}-(p-1)it\right)} \\[2mm]
& \times \frac{\Gamma\left(\frac{n-1}{2}\right)\Gamma\left(\frac{n-2}{2}-it\right)}{\Gamma\left(\frac{n-2}{2}\right)\Gamma\left(\frac{n-1}{2}-it\right)} \\[2mm]
= {} & \left\{\prod_{j=0}^{\frac{q-2}{2}-1}\left(\frac{n-q}{2}+j\right)\left(\frac{n-q}{2}+j-it\right)^{-1}\right\} \\[2mm]
& \times \left\{\prod_{j=0}^{\frac{(q-1)(p-1)}{2}}\left(\frac{(n-q)(p-1)}{2}+j\right)\left(\frac{(n-q)(p-1)}{2}+j-(p-1)it\right)^{-1}\right\} \\[2mm]
& \times \frac{\Gamma\left(\frac{n-1}{2}\right)\Gamma\left(\frac{n-2}{2}-it\right)}{\Gamma\left(\frac{n-2}{2}\right)\Gamma\left(\frac{n-1}{2}-it\right)}
\end{aligned}
$$

$$
= \left\{ \prod_{j=0}^{\frac{q-2}{2}-1} \left(\frac{n-q}{2} + j \right) \left(\frac{n-q}{2} + j - it \right)^{-1} \right\}
$$

$$
\times \left\{ \prod_{j=0}^{\frac{(q-1)(p-1)}{2}} \left(\frac{n-q}{2} + \frac{j}{p-1} \right) \left(\frac{n-q}{2} + \frac{j}{p-1} - it \right)^{-1} \right\}
$$

$$
\times \frac{\Gamma\left(\frac{n-1}{2}\right) \Gamma\left(\frac{n-2}{2} - it\right)}{\Gamma\left(\frac{n-2}{2}\right) \Gamma\left(\frac{n-1}{2} - it\right)}
$$

$$
= \underbrace{\left\{ \prod_{j=1}^{(q-1)(p-1)/2} \left(\frac{n-q}{2} + \frac{j-1}{p-1} \right)^{r_j^*} \left(\frac{n-q}{2} + \frac{j-1}{p-1} - it \right)^{-r_j^*} \right\}}_{\Phi_{W,1}(t)} \tag{16}
$$

$$
\times \underbrace{\frac{\Gamma\left(\frac{n-1}{2}\right) \Gamma\left(\frac{n-2}{2} - it\right)}{\Gamma\left(\frac{n-2}{2}\right) \Gamma\left(\frac{n-1}{2} - it\right)}}_{\Phi_{W,2}(t)},
$$

with the r_j^* defined in a similar manner to that in (15), now going through $(q-1)(p-1)/2$, that is, with

$$
r_j^* = \begin{cases} 1, & j = 1, \ldots, (q-1)(p-1)/2 \\ & j \neq (\ell-1)(p-1)+1 \text{ for } \ell = 1, \ldots, (q-2)/2 \\ 2, & j = (\ell-1)(p-1)+1 \text{ for } \ell = 1, \ldots, (q-2)/2. \end{cases} \tag{17}
$$

In (16) $\Phi_{W,1}(t)$ is now the c.f. of a GIG distribution of depth $(q-1)$ $(p-1)/2$ with shape parameters r_j^* and rate parameters $\frac{n-q}{2} + \frac{j-1}{p-1}$ $(j = 1, \ldots, (q-1)(p-1)/2)$ and, similarly to what we did before, will be left untouched. Once again based on the results in Sect. 5 of [11], we will asymptotically approximate $\Phi_{W,2}(t)$ which is the c.f. of a random variable whose exponential has a Beta distribution with a second parameter equal to $1/2$, by

$$
\Phi_2^*(t) = \sum_{k=0}^{m^*} \pi_k \, (\lambda^*)^{k+1/2} (\lambda^* - it)^{-(k+1/2)}
$$

which is the c.f. of a finite mixture of $Gamma\,(k+1/2, \lambda^*)$ distributions, where λ^* may be either taken as $(n-2)/2$, or alternatively, be computed in a similar manner to that used for even q and even p. This second choice would, mainly for values of p higher than 3, give near-exact distributions that will lie a little bit closer to the exact distribution.

By proceeding in this way we obtain

$$
\Phi_W^*(t) = \Phi_{W,1}(t) \, \Phi_2^*(t)
$$

as a near-exact c.f. for W, which will now yield as near-exact distributions for W mixtures with $m^* + 1$ components, each of which is a GNIG (Generalized Near-Integer Gamma) distribution of depth $(q-1)(p-1)/2 + 1$, with shape parameters r_j^* $(j = 1, \ldots, (q-1)(p-1)/2)$ and a last one equal to $k+1/2$, and corresponding rate parameters $(n-q)/2 + (j-1)/(p-1)$ and λ^*. See [4] and [9, Appendix B] for the GNIG distribution and the expressions for its p.d.f. and c.d.f..

This gives near-exact distributions for Λ with p.d.f.

$$f_\Lambda(z) = \sum_{k=0}^{m^*} \pi_k f^{GNIG}\left(\log z \,\middle|\, \{r_j^*\}_{j=1,\ldots,g}, k+\tfrac{1}{2}; \left\{ \frac{n-q}{2} + \frac{j-1}{p-1} \right\}_{j=1,\ldots,g}, \lambda^*; g+1 \right) \frac{1}{z}$$

and c.d.f.

$$F_\Lambda(z) = \sum_{k=0}^{m^*} \pi_k \left(1 - F^{GNIG}\left(\log z \middle| \{r_j^*\}_{j=1,\ldots,g}, k+\tfrac{1}{2}; \left\{ \frac{n-q}{2} + \frac{j-1}{p-1} \right\}_{j=1,\ldots,g}, \lambda^*; \right. \right.$$
$$\left. \left. g+1 \right) \right),$$

for $g = (q-1)(p-1)/2$ and r_j^* given by (17).

6 Numerical Studies

In order to evaluate the proximity of the near-exact distributions to the exact distribution we will use the measure

$$\Delta = \frac{1}{2\pi} \int_{-\infty}^{+\infty} \left| \frac{\Phi_W(t) - \Phi_W^*(t)}{t} \right| dt \tag{18}$$

Table 1. Values of the measure Δ in (18) for increasing values of p and increasing sample sizes $n = pq + \{2, 102, 502\}$, for near-exact distributions which match m^* exact moments

p	q	n	m^*			
			2	4	10	20
4	6	26	3.70×10^{-8}	1.05×10^{-11}	3.47×10^{-20}	6.24×10^{-28}
		126	3.29×10^{-10}	4.05×10^{-15}	1.11×10^{-26}	2.76×10^{-42}
		526	4.50×10^{-12}	3.14×10^{-18}	1.64×10^{-33}	5.32×10^{-55}
10	6	62	1.06×10^{-9}	8.14×10^{-15}	4.89×10^{-25}	7.13×10^{-39}
		162	5.98×10^{-11}	5.90×10^{-17}	1.22×10^{-29}	4.87×10^{-47}
		562	1.44×10^{-12}	1.09×10^{-19}	1.27×10^{-35}	2.19×10^{-58}
30	6	182	9.06×10^{-12}	2.98×10^{-19}	1.27×10^{-32}	3.05×10^{-52}
		282	2.44×10^{-12}	2.30×10^{-20}	9.77×10^{-35}	3.07×10^{-56}
		682	1.73×10^{-13}	1.42×10^{-22}	5.54×10^{-39}	2.42×10^{-64}

with

$$\Delta \geq \max_{w>0} |F_W(w) - F_W^*(w)| \quad \text{and} \quad \Delta \geq \max_{0<z<1} |F_{\Lambda^*}(z) - F_{\Lambda^*}^*(z)| , \quad (19)$$

and where $\Phi_W(t)$ and $\Phi_W^*(t)$ represent respectively the exact and the near-exact characteristic functions of W and $F_W(\cdot)$ and $F_W^*(\cdot)$ the corresponding cumulative distribution functions. For the derivation of the measure Δ in (18) and the relation in (19) see [7, Appendix A].

In Tables 1 and 2 we may analyze the values of the measure Δ in (18) for different even values of p and q and different sample sizes, and in Tables 3 and 4 the values of this measure for different odd values of p, with smaller values of Δ

Table 2. Values of the measure Δ in (18) for increasing values of q and increasing sample sizes $n = pq + \{2, 102, 502\}$, for near-exact distributions which match m^* exact moments

p	q	n	m^*			
			2	4	10	20
4	6	26	3.70×10^{-8}	1.05×10^{-11}	3.47×10^{-20}	6.24×10^{-28}
		126	3.29×10^{-10}	4.05×10^{-15}	1.11×10^{-26}	2.76×10^{-42}
		526	4.50×10^{-12}	3.14×10^{-18}	1.64×10^{-33}	5.32×10^{-55}
4	16	66	3.55×10^{-10}	5.37×10^{-15}	4.01×10^{-26}	3.42×10^{-40}
		166	2.63×10^{-11}	6.93×10^{-17}	3.05×10^{-30}	3.12×10^{-48}
		566	7.08×10^{-13}	1.66×10^{-19}	5.14×10^{-36}	3.95×10^{-59}
4	36	146	8.47×10^{-12}	1.10×10^{-17}	7.06×10^{-32}	4.45×10^{-51}
		246	2.07×10^{-12}	1.04×10^{-18}	3.92×10^{-34}	2.95×10^{-55}
		646	1.30×10^{-13}	1.02×10^{-20}	1.46×10^{-38}	1.09×10^{-63}

Table 3. Values of the measure Δ in (18) for even q, increasing odd values of p and increasing sample sizes $n = pq + \{2, 102, 502\}$, for near-exact distributions which match m^* exact moments

p	q	n	m^*			
			2	4	10	20
5	6	32	1.06×10^{-8}	2.54×10^{-12}	5.90×10^{-21}	1.30×10^{-30}
		132	1.47×10^{-10}	2.07×10^{-15}	2.74×10^{-27}	3.02×10^{-43}
		532	2.22×10^{-12}	1.90×10^{-18}	5.87×10^{-34}	1.05×10^{-55}
11	6	68	3.44×10^{-10}	9.27×10^{-15}	1.03×10^{-25}	1.07×10^{-39}
		168	2.25×10^{-11}	9.86×10^{-17}	5.47×10^{-30}	7.98×10^{-48}
		568	5.76×10^{-13}	2.20×10^{-19}	8.18×10^{-36}	8.44×10^{-59}
31	6	188	3.44×10^{-12}	4.56×10^{-18}	8.69×10^{-33}	8.83×10^{-53}
		288	9.54×10^{-13}	5.37×10^{-19}	7.97×10^{-35}	1.36×10^{-56}
		688	6.97×10^{-14}	6.86×10^{-21}	5.46×10^{-39}	1.68×10^{-64}

showing a better agreement between the near-exact and the corresponding exact distribution.

We may see how all the near-exact distributions exhibit extremely low values of the measure Δ and how they display a clear asymptotic behavior not only for increasing sample sizes but also for increasing values of p, the number of variables involved, as well as for increasing values of q, the number of populations involved.

Noticeably, even for very small sample sizes the near-exact distributions exhibit extremely low values of Δ, showing their extreme closeness to the exact distribution, even for these very small sample sizes.

As expected, near-exact distributions with higher values of m^* show lower values of the measure Δ, given that m^* is the number of exact moments of W that are matched by these near-exact distributions.

Table 4. Values of the measure Δ in (18) for odd p, increasing even values of q and increasing sample sizes $n = pq + \{2, 102, 502\}$, for near-exact distributions which match m^* exact moments

p	q	n	m^*			
			2	4	10	20
5	6	32	1.06×10^{-8}	2.54×10^{-12}	5.90×10^{-21}	1.30×10^{-30}
		132	1.47×10^{-10}	2.07×10^{-15}	2.74×10^{-27}	3.02×10^{-43}
		532	2.22×10^{-12}	1.90×10^{-18}	5.87×10^{-34}	1.05×10^{-55}
5	16	82	1.00×10^{-10}	1.24×10^{-15}	1.61×10^{-27}	2.05×10^{-43}
		182	1.02×10^{-11}	2.74×10^{-17}	3.85×10^{-31}	7.90×10^{-50}
		582	3.30×10^{-13}	8.90×10^{-20}	1.28×10^{-36}	3.42×10^{-60}
31	6	188	2.40×10^{-12}	2.53×10^{-18}	2.57×10^{-33}	1.05×10^{-53}
		288	7.15×10^{-13}	3.35×10^{-19}	2.99×10^{-35}	2.45×10^{-57}
		688	5.58×10^{-14}	4.77×10^{-21}	2.54×10^{-39}	4.32×10^{-65}

7   Conclusions

The method used to analyze and factorize the characteristic function of the negative logarithm of the likelihood ratio statistic, with the help of the relation (12), proved itself extremely useful. It not only enabled us to obtain, for odd q, that is, for an odd number of the populations involved, the exact distribution of the negative logarithm of the likelihood ratio statistic as a GIG distribution, which is a very manageable distribution, but also allowed for the development of very sharp near-exact distributions for even q. As noted in Subsect. 5.2, when q is even and p is odd, it is possible to obtain even sharper near-exact distributions than those obtained in Subsect. 5.1 for even p and even q. Although, as expected, the near-exact distributions display a much better closeness to the exact distribution as the value of m^*, the number of exact moments of W matched by these near-exact distributions, increases, even for very small values of m^* the near-exact distributions display a great closeness to the exact distribution and a clear asymptotic behavior not only for increasing sample sizes but also for increasing values of the number of populations involved, and opposite to the common asymptotic distributions, also for increasing numbers of variables involved, always with very good performances for very small samples sizes, even for large values of p, the number of variables involved.

Acknowledgements. Research supported by FCT–Fundação para a Ciência e a Tecnologia (Portuguese Foundation for Science and Technology), project UID/MAT/ 00297/2013, through Centro de Matemática e Aplicações (CMA/FCT-UNL).

References

1. Anderson, T.W.: An Introduction to Multivariate Statistical Analysis, 3rd edn. Wiley, Hoboken (2003)
2. Arnold, B.C., Coelho, C.A., Marques, F.J.: The distribution of the product of powers of independent Uniform random variables - a simple but useful tool to address and better understand the structure of some distributions. J. Multivariate Anal. **113**, 19–36 (2013)
3. Coelho, C.A.: The generalized integer Gamma distribution - a basis for distributions in Multivariate Statistics. J. Multivariate Anal. **64**, 86–102 (1998)
4. Coelho, C.A.: The generalized near-integer Gamma distribution: a basis for ear-exactapproximations to the distribution of statistics which are the product of an odd number of independent Beta random variables. J. Multivariate Anal. **89**, 191–218 (2004)
5. Coelho, C.A., Arnold, B.C., Marques, F.J.: Near-exact distributions for certain likelihood ratio test statistics. J. Stat. Theory Pract. **4**, 711–725 (2010)
6. Coelho, C.A., Roy, A.: Testing the hypothesis of a block compound symmetric covariance matrix for elliptically contoured distributions. TEST (in print)
7. Grilo, L.M., Coelho, C.A.: The exact and near-exact distributions for the statistic used to test the reality of covariance matrix in a Complex Normal distribution. In: Bebiano, N. (ed.) Applied and Computational Matrix Analysis, pp. 295–315. Springer, New York (2017)
8. Kshirsagar, A.M.: Multivariate Analysis. Marcel Dekker, New York (1972)
9. Marques, F.J., Coelho, C.A., Arnold, B.C.: A general near-exact distribution theory for the most common likelihood ratio test statistics used in Multivariate Analysis. TEST **20**, 180–203 (2011)
10. Muirhead, R.J.: Aspects of Multivariate Statistical Theory, 2nd edn. Wiley, Hoboken (2005)
11. Tricomi, F.G., Erdélyi, A.: The asymptotic expansion of a ratio of gamma functions. Pacific J. Math. **1**, 133–142 (1951)

Approximating a Retarded-Advanced Differential Equation Using Radial Basis Functions

M. Filomena Teodoro[1,2(✉)]

[1] CEMAT, Instituto Superior Técnico, Lisbon University,
Av. Rovisco Pais, 1, 1048-001 Lisbon, Portugal
maria.alves.teodoro@marinha.pt
[2] CINAV, Naval Academy, Base Naval de Lisboa, Alfeite, 1910-001 Almada, Portugal

Abstract. In last years we have got the approximation of the solution of a linear mixed type functional differential equation, considering the autonomous and non-autonomous case by collocation, least squares and finite element methods considering a polynomial basis. The present work introduces a numerical scheme using collocation and radial basis functions to solve numerically the non-linear mixed type equation with symmetric delay and advance. The results are similar using collocation, B-splines and exponential radial functions. The preliminary results are promising, but more simulations using different basis of radial functions are needed.

Keywords: Mixed type functional differential equation · Numerical approach · Numerical solution · Radial basis function

1 Introduction

In applied sciences, many mathematical models show up functional differential equations with delayed and advanced arguments, the mixed type functional differential equations (MTFDEs). In this class of functional differential equations with delay-advanced argument, the derivative of unknown function depends on itself evaluated in delayed, advanced and on time values of argument.

MTFDEs appear in a wide array of different areas of knowledge such as optimal control [18,19], economic dynamics [20], nerve conduction [3,4,7,14,22], traveling waves in a spatial lattice [1,17], aeroelastic oscillatory phenomena [11,15,34] which often appear in physiology (e.g. human phonation), quantum photonic systems [2]. We are particularly interested in the numerical approximation of the multi-delay-advance differential equation

$$x'(t) = F(t, x(t), x(t - \tau_1), \ldots, x(t - \tau_n)), \qquad \tau_i \in \mathbb{R}, \qquad i = 1, \ldots, n, \quad (1)$$

where the shifts τ_i may take negative or positive values.

© Springer International Publishing AG 2017
O. Gervasi et al. (Eds.): ICCSA 2017, Part V, LNCS 10408, pp. 33–43, 2017.
DOI: 10.1007/978-3-319-62404-4_3

Some numerical methods to approximate the solution of a linear MTFDE were introduced in [8,9] and improved in [12,30,31]. More recently, these methods were adapted and used to solve numerically a nonlinear MTFDE [14,24,29], the FitzHugh-Nagumo equation.

Actually, we pretend to calculate numerical solutions of a particular case of a nonlinear MTFDE which models the vibration of some elastics tissues, by the interaction of a flowing fluid (air, blood,...) with an elastic structure tissue, denominated aeroelastic oscillatory phenomena (AOP). The AOP occurs frequently in physiology. Particularly, the considered model characterizes the oscillation superficial wave propagating through the tissues in the direction of the flow. This model was initially introduced by the author of [33,34]. He proposed a mucosal wave model where a surface wave represents the motion of vocal tissues. Some variants of the this model were presented in several studies in phonation dynamics. In [23], a preliminary approach was introduced where a numerical scheme was adapted from algorithms resulting from earlier work in [14,29]. In [25,27] the previous results were extended using collocation (COLL), finite element method (FEM), method of steps (MS) and Newton method (NM) to obtain the approximate solution of the mucosal wave model. Using some ideas presented in [6,21], where homotopy analysis method (HAM) is used to solve linear and non linear delay differential equations, the work in [26] describes a preliminary approach where HAM is applied to get the solution of the mixed type differential equation under study.

The outline of this work consists in seven sections. Section 2 presents some preliminaries results, namely the method of steps theorem relatively to an autonomous mixed-type functional differential equation. Section 3 introduces the problem to solve, the mucosal wave model. Some radial basis functions are detailed in Sect. 4. The method is described in Sect. 5. In Sect. 6 we make some discussion about the results and get some conclusions. The ackowledgements are done in last section.

2   Preliminaries

In present section, we revisit the MS for a linear non-autonomous MTFDE with the form

$$x'(t) = \alpha(t)x(t) + \beta(t)x(t-1) + \gamma(t)x(t+1), \tag{2}$$

where x is the unknown function, α, β and γ are known functions. In order to analyze and solve this BVP of (2) which satisfies the boundary conditions

$$x(t) = \begin{cases} \varphi_1(t), & \text{if } t \in [-1,0], \\ f(t), & \text{if } t \in (k-1,k], \end{cases} \tag{3}$$

where φ_1 and f are smooth real-valued functions, defined on $[-1,0]$ and $(k-1,k]$, respectively ($1 < k \in \mathbb{N}$), one solves the equation over successive intervals of unitary length. We need to assume the non-degeneracy condition that $\gamma(t) \neq 0$, for $t \geq 0$, so that Eq. (2) can be rewritten in the form

$$x(t+1) = a(t)x'(t) + b(t)x(t-1) + c(t)x(t), \quad t \geq 0 \tag{4}$$

where $a(t) = \frac{1}{\gamma(t)}$, $b(t) = -\frac{\beta(t)}{\gamma(t)}$ and $c(t) = -\frac{\alpha(t)}{\gamma(t)}$.

MS is used usually in delay differential equations (DDEs) which extend a known solution of equation in an interval to a larger interval. Its a way to increase our knowledge about the solutions of (2) as well as it provides us sufficient conditions for the existence of solution for this kind of MTFDE. We have looked for a differentiable solution x on an interval $[-1, k]$, $k \in \mathbb{N}$, given its values on the intervals $[-1, 0]$ and $(k-1, k]$. In next theorem is formulated this result in more precise terms. The main idea of the Theorem 1 is to get a particular solution x of Eq. (2) such us

$$x(t) = \varphi(t), \quad t \in [-1, 1], \tag{5}$$

where the function φ is defined by

$$\varphi(t) = \begin{cases} \varphi_1(t), & \text{if } t \in [-1, 0], \\ \varphi_2(t), & \text{if } t \in (0, 1], \end{cases} \tag{6}$$

constructed using the MS, becomes *less smooth* as time increases. The conclusions on smoothness for the solution constructed using the MS is summarized in the Theorem 1.

Theorem 1. *Let x be the solution of problem (4), (6), where*

$$\alpha(t), \quad \beta(t), \quad \gamma(t) \in C^{2L}([-1, 2L+1]), \quad \gamma(t) \neq 0, \quad t \in [-1, 2L+1], \tag{7}$$
$$\varphi_1(t) \in C^{2L+1}([-1, 0]), \quad \varphi_2(t) \in C^{2L+1}([0, 1]) \quad \text{for some } L \in \mathbb{N}.$$

Moreover, suppose that

$$\varphi_1^{(\ell)}(0^-) = \varphi_2^{(\ell)}(0^+),$$
$$\varphi_2(1) = a(0)\varphi_1'(0^-) + b(0)\varphi_1(-1) + c(0)\varphi_1(0);$$
$$\varphi_2^{(\ell)}(1^-) = \frac{d^\ell}{dt^\ell}\left(a(t)\varphi_1'(t) + b(t)\varphi_1(t-1) + c(t)\varphi_1(t)\right)\big|_{t=0^-}, \ell = 0, 1, 2, \ldots, 2L+1. \tag{8}$$

Then there exist functions $\delta_{i,l}$, $\epsilon_{i,l}$, $\bar{\delta}_{i,l}$, $\bar{\epsilon}_{i,l} \in C([-1, 2L+1])$, $l = 1, \ldots, L$, $i = 0, 1, \ldots, 2l$, such that the following formulae are valid:

$$x(t) = \sum_{i=0}^{2l-1} \delta_{i,l}(t)\varphi_1^{(i)}(t-2l) + \sum_{i=0}^{2l-1} \epsilon_{i,l}(t)\varphi_2^{(i)}(t-2l+1), \quad t \in [2l-1, 2l];$$
$$x(t) = \sum_{i=0}^{2l} \bar{\epsilon}_{i,l}(t)\varphi_2^{(i)}(t-2+l) + \sum_{i=0}^{2l-1} \bar{\delta}_{i,l}(t)\varphi_1^{(i)}(t-2l-1), \quad t \in [2l, 2l+1]$$
$$l = 1, 2, \ldots. \tag{9}$$

Moreover, the solution x, constructed according to the formulae (9), belongs to the class

$$C^{2L+1}([-1, 1)) \bigcap C^{2L}([-1, 2)) \bigcap \cdots \bigcap C^1([-1, 2L+1)). \tag{10}$$

A detailed proof by induction was provided in [28].

3   The Problem

We intend to compute the numerical solution of an equation from acoustics which is associated to mucosal wave model of the vocal oscillation during phonation. As described in [34], the first principle is that vocal fold oscillation is flow induced. The glottal airstream and the yielding duct wall, the vocal folds, consist in a mechanical system which can show some instability under some flow conditions. In this situation, a transfer of energy from the glottal airstream to the tissue will overcome frictional energy losses. The range of oscillation is determined by combination of inertial and elastic properties (mass and stiffness) and geometry of vocal folds. When the net aerodynamic driving force has a component in phase with tissue velocity, it is realized a positive flow of energy from the airstream. If we take a system which consists in a mass-spring oscillator

$$M\xi'' + B\xi' + K\xi = f(\xi', \xi, t), \tag{11}$$

where t is the time, M, B and K are mass, damping and stiffness, respectively, ξ, ξ' and ξ'' are displacement, velocity and acceleration respectivelly, f the diving force. The situation of interest is when we get an autonomous differential equation. It occurs when f does not depend on time. In such case the system oscillates by itself. Another important issue for oscillation is how f is related with ξ'. If f and ξ' have the save direction, as illustrated in the scheme represented in Fig. 1, energy is transmitted to the mass, in the opposite situation, the energy is taken out the mass.

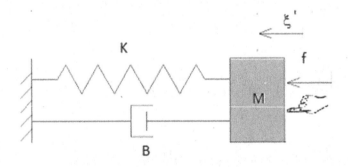

Fig. 1. Mechanical oscillator. Velocity ξ' and driving force f in same direction.

In [11], Libermann describes some ways in which the glottal airstream can provide a driving force that depends on velocity. In some way, the system needs to change the effective driving force on alternate cycles. The same force sucks the vocal folds together prior to closure works and invert direction so it can cancel partially the impulse resulting from prior to closure. This process of reverting the driving force direction is done using different mechanisms which can be simultaneous: deforming the glottal geometry so can exist different intraglottal pressure distributions or making use of the oppositely phased supraglottal and subglottal pressures.

Returning to our objective, we intend to compute the numerical solution of the equation which is associated to mucosal wave model of the vocal oscillation during phonation. The model was proposed in [33] and it can be represented by a geometric scheme where the vocal fold is represented by a trapezoidal glottal configuration associated to mucosal wave model of the vocal fold oscillation during phonation.

It is assumed left-right symmetry and the motion of tissues is done in the horizontal direction. Can be shown that the wave propagates through the superficial tissues, in the upward direction of the airflow. In the simplest case, these waves can be represented using an one-dimensional wave equation with wave velocity c, $\frac{\partial^2 \xi}{\partial t^2} = c^2 \frac{\partial^2 \xi}{\partial z^2}$ with solution given by the general d'Alembert solution. The expression of tissue displacement is given by

$$\xi(z,t) = x(t - \frac{z}{c}), \tag{12}$$

where $x(t) = \xi(0,t)$ is the tissue displacement at midpoint of glottis. We can notice from (12) that the propagation of mucosal wave causes a time delay from bottom to top of vocal fold. In [33] Titze verifies that this delay helps to get some necessary instabilities for the oscillation of vocal fold.

If the prephonatory glottis has a linear (trapezoidal) dependence, we get

$$\xi_0(z) = \frac{(\xi_{01} + \xi_{02})}{2} - (\xi_{01} - \xi_{02})\frac{z}{T}, \tag{13}$$

where ξ_{01} and ξ_{02} are the inferior and superior glottal half widths; T is the vocal fold thickness.

The wave travels to the edges of vocal fold at $z = \pm T/2$, upper and lower edges respectively, the time delay τ is given by $\tau = T/2c$, which conduces to glottal upper and lower areas

$$a_1 = 2L[\xi_{01} + x(t + \tau)], \ a_2 = 2L[\xi_{02} + x(t - \tau)]. \tag{14}$$

Equations (14) are defined at glottis midpoint (it means that the biomechanical properties of the tissues are lumped at midpoint of the glottis).

When a general trapezoidal glottal configuration is replaced by the rectangular case, the prephonatory glottis has no linear dependence on z, being constant in any point of glottis where $\xi_{01} = \xi_{02} = x_0$.

Geometrically, it is assumed a very simple case, where the vocal fold width is constant along glottis when in rest position, with cross sectional area given by $a = 2L(x_0 + \xi)$.

With rectangular glottal configuration, Eqs. (14) are rewritten as follows. The time delay τ is the time that the wave travels to the edges of vocal fold at $z = \pm T/2$ (upper and lower edges respectively) which conduces to glottal upper and lower areas, it is given by $\tau = T/2c$ and we get

$$a_1 = 2L[x_0 + x(t + \tau], \ a_2 = 2L[x_0 + x(t - \tau]. \tag{15}$$

The mathematical model which describes the displacement of tissue is obtained imposing the assumptions:

(i) The pressure at exit of glottis (P_g) equals the atmospheric pressure;
(ii) The sub-glottal pressure equals the lung pressure (P_l);
(iii) The air flow is incompressible, frictionless and stationary;
(iv) The glottis is open ($a_1 > 0$).

We consider the mechanical behavior of tissues focused at mid point of glottis. $x(t)$ is the displacement of tissues at the midpoint of the glottis. The equation of motion, a nonlinear MTFDE with deviating arguments, has the form

$$Mx''(t) + Bx'(t) + Kx(t) = P_g, \tag{16}$$

or

$$Mx''(t) + Bx'(t) + Kx(t) = \frac{P_L}{k_t} \frac{x(t-\tau) - x(t+\tau)}{x_0 + x(t+\tau)}, \tag{17}$$

where P_g is the average glottal pressure, k_t is the transglottal pressure coefficient and $x_0 + x(t+\tau) > 0$. The parameters M, B, K, are, respectively, the effective mass, damping and stiffness per area unit of vocal fold medial surface. The model (17) is also applied in other physiological systems such as avian syrinx, snore, or a flow passing a constricted channel (artery, lips, soft palate, nostrils).

An advantage of the rectangular glottis configuration is that it can clarify the importance of prephonatory glottal width x_0 for oscillation threshold: the closer the vocal folds are brought together, the easier is to begin a small amplitude oscillation. In [33] Titze assumes small values of τ, making possible to consider the first order (linear) approximation of the expansion of solution (12) in a Taylor series around glottis midpoint ($z = 0$). When we consider that mucosal wave has a small time delay [33], Eq. (17) becomes an autonomous ordinary differential equation, analytically solvable for some values of parameters. This model is similar to the one introduced in [10]. The author of [15,16] considered a more realistic issue: an arbitrary time delay for mucosal wave.

4   Radial Basis Functions

Radial basis functions are those functions which have radial symmetry, that is, depend on only (beyond some known parameters) of the distance $r = \|x - x_j\|$, between the center of the function x_j, $j = 1, \ldots, N$, $N \in \mathbb{N}$ and the generic point x, and can be written generically in the form $\phi(r)$.

With such a general definition there will, therefore, be infinite functions of this kind. These functions can be classified as global (said to have global support) or local (Compact or local support) depending on whether they are defined in the entire domain or only partially of this [5].

The types of global support functions $\phi(r)$ include:

– Multiquadrics (MQ):

$$\sqrt{(x - x_j)^2 + (c_j^2)}, \qquad c_j \geq 0; \tag{18}$$

- Inverse Multiquadrics (IMQ):

$$((x - x_j)^2 + (c_j^2))^{-\frac{1}{2}}, \ c_j \geq 0; \tag{19}$$

- Inverse Multiquadratics (IMQT):

$$((x - x_j)^2 + (c_j^2))^{-1}, \ c_j \geq 0; \tag{20}$$

- Gaussians (G):

$$e^{(-c\ r^2)}, \ c > 0; \tag{21}$$

- Polyharmonic Splines (PS):

$$\phi(r) = r^k, \ k = 1, 3, 5, \ldots; \tag{22}$$
$$\phi(r) = r^k \ln(r), \ k = 2, 4, 6, \ldots; \tag{23}$$

- Thin plate splines (TPS): Particular case of PS, for $k = 2$,

$$r^{2\beta} lnr, \quad \beta \in \mathbb{N}. \tag{24}$$

Compact support radial basis functions are, for example, those of

- Wu and Wendland:

$$(1 - r)^n_+ + P(r) \tag{25}$$

where $P(r)$ is a polynomial and $(1 - r)^n_+$ is 0 for r greater than the support;
- Buhmann:

$$\frac{1}{3} + r^2 - \frac{4}{3}r^3 + 2r^2 lnr. \tag{26}$$

Radial basis functions are typically used to build up function approximations of the form

$$y(x) = \sum_{j=1}^{N} w_j \, \phi(\|x - x_j\|), \tag{27}$$

where the approximating function $y(x)$ is represented as a sum of N radial basis functions, each associated with a different center x_i, and weighted by an appropriate coefficient w_i, $j = 1, \ldots, N$, $N \in \mathbb{N}$. The weights w_j, $j = 1, \ldots, N$, $N \in \mathbb{N}$ can be estimated [32] using the matrix methods of linear least squares, COLL, FEM (the approximating function is linear in the weights).

5 Numerical Approach

Previously, distinct computational methods to get the numerical solution of autonomous and non-autonomous linear MTFDEs (2) with symmetric delay and advance, using COLL, least squares and FEM described in [12,13,31], using B-splines as basis of functions. In [14,22,29], it was studied the numerical solution of a nonlinear MTFDE with deviating arguments from nerve conduction theory, with the form (1).

Recently [26], a preliminary approach introduced a numerical scheme using the work presented in [12, 13, 22] to solve numerically (17) applying the generalization of MS to the case using the formula (9) whose demonstration was done in [28], based on Bellman's MS for delay differential equations. In [12], one solves a linear equation over successive unitary intervals. In the case of [22], the equation is solved for successive intervals of length τ. Doing some algebraic manipulation and simplification, we get the following formula

$$u(t + \tau) = -p_n(t)(u''(t) + \alpha u') + u(t - \tau) + g(u(t)), \qquad (28)$$

where $u = x/x_0$, $g(u(t)) = -p_n(t)\omega^2 u(t)$ and $p_n(t)$ a polinomial function with order $n \in \mathbb{N}$. Supposing that all the derivatives of u exist in $(a - 2\tau, a]$, in order to simplify the calculations, we can use the formula (28) to extend the solution for Eq. (17) to an interval $[a, a + k\tau]$ (where k is an integer and a some adequate value), starting from its initial values in $[a - 2\tau, a]$; these starting values are calculated using the solution of Eq. (17) taking into account the small amplitude approximation, which can be found in formula (25) of [33]. After some computation, we may obtain explicitly the expressions for the solution in successive intervals $(a, a + \tau]$, $(a + \tau, a + 2\tau)$, …… Using this process, we can extend the solution to any interval, provided that the initial functions in the first two intervals with length τ are smooth enough functions and satisfy some simple relationships.

The numerical schemes described in [25] are generalizations from the algorithm presented in [14, 22], using a uniform mesh. They can be summarized in three steps:

1st- The initial boundary functions are essential to proceed and implement the numerical approach. The initial step consists in the determination of the boundary conditions using the Titze approximation [33]:

$$\begin{cases} u(t) = \phi_0(t), & t \in [-R - \tau, -R]; \\ u(t) = \phi_1(t), & t \in [R, R + \tau], \end{cases} \qquad (29)$$

where $\phi_0(t)$ and $\phi_1(t)$ are the boundary functions, the solution of (17) using the small amplitude delay approximation (formula (25) in [33], R some positive real multiple of τ. Once the boundary functions are defined, we are able to apply the more recent approaches and techniques using the adapted MS for the nonlinear case (17). Using MS, we can extend the solution to any interval, provided that the initial functions in the first two intervals with a specific length (τ) are smooth enough functions and satisfy some simple relationships.

2nd - Reduction the nonlinear Eq. (17) to a sequence of linear equations using NM.

3rd - The COLL and FEM are applied separately to linearized equation using B-Splines as basis functions. In work presented in [26], 3rd step which corresponds to COLL or FEM implementation, we do not apply B-splines as basis of the approximating function. Instead, we apply HAM to linearized equation, similarly to [6] or to nonlinear equation (17), like the authors of [21]. The ongoing work evaluates the results obtained when we use another kind of basis functions: the radial basis functions. We still are comparing the different available sets performance.

6   Conclusion and Final Remarks

The parameters of model were chosen accordingly with [33], page 1543. The authors of [25] determined the absolute error ϵ_N (2-norm) and the estimated order of convergence $p = log_2\epsilon_{2N}/log_2\epsilon_N$ of approximate solution of (17), when it was considered an uniform mesh, $x_0 = 0.04$ cm and $x_0 = 0.16$ cm. ϵ_N and p were estimated using COLL and FEM methods. The accuracy of numerical results was adequate for both set of parameters and for both methods. The estimated order of convergence p is compatible with the expected one, $p \approx 2$ in COLL case, but it is lower, $p \approx 2$, in FEM case, for the two set of parameters. In the present, the results obtained using radial basis functions set have enough accuracy when compared with the results in [25]. The results are similar using COLL, B-splines and exponential radial functions. The preliminary results are promising, but more simulations using different basis of radial functions are needed.

Acknowledgements. This work was supported by Portuguese funds through the *Center for Computational and Stochastic Mathematics* (CEMAT), *The Portuguese Foundation for Science and Technology* (FCT), University of Lisbon, Portugal, project UID/Multi-/04621/2013, and *Center of Naval Research* (CINAV), Naval Academy, Portuguese Navy, Portugal.

References

1. Abell, K., Elmer, C., Humphries, A., Vleck, E.V.: Computation of mixed type functional differential boundary value problems. SIADS - SIAM J. Appl. Dyn. Syst. **4**, 755–781 (2005)
2. Alvarez-Rodriguez, U., Perez-Leija, A., Egusquiza, I., Grfe, M., Sanz, M., Lamata, L., Szameit, A., Solano, E.: Advanced-retarded differential equations in quantum photonic systems. Sci. Rep. **7** (2017). Art. no. 42933
3. Bell, J.: Behaviour of some models of myelinated axons. IMA J. Math. Appl. Med. Biol. **1**, 149–167 (1984)
4. Bell, J., Cosner, C.: Threshold conditions for a diffusive model of a myelinated axon. J. Math. Biol. **18**, 39–52 (1983)
5. Buhmann, M.: Radial Basis Functions: Theory and Implementations. Cambridge University Press, Cambridge (2003)
6. Caruntu, B., Bota, C.: Analytical approximate solutions for a general class of nonlinear delay differential equations. Sci. World J. **2014**, 6 (2014). iD 631416
7. Chi, H., Bell, J., Hassard, B.: Numerical solution of a nonlinear advance-delay-differential equation from nerve conduction. J. Math. Biol. **24**, 583–601 (1986)
8. Ford, N., Lumb, P.: Mixed-type functional differential equations: a numerical approach. J. Comput. Appl. Math. **229**(2), 471–479 (2009)

9. Iakovleva, V., Vanegas, C.: On the solution of differential equations withe delayed and advanced arguments. Electron. J. Differ. Equ. Conf. **13**, 57–63 (2005)
10. Ishizaka, K., Matsudaira, M.: Fluid Mechanical Considerations of Vocal Cord Vibration. Speech Communications Research Laboratory, monography 8 (1972)
11. Ishizaka, K., Matsudaira, M.: Speech Physiology and Acoustic Phonetics. MacMillan, New York (1977)
12. Lima, P., Teodoro, M., Ford, N., Lumb, P.: Analytical and numerical investigation of mixed type functional differential equations. J. Comput. Appl. Math. **234**, 2732–2744 (2010)
13. Lima, P., Teodoro, M., Ford, N., Lumb, P.: Finite element solution of a linear mixed-type functional differential equation. Numer. Algorithms **55**, 301–320 (2010)
14. Lima, P., Teodoro, M., Ford, N., Lumb, P.: Analysis and computational approximation of a forward-backward equation arising in nerve conduction. In: Pinelas, S., Chipot, M., Dosla, Z. (eds.) Differential and Difference Equations with Applications. Springer Proceedings in Mathematics & Statistics, vol. 47, pp. 475–483. Springer, New York (2013)
15. Lucero, J.: Advanced-delay equations for aerolastics oscillations in physiology. Biophys. Rev. Lett. **3**, 125–133 (2008)
16. Lucero, J.: A lumped mucosal wave model of vocal folds revisited: recent extensions and oscillation hysteresis. J. Acoust. Soc. Am. **129**, 1568–1579 (2011)
17. Mallet-Paret, J.: The global structure of traveling waves in spatially discrete dynamical systems. J. Dyn. Differ. Equ. **11**, 49–128 (1999)
18. Pontryagin, L., Boltyanskii, V., Gamkrelidze, R., Mishchenko, E.: The Mathematical Theory of Optimal Process. Interscience, New York (1962)
19. Rustichini, A.: Functional differential equations of mixed type: the linear autonomous case. J. Dyn. Differ. Equ. **1**, 121–143 (1989)
20. Rustichini, A.: Hopf bifurcation for functional differential equations of mixed type. J. Dyn. Differ. Equ. **1**, 145–177 (1989)
21. Shakery, F., Dehghan, M.: Solution of delay differential equations via a homotopy perturbation method. Math. Comput. Model. **48**, 486–498 (2008)
22. Teodoro, M.F.: Numerical solution of a forward-backward equation from physiology (accepted for publication in Applied Mathematics and Information Sciences)
23. Teodoro, M.F.: Numerical approximation of a delay-advanced equation from acoustics. In: Vigo-Aguiar, J., et al. (eds.) Mathematical Methods in Science and Engineering, pp. 1086–1089. CMMSE, Spain (2015)
24. Teodoro, M.F.: Numerical approach of a nonlinear forward-backward equation. Int. J. Math. Comput. Methods **1**, 75–78 (2016)
25. Teodoro, M.F.: Numerical solution of a delay-advanced equation from acoustics. Int. J. Mech. **11**, 107–114 (2017)
26. Teodoro, M.: Approximating a nonlinear advanced-delayed equation from acoustics. In: Sergeyev, Y.D., Kvasov, D.E., Accio, F.D., Mukhametzhanov, M.S. (eds.) AIP Conference Proceedings. Numerical Computations: Theory and Algorithms. vol. 1776. AIP, Melville (2016)
27. Teodoro, M.: Modelling a nonlinear mtfde from acoustics. In: Simos, T., Tsitouras, C. (eds.) AIP Conference Proceedings. Num. Anal. and App. Math., vol. 1738. AIP, Melville (2016)
28. Teodoro, M.: An issue about the existence of solutions for a linear non-autonomous MTFDE. In: Pinelas, S., Došlá, Z., Došý, O., Kloeden, P. (eds.) Differential and Difference Equations with Applications. Proceedings in Mathematics &Statistics, vol. 164. Springer, Cham (2016)

29. Teodoro, M., Lima, P., Ford, N.J., Lumb, P.: Numerical approximation of a non-linear delay-advance functional differential equations by a finite element method. In: Simos, T., Psihoyios, G., Tsitouras, C., Anastassi, Z. (eds.) AIP Conference Proceedings. Num. Anal. and App. Math., vol. 1479, pp. 406–409. AIP, Melville (2012)

30. Teodoro, M., Lima, P., Ford, N., Lumb, P.: Numerical modelling of a functional differential equation with deviating arguments using a collocation method. In: Simos, T., Psihoyios, G., Tsitouras, C. (eds.) AIP Conference Proceedings. Num. Anal. and App. Math., vol. 1048, pp. 553–557. AIP, Melville (2008)

31. Teodoro, M., Lima, P., Ford, N., Lumb, P.: New approach to the numerical solution of forward-backward equations. Front. Math. China **4**, 155–168 (2009)

32. Tiago, C., Leitão, V.: Utilização de funções de base radial em problemas unidimensionais de análise estrutural. In: Goicolea, J.M., Soares, C.M., Pastor, M., Bugeda, G. (eds.) Métodos Numéricos em Engenieria, vol. V, SEMNI (2002). (in Portuguese)

33. Titze, I.: The physics of small amplitude oscillation of the vocal folds. J. Acoust. Soc. Am. **83**, 1536–1552 (1988)

34. Titze, I.: Principles of Voice Production. Prentice-Hall, Englewood Cliffs (1994)

Questioning Caregivers About Pediatric High Blood Pressure

M. Filomena Teodoro[1,2(✉)], Carla Simão[3,4], and Andreia Romana[4]

[1] CINAV, Portuguese Naval Academy, Portuguese Navy, Base Naval de Lisboa,
Alfeite, 2810-001 Almada, Portugal
maria.alves.teodoro@marinha.pt
[2] CEMAT - Center for Computational and Stochastic Mathematics,
Instituto Superior Técnico, Lisbon University,
Avenida Rovisco Pais, n. 1, 1048-001 Lisboa, Portugal
[3] Medicine Faculty, Lisbon University,
Avenida Professor Egas Moniz, 1600-190 Lisboa, Portugal
[4] Pediatric Department, Santa Maria's Hospital, Centro Hospitalar Lisboa Norte,
Avenida Professor Egas Moniz, 1600-190 Lisboa, Portugal

Abstract. Children caregivers must know the pediatric high blood pressure existence, the consequences associated with it, the risk factors and it's prevention. In [12,13] can be found a statistical data analysis using a simpler questionnaire introduced in [4] under the aim of a preliminary study about pediatric arterial hypertension caregivers acquaintance. The present article presents a preliminary analysis of a questionnaire applied to children caregivers and filled online. The questionnaire structure consists in 15 questions which were built under the aim of easy and quick answer. We have developed multivariate techniques to get models with enough explication of the data.

Keywords: Pediatric hypertension · Caregiver · Questionnaire · Statistical approach · Factorial analysis

1 Introduction

The Pediatric arterial hypertension (PAH) is a severe public health difficult occurrence present since childhood [2], with no visible symptoms at first sight, and an early diagnosis is got by the measurement of regular blood pressure (BP) in regular consultations. PAH complicates numerous functions in the body of the children still in development. A clinical and therapeutic approach to the family, instead of a focused intervention only for the patient, it is commonly more efficient [10].

The diagnosis of pediatric hypertension (PH) should be based on multiple measurements of BP in medical office environment and at different times [8]. The current recommendation of the European Society of Hypertension (ESH) [8] is the inclusion of the practice assessment arterial blood pressure (ABP) in

© Springer International Publishing AG 2017
O. Gervasi et al. (Eds.): ICCSA 2017, Part V, LNCS 10408, pp. 44–53, 2017.
DOI: 10.1007/978-3-319-62404-4_4

all children above three years of age, in all health surveillance pediatric attendees, and below this age, if there exist risk factors. The access of these standards guides enabled the detection of cases of secondary asymptomatic hypertension, which otherwise would be hidden. On the other hand, moderate elevations in BP during childhood are more usual than it was thought, particularly in teenagers. In [1] Ahern highlights PH as a growing problem in health care, which is under-diagnosed [6, 7].

The description of actual ongoing work, firstly was introduced in [14], consists in five sections. Section 2 describes some questionnaire details. Section 3 introduces factorial analysis as a statistical method to reduce the dimension (the number of variables). Data handling is done in Sect. 4. A random sample of 182 individuals were given out and 178 were selected. In last Sect. 5 we make some discussion about the results and get some conclusions.

2   Questionnaire

An observational and descriptive study was carried out, with the target population being the students caregivers of a group of schools from first year until 12nd year of schooling in Telheiras, Lisbon. This group of schools has a population of about 3917 students, between 5 of and 18 years old. Through the application of a simple and closed experimental questionnaire by electronic form, the data collection occurred between November and December 2016, after adequate approval.

In questionnaire, the information requested was:

- Some socio-demographic characteristics such as age, sex, residence area, level of education, profession;
- Fifteen dichotomous questions in order to be easily answered (Yes/No) by the caregivers about acquaintance of PAH and connections with child weight, stature, birth weight, mothers health at child birth, physical activity, some risk factors, etc.;
- A control question to evaluate if an European recommendation about children blood pressure measurement in health surveillance visits is fulfilled.

3   Methodology

Factor analysis (FA) is technique often used to reduce data. The purpose is to get a reduced number of variables from an initial big set of variables and get easier interpretations [5]. The FA computes indexes with variables that measures similar things. There are two types of factor analysis: exploratory factorial analysis (EFA) and confirmatory factorial analysis (CFA) [15]. It is called EFA when there is no idea about the structure or the dimension of the set of variables. When we test some specific structure or dimension number of certain data set we name this technique the CFA. There are various extraction algorithms such as principal axis factors, principal components analysis or maximum likelihood (see [3] for example). There are numerous criteria to decide about the number of factors and theirs significance. For example, the Kaiser criterion proposes to keep the factors that correspond to eigenvalues greater or equal to one. In the classical model, the original set contains p variables $(X_1, X_2, \ldots, X_p)$ and m factors $(F_1, F_2, \ldots, F_m)$ are obtained. Each observable variable X_j, $j = 1, \ldots, p$ is a linear combination of these factors:

$$X_j = \alpha_{j1} F_1 + \alpha_{j2} F_2 + \cdots + \alpha_{jm} F_m + e_j, \qquad j = 1, \ldots, p, \qquad (1)$$

where e_j is the residual. The factor loading α_{jk} provides an idea of the contribution of the variable X_j, $j = 1, \ldots, p$, contributes to the factor F_k, $k = 1, \ldots, m$. The factor loadings represents the measure of association between the variable and the factor [5, 15].

FA uses variances to get the communalities between variables. Mainly, the extraction issue is to remove the largest possible amount of variance in the first factor. The variance in observed variables X_j which contribute to a common factor is defined by communality h_j^2 and is given by

$$h_j^2 = \alpha_{j1}{}^2 + \alpha_{j2}{}^2 + \cdots + \alpha_{jm}{}^2, \qquad j = 1, \ldots, p. \qquad (2)$$

According with the author of [9], the observable variables with low communalities are often dropped off once the basic idea of FA is to explain the variance by the common factors. The theoretical common factor model assumes that observables depend on the common factors and the unique factors being mandatory to determine the correlation patterns. With such objective the factors/components are successively extracted until a large quantity of variance is explained. After the extraction technique be applied, it is needed to proceed with the rotation of factors/components maximizing the number of high loadings on each observable variable and minimizing the number of factors. In this way, there is a bigger probability of an easier interpretation of factors 'meaning'.

4   Empirical Application

The first step organizes the data and get some simple measures by descriptive statistic techniques (see [11]). In a preliminary data analysis and taking into account the non-quantitative nature of the involved variables, were calculated measures of association, nonparametric Spearmann correlation coefficient, nonparametric test of Friedman for paired samples, etc. In Fig. 1 is summarized the questionnaire answers count of the selected 178 participants. About 96, 1% of participants know that the PAH may appear in pediatric age, 69% take into account that, frequently, hypertension has no visible symptoms, summarizing, the majority of caregivers are aware about some risk factors that may be associated with hypertension. The control question to evaluate if the regular measurement of the PBP is done from 3 years age in health surveillance visits (according to current European recommendations) has 44.75% of "No" answers.

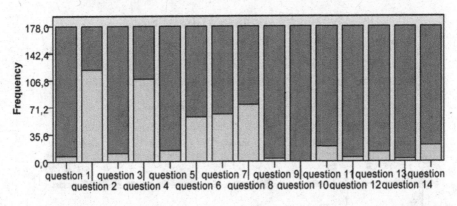

Fig. 1. Questionnaire responses count. Questions 1 to 15. 'Blue' = Yes; 'Green' = No. (Color figure online)

We measure the homogeneity and internal consistence of questionnaire and respective validation. The alpha-Cronbach coefficient was lower than expected, giving the indication of sufficient, but not good internal consistency. This measure of questionnarie reability is improved when question 2 is dropped. The same issue is confirmed when were performed several tests to compare the answers of questions 1 to 15: the paired T-test, McNemar's test for frequencies comparison, Crochan's Q test for binary variables comparison. In Fig. 3 and Table 1 were performed the Friedman test ($p - value = 0.000$) and kendall's coefficient of concordance test ($W = 0.294$) which were statistically significants meaning that questions do not have the same distribution. All tests conduced to the same conclusion: the distributions of questions 1 to 15 are not the same. Notice that the Spearmann correlation coefficient conduces to significant relations between some questions but, in some cases, Friedmann's tests doesn't corroborated. In Fig. 2 we can observe the mean ranks associated to each question response.

The question 2 is correlated with question 4 and also has no statistical difference, questions 4 and 5 are correlated with several others. All details suggests do not consider these 2 questions in our estimation. We also evaluate association

Table 1. Anova with Friedman's Test. Grand Mean = 0.80; Kendal's Coefficient $W = 0.294$.

		Sum of squares	df	Mean square	Fried. Chi-square	Sig.
Between people		39.483	177	0.223		
Within people	Between items	119.120	13	9.163	752.833	0.000
	Residual	247.022	2301	0.107		
	Total	366.143	2314	0.158		
Total		405.626	2491	0.163		

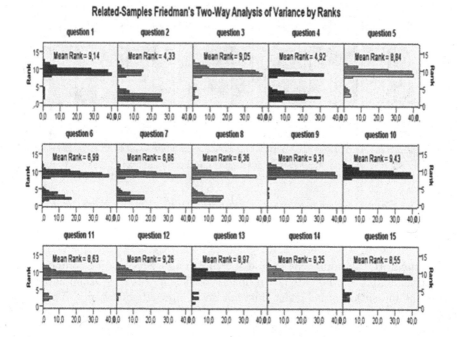

Fig. 2. Friedman nonparametric test. Related-sample Friedman's analysis of variance by ranks.

of the questionnaire answers with socio-demographic characteristics of participants. The Spearmann coefficient and the Kruskal-Wallis test were used for such purpose. The results will be described in the extended version of this article.

The next step of process applies a FA. For such purpose we estimate the communality for the factors, analyzed the significance of R-matrix, test the multicollinearity or singularity. The Bartlett's sphericity test provided a strongly significant level p, so we confirmed the existence of patterned relationships. Also, the Kaiser-Meyer-Olkin measure (KMO) of sampling adequacy conduced to $KMO = 0.67$, so the data is appropriate to apply an EFA.

In Table 2 are presented the eigenvalues and total variance accounted by each factor by descendent order. The ith line corresponds to cumulative variance percentage explained by the first i factors. Notice that Table 2 contains information after extraction and after rotation relative to scaled data.

If we consider the Kaiser criterion for simplicity, we retain the first 5 factors (eigenvalues great or equal to one). Other criteria may be applied, for example using the scree plot or using the average of extracted communalities[1] to determine the eigenvalue cutt-off (see Table 3). The varimax algorithm, which produces orthogonal factors, was applied after the extraction process. This technique

---

[1] The variance in observed variables which contribute to a common factor is defined by communality.

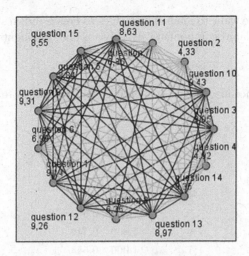

Fig. 3. Parwise comparision. Each node shows the sample average rank. Significant (no significant) pairs in yellow (black). (Color figure online)

Table 2. Total variance accounted for each factor.

Component	Extraction sum of squares loadings			Rotation sum of squares loadings		
	Total	% of variance	Cumulative %	Total	% of variance	Cumulative %
1	2.284	17.509	17.509	1.728	13.282	13.282
2	1.472	11.324	28.894	1.548	11.906	25.198
3	1.357	10.436	39.339	1.420	10.923	36.121
4	1.211	9.317	48.647	1.416	10.891	47.012
5	1.176	9.049	57.676	1.389	10.685	57.696

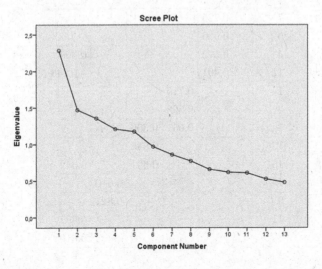

Fig. 4. Scree plot. Total variance accounted for each factor. One dominant factor.

is adequate when we want to identify variables to create indexes or new variables without inter-correlated components. We obtain one dominant factor as can be see in Fig. 4.

Table 3. The variance in observed variables X_j that contribute to a common factor (communalities).

Question	Initial	Final
1	1.000	0.561
3	1.000	0.506
4	1.000	0.481
5	1.000	0.603
6	1.000	0.544
7	1.000	0.555
8	1.000	0.415
9	1.000	0.708
11	1.000	0.563
12	1.000	0.466
13	1.000	0.731
15	1.000	0.731

Table 4. Rotated component matrix. Extraction method: Principal Components Analysis. Rotation method: Varimax with Kaiser normalization.

Question	Component				
	1	2	3	4	5
7	0.725				
6	0.689				
4	0.572				0.368
12	0.491				−0.443
1		0.716			
3		0.698			
5		0.651	0.306		
13			0.845		
15			0.691		0.342
14				0.840	
9				0.821	
11					0.697
8					0.610

Table 5. Spearmann correlation coefficient. Association between factors and socio-demographic variables.

Correlations

		BART factor score 5 for analysis 2	BART factor score 4 for analysis 2	BART factor score 3 for analysis 2	BART factor score 2 for analysis 2	BART factor score 1 for analysis 2	Género	Idade	Prof
Spearman's rho									
BART factor score 5 for analysis 2	Correlation Coefficient	1,000	-,610	-,229	,064	,172	,001	-,010	-,101
	Sig. (2-tailed)	.	,000	,002	,397	,022	,986	,894	,182
	N	178	178	178	178	178	178	175	177
BART factor score 4 for analysis 2	Correlation Coefficient	-,610	1,000	,312	-,082	-,127	-,031	-,066	,028
	Sig. (2-tailed)	,000	.	,000	,274	,092	,685	,388	,708
	N	178	178	178	178	178	178	175	177
BART factor score 3 for analysis 2	Correlation Coefficient	-,229	,312	1,000	-,234	-,247	-,036	-,152	,064
	Sig. (2-tailed)	,002	,000	.	,002	,001	,630	,044	,396
	N	178	178	178	178	178	178	175	177
BART factor score 2 for analysis 2	Correlation Coefficient	,064	-,082	-,234	1,000	-,154	-,117	,015	-,029
	Sig. (2-tailed)	,397	,274	,002	.	,040	,121	,844	,704
	N	178	178	178	178	178	178	175	177
BART factor score 1 for analysis 2	Correlation Coefficient	,172	-,127	-,247	-,154	1,000	,062	-,052	-,158
	Sig. (2-tailed)	,022	,092	,001	,040	.	,412	,492	,036
	N	178	178	178	178	178	178	175	177
Género	Correlation Coefficient	,001	-,031	-,036	-,117	,062	1,000	,000	-,102
	Sig. (2-tailed)	,986	,685	,630	,121	,412	.	,995	,176
	N	178	178	178	178	178	178	175	177
Idade	Correlation Coefficient	-,010	-,066	-,152	,015	-,052	,000	1,000	-,076
	Sig. (2-tailed)	,894	,388	,044	,844	,492	,995	.	,316
	N	175	175	175	175	175	175	175	174
Prof	Correlation Coefficient	-,101	,028	,064	-,029	-,158	-,102	-,076	1,000
	Sig. (2-tailed)	,182	,708	,396	,704	,036	,176	,316	.
	N	177	177	177	177	177	174	174	177

**. Correlation is significant at the 0.01 level (2-tailed).

*. Correlation is significant at the 0.05 level (2-tailed).

The analysis of the component matrix displayed in Table 4 allows the interpretation of the obtained factor conducing to a 'meaning' of each one. Namely each factor is related with:

F_1- Race, prematurity, weight at birth, between others;
F_2- PAH, family history;
F_3- Sports supplements, medicines;
F_4- Feeding, tobacco, alcohol;
F_5- Sleep time and quality, physical exercise practice.

Another idea is to reduce the number of selected factors using the same criteria. It can be done applying an EFA using the raw data. Is this way is possible to extract the maximum possible variance with fewer factors.

Considering raw data, we can observe that the first five components can extract 77.4% of total variance, when we take four components we have 62.8% of accounted variance, more than the extracted variance by the first five components for scaled data case.

Also, when we try to give a 'meaning' for each factor, we identify that each factor is associate to

F_1^*- weight at birth; prematurity;
F_2^*- race, gender, prematurity;
F_3^*- PAH symptoms, race;
F_4^*- breast-feeding.

5   Results and Final Remarks

It was built and applied an experimental questionnaire for survey purposes of PAH literacy. In an earlier work [4,12,13] was applied a simpler questionnaire with 5 questions. The descriptive and univariated analysis was done, also was performed a general linear models approach where some conclusions were obtained. In the present article an EFA was applied. The statistical process was explained, but not detailed. It is still going on the naming of selected factors, the obtained results and factors scores will be described in detail on an extended version of this article. The number of selected factors are (at most) 5, which corresponds to an explained variance 60% approximately considering scaled data. The number of components to consider, when we use raw data, is smaller for the same level of variance explanation. The meaning of each factor is related with feeding habits, medicines and supplements, family history, etc. We can apply other techniques to the selected factors, complementing and improving the statistical approach. For example, analyzing Table 5, we can find interesting and statistically significant associations between some factors and socio-demographics variables, that can be explored using some statistical techniques like generalized linear models.

Acknowledgements. This work was supported by Portuguese funds through the *Center for Computational and Stochastic Mathematics* (CEMAT), *The Portuguese Foundation for Science and Technology* (FCT), University of Lisbon, Portugal, project UID/Multi-/04621/2013, and *Center of Naval Research* (CINAV), Naval Academy, Portuguese Navy, Portugal.

References

1. Ahern, D., Dixon, E.: Pediatric Hypertension: a growing problem. Prim. Care Clin. Off. Pract. **42**(1), 143–150 (2015)
2. Bassareo, P.P., Mercuro, G.: Pediatric hypertension: an update on a burning problem. World J. Cardiol. **6**(5), 253–259 (2014)
3. Child, D.: The Essentials of Factor Analysis. Continuum International Publishing Group, New York (2006)
4. Costa, J.R.B.: Hipertensão arterial em idade pediátrica: que conhecimento têm os prestadores de cuidados sobre esta patologia? Master thesis, Medical Faculty, Lisbon University (2005). (In portuguese)
5. Harman, H.H.: Modern Factor Analysis. University of Chicago Press, Chicago (1976)
6. Flynn, J.: Pediatric hypertension: recent trends and accomplishments, future challenges. Am. J. Hypertens **21**, 605–612 (2008)
7. Hansen, M.L., Gunn, P.: Underdiagnosis of hypertension in children and adolescents. J. Am. Med. Assoc. **298**, 874–879 (2007)
8. Lurbe, E., Cifkovac, R.F.: Management of high blood pressure in children and adolescents: recommendations of the European Society oh Hypertension. J. Hypertens. **27**, 1719–1742 (2009)
9. Marôco, J.: Análise Estatística com o SPSS Statistics. Report Number, Pêro Pinheiro (2014). ISBN: 9789899676343
10. National High Blood Pressure Education Program Working Group on High Blood Pressure in Children, Adolescents: The fourth report on the diagnosis, evaluation and treatment oh high blood pressure in children and adolescents. Pediatrics **114**, 555–576 (2004)
11. Tamhane, A.C., Dunlop, D.D.: Statistics and Data Analysis: From Elementary to Intermediate. Prentice Hall, New Jersey (2000)
12. Teodoro, M.F., Simão, C.: Perception about pediatric hypertension. J. Comput. Appl. Math. **312**, 209–215 (2017)
13. Teodoro, M.F., Simão, C.: Completing the analysis of a questionnaire about pediatric blood pressure. Trans. Biol. Biomed. World Sci. Eng. Acad. Soc. **14**, 56–64 (2017)
14. Teodoro, M.F., Romana, A., Simão, C.: An issue of literacy on pediatric hypertension. In: Simos, T. et al. (eds.) Computational Methods in Science and Engineering, AIP Conference Proceedings (to appear)
15. Young, A.G., Pearce, S.: A beginners guide to factor analysis: focusing on exploratory factor analysis. Tutorial Quant. Methods Psychol. **9**(2), 79–94 (2013)

Workshop on Land Use Monitoring for Soil consumption reduction (LUMS 2017)

Soil Erosion Modelling on Arable Lands and Soil Types in Basilicata, Southern Italy

Dimotta Antonella[1,2], Lazzari Maurizio[2(✉)], Cozzi Mario[1],
and Romano Severino[1]

[1] SAFE - School of Agricultural, Forestry, Food and Environmental Sciences,
University of Basilicata, 85100 Potenza, Italy
antonella.dimotta@unibas.it
[2] CNR IBAM, C/da S. Loja Zona Industriale, 85050 Tito Scalo, PZ, Italy
m.lazzari@ibam.cnr.it

Abstract. Evaluating the impact and the incidence of the erosive phenomenon affecting the Basilicata region in 2012 - in particular, the agricultural areas used for the arable lands cultivation -, is an important goal aimed at correlating the erosion process – evaluated through the USPED method application (2012) - with the main characteristics related to soil and the areas interested, such as: soil types, with particular attention to two physical-chemical characteristics, such as: total CaCO3 (%) and soil organic matter content (SOM, %) -, land uses and the spatial distribution of arable lands at municipal scale. The correlation is intended to give an overview of geological and agricultural of amount of the areas affected by this phenomenon, since it aims to analyze and evaluate the agrarian framework in relation to the state of erosion in 2012 by assessing the incidence of the erosion process at regional and municipal scale in relation to the different scenarios deriving from the land use and soil types and choosing the most efficient land management strategy in terms of potential policies to communicate to the final decision makers.

Keywords: Soil erosion · USPED method · Soil types · Land use · Arable lands · Basilicata · Southern Italy · Land use policy

1 Introduction

Soil is one of the most important and most complex natural resources, but current developments (climate change, soil erosion and urbanization) increasingly threaten this valuable resource in Europe and worldwide [1]. In addition, it is important to remember that soil is a fragile resource that can be lost by erosion or degrade to such an extent as not to be more useful to support the crops Some analyses carried out by Boardman and Poesen [2] and Benchmann [3] describes erosion process formation events in agricultural lands in European countries. Also, as stated in different sources in literature, the aspect related to the cover crops can improve water infiltration, reduce water runoff, and slow down erosion [4, 13]. Indeed, as argued by Cerdan et al. [14] and Kinderiene, Karcauskiene [15], the soil parameters come into a play – along the factors related to the slope, the incorrect land use and natural rich rainfall – in the induction of the

© Springer International Publishing AG 2017
O. Gervasi et al. (Eds.): ICCSA 2017, Part V, LNCS 10408, pp. 57–72, 2017.
DOI: 10.1007/978-3-319-62404-4_5

erosion process. For this purpose, one of the most interesting aspect to analyze in terms of economic-agrarian impacts, as reported by Dimotta et al. [16], regarding the Bakker et al.'s analysis [17], is fundamental to mention the important role given by the well-known erosion-productivity scenario, characterized by the following effects:

(a) topsoil removal may often result in a nutrient deficit;
(b) erosion may also lead to physical hindrance to root growth.

In addition, as argued by Lal [18] these effects might be induced by several interacting factors, such as reduction of soil organic carbon (SOC), loss of plant nutrients, decline in soil structure, loss of effective rooting depth and decrease in available water capacity (AWC). Another important element coming into a strategic role in the soil fertility consists of SOM (soil organic matter). SOM plays a major role in maintaining soil quality, since it can positively influence a wide range of soil properties such as the provision of nutrients, water retention and release, as well as reducing the risks of soil compaction, surface crusting and soil erosion. In order to describe and define this important element, it is fundamental to mention that well-known factors are able to influence the rate of decline of soil organic matter levels including soil type and physical properties, climate, topography, vegetation and land management practice, as argued in *Maintenance of soil organic matter* guideline – available on www.agriculture.gov.ie [19]. In this regard, as shown by Jenny (1941), the factors affecting SOM consist of the amount of organic matter in surface, mineral soils can vary from less than 1% in coarse-textured, sandy soils to more than 5% in fertile, prairie grasslands [20]. The amount is influenced by all soil forming factors. Jenny arranged the order of importance of these factors in this priority list: Climate > vegetation > topography = parent material. Some general statements about SOM levels in virgin soils can be made based upon Jenny's work [21]:

1. Grassland soils have higher SOM than forest soils.
2. SOM increases with increasing precipitation and decreases with increasing temperature.
3. Fine-textured soils have higher SOM than coarse-textured soils.
4. Somewhat poorly and poorly drained soils have higher SOM than well- drained soils.
5. Soils in lowlands have higher SOM than soils on upland positions. Most SOM is found in the zone of maximum biological activity, the topsoil or plow layer. Anything done to this layer will influence long-term buildup or depletion of SOM (e.g., tillage, crop rotation, erosion, cover crops, crop residue management, fertilization, organic amendments, etc.).

Important to highlight that, as stated by van der Keur and Iversen [22], soil properties can vary over time as a result of impact by climate and land management. That's why two soil characteristics has been chosen in order to characterize the soil types present in the Basilicata region at municipal scale.

In order to reason on a SOM's minimum threshold, as reported by Plunkett and Castle [23], it is very useful to report that the soils characterized by organic matter levels above 3.4% are not considered to be vulnerable. Indeed, as resulting from the

Plunkett and Castle's analysis, various benefits can contribute to making less vulnerable a soil, such as:

1. Enhanced soil fertility
2. Improved in soil structure
3. Ease of workability
4. More active soil
5. Yield benefits.

Considering, now, the Ca-carbonate, as an important chemical factor of soil properties, an analysis carried out by Hassan and Agha [24], the influence of the changes in soil of CaCO3 content can cause some changes in soil erodibility factor (K USLE). Soil texture modification due to Ca-carbonate was the main factor affecting soil erodibility.

So, reasoning on the erosion effects on the soil structure and quality, as reported by Guimaraes et al. [25], it is very interesting to focus on the fact that exposing the soil surface to higher levels of energy and erosivity makes them susceptible in terms of structural degradation. This aspect is strictly demonstrated by a Lal's analysis, in which the importance and the related influence of the vegetation have been made evident in the agricultural sector, since the soil is more exposed and susceptible to damage, often resulting in lower SOM levels and lower aggregate stability, depending on the use and management [26]. Logically, maintaining the vegetative cover and/or the addition of organic residues to increase SOM are vital to maintaining soil aggregate stability [25].

The strategic and great importance related to soil resilience in responding positively to the changes of land uses and other aspects coming into a play in the ecosystem context, is well-described by the figure below reported (Fig. 1). Regarding the soil resilience, intended as a potential *soil conservation tool*, it is clearly expressed – by observing the Fig. 1, the balance existing between soil formative and degradative processes, in order to relate the soil properties and the abovementioned balance [27].

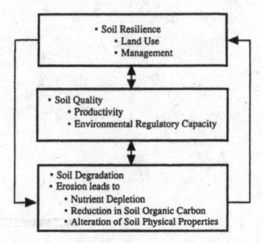

Fig. 1. Interactive effects of soil resilience and degradative processes on soil quality (Lal 1999).

Focusing the attention on the assessment of the soil types, land uses and the areas of the arable lands subjected to the erosion process and putting in relation the soil types and the croplands with this phenomenon at municipal scale, it is possible to obtain an environmental characterization of the territory – by considering geological and agricultural contexts - and the assessment of the areas – at regional and municipal scale – interested and affected by this typology of geomorphologic instability by applying the well-known empirical method - *Unit Stream Power Erosion Deposition* – USPED.

2   Materials and Methods

This section of the work deals with the methods applied in order to assess the quantitative aspect in terms of the arable land areas of the region Basilicata - at municipal scale – affected by soil erosion. The contribute related to the soil erosion derives from a previous output obtained through the USPED method application (Fig. 2). This contribute - taken from a previous study [16] -, has been reclassified into three classes in

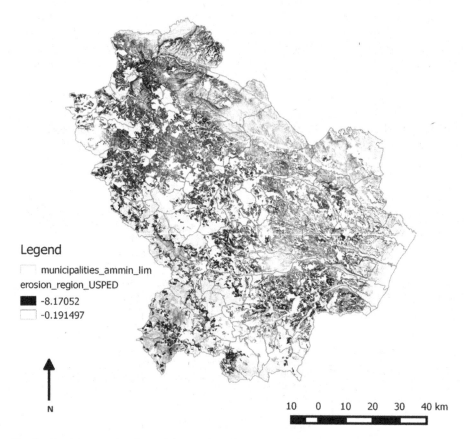

Fig. 2. Spatial representation of the erosive phenomenon affecting the total area size of the Basilicata region (USPED method application) [16].

relation to the potential erosivity (from the highest to the lowest degree), in order to evaluate the areas of arable lands interested by a potential erosion process (Fig. 3). In order to carry out the present analysis, different databases have been used, such as:

a. **Database (1): Utilized Agricultural Area (UAA) and available period:**
   Utilized Agricultural Area (UAA) – Arable lands - dataset coming from ISTAT – National Institute of Statistics - 6th Italian Agriculture Census, year 2010.
b. **Database (2): GIS geodatabase: Corine Land Cover 2012–4th level** – shapefile coming from ISPRA – Superior Institute of Environmental Protection and Research, Italy.
   Layer derived: layer of the Basilicata region used to extrapolate the different croplands areas/polygons of arable lands designed by the CLC code "*211*".
c. **Database (3): GIS geodatabase: Pedological Map of the Basilicata region 2006** (*"I suoli della Basilicata"*, http://www.basilicatanet.it/suoli/comuni.htm)

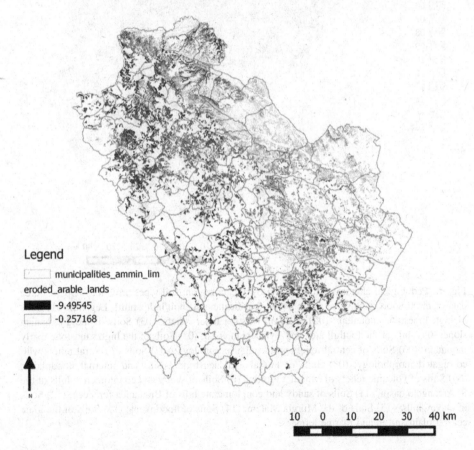

Fig. 3. Spatial representation of the eroded arable lands interesting the municipalities of the Basilicata region (USPED method application).

shapefile coming from Open Source Data by Basilicata Region Office containing spatial information about the soil types in the region (Fig. 4).

d. **Database (4): GIS geodatabases: total and eroded areas of the arable lands at regional scale.**
Layers derived: raster file resulting from the USPED method application of the year 2012 - coming from a previous spatial analysis carried out by Dimotta et al. [16].

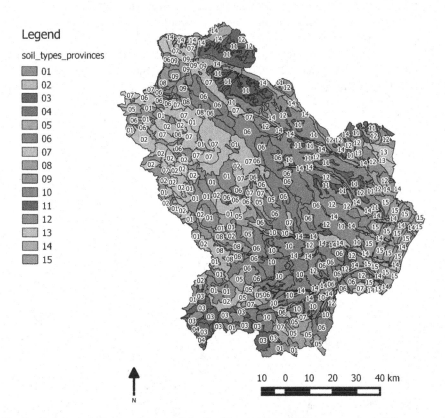

Fig. 4. Pedological characterization of the Basilicata region: soil types provinces [Open source data of the Region of Basilicata http://www.basilicatanet.it/suoli/index.htm]. Legend: (01) Soils of high limestone mountain; (02) Soils of Western inner reliefs; (03) Soils of the Tyrrhenian slope; (04) soils of the foothill area and Tyrrhenian coast; (05) Soils of the high sandstone marly mountain; (06) Soils of central reliefs with rough morphology; (07) Soils of central reliefs with corrugated morphology; (08) Soils of fluvial and lacustrine basins and internal floodplains; (09) Soils of volcanic reliefs of Mount Vulture; (10) Soils of sandy and conglomerate hills of the S. Arcangelo basin; (11) Soils of sandy and conglomerate hills of Bradanica foredeep; (12) Soils of clayey hills; (13) Soils of the Murgia Matera; (14) Soils of floodplains; (15) Soils of the ionic coastal plain and inland marine terraces.

3 Data Analysis

Premised that, as a background of this analysis, two assessments have been carried out by operating the partialization of the areas at municipal scale characterized by a specific land use, such as arable lands.

These assessments have been performed in order to obtain the following outputs:

1. Soil types affected by erosive phenomenon at municipal scale. In order to obtain this output, it has been necessary to use the Regional Pedological Map. This elaboration has been performed in the GIS environment – since it has been necessary to implement the attributes table of the map by adding two data related to the physical-chemical information, such as CaCO3 and SOM content. Then, it has been possible to extrapolate and intersect the different databases coming from different attribute tables: one related to the soil types containing soil characteristics - CaCO3 total and SOM (%) - and the other one containing the dataset of the potential erosivity - interested the areas of the arable land - obtained by the vectorizing process of the raster file generated by the previous application of the USPED method of the year 2012, evaluation deriving from a previous analysis [16].

2. The arable lands areas in hectares – in terms of Utilized Agricultural Area (UAA – source: ISTAT, Italy) - affected by the potential erosion process – classified into the three classes - in each municipality of the Basilicata region.

3. The arable lands affected by soil erosion process at regional scale: this output has been taken through the USPED method application of the year 2012 (Fig. 3) evaluated in the Basilicata region [16].

These outputs have been obtained by operating through two main geoprocessing tools, such as vectorizing and intersection operations followed by appropriate computational operations aimed at calculating the effective areas of interest. Thus, both of these tools allowed to obtain the partialization - in qualitative and quantitative terms -of the areas interested by this analysis.

Describing the steps developed, in order to realize the different scenarios containing the abovementioned results, it has been carried out the following methodologies process:

1. First of all, some data gaps related to the total CaCO3 (%) and the SOM contents (%) have been bypassed by transferring the qualitative data into quantitative terms, by associating an average value aimed at defining the both contents into the correlated value range. Explicating the reasoning: the classes of the value ranges have been considered and the average value has been calculated by applying the well-known analytical relation used for calculating the medium:

$$(max\,value - value\,min)/2 = average\,value$$

2. The utilization of the Corine Land Cover 2012 has made the individualization of the arable lands possible, in order to extrapolate the spatial data related to the areas interested by this specific land use. In fact, this layer has played an important role in

this analysis, by making a biunivocal correspondence evident between the information regarding the land use and the municipal areas interested.

3. The pedological characterization in terms of soil type and the two physical-chemical parameters (total CaCO3 and SOM contents), considered in this evaluation, has been associated to each municipality of the region and, consequently, a sum of the contributes of area - belonging to each soil type - interested to the erosion process, has been calculated. Thus, through this assessment, a *soil type scenario* of the spatial distribution of the areas characterized by different soil types in each municipality and a correlated quantitative result of the areas assessment has highlighted the incidence of the erosion process in the different soil types "districts", by observing the pedological provinces and units more exposed to this phenomenon.

4. The layer "arable lands areas" deriving from the raster obtained through the previous spatial analysis – by USPED method [16] – has allowed to obtain, by a specific assessment, the incidence of the erosive phenomenon in the area interested by arable lands of the Basilicata region (Fig. 3).

5. The operation of intersection, the most strategic '*tool*' used in this analysis, in order to let the different scenarios create geographic, qualitative and quantitative relationships, has been useful to create a complete database – by using the DBF file as a computational sheet in excel environment. This DBF source, taken from the shapefiles generated by the intersection operation, has been used in excel environment, as a computational sheet of great importance aimed at evaluating the different thematisms and parameters coming into a play in this analysis.

6. From the computational operations performed in excel environment on the DBF files deriving from the database generated in the GIS environment, a histogram has been developed in order to illustrate the incidence of the erosion process at municipal and regional scale, in relation to the soil types characterizing the regional and municipal areas affected by soil erosion and a GIS representation related to the incidence of the erosive phenomenon at municipal scale in relation to the land use considered, such as the arable lands.

4   Results

From the analysis carried out, the different outputs resulting have been the following:

1. Assessment related to the areas affected by erosive phenomenon in relation to the soil type more exposed and affected.

2. *GIS elaborations*: a map representative of the erosion process affecting the arable lands evaluated for each municipality and the map representing the erosion process affecting the total pattern of the region, the pedological characterization of the Basilicata's soils and the pedological units interested by the erosion phenomenon affecting the arable lands, the spatial distribution of the SOM and $CaCO_3$ content (%) in the region in relation to the erosion process affecting the arable lands.

By observing the GIS elaboration, deriving from the computational analyses carried out through the attribute table coming from the combination between the municipalities and the excel sheet related to the eroded arable lands evaluated at municipal scale (Fig. 5), it is possible to individuate the most exposed areas to the erosion phenomenon. About the same representation, the intersection tool – GIS operations context – allowed to highlight that the most extensive arable land area affected by soil erosion is the one interesting the territory of Potenza, amounts to 25515.03 ha. On the opposite, the less extensive one amounts to 32.90 ha and is located in Maratea.

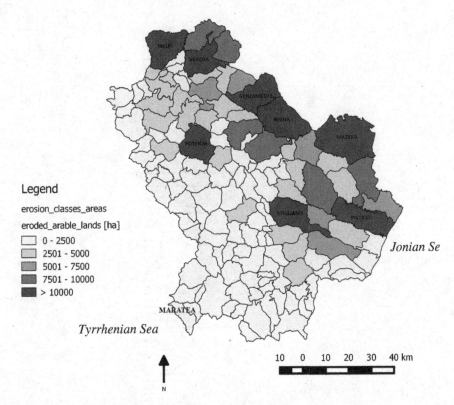

Fig. 5. Spatial distribution of the eroded arable lands evaluated for each municipality in the Basilicata.

By analyzing the assessment related to the soil types more exposed to the erosion process deriving from the histogram – Fig. 6, it is evident to notice that the soil type afferent to the pedologic unit *12.1*, belonging to the pedological province No. 12 defined as "*Soils of the clayey hills*", results to be much more exposed to this instability. The soils belonging to this soil type are called "*Suoli Elemosina*" and "*Suoli Mattina Grande*". This soil type interests different municipalities, such as Acerenza, Banzi, Calciano, Forenza, Genzano di Lucania, Grassano, Grottole, Irsina, Matera, Miglionico, Montemilone, Montescaglioso, Oppido Lucano, Palazzo San Gervasio, Pomarico, San Chirico Nuovo, Tolve and Tricarico. The total arable land – belonging to this pedologic unit – subjected to the erosive phenomenon amounts to 46646.89 ha,

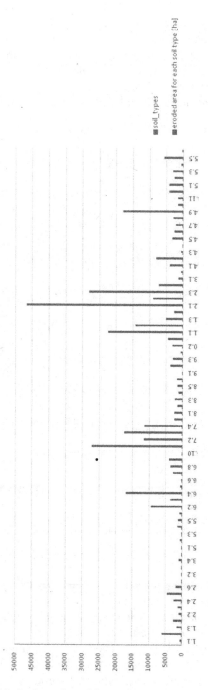

Fig. 6. Eroded arable lands evaluated for each soil type interesting the Basilicata.

calculated by summing the contributions of the eroded arable lands [ha] interesting each municipality characterized by that soil type.

On the other hand, the soil type less exposed to soil erosion consists of the one afferent to the pedological unit *6.10*, belonging to the pedological province No. 6 defined as *"soils of the central mountains in harsh morphology"* characterized by a soil called *"Suoli Arca dei Monaci"* [see *"I suoli della Basilicata"*, Pedological Map of the Basilicata region]. This soil type interests the municipality of Rapone and the related area subjected to the erosive phenomenon amounts to 7.45 ha.

The GIS representations of these elaborations has shown by the Fig. 7.

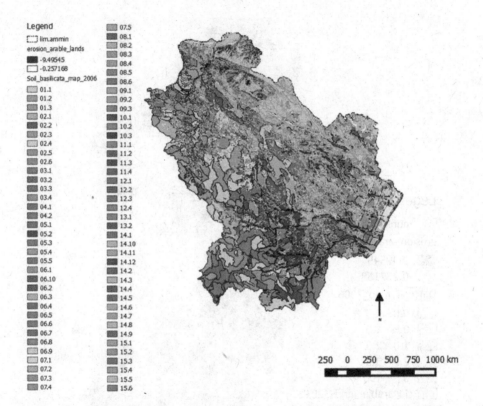

Fig. 7. Spatial distribution of the erosive phenomenon affecting the arable lands in relation to the soil types of the region

The characteristics, emerging from these soil types, highlight a different percentage between both of them: the soil type more exposed to the erosion phenomenon (soil type 12.1) results to contain a total $CaCO_3$ content of 3.7% and SOM of 1.9%; while, the soil type less exposed to the same phenomenon (soil type 6.10) is characterized by a total $CaCO_3$ content of 9.9% and a SOM content of 1.2%.

In relation to the assessment of the areas more exposed and affected by the erosion process, at municipal scale, it is possible to notice and highlight that, in correlation to the total area of each municipality and the area affected by soil erosion, the incidence of the occurrence of the phenomenon is correlated to the aspect related to the soil type characterization (Fig. 8).

This difference of the total $CaCO_3$ content (%) and the SOM content (%) in the two soil types reports a strong correlation with the amount of the areas interested by the land cover considered (arable lands) and the area size in relation to the municipality areas. It is evident that the soil characterized by a SOM content <1.9% is affected by a higher erosion.

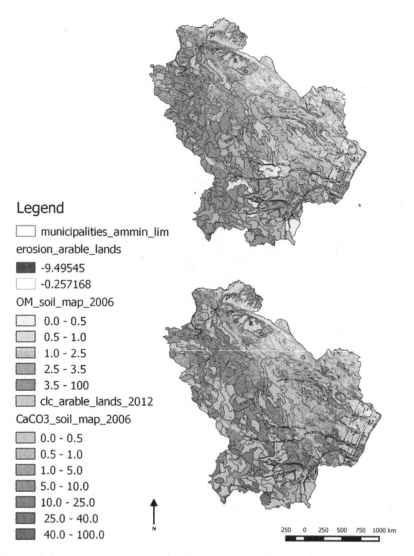

Fig. 8. Spatial distributions of the SOM content (%) and CaCO3 content (%) – respectively - in the Basilicata region in relation to the arable lands affected by soil erosion.

5   Discussion and Final Remarks

From this analysis carried out on different thematisms resulting from different aspects considered, it was possible to make this vision emerge: the areas interested by the erosive phenomenon, both in relation to its own geographical area and the magnitude of the erosion process, belong to a pedological framework that, in relation to the topographic, climatic and land cover features, need to be monitored through a singular and strategic territory monitoring plan, aimed at preventing the potential erosive phenomenon and, if it has already happened, able to mitigate it by reducing the direct and indirect effects on the regional environment.

As the literature demonstrates, the erosion process is able to change soil physical properties, mainly because of the removal (soil profile truncation) of surface soil rich in organic matter and exposure of lower soil layers [28]. Arriaga (2003) indicated that the bulk density and hydraulic conductivity of saturated soil increased slightly with erosion severity [29]. In relation to the soil organic matter influence, it is interesting to mention, as stated by Boyle (2002), this soil parameter, in eroded soil, decomposes at a greater rate than in intact soil. [30]. Numerous field and laboratory studies have shown that soils with low SOM contents are more erodible than soils characterized by a high SOM content, and generally soils with <2% SOM content by weight are highly erodible [31]. Obviously, this aspect can not be considered by itself, given that the various relationships and interrelations among the different land managements and conservation strategies focus on several contributes deriving from the most influencing factors, such as physical, hydrological, geological and pedological characteristics of the area considered.

In the literature, regarding the mitigation of land degradation, several studies have indicated that application of suitable cropping systems (crop rotations) significantly can mitigate this phenomenon of instability in sloping areas [14, 32]. One of the most influencing factors enable to mitigate the land degradation process activated by soil erosion, is the vegetation cover, because it is able to reduce runoff and nutrient losses [33]. For this purpose, it is very important to consider that different plant covers are characterized by different resistance to erosion and can afford soil protection differently [34]. Thus, a constant conservation of these vital resources needs to receive high priority to ensure the effective protection of managed and natural ecosystems [35].

The best management practice in crop and land management is important because, in this way, it is possible to reduce the soil erosion and minimize the leaching of nutrients and increase soil productivity [36].

For this purpose, it is very interesting to focus on one of the most efficient environmental approach described by applying the ratio of *engineering resilience* and *ecological resilience*. Two mean concepts - belonging to this approach -, play an important and strategic role in this context: *recovery duration* (RD) – defined as a measurement of the capacity of land to recover its original state when disturbed – and *recovery effort* (RE), considered in terms of social-ecological resilience, is characterized by the measurement of the land's anthropogenic potential to recover its original state or to prevent damage caused by the same type of disturbance in the future [37, 38].

References

1. Morgan, R.P.C.: Soil erosion and conservation, 3rd edn. Blackwell Publishing, National Soil Resources Institute, Cranfield (2006)
2. Boardman, J., Poesen, J.: Soil erosion in Europe: major processes, causes and consequences. In: Boardman, J., Poesen, J. (eds.). Soil Erosion in Europe, pp. 479–488 (2006). http://dx. doi.org/10.1002/0470859202.ch36
3. Bechmann, M.: Effect of tillage on sediment and phosphorus losses from a field and a catchment in south eastern Norway. Acta Agriculturae Scandinavica, Section B: Soil Plant Sci. Soil Eros. Nordic Countries (spec. iss.), 62(2), 206–216 (2012)
4. Csepinszky, B., Jakab, G.: Pannon R-02 Esőszimulator a Talajerozio Vizsgalatara. XLI. Georgikon Napok, Keszthely, pp. 294–298 (1999)
5. Dabney, S.M., Delgado, J.A., Reeves, D.W.: Using winter cover crops to improve soil and water quality. Commun. Soil Sci. Plant Anal. 32(7), 1221–1250 (2001). doi:10.1081/CSS-100104110
6. Kertész, Á., Tóth, A., Jakab, G., Szalai, Z.: Soil erosion measurements in the Tetves Catchment, Hungary. In: Helming, K. (ed.) Multidisciplinary Approaches to Soil Conservation Strategies. Proceedings, International Symposium, ESSC, DBG, ZALF, Müncheberg, Germany, 11–13 May 2001. ZALF-BERICHT Nr. 47, pp. 47–52 (2001)
7. Pardini, G., Gispert, M., Dunjò, G.: Runoff erosion and nutrient depletion in five Mediterranean soils of NE Spain under different land use. Sci. Total Environ 309, 213–224 (2003)
8. Nearing, M.A., Jetten, V., Baffaut, C., Cerdan, O., Couturier, A., Hernandez, M., Le Bissonnais, Y., Nichols, M.H., Nunes, J.P., Renschler, C.S., Souchere, V., van Oost, K.: Modeling response of soil erosion and runoff to changes in precipitation and cover. CATENA 61(2–3), 131–154 (2005)
9. García-Ruiz, J.M.: The effects of land uses on soil erosion in Spain: a review. CATENA 81, 1–11 (2010)
10. Jakab, G., Centeri, C., Kiss, K., Madarász, B., Szalai, Z.: Erózió és művelés okozta anyagvándorlás szántóföldön. In: Dobos Endre, Bertóti Réka Diana, Szabóné Kele Gabriella (szerk.): Talajtan a mezőgazdaság, a vidékfejlesztés és a környezetgazdálkodás szolgálatában. Talajvédelem (különszám), Budapest, Talajvédelmi Alapítvány; Magyar Talajtani Társaság, pp. 283–292 (2013)
11. Madarász B – Kertész Á.: A gyepes sávok szerepe a talaj, víz és természetvédelemben. In: Zákányi Balázs, Faur Krisztina Beáta (szerk.) IX. Kárpát-medencei környezettudományi konferencia: Konferencia kiadvány. Miskolc, Magyarország, 2013.06.13–2013.06.15. Miskolci Egyetem Műszaki Földtudományi Kar, pp. 24–29 (2013)
12. Madarász, B., Bádonyi, K., Csepinszky, B., Mika, J., Kertész, Á.: Conservation tillage forrational water management and soil conservation. Hung. Geograph. Bull. 60(2), 117–133 (2011)
13. Madarász, B., Csepinszky, B., Benke, S.: Gyepes sávok szerepe a talajerózió elleni védekezésben. In: Jakab, G., Szalai, Z., (szerk.) Talajpusztulás térben és időben: az "Eróziós kerekasztal 2013" közleményei. Budapest, Magyarország, 2013.12.12., MTA CSFK Földrajztudományi Intézet, pp. 32–39 (2014)
14. Cerdan, O., Govers, G., Le Bissonnais, Y., Van Oost, K., Poesen, J., Saby, N., Gobin, A., Vacca, A., Quinton, J., Auerswald, K., Klik, A., Kwaad, F.J.P.M., Raclot, D., Nonita, I., Rejman, J., Rousseva, S., Muxart, T., Roxo, M.J., Dostal, T.: Rates and spatial variations of soil erosion in Europe: a study based on erosion plot data. Geomorphology 122(1–2), 167–177 (2010). doi:10.1016/j.geomorph.2010.06.011

15. Kinderiene, I., Karcauskiene, D.: Effects of different crop rotations on soil erosion and nutrient losses under natural rainfall conditions in Western Lithuania. Acta Agriculturae Scandinavica, Section B: Soil Plant Sci. **62**(2), 199–205 (2012)

16. Dimotta, A., Cozzi, M., Romano, S., Lazzari, M.: Soil Loss, productivity and cropland values gis-based analysis and trends in the Basilicata region (Southern Italy) from 1980 to 2013. In: Gervasi, O., et al. (eds.) ICCSA 2016. LNCS, vol. 9789, pp. 29–45. Springer, Cham (2016). doi:10.1007/978-3-319-42089-9_3

17. Bakker, M.M., Govers, G., Rounsevell, M.D.A.: The crop productivity-erosion relationship: an analysis based on experimental work. CATENA **57**(1), 55–76 (2004)

18. Lal, R., Kimble, J.M., Follett, R.F., Stewart, B.A.: Soil Processes and the Carbon Cycle, p. 609. CRC Press, Boca Raton (1998)

19. Maintenance of soil organic matter. Guidelines. www.agriculture.gov.ie

20. Jenny, H.: Factors of Soil Formation. McGraw-Hill, New York (1941)

21. Rasmussen, P.E., Collins, H.P.: Long-term impacts of tillage, fertilizer, and crop residue on soil organic matter in temperate semiarid regions. Adv. Agron. **45**, 93–134 (1991)

22. van der Keur, P., Iversen, B.V.: Uncertainty in soil physical data at river basin scale – a review. Hydrol. Earth Syst. Sci. **10**, 889–902 (2006)

23. Plunkett, M., Castle, J.: Soil Organic Matter and Nutrients Analysis. Agriculture and Food Development Authority. Teagasc (2010)

24. Hassan, K.F., Agha, M.D.: Effects of calcium carbonate on the erodibility of some calcareous soils by water erosion. Mesopotamia J. Agri. **40**(4) (2012)

25. Guimaraes, D.V., Gonzaga, M.I.S., da Silva, T.O., da Silva, T.L., da Silva, D.N., Matias, M.I.S.: Soil organic matter pools and carbon fractions in soil under different land uses. Soil Tillage Res. **126**, 177–182 (2013)

26. Lal, R.: Soil quality and sustainability. Methods for assessment of soil degradation (1997)

27. Lal, R., Mokma, D., Lowery, B.: Relation between soil quality and erosion. In: Rattan, L. (ed.) Soil Erosion and Productivity. Section IV. Handbook: Soil Quality and Soil Erosion. Soil and Water Conservation Society. Ankeny, Iowa. CRC Press, NY (1999)

28. Jankauskas, B., Jankauskiene, G., Fullen, A.M.: Relationships between soil organic matter content and soil erosion severity in Albeluvisols of the Zemiciai Uplands. Ekologija **53**(1), 21–28 (2007)

29. Arriaga, F.: Soil physical properties and crop productivity of an eroded soil amended with cattle manure. Soil Sci. **168**(12), 888–899 (2003)

30. Boyle, M.: Erosion's contribution to greenhouse gases. Erosion Control. Features. January/February, pp. 21–29 (2002)

31. Fullen, M.A., Catt, J.: Soil Management: problems and solutions, p. 269. Arnold, London (2004)

32. Feiza, V., Feizienė, D., Jankauskas, B., Jankauskienė, G.: The impact of soil management on surface runoff, soil organic matter content and soil hydrological properties on the undulating landscape of Western Lithuania. Zemdirbyste-Agric. **95**(1), 3–21 (2008)

33. Morgan, R.P.C.: Vegetative-based technologies for erosion control, in eco- and ground bio-engineering: the use of vegetation to improve slope stability. Dev. Plant Soil Sci. **103**, 265–272 (2007). doi:10.1007/978-1-4020-5593-5_26

34. Račinskas, A.: Soil erosion, p. 136. Vilnius, Lithuania (1990)

35. Zuazo, V.H.D., Pleguezuelo, C.R.R.: Soil erosion and runoff prevention by plant covers. a review. Agron. Sustain. Develop. **28**(1), 65–86 (2008). doi:10.1051/agro:2007062

36. Szabò, B., Centeri, C., Szalai, Z., Jakab, G., Szabò, J.: Comparison of soil erosion dynamics under extensive and intensive cultivation based on soil parameters. In: 14th Alps – Adria Scientific Workshop, Neum, Bosnia and Herzegovina (2015)
37. Holling, C.S., Engineering resilience vs. ecological resilience. In: Schulze, P. (ed.) Engineering within Ecological Constraints, pp. 31–44. National Academy, USA (1996)
38. Wuang, S.-H., Huang, S.L., Budd, W.W.: Resilience analysis of the interaction of between typhoons and land use change. Landscape Urban Plann. **106**, 303–315 (2012)

An Estimate of Land Take in Municipal Planning of the Campania Region

Massimiliano Bencardino[✉]

Department of Political, Social and Communication Sciences,
University of Salerno, Via Giovanni Paolo II, 132, 84084 Fisciano, SA, Italy
mbencardino@unisa.it

Abstract. The issue of land take is characterized by analytical complexity and legislative effectiveness. So, in dealing with this question, several aspects have to be evaluated.

This project aims at a quantitative assessment of the municipal urban planning in terms of land take, in the context of the Campania region. To make this, the Master Plans of many municipalities are examined. Therefore, the housing needs outlined in the municipal Plans are compared with the trends in population growth. Through this analysis, the municipalities are classified into three groups: virtuous municipalities, growing municipalities e uncontrolled municipalities. Moreover, a quantitative analysis of urban planning standards is taken into account. Then, by describing the obtained results, this work tries to define a synoptic view of municipal planning in Campania region, its critical points and the contrasting actions that can be implemented in regional and national legislations.

Keywords: Land take · Demographic changes · Municipal plans · Housing needs · Large-area administration

1 Object of the Analysis

The aim of this work is to provide a quantitative measurement of the housing needs defined in the Municipal Urban Plans (PUC) of the Campania region.

For this purpose, a list of 118 municipalities, whose Master Plan is submitted to the Strategic Environmental Assessment (SEA) procedure, has been extracted from the website of the Campania Region[1] dedicated to the consultation of the approving results. So, two conditions have been verified for each of them:

1. if the documentation of the Plan and in particular the Technical Report (or the General Report) were published on the official website of the Municipality.
2. if a quantification of the housing needs resulted from published documents, when the first hypothesis was verified.

The 118 investigated municipalities are well distributed among the classes by population size [1]. There are no large towns or cities, lacking Naples in the analysis.

---

[1] The web page from which the list of municipalities has been extracted is: http://viavas.re-gione.campania.it/opencms/opencms/VIAVAS/VAS.

© Springer International Publishing AG 2017
O. Gervasi et al. (Eds.): ICCSA 2017, Part V, LNCS 10408, pp. 73–88, 2017.
DOI: 10.1007/978-3-319-62404-4_6

Six of 18 medium-sized towns of the Region (33%), 17 of the 63 small towns (27%), 30 of the 134 minor small towns (22%), 57 of the 270 villages (21%) and 8 of the 65 small villages (12%) are included. Therefore, the sample of the detected municipalities is well-representative of all classes of cities, as it appears in Table 1.

Table 1. Distribution classes of 118 municipalities by population size.

Class	Population class (inhabitants)	Investigated Municipalities	Municipalities of the Region	Percent
Big cities or Metropolises	>500,001	0	1	0%
Middle-sized towns	100,001–500,000	0	2	33%
	50,001–100,000	6	16	
Small-sized towns	15,001–50,000	17	63	27%
	5,001–15,000	30	134	22%
Village	2,001–5,000	26	150	17%
	1,001–2,000	31	120	26%
Small village	501–1,000	7	55	13%
	≤ 500	1	10	10%
Totale		118	551	21%

Similarly, the sample appears sufficiently representative in its spatial articulation. In fact, we can find 28 municipalities belonging to the province of Avellino, 19 to Benevento, 20 to Caserta, 21 to Naples and 30 to Salerno[2].

It turned out that, among the 118 municipalities for which the SEA procedure was published on the regional website[3] between 2008 and 2015 (in particular between 06/02/2008 and 15/12/2015), only 67 of them (56%) had available information about the planning on own website. In addition, 40 of them (34%) provided documents with accurate information on the housing needs and only 26 (22%) showed an assessment on planning standard (according to D.M. 1444/68). Therefore, the quantitative analysis just focused on the group of 40 municipalities.

The so poor attention to the publication of the planning documents is a first point on which to focus. In fact, the presence or absence of information does not appear a matter of time, because it's not connected to the starting date of the SEA procedure. Therefore, it represents a lack of administrative capacity to complete the Plan process at the right time[4] or a municipal transparency deficit towards their citizens.

---

[2] The sample represents 21.2% of the 551 municipalities in the Campania Region.

[3] It refers to 115 requests for PUC evaluation and 3 cases related to PRG variant. So, all the others procedures related to different type of plan and program have been excluded.

[4] For some of these municipalities, the PUC resulted not yet approved or approved only in preliminary form.

2 Land Take: From Analytical Problems to Contrasting Policies

In Italy, the issues of land take and urban sprawl have for years been the focus of policy makers, scientific community and research institutes [2–16]. Nevertheless, there is no scholarly consensus on these questions which is still dealt with heterogeneous interpretations and perspectives [1].

The problem of quantification can be traced back to two key issues. The first is related to the complexity of the measuring of land use and the difficulty of identifying homogeneous and comparable measurement methods: see the European project Corine Land Cover (CLC), the Land and Ecosystem Accounts (LEAC) or the methodologies applied in Italy by ISPRA or by ISTAT. The second, more important, is related to the definition of the drivers that move the land take, the most appropriate analytical scale and, then, the most effective contrasting actions [1, 3, 4].

Recent studies [17], have shown that, for each new inhabitant, the phenomenon of land take in the villages and small villages is significantly higher than in the cities or middle towns, and the real estate overvaluation has generated a *decoupled land take* not proportional to the real housing or the productive demand. This occurs because the purchase of the house is still a haven investment [18–20] and because there is a significant imbalance between public and private operators in the redistribution of the increase in the ground rent that urban transformation provides [21, 22].

Previous works of the Autor [3–5] showed how some Italian cities tend to occupy new spaces and draw new residential and industrial areas in the absence of a demographic evidence that justifies such choices, analyzing them both at the urban scale and at territorial system scale.

Therefore, in this work the ways that lead to this excessive quantification of housing needs were investigated, taking into account the planning instruments of the Municipalities in the Campania Region. Through this detailed analysis, we want to highlight how the directives that contrast the land use are evaded and the oversizing of housing needs is defined.

3 Population Dynamics in Campania Region

This analysis moves in the context of the Campania region, of which the demographic dynamics will be here represented. The change in population, from 1981 until 2011, of the about 550 municipalities in the Region is analyzed through four ISTAT statistics surveys (Table 2), and through the construction of three changing maps that well represent the demographic dynamics in the reference area (Fig. 1).

Campania region is characterized by a strong polarization around its capital, Naples [23], and by a strong population growth during the decade 1981–1991 (Table 2). This increase, which mainly concerned the metropolitan areas of Naples and Salerno [24], is a clearly consequence of the Fordist industrialization phase, due to the investments of

Table 2. Change in population in the five provinces of the Campania Region

Province of	Pop 1981	Pop 2011	ΔPop 81-91	ΔPop 91-01	ΔPop 01-11
Caserta	755,628	904,921	+60,187	+37,057	+52,049
Benevento	289,143	284,900	+3,883	−5,984	−2,142
Napoli	2,970,563	3,054,956	+45,463	+43,170	−4,240
Avellino	434,021	429,157	+4,791	−9,634	−21
Salerno	1,013,779	1,092,876	+52,822	+7,042	+19,233
Campania Region	5,463,134	5,766,810	+167,146	+71,651	+64,879

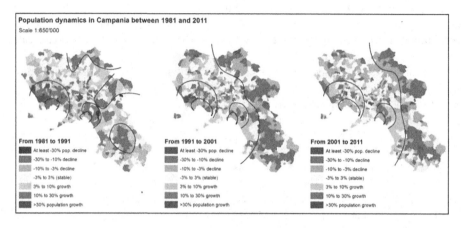

Fig. 1. Population dynamic in Campania between 1981 e 2011, in three steps: (a) 1981–1991; (b) 1991–2001; (c) 2001–2011 (Our elaboration)

the *Cassa del Mezzogiorno*[5], especially for the city of Naples. After the thirty years of extraordinary intervention, Naples, strongly urbanized, enters into a full phase of suburbanization (well represented in Fig. 1a). Here, we can see the strong population growth of urban rings of Naples and Salerno, to the detriment of the core that are in demographic decline.

Alongside these urban dynamics, in the decade 1981–1991, there has been a limited demographic decline of the inner areas, in particular in the Samnite areas of Upper Tammaro and Fortore, in the Upper Irpinia, in the Alburni Mountains and Upper Calore of Salerno.

Overall, in the decade, the region has increased by more than 160 thousand inhabitants, revealing that the attractiveness of urban areas of Naples and Salerno has gone far beyond the regional context and has spread to other regions of southern Italy.

The suburbanization in the metropolitan areas of Salerno and Naples continues up to date (as shown in Fig. 1b and c), but in a more and more rarefied way.

---

[5] It was a Government Agency for extraordinary public investments in Southern Italy from 1950 to 1984. It will be replaced until 1992 by an Agency for the promotion and development of the South.

Instead, over the past two decades, from 1991 to 2011, a stronger depopulation phenomenon has had in the inland areas, up to involve the two provincial capitals of Benevento and Avellino. The population decline has been very strong in the decade 1991–2001, investing the areas of Matese, of Ufita, Terminio, Upper Sele, Tanagro and the totality of the inner areas of Cilento, as well as the Diano and Bussento valleys, in addition to the areas already affected by depopulation.

In the following decade, the decline is smaller but equally significant. Overall, the regional demographic balance remained positive because the depopulation of inland areas is associated with the growth of the Domitian coast and the main axes of Salerno along the Irno and the Sele.

Therefore, the scenario is a region in two demographic dynamic speeds: a thirty-year population decline that runs through all internal areas and a growth in the rings of the urban areas of Naples and Salerno. So, if the construction of new residential volumes cannot be justified in all inner areas of the region, policies for containment of sprawl are particularly urgent and necessary in the suburbs of Naples and Salerno, in order to contain the unsustainable housing development.

4 The Sample of 40 Municipalities Under Analysis

Henceforth, the quantitative analysis will be carried out on the second smaller sample, represented by the already mentioned 40 municipalities that provide accurate information on the housing needs. Like the previous sample (Table 1), also this group of 40 is sufficiently distributed among the classes by population size (Table 3). Here, there are: 2 middle-sized towns, 6 small towns, 12 minor small town, 18 villages and 2 small villages.

Table 3. Distribution classes of the 40 municipalities under analysis by population size

Class	Sample under analysis	Municipalities with a PUC	Percent	M. in the Region	Percent
Big cities or Metropolises	0	0	0%	1	0%
Middle-sized towns	0	0	0%	2	11%
	2	6	33%	16	
Small-sized towns	6	17	35%	63	10%
	12	30	40%	134	9%
Village	11	26	42%	150	7%
	7	31	23%	120	6%
Small village	2	7	29%	55	4%
	0	1	0%	10	0%
Totale	40	118	34%	551	7%

5 The Municipal Planning Assessment

For an efficacy analysis of the planning, the PUC of 40 municipalities will be here examined according to three variables: (a) the number of newly identified housing needs; (b) the change in the population into 2001–2011 decade; (c) the square meters allocated to the equipment for urban standards.

Referring to the first two variables, 3 classes of municipalities can be identified:

1. the municipalities for which no new housing needs are provided ($F_a = 0$); they will be here defined *virtuous municipalities*.
2. those for which new housing needs are expected, consistently with a population growth in the last decade ($F_a > 0$; $\Delta P > 0$): here defined *growing municipalities*.
3. those in which new housing needs are provided in front of a decrease of the population in the last decade ($F_a > 0$; $\Delta P < 0$): here defined *uncontrolled municipalities*.

where F_a is the housing needs and ΔP the change in the population into 2001-2011 decade. Moreover, an analysis of the third variable, that is the deficit of planning standards, is added (Y when the deficit is quantified, N when the standards are enough, and *not det.* when the information is not detectable). The determined scenario is shown in the following Table 4.

Table 4. Summary table of the municipal planning assessments.

Class of municipalities	Number	Planning standard deficit
Virtuous municipalities ($F_a = 0$)	4	3 Y
		1 not det.
Growing municipalities ($F_a > 0$; $\Delta P > 0$)	19	13 Y
		6 not det.
Uncontrolled municipalities ($F_a > 0$; $\Delta P < 0$)	17	10 Y
		6 not det.
		1 N

5.1 Virtuous Municipalities

In this category, only four municipalities are present: one of these is Amalfi, coastal municipality in the province of Salerno; the other three municipalities belong Neapolitan hinterland. Among all, the only municipality of Ottaviano sets do not need any new housing even if with a positive population growth. For the others, the population decline, between −4% and −5.4%, appears a strong deterrent to the new building (Table 5 below).

Regarding **Amalfi**, the planning requirements are not derived from the Provincial Plan (PTCP) but from the Territorial Master Plan (PUT) of Sorrento-Amalfi Peninsula, approved as a regional law (Campania Regional Law no. 35/1987) and still effective. This legislation is binding on the Municipality. The only area where the PUT admits additive transformations is a very small portion on the municipal boundary.

Table 5. The virtuous municipalities

Municipality	Housing needs	Pop 2001	Pop 2011	Δpop	Δpop (%)
Amalfi	0	5,428	5,163	−265	−4.9%
Casoria	0	81,888	78,647	−3,241	−4.0%
Massa di Somma	0	5,908	5,587	−321	−5.4%
Ottaviano	0	22,670	23,543	+873	+3.9%

Then, according to Art. 9 of the same Act, the potential needs for new residences is derived from the sum of three components: (a) the need by population growth, (b) the needs for the reduction of the crowding index and (c) the need for the replacement of unhealthy and not reparable dwellings. So, having to operate on the share of not repairable dwellings, the Municipality of Amalfi approves the requalification of the unused former public factory Pansa, not creating any new volumes.

The choice of no new building areas lies in the geographical position of the other three municipalities (Casoria, Massa di Somma and Ottaviano), because they are included in the fully congested Neapolitan hinterland.

In fact, despite the presence of unhealthy housing, the PUC of **Casoria** indicates «that the strategy of the Plan can only be oriented to a recycling of existing buildings (also including non-residential volumes, often abandoned), avoiding additional taking of non-urbanized land (a rare resource in Casoria) and giving priority restructuring of existing buildings, mostly dating from the years 60 and 80 of the twentieth century».

The town of **Massa di Somma** has drawn a plan of requalifications, demolitions and of tourism development, referring to the indications of the Territorial Landscape Plan, where the will to make urban regeneration and renovation of the existing buildings is declared.

Finally, with reference to housing decompression program of Regional Law 21/2003, the municipality of **Ottaviano** recalls the not needing of new residential housing and foresees a re-functioning of residential buildings in favor of production activities, tourist accommodation, tertiary and public interest.

5.2 Growing Municipalities

To obtain an indirect estimate of the land take in each single PUC, all these municipalities are classified according to the ratio of new housing needs (F_a) and the change in the population into 2001–2011 decade (ΔP):

$$\text{Oversizing index} = \frac{F_a}{\Delta P} \tag{1}$$

This formula (1) assumes that the population trend of the last decade will repeat itself identically in the subsequent period. Accordingly, the majority of the municipalities amounted to a ratio of between 0.2 and 3.8 housing for each new inhabitant, but instead two have a significantly higher ratio, Melizzano (Bn) with 6.8 and Grottaminarda (Av) with 30.0, as shown in the following table (Table 6):

Table 6. More growing municipalities

Municipality	Housing needs	Pop 2001	Pop 2011	Δpop	Δpop(%)	Oversizing index
Melizzano	184	1,865	1,892	+27	+1.4%	6.8
Grottaminarda	691	8,274	8,297	+23	+0.3%	30.0

It is important to note that, according to the regional legislation[6], each municipality calculates the housing needs in its two components:

- *previous needs*, due to the presence of unhealthy and not reparable dwellings and housing with high crowding index;
- *future needs*, connected to the demographic dynamics and new housing demand.

So, despite the choice of a very simplified demographic prediction, this procedure allows to have a comparative measurement, otherwise impossible, and highlights the municipalities with the most critical index.

To the share of new rooms due to the slight population increase (81), the municipality of **Melizzano** adds the needs due to non-domiciled residents (358), returning emigrants (58), for urban decentralization (100), industrialization (70), tourist attractiveness (100), coming to a need of 829 new rooms by 2020, corresponding to approximately 184 new appartaments (considering the average ratio of 4.5 rooms per unit).

Likewise, the municipality of **Grottaminarda** arrives to predict the *monstre* sum of 691 apartments, against a growth of only 23 units in the last decade. This data is justified by the population growth, by an employment increase expected to 2021[7] (capable of generating 608 new residents and then 234 apartments) as well as by the return of emigrants and the requirement resulting from overcrowded housing, cohabitations and improper housing.

The housing needs of other municipalities appear equally oversized: Casalnuovo di Napoli provides 1,101 new housing in the same fully congested area of Casoria and Ottaviano; Montecorvino Rovella, Campagna e Baronissi respectively predict 1,180, 1,207 and 2,373 housing needs, having a not so high growth trend (between 4% and 10%), and finally Sorrento which provides a need of 100 new apartments in an area of great environmental value.

5.3   Uncontrolled Municipalities

Lastly, the municipalities are defined uncontrolled when they declare a new housing need in their Master Plan despite a negative demographic balance in own territory.

---

[6] In 2009, the Planning Department of Campania Region has issued a document entitled *"The estimate of housing needs and the definition of guidelines for the determination of settlement weights in Ptcp"*, to which an update note was followed in 2010 [25].

[7] This employment increase would be given by the investments in the 2007–2013 European Social Fund (FSE), the 2007–2013 Rural Development Programme (PSR) of Campania Region, the Less developed regions Funds (FAS) and the Community Initiatives program (PIC) named Leader +.

Among the municipalities where a higher housing need results, we analyze: Vallo della Lucania, Guardia Lombardi, Caposele and Benevento (Table 7).

Table 7. More uncontrolled municipalities

Municipality	Housing needs	Pop 2001	Pop 2011	Δpop	Δpop (%)
Vallo della Lucania	617	8,818	8,680	−138	−1.6%
Guardia Lombardi	947	2,029	1,803	−226	−11.1%
Caposele	1,594	3,797	3,537	−260	−6.8%
Benevento	2,066	61,791	61,489	−302	−0.5%

The urban Plan of **Vallo della Lucania** is of 2013. The population trend is presented as «substantially constant» and similar to those of the entire province. In addition, the Plan notes that the number of households is growing due to the reduction in their average composition. Therefore, three scenarios are shown: (a) an increase in households of +411 to 2021, (b) an increase of +896, (c) an average increase between the previous two scenarios. The last option is adopted in the Plan

The municipality of **Caposele** has published an updated of Municipal Urban Plan in April 2010. While noting a steady and progressive decrease of the population, the PUC said that the forecast «can not ignore the factors related to the development of commercial, tourist and productive planned at the municipal level, and even less the factors related to regional planning and infrastructural upgrade of the whole province of Avellino and finally the tourist flows linked to the religious cult of San Gerardo».

In this way, it provides for a huge housing demand compared to the population size, due to the change in the average number of household members, to the employment increase determined by various development programs[8] and to the policies for reducing the crowding index. Adding the effects of Regional Law 2/96 "Regional measures in favor of the Campania citizens living abroad", the municipality defines a housing need *monstre* of 1,594 units.

Similarly, in the PUC of **Guardia Lombardi**, an employment increase is expected because of various development programs[9]. To these, the effects of initiatives aimed at the restoration and enhancement of historical centers and of environmental, architectural and touristic interest are added in the analysis. Lastly, combining the housing needs derives from the previously described employment increase, the needs resulting from the return of residents abroad and that deriving from policies for reducing

---

[8] They are: the 2007–2013 European Regional Development Fund, the 2007–2013 European Social Fund (FSE), the 2007–2013 Rural Development Programme (PSR) of Campania Region, the integrated Projects of Monti Picentini and Sele-Tanagro Park, and the programming established in the Regional Finance Act 8/2004, art.6).

[9] In particular: the 2007–2013 European Regional Development Fund, the 2007–2013 European Social Fund (FSE), the 2007–2013 Rural Development Programme (PSR) of Campania Region, the Community Initiatives program (PIC) named Leader +, the Integrated Project il P.I. "Tourist and Eno-gastronomic Chain", the Territorial Pact of Baronia and the Baronia Contract Program for Business Development.

overcrowding in existing housing, the municipality estimates the overall figure of 947 new apartments, despite a substantial process of depopulation in place.

In the context of this analysis, the municipality of **Benevento** has the highest housing dimensioning, by drawing 2,066 new housing units, but with a very low average number of square meters (79 m^2). This low figure is dictated precisely by the forecasts described in the Plan. Therein, it is explained that «to understand what might seem like a paradox, i.e. the increased needs», the fragmentation of families due to separations and divorces should be taken into account. For this purpose, the annual rate of change in household members is calculated, so as to give rise to a considerable increase in housing needs.

5.4 Planning Standars, Manufacturing and Commercial Surfaces

The dimensioning of an urban plan is the result of a complex of considerations that lead to the definition of strategic and operational decisions. To the analysis of the housing needs, the analysis on urban standards and the needs of new areas for production, trade and generally for the tertiary sector are always associated.

With regard to urban standards, the study found a significant and generalized shortcoming in surfaces. In complex of only 40 municipalities of the sample, a gap of about 2,050,000 m^2 is detected, thus equal the Principality of Monaco or about 300 football pitches.

The need is very variable. In fact, if on one hand the municipality congested of Ottaviano declares a deficit of about 300,000 m^2, on the other there are twelve municipalities that declare that current planning standards are satisfactory. Five of these belong to the province of Benevento. Instead, other municipalities such as San Prisco (Ce) and Cimitile (Na) declare needs respectively of 283,000 and 214,000 m^2.

This scenario of municipalities with a reduced endowment of public areas confirms the difficulties of the Local Authorities not only to identify free lands but also to carry out projects, because of the poor financial capacity often date from the non- payment of urbanization costs by citizens. The non-payment of urbanization costs weighs on the municipal budget and often leads to the failure to complete the secondary urbanization works planned in the planning stage.

With regard to production and commercial areas, only a few municipalities (such as Perito, Vallo della Lucania and Visciano) specifically highlight the need for non-residential surfaces.

In particular, the service sector is regulated by article 10 of the Regional Law 35/87, which stipulates that the areas to be allocated to private tertiary uses (like commecio, offices, leisure, tourism, etc.) may not exceed 3 m^2 per inhabitant. Often, this limit is already far exceeded by the existing surfaces, making it impossible to provide for new areas to commercial use. Specifically, this law is criticized in the PUC of Minori, defining it anachronistic. It points out that the existence of such a threshold involves problems in enhancement of services to households and businesses and in the expansion of tourism services, strategic sector for a town in the Amalfi Coast.

6 Open Issues

The work shows that the dimensioning are often the result of incorrect or excessive evaluations, for three reasons: the first concerns the estimation of the real housing needs, the second regards the overestimation of increasing employment, the third refers to the correct analytical scale where the population dynamics are observed.

Looking to the first aspect, according to the legislation of the Campania Region [25], the municipalities have to calculate the housing needs in its two components, for the programmatic provisions of Puc (Sect. 5.2): previous needs and future needs. The ratio of one lodging for each family is to be calculated on the effective presence and not on residential presence and considering the composition and social morphology of the family unit. In addition, it must consider the balance between existing and planned housing for the future needs.

According to the above, we have found that often the data concerning the actual presence is evaded and an improper correspondence between present and residents is established (as in the PUC of Baiano). Also, the reduction of the average composition of families, at times remarked (Sect. 5.3 Vallo della Lucania or Benevento), is not always sufficient condition for the definition of new needs, when many vacant rooms are present.

The lack of a formal monitoring of vacant rooms is an important issue. In fact, several civic initiatives go in this direction. We remember the campaign "Save the Landscape", carried out in 2012 by the homonymous Forum and addressed to all Italian municipalities, which asked for making public the number of unused, abandoned or vacant homes and industrial buildings, or the campaign "We reuse Italy" promoted by the WWF and aiming at achieving a census of brownfield sites, susceptible to transformation. The key concept of these civil actions was centered on the involvement of local Communities, invited to identify sites and to suggest possible strategies for reuse.

In the same way, it would be important to fully implement what the Article 42 of the Italian Constitution, that states about the expropriation for reasons of general interest. In this way, many empty urban spaces could be reused [1].

As regards the second point, the municipalities overemphasize employment forecasts on the basis of development programs, whose impact on employment is uncertain and needs to be verified. (Sect. 5.2, Grottaminarda and Sect. 5.3, Caposele e Guardia Lombardi). So, the employment estimates should be placed under really reached agreements, rather than only on the hypothesis of development.

This is well done in a Norwegian study [26], where the housing forecasts of all the municipalities are related to the local labor markets with a closer quantitative relationship. In this study, the large urban areas are distinctly analyzed, classifying them according to the economic base, as well as analyzing the migration flows due to university study and the population structure. Therefore, housing needs are not left to the markets alone but are identified on the basis of a precise design of future regional demand.

Finally, with regard to the third reason, the present analysis shows that the planning limits should be imposed and checked at a different scale from the municipal one and, at the same time, the definition of a limit for each area (as happens in the PTCP) is insufficient if it is not accompanied by a serious development analysis of the same, by a detailed analysis of population trends, and then, of the real needs.

Previous studies have shown that the choice of a different analytical scale, such as the large area or the urban system, allows a deeper analysis, for example contextualizing the measurement of the urban evolution to a specific phase of the urban life cycle of van den Berg model [3–5].

In France, for example, as already analyzed by the same author [1], a legislation that stimulates large-scale studies has been introduced already since 2000. With the establishment of the *Solidarité et Renouvellement Urbain*, the SCOTs (*Schémas de la COhérence Territorial*) are instituted, in order to coordinate the housing construction at an inter-municipal level [27]. Subsequently, the article L. 123-1-7 of the Urban Code (introduced by Law n. 2010-788 of 12 July 2010 on the national commitment to the environment called "Grenelle II" Law) provides for the possibility of developing a PLUi (Intermunicipal Local Urban Plan) with the effects of a SCOT[10]. So, since 2010, the Ministry of Territorial Equality and Housing has been offering € 50,000 grants to inter-municipal associations involved in developing a PLUi.

Afterwards, the legislature reinforced the article L. 122-2 (the principle of urbanization prohibition in the absence of SCOT) by Law n. 2014-366 of 24 March 2014, totally demanding the containment of land take at an over-municipal scale and focusing on the large-area administration, with the law of 7 August 2015 concerning the new territorial organization of the Republic.

So, in the SCOT of the Agglomeration of Lyon, we can observe a large area analysis[11] where a unique and homogeneous prediction of new inhabitants is carried outfor all 59 municipalities of the agglomeration, based on a preventive economic analysis (Fig. 2).

The doing analysis at regional level (Fig. 3) shows how an extended depopulation of inland areas does not match with a proportional definition of housing needs, with the result that whole portions of these areas are unnecessarily cemented. The population growth only crosses a narrow intermediate strip of the region (Fig. 1), where sometimes the Plans do not allow new residential areas, because the territory is completely congested [29]. By contrast, the availability of free lands seems to be the major driver for the constructive speculation of internal peripheries and inland areas [4].

So, this study confirms that the decoupled land take in the inland areas is a very urgent problem, to be addressed with multiple and coordinated instruments.

---

[10] See: https://www.data.gouv.fr/en/datasets/plans-locaux-durbanisme-intercommunal-plui-valant-scot-en-franche-comte/.

[11] See: SCOT 2030 Agglomération Lyonnaise at https://www.scot-agglolyon.fr/lagglomeration-lyonnaise-coeur-de-laire-metropolitaine/.

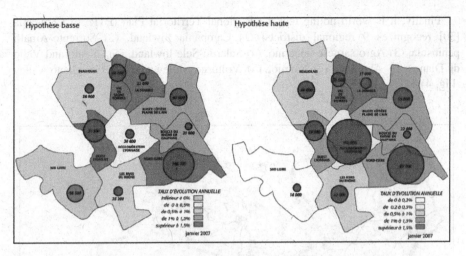

Fig. 2. Number of additional residents between 1999 and 2030 in the SCOT Agglomeration Lyon [28]. Source: https://www.scot-agglolyon.fr/espace-documentaire/

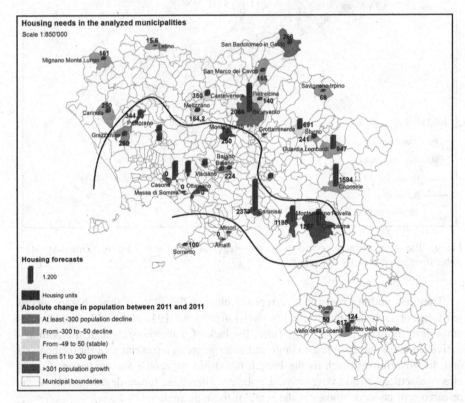

Fig. 3. Housing needs and population changes in the sample of 40 municipalities of Campania Region. (Our elaboration)

Finally, it is worth noting that the Regional Territorial Plan (PTR) of Campania [30] recognizes 9 regional districts: (1) Campania lowland, (2) Sorrento-Amalfi peninsula, (3) Agro sarnese-nocerino, (4) Salerno-Sele lowland, (5) Cilento and Vallo di Diano, (6) Avellino, (7) Sannio, (8) Volturno valley and (9) Gargliano valley (Fig. 4).

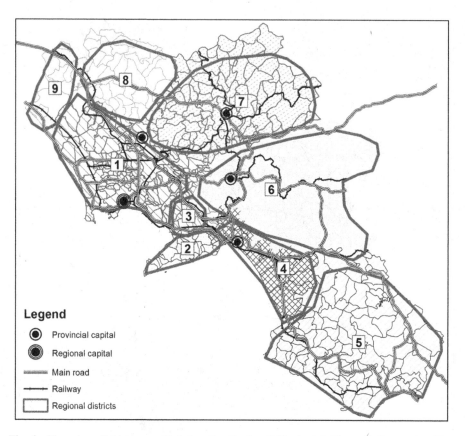

Fig. 4. The nine districts provided by the Regional Territorial Plan of Campania. (Our elaboration based on PTR mapping)

They are nothing more than a repositioning in the Plan of those homogeneous territories of analysis which were also envisioned by the 1942 National Urban Law but never fully implemented in Italy. Here, the lack of a reorganization of the administrative structure that gave rise to large and homogeneous territorial area for the analysis and the government (such as the French ones) has prevented the implementation of effective settlement and development policies. Therefore, future developments of the research will concern studies at the scale of the nine regional districts.

References

1. Bencardino M.: Land take and urban sprawl: drivers e contrasting policies. In: Bollettino, S. G.I. (ed.) Serie XIII, vol. VII(2), pp. 217–237. SGI, Roma (2015). ISSN: 1121-7820, http://societageografica.net/wp/wp-content/uploads/2016/08/bencardino_eng.pdf
2. Arcidiacono, A., Di Simine, D., Oliva, F., Ronchi, S., Salata, S.: Rapporto 2016: Nuove sfide per il suolo. INU Edizioni, Roma (2016)
3. Bencardino, M.: Demographic changes and urban sprawl in two middle-sized cities of campania region (Italy). In: Gervasi, O., Murgante, B., Misra, S., Gavrilova, Marina L., Rocha, A.M.A.C., Torre, C., Taniar, D., Apduhan, Bernady O. (eds.) ICCSA 2015. LNCS, vol. 9158, pp. 3–18. Springer, Cham (2015). doi:10.1007/978-3-319-21410-8_1
4. Bencardino, M.: Un'analisi comparativa dello sprawl nei sistemi urbani di Avellino e Benevento. Bollettino AIC 157, 27–40 (2016). OpenstarTs, Trieste, doi:10.13137/2282-472X/13569, e-ISSN: 2282-472X. https://www.openstarts.units.it/dspace/handle/10077/13569
5. Bencardino, M., Valanzano, L.: Una misura dello sprawl urbano nelle aree interne della Campania: i casi di Benevento, Avellino e Battipaglia. In: Munafò, M., e Marchetti, M. (eds) Recuperiamo Terreno. Analisi e prospettive per la gestione sostenibile della risorsa suolo. Franco Angeli Editore, Milano, pp. 73–88 (2015)
6. Bonora, P.: Atlante del consumo di suolo per un progetto di città metropolitana, Il caso Bologna. Baskerville, Bologna (2013)
7. Centro di Ricerca sui Consumi di Suolo: Rapporto 2009. INU Edizioni, Roma (2009). http://consumosuolo.org/pubblicazioni/rapporti-crcs/
8. CRCS: Rapporto 2010. INU Edizioni, Roma (2010)
9. CRCS: Rapporto 2012. INU Edizioni, Roma (2012)
10. CRCS: Rapporto 2014. INU Edizioni, Roma (2014)
11. Ferrara, A., Salvati, L., Sabbi, A., Colantoni, A.: Soil resources, land cover changes and rural areas: towards a spatial mismatch? Sci. Total Environ. 478, 116–122 (2014). Elsevier B.V., Amsterdam, doi:10.1016/j.scitotenv.2014.01.040
12. ISPRA: Il consumo di suolo in Italia – Edizione 2014, 195/2014. ISPRA Rapporti, Roma (2014). http://www.isprambiente.gov.it/it/pubblicazioni/rapporti/il-consumo-di-suolo-in-italia
13. ISPRA, Il consumo di suolo in Italia – Edizione 2015, 218. ISPRA Rapporti Roma (2015)
14. ISPRA, Consumo di suolo, dinamiche territoriali e servizi ecosistemici - Edizione 2016, 248. ISPRA Rapporti, Roma (2016)
15. Munafò, M., Marchetti, M.: Recuperiamo terreno. FrancoAngeli, Milano (2015)
16. Salvati, L.: Monitoring high-quality soil consumption driven by urban pressure in a growing city (Rome, Italy). Cities, 31, 349–356 (2013). Elsevier, doi:10.1016/j.cities.2012.11.001
17. Pileri P.: La frammentazione amministrativa consuma suolo. In: Convegno ISPRA, CRA e Università La Sapienza, Il Consumo di suolo, lo stato, le cause e gli impatti, 5 February 2013. ISPRA, Roma (2013)
18. Bencardino, M., Nesticò, A.: Demographic Changes and Real Estate Values. A Quantitative Model for Analyzing the Urban-Rural Linkages. Sustainability 9(4), 536 (2017). doi:10.3390/su9040536
19. Nesticò, A., Macchiaroli, M., Pipolo, O.: Costs and benefits in the recovery of historic buildings: the application of an economic model. Sustainability 7(11), 14661–14676 (2015). MDPI AG, Basel, doi:10.3390/su71114661
20. Nesticò, A., Pipolo, O.: A protocol for sustainable building interventions: financial analysis and environmental effects. Int. J. Bus. Intell. Data Mining 10(3), 199–212 (2015). doi:10.1504/IJBIDM.2015.071325. Inderscience Enterprises Ltd., Genève

21. Camagni, R., Gibelli, M.C., Rigamonti, P.: I costi collettivi della città dispersa. Alinea, Firenze (2002)
22. Camagni, R., Modigliani, D.: La rendita fondiaria/immobiliare a Roma: 6 studi di caso, XXVIII Congresso INU - Istituto Nazionale di Urbanistica, Città come motore di sviluppo del Paese, Salerno, 24–26 ottobre 2013
23. Bencardino, M., Greco, I., Ladeira, P.R.: The Comparative Analysis of Urban Development in Two Geographic Regions: The State of Rio de Janeiro and the Campania Region. In: Murgante, B., Gervasi, O., Misra, S., Nedjah, N., Rocha, Ana Maria A.C., Taniar, D., Apduhan, Bernady O. (eds.) ICCSA 2012. LNCS, vol. 7334, pp. 548–564. Springer, Heidelberg (2012). doi:10.1007/978-3-642-31075-1_41
24. Bencardino, M., Greco, I.: Processes of adaptation and creation of a Territorial Governance. The experience of the cities of Benevento and Salerno (Campania region, Italy). J. Sociol. Study, 2(11), 819–833 (2012). ISSN: 2159-5526, David Publishing Company, USA, http://www.davidpublishing.com/show.html?11206
25. Regione Campania: La stima del fabbisogno abitativo e la definizione degli indirizzi per la determinazione dei pesi insediativi nei Ptcp" (2009). http://burc.regione.campania.it/eBurcWeb/directServlet?DOCUMENT_ID=41908&ATTACH_ID=53745
26. Luksas, S.: Demographic changes, housing policies and urban planning. Nordregio Working Paper, 4, 1–48 (2013). Stockholm, Sweden
27. Prevost, A., Molines, N., Dehan, P., Bandet, J.: The urban planning of French cities and the challenge of sustainable town planning: improvement and limits. In: AESOP 26th Annual Congress, Ankara, Turkey, July 2012
28. SCOT de l'agglomération Lyonnaise: Rapport de presentation. https://www.scot-agglolyon.fr/espace-documentaire/
29. Bencardino, F., Greco, I.: Politiche di sviluppo regionale e assetto territoriale in Campania. Alcune riflessioni. Rivista Documenti Geografici, 2 (2016). doi:10.19246/docugeo2281-7549/201602_02. DSSF, Università di Roma, Tor Vergata
30. Regione Campania: PTR Cartografia di Piano. http://www.sito.regione.cam-pania.it/PTR2006/PTRindex.htm

Construction Costs Estimate for Civil Works. A Model for the Analysis During the Preliminary Stage of the Project

Antonio Nesticò[✉], Gianluigi De Mare, Biagino Frusciante, and Luigi Dolores

Department of Civil Engineering, University of Salerno, Via Giovanni Paolo II, 132, 84084 Fisciano, SA, Italy {anestico, gdemare}@unisa.it, gino.frusciante@alice.it, doloresl@hotmail.it

Abstract. In order to estimate the cost of construction it is necessary to identify all the elements having expense and to provide the corresponding economic values accordingly to the level of detail of the project. Given the high number of variables characterizing the engineering project, it is required to have simplified schemes able to facilitate the study and management of the project. In particular, a civil work needs to have a concise representation through a suitable classification system, which allows to identify sets of homogeneous elements such that the complexity of the analysis is reduced. The classification systems commonly treated in literature are indeed based on the assumption that the building process can be broken down into simple elements able to give an efficient representation of the whole project.

In the present paper, we first analyze the main classification systems of civil works, highlighting features, advantages and problems. Then, starting from the classification system proposed in Italy by the UNI 8290 regulation, which has been implemented and extended to multiple levels of detail, it is defined a Work Breakdown Structure (WBS) with the aim to be the reference for the description, the economic analysis and the management of the project already in the preliminary design stage and, later, also in its final planning stages and execution. Operationally, the decomposition of the project, aimed at identifying the processes needed to ensure the production of the work site, is the first step of the procedure, which is then followed by the quantification and the subsequent allocation of unit prices resulting from price lists. In these additional steps, we resort to semi-analytical estimation procedures, which allow us to draw up the Metric Computation (MC) and the Estimate Metric Computation (EMC) also in the preliminary design phase.

The use of a simplified base model for the decomposition of the project at the stage of preliminary analysis, can improve the accuracy of cost estimates, otherwise based on rough and often significantly approximate evaluations which follow from baseless estimates when compared to the macro-processing items. Increasing the accuracy of the cost estimates is of primarily interest as it can ensure higher margins of investments in the technical and economic feasibility

---

The authors equally contributed to this paper.

© Springer International Publishing AG 2017
O. Gervasi et al. (Eds.): ICCSA 2017, Part V, LNCS 10408, pp. 89–105, 2017.
DOI: 10.1007/978-3-319-62404-4_7

of the project on the territory, which may cover the infrastructures, the urban planning, the implementation of new technologies for the environment and the rational use of the land. In this way, it is possible to reduce the risk associated to the project initiative, also allowing a unique decomposition scheme of the project. Such scheme, adopted since the preliminary study, can be then integrated through the following phases of the final and executive project.

Keywords: Cost estimate · Planning levels · UNI 8290 · Uniformat II · Standard form of cost analysis · Work breakdown structure · Quantity takeoff · Bill of quantity

1   Relationship Between the Costs Estimate and the Project Levels

In order to realize a project that stays within the limits of planned expenses, it is necessary to estimate, check and manage the execution costs of the works throughout the whole design path [1–3]. The estimation process advances accordingly to the levels of details reached by the project, resulting from the available technical documents. There is a definite correlation between the level of details of the project and the accuracy of the economic costs [4]. The *American Association of Cost Engineering* (AACE) developed a classification matrix, defined within the recommended practice N.56R-08 which well shows this correlation [5, 6]. AACE establishes five classes of cost estimates, numbered from 5 to 1 accordingly to the information about the project, where the Class 5 – the lower level of information – is a rough estimate, obtained by analogy with other cases, while Class 1 is an analytical estimate, based on a detailed knowledge of all the parts of the project (Table 1).

Then, the construction costs estimate results to be closely related to the availability of the data of a project, as they allow to properly apply the estimation method. Such method relies on the following procedures [7–10]:

– *direct or comparatives estimation*, which identifies one or more parameters representing the elements of the general construction;
– *indirect or analytical procedures*, which make use of many parameters representing in details the quality and quantity of the elements of the project.

The direct method plays a key role during the early stages of the project. The representation of the project passes through the identification of a set of parameters intended to parameterize the elements of the project in a concise way, thus allowing to develop the estimate in the absence of the advanced project. Moreover, these parameters have to ensure an effective comparison between the project under analysis, whose technical details are known, and a collection of similar projects for which the technical details and costs of construction are already well known. To do this, one has to refer to projects as much as possible close to the one under analysis in relation to the intended use, architectural style, technological and construction specifications. The non perfect homogeneity among the projects imposes, in practice, the use of correction factors.

Table 1. Cost estimate classification matrix for building and general construction industries.

Estimate class	Primary characteristic	Secondary characteristic		
	Maturity level of project definition deliverables	End usage	Methodology	Expected accuracy range
	Expressed as % of complete definition	Typical purpose of estimate	Typical estimating method	Typical variation in low and high ranges[a]
Class 5	0% to 2%	Functional area, or concept screening	SF or m^2 factoring, parametric models, judgment, or analogy	L: −20% to −30% H: +30% to +50%
Class 4	1% to 15%	or Schematic design or concept study	Parametric models, assembly driven models	L: −10% to −20% H: +20% to +30%
Class 3	10% to 40%	Design development, budget authorization, feasibility	Semi-detailed unit costs with assembly level line items	L: −5% to −15% H: +10% to +20%
Class 2	30% to 75%	Control or bid/tender, semi-detailed	Detailed unit cost with forced detailed take-off	L: −5% to −10% H: +5% to +15%
Class 1	65% to 100%	Check estimate or pre bid/tender, change order	Detailed unit cost with detailed take-off	L: −3% to −5% H: +3% to +10%

Note: [a]The state of construction complexity and availability of applicable reference cost data affect the range markedly. The ± value represents typical percentage variation of actual cost from the cost estimate after application of contingency (typically at a 50% level of confidence) for given scope.

In Italy the direct processes can be implemented during the phase of «technical and economical feasibility project» (Art.23 Decree n.50/2016).

The accuracy in estimating the costs of construction can increase once the next levels of the project have been specified (e.g. final and executive projects according to the Italian regulations), where the analytical estimation methods are used. With those, one proceeds to the analysis of the production cycle which is necessary for the development of the project. This is done through the identification, quantification and subsequent exploitation of the works needed to realize the construction. The document that let us give a concrete representation to these phases is the Estimative Metric

Computation (EMC) which is made by two parts. The first part, the so called Metric Computation (MC), allows to identify the amount of materials, given the project, by using geometric criteria. The second part leads to the determination of the cost of the project, associating to the amount of materials, defined in the CM, their respective unit prices. The sum of the results provides the total cost [11].

For simplicity, in the preliminary stage of the project, one often proceeds without developing the classification of the elements of the building project, thus excluding the use of the analytical method. In this case, the costs estimate is based on direct procedures which mostly use mono-parameters. Usually, this entails low reliability of the evaluation process and also determines the inability to correlate the direct estimate of the first level with the analytical estimates developed during the final and executive phases of the project.

The use of the classification methods during the preliminary phase is already practice in some international contexts, and it allows to build economic models capable to improve the reliability of estimated cost.

2   Overview on the International Classification Systems

For the rigorous estimation of the construction cost of the building, it is of preliminary importance the classification of the project, i.e. its breakdown, which aims at identifying the necessary works items needed for the construction site. Considering that the building is a structured system of elements, the breakdown system provides a reference for its description and economic and management analysis.

Operationally, the project breakdown can be done accordingly to the national regulation UNI 8290, and in international contexts accordingly to the classification systems *UNIFORMA II* and *ELEMENTAL STANDARD FORM OF COST ANALYSIS*.

2.1   The UNI 8290 Regulation

The UNI 8290 regulation proposes the classification of the building system in several levels, according to rational and homogeneous criteria. Therefore, the elements of the building system are identified and placed in a hierarchical scheme that provides three levels of detail. The main criterion is the capability to trace back the sequential stages that mark the progress in the construction of the building, recovering the technical elements involved in each phase, i.e. prefiguring a classificatory sequence that decomposes the building in: firstly in classes of technological units; then, each class of technological unit is in turns decomposed into technological units; finally, each technological unit is decomposed into classes of technical elements. This classification is then divided in three levels:

1. *Classes of technological units* (first level of detail). At this level belongs the more complex elements of the project: structures, closures, exterior and internal partitions, service delivery systems, security systems, internal and external equipments;

2. *Technological units* (the second level of detail). To this level belongs the building blocks of individual technological units. The complexity decreases disaggregating individual classes in entities with more detailed properties;
3. *Classes of technical elements* (third level of detail). At this level belongs those elements for which the complexity is further reduced while increasing the level of detail. The decomposition in classes of technical elements allows to identify general technological requirements.

The UNI 8290 regulation provides the option to implement additional levels accordingly to the choices of the project. For the identification of the fourth and the subsequent levels, it establishes some criteria such that the levels of decomposition gradually foreshadow more and more details. Obviously, it is necessary that the requirements of each level have to be homogeneous among them.

Let us note that the UNI 8290 regulation also has some limitations, such as the lack of some steps, mostly related to the preliminary stage of the project, such as the set up of the building site work, which is a fundamental element to which often corresponds a significant financial effort.

2.2   Uniformat II and Elemental Standard Form of Cost Analysis

The *National Institute of Standards and Technology* (NIST) of the Department of American Commerce describes Uniformat II as a classification system of the technical and technological elements, intended as the most common elements for most of the buildings, and which defines both the building and the construction site [12]. Uniformat II identifies the functional elements of a general construction and organizes them according to a scheme referring to the role that the single element has to perform. It identifies two distinct systems:

– Technological system (Building Elements, item A ÷ F);
– Environmental system (Building Related Site work, item G).

Uniformat II defines in the classification of building elements also those elements that belong to the environment in which the building is located, such as contextual situation, the distinctive characteristics of the construction site and preliminary works in the site work [13], allowing some improvement in the ability to represent the project process compared to the national classification system (UNI 8290). Uniformat II is the result of an upgrade of the original model Uniformat, through the addition of further factors which have to be taken into account during the analysis and of more detailed descriptions of the elements already present in the original document. Therefore, instead of only three levels of initial hierarchical classification, the new report provides four levels of definition and division:

– *Major Group Elements (Level 1)*, which includes the largest number of elements and identifies more precisely the substructure, the shell and the interiors;
– *Group Elements (Level 2)*, which divides and describes in more detail the elements of the Level 1. The shell includes, for example, the external closures and the roof;

- *Individual Elements (Level 3)*, which represents a further step of decomposition of the elements of the building. At this level the external closures include external walls, windows and doors;
- *Sub Elements (level 4)*, proposed by Uniformat version II. It further divides the single elements in several sub-elements. For example, as sub-elements of the foundations one can consider: the foundation walls, the pillars, insulation and protection of the walls against the ground.

A similar classification system has been proposed by the Building Cost Information Service (hereafter BCIS), in order to plan the cost and to control the construction costs in the UK [14].

BCIS developed in 2012 an elemental classification scheme, namely the Standard Form of Cost Analysis (SFCA), which attempted to take charge of the technical and methodological innovations, involving all the areas of interest that characterize the construction industry [15–18]. The hierarchical structure provided by the BCIS can be seen both as a work breakdown structure and as a cost breakdown structure. It is divided in four levels:

1. Group elements: 0 Facilitating works; 1 Substructure; 2 Superstructure; 3 Internal finishes; 4 Fittings, furnishings and equipment; 5 Services; 6 Prefabricated buildings and building units; 7 Work to existing buildings; 8 External works;
2. Elements;
3. Sub-elements;
4. Components.

The extension to the Level 4, for the two proposed systems, allows to complete the description of the building system and it can also be used to proceed, with suitable adjustments, to the extension of the UNI 8290 regulation.

The classification systems based on the UNI 8290 regulation, Uniformat II and SFCA, although they are all hierarchical schemes, exhibit some differences. The first difference is in the number of levels which the system is made of. Indeed, the UNI 8290 regulation presents three levels while the other two have four.

This means that in the classification used in the US and in the UK, an higher level of details is defined. The second difference lies in the number of work items in each level; Uniformat II and SFCA are more complete than the system introduced by the UNI 8290, regardless of the level considered, since they do not just handle with elements physically making up the building, but they also define the elements that affect its construction. These differences make that among the three hierarchical systems analyzed, the English and American ones are more complete and with a wider range of applicability than the system proposed by the Italian regulations. That is because the classification system proposed by the UNI 8290 regulation has been realized to account only for the decomposition and classification of the building and it is not expected to be used in the phase of design and management. While, international models simultaneously allow to represent both the technical aspects and the more significant costs of the project. Moreover, they are able to satisfy the necessary requirements for the development of the estimate of the costs also during the phase of technical and economic feasibility of the project.

In light of the international classification systems, in the present paper we will define a classification model based on the UNI 8290 regulation which will be then supplied with some additional items following the Uniformat II and SFCA. This is in order to ensure on one hand the easy compilation of the CME already in the preliminary planning stage, and on the other hand the construction of an informative system able to define all the elements of the project.

3 An Economic Model to Estimate the Cost of Construction in Building Industry

The EMC requires the adoption of a classification for the construction materials articulated on one level of detail, from the project to the list of work items. It is possible to develop a system of classification characterized by increasing levels of details, able to connect the different stages of development of the project within a single classification system that requires only adjustments during the progress of the technical project.

The decomposition criterion of the project on several levels has to represent the work in all its aspects, it has to be understandable and has to ensure clarity in tracing back to the choices made at different stages of the project. The final objective is to develop a read-model project able to represent the whole project in all the developing stages with unitary logic [19–21].

The logical path to estimate the cost of construction, during the preliminary stage of technical and economic feasibility study, passes through three specific documents:

1. Work Breakdown Structure (WBS);
2. Metric Computation for Classes of Technical Elements, MC_{CTE};
3. Estimate Metric Computation for Classes of Technical Elements, EMC_{CTE}.

Practically, once the classification structure has been defined, one can proceed with the quantification by using the MC_{CTE}, on the basis of the geometric analysis of the planivolumetric. Subsequently, the application of the unit price, obtained from the Price list, to each element of the MC_{CTE}, allows to process the EMC for classes of technical elements EMC_{CTE}.

Here, we propose the WBS model that implements the classification system UNI 8290 through Uniformat II and SFCA.

The representation models of the building system, on which national and international regulations are applied, are constructed on a generic project. This means that the classification systems mentioned before have to be properly modified in order to accurately represent a specific project. Moreover, the levels of detail of the UNI8290 regulation are not sufficient to provide a complete description of the project, which requires the identification of additional levels of details to fully represent it.

The classification criteria analyzed are based on the assumption that a building process can be divided into simple elements. This implies that a generic project can be seen as the sum of all its basic components [22–25].

The WBS is the first and basic support tool for the project planning [26–29] and it allows to view the entire project breaking down into steps. Each steps, in turn, will be

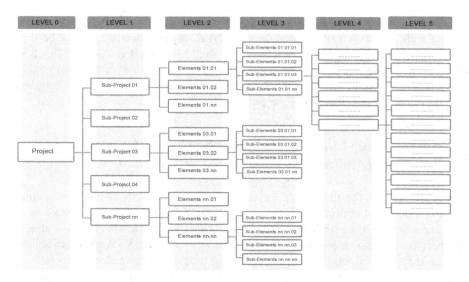

Fig. 1. Levels of detail of a work breakdown structure.

divided into more elementary activities, with a hierarchical structure, from the general (work to be executed) to the particular (processing) (Fig. 1).

The detailed analysis of each steps will allow to view the whole process with all its features. The basic structure may refer to generic or standard models. What matters in defining the project, its general features and details, is to set properly this tool through:

- rational breakdown of the project;
- structuring the analysis through multiple levels of detail, accordingly to the result one wants to achieve and on the contents in the project's documentation;
- hierarchical representation of the project contents.

Starting from a general classification system one proceeds by subtraction of the elements that do not belong to the project under consideration, eventually adding those elements that the standard regulation does not provide. Figure 2 accounts of the need to introduce, in the first level of the project breakdown in the UNI 8290, additional components of the project that are considered in Uniformat II and SFCA and that UNI 8290 does not include.

The well-defined scheme of WBS outlines a representation of the project's structure which also contains items related to preliminary work (building site work), the technical and methodological innovations (Prefabricated building; Special construction), then involving all the areas of interest that characterize the construction industry.

This aspect allows an improvement in the ability to represent the project's process compared to the national classification systems (UNI 9280).

This initial procedure outlines a scheme defined "primary", which is followed by a further breakdown of the identified components. The process continues iteratively, identifying all the necessary levels up to the lowest level of detail desired. The formulation of a WBS, for the design of a generic building, can be organized according to the following scheme (Fig. 3):

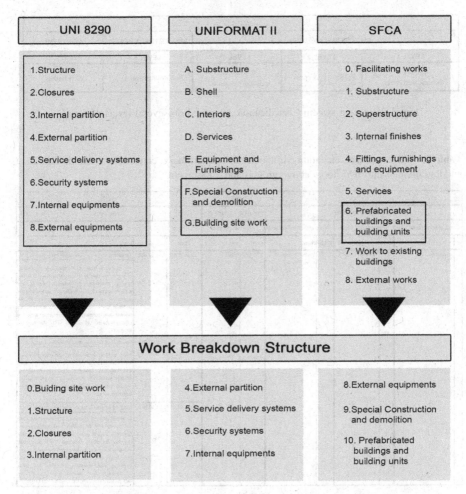

Fig. 2. WBS simplified diagram obtained by implementing the UNI 8290.

- Class of technological units;
- Technological units;
- Class of technical elements;
- Technical elements;
- Work items.

The UNI 8290 regulation divides the building system according to the criteria defining three levels of breakdown, then being a pre-WBS. The classes of technical elements can be divided through the identification of technical elements and price items (Table 2).

The design choices identify the level 4 (technical elements), while the breakdown leads to Level 5 (work items) which is required because the available data in literature

WBS				
UNI 8290 IMPLEMENTED			PROJECTUAL CHOICES	WORKINGS
LEVEL 1	LEVEL 2	LEVEL 3	LEVEL 4	LEVEL 5
Classes of technological units	Technological units	Classes of technical elements	Technical elements	Work Items

Fig. 3. Building system Classification structured on several levels of detail.

Table 2. WBS: vertical elevation structures for an ordinary construction identifiable in a building divided into two floors above ground and a basement.

WBS								
UNI 8290 IMPLEMENTED					PROJECTUAL CHOICES		WORKINGS	
Classes of technological units		Technological units		Classes of technical elements	Technical elements		Work Items	
ID	Name	ID TU	Name	ID CTE	Name	ID TE	Name	ID WI	ID price list	Name
1	Structures	1.2	Elevated structures	1.2.01	Vertical elevation structures	1.2.01.01	Pillars	1.2.01.01.01	E.03.30.10.b	Formwork for vertical elevation structures
										Formwork any straight or arched type for castings of simple or reinforced concrete mixes including arming, disarming, disarmament, shoring and support works up to a height of 4 meters and the supporting surface, and the cleaning of the material for re-use; carried out in a workmanlike manner and measured in accordance with the effective surface of contact with the concrete formwork.
								1.2.01.01.02	E.03.40.10.a	Structural steel for vertical elevation structures
										B450C steel reinforced concrete, in accordance with applicable technical standards, cut to size, shaped and installed, including scrap, ligatures, the charges for the required checks and anything else necessary to give the finished work to the highest standards in 'art.
								1.2.01.01.03	E.03.10.30.a	Concrete structures for vertical elevation Rck 30
										Concrete durable guaranteed performance with consistency class S4, with a maximum aggregate size of 32 mm, in accordance with the applicable technical standards. Provided and implemented, including the use of the pump and the vibrator, and the offcuts and costs of controls provided and anything else necessary to give the work completed in a professional manner. They are excluded formwork and the reinforcement rods.

refer to the work items and not to the technical elements. In this way it is possible to identify those elements of the project that are able to express the costs.

In order to identify the conventional work items, one starts from the general considerations that, through the analysis of the needs of the construction site for the realization of the single technical element, lead to the identification of the necessary product classes, and then look within these to find the appropriate processing. This step has to be extended to each technical element up to complete the analysis for the whole Level 5, with the identification of all work items.

The structured analysis through WBS allows to create an understandable and concise format, which is useful in defining all the technical aspects and the most significant costs of the project. These are essential data if one wants to develop the cost estimate, which reliability improves during the phases of definition of the project.

The following section explains the procedure leading to filling in the MC and EMC documents.

4 Semi-analytical Estimates Procedure: MC and EMC for Classes of Technical Elements

Once the classification procedure of the project is complete, one can proceed filling in the MC and then the EMC based on the level of details of classes of technical elements. During the preliminary phase, the informative content of the technical and economical feasibility study does not allow the analytical calculation of the quantities to be assigned to the components of the detail. That is because of the lack of the project documentation, which will be available only during the executive phase or at least partially during the final one. Based on the low information available at the lowest level of the project (such as the contents of the preliminary project document, the general project solutions and the geometric data of the planivolumetric), one can proceed to measure the classes of technical elements. From a practical point of view, it is necessary to identify sustainable rules for estimating the quantities solely on the basis of the available geometric contents. In this regards, it is possible for some classes of technological units to estimate their quantity through the general geometry of the project, as for example in the case of the shell and for the interior spaces (both vertical and horizontal surfaces). For other classes of technological units one should try to build a rational link between the geometrical information, defined by the planivolumetric, and the class of technical elements under analysis, such as the amount of steel for the reinforced concrete structures, which can be deduced from tabulated values and statistical data (Table 3).

Table 3. Parameterization of the ordinary requirements of steel for reinforced concrete works, ordinary values (source: Utica G. 2011).

Quantity of steel for m^3 of concrete	$[kg/m^3]$
Plinth	$40 \div 50$
Walls against ground	$60 \div 70$
Walls of elevation	$75 \div 85$
Direct foundations	$60 \div 70$
Pillars	$75 \div 85$

Once identified a relation between the classes of technical elements and the information about the project, it is possible to use the appropriate tools which are necessary to set up a quantitative analysis during the preliminary stage of the project [30]. The following example (see Table 4) will make a better understanding of the overall logic of the procedure.

Let us consider a building with two basement floors and one ground floor. The elevation vertical structures are the pillars and partition walls made of reinforced concrete, built with concrete Rck 30, formwork panels of wood and steel reinforcement

Table 4. Metric Computation for classes of technical elements: the vertical elevation facilities for ordinary construction identifiable in a building divided into two floors above ground and a basement.

		K	Length	Width	Height	Coeff.	U.m.	Results
METRIC COMPUTATION for Classes of Technical Elements CM$_{CTE}$								
	Note	K	Length	Width	Height	Coeff.	U.m.	Results
01.02.00 VERTICAL ELEVATION STRUCTURES								
01.02.01 Vertical elevation structures : concrete								
Basement pillars	GFA cellar		15.95	6.60	2.70	4.00%	[m³]	11.37
	to deduct stairway	-1.00	4.20	1.80	2.70	4.00%	[m³]	-0.82
	Total basement						[m³]	10.55
Pillars ground floor	ground floor		15.95	6.60	3.00	4.00%	[m³]	12.63
	to deduct stairway	-1.00	4.20	1.80	3.00	4.00%	[m³]	-0.91
							[m³]	11.73
Pillars first floor 1 P.	first floor		15.95	6.60	3.00	4.00%	[m³]	12.63
	to deduct stairway	-1.00	4.20	1.80	3.00	4.00%	[m³]	-0.91
							[m³]	11.73
	Total vertical elevation structures: concrete						[m³]	34.00
01.02.02 Vertical elevation structures: formwork								
Basement pillars							10.00	[m²]	105.53
Pillars ground floor							10.00	[m²]	117.25
Pillars first floor 1 P.							10.00	[m²]	117.25
	Total vertical elevation structures: formwork						[m²]	340.03
01.02.03 Vertical elevation structures: structural stell work								
Basement pillars							80.00	[kg]	844.21
Pillars ground floor							80.00	[kg]	938.02
Pillars first floor 1 P.							80.00	[kg]	2,720.25
	Total vertical elevation structures: structural stell						[kg]	4,502.48
VERTICAL ELEVATION STRUCTURES: estimated quantities								
	Concrete for vertical elevation structures						[m³]	34.00
	Formwork for vertical elevation structures						[m³]	340.03
	Structural stell for vertical elevation structures						[kg]	4,502.48

B450C. The vertical structures have a base area which occupies a percentage of the surface of the deck. By analyzing the statistical restriction of geometric data on multiple projects with a bearing structure of reinforced concrete, this percentage can be reasonably estimated to be about 4.00%. The interstorey and the perimeter of the elements to be estimated can be deduced from the planivolumetric. This information allows to directly quantify the required amount of concrete. By using tabulated values available in literature, one can determine the amount of required formwork (7.00–12.00 m^2 of formwork/m^3 concrete) and of round steel (75–85 kg steel/m^3 concrete). Extending the process to all classes of technical elements defined in the WBS, the geometric quantities are estimated.

To estimate the cost of construction will be necessary to associate to each class of technical elements the corresponding price. As it can be seen from Table 5, one first has to identify a stratigraphy of all work items which are necessary for the development of the production process associated to each class of technical elements, and to assign to each item the unit price derived from informative Price lists [31].

Table 5. Estimate Metric Computation for classes of technical elements: the vertical elevation facilities for ordinary construction identifiable in a building divided into two floors above ground and a basement.

WBS	Code	Work Items	K	Weight	U.m.	Price List €	Weighted price €	Quantity	Amount €
		ESTIMATE METRIC COMPUTATION for Classes of Technical Elements CM$_{GTE}$							
1.2.01	VERTICAL ELEVATION STRUCTURES								
	Concrete for vertical elevation structures								
	Stratigraphy cost								
	E.03.10.30.a	Concrete structures for vertical elevation Rck 30			[m³]	130.56	130.56		
	Total cost stratigraphy						130.56	34.00	4,439.04
	Formwork for vertical elevation structures								
	Stratigraphy cost								
	E.03.30.10.b	Formwork for vertical elevation structures			[m²]	30.18	30.18		
	Total cost stratigraphy						30.18	340.03	10,262.11
	Structural stell for vertical elevation structures								
	Stratigraphy cost								
	E.03.40.10.a	Structural stell for vertical elevation structures			[kg]	1.43	1.43		
	Total cost stratigraphy						1.43	4,502.48	6,438.55
	VERTICAL ELEVATION STRUCTURES: estimated cost								21,139.69

The cost of construction obtained through this estimation procedure identifies the costs defined as "obvious value" (Table 6). This constitutes a possible underestimation of the cost value because the classes of technical elements considered at this level of the project represent the items that have the most economic impact. One can overcome it by applying the ABC analysis, which allows to assign the project costs to three possible classes of membership, namely A, B and C, in relation to the contribution given by the cost value. In general the 10% of the quantities belong to Class A which represent 70%

Table 6. Summary of the construction cost framework for an ordinary construction identifiable in a building divided into two floors above ground and a basement.

Summary framework			
Building site work: Estimated cost	€	9,039.62	3.06
Direct foundations: Estimated cost	€	6,653.68	2.25
Vertical elevation structures: Estimated cost	€	21,139.69	7.15
Elevation horizontal structures: Estimated cost	€	7,022.66	2.38
Containment structures: Estimated cost	€	17,246.21	5.84
Closing basic horizontal: Estimated cost	€	6,634.28	2.25
Closure vertical matt: Estimated cost	€	67,847.94	22.96
Closure vertical transparent: Estimated costo	€	22,911.94	7.75
Upper closure: Estimated cost	€	24,933.00	8.44
Closure of open spaces: Estimated cost	€	6,098.90	2.06
Vertical partitions internal matt: Estimated cost	€	17,444.25	5.90
Partitions internal vertical transparent: Estimated cost	€	7,998.00	2.71
Closures internal horizontal: Estimated cost	€	21,994.25	7.44
Internal divisions inclined: Estimated cost	€	9,381.61	3.18
Plumbing: Estimated cost	€	8,167.95	2.76
Heating system: Estimated cost	€	23,155.30	7.84
Electrical system: Estimated cost	€	17,803.93	6.03
Total estimated cost of construction (class a, b)	€	**295,473.21**	100.00
Costs in class c 10.00%	€	**29,547.32**	
Estimated cost of construction	€	**325,020.53**	
Total cost of construction unit	€/[m³]	**382.38**	

of the total value. Belong to Class B the 20% of the quantities that represent the 20% of the total value. The remaining quantities are placed in class C which, although representing the remaining 70% of the quantities, collect the remaining 10% of the total value.

In connection with the ABC analysis, one can consider that the procedure for filling in the EMC for classes of technical elements EMC_{CTE} enhances the costs of the classes A and B. For the correct estimation of construction costs, it will be necessary to enhance the outcome of EMC_{CTE} of 10% share of the value representative of the class C that is excluded from EMC_{CTE} because of the approximations that necessarily accompany the preliminary project [20, 21].

5 Conclusion

On the basis of the methodologies established in international literature, the paper proposes a classification system for technical elements of the project, which has to be implemented according to the increasing levels of detail, since the preliminary stage up to the final and executive ones. The UNI 8290 regulation, in force in Italy, is the basic reference for the structured analysis, which has been integrated in order to obtain a Work Breakdown Structure able to account for the technical innovations and to involve all the areas of interest for the construction industry. Essentially, the goal is to properly consider in the WBS: new materials and manufacturing processes; the different types of constructions; all the components producing expenses; the whole process of the project's definition, which starts since the preliminary study, now called techno-economic feasibility study.

Downstream of the WBS characterization, the use of semi-analytical estimation procedures can help, since the initials stages of design, to define guidelines that, during the subsequent stages of detailed development of the project, have to be reasonably (only) confirmed. Mostly, it allows an improvement in the reliability of economic estimation, thus reducing the risk related to the actual feasibility of investment projects [32–34]. Of course, it has a strong impact on the community, in terms of positive feedback about the execution of both public and private works, which may relate to urban renewal, urban development planning, the implementation of new technologies for the environmental sustainability and the rational use of the land [35–40].

In light of the positive impact that careful estimates of costs can produce at an early stage of the project, the model of analysis shown in this paper may become operational practice. Checks on specific projects may outline interesting research developments.

References

1. Ashworth, A., Perera, S.: Cost Studies of Buildings. Routledge, London (2015)
2. Galli, D., Gentile, D., Gualandi, V.P.: Appalti Pubblici. IPSOA, Milano (2015)
3. Washington State Department of Transportation: Cost Estimating Manual for Project. WSDOT publications, USA (2015)
4. Oberlender, G.D.: Project Management for Engineering and Construction. McGraw-Hill, New York (1993)
5. AACE International: Recommended Practice No. 18R-97, Cost Estimate Classification System – as Applied for the Building and General Construction Industries. AACE International, USA (2011)
6. AACE International: Recommended Practice No. 56R-08, Cost Estimate Classification System – as Applied for the Building and General Construction Industries. AACE International, USA (2012)
7. Phaobunjong, K.: Parametric cost estimating model for conceptual cost estimating of building construction projects. Dissertation presented to the Faculty of the Graduate School of The University of Texas, Austin (2002)
8. Niazi, A., et al.: Product cost estimation: technique classification and methodology review. J. Manuf. Sci. Eng. **128**(2), 563–575 (2006)
9. USD (AT&L): Handbook: Construction Cost Estimating, Department of Defense, USA (2011)
10. Mislick, G.K., Nussbaum, D.A.: Cost estimation: methods and tools. Wiley, Hoboken (2015)
11. De Mare, G., Morano, P.: La stima del costo delle opere pubbliche. Utet, Torino (2002)
12. Charette, R.P., Marshall, H.E.: UNIFORMAT II Elemental Classification for Building Specifications, Cost Estimating, and Cost Analysis. NIST, USA (1999)

13. ASTM E 1557-97: Standard Classification for Building Elements and Related Sitework - UNIFORMAT II. American Society for Testing and Materials, West Conshohocken, PA (1997)
14. Akintoye, A., Fitzgerald, E.: A survey of current cost estimating practices in the UK. Constr. Manage. Econ. **18**(2), 161–172 (2000)
15. Benge, D.P.: NRM1 Cost Management Handbook. Routledge, London (2014)
16. Royal Institution of Chartered Surveyors: New Rules of Measurement. Order of Cost Estimating and Cost Planning for Capital Building Works. 2nd edn. RICS, Coventry, UK (2012)
17. Royal Institute of British Architects: RIBA Plan of Work 2013. RIBA, London (2013)
18. Building Costs Information Service: Elemental Standard Form of Cost Analysis, 4th edn. BCIS, London (2012)
19. Utica, G.: Ingegnerizzazione e gestione economica del progetto, vol. 1. Maggioli Editore, Rimini, Italy (2008)
20. Utica, G.: Tecniche avanzate di Analisi e gestione dei progetti. McGraw-Hill, Milano (2010)
21. Utica, G.: La stima sintetica del costo di costruzione, Il computo metrico e il computo metrico estimativo per classi di elementi tecnici. Maggioli Editore, Rimini, Italy (2011)
22. Tausworthe, R.C.: The work breakdown structure in software project management. J. Syst. Softw. **1**, 181–186 (1980)
23. Haugan, G.T.: Effective Work Breakdown Structures. Management Concepts Inc., Vienna, VA (2002)
24. Jung, Y., Woo, S.: Flexible work breakdown structure for integrated cost and schedule control. J. Constr. Eng. Manage. **130**(5), 616–625 (2004)
25. Miti, G.: Stima del costo di costruzione nelle opere di ingegneria civile, 2nd edn. Legislazione Tecnica, Roma (2016)
26. Nesticò, A., Pipolo, O.: A protocol for sustainable building interventions: financial analysis and environmental effects. Int. J. Bus. Intell. Data Min. **10**(3), 199–212 (2015). doi:10.1504/IJBIDM.2015.071325. Inderscience Enterprises Ltd., Genève, Switzerland
27. Nesticò, A., Macchiaroli, M., Pipolo, O.: Costs and benefits in the recovery of historic buildings: the application of an economic model. Sustainability **7**(11), 14661–14676 (2015). doi:10.3390/su71114661. MDPI AG, Basel, Switzerland
28. Bottero, M., Ferretti, V., Mondini, G.: How to support strategic decisions in territorial transformation processes. Int. J. Agric. Environ. Inf. Syst. **6**(4), 40–55 (2015). doi:10.4018/IJAEIS.2015100103. IGI Global Publishing, United States
29. Morano, P., Tajani, F.: The break-even analysis applied to urban renewal investments: a model to evaluate the share of social housing financially sustainable for private investors. Habitat Int. **59**, 10–20 (2017). doi:10.1016/j.habitatint.2016.11.004
30. Kim, G.H., An, S.H., Kang, K.I.: Comparison of construction cost estimating models based on regression analysis, neural networks, and casebased reasoning. Build. Environ. **39**(10), 1235–1242 (2004)
31. Campania, R.: Prezzario dei lavori Pubblici. DEI Tipografia del Genio Civile, Roma (2015)
32. Mare, G., Manganelli, B., Nesticò, A.: The economic evaluation of investments in the energy sector: a model for the optimization of the scenario analyses. In: Murgante, B., Misra, S., Carlini, M., Torre, C.M., Nguyen, H.-Q., Taniar, D., Apduhan, B.O., Gervasi, O. (eds.) ICCSA 2013. LNCS, vol. 7972, pp. 359–374. Springer, Heidelberg (2013). doi:10.1007/978-3-642-39643-4_27

33. Calavita, N., Calabrò, F., Della Spina, L.: Transfer of development rights as incentives for regeneration of illegal settlements. In: 1th International Symposium New Metropolitan Perspectives (ISTH 2020). Advanced Engineering Forum, vol. 11, pp. 639–646. Trans Tech Publications, Switzerland (2014). doi:10.4028/www.scientific.net/AEF.11.639

34. Nesticò, A., Galante, M.: An estimate model for the equalisation of real estate tax: a case study. Int. J. Bus. Intell. Data Min. **10**(1), 19–32 (2015). doi:10.1504/IJBIDM.2015.069038. Inderscience Enterprises Ltd., Genève, Switzerland

35. Aragona, S., Calabrò, F., Della Spina, L.: The evaluation culture to build a network of competitive cities in the mediterranean. In: 1th International Symposium New Metropolitan Perspectives (ISTH 2020). Advanced Engineering Forum, vol. 11, pp. 476–482. Trans Tech Publications, Switzerland (2014). doi:10.4028/www.scientific.net/AEF.11.476

36. Greco, I., Bencardino, M.: The paradigm of the modern city: *SMART and SENSEable Cities* for smart, inclusive and sustainable growth. In: Murgante, B., Misra, S., Rocha, A.M.A.C., Torre, C., Rocha, J.G., Falcão, M.I., Taniar, D., Apduhan, B.O., Gervasi, O. (eds.) ICCSA 2014. LNCS, vol. 8580, pp. 579–597. Springer, Cham (2014). doi:10.1007/978-3-319-09129-7_42

37. Bencardino, M.: Demographic changes and urban sprawl in two middle-sized cities of campania region (Italy). In: Gervasi, O., Murgante, B., Misra, S., Gavrilova, M.L., Rocha, A. M.A.C., Torre, C., Taniar, D., Apduhan, Bernady O. (eds.) ICCSA 2015. LNCS, vol. 9158, pp. 3–18. Springer, Cham (2015). doi:10.1007/978-3-319-21410-8_1

38. De Mare, G., Granata, M.F., Nesticò, A.: Weak and strong compensation for the prioritization of public investments: multidimensional analysis for pools. Sustainability **7** (12), 16022–16038 (2015). doi:10.3390/su71215798. MDPI AG, Basel, Switzerland

39. Bencardino, M., Nesticò, A.: Demographic changes and real estate values. A quantitative model for analyzing the urban-rural linkages. Sustainability **9**(4), 536 (2017). doi:10.3390/su9040536

40. Guarini, M.R., Buccarini, C., Battisti, F.: Technical and Economic Evaluation of a Building Recovery by Public-Private Partnership in Rome (Italy). In: Stanghellini, S., Morano, P., Bottero, M., Oppio, A. (eds.) Appraisal: From Theory to Practice. GET, pp. 101–115. Springer, Cham (2017). doi:10.1007/978-3-319-49676-4_8

Assessing the Effect of Land Use Planning on Soil Savings by SEA

Carmelo Maria Torre[1(✉)], Tommaso Passaro[1],
and Valentina Sannicandro[2]

[1] MITO Lab, Department of Civil Engineering Sciences and Architecture,
Polytechnic University of Bari, Via Orabona 4, Bari, Italy
carmelomaria.torre@poliba.it,
tommaso.passaro@gmail.com
[2] Department of Architecture, University Federico II,
Via Forno Vecchio 12, Napoli, Italy
sannivale@gmail.com

Abstract. The paper tells about the activity of the Observatory for Soil Saving at the MITO Lab of Bari Polytechnic, with special regard to one piece of a research project, named cs@monitor, devoted at studying the effectiveness of planning regulation against excessive urban expansion. The cs@monitor Project is aiming to support policy of soil preservation, in the context of the Apulian Region. Coherently with such aim, the paper shows a meta-appraisal of regulations and evaluation in land-use planning, referring not only to the articulations of plans and norms, but attempting to consider as well a most truthful analysis of the state of soils, devoted to discover countermeasures versus the process pressure-fragility-impact described in SEA procedure. The main scope is the discover of the potential of analyzing land-take as first step of Environmental Assessment of Urban Plans, as frequently discussed in literature [1–3].

Keywords: SEA · Soil sail · Soil savings · Planning regulation · Sustainability

1 Introduction

The Italian planning system, despite any try of renovation, still rules most of the urban transformation, mainly on land-use provision and on the forecast of further growth of built environment due to future needs. The institutional framework in which planning rules decide the land-use change (and its economic value) is mainly that of Municipality. More general changes are decided at upper level as well, but, in any case, they must be conformed, in volumes, land uses, and infrastructure, by the urban local government. The decision to assign a development right increases the land value, generating the consequent satisfaction of owners.

This is one of the main reasons for which all debates on soil sailing [4], urban sprawl and sprinkling [5], (except when the upper institutional level is responsible for policies of preservation), find their main scene in the City Council, during the decision-making process [6] related with the approval of a city master plan (CMP).

O. Gervasi et al. (Eds.): ICCSA 2017, Part V, LNCS 10408, pp. 106–117, 2017.
DOI: 10.1007/978-3-319-62404-4_8

A second crucial aspect is related with the way the urban sprawl can be assessed during the redaction of the CMP [7, 8].

As regards Italy, only seven years since the European Directive on Strategic Environmental Assessment (SEA) n. 42, 2001, June, 27, the Italian Government assumed by the Legislative Decrees n. 4, 2008, January, 16, the obligation of accompanying the CMP process at the Municipal level with the SEA process. This means therefore that, only seven years later, since the promotion of European Directive 42, 2001, Italy took in consideration the environmental effects of land-use planning at the Municipal level. Since the strict relationship between land-use and soil take, most of the environmental effects due to CMP's implementation, can be read through the account of the loss of natural soils, and more generally the loss of untouched land. According to the Directive, a main criterion "to assess the likely significance of effects on environment to be taken in account and to inform about, is "the value and vulnerability of the area" likely to be affected due to:

1. special natural characteristics or cultural heritage,
2. exceeded *environmental quality standards* or limit values,
3. Last, but not least the fragility respect to *intensive land-use*.

The concept of "intensive", should be intended as a degree of use that creates irreversible effects on environment, assessed per its rural peculiarity [9, 10], amenity [11, 12], natural character etc. often preferring an inefficient urban transformation instead of reuse [13, 14]. The paper tells about how the activity of the Observatory for Soil Saving at the MITO Lab of Bari Polytechnic intersects these themes, with special regard to one piece of a research project, named cs@monitor, devoted at studying the effectiveness of planning regulation against excessive urban expansion. Cs@monitor aims to support policy of soil preservation, in Apulian Region, supporting an "Open Data" Approach. Coherently with such aim, the paper shows a meta-appraisal of regulations and evaluation in land-use planning, referring not only to the articulations of plans and norms, but attempting to consider as well a most truthful analysis of the state of soils, devoted to discover countermeasures versus the process pressure-fragility-impact described in SEA procedure.

2 Facts and Data

Apulia accounts 258 Municipalities, that rule their territories with a wide range of planning instrument, differently aged, referring differently to laws, differently conformed, since the law system, in the meanwhile, changed simpler regulations to more complex forms of land-use planning.

The 258 Municipalities in the Apulian Region, have different typologies of planning regulations, referring to different law systems, due to the wide range of years during which CMPs with their planning regulation have been approved. Thirty-eight municipalities have approved a "General Urban Plan" (GUP), that is the CMP as intended by the Regional Act n. 20, 2001, July, 27, but only 18 plans have been developed following the Regional Guidelines of 2007. Further four plans are near to be approved. On the opposite side, about fifty municipalities still keep the "Program for

Constructions", that is to say the oldest planning instrument for land use regulation, (used in Seventies in substitution of Master Plan). Only during the most recent eighteen GUP have been submitted to a SEA procedure. The regional surface interested by the newest planning regulations, including SEA procedure, therefore, amounts only at the 6,8% on the total: 133293.51 ha on 1933319.8 ha for the whole region.

Among these group of recent Plans, our sample is composed by three GUP: (i) the General Urban Plan of Adelfia, (ii) the General Urban Plan of Monopoli, and (iii) the General Urban Plan of San Marco in Lamis. The main aspects of a municipal land-use masterplan that affects the soil saving/sailing are: the demand of volumes for urban activities, and the sizing future urban soils having a formal utilization. To develop the consciousness of some rules that seem to be ineffective in containing the urban sprawl, one of the main step of the research is a comparative assessment among a sample of different land-use plans that look as typologically significant. The main issues of the sample of plans are:

– the resonance with the recent norms on land use planning (the most recent Regional Act n. 20, 2001, July, 27, on planning instruments, and its guidelines of 2007)
– the development of the plan committed to professionals/research bodies having strong experience on the field
– the territories of the sample should cover a variety of aspects representing the multiplicity of environments inside the Apulian Region
– the conformity of the elected CMP with the Legislative Decree n. 4, 2008, January, 16, that means that there is the obligation of accompanying the plan development with a local institutional process of SEA.

The "Environmental Report" (ER), accompanying and describing the SEA procedure, becomes the main knowledge base for assessing the effect of the GUP on the natural resources. The ER, moreover, develop the quantitative and qualitative information to understand the effectiveness of the pan to favor social and economic development with the lowest possible cost of natural resources. The environmental system, passes from a pre-planning status to a post-planning through the implementation of GUP provision. Environmental status is described by a set of indicators, that should be the bases of a "Monitoring Program" (MP), in order to follow the ex post stage after the institutional approval of the GUP. Since its persistent intrinsic nature of land use plan, the effect of GUP can be read by accounting the change of land-uses and by giving to them a quali-quantitative dimension. The main information and documents accompanying the Technical Reports of GUP provide barely location and quantity of soil devoted to industry, commerce, tourism and residential activities and, moreover devoted to facilities, artificial green, urban services and bureaus. In addiction the Plan identifies some conservation areas due to hydraulic risks and natural values.

According with the recent data (2016) Adelfia, the less extended municipality in the sample, accounts a population of 17184 inhabitants on 2972.96 ha; Monopoli is the most populated of the group (49133 inhabitants on 15654.94 ha, with a density of 311.19 ab./km^2) and San Marco in Lamis accounts 14444 inhabitants on the widest territory (23344.8 ha, mainly inside the National Park of Gargano).

Following a rough quantitative approach, the highest density 576.45 inhab/km^2 characterizes Adelfia, that consequently does not have great possibility of expanding its urban belt. On the other side, Monopoli is characterized by a relevant sprinkling in countryside, and san Marco in Lamis, despite is density of 58.6 inhab/km^2 is attained by the limits of hydrological basins and surrounded by a relevant Protected Natural sub-region, as the Park of Gargano is. In Fig. 3, in fact, it is evident just looking to the absence of a (usually existing) dense road network at the North of the urban center, shows a clear wideness of untouched terrains in San Marco in Lamis more than other Municipalities (Figs. 1 and 2).

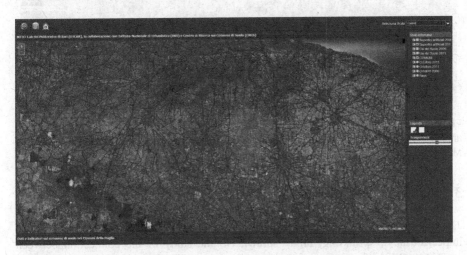

Fig. 1. The extension of Adelfia: note the limited municipality surface (Source: MITOcs SDI)

Fig. 2. Monopoli: high density of infrastructure and settlements on countryside and coastline (Source: MITOcs SDI)

Fig. 3. The extension of San Marco in Lamis: note that the northern part of the territory is unprovided by infrastructure, due to the existence of the Nature Park of Gargano (Source: MITOcs SDI)

3 Materials and Methods

The objects of the research project are several: (i) the seek for realistic measures of imperviousness, sprinkling, urban sprawl; (ii) the study of the connection between property value and pressures for urban expansion; (iii) the analysis of the effective impact of land use planning on soil saving. The case of study have been chosen in order to represent three different typology of planning according to needs of development, conservation, and efficient utilization of land. The need of efficient utilization of land, means that available soil obviously should not be artificialized more than the necessary. "Available soil" does not means "a simply free soil from natural constrain", but "a the soil not interested by natural constrain or planning constrain for conservation".

The aim of the analyses, therefore, is to test useful indicators to exploit the possible eventual unearned soil take, meaning that, respect to the demand of land for urban economic and human activities, the GUP could provide an over-dimensioned transformation and artificialization of surface. The efficient plan should respect the right equilibrium among preservation and development. As a consequence, the measure of over/under sizing of plans can be expressed by identifying unitary needs (demand of artificial surface per inhabitant, or per manpower unit, or demand of surface for housing volumes and so on). The numerous measures of GUP showed by ER, have been classified in two distinguished groups: Basic indicators and derivate indicators.

Basic indicators. They are coming from direct measures:

- directly connected with the current conditions of municipal territory,
- referring to spatial qualities,
- referring to inhabitant's needs and demand of volumes and surfaces,
- related with offer of available land, and need of preserving some natural areas.

Derivate indicators. Such indicators express the sizing of spaces for future developments, transformations and conservation per unit of

- sacrificed natural space, or
- transformed land
- per user (inhabitant, tourist, workers, etc.).

The comparison has been helpful to better describe and understand some dynamics. Monopoli represent the urban model devoted to attract commercial and industrial activities connected with road networks and port areas. San Marco in Lamis, instead represents a small urban reality immerged in a natural environment that provides in the same time constrains and opportunities: constrains for placing solar or wind farms [15, 16], or heavy touristic settlements, and opportunities for being a major node of a network for light nature tourism. A brief analysis of derivate indicators puts on evidence the usefulness of some measures. Firstly, those indicators that allow to compare the current state of land use with future scenarios, supporting a measure of future effects of soil take by a quali-quantitative analysis. Looking at Table 1 the main indicators are as follows:

- the Current Artificial Use Index (CAU Index - identified by O in Table 1), as due to the current Artificial Surface (N in Table 1) per inhabitants (A in Table 1)
- the Potential Artificial Surface (PAS - identified by P in Table 1) that is the result of a theoretical total artificialization of the territory (C) less the preservation areas, such as sites included in EU program Nature 2000, centennial olive groves and coastlines (M in Table 1)
- the Virtual Artificial Use Index (VAU Index - identified by Q in Table 1), that is Potential Artificial Surface (O) per inhabitant (A in Table 1)
- the Post-Plan Artificial Use Index (PAU index, identified by R in first column of the table), and proportioned at the demand of new artificial soil due to new inhabitants and workers (it is assumed a coefficient of 0.8 inhabitants equal to 0,8 rooms and 30 square meters for surface covered by housing and productive areas)
- the Average Housing Property Value in € per square meters (AHPV-identified by S in Table 1) Yearly Income per Capita in € per inhabitant (YIC-identified by T in Table 1)

The surface is mostly interested by rural land uses and preservation areas. The potential land use of rural areas depends on the sizing of new demand of soil. Just for this reason, the most interesting information have been provided by indicators P, Q and R. Q represent the post plan implementation, that shows an intermediate condition of soil take between the current land use (O) with the maximum possible use in case of complete implementation of the plan (R). The measures are standardized by dividing the surfaces for the number of inhabitants, with the aim to support the comparison of various municipalities. Calculation have been provided by the MITOcs SDI: looking at Fig. 4, it is possible to see the different character of non artificial surfaces in the three Municipalities: high presence of woodlands in the north area of San Marco in Lamis,

Table 1. Basic and derivate indicators of land-use management and development

	Basic indicators (source: GUP)		San Marco in Lamis	Monopoli	Adelfia
A	Inhabitants (Units)	A	13725	49133	17184
B	Surface area (km²)	B	234.20	157.89	29.81
C	Surface area (Ha)	C	23420	15789	2981
D	Productive areas (Ha)	D	44	162	18
E	Man power (Units)	E	1780	7847	4922
F	Productive areas (Ha/inhab)	D/A	0.0032	0.0033	0.001
G	Overall productive areas Ha/Ha	D/B	0.0019	0.0103	0.0060
H	Residential areas (Ha)	H	178	1500	140
I	Residential rooms demand (1 room = 0.8 inhabitants = 30 m² of surface)	I	4000	14676	6400
L	Residential areas per capita (Ha/inhab)	H/A	0.0130	0.0305	0.0081
	Basic Indicators (source: RLUM)		San Marco in Lamis	Monopoli	Adelfia
M	Woody/natural surfaces (Ha)	M	14772.25	8186.4900	98.7700
N	Artificial surfaces (Ha)	N	521.41	1873.8800	281.5800
	Derived Indicators		San Marco in Lamis	Monopoli	Adelfia
O	CAU - Current Artificial Use Index (Ha/inhab)	N/A	0.0380	0.0381	0.0164
P	PAS - Potential Artificial Surfaces (Ha)	$C - (M + N)$	8126.34	5728.6300	2600.6500
Q	VAU - Virtual Artificial Use Index (Ha/inhab)	P/A	0.5921	0.1166	0.1513
R	PAU - Post-plan Artificial Use Index (Ha/inhab)	$P/[A + (0.8 \times I)]$	0.4801	0.0898	0.1103
S	AHPV - Average Housing Property Value (€/m²)	S	1050	1600	1350
T	YIC - Yearly Income per Capita (€/inhab)	T	14102	14533	14763

Fig. 4. The land use of San Marco in Lamis, Adelfia, Monopoli (on different scales, from the right to the left): note the presence of a different mix in crops and green-lands (Source: MITOcs SDI)

grasslands and steppe rocks in Adelfia, a mix of woodlands, grasslands, centennials trees and sandy coastlines in Monopoli.

The first set of basic indicators give and idea of the kind of current land use and future demand each GUP is providing. As regards the state of the art, the GUP of Monopoli keeps a surface for industrial and commercial land use that is four times greater of the same land-use in San Marco in Lamis, and ten times greater than Adelfia. Proportions change when looking at residential activities: in this case the area for housing is more less eight times greater if compared to San Marco in Lamis, and ten time greater if compared with Adelfia. The demographic size of San Marco in Lamis and Adelfia is moreless the same (13 thousands and 17 thousands, respect the 50 thousands of Monopoli).

4 Discussion

The plans, therefore evidence a various idea of development. It is believable that the Strategic Environmental Assessment has been consistent with the environmental characterization of the territories, as it has increased the attention to the complexity of the natural system to the town of San Marco in Lamis, consistent with the environmental characteristics of the site; it emphasized the urban transformation in the case of Monopoli, in line with the idea of the Plan and the characteristics of the territory; It treated in a quantitative way (more simplified compared to the rating that was done in Monopoli ER), consistent with the spatial characteristics of Adelfia. The rurality of Monopoli is strongly different if compared with San Marco in Lamis. The debate on landscape faces in a different way with energy management and traditional agriculture, as mainstream of modern conflicts on rural platforms [17]. On one side, San Marco is considered a seat for windfarms, in the small rural southern area, that is the only one able to guest turbines. On the other side, Monopoly is a place where all activities can exist and generate conflicts. In the productive areas, you see a power-station based on the use of scraps from rural production. On one saide this activity produces a long-life cycling of rural activities, but in the other side, such activity can devaluate the rural settlements and landscapes, for a perception of pollution as, well demonstrated in literature [17, 18].

Why does it mean? In absolute value, the loss of environmental resources is more impactive in Monopoli; nevertheless, the surface in Adelfia is so limited that the local environmental cost is more incisive. This means that the choice of looking between the local scale and the global scale represents a strong and discriminative question. In some way this becomes a question of "environmental democracy". The local community can consider the local environment as its own resource, just because the preservation it is on its own responsibility and on its own costs.

As regards the use of indicators that can derive from study on land use and soil consumption, as descriptors of overall environmental issues, we can reconduct the meaning of efficiency in using the land, maximizing positive effects with minimum land use, or minimize negative effect, with bigger land use. The indicators of different Municipalities measure the unsustainability of Monopoli's development, near to the limit of every possible expansion, if compared with San Marco in Lamis and Adelfia. In fact the Post-PAUA is the most limited (0,0898 Hectares per inhabitant, against 0,4801 for San Marco in Lamis and 0,1103 for Adelfia). The increase of population, and the consequent new demand of transformable surfaces, should be widely argued, to justify the required environmental costs. Furthermore, the shift from the ex-ante to the ex-post of each context should be assessed: the 19% of loss of non-artificial surfaces in San Marco in Lamis, the 23% in Monopoli and the 27% in Adelfia.

Figure 5 shows a way to use land take as a metric to position the balance between the three pillar of sustainability (Environment, Economic Welfare, Social Equity). The diagram in the figure represents the well-known "Triangle of Serageldin" [19] with the

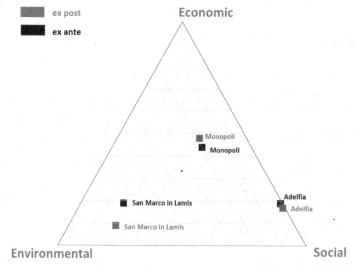

Fig. 5. The position of the three Plans according the Serageldin Triangle

three dimensions (environmental, social and economic). The black dots identify the state of the three Municipalities before the implementation of the plan, and the light blue dots represent he state of the Municipalities after the implementation of the Plan.

The position is given by the variation of surface as regards nature areas (environmental dimension), the artificialization due to residential neighborhood having area for housing and facilities (social dimension), and the artificialization due to industrial-commercial districts (economic dimension). The indicator is obtained by multiplying the variation in surface (natural, artificial for social uses, and artificial for economic uses) per the new post-plan property values.

The shift of the dots representing the status referred to "pre and post" implementation of the plan, shows a coherent connection between metrics, positions and economic/environmental impacts. In fact, San Marco in Lamis is more forwarding the environmental dimension, Monopoli is close to the vertex of the economic dimension, and Adelfia privileges the social one. The effects of plan change radically the position of Monopoli (as regards production and economy) and of San Marco in Lamis (as regards environment and Nature).

5   Conclusions

After the comparison of valuations operated within ER we can answer the following questions:

- with reference to the contents of ER (as defined by legislative framework and method), can we express a judgment on the approaches of the three plans?
- as regards the specific environmental characterization of the three territories, how much their peculiarities appears evident inside the SEA process?

It is believed that the Strategic Environmental Assessment has been consistent with the environmental characterization of the territories, as it has increased the attention to the complexity of the natural system to the town of San Marco in Lamis, consistent with the environmental characteristics of the site; it emphasized the urban transformation in the case of Monopoli, in line with the local economic idea of development that the GUP should support.

We should consider some peculiarities about the process of our sample of planning procedures. In chronological order the first SEA in the time-line is that of the Monopoli Masterplan (2007); Adelfia's GUP follows (2009) and San Marco in Lamis is the earliest (2009). San Marco in Lamis was the first Municipality to have implemented the directives of the RLP. As consequence, GUP of San Marco in Lamis not only implemented the directives of the RLP among, but furthermore, it is also one of the only two plans to be conformed with RLP in all Apulian Region.

The process of Monopoli SEA began in the occasion of the first institutional examination of plan, that is the "adoption" of the plan, that can be considered a complete and exhaustive draft of the Plan; the inversely-VAS of Adelfia and San Marco in Lamis is simultaneously started to plan the training process (keeping the Art 11 of Legislative Decree 04/2008).

– After the final institutional examination, (the final "approval") the City Council of Monopoli (it was the only one of the three municipalities) approved a resolution which released the Plan for Monitoring the environmental effect of the implementation of the plan (as the EU Directive and the Italian law-system provide).

The best plan in terms of environmental protection is to San Marco in Lamis; by contrast, seems to be the worst in terms of urban development (the same people who collaborated express doubts about whether that the plan will allow a development). This apparent contradiction may lead you to think that the compromise between conservation and development is very difficult.

References

1. Khakee, A.: Evaluation and planning: inseparable concepts. Town Plan. Rev. **69**, 359–374 (1998)
2. Dimotta, A., Cozzi, M., Romano, S., Lazzari, M.: Soil loss, productivity and cropland values GIS-based analysis and trends in the Basilicata region (Southern Italy) from 1980 to 2013. In: Gervasi, O., et al. (eds.) Computational Science and its Applications – ICCSA 2016. LCNS, vol. 9789, pp. 29–45. Springer, Heidelberg (2016)
3. Cerreta, M., De Toro, P.: Urbanization suitability maps: a dynamic spatial decision support system for sustainable land use. Earth Syst. Dyn. **3**, 157–171 (2012)
4. Keesstra, S.D., Bouma, J., Wallinga, J., Tittonell, P., Smith, P., Cerdà, A., Montanarella, L., Quinton, J.N., Pachepsky, Y., van der Putten, W.H., Richard, D., Bardgett, R.D., Moolenaar S., Mol, G., Jansen, B., Fresco, L.O.: The significance of soils and soil science towards realization of the United Nations Sustainable Development Goals. Soil **2**, 111–128 (2016)
5. Munafò, M. (ed.) Il Consumo di Suolo dinamiche territoriali e servizi ecosistemici, Ispra, Rome (2016)
6. Bouma, J.: The role of soil science in the land use negotiation process. Soil Use Manag. **17**, 1–6 (2001)
7. Torre, C.M., Morano, P., Tajani, F.: Saving soil for sustainable land use. Sustainability **9**(3), 350 (2017)
8. Modica, G., Laudari, L., Barreca, F., Fichera, C.R.: A GIS-MCDA based model for the suitability evaluation of traditional grape varieties: the case-study of "Mantonico" grape (Calabria, Italy). Int. J. Agric. Environ. Inf. Syst. **5**, 1–16 (2014)
9. Modica, G., Zoccali, P., Di Fazio, S.: The e-participation in tranquillity areas identification as a key factor for sustainable landscape planning. In: Murgante, B., Misra, S., Carlini, M., Torre, C.M., Nguyen, H., Taniar, D., Apduhan, B.O., Gervasi, O. (eds.) Computational Science and its Applications – ICCSA 2013. LNCS, vol. 7973, pp. 550–565. Springer, Heidelberg (2013)
10. Vizzari, M., Modica, G.: Environmental effectiveness of swine sewage management: a multicriteria AHP-based model for a reliable quick assessment. Environ. Manage. **52**, 1023–1039 (2013)
11. Cerreta, M., Fusco Girard, L.: Human smart landscape: an adaptive and synergistic approach for the National Park of Cilento, Vallo di Diano and Alburni. Agric. Agric. Sci. Procedia **8**, 489–493 (2016)

12. Amato, F., Martellozzo, F., Nolè, G., Murgante, B.: Preserving cultural heritage by supporting landscape planning with quantitative predictions of soil consumption. J. Cult. Herit. **23**, 44–54 (2017)

13. Tajani, F., Morano, P.: Evaluation of vacant and redundant public properties and risk control. A model for the definition of the optimal mix of eligible functions. J. Prop. Invest. Financ. **35**(1), 75–100 (2017)

14. Morano, P., Tajani, F.: The break-even analysis applied to urban renewal investments: a model to evaluate the share of social housing financially sustainable for private investors. Habitat Int. **59**, 10–20 (2017)

15. Scorza, F.: Towards self energy-management and sustainable citizens' engagement in local energy efficiency. Int. J. Agric. Environ. Inf. Syst. **7**(1), 44–53 (2016)

16. Morano, P., Tajani, F., Locurcio, M.: GIS application and econometric analysis for the verification of the financial feasibility of roof-top wind turbines in the city of Bari (Italy). Renew. Sustain. Energy Rev. **70**, 999–1010 (2017)

17. Donnat, E., Boffety, D., Bimonte, S., Chanet, J.: Du capteur à l'indicateur: les entrepôts de données spatiales au service d'une meilleure maîtrise des consommations énergétiques des entreprises agricoles. Innovations Agronomiques **55**, 201–214 (2017)

18. Torre, C.M., Balena, P., Ceppi, C.: The devaluation of property due to the perception of health risk in polluted industrial cities. Int. J. Bus. Intell. Data Min. **9**, 74–90 (2014)

19. Serageldin, I., Steer, A.: Making Development Sustainable: From Concepts to Action. The Word Bank, Washington (1994)

Pollination and the Integration of Ecosystem Services in Landscape Planning and Rural Development

Alessandro Bonifazi[1,2](✉) ⓘ, Pasquale Balena[1] ⓘ,
and Carlo Rega[1,3] ⓘ

[1] ITERAS – Research Centre for Sustainability and Territorial Innovation,
Via C. Colombo, 70126 Bari, BA, Italy
alessandro.bonifazi@iteras.org,
pasquale.balena@poliba.it, carlo.rega@ec.europa.eu
[2] Polytechnic of Bari, Via Orabona 4, 70125 Bari, BA, Italy
[3] European Commission - Joint Research Centre,
Directorate D - Sustainable Resources, Via E. Fermi 2749, 21027 Ispra, VA, Italy

Abstract. Mapping and assessment of Ecosystem Services (ES) is a promising field of inquiry that aims to bridge the gap between nature conservation and policy making in different sectors and contexts. Within the class of *Regulating and maintenance* ES, pollination has recently been the target of great interest on the side of ecologists, planners, farmers and the media alike. In this paper, we adapted a wild pollination model by: scaling it down to fit the study context (the Italian region of Puglia); testing different approaches to refine the forest, road side, semi-natural vegetation and olive farming intensity components and; discussing the spatially explicit outcomes (Pollination potential, service and deficit maps) with regard to rural development programming and landscape planning. Findings point to a mismatch between demand and supply of the pollination ES, and help shed light on some spatial configurations that either mitigate or sharpen it. The prospects of mapping and assessment of pollination as a planning-support tool seem to depend critically on input data availability and accuracy, on fine-tuning models – as well as on establishing stronger links between the ecological functions that underpin pollination, the policy measures that might enhance them (be that binding regulations, agri-environmental schemes or spatial strategies) and the socio-economic practices (e.g., farming) that interact with both.

Keywords: Ecosystem services · Pollination · Landscape panning · Rural development

1 Introduction

The concept of ecosystem services (ES) has been steadily gaining momentum over decades at the science/policy interface, along with other approaches to reconcile socio-economic development and nature conservation. Simply defined, ES are "the conditions and processes through which natural ecosystems, and the species that make

© Springer International Publishing AG 2017
O. Gervasi et al. (Eds.): ICCSA 2017, Part V, LNCS 10408, pp. 118–133, 2017.
DOI: 10.1007/978-3-319-62404-4_9

them up, sustain and fulfil human life" [1: 2] or, even more concisely, "[...] the benefits people obtain from ecosystems" [2: 38].

At the core of the concept, there stands an overarching aim to better bridge the ecological processes that underpin life on Earth and the values (however defined) human societies attach to, or derive from, them. The underlying logical and operational foundations may be modelled around the relationships between a limited set of central elements [3, 4]:

- the complexity of natural and semi-natural ecosystems is described in terms of structures (e.g., a coral reef) and processes (e.g., carbon cycling) that are translated into
- a limited number of ecosystem functions (e.g., climate regulation) that have the capacity to provide
- the actual services (e.g., maintenance of a favorable climate for cultivation) that directly or indirectly
- provide benefits or goods that affect human well-being.

Variations on this conceptual framework abound, pointing for instance to the role of landscapes (along with ecosystems) as providers of potential supply of those services, whose actual demand or use should moreover be carefully ascertained, to yield more accurate valuations [5]. However, a growing consensus has been building up around a framework for the classification of ES wherein [2, 6]:

- both natural and human-modified ecosystems are considered as sources of services
- both tangible (i.e., goods) and intangible (i.e., services) benefits are covered and
- a functional grouping of ES is adopted, by discriminating (for operational purposes only, and with due consideration of overlaps) between:
  - Provisioning ES – food, fuel, fresh water, *etc.*
  - Regulating and maintenance ES – e.g., climate regulation, erosion control, water purification, pollination
  - Cultural ES – which are understood as the "nonmaterial benefits people obtain from ecosystems through spiritual enrichment, cognitive development, reflection, recreation, and aesthetic experiences" [2: 58].

ES have brought about multiple and diverse opportunities to advance the knowledge and better management of the interlinkages between natural ecosystems and human societies, and yet value conflicts and scientific controversies have focussed on ES's economic valuation in monetary terms. On the other hand, it is exactly the ability to attach a money figure to virtually any ecosystem structure, function or process (although neither mandatory nor desirable under most studies or policy recommendations) that significantly helped mainstream ES into public policy agendas [7]. According to a powerful underlying theme, for the ecological foundations of human well-being to stimulate policy response and redress business strategies and consumer behaviour, they ought to be translated into the "language of the world's dominant economic and political model" [8: 2–3].

Not surprisingly then, the economics of ES seems to be plagued by the same critiques that have been addressed at cost-benefit analysis, as they tend to be framed as sources of benefits that fall outside of the scope of market transactions – and therefore need to be internalised. Scholars are however particularly wary of a process of commodification, assumed to be lurking in the Payment for Ecosystem Services (PES) approach [9], which would entail [10]:

- simplifying the complexity of natural ecosystems by singling out individual ES
- prioritising a single exchange-value for ES
- masking the social relations underpinning the production and consumption of ES.

This work is in tune with an understanding of the role and purpose of ES that stresses its learning potential (e.g., by unravelling the interdependencies between ES, some neglected ecological functions may move to the foreground), raises awareness on the irreplaceable role of the biota in supporting human well-being, and provides decision-making processes with quantitative, spatially explicit – and sometimes monetary – indicators to allow better evaluation of alternative policies [11, 12].

Despite a lack of consensus on definitions and procedures, the advances in mapping and assessing ES have attracted a great interest from planning scholars and practitioners, following the unprecedented opportunities they offer to frame ecological processes, match them to places or land-use types, and integrate them in a multidimensional evaluation of the implications of options and alternatives on social, economic and environmental dynamics. This interest ranges from landscape planning [5], through rural development [13], to spatial strategies [11, 14] and urban planning [15].

The use of spatial models to map and assess the flow/stock of ES in a spatially explicit fashion is considered a key support to policy making, as reflected in the current EU Biodiversity Strategy [16] (Action 5). Maps are of pivotal importance to prioritise areas in policy interventions – e.g., where there is a mismatch between the demand and supply of a certain ecosystem service – but also to identify possible synergies and trade-offs between ecosystem services or among stakeholder groups.

Building on this broad and diversified background, this work aims to investigate the bridging potential of ES across different planning sectors that have a bearing on biodiversity conservation and land use management, with a view to enhancing their mutual coordination. To do so, we carry out an exploratory analysis of the relationships between a Regulating ES (pollination) and two planning tools, namely landscape and rural development planning, in an Italian region by:

- scaling down to the regional level (where planning in the selected sectors occurs) the methods for pollination's mapping and assessment
- identifying the planning tools that interact with the ecological structures and processes that underpin pollination
- discussing the bridging potential of pollination by dwelling on the synergies and friction between rural development programmes and landscape planning.

To put the remainder of the paper into context, the next Section includes basic information on pollination as a regulating ES, and provides insights into the geography and the planning framework in the study region. Section 3 covers research design, while Sect. 4 is about results. We conclude by discussing the empirical material, working out tentative recommendations, and envisaging future research themes.

2 Setting the Context

Within the conceptual and methodological frameworks that are briefly summarized in, respectively, the previous and the following Section, this research has focussed on a specific ES, and has accordingly investigated the interplay between a mapping and assessment exercise on pollination and two planning tools (a landscape plan and a rural development programme) in the Italian region of Puglia. Hence, this Section provides readers with background information on the chosen fields and context.

Pollination is at the same time a fascinating ecological process and a copybook example of the combination of economic relevance and social neglect that the ES approach is aiming to redress. Key to sexual reproduction in seed plants, pollination consists in the transfer of pollen, which – in flowering plants – is moved from the stamen to the pistil. Pollination may involve the same flower, or two different flowers in either the same plant or different plants (the latter process being defined as cross-pollination vis-à-vis the others, both falling in the category of self-pollination). Together with the wind, animal pollinators (such as bees, butterflies, hummingbirds, and nectar feeding bats) contribute to moving pollen. Indeed, not only are most flowering plants depending on pollination for their reproduction, but animal pollinators have also been found to be beneficial to the majority of the global plant produce, and crucial to a significant share of human food supply [17]. Among pollinators, bees play a prominent role in most ecological regions of the world and, through the interaction between nesting siting and foraging distance, they interfere not only with the genetic structure of plant populations, but also with the spatial configurations of other ecosystem-level processes – such as nutrient transfer, biological dispersal and predation [17].

As a Regulating ES, animal pollination is therefore key to both food security and biodiversity conservation [18] but it is threatened by global change in terms of:

- land-use changes (primarily urbanization) that reduce floral and nesting resources, and
- agriculture intensification, which has both a direct effect (e.g., increased mortality because of pesticides) and indirect effects (as herbicides, fertilizers or tillage decrease plant diversity or interfere with nesting).

Moreover, the effects of the above-mentioned pressures on pollinator occurrence and abundance appear to be critically influenced by each species' ecological traits – including flight season duration, foraging range, reproductive strategy and sociality (ibid.).

The study region, Puglia, lies at the south-easternmost end of Italy, covering 20.000 km^2, stretching along almost 900 km of coastline (surrounded by the Adriatic and Ionian Seas), and hosting around 4 million inhabitants. It is mostly a flat area, except in the North – where the Monti Dauni range and the Gargano headland face each other across the main plain (Tavoliere). Once dominated by extensive agriculture and few prominent trading ports, Puglia evolved into a mixed-economy with a growing service sector and few large industrial poles. Its 258 municipalities are mainly medium to small towns, with only about 15 cities having a population greater than 50.000 inhabitants.

Arable land and permanent crops represent the dominant land uses, accounting for almost 50% of the overall area, whilst forests and other semi-natural ecosystems are to be found on a limited share of the region. Olive groves extend over roughly 4.000 km^2 and constitute a major hallmark in both landscape and agriculture production terms. Recently, the first outbreak in Europe of the so-called 'olive quick decline syndrome' (caused by insect vector borne bacterium *Xylella fastidiosa*) has affected the southern tip of the region, which has eventually been declared a reservoir for the pest [19].

Until the second half of the 20th century, population used to be highly concentrated in towns rather than in small villages or isolated settlements: following a countertrend, urban sprawl is now remarkable in Puglia, with the affected area ranging from 6 through 9%, depending on the focus being, respectively, on soil sealing or land take [20, 21].

Two public policy may be singled out for their relevance to the integration of pollination into planning rationales and operations:

- the Rural Development Programme (RDP), updated every eighth year within the general framework of the European Union (EU) Common Agricultural Policy;
- the Regional Landscape Plan (RLP), adopted in 2015 and fully compliant to the European Landscape Convention.

Within the previous RDP, effective from 2007 through 2013, the regional territory was sorted into four classes ("urban agglomerations", "rural areas with intensive specialized agriculture", "marginal rural areas", and "intermediate areas") to address four main objectives through tailored strategies: agriculture competitiveness; rural environment protection and enhancement; well-being of rural populations and; collaborative rural development. Among the many policy measures of interest, under agri-environmental schemes (AES) farmers are expected to voluntarily implement environment-friendly practices, in exchange for financial incentives [13]. In the context of this paper, at least three elements of the recently adopted RLP are worth highlighting:

1. the inclusion of grasslands, transitional woodland-shrub and forest buffers within the areas that are subject to binding conservation regulations;
2. the "City-Countryside Agreement" – a spatial strategy that stresses the role of agricultural parks as an implementation tool;
3. the promotion of multifunctional ecological networks, intertwined in a regional green and blue infrastructure.

In the following Section, we introduce the methodology we have adapted to map and assess the Pollination ES in Puglia.

3   Research Design

The pollination model used in the present study is based on the conceptual framework originally proposed by Lonsdorf and co-workers [22], as subsequently refined by Zulian *et al.* [23]. The aim of the model is to measure the potential pollination service supplied to crops by specific landscape types and areas, based on the overall capability of its features to support the presence and activity of pollinators. The model considers wild pollinators only (and bees, in particular), as domestic honeybees are mainly managed and hence can be displaced across the territory.

According to the model, the landscape is subdivided in a grid of square cells; each cell has a certain potential to support pollinators, given by the combination of two factors: its suitability as a nesting site (Nesting suitability - NS) and; the availability of nutrient (nectar and pollen) for pollinators (Floral Availability-FA). Each cell is assigned two different scores based on expert judgement, depending on its land cover and ancillary characteristics.

Wild bees are central foragers, i.e., they establish their nest at a suitable site and disperse in the surrounding landscape in search of food. The overall suitability of a given patch to support bees' presence thus depend on its intrinsic NS and FA scores, but also on the FA of the surrounding cells that can be reached by foragers. The foraging ranges of wild bees greatly varies from species to species [17]: for the most common species in Europe, the reported foraging is approximately 100–600 m. In the present application, we assumed a foraging range of 400 m. The probability that a single bee would visit a cell at distance d from its nest is a monotonically decreasing function of d, termed a kernel function. Following Lonsdorf et al. [22] and Zulian et al. [23], we used a negative exponential function as kernel, such that it has a value of 1 at the nesting pixel and it nullifies for distances longer than 400 m, as expressed by Eq. 1.

$$f(r) = \exp(-d/200), \text{ for } d \leq 400; \qquad (1)$$

where $f(r) = 0$, for $d > 400$, and d is the distance between cells.

The potential suitability of a cell to support pollinators, which is here defined as *Pollinator abundance*, is expressed by Eq. 2:

$$P_x = N_x \frac{\sum_{m=1}^{M} Fm * f(Dm, \alpha)}{\sum_{m=1}^{M} f(Dm, \alpha)} \qquad (2)$$

where:

- P_x is the Pollinator abundance;
- N_x is the Nesting suitability (NS) score of cell x;
- $f(Dm, \alpha)$ is the kernel function (a negative exponential);
- M is the number of cells within the maximum distance from cell x, determined by the kernel function and including x itself;
- Fm is the Floral availability (FA) score of cell m;
- Dm is the Euclidean distance between cell m and cell x (meters);
- α is the length scale parameter, governing the distance-weighted decline in influence (set to 200 m).

In practice, for each cell x in the landscape, the kernel function weights the contribution of the surrounding cells to support the presence of bees in that cell, which is proportional to their FA and decreases with their distance following Eq. 1. The denominator in Eq. 2 is a scalar used to normalize the values (from 0 to 100).

· To run the model in a Geographic Information System (GIS) environment, the main required input data are a land cover/land use map and two lookup tables associating the values of FA e NS to the different land cover class. We used the 2011 Regional Thematic Land Use Map of Puglia[1], a vector map with a minimum mapping unity (mmu) of 2.500 m^2 and a classification that is consistent with the Corine Land Cover (CLC) nomenclature, extended for most classes to the 4th level. We then converted it to a regular square grid raster with 50 m × 50 m cells, compliant to the reference Infrastructure for Spatial Information in Europe (INSPIRE) grid.

We assigned NS and FA values to the different land cover classes (Table 1) using as baseline the scores reported in [23]. We resorted to additional spatial information to refine those scores by considering more in detail the following components:

- Forest type and morphology
- Road sides
- Semi-natural vegetation in arable land
- Intensity of management of olive groves.

Table 1. The baseline scores of Floral availability (FA) and Nesting suitability (NS) in a sample of land cover classes, along with indications of further refinement – when relevant. * Refined following road verges' density. # Refined based on the presence of semi-natural vegetation. § Score varies according to olive groves' farming intensity. ° Score depends on forest type and morphology (core/edges). Explanations in the text.

CLC code	Description	FA	NS
111	Continuous urban fabric	5	10
112	Discontinuous urban fabric	30	30
142	Sport and leisure facilities	5	30
2111	Non-irrigated arable land*#	20	20
2112	Vegetables (outdoor or under glass) in non-irrigated land*#	20	20
222	Fruit trees and berry plantations*	90	40
223	Olive groves*§	20–60	40–60
231	Pastures*	20	30
241	Annual crops associated with permanent crops*	50	40
242	Complex cultivation patterns*	40	40
311	Broad-leaved forest°	0–100	70–90
312	Coniferous forest°	0–40	70–90
321	Natural grasslands	100	80
324	Transitional woodland-shrub	85	100
331	Beaches, dunes, sands	10	30
411	Inland marshes	75	30
422-3	Salines and Intertidal flats	0	0
521	Coastal lagoons	0	20

[1] Available at http://www.sit.puglia.it.

Since forest edges are more suitable habitats for pollinators [23], and floral availability decreases towards forest cores, the FA and NS of forest pixels depend on both forest type and morphology. We therefore carried out a Morphological Spatial Pattern Analysis (MSPA) [24] of forest covers with the GUIDOS software [25].

MSPA is a sequence of morphological operators targeted at the description of the geometry and connectivity of the image components. It can be applied at any scale on a binary map (background/foreground, in this case non-forest/forest), to categorize the foreground into mutually exclusive classes (in this case, cores and edges). We assumed FA scores in forest to decline with distance from the edge according to a negative exponential function, up to a maximum distance of 250 m, after which the FA score is set to 0. We therefore calculated the Euclidean distance of each core cell to the nearest edge and assigned them the values reported in Table 2 below, as illustrated by Fig. 1.

For arable land, we adjusted the baseline values of FA and NS by taking into account the presence of semi-natural vegetation in the dominant land cover. We used the 2012 Copernicus Forest High Resolution Layer (spatial resolution = 25 m) to calculate the abundance of trees in arable land cells. We assigned an extra score to arable cells where

Table 2. Floral Availability (FA) and nesting suitability (NS) scores assigned to forest pixel based on forest type and morphology; w(d) is the weighting factor decreasing with distance as a negative exponential.

Forest type	FA edge	FA core	NS edge	NS core
Deciduous forest	100	90*w(d)	90	70
Coniferous forest	40	30*w(d)	90	70
Mixed forest	70	60*w(d)	90	70
Grasslands with trees and shrubs	100	80*w(d)	90	70

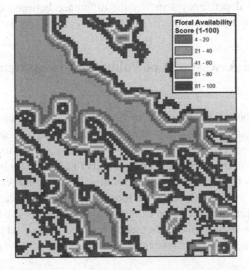

Fig. 1. A sample map of Floral availability scores assigned to forest cells based on forest type, forest morphology (Cores/Edges) and distance of core cells from the nearest edge.

trees occurred, directly proportional to the share of 25 m forest pixels falling within the 50 m pixels. As regards the olive grove component, we followed Weissteiner et al. [26] who assessed olive farming intensity in Euro-Mediterranean countries, and adjusted the final FA and NS scores so that they ranged, respectively, from 20 to 60 and from 40 to 60, ordered according to decreasing farming intensity.

Finally, we increased the scores in cells intersected by roads, as road verges show higher plant diversity (due to mowing, specific maintenance regulation, lower to no use of chemicals, *etc.*) [27–29]. We considered only roads in agricultural land and applied the same method used in [23] to the OpenStreetMap dataset.

Once the Pollinator abundance is calculated – Px in Eq. 2 –, the *pollination potential* (PP), that is, the potential service provided to each cell (that may be conceptualized as the of number visits by bees to a certain farming site) is calculated by combining the contribution of all surrounding cells, according to Eq. (3) [22].

$$P_o = \frac{\sum_{m=1}^{M} Pxm * f(Dm, \alpha)}{\sum_{m=1}^{M} f(Dm, \alpha)} \tag{3}$$

where:

- P_o total (potential) pollination service delivered to cell o;
- P_{xm} is Pollinator abundance, as defined in Eq. (2), for cell m;
- all other parameters and variables are the same as in Eq. (2)

We calculated Crop dependency at grid level by combining information on crop production shares at either municipal or provincial level[2] with the land cover classes, using the dependency scores reported in [23]. We then estimated the actual pollination service, in terms of yield share attributed to pollination, by multiplying the crop dependency scores by the PP. Similarly, a *Pollination deficit* could be calculated by multiplying the crop dependency score by the difference between the maximum possible pollination score under the model (100) and the actual PP for each cell.

4 Mapping and Assessment of Pollination Ecosystem Service in Puglia

By applying the methodology illustrated in the previous Section, we obtained a map of the PP-ES in Puglia (shown in Fig. 2). At the regional level, a few observations may be formulated. A clear majority of the territory is characterized by low or very low PP values, which is consistent with arable land and olive groves being by far the dominant agricultural land uses in Puglia. More interestingly, the maximum value being 90 (on a scale ranging from 0 to 100) it appears that there is no single landscape configuration in the region allowing for a full PP to be expressed. Higher values are to be found where forest covers are prevalent – within the main protected areas – whilst lower ones are associated with arable land (e.g., in the north-western plain) or olive groves with higher

---

[2] Retrieved from the national statistics office's data warehouse (available at: http://en.istat.it).

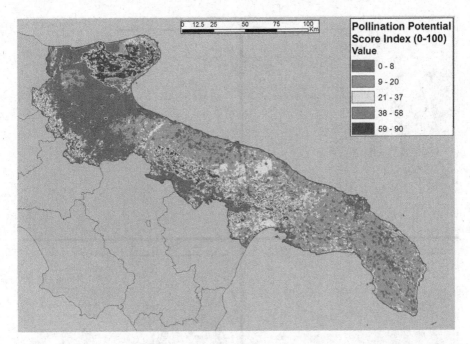

Fig. 2. A map of the Pollination potential in Puglia, understood as an abundance index of visiting pollinators, by using pollinator abundance in each cell, adjusted according to flight ranges of pollinator species to simulate their foraging form nearby cells.

farming intensity (in the northern side of the central part of the region). The null values (which have been excluded from the classification in Fig. 2) are limited to water bodies and forest cores (consistently with the MSPA methodology illustrated in Sect. 3).

A better insight into the main steps of the model implementation, and the sensitivity of the outcomes to its specific components, may be attained by comparing the images included in Fig. 3. Moving from the bottom-right, where a simplified land cover map is shown, one may note that FA scores depend on land covers (bottom-left) but are not univocally determined by them – partly because of the aggregation in the map of land covers having different FA, partly because the other components of the model introduce variations that are specific to certain spatial configurations.

This effect becomes increasingly evident as the kernel function included in Eqs. 2 and 3 (which mirrors the assumed flight range of pollinators) is applied twice, first to calculate Pollinator abundance (top-right), and then to deliver the PP values (top-left). By combining the PP values with Crop dependency ratios, the actual ecosystem service offered by pollinators was calculated and mapped, showing similar spatial patterns to those illustrated in Fig. 4.

At least two aspects are worth being highlighted when assessing the PP-ES map. Firstly, pollination plays a minor role in most part of the region in providing benefits to agriculture, save in areas where fruit trees and vegetables account for a significant share of land covers. On the other hand, the spread of very low crop yield shares depending on pollination over large areas appears to be related to the use of a

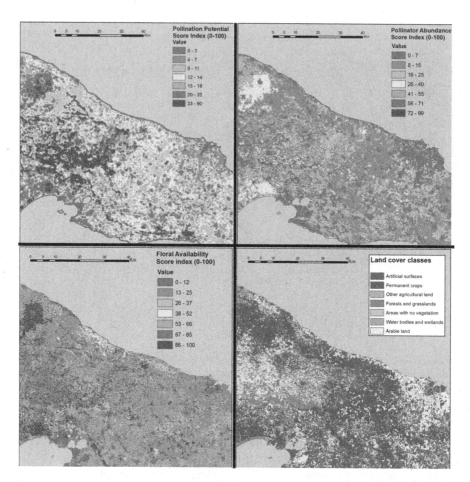

Fig. 3. A more detailed map of a central area in Puglia, where: top-left is the Pollination potential as in Fig. 2; top-right is the Pollinator abundance index (see Eq. 2); bottom-left is one of the basic indicators – namely, Floral Availability and; bottom-right is the land cover map.

weighted average between different crops (e.g., pulses and sunflower vs. durum wheat and potatoes) falling in the arable land classes, whose aggregate yields at municipal level could not be exactly attributed to specific cells.

A *Pollination deficit*, understood as the percentage of crop that may be considered lost because of sub-optimal PP-ES, was also computed; following the relative distribution of PP-ES and crop dependency values, the map in Fig. 4 shows that there are at least three areas of greater importance (between almost 30 and 65% of crop yield being potentially lost):

- a hotspot overlapping with districts where fruit trees dominate (in central Puglia) and

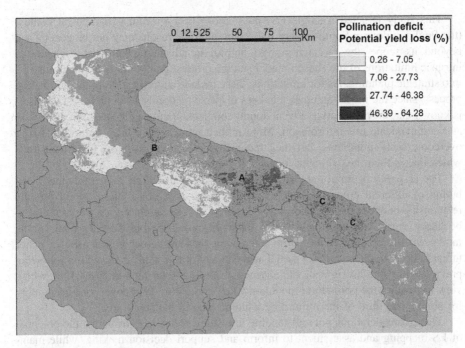

Fig. 4. A map of Pollination deficit, expressed in terms of the percentage of crop yields that may be lost because of a PP-ES deficit, according to crop dependency on wild pollination. A: deficit hotspot in central Puglia; B and C: areas where highly dependent crops are interspersed with, respectively, arable land (Ofanto Valley) or olive groves (province of Brindisi).

- two areas where patches of highly pollination-deficient orchards are interspersed within a background of either arable land (along the Ofanto Valley) or olive groves with relatively high farming intensity (in the province of Brindisi).

5 Discussion and Conclusions

The application of ES modelling presented in this paper aims at contributing to the integration between biodiversity conservation and strategic planning in the fields of rural development and landscape protection and enhancement. Such objective is consistent with the emerging policy frameworks worldwide and in the EU context, where the research was carried out. Under Target 3, the EU Biodiversity Strategy [16] stresses the potential contribution of the Common Agricultural Policy (CAP) to both the maintenance of biodiversity and the supply of a wide range of ES – beyond food provision. Moreover, under its "Partnership for biodiversity" section, the Strategy aims to "further encourage collaboration between researchers and other stakeholders involved in *spatial planning and land use management* in implementing biodiversity strategies at all levels, ensuring coherence with relevant recommendations set out in the European Territorial Agenda" (*ibid.*, p. 8, *emphasis added*).

This study targeted a single ES (pollination) in a specific geographical context (the Puglia region, in South-eastern Italy); although the results may not be generalised beyond its scope, the research proved helpful in advancing knowledge about the intrinsic limitations of the chosen model and the promises and pitfalls of integrating ES into strategic planning. As for limitations, these include simplification of the pollination process, since the model assumes that bees disperse randomly from their nest, whilst it is known that they do feature a behavioural component and can locate sources of food and communicate this information. More refined models have been proposed [30] to overcome such limitations, but they require detailed data on bees' functional traits which makes them less suitable for mapping at large scales.

The accuracy of input data is another key issue, particularly as regards the distribution of different crops that fall within the same land cover class. Moreover, the relationship between the PP index and the estimated pollination service was assumed to be linear, whilst a saturating function might be more appropriate [17]. Finally, the model would certainly benefit from integrating data on agrochemical use – a major threat to bees. In this respect, a partial achievement of this study consisted in following previous efforts to discriminate olive groves according to farming intensity [26], with a view to refining the pollination model on a key agriculture land cover, one accounting for almost one third of the utilised agricultural area in the study area.

These considerations notwithstanding, the study seems to corroborate the potential of ES mapping and assessment to inform and support decision making, while mainstreaming the links between nature conservation and spatially-targeted socio-economic policies. In Puglia, the areas where a remarkable pollination deficit is likely to occur (read the comments to Fig. 4) may be the target of specific interventions to enhance the ecological equipment of agricultural land, for instance by means of spatially tailored agri-environmental schemes under the RDP. Indeed, there seem to be some interesting patterns when comparing the pollination service and deficit maps with the implementation sites of a specific financial scheme supporting organic farming, under the latest RDP (2007-13): interventions are likely to reinforce PP in few areas (e.g., the main protected area in the central part of the region) but in general there is a poor match with the pollination deficit hotspots, thus pointing to an untapped opportunity to harness the potential of ES assessment in improving rural development policy's effectiveness.

More in general, the application of specific conservation measures to landscape areas could be refined if their potential to supply certain ES were fully considered. This, for instance, would imply that zoning in landscape planning were not exclusively based on established taxonomies of land covers, but also considered ecological functions at landscape level. In that respect, pollination is exemplary of all mobile agents-mediated ecosystem services (e.g., biological control or seed dispersion) and of some other regulating ES, such as water purification – in that it depends on larger-scale spatial configurations and dynamics across landscape areas. Puglia's RLP might be a promising application case, given it has already expanded the scope of its binding conservation measures (to include landscape areas that either show low PP-ES values or encroach upon PP deficit hotspots), while promoting a regional ecological network by mapping a system of interconnected landscape features (mixing natural- and agro-ecosystems) under a multifunctional conceptual framework. In this perspective, maps of PP and other ES might significantly help the regional ecological network evolve towards a *"strategically planned network* of natural and semi-natural areas with other environmental features designed and managed to deliver a wide range of ecosystem services" [30, p. 3, *emphasis added*]. Such role may hinge upon the ability of ES-based approaches to improve coordination between planners and land managers (including farmers), and strengthen policy coherence across sectors and governance levels [32]. Mapping and assessment tools may accordingly be used to devise cost-effective measures to reconcile agricultural yields with nature conservation, for example by quantifying the gains in food provision within the agricultural parks to be established under the new RLP, or by reframing the biodiversity trade-offs in rural development policies in terms of their contribution to farming competitiveness.

Agroecosystems are changing swiftly worldwide [7, 16], under the thrust of global economic, technological and environmental change. It is stimulating to notice, based on the present study, that even in landscape areas dominated by crops that have no dependency on wild pollination – such as olive groves – an ES-based approach to strategic planning may be key in providing evidence that anticipated losses from lower farming intensity may be compensated by gains in other crop yields at landscape level, or even at farm scale, in the ever more frequent cases where mixed farming structures that include horticulture are to be found.

Author Contributions. All authors contributed equally to design and conceptual background. As for data processing, C.R. took care of the forest and arable land components and of the aggregate indexes, P.B. of the olive grove and road side modules, and A.B. of crop dependency scores and regional policy assessment. Sections 1 and 2 were drafted by A.B., Sect. 3 by C.R. and Sect. 4 by P.B., while Sect. 5 was jointly written by all, who have read and approved the final manuscript.

References

1. Daily, G., Alexander, S., Naeem, S., Ehrlich, P.R., Goulder, L., Lubcheco, J., Matson, P., Mooney, H., Postel, S., Schneider, S., Tilman, D., Woodwell, G.: Ecosystem service: benefirs supplied to human societies by natural ecosystems. Issues Ecol. **4**, 1–12 (1997)
2. World Resources Institute: Ecosystems and Human Well-being: A Framework for Assessment - Millennium Ecosystem Assessment. Island Press, Washington, D.C. (2003)
3. De Groot, R.S., Wilson, M.A., Boumans, R.M.J.: A typology for the classification, description and valuation of ecosystem functions, goods and services. Ecol. Econ. **41**, 393–408 (2002)
4. Haines-Young, R., Potschin, M.: The links between biodiversity, ecosystem services and human well-being. In: Raffaelli, D.G., Frid, C.L.J. (eds.) Ecosystem Ecology: A New Synthesis, pp. 110–139. Cambridge University Press, Cambridge (2010)
5. Bastian, O., Haase, D., Grunewald, K.: Ecosystem properties, potentials and services – the EPPS conceptual framework and an urban application example. Ecol. Indic. **21**, 7–16 (2012)
6. Haines-Young, R., Potschin, M.: Common International Classification of Ecosystem Goods and Services (CICES): Consultation on Version 4, August–December 2012. EEA Framework Contract No EEA/IEA/09/003 (2013)

7. Costanza, R., D'Arge, R., de Groot, R., Farber, S., Grasso, M., Hannon, B., Limburg, K., Naeem, S., O'Neill, R.V., Paruelo, J., Raskin, R.G., Sutton, P., van den Belt, M.: The value of the world's ecosystem services and natural capital. Nature **387**, 253–260 (1997)
8. TEEB: The Economics of Ecosystem and Biodiversity for local and regional policy makers. Report 207 (2010)
9. Kinzig, A.P., Perrings, C., Chapin, F.S., Polasky, S., Smith, V.K., Tilman, D., Turner, B.L.: Sustainability. Paying for ecosystem services–promise and peril. Science **334**, 603–604 (2011)
10. Kosoy, N., Corbera, E.: Payments for ecosystem services as commodity fetishism. Ecol. Econ. **69**, 1228–1236 (2010)
11. Wilkinson, C., Saarne, T., Peterson, G.D., Colding, J.: Strategic spatial planning and the ecosystem services concept - an historical exploration. Ecol. Soc. **18**, 37 (2013)
12. Balena, P., Sannicandro, V., Torre, C.M.: Spatial multicrierial evaluation of soil consumption as a tool for SEA. In: Murgante, B., Misra, S., Rocha, A.M.A.C., Torre, C., Rocha, J.G., Falcão, M.I., Taniar, D., Apduhan, B.O., Gervasi, O. (eds.) ICCSA 2014. LNCS, vol. 8581, pp. 446–458. Springer, Cham (2014). doi:10.1007/978-3-319-09150-1_32
13. Rega, C., Spaziante, A.: Linking ecosystem services to agri-environmental schemes through SEA: a case study from Northern Italy. Environ. Impact Assess. Rev. **40**, 47–53 (2013)
14. Scolozzi, R., Morri, E., Santolini, R.: Delphi-based change assessment in ecosystem service values to support strategic spatial planning in Italian landscapes. Ecol. Indic. **21**, 134–144 (2012)
15. Woodruff, S.C., BenDor, T.K.: Ecosystem services in urban planning: Comparative paradigms and guidelines for high quality plans. Landsc. Urban Plan. **152**, 90–100 (2016)
16. European Commission: Our life insurance, our natural capital: an EU biodiversity strategy to 2020. COM/2011/244, Brussels (2011)
17. Greenleaf, S.S., Williams, N.M., Winfree, R., Kremen, C.: Bee foraging ranges and their relationship to body size. Oecologia **153**, 589–596 (2007)
18. De Palma, A., Kuhlmann, M., Roberts, S.P.M., Potts, S.G., Börger, L., Hudson, L.N., Lysenko, I., Newbold, T., Purvis, A.: Ecological traits affect the sensitivity of bees to land-use pressures in European agricultural landscapes. J. Appl. Ecol. **52**, 1567–1577 (2015)
19. Strona, G., Carstens, C.J., Beck, P.S.A.: Network analysis reveals why Xylella fastidiosa will persist in Europe. Sci. Rep. **7**, 71 (2017)
20. Bonifazi, A., Sannicandro, V., Attardi, R., Cugno, G., Torre, C.M.: Countryside vs city: a user-centered approach to open spatial indicators of urban sprawl. In: Gervasi, O., Murgante, B., Misra, S., Rocha, A.M.A.M.A.C., Torre, C.M.M., Taniar, D., Apduhan, B.O.O., Stankova, E., Wang, S. (eds.) ICCSA 2016. LNCS, vol. 9789, pp. 161–176. Springer, Cham (2016). doi:10.1007/978-3-319-42089-9_12
21. Morano, P., Tajani, F., Locurcio, M.: Land use, economic welfare and property values: an analysis of the interdependencies of the real-estate market with zonal and socio-economic variables in the municipalities of Apulia region (Italy). Int. J. Agric. Environ. Inf. Syst. **6**, 16–39 (2015)
22. Lonsdorf, E., Kremen, C., Ricketts, T., Winfree, R., Williams, N., Greenleaf, S.: Modelling pollination services across agricultural landscapes. Ann. Bot. **103**, 1589–1600 (2009)
23. Zulian, G., Maes, J., Paracchini, M.: Linking land cover data and crop yields for mapping and assessment of pollination services in Europe. Land **2**, 472–492 (2013)
24. Soille, P., Vogt, P.: Morphological segmentation of binary patterns. Pattern Recogn. Lett. **30**, 456–459 (2009)
25. Vogt, P.: GuidosToolbox - (Graphical User Interface for the Description of image Objects and their Shapes). http://forest.jrc.ec.europa.eu/download/software/guidos

26. Weissteiner, C.J., Strobl, P., Sommer, S.: Assessment of status and trends of olive farming intensity in EU-Mediterranean countries using remote sensing time series and land cover data. Ecol. Indic. **11**, 601–610 (2011)

27. Henriksen, C.I., Langer, V.: Road verges and winter wheat fields as resources for wild bees in agricultural landscapes. Agric. Ecosyst. Environ. **173**, 66–71 (2013)

28. Hopwood, J.L.: The contribution of roadside grassland restorations to native bee conservation. Biol. Conserv. **141**, 2632–2640 (2008)

29. Svensson, B., Lagerlöf, J., Svensson, B.G.: Habitat preferences of nest-seeking bumble bees (Hymenoptera: Apidae) in an agricultural landscape. Agric. Ecosyst. Environ. **77**, 247–255 (2000)

30. Olsson, O., Bolin, A., Smith, H.G., Lonsdorf, E.V.: Modeling pollinating bee visitation rates in heterogeneous landscapes from foraging theory. Ecol. Modell. **316**, 133–143 (2015)

31. European Commission: Green Infrastructure - Enhancing Europe's Natural Capital. COM 2013 249 final, Brussels (2013)

32. Estreguil, C., Caudullo, G., Rega, C., Paracchini, M.L.: Enhancing connectivity, improving green infrastructure. Cost-benefit solutions for forest and agri-environment. A pilot study in Lombardy. Office for Official Publications of the European Union, Luxembourg (2016)

Workshop on Mobile Communications (MC 2017)

On Evaluating IoTivity Cloud Platform

Thien-Binh Dang, Manh-Hung Tran, Duc-Tai Le, and Hyunseung Choo[(✉)]

College of Software, Sungkyunkwan University, Seoul, Korea
{dtbinh,hungtm,ldtai,choo}@skku.edu

Abstract. Accompanying the Internet of Things (IoT) is a demand of advanced applications and services utilizing the potential of the IoT environment. Monitoring the environment for a provision of context-aware services to the human beings is one of the new trends in our future life. The IoTivity Cloud is one of the most notable open-source platform bringing an opportunity to collect, analyze, and interpret a huge amount of data available in the IoT environment. Based on the IoTivity Cloud, we aim to develop a novel platform for comprehensive monitoring of a future network, which facilitates on-demand data collection to enable the network behavior prediction and the quality of user experience maintenance. In consideration of performance evaluation of the monitoring platform, this paper presents results of a preliminary test on the data acquisition/supply process in the IoTivity Cloud.

Keywords: Internet of Things · Monitoring platform · Publish-subscribe pattern · Message queue · Performance evaluation

1 Introduction

A number of significant technology changes have come together to enable the rise of the Internet of Things (IoT) [1–3]. IoT is envisioned to contain billions of devices, including RFID devices, sensors, smartphones, cars and so on, in the near future. To make variety of smart systems such as smart city, smart health care, smart transportation and smart manufacture feasible in the IoT environment, such devices are required to generate a large amount of data and communicate together [4]. There emerges the development of software frameworks to allow the heterogeneous IoT devices to communicate and leverage common software applications.

IoTivity open-source software framework has been developed to enable seamless device-to-device connectivity to address the emerging needs of the IoT [4]. The project, sponsored by the Open Connectivity Foundation (OCF) [6], aims to create a new standard and an open source implementation, which will help ensure interoperability among products and services regardless of makers and across multiple industries, including smart home, automotive, industrial automation, and health-care. The goal of the framework is an extensible and robust architecture that can works on smart and thin devices. As being sponsored by a group

O. Gervasi et al. (Eds.): ICCSA 2017, Part V, LNCS 10408, pp. 137–147, 2017.
DOI: 10.1007/978-3-319-62404-4_10

of industry leaders, it is expected to become a standard specification and certi-
fication program to ensure secure and reliable connections between IoT devices
and the Internet.

Recently, the IoTivity Cloud open-source platform [7] has been developed
based on the IoTivity framework. The platform brings an opportunity to collect,
analyze, and interpret a huge amount of data available in the IoT environment.
The processed data is then required to be available for a provision of smart
services to human beings. All these data should be acquired in real-time, stored
for a long period and analyzed in a proper way. To this end, we aim to develop a
high scalability and low overhead monitoring platform. The monitoring platform
will be designed in a way of collecting any type of data into a cloud database
by utilizing IoTivity Cloud. This feature opens many opportunities for network
operators to customize the monitoring system based on their demands in target
deployment area.

In the scope of this paper, we study the stability and scalability of the IoTivity Cloud, which is the most essential component of our monitoring platform.
Particularly, we measure throughputs of Cloud Interface and Message Queue
servers in the IoTivity Cloud under different network loads, in a simple testbed
with single-machine-based deployment. The main goal of this work is to generate
a baseline that we can use to re-evaluate the performance of the whole platform
in a cloud-based deployment. For the rest of the paper we use the terms framework and platform to refer to the IoTivity framework and the IoTivity Cloud
platform, respectively.

The rest of the paper is organized as follows. In Sect. 2, some popular IoT
platforms are reviewed. Section 3 provides detail information of components in
the IoTivity Cloud platform. Our testbed, testing scenarios, and performance
evaluation results are presented in Sect. 4. Finally, we conclude our paper, and
discuss our future work in Sect. 5.

2   Related Work

There exist many open-source platforms now a day, that can support entire
development of IoT applications and systems [8]. In this section, we review some
popular IoT platforms. ThingWrox [9] is one of the earliest software platforms
designed to build and run the IoT applications. It focuses on rapid development of IoT applications such as Smart Home, Smart City, Smart Agriculture,
Smart Grid, and Smart Water. ThingWrox is a complete development suite that
enables application design, runtime, and intelligence environment. ThingWrox
uses REST, MQTT and sockets for data communication. The strong features of
ThingWrox include modern and complete platform provisioning, faster deployment and search-based intelligence.

ThingSpeak [10] is an IoT application platform for the development of IoT
systems. With ThingSpeak, users can develop applications which can collect
data from sensors, such as an application of location tracking, controlling, and
monitoring home appliances. The key features of the platform include real time

collection of data storage, data analytics and visualization using MATLAB, open API supporting and providing geolocation data. In addition, it enables an integration with Tweeter, i.e. users can get update status of their devices from tweets. The HTTP protocol is utilized to store or retrieve data from things over the Internet or via a Local Area Network.

Google Cloud platform [11] enables developers to code, test and deploy their IoT applications with highly scalable and reliable infrastructure. The developers now just focus on the programming work and Google handles issues regarding infrastructure, scalability, computing power and data storage. What make Google Cloud platform become one of the most popular IoT platforms are fast global network, higher performance, environment safe cloud, Googles big data tool, supporting of various available cloud services like BigQuery, PubSub, Connecting Arduino, RiptideIO and many more.

A common theme among the above platforms is that there is no performance evaluation report apart from general statements about their stability, scalability, and cloud deployment ability. Recently, Vandikas et al. [12] have evaluated the performance of their platform, called IoT-Framework [13]. The work of these authors is our inspiration to evaluate the performance of the IoTivity Cloud platform.

3   IoTivity Cloud Platform

IoTivity is an open source framework implementing OCF standards for the IoT software developments. The framework operates as middleware across all operating systems and connectivity platforms. It consists of four key components including (1) device and resource discovery, (2) data transmission, (3) device management and (4) data management, as shown in Fig. 1 [5].

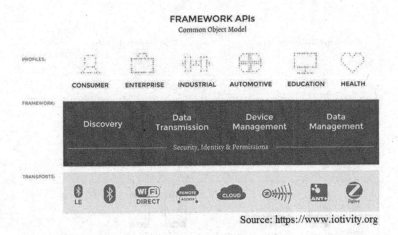

Source: https://www.iotivity.org

Fig. 1. IoTivity common object model.

The IoTivity discovery component supports multiple discovery mechanisms for devices and resources in proximately and remotely. IoTivity adopts the Constrained Application Protocol (CoAP) [14] defined by the Internet Engineering Task Force (IETF) [8] as a data transmission protocol. As CoAP is a lightweight alternative to Hypertext Transfer Protocol (HTTP), it can work with HTTP by using intermediaries to translate between two protocols. While the data management component supports the collection, storage and analytics of data from various devices, the device management component aims to provide a one-stop-shop that supports the configuration, provisioning and diagnostics of devices in an IoT network.

IoTivity Cloud is an open-source platform that aims to extend accessibility of IoTivity devices. The IoTivity Cloud supports techniques such as HTTP to CoAP proxy and OAuth2 [16] over CoAP to enable users to access their devices under their preference accounts over the cloud. Architecture of the IoTivity Cloud is depicted in Fig. 2. The platform includes IoT controllers who own IoT devices. To be widely used over the cloud, both controllers and devices must be registered to the cloud first. The devices read sensory data of the physical world, and then send the data to IoTivity cloud servers. Once the data have been published, IoT controllers can access them even they are not co-located.

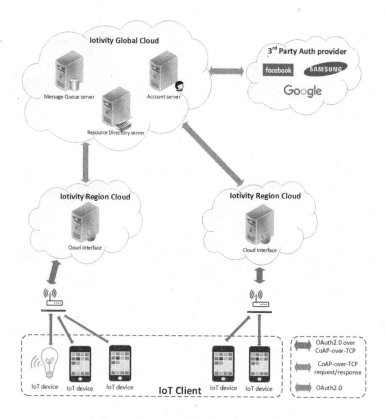

Fig. 2. IoTivity Cloud architecture.

Most of IoTivity framework core components are developed in C and C++, but the IoTivity Cloud is developed in Java. In the platform, servers are separated into two levels: IoTivity Region Cloud (IRC) and IoTivity Global Cloud (IGC). IRC includes regional Cloud Interface servers that accept connections from both IoT devices and IoT controllers, receive sensory data and sends RESTful messages through connected pipelines to IGC. The IGC is the global cloud that includes Message Queue, Resource Directory, and Account servers. The functionality of each component is explained as follows:

- **Cloud Interface (CI)**: a server acts as an interface of IGC. It is basically a proxy of Message Queue, Resource Directory, and Account servers. Additionally, CI handles the server side OAuth2.0 handshake protocol and the keep-alive messages from IoT devices to ensure the connectivity between the devices and the cloud. Last but not least, CI relays handler such that IoT devices and IoT controllers can communicate when they are connected to different regional clouds.
- **Resource Directory (RD)**: a server supports device registration, discovery, updating, or deleting to IoTivity Cloud. It deploys MongoDB to manage the database of IoT device information.
- **Account server**: a server supports third party OAuth2.0 enabled authentication providers like Google, Facebook, and Github extending their users identity to IoTivity Cloud. After a user signs up to the Account server, his/her information and a corresponding access token will be stored in a database. Consequently, the user can register his/her devices to IoTivity Cloud for future use.
- **Message Queue (MQ)**: a broker exposes an interface for clients to initiate a publish/subscribe interaction. The server is built on the top of Apache Zookeeper [17] and Apache Kafka [18]. Apache Zookeeper is an open source providing high performance coordination service for distributed applications. It is mainly used to track status of nodes, content topics, and messages, stored in an Apache Kafka cluster. Apache Kafka is a distributed publish/subscribe messaging system. It is written in Scala programming language and designed for processing of real time activity stream data, e.g. logs and metrics collections.
- **IoTivity client**: IoTivity client consists of IoT devices and IoT controllers. An IoTivity client handles the client side OAuth2.0 handshake protocol and sends keep-alive messages to CI periodically. The client is also able to send resource registration/discovery requests to the cloud.

4   Performance Evaluation

In this section, we describe performance evaluation of the IoTivity Cloud. We start by depicting our testbed, and then describing the testing scenarios. Finally, we discuss on selected evaluation metrics and obtained evaluation results.

4.1   Testbed Setting

Our testbed consists of four physical nodes as shown in Fig. 3. IoT device node is a Mid-2010 MacBook Pro with 4 GB RAM and an Intel Core 2 duo CPU 2.4 GHz. IoT controller node is hosted in a laptop computer with 8 GB RAM and an Intel Core i5 duo CPU 2.3 GHz. The CI is hosted in a desktop computer with 3 GB RAM and an Intel Core i5-2500 CPU 3.3 GHz. The IGC with three components of MQ, Account, and RD servers is set up in a single desktop computer. The computer has 16 GB RAM and Intel Core i7 CPU 3.60 GHz. All the computers run the Ubuntu 16.04 LTS operating system, and support IoTivity framework 1.2.0. The IoTivity Cloud is deployed on the testbed similar to its architecture. We have added Java hooking scripts into source code of the CI and the MQ to measure the performance of these servers. The size of requests/responses are set in the simplest case where a message contains only one character. The number of devices are varied to identify maximum capacity of the system.

4.2   Testing Methodology

We are interested in how the IoTivity platform operates under stress testing with different number of IoT devices and IoT controllers. In our testing, we generate multiple threads on the IoT device node, each of them represents for

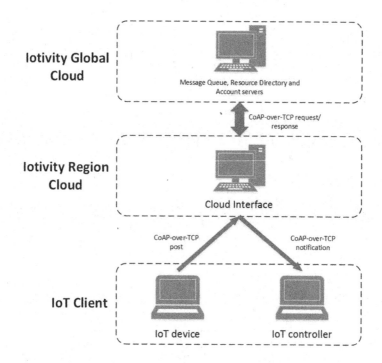

Fig. 3. Testbed model.

a device which generates data. Similarly, multiple processes of controller, which receives data, run in the IoT controller node. Recall that we especially focus on the throughput of individual components: the CI and the MQ. Even though the IoTivity Cloud is designed to deploy on a cluster of nodes, the test we have conducted is intentionally narrowed to a single node for the IRC and a single node for the IGC.

We consider two testing scenarios. The first scenario uses various number of IoT devices on producing side and no IoT controllers. In this scenario, the CI is tasked to only process a large number of post requests from IoT clients without disseminating these post requests to IoT controllers. The second testing scenario is similar to the first one but adding various number of IoT controllers. In both testing scenarios, the IoT devices generate post requests in a Poisson process [20]. The number of IoT devices and the arrival rate λ (msg/sec) determine the level of stress testing that the higher value of λ or the greater number of IoT devices means more post requests arrive at the CI in a period of time. The value of λ is set equally to all IoT devices for an individual test. Donald Knuth describes a method to generate random timings for a Poisson process in [21]. In this method, the exact amount of time until the next event is determined by the formula:

$$ nextTime = \frac{-\ln p}{\lambda}, $$

where p is a random value between 0 and 1.

The algorithms to generate random timings for a Poisson process are demonstrated in the Algorithms 1 and 2. All source code for the simulation, customized CI and customized MQ are available on the Github in order to make the simulation and evaluation are accessible and reproducible to wider audience.

Algorithm 1. Calculate the time for next event

1: **procedure** NEXTTIME(λ)
2:     p = random()
3:     Return -ln(p)/λ
4: **end procedure**

Algorithm 2. Checking timer to generate events

1: **procedure** CHECK(λ,*timer*,*deltaSecond*,*endInterval*)
2:     *timer* = *timer* + *deltaSecond*
3:     **if** *timer*>*endInterval* **then**
4:         timer = 0
5:         endInterval = nextTime(λ)
6:         doEvent()
7:     **end if**
8: **end procedure**

4.3   Testing Scenarios and Results

No Consumers

The first scenario uses a C++ program which generates a maximum number of 25000 CoAP_over_TCP post requests from IoT client towards the CI. These requests are sent by IoT devices which are represented by C++ threads. The number of IoT devices is set to 1, 10, 100, 500 and 1000. The size of one CoAP_over_TCP post request is 0.109 KB and the size of one CoAP_over_TCP response is 0.087 KB. Each post request contains sensory data in Cbor [19] format which is the data read from IoT devices. λ is set to 15000 (req/sec). When the CI received a CoAP_over_TCP post request:

(a) It forwards the request to the MQ
(b) The MQ extracts sensory data from the payload of the request
(c) The MQ pushes sensory data into corresponding queue in Kakfa publish/subscribe messaging system in order to make it available to subscribers who have subscribed to the same queue (in this first testing scenario, there are no subscribers)

An optimization has been made on producing side is using a single sign-in connection for all IoT devices. Since this optimization does not set at the CI and the MQ broker, the evaluation results will not be impacted.

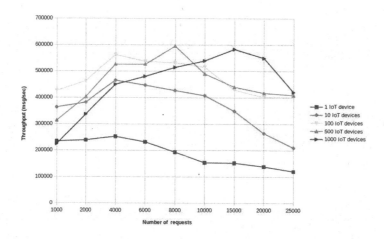

Fig. 4. Throughput of CI server.

Figure 4 illustrates similar trends of throughputs with different numbers of IoT devices. It gradually increases and reaches the maximum value before starting decreasing as the number of requests continues to increase. The increase of throughput can be justified by the fact that a greater number of requests is introduced into the system and the system uses more CPU utilization for handle those requests. On the other hand, the throughput decreases when the number of requests is large enough and impacts the processing capacity of the system. The throughput increases from 252269.2 (msg/sec) for one IoT device setup to 465519.2 (msg/sec) for 10 IoT devices setup, to 562967.7 (msg/sec) for 100 IoT devices setup and to 595406.2 (msg/sec) for 500 IoT devices setup. In other words, the throughput increases at 343137 (msg/sec) which is almost a 57.63% increase. However, the maximum throughput lightly decreases to 583455.1 (msg/sec) with the 1000 IoT devices setup. The maximum throughput of the CI reaches 595406.2 (msg/sec) for 500 IoT devices setup in the scope of our testbed configuration.

As shown in Fig. 5, throughput of the MQ has a similar trend to that of the CI. However, throughputs for setups with different numbers of IoT devices converge to approximate 3640 (msg/sec) when the number of requests passes 4000 (msg/sec). The maximum throughput increases from 4266.4 (msg/sec) for one IoT device setup to 4926.8 (msg/sec) for 10 IoT devices setup before going down to about 4772.2 (msg/sec) with 100 IoT devices setup and 500 IoT devices setup, and to 4610.5 (msg/sec) with 1000 IoT devices setup. The maximum throughput of the MQ reaches 4926.8 (msg/sec) which is much smaller than the throughput of the CI. This can be justified by the fact that the CI is tasked to only forward requests of IoT devices to the MQ while the MQ has to detaches the requests and then constructs the Kafka messages before pushing them into the Kafka message queue. In case the number of generated requests is less than the number of IoT devices, there will be some IoT devices do not generate requests but we still create these IoT devices (C++ threads) and make them connect to the CI to experience various testing cases.

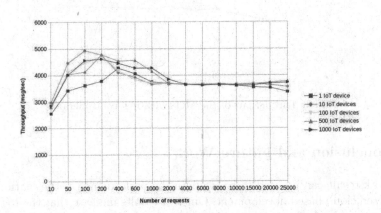

Fig. 5. Throughput of the MQ (no IoT controllers).

With Consumers

The second scenario is the generalized case of the first scenario in terms of the functionality. What is added into this scenario is the different number IoT controllers which are 1, 10, 50, 100, 200 for different tests. Unlike the simulation method of IoT devices, the different numbers of IoT controllers are introduced by using independent processes instead of using threads. A process is a compiled C++ program which is implemented by using IoTivity framework APIs. All IoT controllers subscribe to the same topic of the MQ; therefore, they receive the same notification when a post request is published to the MQ broker. The purpose of using different processes is that we want to duplicate the notification corresponding to the number of subscribers. This cannot be done with a single process having multiple threads to our knowledge about IoTivity framework APIs. Testing result from the first scenario shown that throughput of the CI is much higher than throughput of the MQ so the bottleneck of the throughput of the overall architecture is at the MQ. For this reason, we only focus on measuring the throughput of the MQ in this scenario. Testing results of the second scenario are shown in the Fig. 6.

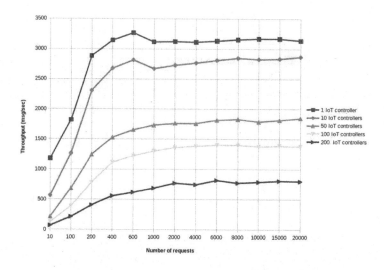

Fig. 6. Throughput of the MQ (with IoT controllers).

5   Conclusion and Future Work

This work result can be used to re-evaluate the performance of the platform in a clustered cloud based development. Our test results indicate that the IoTivity Cloud is a stable platform since no drops of messages have been found under the stress testing. Moreover, the testing results show that the CI can handle a load of 1000 IoT devices simultaneously and the maximum throughput reaches 595406.2 (msg/sec). The maximum throughput of the MQ is 4926.8 (msg/sec) which is much smaller than the throughput of the CI. What can be learned from this is the overall throughput of the architecture is mainly depended on the performance of the MQ. In addition, the throughput of the MQ drops significantly when we introduce a large number of IoT controllers into the system.

Our next step is to continue this evaluation work regrading memory consumption of the CI and the MQ. Moreover, we plan to use a number of computers to generate heavy load instead of using a single computer as this testbed did and then compare the results to the results of this work. Furthermore, we will develop our IoT monitoring platform based on the IoTivity Cloud and re-use this work for performance evaluation.

Acknowledgment. This research was supported in part by Korean government, under G-ITRC support program (IITP-2016-R6812-16-0001) supervised by the IITP, Priority Research Centers Program (NRF-2010-0020210) and Basic Science Research Program (NRF-2016R1D1A 1B03934660) through NRF, respectively.

References

1. Ashton, K.: That Internet of Things thing. RFID J., June 2009
2. Atzori, L., Iera, A., Morabito, G.: The internet of things: a survey. Comput. Netw. **54**(15), 2787–2805 (2010), doi:10.1016/j.comnet.2010.05.010
3. Alcaraz, C., Najera, P., Lopez, J., Roman, R.: Wireless sensor networks and the Internet of Things: do we need a complete integration? In: Proceedings of the 1st International Workshop on the Security of the Internet of Things (SecIoT 2010). IEEE, Tokyo, December 2010. https://www.nics.uma.es/pub/papers/calcaraz10.pdf
4. Miorandi, D., Sicari, S., Pellegrini, F.D., Chlamtac, I.: Internet of Things: vision, applications and research challenges. Ad Hoc Netw. **10**(7), 1497–1516 (2012). http://www.sciencedirect.com/science/article/pii/S1570870512000674
5. IoTivity software framework. https://www.iotivity.org
6. Open Connectivity Foundation. https://openconnectivity.org
7. IoTivity Cloud. https://wiki.iotivity.org/iotivity_cloud_-_programming_guide
8. Nakhuva, B., Champaneria, T.: Study of various Internet of Things platforms. Int. J. Comput. Sci. Eng. Surv. (IJCSES) **6**(6), 61–74 (2015), doi:10.5121/ijcses.2015.6605
9. ThingWorx: Enterprise IoT Solutions and Platform Technology. https://www.thingworx.com
10. ThingSpeak: IoT Analytics. https://thingspeak.com
11. Google Cloud Platform: Google Cloud Computing, Hosting Services & APIs. https://cloud.google.com
12. Vandikas, K., Tsiatsis, V.: Performance evaluation of an IoT platform. In: Proceedings of 2014 Eighth International Conference on Next Generation Mobile Apps, Services and Technologies. IEEE (2014)
13. IoT-Framework. https://github.com/projectcs13
14. RFC 7252 Constrained Application Protocol. http://coap.technology
15. The Internet Engineering Task Force (IETF). https://www.ietf.org
16. OAuth 2.0. https://oauth.net/2
17. Zookeeper. http://zookeeper.apache.org
18. Kafka. http://kafka.apache.org
19. Cbor Concise Binary Object Representation. http://cbor.io
20. Poisson point process. https://en.wikipedia.org/wiki/Poisson_point_process
21. Knuth, D.E.: The Art of Computer Programming, vol. 1. Addison-Weseley Publ. Co., Boston (1968)

Partial Switching Based MBMS Bearer Management Architecture and Procedure for V2N Services with High-Speed Mobility

Jun Suk Kim and Min Young Chung[✉]

College of Information and Communication Engineering, Sungkyunkwan University,
2066, Seobu-Ro, Jangan-Gu, Suwon-Si, Gyeonggi-Do 16419, Republic of Korea
{jsk7016,mychung}@skku.edu

Abstract. A Multimedia broadcast/multicast service (MBMS) architecture can be considered for enabling multimedia vehicle-to-everything (V2X) services for mobile communication networks. However, since the MBMS architecture is designed for transmitting data to stationary users, it is inefficient in providing network services to moving vehicular users. Therefore, in this paper we propose a novel MBMS architecture which simultaneously utilizes both serving communication path and preconfigured communication path called as MBMS bearer. In the proposed scheme, parameters used for establishing MBMS bearer are previously stored into the candidate service area that expected to be used in the future. When the vehicular users actually move to the candidate service area, the proposed scheme activates the stored parameters and switches the conventional communication path into the newly established one. By using the proposed MBMS architecture, we expect that the vehicular users can be effectively supported by multimedia MBMS services from the mobile networks.

Keywords: Vehicle-to-everything communications · Multimedia broadcast/multi-cast service · Service area management · Bearer management · High-speed mobility

1 Introduction

Recently, autonomous driving or self-driving, in which a vehicle can move and head for its destination by itself with rare or no human intervention, is being considered as a primary service scenario for V2X communications [1,2]. Since passengers including a driver owning the vehicle are free from controlling the vehicle during the autonomous driving, they can have considerable amounts of spare time for doing other things. As a result, demand for various types of services to spend their spare time are consequently expected to increase from

This work was partially supported by Samsung Electronics and by Basic Science Research Program through the National Research Foundation of Korea (NRF) funded by the Ministry of Education (NRF-2010-0020210).

© Springer International Publishing AG 2017
O. Gervasi et al. (Eds.): ICCSA 2017, Part V, LNCS 10408, pp. 148–160, 2017.
DOI: 10.1007/978-3-319-62404-4_11

the passengers using autonomous driving services. For example, the passengers can use high-definition multimedia content through streaming from mobile networks, and these service scenarios are valid for both the personal car and public transportation such as bus and train. In general, these streaming services provide users with the contents by using broadcast or multicast transmissions for effective usage of a radio resource in mobile communications. Moreover, fleet management, which multiple vehicles cruise together as a group, can be considered as a derived service from autonomous driving service. When the centralized instructions are given to the fleet of the vehicles via multicast communication, the fleet of the vehicles can be effectively controlled by the networks.

In order to effectively support these services based on broad- and multicasting, multimedia broadcast/multicast service (MBMS) architecture has been introduced to the mobile networks [3,4]. In MBMS architecture, radio resources used for data transmissions are commonly used by multiple users if the users can experience the channel quality better than that of the minimum level. When the users desire the same contents, the mobile networks deliver the contents by using common resources assigned for MBMS and the users requesting the contents can simultaneously receive the contents by listening to the common MBMS resources. Therefore, the mobile networks enable to reduce the number of radio resources used for transmissions, and the resource efficiency can be improved.

As a solution for delivering multimedia contents in V2X communications, 3rd Generation Partnership Project (3GPP) has considered utilizing MBMS architecture as shown in Fig. 1 [5,6]. Since the MBMS architecture enables the contents stored in a V2X application server to be accessed by multiple users simultaneously, the MBMS architecture can be an effective solution for supporting the V2X service scenarios including vehicle-to-networks (V2N) communications. However, the vehicular users targeted for V2N communications have higher speed than that of the conventional users. This may make the amount of time remaining in an MBMS service area decrease and the served MBMS service area frequently changed. As a result, the burden of providing network services and delivery costs for MBMS based V2N services will increase due to the vehicles' mobility. In addition, the MBMS contents transmitted during the changes of service area should be avoided to be delayed and lost. Therefore, it

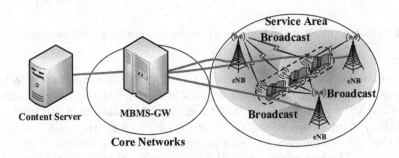

Fig. 1. V2X communication network with MBMS architecture.

is required for MBMS architecture to effectively support vehicular users having high-speed mobility for MBMS based V2N services.

The vehicular devices traveling on roadways can be approximately predicted of their moving directions when the road structure is known in the MBMS architecture. By using the predictable moving directions of the vehicular devices, we propose a novel MBMS architecture which enables to effectively manage MBMS bearers, which is the paths delivering contents to the devices for MBMS services. We introduce the concept of the proposed MBMS architecture and detailed procedures for its operations. The remainder of this paper is organized as follows. Section 2 provides overall descriptions and related works for MBMS architecture. The proposed concept is introduced in Sect. 3, and the detailed procedure and design considerations are covered in Sect. 4. Finally, we conclude our work in Sect. 5.

2 Preliminaries

Figure 2 shows MBMS architecture and interface between its component entities in V2N communication scenarios [7]. In MBMS architecture, a component entity, which plays an important role in operating MBMS services in 3GPP mobile networks, is broadcast and multicast service center (BM-SC). BM-SC takes charge of initiating MBMS services or relying on V2N contents from the V2X application server (V2X AS) to MBMS gateway (MBMS-GW). In order to do this, BM-SC supervises the initiation and releasing procedure for session and bearer which are the communication path for transmission of MBMS contents. In addition, BM-SC administrates authorization for participating in MBMS services and schedules the MBMS transmissions passing through each MBMS bearer.

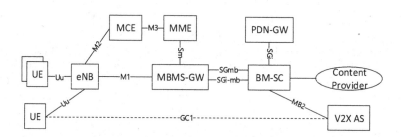

Fig. 2. MBMS architecture and interface between its entities in V2N communications.

In order for 3GPP mobile networks to convey MBMS contents to vehicular users, it is required to establish an MBMS bearer which is the connectivity from V2X AS to end mobile users. In addition, the established MBMS bearer should be updated when quality of services (QoS) level for the MBMS service is changed or the communication path is changed according to users' position or situation [8]. The procedure for initially establishing an MBMS bearer and for updating the bearer is shown in Fig. 3. V2X AS provides BM-SC with the service related parameters such as QoS values, information on the area where MBMS contents are broadcasted. When receiving the parameters from the V2X AS, BM-SC firstly determines which cell is related to the broadcasted service area. By mapping the received service area identifier into the cell identifiers indexed as E-UTRAN cell global identifiers (ECGIs), BM-SC distinguishes its counterpart MBMS-GW covering the target eNBs mapped by the ECGIs. Internet protocol (IP) address of the MBMS-GW is given to the V2X AS to establish a connection between them. Then, BM-SC initiates the procedure for establishing an MBMS bearer by sending a session to start request message. The parameters for the MBMS bearer to be established are sequentially conveyed from BM-SC to the selected MBMS-GW and eNBs, and the partial connections between intermediate entities are established. After establishing all the partial connections with the given parameters, the establishment procedure of the MBMS bearer, which consists of the partial connections, is completed. For effectively managing eNBs in the MBMS architecture, multi-cell coordination entity (MCE) can be considered between MBMS-GW and eNBs. When V2X AS newly gives the changed parameters including MBMS service area, ECGI list, and QoS values to the established MBMS bearer, BM-SC updates the related parameters by using the same procedure of the bearer establishment. If the changed parameters can not be accepted into the conventional bearer, BM-SC creates a new bearer with the parameters and releases the conventional bearer by using session start/stop/update procedure.

In order to manage MBMS service area for V2N communications, two types of solutions mapping between MBMS service area and a cell identifier of eNB are discussed in 3GPP specification [9–11]. To map the service area into the cell identifier, the geo-location information contained in V2X application message is considered to be used in these schemes [12]. In the BM-SC based solution, V2X AS, which is located at out of mobile networks, just manages service area information, and BM-SC determines the cell list related to the service area given from the V2X AS. Since the cell deployment information is generally stored in the mobile networks, BM-SC can organize the cell list for each service area with consideration of the cell deployment. Whereas, the V2X AS based solution determines all the mapping relation in the V2X server and BM-SC simply intermediate the information between the entities in the mobile networks and the V2X server. Since the current geo-location is contained the V2X application message, the V2X server can be easily informed the latest location of the target vehicular users, and effectively links the cell identifier into the serving service area. However, the sensitive information on the cell deployment needs to be leaked to V2X server, which is located at outside of the mobile networks.

For simultaneously providing various V2X services, multiple service areas for different groups of users are allocated although the user groups are geographically located at the neighbor area. In particular, the service areas can be made overlapped due to their proximity because a lot of V2X services are aiming to acquire the network services in a small service area. Therefore, in order to discriminate the groups of users served by different V2X services in the overlapped

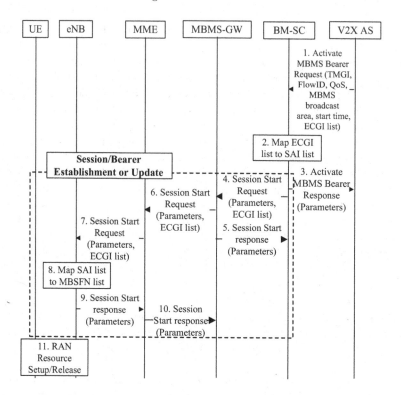

Fig. 3. The initial establishment and update procedures for MBMS bearer.

service area, the use of different temporary mobile group identity (TMGI) are proposed for the user groups, respectively [13]. For more efficient management of the TMGIs, a common serial bit pattern is considered to be inserted in the part of TMGIs, which are assigned to the users receiving the different services in the overlapped service area.

3   Novel MBMS Bearer Management Architecture for V2N Services

3.1   Problem Definition

In the MBMS architecture, MBMS bearer is established from the V2X AS to multiple eNBs belonging to a certain service area. While a user moves only in the service area, there is no need for the MBMS bearer to be updated in order for the user to continually receive the MBMS service. However, if the user migrates from eNBs in the current service area to those in the others, the established bearers should be changed into new eNBs belonging to a new service area which the user migrates. In particular, since a lot of vehicles can have high-speed mobility in V2N communication scenarios, the user can frequently get out of the current service area and can often migrate to the eNBs in another service area. Therefore, for reliable use of the MBMS services, it is required for the established MBMS bearer to be effectively updated according to the mobility of the user.

For guaranteeing the service continuity of MBMS transmissions, it is considered that the path in which an MBMS content are delivered are switched into an ordinary downlink unicast channel until the user deviating from the current service area enters the new service area and establishes new MBMS bearer for its service [14]. In this scheme, when a user changes its services area into others, the MBMS service for the user is temporarily converted into normal unicast service and the MBMS service is recovered as soon as the user can be available to use the MBMS service. The time for switching from the MBMS service to the unicast service and the opposite is determined according to the signal quality in radio access network from the attached eNB in terms of the reference signal received power (RSRP) and signal-to-interference and noise ratio (SINR).

As another method for improving MBMS service continuity, information sharing about the used MBMS channels between neighboring eNBs is proposed [15]. In this scheme, each eNB in the same service area exchanges its MBMS channel information with neighboring eNBs before a user performs its handover. And then, when a user requests handover into another eNB, the eNB gives the MBMS channel information to the user in order for the user to immediately listen to the MBMS channel of the neighbor eNB after completing its handover. Without receiving system information block broadcasted from the neighbor eNB, the user can be delivered MBMS contents through the MBMS channel of the newly attached eNB. This MBMS channel information contains identification of a service area, cell, the MBMS channel and the related parameters.

Although these conventional schemes support the MBMS services, the current MBMS system is architecturally inefficient to provide its services to the vehicular user which frequently requires handover due to its mobility. In the current MBMS architecture, MBMS bearer, which is established from the V2X AS to the eNBs corresponded by the MBMS service area, should be fully updated even though only partial parts of the MBMS bearer are changed. This is because the BM-SC takes care of and centrally manages all the things of MBMS bearer. During the procedure for fully updating the entire MBMS bearer, all the entities located on the communication path of the MBMS bearer should exchange signaling messages between them. Since vehicular users can frequently migrate between different cells or service areas with causing many MBMS bearer updates, the signaling overload for the bearer updates largely increases and it will consume considerable capability of the BM-SC entity. Therefore, in order to effectively enable the MBMS based V2N services, it is required for redesign the procedure for MBMS bearer update to be simplified and to reduce its number of phases.

3.2   Switching Based Bearer Management Procedure

For solving above mentioned problem, we propose a novel bearer management scheme, which uses double MBMS bearers not only the current serving service area but also the candidate service area which is expected to be entered by a vehicular after a while. In order to reduce the number of execution of MBMS bearer update procedure, the BM-SC in the proposed MBMS architecture simultaneously creates an extra MBMS bearer for candidate service area when the MBMS bearer for the currently targeted service area is being established. Each entity corresponding the candidate service area just stores the information on the candidate MBMS bearer as deactivated. Since an MBMS-GW covers a number of service areas, communication path between V2X AS and MBMS-GW is common, but the path from MBMS-GW to eNBs are different between those of the current and the candidate MBMS bearers. Therefore, when the vehicular user migrates the current service area to the candidate service area, the established MBMS bearer is partially modified between MBMS-GW and eNBs.

Figure 4 represents the concept of the proposed MBMS bearer management partially switching the established bearer. In the proposed MBMS architecture, BM-SC receives the current and candidate service areas of the vehicular user which requests initiation of the MBMS service. By mapping these service areas into the cell identifiers, the BM-SC finds out the eNBs matched to the current and candidate service areas. For the eNBs related to the current service area, the MBMS bearer is sequentially established from the BM-SC to the eNBs as an activated mode. On the other hand, for the eNBs covering the candidate service area, the MBMS bearer is partially stored in the bearer context of the MBMS-GW and the related eNBs as a deactivated mode. Until the vehicular user penetrates into one of the eNBs belonging to the candidate service area, the candidate MBMS bearer is disabled. If the handover is needed, mobility management entity (MME) generates a triggering event and gives the message to the MBMS-GW in order to request the current MBMS bearer to be modified. As the triggering message from MME, MBMS-GW internally decides to switch the serving MBMS bearer into the candidate one instead of forwarding the request to the BM-SC for fully updating the entire bearer. This operation

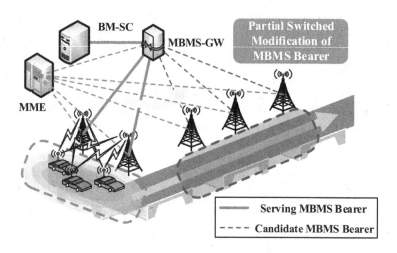

Fig. 4. The proposed partial-switching based MBMS bearer modification by MME.

is simply performed by using small-scale signaling between MBMS-GW and the corresponded eNBs. Therefore the proposed MBMS bearer management scheme can decrease the interrupted time for bearer update, the number of full update of the entire MBMS bearer can be reduced in proportion to the number of predicted candidate service area. After switching, the conventional MBMS bearer is deactivated and the candidate MBMS bearer is activated.

4 Design of the Switching Based Bearer Management Scheme

4.1 Estimating the Candidate Service Area

For operating the proposed partial-switching based MBMS bearer management, V2X AS should provide additional information on the candidate service area, which means the service area for the serving vehicular users to be accessed, to the BM-SC. In order to predict the candidate service area, V2X AS can utilize the information stored in the V2X message generated from the vehicular user, of which the message contains an identifier of the currently positioned the serving cell. In addition, we consider that the V2X AS has a road map and a plan of cell deployment. As shown in Fig. 5, since the vehicular user generally moves along the road excepting special cases, V2X AS can predict the candidate service area by counterpointing the cell planning map against the road map. In particular, the highway, which is straight and has rare exit, can make V2X AS to predict the candidate area without difficulty.

Estimating the candidate service area may be difficult for the V2X AS when the vehicular user is moving on the road in the downtown area. Since there are lots of intersections on the roads in the downtown area, it is difficult for V2X AS to predict where the user will move and in case of wrong prediction, the candidate service area will mislead all the entity related the MBMS bearer into

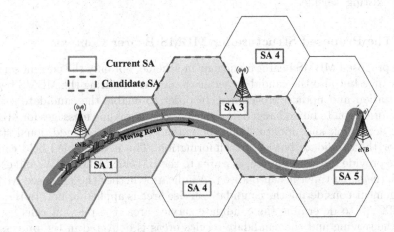

Fig. 5. An example of predicting candidate service area by considering road structure.

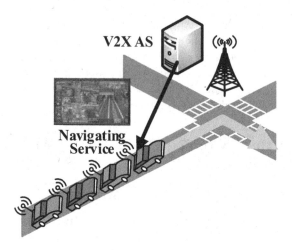

Fig. 6. Prediction scenario for driven path by using network based navigation service.

performing unnecessary bearer management scheduling. To solve this problem, we propose that V2X AS revises the result by using the destination information obtained by a cooperation with other AS. In the case of public transportation such as bus and train, of which the progress path is fixed, the candidate service area can be predicted by using route map information stored in the AS. In addition, when the terminal uses a network-based navigation service, the path information from the AS providing navigation service can be used for V2X AS to exactly predict the candidate service area as shown in Fig. 6. If the V2X AS is unable to predict the candidate service area due to no assistance of other AS, the V2X AS only establishes the MBMS bearer for the serving service area by using the existing procedure. This can eliminate the unnecessary overhead for bearer management from the related entity with the same level of performance of the existing scheme.

4.2   The Proposed Structure for MBMS Bearer Context

In the proposed MBMS bearer management scheme, not only the current serving service area but also the candidate service area is used during the MBMS bearer initialization and update procedures. In order to enable the candidate service area information to be exchanged, the conventional signaling messages for MBMS bearer activation and update should be extended to have an additional string field for the candidate service area information. The newly added field can be used to provide the candidate service area to the BM-SC, MBMS-GW, and eNBs, and at the same time, it can be used to indicate whether the proposed MBMS management considering the candidate service area is applied or not. In the case for V2X AS to determine the candidate service area, the relevant cells list for both the serving and the candidate service areas is delivered in the process for establishing or updating the MBMS bearer. On the other hand, if the V2X AS cannot determine the candidate service area, the signaling message is delivered as the serving service area information is filled and the candidate service area field remains blank.

In initiating and updating the MBMS bearer, all the involved entities including eNB, MME, and MBMS-GW store the delivered serving and candidate service areas into the MBMS bearer context, respectively. During the procedures, the intermediate entity such as BM-SC and MBMS-GW branches the signaling message and its contained information, especially related to the serving and candidate service area, by considering the communication path determined by the service area. In addition, in order to effectively adjust delivered route on the MBMS bearer according to the stored information, an activation flag is introduced in the proposed MBMS bearer context. The activation flag is used to separate the activated communication path on MBMS bearer for the serving area and that for the candidate service area which is just stored for quick bearer update. As shown in Fig. 7, all the information for the serving candidate service areas is identically stored in MBMS bearer context of each entity, and each entity has an activation type flag to switch the communication path of the established MBMS bearer according to the vehicular devices' location. Parameters for the candidate service area are kept stored only in the MBMS bearer context, and these are activated only when the activation flag is changed into the candidate mode by triggering event from MME.

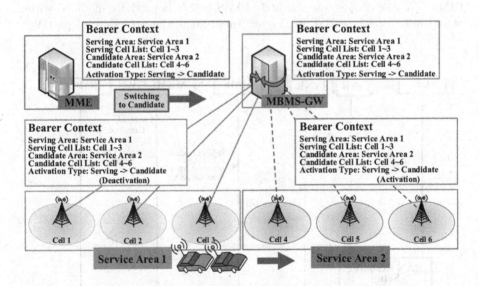

Fig. 7. Switching scenario to the candidate mode triggered by MME and an example of bearer context for each entity.

4.3 Procedure for Partially Switching MBMS Bearer by MME Triggering

In the proposed MBMS bear management architecture, MBMS bearer context for each entity is initially configured following the procedure as shown in Fig. 8. When initially requesting MBMS bearer establishment, the BM-SC provides the target MBMS-GW with session initiation/update request message containing both the serving service area and the candidate service area. The target MBMS-GW replies response message to the BM-SC, and forwards the received the update request message to MME. The MME reconstitutes the session initiation/update request with two types of a message containing the serving and candidate service area, respectively. The reconstituted messages for the serving and candidate service area are delivered to the eNBs belonging to them, respectively. The eNBs of the serving service area store the received information in their MBMS bearer context, and configure radio resources for MBMS service in radio access network (RAN). Whereas, the eNBs belonging to the candidate service area simply store the received parameters for MBMS bearer as deactivated. Both eNBs for the serving and candidate service area use the activation flag to represent their operation mode.

In general, MBMS contents are delivered through MBMS bearer from BM-SC to eNBs of the serving service area. In the proposed MBMS architecture, when the vehicular user migrates into the candidate service area, the part between MBMS-GW and eNBs of established MBMS bearer is partially modified without the intervention of BM-SC. Figure 9 represents the procedure of partially

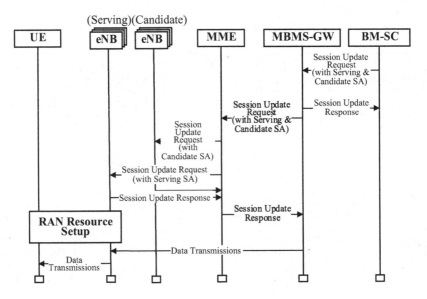

Fig. 8. Initial MBMS bearer establishment for the eNBs belonging to the serving and candidate service area.

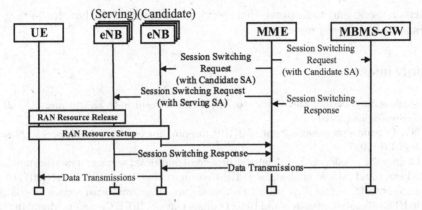

Fig. 9. MME triggering based partial communication path switching on the established MBMS bearer.

switching MBMS bearer by MME Triggering. The eNBs of the serving service area firstly request the bearer switching to the MME. If the MME is informed that the vehicular user moves from the serving service area to the candidate one, the MME requests the MBMS-GW to switch the communication path from the eNBs of the serving service area to those of the candidate service area. And the MME simultaneously gives the eNBs of the candidate service area with an order to activate the stored bearer parameters for its MBMS service. After completing the request, the MME responses to the eNBs of the serving service area in order for the eNBs to deactivate the established MBMS bearer for the vehicle user. By using the previously stored MBMS parameters, the eNBs of the candidate service area allocate radio resources to the activated MBMS bearer and prepare to forward the MBMS contents from MBMS-GW to RAN. The MBMS-GW restart to transmit the MBMS contents buffered during the switching procedure until the vehicular user moves to other MBMS service area.

5   Conclusion

In this paper, we proposed a novel MBMS bearer management scheme in which part of the whole MBMS bearer is switched between eNBs for the serving and candidate service areas. In order to activate the previously stored MBMS bearer, in the proposed management scheme, the MME only exchanges the signaling message with neighboring MBMS-GW and eNBs. As a result, the proposed management scheme can decrease the overall processing time to update the MBMS bearer and can reduce the time where the MBMS contents are queued in MBMS-GW during the update procedure. In addition, the proposed scheme can simplify the MBMS bearer update procedure and can reduce the number of fully modifying the MBMS bearer controlled by BM-SC. Therefore, the proposed scheme is expected to effectively support the MBMS based V2N services specialized for vehicular users, and to improve their service continuity even though the target users have high-speed mobility.

References

1. Qualcomm: Leading the World to 5G: Cellular Vehicle-to-Everything (C-V2X) Technologies (2016)
2. 3GPP: Study on enhancement of 3GPP Support for 5G V2X Services. TR 22.886 V15.1.0 (2017)
3. Gruber, M., Zeller, D.: Multimedia broadcast multicast service: new transmission schemes and related challenges. IEEE Commun. Mag. **49**(12), 176–181 (2011)
4. Lecompte, D., Gabin, F.: Evolved multimedia broadcast/multicast service (eMBMS) in LTE-advanced: overview and Rel-11 enhancements. IEEE Commun. Mag. **50**(11), 68–74 (2012)
5. 3GPP: Study on architecture enhancements for LTE support of V2X services. TR 23.785 V1.1.0 (2016)
6. Seo, H., Lee, K.-D., Yasukawa, S., Peng, Y., Sartori, P.: LTE evolution for vehicle-to-everything services. IEEE Commun. Mag. **54**(6), 22–28 (2016)
7. 3GPP: Multimedia Broadcast/Multicast Service (MBMS); Architecture and Functional Description. TS 23.246 V13.3.0 (2015)
8. 3GPP: Study on enhancements to Multimedia Broadcast/Multicast Service (MBMS) for LTE. TR 23.741 V13.0.0 (2015)
9. 3GPP SA WG2 Meeting #115: MBMS Service Area Mapping. S2–162563 (2016)
10. 3GPP SA WG2 Meeting #115: MBMS Service Area Mapping for V2X. S2–162861 (2016)
11. 3GPP SA WG2 Meeting #115: Solution on the MBMS Service Area Mapping. S2–162862 (2016)
12. 3GPP SA WG2 Meeting #116: Geo Location Handling in V2X Server. S2–163310 (2016)
13. 3GPP SA WG2 Meeting #116: Overlapping MBMS Service Areas. S2–163709 (2016)
14. KR Application: Base Station, Mobile Station, and Method for Providing Service Continuity between MBMS Areas in Mobile Telecommunication System. KR20110071814A (2009)
15. 3GPP: Group Communication System Enablers for LTE (GCSE_LTE). TS 23.468 V13.3.0 (2015)

Service Area Scheduling in a Drone Assisted Network

Yunmin Kim and Tae-Jin Lee[✉]

College of Information and Communnication Engineering,
Sungkyunkwan University, Suwon 16419, South Korea
{kym0413,tjlee}@skku.edu

Abstract. We consider a wireless network using a drone as a sink node collecting data from sensor nodes is considered. Since a drone is expected to cover the large area, the scheduling of the service area is essential. In this paper, we propose an optimal service area scheduling for a drone network. The service area is divided into sections and the effect of such scheduling is analyzed. Simulation results show that our optimization algorithm can find the optimal scheduling policy to maximize the network throughput.

Keywords: Drone network · Service area scheulding · Optimization

1 Introduction

Drones, Unmanned Aerial Vehicles (UAVs), have been used in the military area for tactical missions [1] expanding to the civilian area such as leisure and broadcasting [2]. For example, a medias can obtain great views for the scenes using drones embedded with cameras for broadcasting. Enjoying Remote Controller (RC) with drones is becoming popular because of easy control. Drone racing competitions attached with the Virtual Reality (VR) devices draw attentions.

Recently, drones are actively used in the wireless communication area [3,4]. Drone has some interesting characteristics to expand and assist wireless communications. First of all, drones can move to a target point without geographical constraint. This fast and flexible deployment of drone can reduce the shaded area and reconstruct the service area for disaster site. Also, drones are relatively cheap and safe. Without human pilots, multiple drones can be deployed for constructing networks.

There have been some researches on wireless networks with drones. In [5], drone assisted multi-hop Device-to-Device (D2D) communication is considered. A drone, which acts as a relay node, delivers data from a mobile device to the base station to extend network coverage. The authors investigate the optimal distances between the base station and the device to ensure maximal data rate. Achievable data rate is analyzed considering a realistic channel model. Then, the optimization problems are defined for time and frequency resource allocation. Using the results, drone can be located between a mobile device and the base

© Springer International Publishing AG 2017
O. Gervasi et al. (Eds.): ICCSA 2017, Part V, LNCS 10408, pp. 161–171, 2017.
DOI: 10.1007/978-3-319-62404-4_12

station optimally. In [6], an optimal placement and distribution of cooperative drones in a heterogeneous network is studied. Considering the delay and the user request, a positioning issue of drones is formulated by a minimax facility problem. Then, using the entropy networks, the optimal placement algorithm is provided. Performance evaluation shows that the proposed approach is capable of optimizing the delay. In [7], a network of Drone Small Cells (DSC) with multiple drones is considered. Drones provide connectivity to devices in the ground area while it is connected with the satellite. Drones induce devices using beaconing and they can communicate after a successful encounter with the device. An optimal beaconing period in terms of energy efficiency and encounter rate for two competing drones is presented. Authors propose a game theory model for beaconing period choice. Then, a learning framework for drones to discover the optimal beaconing period is provided.

The previous works focus on the optimal location, placement, and beaconing period of drones. However, the relationship between a drone and its service area needs to be covered by a drone has been not studied. In this paper, a novel service area scheduling method for drones for efficient drone service is presented. We target for a drone collecting sensor data from the nodes deployed in a large area. Since a drone has a limited transmission range, the area is divided into sections. To efficiently collect data, a drone is required to construct an optimal section division strategy for enhancement of computational capability. We first develop a communication framework for a drone to support multiple sections. Then, the effect of section scheduling is analyzed in terms of channel errors and transmission opportunity. To maximize the network throughput, optimization of section scheduling is provided. Simulation results show that an optimal number of sections can be derived.

2   Proposed MAC Protocol and Service Area Scheduling

We introduce an environment of a drone assisted network. Then, we propose a data collecting framework. The effect of service area scheduling is explored in terms of channel error rate and transmission opportunity. Optimization of service area scheduling is presented to maximize the throughput.

2.1   Drone Assisted Network Environment

A drone capable of wireless communications provide service to the sensor nodes in a target area, i.e., *service area*. The service area is defined as a square area which has the area of $(L \times L) \, \mathrm{m}^2$. In the service area, N sensor nodes are deployed and try to transmit data to the drone.

To efficiently collect data from the service area, drone divides the service area into $k \times k$ grids. Then, each grid becomes a *section*. Assuming that the nodes are uniformly distributed in the service area, the number of nodes reside in each section is

$$N_s = \frac{N}{k^2}. \tag{1}$$

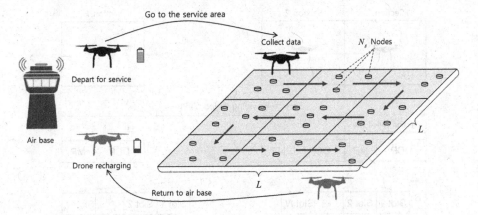

Fig. 1. Example of a drone collecting data in service area.

In a section, the drone collects data from nodes flying at the central point of the section. After that, the drone moves to the next section. To visit every sections, the flight pattern of the drone follows the creeping line. It can fly around the service area during the predefined time T_f, which is *duration of flight*. So, the duration of flight is divided equally to each section for providing full service. After collection of data in the last section, the drone returns to the air base for recharging. Then, a newly charged drone will replace the service area. Figure 1 shows the example of the drone assisted network to provide service to the service area consisting of 3×3 sections.

2.2   Proposed Data Collecting Framework of Drone

We propose a communication framework for a drone to collect data in the service area. For a single drone, the available service time is the duration of flight T_f. The drone utilizes T_f as a whole Service Providing Period (SPP). Since the service area is divided into $k \times k$ grids, SPP consists of k^2 Section Periods (SPs). An SP is further divided into the Data Collection Period (DCP) and the Moving Period (MP) (see Fig. 2).

Data Transmission in DCP. In the DCP, a drone receives information from the transmission of nodes. At the beginning of the DCP, the drone sends a beacon message that includes the number of frames and the frame size. A frame is consists of multiple time slots and the frame size indicates the number of time slots in a frame. An appropriate frame size can be determined by the number of nodes in a section.

Nodes are aware of the existence of the drone by receiving the beacon message and prepare for the transmission. The data transmission procedure is performed using the Frame Slotted ALOHA (FSA). Nodes randomly select their time slots within a frame and send data. The drone receives signals of nodes in each time slot. If the Signal-to-Interference-plus-Noise Ratio (SINR) of the received signal

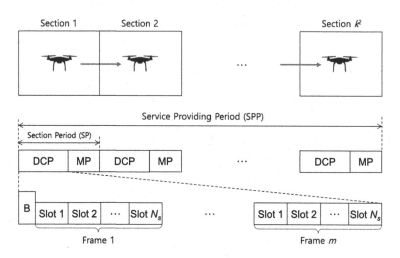

Fig. 2. The proposed data collection framework.

is greater than a certain threshold, drone can successfully decode the signal. Otherwise, it cannot properly receive the message due to low SINR. This procedure repeats until the predefined number of framed indicated in the beacon message.

After DCP, the drone moves from the current section to the next section during the MP. Then, it performs another data collecting process in the next section.

Scheduling of Communications. The drone can schedule SPP according to the number of sections as follows. Considering the number of sections, the duration of SP is

$$T_{SP,k} = \frac{T_f}{k^2}. \tag{2}$$

Here, we set k^2 number of MPs instead of $(k^2 - 1)$ MPs, since after the last DCP, the drone returns to the air base and a new drone enters the Sect. 1. So, we have to take k^2-th traveling time into consideration. To determine the length of DCP, drone first calculates the entire time required for moving. The drone moves from the central point of current section to that of the next section. Then, the traveling distance from the center of the current section to the border of the next section is $L/2k$. The entire time for moving between sections can be calculated as

$$T_{mov,k} = \frac{L/2k}{v_d} \cdot k^2 = \frac{Lk}{2v_d}, \tag{3}$$

where v_d is the speed of a drone.

During the time of SPP, the drone can utilize the DCP except the travel time. Then, duration of DCP and MP can be computed as

$$T_{DCP,k} = \frac{T_f - T_{mov,k}}{k^2}. \tag{4}$$

$$T_{MP,k} = \frac{T_{mov,k}}{k^2}.$$ (5)

Note that the duration of DCP decreases as the number of sections increases. In the determined DCP interval, the drone allocates frames for collecting data from nodes by contention. Since the frame size is optimal when it is N_s [8], the number of frames in each DCP is then

$$m_k = \left\lfloor \frac{T_{DCP,k}}{N_s T_{slot}} \right\rfloor,$$ (6)

where T_{slot} is the duration of a time slot. The drone includes the frame size (N_s) and the number of frames (m_k). When the nodes receive the beacon, they transmit data by contention for m_k frames.

2.3   Effect of the Service Area Scheduling

The proposed framework targets the service area scheduling with $k \times k$ sections. Naturally, the problem is associated with how to divide the service area. We consider two main factors related to the performance of a network.

Channel Error Rate. The service area is scheduled to serve the smaller sections considering the receiver sensitivity of a drone. In each slot in a frame, a drone may receive the signals from nodes. For successful reception, the SINR of the received signal at a drone should be greater than a certain threshold. So, the probability of successful reception of a drone for $k \times k$ sections is

$$p_{succ,k} = \Pr[SINR > \zeta] = \Pr\left[\frac{P_{rx}}{P_I + P_N} > \zeta\right],$$ (7)

where P_{rx}, P_I, P_N, and ζ are the received signal power, the interference power, noise power, and the SINR threshold of a drone. The interference signal is caused from the other transmitting nodes. Channel error rate can be defined as $1 - p_{succ}$. The transmitted signal from the nodes suffer from the path loss and fading. Then, the received signal power at the drone is further expressed as

$$P_{rx} = P_{tx} h r^{-\alpha},$$ (8)

where P_{tx}, h, r and α are the transmission power of a node, Rayleigh fading, distance between a drone and a node, and the pathloss exponent. We use a Rayleigh fading model with the mean of 1.

The size of a section becomes smaller as the number of sections increases. Nodes are relatively near the drone when the size of a section area is scheduled to be small. Therefore, the channel error rate is expected to be low as the number of sections increases.

Data Transmission Opportunity. As in Eq. (4), the duration of DCP becomes shorter as the number of sections increases. As the number of sections increases, the drone should move around sections move frequently. Then, the time required for traveling the service area becomes more. Consequently the duration of DCP which can be utilized for communications of the drone and nodes will decrease. This indicates that within the SPP, the portion of time for data transmission becomes smaller. Therefore, the transmission opportunity decreases as the number of sections increases.

The network throughput can be defined as the number of successful receptions during the SPP.

$$S_k = \frac{k^2 \cdot m_k \cdot (N_s \cdot p_{succ,k})D}{T_f},\tag{9}$$

where D is the payload size in bits. The network throughput is affected by both channel error rate and the transmission opportunity. The throughput will degrade when the channel error rate $(1 - p_{succ,k})$ is high. On the other hand, the throughput will improve if the transmission opportunity m_k is high. As as result, the optimal service area scheduling is required. Figure 3 summarizes the relationship between the number of sections and the channel error rate and the transmission opportunity.

Section scheduling: large section area

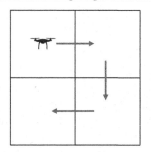

- Nodes are relatively far from the drone
- Channel error occurs frequently

- Travel time is relatively short
- Transmission opportunity is large

Section scheduling: small section area

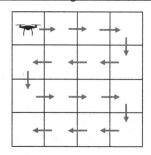

Nodes are relatively near the drone

Channel error occurs sporadically

- Travel time is relatively long
- Transmission opportunity is small

Fig. 3. Effect of section area scheduling: the channel error rate and the transmission opportunity.

2.4   Optimal Section Area Scheduling by Searching

To find the optimal number of sections, a drone needs to estimate the throughput according to the varying k. First of all, a drone needs to narrow down the search space using the constraint on the duration of flight. Since the length DCP decreases as k increases, there exists the maximum number of sections. A drone should reserve the minimum length of DCP to ensure the data transmission. The maximum number of sections can be calculated as

$$k_{max} < \left\lfloor \frac{2T_f \cdot v_d}{L} \right\rfloor. \tag{10}$$

Then, the searching space becomes $k \in [1, k_{max}]$ where k is integer. However the area searching time for each section is expected to $k_{max}^2 T_f$ which is too long. So, we propose a area searching algorithm which differentiates the section parameter during an SPP.

Specifically, drone starts from $k = 1$ and measures the $p_{succ,1}$. Then, it calculates the network throughputs S_k as in Eq. (9). Since m_k frames exist in a single DCP, an average $p_{succ,k}$ can be obtained. By comparing the S_k with the candidate optimal value S_k^*, which initialized as zero, drone can find the optimal k. Figure 4 shows an example of area searching for appropriate k during an SPP. The drone changes k from 1 to 4 and measures the probability of successful reception for each k.

After obtaining the optimal number k^* of sections, the drone provides service to nodes with the $k^* \times k^*$ sections. The entire algorithm to optimize the number sections is indicated in Algorithm 1.

Algorithm 1. Optimization of the number of sections

1: Compute k_{max} by Eq. (10)
2: $S^* = 0$
3:
4: **for** $k = 1$ to k_{max} **do**
5:
6:    Compute $T_{DCP,k}$ by Eqs. (3) and (4)
7:    Compute m_k by Eq. (6)
8:    Measure $p_{succ,k}$
9:    Compute network throughput S_k by Eq. (9)
10:
11:    **if** $S_k > S^*$ **then**
12:       $k^* = k$
13:       $S^* = S_k$
14:    **else**
15:       Break
16:    **end if**
17:
18: **end for**

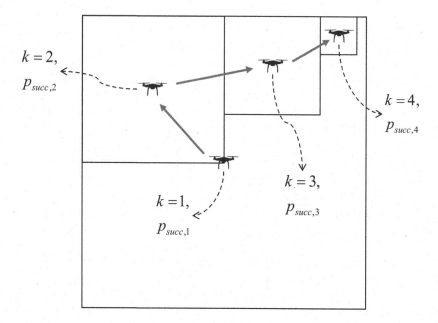

Fig. 4. Searching of optimal section area scheduling.

3   Performance Evaluation

We perform simulations to verify the effect of the service area scheduling in the drone network. The channel error rate and the network throughput is evaluated for varying number of sections. The channel error rate is the ratio between the number of unsuccessful receptions and the entire transmission opportunities. The network throughput can be measured as the number of transmitted bits during the simulation time. Transmitted bits be measured from the number of successful receptions by a drone. Using the number of successful and unsuccessful receptions, the channel error rate and the network throughput can be obtained. The parameters used in the simulations are shown in Table 1.

Figure 5 shows the measured channel error rate $(1 - p_{succ,k})$ for varying number of sections. The channel error rate decreases as the number of sections increases. This phenomenon matches with the expectation in the previous section. As the size of a section becomes smaller, the distance between a drone and the nodes will be smaller. Then, the received signal at the drone is more likely to satisfy the threshold condition. For a smaller service area $(10 \times 10\,\text{km}^2)$, the channel error rate tends to be lower than that of the larger service area $(15 \times 15\,\text{km}^2)$. This also follows from the relative distance between the drone and the nodes. It is shown that the speed of the drone has no effect on the channel error rate. The channel error rate depends on the signal power rather than the transmission opportunity which is related with the duration of DCP.

Table 1. Simulation parameters

Parameter	Value
Size of service area (L^2)	10×10 km^2, 15×15 km^2
Number of sections (k^2)	$(1 \times 1) \sim (15 \times 15)$
Speed of a drone (v_d)	100, 200 km/h
Duration of flight (T_f)	7200 sec
Number of nodes (N)	100,000
Tx power of a node (P_{tx})	23 dBm
Noise power (P_N)	6 dBm
Threshold (ς)	0 dB
Data size (D)	800 bits

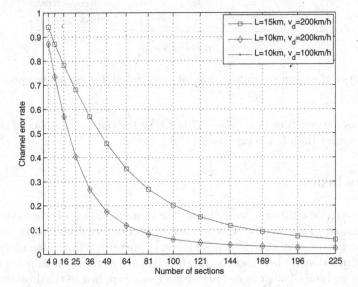

Fig. 5. Channel error rate for varying number of sections.

Figure 6 shows the network throughput for varying number of sections. We consider three different cases, case 1: $L = 15$ km, $v_d = 200$ km/h, case 2: $L = 10$ km, $v_d = 200$ km/h, and case 3: $L = 10$ km, $v_d = 100$ km/h. In the first case, the optimal number of sections is verified as a 100. Also, the network throughput is maximized at the number of sections of 100 in the second case. However, the network throughput is shown to be larger in the second case than that in the first case. Since the size of the service area is smaller in the second case, the throughput shows better. In the third case, the optimal number of sections is 49. The duration of DCP is the shortest in the third case because of the relatively low speed of a drone. So, small area scheduling is limited because

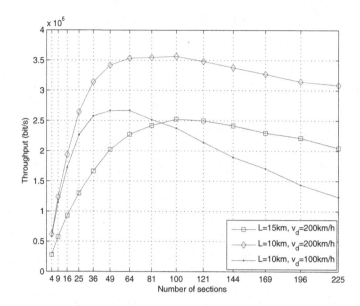

Fig. 6. Effect of section scheduling: channel error rate and transmission opportunity.

of the longer travel time of a drone. That's why the optimal number of sections is shown earlier than the other cases.

4   Conclusion

In this paper, the optimization of the service area scheduling of a drone network is investigated. The effect of the number of sections is discussed in terms of the channel error rate and the transmission opportunity. In the simulation, we verify the mentioned phenomenon and the existence of the optimal point for the number of sections. The proposed algorithm can be applied to the drone network to maximize the network throughput.

Acknowledgments. This work was supported by the National Research Foundation of Korea (NRF) grant funded by the Korean government(MSIP) (2015R1A2A2 A01004067) and Basic Science Research Program through NRF of Korea, funded by MOE(NRF-2010-0020210).

References

1. Drones: What are they and how do they work? http://www.bbc.com/news/world-south-asia-10713898
2. A Field Guide to Civilian Drones. https://www.nytimes.com/interactive/2015/technology/guide-to-civilian-drones.html?_r=0

3. Mozaffari, M., Saad, W., Bennis, M., Debbah, M.: Drone small cells in the clouds: design, deployment and performance analysis. In: IEEE GLOBECOM (2015). doi:10.1109/GLOCOM.2015.7417609

4. Rahman, A.: Enabling drone communications with WiMAX technology. In: International Conference of Information, Intelligence, Systems and Applications (IISA) (2014). doi:10.1109/IISA.2014.6878796

5. Li, X., Guo, D., Yin, H., Wei, G.: Drone-assisted public safety wireless broadband network. In: IEEE Wireless Communications and Networking Conference (WCNC), pp. 323–328 (2015). doi:10.1109/WCNCW.2015.7122575

6. Sharma, V., Sabatini, R., Ramasamy, S.: UAVs assisted delay optimization in heterogeneous wireless networks. IEEE Commun. Lett. 20(12), 2526–2529 (2016). doi:10.1109/LCOMM.2016.2609900

7. Koulali, S., Taleb, T., Azizi, M.: A green strategic activity scheduling for UAV networks: a sub-modular game perspective. IEEE Commun. Mag. 54(5), 58–64 (2016). doi:10.1109/MCOM.2016.7470936

8. Eom, J., Lee, T.-J.: Accurate tag estimation for dynamic framed-slotted ALOHA in RFID systems. IEEE Commun. Lett. 14(1), 60–62 (2010). doi:10.1109/LCOMM.2010.01.091378

Throughput Analysis of a SWIPT Enabled Two-Way Decode-and-Forward Cognitive Relay Network

Syed Tariq Shah and Min Young Chung[✉]

College of Information and Communication Engineering, Sungkyunkwan University,
Natural Sciences Campus, 2066, Seobu-ro, Jangan-gu, Suwon-si, South Korea
{syed.tariq,mychung}@skku.edu

Abstract. Wireless energy harvesting has emerged as an efficient technique to prolong the network life time of energy constrained network. In this paper, we propose a simultaneous wireless information and power transfer (SWIPT) based decode-and-forward (DF) cognitive two-way relay network. In our proposed network the primary nodes communicate with each other via an energy constrained intermediate DF relay. The relay node first harvests the energy from the source signals and then uses this harvested power to decode-and-forward these received primary signals to their respective destinations. In addition to primary signals relay also utilizes some portion of the harvested power to transmit its own information signal to a secondary node. Our simulation result shows that the proper setting of energy harvesting and power allocation parameters can significantly improve the overall network throughput. We also show the effect of various system parameters on overall system performance.

Keywords: Simultaneous wireless information and power transfer (SWIPT) · Decode-and-forward relay · Cognitive relay networks · Wireless energy harvesting · Two-way relay network

1 Introduction

The idea of wireless radio frequency (RF) energy harvesting has gained significant attention in recent years [1]. The main goal of the RF energy harvesting is to prolong the lifetime of low power nodes (LPNs) based energy constrained wireless networks through wireless energy transfer instead of using inconvenient conventional techniques such as physically recharging or replacing batteries. Several other legacy methods for ambient energy harvesting such as thermoelectric effects, wind, solar, and vibration, can also be used to recharge these LPNs. However, since the sources of these legacy ambient energy suppliers are unreliable and highly fluctuating, they cannot be fully adopted as a power source in wireless networks. Another major advantage of RF energy harvesting is that RF signal can simultaneously carry both information and power (SWIPT) [2–4]. Therefore, LPNs in energy-constrained networks can simultaneously harvest energy

© Springer International Publishing AG 2017
O. Gervasi et al. (Eds.): ICCSA 2017, Part V, LNCS 10408, pp. 172–182, 2017.
DOI: 10.1007/978-3-319-62404-4_13

and process information [5]. This idea of SWIPT was first proposed by Varshney in [3], where the author have assumed an impractical ideal receiver architecture.

It is a well-established fact that dividing a single imperfect communication channel (source to destination) into two (or more) useful communication paths (i.e. source to relay and relay to destination) can significantly improve the overall capacity, coverage, and quality of service (QoS) of the network [6]. Recent state-of-the-art studies have shown the feasibility of wireless energy cooperation in energy-constrained networks [7,8]. The performance of a relay network with wireless-powered nodes is studied in [7]. An amplify-and-forward relay based one-way cooperative relay network is studied in [8]. A greedy switching policy where the relay node transmits when its residual energy ensures decoding at the destination is investigated.

For RF energy harvesting in SWIPT based point-to-point cooperative network, time switching (TS) and power splitting (PS) receiver architectures have been proposed in [9,10]. Based on [9,10], Nasir et al. in [11] have proposed two relaying protocols, namely, time switching based relaying (TSR) and power splitting-based relaying (PSR). According to TSR protocol, the energy-constrained relay node switches in time between energy harvesting mode and information processing mode. Likewise, in PSR protocol the relay node splits the power of the received signal into two parts, one is used for energy harvesting and the remaining is used for information processing. In [11], the authors have considered an AF based one-way relay network and they concluded that at high SNR and low transmission rate the PSR protocol outperforms the TSR protocol.

The performance of a one-way DF based energy harvesting relay network is studied in [12]. It has been shown that in a DF relay based network, the PSR protocol outperforms the TSR protocol. Throughput analysis of a two-way AF relay network with SWIPT capabilities is studied in [5,13]. A multiplicative relay based two-way SWIPT network is studied in [14]. The authors shows that the multiplicative relay can outperform AF relay in SWIPT based cooperative networks. Wang et al. in [15] have studied the performance of an SWIPT based one-way AF cognitive relay network. In their proposed network the SWIPT operation is performed during both primary and secondary transmissions. A rate-energy trade-off between ergodic capacity and energy harvesting is analyzed and it is concluded that such a network can achieve satisfactory performance for both secondary and primary transmissions. An AF based two-way energy-constrained cognitive relay network is studied in [16]. Unlike [15], the SWIPT operation in [16] is only performed during primary transmission. The authors concluded that by setting proper parameters, maximum energy efficiency can be achieved.

In this paper, we have studied the performance of DF relay based two-way cognitive relay network where the energy harvesting procedure is only performed at the relay node. In our proposed scheme, the time block is divided into three slots. During first two slots the relay node decodes and harvests the energy from the primary signals and during the third phase, the relay forwards the decoded primary signals along with a secondary signal. The relay node harvests energy based on PSR protocol [11]. Detailed expressions for SNR/SINR, throughput, and sum-rates are derived. With the help of simulation results, it has been shown that with proper setting of parameter, a reasonable throughput from both primary and secondary transmissions can be achieved.

The organization of rest of the paper is as follows. Section 2 provides the details about our considered system model and necessary assumptions. Section 3 explains the proposed energy harvesting and information processing procedures for PSR protocol in two-way DF cognitive relay network. The simulation results and conclusion of the paper are provided in Sect. 4 and Sect. 5, respectively.

2   System Model

This paper considers a network which consists of 4 nodes, A, B, R, and S. The first two nodes (A and B) are primary transceiver nodes, and the other two nodes, R and S are relay node and secondary node, respectively. It is assumed that there is no direct communication link between the primary nodes A and B and the signal-to-noise-ratio (SNR) of this link is less than the minimum required threshold SNR for effective communication. Consequently, a secondary node R acts as a relay to assist the primary transmission between primary nodes A and B. Since the relay node R is a wireless-powered node (energy constrained), it first harvests the energy from the received primary signals using PS technique and then uses this harvested energy to decode and forward the received primary signals to their respective destinations.

In addition to primary signals, relay node R has some of its own information which it wants to send to a secondary node S. Thus, the relay node R broadcasts both the received primary information and its own secondary information. Note that the secondary node S also receives the primary information signals transmitted by both primary nodes A and B. This received primary information signals are later used by node S to cancel out the interference from the combined signal broadcasted by relay node R. Furthermore, the half-duplex constraint is taken into account [17] for all nodes and it is assumed that nodes are equipped with a single antenna.

The basic architecture of our proposed network is shown in Fig. 1. The whole communication procedure can be divided into three main steps.

- Step 1: In step 1 primary node A transmits its information signal to relay node R, where the energy harvesting and information decoding operation are performed.
- Step 2: Similar to step 1, the primary node B transmits its information signal to relay node R and both energy harvesting and information decoding procedures are performed.
- Step 3: After successful operations in step 1 and step 2, the relay node adds its secondary information signal to the decoded primary signals and broadcasts the resultant signal.

The channel coefficients and distances between primary nodes and secondary nodes are shown in Fig. 1. More specifically, g_1, h_1, g_2, h_2, and h_3 are the channel

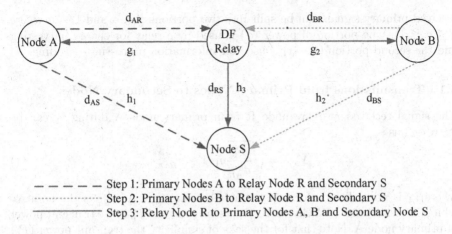

Step 1: Primary Nodes A to Relay Node R and Secondary S
Step 2: Primary Nodes B to Relay Node R and Secondary S
Step 3: Relay Node R to Primary Nodes A, B and Secondary Node S

Fig. 1. System model of a two-way SWIPT based cognitive DF relay network.

coefficients of A-to-R, A-to-S, B-to-R, B-to-S, and R-to-S links, respectively. Likewise, the distances between node A-to-R, A-to-S, B-to-R, B-to-S, and R-to-S are depicted as d_{AR}, d_{AS}, d_{BR}, d_{BS}, and d_{RS}, respectively.

The channel coefficients between nodes are assumed to be quasi-static block-fading channels, which means that the channel constant over the transmission block time T. The channels are independent and identically distributed (iid) in each time block following a Rayleigh distribution [18]. Furthermore, path loss model is considered to be distance-dependent with rate d_{ij}^{-k}, where d_{ij} is the distance between node i and j and k is the path loss exponent, respectively.

3   SWIPT in Two-Way DF Cognitive Relay Network

As shown in Fig. 2, for information exchange in our proposed two-way DF relay scheme, the transmission block time T is divided into three time slots t_1, t_2, and t_3. For energy harvesting at relay node R, power splitting based relaying protocol (i.e. PSR) is assumed [10,11]. According to PSR protocol, the power of

EH (αP_p) at Relay R	EH (αP_p) at Relay R	Relay R to Nodes A, B and S
Node A to Relay R $((1-\alpha)P_p)$	Node B to Relay R $((1-\alpha)P_p)$	
Time slot t_1	Time slot t_2	Time slot t_3
←——— T/3 ———→	←——— T/3 ———→	←——— T/3 ———→
←—————————————— T —————————————→		

Fig. 2. Transmission time-block structure of proposed scheme for PSR protocol.

received primary signals can be split into two portions (i.e. α and $1 - \alpha$, where $0 \leq \alpha \leq 1$). One portion of power (α) is used by a relay for energy harvesting and the second portion ($1 - \alpha$) is used for information processing/decoding.

3.1   Transmissions from Primary Nodes to Secondary Nodes

The signal received at relay node R from primary node A during t_1 can be expressed as

$$Y_{R_{t_1}} = \sqrt{\frac{P_p}{d_{AR}^k}} g_1 i_A + n_{Ra}^{t_1}, \tag{1}$$

where i_A is normalized information symbols from node A, $n_{Ra}^{t_1}$ is the additive white Gaussian noise (AWGN) at receiving antenna and P_p is the transmit power of primary node A. Note that for the sake of simplicity the transmit power (P_p) of both primary nodes A and B is assumed to be equal and constant. After energy harvesting and baseband conversion the received signal can be written as

$$\sqrt{(1 - \alpha)} Y_{R_{t_1}} = \sqrt{\frac{(1 - \alpha) P_p}{d_{AR}^k}} g_1 i_A + \sqrt{(1 - \alpha)} n_{Ra}^{t_1} + n_{Rc}^{t_1}, \tag{2}$$

where $n_{Rc}^{t_1}$ is the AWGN due to RF-to-baseband conversion. The energy harvested from received primary signal at node R during t_1 can be expressed as:

$$EH_R^{t_1} = \frac{\eta \alpha P_p \mid g_1 \mid^2}{d_{AR}^k} (T/3). \tag{3}$$

where $0 < \eta < 1$ is the energy conversion efficiency and $T/3$ is the time duration of harvesting. Similar procedure applies at node R when primary node B transmits during t_2. After energy harvesting and down-conversion the received primary signal at relay node R from node B during t_2 can be expressed as

$$\sqrt{(1 - \alpha)} Y_{R_{t_2}} = \sqrt{\frac{(1 - \alpha) P_p}{d_{BR}^k}} g_2 i_B + \sqrt{(1 - \alpha)} n_{Ra}^{t_2} + n_{Rc}^{t_2}, \tag{4}$$

where $n_{Ra}^{t_2}$ and $n_{Rc}^{t_2}$ are the AWGN at receiving antenna and AWGN due to RF-to-baseband conversion at relay node R. The total harvested energy after t_1 and t_2 can be expressed as:

$$EH_R = \left(\frac{\mid g_1 \mid^2}{d_{AR}^k} + \frac{\mid g_2 \mid^2}{d_{BR}^k} \right) \eta \alpha P_p (T/3). \tag{5}$$

Based on (2) and (4), the signal-to-noise-ration (SNR) at relay node R durinf t_1 and t_2 can be respectively calculated as

$$SINR_R^{t_1} = \frac{(1 - \alpha) P_p \mid g_1 \mid^2}{d_{AR}^k \sigma_{R_{t_1}}^2}, \tag{6}$$

and

$$SINR_R^{t_2} = \frac{(1-\alpha)P_p \mid g_2 \mid^2}{d_{BR}^k \sigma_{R_{t_2}}^2}, \tag{7}$$

where $\sigma_{R_{t_l}}^2$ for $l = 1, 2$ is the combined noise variance of AWGNs $\sqrt{(1-\alpha)}n_{Ra}^{t_1}$ and $n_{Rc}^{t_1}$.

In case of secondary node S, after baseband conversion the received primary signal from node A and node B during time slot t_1 and t_2 can respectively be written as

$$Y_{S_{t_1}} = \sqrt{\frac{P_p}{d_{AS}^k}}h_1 i_A + n_{Sa}^{t_1} + n_{Sc}^{t_1}, \quad and \quad Y_{S_{t_2}} = \sqrt{\frac{P_p}{d_{BS}^k}}h_2 i_B + n_{Sa}^{t_2} + n_{Sc}^{t_2}, \tag{8}$$

where $n_{Sa}^{t_l}$ and $n_{Sc}^{t_l}$ for $l = 1, 2$ are the receiving antenna noise and RF-to-baseband conversion noise at node S. Note that the secondary node S does not harvest any energy and utilizes all of the received signal power for information decoding.

3.2 Transmissions from Relay to Primary and Secondary Nodes

In time slot t_3 the relay node R forwards the received primary signals $\sqrt{(1-\alpha)}Y_{R_{t_i}}$ for $i = 1, 2$ along his own secondary information i_S. The total harvested power at relay (i.e. $P_R = \frac{EH_R}{T/3}$) is divided in two parts ρP_R and $(1-\rho)P_R$. The first part ρP_R is used to transmit the decoded primary information signals to their respective destinations (A and B) and the second part is used to transmit the secondary information to node S. The signal broadcasted by the relay node R can be expressed as:

$$x_{R_{t_3}} = \sqrt{\rho P_r}i_R + \sqrt{(1-\rho)P_r}i_S. \tag{9}$$

After RF-to-baseband conversion, the received signal at primary destination node A from relay node R during t_3 can be written as

$$Y_{A_{t_3}} = \sqrt{\frac{\rho P_r}{d_{AR}^k}}g_1 i_R + \sqrt{\frac{(1-\rho)P_r}{d_{AR}^k}}g_1 i_S + N_A^{t_3}, \tag{10}$$

where $i_R = i_A \oplus i_B$ (XOR operation) and $N_l^{t_3}$ for $l = A, B, R, S$ is the combined AWGN due to receiving antenna and RF-to-baseband conversion. Since the primary node A already knows its self-interfering term i_A, it can simply cancel this self-interference term (i.e. $i_B = i_A \oplus i_R$) and the resulting received signal-to-noise-plus-interference ratio (SINR) at node A can be expressed as

$$SINR_A^{t_3} = \frac{\rho P_r \mid g_1 \mid^2}{(1-\rho)P_r \mid g_1 \mid^2 + d_{AR}^k \sigma_{A_{t_3}}^2}, \tag{11}$$

where $\sigma_{lt_3}^2$ for $l = A, B, S$ is the variance of AWGNs $N_l^{t_3}$. Furthermore, the SINR at primary node B can be calculated as

$$SINR_B^{t_3} = \frac{\rho P_r \mid g_2 \mid^2}{(1 - \rho)P_r \mid g_2 \mid^2 + d_{BR}^k \sigma_{Bt_3}^2}. \tag{12}$$

On the other hand, after RF-to-baseband conversion the received signal at secondary node S from relay node R during t_3 can be written as

$$Y_{S_{t_3}} = \sqrt{\frac{(1 - \rho)P_r}{d_{RS}^k}} h_3 i_S + \sqrt{\frac{\rho P_r}{d_{RS}^k}} h_3 i_R + N_S^{t_3}. \tag{13}$$

In above Eq. (13) the second term (i.e. $\sqrt{\frac{\rho P_r}{d_{RS}^k}} h_3 i_R$) is an interference term. Since i_R is the XOR of two primary information symbols i_A and i_B, and both these terms are already known to secondary node S (see (5)), therefore, they can easily be canceled out and the SNR from resultant signal can be written as

$$SNR_S^{t_3} = \frac{(1 - \rho)P_r \mid h_3 \mid^2}{d_{RS}^k \sigma_{St_3}^2}. \tag{14}$$

In worst case scenario, if secondary node S fails to receive one or both of the primary transmissions from nodes A and B during t_1 and t_2, the resulting SINR can be written as

$$SINR_S^{t_3} = \frac{(1 - \rho)P_r \mid h_3 \mid^2}{\rho P_r \mid h_3 \mid^2 + d_{RS}^k \sigma_{St_3}^2}. \tag{15}$$

3.3   Throughput Calculation

Based on (6), (7), (11), (12), and (14), the throughput at primary nodes A, B and secondary node S can be calculated as

$$\mathcal{T}_A = \frac{T/3 \log_2 \left(1 + \min\{SINR_R^{t_1}, SINR_A^{t_3}\}\right)}{T}, \tag{16}$$

$$\mathcal{T}_B = \frac{T/3 \log_2 \left(1 + \min\{SINR_R^{t_2}, SINR_B^{t_3}\}\right)}{T}, \tag{17}$$

and

$$\begin{aligned}
\mathcal{T}_S &= \frac{T/3 \log_2 \left(1 + SNR_S^{t_3}\right)}{T} \\
&= \frac{1}{3} \log_2 \left(1 + \frac{(1 - \rho)P_r \mid h_3 \mid^2}{d_{RS}^k \sigma_{St_3}^2}\right),
\end{aligned} \tag{18}$$

or, in the worst case scenario,

$$\begin{aligned}
\mathcal{T}_S &= \frac{T/3 \log_2 \left(1 + SINR_S^{t_3}\right)}{T} \\
&= \frac{1}{3} \log_2 \left(1 + \frac{(1 - \rho)P_r \mid h_3 \mid^2}{\rho P_r \mid h_3 \mid^2 + d_{RS}^k \sigma_{St_3}^2}\right),
\end{aligned} \tag{19}$$

where, $\frac{T}{3}$ is the effective information transmission time from source to destination nodes in a time block of T seconds. It can be observed from the above equations that in our derivation process, we have used natural log, therefore, the sum-rates and throughputs in our paper are in *nat per channel use (npcu)*. The term sum-rate means the combined throughput of primary nodes or the combined throughput of overall network and it can be expressed as

$$Sum - rate \ of \ Primary \ Transmissions = T_A + T_B, \tag{20}$$

$$Sum - rate \ of \ Overall \ Network = T_S + T_A + T_B. \tag{21}$$

4   Performance Evaluation

In this section, the throughput analysis and insights into different design choices of our proposed SWIPT enabled two-way DF cognitive relay network are provided. Based on our derived expressions in Sect. 3, we evaluate the sum-rate performance of our proposed two-way DF cognitive relay network. Unless otherwise stated the values of different parameters in our considered system model are as follows: we assume that the transmit power P_p of primary nodes (A and B) is set to unit Joules/sec, the distances between nodes are assumed to be equal (i.e. $d_{AR} = d_{AS} = d_{BR} = d_{BS} = d_{RS}$) and normalized to unit value. Furthermore, the value of path loss exponent k is set to 2.7 and for the sake of simplicity, it is assumed that the noise factors and their variances at all nodes are equal to each other (i.e. $\sigma_a^2 = \sigma_c^2 = 0.01(-20dB)$).

The sum-rate of only primary transmissions with varying values of power splitting factor (α) is depicted in Fig. 3. Note that in cognitive networks, the

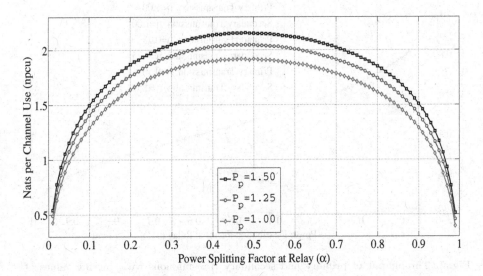

Fig. 3. Sum-rate of primary transmissions with varying values of power splitting factor (α) when, $\rho = 1$, $\sigma_a^2 = \sigma_c^2 = 0.01$ and $\eta = 1$.

primary transmissions usually have higher priority. Therefore in order to find the optimal value of α, the value of relay power distribution factor ρ is set to 1, which means that all the harvested energy at relay is used for primary transmission and no secondary transmission exists. It can be observed that the maximum sum-rate is achieved when the value of $\alpha = 0.48$, which is near to optimal value. Furthermore, it can be observed that the sum-rate increases as the value of α increases and then after a certain point the sum-rate starts decreasing. It is due to that fact that for smaller values of α, relay node harvests small amount of energy which yields to lower relay transmission power P_r and throughput at destination. On the other hand for larger values of α, more energy is harvested and small portion of energy is used for information decoding which eventually results in lower SNR and throughput/sum-rate at relay/destination (see 11, 12, 16, and 17). It can also be observed form Fig. 3 that the overall sum-rate of primary transmission increases as the transmit power of primary nodes (P_p) increases. It is due to the simple fact that the higher values of P_p results in higher harvested energy and improved SNR at receiving node.

Figure 4 depicts the throughput of primary and secondary transmissions with varying values of relay power distribution factor (ρ) when the value power splitting factor α is set to optimal (i.e. $\alpha = 0.48$). It can be observed that the throughput of secondary transmission decreases as the value of ρ increases where on the other hand, the throughput of primary transmission increases as the value of ρ increases. It is because, for higher values of ρ, the relay allocates the higher proportion of harvested power to primary transmission and a small portion of harvested energy is allocated to secondary transmission (see 11, 12, 14, and 21).

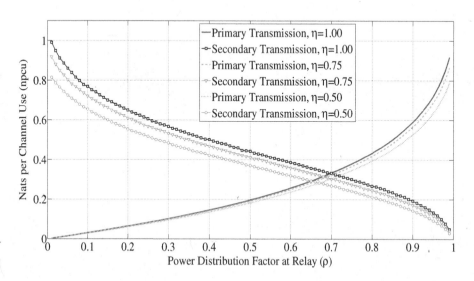

Fig. 4. Throughput of primary and secondary transmissions with varying values of relay power distribution factor (ρ) when, $\alpha = 0.48$, $\sigma_a^2 = \sigma_c^2 = 0.01$, and $P_p = 1$.

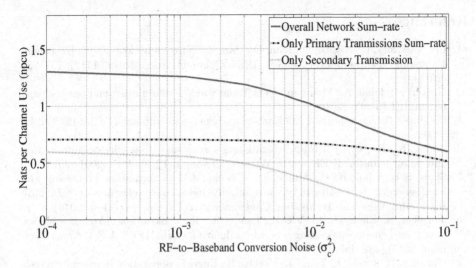

Fig. 5. Sum-rates with varying values of RF-to-baseband conversion noise (σ_c^2) when, $\alpha = 0.48$, $\rho = 0.7$, $\sigma_a^2 = 0.01$, $\eta = 1$, and $P_p = 1$.

It can also be observed from Fig. 4 that for $\eta = 1$ the crossover between primary and secondary transmissions occur when the value of $\rho = 0.7$. It means that at this point the throughput of both primary and secondary transmissions becomes equal. This value of ρ at crossover point (i.e. $\rho = 0.7$) is used in the rest of the paper. Figure 4 also shows the throughput of both primary and secondary transmissions increases as the value of energy conversion efficiency increases.

The impact of AWGN due to RF-to-baseband conversion on overall network sum-rate, primary transmission sum-rate and secondary transmission throughput is provided in Fig. 5. It is obvious from Fig. 5 that the overall network performance decreases as the amount of noise increases.

5   Conclusion

In this paper, a performance analysis of a DF based cognitive relay network with SWIPT capabilities is provided. In the proposed scheme, relay node R is energy constrained, therefore, it first harvests the energy from received primary signals using PSR protocol and then utilizes the harvested energy to forward the received primary signals along with a secondary signal of its own. Detailed expressions for SNR/SINR, throughput, and sum-rates are derived. With the help of simulation results, it has been shown that with proper setting of parameter, a reasonable throughput from both primary and secondary transmissions can be achieved.

Acknowledgment. This work was supported by the National Research Foundation of Korea (NRF) grant funded by the Korean government (MSIP) (2014R1A5A1011478). Prof. Min Young Chung is corresponding author.

References

1. Lu, X., Wang, P., Niyato, D., Kim, D., Han, Z.: Wireless networks with RF energy harvesting: a contemporary survey. IEEE Commun. Surv. Tutor. **17**(2), 757–789 (2015)
2. Grover, P., Sahai, A.: Shannon meets Tesla: wireless information and power transfer. In: IEEE ISIT (2010)
3. Varshney, R.: Transporting information and energy simultaneously. In: IEEE ISIT (2008)
4. Zhang, R., Ho, C.K.: MIMO broadcasting for simultaneous wireless information and power transfer. IEEE Trans. Wireless Commun. **12**(5), 1989–2001 (2013)
5. Shah, S.T., Choi, K.W., Munir, D., Chung, M.Y.: Information processing and wireless energy harvesting in two-way amplify-and-forward relay networks. In: 2016 IEEE 83rd Vehicular Technology Conference (VTC Spring), pp. 1–6 (2016)
6. Jangsher, S., Zhou, H., Li, V.O.K., Leung, K.: Joint allocation of resource blocks, power, and energy-harvesting relays in cellular networks. IEEE J. Sel. Areas Commun. **33**(3), 482–495 (2015)
7. Gurakan, B., Ozel, O., Yang, J., Ulukus, S.: Energy cooperation in energy harvesting wireless communications. In 2012 IEEE International Symposium on Information Theory Proceedings, pp. 965–969 (2012)
8. Krikidis, I., Timotheou, S., Sasaki, S.: RF energy transfer for cooperative networks: data relaying or energy harvesting? IEEE Commun. Lett. **16**(11), 1772–1775 (2012)
9. Xu, J., Zhang, R.: Throughput optimal policies for energy harvesting wireless transmitters with non-ideal circuit power. IEEE J. Sel. Areas Commun. **32**(2), 322–332 (2015)
10. Zhou, X., Zhang, R., Ho, C.K.: Wireless information and power transfer: architecture design and rate-energy tradeoff. IEEE Trans. Commun. **61**(11), 4754–4767 (2013)
11. Nasir, A.A., Zhou, X., Durrani, S., Kennedy, R.A.: Relaying protocols for wireless energy harvesting and information processing. IEEE Trans. Wirel. Commun. **12**(7), 3622–3636 (2013)
12. Nasir, A.A., Zhou, X., Durrani, S., Kennedy, R.A.: Throughput and ergodic capacity of wireless energy harvesting based df relaying network. In: IEEE ICC-Selected Areas in Communications Symposium, pp. 4077–408 (2014)
13. Shah, S.T., Choi, K.W., Hasan, S.F., Chung, M.Y.: Throughput analysis of two-way relay networks with wireless energy harvesting capabilities. Ad Hoc Netw. **53**, 123–131 (2016)
14. Shah, S.T., Choi, K.W., Hasan, S.F., Chung, M.Y.: Energy harvesting and information processing in two-way multiplicative relay networks. Electron. Lett. **52**(9), 751–753 (2016)
15. Wang, Z., Chen, Z., Luo, L., Hu, Z., Xia, B., Liu, H.: Outage analysis of cognitive relay networks with energy harvesting and information transfer. In: IEEE International Conference on Communications (ICC), pp. 4348–4353 (2014)
16. Wang, Z., Chen, Z., Yao, Y., Xia, B., Liu, H.: Wireless energy harvesting and information transfer in cognitive two-way relay networks. In: IEEE Global Communications Conference, pp. 3465–3470 (2014)
17. Chen, Z., Liu, H., Wang, W.: A novel decoding-and-forward scheme with joint modulation for two-way relay channel. IEEE Commun. Lett. **14**(12), 1149–1151 (2010)
18. Xia, B., Wang, J.: Effect of channel-estimation error on QAM systems with antenna diversity. IEEE Trans. Commun. **53**(3), 481–488 (2005)

Workshop on Mobile-Computing, Sensing, and Actuation - Fog Net-working (MSA4FOG 2017)

Towards a Model of Enhancing Safety Fishing in South Africa

Thanyani Netshisumbewa[✉], Okuthe P. Kogeda, and Manoj Lall

Department of Computer Science, Faculty of ICT,
Tshwane University of Technology,
private bag X680, Pretoria 0001, South Africa
{netshisumbewaT,kogedaPO,lallM}@tut.ac.za

Abstract. In South Africa, fishing industry helps reduce poverty, famine and crime by providing jobs to citizens. Fishing industry also contributes to income generation of the country through export markets, investments from private companies, etc. However, the industry faces a mirage of challenges due to unsafe fishing conditions caused by weather, criminals, wild animals, faulty boats, etc. In other words, the benefits we get from fishing are affected by these unsafe conditions. We intend to implement a system that would enhance safe fishing by reducing unsafe fishing conditions using Java, Android, MySQL, and Toad technologies. In order to model our system, we went to Eastern Cape, Limpopo, Mpumalanga, Western Cape, Northern Cape and Kwazulu Natal provinces to collect data using questionnaires. Research questions included, what methods fishermen use to catch fish, what challenges fishermen face while fishing, etc. After collecting all the required data, we modelled the system using UML diagrams. The results show real challenges and safety concerns for fishermen in South Africa.

Keywords: Fishing · Fishermen · Java · Toad · Android · MySQL GPS · Safety · GPRS · UML · Mobile system

1 Introduction

Fisheries support the livelihoods of an estimated 540 million people in South Africa, in march 2013 the government launched the R800 million aquaculture development enhancement program, which offers cost-sharing grants of R40 million per company with the aim to create more jobs in the sector and the grants are made available for machinery, equipment, infrastructure, commercial vehicles and work boats, in pursuing of boosting competition in the industry [1].

However, unsafe fishing conditions are causing challenges to the fishing industry ascribed to weather, criminals, wild animals, faulty boats, etc.

Fishermen may get mauled by dangerous animals such as crocodiles, snakes, and whales. Fishermen may lose their lives as a result of lack of information about weather, animal predators, criminals and boats [2]. The deaths of fishermen at sea is characterizing the South African fishing industry of the new political dispensation in a bad light [3].

© Springer International Publishing AG 2017
O. Gervasi et al. (Eds.): ICCSA 2017, Part V, LNCS 10408, pp. 185–199, 2017.
DOI: 10.1007/978-3-319-62404-4_14

Accidents at fishing places are usually due to a lack of life-saving equipment (for example, lifesaving jackets), faulty or improperly maintained fishing tools and faulty boats [4]. Fishermen without licenses may not get support from the government such as training, exhibitions, weather updates, etc. This may also result in loss of fishermen's lives. Other fishermen are not licensed to fish ascribed to lack of information about the process involved on how to obtain fishing licenses.

In this study, six different provinces were visited in South Africa to collect data on what methods fishermen use to do their fishing activities, what are the challenges they are currently facing while fishing, etc. Therefore, we modelled a system that can help enhance safe fishing using system design diagrams. The system notifies users with weather conditions and by ensuring that people do their fishing activities at safe areas. Also, it identifies electrical faults like lights, starter, and radio signals that can fail to function on the boats while fishermen are doing their fishing activities. It also enhances safe fishing by tracking fishermen's boats/trawlers and ensures that the boats/trawlers are moving around safe areas only. This helps us rescue fishermen if there are any faults with the boats/trawlers that can cause them to sink. The systems also provide fishermen on where and how to get fishing licenses and also provide fishermen with fishing regulations.

It is very important for fishermen to know and obey the fishing regulations. This may reduce the number of deaths at sea. For example, there are several types of areas in the marine and coastal environment where special regulations apply for conversation, fishery management and promotion of tourism. These include: Marine Protected Areas, declared under section 43 of the Marine Living Resources Act [5]. In general no fishing (at least in certain zones), construction work, pollution, or any form of disturbance is allowed here unless written permission (which could be in the form of a permit or exception issued by the department of environmental affairs) has been granted by the minister [5]. As one of the Information Communication and Technology for Development (ICT4D) projects, we seek to improve the safety, economic gain and in turn prevent criminal activities. This is also the aim of other projects in this umbrella including agriculture [6], SMEs [7], social grants [8].

The remainder of this paper is organized as follows: In Sect. 2, we provide a brief overview of fishing. In Sect. 3 we provide spatial distribution of fishing activities in South Africa, In Sect. 4, we provide background and related work. In Sect. 5, we describe the system design and architecture. In Sect. 6, we describe the methodology. In Sect. 7, we provide data analysis and results. In Sect. 8, we provide conclusion.

2   Fishing

Fishing is an activity of catching fish from water using nets or fishing lines, either for commercial or recreational use. Commercial fishing is to catch a fish and sell it. Recreational fishing is catching fish for personal use or for the sport of catching fish. Recreational caught fish are eaten by the person catching them, they are not sold [9].

Fishing is also called angling, the sport of catching fish typically with rod, line and hook. Fishing originated as a means of providing food for survival. Fishing is one of the most relaxing sports at times. It gives our bodies and minds a chance to relax and rebuild from our stressful lives. Fishing offers us a time to de-stress from all of the concerns and worries we have in our professional and family lives.

Some fishermen may actually pursue fishing for the exact opposite reason like seeking excitement from a boring week at work [10].

2.1 Types of Fishing

- Ice fishing – ice fishing is to catch fish in the ice on a frozen body of water.
- Fly fishing – fly fishing is to catch fish using a rod and an artificial fly as bait.
- Saltwater fishing – saltwater fishing is a method of fishing in the ocean. It is usually done using boats.
- Freshwater fishing – freshwater fishing is a method of fishing at rivers, lakes and dams.

2.2 Methods of Fishing

- Saint netting – this method is usually used at rivers, lakes and dams where fishermen walk inside water and put the nets and leave them inside water until fish get stuck into the nets and then they go back and take out the nets.
- Fishing rods/lines standing next to water – fishermen who use this method stand next to water (usually on the bridge) and throw fishing lines inside water baited with hooks.
- Netting using boat/trawler – fishermen go to sea using a boat, while at sea they throw the nets deep into water and then fish will get stuck onto the nets while the boat is moving.
- Fishing rods/lines using boat/trawler – fishermen go to sea using a boat, while at sea they throw the fishing lines into water while standing on the boat.

2.3 Advantages of Fishing

- Income generation – 46 registered fishing companies in south Africa are currently on R5 billion annual sales and receive R5.9 billion from investments for fishing vessels and processing assets. 55% of the catch is exported to developed countries including Europe, Australia and the United States [11].
- Stress relief and self-fulfillment – fishing helps reduce stress by exposing you to beauties of the natural world, by giving you time alone with your thoughts, by giving you a reason to explore your local areas and by demanding heavy concentration and investment [12].
- Unemployment, poverty, famine and crime reduction – fishing industry provided employment to 7050 south Africans between 2015 and 2016, 37% are female and 63% are male. Employees are offered a range of benefits and scope for career progression. The monthly wage bill of fishermen in south Africa is R84.5 million [13].

2.4 Challenges of Fishing

- Dangerous animals and Criminals – fishermen may lose their lives while they are doing their fishing activities due to dangerous animals (like snakes, crocodiles, whales, sharks, etc.) or criminals. Fishermen may get attacked and killed by dangerous animals while fishing. Criminals may target fishermen for money, fish, etc.
- Faulty boats – a boat may start malfunctioning while in sea due to electrical faults like starter, lights etc. For example, if a boat starts malfunctioning due to starter, fishermen may get stuck in sea until the problem is fixed or when they get rescued. While they are stuck, they may get mauled by dangerous animals (like sharks, crocodiles, etc.) or they may get drowned into sea.
- Fights – fishermen may start fighting while doing their fishing activities. They may fight over fish, fishing spot, etc. It is difficult for other people to spend their time at a place where people fight. In other words, fighting may reduce a number of fishermen and this may increase unemployment rate, poverty, famine, etc.
- Bad weather – fishing in a bad weather (in storm, heavy rain, etc.) may cause deaths to fishermen. Dangerous water waves may cause boats to sink or fishermen may get drowned into sea. Nations needs to come to an agreement to monitor fishermen during heavy storm weather using Global Monitoring for Environment and Security (GMES) technology [14].

Each fishing type and method is used at certain fishing places, as shown in Table 1. For example, saltwater fishing is done at sea, freshwater fishing is done at rivers and dam, netting method is used at rivers and dams.

Table 1. Types of fishing and methods of fishing used at a specific fishing place

Fishing place	Type of fishing	Method of fishing
Sea	Fly fishing	Fishing rods/lines
	Saltwater fishing	Netting using boat/trawler
		Fishing rods/lines using boat
River	Fly fishing	Netting
	Freshwater fishing	Fishing rods/lines
Dam	Fly fishing	Netting
	Freshwater fishing	Fishing rods/lines
		Netting using boat/trawler
		Fishing rods/lines using boat/
Lake	Ice fishing	Fishing rods/lines
	Freshwater fishing	

3 Spatial Distribution of Fishing Activities in South Africa

South Africa consists of 9 provinces governed by provincial governments headed by Premier [8]. These provinces include: Eastern Cape (EC), Free State (FS), Gauteng Province (GP), Kwazulu Natal (KZN), Limpopo Province (LP), Mpumalanga province (MP), North West (NW), Northern Cape (NC), and Western Cape (WC). At some provinces exports income is low because of low number of fishing places or because of low number of catch, as shown in Fig. 1. For example, between 2009 and 2011 Limpopo generated low exports income of R1 561 from 7 fishing places whilst Western Cape generated R8 517 041 from 38 fishing places, as shown in Table 2.

For safety support and monitoring of data in all 9 provinces of South Africa, a website may be implemented to monitor the number of catches, number of fishing places and exports income. The system may allow all fishermen from different provinces to enter the number of catches and the provincial governments to enter all legal fishing places and exports income for each province. The system would also help introduce communication or strengthen existing communication between all the provinces.

Table 2. Number of fish caught, fishing places and exports income as from 2009 to 2011 [15, 16]

Region	Catch	Fishing places	Exports income (R)
EC	1212915	20	1103362
FS	3610	12	0
GP	456112	19	305080
KZN	230776	58	129414
LP	36581	7	1561
MP	63980	12	8521
NW	34256	28	4905
NC	16936	8	3004
WC	8790405	38	851704
Total	10845571	202	10072888

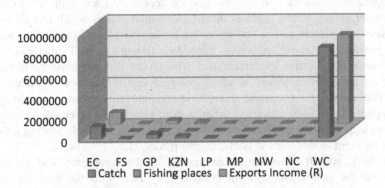

Fig. 1. Spatial distribution of fishing activities in South Africa

4 Related Work

The work in [17] implemented safety at the sea project in close cooperation with regional fisheries bodies such as the Sub-Regional Fisheries Commission (SRFC) in West Africa, and the Bay of Bengal Program Inter-Governmental Organization (BOBP-IGO) in South Asia. They have identified 7 types of fisheries: trawl netting, seining, set netting, dredging, line fishing, pot fishing and diving. For each type of fishing there is a range of possible environmental impact classes: bottom/sea bed disturbance, non-fish by-catch, non-target fish by-catch and pollution. Potential mechanisms for internalizing the externalities from commercial fishing have been identified. They identified and developed a wide range of criteria that can be used to determine which policy mechanisms are best suited to resolving the environmental externalities. The principal decision criteria are those based on the Fisheries Act, i.e., the environmental Principles. They implemented the system to improve safety fishing by strengthening fishing management cycle and coming up with new fishing regulations. However, our system goes further to help providing the fishing regulations documents electronically to fishermen.

The work in [18] developed a system that helps with fisheries management by integrating different databases. Their system integrates the catch registration and fisheries licensing system databases. Their paper discusses the process of data registration related with fishing activities. They were able to describe an information technology application in fisheries management. By the use of literature study, they were able to describe issues concerned with construction of fisheries system and computer applications support. Their work manages fisheries data including catch registration, fishing vessel register and licensing systems. However, our work helps fisheries management to track and keep record of faulty boats, predator animals, etc.

The work in [19] developed a decision support system for fisheries management using operations research and systems science approach. Their approach to fishing management system linked together three fundamental phases which are: (i) System description which includes the collection and processing of data (ii) System analysis which provides parameter estimates from data through a well-structured format (iii) Systems optimization-implementation which uses the estimated parameters to provide the means of enactment of fishing policy designed to achieve optimal harvest levels. They provided a systematic quantitative and innovative decision support system that supports the decision-makers in fisheries management. However, our system goes further to help fisheries management make safe decisions by implementing a system that allows them to monitor the boats, fishing places, etc.

The work in [20] addressed issues created by the complexity and uncertainty inherent in the fishery management system. They developed the decision support system and the following mechanisms were included to help accomplish management objectives. (i) Fishing effort restriction, which limits the number of fishing vessels, and the number of days at sea, (ii) Gear restrictions, which involves the type and size of nets to avoid catch of dangerous animals, (iii) Area specific restrictions, which controls where fishing can take place at any given time in the year. The system is also used to quantify the possible impacts of certain policy instruments, especially the utilization of the area management approach. Furthermore, the system suggests the best policies to achieve a set of management objectives. Also, they defined decision variables as the instruments used by fisheries regulators in controlling fishing effort or landings to obtain the maximum objective function value. They also defined the essential fish habitat using a model-based approach. Their system implemented new fishing regulations, however, our research enhances safety fishing by implementing a system that makes it easier for fishermen to obey the regulations.

5   System Design and Architecture

Our database design is shown in an entity relationship diagram in Fig. 2. Our system requires users' login details to be validated before they can use the system. When the user enters their login details, the system validates the entered username and password with the ones in the Administrator and Fisherman entities in the database. If the user's details are valid, then the system grants them access.

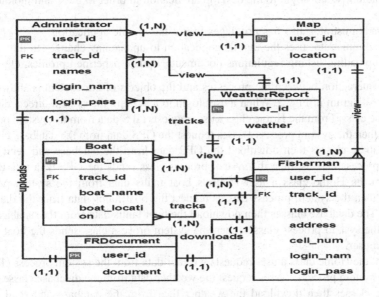

Fig. 2. Entity relationship diagram

Google weather services automatically update WeatherReport entity with weather information. When a user request weather information, the system downloads the information from WeatherReport entity.

The FRDocument entity stores the fishing regulation document. Administrator updates the entity with the recent version of the document. When fishermen request the document, the system downloads the document from the FRDocument entity.

Both administrator and fisherman uses the Boat entity to monitor the boats. Google services updates the Boat entity with the GPS information of a boat. When a user request a location of a boat, the system downloads the information from the Boat entity.

Google maps services updates the Map entity with directions to fishing areas. When a user requests directions to fishing areas, the system downloads information from the Maps entity.

5.1   Business Rules of the System

- The system requires fishermen to login to the mobile application in order to access weather, maps, fishing regulations documents, etc.
- If the fisherman is not registered, he/she has to register in order to gain access to the application.
- Fishermen only have access to the mobile application. They won't be granted access to the desktop application.
- The administrator login to the desktop application in order to track and monitor the boats.
- The administrator also has privileges to use the mobile application.
- The administrator uses the mobile application to update any changes to the system i.e., uploading fishing regulations documents, update fishermen profiles, etc.

The interaction between the processes and the objects of our system is shown in a sequence diagram in Fig. 3. When a user login to a system, the system directs them to the Home class. From the Home class a user requests GPS data from the system process classes, then the system process classes request the GPS data from the database classes. The database classes then download the GPS data from the database and send it the system process classes, then the system process class sends the GPS data to a user.

From the Home class a user requests boat faults data from the system process classes, then the system process classes request the boat faults data from the database classes. The database classes then download the boat faults data from the database and send it the system process classes, then the system process class sends the boat faults data to a user.

From the Home class a user requests weather data from the system process classes, then the system process classes request the weather data from the database classes. The database classes then download the weather data from the database and send it the system process classes, then the system process class sends the weather data to a user.

From the Home class a user requests google map data from the system process classes, then the system process classes request the google map data from the database classes. The database classes then download the google map data from the database and send it the system process classes, then the system process class sends the google map data to a user.

From the Home class a user requests FR document from the system process classes, then the system process classes request the FR document from the database classes. The database classes then download the FR document from the database and send it the system process classes, then the system process class sends the FR document to a user.

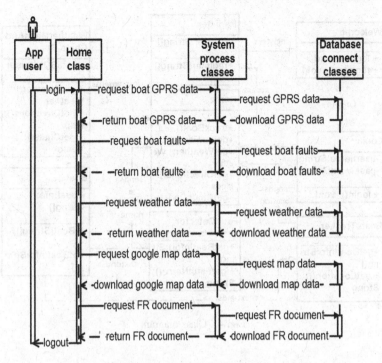

Fig. 3. Sequence diagram

The design of our application classes is shown in a class diagram in Fig. 4. When a user starts the system, the Welcome class opens. From the main screen, a user gets an option to login or to register if they are not yet registered in the system. After a user has login to the system, they are redirected to the Home class where they have options to go to:

BoatsTracker class – in this class, users track a boat by viewing the boat on a google map.

FaultDetector class – users use this class to view faults on a boat. This class checks if there is any electrical fault on a boat.

WeatherMapsAndChats – this class is used to enable users to get directions to fishing areas, get weather updates and to chat to each other.

The interaction between users and the system is shown in a use case form in Fig. 5. The administrator operates a system using a computer or a mobile device (like phone, Personal digital assistance, etc.) monitors boats, view weather, manage user accounts and upload FR document. Fisherman register uses a mobile application on mobile devices to create an account, monitor boats, view weather, view directions and download FR document (Fig. 6).

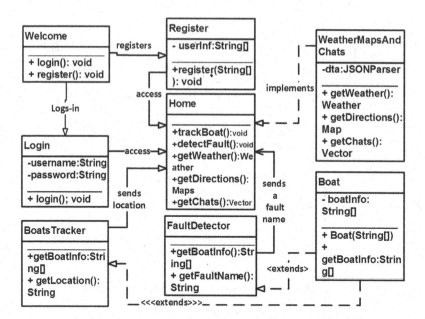

Fig. 4. Class diagram

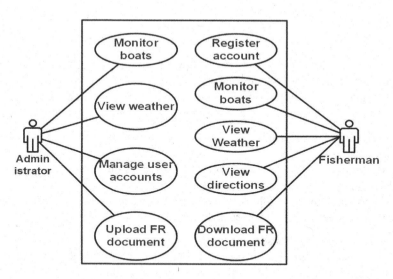

Fig. 5. Use Case diagram

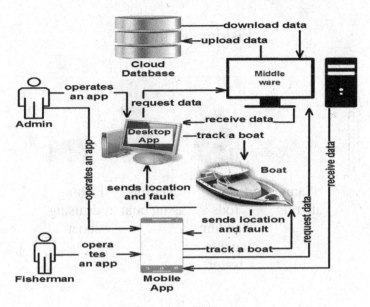

Fig. 6. System architecture

6 Methodology

We collected all required data from fishermen by making use of questionnaires. We went to Western Cape, Northern Cape, Eastern Cape, Limpopo, Kwazulu Natal and Mpumalanga provinces in South Africa to collect data from fishermen.

In order to ascertain what methods fishermen use to catch fish and what challenges they face while fishing, we gave them the questionnaires to answer the research questions. The questions were both structured and unstructured. It was open-ended questionnaires. The Questionnaires were handed to fishermen to answer the research questions, before we handed the questionnaires to them, we first explained our research to them, why is it necessary for us to collect data from them, etc. We gave the questionnaires to fishermen: (i) who fish at sea using boats/trawlers (ii) fishermen who fish at sea standing on bridges or next to water to catch fish using fishing rods (iii) fishermen who fish at rivers and dams using fishing rods and (iv) fishermen who fish at rivers and dams using nets. We gave the questionnaires to both commercial and non-commercial fishermen. After collecting all required data, we modelled our system using system design diagrams.

7 Data Analysis and Results

This data analyses involve the use of some technical tools for weighing evidence and they also provide easily understandable and precise answers to questions of study. To design our system properly it was necessary to analyze the data before we model our system. We present the results of the study to our readers in an understandable and convincing form.

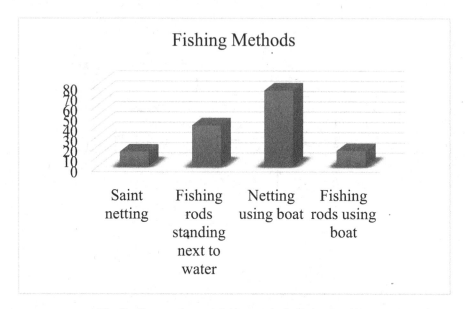

Fig. 7. Commonly used fishing methods in South Africa

There are 56 fishermen that use a netting method using a boat, followed by 15 fishermen who use fishing rods standing next to water, followed by 14 fishermen who use fishing rods while in a boat, and followed by the lowest number of 11 fishermen who use the saint netting method by walking into water and leave the nets inside, as shown in Fig. 7. 4 fishing companies uses Radar, Cavin com and Fish finder technologies to locate fishing spots where there are fishes.

Fishermen that use fishing rods/lines standing next to water face challenge of strong water waves.

Fishermen that use saint netting method are at risk of being attacked by animals (like crocodiles, sharks, whales, etc.). Fishermen that use nets using boats complained about bycatch, their nets usually catch unwanted fish.

The highest number of 74 fishermen face weather challenge, followed by 40 fishermen who fight each other while fishing, followed by 15 fishermen who struggle with directions to fishing places, followed by 5 fishermen who face boat sinking challenge, and then followed by 3 fishermen who faced boat hijacking challenge, as shown in Fig. 8. Weather challenges that fishermen are facing are storm, fog and hail.

There are 4 fishing companies that use Weather guru and Wind guru technologies to get weather data using their computers or mobile devices. This helps them do their fishing activities safely in good weather. These companies also have trawlers that have a built-in weather systems that get weather data from weather satellites, every time when a trawler go out to sea, weather data is sent to the system. Every time when a weather changes, the updates are sent to the trawlers.

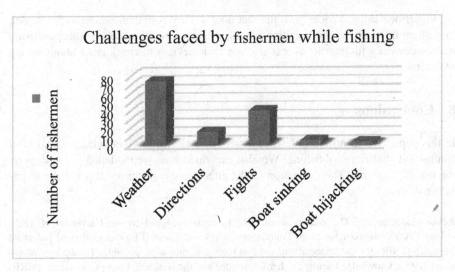

Fig. 8. Challenges faced by fishermen

In 2016 between January and September, South Africa lost 17 fishermen due to heavy storm weather, out of 17 that died, 11 fishermen died while fishing using fishing lines standing on bridges at sea. The other 6 died due to boat sinking in a storm weather while fishing at sea.

All 40 fishermen that fight while fishing, they fight over fishing spots. All these fishermen do not have fishing licenses and they fish using fishing lines standing on bridges next at sea.

56 fishermen are using mobile devices that cannot access the internet and 40 fishermen are using the mobile devices that can access the internet, as shown in Fig. 9.

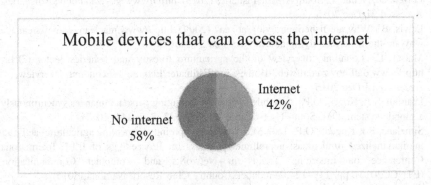

Fig. 9. Mobile devices that can access internet

We noticed that fishermen using mobile devices without internet access are more than fishermen using mobile devices with internet access. Fishermen that cannot access the internet are at risk of losing their lives due to bad weather because they hardly get weather updates.

Fishermen using devices with internet access, they communicate through internet, they share information about fishing places, weather conditions, etc. Fishermen using mobile devices with internet access also use their devices to check news about fishing on internet.

8   Conclusions

In this paper, we identified different types of fishing, fishing methods, advantages of fishing and challenges of fishing. We also explained how we modelled our system by the use of diagrams. The evaluation of the effectiveness of our system will be in our future work.

Acknowledgements. The authors would like to acknowledge Tshwane University of Technology (TUT), National Research Foundation (NRF) and Council for Scientific and Industrial Research (CSIR) for the financial support that has made this work possible. The authors would also like to acknowledge Faculty Higher Committee and the Research Ethics Committee (FCRE) of TUT for ethical approval (Reference Number: FCRE/ICT/2016/05/003(2)).

References

1. Johnson, L.: Ongoing deaths of fishermen unacceptable (2012). http://www.gov.za/. Accessed 12 Nov 2016
2. Netshisumbewa, T., Lall, M., Kogeda, O.P.: A model of ensuring safety for fishermen in South Africa. In: Proceedings of Southern Africa Telecommunication Networks and Applications Conference (SATNAC), George Western Cape, South Africa, pp. 86–87 (2016)
3. Lorren, D., Ncube, I.: South African Fisheries (2013). http://www.gov.za/about-SA/fisheries/. Accessed 21 Dec 2016
4. Lewis, B.: Why are fishermen dying at sea? (2009). http://www.macleans.ca/news/canada/why-are-the-fishermen-dying-at-sea. Accessed 24 Nov 2016
5. Matsei, E.: Economic overview of the agriculture forestry and fisheries sector (2012). http://www.daff.gov.za/daffweb3/Home/Crop-Estimates/Economic/Economic-Overview. Accessed 13 Dec 2016
6. Dlamini, S.J., Koged, O.P.: A mobile system for managing personal finances synchronously: a mobile system. Des. Solut. User-Centric Inf. Syst. **37**, 317–344 (2017)
7. Simelane, S.J, Kogeda, O.P., Lall, M.: A cloud computing augmenting agricultural activities in marginalized rural areas: a preliminary study. In: Proceedings of IEEE International Conference on Emerging Trends in Networks and Computer Communications (ETNCC2015), pp. 119–124. Windhoek Country Club Resort, Namibia (2015)
8. Cwayi, Q.S., Kogeda, O.P.: A model of controlling utilization of social grants in South Africa. In: Murgante, B., Misra, S., Carlini, M., Torre, C.M., Nguyen, H.-Q., Taniar, D., Apduhan, B.O., Gervasi, O. (eds.) ICCSA 2013. LNCS, vol. 7972, pp. 677–692. Springer, Heidelberg (2013). doi:10.1007/978-3-642-39643-4_49
9. Garrison, R.: What is fishing? (2009). http://fishing.about.com/od/gettingstartedfishing/a/Fishing.htm. Accessed 24 Nov 2016

10. Anderson, J.: What is fishing? and why go fishing? (2009). http://www.angelfire.com/ia3/fishing/whatisfishing.htm. Accessed 03 Dec 2016
11. Payne, A.I.L., Punt A.: South African deep sea trawling industry association (2016). http://www.sadstia.co.za/fishery/facts-and-figures. Accessed 08 Jan 2017
12. Pickhartz, E.: 8 ways fishing relieves stress (2014). http://www.wideopenspaces.com/8-ways-fishing-relieves-stress. Accessed 08 Jan 2016
13. Payne, A.I.L., Punt A.: South African deep sea trawling industry association (2016). http://www.sadstia.co.za/fishery/facts-and-figures. Accessed 03 Jan 2017
14. Johannessen, J.A., Le Traon, P.Y., Robinson, I., Nittis, K., Bell, M.J., Pinardi, N., Bahurel, P.: Marine environment and security for the European area: toward operational oceanography. Bull. Am. Meteor. Soc. **87**(8), 1081–1090 (2006)
15. Limam, S.: The best fishing spots (2014). http://www.bestfishingspots.co.za/contact.php. Accessed 12 Nov 2016
16. Richardt, D.: Agriculture, forestry and fisheries (2017). http://www.nda.agric.za/. Accessed 12 Jan 2017
17. Danielsson, P., Ravikumar, R., Westerberg, A., Yadava, Y.: Safety at sea for small-scale fisheries in developing countries. Food Agric. Organ. United Nations **71**, 50–75 (2009)
18. Azadivar, F., Truong, T., Jiao, Y.: A decision support system for fisheries management using operations research and systems science approach. Expert Syst. Appl. **38**, 2971–2978 (2009)
19. Tansel, Y., Yurdakul, M.: Development of a decision support system for machining center selection. Expert Syst. Appl. **5**, 59–71 (2008)
20. Marciniak, M., Szczecin, Z.: Information technology application in fisheries management. Zakład Analizy Systemowej **31**, 92–109 (2009)

Analysis of Impact of RSS over Different Time Durations in an Indoor Localization System

Abdulraqeb Alhammadi[1(✉)], Fazirulhisyam Hashim[1],
Mohd Fadlee A. Rasid[1], and Saddam Alraih[2]

[1] Faculty of Engineering, Universiti Putra Malaysia,
Serdang, Selangor, Malaysia
Abdulraqeb@ieee.org, {Fazirul,Fadlee}@upm.edu.my
[2] Faculty of Engineering, Multimedia University, Cyberjaya, Selangor, Malaysia
eng.alraih@hotmail.com

Abstract. As localization systems have recently increased in popularity, several different techniques and algorithms have been proposed by researchers and developers to achieve high accuracy and an effective localization system. However, there are certain factors that can directly affect the system's accuracy, regardless of the proposed model or algorithm, such as variation of the environment's structure and received signal strength (RSS) data over long time durations. In this paper, we analyse the impact of RSS over a long time duration to predict the user location in indoor environments using a Bayesian network. The results show the average of the distance errors of different time durations of RSS is inconsistent, due to the multipath effect, and the structure of the indoor environment. However, the overall system accuracy is 3.6 m using 15 training points for both time durations.

Keywords: RSS · RF fingerprinting · Bayesian network

1 Introduction

A localization system is a technology which is used to predict the location of objects, such as devices and people. Global positioning system (GPS) is the most popular system used for positioning and navigation purposes. GPS is used in many different applications such as navigation, mapping, timing, tracking and positioning, in both military and civilian fields. Despite all of these applications and features, but GPS does not always work effectively, due to the absence of a non-line-of-sight (NLOS) channel. Thus, researchers and developers have come up with a solution which is called an indoor localization system.

The indoor localization system is a system which can work in an indoor environment in order to locate objects. Many technologies and techniques are used for indoor localization. Bluetooth [1], Wi-Fi [2], Ultra-Wide Band (UWB) [3], ZigBee [4], Lateration [5] and Fingerprinting [6] are all localization systems for indoor environments. Bluetooth is a technology which is used to exchange data over a short distance at a frequency band between of 2400 MHz and 2480 MHz, and uses low power. Wi-Fi is the most popular technology used for the localization systems, since it is widely available in

© Springer International Publishing AG 2017
O. Gervasi et al. (Eds.): ICCSA 2017, Part V, LNCS 10408, pp. 200–211, 2017.
DOI: 10.1007/978-3-319-62404-4_15

indoor environments such as universities, hospitals and malls. This technology can achieve high accuracy with a low-complexity system. Although, technology such as UWB and Zigbee achieve better accuracy than Wi-Fi, they require additional hardware to be attached to the mobile device, which makes the system more complicated.

A lateration technique must have at least three fixed reference points (RPs) to be able to predict a target location. The determination of the target location could be performed by calculating the distance of between the access point (AP) and the target device, based on the signal properties such as received signal strength (RSS), time of arrival (TOA), phase of the arrival (POA) or angle of arrival (AOA).

The fingerprinting technique based on RSS has become the most popular technique to determine the target location in any particular environment. It does not use radio signal propagation geometry, but requires data collection and a radio map built in during the offline phase. It consists of two main phases which are called the offline phase and online phase. In the first, offline, phase, the RSS data are collected from each AP [7]. The RSS data associated with its coordinates are then stored in a server, which builds the radio map. In the online phase, the RSS data being currently received are matched with the stored data in the radio map, which determines the location of the mobile device based on Euclidean distance. The effects of the RSS in an indoor environment were investigated by [8], who introduced three types of RSS data that might have an effect on prediction of every single location. However, the prediction of any user's location in any particular area was found to be significantly affected by the environment's structure. In other words, any change in the environment's structure after collecting RSS data will have a negative impact on system accuracy. Thus, the investigation of RSS during different time periods is required to observe if any there is any change in the system accuracy.

In this research work, an extensive investigation into the impact of RSS over a long time duration was undertaken. The system model for this study is based on a finger-printing technique using Bayesian networks. This study involved obtaining the measurement and characterization of RSS behavior for varying time periods an indoor environment. The effect RSS on prediction of user location was also investigated. This paper is organized as follows. Section 2 presents the system model based on a Bayesian network which was used to estimate the user location with a given RSS. Section 3 describes and explains the experimental testbed used for a measurement campaign at different times. Section 4 provides an analysis of the results regarding RSS over long time durations and its impact on the prediction of user location of the mobile device. Finally, the paper concludes and proposes some of the future work in Sect. 5.

2   System Model

In this work, the localization system is based on Bayesian inference, which depends on a probabilistic model to determine the location of the mobile device at any point in the indoor environment. This model is based on the probabilistic algorithm which depends on the conditional probability of the location. The distribution of conditional probability to estimate an unknown location can be given by Bayes' theorem. The Bayes' theorem in localization describes the probability of the current location based on prior knowledge of the collected RSS. It can be stated mathematically as follows:

$$P(UL|RSS) = \frac{P(RSS|UL)P(UL)}{P(RSS)} \tag{1}$$

where $P(UL|RSS)$ is a posterior distribution for user location, UL, given the prior knowledge of RSS that has been collected in the offline phase. $P(RSS|UL)$ is the likelihood function that is used to build the radio map. $P(UL)$ and $P(RSS)$ are the probability of observing location UL and RSS.

Bayesian probability interprets the theorem's expression in terms of the inference of user location. One of the Bayesian systems using inference of the unknown variable is a single Bayesian system [9], which considers the indoor location system based on Bayes' theorem. It uses a Gibbs sampling algorithm introduced by [10] to draw samples from the highly complex probability based on the prior distribution.

Gibbs sampling algorithm

Initialize the initial values $s^{(0)} = (s_1^{(0)} \ldots \ldots, s_k^{(0)})$

for loop (i: 1:N)

    Drawing samples of s $s_1^{(i+1)}$ from $P(s_1|s_2^{(i)}, s_3^{(i)} \ldots \ldots, s_k^{(i)})$

    Drawing samples of s $s_2^{(i+1)}$ from $P(s_2|s_1^{(i+1)}, s_3^{(i)}, s_k^{(i)})$

        Drawing samples of s

$s_k^{(i+1)}$ from $P(s_k|s_1^{(i+1)}, \ldots ., s_{k-1}^{(i+1)})$

    Return the values $\{ s^{(1)}, s^{(2)} \ldots \ldots, s^{(k)}\}$

Gibbs sampling is used to draw samples $s_k^{(i+1)}$ from the conditional probability, given the initial value $s^{(0)}$. Consequently, a huge number of samples will be drawn, which represent the posterior distribution of the unknown location. The first Bayesian system mainly consists of nodes which represent the variables related to certain parameters which could be used for a localization system, such as distance between the mobile device and APs.

In the equations below, D_i represents the dimensions of the testbed (LxW) and RSS from AP_i. In addition, there are four independent variables, namely initial values of the system, b_{i0} and b_{i1}, and variance, τ_{b0} and τ_{b1}. The nodes and parameters of the single Bayesian system are defined as follows:

$$X \sim Uniform(0, L) \tag{2}$$

$$Y \sim Uniform(0, W) \tag{3}$$

$$D_i = \text{Log}\left(1 + \sqrt{(X - x_i) + (Y - y_i)}\right) \tag{4}$$

$$S_i \sim N(b_{i0} + b_{i1}logD_i, \tau_i) \tag{5}$$

$$b_{i0} \sim N(b_0, , \tau_{b0}), b_0 \sim N(0.001), \qquad \tau_{b0} \sim Gamma(0.001, 0.001)$$
$$b_{i1} \sim N(b_1, , \tau_{b1}), b_1 \sim N(0.001), \qquad \tau_{b1} \sim Gamma(0.001, 0.001)$$

where X and Y is uniformly distributed for length $(0, L)$ and width $(0, W)$, S_i represents the RSS of each AP, which is normally distributed with respect to the distance, D_i.

2.1 System Operation

This system, called the off-the-shelf localization system, is capable of predicting the unknown location using existing APs in any particular indoor environment. The indoor localization system based on the fingerprinting technique consists of two operational phases, namely the offline phase and online phase. Figure 1 shows the operation of the indoor localization system based on the fingerprinting technique.

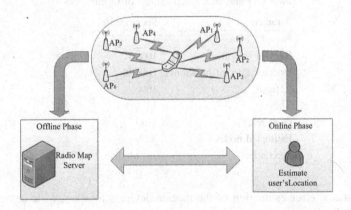

Fig. 1. System operation based on fingerprinting technique

- *In the offline phase*, a mobile device associated with Wi-Fi network, such as a smart phone or laptop is used to collect RSS fingerprints at random RPs

$$\rho = (x_i, y_i) \forall_i = 1, 2, \ldots, N$$

where ρ denotes a set of RPs in Cartesian coordinates x_i, y_i.

The RSS is recorded at every single point in time t_m (one sample per second) where $m = 1, 2, \ldots M$ for $A = AP^1, \ldots, AP^K$. The radio map contains all the RSS fingerprints in terms of $K \times N \times M$, where the time averaged can be represented by the following matrix:

$$\chi = (\chi_1, \ldots, \chi_N) \begin{bmatrix} \chi_1^1 & \cdots & \chi_N^1 \\ \vdots & \ddots & \vdots \\ \chi_1^K & \cdots & \chi_N^K \end{bmatrix} \tag{6}$$

where χ_i represents the fingerprint measurement at each ρ with $\chi_i = [\chi_i^1, \ldots, \chi_i^k]^T$ and $\chi_i^1 = \frac{\sum_{m=1}^M t_m}{M}$

The data collection can be carried out by using software known as WiFi Scanner. At the end of this phase, the system builds a radio map which contains the specific information that will be used in the online phase.

- **In the online phase** the unknown location is determined based on a single Bayesian system [9] and data collection in the offline phase. OpenBUGS program [11] is used to design a Bayesian network and estimate the user location based on Gibbs sampling. It has the capability to draw a huge number of samples based on the Bayesian model and radio map. Table 1 shows the specifications of the system's parameters used for this study.

Table 1. Parameter specifications of OpenBUGS

Parameter	Specification
No. of Chain	1
Burn-in samples	10000
Updates (No. of iterations)	100000
Refresh	100
Thin	1
Over-relax	Yes
Estimated nodes	X, Y
Percentiles	25, Median, 97.5

The distance error estimation of the mobile device's location, $\widehat{l}_i$, is calculated by using the following equation:

$$\epsilon_i = \sqrt{\sum_i (l(x_i, y_i) - \widehat{l}(x_i, y_i))^2} \tag{7}$$

where $l(x_i, y_i)$ and $\widehat{l}(x_i, y_i)$ are the actual and estimated locations of the mobile device in the testbed, respectively, while the overall system accuracy is given by the following equation:

$$\epsilon = \frac{\sum_{i=1}^n \epsilon_i}{n} \tag{8}$$

3   Experimental Testbeds

The measurement campaign was conducted at the Faculty of Engineering with a physical dimension of 52×22 m^2. There were four APs with operating frequency of 2.4 GHz, which were deployed at four different places on the testbed, as shown in Fig. 2. Table 2 shows the specifications of the testbed and AP. The deployment places of the APs were selected according to [12], by which the transmitted signal able to cover the whole entire area. This helps to improve the system accuracy by reducing the average error of user location. The RSS data were collected using a laptop running with a Wi-Fi scanner software [13], along a corridor. The Wi-Fi scanner is an open source software which provides five types of information: RSS, X and Y coordinates, channel number, SSID and time stamp for each AP. The collected data contained 50 RPs along the corridor, and was divided into two groups. Each group contained 25 RPs were separated by a distance of 2 m along the x axis, with a starting point ($x = 1, y = 10$) and ($x = 2, y = 9$), respectively. Each RP consists of 30 samples of RSS with one sample per second.

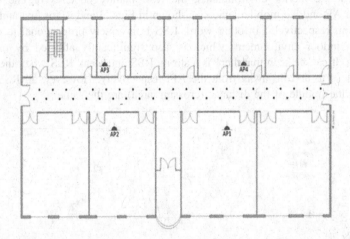

Fig. 2. Floor structure with the four deployed APs

The experiments were conducted to collect RSS data over two different duration times, with a time gap of 3 years to investigate the multipath effect in the indoor environment. Both experiments were conducted at the same place, with same number of APs and the same mobile device.

Table 2. Specifications of the testbed and AP

Type	Parameter	Specification
Testbed	Testbed dimensions	52×22 m^2
	Corridor width	3 m
	Number of APs	4
	Walls type	Concrete, Glass and some plasterboard walls
	Interior wall thickness	15 cm
	Exterior wall thickness	20 cm
AP	Model	Linksys-Cisco
	Operating frequency	2.4 GHz
	Transmitted power	18 dBm

4 Results Analysis

Generally, the radio frequency signal is gradually losing strength over a given distance. Therefore, in the indoor environments, the RSS mainly depends on the distance between the AP and the mobile device, as shown in Figs. 3 and 4, for first and second time-duration, respectively. In other word, RSS is inversely proportional to distance travelled in indoor environment, which is also significantly affected by multipath propagation. It can be seen that there is a strong RSS and weak RSS when the mobile device is close to and far away from the AP, respectively. However, all RSS values obtained in the middle of the distance (crossing area) are the same.

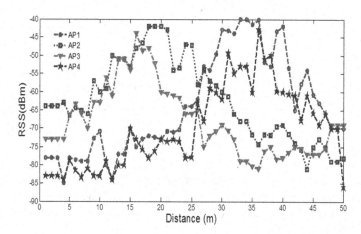

Fig. 3. Average of RSS along the corridor for 4 APs (first time duration)

In this localization technique, the average value of RSS is considered as a unique fingerprint that corresponds to each location in the offline phase. In addition, the unique fingerprint is available in any indoor environment where Wi-Fi networks are deployed. Therefore, the fingerprinting technique is considered to be the best technique to predict the user location.

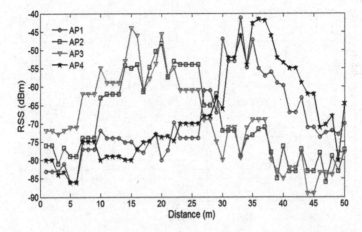

Fig. 4. Average of RSS along the corridor for 4 APs (second time duration)

Figure 5 shows the cumulative distribution function of the standard deviation over time. It can be observed that AP2 has the greatest effect on RSS; this might be due to some changes in the environment's structure compared to AP1, which has less effect.

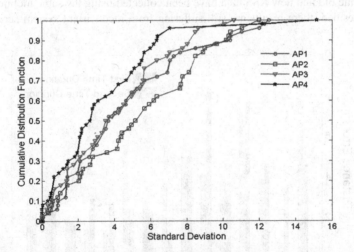

Fig. 5. Effect of standard deviation on RSS data over different time durations

Figure 6 shows the autocorrelation function with a duration of time (20 min). It can be seen that the collected RSS data have different levels of strength, since the mean and variance changes over time. In other words, the autocorrelation function has different levels of RSS during that particular time (20 min). This variation of RSS leads to the large distance error of user location which, negatively affects to the system's accuracy.

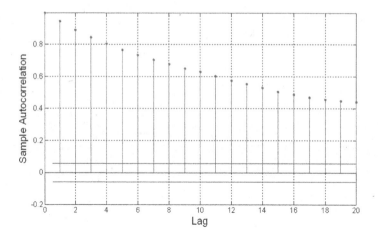

Fig. 6. Autocorrelation function for 20-minute time interval

Figure 7 shows the variation of a distance error caused by different RSS data over a specific time. It can be seen that the old and new RSS data for each training point are given a different distance error, due to the multipath effect in the indoor environment. Although the old and new RSS data have been collected using the same mobile device, APs and testbed, there results are still suffering from inconsistent system accuracy.

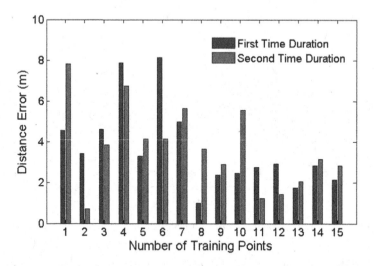

Fig. 7. Effect of different RSS data on system accuracy over a specific time

Figure 8 shows the boxplot illustrates certain parameters, including maximum, minimum and median of the two different data. The two different RSS data have almost the same maximum and minimum distance errors. However, they have different median and variance, due to the variety of signals being received.

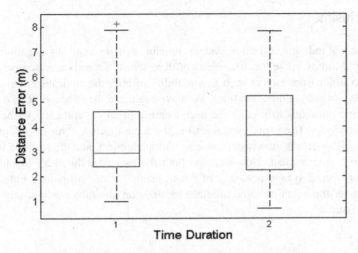

Fig. 8. Effect of different RSS data on distance error

Figure 9 shows the cumulative distribution function of the first and second time durations versus the location error. It can be seen that the first and the second time durations have a different location error over 15 training points, due to the fluctuating RSS during these periods. However, the system achieved an overall system accuracy of 3.6 m for both time durations.

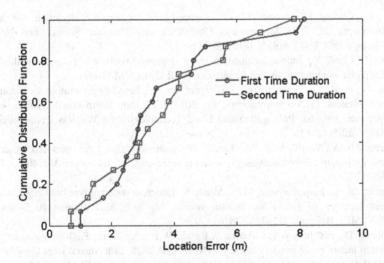

Fig. 9. Cumulative distribution function of first and second time duration

5   Conclusion

The accuracy of indoor localization systems remains a major issue in navigation system technology. Moreover, the localization algorithms which depend on experimental data continue to suffer from factors such as variability of both the environment's structure and RSS data over long time durations. We have evaluated the effects of RSS data over different time durations to predict the user location in an experimental testbed using Bayesian networks. The experimental results show the distance error of different time durations of RSS data is inconsistent, due to multipath effect, and the variable structure of the indoor environment. However, the both the two time durations in these tests obtained an overall system accuracy of 3.6 m using 15 training points. Future work could consider the effect of some different localization algorithms which might overcome this issue.

References

1. Oksar, I.: A Bluetooth signal strength based indoor localization method. In: 2014 International Conference on Systems, Signals and Image Processing (IWSSIP). IEEE (2014)
2. Yang, C., Shao, H.-R.: WiFi-based indoor positioning. IEEE Commun. Mag. 53(3), 150–157 (2015)
3. Gonzalez, J., et al.: Combination of UWB and GPS for indoor-outdoor vehicle localization. In: IEEE International Symposium on Intelligent Signal Processing 2007, WISP 2007. IEEE (2007)
4. Hu, X., Cheng, L., Zhang, G.: A Zigbee-based localization algorithm for indoor environments. In: 2011 International Conference on Computer Science and Network Technology (ICCSNT), vol. 3. IEEE (2011)
5. Yang, J., Chen, Y.: Indoor localization using improved rss-based lateration methods. In: Global Telecommunications Conference 2009, GLOBECOM (2009)
6. Ding, G., et al.: Overview of received signal strength based fingerprinting localization in indoor wireless LAN environments. In: 2013 IEEE 5th International Symposium on Microwave, Antenna, Propagation and EMC Technologies for Wireless Communications (MAPE). IEEE (2013)
7. Alhammadi, A., Yusoff Alias, M., Tan, S.-W., Sapumohotti, C.: An enhanced localisation system for indoor environment using clustering technique. Int. J. Comput. Vis. Robot 7(1/2), 83–98 (2017)
8. Alhammadi, A., Fazirulhiysam, M.F., Alraih, S.: Effects of different types of RSS data on the system accuracy of indoor localization system. In: 2016 IEEE Region 10 Symposium (TENSYMP), Bali, pp. 311–314 (2016)
9. Madigan, D., Einahrawy, E., Martin, R.P., Ju, W.H., Krishnan, P., Krishnakumar, A.S.: Bayesian indoor positioning systems. In: INFOCOM 2005, 24th Annual Joint Conference of the IEEE Computer and Communications Societies. Proceedings IEEE, 13–17 March, vol. 2, pp. 1217–1227 (2005)
10. Gelfand, A.E., Smith, A.F.M.: Sampling-based approaches to calculating marginal densities. J. Am. Stat. Assoc. 85(410), 398–409 (1990)

11. Thomas: OpenBUGS (2004). http://www.openbugs.net/w/FrontPage
12. Baala, O., You, Z., Caminada, A.: The impact of AP placement in WLAN-based indoor positioning system. In: Eighth International Conference on Networks, ICN 2009, 1–6 March, pp. 12–17 (2009)
13. Al-Ahmadi, A., Omer, S.M., Kamarudin, A.I., Rahman, T.A.: Multi-floor indoor positioning system using Bayesian graphical models. Prog. Electromagnet. Res. B **25**, 241–259 (2010)

Fog Networking for Machine Health Prognosis: A Deep Learning Perspective

Saad Bin Qaisar and Muhammad Usman[✉]

National University of Sciences and Technology, Islamabad, Pakistan
musman.msit15seecs@seecs.edu.pk

Abstract. Ensuring machine health and predicting failures beforehand is of utmost importance. Fog networking is an emerging paradigm of computing. Advances in neural networks research and their benefits in accurate classification make them best candidate for application to prognostics. Ubiquity of smartphones, wearables and sensors is giving rise to tremendous amount of data necessitating intelligent data analytics at the data center. Various researches have focused on compression of large deep models for inferencing on smart devices in order to seek answers to issues like reducing the enormity of computation, decreasing the power and memory requirements on these devices. At this point in time, state of the art in inference such as recurrent neural networks (RNN) seem impossible to be implemented on resource constrained devices. Cloud based inference incurs cost in terms of power as more energy is depleted to access infrastructure via technologies such as 3g/4g networks while also witnessing latency issues due to network congestion. A few real world situations offload inferencing to network edge as it is more beneficial to solve many issues like security, privacy of users, redundancy rather than uploading enormous volume of data on cloud. The paradigm, known as Fog Computing, is a hot topic in research facilitating edge analytics by overcoming constraints and shortcoming of cloud enabling quality of service (QoS) required in some real world applications such as Industrial Internet of Things (IoT). Fog acts as a medium between edge device and cloud. In this paper, we propose a hybrid approach of using Fog in conjunction with deep neural nets for inferencing. We propose how neural nets exploited by Fog/Cloudlet can provide computational and storage services to nearby devices and it will also put a barrier by filtering the voluminous data to a reduced form for cloud.

Keywords: CNN · RNN · LSTM · Fog computing

1 Introduction

Deep Learning is playing an important role in different walks of life due to automatic feature extraction [1] which were human selected in past and merely a difficult job. Prediction is based on using whole to coarser level feature decisions [2]. But deep learning entails a huge amount of resources in terms of computation and memory as happened in alexnet, vgg net and google inception model for ImageNet Classification [3]. Even for inference, it uses a pretrained model of weights and then it passes the input data (Tensor) to flow among the overall models to give final decision [2–4].

© Springer International Publishing AG 2017
O. Gervasi et al. (Eds.): ICCSA 2017, Part V, LNCS 10408, pp. 212–219, 2017.
DOI: 10.1007/978-3-319-62404-4_16

In this age, tremendous research is going on network optimization, energy efficient devices and development of tensor processing units for support of deep learning on ASIC based systems [5]. Modern age is compelling us toward use of smartphones, wearable devices, sensors andraspberries. Since the world is transforming towards IoT, and industry is also moving toward Industrial IoT 4.0. All these are producing data at a huge level, placing a barrier on human based inference even just skimming the data [6]. Cyber Physical Systems demand a timely inference and control as well as security to proper functioning of the system [7]. Deep learning models have proven to be effective in health prognosis and fault diagnosis systems [1, 8]. There is a need to implement these algorithms onhand held resource constrained devices which are resource constraint devices. Many researchers have focused on compression of these models upon sacrificing certain level of accuracy. Some are taking into consideration of scaling down the layer model. Since deep learning has two phases, training and testing. Research has been done in carrying out training phase using parallel and distributed computing but still testing has not been done in parallel [9]. Therefore, some software level research has been done by Nicholas Di Lane et al. about reduction of computation by introducing new layers in the model using SVD and Tucker Decomposition. Since Edge analytics demands offline inference as low latency is imperative in critical applications but not on the sacrifice of model reduction or accuracy [6]. In the proposed solution we have introduced fog which is trustworthy to all the nearby IoT devices after successful cooperation on communication. The inference will be done by Fog as this entity has sufficient resources for memory and computation [10]. The fog is also responsible to track new data sets with wrong prediction and send only these datasets to cloud for some update in weights. This will result in drastic reduction in traffic on Cloud. We presented a hybrid approach of compression of neural nets and fog computing to be applicable in next generation of Fog Computing, Industrial IoT and Data Analytics. The novelty in our solution is that it combines both compression and incorporation of fog which is cost effective in terms of communication, security, privacy and delays. Our proposed model will also best fit in future when we will have more powerful devices with multiple CPUs and GPUs. Since camera based sensors are placing plethora of images and video to sort out and extract some information to be utilized for further decision [6]. It is need of the day to address this huge traffic on Internet. Fog Computing is still in infancy and advocated by many researchers to give solutions for next generation networking and computing problems [10]. We discuss in detail our approach to be used in different scenarios and how can we get maximum benefit out of it. Convolutional Neural Networks (CNN) have proved beneficial not only for classification of images but also in health prognosis of machines [11, 12]. In this work, we discuss a use case of fog computing using neural networks for Industrial IoT and machine health prognosis. Currently, Industry employs Cyber Physical System based solutions which constantly requires access to the Internet. Similarly, applications like text to speech and speech to text as well as language translation are carried out using Hidden Markov Models. Advancement in deep learning has shown its effectiveness in all the areas of inference [13]. Recurrent Neural Nets are commonly used to address problems of classification, though, due to their complexity, they are still not implemented on smart devices as they involve input from each hidden layer to generate more likeness for further output. This involves enormous computation again and again, so seems nearly impossible to implement as such on a single device within limited time and limited resource [14]. However, fog provides better support for implementing RNN with a lot of storage and computation resources near to end device.

2 Literature Reviews

Machine health prognosis is gaining attention not only in machines but also in medical field. In machines, prognostics focus on different approaches mostly comprising rule and data driven techniques [15]. The former became less used due to criticism on lesser domain knowledge and hard fixed rules. The latter was adopted due to its effectiveness and accuracy. In the past, there was a gap on inferencing the huge amount of data both in spatial and temporal dimensions. Traditional machine learning classifiers and regressors were in common use.

Due to advancement in deep learning, computer Vision based models in machine learning for classification and regression, these models are performing well in extracting new and hidden facts [2]. We have clouds for intensive computation and data storage. Clouds provide different services like SaaS, PaaS and IaaS to end users by means of Internet [16]. The latency and traffic is increased up to such an extent due to multiple devices used by a single person. This situation creates bottleneck on clouds for inference on some new test data in deep learning problem. We need either to compress our layered model or enhance our computation near the edge device. Fog will serve as a medium between edge device and cloud to serve with minimal latency providing needed computation, storage, privacy, security and most importantly, fast inference. Fog will serve as a medium between edge device and cloud to serve with minimal latency providing needed computation storage privacy security and fast inference. Fog based models are in demand in modern era of technology [10]. Since in all type of neural networks, whether it is CNN, DNN, RNN, the main problem in adoption on smartphone and edge devices is due to high computation needed for deeper models [3]. Leroux et al. proposed an architecture in which adoption of deep learning in smart devices is done by placing a fully connected layer after each hidden layer and calculating confidence. If confidence is high, truncate the later layers, otherwise bring new layers from cloud and compute further. According to their findings, in most of the classification problems, their model ends up in few layers. In rare cases, there is a need of fetching rest of the layers from cloud and this incurs a great cost in terms of latency. To use these deep learning approaches on handheld devices in era of IoT, some researchers advocate compression on deep learning models by introducing new layers which use tucker and SVD compression on parameters as it is proposed by Nicholas lane et al. However, software based compression approach is also adopted in [17] in which compression is done variably upon a certain threshold and on allocating an intermediate layer using either tucker or SVD approach to reduce the number of neurons resulting in a lot of reduction in parameters. The gain in computation reduction makes it possible to fit for execution on end devices. Similar kind of work is also carried out by Yong-Deok Kim et al. by compression of any deep learning model. Authors implemented their proposed solution using convolutional neural networks (CNN). The authors adopt a variation of Singular Value Decomposition (SVD) using tucker decomposition and one shot compression of whole network [18]. Since huge computation and storage is supported by Cloud, a cost is incurred on utilizing cloud. Due to plethora of data produced using video streams and almost 85% of current data being visual, this enormous content leads to congestion on networks. In the current decade, every person is expected to be equipped with 3 to 4 devices on average and in future, as wearable sensor devices gain on popularity, we expect them to contribute to huge data and traffic on cloud [6]. There is a dire need for a reliable solution. Fog is nowadays hot area of research which is addressing many problems of modern Mobile Cloud Computing [19, 20]. Some researchers use cloudlet instead of Fog, but fog seems to be more than a cloudlet [16]. Fog computing is playing inevitable role in Cyber Physical Systems and IoT[19]. But Fog Computing is still in implementation phase in all areas where cloud computing is involved [10]. Since Fog is a new architecture which is an intermediary between cloud and end device, hence facilitates the end device by providing its computation, storage, control and networking services to the end devices [10, 19]. New building automation applications and cyber physical system are now adopting this new architecture to best suit the new demands of modern world.

3 Proposed Method

We have proposed the use of fog to support deep learning by running different neural networks on Fog to facilitate both end user and Cloud. The novelty in our work is that through application of this approach, end user will be benefitted due to local heavy computation and storage node is available to him. We propose our solution to a number of different approaches of deep learning and show how this new architecture is helpful by introducing fog in these deep learning models. Since CNN is mostly used for image classification and as it is discussed in introduction, how CNN is having an impact on machine health prognosis, therefore, we discuss how our proposed architecture will exploit both fog and compression on CNN for inference and prediction.

CNN using Fog: Convolutional Neural Network is widely accepted deep neural network for image classification after Alexnet in 2012. In our suggested model, we incorporate Fog in such a way that it responds in real time and all the sensors and other edge devices are feeding this fog, whereas fog is attached through wire or wirelessly. In our model, first of all, one device will be designated as fog and it will first search all other nearby devices which can run CNN model on their own if the designated fog will not find any nearby devices free, then it will support its own CNN inference. However, if it has found some devices which have enough resources to run the model, it will assign the task with a different setting (e.g. activation, initialization, optimizer, layers and number of filters according to this node), and after the result will depend on averaging all the individual results, so this approach is called ensemble and previous research has shown up to 5% improvement in accuracy while applying ensemble model. Hence this approach is not the static rather it dynamic. Chong Zhang et al. has discussed about the ensemble model for Remaining Useful Life using MODBE approach. Since a single model doesn't fit to multiple applications and to find out the best ensemble is not an easy job. However if these model are accurate and diversified than their ensemble will be better. To achieve the accuracy of a model in deep learning model should very deep making it impossible to fit on smart device. In our solution this problem is addressed using compression of the model. The pseudo code of device search and model selection is also given and one can easily understand model.

1. While(1)
2. Add self to q[]
3. Search nearby devices with add to queue q[]
4. Assign a different model to all the devices in queue q[]
5. Broadcast data to all the devices for inference
6. Broadcast result of inference to all devices
7. Action will be taken by the device which is near to controller(optional)

The proposed model can also be depicted in the given Fig. 1.

Research has shown the importance of CNN model not only in image classification but also in health prognosis. Now some of the examples how Fog based CNN will benefit different real time road, traffic management, industrial IoT etc.

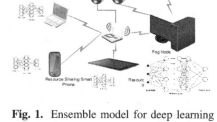

Fig. 1. Ensemble model for deep learning using fog

1. By taking different images of the same machine part and sending them on different available nodes in Fog based model and predicting their health as an ensemble on fog would yield better and timely result.
2. A Japanese engineer used Arduino for controllers and raspberries for image capturing and data sending to cloud for sorting cucumbers which seems to be a difficult task as sorting is not only on size or weight rather it involves detecting textures to identify scratches and prickles. So here CNN even surpassed human. However if we apply Fog based CNN model then we will not only prevent uploading image based data on our cloud so it will be cost effective both for cloud and for end user.
3. Since the automobiles are generating Gigabytes of data on clouds by continuously uploading video streams and then cloud extract metadata for traffic congestion etc. But in our proposed Fog based model Fog will reside in Car and only sends metadata about traffic to cloud. Since this inferencing is Fog based so it is cost effective in terms of power (as 3g/4g consume more power), with minimum latency due to local ad-hoc network.
4. Similarly our proposed Fog based CNN model will also beneficial in MRI and different medical image analysis.
5. In case of rotating machine health prognosis the data is acquired using sensors and feed into deep learning model for in time health prognosis as shown in Fig. 2.

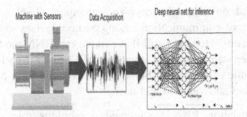

Fig. 2. Machine health prognosis using deep learning

6. When the fog is incorporated in cyber physical system, real time data will be acquired from sensors and feed into local node (fog), inference will be done in no time and action be taken using actuator. This approach can easily be observed in Fig. 3 which is divided into three areas. Edge area which have sensors and actuators, connected to fog area, for inference and only the required data is transferred to cloud which can be accessed by any online users.

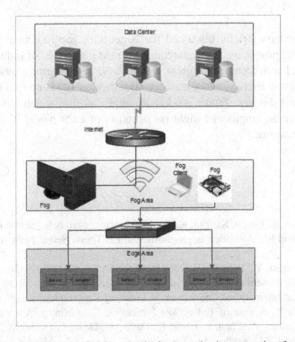

Fig. 3. Division of cyber physical system by incorporating fog.

RNN using Fog: Recurrent Neural Network has shown great impact on language processing, speech recognition, text to speech and speech to text type tasks. Similarly RNN best perform where there is time series data. Since in RNN results of previous states are feed along input to next layer neurons to predict the next possible occurrence on the basis of previous state however due to enormous computation it is still not implemented on smart devices. To implement RNN using Fog we must overcome the latency of communication among ad-hoc devices so that they can share their intermediate results. However still if we move our RNN model near end device and run it on Fog then still we get the advantage of Fog and deep learning in terms of cost and network traffic optimization. Some of the example from daily life where this fog based RNN would add value to end user.

1. In language translation RNN has played a fabulous role so any application involving translation from one language to another developed for smart phone will surely beneficial to end user. Since using Fog model we are translating offload.
2. In stock market where the user is getting continuous data from some web feed. For next predicted target value he may use regression by using LSTM(Long Short Term Memory) a special type of memory cell for implementation of RNN.
3. Text to speech and speech to text are two facilities needed by common man, to make it available on hand held device is really helpful.

4 Conclusion

In this study we have briefly discussed the benefits of incorporating Fog and deep learning for health prognosis, edge analytics, and next generation of Industrial IoT. We proposed a novel architecture in current cloud based deep learning model to be cost effective, secure, low latency, better network optimization and beneficial to end user by applying on smart devices. Future work is to apply all the models discussed in this work and to have an empirical insight on adoption of each model in different fields along with their accuracy.

References

1. Zhang, C., Lim, P., Qin, A.K., Tan, K.C.: Multiobjective deep belief networks ensemble for remaining useful life estimation in prognostics. IEEE Trans. Neural Netw. Learn. Syst. **99**, 1–13 (2016)
2. Lecun, Y., Bengio, Y., Hinton, G.: Deep learning. Nature **521**(7553), 436–444 (2015)
3. Simonyan, K., Zisserman, A.: Very deep convolutional networks for large-scale image recognition. In: International Conference on Learning Representations, pp. 1–14 (2015)
4. Goldsborough, P.: A Tour of TensorFlow Proseminar Data Mining. Arxiv (2016)
5. Abadi, M., Barham, P., Chen, J., Chen, Z., Davis, A., Dean, J., Devin, M., Ghemawat, S., Irving, G., Isard, M., Kudlur, M., Levenberg, J., Monga, R., Moore, S., Murray, D.G., Steiner, B., Tucker, P., Vasudevan, V., Warden, P., Wicke, M., Yu, Y., Zheng, X., Brain, G., Osdi, I.: TensorFlow: a system for large-scale machine learning (2016)
6. Satyanarayanan, M., Simoens, P., Xiao, Y., Pillai, P., Chen, Z., Ha, K., Hu, W., Amos, B.: Edge analytics in the internet of things. IEEE Pervasive Comput. **14**(2), 24–31 (2015)
7. Zhang, Y., Qiu, M., Tsai, C.W., Hassan, M.M., Alamri, A.: Health-CPS: healthcare cyber-physical system assisted by cloud and big data. IEEE Syst. J. **99**, 1–8 (2015)

8. Zhao, G., Zhang, G., Ge, Q., Liu, X.: Research advances in fault diagnosis and prognostic based on deep learning, pp. 1–6 (2016)
9. Chilimbi, T., Suzue, Y., Apacible, J., Kalyanaraman, K.: Project Adam: building an efficient and scalable deep learning training system. In: 11th USENIX Symposium on Operating Systems Design and Implementation, pp. 571–582 (2014)
10. Chiang, M., Zhang, T.: Fog and IoT: an overview of research opportunities. IEEE Internet Things J. **4662**(c), 1 (2016)
11. Sateesh Babu, G., Zhao, P., Li, X.-L.: Deep convolutional neural network based regression approach for estimation of remaining useful life, pp. 214–228 (2016)
12. Zhao, R., Yan, R., Wang, J., Mao, K.: Learning to monitor machine health with convolutional bi-directional LSTM networks. Sensors **17**(2), 273 (2017)
13. Com, S.B., Com, G.B., Com, M.B.: Deep voice: real-time neural text-to-speech. In: ICML (2017)
14. Karpathy, A., Johnson, J., Fei-Fei, L.: Visualizing and understanding recurrent networks. In: ICLR, pp. 1–13 (2016)
15. Peng, Y., Dong, M., Zuo, M.J.: Current status of machine prognostics in condition-based maintenance: a review. Int. J. Adv. Manuf. Technol. **50**(1–4), 297–313 (2010)
16. Fernando, N., Loke, S.W., Rahayu, W.: Mobile cloud computing: a survey. Future Gener. Comput. Syst. **29**(1), 84–106 (2013). Elsevier B.V.
17. Lane, N.D., Bhattacharya, S., Georgiev, P., Forlivesi, C., Jiao, L., Qendro, L., Kawsar, F.: DeepX: a software accelerator for low-power deep learning inference on mobile devices, vol. 1
18. Kim, Y., Park, E., Yoo, S., Choi, T., Yang, L., Shin, D.: Compression of deep convolutional neural networks for fast and low power mobile applications. In: ICLR, pp. 1–16 (2016)
19. Stojmenovic, I., Wen, S.: The fog computing paradigm: scenarios and security issues. In: Proceedings of the 2014 Federated Conference on Computer Science and Information Systems, vol. 2, pp. 1–8 (2014)
20. Bonomi, F., Milito, R., Zhu, J., Addepalli, S.: Fog computing and its role in the internet of things. In: Proceedings of the First Edition of the MCC Workshop on Mobile Cloud Computing, pp. 13–16 (2012)

A Survey on Bus Monitoring Systems

Jessica Castro, Iury Araujo, Eudisley Anjos[(✉)], and Fernando Matos

Ubiquitous and Mobile Computing Laboratory (LUMO), Informatics Center,
Federal University of Paraíba, João Pessoa 58051-900, Brazil
jesscmaciel@gmail.com, iuryrogerio@gmail.com,
{eudisley,fernando}@ci.ufpb.br

Abstract. With the growing interest in Smart City using Internet
of Things (IoT) the focus in Wireless Sensor Networks (WSN) has
increased, and consequently has been used to monitor numerous environments, such as health, habitat control, houses and public transportation.
Due this expansion, the numbers of technologies and researches on bus
monitoring systems has increase. Thereby, this survey provides information about researches, used technologies, implementation, difficulties and
problems on bus monitoring systems.

Keywords: Bus monitoring system · Intelligent transportation system ·
Smart city · Internet of Things · Wireless Sensor Network

1 Introduction

Researches based in Wireless Sensor Networks (WSN) spread worldwide in the
last years, being the increase interest on Smart Cities, Internet of Things (IoT)
and in technologies with a reduced size, which are now capable to gather, process
and transmit data, some of the reasons of this spread [14,27]. WSN is a important
technology used in researches on monitoring systems, for example on the monitoring of, habitat, air or health systems [15,16]. Besides the previous research
fields WSN was broadly used in vehicles monitoring, assisting to develop systems
to monitor public transportation in smart cities.

In the nowadays cities, users unsatisfied with the public transportation has
chosen to buy theirs own car and because of it the numbers of vehicles in urban
areas has increased, bringing problems as traffic jam, air pollution and accidents become more frequents [27]. One solution to minimize these problems is
to make the public transportation more attractive, therefore people would use
less private cars, decreasing thus the number of vehicles in the streets. Thereby,
several bus companies and researches have done the best to improve the public
transportation system [1]. Using IoT with WSN to create Intelligent Transportation System (ITS) is the solution which the majority of researches have used to
reduce the problems regarding public transportation. Examples of those systems
can be seen in cities as Nis, Serbia [2], Beijing, China [3] and Rio de Janeiro,
Brazil [11].

© Springer International Publishing AG 2017
O. Gervasi et al. (Eds.): ICCSA 2017, Part V, LNCS 10408, pp. 220–231, 2017.
DOI: 10.1007/978-3-319-62404-4_17

To create good solutions and systems to monitor the public transportation in big cities is important to analyze the main projects, the used technologies and the evolution stage in the already developed systems and researches. Therefore, this survey shows the most evident technologies, algorithms and problems to the intelligent monitoring urban bus. The paper is structured as follow: The technologies for bus monitoring systems are presented in Sect. 2, the bus monitoring researches and systems are reviewed in Sect. 3, Sect. 4 is about algorithms used in bus monitoring systems, the problems are showed in Sect. 5 and in Sect. 6 the paper is concluded.

2 Technologies

2.1 GPS

GPS is the most popular and used positioning system technology and was developed by the U.S. Department of Defense. Initially, they used 24 satellites at approximated 20000 Km above earth's surface, as shown in Fig. 1. Currently, there are 31 operational satellites orbiting around the earth. It is needed a clear line of sight to three GPS satellites to get a 2-D position (latitude and longitude), but for 3-D position (latitude, longitude and altitude) is necessary the signal of at least four. On average, they provide accuracy of 15 meters. Besides position, the GPS also transmitted current data and time [1,7].

Fig. 1. GPS satellites. (Source: Garmin).

GPS advantages is its accuracy, low-power and popularity, since great part of the population has access to GPS embedded in their smart-phones. However, there are factors that may decrease its accuracy for example, it is possible to loose the signal when it does not have a clear line of sight to the satellites due obstacles such as, tunnels and city buildings. Electronic interference and multipath error, which is the increase of signal path when it is reflected off

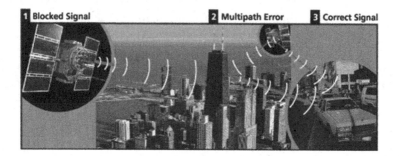

Fig. 2. GPS signal been blocked or reflected off objects. (Source: Garmin).

obstacles, as demonstrate in Fig. 2 are other problems with GPS [9,10]. A minor problem is the Ionosphere and troposphere delays, which happens when the signal is passing through the atmosphere and takes more time to reach the destination (GPS try to prevent this error) [7].

2.2 RFID

RFID is a identification technology based on the detection of electromagnetic signal. [1] The system is composed by three components: an antenna, a tag(transponder) and a reader(transceiver), see in Fig. 3 a example of RFID. The antenna is integrate with the reader and it transmits a radio frequency signal that activate the tag when detected, when it happens, the tag send data to the reader through the antenna. There are low-frequency RFID systems and high-frequency RFID systems, the range is proportional to the frequency as well as the price, in other words, a low-frequency system has less range and is cheaper than a high-frequency system [17].

Fig. 3. RFID reader and RFID tag. (Source: gaorfid and idtechex).

RFID is largely used in different applications around the world, for example in libraries, payment, stores, vehicles, human identification, ticketing, livestock, parking control, also as a better alternative to bar code. RFID tag does not need to be in a line of sight of a RFID reader to be read, being able to put it inside others objects, what is possible due its small size. However, the RFID maximum range is short to the need of some application and increasing the range, consequently it increases the system cost. A concern is about the security, a RFID tag can be read for any RFID reader, whereas RFID tag does not have intelligence to identifying readers. RFID Reader collision is another concern about RFID, it happens when two RFID readers try to read the same tag at the same time and they overlap because the tag can not respond requests simultaneously [13].

2.3   ZigBee

ZigBee protocol is a wireless communication technology to diverse systems types. ZigBee is a WSN with low-cost, low-power, low-complexity and, highly scalable, because of it and its facility to work with other technology what is perfect to Smart Cities applications, the use of ZigBee is increasing in the last years, some applications areas are building automation, industrial control and home control. The distance transmission is around 10–100 m because of the low-power consumption, but ZigBee modules can propagate the data trough others ZigBee until the final destination. ZigBee can identify each other and it is possible to program the Zigbee to only exchange data with permitted Zigbee what increase and guarantee more secure to data transactions. A ZigBee disadvantage is low data transfer rate which can derail the ZigBee use even for simplistic application [12, 21, 23, 24], Fig. 4.

Fig. 4. ZigBee module. (Source: EmbSys Labs).

2.4 Other Communication Technologies

GSM/GPRS. Global System for Mobile Communication(GSM) is the most popular technology for mobile cellphones communications used to transmit mobile voice and data service, and General Packet Radio Service (GPRS) is a upgrade of the basics features of GSM, enabling more speed and possibilities in the data exchange. GPRS is widely covered with a fast access, thus the users can be always online with real-time data exchange [5, 17].

WiFi. WiFi is one of the most used WSN and growing its popularity and availability around the globe. Generally used to local wireless network because it provides access up to 100 m and can suffer problems such as range limit or interference if there is more than one device in the same area.

WiMax. Worldwide Interoperability for Microwave Access (WiMax) is a telecommunication protocol which offers access to broadband wireless internet. Mobile stations can provide access about 5–15 km and fixed station up to 50 km [26].

3 Bus Monitoring Researches

Countless researches have used the technologies described in the Sect. 2 to create their own architecture and implement a bus monitoring system to be used by the inhabitants, encompassing residents, workers, and visitors in the tested areas. These researches have in common the fact that each bus monitoring system needs to adapt to the reality of the community where it will be installed, social and economic factors, however it is necessary to keep in mind that some of these countries also have different characteristics in some areas and some of theses system will need to be adapt to fulfill their task.

Although the smart cities and correlate topics are quite fresh some of the researches trying to create and implement new systems are dated before 2010. In the city of Nis, Serbia, a research from 2007 developed a bus monitoring system based in GPS as the tracking technology and General Packet Radio Service (GPRS) to send data from the bus to the server [2]. The system worked using real time location gathered by the GPS and also with stored data, as timetables and traffic conditions between some periods of the day. With all this data was possible to determine the location of the buses and their arrival time at station through the city [2].

With the arrival of the 2008 Olympic games hosted in Beijing, China, the city received thousands of tourists, who come to prestige the games. This was considered as a problem owing to the already gigantic population of the city and the problems a great number of people would create to flow between gyms. As a solution to the problem was created especial lines for the Olympic games and also a bus monitoring system was implemented to ensure trip safety, emergence handling and rational dispatching [3]. The system was based in GPS to gather the location of the buses with some delay between the requests and after send the location through GPRS, the control room could verify the position and send messages to the buses if necessary [3].

It is interesting to notice that the two systems above used GPS as tracking technology. This happens because it is a cheap technology and is already largely use worldwide. The bus monitoring systems who is based in GPS are quite simple in comparing with other technologies, commonly these systems are only interested in geographically location to determine the bus arrival time prediction [2–6,11]. However there are some researches who use another technology in group with GPS to accomplished other goals. In India a research created a bus monitoring system that besides gather geographically location uses other technologies as Arduino and sensors to receive climate information from the bus, the researchers also implemented a near field communication (NFC) to control the selling of tickets [8].

The increase of the desire to construct smart cities through the internet of things had a effect in the researches about bus monitoring system, it is more interesting to construct and implement systems who can do beyond gather the location of a bus and calculate its arrival time, but also provide new services for passengers and controllers [9]. To construct these types of systems is important to use new technologies who can permit to create more sophisticated systems. Technologies as RFID and ZigBee, types of WSN, are being used with more frequently to mold the systems [1,12].

Using RFID a interesting bus monitoring system was implemented inside the national university of Malaysia (UKM) campus [20]. The system was created to help the students who need to flow between buildings of the university who are spreed through the city and because of the lack of reliability at the university bus were forced to spend money in other transports to not be late for some classes. The system was based in RFID as a trigger to the system, when a bus with a RFID reader, nears a station with a RFID tag, the system send data to the server using a GPRS network and the server can visualize the location of the bus in a map using a Geographical Information System (GIS) software [17–19].

Another example of RFID use is a bus monitoring system carried out in the city of Jabalpur, India. The system was developed using RFID in the bus and in the station. Also the bus had a controller who was responsible to send and receive data from the server [1]. This controller is important because upon receiving data some of this data send by the server could be show into the bus to the passengers through a LED display, for example information about time schedule or the time to arrival into some destination. Besides that the system also have LED displays installed in the main stations in the city to send information about the buses who will arrive in that stop [1].

Other technology already talked about is the ZigBee. The architecture using ZigBee come from a solution where the bus and also the stop have ZigBee modules attach to them. This is important because each module has its own identification code, thus it is possible to locate where is a bus just receiving the code of the station module [9]. The interesting thing about system implement with ZigBee it is the possibility to extend the system further in the future as long the passengers and controllers will be needing new types of data.

A research at ChongQing University of Post and Telecommunication, China created a architecture who uses ZigBee to create a WSN, where a bus transport a ZigBee coordinator who waits to connect to other module, a verification is made to detect if this module is part of this system, its id is send to the server through a GPRS network and if the module belongs to the system it is aloud to send data over the GPRS connection [21]. Another example also from China, is the creation of a bus monitoring system who also wants to gather information inside the bus, as temperature, passenger volume, vehicle speed and stop reports [12]. The system was developed to have a borne terminal in the bus who has a ZigBee module and sensors who can detect some of the needing data, all this parts were controlled by a microcontroller who seeded and received data using a mobile network.

Table 1. Table summarizing the researches presented in this section.

Research paper	Publication year	Test location	Tracking technology	Communication technology
[1]	2011	Jabalpur, India	RFID	GSM
[2]	2007	Nis, Serbia	GPS	GPRS
[3]	2009	Beijing, China	GPS	GPRS
[4]	2014	Dugarpur, India	GPS	Data manually retrieved
[5]	2014	Chennai, India	GPS	GSM
[6]	2014	Nicosia, Cyprus	GPS	Cellular Communication
[8]	2014	Ooty and Nundhala, India	GPS	GSM
[9]	2015	João Pessoa, Brazil	ZigBee	ZigBee and WiMAX
[11]	2014	Rio de Janeiro, Brazil	GPS	IEEE 802.11 Networks
[12]	2012	–	ZigBee	ZigBee and IEEE 802.15.4
[17]	2011	Bangi, Malaysia	GPS	RFID and GPRS
[18]	2011	Bangi, Malaysia	GPS	RFID and GPRS
[19]	2010	Bangi, Malaysia	GPS	RFID and GSM
[20]	2009	Bangi, Malaysia	RFID	RFID and GSM
[21]	2012	–	ZigBee	ZigBee and GPRS

A interesting research using ZigBee and collecting another information was developed in João Pessoa, Brazil. The system called UrbemBee (Muv-Bee) is a bus and environment monitoring system [9]. The system is based on ZigBee protocol to create a WSN between the bus and the stations. Whit the id of each module is possible to get the bus localization through the city, also the system collects with sensors some data about environment, as temperature, humidity, levels of pollutant gases. Theses data are important to create important reports about the air condition of the city. The idea of the project is to gather these information more cheaply than the actual solution, who is to create fix environment monitoring stations, because a bus would track a big part of the city [9]. Other characteristic of this system is the possibility to extend their functionality, adding new modules to the current software and hardware.

The Table 1 presents a summarization of the researches used in this article, it is composed by the research paper reference, publication year, test location, tracking and communication technologies. This table can be used to compare the technologies used in other researches and where this kind of research is being developed.

4   Bus Monitoring System Algorithms

Inside each bus monitoring system there is a algorithm running and doing everything works as planned. This algorithm can be implemented by several forms, however theses forms always try to archive the optimal stage, this is, running with the minimal waste of resources and time. Normally the sequence of these algorithms is to wait for the connection with a bus through the chosen network, verify if the bus connection attempt is legal, receive data from the bus module and finally process that information. Variations of this sequence are possible depend on each individual architecture, although all this steps will continually existing. Some of the variations are related to the technology used in the system. For example systems who use GPS as tracking technology and are interesting only in geographically location will follow the steps already presented and illustrated by the state machine in Fig. 5, [2–4].

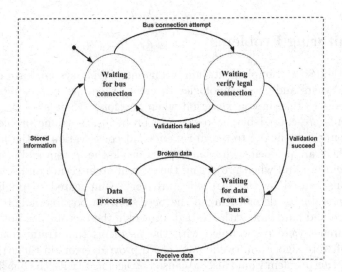

Fig. 5. A simple state machine of a bus monitoring system algorithm using GPS.

The use of another technology can change the algorithm and its steps. For example if some WSN is used, as RFID or ZigBee, to connect the bus to the station it is necessary in those steps to verify if the module in the station is also part of this system. This step is important to exclude interference from another systems and false data [9, 12, 20, 21]. Furthermore the type of network chosen to be used to connect the bus module and the server can interfere on the steps because of the quality of the signal and its speed. As a example is possible to the bus module have a list of aloud station modules and the verification of the legal connection stays in the bus, withdrawing the station connect verification from the server, as on the Fig. 6.

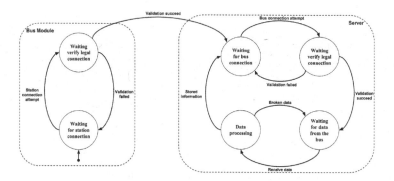

Fig. 6. A simple state machine of a bus monitoring system algorithm using WSN and verify the station on the bus module.

5   Monitoring Problems

Although the use and implementation of bus monitoring system have increased in the past years and the technologies to create them are improving, there is still problems to take in consideration when developed these systems. Some of the problems are caused by the real world problems, as traffic problems, bad network connection in the tested areas and bad conservation of the hardware. However there are problems who can happen inside the system and is necessary to keep them in mind when projecting the system architecture and software.

Problems caused by the real word are very complicated to predict. It is almost impossible to deter them, so the best solution possible it is to prepare the software and hardware with strategies to solve these problems. For example some researches were preoccupied with the problems that traffic could cause into the software algorithm, traffic jams could provoke errors in the arrival time prediction, this problem would also be caused by accidents with the bus [6,11,22]. One of the solutions was to create a system who has a fix timetable to the bus routes and when the software detects a event who will change that prediction the module on the bus send its actual location to the server, although this is a good strategy because reduces the transmission of insignificant data, it requires a technology who can detect location in any point of the tested area, as GPS [6]. Other solution used to some researches is to create a arrival time prediction algorithm who will detect the possible problems in the trajectory, this can be achieved with information stored from other executions of system, for example in China on research reach this goal using a neural network [22].

Another concern is the network connection, the system can not fulfill the tasks without one and if this network has bad signal reception in some parts of the tested area or has a speed drop, it will interfere on the server ability to receive and send data. Unfortunately there no way to ensure that the network will be free of this problems all the time, however some researches have try to minimize this problem reduce the amount of data sent to the server or to the bus module. Besides that the systems are preoccupied with how often it is necessary to send data, because of this reason systems who use WSN normally only send data when a bus module and a station module are connected [9]. Other idea to solve the problem is to evolve the hardware responsible to connect the bus module with the server through the network, in Korea one of the ideas was to construct a LTE antenna specially made for bus monitoring systems [25].

Finally a bus monitoring system can have a expensive cost to be implemented, this is determined by the technologies used in the system, the amount of data transiting the network, the maintenance cost of the system, the number of vehicles and by the size of the implementation area. Because of this cost the researches are always trying to create a cheap system and still provides the require features. Numerous research presents system who uses new technologies to lower the costs or present new ways to use a already used technology in a cheaper way [4,5,9,12,17,21].

6 Conclusion

The bus monitoring systems are increasing in number and quality all around the world. New technologies are being crucial to create cheaper and more reliable systems, furthermore researches are trying to use the old technologies in different and cheaper ways to achieve the sames goals. New systems are not only worried with the monitoring of bus, but also with what they can provide to the passengers and controllers to make their decisions easier. For example a passenger do not need to wait more time that he wants in a bus stop, because he knows the bus arrival time. A controller can decide if is necessary to increase the number of bus in a route in some hour of the day. These kind of information is important to all the users and makes monitoring systems in general to be extremely required in a smart city.

Even if the great possibilities of these systems can offer, there are numerous problems to implement them in the cities. Unfortunately the cost of this type of system need to be thought by the researches, who are trying to find cheaper solutions to construct them. Other problems also need to be watched, as network infrastructure and real word interference. These problems are some of the reason why each system can have a different architecture and algorithm, because it is necessary to analyze the conditions of the area where the system will act, whether they social, economic or traffic.

The interesting thing about the current bus monitoring systems is that their developers are not only worried to create a tracking system who can find where a bus is and the time it will need to arrive at a station, they are trying to create systems who can provide new types of services to the users, whether they users or controllers. The bus monitoring systems are being influenced by the smart cities characteristics and by the concepts of the internet of things, the goal is not only monitor the bus, but also integrate it and their users in a big information ecosystem where they are provided with the information necessary to make smart decisions.

References

1. Vasal, A., Mishra, D., Tandon, P.: Deployment of GSM and RFID technologies for public vehicle position tracking system. In: Meghanathan, N., Kaushik, B.K., Nagamalai, D. (eds.) CCSIT 2011. CCIS, vol. 132, pp. 191–201. Springer, Heidelberg (2011). doi:10.1007/978-3-642-17878-8_20
2. Predic, B., Stojanovic, D., Djordjevic-Kajan, S., Milosavljevic, A., Rancic, D.: Prediction of bus motion and continuous query processing for traveler information services. In: Ioannidis, Y., Novikov, B., Rachev, B. (eds.) ADBIS 2007. LNCS, vol. 4690, pp. 234–249. Springer, Heidelberg (2007). doi:10.1007/978-3-540-75185-4_18
3. Niu, H., Guan, W., Ma, J.: Design and implementation of bus monitoring system based on GPS for Beijing Olympics. In: 2009 WRI World Congress on Computer Science and Information Engineering, vol. 7, pp. 540–544. IEEE (2009)
4. Mandal, R., Agarwal, N., Das, P., Pathak, S., Rathi, H., Nandi, S., Saha, S.: A system for stoppage pattern extraction from public bus GPS traces in developing regions. In: Proceedings of the Third ACM SIGSPATIAL International Workshop on Mobile Geographic Information Systems, pp. 72–75. ACM (2014)
5. Janarthanan, B., Santhanakrishnan, T.: Real time metroplitan bus positionin system desing using GPS and GSM. In: 2014 International Conference on Green Computing Communication and Electrical Engineering (ICGCCEE), pp. 1–4. IEEE (2014)
6. Antoniou, A., Georgiou, A., Kolios, P., Panayiotou, C., Ellinas, G.: An event-based bus monitoring system. In: 2014 IEEE 17th International Conference on Intelligent Transportation Systems (ITSC), pp. 2882–2887. IEEE (2014)
7. Garmin, What is GPS? http://www8.garmin.com/aboutGPS/index.html
8. Bojan, T., Kumar, U., Bojan, V.: An internet of things based intelligent transportation system. In: 2014 IEEE International Conference on Vehicular Electronics and Safety (ICVES), pp. 174–179. IEEE (2014)
9. Araujo, I., Castro, J., Matos, F., Anjos, E.: MUV-Bee: using WSN to monitoring urban vehicles. In: Network Operations and Management Symposium (LANOMS). Latin American, pp. 99–102. IEEE (2015)
10. Milans, V., Naranjo, J.E., Gonzlez, C., Alonso, J., de Pedro, T.: Autonomous vehicle based in cooperative GPS and inertial systems. Robotica **26**(05), 627–633 (2008)
11. da Silva, V.B.C., Sciammarella, T., Campista, M.E.M., Costa, L.H.M.: A public transportation monitoring system using IEEE 802.11 Networks. In: 2014 Brazilian Symposium on Computer Networks and Distributed Systems (SBRC), pp. 451–459. IEEE (2014)
12. Cai, C.Q., Zhang, Z., Ji, S.D.: The intelligent bus scheduling based on zigbee. In: 7th International Conference on Computer Science & Education (ICCSE), pp. 1002–1005. IEEE (2012)

13. Technovelgy, What is RFID? http://www.technovelgy.com/ct/Technology-Article. asp
14. Zanella, A., Bui, N., Castellani, A., Vangelista, L., Zorzi, M.: Internet of things for smart cities. Internet Things J. **1**(1), 22–32 (2014). IEEE
15. Paek, J., Chintalapudi, K., Caffrey, J., Govindan, R., Masri, S.: A wireless sensor network for structural health monitoring: Performance and experience. Center for Embedded Network Sensing (2005)
16. Mainwaring, A., Culler, D., Polastre, J., Szewczyk, R., Anderson, J.: Wireless sensor networks for habitat monitoring. In: Proceedings of the 1st ACM International Workshop on Wireless Sensor Networks and Applications, pp. 88–97. ACM (2002)
17. Hannan, M.A., Mustapha, A.M., Hussain, A., Basri, H.: Communication technologies for an intelligent bus monitoring system. In: 2011 World Congress on Sustainable Technologies (WCST), pp. 36–43. IEEE (2011)
18. Mustapha, A.M., Hannan, M.A., Hussain, A., Basri, H.: Implementing GIS in bus identification and monitoring system. In: 1st International Conference on Electrical, Control and Computer Engineering 2011, InECCE (2011)
19. Mustapha, A.M., Hannan, M.A., Hussain, A., Basri, H.: UKM campus bus monitoring system using RFID and GIS. In: 6th International Colloquium on Signal Processing and Its Applications (CSPA), pp. 1–5. IEEE (2010)
20. Mustapha, A.M., Hannan, M.A., Hussain, A., Basri, H.: UKM campus bus identification and monitoring using RFID and GIS. In: IEEE Student Conference on Research and Development (SCOReD), pp. 101–104. IEEE (2009)
21. Feng, H., Lulu, L., Heng, Y., Xia, H.: Bus monitoring system based on ZigBee and GPRS. In: 2012 International Conference on Computer Distributed Control and Intelligent Environmental Monitoring (CDCIEM), pp. 178–181. IEEE (2012)
22. Wang, L., Zuo, Z., Fu, J.: Bus arrival time prediction using RBF neural networks adjusted by online data. Procedia Soc. Behav. Sci. **138**, 67–75 (2014)
23. DainTreeNetworks Applying Mesh Networking to Wireless Lighting Control
24. Alliance, What is ZigBee? http://www.zigbee.org/what-is-zigbee/
25. Shin, D.K., Jung, H., Chung, K.Y., Park, R.C.: Performance analysis of advanced bus information system using LTE antenna. Multimed. Tools Appl. **74**(20), 9043–9054 (2015)
26. Bhambri, A., Kansal, N.: Survey on WiMAX Technology and its protocol-a review
27. Yick, J., Mukherjee, B., Ghosal, D.: Wireless sensor network survey. Comput. Netw. **52**(12), 2292–2330 (2008)

Workshop on Physiological and Affective Computing: Methods and Applications (PACMA 2017)

Analysis of Keystroke Dynamics for Fatigue Recognition

Mindaugas Ulinskas[1], Marcin Woźniak[2],
and Robertas Damaševičius[1(✉)]

[1] Department of Software Engineering, Kaunas University of Technology,
Kaunas, Lithuania
robertas.damasevicius@ktu.lt
[2] Institute of Mathematics, Faculty of Applied Mathematics,
Silesian University of Technology, Gliwice, Poland

Abstract. The paper analyses the problem of fatigue recognition using keystroke dynamics data. Keystroke dynamics provides the time data of key typing events (press-press, press-release, release-press and release-release time). We propose using statistical features and k-Nearest Neighbour (KNN) classifier to discriminate between different consecutive key typing sessions. The presented approach allows to recognize the state of increased fatigue with an accuracy of 91% (using key release-release data).

Keywords: Keystroke dynamics · Typing behaviour · Fatigue recognition

1 Introduction

Fatigue monitoring is increasingly important in the industrialized world because working tasks are becoming increasingly monotonous and less physically exhausting, resulting in a high risk of losing attention and unintentional accidents [1]. We can recognize human fatigue by observing human actions. The fatigued person lacks of energy and motivation, cannot achieve typical work performance, shows signs of deteriorating memory. Fatigue can lead to poor communication and decrease vigilance, which are very important in everyday life and are essential for people of selected professions (e.g., passenger bus and long-distance lorry drivers) as well as decrease productivity and self-motivation of office employees, and, especially, shift workers [2]. The most often fatigue determinants include: difficulty of sleeping, vitamin deficiency, age, lack of physical activity, monotony, and erratic work schedules. Fatigue also can be caused by boredom or monotonous works, which have been demonstrated to reduce driver attention [3]. The reduction of monotony, e.g., by work breaks, can have a positive influence in reducing fatigue [4].

Fatigue can be identified externally by observing certain externally observable psychophysical signs or symptoms such as involuntary winking. Several approaches have been used previously such as based on gaze tracking [5], electromyography (EMG) [6], heart-rate variability [7], and electroencephalography (EEG) [8]. A number of tests can be used to assess the effects of fatigue on vigilance of a person: such as visual tracking of a small object displayed on a computer screen or words appearing

© Springer International Publishing AG 2017
O. Gervasi et al. (Eds.): ICCSA 2017, Part V, LNCS 10408, pp. 235–247, 2017.
DOI: 10.1007/978-3-319-62404-4_18

randomly on a screen [7] aiming to measure the reaction time of a subject; Mackworth clock vigilance test for measuring reaction time to flashing dot sequences with a missing dot, spatial memory tasks measuring how fast the subject can find and identify visual information, grammatical reasoning tasks as well as subjective fatigue self-rating questionnaires based on visual analogue scales (VAS) [9].

Any test for fatigue assessment must satisfy the fundamental requirement of objectiveness to prevent voluntary manipulation by the test subject. Biometrics are physical or behavioural traits (such as gait [10]) that make each person unique and hardly changeable, which can be used for evaluation of psychophysical state of a person. The behavioural characteristics attributed to the dynamics of typing the computer keyboard keys (Keystroke Dynamics, KD) is one of such biometric characteristics based on unique personal neuro-physiological factors that also make written signatures unique [11]. As opposed to physiological biometrics such as fingerprints, retinal blood vessel patterns and iris patterns, KD is one of behavioural biometrics, which is based on one of externally observable and measurable aspects of human behaviour.

KD monitors the keyboard input and analyses how users type. It is based on the assumption that different people have different manners of typing, which may include variability in keystroke time and key pressure [12]. KD data yields quantitative information with respect to hold/dwell (or press-release) time and time-of-flight (release-press time). When a person types, the latencies between successive keystrokes, keystroke durations, finger placement and applied pressure on the keys can be used to construct a unique profile for that individual and also can be used to track changes of his psycho-physical (e.g., affective) state such as stress [13]. While keystroke dynamics as a behavioural biometry, has been shown to be often unstable and unreliable to be used for user authentication [14] as it can vary from time to time, this feature can still be used to evaluate the changes in human state. Furthermore, recognition based on keystroke dynamics is not intrusive as, e.g., Brain-Computer Interface (BCI) requiring to attach sensors to subject's body.

KD also can be applied in the context of e-Learning, for example, for nonstop biometric user authentication in an online-exam [15], monitoring student's performance in real time and measure the effect of prolonged attention, stress and mental fatigue on students [16]. It has been noted that writing velocity tends to decrease and time between keys tends to increase, i.e., students write slower as activities progress throughout the day [17]. The changing of keystroke rhythm is a crucial factor to be considered in stress analysis. Using this information, the teacher has the possibility to assess the performance of students individually, in real time. Keystroke data also can be used as an indirect indicator of affective states (e.g., happy, sad or frustrated) [18, 19]. Furthermore, the analysis of keyboard interaction data is important in the medical domain as well, where it can serve as an indicator of early Parkinson's disease [20], while key strike force has been related to musculoskeletal symptoms (MSS) [21].

The aim of this paper is to explore the possibility to use KD for evaluating the onset of fatigue. The structure of the paper is as follows. Section 2 provides the methodological background. Section 3 describes the results of our experiments with KD data. Finally, Sect. 4 evaluates the results and presents conclusions.

2 Methodological Backgrounds

2.1 Data

We can use a number of measurements to characterize a user's typing pattern. These measurements can be derived from the raw data of key press times, key release times, and the identity of the keys pressed. From key-press and key-release times a feature vector, often consisting of press hold (PH), press-to-press (PP), press-to-release (PR), release-to-press (RP), and release-to-release (RR) keystroke duration times can be created. The keystroke dynamics data is extracted from a sequence of events, which contains the time stamp of every key-press and key-release event (see Fig. 1).

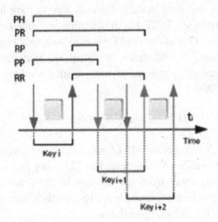

Fig. 1. Illustration of keystroke dynamics: duration times of press hold (PH), press-to-press (PP), press-to-release (PR), release-to-press (RP), and release-to-release (RR) keystroke events

Given a sequence of keystroke times $N = (t_1; t_2 \ldots t_n)$, where t_i is a 2-dimensional vector $t_i = [t_i^p; t_i^a]$, t^p is press time, and t^a is release time, one can define $t_i^{pp} = t_i^p - t_i^a$ as PH time (difference between the press time and the release time of the i-th key), $t_i^{pp} = t_i^p - t_{i-1}^p$ as PP time (difference between the press time of (i + 1)th key and press time of the i-th key), $t_i^{ap} = t_i^p - t_{i-1}^a$ as PR time (difference between the release time of the (i + 1)th key and the press time of the ith key), $t_i^{pa} = t_i^a - t_{i-1}^p$ as RP time (difference between the press time of the (i + 1)th key and the release of the i-th key), and $t_i^{aa} = t_i^a - t_{i-1}^a$ as RR time (difference between the release time of the (i + 1)th key and release time of the i-th key).

2.2 Dataset

We used the RHU Keystroke dataset of keystroke data collected by El-Abed *et al.* [22]. The dataset consists of keystroke data from 53 individuals have participated in the acquisition process by typing the password "rhu.university" 15 times (3 sessions, 5 trials each) with 3 to 30 days separating each session. The data sample was small: size of input is only 13 characters for each trial.

2.3   Data Pre-processing

Two preprocessing steps are performed on the feature measurements, outlier removal and feature standardization. Data preprocessing and cleaning can be done to improve the system's performance to remove obvious outliers, when, e.g., the person has become distracted and stopped typing. Outlier removal is particularly important for these features because a keyboard user could have been distracted and paused typing for some reason, and the resulting outliers (usually overly long transition times) could skew the feature measurements. Different outlier removal schemes can be used, but we use the Median Absolute Deviation (MAD) based method. First, the median of the values is calculated. Then, the difference is calculated between each value and this median. These differences are expressed as their absolute values, and a new median is calculated to yield MAD:

$$MAD = median(|X_i - median(X)|) \tag{1}$$

If a value is a certain number of MAD away from the median of the values, that value is classified as an outlier. As suggested in [23], any feature value, which is 3.5 times the MAD, or more, away from the median of the feature values, can be considered an outlier. This method is generally more effective than the mean and standard deviation based method for detecting outliers.

2.4   Feature Generation

We use a combination of statistical and information-theoretic measures generated fron keystroke time series as follows (with abbreviations given in parentheses): autocorrelation at lag 1 (*ar1*), first zero crossing of the autocorrelation functions (*acf1*), entropy (*entr*), energy aka sum of squares (*ener*), mean (*avg*), median (*mdn*), skewness (*skew*), kurtosis (*kurt*), standard deviation (*std*), median absolute deviation (*mad*), interquartile range (*iqr*), maximum (*max*), minimum (*min*), 1st, 5th, 10th, 25th, 50th, 75th, 90th, 95th and 99th percentiles (*p1 ... p99*), 1st and 3rd quantiles (*q1, q3*), number of outliers (*num*), number of mean crosses (*zcr*), 3rd and 4th statistical moments (*m3, m4*), Hjorth's mobility (*mob*) and complexity (*comp*), peak frequency from coefficients of Dicrete Cosine Transform (*pf*),waveform length aka sum of absolute differences between adjacent values (*len*), standard deviations of absolute differences between adjacent values (*lens*), sum of squares between adjacent values (*len2*), range (*ran*), 2nd-6th L-moments (*lm2 ... lm6*), 2nd-5th cumulants (*cum2 ... cum5*), norm (*norm*), root mean square (*rms*), difference between the 95th and the 5th percentile values (*iqr90*), difference between 99th and 1st percentile values (*iqr98*).

2.5 Feature Ranking and Selection

Keystroke dynamics suffer from high dimensionality and a huge number of irrelevant and dependant features, which may degrade the classification accuracy and efficiency. Feature selection is used as a pre-processing step in order to select a subset of the most informative or discriminative features from the original feature set and eliminate redundant or irrelevant features from large-scale keystroke dynamics.

For feature ranking, we use the Student's t-test. The features are ranked by values of the test obtained by comparing a vector of single variable values corresponding to positive cases (increase of fatigue) and that corresponding to negatives cases (no increase of fatigue). Final subset of features can be than selected according to the predefined p-value.

Next, we apply Principle Component Analysis (PCA) to select and aggregate features. We select features, which allow to explain 99% of variability. In most cases, only two feature dimensions are enough to achieve this result.

2.6 Dataset Balancing

Often classification problems are ill-balanced, i.e., there is a significant disparity between the number of instances in classes. Such misbalance may lead to poor classification results as the classifier may just focus on the dominating class with the largest number of instances. The class imbalance negatively affects the performance of all common classifiers, such as SVM, decision trees and ANN. They usually correctly classify most of the instances belonging to the largest class but obtain poor performance on the minority class. This undesirable result is caused by the rarity of the minority class, which prevents the correct separation from the majority class [24]. To deal with this problem, we employ the random undersampling [25] to resample the instances from the largest class randomly to make the number of instances in both positive and negative classes equal. While this approach can lead to loss of potentially useful data, we employ it during the cross-validation stage. Therefore, the data lost during one cross-validation stage is still retained during other stages.

2.7 Classification

Depending on the study, different classification algorithms can be used during the learning procedure such as Support Vector Machine (SVM), K-nearest neighbour (KNN), K-means, Bayesian classification, Artificial Neural Networks (ANN), Random forest, etc. Here we use KNN classification, when an object is classified by a majority vote of its neighbours, with the object being assigned to the class most common among its k nearest neighbours. In order to define the 'nearest neighbour', one needs to determine the distance between two items. We use the Cityblock (Manhattan) distance and 10 neighbours for classification.

2.8   Evaluation Criteria

In order to evaluate the performances of the classifiers, we have calculated the following measures:

Accuracy (ACC) is the ratio of correctly classified instances to the total number of instances.

Area Under Curve (AUC) is the are under the ROC (Receiver Operating Characteristic) curve, created by plotting True Positives (TP) rate (TPR) against False positives (FP) rate (FPR) at various threshold settings and illustrates the performance of a binary classifier as the discrimination threshold is varied. AUC is an important measure for commercial settings, where cost of misclassifying is high [26].

F-measure: harmonic mean of recall and precision defined as:

$$F = \frac{2TP}{N_{POS} + TP + FP} \tag{2}$$

here N_{POS} is the size of the positive class.

Kappa statistic compares accuracy of a system to accuracy of a random system:

$$kappa = \frac{ACC - ACC_{random}}{1 - ACC_{random}} \tag{3}$$

Matthews Correlation Coefficient (MCC) is a measure of the quality of binary classification, which takes into account the number of true and false positives (TP and FP) as well as true and false negatives (TN and FN), and is often regarded as a balanced measure, which can be used in case of ill-balanced classes.

$$MCC = \frac{TP \times TN - FP \times FN}{\sqrt{(TP + FP)(TP + FN)(TN + FP)(TN + FN)}} \tag{4}$$

3   Results

All programs for the statistical evaluation and computation were created by using MATLAB. First, we perform data cleaning (remove session data, which contains some missing data). Our keystroke feature extraction did not take into account large pauses in typing, when a user might have switched to another mode of input (e.g. mouse) or have taken a break from the computer. Outliers were removed by calculating the median and MAD for all keystroke timing features for each session and then removing the samples from each session which contain outliers. This resulted in the removal of 10.68% of the samples collected. The distribution of the cleared data is given in Fig. 2. We then calculated all of features using the filtered dataset. Feature values in each session were normalized to zero mean and 1 unit of standard deviation to facilitate analysis.

The most important features according to Student's t-test (for unequal variances) are presented in Fig. 3. These are: autocorrelation at lag 1 (for PP), mean zero-crossing rate (for PR), 5th L-moment (for RP), and number of outliers (for RR).

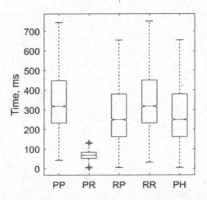

Fig. 2. Distribution of the data for the PP, PR, RP and RR time values

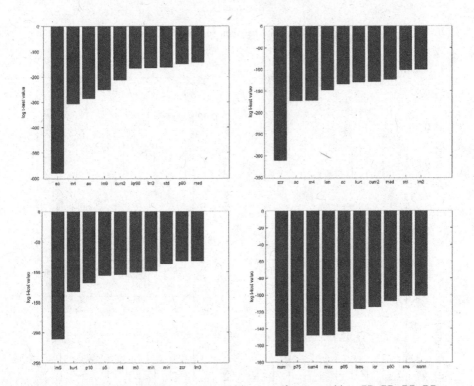

Fig. 3. Top-ranked variables as suggested by t-test feature ranking: PP, PR, RP, RR

We have transformed the keystroke data to the binary classification problem as follows. Let $S = \{S_1, \ldots, S_5\}$ be a session consisting of 5 consecutively performed trials without any interruption or break, and Δ be a difference between different trials during the same session, i.e. $\Delta = i - j, i > j$, here i and j are trial indices, and S_i was performed later than S_j thus implying that the level of subject's fatigue has increased as the subject was typing keys in-between. Then $S_i \in$ positive class and $S_j \in$ negative class.

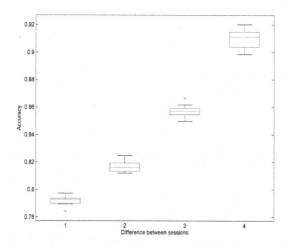

Fig. 4. Difference between sessions: accuracy

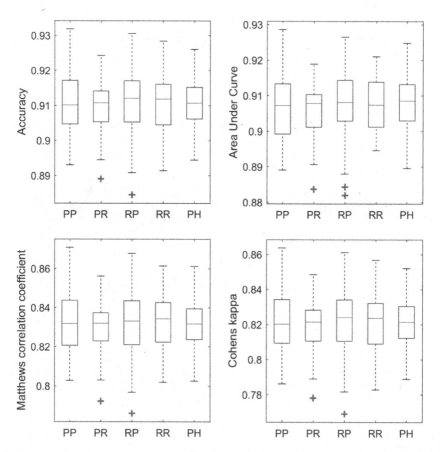

Fig. 5. Classification results (accuracy, AUC, MCC, kappa) for PP, PR, RP, RR and PH ($\Delta = 4$)

The performed classification for each $\Delta = 1..4$, where $\Delta = 1$ for adjacent trials where the least difference in fatigue level is expected and $\Delta = 4$ for most separated trials where the largest difference in fatigue level is expected

We have used 10-fold cross-validation from the stratified training results to evaluate our models, which is standard practice when the data set's size is limited. The classification accuracy (ACC) for different Δ values is presented in Fig. 4, while the detailed look at classification results $\Delta = 4$ for PP, PR, RP, RR and PH data is presented in Fig. 5 (kappa values are shown).

The summary of the classification results is presented in Table 1.

Table 1. Summary of results (best values in bold)

Data	Metric	Δ /99% confidence interval			
		1	2	3	4
PP	Acc	0.7942	0.8172	0.8542	0.9098
		0.7884–0.8000	0.8107–0.8238	0.8328–08756	0.8881–0.9316
	AUC	0.6522	0.7600	0.8358	0.9060
		0.6431–0.6613	0.7517–0.7683	0.8126–0.8591	0.8832–0.9288
	F	0.8725	0.8714	0.8840	0.9201
		0.8684–0.8766	0.8655–0.8773	0.8677–0.9004	0.9007–0.9395
	Kappa	0.5884	0.6344	0.7084	0.8196
		0.5767–0.6001	0.6213–0.6476	0.6657–0.7512	0.7761–0.8631
	MCC	0.4851	0.6332	0.7288	0.8312
		0.4700–0.5001	0.6223–0.6441	0.6925–0.7651	0.7931–0.8693
PR	Acc	0.8112	0.8186	0.8437	0.9108
		0.7979–0.8244	0.8122–0.8250	0.8331–0.8543	0.8917–0.9299
	AUC	0.7345	0.7829	0.8282	0.9080
		0.7202–0.7489	0.7741–0.7916	0.8172–0.8391	0.8894–0.9266
	F	0.8726	0.8642	0.8728	0.9200
		0.8629–0.8824	0.8594–0.8689	0.8635–0.8821	0.9023–0.9378
	Kappa	0.6223	0.6371	0.6874	0.8216
		0.5959–0.6487	0.6244–0.6499	0.6662–0.7086	0.7834–0.8599
	MCC	0.5283	0.6123	0.6917	0.8324
		0.4971–0.5595	0.5967–0.6278	0.6720–0.7114	0.7986–0.8662
RP	Acc	0.7749	0.7436	0.7413	0.9116
		0.7638–0.7860	0.7290–0.7582	0.7309–0.7518	0.8877–0.9356
	AUC	0.6769	0.6998	0.7241	0.9087
		0.6657–0.6881	0.6856–0.7140	0.7127–0.7355	0.8846–0.9328
	F	0.8515	0.8102	0.7900	0.9207
		0.8431–0.8598	0.7979–0.8225	0.7769–0.8031	0.8987–0.9428
	Kappa	0.5498	0.4872	0.4827	0.8232
		0.5276–0.5720	0.4580–0.6164	0.4618–0.5036	0.7554–0.8711
	MCC	0.4217	0.4412	0.4750	0.8334
		0.3935–0.4499	0.4115–0.4709	0.4550–0.4949	0.7905–0.8463
RR	Acc	0.7915	0.8228	0.8610	**0.9121**

(continued)

Table 1. (*continued*)

Data	Metric	Δ /99% confidence interval			
		1	2	3	4
		0.7851–0.7980	0.8093–0.8363	0.8512–0.8708	0.8933–0.9309
	AUC	0.6530	0.7681	0.8420	**0.9089**
		0.6463–0.6598	0.7587–0.7774	0.8292–0.8548	0.8898–0.9281
	F	0.8703	0.8746	0.8895	**0.9215**
		0.8658–0.8749	0.8629–0.8863	0.8812–0.8979	0.9042–0.9388
	Kappa	0.5831	0.6456	0.7220	**0.8241**
		0.5701–0.5961	0.6186–0.6726	0.7024–0.7415	0.7866–0.8617
	MCC	0.4855	0.6452	0.7397	**0.8354**
		0.4737–0.4973	0.6280–0.6625	0.7222–0.7573	0.8030–0.8679
PH	Acc	0.7775	0.7411	0.7427	0.9122
		0.7706–0.7843	0.7278–0.7545	0.7096–0.7759	0.8915–0.9329
	AUC	0.6789	0.6971	0.7240	0.9083
		0.6716–0.6862	0.6807–0.7136	0.6912–0.7569	0.887–0.9278
	F	0.8534	0.8085	0.7927	0.9221
		0.8473–0.8595	0.7989–0.8180	0.7652–0.8202	0.9021–0.9421
	Kappa	0.5549	0.4823	0.4854	0.8244
		0.5412–0.5686	0.4556–0.5089	0.4192–0.5517	0.7830–0.8658
	MCC	0.4254	0.4360	0.4766	0.8342
		0.4069–0.4439	0.4048–0.4671	0.4091–0.5442	0.7976–0.8708

The best results in terms of accuracy metrics were achieved for the RR data, though the difference is quite small. The results can be evaluated as follows. Landis and Koch [27] defines kappa values <0.20 as slight, 0.21–0.40 as fair, 0.41–0.60 as moderate, 0.61–0.80 as substantial, and >0.80 as almost perfect. Fleiss [28] describes kappa values <0.40 as poor, 0.40–0.75 as fair to good, and >0.75 as excellent. The results for MCC can be interpreted in the same as Pearson correlation coefficient, i.e., values larger than 0.7 may be interpreted as "very strong". Based on it, we can evaluate our classification results as excellent.

We have not found any similar work, which focuses on fatigue detection using KD. Somewhat similar work [29] focuses on boredom and frustration, i.e., affective states related to mental fatigue. Specifically, accuracies of the boredom and frustration classifiers using kNN, were 83.81% ± 5.51%, and 74.00% ± 6.07%, respectively.

4   Conclusion

The ability to recognize the psychophysical state of a person is an important part of developing Assisted Living Environments and intelligent systems, as well as increasing the ergonomics of a workplace and productivity of a worker [30]. In this paper, we have analysed the use of keystroke dynamics to recognize the signs of user fatigue. Our work is one of the first in the domain of fatigue recognition using typing behaviour data.

This work is important as it moves us closer to creating affectively-aware computer systems that can be widely deployed for effective management of office working and learning processes.

The method proposed in this work has allowed us to obtain very satisfactory results. Our results show, that we can achieve up to 91% accuracy (using key release-release (RR) data) in recognizing the relatively higher state of fatigue (in binary classification setting). Using statistical tests (two-tailed t-test), we have identified the most relevant features for analysing and using the keystroke dynamics data (press-press, press-release, release-press and release-release time series data) for identifying most statistically significant features (autocorrelation at lag 1, zerocrossing rate, 5th L-moment and the outlier rate). Adding other interaction-based features such as linguistic features of typed text could further improve the classification results.

However, for short input such as passwords, however, the lack of sufficient measurements presents a problem when evaluating the results statistically, because keystrokes, unlike other biometric features, provide a small amount of information about behaviour of an individual. Moreover, a care should be taken when the results are aggregated as the keystroke dynamics depends greatly upon keyboards used, environmental conditions, and entered texts.

With the preliminary models provided by our work, we plan to implement an adaptive version of the software that conducts modelling of user's state in the background and displays a notice suggesting to take a break or perform relaxation exercises when it detects that the user might be in a higher state of fatigue.

We have demonstrated the efficacy of this technique, which opens up opportunities for future research to refine, improve, and utilize this approach. In future work, more extensive experiments to collect more keystroke dynamics data with different people over an extended period under different stress conditions to achieve higher levels of fatigue and to increase our data set size will be performed aiming to develop user-specific models of fatigue.

Acknowledgements. The authors also would like to acknowledge the contribution of the COST Action IC1303– Architectures, Algorithms and Platforms for Enhanced Living Environments (AAPELE).

References

1. Canisius, S., Penzel, T.: Vigilance monitoring – review and practical aspects. Special Issue: Biosignal Processing (Part 3). Biomedizinische Technik **52**(1), 77–82 (2007)
2. Knauth, P., Hornberger, S.: Preventive and compensatory measures for shift workers. Occup. Med. **53**(2), 109–116 (2003)
3. Brandt, T., Stemmer, R., Rakotonirainy, A.: Affordable visual driver monitoring system for fatigue and monotony. In: IEEE International Conference on Systems, Man and Cybernetics, vol. 7, pp. 6451–6456 (2004)
4. Thiffault, P., Bergeron, J.: Monotony of road environment and driver fatigue: a simulator study. Accid. Anal. Prev. **35**(3), 381–391 (2003)

5. Vasiljevas, M., Gedminas, T., Ševčenko, A., Jančiukas, M., Blažauskas, T., Damaševičius, R.: Modelling eye fatigue in gaze spelling task. In: 12th IEEE International Conference on Intelligent Computer Communication and Processing (ICCP), pp. 95–102 (2016)
6. Wang, H.: Detection and alleviation of driving fatigue based on EMG and EMS/EEG using wearable sensor. In: Proceedings of the 5th EAI International Conference on Wireless Mobile Communication and Healthcare (MOBIHEALTH 2015), pp. 155–157 (2015)
7. Mascord, D.J., Walls, J., Starmer, G.A.: Fatigue and alcohol: interactive effects on human performance in driving-related tasks. In: Hartley, L.R. (ed.) Fatigue and Driving: Driver Impairment, Driver Fatigue and Driving Simulation. Taylor & Francis, pp. 189–205 (1995)
8. Trejo, Leonard J., Knuth, K., Prado, R., Rosipal, R., Kubitz, K., Kochavi, R., Matthews, B., Zhang, Y.: EEG-based estimation of mental fatigue: convergent evidence for a three-state model. In: Schmorrow, Dylan D., Reeves, Leah M. (eds.) FAC 2007. LNCS, vol. 4565, pp. 201–211. Springer, Heidelberg (2007). doi:10.1007/978-3-540-73216-7_23
9. Williamson, A.M., Feyer, A.M., Mattick, R.P., Friswell, R., Finlay-Brown, S.: Developing measures of fatigue using an alcohol comparison to validate the effects of fatigue on performance. Accid. Anal. Prev. **33**, 313–326 (2001)
10. Damasevicius, R., Maskeliunas, R., Venckauskas, A., Wozniak, M.: Smartphone user identity verification using gait characteristics. Symmetry **8**(10), 100 (2016)
11. Monrose, F., Rubin, A.D.: Keystroke dynamics as a biometric for authentication. Future Gener. Comp. Syst. **16**(4), 351–359 (2000)
12. Pisani, P.H., Lorena, A.C.: A systematic review on keystroke dynamics. J. Braz. Comp. Soc. **19**(4), 573–587 (2013)
13. Kolakowska, A.: Towards detecting programmers' stress on the basis of keystroke dynamics. In: Proceedings of Federated Conference on Computer Science and Information Systems (FedCSIS), pp. 1621–1626 (2016)
14. Douhou, S., Magnus, J.R.: The reliability of user authentication through keystroke dynamics. Stat. Neerl. **63**, 432–449 (2009)
15. Flior, E., Kowalski, K.: Continuous Biometric User Authentication in Online Examinations. In: 2010 Seventh International Conference on Information Technology: New Generations, Las Vegas, NV, pp. 488–492 (2010)
16. Rodrigues, M., Gonçalves, S., Carneiro, D., Novais, P., Fdez-Riverola, F.: Keystrokes and clicks: measuring stress on e-learning students. In: Casillas, J., Martínez-López, F., Vicari, R., De la Prieta, F. (eds.) Management Intelligent Systems. AISC, vol 220, pp. 119–126. Springer, Heidelberg (2013). doi:10.1007/978-3-319-00569-0_15
17. Gonçalves, S., Rodrigues, M., Carneiro, D., Fdez-Riverola, F., Novais, P.: Boosting learning: non-intrusive monitoring of student's efficiency. In: Mascio, T.D., Gennari, R., Vittorini, P., De la Prieta, F. (eds.) Methodologies and Intelligent Systems for Technology Enhanced Learning. AISC, vol. 374, pp. 73–80. Springer, Cham (2015). doi:10.1007/978-3-319-19632-9_10
18. Zimmermann, P., Guttormsen, S., Danuser, B., Gomez, P.: Affective Computing - A rationale for measuring mood with mouse and keyboard. Int. J. Occup. Saf. Ergon. **9**(4), 539–551 (2003)
19. Epp, C., Lippold, M., Mandryk, R.L.: Identifying emotional states using keystroke dynamics. In: Proceedings of the SIGCHI Conference on Human Factors in Computing Systems (CHI 2011). ACM, New York, pp. 715–724 (2011)
20. Giancardo, L., Sánchez-Ferro, A., Arroyo-Gallego, T., Butterworth, I., Mendoza, C.S., Montero, P., Matarazzo, M., Obeso, J.A., Gray, M.L., Estépar, R.S.J.: Computer keyboard interaction as an indicator of early Parkinson's disease. Sci. Rep. **6**, 34468 (2016)
21. Levanon, Y., Gefen, A., Lerman, Y., Portnoy, S., Ratzon, N.Z.: Key strike forces and their relation to high level of musculoskeletal symptoms. Saf. Health Work **7**(4), 347–353 (2016)

22. El-Abed, M., Dafer, M., Khayat, R.E.: RHU keystroke: a mobile-based benchmark for keystroke dynamics systems. In: 2014 International Carnahan Conference on Security Technology (ICCST), pp. 1–4 (2014)
23. Iglewicz, B., Hoaglin, D.: How to detect and handle outliers. ASQC Quality Press (1993)
24. Cateni, S., Colla, V., Vannucci, M.: A method for resampling imbalanced datasets in binary classification tasks for real-world problems. Neurocomputing 135, 32–41 (2014)
25. Kotsiantis, S., Kanellopoulos, D., Pintelas, P.: Handling imbalanced datasets: a review. GESTS Int. Trans. Comput. Sci. Eng. 30, 25–36 (2006)
26. Gomez, J.C., Boiy, E., Moens, M.F.: Highly discriminative statistical features for email classification. Knowl. Inf. Syst. 31, 23 (2012)
27. Landis, J.R., Koch, G.G.: The measurement of observer agreement for categorical data. Biometrics 33(1), 159–174 (1977)
28. Fleiss, J.L.: Statistical methods for rates and proportions, 2nd edn. John Wiley (1981)
29. Hernandez-Aguila, A., Valdez, M.G., Mancilla, A.: Affective states in software programming: classification of individuals based on their keystroke and mouse dynamics. Res. Comput. Sci. 87, 27–34 (2014)
30. Raudonis, V., Maskeliūnas, R., Stankevičius, K., Damaševičius, R.: Gender, age, colour, position and stress: how they influence attention at workplace? In: Gervasi, O., et al. (eds.) ICCSA 2017, Part V. LNCS, vol. 10408, pp. 248–264. Springer, Cham (2017)

Gender, Age, Colour, Position and Stress: How They Influence Attention at Workplace?

Vidas Raudonis[1], Rytis Maskeliūnas[2], Karolis Stankevičius[1],
and Robertas Damaševičius[3(⊠)]

[1] Department of Automation, Faculty of Electrical and Electronics Engineering,
Kaunas University of Technology, Kaunas, Lithuania
[2] Department of Multimedia Engineering, Faculty of Informatics,
Kaunas University of Technology, Kaunas, Lithuania
[3] Department of Software Engineering, Faculty of Informatics,
Kaunas University of Technology, Kaunas, Lithuania
robertas.damasevicius@ktu.lt

Abstract. We explore the relationship between attention and action, and focus on human reaction to stress in the Supervisory Control and Data Acquisition (SCADA) based Human Computer Interface (HCI) environment aiming to measure the reaction time and warn against attention deficit. To provoke human reaction we simulate several provocative situations mimicking real-world accidents while working on the industrial production line. During the simulation of the industrial line control, the subjects are presented on screen with affective visual stimuli imitating the possible accident and the reaction of subjects is tracked with a gaze tracker. We measure a subjects' response time from stimuli onset to the eye fixation (gaze time) and to the pressing of "line stop" button (press time). The reaction time patterns are analysed with respect to subject's gender, age, colour and position of stop sign. The results confirm the significance of gender, age, sign colour and position factors.

Keywords: Attention focus · Stress · Gaze-tracking · Cognitive · SCADA HCI

1 Introduction

Exploring the attention deficit and the relationship between attention and action is critical to designing modern pervasive computing systems [1] as well as safer industrial production systems. Human attention model covers the path from the perception of signals of attraction and the filtering of stimuli to the alteration of the motivation chain and allocation of attention resources to the execution of related plans to satisfy underlying motivations [2]. With computing technology becoming ubiquitously present, everyday routine interactions with technology should fit seamlessly and Human Computer Interfaces (HCI) should facilitate interaction at various levels of attention [3]. While in the industrial domain, the focus of human work has shifted from manual work to control and supervision of industrial lines and production processes, the problems of boredom and mental fatigue caused by low task loading in the monitoring of such systems still remain [4]. There is an increasing amount of evidence that during

© Springer International Publishing AG 2017
O. Gervasi et al. (Eds.): ICCSA 2017, Part V, LNCS 10408, pp. 248–264, 2017.
DOI: 10.1007/978-3-319-62404-4_19

mental fatigue, shifts in motivation may lower performance, making it very important to identify whether attention is diverted to stimuli that are unrelated to the task, or whether fatigued individuals are still focused on the task [5]. Furthermore, the individual differences in attention of workers can be used to adapt and optimize the industrial process to increase performance and minimize the risk of accidents [6].

Identifying human gaze or eye-movement ultimately serves the purpose of identifying an individual's focus of attention [7]. There is a known hypothesis that a human gaze is attracted to the scenes, which contain discontinuities in image features such as motion, colour, and texture [8]. Attention span can be provoked by new colour, and deprioritized by familiar colour [9]. Data from eye movements reveal that depending on the information displayed people tend to adapt to time pressure by accelerating visual scanning, by filtering information and by changing their scanning strategy [10]. Analysis of an attention bias in fear-relevant stimuli has shown that it can amplify the reaction time and response accuracy [11]. Fear of pain affects the bias of attention and can be detected by eye tracking [12] as test subjects direct immediate visual attention towards the location of sensory pain. A study of employing eye tracking methods to investigate attentional biases in contamination fear confirmed the hypothesis [13] as individuals had increased the duration of gaze fixation on the disgusted and fearful expressions. Increased dominance traits predict a more prolonged gaze towards masked anger [14]. Authors [15] investigated age factors and found that older adults showed an attentional preference toward happy faces, while young adults showed preference only toward afraid faces. Similar trend was noticed in [16] as adults (but not adolescents) have avoided the threatening images when collapsed across anxiety. Ocular behaviour was different in groups that possessed varying levels of performance in dynamic control tasks with complex visual components [17]. Visual attention can be identified using a velocity-threshold based fixation identification algorithm to identify fixations and divide them into different attention clusters [18]. Analytical eye fatigue models can be used to evaluate individual muscular eye fatigue and suggest time breaks required to regain performance of visual tasks [19].

These ideas motivated the introduction of 'shocking' (stressful) images to the industrial standard, SCADA (Supervisory Control and Data Acquisition), based HCI scenarios, refocusing a user on the control task in the high attention spanning industrial line applications, which currently are still very conservative and lack of proper usability design and user experience engineering, especially in the context of Industry 4.0 [20]. Additionally, we investigate the influence of age, gender, colour and location factors on human reaction times.

2 Gaze Point Detection

To perform the required experiments we have used a custom eye tracking system developed by the UAB "Power of Eye" company. The gaze-tracking device is equipped with a near infrared light (NIR) source and the camera that is capable to detect NIR light (see Fig. 1). The eye images captured in NIR have a very clear region of the eye pupil and corneal reflection [21]. The gaze detection algorithm is built

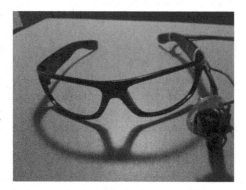

Fig. 1. The developed eye gaze tracking system

around the detection of the eye pupil and the points of corneal reflections (see Fig. 2) as explained in detail below.

The coordinates of the mentioned regions correlate linearly with the gaze point [22]. Gaze point is the intersection point of a gaze vector with the surface of the computer screen [23]. The pupil of the user's eye is detected by computing the average intensity value and the standard deviation of each new eye image $\Gamma_k(u,v)$, where $k = 1, 2, 3$ is a colour channel, and u and v are the positions of the pixel in the image matrix. The pixel value of the grayscale image is acquired by computing the mean colour of the three colour channels:

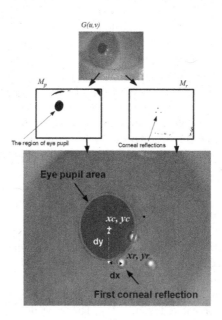

Fig. 2. The measurements needed for gaze point mapping

$$G(u, v) = \frac{1}{3} \sum_{k=1}^{3} \Gamma_k(u,v) . \tag{1}$$

Mean intensity and standard deviation of the grayscale image is calculated using Eqs. 2 and 3:

$$\mu = \frac{\sum_{u=1}^{U} \sum_{v=1}^{V} G(u, v)}{U \cdot V} , \tag{2}$$

$$\sigma = \sqrt{\frac{\sum_{u=1}^{U} \sum_{v=1}^{V} (G(u, v) - \mu)^2}{U \cdot V - 1}} . \tag{3}$$

The image matrix $G(u, v)$ is indexed according to the estimated statistical values based on the condition shown in Eqs. 4 and 5. Mapping image M_P is computed using Eq. 4 and used for accurate pupil detection, while mapping image M_R is estimated using Eq. 5 and used for detection of the corneal reflection points as follows:

$$M_P(u, v) = \begin{cases} 1, & \text{if } G(u, v) < \mu - 2\sigma \\ 0, & \text{otherwise} \end{cases} , \tag{4}$$

$$M_R(u, v) = \begin{cases} 1, & \text{if } G(u, v) > \mu + 3\sigma \\ 0, & \text{otherwise} \end{cases} . \tag{5}$$

The task of the eye pupil detection is reduced to the search of a round dark region in the mapping image M_p. The geometrical centre and area of each dark region are measured in the mapping image. The geometric centre of the non-overlapping closed polygon by N vertices $(x(i), y(i))$ is calculated using Eqs. 6, 7 and 8. The area of the non-self-intersecting polygon is:

$$A(j) = \frac{1}{2} \sum_{i=0}^{N-1} (x_j(i)y_j(i+1) - x_j(i+1)y_j(i)) . \tag{6}$$

The coordinates of the geometrical centre of the polygonsis $C = (C_x, C_y)$, here:

$$C_x(j) = \frac{1}{6A} \sum_{i=0}^{N-1} (x_j(i) + x_j(i+1)) (x_j(i)y_j(i+1) - x_j(i+1)y_j(i)) , \tag{7}$$

$$C_y(j) = \frac{1}{6A} \sum_{i=0}^{N-1} (y_j(i) + y_j(i+1)) (x_j(i)y_j(i+1) - x_j(i+1)y_j(i)) . \tag{8}$$

In Eqs. 8, 9 and 10, the vertices are assumed to be numbered by the order of their occurrence along the polygon's perimeter, and the vertex $(x(N), y(N))$ is assumed to be the same as $(x(0), y(0))$. The j-th region is indexed as the region of the eye pupil if it satisfies the following condition:

$$x_c, y_c = C_x(j), \ C_y(j) \ if \ A_{min} \leq A \leq A_{max} \,. \tag{9}$$

here $A_{min} = \pi R_{min}^2$ is the minimal limit and $A_{max} = \pi R_{max}^2$ is the maximal limit of the pupil size, and x_c and y_c are the coordinates of the detected eye pupil centre.

When the pupil centre is detected, the first closest reflection point is searched in the mapping image M_R. Usually, it is the lower right corner of the triangle. Euclidean distance D_r is estimated to the mapping image M_R points, if these points form a triangle pattern. There are k points in M_R and the distance to each point is expressed as:

$$D_r(k) = \sqrt{(x_c - u_r)^2 + (y_c - v_r)^2}, \ if \ M_R(u, v) = 1. \tag{10}$$

The coordinates of the corneal reflection x_r and y_r are estimated by finding the minimal distance D_r using Eq. 11:

$$x_r, y_r = \min_k(D_r(k)) \,. \tag{11}$$

The resulting gaze point on the computer screen is obtained by interpolating the positions of the pupil centre and the first corneal reflection. The displacements along horizontal axis and vertical axis are expressed as follows:

$$dx = x_c - x_r, \ dy = y_c - y_r \,. \tag{12}$$

The linear approximation to gaze point can be expressed as:

$$X = a_{11} + a_{12}dx, \ Y = a_{21} + a_{22}dy \,. \tag{13}$$

here X and Y are the coordinates of the mouse cursor on the computer screen. Using the least squares method the coefficient is calculated by minimizing the error functions $E_x(a)$ and $E_y(a)$:

$$E_x(a) = X - (a_{11} + a_{22}dx), \ E_y(a) = Y - (a_{21} + a_{22}dy) \,. \tag{14}$$

The system calibration procedure is executed each time, when a user starts working with the gaze tracking system. Custom made program plots 9 target points on the computer screen in the sequence. The mean absolute difference between the target and estimated gaze points is used as an efficacy measure.

3   Experiment Settings

For experiments we use a portable DELL Notebook Inspiron N5110 computer with 15.6" HD LED screen, Intel Core i7 2670QM 3.1 GHz CPU, 8 GB DDR3 RAM, 500 GB HDD, and GeForce GT525 1 GB graphics card.

For simulation of an industrial process, we use Wonderware InTouch, an industrial automation and information management software that can create a variety of SCADA environments. Here the InTouch software is used to imitate dangerous accidents in the

Fig. 3. Hardware and software user interface used in the experiments

industrial production process, and invoke human reaction to stressful situations (see Fig. 3).

We have modelled three industrial processes, which may result in accidents: drilling with automatic drill, crushing of hard materials and sawing. In all cases, the accidents while working may include severe injuries, dismemberment or even death.

The collection of data was carried out in a normal environment, while sitting at the ergonomic desk. As the gaze tracking device used an infrared camera, which is not sensitive to the light intensity, the backlight was not important. The data from 20 subjects (18 men and 2 women), aged from 20 to 31 (mean = 24.4) years was collected. The subjects were introduced with the rules: the mouse is always considered to be roughly in the middle of the screen. In case of an accident, the subject has as quickly as possible to press the STOP button or any of the STOP buttons if more than one is shown. All STOP buttons are active regardless of their on-screen position and colour. The simulation program displays a worker and an object that is moved on the conveyor belt to be processed until an accident occurs. Then, the program displays the shock-inducing picture (e.g., the real-world photo of the cut-off human hand) and animated picture of an injured worker standing next. The subject (imitating the work of an operator of an industrial line) has to press the STOP button to stop the machine. The time required to take notice of an accident (gaze time) and to press the button (press time) is recorded. Each trial is repeated for 5 times, and the average result is saved. The following scenarios described below were considered.

3.1 Human Reaction Time Testing

The STOP button is shown to the subject at random positions of the screen and his/her reaction time (both visual (gaze landing) and muscular (button pressing)) is measured. Each trial is repeated for 5 times, and an average value is recorded.

3.2   Simulation of Drilling Accident

The software simulates the work of an industrial drill. An object arrives by the conveyor belt, the drill drills a hole in it, and a simulated worker must take the object off the conveyor belt. If a drill injures his hand, a real accident photograph is shown and the subject must press the STOP button. The scenario is illustrated in Fig. 4.

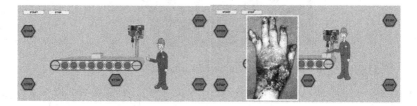

Fig. 4. Simulation of drilling accident (before and after an accident)

3.3   Simulation of Crusher Accident

The software simulates the work of an industrial crusher. Solid materials (such as wood) are shown being thrown into the crusher. Next, an animated worker is shown coming to check the machine, but he/she slips accidentally and falls into the crusher. A real-world accident photograph is shown and the subject should press the STOP button. The scenario is illustrated in Fig. 5.

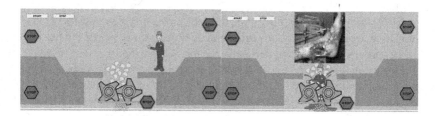

Fig. 5. Simulation of crusher accident (before and after an accident)

3.4   Simulation of Saw Accident

The software simulates the work of an industrial saw. An object arrives by the conveyor belt and is cut in half by the saw. Next, a simulated worker comes to check if everything is working well, but the saw catches his/her clothing sleeve, and cuts off the human hand. A real-world accident photograph is shown and the subject should press the STOP button. The scenario is illustrated in Fig. 6.

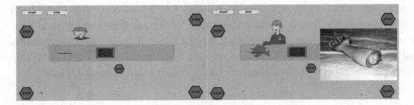

Fig. 6. Simulation of saw accident (before and after an accident)

3.5 Simulation of Effects of STOP Sign Colour and Placement Position

In this scenario, three STOP signs of different colour (red, yellow and green) are placed at different positions (left, right, top, bottom and near the industrial machine) on the screen (see Fig. 7). The industrial accident scenario (drilling, crusher or saw) is simulated and the selections of subjects is analysed with respect to colour and location preferences.

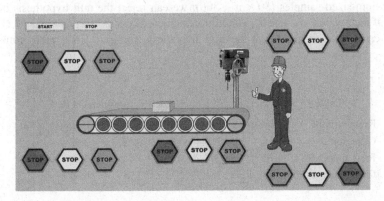

Fig. 7. Color and position of STOP signs in simulation experiments (drilling is shown) (Color figure online)

4 Hypotheses

We formulate the following hypotheses for our research:

H1. Men have better reaction time than women.
H2. Younger people have better reaction time than older people.
H3. Stress increases the reaction time.
H4. The selection of colour can influence the reaction time.
H5. The placement of interface elements can influence the reaction time.

We evaluate each hypothesis using paired t-test on the null hypothesis that population samples have equal means without assuming equal variances as well as using the random permutation test to evaluate probability that a random value taken from one population is smaller than a random value taken from another population.

For statistical processing of results we use the z-test to check for data normality, the paired t-test to determine if compared sample have equal means and bootstrapping (random permutation with replacement) for calculating standard deviations.

5 Results

The results are presented for different experiment scenarios described in the previous section

5.1 Measurement of Human Reaction Time

The statistical characteristics of the reaction time data is presented in Table 1. The distribution of values was evaluated using normality based on skewness and kurtosis [24]. Skewness is a measure of the lack of symmetry. Kurtosis is a measure of outlier. For medium-sized samples ($50 < n < 300$), we can reject the null hypothesis of normality, if the z-value of z-test is over 3.29, which corresponds with an alpha level 0.05. In our case, we can not reject the null hypothesis for gaze time, press time, and gaze-to-press time.

Table 1. Characteristics of human reaction measurement data

Reaction time	Min	Max	Mean	Std	Skewness	Kurtosis	z-val
Gaze time	151	298	210.48	35.08	0.47	2.52	0
Press time	810	1478	995.25	150.9	1.74	5.89	0
Gaze-to-press time	640	1223	784.77	132.7	1.95	6.45	0

We confirm hypothesis H1 for gaze reaction (t-test p = 0.012; random permutation test p-value = 0.778): men have better reaction time than women (difference is 38 ± 21 ms), see the probability density functions in Fig. 8; but we can not confirm it for press reaction (t-test p = 0.13; random permutation test p-value = 0.611): men have only marginally better reaction time than women (difference is 22 ± 29 ms); and gaze-to-press reaction (t-test p = 0.13; random permutation test p-value = 0.572): the difference is 15 ± 20.66.

There is also a relatively strong (>0.4) correlation of reaction times with the age which is supported by random permutation test p-value: for gaze time, Pearson correlation is 0.45, p-value = 0.967. Assuming linear dependency between age and reaction time, with each year of age, the gaze reaction time increases by 6.8 ± 3.5 ms, press reaction time by 15 ± 10 ms, and gaze-to-press reaction time by 9 ± 7 ms.

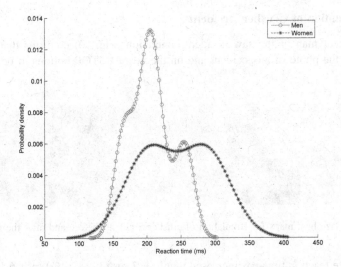

Fig. 8. Visual reaction (gaze) time of men and women

5.2 Simulation of Drilling Accident

The gaze heat map of the drilling process and accident simulation (Fig. 9) shows that the gaze of subjects is attracted by activity and new emerging and eye-catching objects. When an accident is simulated, the gaze focuses on the photo of an accident and on the nearest STOP button to be pressed.

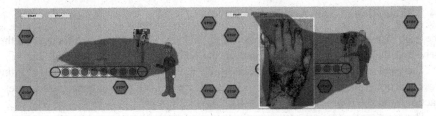

Fig. 9. Gaze heat maps for simulation of drilling accident (before and after the accident)

The gaze reaction time has increased by 71 ± 9 ms ($33 \pm 13\%$) ($p = 5 \cdot 10^{-43}$), the press reaction time by 169 ± 26 ms ($32 \pm 5\%$) ($p = 9 \cdot 10^{-31}$), and the gaze-to-press reaction time by 97 ± 22 ms ($32 \pm 5\%$) ($p = 1 \cdot 10^{-16}$). The reaction time of men has increased more than that of women, for the gaze time 34 ± 24 ms ($p = 0.006$), for press time 147 ± 53 ms ($p = 1 \cdot 10^{-7}$), for the gaze-to-press time 113 ± 41 ms ($p = 1 \cdot 10^{-7}$). The increase of reaction time was larger for older people by 3.3 ± 2.8 ms per each year of age. However, Pearson correlation is weak (0.28) and random permutation test p-value (probability that an older person has longer reaction time) is 0.896. The differences for press and gaze-to-press times were not significant.

5.3 Simulation of Crusher Accident

The gaze heat man of the saw accident simulation (Fig. 10) confirms that the gaze focuses on the photo of an accident and on the nearest STOP buttons to be pressed.

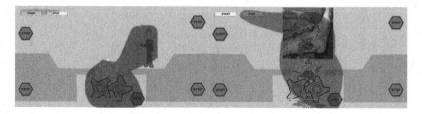

Fig. 10. Gaze heat maps for simulation of crusher accident (before and after the accident)

The gaze reaction time has increased by 66 ± 7 ms ($32 \pm 14\%$) ($p = 6 \cdot 10^{-49}$), the press reaction time by 156 ± 26 ms ($17 \pm 12\%$) ($p = 7 \cdot 10^{-27}$), and the gaze-to-press reaction time by 89 ± 22 ms ($13 \pm 9\%$, $p = 5 \cdot 10^{-14}$). The reaction time of men has increased more than that of women, for the gaze time 31 ± 20 ms ($p = 0.003$), for the press time 139 ± 54 ms ($p = 1 \cdot 10^{-6}$), for the gaze-to-press time 107 ± 42 ms ($p = 1 \cdot 10^{-6}$). The reaction time increase was larger for older people: the increase was larger 3.0 ± 2.6 ms per each year of age. However, Pearson correlation is weak (0.29) and random permutation test p-value is 0.898. Again, the differences were not significant for press and gaze-to-press times.

5.4 Simulation of Saw Accident

The gaze heat map of the saw simulation (Fig. 11) also shows that gaze focuses on the scene and the photo of an accident and on the STOP buttons to be pressed.

The gaze reaction time has increased by 73 ± 9 ms ($34 \pm 13\%$; $p = 2 \cdot 10^{-45}$), the press reaction time by 174 ± 26 ms ($18 \pm 9\%$; $p = 1 \cdot 10^{-32}$), and the gaze-to-press reaction time by 100 ± 22 ms ($p = 1 \cdot 10^{-17}$).

The reaction time of men has increased more than that of women, for the gaze time 36 ± 24 ms ($p = 0.03$), for the press time 150 ± 52 ms ($p = 5 \cdot 10^{-8}$), for the gaze-to-press time 114 ± 40 ms ($p = 1 \cdot 10^{-7}$).

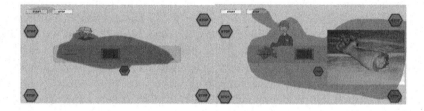

Fig. 11. Gaze heat maps for simulation of saw accident (before and after the accident)

The reaction time increase was larger for older people by 3.4 ± 2.8 ms per each year of age. However, correlation is Pearson correlation is weak (0.28) and random permutation test p-value (probability that an older person has longer reaction time) is 0.899. Again, the differences were not significant for press and gaze-to-press times.

5.5   Simulation of Effects of STOP Sign Colour and Placement Position

The gaze heat map (Fig. 12) shows that the position of the STOP button is more important than the colour of the button in all three simulations.

In this scenario, the gaze time was 277 ± 51 ms and press time was 1128 ± 111 ms (a decrease of 36 ± 22 ms, $p = 3 \cdot 10^{-4}$) for drilling simulation. The gaze time was 279 ± 55 ms and the press time was 1133 ± 136 ms for crusher simulation. The gaze time was 277 ± 47 ms and the press time was 1086 ± 128 ms (a decrease of 82 ± 24 ms, $p = 3 \cdot 10^{-11}$) for saw simulation. Change values for

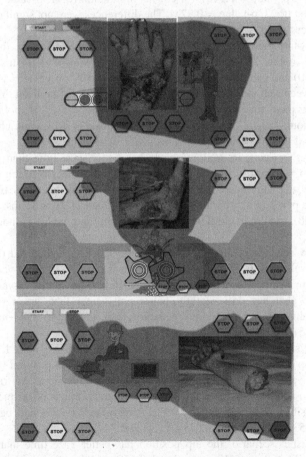

Fig. 12. Gaze heat maps in sign colour and position study (drilling, crusher, saw simulations) (Color figure online)

insignificant p are not given. Differences in reaction times between different scenarios are not statistically significant. In two scenarios out of three, there was a statistically significant decrease in press time, which can be explained by more convenient placement of STOP signs and the use of colours.

The gender related differences remained significant. The gaze time was smaller for men than for women: 27 ± 28 ms (p = 0.04; p-value = 0.638) for drilling scenario, 38 ± 28 ms (p = 0.009; p-value = 0.722) for crusher scenario, 50 ± 15 ms (p = $1 \cdot 10^{-8}$; p-value = 0.833) for saw scenario. The press time was smaller for men than for women: 34 ± 26 ms (p = 0.01; p-value = 0.688) for drilling simulation, insignificant for crusher simulation, 220 ± 20 ms (p = $1 \cdot 10^{-42}$; p-value = 0.950) for saw simulation.

Assuming linear dependency between age and reaction time, with each year of age, the gaze reaction time increases by 8.4 ± 5.7 ms (standard deviation calculated by bootstrapping) for drilling simulation and by 9.4 ± 4.9 ms for crusher simulation. For age-related gaze time reaction, Pearson correlation was weak to strong: for drilling simulation (0.37, p-value = 0.946), for crusher simulation (0.41, p-value = 0.963) and for saw imitation (0.22, p-value = 0.827). The differences were not significant for press and gaze-to-press times.

When analysing the reaction data by the colour of the STOP sign, for the drilling scenario yellow colour has better gaze time than red colour(48 ± 14 ms; p = $1 \cdot 10^{-9}$; p-value = 0.850) and green colour (59 ± 19 ms; p = $1 \cdot 10^{-8}$; p-value = 1.0), while the difference between red and green colours is not statistically significant. Yellow colour also has smaller press time than red colour (48 ± 30 ms; p = 0.001; p-value = 0.627) and green colour (83 ± 49 ms; p = 0.001; p-value = 0.70), while the difference between red and green colours is not statistically significant.

For the crusher scenario, yellow colour has better gaze time than green colour (27 ± 19 ms; p = 0.01; p-value = 0.613), while the differences between other colours are not statistically significant. Yellow colour also has better press time than red (159 ± 38 ms; p = $2 \cdot 10^{-13}$; p-value = 0.814) and green (186 ± 51 ms; p = $1 \cdot 10^{-10}$; p-value = 0.790), while the difference between red and green is not statistically significant.

For the saw scenario, yellow colour has better gaze time than red (29 ± 16 ms; p = $6 \cdot 10^{-4}$; p-value = 0.632) and green (55 ± 16 ms; p = $7 \cdot 10^{-10}$; p-value = 0.794), while red colour scores better than green (26 ± 16 ms; p = 0.002; p-value = 0.750). Yellow colour also has only slightly better press time than green (65 ± 64 ms; p = 0.04; p-value = 0.555), and red is better than green (46 ± 41 ms; p = 0.02; p-value = 0.625).

When analysing the reaction data by the position of the STOP sign, for the drilling scenario the top position has better gaze time than the bottom position (61 ± 22 ms; p = $9 \cdot 10^{-7}$; p-value = 0.950) and only marginally better than the right position (20 ± 19 ms; p = 0.04; p-value = 0.616). The top position has better press time than the bottom position (61 ± 35 ms; p = $8 \cdot 10^{-4}$; p-value = 0.749) and better than the near position (53 ± 41 ms; p = 0.01; p-value = 0.749).

For the crusher scenario, the top position has better gaze time than the bottom position (44 ± 20 ms; p = $5 \cdot 10^{-5}$; p-value = 0.650) and the near position is better than the right position (42 ± 19 ms; p = $2 \cdot 10^{-5}$; p-value = 0.733). The top position has lower press time than the bottom position (112 ± 35 ms; $p = 1 \cdot 10^{-7}$; p-value = 1.0) and lower press time than the near position (60 ± 51 ms; $p = 0.02$; p-value = 0.583).

For the saw scenario, the bottom position has better gaze time than the top position (35 ± 19 ms; $p = 4 \cdot 10^{-4}$; p-value = 0.727) and the right position (44 ± 15 ms; $p = 6 \cdot 10^{-8}$; p-value = 0.80).The left position has better gaze time than the bottom position (44 ± 22 ms; $p = 2 \cdot 10^{-4}$; p-value = 0.750), the near position (54 ± 22 ms; $p = 3 \cdot 10^{-6}$; p-value = 0.821) and the right position (88 ± 12 ms; $p = 4 \cdot 10^{-24}$; p-value = 1.0). The bottom position has only slightly better gaze time than the top position (68 ± 65 ms; $p = 0.04$; p-value = 0.626) and the right position (102 ± 60 ms; $p = 0.001$; p-value = 0.733).The left position has better gaze time than the bottom position (135 ± 75 ms; $p = 6 \cdot 10^{-4}$; p-value = 0.733), the near position (222 ± 53 ms; $p = 3 \cdot 10^{-13}$; p-value = 0.955) and the right position (237 ± 53 ms; $p = 2 \cdot 10^{-13}$; p-value = 1.0).

The results show that there is no best position for all considered scenarios, but based on the results of the rank analysis (evaluating the one factor vs. all remaining factors, and ranking the results from best to worst, see Fig. 13), the Left position, on average, is more preferred than other positions.

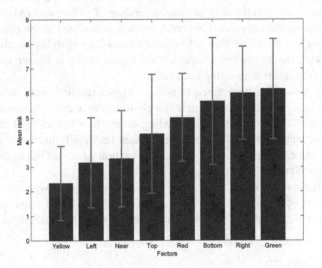

Fig. 13. Mean ranks of colour and position factors

6 Evaluation and Discussion

We have performed the influence of various factors (both subject and interface related) on the reaction times in the simulated context of the industrial workplace. The analysis of data confirmed the gender differences between men and women also noted by other studies, as well as age-related differences, and the influence of stress, colour and position of elements of user interface (confirming the hypotheses H1–H5).

Our results show that men have higher visual reaction times (38 ± 21 ms). The results can explained by the differences between masculine and feminine visual processing systems. In other studies, men also have been demonstrated to exhibit faster reaction times to a visual stimulus with a difference of reaction time ranging between 16 ms [25] and 48 ms [26]. However, men have been shown to cope worse with the increase of visual complexity of tasks, when a stressful image was added to the task.

Assuming linear dependency, reaction time increases with age (6.8 ± 3.5 ms/y for gaze time, 15 ± 10 ms/y for press time), which is consistent with other studies on effects of aging on visual reaction time [26]. Older subjects also had worse reaction time to stress and increased visual complexity of the task than younger subjects.

The introduction of the element of stress (real-world graphic photo of an accident) has reduced the attention and increased the reaction times (by 66–73 ms for gaze time, and by 156–169 ms for press time) in all three industrial simulations. However, the increase in reaction time observed by an introduction of a stress-inducing photo at least in some part may be explained by the increased overall visual complexity of the simulation scene.

The analysis of the effects of colour show that the use of yellow colour for STOP button has allowed to achieve better reaction time than red and green colours. The results are consistent with the common understanding of yellow and red colours as the colours of warning, danger or alert, whereas green is considered as the colour of safety [27]. Yellow may score better than red because of its better visibility because of higher luminosity. Also the sensitivity of the human vision peaks is higher in the yellow portion of the spectrum than in the red one.

The Left position has been noted to achieve higher reaction times as compared to other positions (though the position near the photo of the accident is almost as good). This may be explained by the natural reading order from left to right and common layout order in web-based and computer interfaces (especially on the Windows platform), which place the primary (or confirmatory) action (such as OK) to the left of the secondary (cancellation) action.

Note the limitations of our study: only a minority of subjects were women, and all subjects were of young age (20–31 years, mean = 24.4). A small population size (20 subjects) in some cases did not allow to achieve statistical significance of the results.

7   Conclusions

We simulated real-world accidents while working on the industrial production line and measured the reaction time of subjects. Our results confirm the influence of gender and age, as well as the influence of affective stimuli (stress), and the use of colour and position of graphical elements of user interface on visual reaction times. The results of the paper can be used by HCI designers to design usable industrial accident prevention systems.

References

1. Fersch, A.: Attention, please! IEEE Pervasive Comput. **13**(1), 48–54 (2014)
2. Gollan, B., Ferscha, A.: Directed Effort - a generic measure and for higher level behavior analysis. In: International Conference on Physiological Computing Systems, PhyCS 2014, pp. 83–90 (2014)
3. Bakker, S., Niemantsverdriet, K.: The interaction-attention continuum: considering various levels of human attention in interaction design. Int. J. Des. **10**(2), 1–14 (2016)
4. Cummings, M.L., Gao, F., Thornburg, K.M.: Boredom in the workplace: a new look at an old problem. Hum. Factors **58**(2), 279–300 (2016)
5. Hopstaken, J.F., van der Linden, D., Bakker, A.B., Kompier, M.A.J., Leung, Y.K.: Shifts in attention during mental fatigue: Evidence from subjective, behavioral, physiological, and eye-tracking data. J. Exp. Psychol. Hum. Percept. Perform. **42**(6), 878–889 (2016)
6. Jipp, M.: Reaction times to consecutive automation failures: a function of working memory and sustained attention. Hum. Factors **58**(8), 1248–1261 (2016)
7. Stiefelhagen, R., Finke, M., Yang, J., Waibel, A.: From gaze to focus of attention. In: Huijsmans, D.P., Smeulders, A.W.M. (eds.) VISUAL 1999. LNCS, vol. 1614, pp. 765–772. Springer, Heidelberg (1999). doi:10.1007/3-540-48762-X_94
8. Ballard, D.H., Hayhoe, M.M.: Modelling the role of task in the control of gaze. Vis. Cogn. **17**, 1185–1204 (2009)
9. Horstmann, G., Herwig, A.: Novelty biases attention and gaze in a surprise trial. Atten. Percept. Psychophys. **78**, 69 (2016)
10. Pieters, R., Warlop, L.: Visual attention during brand choice: the impact of time pressure and task motivation. Int. J. Res. Mark. **16**, 1–16 (1999)
11. Rosa, P.J., Esteves, F., Arriaga, P.: Effects of fear-relevant stimuli on attention: integrating gaze data with subliminal exposure. In: IEEE International Symposium on Medical Measurements and Applications (MeMeA), pp. 1–6 (2014)
12. Yang, Z., Jackson, T., Gao, X., Chen, H.: Identifying selective visual attention biases related to fear of pain by tracking eye movements within a dot-probe paradigm. PAIN **153**(8), 1742–1748 (2012)
13. Armstrong, T., Olatunji, B.O., Sarawgi, S., Simmons, C.: Orienting and maintenance of gaze in contamination fear: biases for disgust and fear cues. Behav. Res. Ther. **48**(5), 402–408 (2010)
14. Terburg, D., Hooiveld, N., Aarts, H., Kenemans, J.L., van Honk, J.: Eye tracking unconscious face-to-face confrontations dominance motives prolong gaze to masked angry faces. Psychol. Sci. **22**(3), 314–319 (2011)
15. Isaacowitz, D.M., Wadlinger, H.A., Goren, D., Wilson, H.R.: Selective preference in visual fixation away from negative images in old age? An eye-tracking study. Psychol. Aging **21**(1), 40–48 (2006)
16. Shechner, T., Jarcho, J.M., Wong, S., Leibenluft, E., Pine, D.S., Nelson, E.E.: Threats, rewards, and attention deployment in anxious youth and adults: an eye tracking study. Biol. Psychol. **122**, 121–129 (2017)
17. Du, W., Kim, J.H.: Performance-based eye-tracking analysis in a dynamic monitoring task. In: Schmorrow, D.D., Fidopiastis, C.M. (eds.) AC 2016. LNCS, vol. 9744, pp. 168–177. Springer, Cham (2016). doi:10.1007/978-3-319-39952-2_17
18. Wang, Y., Chen, X., Chen, Z.: Towards region-of-attention analysis in eye tracking protocols. Electron. Imaging **VII**(6), 1–6 (2016)

19. Vasiljevas, M., Gedminas, T., Ševčenko, A., Jančiukas, M., Blažauskas, T., Damaševičius, R.: Modelling eye fatigue in gaze spelling task. In: 2016 IEEE 12th International Conference on Intelligent Computer Communication and Processing (ICCP), pp. 95–102 (2016)
20. Pfeiffer, T., Hellmers, J., Schön, E.-M., Thomaschewski, J.: Empowering user interfaces for industrie 4.0. Proc. IEEE **104**(5), 986–996 (2016)
21. Raudonis, V.: Development and investigation of portable eye tracking system: theory and practice. Lambert, Saarbrucken (2012)
22. Kaklauskas, A., Vlasenko, A., Raudonis, V., Zavadskas, E.K.: Intelligent pupil analysis of student progress system. In: Yang, D. (ed.) Informatics in Control, Automation and Robotics. LNEE, vol 133, pp. 165–168. Springer, Heidelberg (2011). doi:10.1007/978-3-642-25992-0_24
23. Raudonis, V., Paulauskaitė-Taraševičienė, A., Kižauskienė, L.: The Gaze tracking system with natural head motion compensation. Informatica **23**(1), 105–124 (2012)
24. Kim, H.-Y.: Statistical notes for clinical researchers: assessing normal distribution (2) using skewness and kurtosis. Restor. Dent. Endod. **38**(1), 52–54 (2013)
25. Jain, A., Bansal, R., Kumar, A., Singh, K.D.: A comparative study of visual and auditory reaction times on the basis of gender and physical activity levels of medical first year students. Int. J. Appl. Basic Med. Res. **5**(2), 124–127 (2015)
26. Tun, P.A., Lachman, M.E.: Age differences in reaction time and attention in a national telephone sample of adults: education, sex, and task complexity matter. Dev. Psychol. **44**(5), 1421–1429 (2008)
27. Silic, M., Cyr, D., Back, A., Holzer, A.: Effects of color appeal, perceived risk and culture on user's decision in presence of warning banner message. In: 50th Hawaii International Conference on Sciences (HICSS), pp. 527–536 (2007)

Workshop on Quantum Mechanics: Computational Strategies and Applications (QMCSA 2017)

The Astrochemical Observatory: Experimental and Computational Focus on the Chiral Molecule Propylene Oxide as a Case Study

Andrea Lombardi[1]($\boxtimes$), Federico Palazzetti[1], Vincenzo Aquilanti[1,2,3], Fernando Pirani[1], and Piergiorgio Casavecchia[1]

[1] Dipartimento di Chimica, Biologia e Biotecnologie, Università di Perugia, Perugia, Italy
ebiu2005@gmail.com,
{federico.palazzetti,vincenzo.aquilanti,fernando.pirani, piergiorgio.casavecchia}@unipg.it
[2] Istituto di Struttura della Materia, Consiglio Nazionale delle Ricerche, Rome, Italy
[3] Instituto de Fisica, Universidade Federal da Bahia, Salvador, Brazil

Abstract. The recent observation of propylene oxide in the interstellar medium has raised unusually large interest in view of the prototypical role that this molecule plays in chemical and biophysical investigations of chirality, a phenomenon that transversely pervades modern science for implications ranging from the mechanism of the origin and early evolution of life (homochirality) to key aspects of industrial and pharmaceutical chemistry, such as asymmetric synthesis. Here we present a survey of recent advances, designing and illustrating a number of possible experiments for the demonstration of chiral effects in the dynamics of the intermolecular interactions, suggesting a scenario for a stereo-directional origin of chiral discrimination.

Keywords: Scattering experiments · Chirality · Molecular dynamics · Molecular beams · Propylene oxide

1 Introduction

The growth of a new interdisciplinary field of scientific research, astrochemistry [1], as the investigation of the chemical nature of the universe, originates from astronomical and radioastronomical observations, space mission data collections, laboratory experiments, theoretical and computational modeling. This search has already led to the identification of a continuously increasing number of molecules, even complex organic molecules, but progress in space exploration and direct sampling promises further insight into of the chemical evolution of the universe, since its formation. The discovery of amino-acids and other protobiological molecules in meteorites, and possibly in other space environments, has contributed to the debate on the origin of the building blocks of life in the

© Springer International Publishing AG 2017
O. Gervasi et al. (Eds.): ICCSA 2017, Part V, LNCS 10408, pp. 267–280, 2017.
DOI: 10.1007/978-3-319-62404-4_20

universe [2]. In this respect, the recent discovery of propylene oxide in the interstellar medium [3] has induced unusually large interest in spite that it is just a further addition to a now long list of molecules, increasing in number continuously. This molecule is an ideal candidate as a prototype for studies aiming at assessing the role of chirality in chemistry and biophysics, from the origin and early evolution of life, where the initial insurgence of homochirality is particularly intriguing, to asymmetric synthesis and chiral recognition, key aspects of pharmaceutics and materials sciences.

In this paper we focus on chiral discrimination effects in molecular beams, exploiting recent progress coming from extensive molecular beam scattering experiments on intermolecular collisions and interactions [4–6].

2   Stereodynamics and Interactions of Chiral Molecules

The homochirality in the biomolecules – most of the biomolecules in living systems have a specific chirality, and is a striking phenomena: the building blocks in the chemistry of life carry the signature of mechanisms inducing chiral stringent discrimination in chemical processes. Many hypotheses have been proposed to explain the origin of a chiral selectivity in the molecules of life (mostly based on the assumption that homochirality was the consequence of an environment enriched of a specific single enantiomer), such as random fluctuations, enantioselective synthesis, parity violation, circularly polarized light (see for example [7–11], see the collection of papers from two dedicated Symposia "Astrochemistry: molecules in space and in time" [12,13] and "Molecules at the Mirror: Chirality in Chemistry and Biophysics" [14–18]). Of particular interest is the observation that chiral discrimination can be induced by whirling motions in liquids resulting in the prevalent formation of aggregates of achiral porphyrins [19,20] whose handedness is influenced by the sense of the stirring. These effects associated to the true chiral influence of roto-translational motions [7] can be imagined to occur also in gas phase, see for example reports of the observation that the production of enantiomeric excesses of rotamers of substituted alkanes can be induced by roto-translational motions (vortexes), generated by turbomolecular pumping [21–23]. In principle, the sense of rotation of a vortex can act selectively on the direction of a chiral molecular rotation: this affirmation extends the experimental observation that in supersonic beams of gaseous mixtures the component in excess induces directionality and orientation in dragging molecules [24], as amply discussed in previous papers (see [25] and elsewhere).

Besides the stereodynamical aspects related to chirality, another interesting aspect to be investigated comes from the consequences of chirality on the intermolecular pair interactions occurring between chiral molecules of same or different handedness. These effects have been considered so far in terms of chiral recognition in dimers (diastereoisomeric pairs) formed by chiral molecules (e.g. in supersonic molecular beams). The pioneer experimental studies by Giardini-Guidoni and Speranza, by Zehnacker-Rentien and by their collaborators date back to the nineties, when laser-induced fluorescence [26], hole-burning [27] and resonance-enhanced multiphoton ionization spectroscopy [28] were introduced to achieve enantiomeric discrimination. Further work is based on rotational spectroscopic experiments and accompanying ab initio calculations, see specifically Ref. [29] on a study of homochiral and heterochiral dimers of propylene oxide in the gas phase.

Concerning propylene oxide, also known as methyl oxirane, previous work on this molecule has been extensive, by photoionization [30], circular dichroism [31,32], molecular beams with alignment techniques (in view of demonstration of the stereo-directional origin of chiral discrimination [6]) and computational modeling [33], through the quantum chemical search of the intermolecular chirality change mechanism. Remarkably, a strong dichroism effect was observed in the angular distribution of photoelectrons emitted from randomly oriented enantiomers of the propylene oxide by Turchini et al. and Stranges et al. [30,32]. These authors also studied the dynamical behaviour of the chiro-optical property of this molecule in a wide photon energy range, experimentally and theoretically.

Additional progress is within reach. The hypothesis that alignment and orientation in gaseous streams could not only minimize averaging effects of molecular rotations but crucially propitiate chiral effects in the differential scattering of oriented molecules (see Refs. [15,34] and references therein), besides being suggested by analogous effects on scattered electrons [15,35], is supported by indications provided by theoretical studies based on quantum chemistry and dynamics simulations on simple chiral molecules: hydrogen peroxide and persulfide [36–38]. It is to be noted that hydrogen peroxide, which is actually the simplest chiral molecule, had been observed in large quantities in interstellar space since 2011 [39].

3 Molecular Beam Experiments Involving Chiral Molecules

3.1 Spatial Molecular Control

The observation of chiral effects in molecular collisions by molecular beam experiments is optimally performed when the molecules are both translationally directed and aligned or oriented in space (see e.g. [14,22,38]). The techniques of choice we consider are: (i) the exploitation of gas dynamics effects in supersonic expansions and (ii) the use of external fields, such as those produced by electric hexapoles, as sketched in the following.

The spatial control of molecules in connection to the manifestation of signatures of chirality in the collision observables can be realized considering experiments of diffusion of polarized electrons on thin films of chiral molecules, which are imparted a specific orientation, and by the demonstration of stereodynamical effects in the diffusion of electrons from surfaces of aligned molecules [40–42]; the ionization of chiral molecules by collision with electrons was studied theoretically, showing the dependence from the polarization of the incident electron beam (see e.g. Ref. [43] and references therein).

elastic scattering

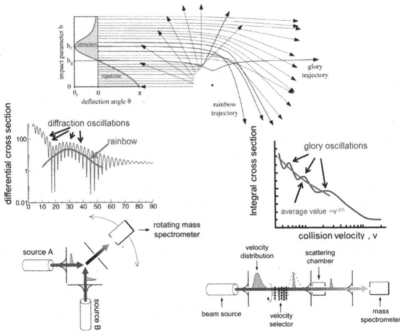

Fig. 1. At the foundations of molecular beam scattering experiments is the formulation of a two-body collisions, in the upper panel illustrated considering classical trajectories for a typical interaction, attractive at long range and repulsive at short range. This feature maps into the nonmonotonic dependence of the deflection angle on the impact parameter b so that trajectories with different b may lead to the same θ, leading to various possible quantum mechanical interference patterns denoted in analogy with those occurring in optics. They are observable in either differential scattering experiments (diffraction oscillations, rainbow effect) or in integral cross section measurements (glory oscillations superimposed to an average velocity dependence $v^{-2/5}$ due to the general R^{-6} of the long range interaction). The corresponding bottom panels give schematically the experimental realizations either the scattering due to the crossing of two beams as a function of θ, or the attenuation of a beam at selected velocities v.

Alignment and orientation are concepts associated to specific polarization of vectors, i.e. to non-statistical distributions of their components with respect to a given quantization axis (usually denoted as the z-axis). Orientation is usually referred to non-statistical distributions in both internal direction and sense, alignment when internal direction only matters. The molecular spatial control of interest can be achieved by alignment of the rotational angular momentum J or the orientation of the molecular axis with respect to z, which is conveniently chosen as the direction and sense of motion. Molecular polarization states are specified by using proper combination of rotational quantum numbers. The generation of naturally aligned or oriented molecular beams is shown in Fig. 1 along with a sketch of the alignment processes. For an extended phenomenology on the alignment in streams of molecules see Refs. [1,12,44–49].

Another effective technique for the control of the spatial orientation relies upon the use of hexapolar electrostatic fields, permitting the alignment and selection of rotational states of supersonic beams of linear, symmetric- and asymmetric-top molecules (see Refs. [6,50] for an account of the application of hexapole state-selection to propylene oxide). Hexapole fields have been applied mostly on linear and symmetric-top molecules (see specifically applications by the Osaka group [50–52]), while in recent years the rising interest for chiral molecules lead us to concentrate our efforts on chiral (and therefore necessarily asymmetric-top) molecules. In previous work, the characterization of supersonic molecular beams of propylene oxide, C_3H_6O, has been performed (see also [33,53] for the calculation of potential energy surface of the isomerization reactions) considering the alignment [50] and the orientational distribution, i.e. the distribution of the angle between the direction of the orienting electric field and the component of the permanent dipole moment with respect to one of the three axes of inertia (see [6] and references therein).

Other methods to induce alignment and orientation make use of lasers as in single-photon excitation (see for example Ref. [54]), high uniform electric fields as in the case of brute force techniques [55] or combination of non-uniform and uniform electric fields to align and consequently orient molecules (see for example Ref. [56]). This latter technique, which was introduced several decades ago for alignment and rotational state-selection, has been largely used to investigate the structure and electrical properties of molecules, and by the Osaka group to prepare intense and continuous beams and high duty cycle for crossed beam experiments (see for example Imura et al. [57–60]).

3.2 Molecular Beam Scattering

A second route to approach the investigation of chiral effects in molecular collisions is based on the probing of intermolecular interactions, as anticipated in previous sections. The difference in the range and strength of such interactions, as they take place in molecular adducts or dimers made up by enantiomers or homochiral molecular pairs, can in principle be studied in accurate collision experiments performed by molecular beams (specifically by beam-gas or crossed beam experimental setups).

In summary, two kinds of molecular beam configurations can be considered experimentally to reveal chiral discrimination effects with the help of the appropriate theoretical modeling.

Measurements of integral and differential cross sections on molecular beams of oriented or aligned chiral molecules. This type of experiments requires the ability of controlling the spatial orientation of molecules in a beam, as a necessary condition to reveal specific effects and possibly chiral selectivity, occurring in collision dynamics, photodissociation and chemical reactivity [61]. The appropriate experimental setups for the measurements of integral and differential cross sections by the molecular beam technique are shown in Fig. 1.

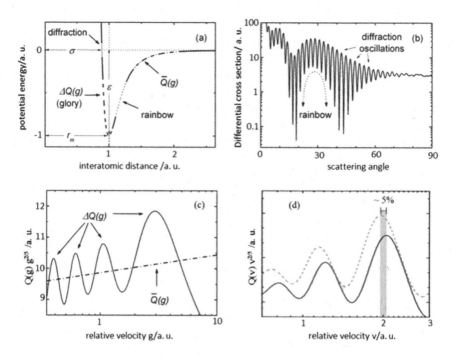

Fig. 2. This figure schematizes the relationship between the features of a generic inter-molecular interaction and the experimental observables alluded to in Fig. 1, attributed each of the latter to specific ranges of distances. Here $Q(g)$ are integral cross sections as a functions of the relative velocity between the velocity selected molecules in the beam and the target ones in the scattering chamber. In the two main high vacuum molecular beam experimental configurations in our laboratory, molecules are detected by ionization and quadrupole mass spectrometry. Panel (d) also reports the observable glory modification for a difference of ∼5 % in the intermolecular interaction, for a quantitative assessment of sensitivity of the experiment to the strength of the interactions.

The apparatus in the left involves two crossed molecular beams and the rotating detector, and under high angular and energy resolution conditions permits the manifestation of rainbow and diffraction quantum interference effects, in the angular dependence of the differential cross sections. The apparatus in the right exploits a single molecular beam velocity selected by a mechanical device consisting of a series of rotating slotted disks, a scattering chamber and a fixed detector. The measurement of the beam intensity with and without the gas target into the scattering chamber allows the determination of the integral cross sections as a function of the collision velocity. This is a quantum mechanical quantity that under favourable conditions can show an oscillatory pattern due to the glory quantum interference. The quantum phenomena can often be understood through analogies with optical phenomena.

Figure 2 illustrates the relationship between experimental resolved quantum interference effects and the features of the interaction being probed. In particular, while diffraction and rainbow oscillations probe the rise of the repulsive wall and the strength of the attraction in proximity of the potential well, the glory pattern is sensitive to depth and position of the potential well itself. Additionally, the absolute value of the average integral cross section is directly related to the strength of the long range attraction (see Fig. 2, panels (a), (b) and (c)). In general, the information that can be extracted requires the assistance of theoretical calculations of scattering observables and the results have to be compared with the measured quantities (for details see Refs. [62,63] and references therein).

3.3 Application to the Propylene Oxide Interactions

We have also estimated the interaction averaged over all the relative orientations of two propylene oxide molecules, which provides an average binding energy of about 3/4 kJ/mol, at equilibrium distances in the range of 4–4.5 Å. Taking into account the information provided by Ref. [29], we have estimated a possible difference of the average interaction between dimers formed by two different combination of the enantiomers, RR and RS (where, as usual, R and S stand for the two mirror forms): they are of the order of ∼0.2 kJ/mol, that is in the range of a difference of about 5% of the total interaction that, as we have seen, amounts to 3–4 kJ/mol. Panel (d) of Fig. 2 gives an idea of the change in the observable in a real experiment, concerning the measurement of the integral cross section associated to such a difference. Effects are expected also to be in principle detectable in the differential cross section for the same estimate of interaction strengths. Techniques of molecular alignment and orientation permits to reduce the averaging effect due to the free rotation of molecules, amplifying the energy differences between RR and RS combinations.

The orientation of propylene oxide has been largely studied by our group, by using hexapolar electric fields [5,6]. Figure 3 reports the appropriate experimental setup for the measurements of the integral cross sections of velocity selected and possibly oriented molecular beams, which is an extension of the previously illustrated integral cross section apparatus. In particular, panel (a) gives a sketch of the microscopic alignment processes promoted by forward collisions in the expansion zone of seeded molecular beam sources. Panel (b) emphasizes the importance of velocity selection in the formed molecular beam and reports a sketch of the experimental probes of the molecular alignment. Panel (c) shows a typical result obtained by the measurement of integral cross sections at different velocities and different alignment degree of projectile molecules. Figure 4 shows the crossed beam apparatus for the measurement of differential cross sections (panel a)).

4   Simulations of the Scattering of Chiral Molecules

For the detailed characterization of the intermolecular interactions and the demanding accuracy required in these problems, we found it necessary to match experimental information to calibrate *ab initio* techniques. Therefore the way

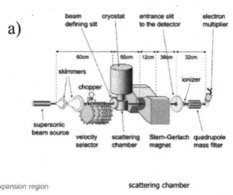

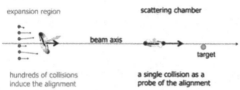

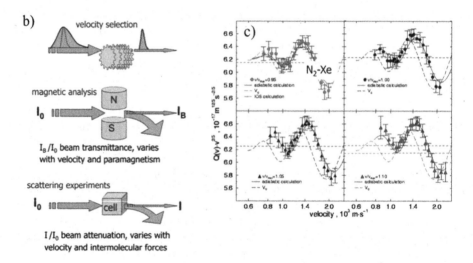

Fig. 3. (a) Experimental apparatus and dependence of the integral cross section measurements on the molecular alignment degree, (b) magnetic analysis of velocity selected beams and scattering of velocity selected beams [62]; (c) total integral cross sections from scattering of rotationally cold supersonic seeded beams of molecular nitrogen by Xe, at four different values of the V/V_{max} ratios. Dashed lines: scattering by the isotropic component of the interaction $V_0(R)$. Dotted lines: Infinite Order Sudden (IOS) calculation; solid lines are calculated according to the adiabatic scheme with nonadiabatic coupling. In each panel the corresponding $Q(v)$s are reported multiplied by $v^{2/5}$. For a more complete description see Ref. [65].

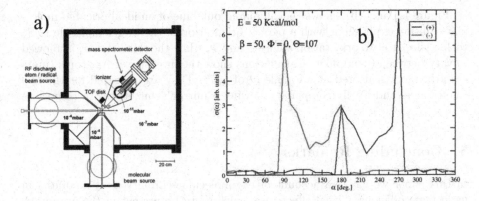

Fig. 4. (a) Crossed molecular beam apparatus with fixed beam sources and rotating mass spectrometer Time of Flight detector [63]. (b) Differential cross section of an oriented collision for different enantiomers (see the main text)

by which we are developing our approach to the characterization of intermolecular interaction potential energy surfaces is essentially an efficient semiempirical method, tested and improved by comparison with results of accurate electronic structure calculations. This procedure enables us to represent in suitable analytic forms the intermolecular interactions, also by explicitly incorporating the interaction parameters coming from the collision observables (see previous sections). Such a formulation correctly reproduces, in an internally consistent way, the interaction in the most significant configurations of the systems, from the least to the most stable one. This condition is crucial to carry out extensive molecular dynamics simulations of collisions involving chiral molecules. This is arguably he best route to a preliminary assessment of the collisional mechanism of chiral discrimination. To this aim, in previous work we performed extensive investigations on the hydrogen peroxide and persulfide molecules, motivated by the interesting problem of large amplitude motions (torsion motion around the O-O [36] and S-S [37] bonds) as a chirality inversion mechanism.

Simulations are described in Ref. [38]. To probe chiral effects in collisions we ideally set the chiral molecule in a flux of atoms coming along a specific direction with respect to the molecular target. The mutual orientation of the molecule and each atom velocity vector can be specified, for example, by Euler angles, say α, β, Φ. If the orientation of the molecules with respect to the velocity vectors of the incoming atoms is restricted into a narrow interval of values of the above angles (sharp molecular orientation distribution), the collisions can be thought of as "oriented". The axial distribution of the molecules in the beam can be prepared by means of the techniques for the orientation control exemplified in previous sections. The experimental observable of oriented collisions, specifically the corresponding differential cross sections, can therefore be labeled by the corresponding orientation angles, the measured cross section being an average over the orientation distribution.

Figure 4, panel (b), shows the simulated outcome of an ideal oriented molecular collision experiment with a perfect orientation of the target molecule H_2S_2 with respect to two orientation angles β and Φ, while the third one, α, is allowed to vary between 0 and $360°$. Calculations show the intensity of Ar atoms (units are arbitrary) scattered at an angle Θ of $107°$. They are repeated for the two enantiomers and finally compared, showing a mirror symmetry with respect to $\Theta = \pi$.

5   Concluding Remarks

In this paper we gave an account of the molecular chirality as it manifests in molecular collisions. Chiral effects are expected to be present in the intermolecular interactions involving homo- and hetero-chiral molecular pairs and in the collision observables connected to the stereodynamics. Best suited experiments and accompanying theoretical approaches are based on molecular beam apparatuses, scattering theory and quantum chemical calculations. The proper experiments along with the corresponding experimental setups, those currently used for elastic and reactive molecular scattering studies, have been described. We are investigating the systems involving propylene oxide interacting with noble gas systems, which can be useful prototypes to define the role of electromagnetic and magnetic interaction components on the collision dynamics. The same method will be extended in future to collisions involving two chiral molecules. As a part of the experimental and theoretical investigations carried on by the "Astrochemical observatory", involving efforts from coordinated research groups and multiple viewpoints of the structure and dynamics of the molecules relevant to the evolution of cosmos, this paper is accompanied by others in this volume of the Lecture Note series dealing with related themes, specifically [64].

Acknowledgement. The authors acknowledge financial support from MIUR PRIN 2010–2011 (contract 2010ERFKXL_002) and from "Fondazione Cassa Risparmio Perugia (Codice Progetto: 2015.0331.021 Ricerca Scientifica e Tecnologica)". They also acknowledge the Italian Ministry for Education, University and Research, MIUR, for financial supporting through SIR 2014 "Scientific Independence for young Researchers" (RBSI14U3VF). Thanks are due to the Dipartimento di Chimica, Biologia e Biotecnologie dell'Università di Perugia (FRB, Fondo per la Ricerca di Base). A. L., P. C., and F. P. acknowledge financial support from MIUR PRIN 2015 (contract 2015F59J3R_002). V.A. thanks Brazilian CAPES for grant as Distinguished Visiting Professor at Universidade da Bahia.

References

1. Palazzetti, F., Maciel, G.S., Lombardi, A., Grossi, G., Aquilanti, V.: The astrochemical observatory: molecules in the laboratory and in the cosmos. J. Chin. Chem. Soc. **59**, 1045–1052 (2012)
2. Pizzarello, S., Groy, T.L.: Molecular asymmetry in extraterrestrial organic chemistry: an analytical perspective. Geochim. Cosmochim. Acta **75**, 645–656 (2011)

3. McGuire, B., Carroll, P.B., Loomis, R.A., Finneran, I.A., Jewell, P.A., Remijan, A.J., Blake, G.A.: Discovery of the interstellar chiral molecule propyleneoxide (ch_3chch_2o). Science **352**, 1449–1452 (2016)
4. Aquilanti, V.: Molecular alignment in gaseous expansions and anisotropy of intermolecular forces. Am. Inst. Phys. **762**, 26–31 (2005)
5. Aquilanti, V., Bartolomei, M., Pirani, F., Cappelletti, D., Vecchiocattivi, F., Shimizu, Y., Kasai, T.: Orienting and aligning molecules for stereochemistry and photodynamics. Phys. Chem. Chem. Phys. **5**, 291–300 (2005)
6. Che, D.C., Kanda, K., Palazzetti, F., Aquilanti, V., Kasai, T.: Electrostatic hexapole state-selection of the asymmetric-top molecule propylene oxide: rotational and orientational distributions. Chem. Phys. **399**, 180–192 (2012)
7. Barron, L.D.: True and false chirality and absolute asymmetric synthesis. J. Am. Chem. Soc. **108**, 5539–5542 (1986)
8. Quack, M.: How important is parity violation for molecular and biomolecular chirality. Angew. Chem. Int. Ed. **41**, 4618–4630 (2002)
9. Rikken, G.L.J.A., Raupach, E.: Enantioselective magnetochiral photochemistry. Nature **405**, 932–935 (2000)
10. Avalos, A., Babiano, R., Cintas, P., Jiménez, J.L., Palacios, J.C.: Absolute asymmetric synthesis under physical fields: facts and fictions. Chem. Rev. **98**, 2391–2404 (1998)
11. Modica, P., Meinert, C., DeMarcellus, P., Nahon, L., Meierhenrich, U.J., Sergeant D'Hendecourt, L.L.: Enantiomeric excesses induced in amino acids by ultraviolet circularly polarized light irradiation of extraterrestrial ice analogs: a possible source of asymmetry for prebiotic chemistry. Astrophys. J. **788**, 79 (2014)
12. Aquilanti, V., Schettino, V., Zerbi, G.: Introduction: astrochemistry-molecules in space and in time. Rend. Fis. Acc. Lincei **22**, 67–68 (2011)
13. Bacchus-Montabonel, M.C.: Radiative and collisional processes in space chemistry. Rend. Fis. Acc. Lincei **22**, 95–103 (2011)
14. Aquilanti, V., Maciel, G.S.: Observed molecular alignment in gaseous streams and possible chiral effects in vortices and surface scattering. Orig. Life Evol. Biosph. **36**, 435–441 (2006)
15. Musigmann, M., Busalla, A., Blum, K., Thompson, D.G.: Enantio-selective collisions between unpolarized electrons and chiral molecules. J. Phys. Chem. B **34**, L79–L85 (2001)
16. Barron, L.D.: True, false chirality, absolute enantioselection. Rend. Fis. Acc. Lincei **24**, 179–189 (2013)
17. Longo, S., Coppola, C.: Stochastic models of chiral symmetry breaking in autocatalytic networks with anomalous fluctuations. Rend. Fis. Acc. Lincei **24**, 277–281 (2013)
18. Ribó, J.M., El-Hachema, I.Z., Crusatz, J.: Effect of flows in auto-organization, self-assembly, and emergence of chirality. Rend. Fis. Acc. Lincei **24**, 197–211 (2013)
19. Ribó, J.M., Crusatz, J., Sagués, F., Claret, J., Rubires, R.: Chiral sign induction by vortices during the formation of mesophases in stirred solutions. Science **292**, 2063–2066 (2001)
20. Matteson, D.S., Ribó, J.M., Crusatz, J., Sagués, F., Claret, J., Rubires, R.: Chiral selection when stirred, not shaken. Science **293**, 1435 (2001)
21. Lee, H.N., Su, T.M., Chao, I.: Rotamer dynamics of substituted simple alkanes. 1. a classical trajectory study of collisional orientation and alignment of 1-bromo-2-chloroethane. J. Phys. Chem. A **108**, 2567–2575 (2004)

22. Lee, H.N., Chang, L.C., Su, T.M.: Optical rotamers of substituted simple alkanes induced by macroscopic translation-rotational motions. Chem. Phys. Lett. **507**, 63–68 (2011)

23. Lee, H.N., Chao, I., Su, T.M.: Asymmetry in the internal energies of the optical rotamers of 1-bromo-2-chloroethane in oriented-molecule/surface scattering: a classical molecular. Chem. Phys. Lett. **i517**, 132–138 (2011)

24. Aquilanti, V., Ascenzi, D., Cappelletti, D., Pirani, F.: Velocity dependence of collisional alignment of oxygen molecules in gaseous expansions. Nature **371**, 399–402 (1994)

25. Aquilanti, V., Grossi, G., Lombardi, A., Maciel, G.S., Palazzetti, F.: Aligned molecular collisions and a stereodynamical mechanism for selective chirality. Rend. Fis. Acc. Lincei **22**, 125–135 (2011)

26. Al Rabaa, A., Le Barbu, K., Lahmani, F., Zehnacker-Rentien, A.: van der waals complexes between chiral molecules in a supersonic jet: a new spectroscopic method for enantiomeric discrimination. J. Phys. Chem. A **101**, 17126–17131 (1997)

27. Le Barbu, K., Brenner, V., Milliè, P., Lahmani, F., Zehnacker-Rentien, A.: An experimental and theoretical study of jet-cooled complexes of chiral molecules: the role of dispersive forces in chiral discrimination. J. Phys. Chem. A **102**, 128–137 (1998)

28. Latini, A., Toja, D., Giardini-Guidoni, A., Piccirillo, S., Speranza, M.: Energetics of molecular complexes in a supersonic beam: a novel spectroscopic tool for enantiomeric discrimination. Angew. Chem. Int. Ed. **38**, 815–817 (1998)

29. Su, Z., Borho, N., Yunjie, X.: Chiral self recognition: direct spectroscopic detection of the homochiral and heterochiral dimers of propylene oxide in the gas phase. J. Am. Chem. Soc. **128**, 17131–17126 (2006)

30. Turchini, S., Zena, N., Contini, G., Alberti, G., Alagia, M., Stranges, S., Fronzono, G., Stener, M., Decleva, P., Prosperi, T.: Circular dichroism in photoelectron spectroscopy of free chiral molecules: experiment and theory on methyl-oxirane. Phys. Rev. A **70**, 014502 (2004)

31. Merten, C., Bloino, J., Barone, V., Yunjie, X.: Anharmonicity effects in the vibrational cd spectra of propylene oxide. J. Phys. Chem. Lett. **4**, 3424–3428 (2013)

32. Stranges, S., Turchini, S., Alagia, M., Alberti, G., Contini, G., Decleva, P., Fronzoni, G., Stener, M.: Valence photoionization dynamics in circular dichroism of chiral free molecules: the methyl-oxirane. J. Chem. Phys. **122**, 244303 (2005)

33. Elango, M., Maciel, G.S., Palazzetti, F., Lombardi, A., Aquilanti, V.: Quantum chemistry of C_3H_6O molecules: structure and stability, isomerization pathways, and chirality changing mechanisms. J. Phys. Chem. A **114**(36), 9864–9874 (2010)

34. Aquilanti, V., Grossi, G., Lombardi, A., Maciel, G.S., Palazzetti, F.: The origin of chiral discrimination: supersonic molecular beam experiments and molecular dynamics simulations of collisional mechanisms. Phys. Scripta **78**, 058119 (2008)

35. Busalla, A., Blum, K., Thompson, D.G.: Differential cross section for collisions between electrons and oriented chiral molecules. Phys. Rev. Lett. **85**, 1562 (1999)

36. Barreto, P.R.P., Vilela, A.F.A., Lombardi, A., Maciel, G.S., Palazzetti, F., Aquilanti, V.: The hydrogen peroxide-rare gas systems: quantum chemical calculations and hyperspherical harmonic representation of the potential energy surface for atom-floppy molecule interactions. J. Phys. Chem. A **111**, 12754–12762 (2007)

37. Maciel, G.S., Barreto, P.R.P., Palazzetti, F., Lombardi, A., Aquilanti, V.: A quantum chemical study of h_2s_2: intramolecular torsional mode and intermolecular interactions with rare gases. J. Phys. Chem. A **129**, 164302 (2008)

38. Lombardi, A., Palazzetti, F., Maciel, G.S., Aquilanti, V., Sevryuk, M.B.: Simulation of oriented collision dynamics of simple chiral molecules. Int. J. Quantum Chem. **111**, 1651–1658 (2011)

39. Bergman, P., Parise, B., Liseau, R., Larsson, B., Olofsson, H., Menten, K.M., Gusten, R.: Detection of interstellar hydrogen peroxide. A&A **531**, L8 (2011)

40. Ray, K., Anathavel, S.P., Waldeck, D.H., Naaman, R.: Asymmetric scattering of polarized electrons by organized organic films of chiral molecules. Science **283**, 814–816 (1999)

41. Kim, J.W., Carbone, M., Dil, J.H., Tallarinda, M., Flammini, R., Casaletto, M.P., Horn, K., Piancastelli, M.N.: Atom-specific identification of adsorbed chiral molecules by photoemission. Phys. Rev. Lett. **95**, 107601–107604 (2005)

42. Gerbi, A., Vattuone, L., Rocca, M., Valbusa, U., Pirani, F., Cappelletti, D., Vecchiocattivi, F.: Stereodynamic effects int the adsorption of propylene molecules on ag(001). J. Phys. Chem. B **109**, 22884–22889 (2005)

43. Musigmann, M., Busalla, A., Blum, K., Thompson, D.G.: Enantio-selective collisions between unpolarized electrons and chiral molecules. J. Phys. B **34**, L-79–L-85 (2001)

44. Aquilanti, V., Ascenzi, D., deCastro Vitores, M., Pirani, F., Cappelletti, D.: A quantum mechanical view of molecular alignment and cooling in seeded supersonic expansion. J. Chem. Phys. **111**, 2620–2632 (1999)

45. Lombardi, A., Maciel, G.S., Palazzetti, F., Grossi, G., Aquilanti, V.: Alignment and chirality in gaseous flows. J. Vac. Soc. Jpn **53**, 645–653 (2010)

46. Pirani, F., Cappelletti, D., Bartolomei, M., Aquilanti, V., Scotoni, M., Vescovi, M., Ascenzi, D., Bassi, D.: Orientation of benzene in supersonic expansions, probed by ir-laser absorption and by molecular beam scattering. Phys. Rev. Lett **86**, 5053–5038 (2001)

47. Pirani, F., Bartolomei, M., Aquilanti, V., Scotoni, M., Vescovi, M., Ascenzi, D., Bassi, D., Cappelletti, D.: Collisional orientation of the benzene molecular plane in supersonic seeded expansions, probed by infrared polarized laser absorption spectroscopy and by molecular beam scattering. J. Chem. Phys. **119**, 265–276 (2003)

48. Pirani, F., Maciel, G.S., Cappelletti, D., Aquilanti, V.: Experimental benchmarks and phenomenology of interatomic forces: open shell and electronic anisotropy effect. Int. Rev. Phys. Chem. **25**, 165–199 (2006)

49. Pirani, F., Cappelletti, D., Bartolomei, M., Aquilanti, V., Demarchi, G., Tosi, P., Scotoni, M.: The collisional alignment of acetylene molecules in supersonic seeded expansions probed by infrared absorption and molecular beam scattering. Chem. Phys. Lett. **437**, 176–182 (2007)

50. Che, D.C., Palazzetti, F., Okuno, Y., Aquilanti, V.: Electrostatic hexapole state-selection of the asymmetric-top molecule propylene oxide. J. Phys. Chem. A **114**, 3280–3286 (2010)

51. Ohoyama, H., Ogawa, T., Kasai, T.: A single rotational state analysis of the state-selected CH_3I beam: a new monte carlo simulation including the second-order stark effect. J. Phys. Chem. **99**, 13606–13610 (1995)

52. Hashinokuchi, M., Che, D.C., Watanabe, D., Fukuyama, T., Koyano, I., Shimizu, Y., Woelke, A., Kasai, T.: Single $\mid J\Omega M_J>$ state-selection of oh radicals using an electrostatic hexapole field. Phys. Chem. Chem. Phys. **5**, 3911–3915 (2003)

53. Elango, M., Maciel, G.S., Lombardi, A., Cavalli, S., Aquilanti, V.: Quantum chemical and dynamical approaches to intra and intermolecular kinetics: the $C_nH_{2n}O$(n = 1, 2, 3) molecules. Int. J. Quantum Chem. **111**, 1784–1791 (2011)

54. Weida, M.J., Parmenter, C.A.: Aligning symmetric and asymmetric top molecules via single photon excitation. J. Chem. Phys. **107**, 7138–7147 (1997)
55. Bulthuis, J., Möller, J., Loesch, H.J.: Brute force orientation of asymmetric top molecules. J. Phys. Chem. A **101**, 7684–7690 (1997)
56. Hain, T.D., Weibel, M.A., Backstrand, K.M., Curtiss, T.J.: Rotational state selection and orientation of oh and od radicals by electric hexapole beam-focusing. J. Phys. Chem. A **101**, 7674–7683 (1997)
57. Imura, K., Kawashima, T., Ohoyama, H., Kasai, T., Nakajima, A., Kaya, K.: Nondestructive selection of geometrical isomers of the $Al(C_6H_6)$ cluster by a 2 m electrostatic hexapole field. Phys. Chem. Chem. Phys. **3**, 3593–3597 (2001)
58. Imura, K., Kawashima, T., Ohoyama, H., Kasai, T.: Direct determination of the permanent dipole moments and structures of $Al-CH_3CN$ and $Al-NH_3$ by using 2-m electrostatic hexapole field. J. Am. Chem. Soc. **123**, 6367–6371 (2001)
59. Imura, K., Ohoyama, H., Kasai, T.: Metal-ligand interaction of $Ti-C_6H_6$ complex size-selected by a 2-m long electrostatic hexapole field. Chem. Phys. Lett **369**, 55–59 (2003)
60. Imura, K., Ohoyama, H., Kasai, T.: Structures and its dipole moments of half-sandwich type metal-benzene (1: 1) complexes determined by 2-m long electrostatic hexapole. Chem. Phys. **301**, 183–187 (2004)
61. Vattuone, L., Savio, L., Pirani, F., Cappelletti, D., Okada, M., Rocca, M.: Interaction of rotationally aligned and of oriented molecules in gas phase and at surfaces. Prog. Surf. Sci. **85**, 92–160 (2010)
62. Pirani, F., Roncaratti, L.F., Casavecchia, P., Cappelletti, D., Vecchiocattivi, F.: Beyond the lennard-jones model: a simple and accurate potential function probed by high resolution scattering data useful for molecular dynamics simulations. Phys. Chem. Chem. Phys. **10**, 5489–5503 (2008)
63. Casavecchia, P.: Chemical reaction dynamics with molecular beams. Rep. Prog. Phys. **63**, 355–414 (2000)
64. Aquilanti, V., Caglioti, C., Lombardi, A., Maciel, G.S., Palazzetti, F.: Screens for displaying chirality changing mechanisms of a series of peroxides and persulfides from conformational structures computed by quantum chemistry. In: Gervasi, O., et al. (eds.) ICCSA 2017, Part V. LNCS, vol. 10408, pp. 354–368. Springer, Cham (2017)
65. Aquilanti, V., Ascenzi, D., Cappelletti, D., Fedeli, R., Pirani, F.: Molecular beam scattering of nitrogen molecules in supersonic seeded beams: a probe of rotational alignment. J. Phys. Chem. **101**, 7648–7656 (1997)

Influence of the Intermolecular Potential Energy on N_2-N_2 Inelastic Collisions: A Quantum-Classical Study

Simone Fioccola[1], Fernando Pirani[2], Massimiliano Bartolomei[3], and Cecilia Coletti[1(✉)]

[1] Dipartimento di Farmacia, Università G. d'Annunzio,
Via dei Vestini, 66100 Chieti, Italy
ccoletti@unich.it
[2] Dipartimento di Chimica, Biologia e Biotecnologie, Università di Perugia,
via Elce di Sotto 8, 06123 Perugia, Italy
[3] Instituto de Física Fundamental, CSIC, C/Serrano 123, Madrid, Spain

Abstract. The study of internal energy transfer processes in N_2-N_2 collisions has found a renewed interest over the last years, in connection with the role such events play in a wide range of temperature regimes, in atmospheric chemistry and physics and in the development of plasma and aerospace technologies. One of the most efficient approaches to calculate vibration to vibration (VV) energy transfer relies on a quantum-classical method, which couples a rigorous quantum mechanical treatment of the vibrations and a quasiclassical description of the other degrees of freedom, allowing for the calculation of energy exchange probabilities for a large body of state selected processes at a reasonable computational cost. The accuracy of the results however depends on the ability of the potential energy surface to correctly describe both long and short range interactions which dominate the outcome of the collisions at different temperatures. In this work we examine the effect of using alternative potential energy surfaces, differing either for the value of the employed parameters and for their formulation, on VV cross sections and rate constants.

Keywords: Inelastic scattering · VV energy transfer · Quantum-classical methods

1 Introduction

The investigation of vibration to vibration (VV) and vibration to translation (VT) energy transfer in molecular collisions is of basic importance for the simulation of non equilibrium environments, which are often encountered in the chemistry of planet atmospheres, the chemistry of plasma, in lasers, etc. [1]. In such situations the population of vibrational states may be quite different from that following a Boltzmann distribution, which in turn can have important consequences on the kinetics of reactive events taking place in such environments.

© Springer International Publishing AG 2017
O. Gervasi et al. (Eds.): ICCSA 2017, Part V, LNCS 10408, pp. 281–296, 2017.
DOI: 10.1007/978-3-319-62404-4_21

Indeed, the speed of many elementary chemical reactions often strongly depends on the vibrational excitation of the reactants [2–5]. A detailed description of non equilibrium and, in general, of gaseous or plasma environments thus relies on the knowledge of rate constants for a large number of VV and VT exchange processes, which allow the solution of the corresponding master equation [6].

Non-equilibrium situations can occur in a wide range of temperature, from few Kelvins to a few hundreds, as is the case for planet atmospheres or laser chemistry, to much higher ones, up to tenths of thousands, like those involved in hypersonic aerodynamics relevant for the design of air and spacecrafts [7]. The correct modeling of the whole set of different conditions requires the knowledge of potential energy surfaces which should be able to accurately describe both long range interactions and dispersion contributions, determining the kinetics at small temperatures, and short range ones, generally accounting for most of the features of the dynamics at larger values of the available energy. Besides, in a high temperature regime, dissociation or reactive events may also occur, even for unreactive species, which should be included in a proper description of the molecular system.

In this sense, the study of N_2+N_2 collisions has become a prototypical example over the last years. Early studies of N_2+N_2 inelastic scattering in the 70's were based on simple model potentials and mainly focused on a temperature range of atmospheric interest (300–1000 K) [8]. Such models were refined over the years and, more recently, the introduction of a potential devoted to an accurate description of long range interactions through the use of an Improved Lennard-Jones potential (ILJ) [9] has allowed the calculation of VV and VT rate constants at lower temperature by using quasi classical and semiclassical methods [10]. This study contributed to unveil the non-Arrhenius behavior of VV rate constants at $T < 100\,\text{K}$, a behavior which found experimental evidence in a recent work [11].

The last years have witnessed a growing interest for N_2+N_2 collisions in a very high temperature regime as well, as this is a key process in hypersonic flows in the atmosphere. At those temperatures highly excited vibrational states are populated and multiple reaction channels are open, which should be considered in the development of the PES. To this purpose, Truhlar and coworkers [12–14] have recently published a series of surfaces describing N_2+N_2 reactive events.

In this work we use the mixed quantum-classical method developed by Billing [15,16] to test: (i) how the introduction of modifications in the electrostatic component of the empirical potential of ref. [17], namely a different value and intra-monomer dependence of the quadrupole moment, can affect cross sections and rate constants for vibrational quanta exchange process; (ii) how VV cross sections calculated with the reactive PES of ref. [14] compare in a high temperature regime with those computed with the previous empirical potential [17].

The paper thus proceeds according to the following scheme: after briefly describing the main features of the mixed quantum-classical method we used to calculate VV cross sections and rate constants (Sect. 2), the potential energy surfaces employed for this study will be introduced (Sect. 3) and technical details on the calculations we carried out are furnished (Sect. 4). A quantitative comparison of these quantities obtained with the investigated surfaces is presented and discussed in Sect. 5, whereas perspectives for future work are illustrated in the final Section.

2   The Quantum-Classical Dynamical Approach for VV Energy Transfer

This approach was introduced and developed by G.D. Billing [15,16] and is still one of the most efficient tools to calculate large bodies of accurate rate constants for processes involving vibrational energy transfer. The present formulation is essentially that used in refs. [6,18–20] with only small technical upgrades to the code. The theoretical foundations of the method will be sketched here, whereas a more detailed description can be found in the above mentioned references.

The mixed quantum-classical model is a time dependent approach where quantum mechanics is employed to describe the degrees of freedom playing the most relevant role in VV quantum energy exchange. Vibrations and roto-vibrational couplings are thus treated quantum-mechanically by close coupled equations, whereas the other degrees of freedom are dealt with classically, by solving the corresponding Hamilton equations. The coupling between the two subsystems is achieved by making use of an Ehrenfest averaged potential (Fig. 1).

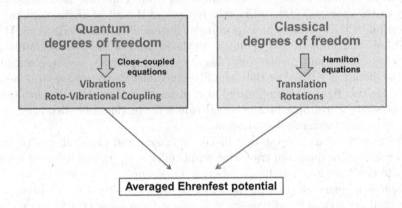

Fig. 1. The Quantum-Classical method

In practice, to solve the quantum mechanical problem, the quantum transition amplitudes $a_{v_a v_b}(t)$ have to be obtained by the following set of equations, whose number depends on the number of vibrational states which we need to include to get convergence:

$$i\hbar \dot{a}_{v'_a v'_b}(t) = \sum \left[\langle \phi^0_{v'_a} \phi^0_{v'_b} | V(r_a, r_b, t) | \phi^0_{v_a} \phi^0_{v_b} \rangle + i\hbar \langle \phi^0_{v'_a} \phi^0_{v'_b} | H_{Co} | \phi^0_{v_a} \phi^0_{v_b} \rangle \right]$$
$$\times a_{v_a v_b}(t) \exp \left[\frac{i}{\hbar} (E_{v'_a} + E_{v'_b} - E_{v_a} - E_{v_b}) t \right] \tag{1}$$

where E_v is the vibrational energy and the quantum vibrational wavefunction (perturbed by the rotational distortion at the first order) is expanded in terms of the product of the oscillator (Morse) wave functions, $\phi_{v_a}(r_a)\phi_{v_b}(r_b)$, of the two isolated diatoms:

$$\Psi = \sum_{v,v'} a_{vv'}(t)\phi_v(r_a)\phi_{v'}(r_b) \exp\left[-i\hbar^{-1}(E_v - E_{v'})t\right] \tag{2}$$

The H_{Co} term in Eq. (1) is the rotational distortion upon the Coriolis centrifugal stretch. The dependence upon time of the coupling terms comes from the time dependence of the coordinates obtained from the classical trajectories. The latter are given by the solution of a set of 18 Hamilton equations of motion obtained through the following Hamiltonian, expressed in Cartesian coordinates:

$$H = \frac{1}{2\mu}(P_x^2 + P_y^2 + P_z^2) + \sum_i \frac{1}{2m_i}(p_{x_i}^2 + p_{y_i}^2 + p_{z_i}^2)$$
$$+ \sum_i \lambda_i(r_i^2 - \bar{r}_i^2) + V_{av}(R(t), r_i, \{\Omega\}) \tag{3}$$

where the effective potential, $V_{av} = \langle\Psi|V(R(t), r_i, \Omega(t))|\Psi\rangle$, is the quantum expectation value of the interaction potential. $\mathbf{R}$ is the distance vector between the centers of mass of the two oscillators, r_a and r_b are the interatomic distances of the diatoms, $\{\Omega\}$ collectively represents the set of angles defining the orientation of the vector r_i in a coordinate system with the z axis along $\mathbf{R}$, $\mathbf{p}_i$ and $\mathbf{P}$ are the momenta corresponding to the motion of the two oscillators and the reciprocal motion, respectively. Lagrange multipliers λ_i are introduced to keep the distances r_i fixed at their equilibrium values $\bar{r}_i$, so to have equations of motion for two rigid rotators located at a distance R. Note that the intramolecular potential depending on the actual values of the diatomic distance is used in the quantum mechanical subsystem.

The simultaneous propagation of the quantum and classical sets of equations produces the quantum transition amplitudes $a_{v_a v_b}(t)$ which can be used to calculate cross sections for the vibrational transitions.

Though in principle this method can be used to obtain cross sections for vibrational/rotational transitions $\sigma_{v_a j_a v_b j_b \to v'_a j'_a v'_b j'_b}$, a Monte Carlo average over the initial Boltzmann distribution of rotational energy is generally introduced to have rate constants for vibrational relaxation. To this purpose an averaged cross section is defined as:

$$\sigma_{v'_a, v'_b}(U, T_0) = \frac{\pi\hbar^6}{8\mu(kT_0)^3 I_a I_b} \times \tag{4}$$

$$\int_0^{l_{max}} \int_0^{j_a\,max} \int_0^{j_b\,max} dj_a\,dj_b\,dl\,(2j_a + 1)(2j_b + 1)(2l + 1)N^{-1}\sum |a_{v'_a v'_b}|^2$$

where T_0 is an arbitrary reference temperature, which cancels out in the formulation of rate constants (Eq. 5), I_i is the moment of inertia for the i-th diatom, U is the classical energy, obtained subtracting from total energy the vibrational energy of the two diatoms, $U = E - E_{v_a} - E_{v_b}$, $j_{a\ max}$ and $j_{b\ max}$ are the upper limit for the randomly chosen rotational quantum numbers for the diatoms and l_{max} the upper limit for the angular momentum.

Rate constants are then calculated through the following equation:

$$k_{v_a' v_b'}(T) = \left(\frac{8kT}{\pi\mu}\right)^{1/2} \left(\frac{T_0}{T}\right)^3 \int_0^\infty d\left(\frac{\overline{U}}{kT}\right) e^{-\overline{U}/kT} \sigma_{v_a', v_b'}(T_0, \overline{U}), \quad (5)$$

which holds for exothermic processes.

$\overline{U}$ is the symmetrized classical energy [21]:

$$\overline{U} = U + \frac{1}{2}\Delta E + \frac{\Delta E^2}{16U} \quad (6)$$

which has been introduced to restore, in an approximate fashion, the quantum mechanical detailed balance principle. A detailed discussion about this issue can be found in refs. [15,16,21]

Note that the anharmonic vibrational energy is here approximated by:

$$E_{v_i} = \hbar\omega_{ei}\left(v_i + \frac{1}{2}\right) - \hbar\omega_{ei}x_{ei}\left(v_i + \frac{1}{2}\right)^2 \quad (7)$$

where ω_{ei} is the wavenumber for the i-th oscillator and x_{ei} is the anharmonicity constant. For the N_2 oscillators, we here use $\omega_{ei} = 2359,60$ cm^{-1}, $x_{ei} = 0,0061$, $\overline{r_i} = 1.098$ Å.

3   Potential Energy Surfaces

As mentioned in the Introduction, a number of potential energy surfaces for N_2-N_2 collisions has been developed, addressing different features of the diatoms interaction and, more recently, the possibility of including reactive channels in the description. As far as inelastic collisions are concerned the surfaces differ for the treatment of short range, long range and dispersion contributions to the potential. Early models made use of simple analytical functions for the three parts, where parameters were usually taken from accurate ab-initio calculations and were refined over the years [8,22].

In this work, the overall interaction V of the diatom-diatom system is as usual partitioned in an *intra* and an *inter* component

$$V = V_{intra} + V_{inter} \quad (8)$$

in which V_{intra} is formulated as in ref. [10], i.e. using a Morse potential energy function $D_e(t^2 - 2t)$, where $t = \exp[-\beta(r - r_e)]$, with $r_e = 1.098$ Å, $\beta = 2.689$ Å^{-1}, $D_e = 9.095$ eV.

V_{inter} is here represented as a combination of an "effective" van der Waals V_{vdW} component and an electrostatic term V_{elect} [17].

$$V_{inter} = V_{vdW} + V_{elect} \quad (9)$$

The V_{vdW} term is formulated as a bond-bond [17] interaction, that is more appropriate than the traditional atom-atom one because it accounts indirectly for three body like effects.

V_{elect} term represents an electrostatic contribution due to the interaction between the molecular permanent multipoles and, as in previous formulations [10,17,23,24,27], only the main quadrupole-quadrupole term is taken into account.

Both V_{vdW} and V_{elect} depend on the intermolecular distance R between the centers of mass of molecule a and b, on the Jacobi angles Θ_a and Θ_b formed by $\mathbf{R}$ with the internuclear vectors $\mathbf{r}_a$ and $\mathbf{r}_b$, respectively, and the angle Φ the dihedral angle formed by the planes $(\mathbf{R}, \mathbf{r}_a)$ and $(\mathbf{R}, \mathbf{r}_b)$.

The formulation adopted for the van der Waals term V_{vdW} is of the Improved Lennard-Jones (ILJ) type [9]:

$$V_{vdW}(R, \gamma) = \varepsilon(\gamma) \left[\frac{6}{n(x) - 6} \left(\frac{1}{x} \right)^{n(x)} - \frac{n(x)}{n(x) - 6} \left(\frac{1}{x} \right)^6 \right] \tag{10}$$

often used in its reduced form

$$f(x) = \frac{V_{vdW}(R, \gamma)}{\varepsilon(\gamma)} \tag{11}$$

where x is the reduced distance of the two bodies defined as

$$x = \frac{R}{R_m(\gamma)} \tag{12}$$

and γ denotes collectively the triplet of angles $(\Theta_a, \Theta_b, \Phi)$, while ε and R_m are respectively the fixed γ well depth of the interaction potential and the equilibrium value of R.

The key feature of the ILJ functional form is the adoption of the additional (variable) exponential parameter n providing a further flexibility thanks to its dependence on both R and γ as [9,10,17]:

$$n(x) = \beta + 4.0 \, x^2 \tag{13}$$

in which β is a parameter depending on the nature and the hardness of the interacting particles leading to a more realistic representation of both repulsion (first term in square brackets of Eq. 10) and attraction (second term in square brackets of Eq. 10). For the present system β has been set equal to 9 (a value typical of van der Waals interactions in neutral-neutral systems) [9].

The other parameters ($\varepsilon(\gamma)$ and $R_m(\gamma)$) needed to define V_{vdW} in the Eq. 10 as well as their dependence on the internal coordinates r_a and r_b are those originally reported in Ref. [17].

As already done in Refs. [10,17], since the mostly probed values of intermolecular distance R are larger than the corresponding intramolecular r, in the present work the V_{elect} term of Eq. 9 is expressed as

$$V_{elect}(R, \gamma) = \frac{Q_a Q_b}{R^5} A^{224}(\gamma) \tag{14}$$

where Q_a and Q_b are the diatomic permanent quadrupole moments and A^{224} is the corresponding bipolar spherical harmonic needed to describe the orientational dependence of their interaction. For Q and its dependence on the intramolecular coordinate r two different estimates have been considered: the first one is the dependence originally obtained in Ref. [25] and also employed in Refs. [10,17]; the second one is a more recent dependence based on accurate ab initio calculations [24,26], which ensures a more reliable behaviour for r up to 2 Å and which has been already used to describe the electrostatic term of the O_2-N_2 interaction [27]. The corresponding profiles as function of r are reported in Fig. 2 by exploiting analytical formulae reported in Refs. [17] and [27], respectively. It can be seen that the more recent estimate [27] provides a slightly larger value than the previous one (-1.123 a.u. versus -1.1 a.u.) at the N_2 equilibrium distance (r_{eq}=1.098Å) and it also better reproduces the reference ab initio data in a wider range of r distances.

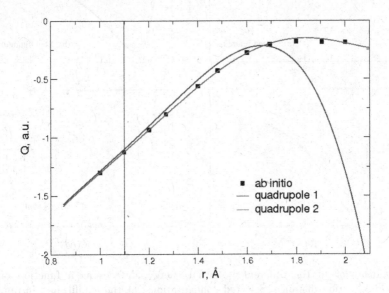

Fig. 2. N_2 quadrupole moment Q as a function of the internuclear distance r. "quadrupole 1" and "quadrupole 2" profiles refer to the analytical formulae reported in Refs. [17,27], respectively. Ab initio reference data are from Ref. [24]. The vertical black line indicates the N_2 equilibrium distance (r_e=1.098Å).

Therefore, in this work two interaction schemes have been taken into account which consider the same V_{vdW} component but two different V_{elect} terms, which are determined by the dependences on r of the molecular quadrupole moment Q shown above. In the following they will be referred to as ILJ-I and ILJ-II, the latter including the most accurate behaviour of Q.

This will allow us to test the effect of such relatively small change on the electrostatic part of the potential upon the value of cross sections and rate constants for VV energy transfer.

The potential as a function of the distance between the two diatoms for some selected geometries can be found in Fig. 3, where it is shown that the modification of the V_{elect} term slightly affects the depth of the interaction well, being less attractive for the ILJ-II PES in the l and H configurations, and, to an even smaller extent, the long range part of the potential.

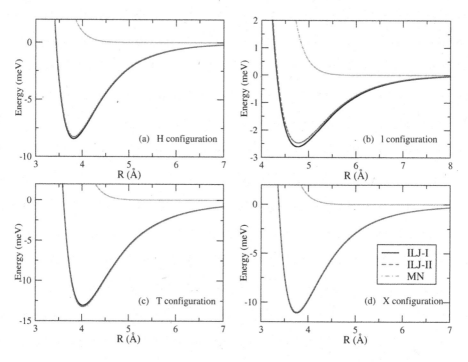

Fig. 3. Behavior of the different potential energy surfaces as a function of the diatoms interaction distance. Selected configurations, at the equilibrium intramolecular diatomic distance of both monomers, are considered: diatoms approaching in a parallel fashion (H configuration, D_{2h} symmetry, panel a); in a collinear configuration, according to l ($D_{\infty h}$ symmetry, panel b); perpendicularly, according to a T orientation (C_{2v} symmetry, panel c); and in a crossed X fashion (D_{2d} symmetry, panel d).

In addition, for preliminary calculations we have used the latest version of the reactive potential energy surface developed at the University of Minnesota (indicated here with MN) [14], based on ab-initio calculations, where, with respect to earlier versions, an effort has been devoted to the description of the long range interaction. Such potential specifically addresses high energy collisions and/or highly excited vibrational states, relevant in the modelling of hypersonic flows.

Figure 3 shows that the interaction wells of this PES are globally much shallower those of the ILJ models, being the corresponding repulsive part much stronger.

4   Computational Details

In this study we focused on the following VV energy exchange processes $(1,0) \rightarrow (0,1)$ and $(25,25) \rightarrow (24,26)$: the first is a resonant process, widely investigated both experimentally [11,28–30] and theoretically [8,10,22]; the second one is a quasi resonant exchange involving highly excited vibrational levels. The investigation was carried out over a wide range of temperatures (60–8000 K) by running trajectories at 40 initial values of total classical energy comprised between $35\,\mathrm{cm}^{-1}$ and $85000\,\mathrm{cm}^{-1}$, with a more frequent sampling directed towards lower energies. For each energy value, 2000 trajectories were considered, which should ensure an accuracy for rate constants of ca. 20 % at lower temperatures and ca. 15% at higher ones. An initial separation of the diatoms equal to 15 Å and an impact parameter randomly chosen between 0 and 9 Å were employed.

For the $(1,0) \rightarrow (0,1)$ process 24 initial vibrational states were considered in the set of coupled time dependent quantum equations to be solved for the vibrational motion (Eq. 1), whereas a larger number, 36, was used for the $(25,25) \rightarrow (24,26)$ transition, due to the closer spacings among vibrational levels.

5   Results and Discussion

The effect of the modification of the electrostatic part in the improved Lennard-Jones formulation of the potential has been examined by comparing the rate constants of the investigated processes in the whole temperature range and is depicted in Fig. 4.

In both cases, the trend of the rate constants as a function of temperature shows a minimum (that is an inversion of the expected increase of rate constants with temperature) at small values of T, $T \leq 460\,\mathrm{K}$ for ILJ-I and $T \leq 390\,\mathrm{K}$ for ILJ-II for the $(1,0) \rightarrow (0,1)$ resonant process and $T \leq 280\,\mathrm{K}$ for ILJ-I and $T \leq 260\,\mathrm{K}$ for ILJ-II for $(25,25) \rightarrow (24,26)$. This behavior was already pointed out by the calculations of ref. [10] and found experimentally in the recent work of ref. [11]. The correct theoretical representation of this feature seems to rely on both the potential, which should accurately reproduce the long range interaction contribution, and the inclusion of quantum effects in the dynamical treatment, as is the case for the present method.

As expected from the fact that multipole moments play an important role on the long range part of the potential, which is determinant for the interaction at small collision energies, it can be noted that at higher temperatures $(T > 4000\,\mathrm{K})$ the rate constants are in practice hardly distinguishable for the two ILJ-I and ILJ-II surfaces in the case of the $(1,0) \rightarrow (0,1)$ transition, and only show very small differences for the $(25,25) \rightarrow (24,26)$ one.

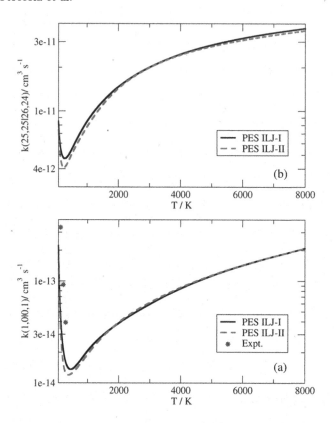

Fig. 4. Rate constants (logarithmic scale) as a function of temperature for the $(1,0) \to (0,1)$ transition (panel a) and for the $(25,25) \to (24,26)$ process (panel b) according the two formulations of the ILJ potential in the 60–8000 K range. For the first process, experimental data [11] are also reported.

The impact of the quadrupole moment modification at smaller temperatures and, particularly, on the position and depth of the minimum of the curve, is, on the other hand, hardly negligible.

In order to look at this effect from a more quantitative point of view, Fig. 5 reports rate constants in a restricted temperature range, where differences are more marked. The ILJ-II surface consistently leads to smaller rate constants than ILJ-I, with differences growing as the temperature decreases. In fact, the slightly larger (in absolute value) quadrupole moment used in the updated PES leads to a less attractive interaction especially evident in the well region for those approaching configurations, as the collinear l (see Fig. 3), for which the V-V energy exchange is expected to be more favourable and thus to give a larger contribution to the corresponding cross sections.

The position of the minimum of the curve for the $(1,0) \to (0,1)$ transition is at 460 K for ILJ-I and at 390 K for ILJ-II, a significant difference even if the minimum is rather shallow, and for the $(25,25) \to (24,26)$ transition is at 280 K

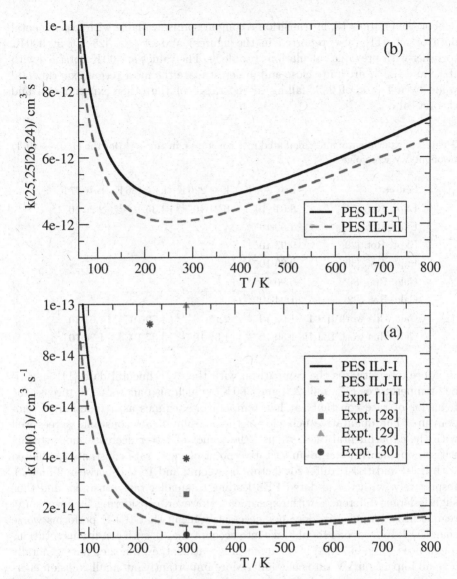

Fig. 5. Rate constants as a function of temperature for the $(1,0) \to (0,1)$ transition (panel a) and for $(25,25) \to (24,26)$ process (panel b) according the two formulations of the ILJ potential in the 60–800 K range. For the first process, experimental data are also reported.

for ILJ-I and at 260 K for ILJ-II. Rate constants in this region are different for ca. 15 % in both cases. At smaller temperature the difference grows: for instance, at 100 K, it is about 25 % for the $(1,0) \to (0,1)$ vibrational exchange.

For the $(1,0) \rightarrow (0,1)$ transition a comparison is available with experimental data of ref. [11] (also reported in the figures) and of refs. [28–30] at 300 K, together with previous calculations (Table 1). The values at 300 K obtained with ILJ-I and ILJ-II are quite close and underestimate the most recent experimental value by a factor of 2–3, falling in the range of the other experimental and theoretical data.

Table 1. Experimental and calculated rate constants, in $cm^3 \, s^{-1}$, for the $(1,0) \rightarrow (0,1)$ resonant VV exchange

Source	k @ 300 K	k @ 226 K	k @ 136 K	k @ 77 K
Expt. Ref. [11]	$3.91 \cdot 10^{-14}$	$9.21 \cdot 10^{-14}$	$3.35 \cdot 10^{-13}$	$2.26 \cdot 10^{-12}$
Expt. Ref. [28]	$2.50 \cdot 10^{-14}$			
Expt. Ref. [29]	$9.93 \cdot 10^{-14}$			
Expt. Ref. [30]	$0.90 \cdot 10^{-14}$			
Calc. Ref. [8]	$0.90 \cdot 10^{-14}$			
Calc. Ref. [22]	$1.94 \cdot 10^{-14}$			
Calc. this work ILJ-I	$1.62 \cdot 10^{-14}$	$2.15 \cdot 10^{-14}$	$4.70 \cdot 10^{-14}$	$1.61 \cdot 10^{-13}$
Calc. this work ILJ-II	$1.30 \cdot 10^{-14}$	$1.56 \cdot 10^{-14}$	$3.37 \cdot 10^{-14}$	$1.20 \cdot 10^{-13}$

More interesting is the comparison with the experimental data [11] at various temperatures (77, 136, 226 and 300 K), which also allows us to discuss the behavior of rate constants at low temperature regimes as a function of temperature. The qualitative behavior of the computed rate constants agrees well with the experimental ones, though the values of latter decrease more steeply with temperature. From a quantitative point of view, rate constants calculated with ILJ-I and ILJ-II differ for factors between 2 and 15 and between 3 and 18, respectively, with the updated PES leading to smaller rate constants and thus slightly larger differences with experiment. However, considering the low energy regime investigated, this does not necessarily mean that ILJ-II performs worse than ILJ-I. Indeed, one should take into account that in such conditions rotations might need to be included in the quantum treatment, even if they have generally a small impact on VV rate constants. More importantly, at small collision energies, symmetry issues, including the population of ortho and para states [31,32] might play a crucial role and thus the corresponding collisions should be treated separately and taken into account. Such effects are usually neglected because they average off at room conditions, however it was shown that they can have a strong impact for the calculations of rate constants at small temperatures [33]. Work to properly include this feature in the calculations is in progress.

We then calculated cross sections for the $(1,0) \rightarrow (0,1)$ energy transfer using the MN potential energy surface. We were not able to scan the whole energy range, as we did for the ILJ type of potentials, because of technical problems encountered running the code at lower collision energies: probably due to the very shallow character of MN potential at long range many of the investigated trajectories failed to converge so that results could not be considered reliable. Cross sections have thus been calculated at values of classical energies $U \geq 5000$ cm^{-1} and are reported in Table 2, together with cross sections obtained with ILJ-I and ILJ-II surfaces.

Table 2. Cross sections for the $(1,0) \rightarrow (0,1)$ energy transfer process at high energy values

Energy (cm^{-1})	$\sigma(\text{Å}^2)$ ILJ-I	$\sigma(\text{Å}^2)$ ILJ-II	$\sigma(\text{Å}^2)$ MN
5000	7.92	6.64	$9.72 \cdot 10^2$
7500	$2.26 \cdot 10^1$	$2.63 \cdot 10^1$	$1.41 \cdot 10^3$
15000	$2.97 \cdot 10^2$	$2.92 \cdot 10^2$	$4.87 \cdot 10^3$
20000	$9.00 \cdot 10^2$	$8.99 \cdot 10^2$	$8.67 \cdot 10^3$
30000	$3.94 \cdot 10^3$	$3.93 \cdot 10^3$	$2.45 \cdot 10^4$
40000	$1.13 \cdot 10^4$	$1.13 \cdot 10^4$	$6.08 \cdot 10^4$
50000	$4.76 \cdot 10^4$	$4.76 \cdot 10^4$	$1.13 \cdot 10^5$
70000	$3.30 \cdot 10^5$	$3.30 \cdot 10^5$	$3.41 \cdot 10^5$
85000	$1.21 \cdot 10^6$	$1.21 \cdot 10^6$	$1.10 \cdot 10^6$

As expected from the above discussion, cross sections obtained at large energy values for the ILJ-type potentials are very close, practically undistinguishble above $10000 \, \text{cm}^{-1}$. Cross sections calculated with the MN potential are instead larger than the ILJ potentails predictions at smaller energies (up to two orders of magnitude), whereas they become comparable at the highest investigated values of U, where the short range contribution to the interaction becomes dominant.

This is an additional indication that the long range interaction in the MN potential energy surface is underestimated and leads to a poor description of inelastic scattering at low temperatures. On the other hand, this PES is bound to produce reliable results when the short range potential drives the dynamics (reactive events, or inelastic scattering at high collision energies).

6   Concluding Remarks and Perspectives

In the present work we used a mixed quantum classical treatment to investigate how the formulation of the potential energy surface and, notably, of the long range interaction, affects the calculation of cross sections and rate constants in a prototypical system, such as N_2-N_2.

It was shown that the modification of the electrostatic component, which is added to an Improved Lennard Jones kind of potential, produces a non negligible difference in the numerical value of rate constants at small temperatures, so that an accurate choice of this parameter might be crucial to quantitatively predict the kinetic behavior of the system.

However, other effects may come into play at low collisional energies. First of all, we are currently considering a separate treatment of ortho and para N_2 collisions, so to be able to deal with the different populations of the two species, which are bound to affect the overall rate constants. Besides, the quantum treatment of vibrations and roto-vibrational coupling might not be sufficient at such low energy values, i.e. the effect of the inclusion of rotations in the quantum subsystem should also be evaluated.

High energy collisions, on the other hand, pose a different kind of questions. In such conditions, reactive channels open and play a role in the dynamics of the system together with inelastic collisions. A potential energy surface able to simultaneously tackle reactive and inelastic scattering (largely dominated by long range interactions, as shown in the present work) with high accuracy is not presently available. Furthermore, one would also wish for a dynamical approach to the problem which allows to obtain reaction and VV/VT probabilities within the same calculations.

In short, notwithstanding the considerable progress achieved in the last years in the direction of accurate potentials and in the ability to perform faster and reliable dynamical computations, very small and very high temperature regimes still represent an open challenge at present.

References

1. Billing, G.D.: Vibration-vibration and vibration-translation energy transfer, including multiquantum transitions in atom-diatom and diatom-diatom collisions. In: Capitelli, M. (ed.) Nonequilibrium Vibrational Kinetics. Topics of Current Physics, vol. 39, pp. 85–112. Springer, Berlin (1986). doi:10.1007/978-3-642-48615-9_4
2. Coletti, C., Billing, G.D.: Quantum-classical calculation of cross sections and rate constants for the H_2+CN $\rightarrow$ HCN+H reaction. J. Chem. Phys. **113**, 11101–11108 (2000)
3. Coletti, C., Billing, G.D.: Quantum dressed classical mechanics: application to chemical reactions. Chem. Phys. Lett. **342**, 65–74 (2001)
4. Martí, C., Pacifici, L., Laganà, A., Coletti, C.: A quantum-classical study of the OH + H_2 reactive and inelastic collisions. Chem. Phys. Lett. **674**, 103–108 (2017)
5. Coletti, C., Billing, G.D.: Quantum dressed classical mechanics: application to the photo-absorption of pyrazine. Chem. Phys. Lett. **368**, 289–298 (2003)
6. Billing, G.D., Coletti, C., Kurnosov, A.K., Napartovich, A.P.: Sensitivity of molecular vibrational dynamics to energy exchange rate constants. J. Phys. B: At. Mol. Opt. Phys. **36**, 1175–1192 (2003)
7. Park, C.: Nonequilibrium Hypersonic Aerothermodynamics. Wiley, New York (1989)
8. Billing, G.D., Fisher, E.R.: VV and VT rate coefficients in N_2 by a quantum-classical model. Chem. Phys. **43**, 395–401 (1979)
9. Pirani, F., Brizi, S., Roncaratti, L.F., Casavecchia, P., Cappelletti, D., Vecchiocattivi, F.: Beyond the Lennard-Jones Model: a simple and accurate potential function probed by high resolution scattering data useful for molecular dynamics simulations. Phys. Chem. Chem. Phys. **10**, 5489–5503 (2008)

10. Kurnosov, A., Cacciatore, M., Laganà, A., Pirani, F., Bartolomei, M., Garcia, E.: The effect of the intermolecular potential formulation on the state-selected energy exchange rate coefficients in N_2-N_2 collisions. J. Comput. Chem. **35**, 722–736 (2014)

11. Martínez, R.Z., Bermejo, D.: Experimental determination of the rate of VV collisional relaxation in $^{14}N_2$ in its ground $(X^1\Sigma_g^+)$ electronic state between 77 and 300 K. Phys. Chem. Chem. Phys. **17**, 12661–12672 (2015)

12. Paukku, Y., Yang, K.R., Varga, Z., Truhlar, D.G.: Global ab initio ground-state potential energy surface of N_4. J. Chem. Phys. **139**, 044309 (2013)

13. Bender, J.D., Doraiswamy, S., Truhlar, D.G., Candler, G.V.: Potential energy surface fitting by a statistically localized, permutationally invariant, local interpolating moving least squares method for the many-body potential: method and application to N_4. J. Chem. Phys. **140**, 054302 (2014)

14. Bender, J.D., Valentini, P., Nompelis, I., Paukku, Y., Varga, Z., Truhlar, D.G., Schwartzentruber, T., Candler, G.V.: An improved potential energy surface and multi-temperature quasiclassical trajectory calculations of N_2+N_2 dissociation reactions. J. Chem. Phys. **143**, 054304 (2015)

15. Billing, G.D.: Rate constants and cross sections for vibrational transitions in atom-diatom and diatom-diatom collisions. Comp. Phys. Comm. **32**, 45–62 (1984)

16. Billing, G.D.: Rate constants for vibrational transitions in diatom-diatom collisions. Comput. Phys. Comm. **44**, 121–136 (1987)

17. Cappelletti, D., Pirani, F., Bussery-Honvault, B., Gómez, L., Bartolomei, M.: A bond-bond description of the intermolecular interaction energy: the case of weakly bound N_2-H_2 and N_2-N_2 complexes. Phys. Chem. Chem. Phys. **10**, 4281–4293 (2008)

18. Coletti, C., Billing, G.D.: Isotopic effects on vibrational energy transfer in CO. J. Chem. Phys. **111**, 3891–3897 (1999)

19. Coletti, C., Billing, G.D.: Rate constants for energy transfer in carbon monoxyde. J. Chem. Phys. **113**, 4869–4875 (2000)

20. Coletti, C., Billing, G.D.: Vibrational energy transfer in molecular oxygen collisions. Chem. Phys. Lett. **356**, 14–22 (2002)

21. Billing, G.D.: The semiclassical treatment of molecular roto/vibrational energy transfer. Comput. Phys. Rept. **1**, 239–296 (1984)

22. Cacciatore, M., Kurnosov, A., Napartovich, A.: Vibrational energy transfer in N_2 N_2 collisions: a new semiclassical study. J. Chem. Phys. **123**, 174315 (2005)

23. Aquilanti, V., Bartolomei, M., Cappelletti, D., Carmona-Novillo, E., Pirani, F.: Dimers of the major components of the atmosphere: realistic potential energy surfaces and quantum mechanical prediction of spectral features. Phys. Chem. Chem. Phys. **3**, 3891–3894 (2001)

24. Lombardi, A., Pirani, F., Laganà, A., Bartolomei, M.: Energy transfer dynamics and kinetics of elementary processes (Promoted) by gas-phase CO_2-N_2 collisions: selectivity control by the anisotropy of the interaction. J. Comput. Chem. **37**, 1463–1475 (2016)

25. Maroulis, G.: Accurate electric multipole moment, static polarizability and hyperpolarizability derivatives for N_2. J. Chem. Phys. **118**, 2673–2687 (2003)

26. Bartolomei, M., Carmona-Novillo, E., Hernández, M.I., Campos Martínez, J., Hernández-Lamoneda, R.: Long-range interaction for dimers of atmospheric interest: dispersion, induction and electrostatic contributions for O_2-O_2, N_2-N_2 and O_2-N_2. J. Comput. Chem. **32**, 279–290 (2011)

27. Garcia, E., Laganà, A., Pirani, F., Bartolomei, M., Cacciatore, M., Kurnosov, A.: Enhanced flexibility of the O_2 + N_2 interaction and its effect on collisional vibrational energy exchange. J. Phys. Chem. A **120**, 5208–5219 (2016)
28. Akishev, Y.S., Demyanov, A.V., Kochetov, I.V., Napartovich, A.P., Pashkin, S.V., Ponomarenko, V.V., Pevgov, V.G., Podobedov, V.B.: Determination of vibrational exchange constants in N_2 from heating of gas. High Temp. **20**, 658 (1982)
29. Valyanskii, S.I., Vereshchagin, K.A., Volkov, A.Y., Pashinin, P.P., Smirnov, V.V., Fabelinskii, V.I., Holz, L.: Determination of the rate constant for vibrational-vibrational exchange in nitrogen under biharmonic excitation conditions. Sov. J. Quantum Electron. **14**, 1229 (1984)
30. Ahn, T., Adamovich, I.V., Lempert, W.R.: Determination of nitrogen VV transfer rates by stimulated Raman pumping. Chem. Phys. **298**, 233–240 (2004)
31. Carmona-Novillo, E., Pirani, F., Aquilanti, V.: Quantum dynamics of clusters on experimental potential energy surfaces: triplet and quintet O_2-O_2 surfaces and dimers of para-N_2 with ortho- and para-N_2 and with O_2. Int. J. Quantum Chem. **99**, 616–627 (2004)
32. Aquilanti, V., Bartolomei, M., Cappelletti, D., Carmona-Novillo, E., Pirani, F.: The N_2-N_2 system: an experimental potential energy surface and calculated rotovibrational levels of the molecular nitrogen dimer. J. Chem. Phys. **117**, 615–627 (2002)
33. Guillon, G., Rajagopala Rao, T., Mahapatra, S., Honvault, P.: Quantum dynamics of the ^{18}O + $^{32}O_2$ collision process. J. Phys. Chem. A **119**, 12512–12516 (2015)

The HI + OH → H$_2$O + I Reaction by First-Principles Molecular Dynamics: Stereodirectional and *anti*-Arrhenius Kinetics

Nayara D. Coutinho[1(✉)], Valter H. Carvalho-Silva[2],
Heibbe C.B. de Oliveira[1], and Vincenzo Aquilanti[3,4]

[1] Laboratório de Estrutura Eletrônica e Dinâmica Molecular (LEEDMOL),
Institute of Chemistry, University of Brasília,
Campus Darcy Ribeiro, Brasília, Brazil
nayaradcoutinho@gmail.com
[2] Grupo de Química Teórica e Estrutural de Anápolis,
Ciências Exatas e Tecnológicas, Universidade Estadual de Goiás,
CP 459, Anápolis, GO 75001-970, Brazil
[3] Dipartimento di Chimica, Biologia e Biotecnologie, Università di Perugia,
Via Elce di Sotto 8, 06123 Perugia, Italy
[4] Istituto di Struttura della Materia, Consiglio Nazionale delle Ricerche,
00185 Rome, Italy

Abstract. Exemplary of four-atom processes, the series of reactions between OH and HX to give H$_2$O + X (here X is a halogen atom) is one of the most studied theoretically and experimentally: the kinetics for X = Br and I manifests an unusual *anti*-Arrhenius behavior, namely a marked decrease of the rate constants as the temperature increases, and this has intrigued theoreticians for a long time. Motivation of the work reported in this paper is the continuation of the investigation of the stereodirectional dynamics of these reaction as the prominent reason for the peculiar kinetics, started in previous papers on X = Br. A first-principles Born-Oppenheimer 'canonical' molecular dynamics approach involves trajectories step-by-step generated on a potential energy surface quantum mechanically calculated on-the-fly, and thermostatically equilibrated in order to correspond to a specific temperature. Previous refinements of the method permitted a high number of trajectories at 50, 200, 350 and 500 K, for which the sampling of initial conditions allowed us to characterize the stereo-dynamical effect. It was confirmed also for X = I that the adjustment of the reactants' mutual orientation in order to encounter the entrance into the 'cone of acceptance' is crucial for reactivity. The aperture angle of this cone is dictated by a range of directions of approach compatible with the formation of the specific HOH angle of the product water molecule; and consistently the adjustment is progressively less effective at higher the kinetic energy. Thermal rate constants from this molecular dynamics approach are discussed: provided that the systematic sampling of the canonical ensemble is adequate as in this case, quantitative comparison with the kinetic experiments is obtained.

© Springer International Publishing AG 2017
O. Gervasi et al. (Eds.): ICCSA 2017, Part V, LNCS 10408, pp. 297–313, 2017.
DOI: 10.1007/978-3-319-62404-4_22

1 Introduction

Reactive halogen species (Cl, Br and I) play a crucial role in the atmospheric chemistry by disturbing the natural equilibrium processes that create and destroy ozone in the stratosphere. For example, depletion of ozone through the reaction with halogen atoms occurs through efficient catalytic cycles. These atoms react with ozone molecules to yield halogen monoxide (XO) and oxygen (O_2) molecules [1, 2].

In particular, the $OH + HX \rightarrow H_2O + X(X = Cl, Br \text{ and } I)$ reactions have been extensively studied because they are major providers for the halogens in the atmosphere. Additionally, these four-body reactions are also of basic relevance for both experimental and theoretical chemical kinetics. The rate constants for most rate processes depend on absolute temperature according to the Arrhenius law: however, for reactions of OH with hydrogen halides, when extended to low temperatures, deviations are observed: the kinetics data available for the reaction with HCl [3, 4] show a strong concave curvature for low temperatures, a phenomenon described as *sub*-Arrhenius behavior, while reactions with HBr [5–11] and HI [12–16] are considered as a typical of processes that exhibit negative temperature dependence of the reaction rate (*anti*-Arrhenius behavior).

In our previous works [17, 18] and as described in Sect. 2, we have approached the study of the *anti*-Arrhenius mechanism of the OH + HBr reaction using first-principles Born-Oppenheimer molecular dynamics. Here, in order to understand the peculiar kinetics of the systems involving hydroxyl radical and hydrogen halides and to continue the previous discussion about *non*-Arrhenius behavior [19–24], we focus on the $OH + HI \rightarrow H_2O + I$ reaction. Work is in progress regarding the Cl case, presenting different behavior to be examined accordingly.

The experimental kinetic data for OH + HI are limited: just a few values are available for rate constants in a narrow range of temperatures [12–16]: under these conditions, the rate constants show a negative temperature dependence. These results are discussed in Sect. 3.

As a contribution to the understanding of the detailed microscopic dynamics of the OH + HI reaction, Moise and collaborators using crossed molecular beam experiments to measure relative state-to-state cross section and steric asymmetries and a comparison was made with the previously studied systems OH-HCl and OH-HBr [25]. They provide an insight on the relevance of the potential energy surface landscape of these molecular systems in the reactive process. From a theoretical perspective, starting in 2010 [26], the direct and reverse reactions have been of interest since some time regarding the potential energy profile of the $I + H_2O$ reaction and showing that the relative energy of products is lower than that of the transition state. Furthermore, quantitative rate constants where determined for the reactions involving iodine-containing species using the canonical transition state theory with a simple Wigner tunneling correction. Recently, the stationary points, zero-point vibrational energies and vibrational frequencies for the $I + H_2O$ potential energy surface have been predicted at high-level *ab initio* CCSD(T) method, with the spin–orbit coupling corrections [27]. However, all previous works neglect the understanding of the *anti*-Arrhenius behavior.

Here, the strategy that we follow to assess to *anti*-Arrhenius mechanism is to use the Born-Oppenheimer molecular dynamics [28–30] technology to carry out numerical experiments that simulate the reaction in a box, which we consider as our first-principles "nanoreactor" [31]: the reactant molecules introduced in the box explore the potential energy surface at a specified temperature, enforced by a Nosé-Hoover thermalizing bath and therefore representing a 'canonical' ensemble [32]. Although computations of the potential energy surface on-the-fly are time-consuming, we can scrutinize trajectories at different configurations and will examine comparatively their behavior at four descriptive temperatures. We show how during trajectories molecular reorientation occurs in order to encounter a mutual approach of reactants favorable for them to proceed to reaction. Besides the demonstration of the crucial role of stereo-dynamics, additional documentation is also provided on the interesting manifestation of the roaming phenomenon, whereby both the search of the reactive configurations sterically favorable to reaction and the subsequent departure involving vibrational excitation, were seen to occur on wandering paths on the potential energy surface not limited to those corresponding to the one of minimum energy. A closer scrutiny is possible thanks to the results of this paper, where a perspective avenue leading to the extraction of quantitative information on reaction rate constants emerges from the analysis of molecular dynamics simulations.

2   Theoretical and Numerical Procedures and Results

2.1   Molecular Dynamics Simulations

The aim of disentangling the basic question concerning the peculiar kinetics of this reaction is approached by molecular dynamics simulations. As noted above (see also Ref. [17]) the technique of choice, the Born-Oppenheimer molecular dynamics (BOMD) [28–30], is suited to follow the evolution of the reaction and therefore to provide a description of its apparently anomalous features. As a result of the various preceding theoretical and computational investigations, a definite role was attributed to the transient aggregate due to van-der-Waals – like interactions, lying at a lower energy than that of the reactants. This feature is so prominent to give to this process an unusual reaction path profile [33, 34] corresponding to essentially a negative activation barrier. The dynamical relevance of this feature is adequately scrutinized under the microscope of the present canonical trajectory simulations. In the HBr case very relevant appeared to us the additional specific goal to provide a link with the available but overlooked experimental stereodynamical studies [35–37].

A previous pioneering investigation [38] of a reactive process where the reactant was the hydroxyl radical, exploited Car-Parrinello molecular dynamics, where motion of the nuclei in the on-the-fly calculated trajectories occurs in the potential generated by the electrons according to classical mechanics. A distinctive feature of the present first-principles Born-Oppenheimer molecular dynamics study is that quantum chemical wavefunctions are converged at every step, making trajectory calculations much more expensive but arguably more accurate.

Electronic structure calculations are essential in molecular dynamics simulations and the reliability of intermolecular forces depends on the quality of the employed quantum chemistry methods and of the dedicated computational effort. Since a reactive process involves the adjustment of the electronic structure according to the evolution of the nuclear positions, reaction mechanisms emerge with no need of computationally prohibitive explorations to find reaction pathways. On the contrary, the exploit of the automatic focusing of trajectories on regions actually sampled during the reaction provides information on parts of the multidimensional potential energy surface which demand more accuracy for improving the realistic simulations of the dynamics. Randomly generated initial conditions and procedures for equilibration with respect to a thermal bath (see the following subsection), permit to efficiently bypass the often severe bottlenecks of computational dynamics, such as both the impact parameter integration to provide total cross sections, and their Boltzmann kinetic energy averaging, allowing the direct specification of the temperature: our previous choice [17] was limited to consider two temperatures only, at the two extremes of the experimentally relevant range, at low (50 K) and high (500 K) temperatures, and the improvements to be described next allow us to explore a total of four temperature by a much higher number of trajectories in both Ref. [18] and in this work.

2.2   Computational Methods

The results from BOMD simulations reported in this paper were obtained utilizing the Car-Parrinello-Molecular-Dynamics CPMD 3.17.1 suite of programs, Copyright IBM, 2012. The electronic structure calculations employed was density functional theory DFT, through the Perdew-Burke-Ernzerhof [39] functional. The plane-wave cutoff was equal to 25 Ry, and the core electrons were described using the Vanderbilt pseudopotential [40]. We used a step size to 0.1 fs and run a total of 2 ps for each trajectory.

The temperatures of the system were controlled by the Nosé-Hoover Thermostats (NVT) scheme [32] at 50, 200, 350 and 500 K. One HI molecule and one OH radical were placed inside a cubic cell having a 6 Å side and periodic boundary conditions were imposed for each trajectory reaching the walls of the cell. The intermolecular orientation of the two molecules in the initial configurations was not optimized; that is, the starting geometries do not represent local minima of the global potential surface.

2.3   Representation of Stereodirectional Dynamics

Figure 1 (upper panel) illustrates the coordinate choice for this discussion of the $OH + HI \rightarrow H_2O + I$ reaction. In a four-body system, the configuration is fixed by six coordinates, two of them are those utilized here for exhibiting the stereodirectional effect on the molecular dynamics: they are the bond length r_1 and the angle θ. Their values are fixed when starting the simulations and serve to identify the trajectories in the following presentation. In order to compare with result for the OH + HBr reaction presents in our previous paper [18], we used the same 60 initial configurations with characteristic values listed in Table 1. The initial settings have been selected according

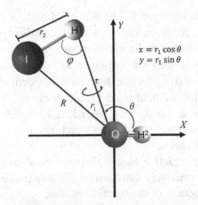

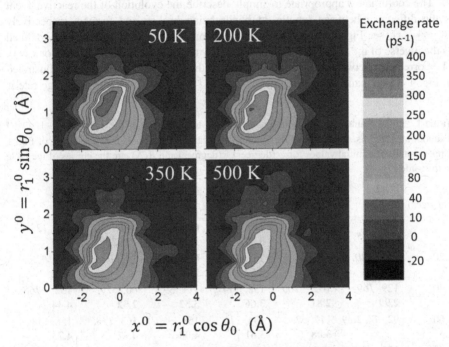

Fig. 1. Upper panel: definitions of geometrical parameters for the configuration of the present four-atom process suited to extract stereodynamical information on the role of the mutual direction between approaching reactants. The origin is on the oxygen atom, the OH bond, of length r_2, lies in the X axis, while Y is the axis perpendicular to X in the IOH^2 plane oriented as in the figure. The initial configurations are identified (Table 1) by a zero affix, namely by the vector length r_1^0 and the angle θ_0 or by the vectors components x_0 and y_0 on the X and Y axes. Lower panel: contour plots of reactivity data, the latter estimated on the assumption that the velocity of reaction can be correlated to the so-called 'switching time', namely to the moment when $r_1 = r_2$. Its inverse (see text), is defined as 'exchange rates', and can be extracted from the entries of Table 2.

to the following criteria: r_1^0 ranging from 1.7 to 3.2 Å with steps of 0.3 Å and θ_0 ranging from 0 to 180° with a 20° increment; all other coordinates were obtained randomly, within limits that guaranteed realistic initial configurations of the system. In Table 1 and in the following ones, they are displayed as labels to a matrix with 60 entries, r_1^0 for the six columns and θ_0 for the ten rows, respectively. In the initial configurations, two other variables are held fixed for all cases, the HI bond length at 1.61 Å and the OH^2 bond length at 1.0 Å. Two other needed coordinates are chosen randomly among the three φ (degrees), τ(degrees) and R(Å), one of them being superfluous but used for internal check.

As the temperature increases, reactive trajectories are found to typically wander around before encountering their relatively narrow road towards product formation and are relatively insensitive to the details of the reaction profile.

The coordinate s appropriate to simply describe the evolution of the reactive event is the difference between lengths of bonds being broken and formed, respectively ($s = r_2 - r_1$, see Fig. 1). The "exchange rate" for the reaction is conveniently defined as the inverse of the "switching" time, defined by the time when either $r_1 = r_2$ or $s = 0$. The correlation between the initial geometry of the propensity to reaction is illustrated in Fig. 1 (lower panel) and in Tables 2, 3, 4 and 5. In the tables, the exchange rate is

Table 1. Initial values of the coordinates for all trajectories for the OH + HI → H$_2$O + I reaction, arranged as a function of the stereodynamical angle, θ_0, and the distance r_1^0 of Fig. 1 (upper panel). The initial values for φ (degrees), τ(degrees) and R(Å), are the entries of the table in this order

θ_0 (degrees)	r_1^0 (Å)					
	1.7	2.0	2.3	2.6	2.9	3.2
0	60, *142*, **1.66**	158, *129*, **3.54**	115, *127*, **3.32**	60, *132*, **2.27**	117, *124*,**3.90**	173, *123*, **4.80**
20	144, *−20*, **3.15**	127, *66*, **3.24**	78, *−28*, **2.52**	60, *132*, **2.27**	107, *0, 3.71*	169, *82*, **4.79**
40	129, *169*, **2.99**	102, *−100*, **2.81**	138, *−14*, **3.66**	111, *39*, **3.52**	60, *−79*, **2.52**	132, *−168*, **4.44**
60	92, *97*, **2.39**	117, *52*, **3.08**	134, *21*, **3.61**	151, *−90*, **4,08**	163, *128*, **4.47**	158, *−60*, **4.73**
80	177, *−148*, **3.31**	167, *114*, **3.59**	179, *47*, **3.91**	168, *120*, **4.19**	60, *113*, **2.52**	60, 28, **2.77**
100	175, *−151*, **3.31**	126, *−5*, **3.23**	145, *157*, **3.73**	60, *−146*, **2.27**	60, *−168*, **2.52**	128, *−158*, **4.37**
120	145, *−107*, **3.16**	162, *20*, **3.57**	60, *−26*, **2.04**	60, *95*, **2.27**	60, *-111*, **2.52**	60, *−21*, **2.77**
140	145, *−147*, **3.16**	121, *97*, **3.14**	117, *−130*, **3.36**	95, *20*, **3.18**	120, *61*, **3.96**	122, *163*, **4.29**
160	173, *−125*, **3.30**	179, *172*, **3.61**	141, *170*, **3.69**	169, *130*, **4.05**	60, *97*, **2.52**	113, *−109*, **4.11**
180	60, *−76*, **1.66**	65, *−82*, **1.97**	*124, 89*, **3.47**	78, *−93*, **2.76**	138, *−110*, **4.24**	160, *171*, **4.75**

Table 2. Exchange rates (ps^{-1}, see Text) for reactive trajectories at 50 K. Zero entries correspond to non-reactive trajectories.

θ_0 (degrees)	r_1^0 (Å)					
	1.7	2.0	2.3	2.6	2.9	3.2
0	0	0	0	0	0	0
20	0	13.48	0	0	0	0
40	28.49	0	0	0	0	0
60	0	46.95	17.89	0	0	0
80	312.50	0	0	0	0	0
100	357.14	32.79	15.48	0	0	0
120	370.37	90.91	0	0	0	0
140	384.62	56.50	28.01	0	7.35	0
160	344.83	9.96	0	0	0	0
180	0	0	17.42	0	0	0

Table 3. Exchange rates (ps^{-1}, see Text) for reactive trajectories at 200 K. Zero entries correspond to non-reactive trajectories.

θ_0 (degrees)	r_1^0 (Å)					
	1.7	2.0	2.3	2.6	2.9	3.2
0	0	0	0	0	0	0
20	0	0	0	0	0	0
40	29.24	0	0	0	0	0
60	0	42.55	17.33	13.33	0	0
80	256.41	3.75	0	0	0	0
100	294.12	24.69	16.16	0	0	0
120	322.58	121.95	0	0	0	0
140	370.37	56.50	29.15	0	10.49	0
160	357.14	17.45	0	0	0	0
180	0	0	22.47	0	0	0

given as a function of r_1^0 and θ_0 and in Fig. 2 in the plane of the Cartesian components of the r_1 vector, $x_0 = r_1^0 \cos \theta_0$ and $y_0 = r_1^0 \sin \theta_0$. For a temperature, e.g. of 50 K the reactivity is seen as largest for x_0 equal to −2 to 0.5 Å range and y_0 equal to 0.5 to 1.5 Å range, manifesting stereodynamical propensity for θ_0 angles in the 80–160° range and for r_1^0 less than 2.3 Å. For values of x_0 larger than 2.3 Å, the reactivity is very low. As the system temperature increases, the dependence of reactivity on the stereodirectionality is lower and other initial conditions can lead to the final product, as can be seen in the corresponding panels at 350 and 500 K and in Tables 3, 4 and 5. For high temperatures the reactivity of the system is less sensitive to the system initial conditions, and the memory of the initial configuration appears to be partially lost during the reactive process, arguably because of the manifestation of the roaming effect, to be discussed next.

Table 4. Exchange rates (ps^{-1}, see Text) for reactive trajectories at 350 K. Zero entries correspond to non-reactive trajectories.

θ_0 (degrees)	r_1^0 (Å)					
	1.7	2.0	2.3	2.6	2.9	3.2
0	0	0	0	0	0	0
20	0	0	0	0	5.63	0
40	28.01	0	0	0	0	0
60	0	29.76	0	0	0	0
80	232.56	0	0	0	0	0
100	263.16	0	15.85	0	0	0
120	294.12	126.58	0	0.75	0	0
140	357.14	54.64	27.62	0	13.81	0
160	357.14	16.13	0	4.36	0	0
180	0	0	23.75	0	0	0

Table 5. Exchange rates (ps^{-1}, see text) for reactive trajectories at 500 K. Zero entries correspond to non-reactive trajectories.

θ_0 (degrees)	r_1^0 (Å)					
	1.7	2.0	2.3	2.6	2.9	3.2
0	0	0	1.52	0	0	0
20	0	0	0	0	0	0
40	26.25	0	3.20	0	0	0
60	0	18.80	0.85	0	0	0
80	217.39	0	0	0	0.71	0.71
100	250	0	17.54	0	0	0
120	270.27	129.87	0	3.45	1.83	0
140	357.14	52.91	23.36	0	14.45	0
160	357.14	0	0.52	0	0	0
180	0	0	24.27	0	0	0

2.4   Delayed Reactivity and Vibrational Roaming of Product Water

The information from Tables 2, 3, 4 and 5 focused on "switching" times along trajectories, identified as the moment when $r_1 = r_2$: they convey the approximate view of the event, as involving the sudden breaking of the reactant HI molecule and the synchronous formation of the H_2O product. Remarkable is the delayed reactivity for trajectories for high temperatures and for high initial stretching of r_1: additionally, this effect appears from emergence of "roaming" in vibrational modes in search of propitious outcomes.

The "roaming" phenomenon has been amply documented as occurring in photodissociation experiments as the emergency of routes to molecular fragmentation channels [41, 42] that circumvent transition-state reaction paths. The presence of these alternative pathways can be inferred by the properties of the translational and internal distribution of the product fragments. Since they involve regions far from the neighborhoods of saddle points along minimum energy paths and lead to avenues to reaction beyond the venerable transition state approach [37, 43–45], they are challenging to theories of chemical kinetics and demand explorations by on-the-fly dynamics, such as the one presented in this work.

Experimental fingerprints of roaming are slow, delayed photodissociation products, as inferred by late arrival of products in time-of-flight measurements. Detailed investigations [41] on the threshold for the opening of the breakdown in three fragments and molecular dynamics simulations pointed out the role of non-adiabatic transitions at a conical intersection between ground state and excited potential energy surfaces [41].

The origin of roaming as a rearrangement between weakly bound reactants is connected to high-lying regions of the ground state potential energy surfaces [46, 47] and indicated in Refs. [42, 48, 49]. Typically, they involve molecular configurations far from the transition state geometry and are propitiated by pronounced bond elongations, such as manifested when emerging from nonadiabatic paths involving conical intersections. From Tables 2, 3, 4 and 5, we observe analogously that in our case "roaming" is favored by starting trajectories at elongated r_1^0.

2.5 Angle of Approach and Excitation of Bending in the Departing Water

In this section, the important role of the stereodynamical angle of approach θ_0 in influencing the reaction is discussed in detail with reference to Fig. 2. The figure shows that when the dynamics is started with those values of θ_0 close to that leading to the formation of the bond angle of water $(\theta_w \sim 104°)$, the system finds an easier way to products, and possible reorientation facilitating the process is hindered as the temperature increases. The specific value of the s coordinate, indicated as $s^{\ddagger}$, marks at each temperature the estimated averaged configuration in terms of new and old bond differences, characterizing the moment in the dynamics when the water molecule can be considered as effectively formed. These values are in general higher than the previously considered values of s corresponding to $r_1 = r_2$, which were used in the preceding estimates of the exchange rates. They decrease from about 1.9 Å at 50 K to 1.6 Å at 500 K. In the following, these values will be correlated to reaction times for each temperature, and will provide further information on the kinetic rate constants (Sect. 3).

In Fig. 2, the trajectories that are visualized are conveniently listed following the initial value of the stereodynamically relevant angle, θ_0, which represents the direction of the approach of the H atom to OH (Fig. 1). Since the process evolves as the H-atom departs from HI and is effectively terminated when it sticks to OH forming a bond angle typical to that of the bending angle for water, the propitious orientation is crucial. It has to be noted here not only again the "roaming" effect as the search of a favorable approaching angle for reactivity, but also that such an effect results more evident at the higher temperature considered, 350 e 500 K. Additionally, it has to be noted how the final energy appears to be disposed of as excitation in the bending mode of the product water, as it is visually clear to a much greater extent again for the higher temperatures (see Ref. [47] for experimental comparisons for an analogous study case). The ranges of values span by the θ angle around 104° as the water molecule departs can be taken as a visualization of the disposal of the energy into the bending mode of the molecular product.

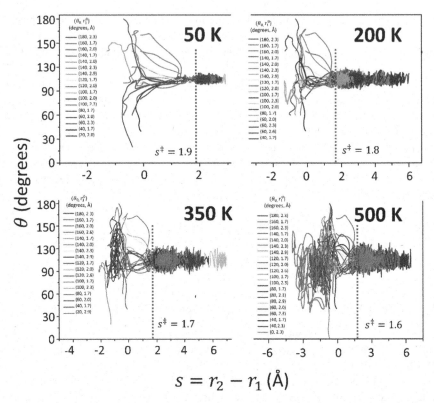

$$s = r_2 - r_1 \,(\text{Å})$$

Fig. 2. Evolution at four temperatures of the stereodynamical angle of approach θ (Fig. 1) for "canonical" trajectories versus the reaction coordinate $s = r_2 - r_1$, conveniently defined as the difference between the lengths of the bond which is broken r_1 and of the bond which is formed r_2. The number of reactive trajectories changes with temperature. The trajectories are distinguished by different colors as listed in the right panel and arranged in decreasing order of θ_0, the initial values for the θ angle; the other value characterizing the trajectory is that of r_1^0; the other parameters defining the initial configurations can be extracted by the corresponding entries in Table 1. Indicated by vertical dashed lines is the value of $s^{\ddagger}$, identified by averaging for all trajectories of a given temperature the values of the reaction coordinate $s = r_2 - r_1$ for which a water molecule can be considered as formed.

3   Rate Constants and Comparison with Experiments

The molecular dynamics investigation reported here has been devoted mostly to the elucidation of the stereodirectional aspects featuring as most relevant in the unusual kinetics of this reaction. In general, the extraction of quantitative information on rate constants from molecular dynamics simulations is an important issue but a very difficult to be tackled.

On the other hand, quantum mechanical benchmark rate constants [50–52] have been so far satisfactorily obtained only for specific three-atom processes, involving great theoretical and computational efforts, and evolving along a series of steps, the first one being the construction or availability of an accurate potential energy surface. In *ab initio* "exact" quantum dynamics, many further other steps are needed to go all the way from the interaction to rate constants. One must proceed through state-to-state coupled-channel Schrödinger dynamics giving scattering matrices (a major step), and then sum over all involved angular momenta, obtaining differential and integral cross sections on a large number of the reactants' kinetic energy values. The integral cross sections have to be obtained in a fine enough grid to finally generate temperature dependent rate constants by computationally demanding averaging on the Maxwell-Boltzmann distribution of the reactants' velocities. As a paradigmatic case, only in the last few years this has been achieved for the triatomic system F + H$_2$ → HF + H, and the predictions [53] have been verified experimentally, in particular from thermal down to the very low temperature reactivity range where tunneling is dominant [54]. For the related isotopic variant F + HD, see Refs. [21, 54].

The present system involves only four atoms, yet its kinetics is unusual and attractive to theorists as archetypal of four-center reactions. As a quantum-mechanical time-independent four-body problem: (i) computation and fitting of multidimensional PES of high accuracy is demanding (six effective degrees of freedom); (ii) exact quantum close coupling state-to-state dynamics is prohibitively expensive, and (iii) even for model PES, benchmark cross sections are difficult to obtain and rate constants out-of-reach (time-dependent techniques typically need calibration against time-independent benchmarks). However, comparison of results for the present four-atom reaction with three-atom processes bearing features in common with this one is interesting: for the reaction OH + HBr, see remarks in Ref. [33]; for the H + HBr reaction, Ref. [55] reports experimental and computational evidence of reactive trajectories far from the minimum energy path, a signature for 'roaming' in the same spirit as our discussion of Fig. 2.

There is ample current activity investigating whether advances in molecular dynamics simulations can provide quantitatively reliable rate constants. Recent Refs. [55–59] indicate that only order-of-magnitude estimates can be currently obtained. Typically, rates are overestimated and accuracy deteriorates considerably with temperature. Uncertainties are often dominated by those in the accurate characterization of transition state features, crucial in applications of TST-type approaches to calculations of rates. Additionally, inherent difficulties of possible direct evaluations from molecular dynamics simulation originate from those regarding the statistical validity of samplings of the system phase space. The latter of course increases enormously with temperature as far as both energy and angular momentum are concerned.

A different approach to estimate rate constants was briefly suggested in the preceding Letter [17] and later expanded in the subsequent work [18] on the basis of a much more detailed information available. The availability of considerably more information from the present results and especially the visualization from Fig. 2 and its discussion of the delayed reactivity leading to emergency of a water molecule, confirm the alternative approach based on the rate of formation of water rather than on the rate of disappearance of reactants. Specifically, for an evaluation of the reaction rate constants we now start from the observation that, being the bimolecular process OH + HI of the second order, the general formula for the rate constant can be written

$$k = \frac{d[H_2O]}{dt} ([OH][HI])^{-1}$$

as the ratio of the rate of formation of water and the product of the initial concentrations of the two reactants. In our numerical experiments, we place one molecule of OH and one molecule of HI in a cubic box of 6 Å in size, amounting to a concentration $[C] \sim 5 \times 10^{21}$ molecules.cm^{-3} for each reactant. The formation of water is "observed" in our first-principles nanoreactor as the appearance of one product molecule in the volume of the box, i.e. [C] times the fraction f of reactive versus total trajectories and emerging at the 'transition time',$t^{\ddagger}$:

$$\frac{d[H_2O]}{dt} = \frac{f[C]}{t^{\ddagger}}$$

The fractional number of reactive trajectories f and the resulting values of the transition time $t^{\ddagger}$ for each temperature can be extracted from Tables 2, 3, 4 and 5. Since the transition time is meant to represent the average time that elapses for the chemical reaction to take place in the nanoreactor, for its present evaluation we searched for the moments along trajectories when the evolution coordinate s corresponded to the emergency of water as a product. Average values of s for each temperature are denoted $s^{\ddagger}$ and highlighted in the plots in Fig. 2 providing the correlation between the angle θ and s.

As documented in other cases, such as the recent ones already considered above [56, 57], and as the HBr system, the rate constant k so obtained were larger than experimental rate constant and the more so the higher the temperature. As discussed there [18], one crucial reason is arguably the fact that the choice of initial conditions (reactants in a small box with close encounters) increases chances of reactive versus total collisions, especially at high temperature. This points out at the general need of calibrating a first-principles nanoreactor against experimental results. Fig. 3 shows that this is not necessary in the present case, due high reactivity between OH and HI compared with HCl and HBr. Indeed, this results is indicative of an at least semi-quantitative route to the extraction of rate constants from first-principles molecular dynamics numerical experiments. The better agreement obtained in this case of larger reactivity can be taken as an indication that calibration may be more needed the rarer are the reactive encounters.

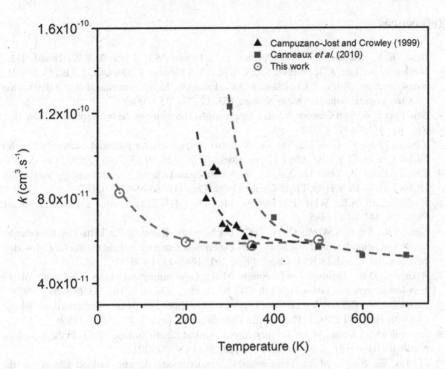

Fig. 3. Reaction rate constants as a function of temperature. We present the estimated rate constant obtained from Born-Oppenheimer molecular dynamics (red circles, see text and Table 6). They are reported together with experimental rate constants from reference [16], and the theoretical values obtained by Canneaux *et al.* [26]. Curves are drawn as aid to the eyes of readers. (Color figure online)

Table 6. Transition times (ps) and rate constants ($10^{-11} cm^3.s^{-1}$) at different temperatures (Kelvin).

T	$t^{\ddagger}$	k
50	0.74	8.25
200	1.09	5.93
350	1.06	5.75
500	1.26	6.00

Acknowledgments. The authors acknowledge grants from Brazilian CAPES, FAPEG, FAPDF, CNPQ and FINATEC. V. H. Carvalho-Silva thanks PrP/UEG for research funding through PROBIP and PRO-PROJETOS programs.

References

1. Read, K.A., Mahajan, A.S., Carpenter, L.J., Evans, M.J., Faria, B.V.E., Heard, D.E., Hopkins, J.R., Lee, J.D., Moller, S.J., Lewis, A.C., Mendes, L., McQuaid, J.B., Oetjen, H., Saiz-Lopez, A., Pilling, M.J., Plane, J.M.C.: Extensive halogen-mediated ozone destruction over the tropical Atlantic Ocean. Nature **453**, 1232–1235 (2008)
2. Saiz-Lopez, A., von Glasow, R.: Reactive halogen chemistry in the troposphere. Chem. Soc. Rev. **41**, 6448–6472 (2012)
3. Zuo, J., Zhao, B., Guo, H., Xie, D.: A global coupled cluster potential energy surface for HCl + OH ↔ Cl + H_2O. Phys. Chem. Chem. Phys. **120**, 3433–3440 (2016)
4. Zuo, J., Zhao, B., Guo, H., Xie, D.: A global coupled cluster potential energy surface for HCl + OH ↔ Cl + H_2O. Phys. Chem. Chem. Phys. **19**, 9770–9777 (2017)
5. Ravishankara, A.R., Wine, P.H., Wells, J.R.: The OH + HBr reaction revisited. J. Chem. Phys. **83**, 447–448 (1985)
6. Sims, I.R., Smith, I.W.M., Clary, D.C., Bocherel, P., Rowe, B.R.: Ultra-low temperature kinetics of neutral-neutral reactions - new experimental and theoretical results for OH + HBr between 295 K and 23 K. J. Chem. Phys. **101**, 1748–1751 (1994)
7. Atkinson, D,B., Jaramillo, V.I., Smith, M.A.: Low-temperature kinetic behavior of the bimolecular reaction OH + HBr (76−242 K). J. Phys. Chem. A **101**, 3356–3359 (1997)
8. Bedjanian, Y., Riffault, V., Le Bras, G., Poulet, G.: Kinetic study of the reactions of OH and OD with HBr and DBr. J. Photochem. Photobiol. A Chem. **128**, 15–25 (1999)
9. Jaramillo, V.I., Smith, M.A.: Temperature-dependent kinetic isotope effects in the gas-phase reaction: OH + HBr. J. Phys. Chem. A **105**, 5854–5859 (2001)
10. Mullen, C., Smith, M.A.: Temperature dependence and kinetic isotope effects for the OH + HBr reaction and H/D isotopic variants at low temperatures (53–135 K) measured using a pulsed supersonic Laval nozzle flow reactor. J. Phys. Chem. A **109**, 3893–3902 (2005)
11. Jaramillo, V.I., Gougeon, S., Le Picard, S.D., Canosa, A., Smith, M.A., Rowe, B.R.: A consensus view of the temperature dependence of the gas phase reaction: OH + HBr → H_2O + Br. Int. J. Chem. Kinet. **34**, 339–344 (2002)
12. Takacs, G.A., Glass, G.P.: Reactions of hydroxyl radicals with some hydrogen halides. J. Phys. Chem. **77**, 1948–1951 (1973)
13. Leod, H. M., Balestra, C., Jourdain, J.L., Laverdet, G., Le Bras, G.: Kinetic study of the reaction OH + HI by laser photolysis-resonance fluorescence. Int. J. Chem. Kinet. **22**, 1167–1176 (1990)
14. Lancar, I.T., Mellouki, A., Poulet, G.: Kinetics of the reactions of hydrogen iodide with hydroxyl and nitrate radicals. Chem. Phys. Lett. **177**, 554–558 (1991)
15. Butkovskaya, N.I., Setser, D.W.: Dynamics of OH and OD radical reactions with HI and GeH4 studied by infrared chemiluminescence of the H_2O and HDO products. J. Chem. Phys. **106**, 5028–5042 (1997)
16. Campuzano-Jost, P., Crowley, J.N.: Kinetics of the reaction of OH with HI between 246 and 353 K. J. Phys. Chem. A **103**, 2712–2719 (1999)
17. Coutinho, N.D., Silva, V.H.C., de Oliveira, H.C.B., Camargo, A.J., Mundim, K.C., Aquilanti, V.: Stereodynamical origin of anti-arrhenius kinetics: negative activation energy and roaming for a four-atom reaction. J. Phys. Chem. Lett. **6**, 1553–1558 (2015)
18. Coutinho, N.D., Aquilanti, V., Silva, V.H.C., Camargo, A.J., Mundim, K.C., de Oliveira, H. C.B.: Stereodirectional origin of anti-arrhenius kinetics for a tetraatomic Hydrogen exchange reaction: Born-Oppenheimer molecular dynamics for OH + HBr. J. Phys. Chem. A **120**, 5408–5417 (2016)

19. Silva, V.H.C., Aquilanti, V., de Oliveira, H.C.B., Mundim, K.C.: Uniform description of non-Arrhenius temperature dependence of reaction rates, and a heuristic criterion for quantum tunneling vs classical non-extensive distribution. Chem. Phys. Lett. **590**, 201–207 (2013)

20. Carvalho-Silva, V.H., Aquilanti, V., de Oliveira, H.C.B., Mundim, K.C.: Deformed transition-state theory: deviation from arrhenius behavior and application to bimolecular hydrogen transfer reaction rates in the tunneling regime. J. Comput. Chem. **38**, 178–188 (2017)

21. Cavalli, S., Aquilanti, V., Mundim, K.C., De Fazio, D.: Theoretical reaction kinetics astride the transition between moderate and deep tunneling regimes: the F + HD case. J. Phys. Chem. A **118**, 6632–6641 (2014)

22. Aquilanti, V., Mundim, K.C., Elango, M., Kleijn, S., Kasai, T.: Temperature dependence of chemical and biophysical rate processes: phenomenological approach to deviations from Arrhenius law. Chem. Phys. Lett. **498**, 209–213 (2010)

23. Aquilanti, V., Mundim, K.C., Cavalli, S., De Fazio, D., Aguilar, A., Lucas, J.M.: Exact activation energies and phenomenological description of quantum tunneling for model potential energy surfaces. The F + H₂ reaction at low temperature. Chem. Phys. **398**, 186–191 (2012)

24. Aquilanti, V., Coutinho, N.D., Carvalho-Silva, V.H.: Kinetics of low-temperature transitions and reaction rate theory from non-equilibrium distributions. Philos. Trans. R. Soc. London A **375**, 20160204 (2017)

25. Moise, A., Parker, D.H., Ter Meulen, J.J.: State-to-state inelastic scattering of OH by HI: A comparison with OH-HCl and OH-HBr. J. Chem. Phys. **126**, 124302 (2007)

26. Canneaux, S., Xerri, B., Louis, F., Cantrel, L.: Theoretical study of the gas-phase reactions of Iodine atoms (2P3/2) with H₂, H₂O, HI, and OH. J. Phys. Chem. A **114**, 9270–9288 (2010)

27. Hao, Y., Gu, J., Guo, Y., Zhang, M., Xie, Y., Schaefer III, H.F.: Spin-orbit corrected potential energy surface features for the I (2P3/2) + H₂O → HI + OH forward and reverse reactions. Phys. Chem. Chem. Phys. **16**, 2641–2646 (2014)

28. Marx, D., Hutter, J.: Ab initio molecular dynamics: theory and implementation. Mod. Methods Algorithms Quantum Chem. **1**, 301–449 (2000)

29. Paranjothy, M., Sun, R., Zhuang, Y., Hase, W.L.: Direct chemical dynamics simulations: coupling of classical and quasiclassical trajectories with electronic structure theory. WIRE Comput. Mol. Sci. **3**, 296–316 (2013)

30. Marx, D., Hutter, J.: Ab Initio Molecular Dynamics: Basic Theory and Advanced Methods. Cambridge University Press, Cambridge (2009)

31. Wang, L.-P., Titov, A., McGibbon, R., Liu, F., Pande, V.S., Martínez, T.J.: Discovering chemistry with an ab initio nanoreactor. Nat. Chem. **6**, 1044–1048 (2014)

32. Martyna, G.J., Klein, M.L., Tuckerman, M.: Nose-Hoover chains: the canonical ensemble via continuous dynamics. J. Chem. Phys. **97**, 2635–2643 (1992)

33. de Oliveira-Filho, A.G.S., Ornellas, F.R., Bowman, J.M.: Quasiclassical trajectory calculations of the rate constant of the OH + HBr → Br + H₂O reaction using a full-dimensional Ab initio potential energy surface over the temperature range 5 to 500 K. J. Phys. Chem. Lett. **5**, 706–712 (2014)

34. de Oliveira-Filho, A.G.S., Ornellas, F.R., Bowman, J.M.: Energy disposal and thermal rate constants for the OH + HBr and OH + DBr reactions: quasiclassical trajectory calculations on an accurate potential energy surface. J. Phys. Chem. A **118**, 12080–12088 (2014)

35. Tsai, P.-Y., Che, D.-C., Nakamura, M., Lin, K.-C., Kasai, T.: Orientation dependence in the four-atom reaction of OH + HBr using the single-state oriented OH radical beam. Phys. Chem. Chem. Phys. **12**, 2532–2534 (2010)

36. Tsai, P.-Y., Che, D.-C., Nakamura, M., Lin, K.-C., Kasai, T.: Orientation dependence for Br formation in the reaction of oriented OH radical with HBr molecule. Phys. Chem. Chem. Phys. **13**, 1419–1423 (2011)
37. Kasai, T., Che, D.-C., Okada, M., Tsai, P.-Y., Lin, K.-C., Palazzetti, F., Aquilanti, V.: Directions of chemical change: experimental characterization of the stereodynamics of photodissociation and reactive processes. Phys. Chem. Chem. Phys. **16**, 9776–9790 (2014)
38. Frank, I., Parrinello, M., Klamt, A.: Insight into chemical reactions from first-principles simulations: the mechanism of the gas-phase reaction of OH radicals with Ketones. J. Phys. Chem. A **102**, 3614–3617 (1998)
39. Perdew, J.P., Burke, K., Ernzerhof, M.: Generalized gradient approximation made simple. Phys. Rev. Lett. **77**, 3865–3868 (1996)
40. Vanderbilt, D.: Soft self-consistent pseudopotentials in a generalized eigenvalue formalism. Phys. Rev. B **41**, 7892–7895 (1990)
41. Tsai, P.-Y., Hung, K.-C., Li, H.-K., Lin, K.-C.: Photodissociation of Propionaldehyde at 248 nm: roaming pathway as an increasingly important role in large Aliphatic Aldehydes. J. Phys. Chem. Lett. **5**, 190–195 (2014)
42. Nakamura, M., Tsai, P.-Y., Kasai, T., Lin, K.-C., Palazzetti, F., Lombardi, A., Aquilanti, V.: Dynamical, spectroscopic and computational imaging of bond breaking in photodissociation: roaming and role of conical intersections. Faraday Discuss. **177**, 77–98 (2015)
43. Bowman, J.M.: Roaming. Mol. Phys. **112**, 2516–2528 (2014)
44. Spezia, R., Martínez-Nuñez, E., Vazquez, S., Hase, W.L.: Theoretical and computational studies of non-equilibrium and non-statistical dynamics in the gas phase, in the condensed phase and at interfaces. Philos. Trans. R. Soc. London A Math. Phys. Eng. Sci. **375**, 20170035 (2017)
45. Ma, X., Hase, W.L.: Perspective: chemical dynamics simulations of non-statistical reaction dynamics. Philos. Trans. R. Soc. London A Math. Phys. Eng. Sci. **375**, 20160204 (2017)
46. Hause, M.L., Herath, N., Zhu, R., Lin, M.C., Suits, A.G.: Roaming-mediated isomerization in the photodissociation of nitrobenzene. Nat. Chem. **3**, 932–937 (2011)
47. Herath, N., Suits, A.G.: Roaming radical reactions. J. Phys. Chem. Lett. **2**, 642–647 (2011)
48. Tsai, P.-Y., Chao, M.-H., Kasai, T., Lin, K.-C., Lombardi, A., Palazzetti, F., Aquilanti, V.: Roads leading to roam. Role of triple fragmentation and of conical intersections in photochemical reactions: experiments and theory on methyl formate. Phys. Chem. Chem. Phys. **16**, 2854–2865 (2014)
49. Lombardi, A., Palazzetti, F., Aquilanti, V., Li, H.-K., Tsai, P.-Y., Kasai, T., Lin, K.-C.: Rovibrationally excited molecules on the verge of a triple breakdown: molecular and roaming mechanisms in the photodecomposition of methyl formate. J. Phys. Chem. A **120**, 5155–5162 (2016)
50. Bonnet, L.: On the dynamical foundations of transition state theory: a semiclassical analysis. Ann. Phys. (N.Y.) **314**, 99–118 (2004)
51. Rayez, J.-C., Bonnet, L., Larrégaray, P., Perrier, A.: Transition state theory: a reaction dynamics tool applied to gas-surface reactions. Mol. Sci. **3**, A0029-1–A0029-10 (2009)
52. Bonnet, L., Rayez, J.-C.: Dynamical derivation of Eyring equation and the second-order kinetic law. Int. J. Quantum Chem. **110**, 2355–2359 (2010)
53. Tizniti, M., Le Picard, S.D., Lique, F., Berteloite, C., Canosa, A., Alexander, M.H., Sims, I. R.: The rate of the $F + H_2$ reaction at very low temperatures. Nat. Chem. **6**, 141–145 (2014)
54. De Fazio, D., Aquilanti, V., Cavalli, S., Aguilar, A., Lucas, J.M.: Exact quantum calculations of the kinetic isotope effect: cross sections and rate constants for the $F + HD$ reaction and role of tunneling. J. Chem. Phys. **125**, 133109 (2006)

55. Pomerantz, A.E., Camden, J.P., Chiou, A.S., Ausfelder, F., Chawla, N., Hase, W.L., Zare, R. N.: Reaction products with internal energy beyond the kinematic limit result from trajectories far from the minimum energy path: an example from H + HBr → H₂ + Br. J. Am. Chem. Soc. **127**, 16368–16369 (2005)
56. Döntgen, M., Przybylski-Freund, M.-D., Kröger, L.C., Kopp, W.A., Ismail, A.E., Leonhard, K.: Automated discovery of reaction pathways, rate constants, and transition states using reactive molecular dynamics simulations. J. Chem. Theor. Comput. **11**, 2517–2524 (2015)
57. Fleming, K.L., Tiwary, P., Pfaendtner, J.: New approach for investigating reaction dynamics and rates with Ab initio calculations. J. Phys. Chem. A **120**, 299–305 (2016)
58. Fu, C.D., Oliveira, L.F.L., Pfaendtner, J.: Assessing generic collective variables for determining reaction rates in metadynamics simulations. J. Chem. Theor. Comput. **13**, 968–973 (2017)
59. Piccini, G., McCarty, J., Valsson, O., Parrinello, M.: Variational flooding study of a SN2 reaction. J. Phys. Chem. A **8**, 580–583 (2017)

Combinatorial and Geometrical Origins of Regge Symmetries: Their Manifestations from Spin-Networks to Classical Mechanisms, and Beyond

Vincenzo Aquilanti[1,2], Manuela S. Arruda[3], Cecilia Coletti[4(✉)],
Robert Littlejohn[5], and Robenilson F. Santos[6,7]

[1] Dipartimento di Chimica, Biologia e Biotecnologie,
Università di Perugia, via Elce di Sotto, 8, 06183 Perugia, Italy
[2] Consiglio Nazionale Delle Ricerche, Piazzale Aldo Moro 7, 00185 Rome, Italy
vincenzoaquilanti@yahoo.it
[3] Centro de Ciências Exatas e Tecnológicas,
Universidade Federal do Recôncavo da Bahia,
Rua Rui Barbosa 710, Cruz Das Almas, BA 44380-000, Brazil
manuelaarruda@gmail.com
[4] Dipartimento di Farmacia, Università G. d'Annunzio,
Via Dei Vestini, 66100 Chieti, Italy
ccoletti@unich.it
[5] Department of Physics, University of California, Berkeley, CA 94720-7300, USA
robert@wigner.berkeley.edu
[6] Instituto de Física, Universidade Federal da Bahia,
Campus Universitario de Ondina, Salvador, BA 40170-115, Brazil
[7] Instituto Federal de Alagoas, Campus Piranhas,
Avenida Sergipe s/n, Piranhas, AL 57460-000, Brazil
roferreirafs@gmail.com

Abstract. Tullio Regge discovered new symmetries in 1958, hidden in formulas for calculations of the coupling and recoupling coefficients of quantum angular momentum theory, as developed principally by Wigner and Racah: the only known (limited) application appeared computational. Ten years later, in a paper with Ponzano, Regge provided a semiclassical interpretation showing relevance to the basic geometry of quadrilaterals and tetrahedra, and opening also a promising road to quantum gravity, still currently being explored. New facets are here indicated, continuing a sequence of papers in this Lecture Notes series and elsewhere. We emphasize how an integrated combinatorial and geometrical interpretation is emerging, and also examples from the quantum mechanics of atoms and molecules are briefly documented. Attention is dedicated to the recently pointed out connection between the quantum mechanics of spin recouplings and the Grashof analysis of four-bar linkages, with perspective implications at the molecular level.

© Springer International Publishing AG 2017
O. Gervasi et al. (Eds.): ICCSA 2017, Part V, LNCS 10408, pp. 314–327, 2017.
DOI: 10.1007/978-3-319-62404-4_23

Keywords: Quantum angular momentum · Semiclassical asymptotics · Wigner-Racah coupling and recoupling · 3j and 6j symbols · Kepler-Coulomb Sturmian orbitals

1 Introduction: Discovery and Developments

On September 23 and October 9, 1958 Tullio Regge (1931–2014) submitted two very brief letters [1,2], where he reported what are now known as Regge symmetries for the Clebsch-Gordan's coupling coefficients and Racah's recoupling coefficients, or respectively the $3j$ and $6j$ symbols of Wigner. Ref. [2], one of the shortest paper ever, consists of only 13 lines of text and of three equations, so that it can be cited practically in full:

We have shown in a previous letter [1] that the true symmetry of Clebsch-Gordan coefficients is much higher than before believed. A similar result has been now obtained for Racah's coefficients. Although no direct connection has been established between these wider symmetries it seems very probable that it will be found in the future. We shall merely state here the results which can be checked very easily with the help of the well known Racah's formula.

(Here, the Racah's formula for $6j$ symbols [3] is given. We will discuss it in Sect. 2). The only citation is to paper [1], which is only slightly longer than [2] and has no citations: it acknowledges discussions and encouragement from Racah. Paper [2] continues:

From the usual tetrahedral symmetry group of the $[6j]$ we know already that: $\begin{Bmatrix} a\,b\,c \\ d\,e\,f \end{Bmatrix} = \begin{Bmatrix} b\,a\,c \\ e\,d\,f \end{Bmatrix} = \begin{Bmatrix} a\,e\,f \\ d\,b\,c \end{Bmatrix} = \begin{Bmatrix} c\,e\,d \\ f\,b\,a \end{Bmatrix} = $ etc.

Our results can be put into the following form:
$$\begin{Bmatrix} a\,b\,c \\ d\,e\,f \end{Bmatrix} = \begin{Bmatrix} a & (b+e+c-f)/(2) & (b+c+f-e)(2) \\ d & (b+e+f-c)/(2) & (c+e+f-b)/(2) \end{Bmatrix} = \text{etc.}$$

Six forms of the new symmetries are given, Sect. 2. The paper concludes:

Only the first of these symmetries is essentially new, the others can be obtained from it and [the permutational symmetries, Sect. 2]. We see therefore that there are 144 identical Racah's coefficients. These new symmetries should reduce by a factor 6 the space required for the tabulation of [the $6j$]. It should be pointed out that this wider 144-group is isomorphic to the direct product of the permutation groups of 3 and 4 objects.

Papers [1] and [2] are reprinted in [4], a collection of articles relevant to quantum angular momentum theory compiled in 1965. At p.12, paper [1] is referred to as a "surprise." In [4], papers [1] and [2] are followed by [5], where Bargmann cites them as "Regge's intriguing discovery of unsuspected symmetries of $3j$ and $6j$ symbols." Although (see above) Regge had the intuition that symmetries in [1] and [2] were connected, early attention was focused on that for $3j$ [1], apparently deceivingly simpler. For example, ten years later, in [6] we read "intriguing symmetry of the Clebsch-Gordan coefficients discovered in 1958 by Regge", that "came as quite a surprise", and "rather bizarre". In the famous 1968 paper, Regge with Ponzano [7] briefly noted that properties of $3j$'s can be obtained by a semiclassical limiting procedure from those of the $6j$'s giving the latter the crucial, basic building role that now they occupy in quantum mechanics.

We present these notes as an ordered series of remarks, exhibiting how the recent results fit into a scheme not necessarily coincident with the chronological succession of events. Sect. 2 is devoted to computational aspects, and more extensively to combinatorial features: for the first time the details of the emergency of the Regge symmetry as a consequence of the triangular and quadrangular inequalities, applied to a tetrahedral structure, is demonstrated. Sect. 3 is concerned with the geometrical perspectives specifically arising from the asymptotic analysis of the semiclassical limit. Important examples of physical implications of the Regge symmetries, encountered principally in atomic theory, are pointed out in Sect. 4. The remarkable connection between the role of the Regge symmetry and that of the classical analysis of a basic mechanical configuration is briefly pointed out in the concluding Sect. 5.

2   Computational and Combinatorial Aspects

2.1   Calculation of $6j$ Symbols

In [2] the application of the new symmetries was indicated to compact tables of $6j$'s: this is actually of a very limited usefulness, now that their calculations and compilations can be carried out routinely. The explicit formulas given by Racah as finite summations [3] can be written in various way, and the same for $3j$ formulas, found by Wigner [8]. A later discovery was the connections of these expressions with generalized hypergeometric series ($_4F_3$ and $_2F_1$ of argument one, for $6j$'s and $3j$'s respectively), as listed in Varshalovich [9], pp. 293–295. They are also related to important classes of orthogonal polynomials of discrete variables, described and classified in books [10,11]. References [7,12–20] report the relationships with spherical and hyperspherical harmonics, and with the orthonormal basis sets as the basic ingredients of quantum mechanical applications to atomic, molecular and nuclear sciences. To be noted is that most of formulas for the calculations as series as listed in the literature are incomplete, because sometimes the summation variable has to be chosen according to rules dictated by Regge symmetries: the precise rules are given on pp. 246 and 259 in [11].

2.2   The Triangle and Polygon Inequalities and the $4j$-model of the $6j$-symbol

We make a remark on a generalization of the triangle inequalities before presenting the $4j$-model of the $6j$-symbol. Here we summarize first the developments in [21], in order to extend it to show its relevance for the Regge Symmetry. If (ℓ_1, ℓ_2, ℓ_3) are three nonnegative lengths, the usual triangle inequalities are $|\ell_i - \ell_j| \leq \ell_k \leq \ell_i + \ell_j$, where $(i, j, k) = (1, 2, 3)$ and cyclic permutations. We generalize these as follows. Let $\{\ell_i, i = 1, \ldots, n\}$ be a set of lengths, $\ell_i \geq 0$, $i = 1, \ldots, n$. Then this set is said to satisfy the "polygon inequality" if

$$\max\{\ell_i\} \leq \frac{1}{2} \sum_{i=1}^{n} \ell_i. \tag{1}$$

This is equivalent to the triangle inequalities when $n = 3$. In general, it represents the necessary and sufficient condition that line segments of given, nonnegative lengths can be fitted together to form a polygon with n sides (in $\mathbb{R}^N$, $N > 0$). An insightful way of writing the $6j$-symbol as a scalar product begins with Fig. 1. With respect to the $6j$ symbols encountered in Sect. 1, we introduce a useful relabeling in Fig. 1 and will refer it as the "asymmetric" labeling, which is more appropriate for the $4j$-model [21].

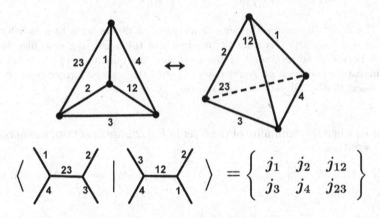

Fig. 1. Asymmetric labeling of the $6j$-symbol, according to the $4j$ model [21]. *Upper*: the plane Yutsis diagram *versus* the Wigner- Regge tridimensional tetrahedron. Note the point-face duality, i.e. triads are represented as points on the left and triangles on the right. *Lower*: Alternative coupling schemes (or spin nets) as labeled trees represented on the left as a bra and a ket, the bracket forming the $6j$ symbol as the simplest of spin network.

The quantum numbers j_{12} and j_{23} of the intermediate angular momenta range in integer steps between the bounds

$$j_{12,\min} \leq j_{12} \leq j_{12,\max}, j_{23,\min} \leq j_{23} \leq j_{23,\max}, \tag{2}$$

where the maximum and minimum values are given in terms of the four fixed $j_r, r = 1, \ldots, 4$ by

$$j_{12,\min} = \max(|j_1 - j_2|, |j_3 - j_4|), \quad j_{12,\max} = \min(j_1 + j_2, j_3 + j_4),$$
$$j_{23,\min} = \max(|j_2 - j_3|, |j_1 - j_4|), \quad j_{23,\max} = \min(j_2 + j_3, j_1 + j_4). \tag{3}$$

Then the dimension D is given by

$$D = j_{12,\text{max}} - j_{12,\text{min}} + 1 = j_{23,\text{max}} - j_{23,\text{min}} + 1. \tag{4}$$

An expression for D can be given that is symmetrical in (j_1, j_2, j_3, j_4). Using the fact that $|x| = \max(x, -x)$, the difference between $j_{12,\text{max}}$ and $j_{12,\text{min}}$ is now computed since $j_{12,\text{min}}$ can be written:

$$j_{12,\text{min}} = \max\{j_1 - j_2, j_2 - j_1, j_3 - j_4, j_4 - j_3\} \tag{5}$$

Then by Eqs. (3) and (5) D is the difference between the minimum of one set of two numbers and the maximum of another set of four numbers, Fig. 2.

$$0$$

$$a_i, \, i = 1, \ldots, N_a \qquad\qquad b_i, \, i = 1, \ldots, N_b$$

Fig. 2. The figure illustrates two sets of numbers as points on a line, in which the maximum of the a-set is less than the minimum of the b-set. In a case like this, the difference between the minimum of the b-set and the maximum of the a-set is the minimum distance between all $N_a N_b$ pairs of points that can be formed from the a-set and the b-set, that is, all pairs of the form (a_i, b_j).

That is, when the minimum of the b-set in Fig. 2 is greater than the maximum of the a-set, then

$$\min\{b_i, i = 1, \ldots, N_b\} - \max\{a_j, j = 1, \ldots, N_a\} = \min\{b_i - a_j, i = 1, \ldots, N_b, j = 1, \ldots, N_a\} \tag{6}$$

When the minimum of the b-set is less than the maximum of the a-set (that is, when the two sets overlap), then the right hand side of Eq. (6) can still be computed, but it is negative. In particular, when $j_{12,\text{max}}$ is greater than or equal to $j_{12,\text{min}}$, the difference $j_{12,\text{max}} - j_{12,\text{min}}$ is given by the minimum value of $2 \times 4 = 8$ numbers,

$$
\begin{aligned}
j_1 + j_2 - (j_1 - j_2) &= 2j_2, \\
j_1 + j_2 - (j_2 - j_1) &= 2j_1, \\
j_1 + j_2 - (j_3 - j_4) &= j_1 + j_2 - j_3 + j_4 = 2(s - j_3), \\
j_1 + j_2 - (j_4 - j_3) &= j_1 + j_2 + j_3 - j_4 = 2(s - j_4), \\
j_3 + j_4 - (j_1 - j_2) &= -j_1 + j_2 + j_3 + j_4 = 2(s - j_1), \\
j_3 + j_4 - (j_2 - j_1) &= j_1 - j_2 + j_3 + j_4 = 2(s - j_2), \\
j_3 + j_4 - (j_3 - j_4) &= 2j_4, \\
j_3 + j_4 - (j_4 - j_3) &= 2j_3.
\end{aligned}
\tag{7}
$$

But if the $j_i, i = 1, ...4$ are all ≥ 0 and if they satisfy the polygon inequality (1), then these eight numbers are all ≥ 0, and so $j_{12,\max} \geq j_{12,\min}$.

Therefore D becomes the shortest distance between one set of four numbers, $\{j_1 - j_2, j_2 - j_1, j_3 - j_4, j_4 - j_3\}$, and another set of two numbers, $\{j_1 + j_2, j_3 + j_4\}$. But this is the minimum of the distance between all eight possible pairs taken from the two sets Eq. (7). Thus

$$D = 2\min(j_1, j_2, j_3, j_4, s - j_1, s - j_2, s - j_3, s - j_4) + 1, \qquad (8)$$

where the list in Eq. (7) is rearranged and given in terms of the semiperimeter s,

$$s = \frac{1}{2}(j_1 + j_2 + j_3 + j_4). \qquad (9)$$

More precisely, if D computed by (8) is ≤ 0, then subspace D is trivial ($D = 0$); otherwise it is crucial for computational purposes.

2.3   Generation of Strings and Matrices of 6j Symbols

The formula (8) not only bears an interesting relationship to the Regge symmetry of the $6j$-symbol (Varshalovich et al. 1988, Eq. (9.4.2.4) [9]), but serves for the best known procedure to obtain whole strings and matrices of the symbols. It is essentially based on a set of 3-term recursion relationships, first suggested by Neville [22], and independently rederived and computationally demonstrated by Schulten and Gordon [14,26].

The derivation in the previous subsection demonstrates that, as in the case of the direct summation formulas (Sect. 2.1). one has to carefully choose which of the two equivalent symbols connected by Regge symmetry has to be chosen for actual calculations. This has been demonstrated and implemented in our papers [23–25,34,38].

3   Semiclassical and Geometrical Aspects

3.1   Visualizations

As explained in [23–25], the use of Regge symmetry, and especially the definition of ranges of the j_{12} and j_{23} variables, permitted to define uniquely the choice of the symbol between the two options. This had been overlooked in previous work, that independently derived [22] or put on a rigorous basis [14,26] the semiclassical treatment developed by Ponzano and Regge [7]. Associating a $6j$ symbol to a Euclidean tetrahedron (Fig. 1) the extraordinary results of [7] are that the symmetry discovered in the quantum mechanical formulas by Regge also holds for properties, (in particular volume, products for face areas, dihedral angles), of the most basic tridimensional geometric object under study since the ancient Greeks and had gone unnoticed for long. For the exploit of Regge symmetry to consistently represent images of computed $6j$ and $3j$ symbols, of use for discussion of properties and for image reconstructions [55], see for example the "screen" representation in Refs. [15,24] i.e. square plots of properties of $6j$'s on the j12, j23 plane. See also [30–33,35–37,56,57]

3.2   The Volume Operator and Non-Euclidean Extensions

The Ponzano-Regge paper played a significant role also in the foam-model and loop-gravity approaches to the still open problem of developing a quantum mechanical foundation to general relativity. Related references are [27,28,42–51,58]. In our current work [29,52] and in preparation, a basic ingredient in the theory, the volume operator, and the representation of its eigenfuntions by discrete polynomial sets, has been recently discussed, and the part played by the Regge symmetries are emerging. Under study is their role in the "regularization", i.e. the removal of divergences in the theory [52] of interest in general for the extension to non-Euclidean elliptic and hyperbolic geometries, see the exploratory study presented in a companion paper in this Lecture Notes Series [53]. The geometrical visualization of the symmetries by projecting a quadrilateral as two hinged triangles inscribed in two confocal conical sections is presented in [29] and will be show elsewhere to be connected to the famous third theorem of Steiner [39].

4   Couplings as Limits of Recouplings

4.1   Regge symmetries and $3nj$ symbols and hydrogenic orbitals

The preceding results can be extended to $3j$ symbols by a limiting procedure illustrated in detail elsewhere [12,13,15] The Regge symmetries for $3js$ play a crucial role in the understanding of the properties of orbitals in quantum chemistry. After Regge discovered it [1], it was realized that it was hidden in the two apparently different formulas for the coupling coefficients given by Wigner and Racah independently (see ref. [59], p. 79).

For instance, Schrödinger equation for the hydrogen atom in configuration space is separable in different coordinate sets [60,61,64,67,69]. Most widely employed are polar coordinates (r, θ, ϕ) for which the separation of variables is always possible in the case of a central symmetric field. The corresponding basis set can be indicated by using Dirac notation and the quantum numbers labelling the wavefunctions as $|nlm\rangle$.

An important alternative set, also leading to analytic close solutions of Schrödinger equation and to the separation of variables, is the parabolic set. This set is particularly advantageous when there is a privileged direction in space, as for atoms in electric or magnetic fields. The notation $|n\mu m\rangle$ can be used for the parabolic wavefunctions, where μ is one among various choices to indicate the parabolic quantum number [61,62,64,67,69].

The connection between the two basis sets is recognized as alternative parametrizations of the hypersphere S^3 embedded in a four-dimensional space (Fock's projection [77]). It is given by a coupling (Clebsch-Gordan) coefficient [63,64]:

$$\langle n\mu m|nlm\rangle =$$
$$(-)^{\frac{1}{2}(n-1)+\frac{m}{2}-\frac{\mu}{2}} \cdot \langle \tfrac{1}{2}(n-1), \tfrac{1}{2}(n-1); -\tfrac{\mu}{2}+\tfrac{m}{2}, \tfrac{\mu}{2}+\tfrac{m}{2}|lm\rangle \tag{10}$$

An interesting representation of these matrix elements was proposed by us making use of the Regge symmetry for Clebsch-Gordan coefficients [69]:

$$\langle \tfrac{1}{2}(n-1), \tfrac{1}{2}(n-1); \tfrac{1}{2}(m-\mu), \tfrac{1}{2}(m+\mu)|lm\rangle = \\ \langle \tfrac{1}{2}(n+m-1), \tfrac{1}{2}(n-m-1); -\tfrac{\mu}{2}, \tfrac{\mu}{2}|l0\rangle \tag{11}$$

Such formulation has the additional advantage of providing a physical meaning for the μ quantum number. A Clebsch-Gordan coefficients with zero projection of the orbital angular momentum l suggests that μ can be interpreted as a helicity quantum number. Indeed, the choice of the reference frame for which the component of the orbital angular momentum vector L is zero is equivalent to change the quantization axis on the plane of the orbit, where the Runge-Lenz vector lies. This interpretation becomes much clearer when analyzed from the momentum space point of view, where the symmetry group for the three-dimensional hydrogen atom manifestly appears to be O(4) [61,63–65,68].

This operation finds its analogues in various contexts: the passage from symmetric and asymmetric coordinates in the hyperspherical treatment of the three body problem [75,76], the space fixed-body fixed transformation in molecular collisions, and the transformation between the Hund's cases $(e) \rightarrow (c)$ in molecular spectroscopy and atomic scattering [73,74].

4.2 Momentum Space Wavefunctions and Sturmian Orbitals

The momentum space perspective allows connecting hydrogenic wave-functions, or specifically Coulomb Sturmian orbitals, with four-dimensional hyperspherical harmonics, as obtained by Fock projection from the Fourier transform of Schrödinger equation in configuration space [77].

Accordingly, the transformation coefficients between alternative Coulomb Sturmians can be calculated as superposition integrals between sets of hyperspherical harmonics pertaining to alternative parameterizations of the four-dimensional sphere S^3 [63,65,68]. This approach has been extended to spaces of any dimension [19,61,64].

In the d-dimensional space the superposition between the two harmonics is essentially a $(d-1)$−dimensional integral over four Jacobi polynomials [11,72] and, apart from a phase factor, can be identified with a Racah orthonormalized coefficient, the discrete analogue of Jacobi polynomials.

In turn, Racah orthonormalized coefficients can also be written as a generalized $6j$ coefficient [66] whose entries can be integers, half integers or proportional to $\tfrac{1}{4}$ depending on the dimensions of the subspaces involved in the construction of the d−dimensional hypersphere.

When such spaces are even in dimension the coefficient reduces to an ordinary $6j$ symbol with integer and/or half integer entries only. In all cases. an alternative expression for the superposition coefficient can be obtained making use of Regge symmetry for $6j$ coefficients by taking care that the selection rules for hyperspherical harmonics still hold valid [61]. In this case in each entry -$i.e.$ for every (hyper-)angular momentum- it appears only a specific quantum number

t_i and the corresponding numbers d_i counting the dimensions of the subgroup reduction chain:

$$T_{t_{12},t_{23}} = (-)^{\frac{t+t_{12}+t_{23}-t_2+d_1+d_2+d_3}{2}} \left[(t_{12} + \frac{d_1+d_2}{2} - 1)(t_{23} + \frac{d_2+d_3}{2} - 1) \right]^{1/2}$$

$$\times \left\{ \begin{array}{ccc} -\frac{t_1}{2} - \frac{d_1}{4} & \frac{t_2}{2} + \frac{d_2}{4} & \frac{t_{12}}{2} + \frac{d_1+d_2}{4} - 1 \\ -\frac{t_3}{2} - \frac{d_3}{4} & \frac{t}{2} + \frac{d_1+d_2+d_3}{4} - 1 & \frac{t_{23}}{2} + \frac{d_2+d_3}{4} - 1 \end{array} \right\} \tag{12}$$

For spaces of low dimensions, hyperspherical harmonics (and the expression of the connecting $6j$ coefficient) may simplify.

For the d-dimensional hydrogen atom, the overlaps between polar and parabolic wavefunctions are generalized $6j$ symbols, which simplify either to a $3j$ coefficient, as seen above in Eq. 10, or to a generalized $3j$ coefficient [12], depending on whether d is even or odd. These functions are relevant as basis sets in quantum chemistry.

5 Connection to a Classical Mechanism and to Molecular Mechanics

Regge symmetries enter also in the discussion of the eigenfunctions of the volume operator. See Ref. [29], where a geometrical picture is presented, as well as relationships with diverse topics, such as hybridization theory in quantum chemistry [70] and quaternion calculus [29,71]. In [29] it was noted that the transformation of a quadrangle involved in the Regge symmetry of a tetrahedron showed analogies to the parametrization of the four-bar linkage mechanism, that accompanied the evolution of mechanics from Watt to robotics: it was a concern for example of Cayley and Grashof, and continues to be currently investigated (see [40,41] and references therein). With the analysis developed here in Sect. 2.2, we are now able to establish the connection between the choice of the convention for the $6j$ according to Regge symmetry, and the Grashof condition written considering four bars of length k, l, m, M where, m is the shortest bar, M is the longest and k, l are the intermediate ones:

$$m + M \le k + l \tag{13}$$

This is the condition for the bar of length m being able to act as a crank, namely to perform a 360° turn: for this mechanism, the dimension D in Eq. 8 can be identified omitting $+1$ since we are dealing with min $(m, s - M)$, with a classical measure of differences in lengths. The identification of m with a in our convention requires $m \le s - m = (m - M + k + l)/2$, rather than on counting number of points in discrete interval. Beyond this application, recently implications for the systematics of the molecular mechanics of chirality changing processes were pointed out and are the subject to a companion note [54].

Acknowledgments. Robenilson Ferreira is grateful to Brazilian CAPES for a sandwich doctoral (PDSE88881.134388/2016-01) fellowship to the Perugia University. Manuela Arruda is grateful to Brazilian CNPq (Conselho Nacional de Desenvolvimento Científico e Tecnológico) for a post doctoral fellowship to the Perugia University. Vincenzo Aquilanti and Frederico Vasconcellos Prudente thank Brazilian CAPES for a Special Visiting Professorship at the Bahia Federal University (PVE 027/2013) and the Italian MIUR for Grant SIR 2014 (RBSI14U3VF).

References

1. Regge, T.: Symmetry properties of Clebsch- Gordan's coefficients. Nuov. Cimento **10**, 544–545 (1958)
2. Regge, T.: Symmetry properties of Racah's coefficients. Nuov. Cimento **11**, 116–117 (1959)
3. Racah, G.: Theory of complex spectra. II. Phys. Rev. **62**, 438–462 (1942)
4. Biedenharn, L.C., Dam, V.H.: Quantum Theory of Angular Momentum. Academic Press, New York (1965)
5. Bargmann, V.: On the representations of the rotation group. Rev. Mod. Phys. **34**, 829–845 (1962)
6. Bincer, A.M.: Interpretation of the symmetry of the Clebsch- Gordan coefficients discovered by Regge. J. Math. Phys. **11**, 1835–1844 (1970)
7. Ponzano, G., Regge, T.: Semiclassical limit of Racah coefficients. In: Bloch et al., F. (ed.) Spectroscopic and Group Theoretical Methods in Physics, pp. 1–58. North-Holland, Amsterdam (1968)
8. Wigner, E.P.: Group Theory: And its Application to the Quantum Mechanics of Atomic Spectra. Academic Press, New York (1959)
9. Varshalovich, D., Moskalev, A., Khersonskii, V.: Quantum Theory of Angular Momentum. World Scientific, Singapore (1988)
10. Koekoek, R., Lesky, P.A., Swarttouw, R.: Hypergeometric Orthogonal Polynomials and Their q-Analogues, 1st edn. Springer, Heidelberg (2010)
11. Nikiforov, A.F., Suslov, S.K., Uvarov, V.B.: Classical Orthogonal Polynomials of a Discrete Variable (Scientific Computation). Springer, Heidelberg (1991)
12. Aquilanti, V., Cavalli, S., De Fazio, D.: Angular and hyperangular momentum coupling coefficients as hahn polynomials. J. Phys. Chem. **99**(42), 15694–15698 (1995)
13. Aquilanti, V., Haggard, H.M., Littlejohn, R.G., Yu, L.: Semiclassical analysis of Wigner 3j-symbol. J. Phys. A **40**(21), 5637–5674 (2007)
14. Schulten, K., Gordon, R.: Exact recursive evaluation of 3j- and 6j-coefficients for quantum mechanical coupling of angular momenta. J. Math. Phys. **16**, 1961–1970 (1975)
15. Bitencourt, A.C.P., Ragni, M., Littlejohn, R.G., Anderson, R., Aquilanti, V.: The screen representation of vector coupling coefficients or Wigner 3j symbols: exact computation and illustration of the asymptotic behavior. In: Murgante, B., Misra, S., Rocha, A.M.A.C., Torre, C., Rocha, J.G., Falcão, M.I., Taniar, D., Apduhan, B.O., Gervasi, O. (eds.) ICCSA 2014. LNCS, vol. 8579, pp. 468–481. Springer, Cham (2014). doi:10.1007/978-3-319-09144-0_32
16. Neville, D.E.: A technique for solving recurrence relations approximately and its application to the 3-J and 6-J symbols. J. Math. Phys. **12**(12), 2438–2453 (1971)
17. Neville, D.E.: Volume operator for spin networks with planar or cylindrical symmetry. Phys. Rev. D **73**(12), 124004 (2006)

18. Aquilanti, V., Capecchi, G.: Harmonic analysis and discrete polynomials from semi-classical angular momentum theory to the hyperquantization algorithm. Theor. Chem. Acc. **104**, 183–188 (2000)

19. Aquilanti, V., Coletti, C.: $3nj$-symbols and harmonic superposition coefficients: an icosahedral abacus. Chem. Phys. Lett. **344**, 601–611 (2001)

20. Lévy-Leblond, J.M., Lévy-Nahas, M.: Symmetrical coupling of three angular momenta. J. Math. Phys. **6**(9), 1372–1380 (1965)

21. Aquilanti, V., Haggard, H.M., Hedeman, A., Jeevangee, N., Littlejohn, R., Yu, L.: Semiclassical mechanics of the Wigner $6j$-symbol. [math-ph], J. Phys. A **45**(065209) (2012). arXiv:1009.2811v2

22. Neville, D.E.: A technique for solving recurrence relations approximately and its application to the 3-J and 6-J symbols. J. Math. Phys. **12**, 2438–2453 (1971)

23. Anderson, R.W., Aquilanti, V., Bitencourt, A.C.P., Marinelli, D., Ragni, M.: The screen representation of spin networks: 2D recurrence, eigenvalue equation for $6j$ symbols, geometric interpretation and Hamiltonian dynamics. In: Murgante, B., Misra, S., Carlini, M., Torre, C.M., Nguyen, H.-Q., Taniar, D., Apduhan, B.O., Gervasi, O. (eds.) ICCSA 2013. LNCS, vol. 7972, pp. 46–59. Springer, Heidelberg (2013). doi:10.1007/978-3-642-39643-4_4

24. Ragni, M., Littlejohn, R.G., Bitencourt, A.C.P., Aquilanti, V., Anderson, R.W.: The screen representation of spin networks: images of $6j$ symbols and semiclassical features. In: Murgante, B., Misra, S., Carlini, M., Torre, C.M., Nguyen, H.-Q., Taniar, D., Apduhan, B.O., Gervasi, O. (eds.) ICCSA 2013. LNCS, vol. 7972, pp. 60–72. Springer, Heidelberg (2013). doi:10.1007/978-3-642-39643-4_5

25. Bitencourt, A.C.P., Marzuoli, A., Ragni, M., Anderson, R.W., Aquilanti, V.: Exact and asymptotic computations of elementary spin networks: classification of the quantum–classical boundaries. In: Murgante, B., Gervasi, O., Misra, S., Nedjah, N., Rocha, A.M.A.C., Taniar, D., Apduhan, B.O. (eds.) ICCSA 2012. LNCS, vol. 7333, pp. 723–737. Springer, Heidelberg (2012). doi:10.1007/978-3-642-31125-3_54

26. Schulten, K., Gordon, R.: Semiclassical approximations to 3j- and 6j-coefficients for quantum-mechanical coupling of angular momenta. J. Math. Phys. **16**, 1971–1988 (1975)

27. Mohanty, Y.: The Regge symmetry is a scissors congruence in hyperbolic space. Algebr. Geom. Topol. **3**, 1–31 (2003)

28. Roberts, J.: Classical 6j-symbols and the tetrahedron. Geom. Topol. **3**, 21–66 (1999)

29. Aquilanti, V., Marinelli, D., Marzuoli, A.: Hamiltonian dynamics of a quantum of space: hidden symmetries and spectrum of the volume operator, and discrete orthogonal polynomials. [math-ph]. J. Phys. A: Math. Theor. **46**, 175303 (2013). arXiv:1301.1949v2

30. Littlejohn, R., Yu, L.: Uniform semiclassical approximation for the Wigner $6j$ symbol in terms of rotation matrices. J. Phys. Chem. A **113**, 14904–14922 (2009)

31. Ragni, M., Bitencourt, A.P.C., da S. Ferreira, C., Aquilanti, V., Anderson, R., Littlejohn, R.: Exact computation and asymptotic approximation of $6j$ symbols. illustration of their semiclassical limits. Int. J. Quantum Chem. **110**, 731–742 (2010)

32. De Fazio, D., Cavalli, S., Aquilanti, V.: Orthogonal polynomials of a discrete variable as expansion basis sets in quantum mechanics. the hyperquantization algorithm. Int. J. Quantum Chem. **93**, 91–111 (2003)

33. Anderson, R.W., Aquilanti, V., Marzuoli, A.: 3nj morphogenesis and semiclassical disentangling. J. Phys. Chem. A **113**(52), 15106–15117 (2009)

34. Anderson, R., Aquilanti, V., da S. Ferreira, C.: Exact computation and large angular momentum asymptotics of $3nj$ symbols: semiclassical disentangling of spin-networks. J. Chem. Phys. **129**(161101), 5 pages (2008)
35. Aquilanti, V., Cavalli, S., De Fazio, D.: Hyperquantization algorithm. I. Theory for triatomic systems. J. Chem. Phys. **109**(10), 3792–3804 (1998)
36. Marinelli, D., Marzuoli, A., Aquilanti, V., Anderson, R.W., Bitencourt, A.C.P., Ragni, M.: Symmetric angular momentum coupling, the quantum volume operator and the 7-spin network: a computational perspective. In: Murgante, B., Misra, S., Rocha, A.M.A.C., Torre, C., Rocha, J.G., Falcão, M.I., Taniar, D., Apduhan, B.O., Gervasi, O. (eds.) ICCSA 2014. LNCS, vol. 8579, pp. 508–521. Springer, Cham (2014). doi:10.1007/978-3-319-09144-0_35
37. Aquilanti, V., Bitencourt, A.C.P., da S. Ferreira, C., Marzuoli, A., Ragni, M.: Combinatorics of angular momentum recoupling theory: spin networks, their asymptotics and applications. Theor. Chem. Acc. **123**, 237–247 (2009)
38. Ragni, M., Bitencourt, A.C.P., Aquilanti, V., Anderson, R.W., Littlejohn, R.G.: Exact computation and asymptotic approximations of $6j$ symbols: Illustration of their semiclassical limits. Int. J. Quantum Chem. **110**(3), 731–742 (2010)
39. Dörrie, H.: 100 Great Problems of Elementary Mathematics: Their History and Solution. Dover Publications, Inc., New York (1965)
40. Khimshiashvili, G., Siersma, D.: Cross- ratios of quadrilateral linkages. J. Singul. **13**, 159–168 (2015)
41. Khimshiashvili, G.: Complex geometry of polygonal linkages. J. Math. Sci. **189**, 132–149 (2013)
42. Biedenharn, L.C., Lohe, M.A.: Quantum group symmetry and q- Tensor algebras. World Scientific, Singapore (1995)
43. Bonatsos, D., Daskaloyannis, C.: Quantum groups and their applications in nuclear physics. Progress Part. Nucl. Phys. **43**, 537–618 (1999)
44. Mizoguchi, S., Tada, T.: Three- dimensional gravity from the Turaev-Viro invariant. Phys. Rev. Lett. **68**, 1795–1798 (1992)
45. Turaev, V.G., Viro, O.Y.: State sum invariants of 3-manifolds and quantum $6j$-symbols. Topology **31**, 865–903 (1992)
46. Izmestiev, I.: Deformation of quadrilaterals and addition on elliptic curves, pp. 1–39 (2015). arXiv:1501.07157v1
47. Taylor, Y.U., Woodward, C.T.: $6j$ symbols for $U_q(sl_2)$ non-euclidean tetrahedra. Sel. Math. New Ser. **11**, 539–571 (2005)
48. Murakami, J.: Volume formulas for a spherical tetrahedron. Proc. Americ. Math. Soc. **140**, 3289–3295 (2012)
49. Taylor, Y.U., Woodward, C.T.: Spherical tetrahedra and invariants of 3-manifolds, pp. 1–18 (2004). arXiv:math/0406228v2
50. Bianchi, E., Modesto, L.: The perturbative Regge- calculus regime of loop quantum gravity. Nucl. Phys. B **796**, 581–621 (2008)
51. Williams, R.M.: $6j$- symbols and discrete quantum gravity. Nucl. Phys. B (Proc. Suppl.) **88**, 124–131 (2000)
52. Aquilanti, V., Marzuoli, A.: Desargues spin networks and their Regge regularized geometric realization (to be published)
53. Anderson, R.W., Aquilanti, V.: Spherical and hyperbolic spin networks: the q-extensions of Wigner-Racah $6j$ coefficients and general orthogonal discrete basis sets in applied quantum mechanics. In: Gervasi, O., et al. (eds.) ICCSA 2017, Part V. LNCS, vol. 10408, pp. 338–353. Springer, Cham (2017)

54. Aquilanti, V., Caglioti, C., Lombardi, A., Maciel, G.S., Palazzetti, F.: Screens for displaying chirality changing mechanisms of a series of peroxides and persulfides from conformational structures computed by quantum chemistry. In: Gervasi, O., et al. (eds.) ICCSA 2017, Part V. LNCS, vol. 10408, pp. 354–368. Springer, Cham (2017)

55. Anderson, R.: Discrete orthogonal transformations corresponding to the discrete polynomials of the askey scheme. In: Murgante, B., Misra, S., Rocha, A.M.A.C., Torre, C., Rocha, J.G., Falcão, M.I., Taniar, D., Apduhan, B.O., Gervasi, O. (eds.) ICCSA 2014. LNCS, vol. 8579, pp. 490–507. Springer, Cham (2014). doi:10.1007/978-3-319-09144-0_34

56. Santos, R.F., Bitencourt, A.C.P., Ragni, M., Prudente, F.V., Coletti, C., Marzuoli, A., Aquilanti, V.: Couplings and recouplings of four angular momenta: alternative 9j symbols and spin addition diagrams. J. Mol. Model. (2017). doi:10.1007/s00894-017-3320-1

57. Arruda, M.S., Santos, R.F., Marinelli, D., Aquilanti, V.: Spin-coupling diagrams and incidence geometry: a note on combinatorial and quantum-computational aspects. In: Gervasi, O., Murgante, B., Misra, S., Rocha, A.M.A.C., Torre, C., Taniar, D., Apduhan, B.O., Stankova, E., Wang, S. (eds.) ICCSA 2016. LNCS, vol. 9786, pp. 431–442. Springer, Cham (2016). doi:10.1007/978-3-319-42085-1_33

58. Carter, J.S., Daniel, E.F., Saito, M.: The Classical and Quantum 6j- Symbols. Princeton University Press, New Jersey (1995)

59. Biedenharn, L.C., Louck, J.D.: Angular momentum in quantum physics. In: Rota, G.-C. (ed.) Encyclopedia of Mathematics and Its Applications, vol. 8. Addison-Wesley Publ. Co., Reading (1981)

60. Calderini, D., Cavalli, S., Coletti, C., Grossi, G., Aquilanti, V.: Hydrogenoid orbitals revisited: from slater orbitals to coulomb sturmians. J. Chem. Sci. **124**, 187 (2012)

61. Coletti, C., Calderini, D., Aquilanti, V.: d-dimensional kepler - coulomb sturmians and hyperspherical harmonics as complete orthonormal atomic and molecular orbitals. Adv. Quantum Chem. **67**, 73 (2013)

62. Aquilanti, V., Cavalli, S., Coletti, C., De Fazio, D., Grossi, G.: Hyperangular momentum: applications to atomic and molecular science. In: Tsipis, C.A., Popov, V.S., Herschbach, D.R., Avery, J.S. (eds.) New Methods in Quantum Theory, pp. 233–250. Kluwer (1996)

63. Aquilanti, V., Cavalli, S., Coletti, C., Grossi, G.: Alternative Sturmian bases and momentum space orbitals: an application to the hydrogen molecular ion. Chem. Phys. **209**, 405–419 (1996)

64. Aquilanti, V., Cavalli, S., Coletti, C.: The d-dimensional hydrogen atom: hyperspherical harmonics as momentum space orbitals and alternative Sturmian basis sets. Chem. Phys. **214**, 1–13 (1997)

65. Aquilanti, V., Cavalli, S., Coletti, C., Domenico, D.D., Grossi, G.: Hyperspherical harmonics as Sturmian orbitals in momentum space: a systematic approach to the few-body Coulomb problem. Int. Rev. Phys. Chem. **20**, 673–709 (2001)

66. Aquilanti, V., Cavalli, S., Coletti, C.: Angular and hyperangular momentum recoupling, harmonic superposition and racah polynomials: a recursive algorithm. Chem. Phys. Lett. **344**, 587–600 (2001)

67. Aquilanti, V., Caligiana, A., Cavalli, S.: Hydrogenic elliptic orbitals, coulomb sturmian sets. Recoupling coefficients among alternative bases. Int. J. Quant. Chem. **92**, 99–117 (2003)

68. Aquilanti, V., Caligiana, A., Cavalli, S., Coletti, C. Hydrogenic orbitals in momentum space and hyperspherical harmonics. Elliptic sturmian basis sets. Int. J. Quant. Chem. **92**, 212–228 (2003)
69. Aquilanti, V., Cavalli, S., Coletti, C.: Hyperspherical symmetry of hydrogenic orbitals and recoupling coefficients among alternative bases. Phys. Rev. Lett. **80**, 3209–3212 (1998)
70. Pauling, L.: The nature of the chemical bond. Application of results obtained from the quantum mechanics and from a theory of paramagnetic susceptibility to the structure of molecules. J. Am. Chem. Soc. **53**, 1367–1400 (1931)
71. Marinelli, D.: Single and collective dynamics of discretized geometries (PhD thesis), University of Pavia, Italy (2013), ISBN: 978-88-95767-73-4
72. Kil'dyushov, M.S.: Hyperspherical functions of tree type in the N-body problem sov. J. Nucl. Phys. **15**, 113 (1972)
73. Aquilanti, V., Grossi, G.: Angular momentum coupling schemes in the quantum mechanical treatment of P-state atom collisions. J. Chem. Phys. **73**, 1165–1172 (1980)
74. Aquilanti, V., Cavalli, S., Grossi, G.: Hund's cases for rotating diatomic molecules and for atomic collisions: angular momentum coupling schemes and orbital alignment. Z Phys. D. **36**, 215–219 (1996)
75. Aquilanti, V., Cavalli, S., Grossi, G.: Discrete analogs of spherical harmonics and their use in quantum mechanics: the hyperquantization algorithm. Theor. Chim. Acta **79**, 283–296 (1991)
76. Aquilanti, V., Cavalli, S.: Discrete analogs of hyperspherical harmonics and their use for the quantum mechanical three body problem. In: Ciofi degli Atti, C., Pace, E., Salmé, G., Simula S. (eds.) Few-Body Problems in Physics. Few-Body Systems, vol. 6, pp. 573–580. Springer, Vienna (1992)
77. Fock, V.: Zur Theorie des Wasserstoffatoms. Z. Phys. **98**, 145–154 (1935)

A Diabatic Electronic State System to Describe the Internal Conversion of Azulene

Shiladitya Banerjee, Dimitrios Skouteris$^{(\boxtimes)}$, and Vincenzo Barone

Scuola Normale Superiore, Pisa, Italy
dimitrios.skouteris@sns.it

Abstract. A diabatic system of two electronic potential energy surfaces as well as the coupling between them is presented. The system is to be used to study the dynamics of the $S_1 \rightarrow S_0$ internal conversion of azulene and is based on single point calculations of the minima of the two surfaces and a dipole-quadrupole (DQ) diabatization. Based on this, a couple of harmonic diabatic surfaces together with a linear coupling surface have been devised. Some preliminary dynamics results are shown.

Keywords: Azulene · Internal conversion · Diabatic states

1 Introduction

Azulene is an isomer of naphthalene. Together with larger polycyclic aromatic hydrocarbons, they are alleged to be precursors of prebiotic molecules and have been identified in several extraterrestrial environments (see for instance [1–3]. The molecule of azulene is a well-known example of an exception to Kasha's rule, according to which fast spontaneous emission is only observed from the lowest excited state. In fact, azulene is known to decay from the first excited singlet state (S_1) to the ground state (S_0) through fast internal conversion induced by nonadiabatic coupling [4].

Internal conversion of azulene has been studied both theoretically and experimentally. A well established means of exploring dynamical processes is through the rate of decay of a state population [5–12]. Rentzepis [5] has determined a lifetime of 7 ps for the S_1 state in solution through a picosecond pump-and-probe experiment. The same lifetime was estimated to be 1.4 ps by Foggi et al. through femtosecond transient absorption. On the other hand, Amirav et al. [13] and Suzuki et al. [14], determined a lifetime of around 1.0 ps for the isolated molecule.

Theoretical calculations on the system include a full-CI optimization by Bearpark et al. [15] where a conical intersection at energies 1–13 kcal/mol above the minimum of the S_1 state was found. The presence of such a conical intersection was strengthened by an increase in the vibronic band broadening observed by Ruth et al. [16] using cavity ring-down absorption spectroscopy at a vibrational excess energy above $0 + 2177$ cm^{-1}. The S_1 state was reported as having a lifetime of 900 ± 100 fs at a vibrational excess energy around 2000 cm^{-1} by

© Springer International Publishing AG 2017
O. Gervasi et al. (Eds.): ICCSA 2017, Part V, LNCS 10408, pp. 328–337, 2017.
DOI: 10.1007/978-3-319-62404-4_24

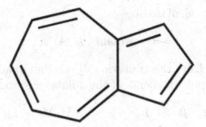

Fig. 1. A representation of the azulene molecule

Zewail and coworkers [17] through femtosecond resolved mass spectrometry in a molecular beam.

In this paper we present a diabatization of the lowest two electronic surfaces of azulene we have recently completed. This diabatization was performed using the dipole-quadrupole (DQ) diabatization method of Truhlar et al. [18]. The two surfaces are assumed to be harmonic while the diabatic coupling is linear. Subsequently, we intend to run quantum dynamics based on our Gaussian Multi-Configuration Time-Dependent Hartree (G-MCTDH) [19–21] algorithm to explore the internal conversion dynamics (the high dimensionality of the problem renders this scheme preferable with respect to others [22–27]). In particular, an exact time-dependent or time-independent calculation would be completely prohibitive, due to the high dimensionality of the problem. On the other hand, the diabatic coupling can be used, together with the calculation of the density of states of the molecule, to calculate an internal conversion rate using Fermi's Golden rule. However, such a calculation furnishes short-time information and does not give any insight on particular vibrational modes that can help or hinder internal conversion. The initial results of a preliminary dynamics calculation are also shown.

2   Calculation of the Electronic PES

The diabatic coupling between the two lowest energy singlet states of azulene has been obtained by maximizing the difference between the dipole and quadrupole moments associated with the two states and the corresponding transition moments, by a rotation of the two states.

For a non-radiative transition between electronic states 1 and 2, the diabatic states can be expressed as a linear combination of two adiabatic states [18]:

$$\Psi_{dia} = \Psi_{adia,1}\, \boldsymbol{T}_1 + \Psi_{adia,2}\, \boldsymbol{T}_2 \tag{1}$$

where $\Psi_{adia,1}$ and $\Psi_{adia,2}$ are the adiabatic states. The $\boldsymbol{T}$ matrices perform the transformation of the adiabatic states to the diabatic ones Ψ_{dia}. In the DQ-diabatization approach, the diabatic states are represented as [18]

$$\begin{pmatrix} \Psi_{dia,1} \\ \Psi_{dia,2} \end{pmatrix} = \begin{pmatrix} \cos\theta & \sin\theta \\ -\sin\theta & \cos\theta \end{pmatrix} \begin{pmatrix} \Psi_{adia,1} \\ \Psi_{adia,2} \end{pmatrix} \tag{2}$$

The mixing angle, θ is calculated by

$$\theta = \arctan(-B/A) \tag{3}$$

A and B are obtained from the transition dipole and quadrupole moments and the dipole and quadrupole moments of the adiabatic states:

$$B = \boldsymbol{\mu}_1 \cdot \boldsymbol{\mu}_t - \boldsymbol{\mu}_t \cdot \boldsymbol{\mu}_2 + \alpha(M_1 M_t - M_t M_2) \tag{4}$$

and

$$A = -\frac{\mu_1^2 + \mu_2^2}{4} + \mu_t^2 + \frac{\boldsymbol{\mu}_1 \cdot \boldsymbol{\mu}_2}{2} - \frac{\alpha M_1^2}{4} + \frac{\alpha M_2^2}{4} - \alpha M_t^2 - \frac{\alpha M_1 M_2}{2} \tag{5}$$

The dipole moments of the two states are represented as $\boldsymbol{\mu}_1$ and $\boldsymbol{\mu}_2$; μ_1 and μ_2 denote their magnitudes. M_1 and M_2 are traces of the quadrupole moments, while $\boldsymbol{\mu}_t$ and M_t are the transition dipole moment and trace of the transition quadrupole moment.

The relative contribution of the quadrupoles to the diabatic coupling is determined by the parameter α. The DQ-formalism reduces to the limit of Boys localisation in the extreme case of $\alpha = 0$. Maximisation of the function F in terms of the adiabatic matrix elements [18] leads to the above relations,

$$F = \mu_1^2 + \mu_2^2 + \alpha(M_1^2 + M_2^2) + A + \sqrt{(A^2 + B^2)}\cos(4(\theta - \gamma)) \tag{6}$$

F being maximum when

$$\theta = \gamma, \gamma + \pi/2, ... \tag{7}$$

At the Franck-Condon level of approximation, the coupling is calculated at the minimum geometry of the final state, *i.e.*, the electronic ground state.

The DFT and TD-DFT levels of theory have been used for obtaining the equilibrium geometries and corresponding force constants, for the ground (S_0) and excited states (S_1) of azulene, using the GAUSSIAN suite of programs [28]. The B3LYP [29] functional and the 6-31G(d) basis set [30] have been used. The dipole and quadrupole moments have been obtained at the TD-B3LYP/6-31G(d) level. All calculations have been done in the gas-phase.

Here, we mention that in a previous study [31] by some of the authors, we computed the temperature dependence of rates of non-radiative transitions where the non-adiabatic, momentum couplings between adiabatic electronic states were used to compute the rates. In that work, azulene was used as the test case to represent rigid molecules to validate the performance of our implementation. The (TD)-B3LYP/6-31G(d) level of theory was used there and showed to be a reliable electronic structure method for the prediction of the rate of S_1 $\rightarrow$ S_0 internal conversion in azulene. Furthermore, the absorption spectrum for the $S_0 \rightarrow S_1$ (Fig. 1) was very well reproduced compared to the experiment [32] at the (TD)-B3LYP/6-31G(d) level of theory, therefore we used the same level of theory in our dynamics study.

Due to a negligible value of the trace of the transition quadrupole moment of azulene, a low value of the parameter alpha was considered, in order to reduce the

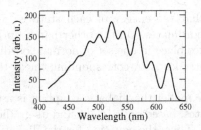

Fig. 2. The vibrationally resolved absorption spectrum for $S_0 \rightarrow S_1$ transition in azulene at the B3LYP/6-31G(d) level of theory. The spectrum compares very well with the experimental spectrum (Fig. 3 in Ref. [32]).

weight of the quadrupole moments on the coupling. Following some test calculations, a 0.1% contribution of the quadrupoles was chosen, effectively reducing the case to the Boys-localization limit.

The diabatic coupling and its derivatives with respect to the normal coordinates have been calculated with a stand-alone code, by displacing each atom 0.001 angstrom to either side of the equilibrium geometry along each Cartesian coordinate.

3 Surface Characteristics

Based on the frequencies of the normal modes around the minima of both ground and excited states, the diabatic surfaces have been modelled as a collection of uncoupled harmonic oscillators. Each surface contains a global minimum and the potential energy is given by a sum of parabolic potentials around it using the calculated frequencies. Besides the frequencies for each state, the system is characterized by the following parameters:

- The adiabatic transition energy between the electronic states, i.e. the difference in energy between the minima.
- The coordinates of the excited state minimum in terms of ground state normal coordinates.
- The Duschinsky matrix, relating the excited state normal coordinates to the ground state ones.

Thus, the energy of both ground and excited states is represented by the formula

$$E^{(s)}(q_1, ..., q_{48}) = E_0^{(s)} + \frac{1}{2} \sum_{k=1}^{48} \omega_k^{(s)} (q_k^{(s)} - q_{k,0}^{(s)})^2 \qquad (8)$$

where q_k denotes the k-th normal mode, its equilibrium position being $q_{k,0}$ (obviously, frequencies are different for ground and excited states). E_0 is assumed to be zero for the ground state, whereas it takes the value of the adiabatic energy difference of the two states for the excited one. The index (s) above the normal coordinates indicates that the energy of each state is expressed with respect to its proper normal coordinates. On the other hand, during a time-dependent propagation (which takes place in one set of normal coordinates), the non-unity of the Duschinsky matrix leads to corresponding linear terms in the potential energy.

Furthermore, in our model the diabatic coupling is assumed to be a linear function of all coordinates, based on its value and its gradient vector around the ground state minimum. Thus, the equation for the diabatic coupling is

$$V(q_1, ..., q_{48}) = V_0 + \sum_{k=1}^{48} V_k(q_k - q_{k,0}) \tag{9}$$

In this equation, V_0 is the value of the diabatic coupling above the ground state minimum, whereas V_k are the derivatives of this coupling with respect to each normal coordinate. At each point, the 2×2 diabatic matrix can be diagonalized, yielding the adiabatic energies. These would be subject to nonadiabatic interaction due to the nuclear kinetic energy, which is difficult to handle computationally.

The frequencies of the 48 normal modes of both ground and excited states are given in Table 1.

4 Preliminary Dynamics

In order to study the dynamics of the internal conversion of azulene, we have used the G-MCTDH code developed previously by us. This code gives us various possibilities to investigate the dynamics of azulene from a quantum mechanical point of view. In particular:

1. A full variational multi-configuration Gaussian (v-MCG) calculation can be performed. In this case, the nuclear wavefunction of the system is written as

$$\Psi(r, t) = \sum_{k=1}^{n} c_k g_k(r_1, r_2, ..., r_{48}, t) \tag{10}$$

where each g_k is a product of Gaussians over the 48 vibrational degrees of freedom. This Gaussian evolves with time, being continually displaced in coordinate and momentum space. This way of expanding the wavefunction corresponds to a linear combination of n trajectories. For $n = 1$ we get an ordinary classical simulation, whereas as n tends to infinity we get convergence to full quantum mechanics.

2. Once a clearer picture of the dynamics is obtained, the vibrational degrees of freedom can be separated into "background" (or "bath") degrees of freedom, which do not have a significant role in the dynamics, and "principal" degrees of freedom. These latter ones need to be described more accurately than the background ones and, as a result, the wavefunction describing them is a linear

Table 1. Frequencies of azulene for both S_0 and S_1 states

Mode	GS frequency (cm^{-1})	ES frequency (cm^{-1})
1	117.981015	163.501597
2	192.662651	170.926311
3	277.256104	322.322986
4	336.034811	340.039919
5	391.897513	413.281252
6	407.212341	430.915084
7	503.395716	499.552709
8	505.41282	576.448949
9	574.103945	614.342818
10	670.849221	680.073437
11	678.597735	728.622826
12	694.762664	742.21335
13	731.621231	746.492958
14	762.735388	787.877933
15	770.800402	804.602064
16	823.313698	833.869817
17	864.009372	883.133207
18	878.618399	919.235272
19	894.605128	946.720822
20	920.960876	961.369049
21	937.590106	984.275191
22	987.607497	1004.03833
23	998.112016	1022.58126
24	1044.6671	1023.18486
25	1083.51897	1065.73774
26	1092.81379	1082.19057
27	1168.64483	1187.29696
28	1222.33232	1242.92626
29	1237.69275	1244.07286
30	1254.14728	1299.15926
31	1275.64852	1324.75001
32	1358.48597	1338.71704
33	1400.16985	1419.94548
34	1423.13679	1430.4382
35	1465.30507	1488.19761
36	1488.96751	1492.02871
37	1535.51969	1527.75368
38	1589.25069	1580.56148
39	1599.63041	1627.64896
40	1682.23746	1640.92519
41	3137.83171	3134.414
42	3141.31682	3136.12121
43	3168.60977	3144.60892
44	3170.11727	3163.53716
45	3181.19379	3172.10287
46	3210.30004	3201.85843
47	3214.09555	3219.14136
48	3244.2273	3227.72017

combination of two or more Gaussians. In other words, the nuclear wavefunction is written (for m principal degrees of freedom) as

$$\Psi(r,t) = \sum_{k=1}^{n} c_k g_k(r_1, r_2, ..., r_m, t) \times g_{bath}(r_{m+1}, ..., r_{48}, t) \qquad (11)$$

where the principal part of the wavefunction is evolved in parallel with a single quantum trajectory.

Moreover, the treatment of the two diabatic surfaces also needs to be considered. The simplest treatment is the complete *single-set* formalism, whereby the same nuclear wavefunction is used for both surfaces. In this case, the complete (including the electronic degree of freedom) wavefunction is given by the formula

$$\Psi = \sum_{k=1}^{n} d_k |s_k> \times \psi_{nuc}(r,t) \qquad (12)$$

Thus the electronic degree of freedom is simply treated as an extra dimension in the G-MCTDH formalism and the calculation is akin to an Ehrenfest one.

Alternatively, the code permits us to propagate a different nuclear wavefunction on each surface, i.e. to use the *multi-set* formalism. Such a treatment is necessary, for example, in dealing with photodissociation problems where dissociation occurs only on one surface. On the other hand, if the issue is simply the time-evolving populations on the surfaces (and the forces on the surfaces are not very different) then an Ehrenfest calculation can at least give a qualitative picture of the dynamics.

We have run a preliminary propagation on the two-surface system. The calculation is a simple Ehrenfest one, where one single Gaussian wavepacket is propagated on both surfaces, its coordinates and surface amplitudes evolving with time in a variational manner. Therefore, the wavefunction propagated is of the form

$$\Psi(r,t) = g[r(t)] \times (c_g(t)|GS> + c_e(t)|ES>) \qquad (13)$$

where $r(t)$ represents the trajectory followed by the wavepacket and c_g, c_e are the coefficients of the ground and excited states respectively. The initial conditions were $c_g(0) = 0, c_e(0) = 1$ (i.e. the wavepacket starts entirely in the excited state), while the coordinates of the wavepacket correspond to the excited state minimum (as it is essentially the zero-level lifetime that has been measured).

In Fig. 2 are shown the results of the propagation for the first 10000 atomic units of time (corresponding to around 0.2 ps). In the lower panel is shown the population of the ground state (initially zero) while in the upper panel is shown the ratio of the diabatic coupling to the energy separation of the two surfaces. If the coupling were zero, there would be no evolution at all as the wavepacket is found above the surface minimum. The diabatic coupling induces a degree of transfer to the lower surface, which causes a displacement of the wavepacket in coordinate space. As can be seen, as time progresses, the wavepacket is gradually exploring regions of higher intersurface coupling. The effect of this can be seen in the lower panel, where the Rabi oscillations between the surfaces gradually rise in amplitude.

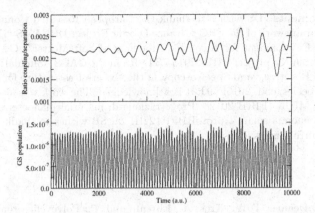

Fig. 3. Small-time dynamics of azulene in a preliminary Ehrenfest calculation

5   Conclusions

Our diabatization scheme, based on dipole and quadrupole moments, has yielded a surface that is expected to reproduce well the first-excited state dynamics of azulene, in particular its internal conversion process from S_1 to S_0. The small degree of intersurface coupling around the minimum of the excited S_1 state implies that

- The diabatic and adiabatic pictures are very close in this region, and therefore the approximation of the initial wavepacket as confined to the upper diabatic state is good.
- The internal conversion dynamics is expected to be well over the picosecond range (as also seen in measurements).

More detailed dynamics calculations, with a view to determine the critical points of the conical intersection seam as well as the particular normal modes governing passage between surfaces, are under way. In particular, possible ways to improve the results include:

1. Simulating the overall wavefunction in a more realistic way, dedicating more Gaussian functions in its description (at least for the principal degrees of freedom), as well as utilizing a multi-set formalism for the two surfaces.

2. Taking into account anharmonicity, simulating the potential energy function with appropriate Morse or Gaussian forms.

Acknowledgements. DS wishes to thank the European Research Council for a fellowship in the framework of the ERC Advanced Grant Project DREAMS "Development of a Research Environment for Advanced Modeling of Soft Matter", GA N. 320951. Contribution from the project PRIN 2015 - STARS in the CAOS - Simulation Tools for Astrochemical Reactivity and Spectroscopy in the Cyberinfrastructure for Astrochemical Organic Species, cod. 2015F59J3R is acknowledged. The work was also supported by the Italian MIUR (FIRB 2012: "Progettazione di materiali nanoeterogenei per la conversione di energia solare", prot.:RBFR122HFZ). SB wishes to thank Dr. Alberto Baiardi for fruitful discussions.

References

1. Groen, J., Deamer, D.W., Kros, A., Ehrenfreund, P.: Polycyclic aromatic hydrocarbons as plausible prebiotic membrane components. Orig. Life Evol. Biosph. **42**, 295–306 (2012)
2. Parker, D.S.N., Zhang, F., Kim, Y.S., Kaiser, R.I., Landera, A., Kislov, V.V., Mebel, A.M., Tielens, A.G.G.M.: Low temperature formation of naphthalene and its role in the synthesis of PAHs (Polycyclic Aromatic Hydrocarbons) in the interstellar medium. PNAS **109**, 53–58 (2012)
3. Balucani, N.: Elementary reactions and their role in gas-phase prebiotic chemistry. Int. J. Mol. Sci. **10**, 2304–2335 (2009)
4. Numata, Y., Toyoshima, S., Okuyama, K., Yasunami, M., Suzuka, I.: S_1-state internal conversion of isolated azulene derivatives. J. Phys. Chem. A **113**, 9603–9611 (2009)
5. Rentzepis, P.M.: Direct measurements of radiationless transitions in liquids. Chem. Phys. Lett. **2**, 117–120 (1968)
6. Hochstrasser, R.M., Li, Y.Y.: Spectral manifestations of nonradiative processes in azulene. J. Mol. Spectrosc. **41**, 297–301 (1972)
7. Ippen, F.P., Shank, C.V., Woerner, R.L.: Picosecond dynamics of azulene. Chem. Phys. Lett. **46**, 20–23 (1977)
8. Schwarzer, D., Troe, J., Schroeder, J.: S_1 lifetime of azulene in solution. ber. Bunsen-Ges. Phys. Chem. **95**, 933–934 (1991)
9. Tittelbach-Helmrich, D., Wagner, B.D., Steer, R.P.: The effect of solvent viscosity on the population relaxation times of the S_1 state of azulene and related compounds. Chem. Phys. Lett. **209**, 464–468 (1993)
10. Wagner, B.D., Szymanski, M., Steer, R.P.: Subpicosecond pump-probe measurements of the electronic relaxation rates of the S_1 states of azulene and related compounds in polar and nonpolar solvents. J. Chem. Phys. **98**, 301–307 (1993)
11. Wurzer, A.J., Wilhelm, T., Piel, J., Riedle, E.: Comprehensive measurement of the S_1 azulene relaxation dynamics and observation of vibrational wavepacket motion. Chem. Phys. Lett. **299**, 296–302 (1999)
12. Foggi, P., Neuwahl, F.V.R., Moroni, L., Salvi, P.R.: $S_1 \rightarrow S_n$ and $S_2 \rightarrow S_n$ absorption of azulene: femtosecond transient spectra and excited state calculations. J. Phys. Chem. A **107**, 1689–1696 (2003)
13. Amirav, A., Jortner, J.: J. Chem. Phys. **81**, 4200–4205 (1984)
14. Suzuki, T., Ito, M.: J. Phys. Chem. **91**, 3537–3542 (1987)
15. Bearpark, M.J., Bernardi, F., Clifford, S., Olivucci, M., Robb, M.A., Smith, B.R., Vreven, T.: J. Am. Chem. Soc. **118**, 169–175 (1996)
16. Ruth, A.A., Kim, E.-K., Hese, A.: Phys. Chem. Chem. Phys. **1**, 5121–5128 (1999)

17. Diau, E.W.-G., Feyter, S.D., Zewail, A.H.: J. Chem. Phys. **110**, 9785–9788 (1999)
18. Hoyer, C.E., Xu, X., Ma, D., Gagliardi, L., Truhlar, D.G.: Constructing diabatic representations using adiabatic and approximate diabatic data - coping with diabolical singularities. J. Chem. Phys. **141**, 114104 (2014)
19. Skouteris, D., Barone, V.: A new Gaussian MCTDH program: implementation and validation on the levels of the water and glycine molecules. J. Chem. Phys. **140**, 244104 (2014)
20. Skouteris, D., Barone, V.: Nonadiabatic photodynamics of phenol on a realistic potential energy surface by a novel multilayer Gaussian MCTDH program. Chem. Phys. Lett. **636**, 15–21 (2015)
21. Skouteris, D.: Time-dependent calculations on systems of chemical interest: dynamical and kinetic approaches. Int. J. Quant. Chem. **116**, 1618–1622 (2016)
22. Skouteris, D., Laganà, A., Capecchi, G., Werner, H.-J.: Wave packet calculations for the $Cl + H_2$ reaction. Int. J. Quant. Chem. **96**, 562–567 (2004)
23. Skouteris, D., Laganà, A., Capecchi, G., Werner, H.-J.: Rotational and alignment effects in a wavepacket calculation for the $Cl + H_2$ reaction. Int. J. Quant. Chem. **99**, 577–584 (2004)
24. Skouteris, D., Laganà, A.: Non-born-oppenheimer MCTDH calculations on the confined H_2^+ molecular ion. Chem. Phys. Lett. **500**, 144–148 (2010)
25. Skouteris, D., Laganà, A., Pirani, F.: An approximate quantum mechanical study of the $N + O \rightarrow NO^+ + e^-$ associative ionization. Chem. Phys. Lett. **557**, 43–48 (2013)
26. Skouteris, D., Laganà, A.: Electronuclear multi-configuration time-dependent Hartree calculations on the confined H atom with mobile electron and nucleus. Int. J. Quant. Chem. **113**, 1333–1338 (2013)
27. Skouteris, D., Laganà, A.: MCTDH calculations on the OH radical moving along a (10,0) nanotube. Chem. Phys. Lett. **575**, 18–22 (2013)
28. Frisch, M.J., Trucks, G.W., Schlegel, H.B., Scuseria, G.E., Robb, M.A., Cheeseman, J.R., Scalmani, G., Barone, V., Mennucci, B., Petersson, G.A., Nakatsuji, H., Caricato, M., Li, X., Hratchian, H.P., Bloino, J., Janesko, B.G., Izmaylov, A.F., Lipparini, F., Zheng, G., Sonnenberg, J.L., Liang, W., Hada, M., Ehara, M., Toyota, K., Fukuda, R., Hasegawa, J., Ishida, M., Nakajima, T., Honda, Y., Kitao, O., Nakai, H., Vreven, T., Throssell, K., Montgomery Jr., J.A., Peralta, J.E., Ogliaro, F., Bearpark, M., Heyd, J.J., Brothers, E., Kudin, K.N., Staroverov, V.N., Keith, T., Kobayashi, R., Normand, J., Raghavachari, K., Rendell, A., Burant, J.C., Iyengar, S.S., Tomasi, J., Cossi, M., Rega, N., Millam, J. M., Klene, M., Knox, J.E., Cross, J.B., Bakken, V., Adamo, C., Jaramillo, J., Gomperts, R., Stratmann, R.E., Yazyev, O., Austin, A.J., Cammi, R., Pomelli, C., Ochterski, J.W., Martin, R.L., Morokuma, K., Zakrzewski, V.G., Voth, G.A., Salvador, P., Dannenberg, J.J., Dapprich, S., Parandekar, P.V., Mayhall, N.J., Daniels, A.D., Farkas, O., Foresman, J.B., Ortiz, J.V., Cioslowski, J., Fox, D.J.: Gaussian Development Version, Revision I.03. Gaussian Inc., Wallingford CT (2014)
29. Lee, C., Yang, W., Parr, R.G.: Development of the Colle-Salvetti correlation-energy formula into a functional of the electron density. Phys. Rev. B **37**, 785–789 (1988)
30. Hariharan, P.C., Pople, J.A.: Influence of polarization function on molecular-orbital hydrogenation energies. Theor. Chem. Acc. **28**, 213–222 (1973)
31. Banerjee, S., Baiardi, A., Bloino, J., Barone, V.: J. Chem. Theory Comput. **12**, 774 (2016)
32. Lou, Y., Chang, J., Jorgensen, J., Lemal, D.M.: J. Am. Chem. Soc. **124**, 15302 (2002)

Spherical and Hyperbolic Spin Networks: The q-extensions of Wigner-Racah $6j$ Coefficients and General Orthogonal Discrete Basis Sets in Applied Quantum Mechanics

Roger W. Anderson[1($\boxtimes$)] and Vincenzo Aquilanti[2,3]

[1] Department of Chemistry and Biochemistry, University of California,
Santa Cruz, CA 95064, USA
anderso@ucsc.edu
[2] Dipartimento di Chimica, Biologia e Biotecnologie,
Università di Perugia, via Elce di Sotto, 8, 06183 Perugia, Italy
[3] Istituto di Struttura Della Materia, Consiglio Nazionale Delle Ricerche,
Piazzale Aldo Moro, 7, 00185 Rome, Italy
vincenzoaquilanti@yahoo.it

Abstract. Discrete basis sets continue to have an important role in mathematics and quantum mechanics. Racah recoupling coefficients or their closely related Wigner $6j$ symbols form a remarkably rich source of such functions, and now their properties are well understood for Euclidean space where $q = 1$. Here we report a unified treatment of their q-extensions to non-Euclidean spaces: hyperbolic, for real q different from 1, and spherical, for $q = r^{th}$ root of unity. We calculate the non-Euclidean coefficients as the eigenvectors of a real symmetric tridiagonal matrix. The eigenvectors form a discrete ortho-normal basis set, and the eigenvalues can be interpreted as energy levels. We provide extensive numerical results, and also show the Neville volume formula for a tetrahedron appears to be valid for both hyperbolic and spherical cases in the semiclassical limit. This q-extended volume is used to scale the magnitude of the eigenvectors in a familiar fashion. We also determine for spherical space that the radius, r, has a sharp minimum value to support all x,y given by triangular relations for a quadrilateral (not necessarily planar) with side lengths a, b, c, d and forming a tetrahedron. The ranges of x and y are truncated for $r < a + b + c + d + 2$.

1 Introduction

This paper explores the extension of tools of importance in quantum science (angular momentum theory, Racah-Wigner algebra, Ponzano-Regge asymptotics, Schulten-Gordon semiclassical analysis) [1] to the non-Euclidean cases, the key is introduction of a parameter denoted as q. In this first publication on q-extensions, we only consider the $6j$ symbol. The $6j$ symbol for $q = 1$ (Euclidean space) with a limiting procedure can be shown to include the $3j$ and $3nj$ [2–4] symbols [5,6] and Wigner rotation matrices [7], the spherical and hyperspherical

© Springer International Publishing AG 2017
O. Gervasi et al. (Eds.): ICCSA 2017, Part V, LNCS 10408, pp. 338–353, 2017.
DOI: 10.1007/978-3-319-62404-4_25

harmonics and practically all orthogonal and complete, discrete and continuous, wavefunction/orbital sets, that can be expressed in close, analytical form, related to hypergeometric polynomials [8–12]. However as we will demonstrate in a future publication that the situation is more complicated for q-extended $6j$.

Progress of these tools in quantum mechanical applications, in theoretical chemistry, in materials science, in biochemical and biophysical simulations, requires computational efforts based on analytical advances: recently, the merging of activities originated from search of basis sets with analytical properties beyond classical (i.e. hyperspherical) special functions and orthogonal polynomials [4,13–20] produced results on Sturmians orbitals, discretization (i.e. hyperquantization) algorithms, imaging reconstruction and so on. The further step, the inclusion of non-Euclidean geometry (i.e. q-extensions) is the main motivation or this paper. For notation and viewpoint, we refer to recent papers in these Lecture Notes Series [21–25] and elsewhere, see also [3,26,27,27–29] in order to generalize, step-by-step $SO(2)$ and $SO(3)$ matrices, of the Euclidean $q{=}1$ case and to extend to the non Euclidean case. References to be consulted are [30–33] and particularly [34,35]. The extensions are presented here to the non Euclidean cases of the 2×2 table (implying interpretation of hyperbolic and spherical angles), and of the 3×3 table. The latter is both basic for recurrence relations and illustrative of the non Euclidean rotation matrices and q-vector couplings as limiting cases.

The following sections deal with explicit calculation by close terminating q hypergeometric series or - numerically better and physically insightful - by derivation of the $q \neq 1$ three term recursions *a la* [36] interpreted as a difference equation and transformed in a matrix diagonalization. Listing the values as entries on a square matrix leads to what we have conveniently defined the screen. Illustrations follow, discussed thanks to our progress in screen representation of caustics as envelopes of turning points in $2D$ wells, delimiting wavelike *vs* decaying or classical *vs* non classical ranges. The key role is played here from analysis originated by Neville [37], Braun [38] and by others [21,22,26,39]. We will point out with little details how to deal with matrix diagonalizations, the discrete quantum and mechanical use of the three-term recurrence relations (crucial for defining orthonormal polynomial sets), the finite difference equations (*e.g.* discrete analogues of Schroedinger-like equations), and the q- Regge-Ponzano asymptotics (*e.g.* to obtain volumes of non-Euclidean tetrahedra (cf. [40]).

2   Background

2.1   Square Matrices of q - $6j$ Symbols. The Screen

In this paper we consider the elements $U_q (abdc; xy)$ of ortho-normal matrices that are related to the q-extended Wigner-Racah $6j$ symbols, here denoted $\begin{bmatrix} a\ b\ x \\ c\ d\ y \end{bmatrix}$. The U_q are proportional to the matrix elements between alternative angular momentum coupling schemes, for $q = 1$ see [1].

$$U_q\left(abdc; xy\right) = \sqrt{[2x+1][2y+1]} \begin{bmatrix} a & b & x \\ c & d & y \end{bmatrix} \tag{1}$$

The terms $[2x+1]$ and $[2y+1]$ are q-numbers for which we specify our choices in the next section. Suffice for now that $[2x+1] = 2x+1$ when $q = 1$, and for given values of a, b, c, d, the U_q will be defined over a range for both x and y.

The screen corresponds to the $6j$ or the U_q values for all possible values of x and y. In previous work [21, 22, 41], we have specified the Canonical form, and this implies that $q-6j$ coefficients in this form are given by:

$$\begin{bmatrix} a & a+\frac{n}{2} & x \\ a+\frac{|m-n|}{2}+k & a+\frac{m}{2} & y \end{bmatrix} \tag{2}$$

where

N is the desired number of values for x or y : $a = \left(\frac{N-1}{2}\right)$.
m , n, and k are non $-$ negative integers.
$m = 0, 1, 2, \cdots$, $n = 0, 1, 2, \cdots$, $0 \le k \le m+n-|m-n|$,

For real q the ranges for x and y are: : $\frac{n}{2} \le x \le 2a+\frac{n}{2}$ $\frac{m}{2} \le y \le 2a+\frac{m}{2}$.
We show in Sect. 4.3 for q the rth root of unity

$$\frac{n}{2} \le x \le 2a + \frac{n}{2} - \Delta \qquad \frac{m}{2} \le y \le 2a + \frac{m}{2} - \Delta,$$

where $\Delta = \max\left(0, a+b+c+d+2-r\right)$.

We see that the number of U elements for real q and for sufficiently large r for root unity q is determined by the magnitude of a. For $a = 1/2$, there are $(2a+1)^2 = 4$ elements. For $a = 1$, there are 9 elements. The range is terminated for $r < a+b+c+d+2$. This general form for q-6j symbols becomes the Canonical form, if $m \ge n$.

2.2   Extended q-Symbols. Various Alternatives and Present Choice

Previous research discussed in the literature has used several choices for evaluating q-numbers, but here we use the definition of a q number as $[n] \equiv \frac{q^n - q^{-n}}{q^1 - q^{-1}}$. However other papers use the definition: $[n] \equiv \frac{q^{n/2} - q^{-n/2}}{q^{1/2} - q^{-1/2}}$. We caution the reader to check the definitions used in other papers because this difference may and has caused errors. We consider three cases for q:

1. Euclidean Space, $q = 1$, and $[n] = n$
2. Hyperbolic Space, $q = e^{\pm \pi n/r}$, and $[n] = \sinh\left(\pi n/r\right)/\sinh\left(\pi/r\right)$
3. Spherical Space, $q = e^{\pm i\pi n/r}$ or the rth root of unity.. and $[n] = \sin\left(\pi n/r\right)/\sin\left(\pi/r\right)$.

The variable r is considered as the curvature of a non-Euclidean space and is a positive integer. We can say that the space becomes more curved as r becomes smaller. Euclidean space results as $r \to \infty$. The values of the q-6j symbols are unchanged when q is replaced by $1/q$, so it does not matter if $q = e^{\pi n/r}$ or $q = e^{-\pi n/r}$.

2.3 The 2×2 and 3×3 Matrices and the Non Euclidean Geometrical Interpretation

We present in Tables I and II the explicit expressions for the canonical form symbols for the cases where the smallest spin is $1/2$ or 1, respectively. Furthermore the four parameters $a = 1/2, b, c, d$ or $a = 1, b, c, d$ of the U must satisfy the restrictions of Sect. 2.1. According to Sect. 2.1 we have arranged them in 2×2 and 3×3 matrices. In view of their importance, the corresponding $q=1$ cases are reported in all books on angular momentum. We make explicit reference to the Tables 9-1 and 9-2 in [1], the main differences being that: (i) the entries have been worked out so that q. numbers appear and they can be explicitly calculated as in Sect. 2.1. (ii) also, they are given with the normalization introduced there that permits to arrange them as elements of orthogonal matrices. As such, associations of their entries to representations of rotations in spaces of dimensions 2 and 3 is transparent [42].

Table II $\sqrt{[2x+1][2y+1]}\begin{bmatrix}1 & b & x \\ c & d & y\end{bmatrix} = \sqrt{[2x+1][2y+1]}\begin{bmatrix}c & d & x \\ 1 & b & y\end{bmatrix}$

y	$x = b+1$
$d+1$ 11	$(-1)^{s+1}\left\{\dfrac{[s-2d][s-2d+1][s-2b+1][s-2b]}{[2b+1][2b+2][2d+1][2d+2]}\right\}^{\frac{1}{2}}$
d 12	$(-1)^{s+1}\left\{\dfrac{[2][s+2][s-2b][s-2d+1][s-2c+1]}{[2b+1][2b+2][2d][2d+2]}\right\}^{\frac{1}{2}}$
$d-1$ 13	$(-1)^{s+1}\left\{\dfrac{[s+1][s+2][s-2c][s-2c+1]}{[2b+1][2b+2][2d][2d+1]}\right\}^{\frac{1}{2}}$
y	$x = b$
$d+1$ 21	$(-1)^{s+1}\left\{\dfrac{[2][s+2][s-2b+1][s-2d][s-2c+1]}{[2b][2b+2][2d+1][2d+2]}\right\}^{\frac{1}{2}}$
d 22	$(-1)^{s}\dfrac{[s-2b][s-2d]-[s+2][2b+2d-s]}{\{[2b][2b+2][2d][2d+2]\}^{\frac{1}{2}}}$
$d-1$ 23	$(-1)^{s}\left\{\dfrac{[2][s+1][s-2d+1][s-2b][s-2c]}{[2b][2b+2][2d][2d+1]}\right\}^{\frac{1}{2}}$
y	$x = b-1$
$d+1$ 31	$(-1)^{s+1}\left\{\dfrac{[s+1][s+2][s-2c][s-2c+1]}{[2b][2b+1][2d+2][2d+1]}\right\}^{\frac{1}{2}}$
d 32	$(-1)^{s}\left\{\dfrac{[2][s+1][s-2d][s-2b+1][s-2c]}{[2b][2b+1][2d][2d+2]}\right\}^{\frac{1}{2}}$
$d-1$ 33	$(-1)^{s+1}\left\{\dfrac{[s-2d][s-2d+1][s-2b+1][s-2b]}{[2b][2b+1][2d][2d+1]}\right\}^{\frac{1}{2}}$

$s = b+c+d = \text{integer}$

Table I. $\sqrt{[2x+1][2y+1]}\begin{bmatrix}1/2 & b & x \\ c & d & y\end{bmatrix} = \sqrt{[2x+1][2y+1]}\begin{bmatrix}c & d & x \\ 1/2 & b & y\end{bmatrix}$

y	$x = b-\dfrac{1}{2}$
$d+\dfrac{1}{2}$	$(-1)^{s+\frac{1}{2}}\dfrac{1}{2}\left\{\dfrac{[2s+3][2s-4c+1]}{[2b+1][2d+1]}\right\}^{\frac{1}{2}}$
$d-\dfrac{1}{2}$	$(-1)^{s-\frac{1}{2}}\dfrac{1}{2}\left\{\dfrac{[2s-4d+1][2s-4b+1]}{[2b+1][2d+1]}\right\}^{\frac{1}{2}}$
y	$x = b+\dfrac{1}{2}$
$d+\dfrac{1}{2}$	$(-1)^{s+\frac{1}{2}}\dfrac{1}{2}\left\{\dfrac{[2s-4d+1][2s-4b+1]}{[2b+1][2d+1]}\right\}^{\frac{1}{2}}$
$d-\dfrac{1}{2}$	$(-1)^{s+\frac{1}{2}}\dfrac{1}{2}\left\{\dfrac{[2s+3][2s-4c+1]}{[2b+1][2d+1]}\right\}^{\frac{1}{2}}$

$s = b+c+d = (\text{odd integer})/2$

2 × 2 Matrix. Table I lists the four terms that form the elements of a 2×2 orthonormal matrix and the transformation can be written as: $\begin{bmatrix} \cos\vartheta & -\sin\vartheta \\ \sin\vartheta & \cos\vartheta \end{bmatrix}$.

We can obtain more geometric insight about the 2×2 matrix, by substituting the definition of s and making the usual semiclassical scaling substitutions: $c = C - \frac{1}{2}$, $b = B - \frac{1}{2}$, $d = D - \frac{1}{2}$. Then we find the following q-extended expressions for $\cos\vartheta$, $\sin\vartheta$, and $\Gamma = \sin\vartheta\cos\vartheta$:

$$\cos\vartheta = (-1)^{B+C+D-1} \frac{1}{2} \left\{ \frac{[2C+2B+2D][-2C+2B+2D]}{[2B][2D]} \right\}^{1/2}$$

$$\sin\vartheta = (-1)^{B+C+D} \frac{1}{2} \left\{ \frac{[2C+2B-2D][2C-2B+2D]}{[2B][2D]} \right\}^{1/2}$$

$$\Gamma = -\frac{\{[2C+2B-2D][2C-2B+2D][2C+2B+2D][-2C+2B+2D]\}^{\frac{1}{2}}}{4[2B][2D]}$$

In Euclidean space where $q = 1$ or $[n] = n$, these equations reduce to the well known formulas for $\cos\vartheta$, $\sin\vartheta$, and the area, Area $= -BD\Gamma$ of a triangle with sides B, C, and D. Also $\sin 2\vartheta$ is exactly given by 2Γ.

3 × 3 Matrix. The nine quantities in Table II are elements of a rotation matrix in three dimensions. The assignment of elements to rows and columns of the matrix is indicated by the bold numbers in the left column of Table II. The matrix is orthonormal and describes a discrete proper rotation as its determinant is 1. Its trace and eigenvectors yield the angle of rotation and the rotation axis. The axes and angles have discrete characterizations determined by the possible values for b, c, and d. These properties hold for both Euclidean and non-Euclidean cases, and their use will provide insight for further analytical work on the geometric interpretation in flat and curved spaces. See [42] for a relevant discussion.

3   Three-term Symmetric Recursion for $U \equiv U_q$

The U values must be calculated by efficient and accurate algorithms, and we have previously used multiple precision arithmetic [3,27,36,43] to evaluate explicit formulas for $3nj$ symbols for the $q = 1$ case [1]. These high accuracy calculations are entirely reliable for all U that we have considered in the past, and the results provide a stringent test for other methods. However recourse to symmetric three term recursion formulas appears most convenient not only for fast and accurate calculations but also for semiclassical analysis, in order to understand high j limit and in reverse to interpret them as discrete wavefunctions obeying Schrödinger type of difference (rather than differential) equations. Also Braun potentials see below can be easily specified for the given screen, and these potentials determine the classical turning points for the screen. We also rely on terms in the recurrence relation to establish the minimum radius of spherical space, Sect. 4.3. We calculated U for $q = 1$ by symmetric recurrence in [21].

Starting with the recurrence relation [21] for $q = 1$ and enforcing consistency with Table II and [37], we can write a three term symmetric recursion relationship for $U(x, y)$ for all relevant q. This is conveniently represented as an eigenvalue equation:

$$g_+ (x) U (x + 1, y) + g_0 (x) U (x, y) + g_- (x) U (x - 1, y) = \lambda (y) U (x, y). \quad (3)$$

where

$$g_+ (x) = \zeta Q (x + 1) [2][2x + 2]^{-1}[2x + 1]^{-\frac{1}{2}}[2x + 3]^{-\frac{1}{2}} \quad (4)$$

$$g_- (x) = \zeta Q (x) [2] [2x]^{-1}[2x + 1]^{-\frac{1}{2}}[2x - 1]^{-\frac{1}{2}} \quad (5)$$

$$g_0 (x) = \zeta_0 P (x) [2x]^{-1}[2x + 2]^{-1} \quad (6)$$

$$\lambda (y) = \zeta_0 ([y + b - c] [c - b + y] - [y + b + c + 2] [b + c - y]), \quad (7)$$

$$P (x) = - \{[a + b - x] [a - b + x] - [b + x - a] [a + b + x + 2]\}$$
$$\times \{[d + c - x] [d - c + x] - [c + x - d] [d + c + x + 2]\}.$$

$$Q (x) = \{[a + b + x + 1] [a + b - x + 1] [a - b + x] [-a + b + x]\}^{\frac{1}{2}}$$
$$\times \{[d + c + x + 1] [d + c - x + 1] [d - c + x] [-d + c + x]\}^{\frac{1}{2}}$$

The quantities, g_+, g_0 and g_- are all real numbers in these equations. Hence the arguments of square roots definiting of g_+ and g_- must be positive. Since $g_+(x, y) = g_-(x + 1, y)$, the recurrence equation defines an eigensystem of a real symmetric tridiagonal matrix. A row of the screen may be efficiently and accurately calculated from these equations. Diagonalization of this matrix with rows given by the $g_-(x)$, $g_0(x)$, $g_+(x)$ provides an accurate check: the eigenvalues of the tridiagonal matrix precisely match those expected from Eq. 7 and eigenvectors generate $U(x, y)$. The U also reproduce $U(x, y)$ calculated in multiple precision with the explicit formula for $q - 6j$ (p. 103: [44]). However a corresponding recurrence relation from a recent paper [34] does not provide agreement between calculated and expected eigenvalues. Stable results are obtained with double precision arithmetic using the Lapack routine *dsetqr*, and the proper phases are applied to the eigenvectors. Both [34,35] give the three term recurrence relations in symbolic form, but we find the algebraic Eq. 3 to be much more useful for numerical work.

Equations (4)–(7), also contain additional parameters, ζ and ζ_0 that were first introduced in [39]. These parameters may have values of ± 1. The eigenvalues of Eq. 3 are unchanged with either sign for ζ, but the eigenvector for smallest λ will have N-1 nodes for one choice of ζ, while the lowest energy eigenvector will have no nodes for the other choice. This device allows the calculation to avoid the "checkerboard" pattern that is generated with the wrong choice for the sign of ζ. The correct node pattern for $U(x, y)$ is found for $\zeta = -1$. The sign of eigenvalues are determined by the parameter, ζ_0. The parameter, ζ_0, also determines whether we should consider the U to be most influenced by which Braun potential, $\mathbf{W}^-(x)$ or $\mathbf{W}^+(x)$.

Braun [38] introduced and defined these potentials as:

$$\mathbf{W}^{\pm}(x) = g_0(x) \pm |g_-(x) + g_+(x)|, \tag{8}$$

for discrete symmetric eigenvalue equations such as Eq. 3, and shows that they can be interpreted as discrete Schrödinger-like equations with a potential energy and a kinetic energy term. The eigenvalue is the energy. Braun shows the important result that two potentials, $\mathbf{W}^{\pm}(x)$, give the turning points for classical motion in the discrete case.

The classical turning points may be determined only by $\mathbf{W}^-(x)$ or only by $\mathbf{W}^+(x)$ or by both. Furthermore the energy (eigenvalue) is bounded by the two potentials, and this is a consequence of the fact that kinetic energy is merely the energy minus the potential energy (whether $\mathbf{W}^-(x)$ or $\mathbf{W}^+(x)$) Braun applies his theory with semiclassical mechanics to calculate the eigenvalues and eigenvectors. We provide an exact calculation of these quantities, but still find great use for the Braun potential functions. Braun also gives some equations for the magnitude of eigenvectors for different eigenvalues and coordinate, x, but we will use the Neville results described in the next section. We have used Braun potential functions in the past with in Ref. [26] where Hamiltonian dynamics is developed for a similar system and in [39]. Braun's potential functions are closely related to the caustics illustrated in [22, 23].

3.1 Neville Volume

In 1971 Neville published a paper [37] where the volume of a tetrahedron is expressed as a function of the coefficients of the three-term recurrence relation for $6-j$ symbols in the asymptotic (semiclassical) limit. We have improved the Neville equation with the introduction of a higher order approximation for the first difference of $6-j$. Neville uses $\delta^{(1)}W(x) \equiv W(x+1) - W(x)$, while we use $\delta^{(1)}W(x) \equiv (W(x+1) - W(x-1))/2$. The resulting volume is determined by the values for a, b, c, d, x, y. With the improvement the Neville volume agrees to order N^{-2} with the well known volume of a physical tetrahedron (See [1]). Although Neville derives his equations for $q = 1$, we have found that his method may also be applied for $q \neq 1$, and hence appears to provide a convenient method to calculate the volume of a non-Euclidean tetrahedron in terms of its edges. The important implication of the Neville volume formula is that it predicts an upper bound on the magnitude of U in the classical region for all values of q. Plots in the last section of this paper provide convincing support for this assertion.

$$s_-^{6j}(x) \begin{bmatrix} a & b & x-1 \\ c & d & y \end{bmatrix} + s_0^{6j}(x,y) \begin{bmatrix} a & b & x \\ c & d & y \end{bmatrix} + s_+^{6j}(x) \begin{bmatrix} a & b & x+1 \\ c & d & y \end{bmatrix} = 0$$

The square of the Neville volume is:

$$V_N^2(x,y) = -\left(s_0^{6j}(x,y) + s_+^{6j}(x) + s_-^{6j}(x)\right)\left(s_0^{6j}(x,y) - s_-^{6j}(x) - s_+^{6j}(x)\right)/48^2.$$

$$s_+ = \sqrt{[2x+3]}g_+\left(x\right), \quad s_- = \sqrt{[2x-1]}g_-\left(x\right), \quad s_0 = \sqrt{[2x+1]}\left(g_0\left(x\right) - \lambda\left(y\right)\right)$$

The $U\left(x,y\right)$ exhibit classical (oscillatory) behavior for $V_N^2\left(x,y\right) > 0$, and non-classical (exponentially small) for negative $V_N^2\left(x,y\right)$. The connected set of points with minimum $\left|V_N^2\left(x,y\right)\right|$ constitute the caustics for the q-6j symbols. A caustic is the dividing line between non-classical and classical behavior.

$$0 \le \sqrt{12\pi V_N}\left\|\begin{bmatrix} a\, b\, x \\ c\, d\, y \end{bmatrix}\right\| \le 1, \qquad V_N^2 > 0 \tag{9}$$

$$\begin{bmatrix} a\, b\, x \\ c\, d\, y \end{bmatrix} = \frac{U\left(x,y\right)}{\sqrt{[2x+1]}\sqrt{[2y+1]}}$$

In the next section we will present plots of $\sqrt{12\pi V_N}\left\|\begin{bmatrix} a\, b\, x \\ c\, d\, y \end{bmatrix}\right\|$ to show that the Neville bounds are accurate.

The Neville theory provides the precise factor 48^{-2} in the volume for flat or curved space tetrahedron. Neville also provides the factor needed to use his method for the projected area of a q-extended 3j coefficient. However we have not tried to extend the Neville analysis to systems other than q-3j and q-6j. Scaling of the magnitude in classical regions for other systems can be obtained by the Braun theory if the normalization constants for discrete semiclassical eigenvector are known for each eigenvalue. This normalization step can be done, but is not needed by the Neville theory for q-6j or q-3j.

The Neville theory is an attractive and simple route for calculating the volume of a tetrahedron in curved space. Murakami and Yano have reported a more complicated analytical formula [40].

4   Images on the Screens and their Discussion

Figures and Captions in this section demonstrate the behavior of screens for $q = 1$, $q = e^{-\pi/r}$, and $q = e^{-i\pi/r}$. For all choices for q we choose only one set of parameter values, $a = b = c = d = 100$, because of limited space. We call this choice for the parameters the degenerate case. We have considered screens and caustics for this case with $q = 1$ in previous work [22,45]. Recalling Sect. 2.2 we deal with the values of $[n]$ as $[n] = n$, $[n] = \sinh\left(\pi n/r\right)/\sinh\left(\pi/r\right)$, and $[n] = \sin\left(\pi n/r\right)/\sin\left(\pi/r\right)$ corresponding to the two non-Euclidean geometries. We will only discuss the most important implications of the cases for q-6j's:

4.1   Reference Euclidean Space, $q = 1$

In this case $[n] = n$. Figure 1a shows the unscaled values of $U(x,y)$, and the classical and non-classical regions. The U are oscillatory in the classical region, and decrease exponentially in the non-classical region. Figure 1b shows that the Braun potentials predict the classical turning points. and Fig. 2b demonstrates that the Neville volume provides the expected scaling for the magnitude of $q-6j$. Figure 2a displays the $U(x,y)$ for various values for y. With the choice that $\zeta = -1$ the lowest eigenvalue has the smallest number of nodes. As expected the U with the largest eigenvalues are clustered at small values of x.

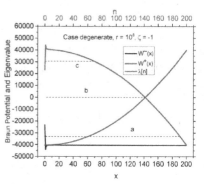

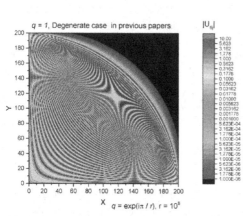

q = exp(iπ / r), r = 10⁸

(a) Contour plot of the log of the magnitude of $U(x,y)$ for $\zeta = -1$ and $\zeta_0 = 1$. The U are oscillatory in the classical region and exponentially decrease (nonclassical) outside what appears as a quarter circular yellow line. The patterns visible in the classical region are caused by the phase evolution of the $U(x,y)$

(b) Plot of the Braun potentials $\mathbf{W}^{\pm}(x)$ and the eigenvalues, $\lambda(y)$. The eigenvalues are plotted as a function of the number of nodes given by the axis at the top of the figure, and the Braun Potentials form upper and lower bounds for the eigenvalues. The dotted guide lines labeled a, b, and c show how the turning points are determined. In each case the left turning point is for $x = 0$ and the right is determined by $\mathbf{W}^{+}(x)$

Fig. 1. $q = 1, a = b = c = d = 100, \zeta = -1, \zeta_0 = 1$

4.2   Hyperbolic Space, Real $q \neq 1$

Here $[n] = \sinh(\pi n/r)/\sinh(\pi/r)$. Figure 3a shows scaled $U(x,y)$ for $r = 200$, and the fact that the Neville volume formula gives the expected scaling. Qualitatively the figure resembles Fig. 2b, but the non-classical region is much larger for $x > y$, and there is more distance between the oscillations for $x < y$. The screen is becoming more diagonally dominated with decreasing r. Figure 3b displays the $U(x,y)$ for various values for y, and shows clearly that the significant values for U are clustering about the diagonal. Figures 4a with $r = 100$ and Fig. 4b with $r = 40$ show further dominance of the diagonal, and expected Neville volume formula scaling. We see that the classical region approaches the diagonal between the (x,y) points $(b-a, d+a+1)$ and $(b+a+1, d-a)$ as the curvature of hyperbolic space increases with decreasing r. This property is predicted in [8]. We have also calculated Braun potentials for the values of r used in these figures, and the results are consistent with the scaled U screens.

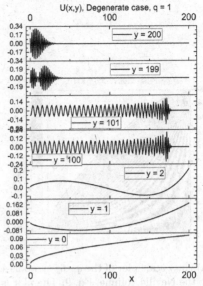

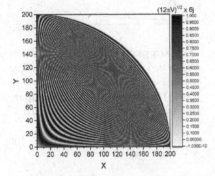

(a) Gray scale plot of the 6j symbols scaled by the Neville volume, Eq. 9. The plot is constucted so that non classical values for 6j are set to zero (white region), and no scaled values in the classical region have a magnitude greater than 1.

(b) Stack plot of $U(x, y)$ for 7 choices of $y = 0, 1, 2, 100, 101, 199, 200$. The number of nodes as a function x in $U(x, y)$ is determined by y. Compare this figure with Figure 1b, see how the Braun potentials determine the turning points. $U(x, y)$ for $y = 0, 1, 2$ have turning points corresponding to guide line a. The $U(x, y)$ for $y = 100, 101$ have turning points corresponding to guide line b. The $U(x, y)$ for $y = 199, 200$ have turning points corresponding to guide line c. The $U(x, 200)$ actually has 200 nodes!

Fig. 2. $q = 1, a = b = c = d = 100, \zeta = -1, \zeta_0 = 1$

4.3 Spherical Space, Imaginary $q = r^{th}$ Root of Unity, Minimum Radius

For spherical space, $[n] = \sin(\pi n/r) / \sin(\pi/r)$, we show four plots that show that the $U(x, y)$ scale as expected by the Neville volume formula. Figure 5a is calculated with $r = 500$ and Fig. 5b with $r = 410$. We note that the classical region for $U(x, y)$ tends to fill more of the screen as r decreases. Figure 6a shows that the classical region completely fills the screen for $r = 401$. Figure 6b for $r = 390$ shows that the screen is truncated for $r \leq 402$ Hence $r = 402$ is a critical value for the radius of spherical space. We show in Sect. 4.3 the important result that a screen of dimension $(2a+1)X(2a+1)$ can only exist if $r \geq a+b+c+d+2$.

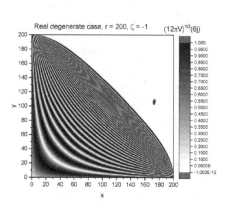

Real degenerate case, r = 200, ζ = -1 $(12\pi V)^{1/2}(6j)$

(a) Gray scale plot of the $q-6j$ symbols scaled by the Neville volume, Eq. 9. The plot is constucted so that non classical values for $6j$ are set to zero (white region), and no scaled values in the classical region have a magnitude greater than 1.

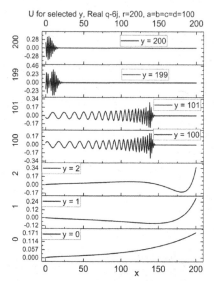

U for selected y, Real q-6j, r=200, a=b=c=d=100

(b) Stack plot of $U(x,y)$ for 7 choices of $y = 0, 1, 2, 100, 101, 199, 200$. The number of nodes as a function x in $U(x,y)$ is determined by y. Compare this figure with Figures 2a and 1b.

Fig. 3. Real q, $[n] = \sinh(\pi n/r)/\sinh(\pi/r)$, $r = 200, a = b = c = d = 100$, $\zeta = -1, \zeta_0 = 1$

The geometric requirement of the critical value for r emerges from a simple argument based on the recurrence relations for U in spherical space. We first rewrite the g_+ and Q parts of the recurrence equations:

$$g_+(x) = \zeta Q(x+1)[2][2x+2]^{-1}[2x+1]^{-\frac{1}{2}}[2x+3]^{-\frac{1}{2}} \tag{10}$$

$$Q(x+1) = \{[a+b+x+2][a+b-x][a-b+x+1][-a+b+x+1]\}^{\frac{1}{2}}$$
$$\times\{[d+c+x+2][d+c-x][d-c+x+1][-d+c+x+1]\}^{\frac{1}{2}}$$

i We see that $g_+(x) \propto Q(x+1) \propto [a+b-x]^{1/2}[d+c+x+2]^{1/2}$

ii For spherical space we have: $g_+(x) \propto \sin(\pi(a+b-x)/r)^{1/2}\sin(\pi(d+c+x+2)/r)^{1/2}$

iii We expect g_+ to be zero for $x = a+b$, and this is satisfied by the fact that $\sin(\pi(a+b-(a+b))/r)^{1/2} = 0$. This is the usual termination for sufficiently large r.

iv But $g_+(x+1)$ will also be zero for $r = a+b+c+d+2$ because then $\sin(\pi(d+c+a+b+2)/r) = 0$ as well.

v If $r = (a+b+c+d+2) - r_0$, then the largest value for x will be $a+b-r_0$, and the screen is truncated per the figures.

This explains the sharp critical value for r.

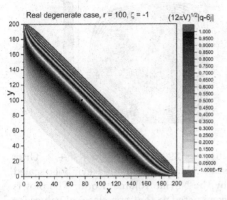

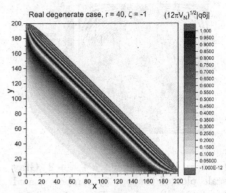

(a) Real q, $r = 100$, Gray scale plot of the $q - 6j$ symbols scaled by the Neville volume, Eq. 9. The plot is constucted so that non classical values for $6j$ are set to zero (white region), and no scaled values in the classical region have a magnitude greater than 1.

(b) Real q, $r = 40$, Gray scale plot of the $q - 6j$ symbols scaled by the Neville volume, Eq. 9. The plot is constucted so that non classical values for $6j$ are set to zero (white region), and few ($< 0.1\%$) of values in the classical region defined by negative V_N^2 have a magnitude greater than 1. These are the blue parts of the plot.

Fig. 4. Real q, $[n] = \sinh(\pi n/r)/\sinh(\pi/r)$, $a = b = c = d = 100$, $\zeta = -1$, $\zeta_0 = 1$.

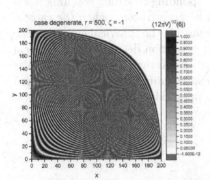

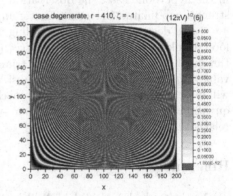

(a) $r = 500 > a + b + c + d + 2$. Gray scale plot of the $q - 6j$ symbols scaled by the Neville volume, Eq. 9. The plot is constucted so that non classical values for $6j$ are set to zero (white region), and no scaled values in the classical region have a magnitude greater than 1.

(b) $r = 410 > a + b + c + d + 2$. Gray scale plot of the $q - 6j$ symbols scaled by the Neville volume, Eq. 9. The plot is constucted so that non classical values for $6j$ are set to zero (white region), and no scaled values in the classical region have a magnitude greater than 1.

Fig. 5. Root of Unity q, $[n] = \sin(\pi n/r)/\sin(\pi/r)$, $a = b = c = d = 100$, $\zeta = -1$, $\zeta_0 = 1$

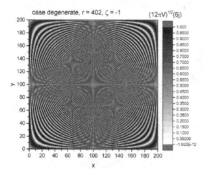
case degenerate, r = 402, ζ = -1 $(12\pi V)^{1/2}(6j)$

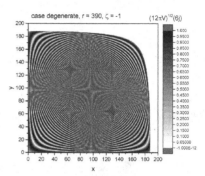
case degenerate, r = 390, ζ = -1 $(12\pi V)^{1/2}(6j)$

(a) $r = 402 = a + b + c + d + 2$. Gray scale plot of the $q - 6j$ symbols scaled by the Neville volume, Eq. 9. The plot is constucted so that non classical values for $6j$ are set to zero (white region), and no scaled values in the classical region have a magnitude greater than 1.

(b) $r = 390 < a + b + c + d + 2$. Gray scale plot of the $q - 6j$ symbols scaled by the Neville volume, Eq. 9. The plot is constucted so that non classical values for $6j$ are set to zero (white region), and no scaled values in the classical region have a magnitude greater than 1.

Fig. 6. Root of Unity q, $[n] = \sin(\pi n/r) / \sin(\pi/r)$, $a = b = c = d = 100$, $\zeta = -1$, $\zeta_0 = 1$

5   Conclusions

The *clous* of the results that are apparent from this exploratory work, are: (1) in the hyperbolic case, the observation that the parameter q acts, as 'coupling strength modulator' between two system corresponding to strong coupling when $q = 1$ and decreasing to full decoupling when it tends to zero, when the caustic loop shrinks to the diagonal unit matrix. (2) regarding the spherical extension the threshold for truncation due to the triangular condition determines the critical value of q for which the matrix shrinks. We anticipate that both of these results will be relevant for applied quantum mechanics, including molecular physics and quantum chemistry and for spin-foam and loop-gravity approaches to general relativity.

References

1. Varshalovich, D., Moskalev, A., Khersonskii, V.: Quantum Theory of Angular Momentum. World Scientific, Singapore (1988)
2. Aquilanti, V., Coletti, C.: $3nj$ symbols and harmonic superposition coefficients: an icosahedral abacus. Chem. Phys. Lett. **344**, 601–611 (2001)
3. Anderson, R.W., Aquilanti, V., Marzuoli, A.: 3nj morphogenesis and semiclassical disentangling. J. Phys. Chem. A **113**, 15106–15117 (2009)
4. Aquilanti, V., Cavalli, S., Coletti, C.: Angular and hyperangular momentum recoupling, harmonic superposition and Racah polynomials. A recursive algorithm. Chem. Phys. Lett. **344**, 587–600 (2001)
5. Aquilanti, V., Haggard, H.M., Littlejohn, R., Yu, L.: Semiclassical analysis of Wigner 3j-symbol. J. Phys. A **40**, 5637–5674 (2007)

6. Bitencourt, A.C.P., Ragni, M., Littlejohn, R.G., Anderson, R., Aquilanti, V.: The screen representation of vector coupling coefficients or wigner 3j symbols: exact computation and illustration of the asymptotic behavior. In: Murgante, B., et al. (eds.) ICCSA 2014. LNCS, vol. 8579, pp. 468–481. Springer, Cham (2014). doi:10. 1007/978-3-319-09144-0_32

7. Littlejohn, R., Yu, L.: Uniform semiclassical approximation for the Wigner 6j symbol in terms of rotation matrices. J. Phys. Chem. A **113**, 14904–14922 (2009)

8. Koekoek, R., Lesky, P., Swarttouw, R.: Hypergeometric Orthogonal Polynomials and Their q-Analogues. Springer, Heidelberg (2010)

9. Nikiforov, A.F., Suslov, S.K., Uvarov, V.B.: Classical Orthogonal Polyomials of a Discrete Variable. Springer, Berlin (1991)

10. Aquilanti, V., Cavalli, S., De Fazio, D.: Angular and hyperangular momentum coupling coefficients as Hahn polynomials. J. Phys. Chem. **99**, 15694–15698 (1995)

11. Aquilanti, V., Capecchi, G.: Harmonic analysis and discrete polynomials. From semiclassical angular momentum theory to the hyperquantization algorithm. Theor. Chem. Accounts **104**, 183–188 (2000)

12. De Fazio, D., Cavalli, S., Aquilanti, V.: Orthogonal polynomials of a discrete variable as expansion basis sets in quantum mechanics. The hyperquantization algorithm. Int. J. Quant. Chem. **93**, 91–111 (2003)

13. Calderini, D., Cavalli, S., Coletti, C., Grossi, G., Aquilanti, V.: Hydrogenoid orbitals revisited: From Slater orbitals to Coulomb Sturmians. J. Chem. Sci. **124**, 187–192 (2012)

14. Coletti, C., Calderini, D., Aquilanti, V.: d-dimensional Kepler-Coulomb Sturmians andHyperspherical Harmonics as Complete Orthonormal Atomic and Molecular Orbitals. Adv. Quantum Chem. **67**, 73–127 (2013)

15. Aquilanti, V., Cavalli, S., Coletti, C., De Fazio, D., Grossi, G.: Hyperangular momentum: applications to atomic and molecular science. In: Tsipis, C.A., Popov, V.S., Herschbach, D.R., Avery, J.S. (eds.) New Methods in Quantum Theory, pp. 233–250. Kluwer (1996)

16. Aquilanti, V., Cavalli, S., Coletti, C., Grossi, G.: Alternative sturmian bases and momentum space orbitals: an application to the hydrogen molecular ion. Chem. Phys. **209**, 405–419 (1996)

17. Aquilanti, V., Cavalli, S., Coletti, C.: The d-dimensional hydrogen atom: hyperspherical harmonics as momentum space orbitals and alternative sturmian basis sets. Chem. Phys. **214**, 1–13 (1997)

18. Aquilanti, V., Cavalli, S., Coletti, C., Di Domenico, D., Grossi, G.: Hyperspherical harmonics as sturmian orbitals in momentum space: a systematic approach to the few-body coulomb problem. Int. Rev. Phys. Chem. **20**, 673–709 (2001)

19. Aquilanti, V., Caligiana, A., Cavalli, S., Coletti, C.: Hydrogenic orbitals in momentum space and hyperspherical harmonics. Elliptic sturmian basis sets. Int. J. Quant. Chem. **92**, 212–228 (2003)

20. Aquilanti, V., Cavalli, S., Coletti, C.: Hyperspherical symmetry of hydrogenic orbitals and recoupling coefficients among alternative bases. Phys. Rev. Lett. **80**, 3209–3212 (1998)

21. Anderson, R.W., Aquilanti, V., Bitencourt, A.C.P., Marinelli, D., Ragni, M.: The screen representation of spin networks: 2D recurrence, eigenvalue equation for 6j symbols, geometric interpretation and hamiltonian dynamics. In: Murgante, B., Misra, S., Carlini, M., Torre, C.M., Nguyen, H.-Q., Taniar, D., Apduhan, B.O., Gervasi, O. (eds.) ICCSA 2013. LNCS, vol. 7972, pp. 46–59. Springer, Heidelberg (2013). doi:10.1007/978-3-642-39643-4_4

22. Ragni, M., Littlejohn, R.G., Bitencourt, A.C.P., Aquilanti, V., Anderson, R.W.: The screen representation of spin networks: images of $6j$ symbols and semiclassical features. In: Murgante, B., Misra, S., Carlini, M., Torre, C.M., Nguyen, H.-Q., Taniar, D., Apduhan, B.O., Gervasi, O. (eds.) ICCSA 2013. LNCS, vol. 7972, pp. 60–72. Springer, Heidelberg (2013). doi:10.1007/978-3-642-39643-4_5

23. Bitencourt, A.C.P., Marzuoli, A., Ragni, M., Anderson, R.W., Aquilanti, V.: Exact and asymptotic computations of elementary spin networks: classification of the quantum–classical boundaries. In: Murgante, B., Gervasi, O., Misra, S., Nedjah, N., Rocha, A.M.A.C., Taniar, D., Apduhan, B.O. (eds.) ICCSA 2012. LNCS, vol. 7333, pp. 723–737. Springer, Heidelberg (2012). doi:10.1007/978-3-642-31125-3_54

24. Marinelli, D., Marzuoli, A., Aquilanti, V., Anderson, R.W., Bitencourt, A.C.P., Ragni, M.: Symmetric angular momentum coupling, the quantum volume operator and the 7-spin network: a computational perspective. In: Murgante, B., Misra, S., Rocha, A.M.A.C., Torre, C., Rocha, J.G., Falcão, M.I., Taniar, D., Apduhan, B.O., Gervasi, O. (eds.) ICCSA 2014. LNCS, vol. 8579, pp. 508–521. Springer, Cham (2014). doi:10.1007/978-3-319-09144-0_35

25. Arruda, M.S., Santos, R.F., Marinelli, D., Aquilanti, V.: Spin-coupling diagrams and incidence geometry: a note on combinatorial and quantum-computational aspects. In: Gervasi, O., Murgante, B., Misra, S., Rocha, A.M.A.C., Torre, C., Taniar, D., Apduhan, B.O., Stankova, E., Wang, S. (eds.) ICCSA 2016. LNCS, vol. 9786, pp. 431–442. Springer, Cham (2016). doi:10.1007/978-3-319-42085-1_33

26. Aquilanti, V., Marinelli, D., Marzuoli, A.: Hamiltonian dynamics of a quantum of space: hidden symmetries and spectrum of the volume operator, and discrete orthogonal polynomials. J. Phys. A: Math. Theor. **46**, 175303 (2013). arXiv:1301.1949v2

27. Ragni, M., Bitencourt, A.C.P., da S. Ferreira, C., Aquilanti, V., Anderson, R.W., Littlejohn, R.G.: Exact computation and asymptotic approximations of 6j symbols: Illustration of their semiclassical limits. Int. J. Quant. Chem. **110**(3), 731–742 (2010)

28. Aquilanti, V., Bitencourt, A., da S. Ferreira, C., Marzuoli, A., Ragni, M.: Combinatorics of angular momentum recoupling theory: spin networks, their asymptotics and applications. Theor. Chem. Acc. **123**, 237–247 (2009)

29. Santos, R.F., Bitencourt, A.C.P., Ragni, M., Prudente, F., Coletti, C., Marzuoli, A., Aquilanti, V.: Couplings and recouplings of four angular momenta: alternative 9j symbols and spin addition diagrams. J. Mol. Model. (2017). doi:10.1007/s00894-017-3320-1

30. Bonatsos, D., Daskaloyannis, C.: Quantum groups and their applications in nuclear physics. Prog. Part. Nucl. Phys. **43**, 537–618 (1999)

31. Mizoguchi, S., Tada, T.: Three- dimensional gravity from the Turaev-Viro invariant. Phys. Rev. Lett. **68**, 1795–1798 (1992)

32. Turaev, V.G., Viro, O.Y.: State sum invariants of 3-manifolds and quantum $6j$ symbols. Topology **31**, 865–903 (1992)

33. Carter, J.S., Daniel, E.F., Saito, M.: The Classical and Quantum $6j$-Symbols. Princeton University Press, Princeton (1995)

34. Taylor, Y.U., Woodward, C.T.: $6j$ symbols for $U_q(sl_2)$ non-Euclidean tetrahedra. Sel. Math. New Ser. **11**, 539–571 (2005)

35. Khavkine, I.: Recurrence relation for the $6j$-symbol of $suq(2)$ as a symmetric eigenvalue problem. Int. J. Geom. Methods Mod. Phy. **12**, 1550117 (2015). (12 pages)

36. Anderson, R., Aquilanti, V., da S. Ferreira, C.: Exact computation and large angular momentum asymptotics of $3nj$ symbols: semiclassical disentangling of spinnetworks. J. Chem. Phys. **129**, 161101 (2008). (5 pages)

37. Neville, D.E.: A technique for solving recurrence relations approximately and its application to the 3-J and 6-J symbols. J. Math. Phys. **12**(12), 2438–2453 (1971)
38. Braun, P.A.: Discrete semiclassical methods in the theory of Rydberg atoms in external fields. Rev. Mod. Phys. **65**, 115–161 (1993)
39. Anderson, R.: Discrete orthogonal transformations corresponding to the discrete polynomials of the askey scheme. In: Murgante, B., Misra, S., Rocha, A.M.A.C., Torre, C., Rocha, J.G., Falcão, M.I., Taniar, D., Apduhan, B.O., Gervasi, O. (eds.) ICCSA 2014. LNCS, vol. 8579, pp. 490–507. Springer, Cham (2014). doi:10.1007/978-3-319-09144-0_34
40. Murakami, J.: Volume formulas for a spherical tetrahedron. Proc. Am. Math. Soc. **140**, 3289–3295 (2012)
41. Bitencourt, A.C.P., Ragni, M., Littlejohn, R.G., Anderson, R., Aquilanti, V.: The screen representation of vector coupling coefficients or wigner $3j$ symbols: exact computation and illustration of the asymptotic behavior. In: Murgante, B., Misra, S., Rocha, A.M.A.C., Torre, C., Rocha, J.G., Falcão, M.I., Taniar, D., Apduhan, B.O., Gervasi, O. (eds.) ICCSA 2014. LNCS, vol. 8579, pp. 468–481. Springer, Cham (2014). doi:10.1007/978-3-319-09144-0_32
42. Kay, D.C.: College Geometry a Unified Development. CRC Press Taylor and Francis Group, Boca Raton (2011)
43. Anderson, R.W., Aquilanti, V.: The discrete representation correspondence between quantum and classical spatial distributions of angular momentum vectors. J. Chem. Phys. **124**, 214104 (2006). (9 pages)
44. Biedenharn, L.C., Lohe, M.A.: Quantum Group Symmetry and q-Tensor Algebras. World Scientific, Singapore (1995)
45. Bitencourt, A.C.P., Marzuoli, A., Ragni, M., Anderson, R.W., Aquilanti, V.: Exact and asymptotic computations of elementary spin networks: classification of the quantum–classical boundaries. In: Murgante, B., Gervasi, O., Misra, S., Nedjah, N., Rocha, A.M.A.C., Taniar, D., Apduhan, B.O. (eds.) ICCSA 2012. LNCS, vol. 7333, pp. 723–737. Springer, Heidelberg (2012). doi:10.1007/978-3-642-31125-3_54

Screens for Displaying Chirality Changing Mechanisms of a Series of Peroxides and Persulfides from Conformational Structures Computed by Quantum Chemistry

Vincenzo Aquilanti[1,2,3], Concetta Caglioti[1], Andrea Lombardi[1], Glauciete S. Maciel[1,4], and Federico Palazzetti[1(✉)]

[1] Dipartimento di Chimica, Biologia e Biotecnologie,
Università di Perugia, Perugia, Italy
federico.palazzetti@unipg.it
[2] Istituto di Struttura della Materia,
Consiglio Nazionale delle Ricerche, Rome, Italy
[3] Instituto de Física, Universidade Federal da Bahia, Salvador, Brazil
[4] Secretaria de Estado da Educação do Distrito Federal, Brasilia, Brazil

Abstract. A great variety of data on molecular structure and changes, accumulated both experimentally and theoretically, need be compacted and classified to extract the information arguably relevant to understand the basic mechanisms of chemical transformations. Here a screen for displaying four-center processes is developed and as an illustration applied to conformations involving torsions around O – O and S – S bonds, extending the structural properties previously calculated in this laboratory. The construction of the screen follows from connections recently established between the classical kinematic mechanism – the four-bar linkage – and the basic ingredient of quantum angular momentum theory – the 6j symbol.

Keywords: Four-center processes · Four-bar linkage · Quantum angular momentum theory

1 Introduction

Peroxidic and persulfidic bonds characterize molecules and intermediates: their role is often crucial in processes of interest in ample areas of chemistry, such as biochemistry, combustion reactions and the chemistry of atmospheres. In the last decade, peroxides [1, 2] and persulfides [3] have been extensively studied in our laboratory, especial motivation being given by the important problem, related to the signature of life in biospheres [4], of the chirality change transitions associated with the torsional motions around the O – O and the S – S bonds. Both H_2O_2 and H_2S_2 are among the simplest examples of chiral molecules and we have studied them systematically, along series of representative substituents, by quantum chemical calculations (see also work on H_2O_2 – rare gas atom [5–7] and H_2S_2 – rare gas atom dimers [8, 9]: the elastic scattering of

© Springer International Publishing AG 2017
O. Gervasi et al. (Eds.): ICCSA 2017, Part V, LNCS 10408, pp. 354–368, 2017.
DOI: 10.1007/978-3-319-62404-4_26

oriented H_2O_2 and H_2S_2 with rare gas atoms has been also investigated by classical trajectory simulations [10]).

The specification of the dynamics of these four-atom molecules (or four-center ones, when atoms are "substituted" by radicals) requires essentially three vectors (nine coordinates), either the mass-weighted Jacobi ones or more simply bond lengths (and their orientation). Excluding the three coordinates accounting for orientation in space, the six remaining ones, in the simplest structural view, are usually three distance coordinates and three angular coordinates [11, 12]. For concreteness, the discussion will regard peroxides, but the extension to persulfides is obvious. The three radial coordinates are the distances between the atom (or group) R_1 and the O_1 atom, between the atoms O_1 and O_2, and between the atom O_2 and the atom (or group) R_2: these distances lie along the three bonds that identify the stereogenic units [13] of peroxides (Fig. 1a). The angular coordinates are defined by the sequence $R_1 - O_1 - O_2$ and $O_1 - O_2 - R_2$, and the dihedral angle $R_1 - O_1 - O_2 - R_2$. Here, we adopt "distance only" coordinate approach, i.e. defining the six distances that bind R_1, O_1, O_2 and R_2. This 6-distance system defines a tetrahedron that, when confined or projected in the plane, results in a "quadrangle", whose joints are precisely the elements of the stereogenic unit. $R_1 - O_1$, $R_1 - O_2$, $R_2 - O_1$, $R_2 - O_2$ define the sides of a "quadrilateral", while the distances $O_1 - O_2$ and $R_1 - R_2$, the diagonals of the quadrilateral, are the variables (Fig. 1b), we denote these distances R_1O_1, R_2O_2, R_1O_1, R_2O_2, R_1O_2 and R_2O_1, respectively. Classification of quadrilaterals are given in the next Section. In this paper, we report diagrams of the permitted geometries of some representative peroxides and persulfides, both organic and inorganic, alternative to the Ramachandran plots for peptides, for which the choice of torsion angles around contiguous bonds may be inappropriate.

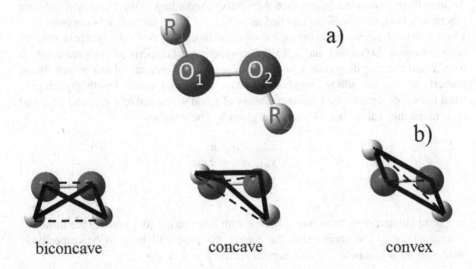

biconcave   concave   convex

Fig. 1. (a) The substituents are labelled by R_1 and R_2, while the oxygen atoms are labelled O_1, the closest to R_1 and O_2 the closest to R_2 (for persulfides O_1 and O_2 are replaced by S_1 and S_2). (b) Classification of the quadrilaterals according to the number of inner and outer diagonals. The sides R_1O_1, O_1R_2, R_2O_2 and O_2R_1 are indicated by continuous lines, while the diagonals O_1O_2 and R_1R_2, x and y respectively, are indicated by dashed lines.

The article is structured as follows: in Sect. 2, we recall some important properties of quadrilaterals, quadrangles and tetrahedra, and their relations with the semiclassical limit of the Wigner – Racah $6j$ symbols; in Sect. 3, we report plots of structures as a function of the "diagonals" of some representative peroxides and persulfides; in Sect. 4, we give the conclusions. An Appendix provides additional information on the proposed representation.

2 Background

2.1 Quadrilaterals, Quadrangles and Tetrahedra

In planar Euclidean geometry, a quadrilateral is defined as a polygon with four sides and four angles, and the sum of the inner angles is 360°. Diagonals are defined as the lines joining the opposite vertices of quadrilaterals. They are classified as convex, if they possess two inner diagonals, concave (one inner and one outer diagonal) and biconcave (two outer diagonals). In projective and affine geometries, considering diagonals as further sides is, gives a complete quadrilateral (four points and six lines), while a complete quandrangle has four lines incident in six points. In projective geometry, duality permits exchange of role of points and lines, so the two complete figures are the same, while they are different from an affine viewpoint. In space, given a tetrahedron's four vertices, one has six edges on three triangular faces; by considering the zero volume situation, or by projection on a plane, one has complete quadrangles; *i.e.* four points and the six joining segments. It can be seen that in the six side of the complete quadrangles there are three ways of choosing couples of diagonals from and defining three four-sided figures (see Appendix). According to the Canonical ordering reported in [14], the edges are labelled as follows: a is the shortest, c is opposite to a, while d is the longest one between the two remaining edges. In the quadrilateral, we define also two diagonals x and y. Thus, the quadrilateral consists of four parameters a, b, c, d and the two diagonals x and y are abscissa and ordinate of our screen, when properly scaled. Regarding the variation range of the diagonals' length, by keeping fixed the edges' length, the minimum values of x and y, respectively x_{min} and y_{min}, and their maximum values, x_{max} e y_{max}, are given by the relations

$$\begin{aligned}
x_{min} &= b - a \\
x_{max} &= b + a \\
y_{min} &= d - a \\
y_{max} &= d + a
\end{aligned} \tag{1}$$

so that to confine the screen into a square with sides in the (0–1) range, the distances corresponding to the shorter and the longer diagonal will have to be respectively shortened by $b - a$ or $d - a$ and normalized by $b + a$ or $d + a$.

2.2   The Screen Representation

The 6-distance system we have discussed shows analogies with the $6j$ symbols of Wigner, or similarly the Racah coefficients. The $6j$ symbols were introduced as matrix elements between different schemes of angular momentum coupling (for the applications of $6j$ symbols, see for example [14, 15]). In their earliest works, Wigner and Racah gave geometrical interpretation of these elements, associating to the six entries of the $6j$ symbols, the lengths of the edges of a generally irregular tetrahedron. In 1968, Ponzano and Regge [16] investigated the functional dependence of the $6\text{-}j$ symbol on their entries, arguing that geometrical properties of tetrahedron, such as volume and dihedral angles, played a role in the amplitude and phase of a semiclassical approximated wave-function. Neville [17] and Schulten and Gordon [18] gave rigorous derivations, also introducing efficient computational procedures [19]. (See also [20–23]).

Littlejohn *et al.* introduce a $4j$ model [22, 23] for the $6j$ symbol, where entries are designated j_1, j_2, j_3, j_4, j_{12}, j_{23}, to represent the allowed range of tetrahedral through plots of the discrete variables, j_{12} and j_{23} (see also [24–30]. The volume V of the tetrahedron can be calculated through the Cailey-Menger determinant. Analogously, we focus here on also-called $4d$ model to represent the 6-distance and geometrical functions of the associated tetrahedron, plotted in a 2-dimensional x-y plane (x and y are continuous variables): the square "screen" of allowed ranges x_{min}, x_{max}, and y_{min}, y_{max} given in Eq. (1) [31–36]. The *caustic* line is the curve corresponding to $V = 0$ (a flattened tetrahedron), while the inside region enclosed by the caustic line is that of a finite volume tetrahedral. The caustic line touches the sides of the screen, *gates*, in four points called North, South, East and West (N, S, E, W). N is the value of x for which y is the maximum; S is the value of x for which y is the minimum; E is the value of y for which x is the maximum; W is the value of y for which x is the minimum. Their locations can be obtained by Stewart theorem and mark points where the ovaloid shape of the caustics, calculate *e.g.* as in [14], touches the frame of the screen.

Ridges are curves that mark configurations of the associated tetrahedron when two specific pairs of triangular faces are orthogonal [14]. In our specific case, ridges connect the geometries of persulfides or peroxides, generally the *cis*, equilibrium and *trans*. In Ref. [37], a series of graphs is reported according to the symmetries of the caustics. In Sect. 3, we classify the plots of the considered peroxides and persulfides according to the symmetric cases shown in Reference [14].

2.3   The Grashof Condition

The 6-distance system recalls a famous problem of kinematics, known as four-bar linkage, a mechanism basic from the early industry revolution (XIX century) to the era of robotics. The system is composed by a chain of three moving bars (assimilated to the distance between centers in the stereogenic unit of peroxides and persulfides. The bar that joins the extremities of the chain is often fixed; the bars are called *ground link* (the fixed bar), *input link* and *output link* (the bars linked to the ground link) and *floating link* the remaining one. Assuming that the ground link is horizontal, the moving bars can rotate according to four different angular intervals: (i) a full rotation of 360° (the *crank*); (ii) rotation ranging from 0° to 180°, both these values being excluded (the *rocker*); (iii) rotation ranging between 0° (included) and 180° (excluded) (0-*rocker*); (iv) rotation ranging between 0° (excluded) and 180° (included) (π-rocker).

The condition of Grashof states that for a four-bar linkage "If the sum of the length of the shortest and the longest bars is lower than the sum of the intermediate bars, than the shortest bar can make a full rotation with respect the adjacent bars". This condition is summarized by the relation

$$s + l \leq p + q \tag{2}$$

Where s is the shortest bar, l is the longest bar, p and q are those of intermediate length. If the Grashof condition is not complied the quadrilateral is not defined within the range of the screen. For the angular momentum analogous case, the Regge symmetry (see for example [37]) can be applied in order to the equivalent alternative quadrilateral (the Regge conjugated) for the analysis of the caustic characterizing by the screen. In the investigations reported in this paper, it is found that most of the systems considered here respect the Grashof condition and a separated discussion deserves to be dedicated to the cases that do not.

3   Screen Representation of Peroxides and Persulfides

The 4d model discussed in the previous section is applied to a series of peroxides and persulfides, whose structures were investigated previously by quantum chemistry codes [1–3]. The examined peroxides are nineteen: HOOH, FOOF, ClOOCl, CH_3OOCH_3, $C_2H_5OOC_2H_5$, FOOCl, FOONO, HOOF, HOOCl, HOOCN, HOONO, CH_3OOH, C_2H_5OOH, iso-C_3H_7OOH, n-C_3H_7OOH, tert-C_4H_9OOH, sec-C_4H_9OOH, n-C_4H_9 OOH, and iso-C_4H_9OOH. The investigated persulfides are twelve: HSSH, FSSF, ClSSCl, CH_3SSCH_3, $C_2H_5SSC_2H_5$, HSSF, HSSCl, FSSCl, CH_3SSH, C_2H_5SSH, CH_3SSCH_3, $C_2H_5SSC_2H_5$. In Figs. 2, 3 and 4, we display the screens for separated classes of peroxides and persulfides and we compare them by also tracing the corresponding caustics according to those reported as an example of various cases in Ref [37]. For each screen the allowed range of x and y is given in normalized distances, while the for the caustics, since they vary slightly for the displayed system, bands of them indicate the semiquantitative behavior. The distances O – O (and S – S), R_1R_2, O_1R_2 (and S_1R_2) and O_2R_1 (and S_2R_1) are given in Tables 1, 2 and 3 to complete the structural information given in Ref [1–3]. For each system the Grashof condition behaviour is also reported; the gates in Figs. 1, 2 and 3 are tested only for those systems that comply the Grashof condition.

In Fig. 3, we report the case of symmetric peroxides and persulhpides, *i.e.* those molecules characterized by identical substituents. For this class of floppy molecules N and W gates coincide in $x = 0$, $y = 1$; as well as S and E gates that coincide in $x = 1$, $y = 0$. This case is ascribable to that reported in Fig. 5(a) of Ref. [37]. In Fig. 2, we report inorganic peroxides and persulphides with non-identical substituents. In this case, the caustic lines are similar to those reported in Fig. 5(a), of Ref. [37]: the N and W gates are very close to the point $x = 0$ and $y = 1$, while the gates S and E are more

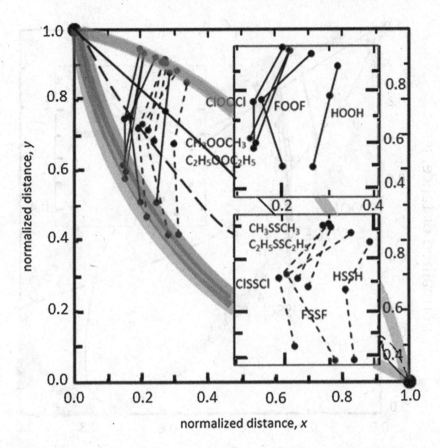

Fig. 2. We report the normalized diagonals x and y of symmetric (identical substituents) peroxides HOOH, FOOF, ClOOCl, CH_3OOCH_3, $C_2H_5OOC_2H_5$, and persulfides, HSSH, FSSF, ClSSCl, CH_3SSCH_3, $C_2H_5SSC_2H_5$. For each molecule, we report up to three geometries (see also Table 1), *cis*, equilibrium and *trans*, connected by a continuous line (peroxides) or a dashed line (persulfides); the geometries are placed in the order *cis*, equilibrium and *trans*, according to the increasing of the y length. CH_3OOCH_3 and $C_2H_5OOC_2H_5$ only present the *cis* and the equilibrium geometry, CH_3SSCH_3 presents the equilibrium and *trans* geometries, while $C_2H_5SSC_2H_5$ only the equilibrium geometry. The gates (indicated by a black dot) N and W coincide in $x = 0$ and $y = 1$; S and E coincide in $x = 1$ and $y = 0$. Insets highlight the features of the considered molecules.

separated and intersect the x-axis at *ca.* $0.8 - 0.9$ and the y-axis at *ca.* $0.1 - 0.2$. It is noteworthy that FOONO and ClOOF, present the most separated S and E gates. In Fig. 4, we conclude the discussion with the organic peroxides and persulphides that present non-identical substituents. This case is similar to that reported in Fig. 2, although the separation of S and E gates is even more pronounced, their range is in fact included between $x = 0.6$ and $x = 0.9$ and $y = 0.1$ and 0.4. The most separated S and E gates are those corresponding to molecules with voluminous substituents.

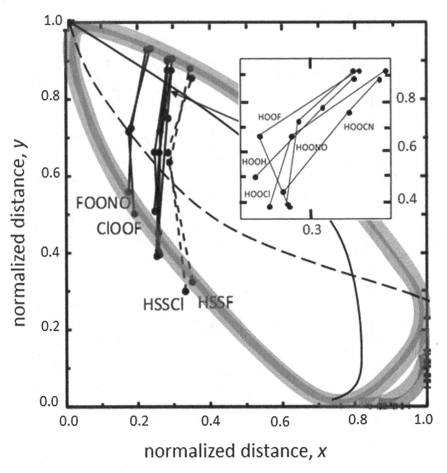

Fig. 3. We report the normalized diagonals x and y of asymmetric (different substituents) inorganic peroxides FOOCl, FOONO, HOOF, HOOCl, HOOCN, HOONO, and persulfides HSSF, HSSCl, FSSCl. For each molecule, we report three geometries (see also Table 2), *cis*, equilibrium and *trans*, connected by continuous line (peroxides) or a dashed line (persulfides); the geometries are placed in the order *cis*, equilibrium and *trans*, according to the increasing of the y length. Insets highlight the features of peroxides.

4   Conclusions

In this paper, we applied the properties of tetrahedral and quadrilaterals to define the structure of peroxides and persulfides investigated previously by our group. The diagonals x or y, respectively the scaled and shifted O – O (or S – S) distance or the distance between the two substituents of the molecule, are the two variables of the tetrahedral structure projected on the square screen, together with a sketch of the qualitative caustic line that define strictly the allowed ranges.

This representation can be applied to other kinds of chiral stereogenic units, such as those characterized by the asymmetric carbon connected to four different ligands or to describe the peptidic bond, by an only-distances reference system. A first information from these displays are the screening of systematics of available data: those used here come from homogeneous source, still the accuracy can be ameliorated and the screen can be checked for regularity. In general, data may have different origins and the screen may serve to evaluate the internal consistency and suggest improvements of the experimental or computational input for the displayed properties, and indeed the proposed frame will be the basis for showing properties other than structural ones. The papers offering data for this exploratory survey, for example contain barrier height information and energetics of the structure, estimated chirality change transition rates, and so on: the display again can screen regularities, trends, accuracies.

The augmentation of data and case studies is to be anticipated as future work, as well as the implementation of similar tools to stimulating problems, notably those associated with conformation changes in aminoacid sequences and in the peptidic bonds, as well as in general with the rearrangements of the four terminal groups bound to tetravalent carbon.

Acknowledgements. The authors acknowledge the Italian Ministry for Education, University and Research, MIUR for financial support through SIR 2014 Scientific Independence for Young Researchers (RBSI14U3VF).

Appendix. Quadrilaterals, Quadrangles, Tetrahedra: The 6-Distance Representation

We extend here geometrical considerations alluded to in Sect. 2.1. The six distances that define the stereogenic unit of peroxides and persulfides, *i.e.* the sequence of bonds $R_1 - O_1 - O_2 - R_2$ (for the sake of simplicity we refer only to the peroxide case, but it can be simply applied to persulfides), individuate a tetrahedron, whose edges are the distances O_1R_1, O_1R_2, O_2R_2, O_2R_1, O_1O_2, and R_1R_2. The planar projection of the tetrahedron permits to define a quadrilateral, whose diagonals can be chosen among the pairs of opposite distances R_1O_1 and R_2O_2; R_1O_2 and R_2O_1; O_1O_2 and R_1R_2. The tetrahedron and quadrilateral coincide when the stereogenic unit has a planar geometry, *e.g.* for the *cis* and *trans* configurations. The length of the diagonals vary within a range, keeping the four sides of the quadrilateral fixed. In these terms, we represent the variation of the diagonals in a two-dimensional diagram, the *screen*. We are here inspired by the Wigner-Racah-Regge approach to theory of the most basic ingredients of quantum angular momentum and of spin networks, the *6j* symbol. In a similar fashion, let's arrange the six distances as follows,

$$\left\{ \begin{matrix} O_1O_2 & O_2R_2 & O_1R_2 \\ R_1R_2 & O_1R_1 & O_2R_1 \end{matrix} \right\}, \tag{A.1}$$

the $6d$ symbols. In the application to peroxides, in the text the diagonals correspond to the first column, since in the specific case of peroxides and persulfides, the variation of R1 – R2 distance is the most suitable to monitor the chirality change transition. Two other choices of diagonals is possible, since by taking into account that the symbol is invariant under permutation of the three columns:

$$\left\{ \begin{matrix} O_1O_2 & O_2R_2 & O_1R_2 \\ R_1R_2 & O_1R_1 & O_2R_1 \end{matrix} \right\} = \left\{ \begin{matrix} O_2R_2 & O_1O_2 & O_1R_2 \\ O_1R_1 & R_1R_2 & O_2R_1 \end{matrix} \right\} = \cdots \qquad (A.2)$$

(there are $3! = 6$ ways identical symbols).

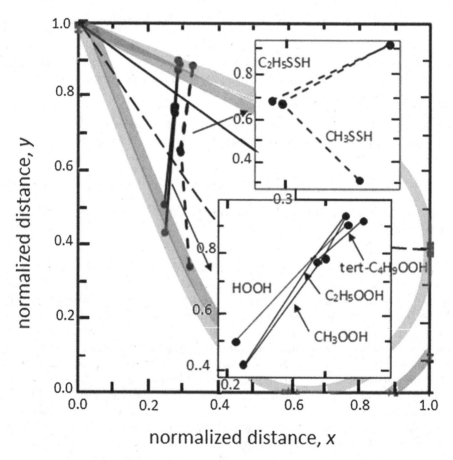

Fig. 4. We report the normalized diagonals x and y of asymmetric (different substituents) inorganic peroxides CH_3OOH, C_2H_5OOH, iso-C_3H_7OOH, n-C_3H_7OOH, tert-C_4H_9OOH, sec-C_4H_9OOH, n-C_4H_9OOH, and iso-C_4H_9OOH, and persulfides CH_3SSH and C_2H_5SSH. For each molecule, we report up to three geometries, *cis*, equilibrium and *trans* (see also Table 3), connected by continuous line (peroxides) or a dashed line (persulfides); the geometries are placed in the order *cis*, equilibrium and *trans*, according to the increasing of the y length. Insets highlight the features of peroxides.

Table 1. The distances O_1O_2 and S_1S_2, R_1O_2, O_1R_2, and R_1R_2 in Å plotted in Fig. 1. Distances R_1O_1 and R_2O_2, R_1S_1 and R_2S_2, are given in Ref. [1–3]. (*) Does not comply with the Grashof condition.

		O_1O_2	R_1O_2	O_1R_2	R_1R_2
HOOH	eq	1.446	1.885	1.885	2.401
	cis	1.457	1.948	1.948	1.964
	trans	1.457	1.872	1.872	2.597
FOOF	eq	1.222	2.245	2.245	3.015
	cis	1.509	2.345	2.345	2.374
	trans	1.474	2.190	2.190	3.362
ClOOCl	eq	1.362	2.580	2.580	3.435
	cis	1.573	2.717	2.717	2.969
	trans	1.506	2.515	2.515	3.997
CH$_3$OOCH$_3$	eq	1.460	2.280	2.280	3.499
	cis	1.481	2.452	2.452	2.721
C$_2$H$_5$OOC$_2$H$_5$	eq	1.462	2.290	2.290	3.517
	cis	1.480	2.486	2.486	2.810
		S_1S_2	R_1S_2	S_1R_2	R_1R_2
HSSH	eq	2.059	2.600	2.600	3.068
	cis	2.111	2.613	2.613	2.394
	trans	2.102	2.537	2.537	3.468
FSSF	eq	1.894	2.864	2.864	3.624
	cis	2.155	2.861	2.861	2.588
	trans	2.108	2.734	2.734	3.975
ClSSCl	eq	1.955	3.221	3.221	4.118
	cis	2.155	3.288	3.288	3.158
	trans	2.095	3.023	3.023	4.699
CH$_3$SSCH$_3$	eq	2.046	2.994	2.994	3.660
	cis	2.090	2.904	2.904	4.363
C$_2$H$_5$SSC$_2$H$_5$	eq	2.052	3.072	3.072	3.863
	cis	2.111	2.977	2.977	4.465

The first row represents a triad (a triangular face of the tetrahedron into a vertex), while the second row exhibits the convergence of three edges of the tetrahedron. One can have four triads, $\{O_1R_1, O_1R_2, O_1O_2\}$, $\{O_2R_2, O_2R_1, O_1O_2\}$, $\{O_1R_1, O_2R_1, R_1R_1\}$, $\{O_2R_2, O_1R_2, R_1 R_2\}$. The invariance with respect to permutations of the four triads and the related triangles generate the invariance of the $6j$ under the interchange of upper and lower arguments of any two columns, for example

$$\begin{Bmatrix} O_1O_2 & O_2R_2 & O_1R_2 \\ R_1R_2 & O_1R_1 & O_2R_1 \end{Bmatrix} = \begin{Bmatrix} R_1R_2 & O_1R_1 & O_1R_2 \\ O_1O_2 & O_2R_2 & O_2R_1 \end{Bmatrix} = \cdots \quad (A.3)$$

(four ways). A total of 24 symmetries can be enumerated in this way. Each symbol has in addition the six Regge symmetries replicas, for a total of 144 symmetries.

Table 2. The distances O_1O_2 and S_1S_2, R_1O_2, O_1R_2, and R_1R_2 in Å plotted in Fig. 2. Distances R_1O_1 and R_2O_2, R_1S_1 and R_2S_2, are given in Ref. [1, 3]. (*) Denotes configurations that do not comply with the Grashof condition.

		O_1O_2	R_1O_2	O_1R_2	R_1R_2
HOOF	eq	1.359	1.851	2.261	2.577
	cis	1.428	1.895	2.269	2.066
	trans	1.441	1.855	2.203	2.989
HOOCl	eq	1.410	1.875	2.580	2.893
	cis	1.454	1.936	2.595	2.385
	trans	1.467	1.859	2.517	3.305
HOONO	eq	1.417	1.876	2.327	2.747
	cis	1.426	1.897	2.315	2.129
	trans	1.436	1.852	2.285	3.061
HOOCN	eq (*)	1.475	1.896	2.248	2.734
	cis (*)	1.481	1.953	2.287	2.194
	trans (*)	1.483	1.880	2.240	2.968
ClOOF	eq (*)	1.281	2.585	2.251	3.231
	cis (*)	1.516	2.666	2.378	2.671
	trans	1.481	2.474	2.221	3.679
FOONO	eq	1.308	2.254	2.397	3.070
	cis	1.365	2.320	2.745	2.917
	trans (*)	1.429	2.203	2.334	3.541
		S_1S_2	R_1S_2	S_1R_2	R_1R_2
HSSF	eq	1.991	2.573	2.863	3.293
	cis	2.102	2.500	2.851	2.381
	trans	2.089	2.489	2.769	3.718
HSSCl	eq	2.013	2.574	3.224	3.589
	cis	2.110	2.556	3.203	2.669
	trans	2.096	2.512	3.077	4.095
ClSSF	eq	2.069	3.239	2.981	3.916
	cis	2.151	3.203	2.924	2.860
	trans	2.024	3.089	2.584	4.346

The important relationship of these quantum mechanically discovered (1959) symmetries were later found. Surprisingly they apply to properties of Euclidean (Ponzano and Regge, 1968) and non-Euclidean tetrahedra and to the operating rules of the most venerable of the kinematic mechanisms. For further discussions, see companion papers in this volume [38, 39].

This "distance only" formulation may be suitable to describe peroxides and similar classes of molecules for which often mapping based on pairs of dihedral angle (*e.g.* Ramachandran plot) is not applicable. In turn, as a viewpoint in the same spirit of the displays on screen examined in the mean text, it can be arguably extendible to other systems, such as molecules characterized by the asymmetric carbon covalently bound to four different ligands, or to describe folding involving the peptidic bonds.

Table 3. The distances O_1O_2 and S_1S_2, R_1O_2, O_1R_2, and R_1R_2 in Å plotted in Fig. 3. Distances R_1O_1 and R_2O_2, R_1S_1 and R_2S_2, are given in Ref. [2, 3]. (*) Does not comply with the Grashof condition.

		O_1O_2	R_1O_2	O_1R_2	R_1R_2
CH_3OOH	eq	1.449	2.299	1.886	2.828
	cis	1.454	2.343	1.940	2.214
	trans	1.459	2.274	1.876	3.045
C_2H_5OOH	eq	1.451	2.320	1.883	2.836
	cis	1.453	2.354	1.938	2.222
	trans	1.459	2.286	1.875	3.055
iso-C_3H_7OOH	eq	1.449	2.338	1.882	2.838
n-C_3H_7OOH	eq	1.457	2.340	1.887	2.869
tert-C_4H_9OOH	eq (*)	1.449	2.371	1.885	2.875
	trans (*)	1.463	2.349	1.867	3.099
sec-C_4H_9OOH	eq (*)	1.449	2.360	1.882	2.853
n-C_4H_9OOH	eq	1.460	2.287	1.876	3.056
iso-C_4H_9OOH	eq	1.459	2.286	1.875	3.005
		S_1S_2	R_1S_2	S_1R_2	R_1R_2
CH_3SSH	eq	2.047	2.600	2.979	3.379
	cis	2.100	2.588	2.976	2.550
	trans	2.091	2.554	2.865	3.894
C_2H_5SSH	eq	2.056	2.620	3.013	3.433
	trans	2.101	2.565	2.900	3.928

References

1. Maciel, G.S., Bitencourt, A.C.P., Ragni, M., Aquilanti, V.: Alkyl peroxides: effect of substituent groups on the torsional mode around the O – O bond. Int. J. Quant. Chem. **107**, 2697–2707 (2007)
2. Maciel, G.S., Bitencourt, A.C.P., Ragni, M., Aquilanti, V.: Quantum study of peroxidic bonds and torsional levels for ROOR' molecules (R, R' = H, F, Cl, NO, CN). J. Phys. Chem. A **111**, 12604–12610 (2007)
3. Aquilanti, V., Ragni, M., Bitencourt, A.C.P., Maciel, G.S., Prudente, F.V.: Intramolecular dynamics of RS – SR' systems (R, R' = H, F, Cl, CH₃, C₂H₅): torsional potentials, energy levels, partition functions. J. Phys. Chem. A **113**, 3804–3813 (2009)
4. Aquilanti, V., Grossi, G., Lombardi, A., Maciel, G.S., Palazzetti, F.: The origin of chiral discrimination: supersonic molecular beam experiments and molecular dynamics simulations of collisional mechanisms. Phys. Scr. **78**, 058119 (2008)
5. Barreto, P.R.P., Vilela, A.F.A., Lombardi, A., Maciel, G.S., Palazzetti, F., Aquilanti, V.: The hydrogen peroxide-rare gas systems: Quantum chemical calculations and hyperspherical harmonic representation of the potential energy surface for atom-floppy molecule interactions. J. Phys. Chem. A **111**, 12754–17762 (2008)
6. Barreto, P.R.P., Palazzetti, F., Grossi, G., Lombardi, A., Maciel, G.S., Vilela, A.F.A.: Range and strength of intermolecular forces for van der waals complexes of the type H2Xn-Rg, with X = O, S and n = 1, 2. Int. J. Quant. Chem. **110**, 777–786 (2010)

7. Barreto, P.R.P., Albernaz, A.F., Palazzetti, F., Lombardi, A., Grossi, G., Aquilanti, V.: Hyperspherical representation of potential energy surfaces: intermolecular interactions in tetra-atomic and penta-atomic systems. Phys. Scr. **84**, 028111 (2011)

8. Maciel, G.S., Barreto, P.R.P., Palazzetti, F., Lombardi, A., Aquilanti, V.: A quantum chemical study of H_2S_2: Intramolecular torsional mode and intermolecular interactions with rare gases. J. Chem. Phys. **129**, 164302 (2008)

9. Barreto, P.R.P., Albernaz, A.F., Palazzetti, F.: Potential energy surfaces for van der Waals complexes of rare gases with H_2S and H_2S_2: Extension to xenon interactions and hyperspherical harmonics representation. Int. J. Quant. Chem. **112**, 834–847 (2012)

10. Lombardi, A., Palazzetti, F., Maclel, G.S., Aquilanti, V., Sevryuk, M.B.: Simulation of oriented collision dynamics of simple chiral molecules. Int. J. Quant. Chem. **111**, 1651–1658 (2011)

11. Maciel, G.S., Bitencourt, A.C.P., Ragni, M., Aquilanti, V.: Studies of the dynamics around the O – O bond: orthogonal mods of hydrogen peroxide. Chem. Phys. Lett. **432**, 383–390 (2006)

12. Palazzetti, F., Munusamy, E., Lombardi, A., Grossi, G., Aquilanti, V.: Spherical and hyperspherical representation of potential energy surfaces for intermolecular interactions. Int. J. Quant. Chem. **111**, 318–332 (2011)

13. Moss, G. P.: Pure Appl. Chem. **68**, 2193–2222 (1996)

14. Bitencourt, A.C.P., Ragni, M., Littlejohn, R.G., Anderson, R., Aquilanti, V.: The Screen Representation of Vector Coupling Coefficients or Wigner $3j$ Symbols: Exact Computation and Illustration of the Asymptotic Behavior. In: Murgante, B., Misra, S., Rocha, A.M.A.C., Torre, C., Rocha, J.G., Falcão, Maria Irene, Taniar, D., Apduhan, B.O., Gervasi, Osvaldo (eds.) ICCSA 2014. LNCS, vol. 8579, pp. 468–481. Springer, Cham (2014). doi:10.1007/978-3-319-09144-0_32

15. Aquilanti, V., Bitencourt, A., da S. Ferreira, C., Marzuoli, A., Ragni, M.: Quantum and semiclassical spin networks: from atomic and molecular physics to quantum computing and gravity. PhysicaScripta **78**, 058103 (2008)

16. Aquilanti, V., Bitencourt, A., da S. Ferreira, C., Marzuoli, A., Ragni, M.: Combinatorics of angular momentum recoupling theory: spin networks, their asymptotics and applications. Theor. Chem. Acc. **123**, 237 (2009)

17. Ponzano, G., Regge, T.: Semiclassical limit of Racah coefficients. In: Bloch, F. et al (eds.) Spectroscopic and Group Theoretical Methods in Physics, pp. 1–58. North Holland, Amsterdam (1968)

18. Neville, D.: A technique for solving recurrence relations approximately and its application to the $3j$ and $6j$ symbols. J. Math. Phys. **12**, 2438 (1971)

19. Schulten, K., Gordon, R.: Semiclassical approximations to $3j$- and $6j$-coefficients for quantum-mechanical coupling of angular momenta. J. Math. Phys. **16**, 1971–1988 (1975)

20. Schulten, K., Gordon, R.: Exact recursive evaluation of $3j$- and $6j$-coecients for quantum mechanical coupling of angular momenta. J. Math. Phys. **16**, 1961–1970 (1975)

21. Ragni, M., Bitencourt, A.C., Aquilanti, V., Anderson, R.W., Littlejohn, R.G.: Exact computation and asymptotic approximations of $6j$ symbols: Illustration of their semiclassical limits. Int. J. Quantum Chem. **110**(3), 731–742 (2010)

22. Aquilanti, V., Cavalli, S., Coletti, C.: Angular and hyperangular momentum recoupling, harmonic superposition and Racah polynomials. A recursive algorithm. Chem. Phys. Lett. **344**, 587–600 (2001)

23. Littlejohn, R.G., Yu, L.: Uniform semiclassical approximation for the Wigner $6j$-symbol in terms of rotation matrices. J. Phys. Chem. A **113**, 14904–14922 (2009)

24. Aquilanti, V., Haggard, H.M., Hedeman, A., Jeevangee, N., Littlejohn, R., Yu, L.: Semiclassical mechanics of the Wigner 6j-symbol. J. Phys. A **45**, 065209 (2012). arXiv:1009.2811v2

25. Aquilanti, V., Capecchi, G.: Harmonic analysis and discrete polynomials. From semiclassical angular momentum theory to the hyperquantization algorithm. Theor. Chem. Accounts **104**, 183–188 (2000)

26. De Fazio, D., Cavalli, S., Aquilanti, V.: Orthogonal polynomials of a discrete variable as expansion basis sets in quantum mechanics. the hyperquantization algorithm. Int. J. Quantum Chem. **93**, 91–111 (2003)

27. Aquilanti, V., Cavalli, S., De Fazio, D.: Angular and hyperangular momentum coupling coecients as Hahn polynomials. J. Phys. Chem. **99**(42), 15694–15698 (1995)

28. Koekoek, R., Lesky, P., Swarttouw, R.: Hypergeometric Orthogonal Polynomials and Their q-Analogues. Springer, Heidelberg (2010)

29. Bitencourt, A.C.P., Marzuoli, A., Ragni, M., Anderson, R.W., Aquilanti, V.: Exact and asymptotic computations of elementary spin networks: classification of the quantum–classical boundaries. In: Murgante, B., Gervasi, O., Misra, S., Nedjah, N., Rocha, A.M.A.C., Taniar, D., Apduhan, B.O. (eds.) ICCSA 2012. LNCS, vol. 7333, pp. 723–737. Springer, Heidelberg (2012). doi:10.1007/978-3-642-31125-3_54

30. Varshalovich, D., Moskalev, A., Khersonskii, V.: Quantum Theory of Angular Momentum. World Scientific, Singapore (1988)

31. Aquilanti, V., Haggard, H.M., Littlejohn, R.G., Yu, L.: Semiclassical analysis of Wigner 3 j - symbol. J. Phys. A **40**(21), 5637–5674 (2007)

32. Anderson, R.W., Aquilanti, V.: The discrete representation correspondence between quantum and classical spatial distributions of angular momentum vectors. J. Chem. Phys. **124**, 214104 (2006). (9 pages)

33. Anderson, R.W., Aquilanti, V., da Silva Ferreira, C.: Exact computation and large angular momentum asymptotics of 3nj symbols: semiclassical disentangling of spin networks. J. Chem. Phys. **129**, 161101–161105 (2008)

34. Anderson, R.W., Aquilanti, V., Bitencourt, A.C.P., Marinelli, D., Ragni, M.: The Screen Representation of Spin Networks: 2D Recurrence, Eigenvalue Equation for 6j Symbols, Geometric Interpretation and Hamiltonian Dynamics. In: Murgante, B., Misra, S., Carlini, M., Torre, C.M., Nguyen, H.-Q., Taniar, D., Apduhan, B.O., Gervasi, O. (eds.) ICCSA 2013. LNCS, vol. 7972, pp. 46–59. Springer, Heidelberg (2013). doi:10.1007/978-3-642-39643-4_4

35. Aquilanti, V., Marinelli, D., Marzuoli, A.: Hamiltonian dynamics of a quantum of space: hidden symmetries and spectrum of the volume operator, and discrete orthogonal polynomials. J. Phys. A: Math. Theor. **46**, 175303 (2013). arXiv:1301.1949v2

36. Arruda, M.S., Santos, R.F., Marinelli, D., Aquilanti, V.: Spin-coupling diagrams and incidence geometry: a note on combinatorial and quantum-computational aspects. In: Gervasi, O., Murgante, B., Misra, S., Rocha, A.M.A.C., Torre, C., Taniar, D., Apduhan, B. O., Stankova, E., Wang, S. (eds.) ICCSA 2016. LNCS, vol. 9786, pp. 431–442. Springer, Cham (2016). doi:10.1007/978-3-319-42085-1_33

37. Ragni, M., Littlejohn, R.G., Bitencourt, A.C.P., Aquilanti, V., Anderson, R.W.: The screen representation of spin networks: images of 6j symbols and semiclassical features. In: Murgante, B., Misra, S., Carlini, M., Torre, C.M., Nguyen, H.-Q., Taniar, D., Apduhan, B. O., Gervasi, O. (eds.) ICCSA 2013. LNCS, vol. 7972, pp. 60–72. Springer, Heidelberg (2013). doi:10.1007/978-3-642-39643-4_5

38. Lombardi, A., Palazzetti, F., Aquilanti, V., Pirani, F., Casavecchia, P.: The astrochemical observatory: experimental and computational focus on the chiral molecule propylene oxide as a case study. In: ICCSA 2017, Part V, LNCS, vol. 10408, pp. 1-14. doi:10.1007/978-3-319-62404-4_20

39 Aquilanti, V., Anderson, R. W.: Spherical and hyperbolic spin network: the q-extensions of wigner racah 6j coefficients and general orthogonal discrete basis sets in applied quantum mechanics. In: ICCSA 2017, Part V, LNCS, vol. 10408, pp. 1-16. doi:10.1007/978-3-319-62404-4_25

Workshop on Scientific Computing Infrastructure (SCI 2017)

Finding Motifs in Medical Data

Vasily Osipov[1], Alexander Vodyaho[2], Elena Stankova[3],
Nataly Zukova[2,4(✉)], and Bassel Zeno[4]

[1] St. Petersburg Institute for Informatics and Automation
of the Russian Academy of Sciences (SPIIRAS), St. Petersburg, Russia
osipov_vasiliy@mail.ru
[2] St. Petersburg State Electrotechnical University, St. Petersburg, Russia
{aivodyaho,nazhukova}@mail.ru
[3] St. Petersburg State University, St. Petersburg, Russia
e.stankova@spbu.ru
[4] St. Petersburg National Research University of Information Technologies,
Mechanics and Optics, St. Petersburg, Russia
basilzeno@gmail.com

Abstract. Nowadays big volumes of medical data are accumulated. So the problem of analysis of these data and mining linked logical structures, defining internal data semantics is an actual one. Solution of this problem allows solve the problem of optimizing intelligent context search. In the article an approach for solving this problem for analyzing processes running in human organism is discussed. Suggested approach is based on building of linked logical structures and assumes finding of motifs in variations of parameters of systems and subsystems. An algorithm of finding of motifs is suggested. The result of algorithm operation is logical structure that reflects internal dependencies which exist in human organism. Nowadays suggested approach is used in Almazov Cardiological Center for medical data processing.

Keywords: Medical data · Linked logical structure · Motifs · Context search

1 Introduction

Large amounts of accumulated medical data require solving the problem of determining the related logical structures that reflect the inner content of the data. Usage of such structures in the process of applied problems solving allows solve the problem of optimization intelligent contextual search. A typical example is the evaluation of the dynamic change of the patient's state in the context of basic and associated diagnoses. As a rule, such a problem can be solved by analyzing the dynamics and coherence of behavior change of the measured parameters.

For evaluation of the dependency of parameter values, both statistical analysis algorithms and the intelligent algorithms are used. Most of them are based on the construction and evaluation of multiparametric functions. The simplest example is an evaluation of regression models of parameters.

Processes that run in a human body are very complex. In order to describe them, a combination of many methods is to be used. As a result, complexity of the problem

© Springer International Publishing AG 2017
O. Gervasi et al. (Eds.): ICCSA 2017, Part V, LNCS 10408, pp. 371–386, 2017.
DOI: 10.1007/978-3-319-62404-4_27

increases significantly. Under real conditions, when high dynamics of data changes is observed, the task becomes too complex. In this case it is possible to limit the scope of the analyzed data. But in this case a limited number of dependencies will be taken into account.

The proposed approach to the construction of related logical structures based on the identification of motifs (tendencies) in changing parameters of the body's systems and subsystems. Novelty motive search algorithm in the data is as follows: algorithm is based on the joint processing of groups of parameters that can detect complex motifs; motives are determined by the dynamics of the parameters behavior. The basis of the algorithm is a procedure of ranking series of parameter values. The resulting logical structure can be represented as a graph which reflects the identified motifs.

2 Description of the Problem and Its Solutions

Let us consider a simple example of the suggested algorithm usage. Suppose that there are values of five parameters which characterize the status of a subsystem. The parameter values are given in the Table 1.

Table 1. Sample of parameters

№	The value of creatinine	The value of RBC	The value of PH	The value of bacteria	The value of urobilinogen
1	5	0.7	1.5	2	0.5
2	2	0.5	2	2	0.5
3	6	0.9	1.4	2	1
4	3	0.6	1.8	2	1

In order to find the motifs in data, firstly, values of parameters are to be sorted. An example is shown in the Table 2.

Table 2. Results of sorting the sample by parameter A

№	The value of creatinine	The value of RBC	The value of PH	The value of bacteria	The value of urobilinogen
1	2	0.5	2	2	0.5
2	3	0.6	1.8	2	1
3	5	0.7	1.5	2	0.5
4	6	0.9	1.4	2	1

The Table 2 shows that the values of the parameter "creatinine" are ordered. In the case when there are multiple values of the same parameter "creatinine", they follow one after another. With such a ranking it is clear that the parameter "RBC" increases continuously, while the parameter "PH" - decreases. The parameter "bacteria" is practically unchanged and parameter "urobilinogen" weakly correlated with "creatinine".

Hence, one can conclude that the parameters "creatinine", "RBC", "PH" are associated. The parameter "bacteria" does not affect "creatinine". Values of parameter "urobilinogen" is random. Thus one can see that the relative difference in values of parameter "RBC" ((0.9 − 0.5)/0.9) is greater than the relative difference in values of parameter "PH" ((2 − 1.4)/2). This may indicate that association of "RBC" with "creatinine" stronger than "PH" with "creatinine" (see Fig. 1).

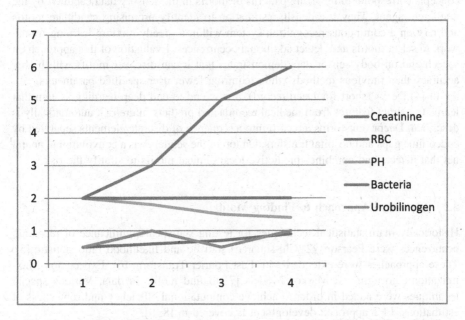

Fig. 1. Association of "RBC" with "creatinine" is stronger than "PH" with "creatinine"

3 Related Work

In this section, we briefly review the common machine learning and statistics approaches to find motifs.

3.1 Machine Learning Methods for Finding Motifs

In [1] a non-supervised method based on motifs to identify events in visual lifelogs is described. It is suggested to use the Minimum Description Length (MDL) method to extract multi-dimensional motifs in time series data, whereas the first step is applying the Symbolic Aggregate approximation (SAX) algorithm for transforming time series into behavior symbol sequences, and the second step is estimating extracted motif candidate based on MDL principle.

In [2] the first application of the use of machine learning to find motifs in wind generation data is described. Authors suggest a techniques of time series analysis to determine if there are motifs. They suggest to convert original time series data into the reduced dimensional piecewise aggregate approximation (PAA) and SAX representations, and for finding the motifs, they considered two approaches: Euclidean distance between subsequences, and Expectation-Maximization to cluster days in the time series.

In [3] authors describe developed intelligent systems that understand their environment by autonomously learning new concepts from their perceptions, where the concepts correspond to recurring patterns or motifs in the sensory data captured by the intelligent agent. They use density estimation to identify promising candidate motifs and rely on a continuous recognition system within a greedy mixture learning framework to select motifs and detect additional occurrences. Evaluation of this approach on speech and on-body sensor data demonstrates that it can discover motifs with higher accuracy than previous methods while requiring fewer user-specified parameters.

In [4] Deepr (short for Deep record), a new end-to-end deep learning system that learns to extract features from medical records and predicts future risk automatically is described. Deepr transforms a record into a sequence of discrete elements separated by coded time gaps and hospital transfers. On top of the sequence is a convolutional neural net that detects and combines predictive local clinical motifs to stratify the risk.

3.2   Statistical Approach to Finding Motifs

Historically main statistical techniques for testing statistical significance of repeating occurrences were Pearson $\chi 2$ (Chi-squared) statistic and likelihood ratio statistic [5]. These approaches were extended with Fast Fourier Transform [6]. Expectation Maximization algorithm and Markov Models [7] to find motifs in data. Various special techniques were added in order to achieve computational efficiency and robustness of estimations. FFT approach development is covered in [8, 9].

Markov models were combined with Monte Carlo method. The result is known as Gibbs sampling method [10]. Another basic statistical technique used for time series exploration is Principle Component Analysis (PCA). Based on matrix singular value decomposition this method initiated SSA. M-SSA [11] and Caterpillar-SSA [12].

These methods designed for time series data, so they are suitable for our medical data, where there is no time series data, so we propose new algorithm based on first and second derivatives for representation data as words of symbols.

3.3   Motifs in Groups of Parameters

Finding motifs algorithms are studied over a decade. The basic idea is identifying similar sequences in a single stream of measurements of some quantity. Important results in the field of the motifs analysis have achieved a research group of the

Universities. They have developed algorithms that allow identify in them rather complex dependencies. The most effectively they are applicable to the ECHO signal processing. In the Fig. 2 a simple example is presented [13].

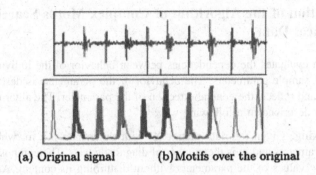

(a) Original signal   (b) Motifs over the original

Fig. 2. Simple example

In order to solve the problem of constructing logical structures for medical data, it is necessary to identify the motifs that are determined by behavior of two or more parameters. In order to solve the problem of identification the motives for the group of parameters it is necessary to use expansion of the original definition of the motif concept.

Under the parameter refers to direct or indirect measurements of a physical quantity, the measurement results are associated with a certain event e, in which the values are ordered in the following way:

$$p = \{p_1 \ldots p_m\} = \{(v_1.e_1) \ldots (v_m.e_m)\}. \tag{1}$$

where m is the number of diagnostic tests (events), V_I value of parameter p at event e_i. Under the fragment sequence refers to a subset s:

$$s = \{p_k \ldots p_l\}.k > 1; l < M.Dim(s) < Dim(p). \tag{2}$$

With regard to the motifs of parameter $t(p) = \{t_1 \ldots t_r\}$. refers to fragments of values that have an identifiable behavior. Motifs are ordered by frequency of occurrence in the original sequence. The most frequent fragment is called the main motif. Complex motif represents dependence between the motifs of several parameters. For two parameters, complex motif is described as:

$$(p_i.p_j) = g(f\Big(t(p_i).f\Big(t\Big(p_j\Big)\Big)\Big), \tag{3}$$

where $g(f(g))$ function of dependency estimation of the structural behavior of parameter descriptions feature f. The algorithm for searching complex motifs adapted to work with medical data is described below.

4 Description of the Algorithm of Complex Motifs Search in Medical Data

The algorithm evaluates the dependencies between behavior of the individual parameter and other sample parameters. The behavior of the parameters is described in the feature space and reflects the general direction of the parameter. The algorithm in more details can be described in a following way:

Step 1. Ranking. Given the data matrix X. with dimension n × m, where n is the number of parameters and m is the number of diagnostic tests. The composition data X allows ranking values of the parameters without disturbing its content. As a result of applying of the procedure of ranking. The skeleton of the structural behavior of a parameter is determined.

For ranking, it is preferable to choose the quantitative attributes. When ranked by the value of a quality attribute may require the definition of additional criteria.

Step 2. Formation piecewise representation of parameter values. Parameters are represented in the form $p = \{x_0.x_{b1}.x_{b2}.....x_{bk}.x_m\}$, $p \in P$, where x_{bi} is the border value that separates the fragment i from fragment $i + 1$. The set X is determined by the points of changing the behavior of the ranked parameter.

Step 3: Building a feature space. Building a feature space F for the behavioral change fragments. Feature space parameter P has the form:

$$F_P = \begin{bmatrix} f_{00} f_{01} \cdots f_{0j} \\ \cdots \\ f_{k0} f_{k1} \cdots f_{kj} \end{bmatrix} \tag{4}$$

where the ith line corresponds to the ith fragment. Generated feature space is determined for each parameter according to the physical meaning of the parameter. The dimension of the feature space $k \times m$. where k is the number of fragments and m is the number of diagnostic studies.

Step 4. Find Motifs. The approach described in [14] uses Euclidean distance as a similarity measure between subsequences, but we suggest to use the same approach with more accurate distance measure. (Cosine distance) This approach requires the setting of a range R, which is a positive real number, such that if the Cosine distance $D(S_i.S_j)$ between two subsequences S_i and S_j is less than R, then S_j is a matching subsequence to S_i. For SAX words, we select R to be 10% of the maximum possible distance between subsequences. Once the most frequent motif, which is the subsequence with the largest number of matches within R, is obtained, the motif and all its matches is removed from consideration and the process is restarted in order to find the next most frequently occurring motif, etc. We expanded this algorithm to find motifs through parameters. We called it shared or complex motifs. Simply we construct new words by appending the words that are facing to each other.

5 Detailed Pseudocode Algorithm

INPUT
   Two dimensional data array $X: n \times m$. where n: number of parameters, m: number of diagnostic studies. The parameters group $P = \{p_1. \dots . p_n\}$. The studied parameter p^*.
OUTPUT
   Behavioral motifs
Method
   Step 1
   Sorting X matrix in an ascending order based on p^* parameter.
   Step 2
Comment   *Finding Fragments*
   for each parameter $p \in P$ do
          $X_b. \ fragmentState_b \leftarrow piecewiseFormation \ (p_i)$
       Where:
   $X_b = \{x_{b1}.x_{b2}. \dots .x_{bk}\}. \ fragmentState_b = \{s_{b1}.s_{b2}. \dots .s_{bk}\}$
   $s = \{'a'.'b'.'c'.'d'.'e'.'f'.'g'.'h'.'i'\}$
   $p = \{x_0.x_{b1}.x_{b2}. \dots .x_{bk}.x_m\}. \ X_b \subseteq p$
   x_{bi} - border value that separate the fragment i from fragment $i + 1$.
   $X_b = \{x_b\}$. determine the points of behavior change of ranked parameter.
   Step 3
Comment *Building Feature Space*
   for each parameter $p \in P$ do
      $F_p = buildFeatureSpace(fragmentState_b.X_b). \ F_p \leftarrow append(F_p)$
          Where
   F_p: two dimensional array $k \times m$. k: number of fragments. the ith line corresponds to the ith fragment. F_P: feature space for all parameters.
   Step 4
Comment *Find behavioral motifs*
   $findBehavioralMotifs \ (L. F_p)$. L: set of parameter indexes. $L \subseteq \{1.2. \dots .n\}$

Piecewise Aggregation Approximation Algorithm

INPUT

Parameter $p \in P$, $p = \{x_0.x_1.....x_m\}$. m: number of diagnostic studies.

OUTPUT

List of points X_b that determine behavior change of the parameter p. $X_b = \{x_{b1}.x_{b2}.....x_{bk}\}$ List of fragments state of parameter p. $fragmentState_b = \{s_{b1}.s_{b2}.....s_{bk-1}\}$. s_{bi} is a letter.

Method

Initialize X_b.

Initialize fragmentState. fragmentStateCurrent . fragmentStatePrev

Find f' the first derivative of p. $f' = \{x_0.x_1.....x_m\}'$

Find f'' the second derivative of p. $f'' = \{x_0.x_1.....x_m\}''$

Comment *First State*

fragmentStatePrev $\leftarrow$ getFragmentState $(f'(x_0).(f''(x_0))$

$X_b \leftarrow$ Append (x_0)

Comment *Rest of States*

    for $k \leftarrow 1$. $k \leq m$. **do**

    fragmentStateCurrent $\leftarrow$ getFragmentState $(f'(x_k).(f''(x_k))$

    if fragmentStateCurrent **NOT EQUAL** fragmentStatePrev **Then**

    $X_b \leftarrow$ Append (x_k)

    fragmentState $\leftarrow$ Append (fragmentStatePrev)

    fragmentStatePrev $\leftarrow$ fragmentStateCurrent

Get Fragment State Algorithm

INPUT

$v1. v2$ First and second derivative of value of parameter p respectively.

OUTPUT

fragmentState.

Method

if $v1 < 0$ *AND* $v2 < 0$ **THEN** fragmentState $\leftarrow a$

if $v1 = 0$ *AND* $v2 < 0$ **THEN** fragmentState $\leftarrow b$

if $v1 > 0$ *AND* $v2 < 0$ **THEN** fragmentState $\leftarrow c$

if $v1 < 0$ *AND* $v2 = 0$ **THEN** fragmentState $\leftarrow d$

if $v1 = 0$ *AND* $v2 = 0$ **THEN** fragmentState $\leftarrow e$

if $v1 > 0$ *AND* $v2 = 0$ **THEN** fragmentState $\leftarrow f$

if $v1 < 0$ *AND* $v2 > 0$ **THEN** fragmentState $\leftarrow g$

if $v1 = 0$ *AND* $v2 > 0$ **THEN** fragmentState $\leftarrow h$

if $v1 > 0$ *AND* $v2 > 0$ **THEN** fragmentState $\leftarrow i$

Build Feature Space Algorithm

INPUT

List of points X_b that determine behavior change of the parameter p. $X_b = \{x_{b1}.x_{b2}.....x_{bk}\}$ List of fragments state of parameter $p.\,fragmentState_b = \{s_{b1}.s_{b2}.....s_{bk}\}$. s_{bi} is a letter.

OUTPUT

F_p Feature space of parameter p. F_p: two dimensional array $k \times m$, k: number of fragments. the ith line corresponds to the ith fragment.

Method

Comments *Currently Each Line Corresponds To State (Letter). Later We Can Use Slope of fragments.*

$$F_p = \{f_{01}.f_{02}.....f_{0k}\} \leftarrow \{s_{b1}.s_{b2}.....s_{bk}\}$$

Find Behavioral Motifs

INPUT

Set of parameter indexes L. $L \subseteq \{1.2.....n\}$

Feature space $F_P = \{F_{p1}.F_{p2}.....F_{pn}\}$. F_{pi}: feature space matrix for ith parameter p.

OUTPUT

Behavioral Motifs

Method

$motifs \leftarrow findMotif(F_{PL}.w.frequency)$.

where

$F_{PL} = \{F_{pi}\} \mid i \in L.w: length\ of\ word(default\ 6).threshold\ (defualt\ 0.1).$ in case of

searching complex motifs : $w = n * length\ of\ word(default\ 6)$.

$n: number\ of\ parameters\ in\ which\ we\ are\ searching\ complex\ motifs.$

6 Recommended Procedure for Finding the Complex Motifs in Medical Data

The procedure is recommended for analysis the measurement results on the circulatory and urinary systems of the body. The peculiarities of the system parameters which define a proposed mathematical tool include slow-changing behavior, relatively narrow range of parameter values.

To highlight the change points of quantitative parameters values, approximation of value series by polynomials was performed. Type of polynomial dependence was determined in the result of approximation error analysis. If the error exceeded the specified limit value, then the degree of the polynomial is increased. The inflection points of the polynomial determine the points of changes of values.

Feature space was restricted to behavioral types of fragments characteristic for a slowly varying parameter value series. Considered the possible combination of values of the first and second derivatives, see Table 3.

Table 3. Behavioral types of fragments of parameter values series

	f' < 0	f' = 0	f' > 0
f" < 0	Decreases concavely	Local maximum	Increases concavely
f" = 0	Decreases linearly	Constant	Increases linearly
f" > 0	Decreases convexly	Local minimum	Increases convexly

In accordance with the fragment types, alphabet for their description is defined can be described as $A = \{a.b.c.d.e.f.g.h.i\}$.

Unlike the existing algorithm, the SAX, the alphabet is determined for behavioral types. The level of values, that defines the alphabet in SAX, is accounted for as associated parameters. The resulting alphabet has the form: A = {ai/bj}/f (xk). where B = {b} is the set of parameter level values. The number of levels is determined by the type of distribution of values f (Xk).

An alternative description of the parameters of the considered body's systems is the vector of coefficients of polynomials obtained by approximating the values of the series.

Considering the possibility of allowing multi analysis, it is possible at first rough to determine the relationships of the parameters at the level of general tendencies in behavior, then perform the refinement by analyzing the weaker links in each level.

7   Experiments

7.1   Dataset

A sample of 13219 urine tests of 4033 patients of Almazov cardiological center was studied. Quantitative parameters taken into account for dependencies finding are the following: Specific Gravity (SG), pH, Glucose and Protein.

There are 9700 tests in dataset after removing missing values and outliers. Tests are considered as outliers with SG > 10 (with reference values between 1 and 1.03) and Glucose > 1000 (only one test is discarded).

7.2   Data Representation

Specific Gravity is chosen as ranking parameter for Step 1 of the proposed algorithm. According to the algorithm the mapping to SAX space is based on parameter derivatives only, not absolute values, so the scales of different parameters are resized for the readability of the plot.

Fragment states are calculated for studied parameters based on finite differences of the first and the second order as estimates for first and second derivatives respectfully. Finite differences are not divided because of the following reasons: only sign of the derivative is important for fragment state calculation, division is interpretable for the ranked data, second order finite difference can be considered as divided by h2 = 1. Estimated derivatives naturally give sequences of behavior states partially shown in Fig. 3.

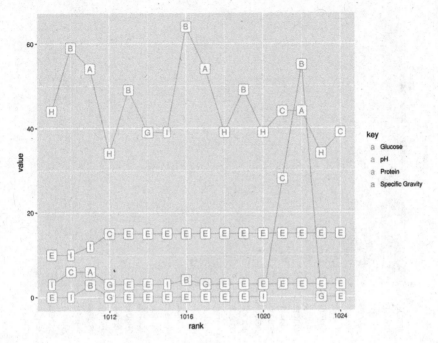

Fig. 3. Behavior states

7.3   Find Motifs in Each Parameter

Fragments of states. Fragments of states are obtained by shrinking down repeated states. Than letter sequences are divided into words based on word length parameter. Words are counted and measured as described above in Step 4 using cosine distance. Words obtained from all parameters are merged into one sequence to find common motifs between parameters thus dependences between parameters can be found.

Using six letter words, filtering frequency of 5 and 10% threshold there are 74 motifs found in the dataset. Thirty most frequent motifs are shown in Fig. 4 counted by parameter. Example of the third most frequent motif is shown over initial data sequence in Fig. 5.

In group of parameters. Keeping repeated states 12 and 18 letter words are generated by gluing 6 letter words of two and three parameters respectively. Glucose and pH are kept as two parameters. In 12 letter case filtering frequency of 5 and 10% threshold is used. 11 motifs found are shown in Fig. 6. An example of 12 letter motif is shown in Fig. 7. In 18 letter case filtering frequency of 2 and 10% threshold is used. 20 motifs found are shown in Fig. 8. An example of 12 letter motif is shown in Fig. 9.

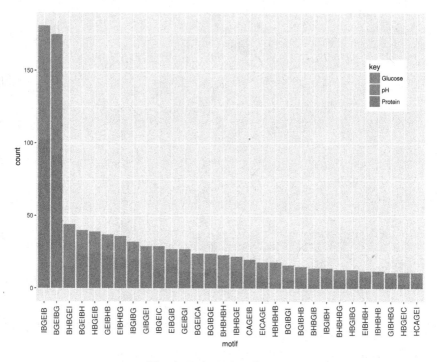

Fig. 4. Frequencies of motifs

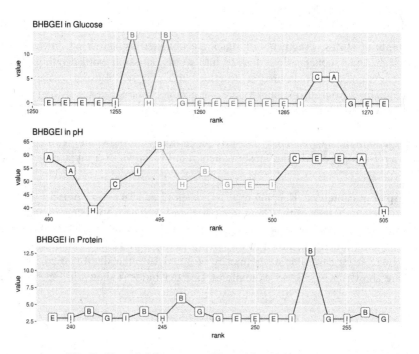

Fig. 5. The third frequent motif over the original sequence

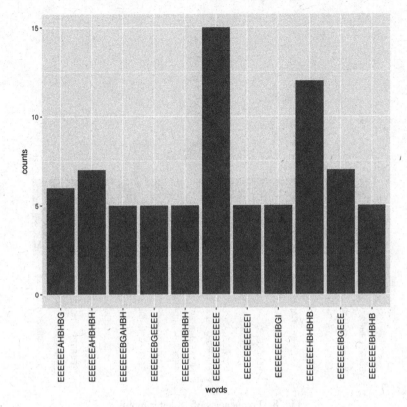

Fig. 6. Frequencies of 12 letter motifs

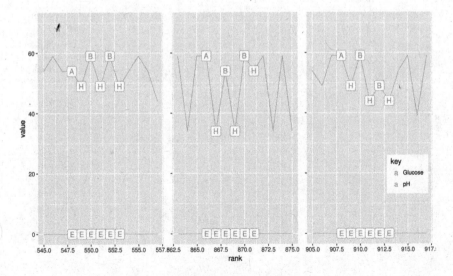

Fig. 7. "EEEEEE AHBHBH" over original series

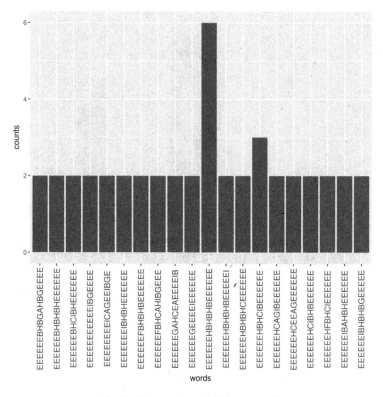

Fig. 8. Frequencies of 18 letter motifs

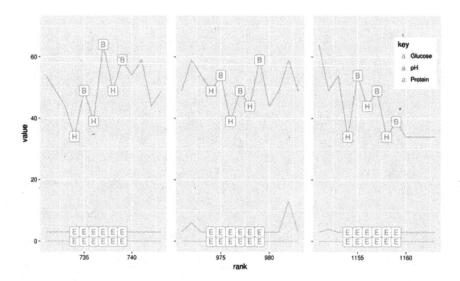

Fig. 9. "EEEEEE HBHBHB EEEEEE" over original series

8   Conclusion

In this paper, we analyzed medical data records in order to identify frequent patterns or motifs. This data is non time series, so in order to approximate the issue to time series data, we have used ranking method of one parameter and then expand it to other parameters.

We proposed new data representation algorithms (Piecewise Aggregate Approximation and SAX) based on first and second derivative. Here there is 9 alphabets, and the algorithm can track the changes in the curve precisely and significantly. We have splitted the PAA alphabets into SAX words, where length of word equals to 6. For finding motifs there are several ways in which we can find the motifs, or the frequently occurring subsequences in the data. We considered one approach by computing the cosine distance between words for each parameter, and when the distance between two words equals or less than 10% of the maximum possible distance between all words, these two words matched as motifs. We also included a constraint that for a word to be considered a motif, there should be at least 5 matches to that word. We also expanded this approach to find complex motifs through parameters. In this case the length of word equals 6 * number of parameters in which we are searching complex motifs. This simple algorithm shows us good results in case of finding simple or complex motifs.

In the future we plan to extend this work by ranking by more than one parameter and by exploring other methods for find motifs like clustering methods.

Acknowledgement. This work was partially financially supported by Government of Russian Federation, Grant 074-U01.

References

1. Li, N., Crane, M., Gurrin, C., Ruskin, H.J.: Finding motifs in larger personal lifelogs. In: 7th Augmented Human International Conference 2016, 25–26 February 2016, Geneva, Switzerland (2016)
2. Kamath, C., Fan, Y.J.: Finding motifs in wind generation time series data. In: 2012 11th International Conference on Machine Learning and Applications (ICMLA), vol. 2, pp. 481–486, December 2012
3. Minnen, D., Isbell, C.L., Essa, I., Starner, T.: Discovering Multivariate Motifs using Subsequence Density Estimation and Greedy Mixture Learning (2007). http://www.cc.gatech.edu/~isbell/classes/reading/papers/minnen-aaai2007.pdf
4. Phuoc, N., Truyen, T., Wickramasinghe, N., Venkatesh, S.: Deepr: A Convolutional Net for Medical Records (2016). https://arxiv.org/pdf/1607.07519v1.pdf
5. Cressie, N., Read, T.: Pearson's $\chi2$ and the log-likelihood ratio statistic g2: a comparative review. Int. Stat. Rev **57**(1), 19–43 (1989)
6. Baglivo, J., Olivier, D., Pagano, M.: Methods for exact goodness-of-fit tests. J. Am. Stat. Assoc. **87**(418), 464–469 (1992)
7. Bailey, T.L., Elkan, C.: Fitting a mixture model by expectation maximization to discover motifs in biopolymers. In: Proceedings of International Conference Intelligent Systems for Molecular Biology, vol. 2, pp. 28–36 (1994)

8. Keich, U.: Efficiently computing the p-value of the entropy score. J. Comput. Biol. **12**(4), 416–430 (2005)
9. Nagarajan, N.: Statistical techniques for biological motif discovery. Cornell University (2007)
10. Lawrence, C.E., Altschul, S.F., Boguski, M.S., Liu, J.S., Neuwald, A.F., Wootton. J.C.: Detecting subtle sequence signals: a gibbs sampling strategy for multiple alignment. Sci. New Ser. **262**(5131), pp. 208–214 (1993)
11. Broomhead, D.S., King, G.P.: Extracting qualitative dynamics from experimental data. Phys. D. **20**, 217–236 (1986)
12. Golyandina, N., Nekrutkin, V., Zhigljavsky, A.: Analysis of Time Series Structure: SSA and Related Techniques. Chapman and Hall/CRC (2001)
13. Gomes, E.F., Jorge, A.M., Azevedo, P.J.: Classifying heart sounds using sax motifs. random forests and text mining techniques. In: Proceedings of the 18th International Database Engineering & Applications (2001). http://repositorium.sdum.uminho.pt/bitstream/1822/33769/1/2001.pdf
14. Lin, J., Keogh, E., Lonardi, S., Patel, P.: Finding motifs in time series. In: Proceedings of the 2nd SigKDD Workshop on Temporal Data Mining 2002, pp. 53–68 (2002)

Distributed Data Processing on Microcomputers with Ascheduler and Apache Spark

Vladimir Korkhov[1]([✉]), Ivan Gankevich[1], Oleg Iakushkin[1],
Dmitry Gushchanskiy[1], Dmitry Khmel[1], Andrey Ivashchenko[1],
Alexander Pyayt[2], Sergey Zobnin[2], and Alexander Loginov[2]

[1] Saint Petersburg State University, 7/9 Universitetskaya nab.,
St. Petersburg 199034, Russia
v.korkhov@spbu.ru
[2] Siemens LLC, St. Petersburg, Russia

Abstract. Modern architectures of data acquisition and processing often consider low-cost and low-power devices that can be bound together to form a distributed infrastructure. In this paper we overview possibilities to organize a distributed computing testbed based on microcomputers similar to Raspberry Pi and Intel Edison. The goal of the research is to investigate and develop a scheduler for orchestrating distributed data processing and general purpose computations on such unreliable and resource-constrained hardware. Also we consider integration of the scheduler with well-known distributed data processing framework Apache Spark. We outline the project carried out in collaboration with Siemens LLC to compare different configurations of the hardware and software deployment and evaluate performance and applicability of the tools to the testbed.

Keywords: Microcomputers · Scheduling · Apache Spark · Raspberry Pi · Fault tolerance · High availability

1 Introduction

The problem of building distributed computing infrastructures for data collection and processing has been around for many years. One of the well-known technologies for building large-scale computing infrastructures is grid computing. It provides means to connect heterogeneous, dynamic resources into a single metacomputer. However, being focused on high-performance computing systems, grid technologies do not suit well other classes of basic hardware. One of such examples are low-performance, low-cost unreliable microcomputers similar to Raspberry Pi or Intel Edison, sometimes also called System-on-Chip (SoC) devices. To be able to execute distributed applications over a set of such devices extensive fault-tolerance support is needed along with low resource usage profile of the middleware.

In this paper we discuss an approach to orchestrate distributed computing and data processing on microcomputers with help of custom scheduler focused on

© Springer International Publishing AG 2017
O. Gervasi et al. (Eds.): ICCSA 2017, Part V, LNCS 10408, pp. 387–398, 2017.
DOI: 10.1007/978-3-319-62404-4_28

fault tolerance and dynamic rescheduling of computational kernels that represent the application. This scheduler, which is named Ascheduler, provides its own low-level API to create and manage computational kernels. Currently the Ascheduler is a closed-source project built on the ideas and approaches presented in [5–7].

In addition, the scheduler has been integrated into Apache Spark [1] data processing framework instead of the default scheduler used by Spark. This opened possibilities to use a wide range of existing Spark-based programs on the underlying microcomputer infrastructure controlled by the Ascheduler. The project aimed to solve the following main tasks:

- Develop automatic failover and high-availability mechanisms for computer system.
- Develop automatic elasticity mechanism for computer system.
- Enable adjusting application algorithm precision taking into account current number of healthy cluster nodes.
- Adjust load distribution taking into account actual and heterogeneous monitoring data from cluster nodes.
- Adjust micro-kernel execution order to minimise peak memory footprint of cluster nodes.

The task of data processing on resource-constrained and unreliable hardware emerges within the framework of sensor real-time near-field data processing. The implementation of the system, allowing to carry out the processing in the field, will allow one to quickly respond to sudden changes in sensor readings and reduce the time of decision-making. The implementation of general-purpose computations in such a system allows one to use the same hardware and software system for a diverse high-tech equipment.

The paper is organised as follows: Sect. 2 presents an overview of related work on using microcomputers for building distributed data processing systems with Hadoop and Spark; Sect. 3 presents the architecture of our solution; Sect. 4 explains how Ascheduler is integrated with Apache Spark; Sect. 5 presents experimental evaluation; Sect. 6 discusses the results and Sect. 7 concludes the paper.

2   Related Work

There are a number of publications which report on successful deployments of Hadoop and Spark on various resource-constrained platforms:

- Hadoop on Raspberry Pi [3];
- Hadoop on Raspberry Pi [4];
- Spark on Raspberry Pi [8];
- Spark on Cubieboard [9].

These papers outline common problems and solutions when running Hadoop/Spark on resource-constrained systems. These are:

- large memory footprint problems,
- too slow/resource-hungry Java VM,
- overheating problems.

These works do not report any particular problem with Java on resource-constrained platforms and all of them use standard JRE. Neither they report any overheating or large memory footprint problems (although, Raspberry Pi, for example, does not have a cooler). However, all the papers deal with system boards in laboratory or similar environments, where these problems are non-existent. Additionally, the authors run only simple tests to demonstrate that the system is working, and no production-grade application is studied nor large-scale performance tests performed. Using Java and standard JRE for scheduler development seems rational for simple workloads, however, large workloads may require additional boards to cope with memory footprint or boost processing power.

3 Architecture

3.1 Architecture Overview

The core concepts and architecture used for the implementation of Ascheduler are described in detail in [5–7]. Here we summarise the most important aspects relevant to the current testbed implementation.

To solve the problem of fault-tolerance of slave cluster nodes we use a simple restart: try to re-execute the task from the failed node on a healthy one. To solve the problem of high-availability of the master node we use replication: copy minimum necessary amount of state to restart the task on the backup node. When the master node fails, its role is delegated to the backup node, and task execution continues. When the backup node fails, the master node restarts the current stage of the task. The most important feature of the approach used in Ascheduler is to ensure master node fault-tolerance without any external controller (e.g. Zookeeper in Hadoop/Spark ecosystem).

Cluster nodes are combined into a tree hierarchy that is used to uniquely determine the master, backup and slave nodes roles without a conflict [7].

Each node may perform any combination of roles at the same time, but can not be both master and backup. The initial construction of the hierarchy is carried out automatically, and the node's position in the hierarchy is solely determined by the position of its IP-addresses in a subnet.

When any cluster node fails or a new one joins the cluster, the hierarchy is rebuilt automatically.

The elasticity of the computer system is provided by dividing each task on a large number of subtasks (called micro-kernels), between which hierarchical links are established. All micro-kernels are processed asynchronously, which makes it possible to distribute them on the cluster nodes and processor cores, balancing the load. Typically, the amount of micro-kernels in a problem exceeds the total number of nodes/cores in the cluster, so the order of their processing can be optimised so as to minimise memory footprint, or to minimise power consumption by grouping all of the micro-kernels on a small number of nodes, or to ensure the maximum speed of task execution, distributing micro-kernels across all nodes in the cluster. If the cluster capacity is not enough to handle the current data flow/volume of data, micro-kernel pools on the cluster nodes overflow, and excessive kernels may be transferred to a more powerful remote server/cluster. The amount of data, that must be replicated to the backup node to ensure the high-availability, equals to the amount of RAM occupied by a kernel, and can be controlled by the programmer.

Figure 1 shows the schematic view of the system.

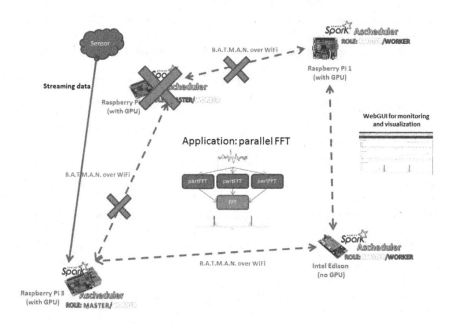

Fig. 1. Schematic view.

3.2 Hardware

Microcomputers used in the testbed:

- Raspberry Pi 3 Model B (2 pieces)
- Raspberry Pi 1
- Intel Edison
- Orange Pi (2 pieces)

3.3 Scheduler Core and API

The Ascheduler has layered architecture, as discussed in [5–7]:

- Physical layer. Consists of nodes and direct/routed network links.

- Daemon layer. Consists of daemon processes residing on cluster nodes and hierarchical (master/slave) links between them.
- Kernel layer. Consists of kernels and hierarchical (parent/child) links between them.

Master and slave roles are dynamically assigned to daemon processes, any physical cluster node may become master or slave. Dynamic reassignment uses leader election algorithm that does not require periodic broadcasting of messages, and the role is derived from node's IP address. Detailed explanation of the algorithm is provided in [5].

Software implementation of Ascheduler consists of three main components (Fig. 2):

- Task scheduler core (which is used to compose distributed applications).
- Scheduler daemon based on the core.
- A driver which integrates scheduler into Apache Spark.

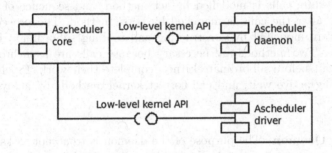

Fig. 2. Scheduler components.

Task Scheduler Core. The core provides classes and methods to simplify development of distributed applications and middleware. The main focus of this package is to make distributed application resilient to failures, i.e. make it fault tolerant and highly available, and do it transparently to a programmer.

All classes are divided into two layers: the lower layer consists of classes for single node applications, and the upper layer consists of classes for applications that run on an arbitrary number of nodes. There are two kinds of tightly coupled entities in the package — *kernels* and *pipelines* — which are used together to compose a programme. Kernels implement control flow logic in their act and react methods and store the state of the current control flow branch. Both logic and state are implemented by a programmer. In act method some function is either sequentially computed or decomposed into subtasks (represented by another set of kernels) which are subsequently sent to a pipeline. In react method subordinate kernels that returned from the pipeline are processed by their parent. Calls to act and react methods are asynchronous and are made within threads spawned by a pipeline. For each kernel `act` is called only once, and for multiple kernels the calls are done in parallel to each other, whereas `react` method is called once for each subordinate kernel, and all the calls are made in the same thread to prevent race conditions (for different parent kernels different threads may be used).

Pipelines implement asynchronous calls to `act` and `react`, and try to make as many parallel calls as possible considering concurrency of the platform (no. of cores per node and no. of nodes in a cluster). A pipeline consists of a kernel pool, which contains all the subordinate kernels sent by their parents, and a thread pool that processes kernels in accordance with rules outlined in the previous paragraph. A separate pipeline exists for each compute device: There are pipelines for parallel processing, schedule-based processing (periodic and delayed tasks), and a proxy pipeline for processing kernels on other cluster nodes.

In principle, kernels and pipelines machinery reflect the one of procedures and call stacks, with the advantage that kernel methods are called asynchronously and in parallel to each other. The stack, which ordinarily stores local variables, is modelled by fields of a kernel. The sequence of processor instructions before nested procedure calls is modelled by act method, and sequence of processor instructions after the calls is modelled by react method. The procedure calls themselves are modelled by constructing and sending subordinate kernels to the pipeline. Two methods are necessary because calls are asynchronous and one must wait before subordinate kernels complete their work. Pipelines allow circumventing active wait, and call correct kernel methods by analysing their internal state.

Scheduler Daemon. The purpose of the daemon is to accept tasks from the driver and launch applications in child processes to run these tasks. Each task is wrapped in a kernel, which is used to create a new child process. All subsequent tasks are sent to the newly created process via shared memory pages, and results are sent back via the same interface. The same protocol is used to exchange kernels between parent and child processes and between different cluster nodes. This allows scheduler daemon to distribute kernels between cluster nodes without knowing exact Java classes that implement kernel interface.

Scheduler daemon is a thin layer on top of the core classes which adds a set of configuration options, automatically discovers other daemons over local area network and launches child processes for each application to process tasks from the driver.

Apache Spark Integration Driver. The purpose of the driver is to send Apache Spark tasks to scheduler daemon for execution. The driver connects to an instance of the scheduler daemon via its own protocol (the same protocol that is used to send kernels), wraps each task in a kernel and sends them to the daemon. The driver is implemented using the same set of core classes. This allows testing the driver without a scheduler (replace integration tests with unit tests) as well as using the driver without a scheduler, i.e. process all kernels locally, on the same node where Spark client runs.

Fault Tolerance and High Availability. The scheduler has fault tolerance and high availability built into its low-level core API. Every failed kernel is restarted on healthy node or on its parent node, however, failure is detected only for kernels that are sent from one node to another (local kernels are not considered). High availability is provided by replicating master kernel to a subordinate node. When any of the replicas fails, another one is used in place. Detailed explanation of the fail over algorithm is provided in [7].

Security. Scheduler driver is able to communicate with scheduler daemons in local area network. Inter-daemon messaging is not encrypted or signed in any way, assuming that local area network is secure. There is also no protection from Internet "noise". Submission of the task to a remote cluster can be done via SSH (Secure Shell) connection/tunnel which is *de facto* standard way of communication between Linux/UNIX servers. So, scheduler security is based on the assumption that it is deployed in secure local area network. Every job is run from the same user, as there is no portable way to switch process owner in Java.

3.4 Ascheduler Integration with Spark

Starting with the version 2.0, custom schedulers can be integrated in Spark via implementation of three interfaces. For better understanding of Spark classes and their interconnections please refer to Mastering Apache Spark 2.0 [10] and source code of Spark classes available at https://github.com/apache/spark, as sometimes there are useful information in code comments. Class diagram of all implemented Apache Spark interfaces as well as wrapper classes is shown in Fig. 3.

3.5 Communication

The aim of the project was to build a wireless microcomputer cluster. To create a Wi-Fi based ad hoc network mesh we have chosen a protocol with a driver and API: B.A.T.M.A.N. (Better Approach To Mobile Adhoc Networking mesh protocol) [2]. B.A.T.M.A.N. helps organizing and routing wireless ad-hoc networks that are unstructured, dynamically change their topology, and are based on an inherently unreliable medium. Additionally, B.A.T.M.A.N. provides means to collect the knowledge about the network topology, state and quality of the links — this information is used by Ascheduler to make scheduling decisions aware of physical network topology and links.

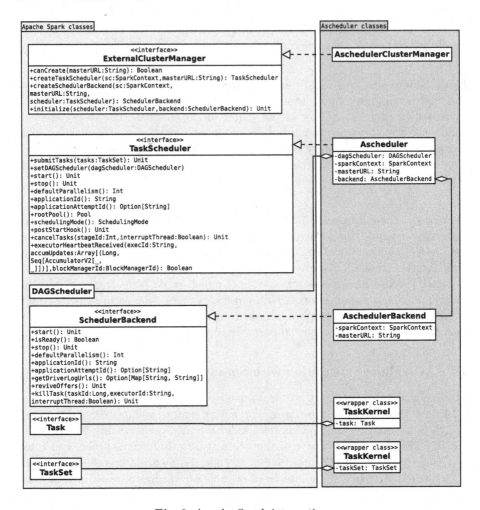

Fig. 3. Apache Spark integration

4   Creating Apache Spark Applications for Running with Ascheduler

Apache Spark connects to Ascheduler via an implementation of interfaces for custom schedulers. Ascheduler works with Spark version 2.0.2 only. Since Ascheduler integration required access to classes and interfaces considered private in Apache Spark, work of Ascheduler with another versions of Spark is not guaranteed.

· Ascheduler integration with Spark has been implemented in a way that allows using Spark functionality disregarding the choice of the scheduler. If Spark is used with several schedulers, the user might want to explicitly choose the scheduling mode. It can be done by creating `SparkContext` from `SparkConf` with method `setMaster(masterURL)` invoked. Here `masterURL` corresponds to particular scheduler with parameters. For Ascheduler string value `ascheduler` could be used for the cluster mode and `ascheduler-local` — for the local mode. Spark driver for Ascheduler has more masterURL options, because of some hard-coded Spark limitations that have to be bypassed:

- `local-ascheduler` for using cluster Ascheduler from Spark shell `
- `local-ascheduler-local` for using local Ascheduler from Spark shell
- `local[0_0]-ascheduler-local` for using Spark Streaming with Ascheduler in local version.

Spark programs running on Ascheduler were tested both on local and cluster versions. Spark with Ascheduler supports a wide range of standard operations and functions, such as:

- running both in Spark shell and as standalone applications;
- operating on Resilient Distributed Datasets (RDDs): mapping, reducing, grouping operations;
- partition-wise transformations on RRDs: controllable re-partitioning, shuffling, persisting RDDs, calling functions for partitions;
- Multi-RDD operations: union, subtracting, zipping one RDD with another;
- Broadcasting shared variables among executors;
- Accumulators and task metrics based on them;
- Spark Streaming with rerunning nodes (master included) in case of failure.

The work of Spark with Ascheduler and any of Spark packages except Spark Streaming is not guaranteed. With those exceptions, any Spark application is expected to work with Ascheduler as a task scheduling base.

5 Evaluation

The application used for evaluation is an example of real-time micro-batch processing using Ascheduler and Apache Spark. The application consists of two entities: a periodic signal generator and its processor. The generator creates batches of values of a superposition of harmonic signals and sends them for processing via a network socket and for output via a websocket. The processor receives the batches from the raw socket, applies adaptive Fast Fourier Transform (FFT) on the signal and sends the result into output via a WebSocket. Both outputs are available on the system monitoring page.

In this experiment we benchmark two implementations of FFT demo application on two platforms using two schedulers (Fig. 4). The first implementation is based on Spark Streaming API, the second is based on Ascheduler API. The first platform (left column) is Intel Edison, the second (right column) is commodity Intel Core i5. The first scheduler is Spark Standalone in local mode, the second scheduler is Ascheduler in local mode. Cluster versions are not benchmarked in this experiment. In each run demo application computes spectrum of 25 KHz signal in real time for 5 min. Time of each spectrum computation is recorded as a point in a graph. Since demo application automatically downsamples input signal when processing is slow, we measure overall throughput by dividing the number of processed points by time taken to process them. The results are presented in Fig. 4 for each run and summarised in Table 1.

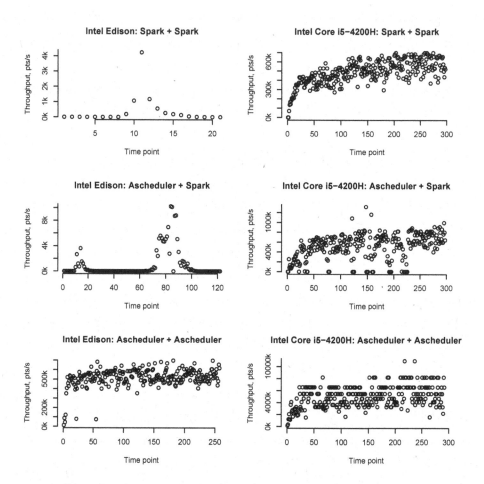

Fig. 4. Comparing performance of Ascheduler and Spark schedulers.

Table 1. Comparing performance of Ascheduler and Spark schedulers.

Platform	Scheduler	API	Average throughput, points/s
Intel Edison	Spark	Spark	375
Intel Edison	Ascheduler	Spark	995
Intel Edison	Ascheduler	Ascheduler	517 676
Intel Core i5-4200H	Spark	Spark	487 594
Intel Core i5-4200H	Ascheduler	Spark	511 618
Intel Core i5-4200H	Ascheduler	Ascheduler	5 046 540

6 Discussion

Graphs show that Spark API is incapable of processing 25 KHz input signal on Intel Edison platform. Ascheduler scheduler outperforms Spark standalone by a factor of 3 on Intel Edison but still more performance is needed to process 25 KHz signal. Direct use of Ashcheduler API on Intel Edison finally solves the problem, allowing to process 500 KHz input signal. On commodity Intel Core i5 platform there is no significant difference between performance of Spark stand-alone scheduler and Ascheduler when using Spark API, however, direct use of Ascheduler API gives tenfold increase in performance: it is capable of processing 5 GHz input signal.

7 Conclusions

The following was achieved as the final outcomes of the project:

- Ascheduler — fault-tolerant scheduler implemented in Java, running stand-alone or with Apache Spark (with Spark Streaming supported)
- Master-node fault tolerance is supported by Ascheduler.
- Dynamic resource discovery, composition and re-configuration of distributed cluster.
- Optimised for running on unreliable and resource-constrained microcomputer hardware.
- Running in heterogeneous and dynamic hardware and networking environment.
- Integrated microcomputer and cluster monitoring API.
- Transparent monitoring and visualization with web-based UI.
- Distributed FFT application (with GPGPU support if available) with streaming input and dynamic graphical output.

Acknowledgments. The research was supported by Siemens LLC.

References

1. Apache spark official website. http://spark.apache.org/
2. B.A.T.M.A.N. official web page. https://www.open-mesh.org/projects/open-mesh/wiki
3. Cox, S.J., Cox, J.T., Boardman, R.P., Johnston, S.J., Scott, M., Obrien, N.S.: Iridis-pi: a low-cost, compact demonstration cluster. Cluster Comput. **17**(2), 349–358 (2014)
4. Fox, K., Mongan, W.M., Popyack, J.: Raspberry hadoopi: a low-cost, hands-on laboratory in big data and analytics. In: SIGCSE, p. 687 (2015)
5. Gankevich, I., Tipikin, Y., Gaiduchok, V.: Subordination: cluster management without distributed consensus. In: 2015 International Conference on High Performance Computing & Simulation (HPCS), pp. 639–642. IEEE (2015)

6. Gankevich, I., Tipikin, Y., Korkhov, V., Gaiduchok, V.: Factory: non-stop batch jobs without checkpointing. In: 2016 International Conference on High Performance Computing & Simulation (HPCS), pp. 979–984. IEEE (2016)

7. Gankevich, I., Tipikin, Y., Korkhov, V., Gaiduchok, V., Degtyarev, A., Bogdanov, A.: Factory: master node high-availability for big data applications and beyond. In: Gervasi, O., et al. (eds.) ICCSA 2016, Part II. LNCS, vol. 9787, pp. 379–389. Springer, Cham (2016). doi:10.1007/978-3-319-42108-7_29

8. Hajji, W., Tso, F.P.: Understanding the performance of low power raspberry pi cloud for big data. Electronics **5**(2), 29 (2016)

9. Kaewkasi, C., Srisuruk, W.: A study of big data processing constraints on a low-power hadoop cluster. In: 2014 International Conference on Computer Science and Engineering Conference (ICSEC), pp. 267–272. IEEE (2014)

10. Laskowski, J.: Mastering apache spark 2.0. https://www.gitbook.com/book/jaceklaskowski/mastering-apache-spark/details

Light-Weight Cloud-Based Virtual Computing Infrastructure for Distributed Applications and Hadoop Clusters

Vladimir Korkhov$^{(\boxtimes)}$, Sergey Kobyshev, Alexander Degtyarev, and Alexander Bogdanov

St. Petersburg State University,
7/9 Universitetskaya nab., St. Petersburg 199034, Russia
v.korkhov@spbu.ru

Abstract. Virtualized computing infrastructures are often used to create clusters of resources tailored to solve tasks taking into account particular requirements of these tasks. An important objective is to evaluate such requirements and request optimal amount of resources which becomes challenging for parallel tasks with intercommunication. In previous works we investigated how light-weight container-based virtualization can be used for creating virtual clusters running MPI applications. Such cluster is configured according to the requirements of particular application and allocates only necessary amount of resources from the physical infrastructure leaving space for co-allocated clusters running without conflicts or resource races. In this paper we investigate similar concepts for MapReduce applications based on Hadoop framework that use Cloudply virtualization tool to create and manage light-weight virtual Hadoop clusters on Amazon cloud resources. We investigate performance of several Hadoop benchmarks in different deployment scenarios and evaluate effects of resource sharing and limitation on application performance.

Keywords: Virtualization · Containers · Virtual cluster

1 Introduction

In this paper we explore possibilities of container-based virtual infrastructures to enable parallel and distributed applications. In previous research [1,2] we examined how flexible configuration of light-weight virtualized computing and networking resources can influence application performance and enable multitenancy with minimal impact of simultaneously running MPI applications on each other. Here we focus on deployment and execution of distributed data processing frameworks in virtual container-based clusters, namely we investigate the dependency of Hadoop benchmarking suite performance on resource restrictions and existence of other simultaneously running applications.

© Springer International Publishing AG 2017
O. Gervasi et al. (Eds.): ICCSA 2017, Part V, LNCS 10408, pp. 399–411, 2017.
DOI: 10.1007/978-3-319-62404-4_29

The driving ideas for this investigation are the following:

- Enable efficient use of available resources (physical machines or VMs) by partitioning them into independent virtual clusters that can be used in parallel
- Allocate just as much resources as needed to solve particular problem
- Limit resource use by simultaneously running clusters with light-weight virtualization technologies

Platform and tools that are used for the experiments:

- Core infrastructure: Amazon cloud
- Fine-grained resource partitioning: Docker containers
- Container management: Docker Swarm
- Resource/application configuration and management: Cloudply
- Distributed computing and data-processing framework: Apache Hadoop
- Benchmarks: TestDFSIO, TeraSort benchmarking suite (TeraGen + TeraSort + TeraValidate), MRBench

Apache Hadoop [3] is a platform for building distributed computing and data processing applications that rely upon massive distributed data storage and distributed computing nodes. Hadoop file system uses data distribution and replication across hosts and racks of hosts to ensure data protection against failures and enable parallel processing of different data blocks located near different computing nodes thus minimizing overheads on sending data across the network.

There are several use-cases that might benefit from Hadoop virtualization. First, some virtualization platforms provide extra capabilities for high-availability and fault-tolerance which can be important to keep Hadoop master daemons alive. For example, such functionality in VMWare is examined in [6]. Another approach to build fault-tolerant frameworks for distributed applications with special attention to master-node fault-tolerance was presented and evaluated in [11,12], however it is not directly applicable to Hadoop clusters. Second, it might be required to deploy dynamic Hadoop clusters of particular size for particular periods of time to solve a particular problem. Such model of using resources on-demand is provided by cloud computing, and major cloud providers offer services of dynamic Hadoop cluster deployment, namely Microsoft Azure HDInsight or Amazon EMR. However, better control on resource utilization and configuration of the cluster according to target application requires involvement into such automatic services. Third, virtualization of the infrastructure helps sharing resources with other Hadoop clusters or other applications which helps better resource utilization. Even in the cloud model computing resources are issued as virtual machines of predefined capabilities which might not be fully utilized by a single application thus fine-grained resource utilization control with light-weight virtualization might be helpful. Some relevant theoretical background and analysis of approaches to build cloud middleware using message passing and scaling control along with scaling in distributed cloud application architecture are given in [13,14].

Moreover, virtualization brings new possibilities to integrate Hadoop work-loads into a datacenter or cloud infrastructure:

- Elasticity allows to grow or shrink clusters as needed in order to release resources to other applications or decrease costs;
- Multi-tenancy enables several virtual clusters share a single physical cluster (or VM-based cluster) and keep high level of isolation;
- In some cases, security requires to distribute computational and data parts of Hadoop (TaskTracker and DataNode) onto separate machines; however keeping them close (e.g. within a single host or VM) increases data locality and performance.

One of the main benefits of virtualized environment is the possibility to tune capacity of every node precisely to suit application needs. In contrast, in a native environment every node has fixed characteristics, and application must be tuned to fit resources. However, some applications are designed to be deployed on small nodes and are not able to use all capabilities of powerful hosts. Another case is using a heterogeneous infrastructure, e.g. mixture of two- and four-core processor hosts; in this case it is reasonable to virtualize four-core hosts as two two-core hosts to make clusters more homogeneous.

The benefits of Hadoop virtualization will only make sense when it will not hamper the performance much. Moreover, it is even more attractive in case it helps to distribute available resources more efficiently between multiple applications or Hadoop clusters: virtualization can provide higher hardware/VM utilization by consolidating multiple Hadoop clusters and other workload on the same physical/VM cluster. In this paper we will evaluate several scenarios of running Hadoop in light-weight container clusters over Amazon cloud virtual machines with a set of benchmarks: MRBench, TestDFSIO, TeraGen, TeraSort, TeraValidate. With these tests we will quantify performance and overheads of running Hadoop in Docker container clusters, especially in case of multiple containers running within a single VM. In our setup container clusters are managed by Docker Swarm, and overall control over infrastructure and application deployment is done by a Cloudply tool. Cloudply takes blueprints of cluster setup and application deployment and with help of Docker Swarm rolls out computing nodes, configures the application, monitors the execution and workload.

The paper is structured as follows: Sect. 2 gives an overview of related work in managing virtual Hadoop clusters; Sect. 3 describes our experimental setup and tools; Sect. 4 shows experimental results for several scenarios of virtual Hadoop cluster deployment; Sect. 5 discusses the results and Sect. 6 concludes the paper.

2   Related Work

There are a number of works that look into running distributed data processing frameworks, in particular Hadoop, in virtual environments. Detailed analysis of virtualized Hadoop performance with VMWare vSphere is presented in [5]. Apache presents discussion on strengths and weaknesses of virtual Hadoop in [4].

Some container-based deployments of Hadoop and their analysis, in particular based on Docker Swarm, appeared in publications recently [7–10]. Most of such works, however, do not focus on evaluation of how we can efficiently utilize available resources by their simultaneous use with several distributed applications, in particular Hadoop clusters, which is the focus of our research.

3 Deploying Hadoop in Virtual Container-Based DCI

In this section we describe the concept of our approach and architecture of our testbed – virtual container-based distributed computing infrastructure (DCI). For the basic infrastructure in our testbed we rely upon Amazon AWS: instances of t2.large and t2.medium virtual machines. Every virtual machine runs one or several Docker containers that are managed by Docker Swarm. Actual configuration of nodes, application deployment and general setup and management is performed by the Cloudply tool (see Fig. 1).

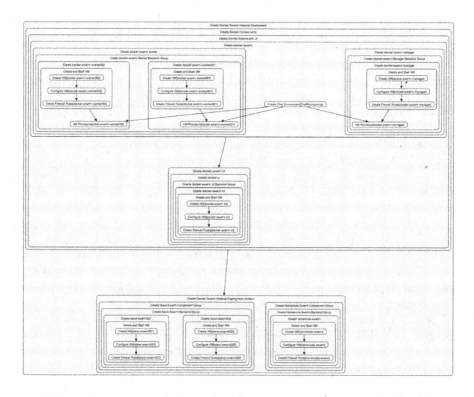

Fig. 1. Schematic view of the application deployment visualized by Cloudply

Cloudply accepts YAML-based descriptions of target infrastructure and applications: Network Blueprint to describe network structure, Security Blueprint to manage application secrets, Application Blueprint to describe application configuration:

```
ApplicationBlueprint:
name: "DockerSwarmHadoop"
description: "DockerSwarmHadoop description"
applicationType: "GENERAL"
componentGroups:
- ComponentGroup:
      name: "Namenode Swarm Component Group"
      description: "hadoop namenode"
      producedServices:
      - Service:
          name: "hdfsUI"
          description: "HDFS web UI"
          portRange:
          - 50070
      - Service:
          name: "yarnUI"
          description: "Yarn web UI"
          portRange:
          - 8088
 - ComponentGroup:
     name: "Slave Swarm Component Group"
     description: "hadoop slave nodes"
```

Application Blueprint describes the high-level architecture of the application: components that will be used, services and their ports. In our case we will use only two component groups: one for Hadoop namenode and another one for Hadoop slave nodes. For the namenode we specify two ports: one for HDFS web interface (port 50070) and another one for YARN web interface (port 8088) Next we need to describe Infrastructure of our application. It contains all information about resources which application requires.

```
infrastructureBlueprints:
- InfrastructureBlueprint:
    name: "DockerSwarmHadoop Infra"
    description: "DockerSwarmHadoop infrastructure"
    agentName: "docker-swarm-agent"
    managedComponents:
    - DockerSwarm:
        name: "docker-swarm"
        agentName: "AWS"
        dockerAgentName: "docker-swarm-agent"
        etcd: "chef01.cloudply.org:2379"
        size:
          cpu: 2
          memory: 4096
          storage: 20
```

```
agentSettings:
    hosted_zone: "cloudply.org."
    subnet: "subnet-eff245a6"
    image: "ami-6d1c2007"
    keypair: "kobyshev.sergey"
    region: "us-east-1"
    instance_type: "t2.medium"
provisionings:
- ChefProvisioning:
    chefServer: "chef01.cloudply.org"
domain: "cloudply.org"
ssh: "kobyshev - centos"
publicIpRanges:
- "0.0.0.0/0"
workerCount: 2
servicePorts:
    docker: 12376
    docker-swarm: 12377
    dockerUI: 19000
    docker-swarm-data-plane: 4789
    docker-swarm-control-plane: 7946
```

In the infrastructure part we describe the Docker Swarm manage component. The manage component prepares templates for some often used components such as gateways, security applications, docker hosts and so on. In our case we need to create Docker Swarm which we will use for deploying a Hadoop cluster; for this we specify an agent which we will use to setup Docker Swarm. In our case we will use Amazon agent (AWS) which contains secrets to work with Amazon API. Next, we specify dockerAgentName. After uploading YAML to Cloudply engine an agent with this name will be created automatically and configured to work with Docker. For Docker Swarm we also specified etcd which contains all information about network using by Swarm. Then we specify hardware parameters for virtual machines: in our example we use t2.medium instances. In agentSettings part we specify parameters which are specific for Amazon cloud. Then we specified Chef server. Applications use Chef for provision, configuring and preparing nodes. We also can use Ansible provisioning system. Next, in Amazon we can specify our private domain, to make all nodes accessible from the same domain. Then we specified ssh key used in keypair. All ssh parameters should be created before. Then we specify Ip ranges that can access Docker Swarm resources. Than we specify the number of swarm workers. Finally, we describe all ports used by Docker Swarm.

After describing Docker Swarm we need to describe Components groups. Most fields the same. As before we describe two component groups, one for Hadoop namenode, second for Hadoop slaves. The last part of application description is deployment part, which integrates all pieces of application together. In our case application is simple and it contains only one infrastructure blueprint.

4   Evaluation of Virtual DCI

For evaluation of the deployment of Hadoop on virtual container-based cluster over Amazon cloud resources we execute a number of standard Hadoop benchmarks: TestDFSIO, TeraSort (including TeraGen and TeraValidate), MRBench.

TestDFSIO benchmark is a read and write storage throughput test for HDFS. It performs stress-testing of the distributed filesystem, discovers performance bottlenecks, in particular in networking as the write test does twice as much I/O as the read test and generates substantial networking traffic. This benchmark gives an overall estimation of how fast the cluster is in terms of I/O.

TeraSort is a benchmark that sorts a large amount of data as fast as possible. It combines testing the HDFS and MapReduce layers of a Hadoop cluster. TeraSort sorts a large number of 100-byte records. It performs significant computation, networking, and storage I/O workloads; it is often considered to be representative of real Hadoop workloads. The benchmark is divided into three parts: generation, sorting, and validation. TeraGen creates the data and is similar to TestDFSIO-write except that large computation is done during generation of random data. The map tasks write directly to HDFS, and there is no reduce phase. TeraSort does the actual sorting and writes sorted data to HDFS in a number of partitioned files. TeraValidate reads all the sorted data to verify that it is in order.

MRBench runs small jobs a number of times and checks whether small jobs are responsive. It is a complimentary benchmark to the large-scale TeraSort benchmark suite to check whether small job runs are running efficiently on the cluster. The test focuses on the MapReduce layer as its impact on the HDFS layer is very limited.

The infrastructure and Hadoop clusters are deployed according to several tests scenarios:

Scenario1: The cluster is composed a set of t2.large VMs (2 vCPUs, 8 GB RAM); every VM runs a single Docker container that uses full VM resources without constraints; Hadoop is deployed with 1 namenode and 2 worker nodes;

Scenario2: The cluster is composed a set of t2.large VMs; every VM runs a single Docker container constrained to use only 4 GB RAM; Hadoop is deployed with 1 namenode and 2 worker nodes;

Scenario3: The cluster is composed a set of t2.large VMs; every VM runs two Docker containers, each constrained to use only 4 GB RAM; two Hadoop clusters are deployed in parallel on containers 1 namenode and 2 worker nodes; thus every VM is shared between two simultaneously running Hadoop clusters.

Figures 2, 3, 4, 5 and 6 illustrate experimental results of running the benchmarks in all 3 scenarios. The following section discusses the obtained results.

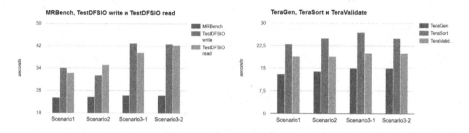

Fig. 2. Benchmark execution time for different scenarios

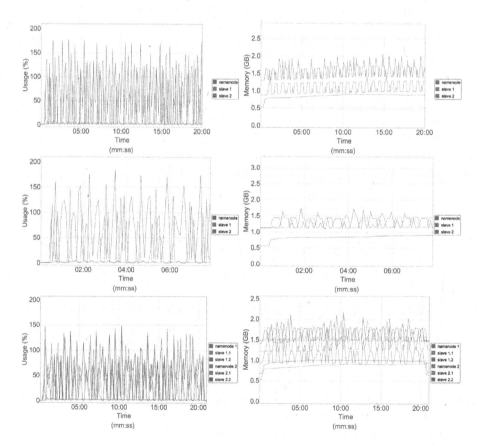

Fig. 3. MRBench: scenario 1, scenario 2, scenario 3

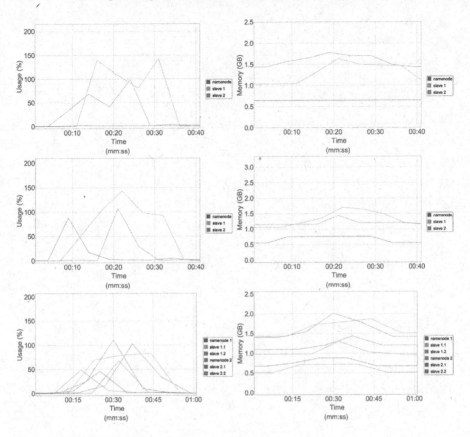

Fig. 4. Terasort: scenarios 1, 2, and 3.

5   Discussion

The goal of the experimental evaluation was to check the efficiency of using resources in distributed virtual Hadoop cluster. We compared several scenarios of infrastructure and application deployment along with running a number of standard benchmarks. Scenarios are explained in the previous section (Scenarios 3-1 and 3-2 in figures mean results for each of Hadoop clusters running in parallel).

Figure 2 shows the runtime of different benchmarks executed in different scenarios. We can see that MRBench performance does not depend on the scenario – indeed, it focuses on MapReduce without much use of HDFS, thus it relies mostly on CPU. In our setup every VM has two vCPUs, thus even in scenario 3 each container gets its own CPU. In turn, we see that the performance if TestDFSIO significantly depends on the scenario: in Scenario 3 both read and write tests perform significantly slower than in Scenarios 1 and 2 – though not

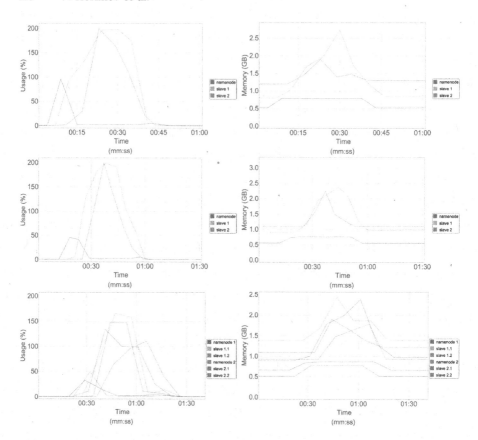

Fig. 5. TestDFSIO read: scenarios 1, 2, and 3.

twice as slow but only about 1.5 times slower, which supports the statement about efficiency of using parallel clusters. TeraSort benchmark shows only a slight decrease of performance in Scenario 3. Again, this is a good evidence that using parallel virtual clusters on a single set of resources (physical hardware or VMs) can increase efficiency of using resources and decrease costs caused by using paid cloud resources for processing workloads. In this case we managed to process twice as much as the original TeraSort workload increasing the overall processing time just for about 15%.

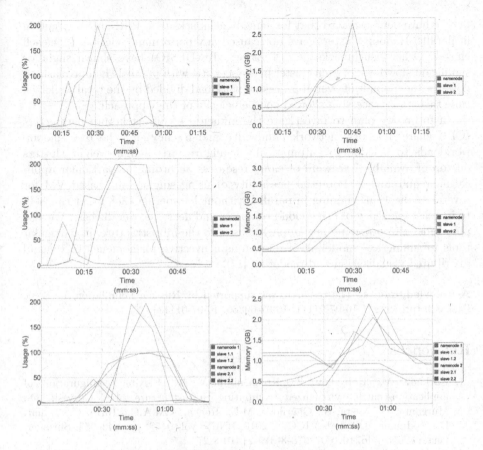

Fig. 6. TestDFSIO write: scenarios 1, 2, and 3.

6   Conclusions and Future Work

In this paper we presented Cloudply – an environment for creating light-weight virtual infrastructures on top of physical or cloud resources. With help of this tool we deployed Hadoop clusters in containers over Amazon VMs and performed experiments to check efficiency of using resources by particular Hadoop workloads. For the workloads we used well-known benchmarks: MRBench, TestDFSIO, TeraSort.

The goal of our experiments was to demonstrate that we can increase efficiency of using distributed resources – even in case of utilizing cloud resources – by simultaneous execution of light-weight virtual clusters. As long as individual requirements of applications are taken into account, we can increase the number of applications occupying a single hardware node or VM by splitting it with help of light-weight virtualization tools. These tools help to control fair resource distribution between parallel applications within a VM (Hadoop clusters in our case) and ensure no significant performance breakdowns for the applications.

We have demonstrated that for some benchmarks (e.g. MRBench) execution in parallel Hadoop clusters have not caused any performance decrease for each cluster. Other benchmarks (e.g. TeraSort, TestDFSIO) have shown slight or significant slowdown of each cluster in the scenario with parallel Hadoop clusters, however the amount of overall processed workload divided by the total wallclock time taken for processing showed good efficiency of this approach.

In future we plan to investigate the influence of infrastructure parameters (CPU share, memory, network bandwidth and latency) for the test Hadoop workloads to be able to automatically configure virtual light-weight clusters on top of available hardware of cloud resources according to particular application requirements. Potential possibility of using single cloud-based VM for several applications running in parallel without hampering each other can help to increase efficiency of using cloud resources and decrease overall costs. We also plan to look into porting new applications onto the infrastructure, in particular tools for numerical modeling of dangerous convective phenomena [15, 16] and distributed visualization and rendering [17].

Acknowledgments. The research was supported by Russian Foundation for Basic Research (projects N 16-07-01111, 16-07-00886, 16-07-01113).

References

1. Korkhov, V., Kobyshev, S., Krosheninnikov, A.: Flexible configuration of application-centric virtualized computing infrastructure. In: Gervasi, O., Murgante, B., Misra, S., Gavrilova, M.L., Rocha, A.M.A.C., Torre, C., Taniar, D., Apduhan, B.O. (eds.) ICCSA 2015. LNCS, vol. 9158, pp. 342–353. Springer, Cham (2015). doi:10.1007/978-3-319-21410-8_27

2. Korkhov, V., Kobyshev, S., Krosheninnikov, A., Degtyarev, A., Bogdanov, A.: Distributed computing infrastructure based on dynamic container clusters. In: Gervasi, O., Murgante, B., Misra, S., Rocha, A.M.A.C., Torre, C., Taniar, D., Apduhan, B.O., Stankova, E., Wang, S. (eds.) ICCSA 2016. LNCS, vol. 9787, pp. 263–275. Springer, Cham (2016). doi:10.1007/978-3-319-42108-7_20

3. Apache Hadoop Project. http://hadoop.apache.org/

4. Apache Wiki: Virtual Hadoop. https://wiki.apache.org/hadoop/Virtual

5. Buell, J.: Virtualized Hadoop Performance with VMware vSphere 5.1. Performance Study. http://www.vmware.com/content/dam/digitalmarketing/vmware/en/pdf/whitepaper/vmware-virtualizing-apache-hadoop-white-paper.pdf

6. Buell, J.: Protecting Hadoop with VMware vSphere 5 Fault Tolerance. VMware Inc. (2012). http://www.vmware.com/resources/techresources/10301

7. Zhang, R., Li, M., Hildebrand, D.: Finding the big data sweet spot: towards automatically recommending configurations for Hadoop clusters on Docker containers. In: 2015 IEEE International Conference on Cloud Engineering, Tempe, AZ, pp. 365–368 (2015)

8. Rey, J., Cogorno, M., Nesmachnow, S., Steffenel, L.A.: Efficient prototyping of fault tolerant map-reduce applications with Docker-Hadoop. In: 2015 IEEE International Conference on Cloud Engineering, Tempe, AZ, pp. 369–376 (2015)

9. Qiao, Y., Wang, X., Fang, G., Lee, B.: Doopnet: an emulator for network performance analysis of Hadoop clusters using Docker and Mininet. In: 2016 IEEE Symposium on Computers and Communication (ISCC), Messina 2016, pp. 784–790 (2016)

10. Ivanov, T., Zicari, R., Izberovic, S., Tolle, K.: Performance evaluation of virtualized hadoop clusters. Technical report No. 2014-1, Frankfurt Big Data Lab oratory. https://arxiv.org/ftp/arxiv/papers/1411/1411.3811.pdf

11. Gankevich, I., Tipikin, Y., Korkhov, V., Gaiduchok, V., Degtyarev, A., Bogdanov, A.: Factory: master node high-availability for big data applications and beyond. In: Gervasi, O., Murgante, B., Misra, S., Rocha, A.M.A.C., Torre, C., Taniar, D., Apduhan, B.O., Stankova, E., Wang, S. (eds.) ICCSA 2016. LNCS, vol. 9787, pp. 379–389. Springer, Cham (2016). doi:10.1007/978-3-319-42108-7_29

12. Gankevich, I., Tipikin, Y., Korkhov, V., Gaiduchok, V.: Factory: non-stop batch jobs without checkpointing. In: 2016 International Conference on High Performance Computing and Simulation, HPCS 2016, Art. no. 7568441, pp. 979–984 (2016)

13. Iakushkin, O.: Cloud middleware combining the functionalities of message passing and scaling control. In: EPJ Web of Conferences, vol. 108, Art. no. 02029 (2016). doi:10.1051/epjconf/201610802029

14. Iakushkin, O.: Intellectual scaling in a distributed cloud application architecture: a message classification algorithm, In: Proceedings of International Conference on Stability and Control Processes in Memory of V.I. Zubov, SCP 2015, art. no. 7342245, pp. 634–637 (2015). doi:10.1109/SCP.2015.7342245

15. Raba, N.O., Stankova, E.N.: On the problem of numerical modeling of dangerous convective phenomena: possibilities of real-time forecast with the help of multi-core processors. In: Murgante, B., Gervasi, O., Iglesias, A., Taniar, D., Apduhan, B.O. (eds.) ICCSA 2011. LNCS, vol. 6786, pp. 633–642. Springer, Heidelberg (2011). doi:10.1007/978-3-642-21934-4_51

16. Raba, N., Stankova, E., Ampilova, N.: On investigation of parallelization effectiveness with the help of multi-core processors. In: Proceedings of 10th International Conference on Computational Science (ICCS) 2010. Procedia Computer Science, vol. 1(1), pp. 2763–2768 (2010). doi:10.1016/j.procs.2010.04.310

17. Bogdanov, A., Ivashchenko, A., Belezeko, A., Korkhov, V., Kulabukhova, N., Khmel, D., Suslova, S., Milova, E., Smirnov, K.: Building a virtual cluster for 3D graphics applications. In: Gervasi, O., Murgante, B., Misra, S., Rocha, A.M.A.C., Torre, C., Taniar, D., Apduhan, B.O., Stankova, E., Wang, S. (eds.) ICCSA 2016. LNCS, vol. 9787, pp. 276–291. Springer, Cham (2016). doi:10.1007/978-3-319-42108-7_21

Prototype of Informational Infrastructure of a Program Instrumentation Complex for Carrying Out a Laboratory Practicum on Physics in a University

N.V. Dyachenko[3], A.V. Barmasov[1,3,4], E.N. Stankova[1,2(✉)],
A.V. Struts[4,5], A.M. Barmasova[3,4], and T. Yu. Yakovleva[3]

[1] Saint Petersburg State University,
7-9, Universitetskaya nab., St. Petersburg 199034, Russia
{a.barmasov,e.stankova}@spbu.ru
[2] St. Petersburg Electrotechnical University "LETI",
5, ul. Professora Popova, St. Petersburg 197376, Russia
[3] Russian State Hydrometeorological University,
98, Malookhtinsky pr., St. Petersburg 195196, Russia
{nat230209,abarmasova,yakovtat}@yandex.ru
[4] St. Petersburg State Pediatric Medical University,
2, Litovskaya ul., St. Petersburg 194100, Russia
struts@email.arizona.edu
[5] The University of Arizona, Tucson, AZ 85721, USA

Abstract. The following article is concerned with the description of the prototype of informational infrastructure of a program instrumentation complex for carrying out a laboratory practicum on physics in a university. The following complex should include: instrumental part for carrying out real physical experiments with the available equipment, program complex of virtual laboratories and a document management system, enabling students to learn the descriptions and to write reports on the laboratories and enabling professors to record student's results and to rate student's work appropriately.

Keywords: Computer technology · Teaching physics · General physics · Laboratory practicum · Virtual laboratories · E-lab

1 Introduction

Nowadays information technology is getting used wider both for teaching and for managing educational process.

Earlier we have discussed the use of computer technologies for increasing the efficiency of physics teaching [1]. Proposed approach included the development of professionally oriented teaching, the use of multimedia lecture courses, the use of Learning Management Systems (such as Blackboard Learn and MOODLE), webinars, etc. It was proposed to organize distributed educational system in a form of Grid infrastructure which should unite facilities of four Russian St. Petersburg Universities.

© Springer International Publishing AG 2017
O. Gervasi et al. (Eds.): ICCSA 2017, Part V, LNCS 10408, pp. 412–427, 2017.
DOI: 10.1007/978-3-319-62404-4_30

This Grid infrastructure could provide equal access to all kinds of resources for the students and lecturers in order to teach and study physics more efficiently. Now University of Arizona (USA) has joined the project.

For several years, authors of this paper have been developing a unique approach of physics and biophysics teaching [2–22] which imlies the development of multimedia support, including presentations with illustrations, animations, video clips, etc., as well as printed manuals [6, 23–41] and webinars [1].

The practice of using this approach has shown that the laboratory studies are the most efficient method of overcoming the "gap" in minds of the majority of students without the necessary skills of the abstract thinking. During these studies students feel the difference between the reality and abstract models directly, not abstractly. Sensible feeling of an object is created during carrying out real experiments.

In our opinion, a good laboratory practicum should demonstrate all phases of a physical research. Limitation of the study time, allocated for laboratory practicum, demands looking for new technological methods of teaching, the main ones are informational technologies. This form implies individual interaction between a student and a computer, laboratory equipment and a lecturer.
Laboratory practicum itself consists of three parts.

- Program instrumental complex, carrying out real experiments.
- Virtual laboratory, carrying out virtual experiments.
- "Digital laboratory" System, which integrates the whole laboratory practicum into a unified educational complex.

The present paper is concerned with the «Digital laboratory» System.

In our opinion, a program instrumental complex (e-lab) should be developed for automation of the laboratory practicum on physics. The complex should be based on web-technologies and mean working with informational content via browser ("thin" client). Using of these technologies in the educational process has following advantages.

- No special technical skills except skills of working with web-sites are required. This is available for the majority of present students. Technology provides unification and intuitive availability of the interface for users of different levels of computer literacy.
- Informational content may include links to other publications, which provides the ability of efficient presentation of the theoretical material.
- Changes made by one user can be instantly available to other users, thereby reacting to the various user's actions in real-time (on-line).
- Maintenance of software and databases is filled in a centralized way.

Depending on the capabilities and policies of the specific university, as well as the presence of specially equipped server room, e-lab may be located in a local network of the university, or in the "cloud".

Laboratory work is carried out on all sections of general physics, including "Mechanics" [42, 43], "Molecular Physics and Thermodynamics" [42–47], "Electricity and Magnetism" [48, 49], "Optics" [50, 51], "Atomic physics, nuclear physics and elementary particles" [51]. The lecture course "Methods of processing the results of measurements of physical quantities" (hereinafter as "Theory of errors") [35] traditionally precedes implementation of the laboratories in the first semester. In 2016, the new course "Integrated laboratory work for the Academic Gymnasium (AG) named after academician Dmitry Konstantinovich Faddeev of St. Petersburg State University" has been developed by one of the authors of the paper and added to the educational process of the St. Petersburg State University. Laboratory works are developed for AG 8th grade students (Physics and Mathematics profile "Convergence and high technologies"). These labs contribute to the realization of continuous natural sciences convergent education in order to develop student's holistic view of the world of natural sciences. Interdisciplinary communication manifests itself in the interaction of physics, biology, anatomy and medicine. Physical methods of research are applied to the study of biological objects in all the works [52].

The following basic steps can be named as the parts of the process of passing real laboratory workshop.

- Colloquium on the course "Theory of errors". It implies solution of the number of practical problems encountered in laboratory practice.
- Receiving of the list of laboratory works.
- Study of a theory of a phenomenon and specific features of an each lab experiment.
- Elimination of uncertainties in the formulas of indirect measurements on laboratory work
- Passing a colloquium concerning a theory of a phenomenon and the features of lab experiment.
- Obtaining access to a laboratory work.
- Carrying out of experimental measurements in the laboratory using the laboratory equipment.
- Carrying out calculations, including calculation of errors and fixing the results.
- Monitoring results by a lab instructor.
- Fixing the results of the implementation of the laboratory work of a student by a lecturer in a laboratory logbook.

The main automated features that should be carried out by the e-lab within these processes are listed below.

2   Automated Features of E-Lab

2.1   Storing

E-lab should provide possibility of storing theoretical material on the theory of errors and on physical phenomena and also of specific features of the experiments conducted in the frame of laboratory work. All the data should be presented in a structured form.

As part of this function, e-lab provides access to training and presentation materials for students, technicians and instructors. Text documents, presentations, audio recordings, video clips, including media with recordings of virtual experiments can serve as such materials. At the same time access to the content across the Internet for home user's computers and mobile devices may be provided according to the policy of certain university.

Search of the materials should be carried out in two modes.

- Automated mode, which is based on user requests expressed in a free form through the search box. The results should be presented in the order of relevance.
- Automatic mode. This mode is used in the case of unsatisfactory results showed by students in the process of computer testing of their knowledge of laboratory materials. In this case, the e-lab provides automatic selection of relevant materials and offers them to the students.

The following types of search are to be implemented in the system.

- Search for details of the material, such as a discipline title, date of last update, lecture name, etc.
- Keyword search, attached to each material when it is loaded into the database.
- Full-text search, i.e. search over the entire content of the materials or a substantial part.

2.2 Checking

E-lab should provide possibility of checking student's knowledge of theoretical material.
This function includes the following tasks.

- Monitoring of student's studying of theoretical material on the theory of errors.
- Control of the correctness of the formulas of errors of indirect measurements derived by students
- Control over student's learning of theory of the phenomenon and the features of the lab experiment.

As a part of the execution of this function, e-lab provides the process of student's testing via solution of control tasks
The choice of a form of control and selection of a specific control task can be carried out in two forms.

- Automatically, depending on the topic of laboratory work and (or) other parameters.
- In the automated mode, that is assigned by a lecturer.

Checking of the control task solution is performed similarly in both modes. In the case of automatic test criteria of successful control task solution are set in advance by a person with administrative rights who is able to provide control tasks management and to set electronic regulations of the laboratory workshops. The criteria are determined by the lecturer if the automated test mode is applied.

E-lab provides automatic selection of theoretical materials on the subject of the lab task if students fulfil a control task unsatisfactory.

A full story of student's control tasks implementation is logged in the e-lab archive via the execution of the application function "Keeping the history of laboratory work and control tasks".

2.3   Control and Monitoring

Electronic regulation of the laboratory practical work is fixed in the system in electronic form as the sequence of stages of a laboratory work implementation and conditions for the transition between the stages.

The main aim of this function is to monitor the student's admission to the next stage of a laboratory practical work on the basis of the results of the previous stage, on the basis of the results of control task implementation.

In addition, some parts of this feature are.

- Control terms of passage by student of all the stages of a laboratory work.
- Automatic generation of notifications to the student, lecturer, technician when approaching or breach of terms.
- Automatic generation of notifications to the student, lecturer, technician during implementation of a laboratory practical work

All control and monitoring parameters are set in the e-lab function "System Setup events, status and service messages".

E-lab should maintain a uniform system of laboratory practical status (a reflection of the results of a student passing his "road map", carried out at any time and for any students) and provide automatic management of the status for each student and for each laboratory practical work. The composition and the status are set within the framework of providing the function "System Setup events, status and service messages".

2.4   Laboratory Work

Transition to the direct fulfilment of a laboratory work is possible only in a case of admission, which is resulted from a student's successful completion of the previous stages of a laboratory practical work, fixed by the e-lab.

Direct implementation of a laboratory work can be done in four ways.

- Setting a virtual experiment. This form does not involve the use of any additional equipment other than a computer.
- An experiment on the equipment, not integrated with the computer. This form assumes that the results of the experiment and the measurement data are recorded in an electronic student's lab manually.
- An experiment on the equipment, integrated with the computer. This form assumes that the results of the experiment and measurement data are recorded in the electronic lab automatically by the interaction of the software (installed on a workstation or as part of hardware and software) with laboratory equipment.
- Mixed form. This form is used for the experiments carried out in several stages, using different means.

As a part of this function, the main objectives of the e-lab are.

- Reception and processing of the experimental results and measurement data.
- Ensuring the correctness of the calculations and monitoring of the experimental results and measurement data.

- Viewing of the results of experiments by a technician from his/her workplace.

As it was noted above the specialized software for setting the virtual experiment ("virtual laboratory") or to integrate with the measuring device (hardware and software laboratory complex) is not a part of e-lab, but should be integrated with it.

2.5 User Interaction

As a part of this function, e-lab should provide interaction of the following main groups of users:

- students;
- lecturers;
- technical assistants.

The work of a lecturer should be organized in such a way that he/she could get in touch with the student at any stage of his work from his workstation, give comments, clarifications and continue monitoring student's work in real-time.

A technical assistant becomes an operator of the e-lab in addition to the usual functions.

When one receives a new message or a comment by another participant of interaction the user must be notified by the system which if necessary should duplicate this message or comment it via user's e-mail.

2.6 Logging

All the stages of a laboratory practical work, including primary and re-commissioning of control tasks, must be logged. This information should be displayed to the students in terms of the progress in implementation of a laboratory practical work, as well as to the lecturers for enabling them possibility to monitor the progress of all students.

2.7 Report Formation

E-lab should provide automated (on request) formation of the following basic types of reports:

- student's report on a laboratory work;
- a general report (for the whole group/all groups) on the current status of students who implement the laboratory works;
- a report on the passage of a students' laboratory practice (history of passage);
- a laboratory sheet (should be prepared according to the approved form), which, if necessary can be automatically upload to the university website.

All reports should be formed with the ability of saving them on personal computer, their e-mailing and printing.

The following minimum set of report parameters must be formed automatically:

- period of the report preparation;
- name of a student and group number;
- name of a lecturer;
- general physics section;
- topic of laboratory work.
- a status of a laboratory practical work.

3 Supporting Functions (Administration)

3.1 Differentiation of Access to the Resources of E-Lab

As a part of this function, e-lab provides:

- identification, authentication, authorization of users;
- creation, redaction and deletion of user's accounts.

3.2 Management of E-Lab Information Content

As a part of this function, e-lab provides:

- creation, redaction and deletion of training and presentation materials.

3.3 Management of Control Tasks and Regulations

As a part of this function, e-lab provides:

- creation, redaction and deletion of control tasks;
- creation, redaction and deletion of control task assessment;
- creation, redaction and deletion of criteria of transition between the stages of a laboratory practical work.

3.4 Adjustment of System Events, Statuses and Service Messages

Adjustment of system events, statuses and service messages
   As a part of this function, e-lab provides:

- creation, redaction and deletion of events, the occurrence of which are monitored by a system during the laboratory work implementation;
- creation, redaction and deletion of statuses of a laboratory work which a monitored by a system;
- creation, redaction and deletion of notifications to users upon the occurrence of certain events.

3.5   Logging of User's Activity

As part of this function, e-lab provides automatic recording of activities of all users of the system.

3.6   Formation and Maintenance of Reference Books and Classifiers

As a part of this function, e-lab ensures the formation and maintenance of intra-directories and classifiers used in completing electronic forms system to ensure the unification of data entered by users.

E-lab customer information space should be divided into the following components.

Open segment. Open segment is data available to an unauthorized user. Depending on the information security policy, adopted at the university, the segment may go or not beyond the restricted or limited authorization form (form for entering the reference name/password).

Closed segment. Closed segment is available only after the user identification, authentication and authorization system. Closed segment includes:

- automated student's workstation (AWS "Student").
  AWS "Student" provides access for a student to:
  - training and presentation materials.
  - his/her personal registration card in the system, including a complete history of the student's progress in laboratory practice;
  - control tasks;
  - laboratory work functionality;
  - tools for generation of laboratory work reports;
  - tools for interaction with a lecturer and a technical assistant.
- automated lecturer workstation (AWS "Lecturer").
  AWS "Lecturer" provides access for a lecturer to:
  - training and presentation materials;
  - his/her personal registration card in the system;
  - control tasks;
  - laboratory work functionality;
  - tools for formation of a general report on a current status of student progress (for the whole group/all groups), of a report on a personal progress of a student in laboratory practical works and the tools for laboratory sheets formation;
  - tools for interaction with students and laboratory assistants.
    Depending on the policy of a university a lecturer may be delegated a part of the system administrator rights, such as follows:
  - management of e-lab information content;
  - management of control tasks and e-lab regulations;
  - formation and maintenance of directories and classifiers.
- automated assistant workstation (AWS "Assistant").

The administrative segment. The administrative segment is available only for the users with system administrator privileges after their identification, authentication and authorization. Administrative segment provides access to the following system:

- Access control to e-lab resources in terms of creating, modifying, deleting user accounts.
- management of e-lab information content;
- management of control tasks and e-lab regulations;
- setting of system events, status and service messages;
- logging user actions;
- formation and maintenance of directories and classifiers.

Currently on the market there are no complete solutions that automate all of these functions. These components are presented separately:

- virtual laboratories (2D, 3D);
- hardware and software laboratory facilities;
- distance education and computer-based testing;
- systems for project and task management (e.g., Redmine);
- electronic document management system (1C, Directum, etc.).

Each of those types of systems automates some of the above e-lab functions, but separately these products do not meet the requirements of automation of laboratory practical works. It should be noted that in case, if the functions implemented in the framework of virtual laboratories, hardware and software laboratory facilities, distance learning systems, and computer-based testing can be used in the electronic laboratory almost completely, the functionality of the system for managing projects and tasks, and electronic document management systems is much redundant. Also it should be noted that, in the case of the acquisition of separate software products for the implementation of certain parts of e-lab, integration and debugging through business processes will not only be expensive and time-consuming, but sometimes will be an impossible task. Thus, it is recommended:

- to use virtual laboratories and laboratory software and hardware systems that are ready-made or developed under the special needs of students;
- to develop e-lab system that automates all of the above functions to be implemented in the universities. This system should be integrated with the software of virtual laboratories and laboratory software and hardware complexes, already used in the universities.

The development of e-lab can be carried out on the basis of open source content management system Alfresco. The main advantages of Alfresco for solving the problems mentioned above are:

- open source, security, scalability;
- a complete web-based interface;
- full-text search of documents;
- integration with LDAP, MS Office, e-mail;

- flexible role-based access to documents and "sites", enabling to share laboratory practice within groups, courses, themes;
- support of the graphical process editor JBoss jBMP;
- workflow support.

In addition to the fact that the Alfresco platform allows to implement the above requirements and has an extensive and fairly universal set of tools for integration with laboratory software, this solution provides the following features that can be used effectively in the learning process.

- Wiki. Wiki environment allows users to edit simultaneously the publication preserving the history of changes The absence of the need to install any other software than the browser on the user's computer is the first advantage of Wiki publications, and the second advantage is the availability of the edited contents to other users in real time. Wiki provides easy cataloguing of information content.
- Blog. Blog is regularly added record having temporal value that can be used for the publication of news, events and general information messages addressed to all students.
- Calendar. Calendar provides the ability to assign and schedule specific dates and times of the events (oral tests, consultations, retakes of the exams, etc.) and notify users of the system about them.
- Links. Links allow keeping a register of references to useful resources.
- Discussion. Discussion allows conducting open discussion of various topics by the users of the system.

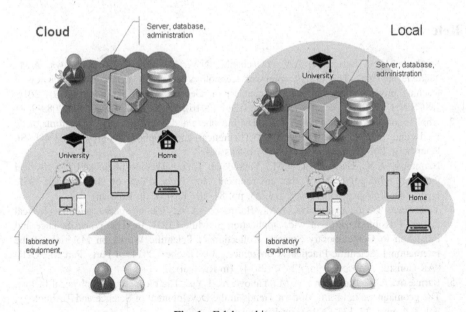

Fig. 1. E-lab architecture

Both medical specialties and the specialties that indirectly use medical and biological knowledge occupy a special place among the many natural sciences and humanities, which contain physics and the concept of modern science in the learning process. Under the proposed approach, the authors have developed multimedia [1] and began to create the proposed e-lab using the facilities of virtual supercomputer and comuper models of real physical objects [53–57].

The proposed e-lab architecture is presented in Fig. 1.

4 Conclusions

Thus, it is suggested to create the prototype of informational infrastructure of a program instrumental complex for carrying out a laboratory practicum on physics in the university (e-lab). This complex includes: the instrumental part for carrying out real physical experiments with the available equipment, the program complex of virtual laboratory works and a document management system, enabling to produce the descriptions and reports on the laboratory practical works and to record student's progress and to estimate student's work appropriately.

Acknowledgment. This research was sponsored by the Russian Foundation for Basic Research under the projects: 16-04-00494 "Research of functioning of rhodopsin as the canonical representative of the class A receptors, which are the G-protein, by the methods of the local selective NMR, optical spectroscopy and numerical simulation" and 16-07-01113 "Virtual supercomputer as a tool for solving complex problems".

References

1. Stankova, E.N., Barmasov, A.V., Dyachenko, N.V., Bukina, M.N., Barmasova, A.M., Yakovleva, TYu.: The use of computer technology as a way to increase efficiency of teaching physics and other natural sciences. In: Gervasi, O., et al. (eds.) ICCSA 2016. LNCS, vol. 9789, pp. 581–594. Springer, Cham (2016). doi:10.1007/978-3-319-42089-9_41
2. Kholmogorov, V.Y., Barmasov, A.V.: The biosphere and physical factors. Electromagnetic fields and life. In: The Problems of Theoretical and Applied Ecology, RSHMU, St. Petersburg, 267 p., pp. 27–47 (2005). (in Russian)
3. Barmasov, A.V., Barmasova, A.M., Yakovleva, T.Yu.: The biosphere and the physical factors. Light pollution of the environment. In: Proceedings of the Russian State Hydrometeorological University, vol. 33, pp. 84–101 (2014). (in Russian)
4. Yakovleva, T.Yu., Barmasova, A.M., Barmasov, A.V.: The biosphere and the physical factors. Possible hazards of wide application of white LEDs. In: The World Science and Education in Contemporary Society: Collection of Scientific Works on Materials of the International Scientific-Practical Conference, 30 October 2014, 4 Part, Part III. OOO "AR-Consult", Moscow, pp. 42–50 (2014). (in Russian)
5. Barmasov, A.V., Barmasova, A.M., Yakovleva, T.Yu.: The biosphere and physical factors. The geomagnetic field. In: Modern Trends in the Development of Science and Technology, vol. 3–4, pp. 127–131 (2015). (in Russian)

6. Barmasov, A.V., Kholmogorov, V.E.: Course of general physics for nature managers. In: Chirtsov, A.S. (ed.) Mechanics 2012, 416 p. BHV-St. Petersburg, St. Petersburg (2008). (in Russian)
7. Barmasova, A.M., Barmasov, A.V., Skoblikova, A.L., et al.: Features of teaching general physics to the students-ecologists. In: The Problems of Theoretical and Applied Ecology. Publishing house RSHU, St. Petersburg, 267 p., 15 p., pp. 226–241 (2005). (in Russian)
8. Barmasova, A.M., Barmasov, A.V., Bobrovsky, A.P., Yakovleva, T.Yu.: To the question about teaching general physics to the students-ecologists. In: Abstracts. Meeting of the Heads of Departments of Physics of Technical Universities in Russia. AVIAIZDAT, Moscow, pp. 46–48 (2006). (in Russian)
9. Barmasova, A.M., Yakovleva, T.Yu., Barmasov, A.V., et al.: An integrated approach to he teaching physics to students-nature managers. In: Spirin, G.G. (ed.) Abstracts of Scientific-Methodical Workshop on "The Physics in the Engineering Education System of the EurAsEC Member States" and the Meeting of Heads of Physics Departments of Technical Universities of Russia. The Scientific Seminar was Held from 25–27 June 2007. Zhukovsky Air Force Engineering Academy, Moscow, 344 p., pp. 40–41 (2007). (in Russian)
10. Barmasova, A.M., Yakovleva, T.Yu., Barmasov, A.V., et al.: Multimedia lecture course on processing of results of measurements of physical quantities for students users. In: Spirin, G. G. (ed.) Abstracts of Scientific-Methodical Workshop on "The Physics in the Engineering Education System of the EurAsEC Member States" and The Meeting of Heads of Physics Departments of Technical Universities of Russia. The Scientific Seminar was Held from, 25–27 June 2007, Zhukovsky Air Force Engineering Academy, Moscow, 344 p., p. 42 (2007). (in Russian)
11. Yakovleva, T.Yu., Barmasova, A.M., Barmasov, A.V.: Problems of pre-university training of students in physics. In: Spirin, G.G. (ed.) Abstracts of Scientific-Methodical Workshop on "The Physics in the Engineering Education System of the EurAsEC Member States" and the Meeting of Heads of Physics Departments of Technical Universities of Russia. The Scientific Seminar was Held from 25–27 June 2007. Zhukovsky Air Force Engineering Academy, Moscow, 344 p., pp. 239–241 (2007). (in Russian)
12. Barmasova, A.M., Yakovleva, T.Yu., Barmasov, A.V., Bobrovsky, A.P.: Independent work of students in the conditions of introduction of profile training in high school. In: Schools and Universities: Achievements and Challenges of Continuous Physical Education: Book of Abstracts of the V Russian Scientific-Methodical Conference of Teachers of Universities and School Teachers. USTU-UPI, Yekaterinburg, 252 p., p. 65 (2008). (in Russian)
13. Yakovleva, T.Yu., Barmasova, A.M.; Barmasov, A.V.: Interdisciplinary connections in teaching general physics to students of science and engineering. In: Spirin, G.G. (ed.) Abstracts of Scientific-Methodical Workshop on "The Physics in the System of Engineering and Pedagogical Education of the EurAsEC Member States". The Scientific Seminar was Held in 2008. Zhukovsky Air Force Engineering Academy, Moscow, 364 p., pp. 355–357 (2008). (in Russian)
14. Bukina, M.N., Barmasov, A.V., Ivanov, A.S.: Modern teaching methods for the teaching general physics and mathematical processing of results of measurements of physical quantities. In: Modern Educational Technology in the Teaching Natural Sciences and the Humanities: Proceedings of the International Scientific-Methodical Conference 27–29 May 2014, Mining University, St. Petersburg, 562 p., pp. 408–414 (2014). (in Russian)
15. Bukina, M.N., Barmasov, A.V., Ivanov, A.S.: Some aspects of teaching physics in high school. In: VIII St. Petersburg Congress "Education, Science, Innovation in the Twenty-First Century". Collection of Works, 24–25 October 2014. Mining University, St. Petersburg, 414 p., pp. 47–49 (2014). (in Russian)

424   N.V. Dyachenko et al.

16. Bukina, M.N., Barmasov, A.V., Lisachenko, D.A., Ivanov, A.S.: Modern methods of teaching physics and the concepts of modern natural science. In: Modern Educational Technologies in Teaching Natural-Scientific and Humane Disciplines: Proceedings of the II International Scientific-Methodical Conference on 09–10 April 2015. Mining University, St. Petersburg, 732 p., pp. 516–520 (2015). (in Russian)

17. Bukina, M.N., Barmasov, A.V., Ivanov, A.S.: Features of general physics teaching to students of natural science specialties in modern conditions. In: The Physics in the System of Modern Education (FSSO-2015): Proceedings of the XIII International Conference, St. Petersburg, 1–4 June 2015, vol. 2, 393 p., pp. 3–6 (2015). (in Russian)

18. Barmasov, A.V., Korotkov, V.I., Kholmogorov, V.Y.: Model photosynthetic system with charge transfer for transforming solar energy. Biophysics **39**(2), 227–231 (1994)

19. Struts, A.V., Barmasov, A.V., Brown, M.F.: Methods for studying photoreceptors and photoactive molecules in biological and model systems: rhodopsin as a canonical representative of the seven-transmembrane helix receptors. Bulletin of St. Petersburg University. Series 4. Physics, Chemistry, vol. 2, pp. 191–202 (2014). (in Russian)

20. Struts, A.V., Barmasov, A.V., Brown, M.F.: Spectral methods for study of the G-protein-coupled receptor rhodopsin. I. vibrational and electronic spectroscopy. Opt. Spectrosc. **118**(5), 711–717 (2015)

21. Bukina, M.N., Bakulev, V.M., Barmasov, A.V., et al.: Luminescence diagnostics of conformational changes of the Hsp70 protein in the course of thermal denaturation. Opt. Spectrosc. **118**(6), 899–901 (2015)

22. Struts, A.V., Barmasov, A.V., Brown, M.F.: Spectral methods for study of the G-protein-coupled receptor rhodopsin. II. magnetic resonance methods. Opt. Spectrosc. **120**(2), 286–293 (2016)

23. Barmasov, A.V., Kholmogorov, V.E.: Course of general physics for nature managers. In: Bobrovsky, A.P. (ed.) Oscillations and Waves. BHV-St. Petersburg, St. Petersburg, 256 p. (2009). (in Russian)

24. Barmasov, A.V., Kholmogorov, V.E.: Course of general physics for nature managers. In: Bobrovsky, A.P. (ed.) Molecular Physics and Thermodynamics 2009, 512 p. BHV-St. Petersburg, St. Petersburg (2012). (in Russian)

25. Barmasov, A.V., Barmasova, A.M., Yakovleva, T.Yu.: The accuracy of definitions in the course of general physics. 1. Material point. In: Spirin, G.G. (ed.) Abstracts of the Meeting of Heads of Physics Departments of Universities of Russia, 344 p., pp. 53–55. APR, Moscow (2009). (in Russian)

26. Barmasov, A.V.; Barmasova, A.M.; Yakovleva, T.Yu.: The accuracy of definitions in the course of General Physics. 2. Simple and physical pendulums. In: Abstracts of the Meeting of heads of physics departments of universities of Russia (Moscow, 2009 г.). Spirin, G.G. (ed.), 344 p., pp. 55–56. APR, Moscow (2009). (in Russian)

27. Barmasov, A.V., Barmasova, A.M., Yakovleva, T.Yu.: The accuracy of definitions in the course of General Physics. 3. Ideal and real gases. In: Spirin, G.G. (ed.) Abstracts of the Meeting of Heads of Physics Departments of Universities of Russia (Moscow, 2009 г.), 344 p., pp. 56–58. APR, Moscow (2009). (In Russian)

28. Barmasov, A.V., Barmasova, A.M., Yakovleva, T.Yu.: The accuracy of definitions in the course of General Physics. 4. Vector and vector variable. In: School and University: Innovation in Education. Interdisciplinary Connections of Natural Sciences: Proceedings of All-Russian Scientific-Practical Internet-Conference. Barmin, A.V. (ed.) OryolSTU, Oryol, 180 p., pp. 18–19 (2009). (in Russian)

29. Barmasov, A.V., Barmasova, A.M., Yakovleva, T.Yu.: The accuracy of definitions in the course of General Physics. 5. Gravitational force, gravity force and weight. In: School and University: Innovation in Education. Interdisciplinary Connections of Natural Sciences: Proceedings of All-Russian Scientific-Practical Internet-Conference. Barmin, A.V. (ed.) OryolSTU, Oryol, 180 p., pp. 20–21 (2009). (in Russian)

30. Barmasov, A.V.: Kholmogorov, V.E.: Course of general physics for nature managers. In: Bobrovsky, A.P. (ed.) Electricity. BHV-St. Petersburg, St. Petersburg 2010, 448 p. (2013). (in Russian)

31. Barmasov, A.V., Barmasova, A.M., Yakovleva, T.Yu.: The accuracy of definitions in the course of General Physics. 6. Point charge and electric dipole. In: Spirin, G.G. (ed.) Abstracts of the International School-Seminar "Physics in Higher and Secondary Education of Russia (Moscow, 2010). APR, Moscow, 328 p., pp. 65–66 (2010). (in Russian)

32. Nordling, C., Österman, J.: Physics Handbook for Science and Engineering. Barmasov, A. V. (ed.) BHV-St. Petersburg, St. Petersburg, 528 p. (2011). (in Russian)

33. Barmasov, A.V., Barmasova, A.M., Yakovleva, T.Yu.: The accuracy of definitions in the course of General Physics. 7. Quasi-elastic forces. In: Spirin, G.G. (ed.) Actual Problems of Teaching Physics in Universities and Schools of Post-Soviet Countries. Proceedings of the International school-seminar "Physics in Higher and Secondary Education" (Moscow, June 2011), 280 p., pp. 46–47. APR, Moscow (2011). (in Russian)

34. Barmasov, A.V., Barmasova, A.M., Yakovleva, T.Yu.: The accuracy of definitions in the course of General Physics. 8. Doppler effect. In: Spirin, G.G. (ed.) Actual Problems of Teaching Physics in Universities and Schools of Post-Soviet Countries. Proceedings of the International School-Seminar "Physics in Higher and Secondary Education" (Moscow, June 2011), 280 p., pp. 47–49. APR, Moscow (2011). (in Russian)

35. Barmasov, A.V., Barmasova, A.M., Struts, A.V., Yakovleva, T.Yu.: Processing of results of measurements of physical quantities. Publishing house of St. Petersburg State Pediatric Medical University, St. Petersburg, 92 p. (2012). (in Russian)

36. Barmasov, A.V., Barmasova, A.M., Struts, A.V., Yakovleva, T.Yu.: Dynamics of rigid body. Elements of the theory and the collection of tasks. Publishing house of St. Petersburg State Pediatric Medical University, St. Petersburg, 28 p. (2012). (in Russian)

37. Barmasov, A.V., Barmasova, A.M., Yakovleva, T.Yu.: The accuracy of definitions in the course of General Physics. 9. Free electrons. In: Spirin, G.G. (ed.) Actual Problems of Teaching Physics in Universities and Schools of Post-Soviet Countries. Proceedings of the International School-Seminar "Physics in Higher and Secondary Education" (Moscow, 2012), pp. 38–40. APR, Moscow (2012). (in Russian)

38. Barmasov, A.V., Barmasova, A.M., Yakovleva, T.Yu.: The accuracy of definitions in the course of General Physics. 10. The equations of state of an ideal gas. In: Spirin, G.G. (ed.) Proceedings of the International School-Seminar "Physics in Higher and Secondary Education" (Moscow, 2014), 278 p., pp. 43–44. APR, Moscow (2014). (in Russian)

39. Barmasov, A.V., Barmasova, A.M., Yakovleva, T.Yu.: The accuracy of definitions in the course of General Physics. 11. Electric potential, potential difference and voltage. In: Physics in the Modern Education System (FSSO-2015): Proceedings of the XIII International Conference, St. Petersburg, 1–4 June 2015, vol. 1, pp. 46–48. Publishing house OOO "Fora-print", St. Petersburg (2015). (in Russian)

40. Barmasov, A.V., Barmasova, A.M., Yakovleva, T.Yu.: The accuracy of definitions in the course of General Physics. 12. Ferroelectrics and antiferroelectrics. In: Science and Education in XXI Century: Collection of Scientific Papers on Materials of International Correspondence Scientific-Practical Conference, 30 January 2015: in 5 parts. Part III: OOO "AR-Consalt", Moscow, 153 p., pp. 91–94 (2015). (in Russian)

41. Barmasov, A.V., Barmasova, A.M., Yakovleva, T.Yu.: The accuracy of definitions in the course of General Physics. 13. Isolated, closed and conservative systems. In: Spirin, G.G. (ed.) Proceedings of the International School-Seminar "Physics in Higher and Secondary Education". International School-Seminar was Held in 2015, 278 p., pp. 40–41. APR, Moscow (2015). (in Russian)

42. Barmasov, A.V., Barmasova, A.M., Belov, M.M., et al.: Laboratory workshop on the subject "Physics". Sections of "Mechanics", "Molecular Physics and Thermodynamics". In: Bobrovsky, A.P. (ed.) Publishing house of RSHU, St. Petersburg, 119 p. (2006). (in Russian)

43. Barmasov, A.V., Barmasova, A.M., Belov, M.M., et al.: Laboratory workshop on the subject "Physics". Sections of "Mechanics", "Molecular Physics and Thermodynamics". Publishing house of RSHU, St. Petersburg, 119 p. (2013). (in Russian)

44. Barmasov, A.V., Barmasova, A.M., Bobrovsky, A.P., et al.: Special laboratory classes on discipline "Physics". Section "Molecular physics and thermodynamics". Publishing house of RSHU, St. Petersburg, 74 p. (2006). (In Russian)

45. Barmasov, A.V., Barmasova, A.M., Bobrovsky, A.P., et al.: Special laboratory classes on discipline "Physics". Section "Molecular physics and thermodynamics". Publishing house of RSHU, St. Petersburg, 74 p. (2013). (in Russian)

46. Bobkova, I.S., Katunin, B.D., Lisachenko, D.A., Barmasov, A.V.: Descriptions of laboratory works of SPSU Physical Department Educational laboratory of physical experiment. In: Zarochentseva, E.P. (ed.) Part II: Molecular Physics: Textbook: VVM, St. Petersburg, 59 p. (2014). (in Russian)

47. Bobkova, I.S., Katunin, B.D., Lisachenko, D.A., Barmasov, A.V.: Descriptions of laboratory works of Educational laboratory of physical experiment. In: Kompaniets, T.N. (ed.) Part III: Molecular Physics: Textbook. VVM, St. Petersburg, 48 p. (2016). (in Russian)

48. Barmasov, A.V., Vysotskaya, S.O., Grishchenko, A.E., et al.: Descriptions of laboratory works of SPSU Physical Department Educational laboratory of physical experiment. Part V: Electricity. Alternating electric current. Korotkov, V.I., Zarochentseva, E.P. (eds.). Publishing house of SPBU, St. Petersburg, 111 p. (2004). (in Russian)

49. Barmasov, A.V., Bobkova, I.S., Vysotskaya, S.O., et al.: Descriptions of laboratory works of SPSU Physical Department Educational laboratory of physical experiment. Part IV: Electricity. Direct electric current. Publishing house of SPBU, St. Petersburg, 93 p. (2007). (in Russian)

50. Barmasov, A.V., Bobkova, I.S., Bukina, M.N., et al.: Descriptions of laboratory works of SPSU Physical Department Educational laboratory of physical experiment. Part VIII: quantum optics. Korotkov, V.I. (ed.) – Publishing house of SPBU, St. Petersburg, 86 p (2009). (in Russian)

51. Barmasov, A.V., Barmasova, A.M., Dyachenko, N.V., et al.: Laboratory workshop on the subject Physics. In: Bobrovsky, A.P. (ed.) Categories: Optics and Nuclear Physics. Course 1, 2. Publishing house of RSHU, St. Petersburg, 111 p. (2016). (in Russian)

52. Bukina, M.N., Barmasov, A.V., Velikorusov, P.V., et al.: Integrated laboratory work for the Academic Gymnasium (AG) named after D.K. Faddeev of St. Petersburg State University (Physics and Mathematics profile "Convergence and high technologies"). (in Russian, in press)

53. Bobrovsky, A.P.; Dyachenko, N.V.: On the role of a real laboratory practical training in physics. In: Spirin, G.G. (ed.) Actual Problems of Teaching Physics in Universities and Schools of Post-soviet Countries. Proceedings of the International School-Seminar "Physics in Higher and Secondary Education" (Moscow, June 2011), Moscow, 280 p., pp. 64–65, April 2011. (in Russian)

54. Gankevich, I., Korkhov, V., Balyan, S., Gaiduchok, V., Gushchanskiy, D., Tipikin, Y., Degtyarev, A., Bogdanov, A.: Constructing virtual private supercomputer using virtualization and cloud technologies. In: Murgante, B., Misra, S., Rocha, A.M.A.C., Torre, C., Rocha, J.G., Falcão, M.I., Taniar, D., Apduhan, B.O., Gervasi, O. (eds.) ICCSA 2014. LNCS, vol. 8584, pp. 341–354. Springer, Cham (2014). doi:10.1007/978-3-319-09153-2_26

55. Gankevich, I., Gaiduchok, V., Gushchanskiy, D., Tipikin, Y., Korkhov, V., Degtyarev, A., Bogdanov, A., Zolotarev, V.: Virtual private supercomputer: Design and evaluation. In: Computer Science and Information Technologies (CSIT), pp 1–6. IEEE Conference Publications (2013). doi:10.1109/CSITechnol.2013.6710358

56. Raba, N.O., Stankova, E.N.: On the problem of numerical modeling of dangerous convective phenomena: possibilities of real-time forecast with the help of multi-core processors. In: Murgante, B., Gervasi, O., Iglesias, A., Taniar, D., Apduhan, B.O. (eds.) ICCSA 2011. LNCS, vol. 6786, pp. 633–642. Springer, Heidelberg (2011). doi:10.1007/978-3-642-21934-4_51

57. Stankova, E.N., Balakshiy, A.V., Petrov, D.A., Shorov, A.V., Korkhov, V.V.: Using technologies of OLAP and machine learning for validation of the numerical models of convective clouds. In: Gervasi, O., et al. (eds.) ICCSA 2016. LNCS, vol. 9788, pp. 463–472. Springer, Cham (2016). http://link.springer.com/chapter/10.1007/978-3-319-42111-7_36

Application of Multi-core Architecture to the Mpdroot Package for the Task Tof Events Reconstruction

Oleg Iakushkin$^{(\boxtimes)}$, Anna Fatkina, Alexander Degtyarev, and Valery Grishkin

Saint-Petersburg State University, St. Petersburg 199034, Russia
o.yakushkin@spbu.ru

Abstract. In this article, we propose an approach that allows acceler- ation of the Time-of-Flight (ToF) event reconstruction algorithm imple- mentation, which is a part of the Multi Purpose Detector (MPD) Root application.

Work on the algorithm was carried out in several stages: the program was assembled on the target devices (Intel Xeon E5-2690v3 and E5-2695 v2); Profiling via Valgrind was performed; We selected a code snippet whose execution takes the longest time; Several algorithms for paralleliz- ing code were investigated and the optimal strategy of code enhancement for the equipment in question was implemented.

Modification of the selected code fragment was carried out using the OpenMP standard. It is widely used in scientific applications, including the reconstruction of events in the PANDA experiment, and has proven to be useful for work in Multi-Core architecture. The standard is sup- ported by the GCC compiler used to build the MpdRoot framework, which makes it possible to integrate this technology into a fragment of the MpdRoot package without changing the structure or build options of the framework.

Due to our optimizations, the algorithm was accelerated on Multi- Core architectures at hand. Paper depicts the direct dependence of the accelerated fragment execution time to the amount of given cores for a given amount of input data. Tests were conducted on the nodes of the heterogeneous cluster JINR "HybriLIT" and cloud node Windows Azure NC12. The paper analyzes the possibilities of optimizing the code for Intel Xeon Phi coprocessors and the problems that we encountered while trying to implement these optimizations.

Keywords: ToF · MPD · Parallel computing · OpenMP · Reconstruction

O. Iakushkin—This research was partially supported by Russian Foundation for Basic Research grant (projects no. 16-07-01113 and no. 16-07-00886).

O. Gervasi et al. (Eds.): ICCSA 2017, Part V, LNCS 10408, pp. 428–437, 2017.
DOI: 10.1007/978-3-319-62404-4_31

1   Introduction

The experimental study of charged particle collision is carried out by means of particle accelerators. The accelerators are complex machines with many components. Among them, a major role is played by particle collision detectors. The detectors have module-based architecture, and each module requires its own piece of programming code that is part of the detectors software. The data obtained by the detector is analysed by a sequence of routines. This highlights the analysis problem and requires to enhance the performance of the basic code fragments [2,4,7,8].

NICA (Nuclotron based Ion Collider fAcility) is one of research centres in this field. It includes the Multi-Purpose Detector (MPD) that obtains experimental data to be further modelled and processed by MpdRoot, a framework developed for the MPD. The MpdRoot is based on FairRoot and ROOT projects that are widely used in nuclear physics research by such centres as CERN and FAIR [1,3]. There is an API available for ROOT that allows to execute algorithms for MpdRoot. The algorithms are implemented as macros that is, special script-containing files that are fed to ROOT as input data.

We focused our attention on the event reconstruction algorithm. After the algorithm is launched, it is executed as follows: first, it reads data modelling results obtained by the MPD; and, second, it uses FairRoot task manager to start a sequence of jobs. Among these jobs, the Time-of-Flight (ToF) matching consumes a major portion of runtime.

This paper examines the ways to optimize the implementation of ToF algorithm in MpdRoot. We propose algorithm modifications that are based on the parallel programming approach.

2   Problem Statement

The algorithm in question has a code fragment whose runtime is a quadratic function of the input data volume, with the input data volume being unknown in advance. This code fragment consumes 47.3% of the algorithms entire runtime. This means that the increase in the input will significantly slow down the processing of the data obtained by the detector.

We examined a number of possible technologies to optimize the code on a variety of devices. The choice was made in favour of multi-core CPUs, because the code transfer to GPU coprocessors would be complicated: the code employs the many data types described in MpdRoot and ROOT, which makes it difficult to copy data on the devices [9,10,12,19]. Furthermore, there is much more memory available in a CPU compared to GPU, which may play the key role when the input data becomes especially large [11,13].

The optimization was carried out on Intel Xeon processors using the OpenMP standard. This standard is widely employed for parallel execution of algorithms, including those in MpdRoot and other packages that are utilized to process data in various nuclear physics experiments (PANDA, CBM) [16]. In addition,

OpenMP is supported by the same compiler that is used to build MpdRoot. We used the implementation of OpenMP compiled by GCC.

We should note that the use of any other compiler for the entire project and its dependences would be complicated, because the source code has a directive that is called many times and contains instructions for GCC ("gcc diagnostic"). The use of a different compiler would result in these instructions being ignored.

The implementation of OpenMP compiled by GCC allows to integrate this technology without making changes in the frameworks structure, which would be necessary if various compilers were used in one project.

3   Analysis

We used Valgrind Callgrind profiler to analyze MpdRoots performance in terms of the bottlenecks that require optimization. This tool allows to build graphs of function invocations taking into account their runtime and number of calls. We obtained profiling data for the event reconstruction algorithm. Then we selected the fragment whose execution was the most time-consuming.

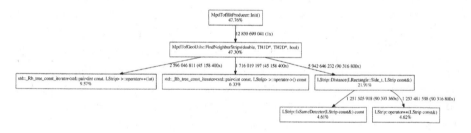

Fig. 1. Part of profiling results for "reco.C" macro.

The profiling results in Diagram 1 show that the longest time is spent on the aggregate of invocations of the FindNeighbourStrips function. We examined the source code to identify that this function contains a nested loop. We further examined the source code of the FindNeighbourStrips function to modify it for parallel processing.

Strips1 and strips2 are local variables. They are defined anew at each iteration of the external and internal loops respectively. The calls of methods for strips1 can result in a conflict. The Diagram 2 also shows calls of ROOTs Fill methods. Here conflicts are also possible, because the source code was made to process the original input data, not its copies. To prevent possible errors, the source code was isolated by means of C++ "mutex" and "lock guard" constructs.

This means that the parallel execution on different cores will not corrupt the result of the method we seek to optimize. In other words, the code fragment in question will be modified for parallel execution, while its result will not be affected.

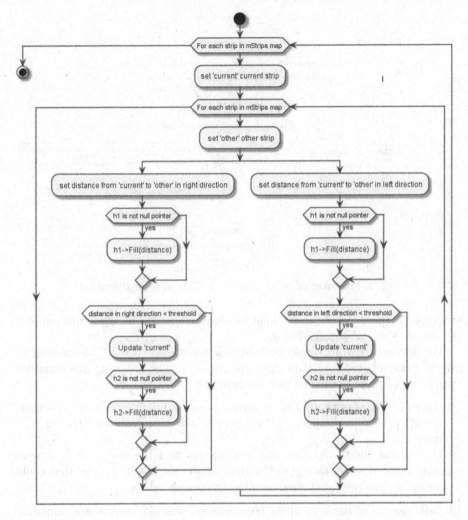

Fig. 2. illustrates the work of the method to be optimized, including the calls of ROOT functions.

3.1   Optimization

We used GCC version 4.9.3 to compile MpdRoots source code. This version supports OpenMP 4.0 and C++. OpenMP 4.0 places restrictions on the type of variables used in loops [17]. They can be integers, random access iterators or variables of a pointer type.

The selected algorithm contains a code fragment that can be optimized for parallel execution. Its implementation uses instances of classes described in Mpd-Root. Specifically, the loop requiring optimization traverses over the instances of MStripIT and MStripCIT classes. The types of data mentioned above serve

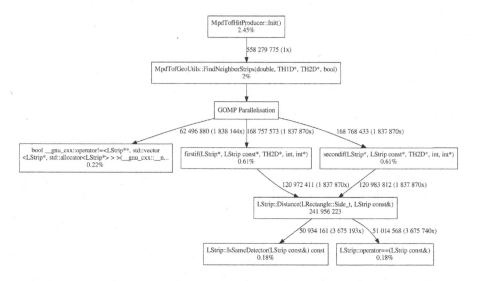

Fig. 3. Fragment of reco.C macro profiling after modification.

as wraps for the iterators and belong to MpdToF class. This structure impedes the use of OpenMP parallel loops.

We decided to wrap the looped over elements into vector. This allowed to use the "range-based for" loop supported in C_{++}. The following modifications were made to prepare the code for optimization:

- The code fragments run at each iteration were subdivided in two parts that, in theory, can be competing. Each part is now represented by the "inline" function.
- The critical code fragments executed at one and the same iteration were supplemented with "lock guard" object to prevent possible errors that could emerge due to several threads processing the same data.

The source code of the loop under consideration was modified to accommodate the said changes. We also added OpenMP directives that allow to run the code in parallel.

We employed two possible ways of using OpenMP. The first way involved the "range-based for" loop. The parallel regions were defined by means of "parallel", "single" and "task" directives. The "task" directive called the code fragment that corresponded to the loop body in the unmodified version of the source code.

The second way involved the iterator variable of integer type. The traversed-over elements had been wrapped into vector, so they were called as vector elements by their number. To allow parallel execution, we used "parallel for" directive with "schedule" option that described the load distribution between the threads. The best result was obtained when the option was defined as "auto".

On average, these two methods of parallel processing yielded the same acceleration. Diagram 3 shows the changes undergone by the call tree of functions in the examined fragment after the described modifications.

After the optimization, we performed data validation by comparing the results returned by the "sequential" and the optimized versions: the results were fully identical.

3.2   Tests

The tests were performed on a heterogeneous cluster HybriLIT and Windows Azure NC12. The following processors were used: Intel Xeon E5-2690v3, E5-2695 v2 and E5-2695 v3.
The parameters of the processors are provided in Table 1:

- E5-2695 v2 - 12 cores, 24 threads;
- E5-2695 v3 - 14 cores, 28 threads;
- E5-2690v3 - 12 cores, 24 threads.

The "libgomp" library allows to define the number of cores that will execute the parallel regions of the code. Furthermore, the library allows to allocate particular threads to be used for processing by their numbers. The diagram below shows the test results obtained on a CPU of cluster HybriLIT and Azure NC12 node. It also shows how the number of threads depends on the runtime of the code being optimized.

The Diagram 4 illustrates the dependence between the acceleration yielded (compared to the sequential processing) and the input data volume. The number of iterations with respect to one loop is shown on the x-axis. The diagram shows that the modified algorithm yields a stably better productivity.

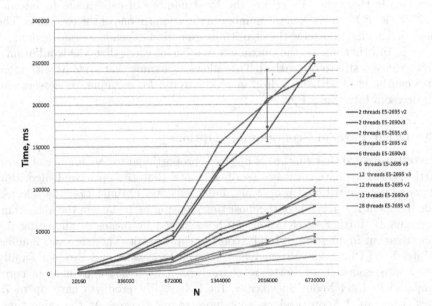

Fig. 4. Dependence between data volume and acceleration.

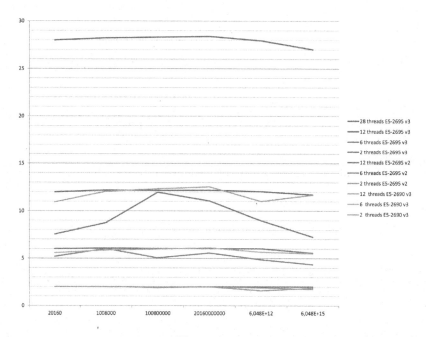

Fig. 5. Tesing.

The next Diagram 5 shows that the best result was obtained by 28 threads of E5-2695 v3 processor. Compared to the sequential version, the runtime improved by 23 times. The loop is nested, and the number of external and internal loop iterations is the same. Therefore, the total number of calls made to internal functions is N*N, where N is the number of iterations in one of the two loops. The curves in the diagram show the algorithms execution dependence on the number of cores. In other words, the maximum number of cores that yields additional productivity is still to be reached. This allows to assume that systems with more cores can be used without a drop in productivity: for example, processors and coprocessors Intel Xeon Phi.

3.3 Other Parallel Programming Options

The tests revealed that runtime is inversely proportional to the number of cores. Furthermore, we have already described above that the optimized algorithm allows to use multithread processing, but even after optimization the selected code fragment remains one of the most time-consuming regions in the algorithm.

Arguably, further acceleration can be achieved by means of allocating the code fragment in question to Intel Xeon Phi coprocessor. There are two families of Intel Xeon Phi [5,20]: Product Family x200 processors and Product Family x100 coprocessors. They both are characterized by a larger number of cores compared to Intel Xeon. Specifically, Intel Xeon Phi products have up to 73 cores, while Intel Xeon products, not more than 24 cores. At the same time, Intel Xeon processors have higher frequency than Intel Xeon Phi, which has an impact on software performance.

The icc compiler developed by Intel is used to work with Intel Xeon Phi coprocessors [15]. The compiler supports the OpenMP standard and provides tools for data exchange between the CPU and coprocessors. There are two ways to copy data to and from the coprocessor:

- by means of "#pragma offload" directive;
- by means of "Cilk" keywords allowing work with Shared Memory.

The use of the former data exchange model is limited by the restrictions on the data types that will be handled by the coprocessor. The data can be copied only if it is represented by arrays, scalars or user data structures without pointers [18].

The selected code fragment uses instances of ROOTs and MpdRoots classes that are not supported by this model. The latter model of data exchange provides better opportunities to work with user-defined classes. We should note, however, that the keywords for a class members and methods whose elements will be copied to the coprocessor must be defined in advance [14].

The algorithm in question uses data types and methods described in ROOT. Therefore, this model cannot be used to transfer data between the processor and coprocessor without changing ROOTs source code by means of including additional keywords, which would, in its turn, necessitate the use of the icc compiler.

However, the use of icc or any other compiler to work with MpdRoot and its dependences is impeded by the directives that specifically address GCC. Therefore, the transfer of data structures and their dependencies constitutes a problem that goes beyond MpdRoot package considered in this paper.

We have analysed another alternative to optimize the code in question the OpenACC standard. OpenACC allows to execute a parallel code not only on a CPU, but also on coprocessors. However, the use of OpenACC and Intel Shared Memory to parallelize loops that call external functions requires special directives to define such functions. This entails modification of a substantial part of MpdRoots and its dependencies source code.

We have earlier considered the possibility of using a GPU with CUDA to accelerate selected fragments of MpdRoot [6]. In particular, we described the ways to optimize a portion of Kalman filter by using CUDA technology. In that case, the optimization was possible, because the data types in ROOT can be easily modified to suite C++ standards. In addition, each iteration required the memory size comfortably available in GPUs.

When optimizing a code fragment in the ToF algorithm, we, conversely, have to deal with a changing size of input data, while the algorithm itself works with complex data structures.

3.4 Conclusions

This paper offers optimization of the ToF event reconstruction algorithms implementation for the MPD in order to allow its execution on multicore CPUs.

We analyzed the available implementation of the fragment in question and described source code modifications that resulted in an up to 23-fold acceleration be means of multithread processing on Intel Xeon processors. The optimization involved the use of OpenMP implementation provided by GCC compiler. We also considered the ways to perform optimization on a GPU and coprocessors and outlined the challenges that emerged when we attempted to port the source code to such devices.

Acknowledgments. This research was partially supported by Russian Foundation for Basic Research grant (projects no. 16-07-01113 and no. 16-07-00886). Microsoft Azure for Research Award (http://research.microsoft.com/en-us/projects/azure/) as well as the resource center "Computer Center of SPbU" (http://cc.spbu.ru/en) provided computing resources. The authors would like to acknowledge the Reviewers for the valuable recommendations that helped in the improvement of this paper.

References

1. Al-Turany, M., Bertini, D., Karabowicz, R., Kresan, D., Malzacher, P., Stockmanns, T., Uhlig, F.: The FairRoot framework. J. Phys. Conf. Ser. **396**, 022001 (2012). IOP Publishing
2. Bogdanov, A.V., Degtyarev, A., Stankova, E.N.: Example of a potential grid technology application in shipbuilding. In: 2007 International Conference on Computational Science and its Applications (ICCSA 2007), pp. 3–8 (2007)
3. Brun, R., Rademakers, F.: Root an object oriented data analysis framework. Nucl. Instrum. Methods Phys. Res. Sec. A: Accelerators, Spectrometers, Detectors and Associated Equipment **389**(1), 81–86 (1997)
4. Chao, A., Mess, K., Tigner, M., Zimmermann, F.: Handbook of Accelerator Physics and Engineering. World Scientific Publishing Company (2013)
5. Chrysos, G.: Intel® xeon phi coprocessor-the architecture. Intel Whitepaper 176 (2014)
6. Fatkina, A., Iakushkin, O., Tikhonov, N.: Application of GPGPUs and multicore CPUS in optimization of some of the MpdRoot codes. In: 25th Russian Particle Accelerator Conference (RuPAC 2016), St. Petersburg, Russia, 21–25 November 2016, pp. 416–418. JACOW, Geneva (2017)
7. Gankevich, I., Gaiduchok, V., Gushchanskiy, D., Tipikin, Y., Korkhov, V., Degtyarev, A., Bogdanov, A., Zolotarev, V.: Virtual private supercomputer: design and evaluation. In: Ninth International Conference on Computer Science and Information Technologies Revised Selected Papers, pp. 1–6, September 2013
8. Gankevich, I., Korkhov, V., Balyan, S., Gaiduchok, V., Gushchanskiy, D., Tipikin, Y., Degtyarev, A., Bogdanov, A.: Constructing virtual private supercomputer using virtualization and cloud technologies. In: Murgante, B., Misra, S., Rocha, A.M.A.C., Torre, C., Rocha, J.G., Falcão, M.I., Taniar, D., Apduhan, B.O., Gervasi, O. (eds.) ICCSA 2014. LNCS, vol. 8584, pp. 341–354. Springer, Cham (2014). doi:10.1007/978-3-319-09153-2_26
9. Grishkin, V., Iakushkin, O.: Middleware transport architecture monitoring: topology service. In: 2014 20th International Workshop on Beam Dynamics and Optimization (BDO), pp. 1–2 (2014)
10. Iakushkin, O.: Cloud middleware combining the functionalities of message passing and scaling control. In: EPJ Web of Conferences, vol. 108 (2016)

11. Iakushkin, O., Grishkin, V.: Messaging middleware for cloud applications: extending brokerless approach. In: 2014 2nd International Conference on Emission Electronics (ICEE), pp. 1–4 (2014)
12. Iakushkin, O., Sedova, O., Valery, G.: Application control and horizontal scaling in modern cloud middleware. In: Gavrilova, M.L., Tan, C.J.K. (eds.) Transactions on Computational Science XXVII. LNCS, vol. 9570, pp. 81–96. Springer, Heidelberg (2016). doi:10.1007/978-3-662-50412-3_6
13. Iakushkin, O., Grishkin, V.: Unification of control in P2P communication middleware: towards complex messaging patterns. AIP Conf. Proc. **1648**(1), 040004 (2015)
14. Iakushkin, O., Shichkina, Y., Sedova, O.: Petri nets for modelling of message passing middleware in cloud computing environments. In: Gervasi, O., Murgante, B., Misra, S., Rocha, A.M.A.C., Torre, C., Taniar, D., Apduhan, B.O., Stankova, E., Wang, S. (eds.) ICCSA 2016. LNCS, vol. 9787, pp. 390–402. Springer, Cham (2016). doi:10.1007/978-3-319-42108-7_30
15. Jeffers, J., Reinders, J.: Intel Xeon Phi Coprocessor High Performance Programming. Elsevier Science, Boston (2013)
16. Kisel, I.: Scientific and high-performance computing at fair. In: EPJ Web of Conferences, vol. 95, p. 01007. EDP Sciences (2015)
17. OpenMP Architecture Review Board: OpenMP application program interface version 4.0 (2013). http://www.openmp.org/wp-content/uploads/OpenMP4.0.0.pdf
18. Rahman, R.: Intel® Xeon Phi Coprocessor Architecture and Tools: The Guide for Application Developers. Expert's Voice in Microprocessors. Apress (2013)
19. Shichkina, Y., Degtyarev, A., Gushchanskiy, D., Iakushkin, O.: Application of optimization of parallel algorithms to queries in relational databases. In: Gervasi, O., Murgante, B., Misra, S., Rocha, A.M.A.C., Torre, C., Taniar, D., Apduhan, B.O., Stankova, E., Wang, S. (eds.) ICCSA 2016. LNCS, vol. 9787, pp. 366–378. Springer, Cham (2016). doi:10.1007/978-3-319-42108-7_28
20. Sodani, A., Gramunt, R., Corbal, J., Kim, H.S., Vinod, K., Chinthamani, S., Hutsell, S., Agarwal, R., Liu, Y.C.: Knights landing: second-generation intel xeon phi product. IEEE Micro **36**(2), 34–46 (2016)

Adaptation and Deployment of PanDA Task Management System for a Private Cloud Infrastructure

Oleg Iakushkin$^{(\boxtimes)}$, Daniil Malevanniy, Alexander Bogdanov, and Olga Sedova

Saint-Petersburg State University, St. Petersburg 199034, Russia
o.yakushkin@spbu.ru

Abstract. Management of computational infrastructure is a complicated task which, often employs user workloads delivery across multiple clusters. Criteria for such tasks distribution may vary: priority, transport costs, utilization of data, node capabilities, etc.

Such process happens to tasks devoted to the simulation and analysis of the results of high-energy physics experiments at CERN. For task distribution on massive data streams obtained during ATLAS experiment, "Production ANd Distributed Analysis system" (PanDA) was developed. It performs management of workloads delivery and execution in a geographically distributed cluster environment. This paper is devoted to the deployment of PanDA server in a private cluster setting.

This paper presents architecture and its implementation that allows, to run and embed PanDA system into existing computational solutions. It consists of a container, that isolates PanDA server its dependencies and environment from other system processes and an embedded Web interface which simplifies task management for end-users. In other words, our approach is focused on PanDA system deployment speed up by means of security layer simplification, containerization and stateless client web service implementation. System was tested on a heterogeneous geographically distributed Azure cloud nodes.

Keywords: Grid computing · User interface · API · Virtualization · Deploying

1 Introduction

The surge in data computation and communication capacity is making big data analytics increasingly accessible. There is a number of notable examples [2, 3, 11, 20]. In trading, a large number of expert opinions and analysis is processed to make stock market forecasts. In medicine, a patients current readings and history are harnessed to calculate risks connected to surgery or infection. Biology taps

---

O. Iakushkin—This research was partially supported by Russian Foundation for Basic Research grant (project no. 16-07-01113).

O. Gervasi et al. (Eds.): ICCSA 2017, Part V, LNCS 10408, pp. 438–447, 2017.
DOI: 10.1007/978-3-319-62404-4_32

into big data when analysing human genome or protein structure. Big data analytics raises two key issues: assigning jobs to computation resources and transferring data that needs to be processed [1,5,6,12]. These challenges have been traditionally actively addressed by particle physicists [7–10].

For instance, Large Hadron Collider particle collision detectors generate great quantities of raw data, which is then stored in a distributed data storage system and analysed using a distributed computing grid cluster [13,15,17,19].

Jobs in particle physics come in the form of code that analyses or models physical processes, links to experimental data input, and output destination in the distributed storage system [4,14,16,18].

There are a number of basic criteria used in assigning jobs, such as: memory size required to perform the job; the jobs focus on either data analysis or data generation; the jobs priority; and specifics of nodes. However, in a geographically distributed system transferring data to the processing site can take considerable time due to the large volume of data. Thus, it becomes a priority to assign jobs to nodes having due regard to the data transfer time. To meet this challenge, the researchers preparing to the ATLAS experiment developed the "Production and distributed analysis system (PanDA)".

PanDA showed an excellent performance when working with data generated by the ATLAS detector during the LHC initial run from 2007 to 2013 and was able to cope with the load increase from 10 thousand to over a million jobs per day. The system received a major upgrade during the collider hiatus of 2013–2014. It gained support for parallel computing with a job being automatically separated into sub-procedures processed at different nodes. Monitoring and assignment systems were also improved. What is more, the developers put ATLAS-specific system components into removable modules, enabling the use of PanDA in other physics experiments.

This paper discusses the PanDA-based software complex aimed at assigning general-purpose computing jobs to geographically distributed cluster nods.

2   Problem Statement

There is a number of distributed computing management systems. Most of them, like PanDA, emerged to manage research data processing. Initially systems like HTCondor and BPS were created to directly manage heterogeneous clusters. They were then followed by globus toolkit and gLite, which are aimed at effectively working with data stored in a distributed system and take the physical location of input data into account when assigning jobs.

PanDA belongs to the latter group. PandDAs development started in 2005, when the scientists were getting ready to process the first batch of ATLAS detector data, and it became apparent that the existing system, Capone, could not effectively harness available resources and had limited scalability.

PanDA enables better collaboration with Rucio, ATLAS distributed data management (DDM) system. PanDA job assignment system relies on assessing data transfer time. Another major feature of the system is that the end user is barely affected by the specific nature of the resources being used. It is also compatible with other grid management systems.

Despite the fact that the system was designed for a particular experiment in particle physics, experiment-specific components were taken out of it during development, and is now ready to be used in other fields. However, its deployment and integration into an existing service infrastructure may still be challenging.

The end user part of the system has not changed significantly since the beginning of PanDA development. To submit a task, the user needs to have the distributed system parts and an SSL certificate signed by a certificate authority (CA) known to the server, which imposes additional constraints on the environments users may work in. Furthermore, the system has no standardized API for working with service methods, making PanDA client harder to integrate with other programs.

Deploying PanDA server affects the working environment, which might be unacceptable in the existing infrastructure. What is more, configuring and debugging the servers available version takes a significant amount of time.

The aim of our project is to solve the issues connected to deploying and accessing this job assigning system for a geographically distributed cluster.

3   Solution Proposed

We have developed: a service interface that enables submitting jobs to the PanDA system; a web interface based on it, and a container-based solution for deploying the PanDA system and integrating it into an existing infrastructure.

We used containerization to develop a solution for prompt deployment of PanDA server in an isolated environment, a job submitting interface and a web user interface based on it. This allowed us to remove requirements for user working environment and expedite the deployment of PanDA in an existing infrastructure.

Let us consider PanDAs minimal configuration as shown in Fig. 1:

– PandaServer is a WSGI application which is connected to an apache server and interacts with users and nodes through the HTTPS protocol.

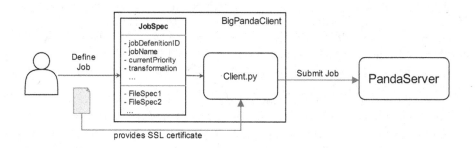

Fig. 1. PanDA component interaction chart.

- PandaPilot is a script running on cluster nodes which requests jobs from the server and executes them.
- BigPandaCient is a client program used to define jobs and submit them to the server.

All the components are written in Python and distributed as source code through PanDA project repository on GitHub.

3.1 PandaServer Deployment

PandaServer is the main system management component which handles all the activities connected to jobs distribution. It processes requests both form programs executing jobs (pilots), giving them access to the data on available jobs, queues, and clusters, and from clients, enabling user authentication and jobs distribution.

Our server deployment solution uses containerization, which allows to isolate the server environment and to ensure that the system is the same in any infrastructure.

The server runs in a container which is based on CentOS 7. When choosing between two database management systems supported by the server, OracleDB and MySQL, we opted for the latter, as it is easy to use and is distributed for free. CentOS uses the community-developed MariaDB version of MySQL. Server deployment process consists of a number of steps:

- The first step is installing the dependencies. Regrettably, they are not listed in PandaServer documentation. By trial and error we came up with the following list of dependencies: apache server; mod_ssl; mod_wsgi; gridsite; lfc-python; MySQL-python; MariaDB-server; pyOpenSSL; rucio-clients. All of them are available as packages in the YUM package-management utility.
- The second step is installing the server. The source code is downloaded from PanDAWMS project repository on GitHub. The server consists of two modules: panda-common and panda-server. The installation process is the same for both of them and is carried out by an installation script created using distutils (Annex I, Para 1).
- The third step is configuring the database. DBMS user rights are configured and ATLAS_PANDA database is created. Its structure is then restored from the dump distributed together with source code (Annex I, Para 2).
- The fourth step is adding the service and modifying crontab. First the scripts carrying out scheduled server tasks are added to the cron table. Then the httpd-pandasrv service is installed. After that, the httpd-pandasrv service runs and starts the system (Annex I, Para 3).

3.2 Server Deployment and Configuration

All server configuration files were removed from the container and are run together with it using Docker Volumes. Their templates may be found in PandaWMS project repository in panda-server package, but require some changes before use. Most of those changes are specifying the user and the group the server is going to run under, database password and server name. In addition to this, modules providing backward compatibility with Apache 2.2 server configuration files need to be connected. This feature is not available in assembled CentOS 7. An SSL certificate and a private key are also necessary to run the server. The modified versions of the configuration files templates are distributed along with the container.

If there is no preexisting CA in the infrastructure the server is deployed in, it will have to be created and the server certificate will need to be signed with it. The container receives configuration files and certificates by accessing the files in the host file system.

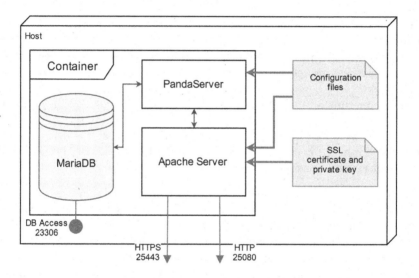

Fig. 2. Host-container interaction chart.

Once all the preliminary steps are taken, PandaServer container is started. It receives $DBUSER and $DBPWD environment variables matching the variables previously specified in the configuration files. The container starts PandaServer and provides three interfaces: open ports 25080 and 25443 bound to the corresponding host ports for HTTP and HTTPS connections to the server and port 23306 for database connection as shown in Fig. 2.

Once the server starts, at least one computing cluster and one queue must be defined in cloudconfig and schedconfig tables. The following fields need to be filled:

- For cloud config:
  - NAME is cluster name;
  - DESCRIPTION is cluster description;

- TIER1 is Tier-1 node of the respective queue. It must have the same value as NICKNAME and SITEID in schedconfig table;
- TIER1SE is the storage unit of the respective Tier-1 in the distributed data storage system;
- SERVER is server name;
- STATUS is queue status. Online means it is ready to accept jobs. Other options are: offline, test, brokeroff.

– For schedconfig:

- NICKNAME is the name of the queue, see TIER1 above;
- SYSTEM & JOBMANAGER is the infrastructure the grid working with the queue is based on: ondor, LSF, CREAM, etc. For virtual queues it is to be set;
- SITE is cluster name;
- STATUS is queue status. Online means it is ready to accept jobs. Other options are: offline, test, brokeroff.

More information on configuring these tables is available in PanDAWMS project documentation.

After these tables have been configured the server is ready. Its status can be checked by opening the http://localhost:25080/server-status page in any browser.

3.3   API and Web User Interface

PanDA takes instances of JobSpec class as input. They contain workload i.e., commands to be executed in the shell environment, the list of files the job will deal with, their location in the distributed data storage system, user name, the virtual organization the user belongs to, and other metadata.

The procedure for submitting jobs to PanDA system is as follows: the user defines the job together with all necessary metadata, then transfers it to the Client.py script which creates an HTTP request to the server, attaching a serialized job and SSL user certificate to it.

Therefore, in order to submit a job to the system, the user must install the BigPandaClient and get a certificate signed by a CA known to the server, which might sometimes be inconvenient as shown in Fig. 3. What is more, an

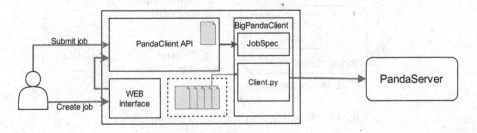

Fig. 3. Submitting a job using BigPandaClient.

intermediate layer translating the jobs into the PanDA standard is needed every time third party software components are integrated into the PanDA client.

We created a job submitting API which does not need the user to have PanDA distributed parts installed in the working environment. It is implemented as a web service written using Flask microframework. We also developed a web interface for submitting and tracking jobs based on it.

Login and password are used to authorize users instead of SSL certificates. The certificate for submitting jobs to PanDA system can be saved in the user profile and then automatically attached to that users jobs.

The jobs the API works with are transferred in HTTP POST request body. They consist of code which includes execution environment, input data location and output destination in the distributed data storage system or, if the volume is low, the data itself, as well as the metadata list. Authentication information is also transferred in the request body. After the user is authorized and the job is submitted, the service converts it into the PanDA server format and, if necessary, uploads the data into the distributed data storage system. It then sends the converted job and the user certificate to BigPandaClient. If the user has not provided a certificate, the job may be sent with the standard service certificate.

This way the user only needs to register in the service and fill in a web interface form in order to submit a job as shown in Fig. 4. It has also become much easier to integrate PanDA job submission feature into other program components: the job only needs to be converted into an appropriate text format, not

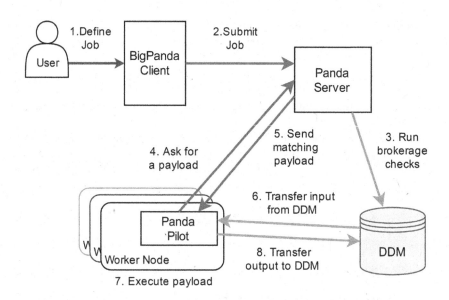

Fig. 4. Submitting a task through our interface.

into a JobSpec instance as before. As a result, we have removed the dependency on PanDA distributed parts.

Attaching a certificate to a user account makes it possible to integrate our interface into existing PanDA user authorization infrastructure. All the features PanDA users have access to, such as access to certain queues and express submission quota, are also available when submitting jobs through our interface. At the same time, the standard service certificate allows users who do not have their own certificate to submit jobs, taking advantage of PanDAs flexible access control. For instance, a separate computing cluster or a queue may be assigned only for the jobs submitted with the standard service certificate.

Implementation was tested on a heterogeneous geographically distributed Azure cloud nodes:

- Workers: Azure General Purpose D2 nodes with 2 vCores, 7 GB RAM, 100 GB SSD on each node in 5 different regions: West Europe; Brazil South; Southeast Asia; Japan West.
- PAnDA Server and UI host - a High Memory D12 node with 2 vCores, 28 GB RAM and 200 GB SSD in South Central US.

Deployment was partly automatic due to containerized infrastructure.

3.4   Conclusions

The solution we developed for integrating the distributed computing management system consists of two parts. The first part is the container-based PandaServer deployment system. It streamlines the installation process and isolates the server from the environment, protecting the operating system from unexpected influence. Users can start with PandaServer minimal configuration image and then expand upon it adding layers with new components to create a configuration which fits a particular application.

The second part is the client service interface with simplified authentication process, which enables integrating PanDA job submission feature into third-party software components without modifying the environment to accomodate BigPandaClient. We also created a clean web interface for submitting simple jobs from a browser working in any environment.

Thus, the PanDA deployment system we developed makes it easy to integrate PanDA into existing service infrastructure, does not prevent subsequent modification and simplifies the use of the system by end users.

Acknowledgments.. This research was partially supported by Russian Foundation for Basic Research grant (project no. 16-07-01113). Microsoft Azure for Research Award (http://research.microsoft.com/en-us/projects/azure/) as well as the resource center "Computer Center of SPbU" (http://cc.spbu.ru/en) provided computing resources. The authors would like to acknowledge the Reviewers for the valuable recommendations that helped in the improvement of this paper.

References

1. Bogdanov, A.V., Degtyarev, A., Stankova, E.N.: Example of a potential grid technology application in shipbuilding. In: 2007 International Conference on Computational Science and Its Applications (ICCSA 2007), pp. 3–8 (2007)
2. Borodin, M., De, K., Garcia, J., Golubkov, D., Klimentov, A., Maeno, T., Vaniachine, A., et al.: Scaling up ATLAS production system for the LHC run 2 and beyond: project ProdSys2. J. Phys. Conf. Ser. **664**, 062005 (2015). IOP Publishing
3. De, K., Klimentov, A., Maeno, T., Nilsson, P., Oleynik, D., Panitkin, S., Petrosyan, A., Schovancova, J., Vaniachine, A., Wenaus, T.: The future of panda in atlas distributed computing. J. Phys. Conf. Ser. **664**, 062035 (2015). IOP Publishing
4. Dworak, A., Ehm, F., Charrue, P., Sliwinski, W.: The new cern controls middleware. J. Phys. Conf. Ser. **396**, 012017 (2012). IOP Publishing
5. Gankevich, I., Gaiduchok, V., Gushchanskiy, D., Tipikin, Y., Korkhov, V., Degtyarev, A., Bogdanov, A., Zolotarev, V.: Virtual private supercomputer: design and evaluation. In: Ninth International Conference on Computer Science and Information Technologies Revised Selected Papers, pp. 1–6 (2013)
6. Gankevich, I., Korkhov, V., Balyan, S., Gaiduchok, V., Gushchanskiy, D., Tipikin, Y., Degtyarev, A., Bogdanov, A.: Constructing virtual private supercomputer using virtualization and cloud technologies. In: Murgante, B., et al. (eds.) ICCSA 2014. LNCS, vol. 8584, pp. 341–354. Springer, Cham (2014). doi:10.1007/978-3-319-09153-2_26
7. Grishkin, V., Iakushkin, O.: Middleware transport architecture monitoring: topology service. In: 2014 20th International Workshop on Beam Dynamics and Optimization (BDO), pp. 1–2 (2014)
8. Iakushkin, O.: Cloud middleware combining the functionalities of message passing and scaling control. In: EPJ Web of Conferences, vol. 108 (2016)
9. Iakushkin, O., Grishkin, V.: Messaging middleware for cloud applications: extending brokerless approach. In: 2014 2nd International Conference on Emission Electronics (ICEE), pp. 1–4 (2014)
10. Iakushkin, O., Sedova, O., Valery, G.: Application control and horizontal scaling in modern cloud middleware. In: Gavrilova, M.L., Tan, C.J.K. (eds.) Transactions on Computational Science XXVII. LNCS, vol. 9570, pp. 81–96. Springer, Heidelberg (2016). doi:10.1007/978-3-662-50412-3_6
11. Iakushkin, O., Grishkin, V.: Unification of control in p2p communication middleware: towards complex messaging patterns. In: AIP Conference Proceedings, vol. 1648, no. 1, p. 040004 (2015)
12. Iakushkin, O., Shichkina, Y., Sedova, O.: Petri nets for modelling of message passing middleware in cloud computing environments. In: Gervasi, O., et al. (eds.) ICCSA 2016. LNCS, vol. 9787, pp. 390–402. Springer, Cham (2016). doi:10.1007/978-3-319-42108-7_30
13. Johnston, W.E., Dart, E., Ernst, M., Tierney, B.: Enabling high throughput in widely distributed data management and analysis systems: lessons from the LHC. In: TERENA Networking Conference (TNC) (2013)
14. Klimentov, A., Buncic, P., De, K., Jha, S., Maeno, T., Mount, R., Nilsson, P., Oleynik, D., Panitkin, S., Petrosyan, A., et al.: Next generation workload management system for big data on heterogeneous distributed computing. J. Phys. Conf. Ser. **608**, 012040 (2015). IOP Publishing

15. Korenkov, V., Pelevanyuk, I., Zrelov, P., Tsaregorodtsev, A.: Accessing distributed computing resources by scientific communities using dirac services (2016)
16. Maeno, T., De, K., Klimentov, A., Nilsson, P., Oleynik, D., Panitkin, S., Petrosyan, A., Schovancova, J., Vaniachine, A., Wenaus, T., et al.: Evolution of the atlas panda workload management system for exascale computational science. J. Phys. Conf. Ser. **513**, 032062 (2014). IOP Publishing
17. Maeno, T., De, K., Panitkin, S.: Pd2p: Panda dynamic data placement for atlas. J. Phys. Conf. Ser. **396**, 032070 (2012). IOP Publishing
18. Maeno, T.: Panda: distributed production and distributed analysis system for atlas. J. Phys. Conf. Ser. **119**, 062036 (2008). IOP Publishing
19. Maeno, T., De, K., Wenaus, T., Nilsson, P., Stewart, G., Walker, R., Stradling, A., Caballero, J., Potekhin, M., Smith, D., et al.: Overview of atlas panda workload management. J. Phys. Conf. Ser. **331**, 072024 (2011). IOP Publishing
20. Shichkina, Y., Degtyarev, A., Gushchanskiy, D., Iakushkin, O.: Application of optimization of parallel algorithms to queries in relational databases. In: Gervasi, O., et al. (eds.) ICCSA 2016. LNCS, vol. 9787, pp. 366–378. Springer, Cham (2016). doi:10.1007/978-3-319-42108-7_28

A Concept of Unified E-Health Platform for Patient Communication and Monitoring

Suren Abrahamyan$^{(\boxtimes)}$, Serob Balyan, Avetik Muradov,
Natalia Kulabukhova, and Vladimir Korkhov

Saint Petersburg State University,
7/9 Universitetskaya nab., St. Petersburg 199034, Russia
suro7@live.com, serob.balyan@gmail.com,
avet.muradov@gmail.com, kulabukhova.nv@gmail.com,
vkorkhov@spbu.ru

Abstract. With the help of Augmentative and Alternative Communication (AAC, which includes all types of communications except oral speech) and modern mobile technologies, it is possible to allow people with speech and language disorders to interact with each other and eliminate the relational barrier.

Also it could be important from doctors' perspective to be informed about condition of patients with such disorders regardless location, make behavioral analysis and organize virtual concilia with other doctors.

So, the combination of this two ideas would allow to create a platform that would solve communication problem for disabled people from one side, and allow doctors to monitor patients' communication, store medical records for organizing group discussions and diagnosis from another side.

In this article we suggest a concept of combination of described two approaches in one unified E-Health platform. We presented architecture of server and mobile applications, optimal choice of data storages and communication protocols for operating in one private network.

Keywords: E-Health · AAC · Real-time messaging · Data storage · Mobile communication · Application server · Communication protocols

1 Introduction

The American Speech and Hearing Association (ASHA) states that communication is the essence of human life and all people have the right to communicate to the fullest extent possible [1]. For people with autism spectrum disorder (ASD) or diseases that cause speech disorders, communication is about having the ability to show people their unique personality, beliefs, feelings and ideas but in order to be successful they must have the right tools and support to develop functional communication skills.

People with autism or with other forms of speech disorders often demonstrate significant challenges in the areas of everyday communication and social interaction. These challenges range from mild to severe, depending on the cognitive abilities of the person. Many people with autism struggle having difficulty effectively using language for the purposes of communication. Some people are nonverbal and unable to speak,

© Springer International Publishing AG 2017
O. Gervasi et al. (Eds.): ICCSA 2017, Part V, LNCS 10408, pp. 448–462, 2017.
DOI: 10.1007/978-3-319-62404-4_33

some have speech that is nonfunctional and other people have extensive vocabularies and are able to talk about certain topics in good detail. They also may have difficulties in nonverbal communication, like through hand gestures, eye contact and facial expressions. Understanding and relating to other people, and taking part in everyday family, school, work and social life, is harder for them usually.

A study published in 2017 by the journal Nature, found that neurotypical peers of people on the autism spectrum often quickly develop a negative bias towards them in face to face social situations [2]. However, these biases were not present when the conversation took place without audio visual cues.

Because many autistic children are delayed in their use of language and some autistic adults don't use speech, therefore, other methods of communication need to be established.

There are many communication solutions and tools available for children with autism and other diseases that cause speech or communication disorders. Current research tells us that children with autism often possess many strengths that allow them to be successful users of symbol and text-based communication strategies.

2   Using Augmentative and Alternative Communication (AAC) and PECS

Augmentative and alternative communication (AAC) includes all forms of communications (other than oral speech) that are used to express thoughts, needs, wants, and ideas. All people use AAC when make facial expressions or gestures, use symbols or pictures, or write.

Although AAC describes any form of language other than speech that helps a person in social-communicative interactions, AAC users are not obligated to stop using speech if they are able to do so. Because autistic sometimes resort to challenging behaviors to meet their needs and express their feelings, the use of an AAC device can give them a primary means of social communicative interactions with interlocutor. AAC aids and devices are used to enhance their intercourse.

AAC can be used at home and when patient goes out. AAC includes

- sign language;
- gestures;
- pictures, photos, objects, or videos;
- written words;
- computer, tablets, mobile phones or other electronic devices.

AAC is divided into two groups: *unaided* and *aided*.

Unaided AAC strategies rely on the user's body to convey messages. Unaided strategies include gestures, body language, and/or sign language. Unaided communication strategies must be understood by others in order to be effective.

Aided strategies require the use of tools and/or equipment in addition to the user's body. Aided communication methods can range from paper and pencil to communication books or boards to devices that produce written output and/or voice output.

Electronic communication aids allow the user to use picture symbols, letters and complete phrases to create messages.

Special augmentative aids, such as picture and symbol communication boards and electronic devices, are available to help people express themselves. This may increase social interaction, school/work performance, and feelings of self-worth.

Here are some of Examples of AAC devices

- Picture Exchange Communication System (PECS), where the person uses a picture to request or express something [3],
- Sign language,
- Communication boards and communication books, where the person can use words, photos and/or symbols,
- Communication cue cards, used primarily with people who are verbal, can be a reminder of what to say and provide an alternative means to communication in stressful situations,
- Conversation books, which can use text, pictures or photographs to support conversation,
- Voice output communication tools like voice synthesizers that generate digitized speech when the person presses a symbol or button.

Current information and communication technologies allow people to interact via both verbal and written speech with the help of internet and telecommunication services like SMS or phone calls. Interacting in a distance for people with autism or others who have speech disorders is still a challenging problem due to limitations of text input and/or speech. According to Newell et al. [4], communication and information technology systems have great potential to enhance the quality of life for people with cognitive disabilities by helping to keep them intellectually and physically active, and by providing methods of communication that reduce social isolation.

Because autistics are not fluent in typing on a computer or on any other handheld devices but still can use them, the simplest solution to express feelings on a distance can be by selection of special symbols or images and sent over the network. For that purpose PECS, and as the easiest, most convenient and suitable option of it - pictograms, selected. The pictogram is a sign that displays the most important recognizable features of an object, an object or phenomenon, to which it indicates, most often in a schematic form.

At present, pictograms have a highly specialized role (for example, road signs, icons-elements of the computer's graphical user interface, etc.), in contrast to the usual alphabetic letter capable of displaying the multilevel character of the natural language. Here are examples of food pictograms (see Fig. 1).

But because Autistic children are very irritable and spend too much attention to secondary aspects of image beside main scope of information. Attributes like color, shapes, form, etc. attract too much attention and children spend lots of time to select an appropriate image to express their feelings or thoughts. That's why the colorful images should be replaced with pictograms that are simpler and clearer for Autistic people (see Fig. 2).

It's widely known that such people conceive such cards information way better than spoken or written language [3].

Fig. 1. Examples of food pictograms

Fig. 2. Dog representation in black-and-white pictogram

Despite "standard" texting and chatting abilities and PECS, there should be provided another form of interaction - synthetic speech. With the help of sounded and expressive pictograms, not only children, but also adults, who are deprived of natural speech for various reasons, can become understood in expressing their needs and desires. On the other hand, for children who received message and then applied for vocal representation, the information became more natural and real-life. The combination of three methods - Text, PECS and voice, can highly eliminate the communication barrier between interlocutors and enhance the quality of the conversation to the highest possible limit.

3 Monitoring and Control

Children with speech and write disorders have to be supervised by their doctors. This kind of supervision can help children treatment and can improve their quality of life. Studies show [5, 6] that significant correlation was found between intensity of supervision and improvement scores in IQ. Intensity of supervision was reliably associated with amount of IQ change between intake and follow-up. These findings show that intensity of supervision together with intensity of treatment, treatment method and pretreatment functioning may affect outcome for children with speech and write disorders, in particular, with Autism Spectrum Disorders (ASD) and may be effective in increasing intellectual and adaptive functioning who receive Early and Intensive Behavioral Intervention (EIBI). The supervision by doctors can be done not only in a traditional way like face-to-face communication, teaching, but also with the help of modern information and communication technologies (ICT) (if child's age and condition allows to use such technologies). Suppose that children and doctors could contact each other and message directly using the familiar PECS system with the help of mobile devices. In this case doctors can use all advantages of remote communication: assign tasks to children, talk to them and analyze answers regardless of location. Also children can contact their doctors and have conversations if needed. This kind of approach can give doctors extra supervision capabilities.

As mentioned studies show intensive intervention affects the outcome in a positive way. So, if children could message each other, then giving doctors access to their conversation (child-child) could enhance potential of supervision and make possible to do analyzes regarding children's behavior and peculiarities of communication that they couldn't do in a traditional approach.

Also, children have to be under certain control by their parents. In addition to messaging, it would be useful for them to know children's geolocation in any moment of time. In this case they could know their children place without additional questions: are they at school or coming home and so on. As children with speech and write disorders have difficulties in communication, they might not contact other people in surrounding if they get lost and could not describe their exact location to their parents so it is important for parents to have information about the location of their children to prevent them to be lost.

Another way of control is to give children possibility to have so-called "alarm or emergency button". When they are in trouble or fill bad or get lost and have not enough time or cannot or don't want to connect parents by writing messages to inform about their condition they could press this button and parents would be immediately informed that something is wrong with the kid and would take further actions.

So, moderate behavior control by doctors as well as by parents could improve quality of life of children and decrease amount of unexpected situations.

4 Group Discussions

Group collaboration and teamwork are widespread not only in modern organizations but also in a medical sphere. Collaboration itself is a key feature of any organizational type. But nowadays modern information and communication technologies (ICT) expand the possibilities of collaborators and give them solutions that they did not have before. E-collaboration enables interaction between people with the help of network services, applications, software or hardware [7]. Doctors could use such IT tools as shared whiteboards, blogs, wikis, online brainstorming during their interactive concilia. Group of doctors who use e-collaboration toolkits for group decision-making purposes, usually requires infrastructure with special hardware and/or software to support data processing, storing, visualization and reliable Internet connection. But this kind of requirements can be eliminated with the help of mobile technologies – if every participant works with his/her own mobile device (smartphone/tablet) and with nothing else (Bring Your Own Device – BYOD). In this case no additional hardware would be needed. This approach could be useful for mobile groups whose tasks can be done without need of traditional office spaces and regardless of location. Previously we had developed such solution called "Teambrainer", which encapsulates such tools and techniques as idea generation, brainstorming, voting, analyzing, data storing and visualization [8]. "Teambrainer" helps to organize meetings, large discussions in a simpler way and regardless of group's location. As it doesn't need any additional network devices to work, it can be used in places without network infrastructures or even electricity. The system consists of different applications each of which has its unique role in whole collaboration process.

As data concerning children sometimes have to be analyzed by a group of doctors, they could use proposed system with all its advantages: organize virtual concilium regardless of location, discuss children's behavioral specificities, make diagnosis, come to a conclusion and store all necessary data into one place – the organizer's tablet. It would be useful if this data, which could be text information or different files, could be uploaded to the centralized server for further analyses and storing, later when there is an opportunity to connect to the Internet.

5 Comparison of Existing Solutions

From touch screen phones to tablet devices, mobile computing power and user-friendly interfaces have never been cheaper or more universally available. That makes possible and bursts creation and spreading of mobile AAC applications. While some of them fulfill voice synthesis, others cover PECS implementation and/or text/emoji-based communication. In this chapter we'll present some examples of such applications and bring out pros and cons of using them.

So, taking into account above mentioned approaches, and the fact that our research area firstly covers Russian audience, we have chosen listed criterias for AAC-enabled applications comparison:

1. Mobile device compatibility
2. Instant messaging
3. Voice synthesizer
4. Available pictogram count
5. Russian localization
6. Parental/doctor monitoring/control

5.1   Avaz App

The app [9] is the world's best speech synthesizer AAC with professional narration for people with speech limitations. It have an easily customizable interface with 15000+ pictures. It have 3 research-based, graded picture vocabularies, and a "Core Words" set that will help a child begin to communicate. Application is keyboard-enabled and has support for saving and loading text, a Quick response feature for frequently-used messages, and a picture-assisted text prediction. Also Avaz has an alarm button. Application do not include remote direct communication, and only for in-room use. Despite application already designated to be used for several major languages, Russian language is not yet supported. Application offers both "lite" version with minimal capabilities which is free, and "Pro" version, that require paid subscription.

5.2   Poymi Menya

The mobile application [10] is an artificial substitute for speech for non-speaking Russian people or for those whose speech is little understood by others. It uses black-and-white pictograms, and pronounces the voice according to formed sentence. Pictograms are divided into 9 thematic palettes. The user has the opportunity to compose three own palettes by choosing them from the application dictionary. The dictionary of the application contains more than 450 words. Voice behind the pictograms narrated by a professional narrator. Like Avaz, this application is also for personal use and cannot involve others to participate remotely and send messages. Application is available for android devices and is paid.

5.3.   SymbolChat

A Finnish application [11] developed in 2012 for personal computers under Windows that supports instant messaging. It features easily customizable interface with 2000 pictograms. Application also have voice narration when user clicks on pictogram from touch screen. SymbolChat do not have mobile compatibility and limited to Windows PC's only. It do not include Russian pictograms and voice output.

5.4   OLA Mundo

The first RAAC (Remote Augmentative and alternative communication) application for Apple mobile devices, with a customizable interface and speech synthesizer [12]. It have advanced Text-To-Speech voice functionality. OLA Mundo allow users to communicate distantly. Application is designated for English audience only, and require subscription to use it.

5.5   Lango

The Lango application [11] developed in 2003 with a pictographic language for users and with more than 300 pictograms. It was released in Java and Brew applications for mobile phones. To communicate, participants used ZLango icon language to create a new type of SMS messages called ZMS and they using ZLango icons instead of words. The icons weren't exact, and most of them had more than one meanings: Each icon meanings that Lango intended for were suggested by interested users who invented own individual meanings for icons. Only mobile network operators were able transmit ZMS, in particular several European ones. How can we assume, there weren't option for voice narration. The project was suspended from 2014.

Summarizing results based on chosen criterias from above described applications, we created Table 1 below:

Table 1. Application comparison based on chosen criterias

	Mobile application	Instant messaging	Voice narrator	Number of pictograms	Russian	Parental control
Poymi menya	+	−	+	450	+	−
Avaz app	+	−	+	15000	−	+
Lango	−	+	−	300	−	−
SymbolChat	−	+	+	2000	−	−
Ola Mundo	+	+	+	500	−	+

As we can see, none of applications from the list supports all the criterias at the same time we highlighted.

6 Concept

Above discussed criterias are functional aspects of our desired AAC-enabled solution. On the other hand, to meet such functionalities, the technical side of solution must support several quality attributes:

- Availability – remote communication regardless time and location,
- Performance – support of network and storage features without terminations and lags,
- Reliability – any data or actions are consistent and stored safely,
- Flexibility – communication should be established regardless of user's device and OS type,
- Accessibility – same data can be accessed both from children and parents/doctors.

Summarizing, we propose concept of unified E-Health platform for patient communication and monitoring that would support functional aspects of our desired AAC-enabled solution and meet technical quality attributes (see Fig. 3).

To support remote communication and data collection for further analysis and history, user's connectivity regardless time/location, the centralized server with Internet access must be established. Client-server architecture based on multiprocessor supercomputers is the basis for different types of telemedicine systems [13]. In this case software like Mosix or FishDirector have to be used to manage resources and monitor overall system [14]. Centralized application server should organize user authentication, handle requests coming from users, log sessions, lead requests to appropriate databases and pull data back to users. For more generic use it should provide API's for client connections.

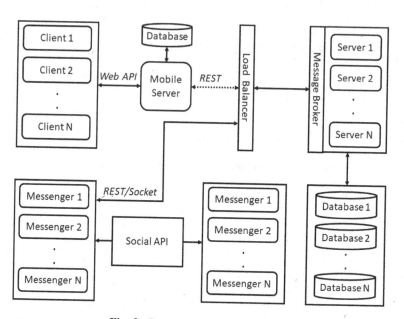

Fig. 3. Proposed system architecture

There are several types of data to store in server – user's personal data, roles, message history, access tokens, geolocation data etc. Main part of data belongs to exact users and there should be a hierarchical and relational model of storing (parents need to have access their children's data, doctors need to know some information of their patients). The best practice of storing relational data is to use SQL database. But some data like access tokens, user credentials needs to be accessed much often than others, so to make server work faster and response users in time, we propose to use in-memory database. Concerning geolocation data – We could save it into SQL database. But this type of data should be sent periodically from all users, and if users' amount is large enough saving geolocation could cause heavy load over physical storage by slowing down SQL database response time and make it a bottleneck for whole system. Thus, to eliminate this kind of problem we need to separate geolocation data from the main database and use another data storage. As this data itself does not have hierarchical construction or any nested information besides geo coordinates, there is no need of SQL storage. In other hand some benchmarks show [15, 16] that due to their non-relational structure some NoSQL document storages act faster on write requests than SQL storages for denormalized data. So the suitable solution is to use NoSQL document storage.

For files it would be more efficient to use object storage than file system. Storing data in an object-oriented structure involves excluding the high-level abstraction provided by the file system and replacing it with an abstraction of a container object. This object contains not only user data and standard attributes, but also metadata – auxiliary and additional information that allows operations on objects more efficiently.

We suggest that server should provide REST [17] API over HTTP for communication, as its main goal is the use of predefined set of stateless operations. Using a stateless protocol and predefined operations REST systems provide high performance, reliability and the ability to grow by reusing components that can be managed without affecting the whole system even during a run-time.

For messaging some message transfer protocol should be chosen. There are two types of such protocols: brokered and brokerless. As clients in our system cannot connect each other directly brokered protocol must be used. Chosen protocol have to be lightweight and use minimum amount of transfer data to reduce energy consumption on mobile devices.

7 Prototype Realization

Using proposed concept we have built system prototype based on open source toolkits for testing efficiency. As a programming language for server application we have chosen NodeJS because of its non-blocking IO, and easy-to-use principles. PostgreSQL was chosen form main SQL database. In comparison with other open-source SQL storages such as MySQL and MariaDB PostgreSQL uses multi-version concurrency control (MVCC) by default and standard row-level locking as an option [18]. PostgreSQL has many of the database features that commercial DBs like Oracle, DB2, or MS-SQL has, including triggers, views, inheritance, sequences, stored procedures, cursors, and user-defined data types. It also supports same replication scenarios as MySQL but also offers additional support for multi master, multi-slave replication from a third-party vendor [18]. PostgreSQL has better support of SQL standards and also, benchmarks show that it has big advantages at complex read query and slight advantages at simple read query (see Fig. 4) [19].

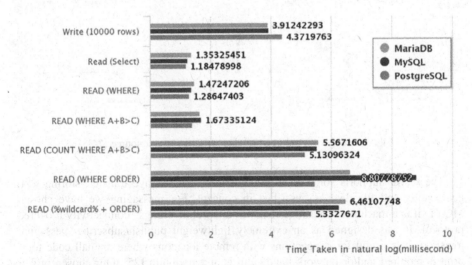

Fig. 4. PostgreSQL, MySQL, MariaDB performance comparison; source [19]

We use redis as an in-memory storage. It does atomic updates by locking, and supports asynchronous replication. It is reported to support about 100K gets/sets per second on an 8-core server and mainly suitable for providing high performance computing to small amount of data [20]. Nowadays it is the most popular key-value store by DB-Engines rating [21].

For document storage we have observed two variants: MongoDB and CouchDB. MongoDB is the most popular document storage. It stores data in a binary JSON-like format called BSON. CouchDB uses text JSON [22]. In MongoDB, unlike CouchDB, it is possible to save part of data in RAM, which increase performance. According to the article [23] MongoDB outperforms CouchDB both in writing and reading speeds. So our choice was made in favor of MongoDB.

Concept proposes to use object storage for storing files of different formats. Therefore we have investigated different object storages, in particular Ceph Object Storage and Openstack Swift. They have different architectures and act in a different way: OpenStack Swift transfers data through proxy servers which then distribute data to the storage nodes. When using multiple proxies load balancer have to be used for distributing workload. In other hand Ceph clients connect directly to the storage nodes eliminating any bottleneck and instead of proxies like Swift, Ceph uses monitors that distribute cluster maps to the clients and storage nodes [24]. It is visible from benchmarks that Swift's performance is higher than Ceph's when the size of transferred data is more than 50–100 MB (see Fig. 5). To reduce response time from storage on high loads (as many doctors can act with files simultaneously) we have chosen Openstack Swift as an object storage for our prototype.

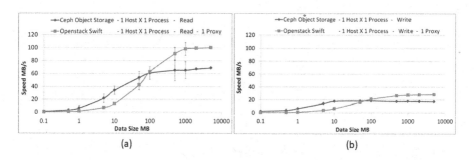

Fig. 5. Swift vs. Ceph read (a) and write (b) speed; source [24]

The server supports some basic functionality like message transfer, storing text, geolocation and file data as described in concept. For messaging we have chosen MQTT. It is a machine-to-machine (M2M)/"Internet of Things" connectivity brokered protocol. It was designed as an extremely lightweight publish/subscribe messaging transport. It is useful for connections with remote locations where a small code footprint is required and/or network bandwidth is at a premium [25]. Our chosen broker library for NodeJS - Mosca [26] supports publish/subscribe mechanism provided by Redis, which makes it to act faster, than with hard-drive database storages.

We have ran the server application on a 4-core machine and tested it to see its maximum capabilities in terms of requests count.

As tests show (see Fig. 6), server works fine when request count is less than 500–600 per second (average response count is less than 100 ms and throughput is equal to request count). After that response time starts slowing down and throughput doesn't change.

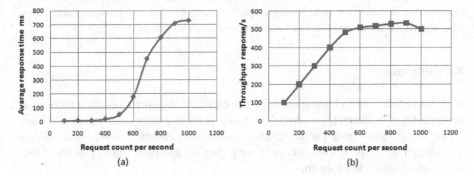

Fig. 6. Server average response time (a) and throughput (b) depending on requests count

Also we have tested Openstack Swift object storage with realistic "CRUD" scenario, during which each connected user sends different count of Create, Read, Update or Delete operation requests to the Swift proxy. In our two test cases users sent 30% of Create, 30% of Read, 15% of Update and 15% of Delete requests with file sizes of 1–5 MB during a fixed period of a time. The first test case was done with 20 concurrent users, the second one with 40. Also the same scenarios were repeated with different replication count (1–3) options of Swift proxy (see Fig. 7).

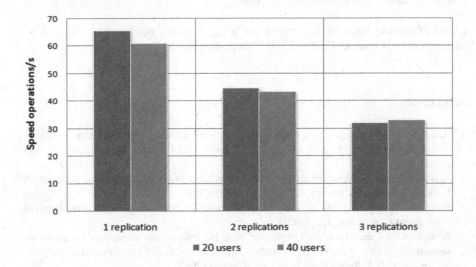

Fig. 7. Openstack swift benchmark depending on concurrent users' and replication count

7.1 Mobile Application Prototype

We have built a prototype of communicator application running on Android OS that allowed children to interact with each other [27]. Initially the application used VK social API for user registration, authentication and transmitting messages. In further releases we implemented also local-server option for registration, message transfer and history based on our proposed concept. Application have 500 black-and-white pictograms that organized in functional groups that represent their common characteristics. Also the application sends device's GPS coordinates to parent every 10 s.

8 Conclusion

With help of modern technologies, AAC can eliminate the communication barrier and allow children to interact. Another challenging point is patient observation and monitoring organization from parents'/doctors' perspective. Studies shown, that children with speech and write disorders could have higher IQ and better quality of life if they are under supervision of doctors.

So we proposed a concept that encapsulates the AAC enabled mobile technologies and patient monitoring opportunity in unified E-Health platform. Based on our suggested concept we developed a provisional mobile application where use of digital analogs of special card-pictograms improves interaction and social involvement of users.

We proffer other stand-alone mobile application system, which helps doctors to organize virtual concilia and analyze information regardless location, without any additional network devices and connections. Later, while there is an internet connection, they could upload necessary data for further storing and accessing to the server. Thus, server prototype was implemented also, for supporting communication between mobile applications. Several tests were conducted to determine peak performance and throughput during normal and extreme loads.

Acknowledgments. Research was carried out using computational resources provided by Resource Center "Computer Center of SPbU" (http://cc.spbu.ru).

References

1. American Speech-Language-Hearing Association: Augmentative and alternative communication: Knowledge and skills for service delivery. ASHA Leader **7**(Suppl. 22), 97–106 (2002)
2. Sasson, N.J., et al.: Neurotypical peers are less willing to interact with those with autism based on thin slice judgments. Sci. Rep. **6**, 40700 (2016)
3. Frost, L., Bondy, A.: PECS: The Picture Exchange Communication System. Pyramid Educational Consultants, Inc. (2002)
4. Newell, A.F., Carmichael, A., Gregor, P., Alm, N.: Information technology for cognitive support. In: Jacko, J.A., Sears, A. (eds.) The Human-Computer Interaction Handbook, pp. 464–481. L. Erlbaum Associates Inc., Hillsdale (2002)

5. Eikeseth, S., Hayward, D., Gale, C., Gitlesen, J.P., Eldevik, S.: Intensity of supervision and outcome for preschool aged children receiving early and intensive behavioral interventions: a preliminary study. Res. Autism Spectr. Disord. **3**, 67–73 (2009)
6. Eikeseth, S., Klintwall, L., Jahr, E., Karlsson, P.: Outcome for children with autism receiving early and intensive behavioral intervention in mainstream preschool and kindergarten settings. Res. Autism Spectr. Disord. **6**, 829–835 (2012)
7. Balyan, S., Abrahamyan, S., Ter-Minasyan, H., Waizenauer, A., Korkhov, V.: Distributed collaboration based on mobile infrastructure. In: Gervasi, O., et al. (eds.) ICCSA 2015, Part IV. LNCS, vol. 9158, pp. 354–368. Springer, Cham (2015). doi:10.1007/978-3-319-21410-8_28
8. Balyan, S., Abrahamyan, S., Korkhov, V., Ter-Minasyan, H., Waizenauer, A.: Teambrainer: network-based collaborative mobile system. In: 2016 International Conference on High Performance Computing & Simulation (HPCS), Innsbruck, Austria, pp. 1009–1012. IEEE (2016). doi:10.1109/HPCSim.2016.7568447
9. Avaz Homepage. http://www.avazapp.com/. Last accessed 15 Apr 2017
10. Understand Me Homepage. http://understandme.su/. Last accessed 15 Apr 2017
11. Keskinen, T., Heimonen, T., Turunen, M., Rajaniemi, J.-P., Kauppinen, S.: SymbolChat: picture-based communication platform for users with intellectual disabilities. In: Miesenberger, K., Karshmer, A., Penaz, P., Zagler, W. (eds.) ICCHP 2012, Part II. LNCS, vol. 7383, pp. 279–286. Springer, Heidelberg (2012). doi:10.1007/978-3-642-31534-3_43
12. Ola Mundo Homepage. https://www.olamundo.com/. Last accessed 15 Apr 2017
13. Guskov, V.P., Gushchanskiy, D.E., Kulabukhova, N.V., Abrahamyan, S., Balyan, S., Degtyarev, A.B., Bogdanov, A.V.: An interactive tool for developing distributed telemedicine systems. Comput. Res. Model. **7**(3), 521–528 (2015)
14. Balyan, S.G., Ralovets, R.V., Abrahamyan, S.A., Yuzhanin, N.V.: Functionalities of virtual cluster management system FishDirector and check of its efficiency. Control Process. Stab. **1**(17), 283–288 (2014)
15. MongoDB vs. SQL Server 2008 Performance Showdown. https://blog.michaelckennedy.net/2010/04/29/mongodb-vs-sql-server-2008-performance-showdown/. Last accessed 15 Apr 2017
16. Is Postgres NoSQL Better than MongoDB? http://www.aptuz.com/blog/is-postgres-nosql-database-better-than-mongodb/. Last accessed 15 Apr 2017
17. Donald Bren School of Information and Computer Sciences, UCI Website, Representational State Transfer (REST). http://www.ics.uci.edu/~fielding/pubs/dissertation/rest_arch_style.htm. Last accessed 15 Apr 2017
18. Conrad, T.: PostgreSQL vs. MySQL vs. Commercial Databases: It's All About What You Need. DevX Journal. http://www.devx.com/dbzone/Article/20743. Last accessed 15 Apr 2017
19. Ng Heng, L.: PostgreSQL [9.5.0] vs. MariaDB [10.1.11] vs. MySQL [5.7.0] year 2016. http://nghenglim.github.io/PostgreSQL-9.5.0-vs-MariaDB-10.1.11-vs-MySQL-5.7.0-year-2016/. Last accessed 15 Apr 2017
20. Cattell, R.: Scalable SQL and NoSQL data stores. Newsl. ACM SIGMOD Rec. **39**(4), 12–27 (2011)
21. DB-Engines: Popularity Ranking of Database Management Systems. DB-Engines. http://db-engines.com/en/ranking/key-value+store. Last accessed 15 Apr 2017
22. Introducing JSON. http://www.json.org/. Last accessed 15 Apr 2017
23. Li, Y., Manoharan, S.: A performance comparison of SQL and NoSQL databases. In: 2013 IEEE Pacific Rim Conference on Communications, Computers and Signal Processing (PACRIM), pp. 15–19. IEEE (2013)

24. Poat, M., Lauret, J., Betts, W.: POSIX and object distributed storage system – performance comparison studies and real-life usage in an experimental data taking context leveraging OpenStack/Ceph. In: 21st International Conference on Computing in High Energy and Nuclear Physics (CHEP 2015). IOP Publishing (2015)

25. MQTT Homepage. http://mqtt.org/. Last accessed 15 Apr 2017

26. Mosca Homepage. http://www.mosca.io/. Last accessed 15 Apr 2017

27. Abrahamyan, S., Balyan, S., Muradov, A., Korkhov, V., Moskvicheva, A., Jakushkin, O.: Development of M-Health software for people with disabilities. In: Gervasi, O., et al. (eds.) ICCSA 2016, Part V. LNCS, vol. 9790, pp. 468–479. Springer, Cham (2016). doi:10.1007/978-3-319-42092-9_36

Preliminary Cleaning and Transformation of Data in Data Mining Using PHP Pthreads Library

Yulia Shichkina[1,2(✉)], Alexander Koblov[1(✉)], Kirill Lysov[2(✉)],
and Oleg Iakushkin[2]

[1] Department of Computer Science and Engineering,
Saint Petersburg Electrotechnical University "LETI", St. Petersburg, Russia
strange.y@mail.ru, koblow.a.a@gmail.com
[2] Saint Petersburg State University, St. Petersburg, Russia
thereis9000@gmail.com, oleg.jakushkin@gmail.com

Abstract. The article deals with a special case of the preparation of data about the vehicles movements which comes in large volumes from the source to the accelerated applied methods of data mining. Data preparation goes through several stages from selecting the necessary fields and records to saving them with modified values into a new data structure. The source data which consist of 18 fields has a share of incorrect information and formats of numerical information that are not suitable for further processing. The source data is large in volume and processing it in the original form takes a very long time. The article shows how to use the pthreads library to organize multi-threaded processing of this data. To confirm the applicability of this library, the article presents the results of numerical experiments.

Keywords: Data mining · Data cleaning · Data transformation · PHP · Pthreads

1 Introduction

The software development industry never stands still. Each year, new technologies, frameworks and new versions of the old ones emerge for public tools which already established on the market and in the mind of their users. The variety of programming languages makes it possible not only to select a solution for a specific task and use the hardware efficiently, but also to benefit from the cost of developing and supporting systems which have already been created.

PHP is one of the most popular languages for creating dynamic web sites. According to the programming languages ranking published by GitHub [3] and based on the number of pull-requests of users of the service PHP takes the fifth place behind JavaScript, Java, Python and Ruby. Studies conducted by the Tagline analytical agency [4] based on a survey of 445 companies working in the field of digital technology also put PHP first as 95% of respondents gave a positive answer to the question of knowing this programming language.

© Springer International Publishing AG 2017
O. Gervasi et al. (Eds.): ICCSA 2017, Part V, LNCS 10408, pp. 463–472, 2017.
DOI: 10.1007/978-3-319-62404-4_34

Popularity is high because of the low entry threshold and it's a huge problem since many novice developers do not even have a special technical education and yet choose PHP as their first programming language. This is what gave PHP the unflattering glory of the tool, suitable only for creating the simplest sites and not capable of more.

Very often the demand for high-loaded solutions does not arise from the very beginning. The transition to radically different technologies in large projects requires huge amount of time and material resources which is not always possible and small project teams may not have the financial opportunity to hire software architects and developers to implement complex functionality. In these cases, you have to work with accessible tools and technologies.

This article shows how you can use PHP to implement a highly loaded solution that implements the process of data cleaning and transformation to prepare for further analysis using Data Mining methods. The solution was tested on test suites of 25,000 and 1,000,000 records.

2   Formulation of the Problem

Probably there are no companies today that would not collect data and information on their activities. Some collect it for reporting, others for interest, but most for analysis and decision making, improving the company's performance. While the information is small in volume company employees are able to recycle it manually, often using spreadsheets, database queries and other software tools. But if the flow of incoming information is significant, then processing information becomes more difficult. It takes a very long time. In these cases, a special methodology is used to extract knowledge from databases (Knowledge Discovery in Databases) [1]. This technique was proposed in the second half of the twentieth century by Grigory Pyatetsky-Shapiro who studied the problem of automating the extraction of knowledge from large databases.

The concept of the methodology for extracting knowledge does not offer specific algorithms, but it represents the order of actions that must be performed to achieve the goal and includes:

• preparing and collecting data from sources;
• cleaning data from abnormal values, gaps and noises and indicators that do not carry a payload within the scope of the task to reduce the amount of information and dimensions;
• transformation of data to bring data to a form suitable for extracting knowledge;
• the actual extraction of knowledge through the use of various algorithms;
• interpretation of the acquired knowledge.

Let's Consider the Task of Extracting Useful Information from the Database Which Contains Data Obtained from Devices that Transmit Their GPS Coordinates.

To solve this task for accelerated usage of the finite methods of Data Mining, preliminary cleaning and transformation of data was implemented in PHP and deeper purification and transformation of data by applying fuzzy cross-sections in databases was implemented in Java. As a repository of information, the noSQL database MongoDB of version 3.2 was used.

More detailed data processing and data transformation processes, as well as results of applying fuzzy cross-sections in databases as a method of deep cleaning are described in [2].

The task considered in this article is a continuation of the task of extracting useful information from the database: we need to examine the performance of PHP7.0 during the preliminary cleaning and transformation of data to determine in what way it is possible to significantly reduce the time of preliminary data cleaning.

3 Multithreading in PHP. Pthreads Library

PHP itself does not support multithreading, but there are several methods for emulating it. The easiest way is to run several copies of the script with the parameters. This approach is unacceptable in highly loaded systems and tasks since it does not allow to control the execution of each instance, allocating memory and resources.

The next approach is PCNTL. This extension allows you to fully work with threads and is fairly simple for those who have mastered multi-threaded computing in C. By using the PCNTL extension the developer can use the function pcntl_fork which is an analog of fork in C and allows generating child processes. But again, this approach is an imitation of multithreading and is not so simple for an unprepared programmer.

Author of the pthreads extension Joe Watkins offers an object-oriented API for implementing truly multi-threaded computing [5]. Pthreads allows an application to perform multi-threaded calculations and synchronize threads with each other. This extension includes several classes:

- Threaded - the main class in pthreads. It allows PHP to run threads in parallel. It contains the synchronized() method for synchronization and many other methods.
- Thread - creates a separate thread by calling the run() method. The run() method starts executing in a separate thread when the start() method is called. This can only be initiated from the context that the thread creates. You can also join threads in this same context.
- Worker - essentially the thread's executor.
- Pool - a pool-container from several Worker instances. As the next Worker is released, the next instance of Threaded is launched.

Thus, pthreads is almost the only way to painlessly organize multi-threaded computing in PHP.

It should be noted that to run pthreads it is necessary to compile PHP with the option – enable-maintainer-zts (Zend Thread Safety). For an experienced system administrator, it won't be a problem. For users of Debian-based Linux systems there is *ppa:ondrej/php-zts* there are two packages *php7.0-zts* and *php7.0-zts-dev*, which add php7.0-zts to the system, which can be launched from the terminal.

4 Preliminary Cleaning and Transformation of Data Without Using the Pthreads Library

The accumulated knowledge of GPS transmitting devices consists of logging information about the device which together, with the coordinates, contains the acceleration, rotation, speed, data on the transmitting and receiving devices, as well as other service information. This set of data is redundant for the task in hand and does not have some derivatives from existing indicators. In order to apply knowledge extraction methods in the future, it is necessary to prepare the available information.

Preliminary cleaning and transformation in our task consists of the following operations:

- During the cleaning phase, it is necessary to exclude the processing of garbage information and data that were obtained by incorrect reception of a signal from GPS satellites. This type of data is geographically located quite far from the rest of the set and can be excluded from processing by calculating the distance to the nearest records of the array sorted by the indexed fields.
- At the transformation stage, it is necessary to make a pass along the two-dimensional array of geographical coordinates and to bind the data related to a certain sector of the geographical coordinate plane to the point in the new coordinate space. Getting from the raw data new features, useful for further processing, is possible by performing simple arithmetic operations.

This set of operations was implemented using PHP 7.0 with the mongodb-1.2 driver on a test setup with the characteristics given in Table 1 without using the PHPLIB library for MongoDB.

Table 1. Test setup characteristics

CPU	
Model name:	Intel(R) Core(TM) i3-4030U CPU @ 1.90 GHz
Socket:	1
Core(s) per socket:	2
Thread(s) per core:	2
Memory	
RAM:	12 GB
Storage:	120 GB (SSD)
OS	
Description:	Linux Mint 18 Sarah
Linux Kernel:	4.4.0-21-generic

One of the main problems associated with processing large data is to get the most out of the hardware on which the information is processed. Despite the fact that most databases easily scale to work with multiple threads, PHP scripts will be executed in a single stream if no additional preparation won't be taken. With this approach, it is

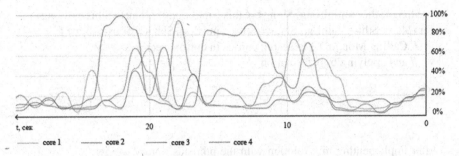

Fig. 1. Logical cores loading graph during processing set of 35,000 entries

impossible to get the maximum efficiency and the loading schedule of logical cores will look something like this (Fig. 1):

As you can see from the graph, all the threads are involved in the processing of data. This is due to the fact that in MongoDB since version 3.0 the new WiredTiger storage engine is used which works with all available threads, but none of the threads is loaded for maximum performance. This indicates the irrational use of available resources.

The only correct way out of this situation is to start the processing in parallel with several threads. You can choose a different programming language for this approach, but for large and complex systems change of technology entails huge overheads and for small projects it is inappropriate to hire new developers to create a solution in another language. For such cases, there are several approaches in PHP for implementing multi-threaded computations.

5 Parallel Implementation of the Preliminary Cleaning and Data Transformation Using the Pthreads Library

During the process of implementing multi-threaded computing, the question arises how to implement the branching with threads and how to ensure the synchronization of these calculations. Since the pthreads library implements the synchronized() method in the Threaded class, it remains to decide at which point it is possible to run a separate thread.

Within the problem of preliminary cleaning and transformation of data such places were:

- Process of cleaning from anomalous values for each coordinate (longitude and latitude). In this case, it is possible to run two threads (one for each of the coordinates).
- Bypassing the coordinate space by longitude and latitude when the embedded for loop is implemented. The inner loop can be run in a separate thread.

After determining such areas, you can start implementing parallel computations. For example, if earlier in the sequential implementation of preliminary cleaning and transformation of data there were two nested loops:

```
for ($long=$this->minLong; $long<=$this->maxLong; $long+=$this->dLong) {
  for ($lat = $this->minLat; $lat <= $this->maxLat; $lat += $this->dLat) {
    // Calling MongoDB to search entries in current sector
    // and applying transformation.
  }
}
```

After implementing this solution with the pthreads library we get:

```
public function run()
{
  do {
    $val = null;
    // Getting object inherited from Threaded
    $prov = $this->worker->getProvider();
    // Synchronizing data
    $prov->synchronized(function($prov) use (&$val) {
      // getNext() implements outer loop
      $val = $prov->getNext();
    }, $prov);
    if ($val['next'] === null) {
      continue;
    }
    // transformation() implements inner loop
    // which is executed in parallel
    $this->transformation($val);
  }
  while ($val !== null);
}
```

In such a simple and beautiful way in PHP you can implement multi-threading.

6   Results

As a result of the research we found out that the pthreads library is very effective for implementing highly loaded systems and computations.

Figure 1 shows a diagram of running PHP code without ZTS and pthreads. Next, the diagrams for loading logical cores will be displayed, depending on the number of running threads. It can be seen that the diagram obtained during performing the sequential solution (Fig. 1) is comparatively similar to the diagram obtained using pthreads with 1 thread (Fig. 2).

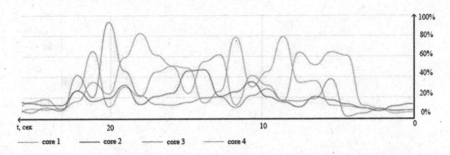

Fig. 2. Logical cores loading graph during processing set of 35,000 entries with pthreads library and 1 thread

After adding second thread the logical cores loading becomes more consistent (Fig. 3):

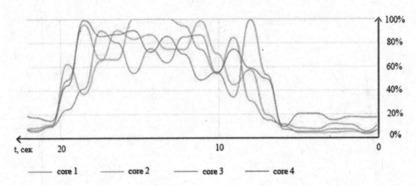

Fig. 3. Logical cores loading graph during processing set of 35,000 entries with pthreads library and 2 threads

After adding the third thread the average loading rate comes to 80% (Fig. 4) and leaves the space for users with less demanding computations, but there's a lot of unused potential left:

After making additional threads, it becomes noticeable that the loading of logical cores grows, and reaches its peak after using all available threads (Fig. 5). It shows that with help of the pthreads extension you can make PHP work quite efficiently not only for web applications, but also for solving problems related to extracting knowledge from large data.

For comparison, we will measure the execution time of a sequential and parallel solutions of the preliminary cleaning task and transformation of data on test sets. To carry out more precise calculations on each set, we performed 100 measurements and average values are listed in the Table 2:

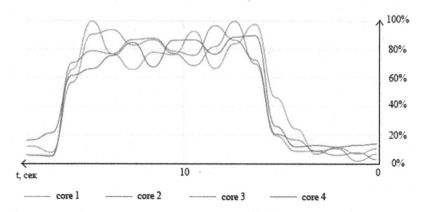

Fig. 4. Logical cores loading graph during processing set of 35,000 entries with pthreads library and 3 threads

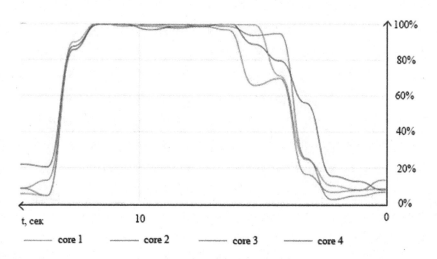

Fig. 5. Logical cores loading graph during processing set of 35,000 entries with pthreads library and 4 threads

Table 2. Test results

Algorithm	Execution time, sec.	
	25,000 entries	1,000,000 entries
Sequential (NTS)	17.09	233.85
Sequential (ZTS)	16.99	228.97
Parallel (1 thread)	17.00	224.94
Parallel (2 threads)	10.01	127.32
Parallel (3 threads)	9.12	98.67
Parallel (4 threads)	8.27	79.67

The results show that the execution time of a sequential solution on a standard PHP7.0 build without using Zend Thread Safety (NTS) is practically the same as for a sequential solution of a task running in PHP using Zend Thread Safety (ZTS) as well as the time of the solution executed with pthreads and creating only one thread. However, if you open more than one thread you get a tremendous performance boost, due to which the execution time of the task decreases with the rate of cubic regression. Figure 6 shows how the execution time of the solution depends on the number of open threads.

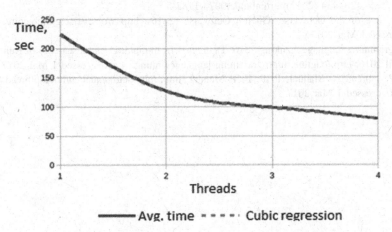

Fig. 6. Dependency of execution time and number of created threads on set of 1,000,000 entries

The results show that with the pthreads library you can force PHP applications to use CPU time more effectively and get a boost in the execution time of the preliminary cleaning task and data transformation more than 2 times on a comparatively weak processor.

In the future work, it is planned to conduct an additional comparative analysis among the software systems of the PHP class, as well as research on the application of additional methods for accelerating the processing of data.

Acknowledgments. The paper has been prepared within the scope of the state project "Initiative scientific project" of the main part of the state plan of the Ministry of Education and Science of Russian Federation (task № 2.6553.2017/BCH Basic Part) as well as supported by grant of Russian Fund for Basic Research (16-07-00886).

References

1. Piatetsky-Shapiro, G., Frawley, W.: Knowledge discovery in databases, 539 p. AAAI Press, December 1991. ISBN: 9780262660709
2. Shichkina, Y., Degtyarev, A., Koblov A.: Technology of cleaning and transforming data using the knowledge discovery in databases (KDD) technology for fast application of data mining methods. In: CEUR Workshop Proceedings. Selected Papers of the 7th International Conference Distributed Computing and Grid-Technologies in Science and Education, vol. 1787, pp. 428–434 (2017). urn:nbn:de:0074-1787-5
3. The state of the Octoverse. GitHub Octoverse (2016). https://octoverse.github.com/. Last accessed 1 Mar 2017
4. Programming languages ranking 2016, Tagline — fresh rankings and researches of Runet, 11 April 2016. http://tagline.ru/programming-languages-rating/. Last accessed 1 Mar 2017
5. PHP: pthreads – Manual, PHP: PHP Manual. http://php.net/manual/en/book.pthreads.php. Last accessed 1 Mar 2017

Problem-Solving Environment for Beam Dynamics Analysis in Particle Accelerators

Nataliia Kulabukhova[✉], Alexander Bogdanov, and Alexander Degtyarev

Saint-Petersburg State University, St. Petersburg, Russia
n.kulabukhova@spbu.ru

Abstract. In particle accelerator physics the problem is that we can not see what is going on inside the working machine. There are a lot of packages for modelling the behaviour of the particles in numerical or analytical way. But for most physicists it is better to see the picture in motion to say exactly what is happening and how to influence on this. The goal of this work is to provide scientists with such a problem-solving environment, which can not only do some numerical calculations, but show the dynamics of changes as a motion 3D picture. To do this we use the power of graphical processors from both sides: for general purpose calculations and for there direct appointment – drawing 3D motion. Besides, this environment should analyse the behaviour of the system to provide the user with all necessary information about the problem and how to deal with it.

1 Introduction

Today accelerator physics is a multidisciplinary kind of science. Not only physicists working in this area. Mathematicians, engineers, programmers are also involved in this process. It is obvious that the progress of further research depends more on new technologies and IT industry, which can be truly helpful for theoretical physics. Of course, all this can be said not only about accelerator physics [1,2].

There are a lot of well known software packages, which are used practically everywhere. Our opinion is that the use of this or that package depends mostly on the laboratory and the research. However, the main are COSY Infinity [3], MaryLie [4], MAD [5], Trace (with different modifications) [6]. Some of them are cross-platform, others not. Though there are a FORTRAN-based applications [7,8] among them, there trustful and stable work is out of doubt. That is the reason why scientists do not want to change anything and start working with other applications. To tell the truth, there is no new modern product that is really different from the old ones. COSY Infinity is working in the field of nonlinear dynamics, where it is used for the computation of perturbation expansions of Poincare maps to high orders. In MaryLia another approach is used. It is based on Lie algebraic methods, which may be used for particle tracking

The work is supported by RFBR 16-07-01113A.

O. Gervasi et al. (Eds.): ICCSA 2017, Part V, LNCS 10408, pp. 473–482, 2017.
DOI: 10.1007/978-3-319-62404-4_35

around or through a lattice and for analysis of linear and nonlinear lattice properties. In addition to single-particle tracking, Lie algebraic methods may also be used to determine how particle phase-space distribution functions evolve under transport through both linear and nonlinear elements. These methods are useful for the self-consistent treatment of space-charge effects and for the study of how moments and emittance evolve. These two approaches are rather quick, but the disadvantage is the need of recalculate all the equations if it is necessary to change the parameter.

Alternative to described above approaches became the Particle-In-cell method [9–11], which came from gas dynamics at the beginning of the 21 century. The main advantage of PIC method is that it does not need to approximate the equation of state. On the other hand, it is very much time depending, because of the amount of data. At present, there are a lot of modifications of PIC method using parallelization on multiple processors [12], hybrid systems [13] and the Intel XEON PHI [14]. But it does not crucially influence on the problem of data sending.

The other idea of helping scientists with there work is to solve the problem of analysing data. There are plenty of works [15–19], where the words "Virtual Accelerator" standing near by with the control system describing. The main task for such environment is to collect data from different detectors and handled them before it can be analysed. On the Fig. 1 the work of such system is shown. The machine operator is the essential component of it. The work of operator is to coordinate the send-received collected data between different detectors and

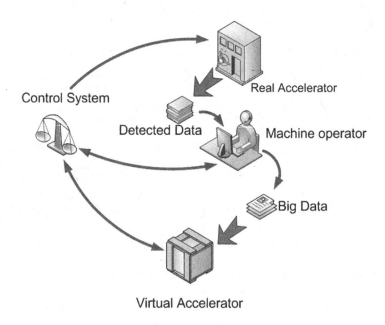

Fig. 1. Working process of virtual accelerator system

the Virtual Accelerator system. Besides, the operator detects the control system to get the instructions for what should be done to fix the errors and improve the results. But all this Virtual Accelerators are just program module working above the real machine. They are rigidly tied to one type of accelerators, and need crucial changes to be used on another.

However, the software packages for modelling beam dynamics and Virtual Accelerator for analysing data are without a doubt an essential part of accelerator physics. On our point of view, it is better to merge these two approaches and make them independent from real facilities.

2   The Main Concept

The idea of using 3D graphics for visualization is a part of a huge project of constructing so called Virtual Accelerator Laboratory (VAL) [20,21]. The idea is to develop a model of real machine and test the behaviour of the beam inside this virtual system of control elements. As it was said above, there are a lot of projects using the words of "Virtual Accelerator" [22] and a number of packages to modelling beam dynamics. The concept of VAL is to provide the user (scientist) with block of different components, such as:

the block of control elements: with the help of it the user can construct the main view of the future accelerator. The general view of circular machine is shown on Fig. 2.

the block of particle distribution: which forms the initial particle distribution coming from the source.

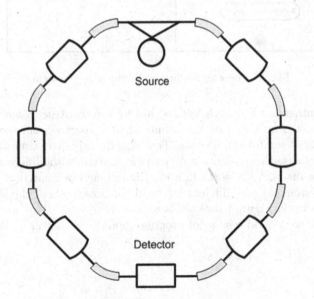

Fig. 2. General view of accelerator ring

the block of data: the data base with all calculated results.

the block of expert system: where the collected data is analysed and the main reasons of received errors are given as a result to user (see Fig. 3).

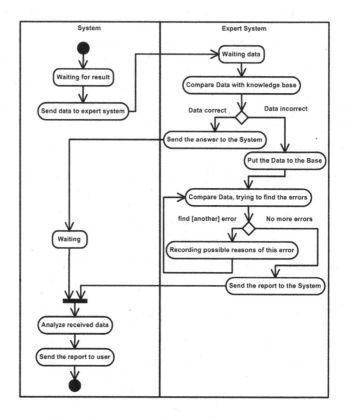

Fig. 3. The working process of the expert system

The advantage of using such VAL is that we can construct a machine before it is really exist. And based on the results of the expert system the advices to build the real accelerator can be done. That significantly saves time and financial resources. Besides, the prediction of particle motion with different nonlinear effects can be made. VAL works in a distributed environment that is why, the user of the system can use different electronic devices to check the intermediate results of the work. Figure 4 shows this idea.

On Fig. 5 the general scheme of program modules is shown.

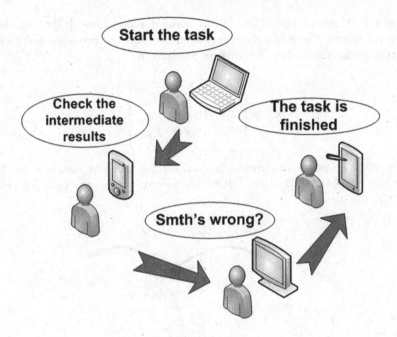

Fig. 4. Distributed environment of VAL

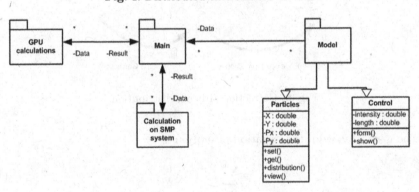

Fig. 5. Main modules of the system

3 About the Approach

The main idea of the method was described in [20]. We have the initial distribution and the control system of elements. If we speak about elements, everything is well known and there are no great problems to construct such system. On the contrary, the difficulty is how to form the initial distribution. There is no proved and stable approach to do this easily.

The easy task is to work with the uniform distribution, but in real case we could not get it from the source. We are trying to use normal and some other distributions, described in [23], to make it more natural. Passing throw the control system the initial distribution, created on the first step and formed as matrix is modified in new intermediate matrix **X**.

$$\mathbf{X}_0 = \begin{pmatrix} X_1 & X_2 & \dots & X_n \\ Y_1 & XY_2 & \dots & Y_n \\ Px_1 & Px_2 & \dots & Px_n \\ Py_1 & Py_2 & \dots & Py_n \\ \dots & \dots & \dots & \dots \end{pmatrix}$$

Following the predictor-corrector algorithm [24] this new matrix is the base matrix to correct the initial distribution and form it for the new turn. The Fig. 6 shows this idea.

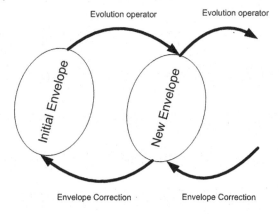

Fig. 6. Correction of beam distribution

The general view of the equation of motion is

$$X = \sum_{i=0}^{k} P^{1i}(t) X_0^{[i]} \tag{1}$$

In the case of space charge, using the described approach [20], Eq. (1) can be rewritten

$$\frac{d\mathbf{X}}{ds} = \sum_{k=1}^{\infty} \left(\mathbb{P}_{ext}^{1k}(s) + \mathbb{P}_{self}^{1k}(s) \right) \mathbf{X}^{[k]} \tag{2}$$

For example, the control matrix $\mathbb{P}^{11}$ in this case can take the following view

$$\mathbb{P}^{11}(s) = \mathbb{P}_{ext}^{11}(s) + \mathbb{P}_{self}^{11}(s)$$

where

$$\mathbb{P}_{ext}^{11}(s) = \begin{pmatrix} 0 & 1 & 0 & 0 \\ -k_x & 0 & 0 & 0 \\ 0 & 0 & 0 & 1 \\ 0 & 0 & -k_y & 0 \end{pmatrix},$$

$$\mathbb{P}^{11}_{self}(s) = \begin{pmatrix} 0 & 0 & 0 & 0 \\ -\eta_x & 0 & 0 & 0 \\ 0 & 0 & 0 & 0 \\ 0 & 0 & \eta_y & 0 \end{pmatrix},$$

If we speak about nonlinear case, the described above equations can be also used with some modifications.

The matrix for **X** is formed by the Kronecker composition:

$$\mathbf{X}^3 = \begin{pmatrix} \mathbf{X} \\ \mathbf{Y} \\ \mathbf{X}^{[3]} \\ \mathbf{X}^{[2]} \otimes \mathbf{Y} \\ \mathbf{X} \otimes \mathbf{Y}^{[2]} \\ \mathbf{Y}^{[3]} \end{pmatrix}.$$

And for matrices $\mathbb{P}$ we add new order:

$$\mathbb{P}^{11} = \begin{pmatrix} \mathbb{P}^{11}_x & \mathbb{O} \\ \mathbb{O} & \mathbb{P}^{11}_y \end{pmatrix},$$

$$\mathbb{P}^{13} = \begin{pmatrix} \mathbb{Q}^{11}_x & \mathbb{O} & \mathbb{Q}^{13}_x & \mathbb{O} \\ \mathbb{O} & \mathbb{Q}^{22}_y & \mathbb{O} & \mathbb{Q}^{24}_y \end{pmatrix},$$

where, for example, elements of $\mathbb{Q}^{11}_x$ can be

$$\mathbb{A}(1,1) = h\frac{13\cos(l\sqrt{|h|}) - \cos(3l\sqrt{|h|}) - 36l\sqrt{|h|}\sin(l\sqrt{|h|})}{192}$$

$$\mathbb{A}(1,2) = \sqrt{|h|}\frac{-5\sin(l\sqrt{|h|}) - 13\sin(3l\sqrt{|h|}) + 12l\sqrt{|h|}cos(l\sqrt{|h|})}{64}$$

$$\mathbb{A}(1,3) = -\frac{\cos(l\sqrt{|h|}) - \cos(3l\sqrt{|h|}) + 12l\sqrt{|h|}sin(l\sqrt{|h|})}{64}$$

$$\mathbb{A}(1,4) = \frac{36l\sqrt{|h|}\cos(l\sqrt{|h|}) + 13\sin(3l\sqrt{|h|}) - 75\sin(l\sqrt{|h|})}{192\sqrt{|h|}}$$

4   Reasons of Using Graphical Processors

As it was said above there are a lot of works describing the parallezation of principally PIC method (see works [12,25]). Though, the approach we use is a matrix based method of Ordinary Differential Equation solving and it gives us some advantages of paralleling them on SMP systems, for example, it became clear that there it is no matter how much resources we have, using only this technologies we a limited. As the method allows to present the intermediate results and the solution of the system in the form of matrices it is better to use the graphical processors [26].

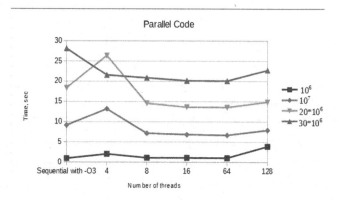

Fig. 7. Parallel code different number of turns using OpenMP concept

The present research shows that there is no great benefit via parallelization of computational code for one particle by using OpenMP library (see Fig. 7). In this case overhead on data sending is significant. On the other hand, we forms the initial distribution and the intermediate results in the form of matrices and that allows us to use GPUs for there direct appointment. But the idea is to use graphical processor not only for general purpose but for drawing as well.

To simplify this process the 3D Virtual Cluster [27] is going to be used. It helps to visualized the results of calculations with some modified based resources.

5   Conclusion

Our goal is to provide the scientist with a clear and easy environment to simulate and predict the behaviour of the beam. The result of the simulation should be shown as a motion picture. We do not guarantee the work of the system in the real time, but it should be the problem-solving environment, that can help the user to construct the needed structure of the accelerator. The previous work was devoted to the particle simulation using matrix approach. Some parallelization of this method was made. But the results showed that there can be some other benefits for modelling beam dynamics using this approach. In this work we sum up all that was done before to transform the simulation method to the problem-solving environment.

Acknowledgements. The authors would like to express gratitude to Vladimir Korkhov for valuable help. And Serge Andrianov for useful explanations of physical processes in accelerators. Scientific research were performed using the equipment of the Research Park of St. Petersburg State University. The work was sponsored by the Russian Foundation for Basic Research under the projects: 16-07-01113 "Virtual supercomputer as a tool for solving complex problems".

References

1. Raba, N.O., Stankova, E.N.: On the problem of numerical modeling of dangerous convective phenomena: possibilities of real-time forecast with the help of multi-core processors. In: Murgante, B., Gervasi, O., Iglesias, A., Taniar, D., Apduhan, B.O. (eds.) ICCSA 2011. LNCS, vol. 6786, pp. 633–642. Springer, Heidelberg (2011). doi:10.1007/978-3-642-21934-4_51
2. Stankova, E.N., Korkhov, V.V., Kulabukhova, N.V., Vasilenko, A.Y., Holod, I.I.: Computational environment for numerical modeling of the results of cloud seeding. In: Gervasi, O., Murgante, B., Misra, S., Rocha, A.M.A.C., Torre, C., Taniar, D., Apduhan, B.O., Stankova, E., Wang, S. (eds.) ICCSA 2016. LNCS, vol. 9788, pp. 454–462. Springer, Cham (2016). doi:10.1007/978-3-319-42111-7_35
3. Makino, K., Berz, M.: COSY INFINITY Version 9. Nuclear Instruments and Methods A558 (2005)
4. Dragt, A.J., Ryne, R.D., et al.: Numerical computation of transfer maps using lie algebraic methods. In: Proceedings of PAC 1987 (1987)
5. Ryne, R.D.: Advanced computing tools and models for accelerator physics. In: Proceedings of EPAC 2008 (2008)
6. http://laacg.lanl.gov/laacg/services/traceman.pdf
7. http://cosyinfinity.org/
8. Dragt, A.J., Ryne, R.D., et al.: MARYLIE 3.0 users manual: a program for charged particle beam transport based on lie algebraic methods. University of Maryland (2003)
9. Paret, S., Qiang, J.: Collisional effects in particle-in-cell beam-beam simulation. In: Proceedings of IPAC 2013. JACOW (2013)
10. Wolfheimer, F., Gjonaj, E., Weiland, T.: Parallel Particle-In-Cell (PIC) codes. In: Proceedings of ICAP 2006. JACOW (2006)
11. Stancari, G., Redaelli, S., Moens, V.: Beam dynamics in an electron lens with the warp Particle-In-Cell code. In: Proceedings of IPAC 2014. JACOW (2014)
12. Giovannozzi, M.: Space-Charge Simulation Using Parallel Algorithms
13. Bowers, K.J.: Accelerating a Paticle-in-Cell simulation using a hybrid counting sort. J. Comput. Phys. **173**, 393–411 (2001)
14. Meerov, I.B., et al.: 3D plasma modelling PIC method on Intel XEON PHI: optimisation and Examples of Use (in Russian), vol. 15. Computational Methods and Programming (2015)
15. Chiu, N.P.C., Kuo, C.H., Chen, J., Cheng, Y.S., Wu, C.Y., Chen, Y.K., Hsu, K.T.: Virtual accelerator development for the TPS. In: Proceedings of IPAC 2010. JACOW (2010)
16. Gu, D., Zhang, M., Gu, Q., Huang, D., Zhao, M.: Development of virtual accelerator environment for beam diagnostics (2014). https://arxiv.org/ftp/arxiv/papers/1401/1401.1889.pdf
17. Gulliford, C., Bazarov, I., Dobbins, J., Talman, R., Malitsky, N.: The NTMAT EPICS-DDS virtual accelerator for the CornellL ERL injector. In: Proceedings of IPAC 2010. JACOW (2010)
18. Malitsky, N., Smith, J., Wei, J., Talman, R.: UAL-based simulation environment for spallation neutron source ring. In: Proceedings of the 1999 Particle Accelerator Conference. JACOW (1999)
19. Sagan, D., et al.: Unified accelerator modeling using the BMAD Software Library. In: Proceedings of IPAC 2011. JACOW (2011)

20. Kulabukhova, N., Andrianov, S.N., Bogdanov, A., Degtyarev, A.: Simulation of space charge dynamics in high intensive beams on hybrid systems. In: Gervasi, O., Murgante, B., Misra, S., Rocha, A.M.A.C., Torre, C., Taniar, D., Apduhan, B.O., Stankova, E., Wang, S. (eds.) ICCSA 2016. LNCS, vol. 9786, pp. 284–295. Springer, Cham (2016). doi:10.1007/978-3-319-42085-1_22

21. Kulabukhova, N.: Software for virtual accelerator environment. In: RuPAC 2012 Contributions to the Proceedings. JACOW (2012)

22. Yamamoto, N.: Use of a virtual accelerator for a development of an accelerator control system (1998). http://accelconf.web.cern.ch/accelconf/pac97/papers/pdf/3P042.PDF

23. Nataliia, K.: Space charge dominated envelope dynamics using GPUs. In: Proceedings of IPAC 2013. JACOW (2013)

24. Kulabukhova, N., Degtyatev, A., Bogdanov, A., Andrianov, S.: Simulation of space charge dynamics on HPC. In: Proceedings of IPAC 2014. JACOW (2014)

25. Qiang, J., Ryne, R.D., Habib, S., Decy, V.: An object-oriented parallel particle-in-cell code for beam dynamics simulation in linear accelerators (2000)

26. Nataliia, K.: GPGPU implementation of matrix formalism for beam dynamics simulation. In: Proceedings of ICAP 2012. JACOW (2012)

27. Bogdanov, A., Ivashchenko, A., Belezeko, A., Korkhov, V., Kulabukhova, N., Khmel, D., Suslova, S., Milova, E., Smirnov, K.: Building a virtual cluster for 3D graphics applications. In: Gervasi, O., Murgante, B., Misra, S., Rocha, A.M.A.C., Torre, C., Taniar, D., Apduhan, B.O., Stankova, E., Wang, S. (eds.) ICCSA 2016. LNCS, vol. 9787, pp. 276–291. Springer, Cham (2016). doi:10.1007/978-3-319-42108-7_21

Best Practices Combining Traditional and Digital Technologies in Education

D.A. Lisachenko[1(✉)], A.V. Barmasov[1,3,4], M.N. Bukina[1],
E.N. Stankova[1,2], S.O. Vysotskaya[1], and E.P. Zarochentseva[1]

[1] Saint Petersburg State University, 7-9, Universitetskaya nab.,
St. Petersburg 199034, Russia
da@fr.spb.ru, a.barmasov@spbu.ru,
mariabukina72@rambler.ru, e.stankova@yandex.ru,
123sony@rambler.ru, lena.strona@gmail.com
[2] St. Petersburg Electrotechnical University "LETI", 5, ul. Professora Popova,
St. Petersburg 197376, Russia
[3] Russian State Hydrometeorological University, 98, Malookhtinsky pr.,
St. Petersburg 195196, Russia
[4] St. Petersburg State Pediatric Medical University, 2, Litovskaya ul.,
St. Petersburg 194100, Russia

Abstract. Recent decades have seen an extensive penetration of computers and social networks into the society, and the information and computer technologies are now widely used at all education levels. Consequently the new generation of students has cognitive functions which strongly differ from those of previous generations. Hence, besides the undoubted advantages of computer and Internet technologies in education, a number of issues arise and require a comprehensive analysis. The authors of the present article giving courses on general physics and concepts of modern sciences to students in natural science and humanities at St. Petersburg State University, Russian State Hydrometeorological University, St. Petersburg State Pediatric Medical University, and St. Petersburg Electrotechnical University "LETI" analyzed the use of information and computer technologies in their teaching experience in recent decades and especially in the last few years and have developed an approach that best combines traditional and innovative learning tools.

Keywords: Education · Computer technology · High school · Physics · General science

1 Introduction

The past decades have seen an overall penetration of computers and social networks into the society at all levels, including in the educative environment. Information and networking technologies are widely used in teaching from primary to high school. It results in the appearance of a new generation of students with cognitive functions strongly different from those of the previous generation.

Along with the undoubted benefits of computer and Internet technologies in the education [1, 2], a number of issues arise that require detailed consideration, similarly

O. Gervasi et al. (Eds.): ICCSA 2017, Part V, LNCS 10408, pp. 483–494, 2017.
DOI: 10.1007/978-3-319-62404-4_36

to the case of previous technological revolutions (for example, the invention of printing some centuries ago was expected not only to result in a dramatic increase in the availability of information, but also to produce an uncontrolled propagation of misunderstandings and errors).

The authors perform all forms of teaching (lectures, seminars, practical courses) on general physics [3–7], biophysics [8–16], concepts of modern science (CMS) [17], language and technical translation [18, 19] for students in natural science and humanities in many faculties of the State University, the Electrical Engineering University and other high schools in St. Petersburg. We analyzed our experience of the use of various information and computer technologies in education over more than past 2 decades (from the pre-computer age till the overall computerization) [20–29] and, taking into account the new trends revealed from these observations, developed and implemented an approach that best combines traditional and innovative educative techniques. New electronic tools strongly differ by their space, time and communicative features, and are appropriate in different situations. We briefly consider them in our article.

2 The Influence of the Information Environment on the Training

A rapid development of computer and information technologies started at the end of the XXth century led to the fact that the new generation of students (formed as personalities in 2000–2015) grew up in an absolutely new information environment. A large number of works has already been published and is rapidly growing devoted to the analysis of the impact of informatics on psychic, physiological and mental characteristics and abilities of this new generation [1, 2]. They note, on the one hand, a positive effect of information technologies: the availability of information increases, its processing is faster, the creative abilities are wider (although somewhat peculiar). On the other hand, the fatigue develops, the concentration decreases, the skills of analysis and understanding of information are weakened, the memory degrades, the thinking becomes mosaic, the knowledge becomes superficial, the inability to perform the easiest operations without computer becomes a common problem. In a whole, there is no definitive answer on the global advantages or shortcomings of the new computerized world. Moreover, the situation changes so rapidly that one person can see several digital revolutions during his life and professional work.

Regarding the educative issues, one of the most important new factors is a free access to huge amounts of information, including texts, photos and videos. Information become the more and more complicated and redundant. However it is not structured, not always objective, often false and tendentious, while its level, quality up-to-dateness are indefinite. This is a problem which is not enough realized by a typical consumer. Thus a first issue faced by the novice users (often at primary school) is an excessive abundance and an unknown reliability of sources of information. A lot of distractions (advertising, chat in a nearby window) disperse the attention and perturb the perception which becomes the more and more superficial, while the memorization becomes quite short-term. Students often cannot stay one hour without Internet or divide 100 by 20 without calculator, or even say how many millilitres contains a litre. They blindly trust the results of the computer calculations, even the most absurd (a molecule larger than a planet). The mining and verifying of information becomes the more and more complicated, while its quality rapidly shuts down.

This is why a primary task of today's teaching is rather not to provide information (which can be easily googled out), but to analyze it, systematize and construct causal relationships on its basis. In other words, we need not raw information but a product of its deep processing that is considered to be a basis of progress in advanced countries. The essence of education is a creation of a high value added information and mental product, but not a waste of primary information resources.

3 The Authors Experience in Informatics for Education

The authors give their courses (physics, CMS, translation and other) to students of many faculties for many years and always were searching for effective methods and used various means.

The use of multimedia greatly expanded the abilities of teachers. The use of presentations with pictures, video clips, animation allows to demonstrate the dynamic processes in the nature. The authors compile and permanently update a database of presentations on different subjects, but also collect new raw digital materials such as links, pictures, text and videos (in order to build new presentations on the fly as required). For example, a data collection on applied physics in dental implantation is based on the last year world leading scientific articles (the information is so rapidly renewed that we design a final presentation at the last moment, and not before, however from blocks preliminarily constructed) and is used in the renewal of the general physics lectures and practical works at the dental faculty. The authors also note that the use of multimedia allows to significantly increase the amount of material demonstrated and studied in the classroom, as well as the intensity of thinking work. However a real rate of understanding cannot be accelerated.

Consider now several activities which differ by the use of a computer due to a different nature of the matters themselves: provide the information, interest the students, calculate. Namely, physics (lectures), physics (practical courses), concepts of modern science (CMS), language and translation. For example, teaching of CMS contains an important component of popularization, so it is important to demonstrate fascinating pictures and inspiring videos, prior to make the students think and analyze, while a professional understanding of physics or other natural sciences is not required. Therefore, in this case we demonstrate modern and attractive objects or phenomena (absolutely unavailable in a real classroom) on the screen. On the contrary, in the course of general physics we demonstrate rather simple tutorial objects. In addition, when studying science (physics, geology, biology) at a professional level it is absolutely necessary to work with a real object (pendulum, stone, flower etc.) thoroughly, and its perception must be real. So in this case the role of a good computer presentation is great but not unique.

4   Lectures: Physics and CMS

As is known, presentation slides should not contain too much information under the form of text and formulas. In our presentations we account either for visual memory (pictures, photos, and video) or invite students to understand a general idea of the deduction of mathematical and physical formulas (for example we write in a presentation a sequence of formulas and decorate them with various fonts, colours, blocks or arrows). However the formulas themselves should appear slowly on a true blackboard, allowing the students to be involved into the process and follow the logics, notice the errors, ask questions, analyze particular cases.

Therefore, when giving a lecture it is better to combine traditional forms of teaching with modern ones, using the computer and multimedia equipment. Note that our students fully agree with this point of view: they all prefer to keep a traditional lecture in a classroom with a live contact to a teacher.

In the case of CMS the computer is widely used to search for information, and, since the Internet contains too much, it is extremely important to know how to deal with it: found, select, analyze, check. However these skills are usually not developed at all. A common issue of this course is that a kind of essay is demanded by the official program, and students use to rapidly copy-paste fragments from everywhere without thinking or fact checking. So in our practice we replaced it by a detailed, informative but brief written plan, followed by an oral presentation. This plan must comply with a lot of strict but reasonable rules (a kind of a checklist is available) and needs a good analytical work under a supervision of a teacher (a email is the most convenient in this case). The Internet is overfilled by such "essays", but "plans" are still not in a common use. This is why we have never seen a notable plagiarism in them.

In addition, lectures on physics and CMS are often held under the form of discussions and conferences where the acquired information must be thoroughly analyzed from different points of view, including non-standard ones.

This is particularly important due to the fact that the main method of knowledge evaluation in secondary school for many years was the multiple choice testing (fortunately, classical exams gradually come back and a good mental work is required again). Note that many students of all faculties (including linguists and journalists) have great difficulties when formulating their ideas in oral presentations or written works, and they often believe that a bibliographic reference can be just a "www.google.com". Such oral presentations, discussed and analyzed word by word, can be performed only in a live classroom.

5   Practical Courses on Physics

The authors give practical courses of physics for students in natural science. Earlier they developed multimedia lectures on mathematical processing of measurement results and on virtual laboratory [1, 2]. Also a good learning effect is obtained when working with numerical models of natural phenomena, for example, a convective cloud [31].

Preparing to a laboratory work and writing reports cause lots of problems for students. Hence we created a virtual group in a social network (vk.com/physlab) where students can found a regularly updated information on the equipment in use, download needed brochures, textbooks and tests, get useful links and other information related to their practical work. They also can contact their teachers by means of chat. Since the problems, questions and answers are often the same, we have created and made available online an "Encyclopaedia of errors". It contains an analysis of all notable mistakes made by hundreds of students for many years in their home preparation, measurements, processing and interpretation of experimental results, writing he reports. At all stages of their practical work students consult it and try to avoid the errors ever done.

By the way the Encyclopaedia allowed to confirm two common conclusions concerning the errors in education:

- Hundreds of errors can be and were done, but their frequencies are very different. If we range the errors by frequency we see that about 5 of most frequent errors cover about 80% of their total number found in the students reports, 10 errors for 90% and so on. So we can say to the students that if they learn to avoid about 10 common errors, an overall number of errors will decrease by one order of magnitude, and the time spent to draw up reports will decrease manyfold. Note that this is a rather general conclusion, valid as well for grammar errors in learning languages [18].
- Different students perform the same errors for many years, and after a comprehensive analysis of several hundreds of reports new mistakes do not appear any more (and any new error becomes an event to be celebrated).

Apart getting the information online on the site, students can communicate with their professors in order to ask questions or to send their reports and get a fast feedback: our teachers are available online every day and at any reasonable time, often under the form of a chat. However, whatever is the mean of electronic communication or the quality and resolution of graphic files, most part of mistakes can easily be shown and explained to the students in the classroom, while it takes much more time to document them under a form clear enough to be sent over the networks and understood.

Concerning the choice of networking media, most part of students and teachers prefer to form their educative communities in their well known social network such as Facebook or VKontakte where all the needed basic functions are found under a familiar and friendly interface. Some of them use also Learning Management Systems (such as Blackboard Learn or MOODLE) [1] which possess their own user-friendly features, especially for very large groups and repetitive works.

On the other hand, in recent years we teach students to process scientific data in MS Excel, Matlab, Origin and other mathematical packages. We noted that many of the 1st year students in natural sciences, despite a regular use of computers and other gadgets, has no data processing skills in Excel, nor in mathematical packages such as Origin, Derive etc. They have mastered the computer in their childhood as a tool of entertainment and friendly chat, but they never had an idea of its initial purpose (military calculations in the middle of the XX century). While working on a practical work report, the students begin to see a computer from a new but realistic and useful point of view and acquire new working skills. Besides, a computer with the mathematical packages provided allows, when the measurements in a practical work are done, to test immediately the consistency of the obtained data (smooth curves, linearity of graphs) prior to go home, already knowing whether the measurements should be redone or not.

For example, if the dependence of resistance on temperature is smooth enough, the experimental points reasonably fit a theoretical curve, the number of measurements is sufficient. This allows to immediately found out crude errors and discuss them with a professor.

6 Inquiry

In order to reveal the attitude of students and professors to the problem under consideration and to better understand the future trends in the use of computer in education an inquiry was conducted. Prior to the inquiry some quantitative conclusions could already be done from our many years experience in various high school, and they were in general confirmed.

About a hundred of students were inquired, and they belonged to different groups, allowing to clearly see the differences. Their number might seem insufficient to reveal fine effects, however it correctly shows main trends and allows for overall conclusions.

Inquiry of students and teachers
A number of questions were formulated concerning the use of various means of e-learning and on their compared effectiveness. The answers given by the students of different age and specialities allowed drawing up several qualitative and quantitative conclusions.

1. Lectures.
   Point of view of students.
   In the case of equal availability a live lecture in the classroom is strongly preferred to any form of video (mentioned by 100% of students), even when a feedback from the students is not very active. Students prefer the classroom lectures because of the opportunity to put questions and discuss immediately after the lectures and even during it. About 20% of them believe that a video translation on Internet could also be acceptable. The students estimate that if needed a small part (25%) of theoretical courses could be given under a video format (but in this case it was not asked to specify if a course is rather of a monologue or dialogue kind). A possible attractive feature of video recorded lectures is a possibility to selectively review or replay them (noted by 25% of students) which could be a good supplement to live courses.
   Point of view of teachers.
   Their points of view are naturally different, since students are the consumers, and teacher are the producers of the educative content. While a student accounts for getting the best of the course, a teacher must create it. For that its very important to get a live reaction, but not to speak to a camera alone. Students have their own preferences, but they are not always conscious of what is really needed and how to do it, while professors can and must use all their experience.

2. Use of Internet and other typical online tools in educative processes.
   All students (100%) use the Internet firstly to search for information and to rapidly dialogue with the teacher about their homework. These two functions are of equal

importance. Other tasks seem to be less important. All students and teachers fluently use e-mail and social networks and spend many hours (5 to 7 h per day) at the computer online-ready, much more than in the secondary school. The commonly used e-mailing and networking tools (the worldwide ones such as facebook and gmail, and the national ones such as vkontakte, mail.ru etc.) are quite familiar and user-friendly and contain virtually all functions needed for communications for educative purposes (this was noted by all respondents). They are widely used for distribution of educational texts and presentations and for quick feedback, much more than special educative systems such as Blackboard Learn or MOODLE [1]. Note again that for the choice and use of the online tools all have the same point of view, professors and students.

3. Progressive and traditional forms.

In spite of the progress in electronics, all students consider that their own paper copybooks and paper textbooks always remain the best essential educational materials. The breakthrough technologies are welcome, but our inquiry shows that we should correctly distinguish and separate classroom and e-learning forms, and concentrate our classroom work on the activities that cannot be done elsewhere. The absolute majority of students believe impossible to replace the traditional forms of teaching by their virtual models. Video lectures and other remote e-learning means will certainly be useful and even vital if a personal presence is impossible (great distances, disabilities).

Note some numerical results.

Seminars: 60% of students stand for classroom, 20% hesitate and 20% allow them to be virtual.

Lectures: 30% for classroom and 70% hesitate.

However tests can be performed via internet (50%: fully, 30%: partially).

Il all cases where virtual educative tools were mentioned as preferred there was a physical impossibility to attend live courses (large distances, intensive work, etc.)

4. Age and profession.

There was no clear difference between students in sciences or humanities. However, the 1st year students were more categorical in their estimations (for example, 100% instead of 60%, "no" instead of "sometimes" etc.).

5. Teachers were also inquired.

As expected, two factors were clearly stressed out. First, in any learning process a teacher has to create a specific psychological ambience that will never be done by a machine. Second, in many cases real objects are studied.

In particular: Teachers in natural sciences reject the substitution of a real object or phenomenon by its digital image (a pendulum in physics, a stone in geology, a flower in botanic) – and not only for the general reasons that an original is better than a digital copy. The problem is that many fundamental and fine aspects of original objects are lost in any digital copy (video, photo, simulation) that is absolutely unacceptable at the professional level (recall, while quite possible in popularisation or CMS). Some specific sciences such as programming might be successfully studied using distant e-learning tools; however for better understanding of the mentality of students a live communication is essential and very desirable prior to e-learning.

Concerning languages and translation, some technical translation courses can be performed online, since a modern technical translation is now rather a database management and data processing in a multi-user environment than a traditional language work, and the computer assisted translation (CAT) tools rapidly migrate to a server-based model [19, 30].

7 Infrastructural Remarks

We believe that all kinds of computer work should originate from real demands and facilities, depending on such parameters as space, time and complexity of work.

As already noted, online/offline techniques strongly depend on a physical availability of the courses. The authors have a teaching experience in various high schools with different conditions. Compare for example such two universities as LETI and SPbU. In LETI all is in the same or next building and instantly available at any moment of every day. In SPbU the faculties are dispersed in the megapolis at the distances of about 50 km, in contrast to most other high schools. So typical space scales can be indicated and correlated to typical works that can or cannot be performed in person due to their typical duration. They are: (a) direct presence, immediate availability; (b) walking distance (same building in winter, next building in summer); (c) back and forth from one building to another during one working day; (d) all day long at the same faculty with no possibility of travel; (e) unavailable within one working day. The bigger is the distance, the more is the role of virtual learning tools, as a student will not lose several hours for a one minute question, and so for other typical time scales.

In LETI a professor can be available for a live contact at any reasonable time, while in SPbU the professors of physics, the students in geology and the laboratory of physics are separated by very large distances, so virtual tools become a unique way to accelerate the educative process.

Consider a case of practical works in physics. They are a good model object, since the work takes much time and consists of all types of works at many stages: introductory lectures, tests on theoretical knowledge, experiments, data processing, drawing a report, corrections, and many of them are repeated many times. Practical works need a real presence in a laboratory under a direct supervision, but writing a report is a long iterative process, with several typical time scales and suitable e-learning tools.

In a whole, social networks such as vk/fb are more suitable for rapid communications at a preliminary stage where a quick and brief answer is required. A mailbox is suitable to receive, classify, store and revise emails with reports. Comparing vk/fb and Blackboard (Bb), we note the advantages of vk/fb such as a well known and friendly interface, and the availability of all main functions: chat, email, file exchange, provided that there are no confidence or copyright problems. In contrast, Bb is better suited for copyrighted internal resources and for administrative management of educative tasks. Thus a natural difference and delimitation between these tools appears. Concerning our practical experience, in general physics and natural science courses there are usually no

Table 1. Works, time scales and usable e-tools

Typical functions and works	Lead time	Best form of contact	E-tool used[a]
Minor corrections, misspellings	Minute	chat	vk/fb
Recalculate or replot some results	Hour	chat, e-mail	vk/fb, gmail
Total rework of a report	Day	e-mail	gmail
Home reading of relevant chapters	Week	download	online archive

[a] vk/fb mean common social networks, gmail is an example of a e-mail tool.

copyright problems, so the convenience of use is a main criterion, and the vk/fb networks are preferred. This was also confirmed by our inquiry and experience.

8 Conclusions

Since all the matters are different, all teachers and students are different and each one comes with his own way of thinking, a high-quality computer formalization of all possible cases seems impossible. The computer is only a good supplement to the reality; it cannot perform all distant functions and cannot replace real objects. However the e-learning is to be permanently enhanced, especially when a classroom work is impossible fore some reasons. So the main task is to clearly separate live and electronic works, each with its own tasks and results.

There is sometimes a logic error: it is presumed that e-learning is a self-evident advantage, while classic human contacts need to be justified to their adversaries. Anyway, a high school menu should certainly offer e-learning and computer-added activities which should be permanently enhanced, but rather as a supplement. On the other hand, the educative market not always follows the point of view of leading teachers. So if the market requires a high-quality multimedia product, this product must be provided. A routine training can be performed on or by the computer, while the true understanding can be acquired only in a personal contact with a teacher.

Acknowledgment. This research was sponsored by the Russian Foundation for Basic Research under the projects: 16-04-00494 "Research of functioning of rhodopsin as the canonical representative of the class A receptors, which are the G-protein, by the methods of the local selective NMR, optical spectroscopy and numerical simulation" and 16-07-01113 "Virtual supercomputer as a tool for solving complex problems".

Authors have a reason to believe that a number of makes mentioned constitute trademarks, but they were not designated as such only to save space.

References

1. Stankova, E.N., Barmasov, A.V., Dyachenko, N.V., Bukina, M.N., Barmasova, A.M., Yakovleva, T.Yu.: The use of computer technology as a way to increase efficiency of teaching physics and other natural sciences. In: Gervasi, O., et al. (eds.) ICCSA 2016, Part IV. LNCS, vol. 9789, pp. 581–594. Springer, Cham (2016). doi:10.1007/978-3-319-42089-9_41

2. Stankova, E.N., Barmasov, A.V., Dyachenko, N.V., et al.: Prototype of informational infrastructure of a program instrumentational complex for carrying out a laboratory practicum on physics in a university. In: Gervasi, O., et al. (eds.) ICCSA 2017, Part V. LNCS, vol. 10408, pp. 412–427. Springer, AG (2017)

3. Barmasov, A.V., Kholmogorov, V.E.: Course of general physics for nature managers. Mechanics, Ed. by Chirtsov, A.S. BHV-St. Petersburg, St. Petersburg. 416 p. (2008, 2012) (in Russian)

4. Barmasov, A.V., Kholmogorov, V.E.: Course of general physics for nature managers. Oscillations and Waves, Ed. by Bobrovsky, A.P. BHV-St. Petersburg, St. Petersburg. 256 p. (2009, 2012) (in Russian)

5. Barmasov, A.V., Kholmogorov, V.E.: Course of general physics for nature managers. Molecular Physics and Thermodynamics, Ed. by Bobrovsky, A.P. BHV-St. Petersburg, St. Petersburg. 512 p. (2009, 2012) (in Russian)

6. Barmasov, A.V., Kholmogorov, V.E.: Course of general physics for nature managers. Electricity, Ed. by Bobrovsky, A.P. BHV-St. Petersburg, St. Petersburg. 448 p. (2010, 2013) (in Russian)

7. Barmasov, A.V., Barmasova, A.M., Struts, A.V., Yakovleva, T.Yu.: Dynamics of rigid body. Elements of the theory and the collection of tasks, 28 p. Publishing House of St. Petersburg State Pediatric Medical University, St. Petersburg (2012). (in Russian)

8. Kholmogorov, V.Ye., Barmasov, A.V.: The biosphere and physical factors. Electromagnetic fields and life. In: The Problems of Theoretical and Applied Ecology, pp. 27–47. RSHMU, St. Petersburg (2005). 267 p. (in Russian)

9. Barmasov, A.V., Barmasova, A.M., Yakovleva, T.Yu.: The biosphere and the physical factors. Light pollution of the environment. In: Proceedings of the Russian State Hydrometeorological University, vol. 33, pp. 84–101 (2014). (in Russian)

10. Yakovleva, T.Yu., Barmasova, A.M., Barmasov, A.V.: The biosphere and the physical factors. Possible hazards of wide application of white LEDs. In: The World Science and Education in Contemporary Society: Collection of Scientific Works on Materials of the International Scientific-Practical Conference, 4 parts, Part III, pp. 42–50. OOO "AR-Consult", Moscow, 30 October 2014. (in Russian)

11. Barmasov, A.V., Barmasova, A.M., Yakovleva, T.Yu.: The biosphere and physical factors. The geomagnetic field. In: Modern Trends in the Development of Science and Technology, (3–4), pp. 127–131 (2015). (in Russian)

12. Barmasov, A.V., Korotkov, V.I., Kholmogorov, V.Ye.: Model photosynthetic system with charge transfer for transforming solar energy. Biophysics **39**(2), 227–231 (1994)

13. Struts, A.V., Barmasov, A.V., Brown, M.F.: Methods for studying photoreceptors and photoactive molecules in biological and model systems: rhodopsin as a canonical representative of the seven-transmembrane helix receptors. Series 4. Physics, Chemistry, (2), pp. 191–202. Bulletin of St. Petersburg University (2014). (in Russian), https://www.journalguide.com/journals/bulletin-of-st-petersburg-university-series-4-physics-chemistry

14. Struts, A.V., Barmasov, A.V., Brown, M.F.: Spectral methods for study of the G-Protein-Coupled receptor rhodopsin. I Vibrational and electronic spectroscopy. Opt. Spectrosc. **118**(5), 711–717 (2015)

15. Struts, A.V., Barmasov, A.V., Brown, M.F.: Spectral methods for study of the G-Protein-Coupled receptor rhodopsin. II Magnetic resonance methods. Opt. Spectrosc. **120**(2), 286–293 (2016)

16. Bukina, M.N., Bakulev, V.M., Barmasov, A.V., et al.: Luminescence diagnostics of conformational changes of the Hsp70 protein in the course of thermal denaturation. Opt. Spectrosc. **118**(6), 899–901 (2015)

17. Bukina, M.N., Barmasov, A.V., Lisachenko, D.A., Ivanov, A.S.: Modern methods of teaching physics and the concepts of modern natural science. In: Proceedings of the II International Scientific-Methodical Conference on Modern Educational Technologies in Teaching Natural-Scientific and Humane Disciplines. Mining University, St. Petersburg, pp. 516–520, 9–10 April 2015. 732 p. (in Russian)
18. Lisachenko, D.A.: Le français par la science: une langue étrangère enseignée par un scientifique aux scientifiques. Le français de spécialité. Enjeux culturels et linguistiques. Comité Éditorial: Olivier Bertrand, Isabelle Schaffner. Paris, Editions de l'Ecole Polytechnique, pp. 141–150 (2008)
19. Lisachenko, D.A., Ibragimov, I.I.: Modern issues in scientific and technical translation and its teaching in the system of higher education. In: Modern Educational Technology in the Teaching Natural Sciences and the Humanities: Proceedings of the IV International Scientific-Methodical Conference. Mining University, St. Petersburg, pp. 106–111, 11–12 April 2017. (in Russian)
20. Barmasova, A.M., Barmasov, A.V., Skoblikova, A.L., et al.: Features of teaching general physics to the students-ecologists. In: The Problems of Theoretical and Applied Ecology, pp. 226–241. Publishing House RSHU, St. Petersburg (2005). 267 p., 15 p. (in Russian)
21. Barmasova, A.M., Barmasov, A.V., Bobrovsky, A.P., Yakovleva, T.Yu.: To the question about teaching general physics to the students-ecologists. In: Abstracts. Meeting of the Heads of Departments of Physics of Technical Universities in Russia, pp. 46–48. AVIAIZDAT, Moscow (2006). (in Russian)
22. Barmasova, A.M., Yakovleva, T.Yu., Barmasov, A.V., et al.: An integrated approach to he teaching physics to students-nature managers. In: Spirin, G.G. (ed.) Abstracts of Scientific-Methodical Workshop on "The Physics in the Engineering Education System of the EurAsEC Member States" and the Meeting of Heads of Physics Departments of Technical Universities of Russia. The Scientific Seminar was Held from 25 to 27 June 2007, pp. 40–41. Zhukovsky Air Force Engineering Academy, Moscow (2007). 344 p. (in Russian)
23. Barmasova, A.M., Yakovleva, T.Yu., Barmasov, A.V., et al.: Multimedia lecture course on processing of results of measurements of physical quantities for students users. In: Spirin, G. G. (ed.) Abstracts of Scientific-Methodical Workshop on "The Physics in the Engineering Education System of the EurAsEC Member States" and the Meeting of Heads of Physics Departments of Technical Universities of Russia. The Scientific Seminar was Held from 25 to 27 June 2007, p. 42. Zhukovsky Air Force Engineering Academy, Moscow (2007). 344 p. (in Russian)
24. Barmasova, A.M., Yakovleva, T.Yu., Barmasov, A.V., Bobrovsky, A.P.: Independent work of students in the conditions of introduction of profile training in high school. In: Schools and Universities: Achievements and Challenges of Continuous Physical Education: Book of Abstracts of the V Russian Scientific-Methodical Conference of Teachers of Universities and School Teachers, p. 65. USTU-UPI, Yekaterinburg (2008). 252 p. (in Russian)
25. Yakovleva, T.Yu., Barmasova, A.M., Barmasov, A.V.: Interdisciplinary connections in teaching general physics to students of science and engineering. In: Spirin, G.G. (ed.) Abstracts of Scientific-Methodical Workshop on "The Physics in the System of Engineering and Pedagogical Education of the EurAsEC Member States". The Scientific Seminar was Held in 2008, pp. 355–357. Zhukovsky Air Force Engineering Academy, Moscow (2008). 364 p. (in Russian)
26. Bukina, M.N., Barmasov, A.V., Ivanov, A.S.: Modern teaching methods for the teaching general physics and mathematical processing of results of measurements of physical quantities. In: Modern Educational Technology in the Teaching Natural Sciences and the Humanities: Proceedings of the International Scientific-Methodical Conference, pp. 408–414. Mining University, St. Petersburg, 27–29 May 2014. 562 p. (in Russian)

27. Bukina, M.N., Barmasov, A.V., Ivanov, A.S.: Some aspects of teaching physics in high school. In: VIII St. Petersburg Congress "Education, Science, Innovation in the Twenty-First Century". Collection of Works, pp. 47–49. Mining University, St. Petersburg, 24–25 October 2014. 414 p. (in Russian)

28. Bukina, M.N., Barmasov, A.V., Ivanov, A.S.: Features of general physics teaching to students of natural science specialties in modern conditions. In: The Physics in the System of Modern Education (FSSO 2015): Proceedings of the XIII International Conference, St. Petersburg, vol. 2, pp. 3–6, 1–4 June 2015. 393 p. (in Russian)

29. Bukina, M.N., Barmasov, A.V., Lisachenko, D.A., Ivanov, A.S.: Modular design of general physics course for students in natural sciences. In: Modern Educational Technology in the Teaching Natural Sciences and the Humanities: Proceedings of the III International Scientific-Methodical Conference, pp. 350–355. Mining University, St. Petersburg, 7–8 April 2016. 814 p. (in Russian)

30. Achkasov, A.V.: If the mountain won't come... translation studies meets localization. J. Siberian Federal Univ. Humanit. Soc. Sci. **9**(3), 568–578 (2016)

31. Raba, N.O., Stankova, E.N.: On the problem of numerical modeling of dangerous convective phenomena: possibilities of real-time forecast with the help of multi-core processors. In: Murgante, B., Gervasi, O., Iglesias, A., Taniar, D., Apduhan, B.O. (eds.) ICCSA 2011, Part V. LNCS, vol. 6786, pp. 633–642. Springer, Heidelberg (2011). doi:10.1007/978-3-642-21934-4_51

Hybrid Approach Combining Model-Based Method with the Technology of Machine Learning for Forecasting of Dangerous Weather Phenomena

Elena N. Stankova[1,2(✉)], Irina A. Grechko[2], Yana N. Kachalkina[2], and Evgeny V. Khvatkov[1]

[1] Saint-Petersburg State University, 7-9, Universitetskaya nab., St. Petersburg 199034, Russia
e.stankova@spbu.ru, e.hvatkov@gmail.com
[2] Saint-Petersburg Electrotechnical University "LETI", (SPbETU), ul. Professora Popova 5, St. Petersburg 197376, Russia
grechko.irinka@gmail.com, yankevich-2502@mail.ru

Abstract. The paper is a continuation of the works [1–4] where has been shown how the technologies of machine learning and online analytical processing (OLAP) could be used in conjunction with the numerical model of convective cloud for forecasting dangerous convective phenomena such as thunderstorm, heavy rainfall and hail. We study specifically the possibility of making predictions via a hybrid approach that combines the predictive numerical model of convective cloud with the modern methods of big data processing. We overview the existing examples of using of machine learning tools for weather forecasting and discuss the range of their applicability.

Keywords: OLAP · Online analytical processing · Machine learning · Validation of numerical models · Numerical model of convective cloud · Weather forecasting · Thunderstorm · Multidimensional data base · Data mining

1 Introduction

Forecasting of the atmospheric phenomena has been always a very sophisticated problem during the whole history of mankind. Low accuracy of meteorological forecasts is connected with the extreme complexity of the Earth's atmosphere as a system, its dynamic variability and the presence of great number of feedbacks, the nature of which is not known to the end.

Weather forecasts are produced on the basis of meteorological data collected by satellites and observation stations around the world. The data are processed in the meteorological centers, and then are used as an input in the forecast numerical models. Systems of the model equations are based on the laws of physics and hydrodynamics and their computational solutions are obtained on the modern computers with the help of complex numerical algorithms. Model output is calculated values of temperature, pressure, wind velocity, precipitation amount and other atmospheric parameters.

© Springer International Publishing AG 2017
O. Gervasi et al. (Eds.): ICCSA 2017, Part V, LNCS 10408, pp. 495–504, 2017.
DOI: 10.1007/978-3-319-62404-4_37

Despite of the long history of numerical models application for weather forecasting, the accuracy of the model based predictions is far from desirable values especially in case of long and medium term period forecasting. The reason lies in the inaccuracy of the input data (the errors in the data of radiosonde sounding can reach the values of 20%) and the uncontrolled numerical errors emerged in long period calculations of the atmospheric process evolution.

Besides, there are a lot of coefficients and constants in the models, which values are either known approximately or obtained during the experiments in conditions far from the atmospheric ones.

Nowadays in conditions of great progress of information technologies and especially the development of the technology of big data processing there is an opportunity to use hybrid approach combining numerical models for calculation of the evolution of the atmospheric parameters with the machine learning methods and the technology of online analytical processing (OLAP) both for validation of the models themselves and for revealing the corridors of the atmospheric conditions where the models produce the most adequate results.

In the next sections of the paper we will overview how the companies, among which are Microsoft [5], Yandex [6], and IBM [7], apply information technologies for weather forecasting. The last sections of the paper concern with the application of machine learning and OLAP for validation of the numerical model of convective cloud with the final aim to improve the quality of dangerous convective phenomena (thunderstorm, hail, heavy rain) forecasting.

2   The Use of Methods of Machine Learning in Meteorology

The use of machine learning methods in meteorology has a dual character. From one side, the pure model of machine learning is developed, where certain atmospheric parameters are predicted on the base of the observational data, obtained at the weather stations, centers and etc. From the other side, machine learning methods are used for identifications of patterns and relationships between the model forecasts and the actual meteorological situation.

The first approach is presented in [8], where an attempt is made to predict the weather of tomorrow based on meteorological observations with the help of machine learning. The author predicts the tomorrow temperature at 12:00 UTC in Oslo, the capital of Norway using Amazon Machine Learning service [9]. The weather observations from five cities in Norway, scattered around the southern half of the country, has been chose as the dataset.

The data was obtained from the Wunderground.com website in json format. Each line consisted of characteristic values in each city at a certain time. On the next day a temperature value was added to each row.

When initializing machine learning model, one can specify in the settings the number of passes through the dataset and the regularization method used. The author used the original settings. Service Amazon divides the input data in a ratio of 70% to 30%, for learning and estimating the accuracy of predictions, respectively.

The Amazon service uses the standard deviation as a parameter to estimate the accuracy of the prediction model. Ideally, the root-mean-square deviation should be small and approaching the target variable should be good.

Amazon also provides the ability to sort data by the extent to which they affect the target variable.

The last step is getting the forecast of the target variable (forecasting the temperature for tomorrow). To do this, the authors set observation obtained during one day, and left blank the value of the target variable.

The output is GZIP archive, which contains a csv file with the result.

Since the author used the data broken down by time, he got 9 temperatures as the output corresponding to each time interval. All of them were in the range from 13 to 14.5 °C. Calculating the average value, he received 13.6.

On this day the real value of the temperature was 12 °C.

Thus, the obtained value fits into the error of 1–2°. The author explains this by a too small test sample (14 days), he believes that it is necessary to use the data throughout a year. Increase of observation places (cities) can also serve as an alternative method of optimization.

The obtained preliminary results look quite optimistic (the error of prognostic temperature does not exceed 1–2°) and the author concludes that Machine Learning is a viable approach to weather forecasting.

IBM Company [7] unveiled a service called Deep Thunder that uses machine learning to help companies optimize operations based on short-term changes in temperature and rainfall. Deep Thunder is a combination of the two models: hyper-local, short-term custom forecasts developed by IBM Research with The Weather Company's global forecast model. According to Mary Glackin, Head of Science & Forecast Operations for The Weather Company, IBM Research has pioneered the development of techniques to capture very small scale features to boost accuracy at the hyper local level for critical decision making.

In November 2015 the Yandex company announced a new technology called Meteum [6, 10]. With the help of the technology, the "Yandex.Pogoda" service builds its own weather forecast. The forecast is hyper local: when the user accesses the service, Meteum recalculates a new forecast. "Yandex.Pogoda" determines where a user is, and shows the fresh forecast for the place of his/her location. Thus, "Yandex. Pogoda" is a service for building the most current weather forecast for given coordinates.

Meteum technology combines traditional meteorological models and technologies of machine learning. Machine learning allows to refine existing numerical models and takes into account local features.

Meteum is a combination of the WRF model [11], which is calculated directly on Yandex clusters, of forecasts for 12,000 cities of Russia provided by Foreca Company, and of detailed information about the global state of the atmosphere provided by the US model GlobalForecastSystem, which is considered to be one of the most accurate global models in the world and has resolution of 0.25°.

As initial information, Meteum uses weather station data and the data from the other sources that can refine the local features of meteorological parameters on the Earth's surface.

As it is stated above numerical models can produce wrong data but it is interesting to state that it is possible to find certain patterns in their mistakes.

The behaviour of these models in different meteorological situations allows Meteum to assess more accurately the forecast adjustments and to choose a correct combination of input data in more optimal way.

Some of the weather forecast models overestimate the number of precipitation on the surface, others underestimate the values of night temperature in the city. If you have an archive of model forecasts, you can allocate a lot of such patterns, including much less obvious. Yandex uses its own Machine learning algorithm Matrixnet [12] for identification of the patterns and relationships between model predictions and real meteorological situation.

Matrixnet uses the revised weather forecast archives as an input data and compares them with the real data observed in the natural meteorological situation. As a real weather data information is used obtained from different sources all around the world.

As a result of such comparisons, an adjustment formula for a forecast is obtained, which, depending on the meteorological situation presents an optimal combination of the forecasts produced by the models.

By its own calculations, Yandex found out that they managed to achieve an accuracy of the temperature forecast which exceeded the accuracy of the corresponding forecast of the nearest competitor by 35%.

Grover et al. [13] uses hybrid approach trying to avoid limitations occurring while using machine learning methods for weather predictions. The limitations concern the absence of exploring the joint spatiotemporal statistic of multiple weather phenomena and the refusal to simulate long-range spatiotemporal dependencies. The authors [13] overcome the limitations by using so called hybrid approach. In [13] individual predictors are discriminatively trained from historic data and local inferences from these models are combined with a deep neural network that overlays statistical constraints among key weather variables.

3   Application of Machine Learning and OLAP for Validation of the Numerical Model of Convective Cloud

The approach proposed by Grover et al. [13] is very promising but at present it is used for predicting a few parameters: wind velocity, pressure, temperature and dew point The number of the parameters is not enough for forecasting thunderstorm, heavy rain or hail.

Yandex approach could be also called 'hybrid' in the sense that it also imply both numerical models and verify their results using machine learning methods. They use so called regional model such as WRF which is able to predict precipitation parameters but is not able to simulate the details of convective cloud microphysical and electrical characteristics.

We develop the scientific direction proposed by Yandex, but apply hybrid methods of numerical calculations and machine learning algorithms for dangerous convective phenomena forecasting with the help of specialized models of convective clouds. Before using for operational forecasts in meteorological centers the models have to be properly validated using real meteorological data. Modern information technologies such as machine learning [14, 15] and OnLine Analytical Processing (OLAP) [16] are effective tools for such validation realization.

In [4] we use three methods of machine learning and OLAP technology for processing the output data of 1.5D cloud model with a detailed description of microphysical processes [17–21]. Machine learning algorithms are applied for distinguishing the cases with dangerous convective phenomenon and without it. OLAP technology is used to differentiate a thunderstorm from hail or heavy rainfall. In the present paper we verify and enhance the results obtained in [4].

We use complex information system [1–3] for obtaining statistically significant amount of meteorological data about the state of the atmosphere in the place and at the time when a dangerous convective phenomenon takes place. Corresponding amount of information has been collected about the state of the atmosphere in cases when no dangerous convective phenomena have been observed. The collected data are used as the initial data for the cloud model for conducting series of model calculations

To implement the methods of machine learning, the Scikit-learn library was used [22]. Scikit-learn is an open source library written in the Python programming language and contains many different machine learning algorithms. It is distributed under the BSD (Berkeley Software Distribution) license, which also allows commercial use of this library.

Machine learning is used to automate the determination of the convective model input data (radiosonde sounding) which correspond to a dangerous convective phenomenon or not correspond. As a result the numerical model with proper initial data can be used for the operational prediction of a dangerous convective phenomenon in various meteorological centers. Results of application of various methods of machine training for classification of soundings through training with the teacher are presented. Our training set consists of numerical parameters simulated by a numerical model of the cloud for each sounding and is manually marked, that is, for each sounding from our set, we know whether any dangerous convective phenomenon was observed or not.

The following cloud parameters are calculated: the vertical and radial components of the velocity, pressure, air density, ambient temperature, temperature excess in the cloud, relative humidity, vertical height of the cloud, mixing ratio of water vapour, mixing ratios of aerosols, water drops, ice particles, graupel and hail.

The following 6 cloud parameters appear to be optimal as a result of feature selection analyses described in [4]. They are: the vertical component of the velocity, temperature excess in the cloud, relative humidity, mixing ratio of water vapour, mixing ratio of water drops and cloud thickness.

The first lines of the model output data set is presented in Fig. 1

The following number of soundings has been considered: 196 cases without any phenomena, 220 cases with thunderstorms, 174 cases with heavy rain, and 86 cases with light rain. To study the results and establish the patterns between the values of each type of phenomena, it was decided to use machine learning methods, namely, the naïve Bayes classifier, the method of the Parsen window, the nearest neighbour algorithm (k-nearest neighbour algorithm). The use of the support vector method (support vector machine) has been considered also [4].

	velocity	velocityU	temperature	deltaT	relativeH	vapor	pressure	density	aerosol	drop	ice	hailAndGrits	targetV
0	-0.000020	-0.000153	251.76141	-0.957136	0.154159	0.000182	58073.802	0.803588	5.660486e-08	0.0	0.0	0.0	0.0
1	-0.000003	-0.000058	256.38289	0.000636	0.385655	0.000672	58636.150	0.796744	5.715156e-08	0.0	0.0	0.0	0.0
2	0.025542	0.095872	264.02576	-0.351798	0.302595	0.000972	59282.891	0.782214	6.129834e-08	0.0	0.0	0.0	0.0
3	-0.000026	-0.000224	248.77804	0.789394	0.480335	0.000443	57008.999	0.798314	5.700730e-08	0.0	0.0	0.0	0.0
4	0.000652	0.008712	251.35257	-1.115117	0.422057	0.000489	57171.311	0.792387	5.166241e-08	0.0	0.0	0.0	0.0

Fig. 1. Model output data set

We have model data, expressed by the sets of cloud parameters and the type of precipitation. There are k neighbours, Euclidean distance to which is minimal for the each set of parameters under consideration. We prescribe the new data to the class which has gained more votes following the results of the neighbour votes.

At first we tried to teach the classifier to determine both the presence and type of phenomenon. The ratio of the train sample to the test sample was set 2 to 1 and was randomly distributed. As it turned out, this ratio strongly affects the accuracy of the obtained results. The number of neighbours k was constantly changed from 5 to 21 to track the change in the results. The probability of forecasting the type of phenomenon varied from 35% to 55%, depending on changes in the train/test ratio and the number of neighbours. This result appeared to be quite unsatisfactory one.

The next step is to simplify the task of the classifier by trying to establish the type of phenomenon. It was manually selected that the optimal ratio of train/test ration is 4 to 1. The number of neighbours changed from 3 to 51. The result was 60–70%, which is also unsatisfactory one.

The calculation of the Euclidean distance between the parameters and the adequacy of the estimation depend also on the ratio of the parameters themselves (some parameters are larger/smaller than the others by an order of magnitude). To solve this problem, normalization was carried out using the standard deviation. Values of the parameters became an order of magnitude closer to each other. This operation increased the accuracy of estimating of the result to 85–95%. 95% was obtained when the ratio train/test was equal 4 to 1 and k = 21.

The accuracy of the assessment depends heavily on how the train/test sample was distributed. Either in train, or in test, in some cases, accidentally, there can be significantly more sets of parameters of one class than the other. This can change the accuracy of the estimation by 5–10% up or down.

The obtained results show that machine learning methods are quite good for distinguishing the cases with dangerous convective phenomenon and without it. To differentiate various types of convective phenomena we have to use OLAP technology.

Multidimensionality in the framework of OLAP technology assumes a conceptual representation of data in the form of a multidimensional data structure, which is called a hypercube (OLAP-cube), although the sides of such a cube are not always equal. The hypercube is viewed as a coordinate system in which the axes are measurements (theoretically, the cube can have any number of measurements). The measurement values will be plotted along the axes. In such a system, each set of measurement values will correspond to a cell in which you can place measures (numerical indicators/facts) associated with the given set. Consequently, a unique relationship is established between the process objects of the process and their numerical characteristics.

Our multidimensional database is a 3-D cube, the axes of which represent the following dimensions: "Dates," "Phenomena," and "Cloud features." The dates of the specific cases when the specific dangerous convective phenomenon has been observed or has not been observed are represented along the "Dates" axis. The types of phenomena (storm, hail, heavy rain, with no events) are located along the "Phenomena" axis. Cloud features selected above are located along the corresponding third axis. The view of the cube is presented on Fig. 2.

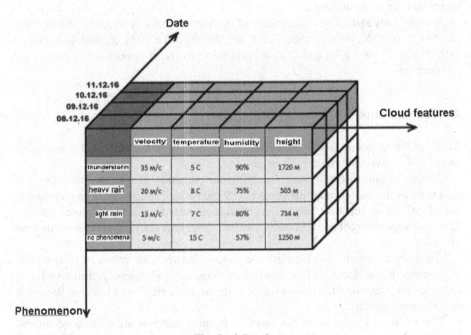

Fig. 2. 3-D cube

We fill in our multidimensional data base with the help of integrated information system, which allow to integrate information about the dates and types of different convective phenomena, about vertical distributions of temperature and relative humidity observed on these dates and cloud features, obtained as a result of numerical experiments by using the cloud model with corresponding input parameters. The values of the calculated cloud features are filled in the cells of the cube at the intersection of corresponding axes.

Technical realization of the development of a multidimensional database, it's filling and multidimensional analysis are carried out using PHP API (Application Program Interface written on PHP language). PHP API is provided by the developers of the Jedox Palo BI Suite system produced by a German company Jedox AG [23].

It has been chosen because Jedox Palo is an open source OLAP-system allowing becoming a client for any outer program or system (e.g. ERP or CRM). Jedox Palo enables to realise statistical processing of the output data of complex models for providing subsequent analysis.

After the data is successfully downloaded in the multidimensional data base one can move to their analysis. Analysis shows, that vertical velocity, temperature excess, mixing ratios of water droplets, ice particles and hail vary in much larger range of values in case of thunderstorm than the corresponding parameters in case of light rain and heavy rain.

However, the data do not allow finding significant differences in the values of the of light and heavy rain parameters. Obviously, this question requires further study using a larger number of input data.

We can only state that if the values of the vertical velocity exceeds 18 m/s, temperature excess $5°$, mixing ratios of water droplets, ice particles and hail exceed $7 \cdot 10-3$ g/kg, $3 \cdot 10-2$ g/kg and $2 \cdot 10-4$ g/kg, respectively, it is possible to predict the thunderstorm.

4 Conclusions

Machine learning and OLAP technologies are used for validation of 1.5 numerical model of a convective cloud.

Integrated information system is applied for gathering of specific meteorological data used as the model input parameters. 289 radiosonde soundings were collected in the place and at the time when dangerous convective phenomena were recorder. 326 soundings were collected in cases when no dangerous convective phenomena were observed.

To study the results and establish the patterns between the values of each type of phenomena, it was decided to use machine learning methods, namely, the naïve Bayes classifier, the method of the Parsen window, the nearest neighbour algorithm (k-nearest neighbour algorithm).

The obtained results show that machine learning methods are quite good for distinguishing the cases with dangerous convective phenomenon and without it. To differentiate various types of convective phenomena we have to use OLAP technology.

Multidimensional data base intended for distinguishing the types of the phenomena (thunderstorm, heavy rainfall and light rain) has been developed where the data have been presented in the form of a cube that contains information about the parameters of the convective clouds obtained by a series of numerical experiments Technical realisation is carried out using PHP API of the Jedox Palo BI Suite system produced by the German company Jedox AG. The range of variation and average values of cloud parameters have been identified typical for different convective phenomena.

Future work includes revealing the existence of the geographical differences in the values of decision functions. It will require the collection of statistically significant initial information about the presence of thunderstorms in different geographical areas and the selection of corresponding radiosonde soundings. We wish to investigate the influence of the moment of cloud evolution when the most representative cloud parameters (features) are selected upon the results of machine learning. Besides we are interested in exploring the number of the "classical" features, already used for thunderstorm prediction while operational forecasting in meteorological centers and airports in Russia. We intend to expand the capabilities of our integrated information system by connecting it to a wider range of sources of meteorological information, as well as to continue filling the multidimensional database and work with it for obtaining more accurate range of cloud parameters typical for various convection phenomena. We plan that our integrated information system will be a consistent part of the Virtual private supercomputer [24, 25], that will enable users to provide forecasts of the dangerous convective phenomena by themselves.

Acknowledgment. This research was sponsored by the Russian Foundation for Basic Research under the projects: No. 16-07-01113.

References

1. Petrov, D.A., Stankova, E.N.: Use of consolidation technology for meteorological data processing. In: Murgante, B., Misra, S., Rocha, A.M.A.C., Torre, C., Rocha, J.G., Falcão, M. I., Taniar, D., Apduhan, B.O., Gervasi, O. (eds.) ICCSA 2014. LNCS, vol. 8579, pp. 440–451. Springer, Cham (2014). doi:10.1007/978-3-319-09144-0_30
2. Petrov, D.A., Stankova, E.N.: Integrated information system for verification of the models of convective clouds. In: Gervasi, O., Murgante, B., Misra, S., Gavrilova, M.L., Rocha, A.M.A. C., Torre, C., Taniar, D., Apduhan, B.O. (eds.) ICCSA 2015. LNCS, vol. 9158, pp. 321–330. Springer, Cham (2015). doi:10.1007/978-3-319-21410-8_25
3. Stankova, E.N., Petrov, D.A.: Complex information system for organization of the input data of models of convective clouds. Appl. Math. Comput. Sci. Control Process. **10**(3), 83–95 (2015). Vestnik of Saint-Petersburg University. (in Russian)
4. Stankova, E.N., Balakshiy, A.V., Petrov, D.A., Shorov, A.V., Korkhov, V.V.: Using technologies of OLAP and machine learning for validation of the numerical models of convective clouds. In: Gervasi, O., Murgante, B., Misra, S., Rocha, A.M.A.C., Torre, C., Taniar, D., Apduhan, B.O., Stankova, E., Wang, S. (eds.) ICCSA 2016. LNCS, vol. 9788, pp. 463–472. Springer, Cham (2016). doi:10.1007/978-3-319-42111-7_36
5. Grover, A., Kapoor, A., Horvitz, E.: A Deep Hybrid Model for Weather Forecasting (2015). http://research.microsoft.com/en-us/um/people/horvitz/weather_hybrid_representation.pdf. Accessed 13 Aug 2016
6. Meteum technology. https://yandex.ru/pogoda/meteum. Accessed 17 Jan 2017. (in Russian)
7. The Weather Company Launches 'Deep Thunder' - the World's Most Advanced Hyper-Local Weather Forecasting Model for Businesses https://www-03.ibm.com/press/us/en/pressrelease/49954.wss. Accessed 15 June 2016
8. Using Amazon Machine Learning to Predict the Weather. https://arnesund.com/2015/05/31/using-amazon-machine-learning-to-predict-the-weather/. Accessed 20 Feb 2017
9. Tutorial: Using Amazon ML to Predict Responses to a Marketing Offer. http://docs.aws.amazon.com/machine-learning/latest/dg/tutorial.html. Accessed 10 Mar 2017
10. How Yandex predicts the weather. https://yandex.ru/company/technologies/meteum/. Accessed 17 Jan 2017. (in Russian)
11. Weather Research and Forecasting Model. http://www.wrf-model.org/index.php. Accessed 7 Mar 2017

12. Matrixnet. https://yandex.ru/company/technologies/matrixnet/. Accessed 26 Nov 2016. (in Russian)
13. Grover, A., Kapoor, A., Horvitz, E.: A Deep Hybrid Model for Weather Forecasting (2015). http://research.microsoft.com/en-us/um/people/horvitz/weather_hybrid_representation.pdf. Accessed 13 Aug 2016
14. Hastie, T., Tibshirani, R., Friedman, J.: The elements of Statistical Learning (2009). http://statweb.stanford.edu/~tibs/ElemStatLearn/. Accessed 15 Feb 2015
15. Mitchell, T.: Machine Learning. Springer, Berlin (2009)
16. Codd, E.: Providing OLAP (on-line analytical processing) to user-analysts: an IT mandate, Technical report, E.F. Codd and Associates (1993)
17. Raba, N., Stankova, E.: Research of influence of compensating descending flow on cloud's life cycle by means of 1.5-dimensional model with 2 cylinders. Proc. MGO **559**, 192–209 (2009). (in Russian)
18. Raba, N., Stankova, E., Ampilova, N.: On investigation of parallelization effectiveness with the help of multi-core processors. Procedia Comput. Sci. **1**(1), 2757–2762 (2010)
19. Raba, N., Stankova, E.: On the possibilities of multi-core processor use for real-time forecast of dangerous convective phenomena. In: Taniar, D., Gervasi, O., Murgante, B., Pardede, E., Apduhan, Bernady O. (eds.) ICCSA 2010. LNCS, vol. 6017, pp. 130–138. Springer, Heidelberg (2010). doi:10.1007/978-3-642-12165-4_11
20. Raba, N.O., Stankova, E.N.: On the Problem of Numerical Modeling of Dangerous Convective Phenomena: Possibilities of Real-Time Forecast with the Help of Multi-core Processors. In: Murgante, B., Gervasi, O., Iglesias, A., Taniar, D., Apduhan, Bernady O. (eds.) ICCSA 2011. LNCS, vol. 6786, pp. 633–642. Springer, Heidelberg (2011). doi:10.1007/978-3-642-21934-4_51
21. Raba, N.O., Stankova, E.N.: On the effectiveness of using the GPU for numerical solution of stochastic collection equation. In: Murgante, B., Misra, S., Carlini, M., Torre, Carmelo M., Nguyen, H.-Q., Taniar, D., Apduhan, Bernady O., Gervasi, O. (eds.) ICCSA 2013. LNCS, vol. 7975, pp. 248–258. Springer, Heidelberg (2013). doi:10.1007/978-3-642-39640-3_18
22. Scikit-learn: Machine Learning in Python. http://scikit-learn.org/
23. Jedox. http://www.jedox.com/. Accessed 21 Nov 2015
24. Gankevich, I., Korkhov, V., Balyan, S., Gaiduchok, V., Gushchanskiy, D., Tipikin, Y., Degtyarev, A., Bogdanov, A.: Constructing virtual private supercomputer using virtualization and cloud technologies. In: Murgante, B., Misra, S., Rocha, Ana Maria A.C., Torre, C., Rocha, J.G., Falcão, M.I., Taniar, D., Apduhan, Bernady O., Gervasi, O. (eds.) ICCSA 2014. LNCS, vol. 8584, pp. 341–354. Springer, Cham (2014). doi:10.1007/978-3-319-09153-2_26
25. Gankevich, I., Gaiduchok, V., Gushchanskiy, D., Tipikin, Y., Korkhov, V., Degtyarev, A., Bogdanov, A., Zolotarev, V.: Virtual private supercomputer: design and evaluation. In: Computer Science and Information Technologies (CSIT), pp 1–6. IEEE Conference Publications (2013). doi:10.1109/CSITechnol.2013.6710358

Acceleration of Computing and Visualization Processes with OpenCL for Standing Sea Wave Simulation Model

Andrei Ivashchenko[✉], Alexey Belezeko, Ivan Gankevich, Vladimir Korkhov, and Nataliia Kulabukhova

Department of Computer Modeling and Multiprocessor Systems, Saint Petersburg State University, Universitetskii prospekt 35, Petergof, Saint Petersburg 198504, Russia
aiivashchenko@cc.spbu.ru, alexey.belezeko@gmail.com, {i.gankevich,v.korkhov,n.kulabukhova}@spbu.ru

Abstract. In this paper we highlight one of the possible acceleration approaches for the standing wave model simulation model with the use of OpenCL framework for GPGPU computations. We provide a description of the wave's mathematical model, an explanation for the technology selection, as well as the identification of the algorithm part that can be accelerated. The text also contains a description of solution's performance evaluation stage being compared with CPU-only program. The influence of OpenCL usage for improvements in rendering process is also shown here. Finally, possible ways of application improvement and further development are also considered.

Keywords: Computing · Mathematical modelling · OpenCL · OpenGL · Autoregressive process · Moving average process · Velocity potential field · Visualisation · Real-time simulation

1 Introduction

In most cases, visualisation of scientific data obtained during simulation or computation process is carried out separately, after all the stages of calculation are completed. This fact is connected with a rather large number of factors: computation process could be executed with CPU-only nodes (however, this should not be considered as a problem since the Mesa 3D graphics library exists); the goal to complete a task as fast as possible could have greater priority, thus, all available resources would be used for this; data could be just difficult to process and synchronise during in runtime, if such a scenario was not assumed by the software solution.

However, on the other hand, during the computation process, especially the long one, there is a need to monitor for performed operations and obtained results. In the case where such a control is possible the calculations could be suspended and the necessary tweaks made with a timely response. This kind of action may also be

© Springer International Publishing AG 2017
O. Gervasi et al. (Eds.): ICCSA 2017, Part V, LNCS 10408, pp. 505–518, 2017.
DOI: 10.1007/978-3-319-62404-4_38

needed while debugging the program or testing a new mathematical model. Thus, in this article we will consider the possibility of interactive control organisation for calculations with a terms of visualisation, which will be performed using the OpenGL API.

Another possible scenario of this approach is an interaction with simulated objects and processes in real-time. So, you can change the initial conditions, add new environmental parameters and observe the system's response immediately from the moment of the effect's influence beginning to its end. In the framework of ocean wave simulation this has educational value, as the effect of every change in the input parameter is immediately visible. In addition to this, instantaneous visualisation of ocean wavy surface brings simulation to a new level, where dynamically changing parameters to arbitrary values within predefined ranges allows to visually verify the model and its numerical code.

For the experiment we have chosen an autoregressive model of standing waves within framework of which we have accelerated velocity potential field computation with the usage of GPGPU technology through the OpenCL framework. Since, data structures that are needed for visualisation are already stored in GPU memory, we take into account that fact and remove unnecessary copying between host and device using OpenGL/OpenCL interoperability API.

2   Related Work

The idea of mixing various computing APIs is not a fresh one, also including for OpenGL/OpenCL interoperability. Nvidia has announced the support for this technology in the 2011, and since then we have been able to observe the related solutions appeared on the market.

The idea of compute API usage was widely spread and adopted by entertainment industry, especially in game development sphere. Ever since the popularisation of the PhysX engine, which uses the capabilities of graphics cards to simulate a certain set of physical phenomena, it was clear that such a technology will find a place to be applied in the future [9]. So, for today, almost all heavy dynamic particle systems you can met are using one of the general compute APIs [15].

Another area of general usage where this technology was introduced is a computer vision. Industry standard library OpenCV has a special OCL module originally provided by AMD, which enables the acceleration for various algorithms, including ones for matrix transformations, image filtering and processing, object detection and many more [3].

However, the situation with scientific calculation is absolutely different. Unlike the entertainment software where the vast of the scene contents in most cases are generated in advance and the number of processes is strictly limited to ones affecting the environment at the current moment, for the scientific simulations almost everything should be calculated from scratch based only on given initial conditions, including the geometry (if it is meant by the process), the particle system, visual effects, etc. In addition, simulations by themselves are much more complicated, and the optimisation for dynamically forming geometric structures is quite difficult to perform.

There is a way to achieve more efficient usage of resources while performing the visualisation of the computational experiment results, which are involving GPGPU to speed up the computation, and it is directly related to the accelerator exploitation. Thus, when graphics cards are used to compute, it is obvious that the data is already allocated on its memory. So, if there is a way to transform the data to the format that can be used by the graphic API, and also the way to transfer it between the compute and graphics contexts, then we will not have to copy it from the memory of GPU to the RAM and vice versa. Thus, the usage of OpenCL, CUDA, or any other compute API can boost the performance not only for the calculations themselves, but also for the results rendering. Thus, we have reviewed several papers which are referring to the stated problem to get a glance whether this approach could be used for the optimisation in our case.

One of the most interesting cases was shown by the research group from Boston Northeastern University [14]. The OpenCL/OpenGL interoperability was applied to five completely different applications related to the different study areas. For example, one of them is a Material Fault Detection program used for fault detection using wave propagation in anisotropic materials, which produces material layer surfaces. They have used a slot-based rendering technique, which means that data is precomputed for several frames in advance before passing it to the rendering context. As a result, they have been able to obtain 2.2 more frames in average with discrete AMD GPUs Radeon 7770 and Radeon 7970 and 1.9 more with AMD Fusion A8 APU.

As for the image processing, we can refer to [12], where the interop technique is used for panorama video image stitching. According to the provided metrics the best result is achieved with involving two buffers for both OpenCL computations and OpenGL rendering, and it is 12 times faster compared to the original CPU based solution. The paper is also showing that the proposed solution is scaled really well when the additional image capturing devices are attached to the system. We should also notice an another closely related case presented by Samsung at SIGGRAPH'13, which talks in general about real time video stream processing on mobile platforms captured by camera module with the usage of OpenCL and OpenGL ES interoperability [4].

All the examples of GPGPU API interoperability mentioned above are proving that the proposed approach could be applied for the various set of problems to achieve the significant results in optimisation of calculations and visualisation itself. However, it should be said that the following solutions has been applied for the particular cases and not showing any general solution, which could be treated as a specificity of the interoperability method. During the study we will try to point out the major improvements made by research groups to complete our solution in a most optimal way.

3   Compute and Graphics Contexts Interoperability

OpenGL itself does not contain any mechanisms that could help to organise the interaction between OpenGL and OpenCL. However, despite the fact that the specified functionality is not available, OpenGL supports the data and message exchange between its own contexts, the fundamental principles of which are laid in CL/GL interoperability [1]. Thus, it would be expediently to consider on this question as it represents the basics we need to understand.

First, the graphics card, which is intended to be used for computation, should be checked for OpenCL shared context mode support. To find this out, the `clinfo` command line utility should be run on the target machine. If the required functionality is supported the `cl_khr_gl_sharing` option will be specified in the "Device Extensions" section [10]. This extension is provided by Khronos group and it is responsible for the interaction between APIs.

The following extension contains all necessary functions for OpenCL, which are defined in `cl_gl.h` header file. In general, they could be divided into three main groups:

- Memory broker functions—acquire and release allocated memory areas represented with OpenGL objects;
- Object transformation functions—create an OpenCL representation for OpenGL object;
- Info functions—provide various information about OpenGL context, like associated devices, object description, etc.

The next thing that should be discussed is data types, which could be driven by the interoperability API. This issue has been partially reviewed in [2] at the discussion about graphics API parallelization. Basically, all OpenGL object are represented with two groups. The first one is a Container Object group the specificity of which lies in the fact that they can not be shared between contexts since they contain references to other objects, and GL standard disallow transfer for objects of that type, i.e. they are not a point of our interest. Another group contains regular Objects, which could be shared between context without any limitations. Since we need to share only the data for now, we should take a look for the Buffer Object, which could actually store an array of unformatted memory allocated by the OpenGL context. Among all Buffer Objects, for the our particular case the Vertex Buffer Object should be used at first to transfer the surface representation data.

Due to the fact that graphics unit could proceed with the single context at once, we will need to manage them manually by alternating them upon request. Following this way we should be able to build a pipeline as it presented in Fig. 1. Here, both contexts controlled by the main process are basically performing eight main steps to achieve the goal:

1. First, check whether the `cl_khr_gl_sharing` is supported by the target GPGPU.

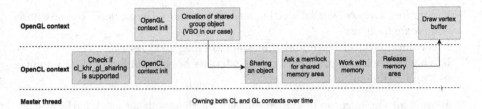

Fig. 1. OpenGL/OpenCL interoperability pipeline.

2. If the previous step succeeds, initialise both compute and graphics contexts.
3. Next, the shared object is created by OpenGL. It will be used later on to pass the data back to graphics context.
4. Then, the control passes to the OpenCL context and the object is registered here for the sharing.
5. Apply a lock for the memory area acquired by the object.
6. Perform all required computations and write the results to the shared memory.
7. Release the lock and pass control to the graphics API.
8. Finally, process and draw geometry.

4 Standing Sea Waves Simulation Model

Our approach to sea waves simulation is based on the autoregressive model—moving average (ARMA) model of sea waves [6,7]. This model was developed as an superior alternative to existing linear Longuet—Higgins model. The new model simulates sea waves without assumptions of linear and small amplitude wave theories, i.e.

– the model generates waves of arbitrary amplitudes,
– period of wavy surface realisation equals the period of pseudo-random number generator (PRNG) and
– it requires less number of coefficients to converge compared to Longuet—Higgins model.

This model allows to generate both propagating and standing sea waves via moving average and autoregressive process respectively, but for the purpose of this paper we narrow the discussion to standing waves and autoregressive (AR) process only.

One implication of turning down the assumptions of linear wave theory is that it is not possible to use linear velocity potential field computation formulae for the new wavy surface, as they were derived under the same assumptions. As a result, the new analytic formula was derived, that determines velocity potential field under arbitrary wavy sea surface. This formula is particularly suitable for computation on GPUs:

– it contains transcendental mathematical functions (hyperbolic cosines and complex exponents);
– it is computed over large four-dimensional (t, x, y, z) region;
– it is analytic with no information dependencies between individual data points in t and z dimensions.

Moreover, for the purpose of the verification of the resulting wavy surface, it is imperative to visualise the surface and velocity potential velocity field in real-time as the computation progresses. Performing two simulations at a time with different velocity potential field formulae allows to spot the difference in computed fields, and to visually compare the size and the shape of regions where the most wave energy is concentrated.

Within the framework of autoregressive model for standing waves we investigate how GPGPU computations can be used to speed-up velocity potential field computation and make real-time visualisation of the surface as computation proceeds.

4.1 Governing Equations for 3-Dimensional AR Process

Three-dimensional autoregressive process is defined by

$$\zeta_{i,j,k} = \sum_{l=0}^{p_1} \sum_{m=0}^{p_2} \sum_{n=0}^{p_3} \Phi_{l,m,n} \zeta_{i-l,j-m,k-n} \epsilon_{i,j,k},$$

where ζ—wave elevation, Φ—AR coefficients, ϵ—white noise with Gaussian distribution, (p_1, p_2, p_3)—AR process order, and $\Phi_{0,0,0} \equiv 0$. The input parameters are AR process coefficients and order.

The coefficients Φ are calculated from ACF via three-dimensional Yule—Walker equations:

$$\Gamma \begin{bmatrix} \Phi_{0,0,0} \\ \Phi_{0,0,1} \\ \vdots \\ \Phi_{p_1,p_2,p_3} \end{bmatrix} = \begin{bmatrix} K_{0,0,0} - \sigma_\epsilon^2 \\ K_{0,0,1} \\ \vdots \\ K_{p_1,p_2,p_3} \end{bmatrix}, \quad \Gamma = \begin{bmatrix} \Gamma_0 & \Gamma_1 & \cdots & \Gamma_{p_1} \\ \Gamma_1 & \Gamma_0 & \ddots & \vdots \\ \vdots & \ddots & \ddots & \Gamma_1 \\ \Gamma_{p_1} & \cdots & \Gamma_1 & \Gamma_0 \end{bmatrix},$$

where $N = (p_1, p_2, p_3)$, σ_ϵ^2 — white noise variance, and

$$\Gamma_i = \begin{bmatrix} \Gamma_i^0 & \Gamma_i^1 & \cdots & \Gamma_i^{p_2} \\ \Gamma_i^1 & \Gamma_i^0 & \ddots & \vdots \\ \vdots & \ddots & \ddots & \Gamma_i^1 \\ \Gamma_i^{p_2} & \cdots & \Gamma_i^1 & \Gamma_i^0 \end{bmatrix} \quad \Gamma_i^j = \begin{bmatrix} K_{i,j,0} & K_{i,j,1} & \cdots & K_{i,j,p_3} \\ K_{i,j,1} & K_{i,j,0} & \ddots & x & \vdots \\ \vdots & \ddots & \ddots & K_{i,j,1} \\ K_{i,j,p_3} & \cdots & K_{i,j,1} & K_{i,j,0} \end{bmatrix},$$

Since $\Phi_{0,0,0} \equiv 0$, the first row and column of Γ can be eliminated. Matrix Γ is block-toeplitz, positive definite and symmetric, hence the system is solved by Cholesky decomposition. White noise variance is estimated by

$$\sigma_\epsilon^2 = K_{0,0,0} - \sum_{i=0}^{p_1}\sum_{j=0}^{p_2}\sum_{k=0}^{p_3} \Phi_{i,j,k}K_{i,j,k}.$$

4.2 Three-Dimensional Velocity Potential Field

The problem of finding pressure field under wavy sea surface represents inverse problem of hydrodynamics for incompressible inviscid fluid. System of equations for it in general case is written as [11]

$$\begin{aligned} & \nabla^2\phi = 0, \\ & \phi_t + \frac{1}{2}|\boldsymbol{v}|^2 + g\zeta = -\frac{p}{\rho}, && z = \zeta(x,y,t), \\ & D\zeta = \nabla\phi\cdot\boldsymbol{n}, && z = \zeta(x,y,t), \end{aligned} \tag{1}$$

where ϕ—velocity potential, ζ—elevation (z coordinate) of wavy surface, p—wave pressure, ρ—fluid density, $\boldsymbol{v} = (\phi_x, \phi_y, \phi_z)$—velocity vector, g—acceleration of gravity, and D—substantial (Lagrange) derivative. The first equation is called continuity (Laplace) equation, the second one is the conservation of momentum law (the so called dynamic boundary condition); the third one is kinematic boundary condition for free wavy surface, which states that rate of change of wavy surface elevation ($D\zeta$) equals to the change of velocity potential derivative along the wavy surface normal ($\nabla\phi\cdot\boldsymbol{n}$).

Inverse problem of hydrodynamics consists in solving this system of equations for ϕ. In this formulation dynamic boundary condition becomes explicit formula to determine pressure field using velocity potential derivatives obtained from the remaining equations. So, from mathematical point of view inverse problem of hydrodynamics reduces to Laplace equation with mixed boundary condition—Robin problem.

Three-dimensional version of (1) is written as

$$\phi_{xx} + \phi_{yy} + \phi_{zz} = 0,$$

$$\zeta_t + \zeta_x\phi_x + \zeta_y\phi_y = \frac{\zeta_x}{\sqrt{1+\zeta_x^2+\zeta_y^2}}\phi_x + \frac{\zeta_y}{\sqrt{1+\zeta_x^2+\zeta_y^2}}\phi_y - \phi_z, \quad z = \zeta(x,y,t).$$

Using Fourier method with some assumptions the equation is solved yielding formula for ϕ:

$$\phi(x,y,z,t) = \mathcal{F}_{x,y}^{-1}\left\{\frac{\cosh\left(2\pi|\boldsymbol{k}|(z+h)\right)}{2\pi|\boldsymbol{k}|\cosh\left(2\pi|\boldsymbol{k}|h\right)}\mathcal{F}_{u,v}\left\{\frac{\zeta_t}{(if_1(x,y)+if_2(x,y)-1)}\right\}\right\}, \tag{2}$$

where $f_1(x,y) = \zeta_x/\sqrt{1+\zeta_x^2+\zeta_y^2} - \zeta_x$ and $f_2(x,y) = \zeta_y/\sqrt{1+\zeta_x^2+\zeta_y^2} - \zeta_y$.

4.3   Architecture

Incorporation of OpenCL version of velocity potential solver into the existing source code reduced to an addition of two subclasses (Fig. 2):

Realtime_solver a subclass of abstract solver that implements computation of velocity potential field on GPU, and

ARMA_realtime_driver a subclass of control flow object—an object that defines the sequence of calls to subroutines—that implements real-time visualisation and stores OpenGL buffer objects that are shared with the solver. These objects are shared with the solver only if the solver is real-time.

The algorithm for computation and visualisation pipeline is presented in Algorithm 1.

Initialise shared OpenCL/OpenGL context.
Generate the first wavy surface realisation time slice.
Compute corresponding velocity potential field.
while *not exited* **do**
| Visualise the current slice of wavy surface and velocity field.
| Asynchronously compute next wavy surface time slice.
| Compute its velocity potential field.
end

Algorithm 1. Main loop of computation and visualisation pipeline.

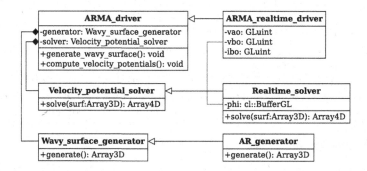

Fig. 2. Classes which implement OpenCL/OpenGL interoperability in the simulation code.

5   Evaluation

For the purpose of evaluation we use simplified version of (2):

$$\phi(x, y, z, t) = \mathcal{F}_{x,y}^{-1}\left\{\frac{\cosh\left(2\pi|\boldsymbol{k}|(z+h)\right)}{2\pi|\boldsymbol{k}|\cosh\left(2\pi|\boldsymbol{k}|h\right)}\mathcal{F}_{u,v}\{\zeta_t\}\right\}$$

$$= \mathcal{F}_{x,y}^{-1}\{g_1(u,v)\mathcal{F}_{u,v}\{g_2(x,y)\}\}. \tag{3}$$

Since standing sea wave generator does not allow efficient GPU implementation due to autoregressive dependencies between wavy surface points, only velocity potential solver was rewritten in OpenCL and its performance was compared to existing OpenMP implementation.

For each implementation the overall performance of the solver for a particular time instant was measured. Velocity field was computed for one t point, for 128 z points below wavy surface and for each x and y point of four-dimensional (t, x, y, z) grid. The only parameter that was varied between subsequent programme runs is the size of the grid along x dimension. A total of 10 runs were performed and average time of each stage was computed.

A different FFT library was used for each version of the solver. For OpenMP version FFT routines from GNU Scientific Library (GSL) [8] were used, and for OpenCL version clFFT library [5] was used instead. There are two major differences in the routines from these libraries.

1. The order of frequencies in Fourier transforms is different and clFFT library requires reordering the result of (3) whereas GSL does not.
2. Discontinuity at $(x, y) = (0, 0)$ of velocity potential field grid is handled automatically by clFFT library, whereas GSL library produce skewed values at this point.

For GSL library an additional interpolation from neighbouring points was used to smooth velocity potential field at these points. We have not spotted other differences in FFT implementations that have impact on the overall performance.

In the course of the numerical experiments we have measured how much time each solver's implementation spends in each computation stage to explain find out how efficient data copying between host and device is in OpenCL implementation, and how one implementation corresponds to the other in terms of performance.

6   Results

The experiments showed that GPU implementation outperforms CPU implementation by a factor of 10–15 (Fig. 3), however, distribution of time between computation stages is different for each implementation (Fig. 4). The major time consumer in CPU implementation is computation of g_1, whereas in GPU implementation its running time is comparable to computation of g_2. GPU computes g_1 much faster than CPU due to a large amount of modules for transcendental mathematical function computation. In both implementations g_2 is computed on CPU, but for GPU implementation the result is duplicated for each z grid point in order to perform multiplication of all XYZ planes along z dimension in single OpenCL kernel, and, subsequently copied to GPU memory which severely hinders overall stage performance. Copying the resulting velocity potential field between CPU and GPU consumes $\approx 20\%$ of velocity potential solver execution time.

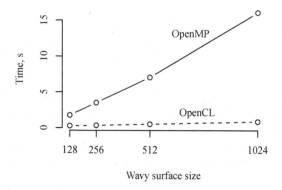

Fig. 3. Performance comparison of CPU (OpenMP) and GPU (OpenCL) versions of velocity potential solver.

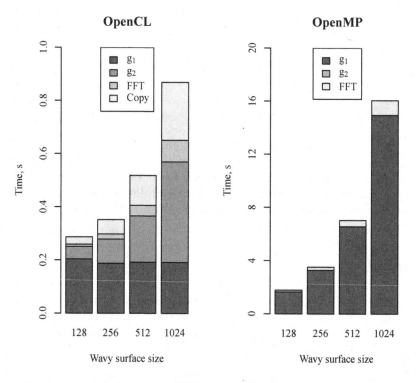

Fig. 4. Performance breakdown for GPU (OpenCL) and CPU (OpenMP) versions of velocity potential solver.

7 Discussion and Future Work

Simplified velocity potential formula (3) lacks $f_{1,2}$ functions which contain spatial derivatives of wavy surface ζ which are inefficient to compute on GPU.

The remaining derivative ζ_t is also computed on CPU for the sake of efficiency. The future work is to find high-performance algorithm for multidimensional derivative computation on GPUs.

OpenGL is still a single-thread library and in most cases of graphics applications only one thread manages the access to the GL context. This could lead to the performance drops, thread interoperability issues and complicated application architecture. Some workarounds could be found yet, like launching multiple processes and switching contexts between them, but it is not solving the problems mentioned about really. Thus, there are some premises exist, which are making sense to investigate on the similar result achievement with the newer APIs, such as a Vulkan and DirectX 12.

Relatively the same statement could be made about the OpenCL toolkit. Despite the fact that general GPGPU computing interface allowed us to achieve some improvements through the waveform computation acceleration and and made a cross-platform execution possible, it still has some disadvantages. E.g., each core should be manually cached after the compilation, which is exactly proceeded over execution time. Moreover, it could happen that other compute APIs could show even better performance rates.

We can also consider experimenting with dual chip GPU boards. The main idea here is to provide for both computing and rendering contexts an exclusive right to use their own dedicated GPU core in every moment of time. This improvement can help for the cases where intensive rendering routines are expected to be applied for the data obtained during the computations. In that way we will not lose the performance and, probably, will achieve even better results.

And the most interesting question here is what should be done when the computing capabilities of the single node will be reached, or simply how do we scale. The part of application connected with direct computations could be handled in a common way by the one of MPI implementations. This method is compatible for both CUDA and CPU driven processes. Some concerns could appear at the stage of visualisation scaling.

The first and simplest way to achieve the desired result is to accumulate data from the nodes after each computation round on the master node to join results and visualise them on it. But if we will make it like this we will lose the benefits of using a shared buffer for OpenCL and OpenGL. In addition, as the number of nodes will increase the bandwidth requirements of the channel will grow too, and in the end we will rest against its limitations.

The second possible method of achieving the result is similar to the first one and has the same problems, but involves the usage of GPUDirect or DirectGMA technology for graphics cards depends on their vendor. The only difference here is that the exchange of data between nodes will be based on peer-to-peer protocol under CUDA context. It means that GPU will receive messages directly.

The last possible way to solve this problem is to use distributed rendering techniques. It is based basically on combination of load distribution and objects

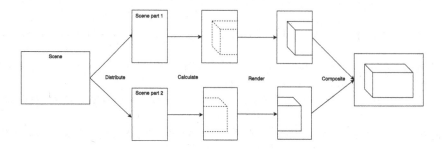

Fig. 5. Sort-first image compositing.

or images composition algorithms, where three main ones can be distinguished: sort-first, sort-middle and sort-last [13].

Sort-first (Fig. 5) assumes that the scene should be divided into a number of zones, each processed on its own hardware. In fact, several cameras/viewports are created in the OpenGL context on different nodes, and then resulting frame buffers are simply merged into a single final frame. Two main problems that could be met here, but can be solved in some way, are artefacts at the joints of frame parts when using lossy compression and desynchronization of frame pieces when there is some motion on the scene.

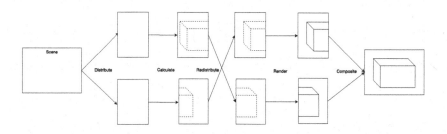

Fig. 6. Sort-middle image compositing.

Sort-middle (Fig. 6) is not widely used in real time applications, due to the fact that it takes an extra time to produce and brings network overheads, but it is the most effective one. First, each node calculates geometry, and then workload is getting redistributed equally among all computing devices.

Both methods described above do not really suit us well, since each of the nodes will process either a single frame, or a part of the total surface, and we will not involve a viewport in a such way, at least for now.

Actually, we are interested in the sort-last method (Fig. 7) most of all. Unlike the previous two, the load distribution here is performed based on the 3D objects grouping and segmentation. Later on, alpha blending of rendered objects is performed to retain the resulting frame. This way may not be optimal in some cases,

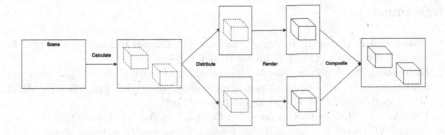

Fig. 7. Sort-last image compositing.

since nodes will have to render parts of objects that will be overlapped at the compositing stage, but still it allows to achieve the desired result.

We can even make some optimisation steps here. For example, to reduce the load on the network channel, we can use an N-ary compositing. In other words, instead of joining all objects on the only node, we can exchange objects between N nodes first and connect them. For example, it can be done on the principle of a binary tree. We can also use various compression algorithms, which show the greatest performance for colour and numeric data.

8 Conclusion

As a result of the investigation, we managed to achieve positive outcome in computation acceleration and its visualisation using interaction mechanisms between the graphics and compute contexts. The joint use of OpenGL and OpenCL allowed us to simultaneously use the shared areas of dedicated GPU memory for calculation and rendering, thereby saving us some time required to copy the data for RAM to the video card memory. Visualisation of real-time calculation results allowed to perform fine-grained control for the process showing us new opportunities for simulation with variable conditions.

Proposed solution could be applied not only for the ocean wavy surface simulation, but for any other iterative computations, which are producing a sane amount of data. For example, we can reuse the result in a similar manner for the costs prediction of monetary assets.

We have also determined the list of possible tasks that could be performed in the future to improve the functionality of the software solution. One of the directions is to experiment on combining various graphics and computing APIs to identify the most optimal solution.

Acknowledgements. Research was supported by grants of Russian Foundation for Basic Research (projects no. 16-07-01111, 16-07-00886, 16-07-01113).

References

1. Board, O.A.R.: OpenGL Reference Manual: The Official Reference Document for OpenGL, Release 1 (OTL). Addison-Wesley (C) (1993)
2. Bogdanova, A., Ivashchenko, A., Belezeko, A.: Creating distributed rendering applications. In: CEUR Workshop Proceedings, vol. 1787, pp. 130–134 (2016). http://ceur-ws.org/Vol-1787/130-134-paper-21.pdf
3. Bradsky, G.: The OpenCV library. Dr. Dobb's J. Softw. Tools (2000)
4. Bucur, A.: OpenCL - OpenGL ES interop: processing live video streams on a mobile device - case study. In: ACM SIGGRAPH 2013 Mobile, SIGGRAPH 2013, NY, USA, p. 15 (2013). http://doi.acm.org/10.1145/2503512.2503532
5. clFFT developers: clFFT: OpenCL Fast Fourier Transforms (FFTs). https://clmathlibraries.github.io/clFFT/
6. Degtyarev, A., Reed, A.: Modelling of incident waves near the ship's hull (application of autoregressive approach in problems of simulation of rough seas). In: Proceedings of the 12th International Ship Stability Workshop (2011)
7. Degtyarev, A.B., Reed, A.M.: Synoptic and short-term modeling of ocean waves. Int. Shipbuilding Prog. **60**(1–4), 523–553 (2013)
8. Galassi, M., Davies, J., Theiler, J., Gough, B., Jungman, G., Alken, P., Booth, M., Rossi, F., Ulerich, R.: GNU Scientific Library Reference Manual, 3rd edn. Network Theory Ltd. (2009). Gough, B. (ed.)
9. Geer, D.: Vendors upgrade their physics processing to improve gaming. Computer **39**(8), 22–24 (2006)
10. Khronos Group: OpenCL API reference (2013)
11. Kochin, N., Kibel, I., Roze, N.: Theoretical hydrodynamics. FizMatLit (1966) (in Russian)
12. Liao, W.S., Hsieh, T.J., Chang, Y.L.: Gpu parallel computing of spherical panorama video stitching. In: 2012 IEEE 18th International Conference on Parallel and Distributed Systems, pp. 890–895, December 2012
13. Molnar, S., Cox, M., Ellsworth, D., Fuchs, H.: A sorting classification of parallel rendering. IEEE Comput. Graph. Appl. **14**(4), 23–32 (1994)
14. Ukidave, Y., Gong, X., Kaeli, D.: Performance evaluation and optimization mechanisms for inter-operable graphics and computation on GPUS. In: Proceedings of Workshop on General Purpose Processing Using GPUs, GPGPU-7, NY, USA, pp. 37–45 (2014). http://doi.acm.org/10.1145/2576779.2576784
15. Unity Technologies: Unity - Manual: Compute Shaders. https://docs.unity3d.com/Manual/ComputeShaders.html

Complexity of the Code Changes and Issues Dependent Approach to Determine the Release Time of Software Product

V.B. Singh[1](✉), K.K. Chaturvedi[2], Sujata Khatri[3],
and Meera Sharma[4]

[1] Delhi College of Arts and Commerce, University of Delhi, Delhi 110023, India
vbsingh@dcac.du.ac.in
[2] ICAR-IASRI, Pusa, New Delhi 110012, India
kkcchaturvedi@gmail.com
[3] DDU College, University of Delhi, New Delhi 110078, India
khatri.sujata@gmail.com
[4] Swami Shraddhanand College, University of Delhi, Delhi 110036, India
meerakaushik@gmail.com

Abstract. Changes in source code of the software products are inevitable. We need to change the source code to fix the feature improvements, new features and bugs. Feature improvements, new features and bugs are collectively termed as issues. The changes in the source code of the software negatively impact its product, but necessary for the evolution of the software. The changes in source code are quantified using entropy based measure and it is called the complexity of code changes. In this paper, we built regression models to predict the next release time of software using the complexity of code changes (entropy), feature improvements, new feature implementation and bugs fixed. The regression models have been built using Multiple Linear Regression (MLR), various kernel functions based Support Vector Regression (SVR) and k-Nearest Neighbor (k-NN) methods. The proposed models have been empirically validated using four open source sub-projects of the Apache software foundation. The proposed models exhibit a good fit. The developed models will assist release managers in release planning of the software.

Keywords: Entropy · Complexity of code change · Release problem · Bug repositories · Source code repositories

1 Introduction

Once the software is ready to use, it can be made available for others to use. The version made available for different users are termed as release of the software. In other terms, the release is a version of the software which makes its availability for external users. The process of software development and its preparation for release is another interesting area of research. The release planning is a key aspect of any software development process, so it is being followed by Apache foundation as well. In some cases, the binary/bytecode packages are produced to build a compiled version of the source and

© Springer International Publishing AG 2017
O. Gervasi et al. (Eds.): ICCSA 2017, Part V, LNCS 10408, pp. 519–529, 2017.
DOI: 10.1007/978-3-319-62404-4_39

released with the same version number as the source release. The Apache software foundation produces various types of releases, namely Test packages, Nightly Builds, Release Candidates and Releases. Releases that are believed to be usable by testers and developers outside the team are usually referred to as "beta" or "unstable" but releases are intended for developers working outside the project are called "alpha" release.

The growth of open source software is being continuously improved with the increasing interest of various companies by involving the participation of contribution from the geographically distributed developers. Primarily, the release of the software is determined based on the fixed time interval, inclusion of specific functional features, platform change, competitive interest of peer groups/organizations and many others depend on the strategy of the mentoring group. The release problem is categorized as a collection of customer's requirements [1]. The issues/requirements are submitted as new feature, feature improvement and bug in bug/issue reporting system. These requirements are assessed and used as an important parameter in deciding the next release of the software. The software consortium releases the software in a timely manner generally on the calendar time basis or periodic basis to evolve the software. But, it is not possible to get the release at a specific time. Open source projects release their software version on the basis of milestone, specific requirement, important patch, fixed time, etc. This requires us to conduct the study that determines the suitable release time of the software based on various types of issues/features and the corresponding changes in the source code.

With the available literature, the release models are developed in isolation with the number of issues fixed. These models did not consider the changes made in the source code due to fixing of these issues. In this paper, release time of software is determined using the entropy and corresponding number of and types of issues fixed. To the best of our knowledge, no authors have applied the entropy and types of issues for determining the time of the next release of the software product.

In this study, our objective is to investigate the impact of entropy and different types of issues, namely bugs, new features and improvements in the next release of the software products.

To empirically investigate the association of release time problem with entropy and various types of issues fixed, we have built various regression models using Multiple Linear Regression (MLR), Support Vector Regression (SVR) and k-Nearest Neighbor (k-NN). The models have been validated using real data from the popularly known sub projects of Apache Software Foundation. The historical changes in the source code and corresponding number of issues have been extracted and arranged with respect to various releases. The rest of the paper is organized as follows:

Section 2 presents the related work. Materials and methods have been described in Sect. 3. Section 4 provides the results and discussion. Finally, the paper is concluded in Sect. 5 with future research directions.

2   Review of Works

The research in software engineering is being taken up in many hot topics related to mining with respect to software evolution, qualities, bug prediction, software change tracking and source code analysis, developers grouping and characterization including their activities, release planning and code cloning identification and analysis [6]. The increasing number of large scale requirements leads to a combinatorial optimization problem, determining the release time is becoming a N-P hard problem even most of the requirements are independent to each other [7]. Researchers made an attempt to study the next release problem using genetic algorithm based approach [8], and extended the study with greedy algorithm and simulated annealing [9].

The time of next release prediction is attempted in previous years to maximize the profits by satisfying larger set of requirements within the limited financial constraints [10]. The modelling was attempted in close source but further extended in open source environment as well because the validation of results are possible with the use of open source software repositories in various forms that contains variety of data and information. The authors attempted using backbone based multilevel algorithm for next release problem but did not take the arrival/fixing of bugs with committed changes occurred in the code [10]. A preliminary study has been conducted to study the next release problem using number of bugs fixed in literature based on multi attribute theory [11].

The entropy based measurement used for bug prediction [2, 3]. Authors attempted and developed various process metrics based on complexity of code changes and established a relationship between entropy/complexity of code changes and fixing of bugs [4]. Further, liner regression and kernel function based support vector regression attempted to study in predicting the occurrence of future bugs based on current entropy [5]. Recently, authors also established software reliability based models to determine the value of decay rate/factor for monitoring the bug detection/occurring process [12]. Maturity time and potential bugs were determined by modeling the complexity of code changes [13] and developed various approaches to model the bug prediction approaches [14]. An effort was also initiated to predict the release time of the software based on the complexity of code changes and bugs fixed [15]. There is no study that has been conducted to study the next release problem using the complexity of code change with the incorporation of various types of issues reported in the system. These issues are addition of new features, enhancement or improvement of the existing features and a number of bugs. A concern has been raised recently for any prediction problem that the approaches are being evaluated and how they are being compared against each other [16].

3 Materials and Methods

In the current study, four subprojects of Apache have been considered for analysis and brief of them are as follows

- Apache Avro (https://avro.apache.org) is a data serialization system and provides rich data structure, various easy to use data formats and easy integration with the dynamic languages.
- Apache jUDDI (https://juddi.apache.org/) is an open source and platform independent implementation of OASIS the Universal Description, Discovery, and Integration (UDDI) specification for web Services in Java language. The jUDDI can be used with any popular relational database.

- Apache Pig (https://pig.apache.org/) provides high level language for analysis of large data sets. The primary feature of Apache Pig includes the parallelization which enables the platform to process and analyze large data sets.
- Apache Whirr (https://whirr.apache.org/) is a rich set of libraries for running cloud services and provides common APIs. This can also be used as a command line tool for cluster deployment.

The issues that are considered as features are new feature, feature enhancement and bug fixes. These issues have been extracted from the issue reporting system and available at Apache web resource (https://issues.apache.org/). The issues related to four sub projects namely Avro, Pig, Whirr and JUDDI have been downloaded. The issues are integrated with the corresponding releases based on the calendar time. The continuous changes are being made to resolve these issues and corresponding changes in the source code are being committed in the repositories. The historical changes of the source code are extracted by writing a script and executed under GitShell. GitShell is a command line utility to provide the extraction of various historical changes, developers, files, number of lines added, removed and modified etc. in terms of numerical values. The summary of the collected data from issue reporting system is shown in Table 1. The issue data are varied from 2009 to 2014 for various types of sub projects. There are 23, 12, 16 and 11 releases for Apache Avro, Apache jUDDI, Apache Pig and Apache Whirr respectively between first and latest (at the time of data collection) releases considered in the study. The time has been calculated as number of months between two subsequent releases.

Table 1. Summary of collected data.

Projects	First release	Time of first release	Last release	Time of last release	Number of releases
Avro	1.0.0	14/07/2009	1.7.7	24/07/2014	23
jUDDI	2.0	02/08/2009	3.2	05/02/2014	12
Pig	0.1.0	11/09/2008	0.12.0	01/04/2013	16
Whirr	0.1.0	20/09/2010	0.8.2	23/04/2013	11

In this study, multiple linear regression (MLR has been applied to model and compare the release planning with the complexity of code change and number of bugs fixed models [15]. The model has been developed to determine the release time of the software (Y) using multiple linear regression by including the number of modifications and number of new features in addition to the existing feature of the existing model, is as follows

$$Y = a_0 + a_1 X_1 + a_2 X_2 + a_3 X_3 + a_4 X_4 \tag{1}$$

Where X_1 shows the complexity of code changes and a_1 shows the contribution of complexity of code changes in determining the release time, X_2 shows the number of bugs and a_2 shows the contribution of bugs in determining the release time, X_3 shows the number of improvements and a_3 shows the contribution of improvements in determining the release time, X_4 shows the number of new features and a_4 shows the contribution of new features in determining the release time, and a_0 shows the intercept or coefficient in determining the release time. The coefficients, a_i where the values of i from 0 to 4 will be estimated using the available data. Once, the parameters or coefficients have been estimated, the time for the next release can be determined easily.

We have also applied four kernel functions (Linear, Polynomial, Radial Basis Function and Sigmoid) based Support Vector Regression (SVR) and k-Nearest Neighbor (k-NN) using four distance measure namely Euclidean, Euclidean squared, Cityblock (Manhattan), Chebychev.

4   Complexity of Code Change

The changes in the source code are required to improve and enhance the software. These changes are termed as issues and categorized as new feature, improvement and bugs. The changes make the code complex as there are many persons involved in incorporating the required changes to fix the issues. The developers rarely meet each other in person in open source software development process as they are not sitting at a single geographical location. The diverse changes in the source code make the code complex and can lead to generate another set of further issues. The information theory based entropy is helpful in determining the complexity of code changes. The Shannon Entropy, H_n is defined as

$$H_n(P) = -\sum_{k=1}^{n} (P_k * \log_2 P_k) \qquad (2)$$

Where $P_k \geq 0$ and $\sum_{k=1}^{n} P_k = 1$

For a distribution P, where all elements have the same probability of occurrence ($P_k = 1/n$; $\forall k \in 1, 2, \ldots, n$). We achieve maximum entropy. On the other hand, for a distribution P where an element i has a probability of occurrence $P_i = 1$ and $\forall k \neq i$, $P_k = 0$, we achieve minimal entropy.

Hassan [3] has firstly used this concept to measure the complexity of code change, where the author has taken P_k as probability which is defined as the ratio of the number of times a file changed during a period and the total number of changes for all files in that period.

For example, suppose that there are 15 changes occurred for four files and three periods. For a first period, there are five changes occurred across all four files. The probability of file F1, F2, F3, and F4 will be 1/5 (= 0.2), 1/5 (= 0.2), 2/5 (= 0.4) and 1/5 (= 0.2) respectively for the first period T1. These probabilities have been shown in Fig. 1.

The entropy for this period can be calculated by substituting the values of these probabilities in the Eq. (2) which is useful in quantifying the code change using this entropy based metric. From the definition, it is clear that the entropy will be maximum,

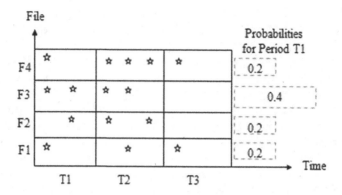

Fig. 1. Number of changes in files with respect to a specific period of time

if there are frequent changes in every file while it will be minimum if the changes are occurring in a single file [3].

The complexity of code change has been calculated using the various complexity of code change metrics [4] and used for modelling the bugs arrival/fixing pattern using kernel based support vector regression [5] that was further used to determine the software quality [5].

5   Results and Discussion

The estimated parameters of the MLR have been documented in Table 2. The effects of the inclusion of improvements are reducing the time of next release due to negative value of coefficients for Improvement in all the four data sets. The negative value of coefficients shows that the parameters will reduce the time for next release of the software. The negative value of coefficients for Improvement shows the decrease in time for release time of the software. Further, the Improvements need modifications that require changes in the source code and the incorporation of these changes will be termed as patch instead of release because it does not consider major feature of the release. As the literature suggests, the improvements in the software are initiated from the main or primary group of developers, thus did not take much time in making the required changes for inclusion of improvements in the software. This is one of the reasons for getting the negative value of coefficients for Improvement in determining the release time of the software. The larger value of coefficients for New Feature signifies that the introduction of New Feature will require discussion and incorporation of new strategy in developing or implementing the fresh code and sometime requires the major changes in the existing code. The new development requires times to implement the innovative things and include the new code development. The inclusion of more number of new features will delay the release of the software. Similarly the coefficient of bugs also requires the modification in existing code and requires intensive debugging of the code to identify the place of code change and inclusion of additional code. The inclusion of bug fixes also delays the release of the software. The complexity of code changes increases as the large number of changes in the source code is required to incorporate the fixing of various types of issues. The increase value of complexity of code changes will also affects the delay in release time of the software.

Table 2. Estimated parameters of multiple linear regression.

Projects	Parameters	Coefficients	Standard Error	t Stat	P-value
Avro	Intercept	0.127	0.206	0.615	0.547
	Entropy	0.886	0.034	25.819	0.000
	Bug	0.007	0.006	1.101	0.286
	Improvement	−0.037	0.010	−3.616	0.002
	New Feature	0.149	0.028	5.404	0.000
jUDDI	Intercept	−0.544	3.243	−0.168	0.872
	Entropy	2.237	0.618	3.622	0.009
	Bug	−0.112	0.082	−1.366	0.214
	Improvement	−0.133	0.740	−0.179	0.863
	New Feature	0.428	1.004	0.427	0.683
Pig	Intercept	0.484	3.047	0.159	0.877
	Entropy	0.088	0.275	0.318	0.757
	Bug	0.042	0.028	1.496	0.166
	Improvement	−0.064	0.072	−0.895	0.392
	New Feature	0.095	0.112	0.856	0.412
Whirr	Intercept	−1.421	0.501	−2.835	0.030
	Entropy	1.754	0.170	10.326	0.000
	Bug	0.078	0.041	1.903	0.106
	Improvement	−0.232	0.070	−3.314	0.016
	New Feature	0.392	0.188	2.087	0.082

The summary statistics of these models are shown in Table 3. The value of R^2 is more than 99% in all the data sets except jUDDI where it is more than 96%. Similarly, the Significance of F values have shown that these results are statistically significant because the value of Sig. F is less than 0.001 in all the cases.

Table 3. Summary statistics for multiple linear regression.

Projects	Mult. R	R^2	Adj. R^2	Std. Error	F	Sig. F
Avro	1.000	1.000	1.000	0.289	17702.771	1.62E-30
jUDDI	0.985	0.969	0.952	3.876	55.581	2.18E-05
Pig	0.994	0.989	0.984	2.004	215.609	1.18E-09
Whirr	0.999	0.999	0.998	0.503	1012.754	1.29E-08

Multi. R – Multiple R, Adj. R^2 – Adjusted R^2, Std. Error–Standard Error, Sig. F – Significance of F

Thus, these analytical results show the significance of the problem and helpful in determining and predicting the release time of the software. These results reveal that the complexity of code changes and introduction of new feature in the software will significantly affect the release time of the software. Further, the goodness of curve has been plotted for all the datasets. The goodness of curve shows the fitness of the developed MLR based models in determining the release time of the software. In Fig. 2, the goodness of fit for Apache Avro and Apache Whirr show significantly similar to the predicted as observed by looking into the trend lines are overlapping with each other. In Apache jUDDI and Apache Pig, the goodness of fit curve between observed and predicted values are deviating with minor deviations.

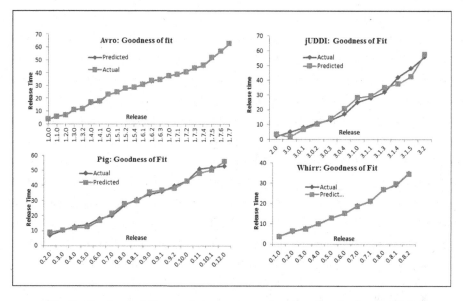

Fig. 2. Goodness of fit curve between observed and predicted values in MLR

The analytical results of the four kernel functions based SVR have also been obtained and summarized in Table 4. The performance of the various kernel functions does not provide significant difference except the Sigmoid where the Correlation has been observed below 70% in Avro and Whirr projects.

There is no significant difference has been observed in varying the distance measures. The Fig. 3 shows that there is very high cross validation error which does not fit the k-NN based models well in this scenario.

The analytical results of the four distance measure in k-NN have also been obtained and summarized in Table 5.

The comparative study shows that the Multiple Linear Regression is effectively models various types of changes as well as complexity of code changes in determining the release time of the subprojects.

Table 4. The performance statistics of SVR.

Projects	Type of kernel	No. of support vectors	C.V. error	Error mean	MSE	S.D. Ratio	Correlation
Avro	Linear	3	0.009	−2.328	6.572	0.1125	0.9976
	Poly	8	0.025	1.850	5.825	0.1622	0.9996
	RBF	3	0.007	−1.876	4.111	0.0805	0.9968
	Sigmoid	15	0.052	2.467	135.483	1.1910	0.5767
jUDDI	Linear	2	0.007	7.784	94.1053	0.5943	0.9646
	Poly	6	0.108	18.363	386.456	0.7206	0.9420
	RBF	3	0.039	7.419	84.1204	0.5536	0.9606
	Sigmoid	3	0.007	7.498	89.5083	0.5923	0.9600
Pig	Linear	2	0.008	8.822	101.548	0.5876	0.9959
	Poly	2	0.125	7.2833	58.2603	0.2755	0.9865
	RBF	3	0.013	1.6575	8.8518	0.2981	0.9982
	Sigmoid	4	0.009	2.419	18.3451	0.4264	0.9980
Whirr	Linear	2	0.014	6.002	66.1093	0.6546	0.9921
	Poly	5	0.053	−1.852	15.1313	0.4082	0.9999
	RBF	3	0.035	3.146	22.8630	0.4297	0.9780
	Sigmoid	6	0.046	7.899	125.195	0.9456	0.6781

Ploy – Polynomial, RBF – Radial Basis Function, C.V. Error – Cross Validation, Error, S. D. Ratio – Standard Deviation Ratio

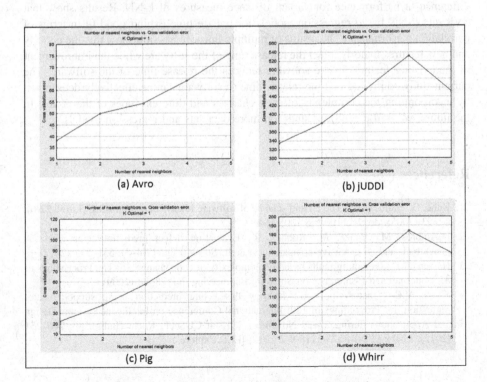

(a) Avro

(b) jUDDI

(c) Pig

(d) Whirr

Fig. 3. Cross validation Error in k-NN for various projects

Table 5. The performance statistics of k-NN.

Projects	C.V. Error	Error Mean	Absolute Error Mean	S.D. Ratio	Correlation
Avro	38.18750	−1.8333	2.5000	0.2374	0.9729
jUDDI	334.33333	7.6667	9.6667	0.8141	0.9679
Pig	22.45455	−0.7500	4.7500	0.6463	0.7741
Whirr	83.00000	4.0000	4.0000	0.3375	0.9563

CV Error – Cross Validation Error, S.D. Ratio – Standard Ratio

6 Conclusion

Now a days to meet user's requirements of new features and improvements, frequent versions of the software need to be released. Traditional methods like a milestone or calendar based and software reliability growth model are not able to handle the frequent nature of releases. These methods need more data to estimate the values of different parameter, but we have less number of data points in frequent releases. Also, these methods are based on only one issue type, i.e. bugs fixed. In this paper, we have considered two more types of issues, namely new feature and improvements in addition to the entropy for release time planning of the software. In case of SVR, the performance of the various kernel functions does not provide significant difference except for Sigmoid kernel function in Avro and Whirr projects. We have observed no significant difference in performance for variant distance measures of k-NN. Results show that SVR and k-NN based regression models for release time exhibit good fit in terms of correlation performance. The results of multiple linear regression show that the entropy and new features majorly affect the release time of the software while the improvement of the existing features in the software reduces the release time of the software. The current study confirmed that the release time of software can be effectively determined by incorporating the complexity of code changes and different types of the issues. In the future, we will extend our study on more data sets and regression models.

References

1. Ruhe, G., Saliu, M.O.: The art and science of software release planning. IEEE Softw. 22(6), 47–53 (2005). doi:10.1109/MS.2005.164
2. D'Ambros, M., Lanza, M., Robbes, R.: Evaluating defect prediction approaches: A benchmark and an extensive comparison. Empir. Softw. Eng. 17(4–5), 531–577 (2012)
3. Hassan, A.E.: Predicting faults based on complexity of code change. In: The Proceedings of 31st International Conference on Software Engineering, pp. 78–88 (2009)
4. Singh, V.B., Chaturvedi, K.K.: Entropy based bug prediction using support vector regression. In: Proceedings of 12th International Conference on Intelligent Systems Design and Applications during 27–29 November 2012 at CUSAT, Kochi (India), pp. 746–751 (2012). ISBN: 978-1-4673-5118-8_c 2012, IEEE Explore

5. Singh, V.B., Chaturvedi, K.K.: Improving the quality of software by quantifying the code change metric and predicting the bugs. In: Murgante, B., Misra, S., Carlini, M., Torre, C.M., Nguyen, H.-Q., Taniar, D., Apduhan, B.O., Gervasi, O. (eds.) ICCSA 2013. LNCS, vol. 7972, pp. 408–426. Springer, Heidelberg (2013). doi:10.1007/978-3-642-39643-4_30

6. Xie, T., Zimmermann, T., van Deursen, A.: Introduction to the special issue on mining software repositories. Empir. Softw. Eng. 18(6), 1043–1046 (2013)

7. Bagnall, A., Rayward-Smith, V., Whittley, I.: The next release problem. Inf. Softw. Technol. 43(14), 883–890 (2001). doi:10.1016/S0950-5849(01)00194-X

8. Glance, D.G.: Release criteria for the linux kernel. First Monday 9(4) 2004

9. Baker, P., Harman, M., Steinhofel, K., Skaliotis, A.: Search based approaches to component selection and prioritization for the next release problem. In: Proceedings of the 22nd International Conference on Software Maintenance (ICSM 2006), pp. 176–185 (2006). doi:10.1109/ICSM.2006.56

10. Xuan, J., Jiang, H., Ren, Z., Luo, Z.: Solving the large scale next release problem with a backbone-based multilevel algorithm. IEEE Trans. Software Eng. 38(5), 1195–1212 (2012)

11. Kapur, P.K., Singh, V.B., Singh, O.P., Singh, J.N.P.: Software release time based on multi-attribute utility functions. Int. J. Reliab. Qual. Saf. Eng. 20(4), 15 (2013)

12. Chaturvedi, K.K., Singh, V.B.: Bug prediction using entropy based measures. Int. J. Knowl. Eng. Data Min. 2(4), 266–291 (2013)

13. Chaturvedi, K.K., Kapur, P.K., Anand, S., Singh, V.B.: Predicting the complexity of code changes using entropy based measures. Int. J. Syst. Assur. Eng. Manage. 5(2), 155–164 (2014). doi:10.1007/s13198-014-0226-5

14. Singh, V.B., Chaturvedi, K.K., Khatri, S.K., Kumar, V.: Bug prediction modeling using complexity of code changes. Int. J. Syst. Assur. Eng. Manage. 6(1), 44–60 (2015). doi:10.1007/s13198-014-0242-5

15. Chaturvedi, K.K., Bedi, P., Misra, S., Singh, V.B.: An empirical validation of the complexity of code changes and bugs in predicting the release time of open source software. In: The Proceedings of 16th IEEE International Conference on Computational Science and Engineering held at University of Sydney, Australia during 3–5th December 2013, pp. 1201–1206 (2013). IEEE Computer Society

16. Lanza, M., Mocci, A., Ponzanelli, L.: The tragedy of defect prediction, prince of empirical software engineering research. IEEE Softw. 33(6), 102–105 (2016)

Workshop on Software Quality (SQ 2017)

Experimental Validation of Source Code Reviews on Mobile Devices

Wojciech Frącz[✉] and Jacek Dajda

AGH University of Science and Technology, al. Adama Mickiewicza 30,
30-059 Kraków, Poland
{fracz,dajda}@agh.edu.pl

Abstract. The practice of code reviews is fundamental for producing and maintaining high-quality source code. However, because it is not the most favourite and enjoyable task of a developer, it is still not acknowledged as the industry worldwide standard. The idea behind this research is to encourage developers by providing them with an accessible way to perform reviews by using mobile devices. This paper presents the results from the experiment-driven investigation aimed at comparative analysis of code reviews performed on a dedicated mobile tool and a desktop application. After comparing results from 79 mobile and 102 desktop reviews and analysing almost 2500 comments we claim that mobile devices can be used to effectively read, understand and review source code of any size.

1 Introduction

The aim of the source code review technique is to maintain the code quality. While some tools are available to automate the process of source code quality assessment, regular code reviews still seem unbeatable in the context of code readability and clarity [10].

The process of reviewing the code is often associated with desktop devices. The available tools and platforms facilitating code reviews such as GitHub or Gerrit Code Review are designed to be used on desktop. While the process of code reviews is constantly evolving (e.g. Modern Code Review Process [4]), the tools used to code reviews seem to be in a stagnation. On the other hand, everything is tempted to be mobile today. Mobile devices and applications facilitate important aspects of our lives, including communication, entertainment, shopping, and work.

This paper contributes to these trends with the idea of code reviews performed on a mobile device such as a smartphone, or better, a tablet. Doing a review while seating on a comfortable sofa in a company social space seem definitely more attractive to a software developer than a typical review performed at his desk. Another important benefit is the higher communication comfort. It is much easier to discuss specific code fragments with nearby developers just by passing them the device instead of inviting them to the reviewer's desk. In addition, mobile code reviews can make the practice more available during

© Springer International Publishing AG 2017
O. Gervasi et al. (Eds.): ICCSA 2017, Part V, LNCS 10408, pp. 533–547, 2017.
DOI: 10.1007/978-3-319-62404-4_40

business trips, especially when offline. These aspects seem significant in encouraging developers to bring more focus to code quality and frequent reviews.

On the other hand, several questions arise whether the physical limitations of mobile devices, in particular the small screens and uncomfortable virtual keyboards, can affect the quality and efficiency of such reviews not to mention other aspects such as developers fatigue and general attitude. The preliminary answers to these doubts have already been provided [8] and proved promising. However, further evaluation in order to confirm these findings is required. This paper describes results from a thorough empirical evaluation of mobile code reviews in comparison to the classic process performed at the desk.

The paper is organized as follows. Below you can find research questions that we are attempting to answer with this paper. Next section presents a few contributions that has been done in a field of mobile source code reviews. Section 3 describes the applied research method including the presentation of the developed tool and organized evaluation experiments. Section 4 provides the experimental results with corresponding figures which are commented in next section. Last section summarizes the conducted research and plans for future work.

1.1 Research Questions

Our overall research goal is to find out whether the source code reviews on mobile devices are as effective in defects detection as they are when performed on large screens. This led to formulating the following research questions.

Research Question 1: Are mobile code reviews as effective in finding *code smells* (defects, poor design and implementation solutions) as reviews performed on desktops?

Research Question 2: Is quality of the remarks added to the code during mobile and desktop code review worse?

While working on mobile application, we have noticed that text input in mobile devices can be really discouraging. Therefore, we have came up with an idea of adding predefined comments to the application to facilitate the process (read more in Sect. 3.1). This decision also led to another research question.

Research Question 3: Are reviewers willing to use predefined comments feature?

2 Related Work

The preliminary experiment concerning this topic has been conducted by [8]. It involved a small group of inexperienced students. It consisted of only one simple review task and it was limited to 7 min only due to organizational issues. The promising results encouraged us to perform a more thorough experiment described in this paper. Table 7 in Sect. 4.6 presents a detailed comparison of both studies.

The method used for assessment of feedback received from reviews has also been tweaked when compared to the previous study. In [8], comments were classified as worthless or valuable only. This decision resulted in confusion where to assign remarks that were partially correct. Current methodology solves this issue by introducing a comment quality (see Sect. 3.4).

Not only the experiment has been extended in this study but also the mobile application for code reviews has been rewritten. The new tool responds to the suggestions and problems found during the preliminary study [8]. The main differences are as follows.

- support for browsing between multiple files in a change that is reviewed
- direct communication with existing online tool - Gerrit Code Review
- removal of voice comments recording feature
- ability to edit predefined comments before adding them to the source code
- long lines of code are not wrapped even on small screens (reviewer can swipe the screen in order to see the rest of the code)

Besides the tool created for this study, a dedicated application called mGerrit is being developed on the GitHub repository [5]. This application is intended to be a mobile client for a Gerrit Code Review tool. However, the authors have yet to launch any results concerning their work.

There are other applications that support reviewing source code on mobile devices, although it is not their main purpose. For example LabCoat [9], mobile client for GitLab, can be used for adding comments to source code in commits in a comfortable way. GitHub, in spite of lack of dedicated mobile application, facilitates browsing and source code reviewing on devices with small screens by serving mobile ready layout directly in the browser.

The source code review practice is constantly evolving in order to both facilitate the process of checking the source code and make it more effective. Such lightweight, tool-based peer reviews are defined as Modern Code Reviews (MCR) [1,4,13]. Performing them on mobile devices is only one of many ways to improve this activity.

A tool that helps the reviewer understand what changes a particular commit introduces is proposed in [2]. A commit that contains more than one logical change can make the review much more difficult. Change clustering technique and a tool that leverages it can serve a tremendous help when reviewing large contributions.

[15–19] investigates a possibility of an automatic selection of the most appropriate reviewer for a particular change, based on the history of the code and activities of team members. Choosing a programmer that can review the given source code faster and more accurate than others can definitely improve the defects detection rate of the whole process.

Support of static code analysis tools seem to be a good idea when it comes to suggesting places that need more attention of a reviewer than others. Although such tools are often launched during continuous integration build, displaying warnings produced by them for reviewers is proved to be a successful technique of indicating suspicious lines of code [14].

Last but not least, [3] states that the non-technical factors like organization of source code review activity or the time required for a change to be reviewed are as important for successful code reviews as the technical factors like a size of the changes or their difficulty. Moreover, [6] states that the current methods of performing Modern Code Reviews unnecessarily block a code submission for a long time. Enabling reviewers to read and assess the code on mobile devices can be treated as another non-technical factor that should lead to shortening the time required for completing a review.

3 Method

To examine the effectiveness of mobile reviews, a comparison of mobile and desktop reviews needs to be performed. That is why the applied research method consists of two following elements:

1. dedicated review tool for mobile device created for the purpose of the research,
2. experimental comparison of the results obtained from mobile reviews and desktop reviews.

Both elements are described in detail in consecutive subsections.

3.1 Tools

A dedicated Android application has been developed for the purpose of checking efficiency of mobile reviews. It targets Android because of its popularity. Application communicates with Gerrit - a well known web based code review system that facilitates online code reviews. Changes from web application can be displayed and reviewed on a mobile. Review results are saved with Gerrit API in server database. An example screenshot of the application with the source code displayed is presented in Fig. 1. The application was developed from scratch, based on the experiences and findings gained from the preliminary study [8].

The mobile application has an ability to input predefined comments. They can be added to the source code with one touch which strongly facilitates the review process on a small screen. Mobile reviewer can choose a comment from a supplied list, such as *Duplicated Code, Find a better name, Magic value, Unused variable*. The list was collected based on own experiences and findings from the previous study [8]. It can be easily extended on demand.

Application features were truncated for the sake of the experiment. The dedicated version for experiment can display only review tasks designed for the study. For a reference desktop review tool, Gerrit seemed a natural choice (the mobile solution was already dependent on it).

The experiment data consisted of comments and remarks entered by participants with the mobile and PC tools. All comments have been collected in a single database for further analysis and assessment.

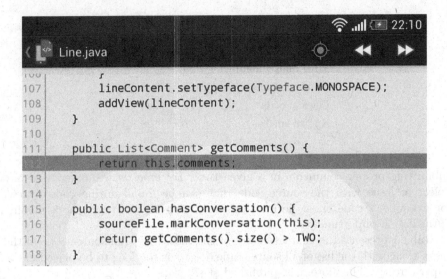

Fig. 1. Source code displayed in the mobile application.

3.2 Participants

The participants were Computer Science students from 1st and 2nd year of MSc studies degree from the University of Science and Technology in Kraków, Poland. The study involved 91 students, 41 of whom performed code reviews using their own mobile devices, mainly smartphones.

The experiment duration was 90 min. All students were educated in the aspect of code reviews and code smells. In addition, most of them have already had industry experience at the time of the experiment.

A short introduction to the Gerrit and the mobile tool has been given prior to the experiment. Students were asked to solve two tasks designed for the experiment (see Sect. 3.3). After each task, students were given time to discuss the code, especially the code smells that they were and were not able to discover in the provided source code.

Students that performed code reviews on mobile devices were chosen based on the types of devices they possessed. Students with Android devices were kindly asked to take part in the experiment as a mobile reviewer. Also, for students without proper device but willing to try mobile review, we had a limited number of devices we could borrow.

To conclude, we put emphasis on obtaining comparable conditions for both desktop and mobile reviews: participants on the same level of education and random distribution among the two tested tools and environments.

3.3 Tasks

Participants were given two review tasks. Each task consisted of source code in which participants were expected to find as many problems as possible by

Table 1. Specification of code review tasks.

Aspect	Task 1	Task 2
Time limit (minutes)	20	20
Number of files/classes	1	5
Lines of code	117	238
Known smells	37	28

submitting proper comments in a given time. By *problem* we understand any defect or issue with the source code that can be found during code review, for example a code smell, formatting or naming inconsistency, or a missing optimization opportunity.

Table 1 presents the characteristics of the tasks. The full source code of the tasks along with the list of all source code defects is too long to be placed in the paper directly. Therefore, it is published at [7].

Both tasks consist of Java source code. Task 1 is a one Java class. Task 2 contains the same class with addition of neighbouring classes. The quality of the source code in Task 1 is really poor. No student should have problems with finding a few defects in it. Task 2 resembles a real production code with bad design choices.

Task 1 is intended to verify effectiveness of reviews concerning problems which are local or minor, such as bad naming, long methods, complex conditions. Task 2 is focused on design problems including several classes. Its idea was, in particular, to verify ability to navigate between several source files on small mobile screens comfortably. Each participant reviewed both tasks with the same review tool. It was not possible to switch the tool between tasks.

The code smells used to assess the reviews are based on the list published in *Clean Code* [12] and on authors' experience.

As for chosen programming language, Java is introduced as one of the first programming languages at our university. Therefore, it is the most common and well known language among the experiment participants. Obviously, this strongly mitigates the risk of discrediting experiment results due to participants' syntax ignorance.

3.4   Assessment

Comments gathered in the described experiment have been carefully analysed. First of all, they have been divided into two categories - *valuable* and *worthless*. A comment has been classified as *valuable* if it could be clearly understood and if it pointed to the known code smell or defect in the reviewed code. It was labelled as *worthless* in other cases.

Having all remarks divided into these two buckets, each of the *valuable* comment has been given a *quality* value. The *quality* is an integer from 1 to 10 indicating how accurate the observation is. Ten (10) means that author of the code reading the comment would undoubtedly know what to fix. *Quality* of one (1) means that author of the code would have problems with identifying targeted defect but it is not impossible. We understand the *quality* as a *possibility of defect being fixed after reading the comment.* We tried to put ourselves in the code author's shoes during this classification – *Would I understand such remark if it was my code?*

The *quality* value has been used to calculate a *quality* of reviews. That is, the average amount of *qualities* of remarks added in a particular session.

4   Results

This section shows the summary of selected results which are further discussed in Sect. 5 and are important for drawing final conclusions.

The experiment resulted in 91 reviews for Task 1 and 90 reviews for Task 2 (one participant had to leave the experiment before its end). The code was given 2426 comments. Every code smell has been found by at least one participant. Overall measures for all reviews are presented in Table 2.

Table 2. Summarized results of conducted experiment.

Aspect	Mobile	PC	Overall
Total number of reviews	79	102	181
Total number of comments	1103	1321	2426
Average number of comments per review	14.0	13.0	13.4
Average number of code smells detected per review	8.9	8.8	8.9
Average number of worthless comments per review	3.9	3.6	3.7
Average reviews quality	6.23	6.51	6.37
Average length of the comment	23	44	35
Average time to the first comment	164s	213s	189s

4.1   Code Smells Finding Frequency

Table 3 shows only the most diversified results concerning the *hit rate* for selected smells for each type of the code review. The results are further discussed in Sect. 5. The numeration of code smells follows the pattern x.y where x is the Task number and y is the number of the code smell in a given task. For example, the number 1.16 denotes 16th smell from Task 1. The number can be used to look up the specific code smell in the full list of code smells available at [7]. However, for the comfort of the reader, the code smells mentioned in the paper are briefly described in the following tables.

The Table 4 presents interesting selected data concerning smells that have been found as the first ones during particular review session.

Table 3. Detected code smells with the biggest diversity between PC and mobile.

Smell no.	Description	Mobile	PC
1.16	Magic value	20	7
1.19	Hidden coupling	0	1
1.20	Long vertical distance	2	4
1.22	Useless comment	26	51
1.24	Code duplication	39	27
1.29	Typographic error	11	4
1.33	Lack of curly braces around if/else blocks	6	18
2.17	Pointless code	33	45
2.27	Design flaw, need for inheritance introduction	41	54

Table 4. The first smell found in the review.

Smell no.	Description	Mobile	PC
1.06	Useless encoding of variable names with_prefix	6	2
1.07	Obsolete comment	2	7
1.23	Inconsistency in method naming	2	0
1.26	Useless condition	1	3
2.26	Lack of synchronization for a method	4	0

4.2 Usage of Predefined Comments

The Table 5 presents the usage of the predefined comments. It shows the numbers of collected comments for particular predefined comment type as well as the average quality of these comments.

Figure 2 shows the proportion of predefined comments count to the count of all remarks that have been typed in.

Table 5. Usage of predefined comments.

Comment	Times used	Average quality	Worthless count
Duplicated code	21	9.7	3
Extract method	64	8.5	10
Find a better name	98	8.4	26
Syntax error	16	10	1
Train wrecks	19	7.1	7
Typo	11	9.1	0
Unhandled exception	16	0	16
Unused variable	9	10	0

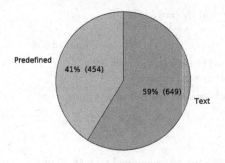 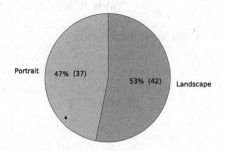

Fig. 2. The type of comments used in mobile reviews

Fig. 3. The device orientation used in mobile reviews.

4.3 Orientation of Mobile Device During the Review

Figure 3 presents the ratio of devices used in portrait and landscape mode during the review. This information has been collected by the mobile application.

If the reviewer held the device in both orientations at different moments of the review, it was classified based on the orientation that was used for a longer time.

4.4 Statistical Significance

The p value has been calculated with t-test (independent, unpaired samples) to compare the PC and mobile datasets containing the number of unique code smells found by single participant during the code review. The results are as follows.

$p_1 = 0.98$
$p_2 = 0.81$
$p_{all} = 0.81$

where p_1 and p_2 are calculated for the data collected during task 1 and 2, respectively. p_{all} is calculated for the all data we have gathered.

4.5 New Defects Detected by the Participants

Interestingly, the full list of code smells available at [7] contains more defects that it had before the experiment. Similar situation has already happened during the preliminary experiment [8]. Some participants managed to find two valid code smells that were not spotted by us during experiment preparation. Table 6 describes them in detail.

4.6 Comparison to the Previous Experiment

As already stated in Sect. 2, the described experiment is a successor of a previous, similar study [8]. We aimed at performing more code reviews that better simulate

Table 6. New defects detected by participants.

Code smell	Description	Found times
1.9	SourceFile class is not Serializable but is used as a field in Line class that is Serializable	2
1.11	Line should refer to AbstractComment instead of Comment	1

real conditions of this activity. The most efficient reviews need to last 40 min per 100 lines of code [11] so extending the experiment time limit was crucial. With a support of a new mobile tool for code reviews that fixes previously spotted issues, we aimed at more accurate and justifiable findings. Table 7 presents all the main differences between these two studies.

Table 7. The differences between the preliminary experiment [8] and the current one

Aspect	The preliminary experiment	The current experiment
Time limit for code review (minutes)	7	40
Lines of code	120	238
Participants	55	91
Reviews	55	180
Mobile reviews	23	79
Comments added to the code	322	2426
Comments added to the code (mobile)	198	1103
Average number of comments per review (mobile)	8	14
Average number of worthless comments per review (mobile)	5	4
Percentage of predefined comments (mobile)	75%	41%

5   Discussion

The summarized results presented in previous section allow to make several interesting observations.

5.1   Mobile Reviews Are as Effective as PC Reviews

The first observation we would like to emphasis is that participants that used mobile devices for the code reviews were as successful in finding code smells in the code as their PC counterparts. This thesis has also confirmation in p values calculated with a t-test. They are much higher than the $p < 0.05$ required to claim that the two datasets are statistically significantly different.

Undoubtedly, reviewing the code on the bigger screen is more comfortable. Nevertheless, our results show that the effectiveness of code reviews were not affected by the tool that has been used to perform the assigned tasks.

These facts also provide an answer to our *Research Question 1: Are mobile code reviews as effective in finding code smells as reviews performed on desktops?* Yes, they are.

5.2 Mobile Devices Need to Provide Friendly Input Method

The quality of mobile reviews are slightly worse than the quality of the PC reviews. This may indicate some problems in the communication between the mobile reviewer and the author of the code.

This leads to a conclusion that the small screens do not limit reviewers in understanding the source code. However, when it comes to the writing of remarks, participants found it really cumbersome to input comprehensive explanation.

We can now answer our *Research Question 2: Is quality of the remarks added to the code during mobile and desktop code review worse?* Yes, they are slightly worse but not to the extent that it would cause significant issues with code reviews.

5.3 The Design of Mobile Application Impacts Code Review Results

In Sect. 2 we enumerated enhancements that have been introduced into the mobile application prepared for this experiment. This involved improvements in source code displaying and ability to edit comments added to the code even if they were chosen from the predefined list.

As can be seen in Table 7, these adjustments resulted in much more careful usage of the predefined comments. Only 4 out of 14 comments added to the source code were considered worthless (not indicating any smell or defect). When compared to the values obtained in the preliminary study [8] (5 worthless comments per 8 added) it becomes clear that the first application suffered from small yet crucial design problems.

5.4 Participants Enjoyed Predefined Comments

It was noticed in the preliminary results [8] that reviewers tend to overuse predefined comments. They prefer to add the predefined comment that somehow indicates the problem instead of write one that would perfectly describe the issue.

Obviously, this is tightly connected with uncomfortable text input method on mobile devices. However, we noticed a major improvement in the quality of predefined comments when compared to the previous experiment. The majority of comments added in mobile reviews were typed in, as shown in Fig. 2.

This may be result of much longer experiment time and greater programming experience of participants. What is more, the new mobile application allowed to expand inserted predefined comment, for example by adding more information or explaining the problem in detail.

Our results presented in Table 5 show that the predefined comments are promising feature of any application for code reviews. However, a special care must be taken by both reviewers and application designers not to misuse them.

The answer for the *Research Question 3: Are reviewers willing to use predefined comments feature?* is: yes, they are. We also think that such functionality could be successfully introduced in desktop tools, but it definitely needs further investigation.

5.5   Mobile Reviewers Pay More Attention to the Details

Besides providing answers to our research questions, we could add four more conclusions from our experiment.

First of all, small screen enables reviewers to see only a few lines of code at a time. We consider this the main disadvantage of mobile reviews. This prevents them from finding code issues that are spread across the whole source file or event multiple files. Table 3 shows that mobile reviewers found such smells less frequent. Examples are: 1.19 (hidden coupling), 1.20 (vertical distance), 2.27 (badly designed class).

However, seeing only a few lines of code encourages mobile reviewers to pay more attention to the code details. Reviewers using mobile devices were able to find typographic (1.29) and syntax (1.16) error more often. They are also able to see such details faster (see 1.06 and 2.26 in Table 4). Last but not least, they needed approximately 1 min less to start the review of given code (see Table 2).

5.6   Participants Did Not Favour Landscape Device Mode

As can be seen on Fig. 3, almost half of the mobile participants used their devices in vertical mode. This surprised us a little, because we expected the majority to use horizontal mode. It enables reviewers to see the whole lines of code without breaking them or needing to swipe the screen.

As we have pointed out a few times already, performing a code review is not only reading but also writing. Text input is considered to be more convenient in vertical mode. The results may indicate that some participants have chosen writing remarks to be more important than reading the code comfortably.

We failed find any correlation between the device orientation and the number of code smells found.

Last but not least, the mobile devices today offer much bigger resolution than it was even a few years ago. Displaying the source code in the vertical mode on such devices is not so inconvenient as one may expect in the beginning.

5.7   There Were No Reviewers' Profiles Among Our Participants

The gathered data has been also analysed with apriori algorithm but we failed to find any valuable frequent itemsets or rules.

By extracting frequent itemsets and rules from the list of found code smells, we were aiming at finding profiles of reviewers. If, for example, someone is a Java expert, he should have definitely found smells 2.6 (incorrect usage of `StringBuffer`) and 2.26 (not synchronized access to `SimpleDateFormat`). If someone pays more attention to the clean code, he should have found all 1.12, 1.13, 1.38, and 2.19 (all concerns code readability).

However, neither frequent itemset nor rule has enough support or confidence to claim such patterns in our results. Nevertheless, we strongly believe such patterns do exist. This must be confirmed by another experiment, though.

5.8   Code Reviews Are Indispensable in Defects Detection

The source code used in the experiment was carefully prepared and checked by a few programmers from the university prior to the research. Still, experiment participants were able to find new defects (see Table 6) which were overlooked during tasks preparation.

Although this conclusion is not related to mobile code reviews in any way, we would like to emphasis one more time that code reviews are incredibly effective in maintaining good code quality.

6   Conclusions and Further Work

The results of the conducted experiment show that the source code can be reviewed on mobile devices. We have proved that the outcomes of reviews performed on mobile devices can not be easily distinguished from the reviews made on desktops.

The obvious fact is that the bigger screen size and resolution the better code reviews comfort is. However, the data we have gathered show that there is a big advantage of small screen size - reviewers pay more attention to details of the code.

Although the dataset we have collected is big enough to notice some interesting observations, it can be argued that obtained results are slightly biased by the university experiment environment. Launching similar research with professional programmers instead of students should be definitely included in future research plan, but it would require some extra resources and preferably a business partner willing to test the mobile review tool in a real industry work environment.

Moreover, the mobile review application needs more tweaking towards easy text input as it seems to be the main obstacle preventing to spread mobile reviews idea across community. The voice comments feature might be reconsidered, although the preliminary results [8] show it has not been used willingly.

Acknowledgements. The research leading to these results has received funding from the Dean's Grant Programme (grant no. 15.11.230.289) funded by Faculty of Computer Science, Electronics and Telecommunications at AGH University of Science and Technology.

References

1. Bacchelli, A., Bird, C.: Expectations, outcomes, and challenges of modern code review. In: Proceedings of the 2013 International Conference on Software Engineering, pp. 712–721. IEEE Press (2013)
2. Barnett, M., Bird, C., Brunet, J., Lahiri, S.K.: Helping developers help themselves: automatic decomposition of code review changesets. In: Proceedings of the 37th International Conference on Software Engineering, vol. 1, pp. 134–144. IEEE Press (2015)
3. Baysal, O., Kononenko, O., Holmes, R., Godfrey, M.W.: Investigating technical and non-technical factors influencing modern code review. Empirical Softw. Eng. **21**(3), 932–959 (2016)
4. Beller, M., Bacchelli, A., Zaidman, A., Juergens, E.: Modern code reviews in open-source projects: which problems do they fix? In: Proceedings of the 11th Working Conference on Mining Software Repositories, pp. 202–211. ACM (2014)
5. Conway, E., Stanford, J., Rettschlag, D., et al.: mGerrit - a Gerrit instance viewer (2016). https://github.com/JBirdVegas/external_jbirdvegas_mGerrit. Accessed 3 May 2017
6. Czerwonka, J., Greiler, M., Tilford, J.: Code reviews do not find bugs: how the current code review best practice slows us down. In: Proceedings of the 37th International Conference on Software Engineering, vol. 2, pp. 27–28. IEEE Press (2015)
7. Frącz, W.: Code review task (2016). https://git.io/code-review-task. Accessed 3 May 2017
8. Frącz, W., Dajda, J.: Source code reviews on mobile devices. Comput. Sci. **17**(2), 143 (2016)
9. Jawnnypoo, M., et al.: Labcoat - gitlab app for android (2017). https://gitlab.com/Commit451/LabCoat. Accessed 3 May 2017
10. Kemerer, C.F., Paulk, M.C.: The impact of design and code reviews on software quality: an empirical study based on psp data. IEEE Trans. Softw. Eng. **35**(4), 534–550 (2009)
11. Mäntylä, M.V., Lassenius, C.: What types of defects are really discovered in code reviews? IEEE Trans. Softw. Eng. **35**(3), 430–448 (2009)
12. Martin, R.C.: Clean Code. A Handbook of Agile Software Craftsmanship. Pearson Education, Inc., Upper Saddle River (2009)
13. McIntosh, S., Kamei, Y., Adams, B., Hassan, A.E.: An empirical study of the impact of modern code review practices on software quality. Empirical Softw. Eng. **21**(5), 2146–2189 (2016)
14. Panichella, S., Arnaoudova, V., Di Penta, M., Antoniol, G.: Would static analysis tools help developers with code reviews? In: 2015 IEEE 22nd International Conference on Software Analysis, Evolution and Reengineering (SANER), pp. 161–170. IEEE (2015)
15. Rahman, M.M., Roy, C.K., Collins, J.A.: Correct: code reviewer recommendation in github based on cross-project and technology experience. In: Proceedings of the 38th International Conference on Software Engineering Companion, pp. 222–231. ACM (2016)

16. Thongtanunam, P., Tantithamthavorn, C., Kula, R.G., Yoshida, N., Iida, H., Matsumoto, K.I.: Who should review my code? A file location-based code-reviewer recommendation approach for modern code review. In: 2015 IEEE 22nd International Conference on Software Analysis, Evolution and Reengineering (SANER), pp. 141–150. IEEE (2015)
17. Xia, X., Lo, D., Wang, X., Yang, X.: Who should review this change?: putting text and file location analyses together for more accurate recommendations. In: 2015 IEEE International Conference on Software Maintenance and Evolution (ICSME), pp. 261–270. IEEE (2015)
18. Yu, Y., Wang, H., Yin, G., Wang, T.: Reviewer recommendation for pull-requests in github: what can we learn from code review and bug assignment? Inf. Softw. Technol. **74**, 204–218 (2016)
19. Zanjani, M.B., Kagdi, H., Bird, C.: Automatically recommending peer reviewers in modern code review. IEEE Trans. Softw. Eng. **42**(6), 530–543 (2016)

Developing Prediction Models to Assist Software Developers and Support Managers

Meera Sharma[1(✉)] and Abhishek Tondon[2]

[1] Department of Computer Science, University of Delhi, Delhi, India
meerakaushik@gmail.com
[2] SSCBS, University of Delhi, Delhi, India
abhishek.tondon@rocketmail.com

Abstract. A huge amount of historical information about the evolution of a software project is available in software repositories, namely bug repositories, source control repositories, archived communications, deployment logs, and code repositories. By mining the evolutionary history of a software, we have designed prediction models to assist software developers by predicting bug attributes like priority, severity, assignee and fix time. We have evaluated the uncertainty in the software in terms of entropy arises due to source code changes done in files of the software to fix different issues. To support software managers, we have designed prediction models to predict potential values of entropy and different issues, namely bugs, improvements in existing features (IMPs) and new features (NFs) over a long run. In this research work, we have developed mathematical models to assist software managers and developers in bug triaging, bug fixing and different software maintenance related tasks. Our work has been validated on issue and code change data of several open source projects, namely Eclipse, Open office, Mozilla and Apache.

1 Problem Statement and Its Importance

Advancement in internet and communication technologies has given impetus to the development and usage of Open Source Software (OSS). Various open source software repositories: source control repositories, bug repositories, archived communications, deployment logs, and code repositories are available online and easily accessible. These repositories help bug triager/developers in the bug resolving process and also in the evolution of the software products. Software repositories are helpful in understanding the development of a software. Different predictions can be made about the development of a software by using the information available in different software repositories. It will be again helpful for planning different aspects of the software evolution. The bug report history is stored in bug reporting and tracking systems (BugZilla, Jira, Mantis, Trac, Gnats, Fossil and Bugtracker.net) separately. Reporting a bug requires several parameters/attributes to be filled at the time of bug submission. Some attributes such as summary, reporter and submission date are entered during the initial submission and remain constant. Other attributes such as severity, priority, resolution, status, assignee and milestone are entered later on in the bug fixing process and can be updated.

© Springer International Publishing AG 2017
O. Gervasi et al. (Eds.): ICCSA 2017, Part V, LNCS 10408, pp. 548–560, 2017.
DOI: 10.1007/978-3-319-62404-4_41

Bug priority describes about the urgency and importance of fixing a bug. It can be assigned into 5 levels from 1 to 5. Priority level 1 is the highest and priority level 5 is the lowest priority. Another important bug parameter is severity. Severity is one of the ordinal attribute which is used to measure the effect of the bug on the software functionality. Open source projects have used seven severity levels from 1 (Blocker) to 7 (Trivial). During bug fixing process, correct bug severity assignment and prioritization help in bug assignment/bug fix scheduling and resource allocation. In case of failure of this, resolution of important bugs will be delayed. A bug priority and severity prediction system will be helpful for software developers to fix reopened or newly reported bugs. In the available literature, several studies have been conducted for the proposal of severity and priority prediction [1–10]. Prediction of bug priority and severity needs historical data on which we can train the classifiers. But, unavailability of bug history for a software, especially for a new one, is a problem. In this situation, building prediction models based on cross project is the solution. No author has attempted to work on cross project validation in case of bug severity and priority prediction. In this paper, we have conducted a study to predict bug priority and severity by using bug summary (a brief description about the bug) in the context of cross project [27, 29, 33].

The absence of Association Rule Mining based study for bug fix time and assignee prediction motivated us to propose bug fix time and assignee prediction models [28, 30, 31]. To assist bug triaging process, Apriori algorithm has been used

- to predict the bug fix time by using the bug severity, priority, summary terms and assignee and
- to predict the assignee of a newly reported bug by using the bug severity, priority and summary terms.

In Open Source Software (OSS), users located at different geographical locations participate in the evolution of the software by reporting bugs and requesting for the new features (NFs) and improvements in the existing features (IMPs). Software developers do source code changes in files of the software to fix bugs or to meet the demands of the users. These source code changes in a given time period can be used to measure the potential complexity of code changes, i.e. possible code changes in the software over a long run. OSS evolves as a result of these modifications. An empirical understanding of different issues fixing and changes done in source code files can help software mangers to plan different evolutionary aspects of a software. We proposed mathematical models for prediction of potential bugs to be detected or fixed [32]. We have also predicted new features and improvements in existing features that can be incorporated in the software over a long run. The code change complexity has been quantified by using entropy based measures. Then, the potential entropy has been predicted by using Cobb-Douglas function [15]. We also extended Cobb-Douglas based diffusion models to incorporate the impact of different issues on the complexity of code changes. The rest of the paper is organized as follows: Sect. 2 gives the related literature. Section 3 presents the research questions deigned for this study. Proposed solution for the research questions and its novelty has been discussed in Sect. 4. Present status and future research plan have been presented in Sect. 5. Finally, the paper has been concluded in Sect. 6.

2   Related Work

In this section, we have presented an overview of the related studies. In text based bug severity assessment, studies have been conducted for bug severity prediction by using textual description, i.e. summary of bug [1–3]. In a study [4], NB, MNB, SVM, k-NN, J48, and RIPPER classifiers have been used for bug severity prediction and results showed that for closed source projects NB worked with significant accuracy performance and For open source projects, SVM worked well. A method has been proposed for the bug triage and the bug severity prediction [5]. The authors used historical bug reports in the bug repository for extracting topic(s) and then map the bug reports related to each topic. The authors identified corresponding reports having similar attributes: component, product, priority and severity, with the newly submitted bug report. After that severity for the bug and the most appropriate developer are recommended. Reference [6] suggested a concept profile-based severity prediction technique which first analyzed historical bug reports in the bug repositories and then build the concept profiles from them. Recently, a new approach has been proposed in [7] which assess the accuracy of bug severity prediction by taking into consideration the unreliable nature of the data. Results of this approach show that current prediction approaches perform well 77–86% agreement with human-assigned severity levels. Reference [22] predicted the priority of a bug during the software testing process using Artificial Neural Network (ANN) and Naïve Bayes classifier. References [9, 10] used a classification based approach to compare and evaluate the Support Vector Machine (SVM) and Naïve Bayes classifiers to automate the prioritization of new bug report by using the categorical and textual attributes of a bug report to train the model. They have shown that SVM performance was better than the Naïve Bayes with textual attributes and Naïve Bayes performance was better than SVM for categorical attributes. But this analysis has been carried out on a limited data and techniques. Cross project bug priority and severity prediction is a new and challenging task. No attempt has been made in available literature to discover association rules for different attributes of bug.

In OSS, source code needs to be changed frequently in order to fix different issues reported by different users. These changes done in the files of the software system makes the source code complex and buggy. Such source code changes can be measured by using various complexity measures proposed in the literature. In a study [23], complexity is defined on the basis of expanded system resources when the system performs a given task by interacting with a part of software. In case of a computer system, the complexity is defined by using the storage needed and execution time required to do the computation. If a programmer is considered as an interacting system then the difficulty faced by him in performing different tasks is used to measure the complexity. The task may be of coding, testing, debugging and modification. According to thermodynamics second law the disorder of a closed system remains constant or it increases, but it never reduces and entropy is defined as a measure of this disorder. The Entropy of an evolving system always increases [24]. As a software is modified or evolved, the source code changes and these changes lead to the uncertainty or randomness in the software which results in complex and buggy code. Entropy of a software is defined as a measure of this uncertainty or randomness or complexity of the source code. The first attempt to predict the bugs by using past defects has been made by [12]. The authors numerically evaluated the process of code change by using entropy based measures. Reference [13] proposed a model which predicts the code change complexity of a software over a long run by using entropy based measures. The authors also determined the rate of code change complexity diffusion. The historical code change data of various components of open source Mozilla wed browser have been used to validate the proposed model. In literature, [25, 26] have used 2-dimensional Cobb-Douglas function for software reliability modeling to consider the impact of efforts used in testing, testing time and testing coverage. The effect of different types of issues: bugs, NFs and IMPs, have not been considered so far for code change complexity prediction.

3 Research Questions

We have designed following research questions for our study

Research Question 1: Does training data from other projects provide acceptable bug priority and severity prediction results?

Research Question 2: Does the combination of training data sets provide better performance than single training data set?

Research Question 3: Can we discover association rules between different bug attributes that will assist the developers in bug assignment and prediction of bug fix time?

Research Question 4: Can we predict the potential entropy that can be diffused in the software over a period of time?

Research Question 5: Can we predict the potential bugs to be detected/fixed and NFs, IMPs that can be incorporated in the software over a long run?

4 Proposed Solution and Its Novelty

Active users located at different geographical locations, participate in the software evolution by reporting bugs and requesting for the new features (NFs) and improvements in the existing features (IMPs) as shown in Fig. 1.

Fig. 1. Issues (bugs/NFs/IMPs) submission in open source software

Prediction models for bug priority and severity assist software developers in bug triaging. The prediction models need historical data on which we can train the classifiers. But, unavailability of bug history for a software, especially for a new one, is a problem. In this situation, building prediction models based on cross project is the solution [17–21]. In answer to Research Question 1, we proposed cross project bug priority and severity prediction models as shown in Fig. 2. We trained the classifiers with summary attribute of fixed bug reports (with known labels of priority and severity) of projects other than the testing projects.

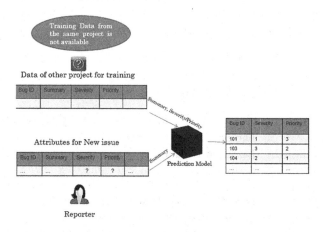

Fig. 2. Cross project bug priority and severity prediction

We have used text mining [1] to extract terms/features of bug summary attributes based on information gain criteria to train the classifiers.

In answer to Research Question 2, we used all the combinations consisting of maximum 3 datasets from projects other than the testing project. During making the combination of training datasets, we have excluded project which is going to be tested. The number of combinations consisting of less than or equal to N datasets for M available datasets/projects can be computed as shown below in Eq. (1).

$$\sum_{j=1}^{N} \frac{M!}{j!(M-j)!} \tag{1}$$

Example of generating training datasets for DB dataset has been shown in Fig. 3 [29].

Based on the accuracy and f-measure performance, the best training candidate for every testing dataset has been identified.

The absence of association rule based bug fix time and assignee prediction models motivated us to design Research Question 3. To assist bug triaging process, we used Apriori algorithm

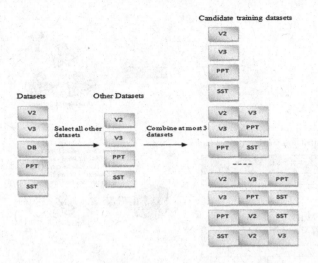

Fig. 3. Procedure of generating training datasets for DB dataset

- to predict the bug fix time by using bug severity, priority summary terms and assignee (Fig. 4) [28] and
- to predict the assignee of a newly reported bug by using bug severity, priority and summary terms (Fig. 5) [30, 31].

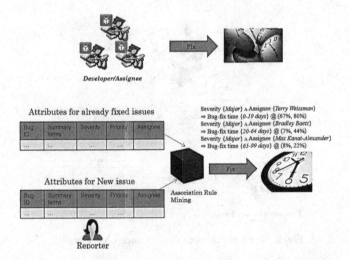

Fig. 4. Association rule Mining based Bug fix time Prediction

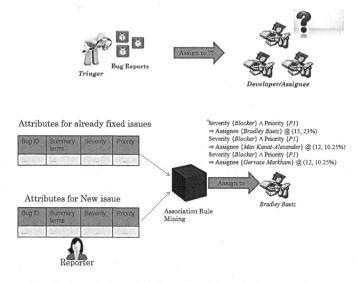

Fig. 5. Association rule Mining based Bug Assignee Prediction

Frequent code changes are required to fix different issues reported by users, which results in complex code as shown in Fig. 6.

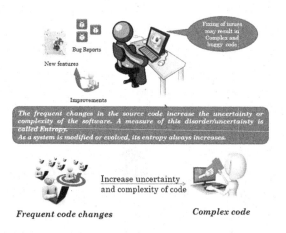

Fig. 6. Frequent changes make source code complex

The source code changes done in the software in order to fix different issues are quantified using entropy based measures and termed as complexity of code changes. The quantification of code changes is based upon the Shannon entropy [11] as given in Eq. (2):

$$E_n(P) = -\sum_{j=1}^{n} (P_j * \log_2 P_j), \quad P_j \geq 0 \quad \sum_{j=1}^{n} P_j = 1 \tag{2}$$

The probability of occurrence of a change is denoted by P_j, where P_j is defined as follows:

$$P_j = \frac{no.\ of\ times\ j^{th}\ file\ changed\ in\ a\ period}{total\ no.\ of\ changes\ done\ in\ all\ the\ files\ in\ that\ period}$$

The concept of entropy to measure the complexity of code changes has been used by [12] as given in Eq. (3).

$$E(P) = \frac{1}{Max\ Entropy\ for\ Distribution} * E_n(P)$$
$$= \frac{1}{\log_2 n} * E_n(P) = \frac{1}{\log_2 n} * -\sum_{j=1}^{n} (p_j * \log_2 p_j)$$
$$= -\sum_{j=1}^{n} (p_j * \log_n p_j) \tag{3}$$

where $p_j \geq 0, \forall j \in 1, 2, \ldots, n \quad and \sum_{j=1}^{n} p_j = 1.$

As the entropy (E) depends on that how many files the system have (n), to prevent the reduction in entropy due to the rarely modified files, to get the effective entropy, the number of recently modified files has been used to divide [12, 13]. Fifty source code changes done in a single file are easy to recall instead of fifty single changes done in fifty different files.

There is a challenge before us to determine the future requests that can come from different users and to determine the potential source code change that can be done in the software over a long run. We need to link all the issue implementations with the source code changes of the software.

In answer of the Research Question 4, we proposed models along the line of [13, 14] for potential entropy prediction. We defined r as the rate at which entropy is diffused in the source code due to NFs or IMPs and s is defined as the rate at which entropy is diffused due to bug fixes.

We have made the following assumptions for the proposed models:

- Potential entropy remains same.
- The effect of NFs/IMPs on entropy is independent and may generate bugs.
- At $t = 0$, entropy is zero.

The entropy diffusion per unit time can be written as follows:

$$\frac{d(E(t))}{dt} = r\left(\overline{E} - E(t)\right) + s\frac{E(t)}{\overline{E}}\left(\overline{E} - E(t)\right) \tag{4}$$

where $\overline{E}$ is the potential entropy to be diffused in software and $E(t)$ is the amount of entropy at any given time t. We solved Eq. (4) with $t = 0$ and $E(0) = 0$, we get

$$E(t) = \overline{E}\left[\frac{1 - e^{-(r+s)t}}{1 + \frac{s}{r}e^{-(r+s)t}}\right]$$

or

$$E(t) = \overline{E}\left[\frac{1 - e^{-\alpha t}}{1 + \gamma e^{-\alpha t}}\right] \tag{5}$$

Here $\alpha = r + s$ is the rate at which entropy is diffused due to source code changes and $\gamma = \frac{s}{r}$ is a constant.

We have extended the Cobb-Douglas type function [15] to consider the effect of NFs and IMPs on the entropy. In Eq. (6), v denotes IMPs and w denotes NFs, and μ is the degree of the impact on the entropy.

$$t \equiv v^{\mu}w^{1-\mu} \quad (0 \leq \mu \leq 1) \tag{6}$$

We have proposed a model to measure the entropy depending on two factors: NFs and IMPs, and for that we extended t of Eq. (5) by using Eq. (6) as

$$E(v, w) = \overline{E}\left[\frac{1 - e^{-\alpha(v^{\mu}*w^{1-\mu})}}{1 + \gamma e^{-\alpha(v^{\mu}*w^{1-\mu})}}\right] \tag{7}$$

We have extended the Cobb-Douglas type function [15] to incorporate the effect of NFs, IMPs and bugs on the entropy of the software. In Eq. (8), v, w and x denote the IMPs, NFs and bugs. α and γ are the effect of NFs and IMPs on the entropy.

$$t \equiv v^{\mu}w^{\lambda}x^{1-(\mu+\lambda)} \quad (0 \leq \mu \text{ and } \lambda \leq 1) \tag{8}$$

We model to measure the effect of NFs, IMPs and bugs on the entropy diffusion simultaneously by extending t of Eq. (5) by using Eq. (8) as

$$E(v, w, x) = \overline{E}\left[\frac{1 - e^{-\alpha(v^{\mu}*w^{\lambda}*x^{1-(\mu+\lambda)})}}{1 + \gamma e^{-\alpha(v^{\mu}*w^{\lambda}*x^{1-(\mu+\lambda)})}}\right] \tag{9}$$

In answer to Research Question 5, we considered 'a' as the potential issues: bug, NFs, IMPs and NFs + IMPs, that are reported in the software over a period of time and this follows nonhomogeneous poison process. In line of [14, 16], the following equation has been written. We considered the logistic rate, i.e. c, for diffusion of NFs/IMPs and bug detection in the software.

$$\frac{d}{dt}m(t) = \frac{c}{1+\gamma\exp\left(-ct\right)}\left(a - m(t)\right)$$

where $m(t)$ is the cumulative value of bug/NFs/IMPs/(NFs + IMPs) at any time t.
In above equation, we take $m(t) = 0$ at $t = 0$, which results in Eq. (10)

$$m(t) = a\left[\frac{1 - \exp(-ct)}{1 + \gamma\exp(-ct)}\right] \tag{10}$$

Above model in Eq. (10) is used for prediction of potential bugs/NFs/IMPs/ (NFs + IMPs) at any given time.

Validation of the proposed prediction models has been done by using historical data for several open source projects, namely Eclipse, Open office, Mozilla and Apache. Results show that bug priority prediction accuracy in cross project context is better than within project. Cross project priority prediction gives accuracy above 72% for SVM, k-NN and NNET. For combined training datasets, we get accuracy which is above 73% for all cases. Combined cross-project datasets result in improved f-measure performance in 12 cases and improved accuracy performance in 11 cases out of 20 total cases across all the 4 classifiers. SVM and NNET are better than k-NN and k-NN is better than Naïve Bayes in terms of accuracy performance.

The results of cross project bug severity prediction show that Combined cross-project datasets result in improved f-measure performance in 12 cases and improved accuracy performance in 10 cases out of 21 total cases across all the 3 classifiers.

Non-parametric Mann-Whitney U test has shown a statistical significant difference in f-measure performance of different training candidates for a particular testing dataset. The two ensemble approaches: *Vote* and *Bagging*, have improved the f-measure performance up to 5% and 10% respectively for the severity levels having less number of bug reports in comparison of major severity level.

Association rule mining based prediction models for bug fix time and assignee predictions reveal rules that will assist developers in bug triaging and fixing process. Results show that proposed models for prediction of entropy and different issues submitted by users give a high goodness of fit for various performance measures, namely R^2, Bias, Variation, MSE and RMSPE.

5   Current Status and Future Plans

All the proposed prediction models have been described in detail in published papers [27–33]. In future, we will propose mathematical models to incorporate the unique paradigms of OSS development, such as the multiple releases property and rate of issues fixed by different types of contributors (innovators and imitators). In OSS, a number of contributors are innovative in nature in the sense that they work without their own implicit requirements, but for the evolution of the software product. We consider them as innovators (core developers) and others may be imitators. Issues are fixed by the innovators and a proportion of issues fixed, also causing to fix more issues by imitators.

A proportion of issues which are fixed by the innovators gave an impetus to fix more issues (imitators). We will also develop a mathematical model to embody the open source software development. The model will be based on the rate at which new features, feature improvements are added and the rate at which bugs are generated from these additions. We will extend the proposed model by considering the complexity of code changes (entropy) and discuss the release time planning of the software using the proposed model by maximizing the user's satisfaction level subject to fixing of issues up to a desired level. The proposed decision model will assist management to appropriately measure the software reliability, i.e. the issues left in the software and to determine the optimal release-update time for open source software.

6 Conclusion

In the paper, prediction models have been proposed to assist software developers and support managers in software maintenance and evolution. Bug reports of open source projects have been analyzed to predict bug severity and priority in cross projects context using text mining and machine learning techniques. We concluded that historical data of other projects developed in open source environment is better priority predictor and priority prediction in cross project context is working well. Results indicate that cross-project bug severity prediction is a serious challenge, i.e. simply using training data from projects in the same domain does not lead to accurate predictions. More research is needed to find out how to best describe the selection of a training project automatically. The association rule mining can be used to mine the association rules for bug fix time and assignee prediction. The proposed models to predict the potential of different issues and the entropy fit the observed data.

References

1. Menzies, T., Marcus, A.: Automated severity assessment of software defect reports. In: International Conference on Software Maintenance, pp. 346–355. IEEE (2008)
2. Lamkanfi, A., Demeyer, S., Giger, E., Goethals, B.: Predicting the severity of a reported bug. In: Mining Software Repositories, pp. 1–10. MSR (2010)
3. Lamkanfi, A., Demeyer, Soetens, Q.D., Verdonck, T.: Comparing mining algorithms for predicting the severity of a reported bug. In: 15th European Conference on Software Maintenance and Reengineering, pp. 249–258. IEEE (2011)
4. Chaturvedi, K.K., Singh, V.B.: An empirical comparison of machine learning techniques in predicting the bug severity of open and close source projects. Int. J. Open Source Softw. Process. 4(2), 32–59 (2013)
5. Yang, G., Zhang, T., Lee, B.: Towards semi-automatic bug triage and severity prediction based on topic model and multi-feature of bug reports. In: Computer Software and Applications Conference (COMPSAC), pp. 97–106. IEEE (2014)
6. Zhang, T., Yang, G., Lee, B., Chan, A.T.: Predicting severity of bug report by mining bug repository with concept profile. In: 30th Annual ACM Symposium on Applied Computing, pp. 1553–1558, April 2015

7. Tian, Y., Ali, N., Lo, D., Hassan, A.E.: On the unreliability of bug severity data. Empirical Softw. Eng. **21**(6), 2298–2323 (2015)

8. Zhang, T., Chen, J., Yang, G., Lee, B., Luo, X.: Towards more accurate severity prediction and fixer recommendation of software bugs. J. Syst. Softw. **117**, 166–184 (2016)

9. Kanwal, J., Maqbool, O.: Managing open bug repositories through bug report prioritization using SVMs. In: Proceedings of the International Conference on Open-Source Systems and Technologies, Lahore, Pakistan (2010)

10. Kanwal, J., Maqbool, O.: Bug prioritization to facilitate bug report triage. J. Comput. Sci. Technol. **27**(2), 397–412 (2012)

11. Shannon, C.E.: A mathematical theory of communication. Bell Syst. Tech. J. **27**(379–423), 623–656 (1948)

12. Hassan, A.E.: Predicting faults based on complexity of code change. In: International Conference on Software Engineering, pp. 78–88 (2009)

13. Chaturvedi, K.K., Kapur, P.K., Anand, S., Singh, V.B.: Predicting the complexity of code changes using entropy based measures. Int. J. Syst. Assur. Eng. Manage. **5**, 155–164 (2014)

14. Bass, F.: A new product growth model for consumer durables. Manage. Sci. **15**, 215–227 (1969)

15. Varian, H.R.: Intermediate Microeconomics — A Modern Approach. W.W. Norton & Company, New York (1991)

16. Bittanti, S., Bolzern, P., Pedrotti, E., Pozzi, M., Scattolini, R.: A flexible modelling approach for software reliability growth. In: Bittanti, S. (ed.) Software Reliability Modelling and Identification. LNCS, vol. 341, pp. 101–140. Springer, Heidelberg (1988). doi:10.1007/BFb0034288

17. Zimmermann, T., Nagappan, N., Gall, H., Giger, E., Murphy, B.: Cross-project defect prediction: a large scale experiment on data vs. domain vs. process. In: Joint Meeting of the European Software Engineering Conference and the ACM SIGSOFT Symposium on the Foundations of Software Engineering (ESEC/FSE), pp. 91–100 (2009)

18. Turhan, B., Menzies, T., Bener, A.: On the relative value of cross-company and within-company data for defect prediction. Empirical Softw. Eng. **14**(5), 540–578 (2009)

19. Ma, Y., Luo, G., Zeng, X., Chen, A.: Transfer learning for cross-company software defect prediction. Inf. Softw. Technol. **54**(3), 248–256 (2011). Science Direct, Elsevier

20. He, Z., Fengdi, S., Ye, Y., Mingshu, L., Qing, W.: An investigation on the feasibility of cross-project defect prediction. Autom. Softw. Eng. **19**, 167–199 (2012). Springer

21. Peters, F., Menzies, T., Marcus, A.: Better cross company defect prediction. In: 10th IEEE Working Conference on Mining Software Repositories (MSR), pp. 409–418. IEEE (2013)

22. Yu, L., Tsai, W., Zhao, W., Wu, F.: Predicting defect priority based on neural networks. In: 6th International Proceedings on Advanced Data Mining and Applications, pp. 356–367, Wuhan, China (2010)

23. Basili, V.R.: Qualitative software complexity models: a summary. In: Tutorial on Models and Methods for Software Management and Engineering. IEEE Computer Society Press, Los Alamitos, California (1980)

24. Jacobson, I., Christerson, M., Jonsson, P., Overgaard, G.: Object Oriented Software Engineering: A Use Case Driven Approach. ACM Press, Addison Wesley, pp. 69–70 (1992)

25. Inoue, S., Yamada, S.: Two-dimensional software reliability measurement technologies. In: IEEE IEEM, pp. 223–227 (2009)

26. Kapur, P.K., Pham, H., Gurjeet, A.G.: Two dimensional multi-release software reliability modeling and optimal release planning. IEEE Trans. Reliab. **61**(3), 758–768 (2012)

27. Singh, V.B., Misra, S., Sharma, M.: Bug severity in cross project context and identifying training candidates. J. Inf. Knowl. Manage. **16**(1), 30 (2017). World Scientific Publishing

28. Sharma, M., Kumari, M., Singh, V.B.: The way ahead for bug-fix time prediction. In: 3rd International Workshop on Quantitative Approaches to Software Quality (QuASoQ), co-located with 22nd Asia-Pacific Software Engineering Conference (APSEC 2015), New Delhi, India, pp. 31–38, 1–4 December 2015

29. Sharma, M., Bedi, P., Singh, V.B.: An empirical evaluation of cross project priority prediction. Int. J. Syst. Assur. Eng. Manage. 5(4), 651–663 (2014). Springer

30. Sharma, M., Singh, V.B.: Clustering-based association rule mining for bug assignee prediction. Int. J. Bus. Intell. Data Min. 11(2), 130–150 (2016)

31. Sharma, M., Kumari, M., Singh, V.B.: Bug assignee prediction using association rule mining. In: Gervasi, O., Murgante, B., Misra, S., Gavrilova, M.L., Rocha, A.M.A.C., Torre, C., Taniar, D., Apduhan, B.O. (eds.) ICCSA 2015. LNCS, vol. 9158, pp. 444–457. Springer, Cham (2015). doi:10.1007/978-3-319-21410-8_35

32. Singh, V.B., Sharma, M.: Prediction of the complexity of code changes based on number of open bugs, new feature and feature improvement. In: 25th IEEE International Symposium on Software Reliability Engineering (ISSRE), WOSD, Neples, Italy, pp. 478–483 (2014)

33. Sharma, M., Bedi, P., Chaturvedi, K.K., Singh, V.B.: Predicting the priority of a reported bug using machine learning techniques and cross project validation. In: International Conference on Intelligent Systems Design and Applications (ISDA), pp. 539–545. IEEE (2012)

Improving Static Initialization Block Handling in Java Symbolic Execution Engine

Edit Pengő$^{(\boxtimes)}$ and István Siket

Department of Software Engineering, University of Szeged, Szeged, Hungary
{pengoe,siket}@inf.u-szeged.hu

Abstract. Runtime exceptions usually cause serious problems during execution, so it is important to focus on them during testing. On the other hand, it is very difficult to discover such problems by static analysis, so most tools are not able to find them. Symbolic execution is applied to verify the possible execution paths of the program without really executing it. Although it is able to detect runtime exceptions, usually it is very slow and requires lots of resources, consequently some trade-offs must be made so that it can be used in practice. But due to the different trade-offs, the results become less precise.

Our static analyzer tool, called RTEHunter, uses a symbolic execution engine to detect runtime exceptions in Java source code but it has limitations as well. One of them is the proper handling of static initialization which is neglected in the latest version of RTEHunter. We provided a heuristical solution for managing static initializer blocks instead of implementing the proper working of the Java ClassLoader, which can be very complex.

The results were tested on more than 200 various sized Java systems. Our solution filtered out more than 200 false positive NullPointerException warnings, which is about 8% of the total number of reported NullPointerExceptions.

Keywords: Symbolic execution · Java · Static initialization block

1 Introduction

Developing a software is a very complex task and the unclear requirements, the underestimated efforts, and the strict deadlines make it even more difficult. Taking all these into account, it is not surprising that every software contains bugs even after its releasing. To decrease the number of bugs, the software has to be tested. Although the resources (computation capacity and human resources together) are limited, the efficiency of testing heavily depends on how it is done. For example, manual testing can discover lots of different kinds of bugs in the software, however it is very expensive to carry out by testers. On the other hand, static code analysis – when the code is automatically analyzed and the potential problematic places are identified by tools – is very cheap and can be applied continuously. Its drawback is that certain kinds of bugs cannot be discovered by

© Springer International Publishing AG 2017
O. Gervasi et al. (Eds.): ICCSA 2017, Part V, LNCS 10408, pp. 561–574, 2017.
DOI: 10.1007/978-3-319-62404-4_42

this way, or its efficiency depends on the quality and the purpose of the static analyzer tool.

Different kinds of static analyzers for Java systems exist but their capabilities differ considerably. For example, besides the error messages, the Java compiler itself gives us warning messages as well. Furthermore several open source and free tools can be used for static source code analysis. CheckStyle [7] verifies whether the Java source code adheres to a coding standard. Although it rarely discovers real bugs, its usage improves the readability and quality of the source code. Another tool is PMD [17] that is able to detect problems like real bugs or dead code in Java source code. FindBugs [10] is also able to discover bugs, but its drawback is that it works on Java bytecode, which means that the source code must be compiled otherwise this tool cannot be used. In addition, the existing commercial tools usually make a deeper static analysis by applying more complex algorithms. For example, the symbolic execution simulates the execution of the program or a part of the program using only the static analysis information. Although this way more serious problems can be found, one of the drawbacks of the approach is that it requires more resources. Besides, there are some language constructions that are difficult to simulate precisely, so some trade-offs must be applied.

In this work, we focus on the symbolic execution engine developed by our team. We first examine how it handles the static initialization blocks of classes and how it influences bug detection accuracy. It has turned out that neglecting static initialization blocks leads to noisy results, therefore we have developed a heuristic to handle it. Its advantage is that it hardly increases execution time or memory usage, while it improves the result. We tested on more than two hundred open source Java systems and it was proven that in practice it worked well because a notable amount of false positive warnings were filtered out.

The rest of the paper is organized as follows. Related work is discussed in Sect. 2. Section 3 introduces the technical background of symbolic execution and our static analyzer tool. Our new approach and the results are presented in Sect. 4. Finally, we conclude the study in Sect. 5.

2   Related Work

The idea of symbolic execution was introduced in the 1970s as an elegant and powerful method for software proving, validation, and test generation. In 1976, King introduced the fundamentals of symbolic execution along with the presentation the EFFIGY system [15]. EFFIGY is one of the first symbolic executor engines. It is written for PL/I programs and handles only integer variables symbolically. With its interactive user interface, EFFIGY lets programmers explore the symbolic executional tree for exhaustive software testing. Another important early work was the SELECT system for systematical debugging of LISP programs. SELECT was published by Boyer et al. in 1975 [3]. Like EFFIGY, it aims at systematical and exhaustive testing, it allows verifications by user supported asserts, and it also provides interactivity in the control of symbolic execution. In his 1988 survey, Coward collected and analysed six symbolic executor systems containing the previously mentioned EFFIGY and SELECT systems too [8]. He compared the investigated systems to an ideal symbolic executor engine revealing the major limitations and challenges like the handling of path explosion and constraint solving, that still have to be faced nowadays. The survey also provided a classification for symbolic engines according to their main purpose: test data generation from constraints applied to symbolic variables, program proving with the use of assertions, program reduction, path domain checking, and symbolic debugging for tracing runtime issues.

Due to the growth in computational power, the interest for symbolic executors was renewed in the 2000s. Two recent surveys in the subject are the work of Cadar and Sen [6] which was presented in 2013, and the detailed paper of Baldoni et al. from 2016 [2]. Both give an overview of the state of the art, the challenges, and their current solutions. The new trend was that the engines did not use pure symbolic execution, instead they relied on hybrid techniques to overcome the limitations of symbolic execution. The mixture of concrete and symbolic execution is called concolic execution, or in other words dynamic symbolic execution. The DART (Directed Automate Random Testing) system introduced by Godefroid et al. [11] was the first to suggest this approach. It performs a directed search in the symbolic execution tree through the iterated executions of the investigated software. The process starts with random input values, then during each execution information is collected about the symbolic variables to produce input data that would force the next execution on a new path. CUTE and jCUTE are also concolic testing systems for C and Java [16,20]. Similarly to the DART system, they collect information about symbolic constraints to produce input data, but they are extended with the capability of handling multithreading. If the constraint solver fails to satisfy a complex expression, the constraints are simplified by replacing some symbolic variables with concrete values. jCUTE can generate JUnit tests for sequential softwares. For .NET programs Pex [22] is used for generating test suites with the help of dynamic symbolic execution. It can be integrated to Visual Studio as an add-in.

EXE (EXecution generated Executions) [5] and its successor, KLEE [4] symbolically executes C programs trying to explore all possible paths. When an error is reached the symbolic constraints are used for test input generation. KLEE is based on the LLVM assembly language and functions as a virtual machine. It powerfully handles environmentally-intensive programs, for example by setting up a symbolic filesystem or by simulating faulty system calls. Similarly, the Java PathFinder (JPF) [12] tool also behaves like a virtual machine and executes the Java bytecode in a special way. JPF is developed at the NASA Ames Research Center for verifying and checking NASA projects. It has an extension, called Symbolic PathFinder (SPF) [18], for performing symbolic execution. SPF supports concolic execution and can be customized with several constraint solvers. However, it can perform symbolic execution starting only from the `main` method, which can have several drawbacks. Kádár et al. created a wrapper for SPF, called JPF Checker [13] that generates classes with a `main` method for each function in the investigated software. SPF is parametrized to run these generated `main` methods from which the function in question is called through reflection. JPF Checker performs the execution in the style of RTEHunter, but with the use of SPF as a symbolic engine. The predecessor of RTEHunter, named Symbolic Checker, was introduced by Kádár et al. in 2015 as a subject for improved constraint solving technique [14]. The performance of the two symbolic engines was compared in this work.

In this 2015 work of Ramos and Engler [19] the basic idea to overcome path explosion is similar to the approach implemented in RTEHuntre and JPF Checker. They created a KLEE based symbolic engine for C/C++ programs but instead of starting the execution only from the `main` function they directly executed individual functions within a program. It is called under-constrainted execution because the function parameters have unknown preconditions which may result in false positive errors.

3 Background

In this section we give a quick insight into the theory of symbolic execution. First, the most important definitions will be discussed, then we show an example of how the execution works and finally we present how it is implemented in our static analyzer tool.

3.1 Symbolic Execution

The basic idea of symbolic execution is that the program is run on symbolic input data instead of actual ones. During regular execution, the variables of the program have concrete values, which means the program follows a specific executional path determined by these values. In contrast to that, symbolic values are the set of concrete values. Without applying any constraint, a symbolic variable can hold every concrete value that is possible for its type. When the symbolic executor cannot determine the exact value of a variable (because, for example, it is a user input or method parameter), a symbolic value is assigned to it. The usage of these symbolic variables becomes interesting when a conditional statement is reached. The result of a logical expression containing symbolic values will be symbolic too, so the symbolic engine has to continue the execution parallel on every branch. This means that during symbolic execution theoretically every possible executional path of a program will be explored allowing to detect runtime failures along those paths. The tree built up from these paths is called the symbolic execution tree (an example is presented in Fig. 2). This is a directed, acyclic graph where each node represents a state of the program. It is clear that some branches of the symbolic execution tree is unreachable even with symbolic values because the concatenation of the conditional statements leading to them are unsatisfiable. Symbolic engines can cut off these unnecessary branches by maintaining and checking the satisfiability of a path condition (PC). The path condition is a quantifier-free logical formula over the symbolic variables. It contains constraints derived from the conditional statements that have to be satisfied in order to reach the investigated executional state. Symbolic engines use constraint solver algorithms to check the satisfiability of the path condition and to decrease the number of possible branches when a conditional statement is reached. On the contrary, if a path condition is satisfiable, assigning the solutions to the symbolic variables as input values will direct the concrete execution to the state of that PC. Therefore, for example, symbolic execution can be a tool for test input generation.

```
1  public static int isTriangleValid(Point p1,Point p2,Point p3){
2      double a = euclideanDistance(p1,p2);
3      double b = euclideanDistance(p2,p3);
4      double c = euclideanDistance(p1,p3);
5      if(a == b+c || b == a+c || c == a+b) {
6          return -1;
7      }
8      if(a > b+c || b > a+c || c > a+b) {
9          return 1;
10     }
11     return 0;
12 }
```

Fig. 1. Sample code that checks if three points can form a triangle.

Figure 1 shows an example function which decides if the three 2-dimensional points given as parameters can form a triangle. There are two erroneous return values: the function returns with -1 if the three points are on a line, and with 1 if the three points are not on one line but the triangle inequality is not satisfied anyway. The return value is 0 if a proper triangle can be composed from the three points. The implementation of the euclideanDistance function is not present but as its name suggests it calculates the distance between two 2-dimensional points with the classic euclidean formula. Suppose that the symbolic execution was started with this function, so the actual value of parameter p1, p2, and p3 are unknown, therefore they must be handled symbolically. It means that the two data members (coordinate x and y) of each Point are symbolic too, so they can hold any value from the domain of their type. Therefore, the value returned by the euclideanDistance function can be symbolic, making local variable a, b, and c also symbolic variables. Theoretically, we have more information about these variables than the parameters of isTriangleValid because the symbolic engine executes their initialization. Nonlinear constraints can be derived from the euclidean formula and then appended to the path condition, however it is clear that doing it programmatically is not a trivial task. Figure 2 shows the symbolic execution tree built up during the execution of the sample code. Each conditional statement at line 5 and 8 can be split up to three sub-expressions, all of them containing symbolic variables. The short circuit evaluation gives an explanation why the two if statements create three-three branching points during the exe-

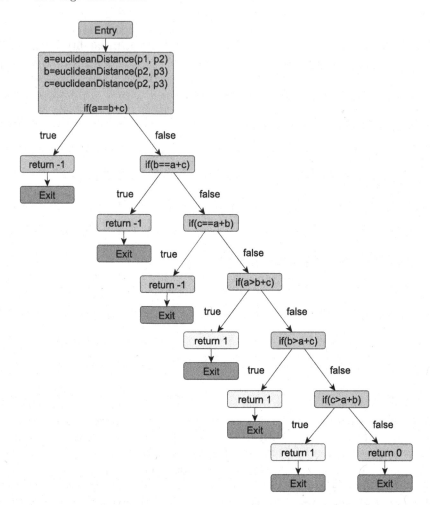

Fig. 2. Symbolic execution tree constructed from `isTriangleValid` (see Fig. 1).

cution, whilst having symbolic variables in the conditions means that both the true and false outcomes of each sub-expression have to be investigated.

Path conditions are not presented in Fig. 2 because - as previously mentioned - the constraints derived from the initialization are non-linear. We assume that symbolic engines will not build up and solve constraints like that on their own, mostly because they treat the `sqrt` function grammatically with symbolic variables and indefinite number of loops instead of using its mathematical meaning. However a developer is able to detect straightaway the three unreachable states, namely the three `return 1` branches (colored with yellow). If three points given on the two dimensional plane are not arranged on a line they definitely form a triangle. Therefore, the `if` condition in line 8 is unnecessary, mathematically infeasible, making the true branches of each sub-expression unreachable.

If an unreachable program state is discovered through unsatisfiable path conditions, the state and the sub-tree derived from it should be pruned from the symbolic execution tree. Not only do we avoid needless computations on that path, but possible false positive warnings will be eliminated.

The example in Fig. 1 gives a quick insight on how the symbolic execution is performed in the classical way. Whilst it is a very powerful tool for detecting runtime failures, it has several limitations. One of them that already occurred in the sample code is related to constraint solving. As the example shows it is not a trivial task to find an efficient solution to reveal unreachable program states. Another major drawback is path explosion. The number of possible executional paths grows with the number of conditional statements almost exponentially. The scenario is even worse with switch statements and loops containing symbolic conditions. Since it is not known in advance how many iterations have to be done in a loop, symbolic engines have to make a guess or unroll the cycle until a limitation is reached, otherwise an infinite number of branches is created. Managing different kinds of features in programming languages symbolically, like static initialization in Java, also gives a room for challenges. For a more detailed summarization of symbolic execution and its difficulties see the survey of Baldoni et al. [2].

3.2 RTEHunter

We[1] are developing SourceMeter [21], a static source code analyzer tool. It analyses C/C++, Java, C#, Python and RPG projects and calculates source code metrics, detects code clones and finds coding rule violations in the source code. RTEHunter (abbreviation of RunTimeException Hunter) is one of the static analyzers of the SourceMeter Java toolchain, and it is designed to detect runtime exceptions in Java source code without actually executing the application in real-life environment. Currently, it can detect four kinds of common failures: *NullPointerException*, *ArrayIndexOutOfBoundsException*, *NegativeArraySizeException*, and *DivideByZeroException*.

RTEHunter performs the analysis by calling the symbolic execution for each method in the program separately. For big systems, this approach is usually a better solution than starting the execution only from the main() method [13,19]. Starting the execution at the entry point of the real-life execution seems like a natural and convenient idea, however it is clear that the practical limitations mentioned in the previous section would be reached very soon leaving many parts of the code unexplored. RTEHunter limits the number of states (nodes) in the symbolic execution tree and the depth of the execution tree as well.

RTEHunter uses the Abstract Semantic Graph (ASG) [9] of the program which is constructed by the analyzer of SourceMeter. The ASG is a language-dependent representation of the source code that contains every detail of the source code in an internal graph representation. It is similar to an Abstract

---

[1] SourceMeter is developed at Department of Software Engineering, University of Szeged.

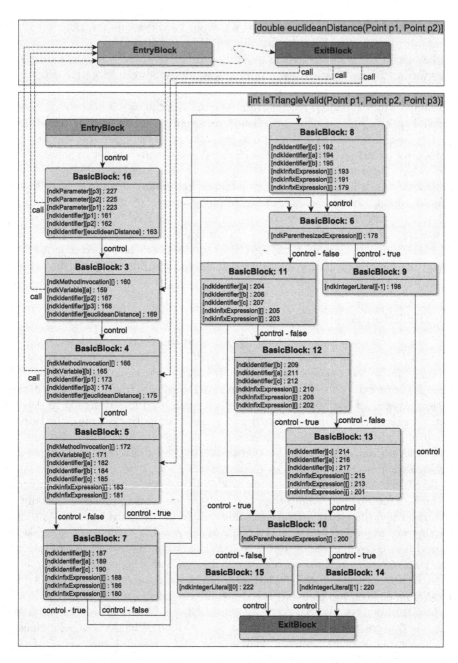

Fig. 3. Control flow graph of isTriangleValid (see Fig. 1).

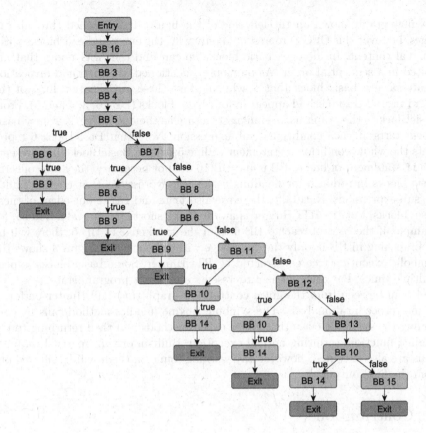

Fig. 4. Symbolic execution tree built by RTEHunter for the sample code at Fig. 1.

Syntax Tree but provides additional semantic information. First, RTEHunter builds a language-independent Control Flow Graph (CFG) [1] based on the ASG, and symbolic execution works on this CFG. In a CFG, each node represents a *basic block*. Basic blocks are the abstraction of straight-line program parts which are guaranteed to be executed sequentially. A jump in the code, like a conditional statement or a return statement, terminates the current basic block and the outgoing edges connect to the basic blocks that are the targets of that particular jump. BasicBlock 5 in Fig. 3 shows an example for a conditional jump with a `true` and `false` outgoing edge. Since RTEHunter performs symbolic execution on each method of the program, a separate control flow graph will be created for all methods. Each CFG for a method contains exactly one entry block and exactly one exit block even if there are more `return` statements in a method (see Fig. 3). The control can enter and can leave the CFG of a method only through these two blocks making them useful for handling function calls and returns.

Figure 3 shows the CFG built up by RTEHunter for the `isTriangleValid` function defined in Fig. 1. The `euclideanDistance` function has a different control flow graph shown on the left side of the figure. It is reached through call edges, however this CFG is represented only with the entry and exit blocks without real content. Inside each basic block, we can find the ASG nodes that are visited in a sequential order. As previously mentioned, each method invocation creates a new basic block that is why the first three initialization lines of the isTriangleValid method appear in four basic blocks (BB 16, 3, 4 and 5). From BasicBlock 5, the graph has a similar structure as the one in Fig. 2. A new basic block starts at each conditional sub-expression. Note that BasicBlock 6 represents the whole conditional statement at line 5, whilst BasicBlock 10 represents the if statement of line 8. BB 6 and BB 10 are not necessary, they are collector basic blocks introduced for handling easier the expressions that contain multiple sub-expressions. Naturally, there are also true and false out-edges of these basic blocks, but the RTEHunter is aware of the short circuit evaluation so, for example, if the control reaches BB 6 from the true edge of BB 5, there will be no branching in BB 6, only the true edge will be continued. Figure 4 shows the symbolic execution tree constructed by RTEHunter. Some basic blocks appear multiple times, but each of them represents a different program state.

It can be seen from the given control flow graph that RTEHunter performs an interprocedural analysis. The symbolic engine handles method calls by continuing the symbolic execution in the called methods and then returning to the original function as during normal execution. Built-in or third-party Java functions are also executed, however any warning found in them will be filtered out from the final output.

4 Contribution

As mentioned in Sect. 3, a symbolic execution engine has to overcome many practical limitations to be able to produce useful results efficiently. Some behaviors are hard to simulate in the synthetic environment of symbolic execution. The handling of the static initialization blocks in Java is a good example. First, we give a short insight into the difficulties of handling the static initialization blocks, then we describe our solution that was implemented in RTEHunter.

4.1 Static Initializer Blocks

A static initializer block is a static{} block of code in a Java class. It is executed only once when the class is loaded and initialized by the ClassLoader. A class can have multiple static initialization blocks which can appear anywhere inside the class body and executed in the order of appearance. Typically, their purpose is the initialization of static class members. Static blocks and initializers are assembled into a compiler generated function. Therefore, we can think about these blocks as a function called automatically during loading the class.

The behavior of the Java ClassLoader is well defined, a class is loaded only when certain circumstances meet: the class is used somehow (e.g. instance creation, usage of a static function or attribute, loaded by reflection) and has not been not loaded before. For a static analyzer tool like RTEHunter that does not actually execute the Java bytecode it is difficult to handle the Java classloading mechanism. The evident solution would be to implement a module similar to the Java ClassLoader itself. This module would produce a CFG composed from the ASG nodes of the static initializer blocks found in a class, then execute it when the engine meets a class for the first time. If we consider that RTEHunter performs a method-by-method execution, it is clear that each class has to be loaded every time when the symbolic engine starts to execute a new function. With this approach, we add not only extra function calls, but execute the initializer method for a class repeatedly. Unfortunately, even with this solution it is not guaranteed that the values of the static variables are correct because in real execution they can be changed since they were given initial values at the time when their classes were loaded.

Figures 5 and 6 show a very simplified example for the static initialization of two classes. Class A uses the static member of class B, therefore there is a dependency between the two static blocks. The sample code also suggests that loading a class and executing its constructed static initializer function might cause the recursive loading of other classes (String and Integer in the example). This recursion may add so many extra nodes to the symbolic execution tree that it can easily reach its limitation before providing any useful result about the examined method.

```
1  class A {
2      public static String STR;
3
4      static {
5          STR = B.NUM.toString();
6      }
7  }
```

```
1  class B {
2      public static Integer NUM;
3
4      static {
5          NUM = new Integer(6);
6      }
7  }
```

Fig. 5. Example class A.   **Fig. 6.** Example class B.

We concluded that this closer-to-reality approach is very powerful and helps detecting runtime issues in connection with static initialization, however it gives an overhead to the symbolic execution. The practical limits like the number of states or the depth of symbolic execution tree would be reached sooner, especially in complex methods, leaving the interpreation of function body unfinished. A natural idea for improving the classloader solution is to run each static initializer block only once before the symbolic execution of methods starts. This technique lessens the overhead and the computational time but does not solve several other considerable problems. A dependency graph is needed for setting up the proper initialization order. Methods can change the value of static member variables making them invalid for other methods, so the symbolic engine should be able to reset the initial values for these fields after each method-execution. This means extra-memory usage and the cautious handling of static class members.

4.2   Our Approach

During the investigation of the two solutions listed in the previous subsection, we found out that integrating one of them to the RTEHunter would provide a system whose overall behavior was still not close enough to the real-life one. For an engine which starts the execution from the `main` method, like the Symbolic PathFinder [18] does, the effort for creating a ClassLoader module might be rewarding. However, for RTEHunter the trade-off between the complexity and the usefulness of such a module is not so promising, therefore, we decided to choose a simpler but still fast and usable approach.

The previous version of RTEHunter neglected the handling of static initializer blocks. Examining the reported warnings showed that this shortage caused many false positive errors. Most of them were `NullPointerExceptions` originated from uninitalized static class members. We decided to work out a solution that would not alter the current computational time and effort needs of RTE-Hunter very much, but would still be capable of eliminating the false positive warnings. Detecting less but almost one hundred percent precise warnings is better from the user point of view than having an output full of incorrect runtime failures.

The result of our idea was a filtering mechanism. Instead of mimicing the behavior of Java ClassLoader, we simply checked when a `NullPointer Exception` arose, if the variable associated with this warning was initialized in the static initializer blocks of its class. If the answer was positive the warning was treated as a false positive.

4.3   Results

We collected 209 open source Java systems to test our solution. These Java systems were various, they were from different domains and their size ranged from a thousand to 2.5 million lines of code. Table 1 shows the minimum, maximum, and the average lines of code and the number of classes metrics of the systems. To see the improvement, we executed both the original and the improved versions of RTEHunter on the Java systems. The results are presented in Table 2. As it can be seen the number of NullPointerException warnings (NPE) decreased by 237, the number of ArrayIndexOutOfBoundsException warnings increased by 2, while the other two remained the same. We compared the warnings and found that in fact 242 NPE warnings were eliminated and 5 new NPE warnings appeared in the results of the improved RTEHunter. RTEHunter stops the execution along a path when a runtime failure is detected, therefore, it is obvious that the 7 new warnings showed up because our filtering mechanism let the engine go deeper in the symbolic execution tree. 10% of the disappeared runtime failures were manually investigated to check whether they were really false positives. The conclusion of the verification was that not only did we eliminate more than two hundred erroneous NPE warnings, but also discovered 7 true positive runtime issues, which is about 7% improvement.

Table 1. The lines of code and number of classes metrics of the examined Java projects.

	Lines of code	Number of classes
Minimum	993	17
Maximum	2,594,569	16,934
Average	~140,653	~1,090

Table 2. The results of the original and improved RTEHunter executions.

RTEHunter	NullPointerE	Negative ArraySizeE	DivideBy ZeroE	ArrayIndex OutOfBoundsE
Original	3,369	24	167	679
Improved	3,132	24	167	681

5 Conclusions

We introduced the basics of classical symbolic execution which simulates the execution of a program using only static analysis results. In spite of the fact that symbolic execution is a powerful tool for bug detection, there are many challenges and practical limitations. Some programming features are very difficult or rather almost impossible to simulate, therefore, some trade-offs or heuristical approaches must be made. In this work, we examined how static initializer blocks can be simulated during symbolic execution and what the advantages and disadvantages of the different approaches are. The previous solution applied in RTEHunter led to many false positive warnings, so we worked out a heuristic which was not the proper simulation of initializer block handling but gave much better results. We tested it on more than 200 open source Java systems, and it eliminated 7% of the total number of warnings and almost all of them were false positive.

In the future, we plan to investigate other weaknesses of the symbolic execution engine implemented in RTEHunter and find more heuristical solutions that will not increase the resource requirements significantly, but improve the efficiency of the algorithm.

Acknowledgment. This research was supported by the EU-funded Hungarian national grant GINOP-2.3.2-15-2016-00037 titled "Internet of Living Things".

References

1. Allen, F.E.: Control flow analysis. SIGPLAN Not. 5(7), 1–19 (1970)
2. Baldoni, R., Coppa, E., D'Elia, D.C., Demetrescu, C., Finocchi, I.: A survey of symbolic execution techniques. arXiv preprint arXiv:1610.00502 (2016)

3. Boyer, R.S., Elspas, B., Levitt, K.N.: SELECT - a formal system for testing and debugging programs by symbolic execution. In: Proceedings of the International Conference on Reliable Software, pp. 234–245. ACM, New York (1975)

4. Cadar, C., Dunbar, D., Engler, D.R., et al.: Klee: unassisted and automatic generation of high-coverage tests for complex systems programs. OSDI **8**, 209–224 (2008)

5. Cadar, C., Ganesh, V., Pawlowski, P.M., Dill, D.L., Engler, D.R.: EXE: automatically generating inputs of death. In: Proceedings of the 13th ACM Conference on Computer and Communications Security, CCS 2006, pp. 322–335. ACM, New York (2006)

6. Cadar, C., Sen, K.: Symbolic execution for software testing: three decades later. Commun. ACM **56**(2), 82–90 (2013)

7. The Checkstyle Homepage. http://checkstyle.sourceforge.net

8. Coward, P.D.: Symbolic execution systems - a review. Softw. Eng. J. **3**(6), 229–239 (1988)

9. Ferenc, R., Beszédes, Á., Tarkiainen, M., Gyimóthy, T.: Columbus – reverse engineering tool and schema for C++. In: Proceedings of the 18th International Conference on Software Maintenance (ICSM 2002), pp. 172–181. IEEE Computer Society, October 2002

10. The FindBugs Homepage. http://findbugs.sourceforge.net

11. Godefroid, P., Klarlund, N., Sen, K.: DART: directed automated random testing. In: Proceedings of the 2005 ACM SIGPLAN Conference on Programming Language Design and Implementation, PLDI 2005, pp. 213–223. ACM, New York (2005)

12. Java PathFinder Tool-set. http://babelfish.arc.nasa.gov/trac/jpf

13. Kádár, I., Hegedűs, P., Ferenc, R.: Runtime exception detection in java programs using symbolic execution. Acta Cybern. **21**(3), 331–352 (2014)

14. Kádár, I., Hegedűs, P., Ferenc, R.: Adding constraint building mechanisms to a symbolic execution engine developed for detecting runtime errors. In: Proceedings of the 15th International Conference on Computational Science and Its Applications, pp. 20–35 (2015)

15. King, J.C.: Symbolic execution and program testing. Commun. ACM **19**(7), 385–394 (1976)

16. Majumdar, R., Sen, K., Hybrid concolic testing. In: Proceedings - International Conference on Software Engineering, pp. 416–425 (2007)

17. The PMD Homepage. http://pmd.sourceforge.net

18. Păsăreanu, C.S., Rungta, N., PathFinder, S.: Symbolic execution of Java Bytecode. In: Proceedings of the IEEE/ACM International Conference on Automated Software Engineering, ASE 2010, pp. 179–180. ACM, New York (2010)

19. Ramos, D.A., Engler, D.: Under-constrained symbolic execution: correctness checking for real code. In: 24th USENIX Security Symposium (USENIX Security 2015), pp. 49–64. USENIX Association, Washington, D.C. (2015)

20. Sen, K., Agha, G.: CUTE and jCUTE: concolic unit testing and explicit path model-checking tools. In: Ball, T., Jones, R.B. (eds.) CAV 2006. LNCS, vol. 4144, pp. 419–423. Springer, Heidelberg (2006). doi:10.1007/11817963_38

21. The SourceMeter Homepage. https://www.sourcemeter.com

22. Tillmann, N., Halleux, J.: Pex–white box test generation for.NET. In: Beckert, B., Hähnle, R. (eds.) TAP 2008. LNCS, vol. 4966, pp. 134–153. Springer, Heidelberg (2008). doi:10.1007/978-3-540-79124-9_10

Applying and Evaluating Halstead's Complexity Metrics and Maintainability Index for RPG

Zoltán Tóth(✉)

Department of Software Engineering, University of Szeged, Szeged, Hungary
zizo@inf.u-szeged.hu

Abstract. Although RPG is an older programming language for developing general-purpose software systems, it is still widely used by many companies due to the many legacy modules written in RPG that are still in use. IBM's RPG programming language has continuously evolved with the new demands. RPG has become a high-level programming language, however its original purpose was only to replicate punched card processing. Whilst RPG went through a bunch of improvements, the methodologies related to code quality assurance for RPG hardly come along. RPG is strongly applied for business applications, yet there is a lack of appropriate research studies and tools in this field. In this study, we first propose an application of Halstead's complexity metrics for RPG/400 and RPG IV. Furthermore, we investigate the usefulness and the impact of Halstead's complexity metrics in RPG programs. We examine the Halstead's complexity metrics and four Maintainability Index metrics in details to get more insight about how they correlate with other software product metrics and how could we use them to improve the quality of RPG software systems. To do so, we used Principal Component Analysis (PCA) to show the dimensionality and behavior of these metrics. We found that Halstead's complexity metrics form a strong metric group that can be used to give more details about RPG software systems.

Keywords: Software quality · Halstead complexity metrics · Maintainability index · IBM RPG

1 Introduction

ISO 25010 standard describes maintainability as one of the eight quality characteristics. Maintainability has become the most important trait related to quality as the cost of maintaining a software system gives the 40–60% of the total costs of a software [4,21]. This is why researchers focus on maintainability and try to discover relationships between maintainability and different characteristics of the system.

IBM RPG is a programming language with a long history. It was first released in 1959 and become quite popular on IBM mainframes. There are numerous business applications having the core written in RPG. Maintainability of legacy business application are likely to be more important. More effort should be

© Springer International Publishing AG 2017
O. Gervasi et al. (Eds.): ICCSA 2017, Part V, LNCS 10408, pp. 575–590, 2017.
DOI: 10.1007/978-3-319-62404-4_43

put into research studies that deal with the legacy systems' maintainability to prevent software erosion.

Halstead metrics are the first complexity measures that were defined by Maurice Halstead [8]. He taught that many characteristics of a software system can be expressed by only using the number of operands and operators occurred in a software. Halstead complexity metrics were first occurred/calculated for IBM RPG systems in 1982 presented by Hartman [9]. At that time the calculation was performed on RPG II and RPG III systems that are rare nowadays.

In this study we propose a definition of Halstead complexity metrics for newer versions of RPG, namely IBM RPG/400 and RPG IV. RPG IV brought new core language features that makes the calculation of Halstead complexity metrics absolutely different than before. Free-form block (column independent) constructions has the most impact on the methodology. We extended our static analysis tool which is called SourceMeter[1] to calculate Halstead complexity measures for RPG. We used this tool to calculate the metrics for 348 RPG programs containing 7475 subroutines. We also applied four Maintainability Index (MI) metrics that are widely used to express the overall maintainability of a software. For instance, Microsoft's Visual Studio is currently using a Maintainability Index definition to provide an overall maintainability/quality measurement for a system. Maintainability Index depends upon Halstead's Volume which motivates us to investigate the Halstead's Complexity metrics to get a deeper insight on how they are related with other software metrics. Similarly, maintainability models are constructed to gain an overall maintainability score by aggregating low-level metric values. In our previous study, we defined a quality model for RPG [12].

To determine which metrics form groups that have strong inner connections, researchers often use the concept of Principal Component Analysis (PCA). PCA is also used to reveal hidden connections from the dataset and to reduce the dimensionality of the data. Based on the Principal Component Analysis, we determined how our previous model could be extended to involve more metrics, thus ensuring a stronger descriptive behavior of our maintainability model.

The rest of this paper is structured as follows. In Sect. 2, we present the most important studies that are related with our research domain. Then in Sect. 3 we describe the background for this study that includes the RPG programming language itself and the software metrics and the maintainability model. In Sect. 4, we present the definitions of the used metrics. Section 5 shows the results of the Principal Component Analysis and we make suggestions for extending the quality model. Finally, we end the paper with summarizing and concluding the results, enumerating the future work possibilities and the threats to validity.

---

[1] https://www.sourcemeter.com.

2   Related Work

In this section we present the most important studies that relate to static source code analysis in RPG systems and software metrics defined for RPG language. The literature is lack of studies that focus on RPG legacy software systems hence we can only enumerate a very limited number of papers that have RPG related research topics. We can hardly identify groups of research areas when RPG is in the spotlight. The first studies that are related to IBM RPG are from 1982. Naib investigates internal (not varying with time - McCabe, Halstead, Lines of Code) and external (varying with time - number of users) metrics on two large RPG packages to see whether the metrics have correlation with error rates [18]. Different internal measures are calculated at module level for which Naib used Hartman's counting tool to support the identification of fault-prone RPG II and RPG III modules [9]. Hartman used the original definitions to calculate McCabe's Cyclomatic Complexity [14] and the Halstead's complexity metrics [8].

The usefulness of metrics are mostly accepted, however sometimes the metrics are criticized rather to pinpoint the weaknesses and add a gentle indication to change or modify the directions of the research areas [23]. These kind of studies often reflect the misuse of metrics in different models. Halstead's complexity metric family as being one of the first complexity metric set is sometimes handled as a golden hammer [5] that is obviously a bad practice. Consequently, more metrics were defined and used for empirical analysis to show different characteristics of the subject systems [2,16]. For evaluating new complexity metrics, sometimes different frameworks are used [15]. Maintainability Index (MI) was first introduced by Oman et al. in 1994 [7,19]. MI was designed to express the maintainability of a system (as its name reflects) with a single value. Its power has become its weakness since it does not provide any information on how the metric value was made up (maybe only one lower level metric is critical) or what changes should be made to improve the system's maintainability [10]. As ISO 25010 describes, maintainability is a derived quality indicator which is comprising modularity, reusability, analyzability, modifiability, testability. However, Maintainability Index is an ideal measurement when one would like to compare the overall maintainability of different software systems. Maintainability models were proposed to overcome the above mentioned problems [11,17] and soon more complex quality models were given birth, [1,20,22].

Bakota et al. presented a probabilistic software quality model where the overall maintainability is derived from analyzability, changeability, stability, testability [1]. They used the ISO 9126 standard which is the ancestor of ISO 25010, thus this model has become quite out-dated and needs to be updated, however it is still usable. In case of RPG we have proposed a similar quality model in our paper [12] which is based on the results of the probabilistic software quality model. In this study we would like to give recommendations for extending the RPG quality model to involve more measurements that reflect the overall quality of a system in a more precise way.

3   Background

3.1   RPG Programming Language

RPG is a high level programming language developed by IBM (first released in 1959) and used in IBM mainframe environment. RPG is still a popular programming language on the IBM i OS. RPG has been continuously developed to fulfill the new demands and capabilities presented in other domain-free languages. These improvements result in multiple versions of the programming language.

Listing 1.1. A simple RPG IV program

```
.....  *. 1 ...+... 2 ...+... 3 ...+... 4 ...+... 5 ...+...
      D Add            pr              15s 2
      D num1                           15s 2
      D num2                           15s 2
      p Add            b                            export
      d Add            PI              15s 2
      d num1                           15s 2
      d num2                           15s 2
      d result         s               6s 0
       /free
               result  = num1 + num2;
               *inlr  = *on;
               return  result ;
       /end−free
      p Add            e
```

Two commonly used versions are RPG/400 (also known as RPG III) and ILE RPG (also known as RPG IV). A simple RPG IV program is shown in Listing 1.1. RPG/400 uses a strict, column-based format that is inherited in RPG IV, but the latter has free-form blocks that makes possible a column-independent programming style which opens a different world for RPG programmers. The sample program consists of a simple procedure declaration (Add) and its definition which returns the sum of two numbers.

RPG has different specifications that are noted with a specified letter in the sixth column. For our investigations we will mainly focus on the Calculation Specifications that indicate the operations to be done on the data.

3.2   Software Metrics and Quality Model

"You can't manage what you can't measure." is an old adage by Peter Drucker that is still accurate. This is why different software metrics became so important in the last decades [6].

We used a tool named SourceMeter which is our own development for static source code analysis. We used this tool to calculate the appropriate software product metrics, thus we can investigate the correlation between the original metrics like LLOC, McCC and the newly added ones (Halstead and Maintainability Index metrics).

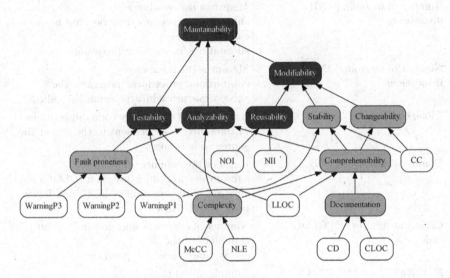

Fig. 1. Quality Model for RPG

The quality model makes use of the software product metrics as shown in Fig. 1. Maintainability as the root node is calculated from testability, analyzability, and modifiability. These metrics are also aggregated from other metrics as depicted. Leaf node metrics are the sensor metrics (which we can directly measure). Every aggregated node is (constructed from sensor metrics - inner nodes) calculated from multiple lower level metrics with different weights (in other words the presented graph is weighted). The quality model is based on the 9126 ISO standard that has become quite obsolete and should be updated.

Table 1 presents the definitions of sensor metrics used in the quality model for RPG. We will later investigate the relationship of these metrics and the Halstead and MI metrics. One can find a more detailed description about the listed metrics on the User's Guide page[2].

---

[2] https://www.sourcemeter.com/resources/rpg/.

Table 1. Definition of source code metrics used in the quality model

Metric name	Abbreviation	Description
Logical lines of code	LLOC	Number of non-empty and non-comment code lines of the subroutine/procedure/program
Number of incoming invocations	NII	Measures the number a subroutine/procedure/program has been called by other subroutines/procedures/programs
Number of outgoing invocations	NOI	Measures the number of subroutines/procedures/programs the subroutine/procedure/program has called
Clone coverage	CC	Ratio of code covered by code duplications in the source code element to the size of the source code element
Comment density	CD	Ratio of the comment lines of the subroutine/procedure/program (CLOC) to the sum of its comment (CLOC) and logical lines of code (LLOC)
Comment lines of code	CLOC	Number of comment and documentation code lines of the subroutine/procedure/program
McCabe's cyclomatic complexity	McCC	Complexity of the subroutine/procedure/program expressed as the number of independent control flow paths in it
Nesting level else-if	NLE	Complexity of the subroutine/procedure/program expressed as the depth of the maximum embeddedness of its conditional, iteration and exception handling block scopes
Warning occurrences	Warnings (P1, P2, P3)	Number of detected coding rule violations with a given severity (P1 - lowest severity, P3 - highest severity)

4   Computing Halstead Metrics and Maintainability Index for RPG

Halstead Complexity metrics [8] are likely to be forgotten that is undeserving in many cases. For instance, Maintainablity Index [7] shows the strength of Halstead's metrics. Coleman et al. used Halstead's Effort metric amongst others to derive the original Maintainability Index (MI) metric. At that time Halstead's volume and effort metrics were considered as the best indicators for predicting the maintainability of a software system.

To produce the necessary metric values, we first present the list of definitions for Halstead metrics. Let us consider the following notations:

- η_1 = number of distinct operators
- η_2 = number of distinct operands
- N_1 = total number of operators
- N_2 = total number of operands

Now we have the definition of the four basic metrics we will use in our further formulas, however there is no intention or concept what should be considered as an operand and an operation. This problem can cause inconsistencies between research papers since they use different interpretations. Furthermore, the calculation of operands and operators can intensely differ by programming languages (mainly comes from the dissimilarities of the languages). Fortunately, in case of RPG we do not have to dig deep to figure out how different source code elements should be treated. We calculated the Halstead's complexity metrics similarly as it was presented by Hartman for RPG III, thus we concentrate on the peculiarities of RPG IV. Now we will present the different source code elements that should be included in the calculations.

Table 2. List of source code elements to be counted as operators

Specification name	Construct name	RPG version
Calculation	Operator	RPG/400 RPG IV
Free-form (C)	Infix expressions	RPG IV
Free-form (C)	Member Selection	RPG IV
Free-form (C)	Array Subscript	RPG IV
Free-form (C)	Parentheses	RPG IV
Free-form (C)	Prefix Expressions	RPG IV

Table 2 summarizes the source code elements in different RPG versions to be counted as operators. Calculation specification is the place where we can specify the operations to be done on the given operands. In RPG IV we use free-form to avoid column-sensitive programming. In free-form section we can use different operators such as infix operators $(+, -, *, /, <, >, \ldots)$, member selection (data structure field select), array subscription (to get elements from an array), parentheses (to modify the operation precedence), and also prefix operations. Most of the free-form statements can be written in calculation specifications, some cannot.

Table 3 shows the RPG constructions to be counted as operands. When we use an operator in Calculation Specification we have to specify operand(s) (if needed) to perform the operation on. These operands should be specified in factor 1 and factor 2. The result of the operation is stored in the given result field. In RPG IV we can use Definition Specification to define variables and

Table 3. List of source code elements to be counted as operands

Specification name	Construct name	RPG version
Calculation	Factor 1	RPG/400 RPG IV
Calculation	Factor 2	RPG/400 RPG IV
Calculation	Result Field	RPG/400 RPG IV
Definition	(Variable) Name	RPG IV
Input	Program Field	RPG/400, RPG IV
Input	Data Structure	RPG/400, RPG IV
Input	Data Structure Subfield	RPG/400, RPG IV
Input	External Record	RPG/400, RPG IV
Input	External Field	RPG/400, RPG IV
Input	Data Structure	RPG/400, RPG IV
Input	Data Structure	RPG/400, RPG IV
Input	Named Constant	RPG/400
Free-form	Literal	RPG IV
Free-form	Identifier	RPG IV
Output	Output External Record	RPG/400, RPG IV
Output	Output External Field	RPG/400, RPG IV
Output	Output Program Field	RPG/400, RPG IV

constants. We use Input and Output Specification to declare the appropriate input and output data structures and their fields (also constants in RPG/400). In RPG IV we can also use literals and identifiers in free-form section which are also counted as operands.

Table 4 introduces the Halstead metrics that are aggregated from the basic ones (η_1, η_2, N_1, N_2). Table 5 presents the different variants of Maintainability Index (MI) metrics.

Table 4. List of the used Halstead metrics

Metric name	Formula
Program vocabulary (HPV)	$\eta = \eta_1 + \eta_2$
Program length (HPL)	$N = N_1 + N_2$
Calculated program length (HCPL)	$\hat{N} = \eta_1 \cdot log_2 \eta_1 + \eta_2 \cdot log_2 \eta_2$
Volume (HVOL)	$V = N \times log_2 \eta$
Difficulty (HDIF)	$D = \frac{\eta_1}{2} \times \frac{N_2}{\eta_2}$
Effort (HEFF)	$E = D \times V$
Time required to program (HTRP)	$T = \frac{E}{18}$
Number of delivered bugs (HNDB)	$B = \frac{E^{\frac{2}{3}}}{3000}$

Table 5. List of the used Maintainablity Index metrics

MI variant	Formula
Original (MI)	$171 - 5.2 \times ln(HVOL) - 0.23 \times McCC - 16.2 \times ln(LLOC)$
SEI (MISEI)	$171 - 5.2 \times log_2(HVOL) - 0.23 \times McCC - 16.2 \times log_2(LLOC) + 50 \times sin(\sqrt{2.4 * CD})$
Visual studio (MIMS)	$max(0, 100 \times \frac{171 - 5.2 \times ln(HVOL) - 0.23 \times McCC - 16.2 \times ln(LLOC)}{171})$
SourceMeter (MISM)	$max(0, 100 \times$ $\frac{171 - 5.2 \times log_2(HVOL) - 0.23 \times McCC - 16.2 \times log_2(LLOC) + 50 \times sin(\sqrt{2.4 * CD})}{171})$

In RPG, we have 3 levels of abstraction, namely subroutine, procedure, and program. We can define a subroutine by writing code between BEGSR and ENDSR operation codes. To call a subroutine we have to use the EXSR operation and specify the name of the subroutine to be called. Unlike subroutines, procedures can be prototyped and have parameters, thus supporting a more flexible way to reuse code portions. Programs are larger building blocks that encapsulate subroutines and procedures as well. In this study, we will only examine subroutines and programs because we accessed a limited set of source code files that mainly contains subroutines instead of procedures.

5 Evaluating the Usefulness of Halstead's and MI Metrics

Principal Component Analysis (PCA) [24] is widely used in many domains to accomplish dimensionality reduction and uncover patterns from the data [3,13]. PCA determines which dimensions are the most important ones and which ones represent the most variation in the data. PCA takes a dataset (a set of metrics in our case) as input and outputs principal components (uncorrelated dimensions) that span the direction of the $1^{st}, 2^{nd}, 3^{rd}, \ldots$ largest variations.

We have performed PCA both at program (RPG file) and subroutine level to see the difference between these levels if any exists. We investigated 348 RPG programs (185 RPG IV and 163 RPG/400 programs) and 7475 RPG subroutines with PCA.

We first present the correlation matrices that can be seen in Tables 6 and 7. We included the Halstead, Maintainability Index metrics and the sensor metrics that are used by the quality model in the correlation matrix to investigate the relationship between them. Values in the table are mapped with color codes to help better understand the correlations between metrics. The color interpolation has three base points: $-1, 0, 1$. The greater the correlation between two metrics (negative or positive correlation) the greener the cell is (1 and -1 values imply pure green color). Red means that two variables are not correlated. One can see clear groups of metrics that correlation coefficients are very high inside the group. In case of programs Halstead metrics form such a group that is not surprising since many of them are calculated with the help of another (See Table 4).

Table 6. Correlation between metrics (Program Level)

Variables	CC	HCPL	HDIF	HEFF	HNDB	HPL	HPV	HTRP	HVOL	MI	MIMS	MISEI	MISM	NLE	PC	NOI	CD	CLOC	TCD	LLOC	Warning Info	Clone Metric Rules	Complexity Metric Rules	Coupling Metric Rules	Doc. Metric Rules	Size Metric Rules
CC	1	0.073	0.162	0.033	0.067	0.066	0.087	0.033	0.055	-0.186	-0.186	-0.156	-0.149	0.090	0.061	0.074	0.083	0.207	0.009	0.145	0.435	0.485	0.658	0.020	0.007	0.079
HCPL	0.073	1	0.811	0.891	0.947	0.970	0.996	0.891	0.965	-0.698	-0.698	-0.662	-0.667	0.521	0.951	0.215	0.076	0.461	-0.417	0.513	0.785	0.712	0.889	0.834	0.789	0.933
HDIF	0.162	0.811	1	0.736	0.865	0.841	0.835	0.736	0.812	-0.673	-0.673	-0.610	-0.627	0.645	0.636	0.346	0.102	0.463	-0.400	0.253	0.771	0.720	0.774	0.609	0.619	0.829
HEFF	0.033	0.891	0.736	1	0.967	0.953	0.808	1.000	0.966	-0.464	-0.464	-0.438	-0.447	0.370	0.949	0.082	0.057	0.502	-0.255	0.334	0.745	0.675	0.871	0.825	0.815	0.847
HNDB	0.067	0.947	0.865	0.967	1	0.992	0.933	0.967	0.990	-0.578	-0.578	-0.539	-0.551	0.481	0.984	0.172	0.091	0.510	-0.330	0.346	0.813	0.744	0.910	0.850	0.813	0.911
HPL	0.066	0.970	0.841	0.953	0.992	1	0.956	0.953	0.998	-0.696	-0.696	-0.567	-0.578	0.483	0.987	0.189	0.090	0.515	-0.350	0.379	0.818	0.746	0.918	0.866	0.821	0.928
HPV	0.087	0.996	0.835	0.808	0.933	0.956	1	0.858	0.946	-0.740	-0.740	-0.700	-0.706	0.554	0.935	0.256	0.088	0.451	-0.442	0.321	0.796	0.715	0.871	0.813	0.764	0.937
HTRP	0.033	0.891	0.736	1.000	0.967	0.953	0.858	1	0.966	-0.464	-0.464	-0.438	-0.447	0.370	0.949	0.082	0.057	0.502	-0.255	0.334	0.745	0.675	0.871	0.825	0.815	0.847
HVOL	0.055	0.965	0.812	0.966	0.990	0.998	0.946	0.966	1	-0.579	-0.579	-0.543	-0.554	0.370	0.966	0.162	0.081	0.514	-0.332	0.380	0.806	0.733	0.919	0.869	0.827	0.918
MI	-0.186	-0.698	-0.673	-0.464	-0.578	-0.696	-0.740	-0.464	-0.579	1	1.000	0.946	0.950	-0.631	-0.572	-0.682	-0.121	-0.360	0.654	-0.680	-0.540	-0.492	-0.546	-0.432	-0.486	-0.716
MIMS	-0.186	-0.698	-0.673	-0.464	-0.578	-0.696	-0.740	-0.464	-0.579	1.000	1	0.946	0.950	-0.631	-0.572	-0.682	-0.121	-0.360	0.654	-0.680	-0.540	-0.492	-0.546	-0.432	-0.486	-0.716
MISEI	-0.156	-0.662	-0.610	-0.438	-0.539	-0.567	-0.700	-0.438	-0.543	0.946	0.946	1	0.995	-0.578	-0.535	-0.421	-0.209	-0.254	0.743	-0.701	-0.496	-0.449	-0.511	-0.406	-0.512	-0.670
MISM	-0.149	-0.687	-0.627	-0.447	-0.551	-0.578	-0.706	-0.447	-0.554	0.950	0.950	0.995	1	-0.583	-0.546	-0.418	-0.180	-0.260	0.743	-0.665	-0.507	-0.459	-0.520	-0.415	-0.510	-0.682
NLE	0.090	0.521	0.645	0.370	0.481	0.483	0.554	0.370	0.370	-0.631	-0.631	-0.578	-0.583	1	0.472	0.380	0.133	0.276	-0.461	0.318	0.443	0.398	0.570	0.366	0.337	0.554
PC	0.061	0.951	0.636	0.949	0.984	0.987	0.935	0.949	0.966	-0.572	-0.572	-0.535	-0.546	0.472	1	0.164	0.088	0.479	-0.319	0.332	0.796	0.724	0.915	0.865	0.807	0.911
NOI	0.074	0.215	0.346	0.082	0.172	0.189	0.256	0.082	0.162	-0.682	-0.682	-0.421	-0.418	0.380	0.164	1	0.164	0.262	-0.205	0.135	0.163	0.142	0.185	0.068	0.112	0.314
CD	0.083	0.076	0.102	0.057	0.091	0.090	0.088	0.057	0.081	-0.121	-0.121	-0.209	-0.180	0.133	0.088	0.164	1	0.305	0.301	-0.094	0.110	0.111	0.064	0.059	-0.102	0.109
CLOC	0.207	0.461	0.463	0.502	0.510	0.515	0.505	0.502	0.514	-0.360	-0.360	-0.254	-0.260	0.276	0.479	0.262	0.305	1	-0.052	0.171	0.171	0.574	0.128	0.384	0.467	0.496
TCD	0.009	-0.417	-0.400	-0.255	-0.330	-0.350	-0.442	-0.255	-0.332	0.654	0.654	0.743	0.743	-0.461	-0.319	-0.205	0.301	-0.052	1	-0.511	-0.228	-0.178	-0.345	-0.222	-0.455	-0.460
LLOC	0.145	0.513	0.253	0.334	0.346	0.379	0.321	0.334	0.380	-0.680	-0.680	-0.701	-0.665	0.318	0.332	0.135	-0.094	0.171	-0.511	1	0.272	0.225	0.385	0.251	0.467	0.449
WarningInfo	0.435	0.785	0.771	0.745	0.813	0.818	0.796	0.745	0.806	-0.540	-0.540	-0.496	-0.507	0.443	0.796	0.163	0.110	0.171	-0.228	0.272	1	0.992	0.737	0.251	0.516	0.748
Clone Metric Rules	0.485	0.712	0.720	0.675	0.744	0.746	0.715	0.675	0.733	-0.492	-0.492	-0.449	-0.459	0.398	0.724	0.142	0.111	0.574	-0.178	0.225	0.992	1	0.654	0.788	0.657	0.668
Complexity Metric Rules	0.658	0.889	0.774	0.871	0.910	0.918	0.871	0.871	0.919	-0.546	-0.546	-0.511	-0.520	0.570	0.915	0.185	0.064	0.128	-0.345	0.385	0.737	0.654	1	0.788	0.801	0.857
Coupling Metric Rules	0.020	0.834	0.609	0.825	0.850	0.866	0.813	0.825	0.869	-0.432	-0.432	-0.406	-0.415	0.366	0.865	0.068	0.059	0.384	-0.222	0.251	0.251	0.788	0.788	1	0.657	0.755
Documentation Metric Rules	0.007	0.789	0.619	0.815	0.813	0.821	0.764	0.815	0.827	-0.486	-0.486	-0.512	-0.510	0.337	0.807	0.112	-0.102	0.467	-0.455	0.467	0.516	0.657	0.801	0.657	1	0.780
Size Metric Rules	0.079	0.933	0.829	0.847	0.911	0.928	0.937	0.847	0.918	-0.716	-0.716	-0.670	-0.682	0.554	0.911	0.314	0.109	0.496	-0.460	0.449	0.748	0.668	0.857	0.755	0.780	1

Table 7. Correlation between metrics (Subroutine Level)

Variables	CC	HCPL	HDIF	HEFF	HNDB	HPL	HPV	HTRP	HVOL	MI	MIMS	MISEI	MISM	McCC	NLE	NII	NOI	CD	CLOC	LLOC	Warning Info	Clone Metric Rules	Complexity Metric Rules	Coupling Metric Rules	Doc. Metric Rules	Size Metric Rules
CC	1	-0.099	-0.047	-0.016	0.045	-0.064	-0.102	-0.016	-0.058	0.100	0.100	0.105	0.105	-0.135	0.015	0.027	0.132	0.142	-0.026	-0.063	0.825	0.902	0.023	0.026	-0.021	-0.050
HCPL	-0.099	1	0.308	0.607	0.728	0.954	0.982	0.607	0.952	-0.684	-0.684	-0.680	-0.680	0.306	-0.188	0.132	-0.509	0.132	0.859	0.952	0.263	0.101	0.208	0.076	0.301	0.671
HDIF	-0.047	0.308	1	0.636	0.798	0.740	0.455	0.636	0.353	-0.589	-0.589	-0.691	-0.690	0.743	-0.650	0.167	-0.633	0.894	0.680	0.451	0.280	0.123	0.622	0.650	0.384	0.358
HEFF	-0.016	0.607	0.636	1	0.922	0.740	0.763	0.922	0.710	-0.492	-0.492	-0.481	-0.482	0.701	-0.226	0.194	-0.332	0.332	0.660	0.734	0.281	0.116	0.388	0.553	0.247	0.560
HNDB	0.045	0.728	0.798	0.922	1	0.827	0.763	0.827	0.768	-0.722	-0.722	-0.716	-0.704	0.750	-0.387	0.158	-0.630	0.553	0.680	0.828	0.352	0.115	0.537	0.087	0.444	0.690
HPL	-0.064	0.954	0.740	0.740	0.827	1	0.925	0.760	0.989	-0.669	-0.668	-0.662	-0.645	0.408	-0.162	0.098	-0.475	0.888	0.888	0.995	0.298	0.121	0.301	0.467	0.331	0.722
HPV	-0.102	0.982	0.455	0.763	0.925	0.925	1	0.601	0.925	-0.798	-0.798	-0.795	-0.784	0.387	-0.289	0.177	-0.831	0.831	0.928	0.928	0.290	0.115	0.330	0.094	0.331	0.679
HTRP	-0.016	0.607	0.636	0.922	0.827	0.760	0.601	1	0.710	-0.892	-0.892	-0.881	-0.892	0.701	-0.228	0.184	-0.332	0.600	0.600	0.734	0.290	0.184	0.347	0.080	0.347	0.670
HVOL	-0.058	0.952	0.353	0.710	0.768	0.989	0.925	0.710	1	-0.580	-0.580	-0.573	-0.554	0.330	-0.111	0.104	-0.393	0.883	0.883	0.983	0.263	0.105	0.240	0.054	0.288	0.670
MI	0.100	-0.684	-0.589	-0.492	-0.722	-0.669	-0.798	-0.892	-0.580	1	1.000	0.998	0.997	-0.584	0.580	-0.543	0.292	0.894	-0.686	-0.087	-0.318	-0.151	-0.472	-0.114	-0.347	-0.528
MIMS	0.100	-0.684	-0.589	-0.492	-0.722	-0.668	-0.798	-0.892	-0.580	1.000	1	0.998	0.997	-0.584	0.580	-0.543	0.292	0.894	-0.686	-0.087	-0.317	-0.151	-0.471	-0.143	-0.347	-0.528
MISEI	0.105	-0.680	-0.691	-0.481	-0.716	-0.662	-0.795	-0.881	-0.573	0.998	0.998	1	1.000	-0.574	0.574	-0.549	0.271	0.916	-0.680	-0.663	-0.309	-0.143	-0.469	-0.130	-0.368	-0.519
MISM	0.105	-0.680	-0.690	-0.482	-0.704	-0.645	-0.784	-0.892	-0.554	0.997	0.997	1.000	1	-0.568	0.549	-0.522	0.271	0.916	-0.663	-0.551	-0.308	-0.143	-0.469	-0.129	-0.367	-0.515
McCC	-0.135	0.306	0.743	0.701	0.750	0.408	0.387	0.701	0.330	-0.584	-0.584	-0.574	-0.568	1	-0.552	0.331	0.281	-0.587	0.307	0.198	0.092	-0.307	0.963	0.062	0.185	0.305
NLE	0.015	-0.188	-0.650	-0.226	-0.387	-0.162	-0.289	-0.228	-0.111	0.580	0.580	0.574	0.549	-0.552	1	0.992	0.019	-0.587	0.101	0.198	0.296	0.591	0.591	0.082	0.185	-0.102
NII	0.027	0.132	0.167	0.194	0.158	0.098	0.177	0.184	0.104	-0.543	-0.543	0.058	0.058	0.331	0.992	1	0.991	0.019	-0.119	0.091	0.092	-0.008	0.091	0.053	0.035	0.016
NOI	0.132	-0.509	-0.633	-0.332	-0.630	-0.475	-0.831	-0.332	-0.393	0.292	0.292	0.271	0.271	0.281	0.019	0.991	1	0.124	0.248	-0.493	0.290	0.137	0.256	0.055	0.068	0.073
CD	0.142	-0.208	0.894	0.493	0.553	0.888	0.831	0.600	0.883	0.894	0.894	0.916	0.916	-0.587	-0.587	0.019	0.124	1	0.248	-0.493	0.187	-0.062	-0.268	-0.187	-0.371	-0.327
CLOC	-0.026	0.859	0.680	0.660	0.680	0.888	0.928	0.600	0.883	-0.686	-0.686	-0.680	-0.663	0.307	0.101	-0.119	0.248	0.248	1	0.890	0.303	0.158	0.237	0.169	0.109	0.652
LLOC	-0.063	0.952	0.451	0.734	0.828	0.995	0.928	0.734	0.983	-0.087	-0.087	-0.663	-0.551	0.198	0.198	0.091	-0.493	-0.493	0.890	1	0.305	0.125	0.324	0.083	0.340	0.722
WarningInfo	0.825	0.263	0.280	0.281	0.352	0.298	0.290	0.290	0.263	-0.318	-0.317	-0.309	-0.308	0.092	0.296	0.092	0.290	0.187	0.303	0.305	1	0.961	0.993	0.288	0.201	0.311
Clone Metric Rules	0.902	0.101	0.123	0.116	0.115	0.121	0.115	0.116	0.105	-0.151	-0.151	-0.143	-0.143	-0.307	0.120	-0.008	0.137	-0.062	0.158	0.125	0.961	1	0.003	0.208	0.099	0.045
Complexity Metric Rules	0.023	0.208	0.622	0.388	0.537	0.301	0.330	0.347	0.240	-0.472	-0.471	-0.469	-0.469	0.963	0.591	0.091	0.256	-0.268	0.237	0.324	0.993	0.003	1	0.208	0.325	0.275
Coupling Metric Rules	0.026	0.076	0.650	0.553	0.087	0.467	0.094	0.080	0.054	-0.114	-0.143	-0.130	-0.129	0.062	0.082	0.053	0.055	-0.187	0.169	0.083	0.288	0.208	0.208	1	0.060	0.340
Documentation Metric Rules	-0.021	0.301	0.384	0.247	0.444	0.331	0.331	0.347	0.288	-0.347	-0.347	-0.368	-0.367	0.185	0.185	0.035	0.068	-0.371	0.109	0.340	0.201	0.099	0.325	0.060	1	0.275
Size Metric Rules	-0.050	0.671	0.358	0.560	0.690	0.722	0.679	0.670	0.670	-0.528	-0.528	-0.519	-0.515	0.305	-0.102	0.016	0.073	-0.327	0.652	0.722	0.311	0.045	0.275	0.340	0.275	1

Maintainability Index metrics has the same characteristics. Their lowest correlation is 0.946 (program level) and 0.997 (subroutine level) that is a very high value. High correlation is caused by the fact that each variant has almost the same core in their formula. A relatively high correlation can be seen in case of the different warnings (avg. correlation: 0.774) at program level but the same cannot be told for subroutines. Warnings are different bad smells that should be reviewed because they can reveal the weak spots of the system.

It is promising that the correlations between Halstead metrics and warnings are high (avg. correlation is 0.812) since we can use the Halstead metrics to predict warnings in the system (at program level). Unfortunately, no valuable correlation found at subroutine level between these metrics. The Halstead complexity metrics are also highly correlated with the McCC metric (we use the Program Complexity (PC) terminology at program level) which means that each complexity measure can express the other. This is partly true at subroutine level since HCPL, HPL, HPV and HVOL have poor correlations with McCC. At program level, the McCabe's Complexity metric also can be used to express the warnings in the system since it has 0.836 avg. correlation coefficient with the warning metrics.

PCA constructs 25 dimensions (factors) from 26 dimensions that is not the best case scenario. However, using the first ten factors will give back 96.865 (program level) and 96.366 (subroutine level) percent of the total variability. Figures 2 and 3 depict the eigenvalues for all the 25 factors and the cumulative variability at program level and subroutine level respectively. The cumulative variability is slightly steeper in case of programs meaning that we can reconstruct the original data by using less dimensions (factors).

Factors are constructed from the original metrics with linear combination. It is important to examine the so called factor loadings which gives us the linear combinations for each factor. We analyzed the factor loadings only for the first

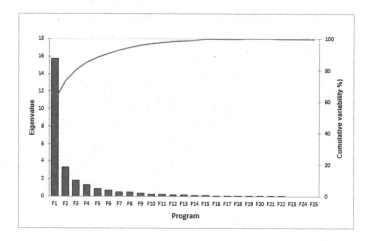

Fig. 2. Eigenvalues and variability of principal components (Program level).

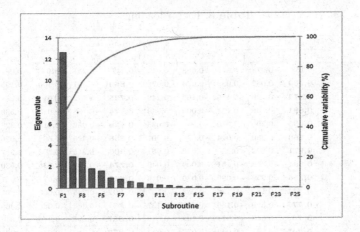

Fig. 3. Eigenvalues and variability of principal components (Subroutine level).

five factors since they retrieve 88.204 and 83.814% of the whole variability at program and subroutine level respectively, thus analyzing the most dominant factors is enough to detect the most dominant original metrics. Table 8 shows the factor loadings for the first five factors both at program and subroutine levels. Values higher than 0.7 are highlighted. It is clearly visible that the first factors are made up from many metrics to caption the maximum possible variability. Both in case of program and subroutine levels the Halstead metrics are the most prominent ones that contribute with the largest weights meaning that they are the most descriptive metrics. Maintainability Index variants are combined with negative weights but they are also significant ones. Further dominant metrics are different at program and subroutine level. The McCabe Cyclomatic Complexity is as strong as the warning occurrence metrics at program level. At subroutine level, the CD, CLOC and LLOC metrics are stronger besides the Halstead and MI metrics which are absolutely dominating.

5.1   Extend Quality Model for RPG

Consider the maintainability model presented in Fig. 1. We can enhance the expressiveness of the model by involving further metrics based on the results of the Principal Component Analysis. PCA showed that the Halstead complexity metrics form an independent group that captures the most information of the system (has the largest weights in factor loadings). Considering the correlation matrix we suggest to involve HNDB metric into the model to contribute to the calculation of fault proneness since it has the largest correlation coefficients with the warning occurrences. Furthermore, we suggest to include the HPV metric to contribute to the Complexity aggregated node since it has low correlation with the McCabe's cyclomatic complexity in case of subroutines but it has a large weight in the linear combination in factor loading (dominant metric) thus

Table 8. Factor loadings

	Program					Subroutine				
	F1	F2	F3	F4	F5	F1	F2	F3	F4	F5
CC	0,153	−0,078	0,616	0,663	0,017	−0,047	−0,081	**0,947**	−0,081	−0,167
HCPL	**0,969**	0,082	−0,090	−0,028	0,072	**0,853**	−0,397	−0,100	−0,193	0,069
HDIF	**0,874**	0,020	0,166	−0,109	−0,249	**0,725**	0,442	0,014	0,291	−0,199
HEFF	**0,891**	0,358	−0,151	−0,009	0,049	**0,774**	−0,198	0,035	0,530	−0,044
HNDB	**0,955**	0,260	−0,070	−0,039	−0,035	**0,928**	−0,052	0,010	0,328	−0,079
HPL	**0,966**	0,230	−0,074	−0,038	−0,007	**0,888**	−0,426	−0,064	−0,026	0,030
HPV	**0,971·**	0,022	−0,055	−0,040	0,051	**0,906**	−0,245	−0,102	−0,237	0,046
HTRP	**0,891**	0,358	−0,151	−0,009	0,049	**0,774**	−0,198	0,035	0,530	−0,044
HVOL	**0,956**	0,259	−0,099	−0,030	0,016	**0,827**	−0,508	−0,071	−0,021	0,053
MI	**−0,771**	0,580	−0,136	0,068	−0,127	**−0,892**	−0,285	0,065	0,305	0,032
MIMS	**−0,771**	0,580	−0,136	0,068	−0,127	**−0,891**	−0,286	0,066	0,309	0,032
MISEI	**−0,736**	0,643	0,071	−0,102	0,010	**−0,887**	−0,297	0,076	0,312	0,058
MISM	**−0,745**	0,631	0,049	−0,072	0,034	**−0,877**	−0,313	0,076	0,323	0,061
NLE	0,602	−0,326	0,186	−0,240	−0,288	0,463	0,664	−0,097	0,035	−0,049
McCC	**0,947**	0,260	−0,090	−0,042	−0,020	0,678	0,393	0,092	0,478	0,044
NOI	0,297	−0,430	0,377	−0,422	−0,281	0,258	0,315	0,203	−0,036	**0,782**
CD	0,072	0,215	0,627	−0,516	0,412	**−0,724**	−0,439	0,155	0,348	0,215
CLOC	0,537	0,185	0,455	−0,065	0,150	**0,771**	−0,455	0,008	−0,108	0,247
NII	-	-	-	-	-	−0,059	0,182	0,047	0,208	0,123
LLOC	0,516	−0,502	−0,180	0,185	0,549	**0,899**	−0,393	−0,059	−0,033	0,046
Warning info	**0,837**	0,206	0,314	0,306	−0,110	0,397	−0,012	**0,897**	−0,088	−0,095
Clone metric rules	**0,768**	0,209	0,379	0,362	−0,125	0,188	−0,029	**0,948**	−0,162	−0,129
Complexity metric rules	**0,899**	0,202	−0,101	−0,068	−0,033	0,538	0,453	0,089	0,311	0,055
Coupling metric rules	**0,813**	0,332	−0,106	−0,008	−0,028	0,156	0,191	0,201	0,028	**0,829**
Documentation metric rules	**0,808**	0,126	−0,312	0,053	0,081	0,439	0,125	0,002	0,199	−0,244
Size metric rules	**0,947**	0,021	−0,030	−0,105	0,001	**0,705**	−0,330	−0,011	0,056	0,001

McCabe's complexity, NLE and HPV forms a unit together to describe the overall Complexity.

6   Conclusion

We have defined the Halstead Complexity metrics for RPG/400 and RPG IV programming languages that has never done before. Furthermore, we have a prototype implementation for these defined metrics. We also work out four different Maintainability Index variants in our static source code analyzer. We performed a Principal Component Analysis on 348 RPG programs and on 7475 subroutines and we investigated the relationships between the calculated metrics. We experienced that the Halstead's Complexity metrics form a disjoint group that can be used to characterize the warning occurrences in the system at program level. Moreover, Halstead metrics can be involved in a maintainability model to improve its usefulness and compactness. We suggest to use the Halstead's

Program Vocabulary (HPV) and the Halstead's Number of Delivered Bugs metrics in the model since these two metrics best expend the model based on our observations.

6.1 Threats to Validity

It is a very challenging task to find any open source software system written in RPG (since RPG is used in business applications). Consequently, it is hard to gather RPG source code sets from different domains that would guarantee the generality. We only have source code from one company and they mostly use subroutines that obviously moderates the generality.

6.2 Future Work

We have calculated four different Maintainability Index metrics for RPG. We plan to compare the MI variants with the Maintainability value obtained from the maintainability model. MI variants only use the subset (McCC, LLOC, CD, HVOL) of metrics we applied in the model thus this kind of research could reveal the possible differences between these maintainability measures.

Gathering RPG source code is a harsh task but we would like to gather more source code from more companies to ensure the generality and also investigate the behavior of Halstead metrics at Procedure level.

Acknowledgment. This research was supported by the EU-funded Hungarian national grant GINOP-2.3.2-15-2016-00037 titled "Internet of Living Things".

References

1. Bakota, T., Hegedűs, P., Körtvélyesi, P., Ferenc, R., Gyimóthy, T.: A probabilistic software quality model. In: 2011 27th IEEE International Conference on Software Maintenance (ICSM), pp. 243–252. IEEE (2011)
2. Baski, D., Misra, S.: Metrics suite for maintainability of extensible markup language web services. IET Softw. **5**(3), 320–341 (2011)
3. Becker, B.A., Mooney, C.: Categorizing compiler error messages with principal component analysis. In: 12th China-Europe International Symposium on Software Engineering Education (CEISEE 2016), Shenyang, China, 28–29 May 2016 (2016)
4. Frederick P Brooks Jr. The mythical man-month (anniversary ed.). 1995
5. Brown, W.H., Malveau, R.C., McCormick, H.W., Mowbray, T.J.: AntiPatterns: Refactoring Software, Architectures, and Projects in Crisis. Wiley, New York (1998)
6. Chidamber, S.R., Kemerer, C.F.: A metrics suite for object oriented design. IEEE Trans. Softw. Eng. **20**(6), 476–493 (1994)
7. Coleman, D., Ash, D., Lowther, B., Oman, P.: Using metrics to evaluate software system maintainability. Computer **27**(8), 44–49 (1994)
8. Halstead, M.H.: Elements of Software Science, vol. 7. Elsevier, New York (1977)
9. Hartman, S.D.: A counting tool for RPG. In: ACM SIGMETRICS Performance Evaluation Review, vol. 11, pp. 86–100. ACM (1982)

10. Heitlager, I., Kuipers, T., Visser, J.: A practical model for measuring maintainability. In: 2007 6th International Conference on Quality of Information and Communications Technology, QUATIC 2007, pp. 30–39. IEEE (2007)

11. Kiewkanya, M., Jindasawat, N., Muenchaisri, P.: A methodology for constructing maintainability model of object-oriented design. In: 2004 Proceedings of the Fourth International Conference on Quality Software, QSIC 2004, pp. 206–213. IEEE (2004)

12. Ladányi, G., Tóth, Z., Ferenc, R., Keresztesi, T.: A software quality model for RPG. In: 2015 IEEE 22nd International Conference on Software Analysis, Evolution and Reengineering (SANER), pp. 91–100. IEEE (2015)

13. Lakshminarayana, A., Newman, T.S.: Principal component analysis of lack of cohesion in methods (lcom) metrics. Technical report TRUAH-CS-1999-01 (1999)

14. McCabe, T.J.: A complexity measure. IEEE Trans. Softw. Eng. 4, 308–320 (1976)

15. Misra, S., Akman, I., Colomo-Palacios, R.: Framework for evaluation and validation of software complexity measures. IET Softw. 6(4), 323–334 (2012)

16. Misra, S., Koyuncu, M., Crasso, M., Mateos, C., Zunino, A.: A suite of cognitive complexity metrics. In: Murgante, B., Gervasi, O., Misra, S., Nedjah, N., Rocha, A.M.A.C., Taniar, D., Apduhan, B.O. (eds.) ICCSA 2012. LNCS, vol. 7336, pp. 234–247. Springer, Heidelberg (2012). doi:10.1007/978-3-642-31128-4_17

17. Muthanna, S., Kontogiannis, K., Ponnambalam, K., Stacey, B.: A maintainability model for industrial software systems using design level metrics. In: 2000 Proceedings of the Seventh Working Conference on Reverse Engineering, pp. 248–256. IEEE (2000)

18. Naib, F.A.: An application of software science to the quantitative measurement of code quality. In: ACM SIGMETRICS Performance Evaluation Review, vol. 11, pp. 101–128. ACM (1982)

19. Oman, P., Hagemeister, J.: Construction and testing of polynomials predicting software maintainability. J. Syst. Softw. 24(3), 251–266 (1994)

20. Ortega, M., Pérez, M., Rojas, T.: Construction of a systemic quality model for evaluating a software product. Softw. Qual. J. 11(3), 219–242 (2003)

21. Parikh, G., Zvegintzov, N.: The world of software maintenance. In: Tutorial on Software, Maintenance, pp. 1–3 (1983)

22. Rawashdeh, A., Matalkah, B.: A new software quality model for evaluating cots components. J. Comput. Sci. 2(4), 373–381 (2006)

23. Shepperd, M., Ince, D.C.: A critique of three metrics. J. Syst. Softw. 26(3), 197–210 (1994)

24. Shlens, J.: A tutorial on principal component analysis. arXiv preprint arXiv:1404.1100 (2014)

A Rigorous Evaluation of the Benefits of Usability Improvements Within Model Checking-Aided Software Inspections

Luciana Brasil Rebelo dos Santos[1(✉)],
Valdivino Alexandre de Santiago Júnior[2], and Albino Vieira Freitas[1]

[1] Instituto Federal de Educação,
Ciência e Tecnologia de São Paulo (IFSP) - Campus Caraguatatuba,
Av. Bahia, 1739, Caraguatatuba, São Paulo, SP, Brazil
lurebelo@ifsp.edu.br, albinofreitas7@gmail.com
[2] Instituto Nacional de Pesquisas Espaciais (INPE),
Av. dos Astronautas, 1758, São José dos Campos, São Paulo, SP, Brazil
valdivino.santiago@inpe.br

Abstract. In this paper, we show the results of a controlled experiment aiming at assessing the benefits of usability improvements for software inspection methodologies that rely on Model Checking. This work has been carried out in the context of the SOLIMVA 3.0 methodology which uses Model Checking to help in the inspection of software designs. A tool, XMITS, has been developed to support SOLIMVA 3.0. Thus, we compared the benefits in terms of cost mainly related to the Modeling activity of SOLIMVA, by using the new (3.0) and the previous (2.0) versions of XMITS. We considered 20 sets of UML behavioral diagrams from two different space application systems and the ATM system. Results backed by statistical analysis show that XMITS 3.0 was better than XMITS 2.0, helping to decrease the total time spent in the Modeling phase. This fact confirms that true usability improvements in software products can have a significant impact on processes such as inspection.

1 Introduction

The scientific community has increased efforts to carry out more rigorous assessments, such as experimental studies and quasi-experiments. One of the main reasons is that 'there is an increasing understanding in the software engineering community that empirical studies are needed to develop or improve processes, methods, and tools for software development and maintenance' [1]. Various surveys with gathered data of an assorted number of papers addressing controlled experiment show the relevance of software engineering experiments to industrial practice and scientific maturity of software engineering research [1–3].

Inspections are used to identify defects in software artifacts. Design documents can be inspected to verify whether software requirements were correctly captured. In this way, inspection methods help to improve software quality, especially when used early in software development. Inspections of software design

O. Gervasi et al. (Eds.): ICCSA 2017, Part V, LNCS 10408, pp. 591–606, 2017.
DOI: 10.1007/978-3-319-62404-4_44

can be especially crucial since design defects, such as problems of correctness and completeness with respect to the requirements or internal consistency, can directly affect the quality and effort required for the software development [4]. Nevertheless, the number of companies where software inspection is part of the culture and organizational process is still small compared to the benefits of its use. Therefore, the development of techniques that are applicable in the scenarios normally found in software companies can make the use of inspection effective.

Model Checking [5–7] is the most popular Formal Verification method which has been receiving much attention from the academic community due to its mathematical foundations. It has been adopted in the industry, as well. Model Checking is a formal automatic verification technique that, given a finite-state model of a system (also known as a Transition System (TS)) and a formal property, systematically verifies whether this property is satisfied by that model [5]. However, despite its benefits, in general, practitioners still avoid using Model Checking in their projects due to aspects such as high learning curve and cost, and the lack of commercially supported tools. Thus, efforts to build tools and automate the process for the use of Formal Verification can facilitate and encourage a wide acceptance of Formal Methods in every day software development. In this line, approaches that translate industry non-formal standards such as UML (Unified Modeling Language) [8] to model checkers notation are a great step towards this goal.

In this context, we had started a work to study, analyze and manipulate UML diagrams to make feasible the use of Model Checking addressing inspection in the software industry. For this, a methodology called SOLIMVA [9] was developed aiming to translate several UML behavioral diagrams (sequence, activity, and state machine) into Transition Systems (TSs) to support Model Checking-aided software inspections. XMITS - XML Metadata Interchange to Transition System [10] - is the tool that supports the conversion of the UML diagrams representation to the input language of NuSMV [11] model checker. The diagrams are processed and converted into Transition System (TS), the basis for Model Checking tool entry. So, basically the main goal of XMITs is to transform the UML diagrams into TSs.

We improved our tool with many important features. Some advancement mainly related to usability aspects are addressed in this new version of XMITS (3.0). The major differences relating to the older version (2.0) are: (i) Interface - the user has an interface where he/she can choose the diagrams and generate the TS or the NuSMV input language. In version 2.0, the user should build a Java class to handle XMITS; (ii) Graph format file - the TS output was a txt file in version 2.0. Now, one can also generate another output file, where it is possible to visualize the Transition System in graph format, observing its states and transitions, which substantially facilitates the system model validation process, before applying Model Checking; and (iii) Installer - an installer was generated to create an executable with any necessary dependencies.

In this paper, we present a controlled experiment, a rigorous evaluation, to realize how usability improvements in software products impact on processes, such as inspections based on Model Checking. This work has been carried out in the context of the SOLIMVA 3.0 methodology which uses Model Checking to help in the inspection of software designs. We compared the benefits in terms of cost, i.e. the amount of time spent, mainly related to the Modeling activity of SOLIMVA, by using the new (3.0) and the previous (2.0) versions of XMITS. Twenty sets of UML behavioral diagrams from two different complex space application systems and the Automated Teller Machine (ATM) case study have been evaluated. Results backed by statistical analysis show that XMITS 3.0 was better than XMITS 2.0, helping to decrease the total time spent in the Modeling phase. We believe that true usability improvements in software products that support Verification & Validation (V&V) processes, such as inspection, can have a significant impact on such efforts.

This paper is structured as follows. Section 2 shows an overview of the SOLIMVA 3.0 methodology and the new version, 3.0, of the XMITS tool. The controlled experiment where we compared the two different versions of our tool in the context of SOLIMVA is in Sect. 3. Section 4 presents related work. In Sect. 5, we state the conclusions and future directions of this research.

2   SOLIMVA and XMITS: Versions 3.0

The verification process established in SOLIMVA 3.0 essentially consists of sequence of scenarios to be checked. Scenarios focus on how the system behaves to implement its functionalities. The analyst gathers requirements from software specifications. In practice, such requirements are generally expressed within UML use case models or simply in Natural Language. SOLIMVA 3.0 suggests using specification patterns [12] to direct the formalization of properties in Computation Tree Logic [5]. The corresponding UML behavioral diagrams that represent the solution to meet the requirements (use cases or pure textual requirements) are taken into account. These UML diagrams (sequence, behavioral state machine, and activity) are input to XMITS. XMITS performs a three-step translation. First, it translates individual types of diagrams (Sequence Diagram, Activity Diagram, Behavioral State Machine Diagram) into a TS in a simple intermediate format. After that, XMITS merges all single TSs into a unified TS. Finally, the tool transforms this unified TS into the notation of the NuSMV model checker. By running NuSMV with the unified TS and the properties in CTL, it is possible to determine if there are defects with the design of the software product. In case the TS does not satisfy a certain property, a counterexample is presented by the model checker. The workflow of SOLIMVA 3.0 is shown in Fig. 1.

XMITS interoperates with two other tools: Modelio 3.2 [13], that is the software used to produce the UML artifacts. The design artifacts are then exported into XMI (XML Metadata Interchange) format, and are inputted to XMITS; and the NuSMV model checker. Currently, XMITS consists of six modules (one more than its older version): the **Reader**, that transforms the XMI file to a list of tags; the **Converter**, that transforms the list of tags to a single TS; the

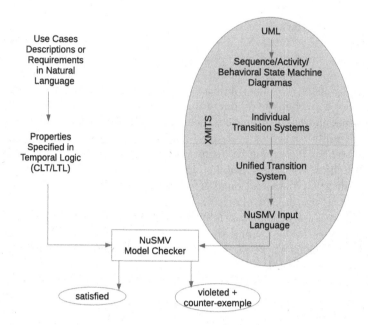

Fig. 1. Schematic view of SOLIMVA 3.0 using XMITS. Adapted from [5].

TUTS (The Unified Transition System), that transforms the single TSs to the unified TS; the **Bridge** module, that transforms the unified TS into the model checker notation; and the **Global** module, which is responsible for several important functions, such as the creation of the TS data structure and the *Printer*, where one can visualize the TS tree. A detailed description of these modules is presented in [10]. And finally, the **Interface** module, which is explained in next subsection.

2.1   The Interface Module

The **Interface** module was developed to support the tool graphical views. This module uses the *JavaFX* API, which in turn, has the purpose to express user interfaces, using a declarative programming style [14]. The module also works with Graphviz, an open source free software for graph visualization [15]. Graphviz uses DOT [16], a language to draw hierarchical or layered directional graphs. In this way, Graphviz can be used for visualization of Transition Systems. The GraphViz Java API is adopted to call Graphviz through the Java application. This module, composed of four classes: the *Main* class, the *Controller* class, the *Graphviz* class, and the *Dot* class.

The **Main** class is responsible for starting the application using *FXML*, a declarative language, XML-based, for constructing a *JavaFX* application user interface; the **Controller** class manages the whole application manipulating the interface and all the tool functionality; the **Graphviz** class is responsible for generating the pdf file with the graphical image of the TS; and the class **Dot** generates the dot file, used for the Graphiviz class to generate the image.

2.2   New Features of XMITS

As stated before, there are three main differences between the two versions, which impacts directly the aspects of usability and cost.

Interface: In the previous version of XMITS the user was required to have a knowledge in programming, as he/she needed to create a project in a Java development environment. The user had to add the Java ARchive (JAR) of XMITS and create a class to manually insert the directory of the UML files to be processed. This process influences directly the usability of the application, since it can cause several errors, such as inserting the wrong UML diagram directory, syntax error in code, JAR import errors, among others.

Thus, an interface, which can be seen in Fig. 2, was developed to solve the issues related above. Following, the description of the actions of each numbered button is explained.

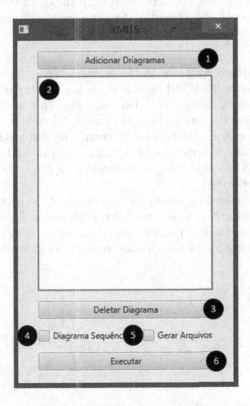

Fig. 2. XMITS graphical interface.

1. (Add Diagrams): This button is used to insert the diagrams that will be processed by the tool. The allowed input formats are XMI, XML and UML. Clicking this button will open a window where diagrams can be selected.
2. (Display List): In this list, the diagrams that are selected will be displayed and processed. The insertion of diagrams with identical names is not allowed.
3. (Delete Diagram): This button allows to delete a diagram from the list, preventing it from being processed. To do this, it is necessary to select a diagram using the mouse click and then press the 3 button or the delete key on the keyboard.
4. (Sequence Diagram): This check box is used to indicate the existence of a sequence diagram and allow the insertion of more diagrams. It was not mentioned, but according to the SOLIMVA methodology, the sequence diagram is mandatory to generate the TS. The description of SOLIMVA is explained in [9].
5. (Generate Files): This check box is used to enable the creation of output files. Three types of files can be created: a text file with the Transition System representation; a file in the pdf extension containing the image of the transition system; and a file in smv format, that is the input for NuSMV.
6. (Execute): This button is used to perform the processing of the input diagrams and generate their respective output. If the check box (Generate Files) is not checked, only the Transition System representation in txt format is displayed on the screen.

Graphical Transition System: In the previous version of XMITS, when the user had to validate the TS model generated, he/she should read the text file, and then generate a graphical representation manually. This action is not a trivial task, since it requires the user to have the knowledge of how the tool generates the output and how it should be read to create the graphical view of the TS. In addition, this task is very time consuming and can lead to several errors, especially when TS has many states. Depending on the number of states, this task can not be performed.

To solve this problem, an automatic generation of the graphical view of the TS was developed. Graphviz is used to perform this action. This software receives as input a file specified in Dot language and then generates an output containing the graphic representation of the specified content, as shown in Fig. 3.

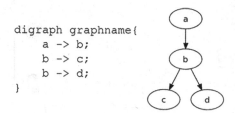

Fig. 3. TS specified in Dot language and its output after being processed by Graphviz.

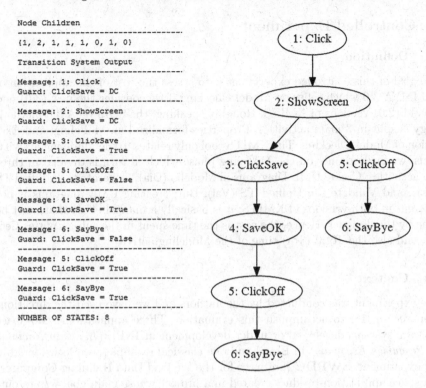

```
Node Children
-----------------------------------
{1, 2, 1, 1, 1, 0, 1, 0}
-----------------------------------
Transition System Output
-----------------------------------
Message: 1: Click
Guard: ClickSave = DC
-----------------------------------
Message: 2: ShowScreen
Guard: ClickSave = DC
-----------------------------------
Message: 3: ClickSave
Guard: ClickSave = True
-----------------------------------
Message: 5: ClickOff
Guard: ClickSave = False
-----------------------------------
Message: 4: SaveOK
Guard: ClickSave = True
-----------------------------------
Message: 6: SayBye
Guard: ClickSave = False
-----------------------------------
Message: 5: ClickOff
Guard: ClickSave = True
-----------------------------------
Message: 6: SayBye
Guard: ClickSave = True
-----------------------------------
NUMBER OF STATES: 8
```

Fig. 4. TS Output of XMITS in both formats.

The Interface module implements the conversion of the TS, which is represented as a linked list in the TUTS module, into a file specified in Dot language. The class *Dot* has a method that traverses the linked list and construct the TS structure specified in Dot language and save it to a String. This String is used later to create the ".dot" file that will be processed by Graphviz. Figure 4 shows the TS represented in both output files. Note that building the TS from the text file is not so easy. It is necessary to follow a heuristic and understand how the text file was constructed.

Installer: To use XMITS, an application JAR was generated and should be run in the same directory as the folder where the Graphviz files and dependencies are located. However, to facilitate the execution of the application and to avoid possible errors caused by the use of Graphviz without installation, an installer was generated through the software Inno Setup [17]. Such software allows to create an executable with any necessary dependencies.

Thus, it was possible to join the Graphviz folder to the generated executable file. Therefore, when the XMITS installation is run, a folder is created on the machine's local disk and the application's JAR and Graphviz folder are extracted to this directory. The user still has the option to save a shortcut of the application executable to the desktop of the computer.

3 Controlled Experiment

3.1 Definition

The goal of this controlled experiment is to assess the cost of the application of SOLIMVA 3.0 which relies on Model Checking if we consider the new (3.0) and the old (2.0) versions of XMITS. Roughly speaking, the SOLIMVA 3.0 methodology is split in 3 main activities: Properties formalization, Modeling, and Execution of Model Checking. The XMITS tool only relates to the Modeling activity. Thus, we focused only on the Modeling phase which in turn is divided in three sub-activities: Create UML Diagrams in Modelio (Dia), Generate the Unified TS (Gen), and Validate the Unified TS (Val). But, creating UML diagrams is not different in both versions of XMITS: it is basically a manual effort that must be done by the designer. Hence, the cost is the time spent in the sub-activities Gen, Val, and also the Total (Tot) time of the Modeling activity.

3.2 Context

The experiment was conducted by the authors and we have used the directions proposed in [18] to accomplish this evaluation. Three applications, two space software systems developed or under development at INPE (*Instituto Nacional de Pesquisas Espaciais*) in Brazil and one classical example, were considered in our experiment. **SWPDC** (Software for the Payload Data Handling Computer) is a space application product created in a project whose main goal was to outsource the development of software embedded in satellite payload. **SWPDCpM** (Software for the Payload Data Handling Computer - protoMIRAX experiment) is an considerably improvement of SWPDC and it has been adapted to protoMIRAX, a hard X-ray imaging telescope under development at INPE. A balloon will launch this instrument and it will operate between 40 to 42 Km of altitude. The third case study is the classical **ATM** (Automated Teller Machine) where the ATM interacts with a customer via a specific interface and communicates with the bank over an appropriate communication link.

For the three software products, several scenarios have been selected. Hence, a sample is precisely a scenario identified in accordance with the guidelines of SOLIMVA 3.0. In total, 20 scenarios (samples) have been analyzed. Each scenario is defined as a set of UML behavioral diagrams, as presented in Table 1. Moreover, in Table 1 the number means how many diagrams of a certain type exist for a scenario.

3.3 Hypotheses

The following hypotheses were considered in this evaluation:

- **Null Hypothesis H1.0:** There is no difference in cost (time spent) related to the Gen sub-activity between XMITS 3.0 and XMITS 2.0;
- **Alternative Hypothesis H1.1:** There is difference in cost (time spent) related to the Gen sub-activity between XMITS 3.0 and XMITS 2.0;

Table 1. Samples for the controlled experiment: scenarios.

Scenario	Sequence	Activity	State machine
SWPDC - 1	1	1	1
SWPDC - 2	2	0	0
SWPDC - 3	1	0	1
SWPDC - 4	1	1	1
SWPDC - 5	3	0	1
SWPDC - 6	1	1	1
SWPDC - 7	2	1	1
SWPDCpM - 1	1	0	0
SWPDCpM - 2	1	0	0
SWPDCpM - 3	1	0	0
SWPDCpM - 4	1	0	0
SWPDCpM - 5	1	0	0
SWPDCpM - 6	1	0	0
SWPDCpM - 7	1	0	0
SWPDCpM - 8	1	0	0
SWPDCpM - 9	1	0	0
SWPDCpM - 10	1	0	0
SWPDCpM - 11	1	0	0
SWPDCpM - 12	1	0	0
ATM - 1	1	1	1

- **Null Hypothesis H2.0:** There is no difference in cost (time spent) related to the Val sub-activity between XMITS 3.0 and XMITS 2.0;
- **Alternative Hypothesis H2.1:** There is difference in cost (time spent) related to the Val sub-activity between XMITS 3.0 and XMITS 2.0;
- **Null Hypothesis H3.0:** There is no difference in cost (time spent) related to the Total (Tot) effort between XMITS 3.0 and XMITS 2.0;
- **Alternative Hypothesis H3.1:** There is difference in cost (time spent) related to the Total (Tot) effort between XMITS 3.0 and XMITS 2.0.

3.4 Variables and Description of the Experiment

The *independent* variables are those that can be manipulated or controlled during the process of trial and define the causes of the hypotheses [19]. In our case, the independent variables are both versions of XMITS (2.0 and 3.0), the selected scenarios/samples and its UML behavioral diagrams, the ability of the professional to model software designs via UML and to validate the unified TS. In the *dependent* variables, we can observe the result of manipulation of the *independent* ones. The time for generating the unified TS, the time for validating the unified TS, and the total time for the Modeling phase are the dependent variables. All time measures were done in minutes (min).

SOLIMVA 3.0 was executed twice considering the 20 scenarios (see Table 1): 19 scenarios refer to the two space systems, and 1 is from the ATM case study. In the first execution we considered the current version, 3.0, of XMITS, and, in the second execution, the previous version of XMITS, 2.0. For each version of XMITS, we measured and recorded the time spent for generating the unified TS (Gen 2.0, Gen 3.0), validating the unified TS (Val 2.0, Val 3.0), and the Total (Tot 2.0, Tot 3.0) time of the Modeling activity. In the first execution, we recorded the respective times due to XMITS 3.0 (Gen 3.0, Val 3.0, Tot 3.0), and, in the second execution, due to XMITS 2.0 (Gen 2.0, Val 2.0, Tot 2.0).

The cost is simply considered as the amount of time spent for each of the tasks: the lower the time, better the cost. XMITS 3.0 and 2.0 ran in a computer with an Intel Core(TM) i3-4005U CPU @ 1.70 GHz Multicore processor, 4 GB of RAM, running Microsoft Windows 10 Professional 64-bit operating system.

A statistical evaluation for verifying data normality has been done in five steps: (i) by using the Shapiro-Wilk test [20] with a significance level $\alpha = 0.05$; (ii) by using the Anderson-Darling test [21] with a significance level $\alpha = 0.05$; (iii) checking the *skewness* of the frequency distribution; (iv) visually inspecting the Q-Q plot; and (v) visually inspecting the histogram. This 5-step verification gives a greater confidence in the conclusion on data normality compared to an approach that is based only on a normality test (e.g. Shapiro-Wilk, Anderson-Darling), considering the effects of polarization due to the length of the samples [22].

If we concluded that data are from a normally distributed population, then the t-test would be applied with $\alpha = 0.05$. Otherwise, we applied the nonparametric Wilcoxon test (Signed Rank) [23] with $\alpha = 0.05$, too. However, if the samples presented ties, we applied a variation of the Wilcoxon test, the Asymptotic Wilcoxon (Signed Rank) [23], suitable to treat ties with significance level $\alpha = 0.05$.

3.5   Validity

The validity evaluation takes into account the risks that may compromise the validity of the experiment.

Threats to internal validity compromise the confidence in stating that there is a relationship between dependent and independent variables [22]. We can not assert that the samples/scenarios were randomly selected because their choice depends on the software products under evaluation. One factor that could compromise the internal validity of the experiment is the professional skills in the validation of the unified TS, since the same TS must be validated twice, one for each version of the tool (3.0 and 2.0). To minimize the effects of this factor, we first performed the experiment with version 3.0 of XMITS, which favors version 2.0, as the professional already knows the TS at the time of its validation when executing version 2.0.

One category of threat to external validity is the population threat. In this threat, we wish to realize how significant is the sample set (scenarios set in our case) of the population used in the study. In this sense, it is pertinent to examine

Table 2. Cost (time spent in min) due to each of the activities: results and mean value.

Scenario	Gen 2.0	Gen 3.0	Val 2.0	Val 3.0	Tot 2.0	Tot 3.0
SWPDC - 1	5	0.5	7	4	34	26.5
SWPDC - 2	5	0.4	1	1	22	17.4
SWPDC - 3	4	0.4	4	8	21	21.4
SWPDC - 4	4	0.5	11	7	32	24.5
SWPDC - 5	5	0.5	11	3	47	34.5
SWPDC - 6	4	0.5	8	6	25	19.5
SWPDC - 7	4	0.6	10	8	42	36.6
SWPDCpM - 1	4	0.3	4	1	13	6.3
SWPDCpM - 2	3	0.3	3	1	13	8.3
SWPDCpM - 3	3	0.3	5	2	17	11.3
SWPDCpM - 4	3	0.3	4	1	11	5.3
SWPDCpM - 5	4	0.3	3	1	11	5.3
SWPDCpM - 6	3	0.3	3	1	10	5.3
SWPDCpM - 7	3	0.3	3	1	11	6.3
SWPDCpM - 8	3	0.3	5	3	18	13.3
SWPDCpM - 9	3	0.3	3	1	11	6.3
SWPDCpM - 10	3	0.3	2	1	10	6.3
SWPDCpM - 11	3	0.3	2	1	10	6.3
SWPDCpM - 12	3	0.3	2	0.5	9	4.8
ATM - 1	3	0.5	11	4	30	20.5
$\bar{x}$	3.6	0.375	5.1	2.775	19.85	14.3

the population used in the experiment. Even though the choice of samples were not random as previously mentioned, altogether the set of UML behavioral diagrams that characterize all scenarios contains most of the important fragments, components, states which define the UML diagrams. Thus, we believe that our choice of the set of samples is considerably satisfactory.

3.6   Results

In this section, we present and discuss the results of our controlled experiment. By using the 5-step approach to check data normality, we concluded that none of the measured data come from a normal distribution. As a matter of record, the greatest *p-value* due to Shapiro-Wilk test was from Val 2.0: 0.004077. And the greatest one due to Anderson-Darling test was from Tot 2.0: 0.002769. We clearly see that these values are below the significance level, α, and hence we reject the null hypothesis that the population is normally distributed. We also checked the *skewness*, Q-Q plot and histograms in accordance with our proposed approach.

Since there are ties, we applied the nonparametric test Asymptotic Wilcoxon (Signed Rank) [23]. In Table 2, we show the time measures (in min) and the

Table 3. Cost (time spent in min) due to each of the activities: Asymptotic Wilcoxon.

Hypothesis	p-value
1: Gen 3.0 ↔ Gen 2.0	$1.907e - 06$
2: Val 3.0 ↔ Val 2.0	0.000679
3: Tot 3.0 ↔ Tot 2.0	$3.815e - 06$

mean value ($\bar{x}$) regarding the six data sets. Thus, for scenario SWPDC - 1, the designer took 5 min to generate the unified TS by using XMITS 2.0 (Gen 2.0) while he/she took 4 min to validate the unified TS via XMITS 3.0 (Val 3.0).

Table 3 shows the p-values due to the Asymptotic Wilcoxon test and the boxplots are in Fig. 5. Based on these results, we conclude that all three null hypotheses (H1.0 to H3.0) were rejected because the p-values are below α. Statistically speaking, there is difference in cost if we apply SOLIMVA 3.0 via the two different versions of the XMITS tool. In a pairwise comparison, i.e. Gen 2.0 × Gen 3.0, Val 2.0 × Val 3.0, Tot 2.0 × Tot 3.0, the mean values ($\bar{x}$) of XMITS 3.0 are all smaller than the respectives mean values of XMITS 2.0. We then conclude that applying SOLIMVA 3.0 with XMITS 3.0 is better than doing the same with XMITS 2.0.

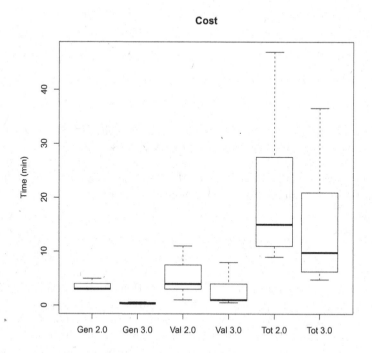

Fig. 5. Cost (time spent in min) due to each of the activities: boxplots.

4 Related Work

This section presents some of the research literature related to this paper (not exhaustive), showing works that deal with software inspections using software support. First, we show some approaches that deal with inspection-aided tools related to software design. Then, works which encompass controlled experiments applied to inspection techniques are addressed.

Taba and Ow [24] developed a web-based tool, ArSeC, to support their proposed model. It is designed to detect and remove the defects in the first two phases of software development. The model suggests designing and using a comprehensive database that contains potential defects and their causes stored. This engine alerts the inspectors about the possible defects and shows the possible causes. The work [25] presents AutoInspect, a tool for semi-automated inspection of design documents. The tool was developed in the context of Turkish Aerospace Industries. The tool facilitates and increases the inspection efficiency in the tasks that in their experience has shown to be tedious and effort intensive, e.g., browsing through a long design Word document and checking formats, etc. As outputs, a list of defects found during inspection, and a design verification report (in PDF format) are created.

A tool-based approach that tries to identify potential document quality defects is presented in [26]. This tool-based analysis relies on best practices for software documentation. The tool checks software development documents against implemented document quality rules. It covers the range from requirements across system, architecture and design, up to test specifications. Sinha et al. [27] have developed an approach for automated and 'edittime' inspection of use cases based on the construction and analysis of models of use cases. The models contain linguistic properties of the use case text along with the functional properties of the system under discussion. The author of the use case enters Natural Language text and issues found with the underlying model are listed by the tool. Li and Liu [28] designed methods of deriving functional scenarios and generating inspection tasks by applying consistency properties to each scenario. They implemented these specific methods in a support tool. The inspector has to derive functional scenarios from specification first. Then, the consistency properties need to be applied to each functional scenario to create inspection tasks, which should be examined by the inspector to ensure the consistency.

The papers presented so far show tools that were developed to support particular techniques/methodologies, normally to deal with issues on specific contexts. We did not find any available tool that could be adapted to our needs. We are interested in a more broad way to perform requirements checking, which can be applied in different contexts. Our approach allows that an informal language (UML), still quite popular, can continue to be used for creating the design of software systems. The complexity for the use of formal methods (Model Checking, in this case) is almost completely hidden from the practitioner, and thus it has a high potential to be applied in practice. SOLIMVA 3.0 can be applied to any software product that uses UML as the modeling specification language.

[29] compared two Inspection Technique, MIT 1 - Model Inspection Technique and UCE - Use Case Evaluation, for Usability Evaluation by means of a controlled experiment that measured efficiency, effectiveness, perceived ease of use, and perceived usefulness. The two techniques aim to support the identification of usability defects through the evaluation of use cases specifications. The results indicate that MIT 1 allows users to find more usability defects in less time than UCE. However, UCE was considered easiest to use and more useful than MIT 1. The work [30] proposed a metric based reading (MBR) technique used for requirements inspections, whose main goal is to identify specific types of defects in use cases. They performed a controlled experiment to ascertain if the usage of MBR really helps in the detection of defects in comparison with a simple Checklist technique. The experiment result revealed that MBR reviewers were more effective at detecting defects than Checklist reviewers, but they were not more efficient, because MBR reviewers took longer than Checklist reviewers on average.

The last two works presented controlled experiments, each one comparing two techniques, the first for usability defects in use cases and the second comparing the reading technique to checklist technique, also related to use cases. We didn't find experiments dealing with Model Checking aiming inspection as our approach does. Besides, SOLIMVA proposes to check requirements not only from use cases, but also requirements expressed in natural language.

5   Conclusions

In this work we presented a controlled experiment aiming at assessing the benefits of usability improvements for software inspection methodologies based on Model Checking. For this, we compared the two versions (2.0 and 3.0) of XMITS, the tool developed to support the SOLIMVA 3.0 methodology, which uses Model Checking to help in the inspection of software designs. The results backed by statistical analysis showed that the cost to perform the Modeling activity of SOLIMVA using the new version of XMITS (3.0) was better than XMITS 2.0. We considered 20 sets of UML behavioral diagrams from two different space application systems and the ATM system to perform the experiment. This fact suggests that usability improvements on software products are valuable and can produce significant impact on process such as inspection, which is strongly dependent on the human factor.

Future directions include advances on usability issues of XMITS, but regarding to another activity of SOLIMVA, the Execution of Model Checking. Such improvements include to inform the user the type of error that is occurring when some inconsistency is found in the model when applying Model Checking. In the current version, the encountered problem is not detailed. Another constraint is related to the counterexample generated, when finding an inconsistency. The model checker shows the state where the requirement (property) was not satisfied within the TS. However, it is necessary to automatically specify the UML diagram where this inconsistency was found and, more than that, the exact point in this diagram where the property was not satisfied. In addition, we will perform another controlled experiment or quasi-experiment, considering these improvements, addressing not only the cost but also the effectiveness relating to the number of encountered defects, since effectiveness is a very important question to be answered.

References

1. Sjøberg, D.I.K., Hannay, J.E., Hansen, O., ByKampenes, V., Karahasanovic, A., Liborg, N.-K., Rekdal, A.C.: A survey of controlled experiments in software engineering. IEEE Trans. Softw. Eng. **31**(9), 733–753 (2005)
2. Zannier, C., Melnik, G., Maurer, F.: On the success of empirical studies in the international conference on software engineering. In: Proceedings of the 28th International Conference on Software Engineering, pp. 341–350. ACM (2006)
3. Lemos, O.A.L., Ferrari, F.C., Eler, M.M., Maldonado, J.C., Masiero, P.C.: Evaluation studies of software testing research in Brazil and in the world: a survey of two premier software engineering conferences. J. Syst. Softw. **86**(4), 951–969 (2013)
4. Travassos, G.H.: Forrest Shull, Jeffrey Carver, and Victor Basili. Reading techniques for OO design inspections. Technical report (2002)
5. Baier, C., Katoen, J.-P.: Principles of Model Checking. MIT Press, Cambridge (2008)
6. Clarke, E.M., Emerson, E.A.: Design and synthesis of synchronization skeletons using branching time temporal logic. In: Grumberg, O., Veith, H. (eds.) 25 Years of Model Checking. LNCS, vol. 5000, pp. 196–215. Springer, Heidelberg (2008). doi:10.1007/978-3-540-69850-0_12
7. Queille, J.P., Sifakis, J.: Specification and verification of concurrent systems in CESAR. In: Dezani-Ciancaglini, M., Montanari, U. (eds.) Programming 1982. LNCS, vol. 137, pp. 337–351. Springer, Heidelberg (1982). doi:10.1007/3-540-11494-7_22
8. The Object Management Group (OMG), Needham, MA, USA. OMG Unified Modeling Language (OMG UML), Superstructure, V2.4.1 (2011)
9. dos Santos, L.B.R., de Santiago, Jr., V.A., Vijaykumar, N.L.: Transformation of UML behavioral diagrams to support software model checking. Electron. Proc. Theor. Comput. Sci. **147**, 133–142 (2014)
10. Eras, E.R., dos Santos, L.B.R., Santiago Júnior, V.A., Vijaykumar, N.L.: Towards a wide acceptance of formal methods to the design of safety critical software: an approach based on UML and model checking. In: Gervasi, O., Murgante, B., Misra, S., Gavrilova, M.L., Rocha, A.M.A.C., Torre, C., Taniar, D., Apduhan, B.O. (eds.) ICCSA 2015. LNCS, vol. 9158, pp. 612–627. Springer, Cham (2015). doi:10.1007/978-3-319-21410-8_47
11. Fondazione Bruno Kessler. NuSMV home page (2015)
12. Dwyer, M.B., Avrunin, G.S., Corbett, J.C.: Patterns in property specifications for finite-state verification. In: Proceedings of the International Conference on Software Engineering, pp. 411–420. ACM, New York (1999)
13. Modeliosoft. Modelio open source community (2011)
14. Weaver, J.L., Gao, W., Chin, S., Iverson, D., Costa, A.G.M.: Plataforma Pro JavaFX Desenvolvimento de RIA para Dispositivos Móveis e para Área de Trabalho por Scripts com a Tecnologia Java, p. 619. Ciência Moderna LTDA, Rio de Janeiro (2010)
15. GRAPHVIZ. Graph visualization software (2017)

16. Gansner, E., Koutsofios, E., North, S.: Drawing graphs with dot: dot users manual (2006)
17. JRSOFTWARE. Inno setup (2016)
18. Wohlin, C., Runeson, P., Host, M., Ohlsson, M.C., Regnell, B., Wesslen, A.: Experimentation in Software Engineering: An Introduction (2000)
19. Campanha, D.N., Souza, S.R.S., Maldonado, J.C.: Mutation testing in procedural and object-oriented paradigms: an evaluation of data structure programs. In: 2010 Brazilian Symposium on Software Engineering (SBES), pp. 90–99. IEEE (2010)
20. Shapiro, S.S., Wilk, M.B.: An analysis of variance test for normality (complete samples). Biometrika **52**(3–4), 591–611 (1965)
21. Stephens, M.A.: Tests Based on EDF Statistics. Marcel Dekker, New York (1986)
22. Balera, J.M., Santiago Júnior, V.A.: A controlled experiment for combinatorial testing. In: Proceedings of the 1st Brazilian Symposium on Systematic and Automated Software Testing (SAST 2016), pp. 1–10. ACM (2016)
23. Kohl, M.: Introduction to Statistical Data Analysis with R. Bookboon.com, London (2015)
24. Taba, N., Ow, S.: A new model for software inspection at the requirements analysis and design phases of software development. Int. Arab J. Inf. Technol. (IAJIT) **13**(6), 51–57 (2016)
25. Coskun, M.E., Ceylan, M.M., Yigitözu, K., Garousi, V.: A tool for automated inspection of software design documents and its empirical evaluation in an aviation industry setting. In: 2016 IEEE Ninth International Conference on Software Testing, Verification and Validation Workshops (ICSTW), pp. 287–294. IEEE (2016)
26. Dautovic, A., Plösch, R., Saft, M.: Automated quality defect detection in software development documents. In: First International Workshop on Model-Driven Software Migration (MDSM 2011), p. 29 (2011)
27. Sinha, A., Sutton, Jr., S.M., Paradkar, A.: Text2Test: automated inspection of natural language use cases. In: 2010 Third International Conference on Software Testing, Verification and Validation (ICST), pp. 155–164. IEEE (2010)
28. Li, M., Liu, S.: Tool support for rigorous formal specification inspection. In: 2014 IEEE 17th International Conference on Computational Science and Engineering (CSE), pp. 729–734. IEEE (2014)
29. Valentim, N.M.C., Rabelo, J., Oran, A.C., Conte, T., Marczak, S.: A controlled experiment with usability inspection techniques applied to use case specifications: comparing the MIT 1 and the UCE techniques. In: 2015 ACM/IEEE 18th International Conference on Model Driven Engineering Languages and Systems (MODELS), pp. 206–215. IEEE (2015)
30. Bernárdez, B., Genero, M., Durán, A., Toro, M.: A controlled experiment for evaluating a metric-based reading technique for requirements inspection. In: Proceedings of the 10th International Symposium on Software Metrics, pp. 257–268. IEEE (2004)

Document-Oriented Middleware:
The Way to High-Quality Software

Jaroslav Král[1], Tomáš Pitner[1], and Michal Žemlička[2,3(✉)]

[1] Faculty of Informatics, Masaryk University, Botanická 68a,
602 00 Brno, Czech Republic
{kral,pitner}@fi.muni.cz
[2] Faculty of Mathematics and Physics, Charles University,
Malostranské nám. 25, 118 00 Praha 1, Czech Republic
zemlicka@sisal.mff.cuni.cz
[3] Závod Technika, AŽD Praha, Žirovnická 2/3146, 106 17 Praha 10, Czech Republic
zemlicka.michal@azd.cz

Abstract. Information systems increase their size and complexity. Users of information systems become rather partners than clients of software developers. Users take increasing part in agile and modifiable business processes supported by software systems. They usually should take part in system development and maintenance and be able to apply their business expertise. We show that the issues can be solved if a document-driven service-oriented software architecture is used. The services forming the architecture are autonomous. They exchange the (business) documents via a network specific (infrastructure) services. It substantially enhances the properties of the virtual middleware and overall quality of the developed system. This solution enables to use, retail, and develop user business knowledge and skills. There are further technical as well as economic advantages like smooth and cheap continuous system maintenance, incremental specification and development, ability to reuse software and to meet planned terms and investments.

The paper is based on our long-term practical experience, research, consulting, and educational activities.

Keywords: Document-oriented services · Documents in SOA · Architectural services · Document interfaces

1 Introduction

Information systems are a crucial part of information technology. Their needs stimulate new software engineering paradigms and gradually influence our public as well as our private world. The resulting software systems might become very large. They are simply so complex that they do not properly fit into any mind, although their development methodology (e.g. quite popular holistic approach) directly or indirectly requires it. Their development and maintenance cost tend to be very high. The giants cannot be developed in time and maintained promptly enough.

© Springer International Publishing AG 2017
O. Gervasi et al. (Eds.): ICCSA 2017, Part V, LNCS 10408, pp. 607–619, 2017.
DOI: 10.1007/978-3-319-62404-4_45

Users must take part in system development and maintenance and should be able to apply their business expertise. They become rather partners than clients of software developers [19]. They also must properly respond to business and system accidents and failures. It is a crucial requirement. The response often cannot be supported by the developed system only. It often must be done in cooperation with users.

Digitalization of existing, often only partly formalized (modelled), business processes becomes crucial [7,8]. Successful solutions in practice often use exchange of digitalized business documents in semi-structured form. The digitalized form can be variously encapsulated and used for communication. It opens new opportunities for the developed system (as shown below).

According [4] the systems must be decomposed and their parts tend to be autonomous and they communicate. We prefer to construct the systems as complex networks of communicating autonomous components [11]. The components need not emerge only via decomposition of an entity but they can also be encapsulated already existing solutions. The development process can be therefore based on decomposition as well as on integration. The parts can be encapsulated services in the sense of service-oriented architecture (SOA, [6,13]).

We show that the issues can be solved if the systems have specific service-oriented architecture (SOA) driven by digitalized documents. A specific feature of our solution is the emphasis on the use of *digitalized business documents*. It in fact generalizes current successful solutions used in practice to digitalize and enhance current business without extensive modelling and formalization. It is an implementation of the second mode in a *bimodal system* [7]. It enables to use existing user knowledge and skills and enhance system usefulness as well as usability.

The solutions are well suited to the needs of small-to-medium software vendors as well as to the needs of small-to-medium enterprise (SME) users. Most of the aspects of our attitude can be well applied in large organizations too. It enables avoidance of negative effects of unnecessary business process reengineering. The documents could be transformed or combined. A typical case is a transformation of the digital document into a paper (printed) form.

The structure of the paper is as follows: In Sect. 2 we discuss examples of simple document-driven patterns. Then (in Sect. 3) we summarize and generalize the practical achievements. We introduce the concept of infrastructure services there. In Sects. 4 and 5 we summarize main benefits and opportunities of decomposition and SOA. Challenges and threats are discussed in Sect. 6. Finally, the conclusions and further research are given in Sects. 7 and 8.

2   Towards Document-Driven Ecosystems

A proper use of digitalized (business) documents is a very powerful design pattern. It enables a smooth digitalization of existing business practices without extensive modelling.

The key aspect of the document-oriented approach is the acceptance of the principle that individual components of software system ask for a service (action) from some other services (processors, service providers) using documents but it need not be prescribed by whom, how, nor when. It is like in real life and it is supported by the fact that it is required or even implemented that the document can be transformed into a paper form. The reason is described in [4,5].

It opens new opportunities for flexibility, prototyping, component replacement, incremental development, and various variants of maintenance.

On the first sight it looks very simple (straightforward) but it is in fact a specific development paradigm different from the frequently applied ones. Our practical experience shows that if it is used, it allows (especially by smaller vendors) to reach interesting results (compare the discussion below).

In the case of large systems we usually must use the philosophy of requests as otherwise we must solve large issues to implement complex systems or to interconnect them. The principle of request is useful also in quite simple cases. Let us discuss typical examples.

2.1 Collaboration of Independent Information Systems

Paper business documents are crucial for classical business and production processes. The activities of business partners can be supported by their business information systems. It can happen that a partner has no ERP or no information system at all, some parties still use paper documents, see [5]. The systems communicate using business documents like invoices. They often have spreadsheet table format.

The messages (documents) can be modified during their transfer and they destinations can be dynamically changed. It is preferable to equip the systems with specific services providing the necessary transformations.

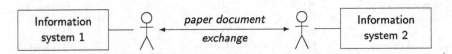

Fig. 1. Classical communication pattern.

Typical situation is that both partners are information systems or autonomous software entities. The collaboration is enhanced if the documents (messages) if Fig. 1 are digitalized. It is often required that proper documents can be alternatively used. Typical situation for collaborating information systems is in Fig. 2.

The digitalized documents must be usually transformed into an agreed (textual, human readable) format to be usable by all cooperating parties. It is highly preferable to use pairs (digital interface, information system) as service in the sense of SOA [6,13].

The preferable solution is to use front-end gate (FEG, [12]) transforming messages into standardized form (agreed document format) and enabling pairs

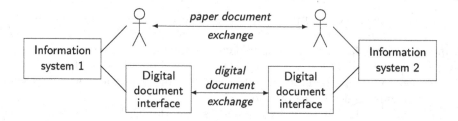

Fig. 2. Combination of classical and digitalized document exchange.

(digital interface, information system) to be used as a service in the sense of SOA. Note that similar turn can be used for software entities simpler than for entire information systems – see below.

In order to increase the flexibility of the networks of software entities the system can be further enhanced.

The messages (documents) being e.g. texts in XML or in another format for semi-structured documents pass gates directing, transforming, and combining the messages documents. It is especially effective if the messages or documents have a proper format. The gates can be influenced by administrators – see [17] and Fig. 3.

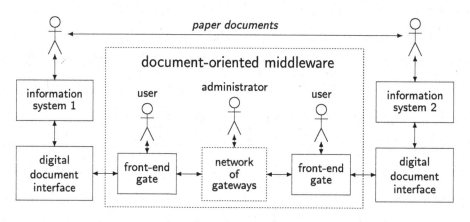

Fig. 3. Complex system of document-oriented communication.

2.2   Cooperation of Business Partners

Cooperation of business partners is based on an exchange of business documents like invoices, bills of delivery, or reminders. The documents can be understood as requests. They can be quite easily digitalized. When properly digitalized (today based on documents in XML formats), it is possible to get further benefits like agility of software and business processes, wide opportunities of user involvement, solution of business trials. It is possible to implement various transformations of the documents during their transfer. Such transformations can be provided by infrastructure services [16]. It opens the way to the full application of the concept of software town (compare [27]) – i.e. a system formed by large software entities (either monolithical or well-structured) connected via infrastructure services. Unfortunately, it is very hard to find practical projects that could be used to teach students how to cope with this approach. It is even harder – we need the projects to be able to clearly demonstrate advantages of the approach.

2.3   Enterprise Systems

Enterprise Systems [23] are large socio-technical economic systems. The situation can be more complicated in the case of networked enterprises or large manufacturing supply chains made of several business entities (e.g. suppliers, manufacturers, assemblers, retailers, . . .) and which become *Systems of Systems* (SOSs) as defined by Ackoff [1]. We use a solution allowing also hierarchical composition of systems as well as of services.

Information systems supporting activities of enterprises have as a rule the form of a collection of autonomous software entities. These systems are usually *enterprise resource planning* systems (ERP).

Enterprise systems must be able to support enterprises having different organization structures. They should support organization changes of enterprises, if needed. The parts of the ERP must be autonomous and can be provided by different vendors. Some parts must be developed from scratch; some can be reused or purchased.

ERP therefore tend to be a network of autonomous entities exchanging documents or sending to or accepting documents from outside world, other ERP inclusive. The communication inside an ERP has features similar to the ones shown in Fig. 1 or Fig. 2. But the communication is more standardized than the one described in Sect. 2.1.

The systems usually enable to modify document paths. User interface is good for the cooperation with whole ERP. The user interface can have the abilities of web application for the users and the abilities of a service for other parts of the system.

It is quite easy to redirect document outside ERP. It is very useful in the case that we want to implement outsourcing and insourcing. It can be also used for very flexible service prototyping [14] and for the solution of business accidents [28].

2.4   Document-Driven SOA

Document-based interfaces enable simple integration of new components with existing systems and replacement of components. It enforces an extended version of Parnas's principle of information hiding [21]. A typical example is a design pattern based on autonomous development of a new service initially connected to a portal. The communication can be then redirected to a system having a document-based interface. It can be ERP of an enterprise or information system of a university. Many students' projects can be implemented this way. The turn can be used also for students practical projects – e.g. for start-ups cooperating with the university. Let us note that it is also training for incremental development.

It is a very powerful tool enabling incremental development as well as incremental specification of software systems. Its full power is – at least in some countries – limited by some legislative restrictions. The legislative restrictions are limiting especially in attempts to reduce total costs and to improve cash flow.

3 Benefits and Opportunities of Decomposition of Large Systems

Development of large monolithic systems cannot be arbitrarily accelerated, see the phenomenon of inaccessible are in the plain of duration and effort [3,10]. The consequence is that large systems are not delivered on time and in sufficient quality. This trend is supported by the dynamics of changes in IT (new paradigm in less than ten years, half of the necessary professional knowledge is in practice younger than five years). There is a strong need for system maintenance. It implies continuous degradation of system quality. The system must be often completely rewritten. This is especially true for small and medium software enterprises. It affects even the large ones. The issue can be solved if we use proper software architecture discussed above. Business document driven SOA allows applying knowledge and skills of users verified and trained for many years, often for many centuries.

There are technical (engineering) advantages. Business document interfaces allows smooth integration of new components into existing systems, replacement of parts, and basically enforcing an improved version of the Parnas principle of information hiding [21]. A typical example is a design pattern based on the autonomous development of new services, originally associated with the portal. The communication of the service is then redirected to the system interface. It may be an enterprise or ERP information system or information system of our university. In both cases we realize many student projects. It also can be used in student projects team for practice – e.g. projects of start-ups cooperating with the universities. According to our experience, in this way it can be applied incremental development in the large.

4 Collaboration of Software Systems

The attitudes described above can be implemented using specific SOA called *software confederations* (or *confederation* for short) [13]. A confederation is a document-oriented SOA. A confederation is formed by application services in common sense and by infrastructure services providing transformation of tuples of input documents into tuples of output documents, routing, and other system structure capabilities. Their activities can be changed in an agile way by their administrators. The service can specify the destinations of output documents and there are rules filtering input documents. The following variants of infrastructure services are typically used (see [17] for details).

- Front-end gate is used as a generalized connector and wrapper. It works as an entry point of the connected service. It changes document formats if necessary. In the case when it is the gate of an application service, it transforms fine-grained and eventually procedure-call-oriented document coming from the application service into document-request oriented ones.
- Portals provide user interfaces wrapped as services. Technically the other services can communicate with it like with other services [20].
- Heads of composite service enables hierarchical composition.

A confederation is a network of wrapped large applications (services) connected by an intelligent middleware that works as infrastructure of the system. If the applications are large, i.e. they are cathedrals in the sense of [22], the whole structure of the system is similar to the structure of a modern town. It is no bazaar. If the system is not too complex, it can be seen as a bazaar of cathedrals. We successfully applied confederations in several practical projects of information as well as control systems [10,16].

It often suffices to apply a SOA having only some features of confederations. We say that such a service-oriented system is confederative. The minimal set of features is:

- service orientation in the broader sense,
- user-understandable problem domain oriented declarative interfaces,
- message/document routing.

Middleware can use various tools. Good experiences are with some document management systems (DMS)[1], e.g. with open source system Alfresco (see below). The concept of metadata in the sense of DMS is very useful.

4.1 Binary Systems

Let us discuss typical document generating services (document generators, DG) are tending rather to produce than to consume documents.

- Wrapped collection of intelligent devices or small subservices, e.g. sensors or simple applications.
- Portal: A service being wrapped user interface used to fill document-like formats. It usually behaves like a thick intelligent client tier. A thick tier is in this case preferable as it prevents snags related to thin client (slow click responses, system failures). Thick document-oriented solution simplifies the application of batch processes. In some situations it can by highly desirable. It is then possible to benefit from the structured analysis and design [25,26].

---

[1] http://www.businessnewsdaily.com/8038-best-document-management-software.html.

– Wrapped collection of small documents, e.g. a collection of payment requests.

We discussed the cases when the services are in peer-to-peer relation technically as well as logically. Information systems can have "binary" architecture when one part (DG) of the system works as a data producing and collecting body. The individual data are encapsulated into documents and sent to the second part which is typically an ERP system. The ERP uses the data from incoming documents to perform financial operations.

It could look very simple. But in the Czech Republic the binary architectures were improperly used in several e-government projects. It caused substantial loses. It is indirectly confirmed by the following fact: A proper reconstruction of a DG serving pre-paid transportation city chip cards used by Prague citizen enabled to reduce construction costs more than ten times.

Binary architecture is quite common as it can be used not only in financial activities. A small modification enables a substantial enhancement of the quality of data coming from different sources having different properties.

Service-oriented architecture is according to [18] seen as a promising technique to bridge the gap between sensor nodes and enterprise applications such as factory monitoring, control, and tracking systems where sensor data are used. A data generator can be a wrapped sensor or a wrapped collection of sensors. For example, wrapped collection of environmental sensors is projected to be implemented in a neighbourhood of Prague by Czech Technical University.

The concept of binary systems was successfully used by the company Business Systems, Inc., Prague for a hospital Na Františku. The DG part of the solution (called Requisitions) used a document management system as a data tier and small part of logic tier. The Requisitions communicate with the hospital's ERP.

5   Crucial Positive Effects of Document SOA

Confederations enable to achieve high levels of many quality aspects [9,14]. Let us discuss some of them.

Autonomy of services is itself a crucial quality aspect. It simplifies enhancements of system modifiability, maintainability, understandability [28]. The most important features are system transparency, the possibility of hierarchical composition, and use of knowledge and skills of the users. The aspects simplify the application of agility of system development processes that can be incremental. It is preferable for the implementation of agile user business processes.

The methodology enables digitalization and easy enhancement of existing intuitive business processes. Existing user knowledge and skills simplifies the system development and reuse of legacy software artefacts. The pace of system changes, coding and maintenance effort can be reduced. The systems need not become obsolete quickly. The threats business process restructuring known from history are practically avoided.

The most visible formal effects of the attitude presented here is that users need not produce a lot of models. It is not wrong as excessive (complex) models are based on techniques developed by large software vendors and intended for large clients (developers). It limits the usability of the tools for smaller software producers.

There are less visible effects. Any system can fail due various reasons including hacker attacks, hardware failures, system overloading, environmental and social catastrophes, etc. Properly constructed confederative service-oriented system can reduce the probability of total system failure. It moreover enables gradual system recovery.

6   Opportunities and Threats

Clouds enable very powerful operations. Developers developing document-driven SOA should retain the autonomy of services. The systems implemented using clouds should enable sourcing.

It is a specific paradigm. It is difficult to learn and must be moreover trained early. The acceptance of this paradigm in practice and often in research is not easy.

Document-based service orientation is a new paradigm. It is the main reason of its power but at the same time there are some issues and challenges: The first challenge is the appreciation of the fact that many things must be done other way than the developers are used to do under object-oriented approach. The object-oriented approach is very well prepared, supported by complex research, and supported by many tools as well as by extensive pedagogical background. If the developed system is not too large, the object-oriented development leads quite quickly to the goal. The danger is that for very complex systems the complexity of development and maintenance of object-oriented development grows dramatically. If the system is of low complexity, then the object-oriented approach is usually more efficient than the service-oriented one.

The principles of the proposed solution are suited to digitalization of existing business processes. The principles are based on long-time practical experience. The processes to be digitalized already exist. Although they are executed informally, they in fact have some (non-formal) model – the existing business processes. They need not be therefore formally modelled. It is advantageous especially for small companies.

The key issue is that if it is not applied in a large company, the users need not be able to comply with the complex models and moreover it is possible that they even do not need them.

6.1   Training Document SOA

Our experience shows that if we want to teach successfully the service-oriented paradigm, we must enable students (or at least to most of them) to be in contact with projects where service orientation has sense. One of the opportunities how to achieve it is to work on projects developing binary systems, e.g. collection of payment requests. Another possibility is writing of add-ons to existing information systems. A good solution can be extensions of information system of the university. The main conclusion from the projects that we have managed up to now [15] the proportion of the students that are able to supervise such project or its design, is smaller than 20%. We can hope for application of our proposal in start-ups as they are usually not burdened with existing practices but the problem is that most of their employees do – they are used to use object-oriented solutions and not the service-oriented ones (at least in the sense mentioned here).

6.2 Standards

The development of standards is a long-term process. It tends to standardize rather the practice of large companies. It implies that there are open questions regarding to standards applicable in document SOA.

The described approach can be often in conflict with existing standards. There are two main groups of issues:

1. The standards are so complex and interrelated with other standards that they cannot be fully implemented by a smaller group of people.
2. The standards were often based on existing (object-oriented) philosophy. Their authors usually did not take into account existing (human-based) solution, nor opportunities of service orientation.

7 Conclusions

Document-driven SOA enables a smooth digitalization of existing business processes in the sense of [8]. Document-driven SOA offers new opportunities for decomposition and integration of systems in the large. The principles can be easily adapted and also successfully used in the case of fine-grained documents in binary systems. It enables to reduce substantially the percentage of failed and challenged projects [24]. The education of students and training of IT experts must be tuned yet. The combinations of object orientation and service orientation must be studied yet.

The described approach is quite general. It can be used in the development of loosely coupled service-oriented systems. Its abilities seem to be very promising for design and implementation of the concept of Industry 4.0.

The results in practice (especially in development and maintenance of systems) are often dramatic. The savings are not in single percent grade. They are often in tens of percent.

8 Further Research

Crucial issue is a prejudice (antipattern) that digitalization of messages brings nothing substantial (compare service-oriented "What's New" Antipattern [2]). Document SOA enables substantial enhancement of the quality of software (like usability, stability, maintainability). Many opportunities are not still met. It holds especially management possibilities offered by attitudes discussed above.

The limits of the applicability of document SOA are not clear yet. Our practical experience shows that the principles of document SOA are well applicable in small information systems as well as in global systems (e.g. in Internet of Things). Our concept of documents seems to be too fine-grained for macroeconomy processes.

IT professionals provide many results in service science. It is open how much service science results are useful for our research of document SOA.

- It is not clear whether the characteristics of software quality from ISO 25010 can be used.
- It appears that services in the sense of service science do not tend to exchange documents.
- It is not clear what is a service in the sense of service science. It appears to be very similar to objects in object orientation.

Another open question is what background is best for people doing the integration. Our long-term practical experience shows that people well trained in object-oriented attitude do not want to work this way. They can be well used in making the integrated parts but not for the integration.

We want to focus in our further research to speeding up the transfer of the results of our research into practice and education.

References

1. Ackoff, R.L.: Towards a system of systems concepts. Manage. Sci. **17**(11), 661–671 (1971)
2. Ang, J., Cherbakov, L., Ibrahim, M.: SOA antipatterns, November 2005. http://www-128.ibm.com/developerworks/webservices/library/ws-antipatterns/
3. Boehm, B.W., Abts, C., Brown, A.W., Chulani, S., Clark, B.K., Horowitz, E., Madachy, R., Reifer, D., Steece, B.: Software Cost Estimation with COCOMO®II. Prentice Hall, Upper Saddle River (2000)
4. Bostrom, R.: A new information systems paradigm: What does a business analyst needs to know? (2012). http://www.modernanalyst.com/Resources/Articles/tabid/115/ID/2293/A-New-Information-Systems-Paradigm-What-does-a-Business-Analyst-Needs-to-Know.aspx
5. Brandon, J.: Why paper still rules the enterprise. CIO Magazine, January 2016. http://www.cio.com/article/3025928/printers/why-paper-still-rules-the-enterprise.html
6. Erl, T.: Service-Oriented Architecture: Concepts, Technology, and Design. Prentice Hall PTR, Upper Saddle River (2005)
7. Foster, M.: Case management part 1: An introduction (2013). http://www.ateam-oracle.com/case-management-part-1-an-introduction/
8. Golluscio, E., Pezzini, M.: Unleash DIY ctizen integration to enable digital business transformation (2011). https://www.gartner.com/doc/3184624/unleash-diy-citizen-integration-enable
9. International Organization for Standardization, International Electrotechnical Commission: ISO/IEC 25010: 2011 systems and software engineering - systems and software quality requirements and evaluation (SQuaRE) - system and software quality models (2011). https://www.iso.org/obp/ui/#iso:std:iso-iec:25010:ed-1:v1:en

10. Král, J.: Informační Systémy, (Information Systems, in Czech). Science, Veletiny, Czech Republic (1998)
11. Král, J., Žemlička, M.: Autonomous components. In: Hlaváč, V., Jeffery, K.G., Wiedermann, J. (eds.) SOFSEM 2000. LNCS, vol. 1963, pp. 375–383. Springer, Heidelberg (2000). doi:10.1007/3-540-44411-4_26
12. Král, J., Žemlička, M.: Component types in software conferations. In: Hamza, M.H. (ed.) Applied Informatics, pp. 125–130. ACTA Press, Anaheim (2002)
13. Král, J., Žemlička, M.: Software confederations - an architecture for global systems and global management. In: Kamel, S. (ed.) Managing Globally with Information Technology, pp. 57–81. Idea Group Publishing, Hershey (2003)
14. Král, J., Žemlička, M.: Service orientation and the quality indicators for software services. In: Trappl, R. (ed.) Cybernetics and Systems, vol. 2, pp. 434–439. Austrian Society for Cybernetic Studies, Vienna, Austria (2004)
15. Král, J., Žemlička, M.: Experience with real-life students' projects. In: Ganzha, M., Maciaszek, L., Paprzycki, M. (eds.) Proceedings of the 2014 Federated Conference on Computer Science and Information Systems. Annals of Computer Science and Information Systems, vol. 2, pp. 827–833. IEEE (2014). http://dx.doi.org/10.15439/2014F257
16. Král, J., Žemlička, M.: Simplifying maintenance by application of architectural services. In: Murgante, B., Misra, S., Rocha, A.M.A.C., Torre, C., Rocha, J.G., Falcão, M.I., Taniar, D., Apduhan, B.O., Gervasi, O. (eds.) ICCSA 2014. LNCS, vol. 8583, pp. 476–491. Springer, Cham (2014). doi:10.1007/978-3-319-09156-3_34
17. Král, J., Žemlička, M.: Novel software engineering attitudes for bussiness-oriented information systems. In: Gervasi, O., Murgante, B., Misra, S., Gavrilova, M.L., Rocha, A.M.A.C., Torre, C., Taniar, D., Apduhan, B.O. (eds.) ICCSA 2015. LNCS, vol. 9159, pp. 193–205. Springer, Cham (2015). doi:10.1007/978-3-319-21413-9_14
18. Kyusakov, R., Eliasson, J., Delsing, J., Van Deventer, J., Gustafsson, J.: Integration of wireless sensor and actuator nodes with IT infrastructure using service-oriented architecture. IEEE Trans. Industr. Inf. 9(1), 43–51 (2013). http://dx.doi.org/10.1109/TII.2012.2198655
19. Merali, Y., Papadopoulos, T., Nadkarni, T.: Information systems strategy: Past, present, future? J. Strateg. Inf. Syst. 21(2), 125–153 (2012). http://doi.org/10.1016/j.jsis.2012.04.002
20. Molnár, B., Benczúr, A.: Facet of modeling web information systems from a document-centric view. Int. J. Web Portals (IJWP) 5(4), 57–70 (2013)
21. Parnas, D.L.: Designing software for ease of extension and contraction. IEEE Trans. Softw. Eng. 5(2), 128–138 (1979). http://dx.doi.org/10.1109/TSE.1979.234169
22. Raymond, E.: The cathedral and the bazaar. Knowl. Technol. Policy 12(3), 23–49 (1999). http://dx.doi.org/10.1007/s12130-999-1026-0
23. Romero, D., Vernadat, F.: Enterprise information systems state of the art: Past, present and future trends. Comput. Ind. 79, 3–13 (2016). http://dx.doi.org/10.1016/j.compind.2016.03.001
24. Standish Group: Chaos manifesto 2013: Thing big, act small (2013). http://versionone.com/assets/img/files/haosManifesto2013.pdf. Accessed 28 Feb 2014
25. Weinberg, V.: Structured analysis. Prentice-Hall Software Series. Prentice-Hall, Englewood Cliffs (1980)
26. Yourdon, E.: Modern Structured Analysis, 2nd edn. Prentice-Hall, Englewood Cliffs (1988)

27. Žemlička, M., Král, J.: Software architecture and software quality. In: Gervasi, O., Murgante, B., Misra, S., Rocha, A.M.A.C.M.A.C., Torre, C.M.M., Taniar, D., Apduhan, B.O.O., Stankova, E., Wang, S. (eds.) ICCSA 2016. LNCS, vol. 9790, pp. 139–155. Springer, Cham (2016). doi:10.1007/978-3-319-42092-9_12

28. Žemlička, M., Král, J.: Flexible business-oriented service interfaces in information systems. In: Filipe, J., Maciaszek, L. (eds.) Proceedings of Enase 2014–9th International Conference on Evaluation of Novel Approaches to Software Engineering, pp. 164–171. SCITEPRESS - Science and Technology Publications (2014). http://ieeexplore.ieee.org/stamp/stamp.jsp?tp=&arnumber=7077131

Modeling Android Fragments and Activities Life Cycles Coordination

Mohamed A. El-Zawawy[1,2]([✉])

[1] College of Computer and Information Sciences, Al Imam Mohammad Ibn
Saud Islamic University (IMSIU), Riyadh, Kingdom of Saudi Arabia
[2] Department of Mathematics, Faculty of Science, Cairo University,
Giza 12613, Egypt
maelzawawy@cu.edu.eg

Abstract. One of the famous software packages for running smart
devices is Android. It is an operating system with middlewares and applications. Android runs most functioning mobile phone and tablet devices,
today. On the top of the stack describing the organization of different
parts of Android is the "applications" component. A main part of an
Android application is activity useful for interaction with users where
each activity can be realized as a single-frame user interface. An important tool for utilizing activities is that of fragment representing slices of
the interface of the activity. Activities and fragments have life cycles.

This paper presents an operational semantics for precisely and efficiently modeling the state transitions within life cycles of activities and
fragments. The semantics considers the effects of the transitions in both
life cycles on each other. Such semantics is necessary for precisely designing important static analyses for Android applications including fragment components.

Keywords: Android · Activities · Fragments · Operational semantics ·
Static analysis

1 Introduction

Android is a software package for running smart devices. Android is mainly an
operating system with main applications and middleware. Android is the operating system running most functioning mobile phone and tablet devices, today. On
the top of the stack describing the organization of different parts of Android is the
"applications" component. Android applications (written using Java) included in
Android are most necessary ones for devices to be useful enough. These applications include browser, e-mail client, contacts, SMS program, maps, and calendar
applications [1,5].

Four components are used in building Android applications: activities, services, content providers, and broadcast receivers. The user or the system may
interact with the application via any of these components which may depend on
each others. Main components to interact with users are activities where each

© Springer International Publishing AG 2017
O. Gervasi et al. (Eds.): ICCSA 2017, Part V, LNCS 10408, pp. 620–634, 2017.
DOI: 10.1007/978-3-319-62404-4_46

of which can be realized as a single-frame user interface. For example, a contact application would include an activity to present list of contacts and another activity to show details of a selected contact. Activities also enable main communications between applications and the system such as enabling the application recovering from the situation of a killed process by the system [1].

Activities have a life cycle composed of different states for activities. Activities transit through these states in response to the user actions of navigating through, leaving, and coming back to the application. Different callback methods are typically included in activity classes supporting state changes such as *creation, stopping, running,* or *destruction* [1].

An important tool for utilizing activities is that of fragment representing slices of the interface of the activity. Fragments are reusable in multiple activities and one activity can host multiple fragments to design a multi-pane UI. Therefore fragments are modular entities with their own life cycles. Fragments have high degree of independence from activities as they hold their input events and can be created or destroyed during the activity run time.

There is a direct effect by the life cycle of an activity on that of each fragment hosted by the activity. This effect has the form of calling a corresponding callback on the fragment when a callback is called for the hosting activity. Hence running the *onResume()* callback for an activity implies running the *onResume()* of each hosted fragment by the activity. It worth noting that a proper interaction between an activity and its hosted fragment requires fragments to have new callback methods that are not included in the life cycle of the activity. *onAttach(), onActivityCreated(),* and *onDetach()* are examples of these new callback methods [1]. The objective of this paper is to model the effect of activity life cycle on that of fragments using means of programming semantics.

This paper presents an operational semantics for precisely and efficiently modeling the effect of the activity life cycle on that of the fragments hosted by the activity. Such semantics is necessary for precisely designing important static analyses for Android applications including fragment components. The semantics proposed in this paper is necessary to model formally the way data are swapped between activities and fragments. Many critical application analyses are based on proper modeling of this swapping. Therefore, these analyses would need to be based on semantics like that presented in this paper. Verifying the content of *bundles* (objects used in communications between activities and fragments) is necessary to ensure correct interaction between fragments and activities. This verification can only be done by an analysis that models the interaction between activities and fragments such as the one presented in this paper.

Motivation

This paper is motivated by the need of an operational semantics to model state transitions of activities and fragments and their effects on each other. Such semantic would be useful to model effects of the following activity-class code that assigns the activity a fragment object (*gameLevelsFragments [GlobalVars.currentLevel]*):

```
FragmentManager fragmentManager =
    getSupportFragmentManager ();
FragmentTransaction fragmentTransaction =
    fragmentManager.beginTransaction ();
fragmentTransaction.add(android.R.id.content ,
    gameLevelsFragments [ GlobalVars.currentLevel ]);
fragmentTransaction.commit ();
```

Paper Outline

The rest of the paper is organized as follows. Section 2 presents the proposed semantics in several subsections. Semantic states, semantic rules for activities, and semantic rules for fragments are shown in Sects. 2.1, 2.2 and 2.3, respectively. Related and future work are discussed in Sect. 3.

2 Semantics

This section presents a precise operational semantics for the necessary coordination between states of life cycles of activities and their fragments in Android applications. Definition 1 presents possible states of activities and fragments in Android applications [5].

Definition 1. – *An activity can be in any of the following states:*

$$actState = \{constructor, onCreate, onStart, onRestart, onResume, running,$$
$$onPause, onStop, onDestroy\}.$$

– *A fragment can be in any of the following states:*

$$frgState = \{constructor, onCreate, onStart, onResume, running, onPause,$$
$$onStop, onDestroy, onAttach, onCreateView, onActivityCreated,$$
$$onDestroyView, onDetach\}.$$

The states of fragments are those of activities plus extra states accounting for the fact that fragments are hosted by activities. Different states transitions allowed during life cycles of activities and fragments in Android applications are presented in the following definition.

Definition 2. – *During the life cycle of an activity the state can change according to the following relationship on actState:*

$$actStateR = \{(constructor, onCreate), (onCreate, onStart), (onRestart,$$
$$onStart), (onStart, onResume), (onResume, running), (running, onPause),$$
$$(onPause, onResume), (onPause, onStop), (onStop, onRestart),$$
$$(onResume, onPause), (onStart, onStop), (onStop, onDestroy)\}.$$

- *During the life cycle of a fragment the state can change according to the following relationship on frgState:*

  frgStateR={(constructor, onAttach), (onAttach, onCreate), (onCreate, onCreateView), (onCreateView, onActivityCreated), (onActivityCreated, onStart), (onStart, onResume), (onResume, onPause), (onPause, onStop), (onStop, onDestroyView), (onDestroyView, onDestory), (onDestroyView, onCreateView), (onDestory, onDetach)}.

Transitions of fragments may be realized as a superset of that of activities due to the extra states fragments have. Each state is associated with a method executed upon reaching the state. These methods are named "callback methods".

2.1   Semantics States

Table 1 presents in details states of the semantic presented in this paper together with all components necessary to build the semantic states. Among the 200+ instructions used by the *Dalvik* virtual machine to run Android applications, Definition 3 presents main instructions considered in this paper.

Table 1. Semantics notations

Notations	Semantics
$l \in \mathcal{L}$	The set of all memory locations
$v \in \mathcal{V}$	The set of all values $= \mathbb{Z} \cup \mathcal{L}$
$a \in \mathcal{A}$	The set of all activities names
$f \in \mathcal{F}$	The set of all fragments names
$r \in \mathcal{A}r$	The set of all arrays names
$i \in DBIs$	The set of all considered Dalvik bytecode instructions
$p \in APs$	The set of all considered Android procedures
$b \in \mathcal{B}$	The set of all sequences (blocks of codes) over DBIs $\cup$ APs
$c \in \mathcal{C}$	The set of all classes names $= \mathcal{A} \cup \mathcal{F}$
$f_c \in \mathcal{F}_c$	The set of all fields of a class c
$o_c \in \mathcal{O}_c$	The set of all objects of class $c = \{o_c \mid o_c : \mathcal{F}_c \to \mathcal{V}\}$
$o \in \mathcal{O}$	The set of all objects $= \cup_{c \in \mathcal{C}} \mathcal{O}_c$
$re_n \in \mathcal{R}e_n$	The set of all n-arrays states $\{re_n \mid re_n : \{0, \ldots, n-1\} \to \mathbb{Z}\}$
$re \in \mathcal{R}e$	The set of all arrays states $= \cup_{n \in \mathbb{N}} \mathcal{R}e_n$
$a_{[]} \in \mathcal{A}_{[]}$	The set of all stacks of activities $\{[o_1; \ldots; o_n] \mid o_i \in \mathcal{O}_a \wedge a \in \mathcal{A}\}$
$s \in r\mathcal{S}$	The set of all register states $= \{s \mid s : \mathbb{N} \rightharpoonup \mathcal{V}\}$
$h \in \mathcal{H}$	The set of all heaps $= \{h \mid h : \mathcal{L} \rightharpoonup \mathcal{O} \cup \mathcal{R}e\}$
$d \in \mathcal{D}$	The set of Dalvik states $= \{(s, h, a_{[]}) \mid s \in r\mathcal{S} \wedge h \in \mathcal{H}, a_{[]} \in \mathcal{A}_{[]}\}$
$t \in \mathcal{T}$	The set of all types $= \mathcal{C} \cup \{int, void, int\ array\}$

Definition 3. *The set of Dalvik bytecode instructions (DBIs) include the following main instructions:*

$$\{nop;\ const\ i,v;\ move\ i,j;\ goto\ \delta;\ new\text{-}array\ i,j,t;$$

$$array\text{-}length\ i,j;\ aget\ i,j,k;\ aput\ i,j,k;\ new\text{-}instance\ i,c;$$

$$iget\ i,j,f;\ iput\ i,j,f;\ invoke\text{-}direct\ m(i_1,\ldots,i_n);$$

$$neg\text{-}int\ i,j;\ add\ i,j,k;\ if\text{-}eq\ i,j,k;\ if\text{-}eqz\ i,j;\ return\ i;\ return\ void\}$$

The formal effect of DBIs on elements of the set of Dalvik states $\mathcal{D}$ (Table 1) is straightforward and can be built with the guidance of [6,14]. These effects on the Dalvik states are restricted to the stack and heap components of the states and do not affect the activity stacks components. We let the binary relation on $\mathcal{D}$ capturing the semantics of DBIs denoted by $\rightrightarrows$. Hence for every $i \in DBIs$ and $(s,h,a_{[]}) \in \mathcal{D}$ either there is $(s',h',a_{[]}) \in \mathcal{D}$ such that $i : (s,h,a_{[]}) \rightrightarrows (s',h',a_{[]})$ or $i : (s,h,a_{[]}) \rightrightarrows abort$. We let *return* denotes any of the *return* instructions: *return i* and *return void*.

Formal definitions of activities and fragments as classes are presented in the following definition.

Definition 4. *– An activity is a class that extends the standard class "App-CompatActivity". We assume that an activity class include the following fields:*

- *layout: contains the activity view structure with addresses of different activity views.*
- *finished: states whether the activity has finished.*
- *backStack: a stack of addresses of fragment objects currently running on the activity.*
- *aFreg: the address of the current active fragment of the activity if any. This field has the value −1 when there is no active fragment in the activity.*
- *status: the state of the activity (running, onPause, onStop,...).*

– A fragment is a class that extends the standard class "Fragment". We assume that a fragment class include the following fields:

- *layout: contains the fragment view structure with addresses of different fragment views.*
- *finished: states whether the fragment has finished.*
- *parent: address of the activity hosting the fragment.*
- *status: the status of the fragment (running, onPause, onStop,...).*

Example 1. – An example of a register state is $s_1 \in r\mathcal{S}$ is defined as $s_1 = \{0 \mapsto l_1, 1 \mapsto l_2, 2 \mapsto l_3\}$.
– An example of a heap $h_1 \in \mathcal{H}$ is defined as follows: $h_1 = \{(l_1,o_1), (l_2,o_2),(l_3,o_3)\}$, where:
1. $o_1.class = A_1$, $o_2.class = A_2$, and $\{A_1,A_2\} \subseteq \mathcal{A}$.
2. $o_3.class = F_1$, and $F_1 \in \mathcal{F}$.
3. We assume all the callback methods of the activities and fragments classes on this example are empty unless specific definitions are given.

4. $o_1 = \{f \mapsto 1,\ backStack \mapsto [],\ aFrag \mapsto -1,\ status \mapsto onCreate\}$.
5. $o_2 = \{f \mapsto 2,\ backStack \mapsto [],\ aFrag \mapsto -1,\ status \mapsto onDestory\}$.
6. $o_3 = \{f \mapsto 3,\ parent \mapsto -1,\ status \mapsto constructor\}$.

- $a_{[]}^1 = [l_1; l_2]$.
- The components $(s, h, a_{[]})$ defined above provide an example of a Dalvik state. The state represents an application with two activities and one fragment.

We assume that each object has a field "class" that defines the object's class. We also assume that the following registers are reserved for holding special values:

- Register number r is reserved for holding the result of the latest method call. The content of this register is -1 in case the latest call returns nothing. Therefore the instruction *return i* is semantically equivalent to the instruction *move* r,i. Also the instruction *return-void* is semantically equivalent to the instruction *const* r,-1.
- Register number t is reserved for holding the address of the currently active object. When no activity is active, the value in t is -1.

Among the Android set of procedures, the focus in this paper is on the set defined in Definition 5. These Android procedures are the most necessary ones to formalize precisely the semantics of coordination between activities and fragments in Android applications.

Definition 5. *The set of Android Procedures (APs) includes:*

1. *startActivity(Activity class object ref l); this method starts running the activity object at reference l. This mainly involves invoking the onCreate method of that activity (Fig. 1 – Rule 1).*
2. *fragmentTransaction.add(Activity class object l_1, Fragment class object l_2); this method links a fragment object at reference l_2 with an activity object at reference l_1. This is modeled in Rule 2 (Fig. 1).*
3. *fragmentTransaction.commit(Activity class object l_1, Fragment class object l_2); this method runs the fragment at reference l_2 within the activity at reference l_1.*
4. *findViewById(view, i); this method search for the reference of a view whose id is in register i.*
5. *inflater.inflate(Activity class object ref l_1, Fragment class object ref l_2);*
6. *setContentView(Activity class object ref l, layout);*
7. *finish;*

Formal semantics and effects of commands of Definition 5 are presented on the semantic states in Fig. 1.

Definition 6. *A block of code (b) is a sequence of DBIs and APs:*

$$b \in \mathcal{B} ::= i \mid p \mid b; b$$

The semantics of composition is defined as usual:

$$\frac{b_1 : (s, h, a_{[]}) \Rightarrow (s'', h'', a_{[]}'') \qquad b_2 : (s'', h'', a_{[]}'') \Rightarrow (s', h', a_{[]}')}{b_1; b_2 : (s, h, a_{[]}) \Rightarrow (s', h', a_{[]}')} \tag{9}$$

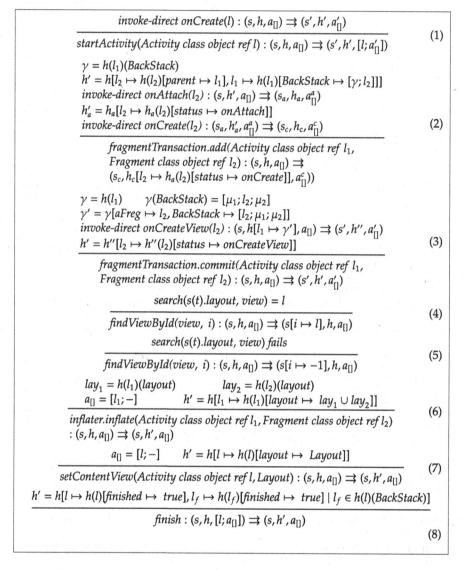

Fig. 1. Semantics rules of the Android procedures presented in Definition 5.

2.2   Activities Life Cycle Transitions with Consideration for Hosted Fragments Life Cycles

Figures 2 and 3 show the semantics of changing activities states during their life cycles. In these rules the effects of the transitions on fragments hosted by the activity are considered. Rule 10 models the situation when the active activity loses focus and no other activity becomes active. Rule 12 captures the action of changing the active activity (which has the focus). We assume that after

$$aRemove : (s, h, [l; a_{[]}]) \Rrightarrow (s, h, a_{[]}) \tag{10}$$

$$aActivation : (s, h, [a_{[]}; l; a'_{[]}]) \Rrightarrow (s, h, [l; a_{[]}; a'_{[]}]) \tag{11}$$

$$aDeActivation : (s, h, [l; a_{[]}; a'_{[]}]) \Rrightarrow (s, h, [a_{[]}; l; a'_{[]}]) \tag{12}$$

$$\frac{\text{the application user did an action Act} \quad a_{[]} = [l; -]}{\text{invoke-direct onActListner}(l) : (s, h, a_{[]}) \Rrightarrow (s', h', a'_{[]})}$$

$$aListner() : (s, h, a_{[]}) \Rrightarrow (s', h', a'_{[]}) \tag{13}$$

$$\begin{aligned}
&a_{[]} = [l] \quad (\xi, \xi') = (running, onPause) \\
&h(l)(status) = \xi \qquad \xi'(l) : (s, h, a_{[]}) \Rrightarrow (s', h', a'_{[]}) \\
&(s_1, h_1, a_{[]}^1) = (s', h'[l \mapsto h'(l)[status \mapsto \xi']], a'_{[]}) \\
&h(l)(BackStack) = [l_1, \ldots, l_n] \\
&\forall i. \begin{cases} \xi'(l_i) : (s_i, h_i, a_{[]}^i) \Rrightarrow (s_{i+1}, h_{i+1}, a_{[]}^{i+1}), h(l_i)(status) = \xi; \\ (s_i, h_i, a_{[]}^i) = (s_{i+1}, h_{i+1}, a_{[]}^{i+1}), \quad\quad otherwise. \end{cases}
\end{aligned} \tag{14}$$

$$aStopping_1 : (s, h, a_{[]}) \Rrightarrow$$
$$(s_{n+1}, h_{n+1}[l_i \mapsto h_{n+1}(l_i)[status \mapsto \xi'] \mid 1 \le i \le n \wedge h(l_i)(status) = \xi], a_{[]}^{n+1})$$

$$\frac{a_{[]} = [l; a'_{[]}] \quad h(l).finished = true \quad h(l).status = onDestroy}{aFinished : (s, h, a_{[]}) \Rrightarrow (s, h, a'_{[]})} \tag{15}$$

$$\begin{aligned}
&a_{[]} = [l; -] \quad (\xi, \xi') \in \{(running, onPause), (onPause, onStop)\} \\
&h(l)(finished) = true \quad h(l)(status) = \xi \quad \xi'(l) : (s, h, a_{[]}) \Rrightarrow (s', h', a'_{[]}) \\
&(s_1, h_1, a_{[]}^1) = (s', h'[l \mapsto h'(l)[status \mapsto \xi']], a'_{[]}) \quad h(l)(BackStack) = [l_1, \ldots, l_n] \\
&\forall i. \begin{cases} \xi'(l_i) : (s_i, h_i, a_{[]}^i) \Rrightarrow (s_{i+1}, h_{i+1}, a_{[]}^{i+1}), h(l_i)(status) = \xi; \\ (s_i, h_i, a_{[]}^i) = (s_{i+1}, h_{i+1}, a_{[]}^{i+1}), \quad\quad otherwise. \end{cases}
\end{aligned} \tag{16}$$

$$aStopping_2 : (s, h, a_{[]}) \Rrightarrow$$
$$(s_{n+1}, h_{n+1}[l_i \mapsto h_{n+1}(l_i)[status \mapsto \xi'] \mid 1 \le i \le n \wedge h(l_i)(status) = \xi], a_{[]}^{n+1})$$

Fig. 2. Formal semantics for activities life cycle transitions (part 1).

executing the last instruction in a block of code the system is in *ideal* status. The system leaves the ideal status to response to an action of the user (such as a mouse click). This is presented in Rule 13.

Example 2. The semantics of executing the command

$$fragmentTransaction.add(l_1, l_3);$$

on the state $(s_1, h_1, a_{[]}^1)$ of Example 1 results (by applying Rule 2) in the state $(s_2, h_2, a_{[]}^2)$ where $s_2 = s_1, a_{[]}^1 = a_{[]}^2, h_2 = h_1[l_1 \mapsto o'_1, l_3 \mapsto o'_3]$ and:

- $o'_1 = \{f \mapsto 1, \; backStack \mapsto [l_3], \; aFrag \mapsto -1, \; status \mapsto onCreate\}$.
- $o'_3 = \{f \mapsto 3, \; parent \mapsto l_1, \; status \mapsto onCreate\}$.

$$\frac{a_{[]} = [l; -] \quad h(l)(BackStack) = [l_1, \ldots, l_n] \quad h(l)(status) = onResume \quad h' = h[l \mapsto h(l)[finished \mapsto true], l_j \mapsto h(l_j)[finished \mapsto true] \mid 1 \leq j \leq n]}{aPressBack : (s, h, a_{[]}) \Rrightarrow (s, h', a_{[]})} \quad (17)$$

$$\frac{\begin{array}{l} a_{[]} = [l; a'_{[]}] \quad h(l)(status) = onDestroy \quad s'' = s \quad h'' = h[l' \mapsto o] \\ o \text{ is a new object of class } h(l).class \text{ at the fresh memory location } l' \\ \text{The backstack of } o \text{ is similar to that of } h(l') \quad h''(l')(BackStack) = [l_1, \ldots, l_n] \\ constructor(l') : (s'', h'', [l'; a'_{[]}]) \Rrightarrow (s_1, h_1, a^1_{[]}) \\ \forall i. \ constructor(l_i) : (s_i, h_i, a^i_{[]}) \Rrightarrow (s_{i+1}, h_{i+1}, a^{i+1}_{[]}) \end{array}}{aResize : (s, h, a_{[]}) \Rrightarrow (s_{n+1}, h_{n+1}, a^{n+1}_{[]})} \quad (18)$$

$$\frac{\begin{array}{l} a_{[]} = [l] \quad (\xi, \xi') = (running, onDestroy) \\ h(l)(status) = \xi \quad \xi'(l) : (s, h, a_{[]}) \Rrightarrow (s', h', a'_{[]}) \\ (s_1, h_1, a^1_{[]}) = (s', h'[l \mapsto h'(l)[status \mapsto \xi']], a'_{[]}) \\ h(l)(BackStack) = [l_1, \ldots, l_n] \\ \forall i. \ \begin{cases} onDestroyView(l_i) : (s_i, h_i, a^i_{[]}) \Rrightarrow (s_{i+1}, h_{i+1}, a^{i+1}_{[]}), \ h(l_i)(status) = \xi; \\ (s_i, h_i, a^i_{[]}) = (s_{i+1}, h_{i+1}, a^{i+1}_{[]}), \quad\quad\quad\quad otherwise. \end{cases} \end{array}}{aStopping_3 : (s, h, a_{[]}) \Rrightarrow (s_{n+1}, H, a^{n+1}_{[]});} \quad (19)$$

$$H = h_{n+1}[l_i \mapsto h_{n+1}(l_i)[status \mapsto onDestroyView] \mid 1 \leq i \leq n \wedge h(l_i)(status) = \xi]$$

$$\frac{a_{[]} = [l; a'_{[]}] \quad h(l)(status) = onDestroy \quad h' = h \setminus \{(l, h(l))\} \quad h(l)(finished) = true}{aRemove : (s, h, a_{[]}) \Rrightarrow (s, h', a'_{[]})} \quad (20)$$

Fig. 3. Formal semantics for activities life cycle transitions (part 2).

Example 3. Suppose that the class F_1 of the object o_3 (of Example 1) has the following definition for the callback method *onCreateView (object reference l)*:

```
onCreateView (object reference l): void
.registers 2
const v1,20;
iput v1,v0,f;
return-void;
```

The semantics of executing the commands

$$fragmentTransaction.commit(l_1, l_3);$$

on the state $(s_2, h_2, a^2_{[]})$ of Example 2 results (by applying Rule 3) in the state $(s_3, h_3, a^3_{[]})$ where $s_3 = s_2, a^3_{[]} = a^2_{[]}, h_3 = h_2[l_1 \mapsto o'_1, l_3 \mapsto o'_3]$ and:

- $o'_1 = \{f \mapsto 1, \ backStack \mapsto [l_3], \ \underline{aFrag \mapsto l_3}, \ status \mapsto onCreate\}$.
- $o'_3 = \{f \mapsto 20, \ parent \mapsto l_1, \ \underline{status \mapsto onCreateView}\}$.

We now assume that the system runs the following callback methods

$$onActivityCreated(l_3); \ onStart(l_1); \ onStart(l_3); \ onResume(l_1); \ onResume(l_3);$$

Then we will have

$-\ o'_1 = \{f \mapsto 1,\ backStack \mapsto [l_3],\ aFrag \mapsto l_3,\ \underline{status \mapsto onResume}\}.$

$-\ o'_3 = \{\underline{f \mapsto 20},\ parent \mapsto l_1,\ \underline{status \mapsto onResume}\}.$

Example 4. Suppose that the class A_1 of the object o_1 (of Example 1) has a method *onPause (object reference l)* whose definition is as follows:

```
onPause (object reference l): void
.registers 2
const v1,30;
iput v1,v0,f;
return-void;
```

Now suppose that another activity rather than o_1 comes into the foreground, hence the status of o_1 changes to *onPause*. This action can be modeled by running Rule 8 followed by Rule 16 on the state $(s_3, h_3, a^3_{[]})$ of Example 3. The result would be the state $(s_4, h_4, a^4_{[]})$ where $s_4 = s_3, a^3_{[]} = a^3_{[]}, h_4 = h_3[l_1 \mapsto o'_1, l_3 \mapsto o'_3]$ and

$-\ o'_1 = \{\underline{f \mapsto 30},\ \underline{finished \mapsto true},\ backStack \mapsto [l_3],\ aFrag \mapsto l_3,\ \underline{status \mapsto onPause}\}.$

$-\ o'_3 = \{f \mapsto 20,\ \underline{finished \mapsto true},\ parent \mapsto l_1,\ \underline{status \mapsto onPause}\}.$

We now assume that the system runs the following callback methods

$$onStop(l_1);\ onStop(l_3);\ onDestory(l_1);\ onDestroyView(l_3);$$

Then we will have

$-\ o'_1 = \{\underline{f \mapsto 30},\ \underline{finished \mapsto true},\ backStack \mapsto [l_3],\ aFrag \mapsto l_3,\ \underline{status \mapsto onDestroy}\}.$

$-\ o'_3 = \{f \mapsto 20,\ \underline{finished \mapsto true},\ parent \mapsto l_1,\ \underline{status \mapsto onDestroyView}\}.$

In case an activity is the only one in the application ($|img(aF)| = 1$), Rule 14 formalizes the transition from *running* state to *onPause* one (γ'). In this case each fragment of the activity (with address in *fList*) must receive *onPause* as well (γ'). Rule 17 models hitting the back button while the activity is running. Rule 16 is similar to Rule 14 but the move happens in case the activity is indicated as finished ($h(s(t)).finished = true$). Rule 19 is similar to Rule 16 except that when the activity transits to the *onDestroy* state each of its hosted fragments must transit to *onDestroyView* state. In case the current activity (pointed to by $s(t)$) is finished and has executed *onDestroy* then Rule 20 removes the address of this activity from the stack of current activities (aF). The system may need to recreate the current active activity due to many reasons (including a change of the screen orientation). This is modeled by Rule 18.

2.3 Fragments Life Cycle Transitions with Coordination for Hosting Activities Life Cycles

Figures 4 and 5 show the semantics of changing fragments states during their life cycles. In these rules the effects of the transitions on hosting activities are considered. Rule 21 models the situation when the active fragment of the activity loses focus and no other fragment becomes active. Rule 22 captures the action of changing the active fragment of the active activity. Rule 23 is the fragment counterpart of Rule 13. All the rules in this section apply when the currently active object is a fragment i.e. when $h(s(t)).class$ is a fragment class.

$$\frac{a_{[]} = [l;-] \quad l_f = h(l)(aFrag) \quad h' = h[l \mapsto h(l)[aFrag \mapsto -1]]}{fDeActivation : (s,h,a_{[]}) \Rrightarrow (s,h',a_{[]})} \quad (21)$$

$$\frac{a_{[]} = [l;-] \quad h(l_f)(BackStack) = [\gamma_1; l'_f; \gamma_2]}{fActivation : (s,h,a_{[]}) \Rrightarrow (s,h',a_{[]})} \quad (22)$$

with $h' = h[l \mapsto h(l)[aFrag \mapsto l'_f, BackStack \mapsto [l'_f; \gamma_1; \gamma_2]]]$

$$\frac{\begin{array}{c} a_{[]} = [l;-] \quad l_f = h(l)(aFrag) \\ \text{the application user did action Action} \\ onActionListner(l_f) : (s,h,a_{[]}) \Rrightarrow (s',h',a'_{[]}) \end{array}}{fListner : (s,h,a_{[]}) \Rrightarrow (s',h',a'_{[]})} \quad (23)$$

$$\frac{\begin{array}{c} a_{[]} = [l;-] \quad l_f \in h(l)(BackStack) \quad (\gamma,\gamma') \in \{(constructor, onAttach), \\ (onAttach, onCreate),(onCreate, onCreateView),(onCreateView, onActivityCreated)\} \\ h(l_f)(status) = \gamma \quad h(l)(status) = onCreate \\ h(l_f).\gamma' : (s,h,a_{[]}) \Rrightarrow (s',h'',a'_{[]}) \quad h' = h''[l_f \mapsto h(l_f)[status \mapsto \gamma']] \end{array}}{fCreation : (s,h,a_{[]}) \Rrightarrow (s',h',a'_{[]})} \quad (24)$$

$$\frac{\begin{array}{c} a_{[]} = [l;-] \quad l_f \in h(l)(BackStack) \quad (\gamma,\gamma') = (onActivityCreated, onStart) \\ h(l_f).status = \gamma \quad h(l)(status) = onStart \quad h(l_f).\gamma' : (s,h,a_{[]}) \Rrightarrow (s',h'',a'_{[]}) \\ h' = h''[l_f \mapsto h(l_f)[status \mapsto \gamma']] \end{array}}{fStart : (s,h,a_{[]}) \Rrightarrow (s',h',a'_{[]})} \quad (25)$$

$$\frac{\begin{array}{c} a_{[]} = [l;-] \quad l_f \in h(l)(BackStack) \quad (\gamma,\gamma') \in \{(onStop, onDestroyView), \\ (onDestroyView, onDestory),(onDestory, onDetach)\} \\ h(l_f)(status) = \gamma \quad h(l)(status) = onDetach \\ h(l_f).\gamma' : (s,h,a_{[]}) \Rrightarrow (s',h'',a'_{[]}) \quad h' = h''[l_f \mapsto h(l_f)[status \mapsto \gamma']] \end{array}}{fStopping : (s,h,a_{[]}) \Rrightarrow (s',h',a'_{[]})} \quad (26)$$

$$\frac{\begin{array}{c} a_{[]} = [l;-] \quad l_f \in h(l)(BackStack) \quad l_f \neq h(l)(aFrag) \\ h(l_f)(finished) = true \quad h(l_f)(status) = onDetach \\ [l_f; BS'] = h(l)(Backstack) \quad h' = h[l \mapsto h(l)[BackStack \mapsto BS']] \end{array}}{fRemove : (s,h,a_{[]}) \Rrightarrow (s,h',a_{[]})} \quad (27)$$

Fig. 4. Formal semantics for fragments moves relative to activities (part 1).

$$a_{[]} = [l; -] \qquad l_f \in h(l)(BackStack) \qquad (\gamma, \gamma') = (onStart, onResume)$$
$$h(l_f)(status) = \gamma \qquad h(l)(status) = onResume$$
$$h(l_f).\gamma' : (s, h, a_{[]}) \rightrightarrows (s', h'', a'_{[]}) \qquad h' = h''[l_f \mapsto h(l_f)[status \mapsto \gamma']] \qquad (28)$$

$$\overline{fOnResume : (s, h, a_{[]}) \rightrightarrows (s', h', a'_{[]})}$$

$$a_{[]} = [l; -] \qquad l_f \in h(l)(BackStack) \qquad h(l_f)(status) = onResume$$
$$h' = h[l_f \mapsto h(l_f)[finished \mapsto true]] \qquad (29)$$

$$\overline{fFinish : (s, h, a_{[]}) \rightrightarrows (s, h', a_{[]})}$$

$$a_{[]} = [l; -] \qquad l_f \in h(l)(BackStack) \qquad (\gamma, \gamma') = (onResume, onPause)$$
$$h(l_f)(status) = \gamma \qquad h(l)(status) = onPause \qquad l_f \neq h(l)(aFrag)$$
$$h(l_f).\gamma' : (s, h, a_{[]}) \rightrightarrows (s', h'', a'_{[]}) \qquad h' = h''[l_f \mapsto h(l_f)[status \mapsto \gamma']] \qquad (30)$$

$$\overline{fOnPause : (s, h, a_{[]}) \rightrightarrows (s', h', a'_{[]})}$$

$$a_{[]} = [l; -] \qquad l_f \in h(l)(BackStack) \qquad h(l_f)(status) = onDestroy$$
$$o \text{ is a new object of class } h(l_f).class \text{ at the fresh memory location } l'$$
$$h'' = h[l' \mapsto o, BackStack \mapsto BackStack.remove(l_f).addTop(l')]]$$
$$h(l)(aFrag) = l_f \Rightarrow h'' = h''(l)[aFrag \mapsto l']] \qquad (31)$$
$$l'.constructor : (s, h'', a_{[]}) \rightrightarrows (s', h', a'_{[]})$$

$$\overline{fResize : (s, h, a_{[]}) \rightrightarrows (s', h', a'_{[]})}$$

$$a_{[]} = [l; -] \qquad l_f \in h(l)(BackStack) \qquad (\gamma, \gamma') = (onPause, onStop)$$
$$h(l)(status) = onStop \qquad h(l_f)(status) = \gamma \qquad l_f \neq h(l)(aFrag)$$
$$h(l_f).\gamma' : (s, h, a_{[]}) \rightrightarrows (s', h'', a'_{[]}) \qquad h' = h''[l_f \mapsto h(l_f)[status \mapsto \gamma']] \qquad (32)$$

$$\overline{fOnStop : (s, h, a_{[]}) \rightrightarrows (s', h', a'_{[]})}$$

Fig. 5. Formal semantics for fragments moves relative to activities (part 2).

Rule 24 expresses the fact that a fragment can do any of the state changes specified in the rule only if the hosting activity was created. This is specified in the rule by the condition: $h(l).parent.status = onCreate$. Rule 26 is similar to Rule 24 and it expresses the fact that a fragment can do any of the state changes specified in the rule only if the hosting activity was destroyed. This is specified in the rule by the condition: $h(s(t)).parent.status = onDestroy$. Rule 25, stresses that a fragment can transit to *onStart* state only if its hosting activity has already done the same. Rules 28, 30, and 32 are similar to 25. In case the current active object is a fragment, it is finished, and has executed the callback method *onDestroy* ($h(s(t)).finished = true$ and $h(s(t)).status = onDestroy$), then Rule 27 removes the fragment from the list of the parent object (which is an activity). Rule 29 models hitting the back button while the fragment is running. The system may need to recreate the current active fragment due to recreating the hosting activity. This is modeled by Rule 31.

Example 5. Suppose that the class F of the object o_3 (of Example 1) has the following definition for the callback method *onDestroy (object reference l)*:

```
onDestroy (object reference l): void
```

```
.registers 2
const v1,-1;
iput v1,v0,f;
return-void;
```

Now suppose that the system changes the status of the fragment o_3 of Example 4 to *onDestroy*. This action can be modeled by running Rule 26 on the state $(s_4, h_4, a_{[]}^4)$ of Example 4. The result would be the state $(s_5, h_5, a_{[]}^5)$ where $s_5 = s_4, a_{[]}^4 = a_{[]}^4, h_5 = h_4[l_3 \mapsto o_3']$ and

$$o_3' = \{f \mapsto -1, \text{ finished} \mapsto \text{true}, \text{ parent} \mapsto l_1, \underline{\text{status} \mapsto \text{onDestroy}}\}.$$

A simple structural induction on the syntax of blocks of codes proves the following theorems.

Theorem 1. *(Preservation) If $(s, h, a_{[]})$ is a well-formed Dalvik state and $X : (s, h, a_{[]}) \rightrightarrows (s', h', a_{[]}')$ using the semantic rules defined above, then $(s', h', a_{[]}')$ is a well-formed Dalvik state.*

Theorem 2. *(Progress) Suppose that $\delta = (s, h, a_{[]})$ is a well-formed Dalvik state. Then δ is a stuck one or there is a well-formed Dalvik state $\delta' = (s', h', a_{[]}')$ such that $X : (s, h, a_{[]}) \rightrightarrows (s', h', a_{[]}')$ using the semantic rules defined above.*

3   Related and Future Work

This section presents the work on Android systems that are most related to the work presented in this paper. There are two types of the reviewed work. The first type is analyses techniques (like taint analysis) that can be formally supported using the semantics presented in our paper [2,3,11,12,16]. The second type is formal techniques like the one presented in our paper. However almost all type two techniques do not account for fragments and their relationship to activities [6,7,10,15].

Operational semantics for android activities is proposed in [14]. The semantics treats Dalvik bytecode and models mechanisms for inter-component communication within applications. The objective in the paper is to provide a formal framework for verifying static analyses techniques of Android applications. However [14] does not provide a model for fragments and their relationship to activities.

A symbolic simulator, SymDroid, that simulates operating on Dalvik bytecode was proposed in [13]. SymDroid uses 16 instructions (of the language μ-Dalvik) to simulate the 200+ instructions of Dalvik. A formalism for this symbolic simulator using operational semantics is also presented in this paper. However, this work does not consider the interaction between fragment and activities life cycles. An operational semantics to formally studying Android security is presented in [4]. Similarly to our strategy, [4] proposes and uses a typed language for denoting Android applications. The purpose in [4] is to reason about applications security-issues related to data-flow.

The work in [17], proposes a malware analysis, DroidScope, that is visualization-based. This analysis establishes both the Java and Android semantics simultaneously. Besides other APIs, DroidScope manipulates the Dalvik Virtual Machine. DroidScope uses taint analysis and gathered traces of Dalvik commands and profile activity to report information drainage.

Another realtime analysis is TaintDroid proposed in [8] as a realtime taint analysis for simultaneously monitoring several repositories of data. One advantage of TaintDroid over related analyses is that it incurs tolerable overhead for most cases. For Android applications, another taint analysis, FLOWDROID, is presented in [2]. This system models life cycles for manipulating callbacks. This analysis is field, flow, context, and object-sensitive.

One direction for extending work presented in this paper is utilizing the formalism presented in the paper to develop formal security models [9]. Therefore the objective would be to develop the system of the current paper so that an Android applications will have a semantics-judgment in the system if and only if the application has no data leakage problems.

References

1. Android developers. http://developer.android.com
2. Arzt, S., Rasthofer, S., Fritz, C., Bodden, E., Bartel, A., Klein, J., Le Traon, Y., Octeau, D., McDaniel, P.: Flowdroid: precise context, flow, field, object-sensitive and lifecycle-aware taint analysis for android apps. ACM SIGPLAN Not. **49**(6), 259–269 (2014)
3. Burguera, I., Zurutuza, U., Nadjm-Tehrani, S.: Crowdroid: behavior-based malware detection system for android. In: Proceedings of the 1st ACM Workshop on Security and Privacy in Smartphones and Mobile Devices, pp. 15–26. ACM (2011)
4. Chaudhuri, A.: Language-based security on android. In: Proceedings of the ACM SIGPLAN Fourth Workshop on Programming Languages and Analysis for Security, pp. 1–7. ACM (2009)
5. Android Developers. What is android (2011)
6. El-Zawawy, M.A.: An operational semantics for android applications. In: Gervasi, O., et al. (eds.) ICCSA 2016, Part V. LNCS, vol. 9790, pp. 100–114. Springer, Cham (2016). doi:10.1007/978-3-319-42092-9_9
7. El-Zawawy, M.A.: A type system for android applications. In: Gervasi, O., et al. (eds.) ICCSA 2016, Part V. LNCS, vol. 9790, pp. 115–128. Springer, Cham (2016). doi:10.1007/978-3-319-42092-9_10
8. Enck, W., Gilbert, P., Han, S., Tendulkar, V., Chun, B.-G., Cox, L.P., Jung, J., McDaniel, P., Sheth, A.N.: Taintdroid: an information-flow tracking system for realtime privacy monitoring on smartphones. ACM Trans. Comput. Syst. (TOCS) **32**(2), 5 (2014)
9. Enck, W., Ongtang, M., McDaniel, P.: Understanding android security. IEEE Secur. Priv. **7**(1), 50–57 (2009)
10. Farzan, A., Chen, F., Meseguer, J., Roşu, G.: Formal analysis of java programs in JavaFAN. In: Alur, R., Peled, D.A. (eds.) CAV 2004. LNCS, vol. 3114, pp. 501–505. Springer, Heidelberg (2004). doi:10.1007/978-3-540-27813-9_46
11. Felt, A.P., Chin, E., Hanna, S., Song, D., Wagner, D.: Android permissions demystified. In: Proceedings of the 18th ACM Conference on Computer and Communications Security, pp. 627–638. ACM (2011)

12. Gibler, C., Crussell, J., Erickson, J., Chen, H.: AndroidLeaks: automatically detecting potential privacy leaks in android applications on a large scale. In: Katzenbeisser, S., Weippl, E., Camp, L.J., Volkamer, M., Reiter, M., Zhang, X. (eds.) Trust 2012. LNCS, vol. 7344, pp. 291–307. Springer, Heidelberg (2012). doi:10.1007/978-3-642-30921-2_17

13. Jeon, J., Micinski, K.K., Foster, J.S.: Symdroid: Symbolic execution for dalvik bytecode. Technical report (2012)

14. Payet, E., Spoto, F.: An operational semantics for android activities. In: Proceedings of the ACM SIGPLAN 2014 Workshop on Partial Evaluation and Program Manipulation, pp. 121–132. ACM (2014)

15. Spreitzenbarth, M., Freiling, F., Echtler, F., Schreck, T., Hoffmann, J.: Mobile-sandbox: having a deeper look into android applications. In: Proceedings of the 28th Annual ACM Symposium on Applied Computing, pp. 1808–1815. ACM (2013)

16. Wu, D.-J., Mao, C.-H., Wei, T.-E., Lee, H.-M., Wu, K.-P.: Droidmat: android malware detection through manifest and API calls tracing. In: 2012 Seventh Asia Joint Conference on Information Security (Asia JCIS), pp. 62–69. IEEE (2012)

17. Yan, L.-K., Yin, H.: Droidscope: seamlessly reconstructing the os and dalvik semantic views for dynamic android malware analysis. In: USENIX Security Symposium, pp. 569–584 (2012)

An Approach for Modularizing Gamification Concerns

Eduardo M. Guerra[1], Gabriel Fornari[1], Wanderson S. Costa[1],
Sandy M. Porto[1], Marcos P.L. Candia[1,2], and Tiago Silva da Silva[2]([✉])

[1] Instituto Nacional de Pesquisas Espaciais - INPE, São José Dos Campos, SP, Brazil
[2] Universidade Federal de São Paulo - UNIFESP, São José Dos Campos, SP, Brazil
silvadasilva@unifesp.br

Abstract. This paper proposes the implementation of Esfinge Gamification framework to modularize the gamification concerns within an application. We carried out a qualitative study to develop a prototype for a classification system of transient luminous events in order to evaluate the proposed approach with regards to the identification of the dependencies that are necessary to instantiate such framework, evaluating the resulting coupling. From the use of a Dependency Structure Matrix, it was shown that Esfinge Gamification does not rely on any information related to the domain-specific application, except in the category of recovering points. Based on that, it is possible to conclude that the framework was able to modularize the gamification features, having dependencies only for configuration and to retrieve gamification data.

Keywords: Java · Code annotation · Metadata · Gamification · Framework

1 Introduction

Combining game elements with non-game applications in a systematic and experiential way has rapidly gained a substantial amount of attention after the second half of 2010. This term was dubbed as gamification and it can be used as a means of enhancing the social interaction and user participation and motivation in execution of several tasks that usually could not be attractive [13]. For example, the success of mobile applications such as Nike+ and Foursquare are often attributed to gamification [24].

Considering the implementation of such applications, the gamification adds an additional complexity in the regular functionality. In other words, in addition to execute the regular functionality, the application should also compute what that action means for gamification logic, such as add points, raise ranks or give trophies. It is important to highlight that it can have complex conditions and triggers. This gamification logic can be considered orthogonal to the application logic. However, most application still embedded gamification concerns into the regular application code. That practice can generate bad consequences for the

© Springer International Publishing AG 2017
O. Gervasi et al. (Eds.): ICCSA 2017, Part V, LNCS 10408, pp. 635–651, 2017.
DOI: 10.1007/978-3-319-62404-4_47

maintenance of both, making hard to manage the application gamification as a whole.

Within this context, we propose the usage of metadata as a solution to modularize the gamification logic. This solution is the core idea of the Esfinge Gamification, a Java metadata-based framework. It can be applicable to systems that needs a gamification logic, regardless of its domain. Generally, the framework uses annotations to configure what is the gamification logic that should be executed for each application method. It allows the configuration of several kinds of achievements and the extension of how these achievements are stored.

Moreover, a prototype system in a real context was implemented to analyse the modularization achieved by the use of Esfinge Gamification. The case study was a citizen science application in the context of a project named LEONA, which is intended to study electrodynamical events at atmospheric layers signalled by Transient Luminous Events (TLEs). In the implemented application, the user analyses and classifies images reporting if the photos contain some TLE or not. The application uses Esfinge Gamification system to receive affordances for the classifications done. Based on that application, a modularization analysis is performed to verify the coupling points between gamification and application concerns.

The paper is organized as follows: Sect. 2 presents the necessary background about gamification and metadata-based frameworks; Sect. 3 presents the proposed framework Esfinge Gamification; Sect. 4 presents the evaluation performed in the LEONA project; Sect. 5 presents other software solutions for gamification presented in the literature; and finally, Sect. 6 concludes the paper and points the direction for future works.

2   Background

The goal of this section is to present the main concepts about gamification and metadata-based frameworks.

2.1   Gamification

During recent years, there has been a growing interest in using game design elements in non-game contexts as a means to enhance the user engagement, retention and activity as well as social interaction [22]. This development of improving services has been named as the term gamification. The term was formerly introduced in the early 2000s [13], but it began to be mentioned and got attention after the second half of 2010 [39].

Thereupon, this concept has already been applied in several areas, including commerce, work, health, education, finance, citizen science, among others. It is predicted that over 50% of organizations will gamify features of their business by 2015 [20]. Furthermore, there is a growing amount of startups whose services are dedicated on adding a gamified layer to a main activity. The concern in gamification is also increasingly in an academic context [22].

Overall, gamification can be defined in two views. The first conceptualization designates the term with the use of game elements in non-game contexts and, regardless of the effects, the achievements implemented in an application must be equivalent as the ones used in games [6]. The latter dubs the term as a process of providing achievements for gameful experiences, which generally stimulate user's value creation [24].

In addition, Huotari and Hamari [24] highlight that participants should first be engaged in gameful experiences for gamification to have a positive outcome on user loyalty and retention. Subsequently, basically inserting game elements does not automatically assure a positive effect. It is important to define tasks for user that are associated to any interest or passion that he has already had in one's everyday activities. Besides, the user has to be confronted with exciting challenges, presented in a clear, visual and structured way, with combined well-defined rules and tasks, varying their difficulty. It is also desirable that the activities are voluntary to incite the motivation so that the user does not feel being controlled and losing autonomy [13].

Gamification in education applications, for example, appears to have potential to raise student motivation, but it is not trivial to accomplish that outcome, and it is necessary a significant work in design and implementation of the experience for it to be completely interesting for users [7]. Nevertheless, in accordance with Hamari, Koivisto and Sarsa [22], it is important to notice that there is a deficiency of understanding on what nature of studies that has been leaded about gamification concept. Regarding user behaviour, there is a dearth of empirical studies investigating the effects from gamifying applications.

Gamification has raised a lot of interest in industry and it is also reflected in the academic context during the last years [24]. Several gamified applications were developed across different domains for improving user activity and retention, including in sharing [29], sustainable consumption [18], innovation/ideation [26,42], data gathering and work [3], with most of the articles related to work conducted in crowdsourcing systems. Other researches involve areas such as commerce [20], intra-organizational systems [9], health/exercise [21] and education/learning [7,19].

Therefore, the application of gamification is not restricted to any particular area and can be used in different contexts. In particular, education is a specific area with high potential for the application of gamification and it was the most common domain of the studied papers. From elementary school to college students, several frameworks have been proposed for its use in learning environments. For example, Simões, Redondo and Vilas [38] built a framework adapted do K-6 education (students from 6 up to 12 years old) that it should enable teachers to organize their contexts, whereas Fitz-Walter, Tjondronegoro and Wyeth [10] created a mobile event application in order to help students at university orientation based on gamification.

Studies in the learning domain show the use of gamification as mostly positive, regarding increased motivation, enjoyment and commitment in the learning tasks. Nonetheless, these papers call attention to negative consequences, such as the effects of increased competition instead of collaboration, design features, and activity assessment difficulties.

Furthermore, the papers combined different achievements to improve user motivation and activity, such as badges, points, leaderboards, levels, rewards, trophies, progress, challenges, stories/themes, clear goals and gifts. In accordance with Hamari, Koivisto and Sarsa [22], points, badges and leaderboards have been the most frequent variants used in the studies.

2.2   Metadata-Based Frameworks

This section aims to describe metadata-based frameworks highlighting their main characteristics and the way that they provide behaviour adaptation. A framework can be considered an incomplete software with some points that can be specialized to add application-specific behaviour, that represents an abstract design for a family of related problems. These classes should be extended and composed with others in order to create a concrete and executable application [25].

Introspection [8] is a technique that can be considered a subset of reflection [11], where a software can access its own runtime structure. It is highly used by recent frameworks to be able to adapt themselves to application classes. However, depending on the framework domain, it might need more than the information existing the class for its processing. Code conventions can add additional semantic to code elements names [4], like on Ruby on Rails [40], but there are some situation where a more complex metadata about the class is necessary.

Metadata-based frameworks can be defined as frameworks that process their logic based on class metadata [17]. It changes the way frameworks are built and how they are used by software developers [31], since the interaction with it is mostly adding domain-specific metadata to the application classes, and not by invoking method and specializing classes as in the traditional framework approach. The basic processing in a metadata-based framework consists in: (a) read metadata from the target object; and (b) process metadata to execute its functionality. The role of metadata is to configure framework behaviour.

In [17], it was defined a pattern language for metadata-based frameworks that identified best practices about this kind of framework. This pattern language was the basis of a reference architecture [14] and of a model for metadata-based frameworks that handles crosscutting concerns [15]. For the present work, it is important to highlight the patterns Delegate Metadata Reader and Metadata Processor that provide a solution that allow the insertion of application-specific metadata. This solution is used in APIs like Bean Validation [2] and frameworks like JColtrane [30].

A popular alternative for metadata configuration are code annotations, that is supported by some programming languages like Java [1] and C# [28]. This language feature allows addition custom metadata directly into code elements. The use of code annotations is referenced by some works as attribute-oriented programming [5,34], which are used with success in domains like serialization, web service endpoints and interface to databases. It was also applied in a fractal component model implementation [33] and in conjunction with Model-driven

Development [41]. A recent experiment about annotations reveals that the use of them in frameworks reduces the application coupling and can increase the team productivity [16].

3   Esfinge Gamification

Based on the concept of gamification and on the model for metadata-based frameworks this work proposes the Esfinge Gamification framework. The main goal of this framework is to decouple the gamification concerns from the application. Its main idea is to allow the developers to focus on the application logic, only adding information on how the gamification should work in each invoked functionality. The framework intercepts these invocations and executes the appropriate gamification logic. It provides extension points that allow the introduction of application-specific gamification behaviour.

The framework defines various types of achievements and different implementations to store gamification information about the users. To register how the gamification should be handled within the application, Esfinge Gamification uses annotations that should be added in the business methods of the application classes. The proposed framework can be easily integrated to any Java application, being responsible to register users' achievements and it does not depend on any information related to the domain-specific of the application. It also provides an API that can be directly accessed by the application to retrieve and show information related to the user achievements, such as how many points a user has or its position in a ranking system.

This section presents the Esfinge Gamification framework, first focusing on how it should be used to be instantiated within an application. Therefore, it is presented details on its internal structure, such as how achievements are defined and managed and the framework extension points.

3.1   Framework Instantiation

The goal of this subsection is to present the steps to instantiate Esfinge Gamification within an application. The first configuration step is to configure the class that should be used to store the gamification information and the current user. Figure 1 presents an example of how this should be done. The configured instance should extend the abstract class *Game*. The framework provides some implementations that store this information in files, memory and database, however the application can create its own implementations for these. This instance is configured by calling the method *setGame()* on the *GameInvoker*.

Another important configuration presented in the previous listing is the current user. The method *setUserID()* in the class *UserStorage* should be called to configure the user to be used by the framework for the current thread. So, all methods invoked in the current thread that trigger a gamification logic will use this user as a reference. The parameter should be any user identification, which will be used for storage and retrieval purposes. For instance, to instantiate the

```
//configure game
Game g = new GameMemoryStorage();
GameInvoker.getInstance().setGame(g);

//current user
UserStorage.setUserID("spider");
```

Fig. 1. Esfinge Gamification instantiations.

framework on a web application, a web filter can be created to configure the current user in every received request.

The next step is to add the appropriate gamification annotations to the application interfaces. The methods chosen to be annotated should represent the action in the application domain that should trigger the gamification logic. Figure 2 illustrates the usage of the annotation *@PointsToUser*. Based on the configuration, when an implementation of the method *answerQuestion()* is invoked, the gamification framework should add 10 ANSWER points to the current user. It is important to highlight that there are other annotations provided by the framework, and it also provides an extension point that allow the creation of custom annotations.

```
public interface Questionnaire {
    @PointsToUser(name = "ANSWER", quantity = 10)
    public void answerQuestion(String answer);
}
```

Fig. 2. The use of the annotation *@PointsToUser*

The final step to instantiate the framework is to allow the interception of the application methods invocation. Esfinge Gamification works with dynamic proxies that encapsulate the application classes to introduce the invocation of the gamification logic based on the configured annotations. To create the proxy, the method *createProxy()* from the class *GameProxy* should be invoked. It receives an instance of the implementation and returns a dynamic proxy that implements all of its interfaces. Figure 3 presents an example of how it should be done. It is advisable to encapsulate this creation logic on a factory class.

```
Questionnaire q = (Questionnaire) GameProxy.createProxy(new
    QuestionnaireImpl());
```

Fig. 3. An example of how to create a dynamic proxy.

Finally, the application can use the framework API to directly access gamification data. This API is available through the implementation of the class Game that can be retrieved using the command *GameInvoker.getInstance().getGame()*. These points, when the application needs gamification information, should be the only business logic that has direct access to the framework.

3.2 Achievement Types

The framework uses a reward system in which the user can receive a certain kind of achievement when a task is performed or accomplished in the application. In Esfinge Gamification, four types of achievements can be found: point, ranking, reward and trophy. The interface *Achievement* can also be extended to include other kinds of rewards.

The *Point* type represents an affordance that contains a discrete number measure such as points or coins, which can be used to reach other achievements, or to use within the system itself. The same system can have different kinds of points.

The *Ranking* type represents a scalar user level and is described by two attributes, a name and level. It can be used to account the user improvement in some task or represent his status. For instance, when a task is successfully completed a certain number of times, the user may up one level in that skill. This encourages the user to explore tasks to be accomplished and also improve the work carried out.

The *Reward* achievement represents something that the user win and can spend. Its attributes are a name and a Boolean variable that indicates if the reward has already been used. The user keeps this reward until he decides to use it for some purpose. For example, if the reward is a discount coupon, it will be available until the user uses it.

The *Trophy* type, which is similar to badge, as in the real world, describes a premium received only once. The user can receive a Trophy for performing a task, but he will not win it again if he repeat the same task.

New kinds of achievements may be added by implementing the Achievement interface. This interface has methods to define what should be done when a new achievement of that kind is added for a user.

3.3 Achievements Management

Besides the interface *Achievement* and its implementations, the framework defines a component which role is to store the achievements. The abstract class *Game* encapsulates the mechanics of Gamification storage. It defines abstract methods that must be implemented in order to give the appropriate actions to assign or remove user's achievements. Currently, three Game subclasses are available: *GameMemoryStorage*, that keeps data stored only in memory; *GameFileStorage*, that stores the achievements in a properties file; and *GameDatabaseStorage*, that saves the data in a SQL database. The methods concerning the achievements storage are: insertAchievement(), deleteAchievement(), updateAchievement(), getAchievement(), and getAchievements().

The concrete subclasses of *Game* should manage the achievements without using their concrete types. This is important to allow the extension of the achievement types.

The implementations of the class *Game* can provide more specific methods for querying the gamification information. For instance, there can be methods to retrieve rankings or to find the user position. In future versions these features should be standardized on the framework API.

3.4   Gamification Metadata

Beyond achievement creation and storage, operations that add or remove achievements can be configured through annotations to be triggered based on the invocation of the application interface methods. Figure 4 exemplifies how some of these annotations should be configured on an interface of the application.

```
public interface ITestAnnotations {

        @PointsToUser(name = "GOLD", quantity = 1000)
        public void doSomething();

        @RewardsToUser(Name = "lunch", used = false)
        public void doSomethingRemarcable();

        @RemovePoints(name = "GOLD", quantity = 500)
        public void doBadThing();

        @RemoveReward(Name = "lunch", used = true)
        public void useReward();

        @PointsToParam (name = "SILVER", quantity = 100, param = "owner")
        public void niceComment(String comment, @Named("owner") String
            owner);

        @PointsToParam (name = "SILVER", quantity = 300, param = "comment"
            prop ="user.login")
        public void niceComment(@Named("comment") Comment c);
}
```

Fig. 4. Example of how the annotations should be configured on an interface.

In the first two methods there is an example of annotations that gives achievements to the current user and in the next two there are examples of annotations that triggers the removal of them. The last two methods presents examples of an annotation that gives points for a user being referenced on a *param*. The annotation attribute *param* refers to the attribute name, labelled by the annotation

@Named, that contains the user id. The attribute *prop* can be used to configure the parameter property that contains that information.

It is important to highlight that there was not a concern to create a large number of annotations that can cover all possible requirements. However, the framework has a mechanism that allows the extension of its annotations, which is presented in the next subsection. The provided annotations aims to exemplify what kind of configurations can be performed.

3.5   Extension Points

Esfinge Gamification framework has two internal extension points: one that configures the persistence and other that allows the addition of new kinds of achievements. The persistence can be extended to be compatible of what is used in the application. This point can be extended by creating a new subclass of the abstract class *Game* and configuring it in the class *GameInvoker*. To create new kinds of achievements, the first step is to create a new implementation of the interface *Achievement*, defining the rules for the addition and removal of such achievements. The persistence mechanism should also be ready to handle these achievements and there should be created annotations to trigger actions for their management. Some details for these extension points were presented in the previous sections.

The creation of new annotations can be seen as the main framework extension point. For each new annotation there should be a class that knows how to interpret its information and execute the action that should be triggered when a method with it is invoked. All gamification annotations should have a *@GamificationProcessor* annotation that configures the related processor class.

The class configured in the annotation should implements the *AchievementProcessor* interface. This interface defines the method *receiveAnnotation()* that is responsible to interpret the annotation, retrieving information from its specific attributes. The method *process()* is responsible to execute the action on the gamification logic related to that annotation.

It is important to highlight that this mechanism can be used to add different application-specific logic to the framework. For instance, an annotation can configure points to the current user, to someone related to the user action, and even to a group or a team in which the user participates. However, by using this approach, the actions related to the gamification are decoupled from the application classes, being related only by its metadata.

4   Approach Evaluation

This section presents an evaluation of the proposed approach, implemented on Esfinge Gamification, to modularize the gamification concerns within an application. The goal of this study is to identify the dependencies that are necessary to instantiate such framework, evaluating the resulting coupling. Based on that, it is possible to analyse how the proposed approach helps in the modularization of gamification concerns.

As part of this evaluation, it was developed a prototype of a citizen science application based on the real needs of a project called LEONA. The gamification will be introduced to the application by using the Esfinge Gamification framework. Afterwards, a modularization analysis using a DSM were used to identify the points in the application that depends on the framework. Based on that, a qualitative coupling analysis is performed to identify how the interaction between the application and the gamification logic happens to fulfill its requirements.

The following subsections describe the case study domain, the implemented application, the modularity analysis and the study conclusions.

4.1   Case Study Domain - LEONA Project

In space geophysics and atmospheric science domain, there are several researches concerned about the comprehension of Transient Luminous Events (TLEs) and their possible consequences to the planet [35]. Discovered by chance in 1989 during astronomical observations [12], these events are consequences of electrical activity in the atmosphere and correspond to short-term luminous emissions that occur in stratosphere, mesosphere and lower portion of the ionosphere [36]. Generally, according to Silva [37], the main events observed are called sprites, halos, elves and jets.

With the aim of performing the classification of images that might contain TLEs, a prototype system was implemented as part of the project *LEONA: Transient luminous event and thunderstorm high energy emission collaborative network in Latin America*. By using the prototype, users can classify images that might contain some of these events. It uses gamification to motivate the user to classify a higher amount of images. Figure 5 presents the system screen that classify an image with a possible TLE.

For each classified image, the user receives a stipulated number of points through framework Esfinge Gamification, using the classes and methods implemented for class Point. Let it be C a TLE chosen by the user in a given image X. For each image X that user classifies, the assigned number of points (in a scale from 0 to 5) given for the user follows the criterion:

$$Points = \left\lfloor \frac{\text{Number of votes of class } C \times 5}{\text{Total number of votes for } X} \right\rfloor$$

The only exception occurs when the user classify the image as "Doubt". In this case, he does not receive any points. By classifying an image, the system automatically updates the amount of user points, which can be seen in the user profile. Additionally, the system also updates the current class occupied by the user, which can be recruit, soldier, lieutenant or expert. These classes are based on the ratio of the user, which is calculated dividing the number of points by the number of images voted. Therefore, a user can increment or decrement his position.

Fig. 5. Classification of TLES by user.

Moreover, information can be extracted from the framework about the user position (score) with regards to all registered users who are also classifying the same images. Through the framework, methods that retrieve the user's position from its points are called and a table with a ranking of system users is created. The table displayed in this features contains the position, ID, name, number of points, total of classified images and the ratio for the top system users.

4.2   Analysis and Discussion

With the purpose of evaluating the dependencies in the instantiation of Esfinge Gamification framework, it was generated a Dependency Structure Matrix (DSM) [43] using IntelliJ IDEA 13 that presents the dependencies in class files of the prototype described in the previous section. A DSM consists of a squared matrix where every row and column with the same number represent a software project artifact, such as a class, an interface or an annotation. For instance, the third row represents the same artifact as the third column. A number in a DSM cell means that the column artifact has that amount of dependencies with the row artifact. As a consequence, considering an artifact, its column shows all dependencies that it has and a row shows all dependencies from other artifacts to it. The DSM is presented in Fig. 6.

To operate the framework without changing the system, some additional packages were added, as a listener, a filter and a new annotation. The listener is responsible to set the initials parameters of the application. For example, define if the application will store the data in a database or a common file. In turn, the filter has the role to set the current user in Esfinge Gamification. At last, a new annotation was created to increment the score following the logic explained in the previous section. The following paragraphs describe each dependence from the application to the framework.

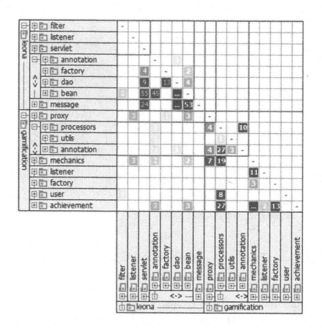

Fig. 6. DSM created from Leona prototype.

It is important to note that no class depends on the package filter, but has two dependencies. It is similar to the package listener that has 6 dependencies. Despite these classes depends on some system classes, the other system classes are independent from it.

The module annotation is an extension of the framework. It can be noted observing its dependencies and influences. Additionally, the package factory is responsible to configure the correct proxy defined by the system. Therefore, the framework can communicate with the system, as we can see in its two dependencies.

At this point, system and framework are not directly dependent. But, as we can see in figure, the package bean, which is part of domain-specific system, has three direct links to framework. It happens because the only way to update user status is retrieving information directly from framework.

Evaluating the dependencies for the gamification framework instantiation, it can be seen that some classes from the application need to invoke some methods to configure the framework, such as the filter and the listener that creates the framework configurations, and the factory that wraps the application classes in the gamification proxy. In the case study, the strongest dependence happened in the package that extended the framework, which was expected. Beyond that, the application classes depend only on framework annotations and in some specific points where gamification information should be retrieved, such as the user ranking.

5   Related Work

This section will present some frameworks for gamification that can be found in the literature. None of the articles found is a generic framework proposal, all actually have some area of interest, whether learning or business. Four frameworks will be referenced below, two of the learning area, one of the business area and one of the geographic information area.

Pivec and Dzianbenko [32] present a framework called "Unigame: Social Skills and Knowledge Training". The developers' proposal is that any tutor or teacher can apply game-based learning using their platform. It is a on-line framework allowing multiple remote groups participate and the teacher is responsible for defining the topic of learning and coordinate and moderate the activities during the game.

The game dynamics divides students into 4 teams who must find the solution to a problem and the team to reach the best one wins. The solution should be found through research on the topic and discussion among participants, all this being facilitated and moderated by the teacher. It is expected that students learn social skills, working collaboratively to find and share information and to develop their argumentation strategies and understanding of the subject area.

The framework presented by Simões et al. [38] also proposes an environment for game-based learning but specialized to children aged 6 to 12. The platform guide teachers to gamify the teaching process through a dashboard that provides the tools for teachers to adapt and customize tasks and rewards such as badges and trophies for students. It is also an on-line framework as the Unigame aforementioned, and in addition to students and teachers, parents also participate in the platform, either watching the children or actively helping the learning process.

Herzig et al. [23] present a generic platform for enterprise gamification. In a business environment, gamification can be used to increase customer engagement and loyalty to the company or to increase employee engagement through performance evaluation. This framework is based on events, so that when an event that attends one of the rules (for example, a customer reaches a minimum number of purchases at a store) immediate feedback is released, giving a badge or points to this user. In the case of employees these points can be used to assign bonus or time off, for customers points can be used as discounts at a next purchase.

Lastly, Martella et al. [27] present a framework to encourage and motivate users to share geographic information. This type of data is known as Volunteered Geographic Information (VGI) and represents data that is gathered via crowdsourcing. Gamification is used to motivate the user to participate, since with crowdsourcing a large amount of data on a relative low cost in a short period of time can be collected.

The article says that there is no established techniques to integrate gamification in VGI applications and therefore they propose a framework for any developer looking to add it in your application to do so. The framework uses points, badges, bonus, virtual goods, avatar, leaderboards, levels, friending, ownership and votes as elements that can be added to an application. Furthermore, there are specific elements of VGI, which are: the Geo-data gathering, the Geo-data validation and the Geo-data integration. The first concerns the insertion, modification or deletion of data, the second is the verification and confirmation of data entered by other users and the third is to identify redundant data.

The authors did not give details on how the framework was developed or how it can be used, but shows the results of a case study when the framework is added in an Android application that already existed, the CampusMapper app.

6   Conclusion and Future Work

Being founded on the conceptualization of gamification, this paper proposed an implementation of a framework called Esfinge Gamification. The framework was used with an application as a case study, a classification prototype system of transient luminous events. From the use of Dependency Structure Matrix, it was shown that Esfinge Gamification does not rely on any information related to the domain-specific application, except in category of recovering points. Based on that, it is possible to conclude that the framework was able to modularize the gamification features, having dependencies only for configuration and to retrieve gamification data.

As a future study, the framework can be incremented to include listeners to gamification events, such as receiving or losing an achievement. Moreover, a controlled experiment could also be performed to verify how intuitive is for developers to use it.

References

1. Jsr 175: a metadata facility for the java programming language (2003). http://www.jcp.org/en/jsr/detail?id=175. Accessed 06 Mar 2015
2. Jsr 303: Bean validation (2009). Accessed 06 Mar 2015
3. Anderson, A., Huttenlocher, D., Kleinberg, J., Leskovec, J.: Steering user behavior with badges. In: Proceedings of the 22nd International Conference on World Wide Web, pp. 95–106. International World Wide Web Conferences Steering Committee (2013)
4. Chen, N.: Convention over configuration (2006). http://softwareengineering.vazexqi.com/files/pattern.html. Accessed 05 Mar 2015
5. Cisternino, A., Cazzola, W., Colombo, D.: Metadata-driven library design. In: Library-centric Software Design Workshop (2005)
6. Deterding, S., Dixon, D., Khaled, R., Nacke, L.: From game design elements to gamefulness: defining gamification. In: Proceedings of the 15th International Academic MindTrek Conference: Envisioning Future Media Environments, pp. 9–15. ACM (2011)
7. Domínguez, A., Saenz-deNavarrete, J., De-Marcos, L., Fernández-Sanz, L., Pagés, C., Martínez-Herráiz, J.J.: Gamifying learning experiences: practical implications and outcomes. Comput. Educ. **63**, 380–392 (2013)

8. Doucet, F., Shukla, S., Gupta, R.: Introspection in system-level language frameworks: meta-level vs. integrated. In: Design, Automation and Test in Europe Conference and Exhibition, 2003, pp. 382–387 (2003)
9. Farzan, R., Brusilovsky, P.: Encouraging user participation in a course recommender system: an impact on user behavior. Comput. Hum. Behav. **27**(1), 276–284 (2011)
10. Fitz-Walter, Z., Tjondronegoro, D., Wyeth, P.: Orientation passport: using gamification to engage university students. In: Proceedings of the 23rd Australian Computer-Human Interaction Conference, pp. 122–125. ACM (2011)
11. Foote, B., Yoder, J.: Evolution, architecture, and metamorphosis. In: Pattern Languages of Program Design 2, pp. 295–314. Addison-Wesley Longman Publishing Co., Inc., Boston (1996)
12. Franz, R., Nemzek, R., Winckler, J.: Television image of a large upward electrical discharge above a thunderstorm system. Science **249**(4964), 48–51 (1990)
13. Groh, F.: Gamification: State of the art definition and utilization. Institute of Media Informatics Ulm University 39 (2012)
14. Guerra, E., Alves, F., Kulesza, U., Fernandes, C.: A reference architecture for organizing the internal structure of metadata-based frameworks. J. Syst. Softw. **86**(5), 1239–1256 (2013)
15. Guerra, E., Buarque, E., Fernandes, C., Silveira, F.: A flexible model for crosscutting metadata-based frameworks. In: Murgante, B., Misra, S., Carlini, M., Torre, C.M., Nguyen, H.-Q., Taniar, D., Apduhan, B.O., Gervasi, O. (eds.) ICCSA 2013. LNCS, vol. 7972, pp. 391–407. Springer, Heidelberg (2013). doi:10.1007/978-3-642-39643-4_29
16. Guerra, E., Fernandes, C.: A qualitative and quantitative analysis on metadatabased frameworks usage. In: Murgante, B., Misra, S., Carlini, M., Torre, C.M., Nguyen, H.-Q., Taniar, D., Apduhan, B.O., Gervasi, O. (eds.) ICCSA 2013. LNCS, vol. 7972, pp. 375–390. Springer, Heidelberg (2013). doi:10.1007/978-3-642-39643-4_28
17. Guerra, E., Souza, J., Fernandes, C.: Pattern language for the internal structure of metadata-based frameworks. In: Noble, J., Johnson, R., Zdun, U., Wallingford, E. (eds.) Transactions on Pattern Languages of Programming III. LNCS, vol. 7840, pp. 55–110. Springer, Heidelberg (2013). doi:10.1007/978-3-642-38676-3_3
18. Gustafsson, A., Katzeff, C., Bang, M.: Evaluation of a pervasive game for domestic energy engagement among teenagers. Comput. Entertainment (CIE) **7**(4), 54 (2009)
19. Hakulinen, L., Auvinen, T., Korhonen, A.: Empirical study on the effect of achievement badges in trakla2 online learning environment. In: 2013 Learning and Teaching in Computing and Engineering (LaTiCE), pp. 47–54. IEEE (2013)
20. Hamari, J.: Transforming homo economicus into homo ludens: a field experiment on gamification in a utilitarian peer-to-peer trading service. Electron. Commer. Res. Appl. **12**(4), 236–245 (2013)
21. Hamari, J., Koivisto, J.: Social motivations to use gamification: an empirical study of gamifying exercise. In: ECIS, p. 105 (2013)
22. Hamari, J., Koivisto, J., Sarsa, H.: Does gamification work?-a literature review of empirical studies on gamification. In: 2014 47th Hawaii International Conference on System Sciences (HICSS), pp. 3025–3034. IEEE (2014)
23. Herzig, P., Ameling, M., Schill, A.: A generic platform for enterprise gamification. In: Proceedings of the 2012 Joint Working IEEE/IFIP Conference on Software Architecture and European Conference on Software Architecture, WICSA-ECSA 2012, pp. 219–223. IEEE Computer Society, Washington, DC (2012)

24. Huotari, K., Hamari, J.: Defining gamification: a service marketing perspective. In: Proceeding of the 16th International Academic MindTrek Conference, pp. 17–22. ACM (2012)
25. Johnson, R.E., Foote, B.: Designing reuseable classes. J. Object-Oriented Program. 1, 22–35 (1988)
26. Jung, J., Schneider, C., Valacich, J.: Enhancing the motivational affordance of information systems: the effects of real-time performance feedback and goal setting in group collaboration environments. Manage. Sci. 56(4), 724–742 (2010)
27. Martella, R., Kray, C., Clementini, E.: A gamification framework for volunteered geographic information. In: Bação, F., Santos, M.Y., Painho, M. (eds.) AGILE 2015. LNGC, pp. 73–89. Springer, Cham (2015). doi:10.1007/978-3-319-16787-9_5
28. Miller, J.S., Ragsdale, S.: The Common Language Infrastructure Annotated Standard. Addison-Wesley Longman Publishing Co., Inc., Boston (2003)
29. Montola, M., Nummenmaa, T., Lucero, A., Boberg, M., Korhonen, H.: Applying game achievement systems to enhance user experience in a photo sharing service. In: Proceedings of the 13th International MindTrek Conference: Everyday Life in the Ubiquitous Era, pp. 94–97. ACM (2009)
30. Nucitelli, R., Guerra, E., Fernandes, C.: Parsing XML documents in java using annotations. In: XATA 2010 XML: Associated Technologies and Applications, pp. 103–114 (2010)
31. O'Brien, L.: Design patterns 15 years later: an interview with Erich gamma, Richard Helm and Ralph Johnson (2009). http://www.informit.com/articles/article.aspx?p=1404056. Accessed 06 Mar 2015
32. Pivec, M., Dziabenko, O.: Game-based learning in universities and lifelong learning: "unigame: Social skills and knowledge training" game concept. J. Univers. Comput. Sci. 10(1), 14–26 (2004)
33. Rouvoy, R., Pessemier, N., Pawlak, R., Merle, P.: Using attribute-oriented programming to leverage fractal-based developments. In: Proceedings of the 5th International ECOOP Workshop on Fractal Component Model (2006)
34. Schwarz, D.: Peeking inside the box: attribute-oriented programming with java 1.5 (2004). http://www.onjava.com/pub/a/onjava/2004/06/30/insidebox1.html. Accessed 06 Mar 2015
35. Sentman, D.D., Wescott, E.M.: Observations of upper atmospheric optical flashes recorded from an aircraft. Geophys. Res. Lett. 20(24), 2857–2860 (1993)
36. Sentman, D.D., Wescott, E.M., Osborne, D., Hampton, D., Heavner, M.: Preliminary results from the sprites94 aircraft campaign: 1. Red sprites. Geophys. Res. Lett. 22(10), 1205–1208 (1995)
37. Silva, C.L.d.: Mecanismo de iniciação de sprites. Master's thesis, Instituto Nacional de Pesquisas Espaciais, São José dos Campos (2011–02–28 2011). http://urlib.net/sid.inpe.br/mtc-m19/2011/02.07.13.17
38. Simões, J., Redondo, R.D., Vilas, A.F.: A social gamification framework for a k-6 learning platform. Comput. Hum. Behav. 29(2), 345–353 (2013)
39. Smith, A.L., Baker, L.: Getting a clue: creating student detectives and dragon slayers in your library. Ref. Serv. Rev. 39(4), 628–642 (2011)
40. Thomas, D., Hansson, D., Breedt, L., Clark, M., Davidson, J.D., Gehtland, J., Schwarz, A.: Agile Web Development with Rails. Pragmatic Bookshelf (2006)
41. Wada, H., Suzuki, J.: Modeling turnpike frontend system: a model-driven development framework leveraging UML metamodeling and attribute-oriented programming. In: Briand, L., Williams, C. (eds.) MODELS 2005. LNCS, vol. 3713, pp. 584–600. Springer, Heidelberg (2005). doi:10.1007/11557432_44

42. Witt, M., Scheiner, C., Robra-Bissantz, S.: Gamification of online idea competitions: insights from an explorative case. Informatik schafft Communities, p. 192 (2011)
43. Yassine, A.: An introduction to modeling and analyzing complex product development processes using the design structure matrix (DSM) method. Urbana **51**(9), 1–17 (2004)

Implementation of Analytical Hierarchy Process in Detecting Structural Code Clones

Mehmet S. Aktas$^{(\boxtimes)}$ and Mustafa Kapdan

Computer Engineering Department, Yildiz Technical University,
Istanbul, Turkey
aktas@yildiz.edu.tr,
mustafa.kapdan@student.yildiz.edu.tr

Abstract. The nature and the size of data plays an important rule at the identification process of similar objects (clones). The type of utilized similarity measures is also an important factor. The nature of data and selecting the right identification algorithm appropriate to type of data should be examined thoroughly when a clone identification technique is applied. This study suggests a new methodology in software systems for minimization/prevention of code cloning. Its main contribution is to propose an Analytical Hierarchy Process based methodology at detection of code clones in object-oriented software systems, in which the software is represented by means of software metrics data at class level. The suggested clone detection model is able to select the most suitable code clone candidates by considering different correlation and distance metrics to identify code clones. To facilitate the testing and the usability of the suggested clone detection model, the system is used for detection of structural code clone. The methodology is validated by comparison with results obtained by human judges as well as by comparison with a plain structural code clone identification approach. The evaluation of the methodology is carried out in terms of accuracy and indicates promising results.

Keywords: Code clone · Analytical hierarchy process · Structural code clone · Soft computing · Software metrics

1 Introduction

Software developers tend to reuse code fragments with or without minor changes in software development process. In turn, this creates software systems with highly similar code fragments. Similar code fragments are often referred as code clones in software engineering. A code fragment is called as structural code clone if it repeats in several levels of software architectural design. Software clones often decreases software quality, since they may cause a number of problems in software systems. Thus, clone detection becomes an important part of tasks in software analysis [1, 2].

A number of various detection methods were suggested based on different clone types. These methods can be broadly categorized under two categories: (a) simple detection of code clones and (b) structural detection of code clones. The former relies on the detection of similarities in source code representations. The latter takes

© Springer International Publishing AG 2017
O. Gervasi et al. (Eds.): ICCSA 2017, Part V, LNCS 10408, pp. 652–664, 2017.
DOI: 10.1007/978-3-319-62404-4_48

similarities in design patterns and/or object relations into consideration within the software structure. In this paper, we focus on structural code clone detection problem. The nature and the size of data plays an important rule at the identification process of similar objects (clones). The type of utilized similarity measures is also an important factor. Recent studies has shown that, it is likely that a similarity measure which is appropriate for one domain is inappropriate for another [3, 4]. For example, some of the similarity measures assign more importance to an absent feature than others [5]. In case the absence of such a particular feature between two entities constitutes a sign of similarity, that similarity measure may be applied in its specific field. However, this seems to be irrelevant in software code clone detection problem domain [2].

Our previous work on structural code clone detection relies upon certain similarity metrics such as Jaccard or Cosine similarity in identifying similar code fragments [2]. Hence, they are only are capable of working in software metric domains, in which these similarity metrics may successfully detect identical code fragments. Hence there is an emerging need for a domain-independent structural detection mechanisms for code clones, in which the appropriate similarity measures can be selected for identifying the best clone candidates.

This research mainly contributes in proposing a methodology for AHP-based class level structural detection of code clones within object-oriented software systems. Hence, in this research three implications were presented: First, our suggested methodology is improving our previous work [2] on structural code clone detection by employing AHP-based multi-criteria selection algorithm. The suggested AHP-based selection algorithm enables us to select the best clone-candidates considering varying correlation and distance metrics. This study presents a new approach, as far as recent studies are considered where code clones are detected using a soft computing technique. Second, the suggested methodology introduces an AHP-based structural code clone detection software solely based on software metrics. In this setting the actual source-code is not used to determine structural code clones. Its computation relies on metadata, namely metric measurements on the source code. Third, the performance of suggested algorithm was evaluated through experiments. We have used the testing data at the comparison of results (i.e. software to be mined for structural code clones) that was previously published in [2]. A comparison of results was performed between our AHP-based algorithm in this study and the results of a Structural Code Clone Detection algorithm that is solely dependent on certain similarity measures.

This article is structured as follows: Related work was reviewed in Sect. 2. The suggested methodology which uses AHP technique for detection of structural code clone is described in Sect. 3. Software details were explained in Sects. 4 and 5 follows it for experimental evaluation. The evaluation is stated in Sect. 6. The article concludes in Sect. 7 and future work is presented.

2 Related Work

In order to have a robust system and lower costs, soft computing consists of techniques that mainly aim to understand imprecision, partial truth, and the tolerance of uncertainty. Soft computing may be viewed as a main component for conceptual intelligence.

Over the years, soft computing community has been published studies using methods that evolved under various categories such as fuzzy logic, neural computing, evolutionary computing and machine learning. We also see that soft computing methods have been applied to varying application domains such as aeronautical applications, telecommunication systems, transportation systems, household appliances, power grid systems, automated manufacturing systems and robotics, and healthcare.

We have particularly focused on using Analytical Hierarchy Process, in this study. This is a soft computing method that has been applied to the multi criteria decision making methods, for structural code clone detection problem. To our best knowledge, soft computing techniques have not been applied in clone detection problem in software engineering area. Hence, this study reports a pioneering approach that leads to better results in discovering structural code clones in software engineering projects.

Saaty first introduced Analytical Hierarchy Process (AHP) in order to exploit complex decision-making problems under uncertainties [6]. AHP is mainly utilized to obtain ranked decisions from both continuous and discrete paired comparisons amongst the candidates. It has a hierarchical structure and divides inputs to layers to simplify a problem. Within the layered structure, each layer has several nodes and weights are used to connect nodes in adjacent layers. Multiple criteria are evaluated by the AHP method; hence it simplifies the decision-making process. It requires a questionnaire to perform pairwise comparison of importance among the variables input. The results of the pairwise comparisons are formulated in a comparison matrix, which is used create ranked decision candidates based on their importance. One of the critical steps in AHP is to set up comparison matrices. If one increases the number of candidates in the hierarchy process, in turn, this requires more comparisons to be made between the alternatives. Because of the excess of questions, a consistency check is necessary for the pairwise comparison matrix. If the comparison matrix is not consistent, elements of comparison matrix need to be adjusted recursively until the comparison matrix becomes consistent.

Under structural analysis, codes of clones were analyzed logically and syntactically. At the analysis of structural clones' software design templates were analyzed for the logical analysis part. Design templates prepared previously lay out the structural system. As in the class structure, design templates provide micro patterns which are abstraction structures at application-level [7]. So, design templates give the possibility to analyze micro-structural clones. Using design templates in source code, Pinot tool executes the clone analysis as suggested by Shi and Olsson [8]. A strategy using the simple clones in a software system as a sign of high level similarities was implemented for syntactic analysis. The Clone Miner tool with the following working principle can be defined as suggested by Basit et al. [9]: (1) Detection of simple clones, (2) Analyzing the code clone structure by clustering the determined simple clones. The approach for detecting structural clones across web pages was suggested by De Lucia et al. [10]. A threshold value is specified for any web page and the page is compared to other web pages. Two pages are allegedly clones of each other, in case others are more similar than this threshold. A different perspective was introduced by Marcus and Maletic [11] through clone detection. This approach works for two different structural code clones with similar identifier names, however, if the identifier names change, it fails to identify structural clones. These approaches have drawbacks because they either need simple clones in the software system or they assume that the system contains design templates. This makes it hard to apply them to software systems without simple clones to be used as a sign for similarities and/or software systems not offering any design templates to provide structural information on the software.

Our previous work used specific similarity metrics to identify structural code clones and showed promising results. However, recent studies has shown that, it is likely that a similarity measure which is appropriate for one domain is inappropriate for another [3, 4]. To this end, in this study, we extend our previous work by using different similarity metrics all-together in decision making process for detecting structural code clones. Here, each similarity metric is considered as a criterion. Likewise, each structural clone candidate is considered as an alternative. Since we intend to identify best alternatives (the structural clones), using different independent criteria (similarity metrics), we formulate this problem as multi-criteria decision making problem. To solve this problem, we utilize AHP technique and introduce an approach that employs multiple similarity metrics and calculates structural code clones. We compare/contrast this methodology against our previous work which primarily focused on using only specific similarity metrics. On two different cases of application we have tested our suggested methodology to figure out the applicability and effectiveness of this approach.

Our previous work focused on metric-based approaches to identify structural code clones [1, 2]. We have shown that software metrics based measurements can be utilized for the detection of structural clones. Actual source-code is used by this methodology for detecting structural code clones. However, its computation is based on metadata, namely metric measurements taken from the source code. The process of identifying together clones depends upon the similarity measures being used.

The utilized metric categories are as follows: Code Size Metrics; Complexity metrics; Object-oriented metrics. Software metrics in this regard, their descriptions and the reason of their preference is summarized and categorically listed in [2]. Possible relationships between objects such as aggregation, dependency, association, composition, and inheritance have been the source of inspiration in this study. We argue that the structure of software systems with object oriented infrastructure is created through these relationships. We also argue that these object relationships may be determined through existing software metrics. In this study, an approach for detecting structural code clones using software metrics was introduced particularly focusing on the object-oriented software metrics, assuming that they would help us identify structural code clones. In structural clone analysis, various software metrics are used depending on the program and the programming language. Various level information of the software are provided by these metrics (particularly, package level and class level). Conditional statements, class and method definitions, loop statements, and block range in Java programming language are some of the examples for metrics in structural clone analysis. Only class level software metrics were used in this study.

In our previous study [2], each class was evaluated for structural code clone analysis using measurements of aforementioned software metric categories. In order to identify structurally similar classes, we have computed the distance between metric measurement vectors. In order to determine the similarity of measurement values, we have used two common similarity functions: cosine similarity and jaccard similarity.

Two classes were called clone pairs, after their similarities were computed. In this study, the term clone-pair was used for class pairs having classes with similar structures identified by both similarity functions.

3   Methodology: AHP Usage in Structural Clone Detection

The structural code clone detection methodologies use similarity metrics between the code clone candidates. Correlation measures, association coefficients, and distance metrics were used extensively to compute the similarity between two objects. Various previous studies have shown that different similarity measures may show different accuracies [3–5]. Since there exists multiple similarity measures with varying accuracies and a number of clone candidates, where the similarities of the clones are computed based on the similarity values, we consider this as a decision-making method consisting of multiple criteria for solving the problem in structural detection of code clones. In our approach, we have introduced an AHP-based code clone identification method, where the candidates for identification are not shown all together or sequentially, but in pairs. The suggested approach uses similarity metrics to detect code clones. Validation of the suggested method in practical testing shows good agreement with actual measured values obtained from human judges.

3.1   AHP Process for Structural Code Clone Detection

To demonstrate how the method works, we will use a numerical illustration given in [2]. This example has a code base comprising 7 classes having 4 interfaces and 3 regular classes. Our previous research showed that Inheritance related metrics show the best accuracy performance in finding the structural code clones. For a class of objects, inheritance is defined as the concept where any subclass may inherit the definitions of one or more upper classes. Our argument is that if inheritance metrics provide close values to each other two objects may be cloned structurally. Inheritance metrics may include *default-abstract$_i$* (total number of abstract methods of class i) and *default-overridden$_i$* (total number of methods that are overridden in class i) for example. In order to demonstrate the usefulness of our research, we use Inheritance related metrics to test whether the AHP approach performs better.

We investigate the structural code clones amongst the regular classes in the example case study given in [2]. We used indexed regular classes as follows, in order to achieve this: *Regular_Class_Index_Vector = {C$_1$, C$_2$, C$_3$}*; here each index corresponds to a class. Let's assume only member functions are considered as software metrics, as an example of detecting structural code clones. The member functions provide measurement vectors with statistical values through this analysis. As a result, we have 3 different measurement vectors each correspond to each Regular Class as following: *Measurement_Vectors = {MV$_1$, MV$_2$, MV$_3$}*. We demonstrate a measurement vector in the example below: *MV$_i$ = {default-abstract$_i$, default-overridden$_i$, private-abstract$_i$, private-overridden$_i$, protected-abstract$_i$, protected-overridden$_i$, public-abstract$_i$, public-overridden$_i$}*. Here, index *"i"* indicates the pair number.

Here, measurement vector values are shown in three classes: C_1, C_2, and C3. MV_1 = {0, 0, 0, 0, 0, 0, 0, 2}, MV_2 = {0, 0, 0, 0, 0, 0, 0, 2}, MV_3 = {0, 0, 0, 0, 0, 0, 0, 0}. Every pair mapping class is included. So, a set with 3 candidate code-clone pairs is formed: $Clon\_Pair\_Set$ = {(C_1, C_2), (C_1, C_3), (C_2, C_3)}. Similarities between the Measurement Vectors for each mapping class pair is computed by different similarity metrics. We use AHP to evaluate the similarity metric factors in clone detection and find the best code clone candidate. We follow the AHP steps for structural code detection as following.

(1) **Define the goal of the decision:** The goal of the suggested AHP approach is to select the best structural code clone candidates considering varying correlation and distance metrics.

(2) **Structure the decision problem in a hierarchy:** Figure 1 represents the structure of the decision problem that work on. As representative of these categories, we use the following similarity metrics: Jaccard similarity, Euclidean distance and Cosine Similarity. Our reasoning for selecting these similarity metrics are discussed in the previous Sect.

(3) **Pair comparison of criteria:** AHP requires a questionnaire on criteria preferences. Hence, it is necessary to identify how much a criterion is preferred over another. For relative comparisons between the criteria Saaty defines a relative importance by employing 1-9 scales. Based on the binary comparison between the values of each similarity metric pair, the local rate of the criteria amongst all the other metrics are computed.

(4) **Calculate the priorities and a consistency ratio:** As demonstrated on Table 1, based on pairwise comparisons, we have computed the resulting priority weights for the criteria. Various previous studies have shown that different similarity measures may show different accuracies [3–5]. Furthermore, these studies have also shown that both Jaccard Coefficient and Cosine Similarity are preferred over Euclidean Distance in terms of accuracy. Therefore, we rely on their findings and utilize their priorities when comparing the similarity metric pairs. However, in order the results of the given set of values to be valid, the results must be consistent. Hence, we also calculate the Consistency Ratio based on the Saaty's Consistency Ratio formula. We should note that, Saaty indicates that if the value of Consistency Ratio is smaller or equal to 1.0%, then the inconsistency is acceptable. Below, Table 2 indicates the ranking results.

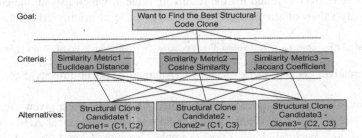

Fig. 1. AHP Structure for Finding the Best Structural Code Clone among three candidates where each candidate is a pair of java classes and there exist total of three classes: C1, C2 and C3.

Table 1. Priorities amongst to alternatives with respect to each criterion (similarity metric)

Criteria1 — importance — or Criteria2?				Equal	How much more?
■ Cosine Similarity		□ Jaccard Coefficient		■ 1	| □ 3 | □ 5 | □ 7| □ 9 |
■ Cosine Similarity		□ Euclidean Distance		□ 1	| □ 3 |■ 5 | □ 7| □ 9 |
□ Jaccard Coefficient		□ Euclidean Distance		□ 1	| □ 3 |■ 5 | □ 7| □ 9 |

Table 2. Priorities amongst the similarity metrics

Category		Priority	Rank
1	Cosine Similarity	45.5%	1
2	Jaccard Coefficient	45.5%	1
3	Euclidean Distance	9.1%	3
Consistency Ratio (CR)		0.0%	

(5) **Evaluate alternatives according to the priorities identified:** At this stage, we investigate the alternative optimum solution to the decision problem, which is finding the best candidate for structural code clone detection. To do this, for each criterion, we compare/contrast the clone candidates and find the priorities amongst them with respect to similarity metrics. First we compute distances for every clone candidate (Clone1 = (C1, C2), Clone2 = (C1, C3), Clone3 = (C2, C3)). Then, we use an algorithm given in Fig. 2 to compute the relative priority values, based on an algorithm that takes minimum, maximum and average distances corresponding to clones as well as the distances of clones that needed to be compared pairwise. Based on this algorithm, the shorter distance is the better. Hence the clones with shorter similarity values get more importance value compared to the clones with higher similarity values. If the values of the similarity distances equal to each other, then the clones are treated with equal importance.

When applying the algorithm to the abovementioned problem, we find the relative importance values amongst the candidate clones with respect to each similarity criteria as shown in Table 3. Then, we calculate the priorities and consistency ratios according to Saaty's AHP approach and list the results in Table 4, which lists all the computed local priority values of alternative Clones for a given local priority criterion.

$$\text{Global \_AHP\_Score}_{\text{Clone\#1}} = (\text{Criteria\_Priority\_Score}) \times [\,(\text{Alternative\_Local\_Priority\_Score}_1)$$

$$+ (\text{Alternative\_Local\_Priority\_Score}_2) + (\text{Alternative\_Local\_Priority\_Score}_3)] \quad (1)$$

We give the equation for calculating Global AHP scores for a given Clone alternative (Clone#1) in Eq. 1. Code Clone Candidates with high global AHP scores are considered as structural-clones. For example, because Clone1 has the highest

```
private Integer giveIntenseValue(double minDistance, double maxDistance, double averageDistance, double prj1, double prj2) {
    int defaultvalue = IntensceValues.Equal;

    if (minDistance == maxDistance) {
        defaultvalue = IntensceValues.Equal;
    } else if (prj1 == prj2) {
        defaultvalue = IntensceValues.Equal;
    } else if (prj1 == minDistance && prj2 == maxDistance) {
        defaultvalue = IntensceValues.ExtremeImportant;
    } else if (minDistance <= prj1 && prj2 < averageDistance) {
        defaultvalue = IntensceValues.LittleImportant;
    } else if (minDistance < prj1 && prj1 < averageDistance && prj2 >= averageDistance && prj2 < maxDistance) {
        defaultvalue = IntensceValues.Important - 1;
    } else if (minDistance == prj1 && prj2 >= averageDistance && prj2 < maxDistance) {
        defaultvalue = IntensceValues.Important;
    } else if (minDistance < prj1 && prj1 < averageDistance && prj2 == maxDistance) {
        defaultvalue = IntensceValues.MoreImportant;
    } else if (averageDistance <= prj1 && prj2 < maxDistance) {
        defaultvalue = IntensceValues.LittleImportant - 1;
    } else if (averageDistance == prj1 && prj2 == maxDistance) {
        defaultvalue = Important;
    } else if (averageDistance < prj1 && prj2 == maxDistance) {
        defaultvalue = IntensceValues.LittleImportant;
    } else {
        defaultvalue = IntensceValues.Equal;
    }

    return defaultvalue;
}
```

Fig. 2. Algorithm for calculating relative importance values amongst clone candidates.

Table 3. Priorities amongst the alternatives with respect to each criterion (similarity metric)

Criteria	Alternative1 — importance — or Alternative2?			Equal	How much more?
Cosine Similarity	☐ Clone1		☐ Clone2	☐ 1	| ☐ 3| ☐ 5| ☐ 7| ■ 9 |
	☐ Clone1		☐ Clone3	☐ 1	| ☐ 3| ☐ 5| ☐ 7| ■ 9 |
	☐ Clone2		☐ Clone3	■ 1	| ☐ 3| ☐ 5| ☐ 7| ☐ 9 |
Jaccard Coefficient	☐ Clone1		☐ Clone2	☐ 1	| ☐ 3| ☐ 5| ☐ 7| ■ 9 |
	☐ Clone1		■ Clone3	☐ 1	| ☐ 3| ☐ 5| ☐ 7| ■ 9 |
	☐ Clone2		☐ Clone3	■ 1	| ☐ 3| ☐ 5| ☐ 7| ■ 9 |
Euclidean Distance	☐ Clone1		■ Clone2	☐ 1	| ☐ 3| ☐ 5| ☐ 7| ☐ 9 |
	☐ Clone1		■ Clone3	☐ 1	| ☐ 3| ☐ 5| ☐ 7| ■ 9 |
	☐ Clone2		☐ Clone3	■ 1	| ☐ 3| ☐ 5| ☐ 7| ☐ 9 |

Table 4. Priority and Consistency Ratios

Criteria	Local priority of criterion	Alternatives	Local priority of alternatives	CR of alternatives	CR of the criterion
Cosine similarity	45.5%	Clone1	91.8%	0.0%	0.0%
		Clone2	9.1%		
		Clone3	9.1%		
Jaccard coefficient	45.5%	Clone1	91.8%	0.0%	
		Clone2	9.1%		
		Clone3	9.1%		
Euclidean distance	9.1%	Clone1	91.8%	0.0%	
		Clone1	9.1%		
		Clone2	9.1%		

Table 5. Evaluation of the Clone Candidates

Alternatives	Cosine similarity	Jaccard coefficient	Euclidean distance	Global AHP priority score	Ranking
Clone1	$0.455 \times 0.918 = 0.418$	$0.455 \times 0.918 = 0.418$	$0.091 \times 0.918 = 0.084$	$0.418 + 0.418 + 0.084 = 0.92$	1
Clone2	$0.455 \times 0.091 = 0.041$	$0.455 \times 0.091 = 0.041$	$0.091 \times 0.091 = 0.008$	$0.041 + 0.041 + 0.008 = 0.09$	3
Clone3	$0.455 \times 0.091 = 0.041$	$0.455 \times 0.091 = 0.041$	$0.091 \times 0.091 = 0.008$	$0.041 + 0.041 + 0.008 = 0.09$	3

Global AHP score, structurally C1 and C2 are evaluated as cloned classes. While the other pair of java classes, i.e. C2 and C3 with their clone having the lowest Global AHP score are not called as structural clones. The results of the evaluation of the clone candidates are listed in Table 5.

4   Software Details

Source codes: For identifying the structure of code clones, source code of the project was to be processed by an analysis tool. Multiple project sources may be processed through the analyzer tool, then follows the analysis of structural code-clones.

Tools: The quality management system Sonar which is an open source software is used to measure the project's software quality. This tool analyzes projects from method to whole project at various levels. In our previous studies, we have added new metrics comprising analysis of structural code-clone to extend the metric capacity of Sonar. In this study, we used the extended version of Sonar tool to analyze different software projects for software metrics for the suggested AHP based structural code clone detection.

Software Metric Collection module: To illustrate the usefulness of suggested methodology, we utilized our previous work [2] on software metric collection, which is a tool that communicates with the tools to collect software metric measurements based on the user requests.

AHP Priority Calculator Module: This module is responsible for calculating priorities based on pairwise comparisons. It computes priorities or weights for a set of criteria based on pairwise comparisons. A model from a vector space was used to store category results. Every class was compared individually to other classes of the project. Section 3 discusses a numerical illustration of the AHP process that is used in detecting structures of code-clones. For varying implementations of similarity metrics, this module interacts with Similarity Library, which implements a number of similarity and distance metrics. After the comparison process, priorities regarding all candidate clone pairs were recorded into the AHP priority results database.

Similarity Library Module This module implements varying similarity and distance metrics. For prototype implementation, we implemented the following metrics: Jaccard coefficient, Cosine similarity, Euclidean distance.

Web UI for AHP based Structural Code Clone Detection: A web based interface was developed for AHP based structural code clone detection. The user interface allows the users input the number of criteria (similarity metrics) and select each criterion.

We make the decision on which of the criteria in each pair is more important and how many times more based on the previous published studies on similarity metrics. By initiating the AHP process, the user will then get the resulting priorities among alternatives, their ranking, and a consistency ratio.

5   Experimental Evaluation

We have used an evaluation method described in [12], for validation of our methodology. During detection of simple code clones, Kim et al. used human judges in different software projects, in order to validate the methodology. We have also used judges in detection of structural code clones and computed the thresholds to be used in evaluating structural similarity of code-clone pairs.

5.1   Control Software Projects for Structural Code Clone Detection

During the evaluation process of our suggested methodology, we have made use of a software metric measurement dataset where the metric values were collected from two different open source projects. The first of them Simpack, generated by Dynamics and Distributed System Laboratory at the Zurich University, aims at similarity detection across ontologies [13]. The next one, DNSjava written by Brain Wellington handles DNS in java [14]. SimPack and DNSJava feature 128 and 165 different classes respectively.

5.2   Control Data Set 1– Human Judge's Result Data Set for Structural Code Clone Detection on Software Projects

We have also used a dataset collected from human judges about the identification of the structural code clone pairs during evaluation of the suggested methodology. To obtain such a dataset, source codes of each project were presented to each human judge and each developer decided if the presented pair was a clone or not. Those pairs selected as clones were maintained in the database. Ten experienced developers have contributed to our study to provide reliable results by human judges. For the Simpack project 718 potential clone candidates were detected on average by the developers. 950 potential clone candidates were detected at the DNSJava project.

5.3   Control Data Set 2– Structural Code Clone Identification Algorithm's Result Data Set for Structural Code Clone Detection on Software Projects

To compare the suggested AHP based approach against the Structural Code Clone Identification Algorithm (introduced in [2]), we used the accuracy result set obtained in that study. The previous work on structural code clone detection was relying on certain similarity metrics, in turn, its results were biased and limited by their accuracies.

In the previous work, the accuracy rate for the Structural Code Clone Identification Algorithm was found by comparing the results against Human Judge's judgement. To find the highest accuracy rate, we investigated the similarity threshold value, which is used to select the structural code clone candidates. By increasing the threshold value from 0.1 to 0.99 (with increments of 0.01) we have observed accordances between the Control data set from Sect. 5.2 and the results Structural Code Clone Identification Algorithm from [2]. For each metric category, we have tried 99 different threshold values. We have detected candidate clone pairs in each try. Then, the accordance between the computed clone-pair set and the clone-pair set detected by human judges was examined. As for the inheritance related software metrics, Table 6 indicates best threshold values and corresponding accuracy values.

Table 6. The Accuracy Results from AHP approach vs. Accuracy Results from Plain Structural Code Clone Detection approach

Metric set	SimPack		DNSjava	
	Similarity metric dependent approach (previous work)	AHP based approach (new approach)	Similarity metric dependent approach (previous work)	AHP based approach (new approach)
Inheritance	72.63%	76.38%	66.31%	73.04%

5.4   Experiment: Accuracy Investigation of the AHP Approach

To illustrate the testing of our AHP approach we also used Inheritance based Software metrics. We apply the AHP process on the Control Software Projects from Sect. 5.1 and compute the ranked list of structural code candidates. We used the Control Data Set-1 to compute the accuracy of our results. Then we compare the accuracy results against the result set from Control Data Set-2, which is obtained by using a Structural Code Clone Identification Algorithm from [2]. When applying the AHP process, for selecting the alternatives to be evaluated, we used the similarity thresholds, from Sect. 5.3, in order to compare the results from AHP approach. We compare the results of AHP based structural code clone detection approach against our previous work that is entirely based on certain similarity metrics. The results are listed in Table 6.

6   Results

We have studied the implementation of AHP in detecting structural code-clones. The motivational reasons were issued as a survey in [1]. An approach using plain similarity metrics in structural code identification was accepted to be published in April issue of International Journal of Software Engineering and Knowledge [2]. The related work was discussed in Sect. 2. Identifying suggested solutions in this regard, we have suggested a methodology for implementing AHP in detection of structural code-clones using software metric measurements. The suggested methodology was discussed in

Sect. 3 and the software architecture and prototype were explained in Sect. 4. The prototype implementation is available at [15]. The empirical evaluation of the methodology was presented in Sect. 5. In order to investigate the accuracy of the methodology in finding the structural code clones using the suggested AHP, we have conducted an accuracy experiment. The accordance of results from another user study along with the results from our suggested methodology was compared for analyzing the accuracy. We compared the resulting accuracy values against accuracy results obtained from our previous study. The AHP-based approach shows promising results better than our results obtained from structural code clone detection that is dependent on some similarity metrics.

7 Conclusion and Future Work

In this study, we investigated the use of AHP approach in structural code-clone detection problem. Introducing an AHP based methodology to detect structural code clones at class level using software metrics, our approach can detect structural code clones by considering a number of different similarity metrics. Our methodology was also implemented as a prototype. In our work, we have extended Sonar, the quality analysis tool which is an open source code and also our previous work on structural code clone detection, which was entirely based on certain similarity metrics. The results of our methodology were compared with those of human evaluators, in order to evaluate our methodology. According to obtained results, AHP based approach performs better compared to plain structural code clone identification approaches which only takes into account certain similarity metrics. Work remains in investigating the use of other similarity metrics integrated to our AHP-based approach for finding the best structural code clone pairs.

References

1. Kapdan, M., Aktas, M., Yigit, M.: On the structural code clone detection problem: a survey and software metric based approach. In: Murgante, B., Misra, S., Rocha, Ana Maria A.C., Torre, C., Rocha, J.G., Falcão, M.I., Taniar, D., Apduhan, Bernady O., Gervasi, O. (eds.) ICCSA 2014. LNCS, vol. 8583, pp. 492–507. Springer, Cham (2014). doi:10.1007/978-3-319-09156-3_35
2. Aktas, M., Kapdan, M.: Structural code clone detection methodology using software metrics. Int. J. Softw. Eng. Knowl. Eng. 26(2), 307–332 (2016)
3. Huang, A.: Similarity measures for text document clustering, In: NZCSRSC 2008, Christchurch, New Zealand, April 2008
4. Xue, Y.: Reengineering legacy software products into software product line, Ph.D. thesis, CS Department, National University of Singapure, January 2013
5. Stherl, A., Ghosh, J., Mooney, R.: Impact of similarity measures on web page clustering, AAAI Technical report WS-00-01, 2000 AAAI (www.aaai.org)
6. Saaty, T.L.: The Analytic Hierarchy Process. McGraw-Hill, New York (1980)

7. Gil, J.Y., Maman, I.: Micro patterns in Java code. In: SIGPLAN Notices, 2005, New York (2005)
8. Shi, N., Olsson, R.A.: Reverse engineering of design patterns from java source code. In: Proceedings of the 21st IEEE/ACM International Conference on Automated Software Engineering, ASE 2006, 18–22 September 2006, Tokyo (2006)
9. Basit, H., Ali, U., Jarzabek, S.: Viewing simple clones from structural clones' perspective. In: Proceedings of the 5th International Workshop on Software Clones, 23 May 2011, Honolulu (2011)
10. De Lucia, A., Francese, R., Scanniello, G., Tortora, G.: Reengineering web applications based on cloned pattern analysis. In: Proceedings of the 12th IEEE International Workshop on Program Comprehension, 24–26 June 2004, Bari (2004)
11. Marcus, A., Maletic, J.I.: Identification of high-level concept clones in source code. In: Proceedings 16th Annual International Conference on Automated Software Engineering, 2001, Chicago (2001)
12. Kim, S., Pan, K., Whitehead, E.J.: When functions change their names: automatic detection of origin relationships. In: Proceedings of the 12th Working Conference on Reverse Engineering, 7–11 November 2005, Pittsburgh (2005)
13. Dynamic and Distributed Information Systems Group, U.o.Z., (2014). "SimPack". https://files.ifi.uzh.ch/ddis/oldweb/ddis/research/simpack/index.html. 15 August 2014
14. Wellington, B.: "DNS Java" (1999). http://www.dnsjava.org/. 15 August 2014
15. GitHub Software Repository address: mkapdan: Mustafa Kapdan Repositories (2014). https://github.com/mkapdan?tab=repositories. 15 August 2014

A Systematic Literature Review: Code Bad Smells in Java Source Code

Aakanshi Gupta[1,2], Bharti Suri[1], and Sanjay Misra[3(✉)]

[1] USICT, Guru Gobind Singh Indraprastha University, Delhi, India
aakankshi@gmail.com, bhartisuri@gmail.com
[2] Amity School of Engineering and Technology, New Delhi, India
[3] Center of ICT/ICE Research, CUCRID, Covenant University, Ota, Nigeria
ssopam@gmail.com

Abstract. Code smell is an indication of a software designing problem. The presence of code smells can have a severe impact on the software quality. Smells basically refers to the structure of the code which violates few of the design principals and so has negative effect on the quality of the software. Larger the source code, more is its presence. Software needs to be reliable, robust and easily maintainable so that it can minimize the cost of its development as well as maintenance. Smells may increase the chances of failure of the system during maintenance. A SLR has been performed based on the search of digital libraries that includes the publications since 1999 to 2016. 60 research papers are deeply analyzed that are most relevant. The objective of this paper is to provide an extensive overview of existing research in the field of bad smells, identify the detection techniques and correlation between the detection techniques, in addition to find the name of the code smells that need more attention in detection approaches. This SLR identified that code clone (code smell) receives most research attention. Our findings also show that very few papers report on the impact of code bad smells. Most of the papers focused on the detection techniques and tools. A significant correlation between detection techniques has been calculated. There are four code smells that are not yet detected are Primitive Obsession, Inappropriate Intimacy, Incomplete library class and Comments.

1 Introduction

An intrinsic property of the object oriented software design process is ease of evolution. In order to preserve this property software system must follow the design principles like: modularity, encapsulation, and data abstraction etc. In the maintenance process of object oriented systems, due to aggressive market conditions and anxiety to meet deadlines, developers are compelled to violate the design postulates. The violation of design principles is termed as 'code smell or bad smell'. Smells are introduced when the operations like: modification and enhancement are performed on the system to meet with new requirements. The code becomes complex and the originality of design is abdicated thereby lowering the software quality. To rout these problems, the concept of bad smell has been

© Springer International Publishing AG 2017
O. Gervasi et al. (Eds.): ICCSA 2017, Part V, LNCS 10408, pp. 665–682, 2017.
DOI: 10.1007/978-3-319-62404-4_49

introduced in Martin Fowler's book called "Refactoring: Improving the Design of Existing Code" [1].

In theory, bad smells are poor implementation of the code or the design defects. Bad smells define common pitfalls in the software designing. Code smells are one of the major threats to the quality of the software. However, the term 'code smell' was first coined by Kent Beck while helping Fowler in his book [1]. Bad smells are not any kind of program bugs, in fact they are not even technically incorrect.

The objective of this work is to analyze the quantitative evidence on the relationship between detection techniques and code smells. A significant correlation between detection techniques and code smells has been performed on the basis of code smells. There are some code bad smells given by Fowler and Beck that have not been detected by any detection technique. Our goal also addresses the challenges and research opportunities in the field of code smell. The authors also explored the impact of code smells on software.

According to Fowler, "A bad code smell is a surface indication that usually corresponds to a deeper problem in the system" [1]. Few of these problems classified so far by Beck and Fowler are most widely known set of 22 smells. In this review, all the 22 code smells are tabulated in the Table 1. All the smells are described in a nutshell with a unique id which is used further in the research.

Motivation for work

- Code smells are present in numerous distinct software artefacts. So, the research on detection techniques goes beyond the source code.
- Upon surveying the literature we realized the lack of systematic literature review.

Contribution of this work

- Calculation of the correlation (positive or negative) between code detection techniques based on bad smells.
- Identification of five code bad smells; their detection techniques are not available in the literature.
- Observing the impact of bad smells on the software.
- Reviewing the different techniques for bad smells.

The rest of the paper is organized as follows. Background of the code smell is described in Sect. 2, research methodology of the systematic literature review and the validity threats are presented in Sects. 3, Sect. 4 demonstrates the result of the research questions with critical analysis and observations. Section 5, discusses the overall findings with future aspects, and Sect. 6, concludes the whole work.

2   Background

Bad smells are found generally in the source code that degenerates the quality of the software. Bad smells indicate the poor structure of the code which violates

Table 1. Code Smells Description

S.no	ID	Name	Description
1	CS1	Duplicate Code	The same expression in two methods of the same class or sibling subclasses
2	CS2	Long method	A method with lots of parameters and temporary variables
3	CS3	Shotgun Surgery	Shotgun surgery is one change that alters many classes
4	CS4	Feature Envy	When a method seems more interested in a class other than the one it actually is in
5	CS5	Data Clumps	When the same three or four data items together in lots of places
6	CS6	Primitive Obsession	Primitive types are building blocks; Overuse of this type can cause this smell
7	CS7	Switch Statements	Find the same switch statement scattered about a program in different places
8	CS8	Parallel Inheritance Hierarchies	When an inheritance tree depends upon another inheritance tree by composition where we create a subclass for a class and need to create a subclass for another class also
9	CS9	Lazy Class	A class that isn't doing enough to pay for itself
10	CS10	Speculative Generality	When there is unused class, field, parameter and method for future flexibility
11	CS11	Large class	When a class is trying to do too much, it often shows up as too many instance variables
12	CS12	Long Parameter List	When a method has too long parameter list
13	CS13	Divergent Change	One class that suffers many kinds of changes
14	CS14	Temporary Field	An object in which an instance variable is set only in certain circumstances
15	CS15	Message Chains	When a series of messages in a chain
16	CS16	Middle Man	At a class's interface half the methods are too much delegating to other class
17	CS17	Inappropriate Intimacy	A class uses the internal field and know too much of other class
18	CS18	Alternative Classes with Different Interfaces	Any methods that do the same thing but have different signatures for what they do
19	CS19	Incomplete Library Class	After sometime library stop to meet use requirements
20	CS20	Data Class	Classes that are just contain the data for other classes and can not control their data independently
21	CS21	Refused Bequest	When the sub classes use only the inherited properties
22	CS22	Comments	To explain a method or variable there are too many comments

the basic design fundamentals that may cause the failure of the system. Bad smells suggest the refactoring technique; and when refactoring performed to remove bad smells, it causes changes in the internal structure of the code, without upsetting the external behavior of the system, with the goal to improve the quality attributes of the system.

Zhang et al. [2] presented the systematic review of all 39 papers published in between 2000–2009. He revealed that the code clone smell has been studied the most. He also stated that the impact of smells is unclear. A. Ouni and M. Kessentini et al. [3] realized that code smells increases the maintenance cost and code smells can be prioritized on the basis of risk and importance of classes. M. Kessentini et al. [4] stated the detection rules using formal definition of defects and R. Mahouachi et al. [5] stated the detection and correction rules with the genetic algorithm. Yamashita et al. [6,7] analyzed that not only the smells but also the interaction between smells also affect the maintenance. There is also uneven coverage of smells in the available literature. Mantyla et al. [8] computed the correlation between the smells. They grouped the smells into six categories and introduced one more code smell; 'Dead code' that is never executed. They have analyzed the detection of code smells subjectively and found that detection of code smells depend on the developers experience and program analysis. Hall et al. [9] reported the relationship between defects and five smells, on the basis of three open source system analysis. Some code smells have no defect-proness whereas some of them increased the number of defects. Li et al. [10] examined three open source systems and found that the detection process of smells could act as a method for identifying and restructuring the problematic classes. N. Moha et al. [11,12] developed a tool which is implemented in the proposed framework. This proposed framework define the code smells in a domain specific language definition of code smells. Fontana et al. [31,60] pointed out that the illustration of the threshold values and magnitude is arduous across tools. They asserted that as the use of different techniques, the outcomes of distinctive tools sometimes distinct. G. Rasool et. al [67] presented an review on several detection techniques and tools for mining code smells.

3   Research Methodology

A systematic literature review (SLR) gathers existing information related to specific research and provide confidence to the author to synthesize conclusion. The steps in performing the SLR are shown in the Fig. 1.

3.1   Research Questions

A Systematic Literature Review (SLR) has been performed on 60 papers. There are some research questions that arise and few of them are given below.

RQ.1 Justify the influence of bad smells on the software?
RQ.2 Are all known bad smells [1] detectable?
RQ.3 What is the correlation between the detection techniques based on bad smells ?

RQ.4 What are the different techniques that are available to detect the bad smells?

The first research question (RQ.1) is motivated by the fact that if the code smell exists in the code snippets then what happens with codes, what is the impact on the whole software. The second research question (RQ.2) has the purpose to identify the code smells that are not detected yet. The third question aims to deduce the relationship between the detection techniques. The fourth question find out the detection techniques to understand how the specific code smell is detected and by which technique, and how many techniques are available for the detection process.

3.2 Search String

("Java" AND "Software" AND ("Code Smell" OR "Code Bad Smell" OR "Bad Smell")

This search string is advance searched in electronic data sources like IEEE Explore, ACM Digital Library etc. And after title, abstract and full text exclusion got 60 papers for reviewing.

3.3 Sources of Information

In the SLR, we searched the electronic sources as recommended by Kitchenham's guidelines [13]. Grey literature (technical report, some workshop reports and work in progress) was not included in the SLR. We also excluded the techniques in the study that focuses only one code smell detection technique. The literature brims over with particular code smell that is 'code clone'. This review deals with the generic aspects of the code smells. The duplicates and overlapping among the papers were also excluded by manual filtering. Study selection is done as given in the Table 2.

Table 2. Defining the extracted Data

Data sources name	Link to access	Total No. of papers	after Title based exclusion	After abstract based	After Full text Reading
IEEEXplore	ieeexplore.ieee.org	343	167	65	25
ACM(DL)	www.acm.org	123	66	34	15
Springer	www.springer.com	249	76	19	10
Wiley Online Library	onlinelibrary.wiley.com	40	11	7	3
Elsevier Science Direct	www.sciencedirect.com	99	35	16	7

3.4 Threats to the Validity

Threats to the validity concern those factors where the conclusion or the answers of the research questions might be biased. Threats to the validity are classified into four categories; Internal, External, Construct and Conclusion.

Internal validity threat is concerned with the actual analysis of the data. In this work, we performed the statistical analysis and found the negative correlation between the detection techniques and the code bad smells. However, employing other statistical analysis may lead to different conclusions.

External validity threat is to generalize the effect of the outcome of the review process on the external world that imply unrelated software. Our review targets only the software developed in Java language. This result can not be generalized for the software in other languages.

Construct validity threat is about the researchers theory and the results investigated related to the research questions (RQ.). Any change in search string can change the results obtained for RQ. 3 and 4. Conclusion validity threat focuses on whether the data is collected and the analysis is conducted for the conclusion and to answer the research questions in a way that it is related to the actual outcome. Statistical correlation between detection techniques based on the code bad smells is negative for Java software and it can be further examined for other systems. The overall structure of the study as well as the criteria of inclusion/exclusion of the papers, classification and quality is totally according to a protocol that is defined in the Kitchenham's guidelines [13].

4 Results

4.1 Primary Research

The objective of this study is to find the detection techniques of bad smells and to summarize the available literature in systematic way. There is lack of availability of systematic reviews on code bad smells. The papers are initially obtained by a broad search, in the five databases that covers the relevant journals and conferences. An ample systematic review process is carried out to distinguish papers describing the code bad smells. The outcome present here, gives an actual picture of the existing facts.

4.2 Analysis of the Primary Research

The distribution of 60 papers, screened out of 854 papers is shown in Table 3. These papers are categorized on the basis of research methodologies. There is only one systematic review paper [2] on code bad smells. Out of 60 papers, 21 papers exist on the detection techniques of the bad smells.

Figure 1 presents the percentage wise research papers distribution of the related code smell. This analyzes that 50% papers are considering all the 22 types of bad smells. Also, the code smell: CS1 (duplicate code or code clone) got the most research attention as 25% papers are available on this single bad

Table 3. Different - different methodologies of the research papers

Sr. No	Motivation of study	Count	Reference
1	Systematic literature review	1	[2]
2	Applications of the code smells	6	[6,14–18]
3	Detection of code bad smells	26	[5,7,11,12,16,19–37,37]
4	Improving the definition/ Understanding of the code bad smells	7	[9,27,38–42]
5	Empirical/ Exploratory study	13	[6,8,14,15,17,43–50]
6	Case study	2	[51,52]
7	Others	7	[3,4,10,53–56]

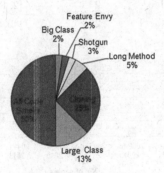

Fig. 1. Percentage of research papers for respective Code Smells

smell, CS4 (feature envy) code smells have the minimum 2% coverage. In Table 4 active authors and co-authors are given with their publication numbers. Authors with more than one publications are listed in this table. M. Kessentini et. al. has 7 publications in this research field. Figure 2 shows the year wise distribution of the research papers. Maximum papers are published on the code bad smells during 2011 to 2013.

Table 5 lists publication fora in which the primary studies have been published. It is worthy to pay attention to the field since, a vast diversity of journals and conference proceedings have published the articles as listed. Total 40% publications are from journals and 42% from conference proceedings. We conclude from this analysis that only a single SLR is available and it is hard to find the a comprehensive comparison between the detection techniques of the bad smells.

Table 4. Active authors and number of publication in the code bad smells

Sr. No	Author name	No. of papers	Reference
1	M. Kessentini	7	[3,11,19,22,36,53]
2	F. Khomh	5	[28,42,44,50,57]
3	A. Yamashita	5	[6,14,15,17,18]
4	A. Chatzigeorgiou	3	[34,38,58]
5	N. Moha	3	[5,20,42]
6	T. Hall	3	[2,41,59]
7	F. A. Fontana	4	[31,37,60,61]
8	F. Palomba	2	[35,62]
9	M. Boussaa	2	[11]
10	A. Ouni	2	[36,53]
11	W. Li	2	[40,47]
12	M. Zhang	3	[2,41,59]
13	S. Olbrich	2	[51,52]
14	N. Baddoo	2	[2,41]
15	R. Shatnawi	2	[40,47]

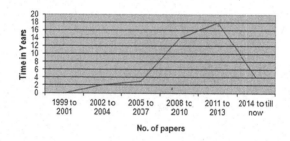

Fig. 2. Year wise distribution of the research papers

The concept has been introduced in 1999 by Fowler and Beck [12], an extensive research had been done during 2011 to 2013.

We conclude from this analysis that only a single SLR is available and it is hard to find the a comprehensive comparison between the detection techniques of the code bad smells. The concept has been introduced in 1999 by Fowler and Beck [12], an extensive research had been done during 2011 to 2013.

In order to explore the research and validate the primary studies, we have specified four research questions, identified related studies and extracted the data to answer these following questions:

RQ1: Justify the Influence of Code Bad Smells on the Software?
Code smells have tremendous influence on the software. The major impact is

Table 5. Research papers with their different- different publication fora

Sr. No	Type	No. of papers	Percentage	Reference
1	Journal	25	39.07	[2–4,6,8,10,14,17,18,20,21,29, 36,38,43–47,53,56,59,60,63,64]
2	Conference	27	42.18	[9,15,16,23–28,30,32– 35,40,42,48– 52,54,55,57,58,61,65]
3	Workshop	4	6.25	[7,31,37,41]
4	Book chapter	8	12.5	[1,5,11,12,19,22,39]
5	Total	64	100	

on the maintenance process. Li and Shatnavi [40,47] investigate the relationship between the class error probability and bad smells based on the 3 versions of the Eclipse. Steffen et. al [51,52] analyze that the class which are infected with code smells have a higher frequency of changes; need more maintenance; compared to the non-infected classes. Foutse Khomh et. al [44,57] identified certain smells that are more correlated than others to change-proneness and the change-proneness affects the maintenance effort. Tracy Hall et. al [9] showed the effect of 5 smells on the number of faults. Steffin Olbrich et. al [51,52] said that infected components with smells need more maintenance. Morden et. al [12] report that code clone can increase the software reliability.

RQ2: Are All Known Code Bad Smells [1], **Detectable?** There are 22 code bad smells defined in Table 1, coined by Fowler and Beck. In the available literature, there are four code smells that are still not detected by any detection technique. These are Primitive Obsession (CS6), Inappropriate Intimacy (CS17), Incomplete library class (CS19) and Comments (CS22). There are 13 different techniques for 21 code bad smells (CS2 to CS22) and 16 techniques for CS1 are available in the literature [66] and none of these detects the above mentioned code smells. The accuracy of the answer can be validated with the help of Fig. 2 and Tables 6,7. We can conclude that not all the code smells are detectable.

RQ3: What Is the Correlation Between Techniques Based on Code Bad Smells? Correlation is a statistical technique that can show, how strongly two variables are related with each other. The correlation analysis can lead to a greater understanding of the collected and analyzed data. We want to determine how the 'r' parameter is affected by the detection techniques with respect to code bad smells. With this parameter we can observe the correlation between the detection techniques. The values are calculated with the help of Fig. 2 and Tables 6,7. In order to answer this question, we determined the Pearson correlation between techniques based on code bad smells. The value of 'r' is calculated with the help of following Eq. 1.

$$r = \frac{n \sum x_i y_i - \sum x_i \sum y_i}{\sqrt{\left[n \sum x_i^2 - (\sum x_i)^2\right]\left[n \sum y_i^2 - (\sum y_i)^2\right]}} \tag{1}$$

where

- x_i and y_i are the variables,
- n is the number of code bad smells.

Table 6. Code smells detection techniques (one part)

Sr. No	Technique name	Code smell									
		CS2	CS3	CS4	CS5	CS6	CS7	CS8	CS9	CS10	CS11
1	Metrics analysis with machine learning	✓		✓					✓		✓
2	Binary logistic regression	✓									
3	Binomial regression model				✓		✓		✓		
4	Algorithm using domain specific language	✓							✓	✓	✓
5	Detection rules using definition			✓					✓		✓
6	Relational association rule mining	✓		✓							
7	Clustering based analysis										
8	Using change history		✓	✓				✓			
9	Using software metrics								✓		
10	Metrics extraction using quantitative information	✓									
11	Cooperative parallel SBSE approach		✓	✓					✓		
12	Software metrics using Eclipse plug-in	✓					✓	✓	✓		✓
13	Weight based distance metrics			✓							

There is negative correlation or inverse correlation between the detection techniques based on code bad smells. It is hence inferred that as one variable increases the other one decreases. The square of the value of r shows that 25 percent variation is related.

RQ4: What are the different techniques that are available, to detect the code bad smells? Detection process for code bad smells is essential with respect to the maintenance of the software. And other reasons of the detection are described in the RQ1 in which the impact of code bad smells on the software are answered. The detection process can be successful with the assistance of a applicable detection technique. In Tables 6 and 7 various detection techniques

Table 7. Code smells detection techniques (second part)

Sr No	Technique name	Code smell										
		CS12	CS13	CS14	CS15	CS16	CS17	CS18	CS19	CS20	CS21	CS22
1	Metrics analysis with machine learning							✓				
2	Binary logistic regression											
3	Binomial regression model				✓	✓						
4	Algorithm using domain specific language	✓									✓	
5	Detection rules using definition	✓										
6	Relational association rule mining											
7	Clustering based analysis									✓		
8	Using change history			✓								
9	Using software metrics			✓								
10	Metrics extraction using quantitative information											
11	Cooperative parallel SBSE approach	✓								✓		
12	Software metrics using Eclipse plug-in	✓								✓		
13	Weight based distance metrics											

are listed to detect 21 code bad smells(CS2 to CS22) and 16 detection techniques for CS1 (duplicate code smell) are available in the literature.

One technique can detect more than one code bad smell. A few techniques like 'Binary logistic regression', 'Clustering based analysis', 'Metrics extraction' using quantitative information and 'Weight based distance metrics' are able to detect smells namely CS2, CS20, CS2, CS4 respectively, single bad smell. Software metrics using Eclipse plug-in, can detect seven smells namely CS2, CS7, CS8, CS9, CS11, CS12 and CS20 bad smells. Phongphan et. al. proposed a tool called BSDT (Bad smell detection tool) [32] which is implemented as Eclipse plug-in. The tool uses the software metrics as threshold values and detect the location of the code bad smells. Other techniques like 'Metrics analysis with machine learning', 'Binomial Regression Model', 'Algorithm using Domain Specific language' and 'Cooperative Parallel SBSE' (Search Based Software Engineering) approach can detect CS2, CS4, CS9, CS11, CS18, CS5, CS7, CS10, CS15, CS16, CS12, CS21, CS3 and CS20 bad smells.

5   Discussion

The overall objective of this research is to identify detection techniques of all the code smells and systematically assess the validation of the collected data. The outcome specify that there is a vast opportunity for further research in the area of code bad smells. This review concludes few of the aspects for further research in this field; undetected code bad smells (CS6, CS17, CS19, CS22) and comparative analysis between detection techniques. There is no literature available with respect to undetected code bad smells and only one research paper compares the code bad smell detection techniques. The future research area could also focus on the attributes considered during design. The research community should concentrate on a general detection techniques rather than on specific code smells, to pay more attention on the undetected code bad smells and to encourage systematic review on the comparative analysis on detection techniques.

5.1   Undetected Code Bad Smells

A brief about the code bad smells is presented in the Table 1. There are a total of 22 bad smells and their detection techniques are described in the Tables 6 and 7. With the help of Tables 6 and 7 we can analyze that there is not any single approach available to detect all the 22 code bad smells [12]. On an average three or four code smells can be detected by the single technique. These undetected code bad smells are: Primitive Obsession(CS6), Inappropriate Intimacy(CS17), Incomplete library class(CS19) and Comments(CS22). The literature does not explain why the researchers did not attempt to detect the for above mentioned undetected code bad smells. Individually, code smells CS1 and CS2 are mostly extracted by the different authors. Specifically code smell CS1 has total 16 detection approaches [66].

5.2 Comparative Analysis Between Detection Techniques

Our investigation indicates that most researchers have explained different detection techniques for bad smells. There is no such literature available that analyze and compare all the detection techniques. Fontana et al. [60] compares only the machine learning techniques for code smell detection. This provide the information that machine learning techniques gives high accuracy (96%), except the support vector machine which provide the worst performance.

5.3 Significance of Targeting Java Source Code

This paper is specifically aimed for the research papers related with only for Java source code. The reasons behind this are: there are about 6,000 research papers and other literature available for code smells so performing systematic review efficiently, it is very difficult process with the huge number of papers. We have to apply a search string to select some specific papers as specify in Kitchenham's guidelines. Another reason is that mainly code smell work is performed on object oriented languages so we have selected the one language Java on which most of the work has been done. The most conveyancing cause is tools performance. There are many tools like PMD, Jdeodarant, Robusta, Sonar, Jsmell etc. available that can detect code smells but very few of them suggest the removing or refactoring method for the specific code smell. PMD, Jsmell and Jdeodarant identify Java code smells with their refactoring methods to remove the code smells. Due to aiming only for Java code the Table. 3 is also different from the distribution in the work of Zhang et al. [2].

6 Conclusion

In this SLR we present the outcome from systematic review of the papers related to Java source code smells. Related to research questions we have analyzed that:

RQ1, The impact of code bad smells are on maintenance process of the software. As the changes increase in the software, maintenance efforts also increase.

RQ2, All the code smells of Fowler are not detectable. Primitive Obsession, Inappropriate Intimacy, Incomplete library class and Comments are undetected code bad smells.

RQ3, There is a statistical negative correlation between the detection techniques based on code bad smells.

RQ4, Thirteen detection techniques with the respective code smells are listed in Tables 6 and 7. All the code smells [1] are listed here except only one code smell (Code Clone) which is detected by 16 detection techniques [66].

This review identified few problems in the code bad smell field which hinders the systematic review of the literature. Firstly there are mainly papers on object oriented languages like: Java, C/C++, C#, Javascript, SOUL. The selection of one language Java is due to the fact that maximum work is done on the

Java software. In addition there is no detection technique available to detect all the 22 code smells. Some smells like duplicate code and long method received more attention of the researchers than other code smells. Thus, it is a rigorous process to collect data for all types of code bad smells. There is a difference between the terms 'antipattern' and 'code bad smells' but few studies show overlapping in their categories. Some times antipattern category is explained as a code smell category.

References

1. Fowler, M.: Refactoring: Improving the Design of Existing Code. Pearson Education, India (1999)
2. Zhang, M., Hall, T., Baddoo, N.: Code bad smells: a review of current knowledge. J. Softw. Maint. Evol.: Res. Pract. **23**(3), 179–202 (2011)
3. Kessentini, M., Mahaouachi, R., Ghedira, K.: What you like in design use to correct bad-smells. Software Qual. J. **21**(4), 551–571 (2013)
4. Rattan, D., Bhatia, R., Singh, M.: Software clone detection: a systematic review. Inf. Softw. Technol. **55**(7), 1165–1199 (2013)
5. Moha, N., Guéhéneuc, Y.-G., Le Meur, A.-F., Duchien, L.: A domain analysis to specify design defects and generate detection algorithms. In: Fiadeiro, J.L., Inverardi, P. (eds.) FASE 2008. LNCS, vol. 4961, pp. 276–291. Springer, Heidelberg (2008). doi:10.1007/978-3-540-78743-3_20
6. Yamashita, A., Moonen, L.: To what extent can maintenance problems be predicted by code smell detection?-an empirical study. Inf. Softw. Technol. **55**(12), 2223–2242 (2013)
7. Kreimer, J.: Adaptive detection of design flaws. Electron. Notes Theoret. Comput. Sci. **141**(4), 117–136 (2005)
8. Mäntylä, M.V., Lassenius, C.: Subjective evaluation of software evolvability using code smells: an empirical study. Empir. Softw. Eng. **11**(3), 395–431 (2006)
9. Murphy-Hill, E., Black, A.P.: An interactive ambient visualization for code smells. In: Proceedings of the 5th International Symposium on Software Visualization, pp. 5–14. ACM (2010)
10. Chen, C.-T., Cheng, Y.C., Hsieh, C.-Y., Wu, I.-L.: Exception handling refactorings: directed by goals and driven by bug fixing. J. Syst. Softw. **82**(2), 333–345 (2009)
11. Boussaa, M., Kessentini, W., Kessentini, M., Bechikh, S., Chikha, S.B.: Competitive coevolutionary code-smells detection. In: Ruhe, G., Zhang, Y. (eds.) SSBSE 2013. LNCS, vol. 8084, pp. 50–65. Springer, Heidelberg (2013). doi:10.1007/978-3-642-39742-4_6
12. Kapdan, M., Aktas, M., Yigit, M.: On the structural code clone detection problem: a survey and software metric based approach. In: Murgante, B., Misra, S., Rocha, A.M.A.C., Torre, C., Rocha, J.G., Falcão, M.I., Taniar, D., Apduhan, B.O., Gervasi, O. (eds.) ICCSA 2014. LNCS, vol. 8583, pp. 492–507. Springer, Cham (2014). doi:10.1007/978-3-319-09156-3_35
13. Keele, S.: Guidelines for performing systematic literature reviews in software engineering. Technical report, Ver. 2.3 EBSE Technical report, EBSE (2007)
14. Yamashita, A., Counsell, S.: Code smells as system-level indicators of maintainability: an empirical study. J. Syst. Softw. **86**(10), 2639–2653 (2013)

15. Yamashita, A., Moonen, L.: Exploring the impact of inter-smell relations on software maintainability: an empirical study. In: Proceedings of the 2013 International Conference on Software Engineering, pp. 682–691. IEEE Press (2013)

16. Van Emden, E., Moonen, L.: Java quality assurance by detecting code smells. In: 2002 Proceedings of Ninth Working Conference on Reverse Engineering, pp. 97–106. IEEE (2002)

17. Yamashita, A.: Assessing the capability of code smells to explain maintenance problems: an empirical study combining quantitative and qualitative data. Empir. Softw. Eng. 19(4), 1111–1143 (2014)

18. Sjoberg, D., Yamashita, A., Anda, B.C.D., Mockus, A., Dyba, T., et al.: Quantifying the effect of code smells on maintenance effort. IEEE Trans. Softw. Eng. 39(8), 1144–1156 (2013)

19. Mahouachi, R., Kessentini, M., Ghedira, K.: A new design defects classification: marrying detection and correction. In: Lara, J., Zisman, A. (eds.) FASE 2012. LNCS, vol. 7212, pp. 455–470. Springer, Heidelberg (2012). doi:10.1007/978-3-642-28872-2_31

20. Moha, N., Guéhéneuc, Y.-G., Le Meur, A.-F., Duchien, L., Tiberghien, A.: From a domain analysis to the specification and detection of code and design smells. Formal Aspects Comput. 22(3–4), 345–361 (2010)

21. Czibula, G., Marian, Z., Czibula, I.G.: Detecting software design defects using relational association rule mining. Knowl. Inf. Syst. 42(3), 545–577 (2015)

22. Kessentini, M., Sahraoui, H., Boukadoum, M., Wimmer, M.: Search-based design defects detection by example. In: Giannakopoulou, D., Orejas, F. (eds.) FASE 2011. LNCS, vol. 6603, pp. 401–415. Springer, Heidelberg (2011). doi:10.1007/978-3-642-19811-3_28

23. von Detten, M., Becker, S.: Combining clustering and pattern detection for the reengineering of component-based software systems. In: Proceedings of the Joint ACM SIGSOFT Conference-QoSA and ACM SIGSOFT Symposium-ISARCS on Quality of Software Architectures-QoSA and Architecting Critical Systems-ISARCS, pp. 23–32. ACM (2011)

24. Santos, J.A., de Mendonça, M.G., Silva, C.V.: An exploratory study to investigate the impact of conceptualization in god class detection. In: Proceedings of the 17th International Conference on Evaluation and Assessment in Software Engineering, pp. 48–59. ACM (2013)

25. Munro, M.J.: Product metrics for automatic identification of "bad smell" design problems in java source-code. In: 2005 11th IEEE International Symposium on Software Metrics, pp. 15–15. IEEE (2005)

26. Dhambri, K., Sahraoui, H., Poulin, P.: Visual detection of design anomalies. In: 2008 12th European Conference on Software Maintenance and Reengineering, CSMR 2008, pp. 279–283. IEEE (2008)

27. de F Carneiro, G., Silva, M., Mara, L., Figueiredo, E., Sant'Anna, C., Garcia, A., Mendonça, M.: Identifying code smells with multiple concern views. In: 2010 Brazilian Symposium on Software Engineering (SBES), pp. 128–137. IEEE (2010)

28. Hassaine, S., Khomh, F., Guéhéneuc, Y.-G., Hamel, S.: IDS: an immune-inspired approach for the detection of software design smells. In: 2010 Seventh International Conference on Quality of Information and Communications Technology (QUATIC), pp. 343–348. IEEE (2010)

29. Liu, H., Ma, Z., Shao, W., Niu, Z.: Schedule of bad smell detection and resolution: a new way to save effort. IEEE Trans. Softw. Eng. 38(1), 220–235 (2012)

30. Maneerat, N., Muenchaisri, P.: Bad-smell prediction from software design model using machine learning techniques. In: 2011 Eighth International Joint Conference on Computer Science and Software Engineering (JCSSE), pp. 331–336. IEEE (2011)

31. Fontana, F.A., Mariani, E., Morniroli, A., Sormani, R., Tonello, A.: An experience report on using code smells detection tools. In: 2011 IEEE Fourth International Conference on Software Testing, Verification and Validation Workshops (ICSTW), pp. 450–457. IEEE (2011)

32. Danphitsanuphan, P., Suwantada, T.: Code smell detecting tool and code smell-structure bug relationship. In: 2012 Spring Congress on Engineering and Technology (S-CET), pp. 1–5. IEEE (2012)

33. Dexun, J., Peijun, M., Xiaohong, S., Tiantian, W.: Detecting bad smells with weight based distance metrics theory. In: 2012 Second International Conference on Instrumentation, Measurement, Computer, Communication and Control (IMCCC), pp. 299–304. IEEE (2012)

34. Ligu, E., Chatzigeorgiou, A., Chaikalis, T., Ygeionomakis, N.: Identification of refused bequest code smells. In: 2013 29th IEEE International Conference on Software Maintenance (ICSM), pp. 392–395. IEEE (2013)

35. Palomba, F., Bavota, G., Di Penta, M., Oliveto, R., De Lucia, A., Poshyvanyk, D.: Detecting bad smells in source code using change history information. In: 2013 IEEE/ACM 28th International Conference on Automated Software Engineering (ASE), pp. 268–278. IEEE (2013)

36. Kessentini, W., Kessentini, M., Sahraoui, H., Bechikh, S., Ouni, A.: A cooperative parallel search-based software engineering approach for code-smells detection. IEEE Trans. Softw. Eng. 40(9), 841–861 (2014)

37. Walter, B., Matuszyk, B., Fontana, F.A.: Including structural factors into the metrics-based code smells detection. In: Scientific Workshop Proceedings of the XP2015, p. 11. ACM (2015)

38. Chatzigeorgiou, A., Manakos, A.: Investigating the evolution of code smells in object-oriented systems. Innov. Syst. Softw. Eng. 10(1), 3–18 (2014)

39. Bakota, T.: Tracking the evolution of code clones. In: Černá, I., Gyimóthy, T., Hromkovič, J., Jefferey, K., Královič, R., Vukolić, M., Wolf, S. (eds.) SOFSEM 2011. LNCS, vol. 6543, pp. 86–98. Springer, Heidelberg (2011). doi:10.1007/978-3-642-18381-2_7

40. Shatnawi, R., Li, W.: An investigation of bad smells in object-oriented design. In: 2006 Third International Conference on Information Technology: New Generations, ITNG 2006, pp. 161–165. IEEE (2006)

41. Zhang, M., Baddoo, N., Wernick, P., Hall, T.: Improving the precision of fowler's definitions of bad smells. In: 2008 32nd Annual IEEE Software Engineering Workshop, SEW 2008, pp. 161–166. IEEE (2008)

42. Vaucher, S., Khomh, F., Moha, N., Guéhéneuc, Y.-G.: Tracking design smells: lessons from a study of god classes. In: 2009 16th Working Conference on Reverse Engineering, WCRE 2009, pp. 145–154. IEEE (2009)

43. Göde, N., Koschke, R.: Studying clone evolution using incremental clone detection. J. Softw.: Evol. Process 25(2), 165–192 (2013)

44. Khomh, F., Di Penta, M., Guéhéneuc, Y.-G., Antoniol, G.: An exploratory study of the impact of antipatterns on class change-and fault-proneness. Empir. Softw. Eng. 17(3), 243–275 (2012)

45. Thummalapenta, S., Cerulo, L., Aversano, L., Di Penta, M.: An empirical study on the maintenance of source code clones. Empir. Softw. Eng. 15(1), 1–34 (2010)

46. Rahman, F., Bird, C., Devanbu, P.: Clones: What is that smell? Empir. Softw. Eng. **17**(4–5), 503–530 (2012)

47. Li, W., Shatnawi, R.: An empirical study of the bad smells and class error probability in the post-release object-oriented system evolution. J. Syst. Softw. **80**(7), 1120–1128 (2007)

48. Guo, Y., Seaman, C., Zazworka, N., Shull, F.: Domain-specific tailoring of code smells: an empirical study. In: Proceedings of the 32nd ACM/IEEE International Conference on Software Engineering, vol. 2, pp. 167–170. ACM (2010)

49. Counsell, S., Hamza, H., Hierons, R.: The deception of code smells: an empirical investigation. In: 2010 32nd International Conference on Information Technology Interfaces (ITI), pp. 683–688. IEEE (2010)

50. Abbes, M., Khomh, F., Gueheneuc, Y.-G., Antoniol, G.: An empirical study of the impact of two antipatterns, blob and spaghetti code, on program comprehension. In: 2011 15th European Conference on Software Maintenance and Reengineering (CSMR), pp. 181–190. IEEE (2011)

51. Olbrich, S., Cruzes, D.S., Basili, V., Zazworka, N.: The evolution and impact of code smells: a case study of two open source systems. In: Proceedings of the 2009 3rd International Symposium on Empirical Software Engineering and Measurement, pp. 390–400. IEEE Computer Society (2009)

52. Olbrich, S.M., Cruze, D.S., Sjøberg, D.I.: Are all code smells harmful? A study of god classes and brain classes in the evolution of three open source systems. In: 2010 IEEE International Conference on Software Maintenance (ICSM), pp. 1–10. IEEE (2010)

53. Ouni, A., Kessentini, M., Bechikh, S., Sahraoui, H.: Prioritizing code-smells correction tasks using chemical reaction optimization. Softw. Qual. J. **23**(2), 323–361 (2015)

54. Parnin, C., Görg, C., Nnadi, O.: A catalogue of lightweight visualizations to support code smell inspection. In: Proceedings of the 4th ACM Symposium on Software Visualization, pp. 77–86. ACM (2008)

55. Macia, I., Garcia, J., Popescu, D., Garcia, A., Medvidovic, N., von Staa, A.: Are automatically-detected code anomalies relevant to architectural modularity?: an exploratory analysis of evolving systems. In: Proceedings of the 11th Annual International Conference on Aspect-Oriented Software Development, pp. 167–178. ACM (2012)

56. Pate, J.R., Tairas, R., Kraft, N.A.: Clone evolution: a systematic review. J. Softw.: Evol. Process **25**(3), 261–283 (2013)

57. Khomh, F., Penta, M.D., Gueheneuc, Y.-G.: An exploratory study of the impact of code smells on software change-proneness. In: 2009 16th Working Conference on Reverse Engineering, WCRE 2009, pp. 75–84. IEEE (2009)

58. Chatzigeorgiou, A., Manakos, A.: Investigating the evolution of bad smells in object-oriented code. In: 2010 Seventh International Conference on Quality of Information and Communications Technology (QUATIC), pp. 106–115. IEEE (2010)

59. Hall, T., Zhang, M., Bowes, D., Sun, Y.: Some code smells have a significant but small effect on faults. ACM Trans. Softw. Eng. Methodol. (TOSEM) **23**(4), 33 (2014)

60. Fontana, F.A., Mäntylä, M.V., Zanoni, M., Marino, A.: Comparing and experimenting machine learning techniques for code smell detection. Empir. Softw. Eng. **21**(3), 1143–1191 (2016)

61. Fontana, F.A., Ferme, V., Zanoni, M.: Filtering code smells detection results. In: Proceedings of the 37th International Conference on Software Engineering, vol. 2, pp. 803–804. IEEE Press (2015)

62. Tufano, M., Palomba, F., Bavota, G., Oliveto, R., Di Penta, M., De Lucia, A., Poshyvanyk, D.: When and why your code starts to smell bad. In: Proceedings of the 37th International Conference on Software Engineering, vol. 1, pp. 403–414. IEEE Press (2015)

63. Kapser, C.J., Godfrey, M.W.: Cloning considered harmful considered harmful: patterns of cloning in software. Empir. Softw. Eng. **13**(6), 645–692 (2008)

64. Walter, B., Alkhaeir, T.: The relationship between design patterns and code smells: an exploratory study. Inf. Softw. Technol. **74**, 127–142 (2016)

65. AyshwaryaLakshmi, S., Mary, S., Vadivu, S.S., et al.: Agent based tool for topologically sorting badsmells and refactoring by analyzing complexities in source code. In: 2013 Fourth International Conference on Computing, Communications and Networking Technologies (ICCCNT), pp. 1–7. IEEE (2013)

66. Aakanshi Gupta, B.S.: A survey on code clone, its behavior and applications. In: Networking Communication and Data Knowledge Engineering- Proceedings of ICRACCCS-2016 (2016)

67. Rasool, G., Arshad, Z.: A review of code smell mining techniques. J. Softw.: Evol. Process **27**(11), 867–895 (2015)

A Requirements Engineering Techniques Review in Agile Software Development Methods

Lizbeth Zamudio[1], José Alfonso Aguilar[2(✉)], Carolina Tripp[2],
and Sanjay Misra[3]

[1] Posgrado en Ciencias de la Información, Facultad de Informática Culiacán,
Universidad Autónoma de Sinaloa, 82120 Mazatlán, Mexico
e.zamudio@uas.edu.mx
[2] Señales y Sistemas (SESIS) Facultad de Informática Mazatlán,
Universidad Autónoma de Sinaloa, 82120 Mazatlán, Mexico
{ja.aguilar,ctripp}@uas.edu.mx
[3] Covenant University, Ota, Nigeria
ssopam@gmail.com
http://sesis.maz.uasnet.mx

Abstract. The first phase in the software development process is the Requirements Engineering (RE). Several methods for software development and RE techniques have been used to extract these users' needs depending on the software complexity. Our goal is to map the evidence available about requirements engineering techniques adopted and challenges faced by agile methods in order to understand how traditional requirements engineering issues are resolved using agile requirements engineering. The agile methods considered for this work are: SCRUM, Dynamic Systems Development Method (DSDM), Adaptive Software Development (ASD) and Crystal Family. The present work is based on the Systematic Literature Review (SLR) method proposed by Kitchenham; we have reviewed publications from ACM, IEEE, Science Direct, DBLP and World Wide Web. From a population of 34 papers, we identified 15 primary studies, which provide information concerning RE used in Agile Software Development Processes.

Keywords: Requirements engineering · Systematic literature review · RE Techniques

1 Introduction

Many companies nowadays do not use formal methodologies in their software development projects [1], they uses intead common sense and its team experience. This issue originates low quality software, which is not allowed in an environment in which the technological and business environment changes rapidly. Methodologies have proven too cumbersome to meet the rapidly changing requirements and short product cycles demanded by business today. To meet these rapidly

© Springer International Publishing AG 2017
O. Gervasi et al. (Eds.): ICCSA 2017, Part V, LNCS 10408, pp. 683–698, 2017.
DOI: 10.1007/978-3-319-62404-4_50

changing requirements, software developers have developed agile software development methodologies utilizing iterative development, prototyping, templates, and minimal documentation requirements [2].

This is the reason why software engineering projects requires the use of methodologies and dynamic processes to develop products and services quickly and reliably. A clear fact is, however, that there is no single methodology that is suitable for any project. This is why it is very important to know the different methodologies that may be applicable to the projects, as well as to manage the tools that will allow them to be selected, adapted or even formulated. These new approaches focus mainly on iterative and incremental development, customer collaboration, and frequent delivery through a light and fast development cycle [3]. Many researchers have reported that agile methods have the potential to provide a higher level of customer satisfaction, lower bug rates, a shorter development cycle, and a quicker adaptation to rapidly changing business requirements.

In this sense, one of the most important facts to achieve a successfull software is the first phase in the software development process: the Requirements Engineering (RE). The main goal of RE is to attempt to fully satisfy users' needs [4]. Therefore, several methods for software development and RE techniques have been used to extract these users' needs depending on the software complexity.

Although claimed to be beneficial, the software development community as a whole is still unfamiliar with the role of the RE practices in agile methods. The term "agile requirements engineering" or ARE is used to define the agile form of planning, executing and reasoning about RE activities. Moreover, not much is known about the challenges posed by collaboration-oriented agile way of dealing with RE activities [5]. Agile methods offer a viable solution when the software to be developed has fuzzy or changing requirements, being able to cope with changing requirements throughout the life cycle of a project. Adoption of agile software development methods enables a software developer to be more flexible and responsive to the changing environments and customer demands [6].

Agile software development processes were developed primarily to support timely and economical development of high-quality software that meets customer needs at the time of delivery. It is claimed by agile process advocates that this can be accomplished by using development processes that continuously adapt and adjust to (1) collective experience and skills of the developers, including experience and skills gained thus far in the development project, (2) changes in softw requirements and (3) changes in the development and targeted operating environments [7].

This paper presents a Systematic Literature Review (SLR) in order to analyze the current state-of-the-art with regard to Requirements Engineering (RE) techniques used in ASD, specifically in agile requirements engineering (ARE), thus revealing the activities that are implemented, such as elicitation, analysis, specification, validation and management. A SLR is a means of identifying, evaluating and interpreting all the available research that is relevant to a particular research question, topic area or phenomenon of interest. It originated in the field of medical research and was successfully adapted to Software Engineering (SE) by Kitchenham [8].

This paper is structured as follows: Sect. 2 presents some background. The SLR is detailed in Sect. 3. The research Questions are answered in Sect. 4, in which and analysis and discussion of this work are also presented. Finally, our conclusions are provided in Sect. 5.

2 Background

This section presents an introduction about the agile methods considered for this work and the Requirements Engineering Concepts for the analysis of Sect. 4.

The agile software development methods analyzed are: SCRUM, Dynamic Systems Development Method (DSDM), Adaptive Software Development (ASD) and Crystal Family. SCRUM is a methodology for the management and control of projects, focused on the construction of software that satisfies the needs of the customer, meets the objectives of the business and the development team that product. Scrum does not require or provide any specific software development methods/practices to be used. Instead, it requires certain management practices and tools in different phases of Scrum to avoid the chaos by unpredictability and complexity [9].

In [10], the author defines SCRUM, as a collection of processes for the management of projects, which in delivering value to the customer and the power- of the equipment to achieve maximum efficiency, within of a continuous improvement scheme. The fundamental idea behind DSDM is that instead of fixing the amount of functionality in a product, and then adjusting time and resources to reach that functionality, it is preferred to fix time and resources, and then adjust the amount of functionality accordingly. Also, the roles defined in that approach were combined and adapted, according to the team structure of the company. Because of its simplicity and being more test-driven, allowing close collaboration and communication [6]. In [11] the author define This is heavier than XP and Scrum. It provides a technique-independent process and is flexible in terms of requirement evolution. It is efficient in terms of budget and time. But It is based on user involvement which is not possible in every project.

Adaptive Software Development (ASD) is a framework for the iterative development of large, complex systems. The method encourages incremental, iterative development with constant prototyping [12]. ASD highlights that a sequential waterfall approach only works in well-understood and well-defined environments. But as changes occur frequently in software development, it is important to use a change-tolerant method. The first cycles of an ASD project should be short, ensure that the customer is strongly involved and confirm the project's viability. ASD focuses more on results and their quality than the tasks or the process used for producing the results [9].

Crystal Family method is based on the concept Rational Unified Process [RUP] and is composed by Crystal Clear, Crystal Yellow, Crystal orange and Crystal Red, important, the level of color opacity in the name indicates a greater number of people involved and the size of the project, therefore, the need for greater control in the process [13]. The values shared by members of the Crystal family are focused on people and communication, its principles indicate that: the team can reduce intermediate work to the extent that it produces code with greater frequency and uses better channels of communication between people.

On the other hand, there are interesting works about reviews in agile software developments methods such as [7,9,11,14–17], but these works regrettably does not point out the gaps regarding to requirements engineering techniques applied on each method and how to address their limitations in order to improve software development. In this sense, Requirements Engineering (RE) is the process of establishing the services that the customer requires from a system and the constraints under which it operates and is developed [18]. Various approaches have been used to define RE activities, such as those proposed in [19], and these activities widely differ from each other for several reasons, e.g., depending on the application domain, the people involved and the organization developing the requirements. Requirements Engineering (RE) is concerned with the elicitation, analysis, specification, validation and management of software requirements [20]. These are detailed as follows:

- Elicitation, whose goal is to discover what problems need to be solved [21], and to identify the stakeholders, and the objectives that a software system must attain. It is carried out through the application of various techniques [22], such as questionnaires, brainstorming, prototyping and modeling techniques, e.g., goal oriented based methods [23].
- Analysis, which includes the creation of conceptual models or prototypes with which to achieve the completeness of the requirements and deals with understanding an organization's structure, its business rules, goals and tasks, and the data that is needed.
- Specification, which is an integral description of the behavior of the system to be developed. The most widely used techniques are templates, scenarios, use case modeling, and natural language [24].
- Validation. The aim of this phase is to establish whether the requirements elicited provide an accurate representation of the actual stakeholder requirements. Some of the techniques employed are reviews and traceability [25].
- Management, which consists of recognizing changes through the use of continuous requirements elicitation, and includes techniques for configuration management and version control [26].

With regard to RE techniques, we have Interviews, Documentation Study, On-site observation, Use Cases, Scenarios, Focus Groups, Brainstorming, Prototyping, Questionnaire, Natural Language and Form of contract, these are detailed next.

- Interviews. Interviewing is a method for discovering facts and opinions held by potential users and other stakeholders of the system under development. There are two different kinds of interviews: (i) the closed interview, where the requirements engineer has a pre-defined set of questions and is looking for answers and (ii) the open interview, without any pre-defined questions the requirements engineer and stakeholders discuss in an open-ended way what they expect from a system. The advantage of interviews is that they help the developer to get a rich collection of information. Their disadvantage is that this amount of qualitative data can be hard to analyze and different stakeholders may provide conflicting information [25].

- Documentation study. The documentation study consists of an in-depth reading based on documents on the domain of the problem of the system to be developed. These documents will deal with aspects related to the business objectives of the organization or its professional practices. Some of the main documents that can be consulted and analysed are: manuals of procedures and functions, reports generated by the current system, regulations and legislations, user manuals of the current system, etc.
- On-site observation. The in situ observation consists of the direct observation of the professional practices that are usually carried out in the organization for which the software will be developed. Before conducting an on-site observation session, a set of practices representative of the rest should be chosen, which are carried out relatively often or have a certain complexity of understanding.
- Use cases. This technique intends at defining the requirements by portraying complete flow of events to the stakeholders in the form of a story telling style. Use cases are informal and easy to use that help understanding the requirements and validating them with stakeholders [27].
- Scenarios. Scenarios are commonly used after collecting the initial requirements. Scenarios also define the actions and interactions between user and the system. Scenarios are useful to validate requirements and develop test cases [27].
- Focus Groups. This technique is effective to elicit requirements and resolving conflicts among the stakeholders by discussing all aspect of requirements with proper suggestions by the group members in a cooperative environment. However, it requires a lot of effort to conduct such meeting as it is always difficult to get hold of all the stakeholders at the same time [27].
- Brainstorming. Brainstorming is a technique of group meetings whose purpose is to generate ideas in an environment free of criticism or judgment. As a technique for collecting requirements information, brainstorming can help generate a wide variety of views of the problem and formulate it in different ways, especially at the beginning of the requirements engineering process, when the requirements are still very diffuse [28]. The key disadvantage of brainstorming is that it cannot be effectively used to resolve major issues [27].
- Prototyping. Prototyping is a useful technique to develop novel applications and to build GUI interface. This technique is used with the combination of other requirement engineering techniques like interviews and JAD. Conversely, potential hazards in prototyping are that the user often resist changes if they had become used to a specific kind of the system as well as it is also expensive in terms of time and cost [27].
- Questionnaire. The questionnaire is a method of requirement elicitation which is simple and requires lesser time and cost. To get precise results, the questionnaire should be clear, concise and structured to obtain genuine user require-

ments, objective and constraints However, this technique lacks in the mechanism to seek users clarification on the topic [27].

- Form of contract. Consists of filling forms or contracts indicating the requirements. It can be extensive according to the size of the Project and therefore tends to be tedious its use within software development [29].
- Natural Language. Natural language is an important source of information, because in most domains it is the most common mode of knowledge representation. There are two categories: direct interaction with the user using natural language and elicitation of requirements from a natural language document. The greatest appeal of natural language lies in its preexisting vocabulary, informality and syntax. The existence of a vocabulary of thousands of predefined words used to describe any possible concept makes natural language an efficient means of communication. It is familiar to both the user and the analyst and does not require learning time. However, there are two clear limitations: natural language is very complex and ambiguous [30].

Summarizing, the use of techniques in the RE process is important since this helps software engineers to avoid errors in the definition of the requirements due to it can be very expensive to correct once the system has been developed. In this paper the traditional techniques that are used in the RE applied by the traditional methodologies are mentioned adding to this the process with which each method counts helps to strengthen and in this way to obtain products to develop with a higher quality. Agile methods are the solution to the problems that can be caused by traditional methodologies. These methodologies emphasize that responsiveness to change is more important than strict adherence to a plan.

3   The Systematic Literature Review

The goal of this SLR is to analyze the current state-of-the-art with regard to Requirements Engineering (RE) techniques [21] used in ASD, specifically in agile requirements engineering (ARE), thus revealing the activities that are implemented, such as elicitation [22], analysis [19], specification [31], validation [24] and management [25] in order to detect avenues for future research.

3.1   Research Questions

According to [8], the question structure is divided into four aspects known as PICO (Population, Intervention, Comparison and Outcomes). The term Population refers to the people, projects and application types affected by the intervention. Intervention concerns the software technology, tool or procedure that generates the outcomes. Comparison refers to another type of intervention – if applicable – while Outcomes are the technological impact on relevant information terms for practical professionals. This PICO strategy has been used as the basis for our research and is use in this context is described as follows:

- Population: the population is composed of developers who request a method in order to obtain more robust process support.
- Intervention: this review must search for indications that the development of software can be fully supported by an agile method supporting requirements engineering techniques.
- Comparison: not applicable.
- Outcomes: the objective is to demonstrate how a systematic process supports the development software and whether or not the process is fully supported with RE techniques.

Our research questions (RQ), which are based on the aforementioned strategy, are:

- RQ1.- What agile approaches exist applying traditional RE techniques in their agile development processes?
- RQ2.- Which RE techniques are commonly used to obtain the users' needs in their agile development processes?

3.2 Search Strategy

The search strategy should be systematic. According to [8], it is necessary to use search engines by applying a combination of search terms (keywords) extracted from RQ's. Experts should then verify and review the search results. Once the steps to be followed in the search process have been defined, it is necessary to state the resources that are available to conduct the review of primary studies (individual studies contributing to an SLR). The research sources used are repositories with restricted access such as: ACM, IEEE, Science Direct, DBLP Computer Science Bibliography, World Wide Web: Google Scholar. In accordance with Brereton [32], these libraries were chosen because they are some of the most relevant sources in SE. Furthermore, Google Scholar was selected to complete the set of conferences and workshops searched and to seek grey literature in the field (white papers, PhD theses), and the results obtained were then compared with the works found using the search strings.

3.3 Inclusion and Exclusion Criteria

Essentially, only those publications from the RE literature regarding the RE activities for specific use in the ASD field were considered. Although our research questions are related only to techniques, this SLR includes the primary studies related to the RE in the agile methods field and we therefore deemed that at least the part related to the use of one of the RE activities in ASD must be present in each primary study, since we assumed that not all methods implement another RE phase. We chose the following inclusion criteria in order to select the relevant publications required to answer our research questions: (i) Publication date between 01/01/2006 – 01/01/2016, (ii) Requirements phase of the development process, (iii) Explicit mention of agile software development and (iv) Relevance with regard to research questions. The exclusion criteria were: (i) Topics that do not match the RE activities implemented in ASD methods and (ii) Duplicated documents from the same study.

3.4 Study Quality Assessment

The place of publication and the diffusion of the papers were used as indicators when performing the quality assessment. The place of publication refers to the journals and conferences in which the primary studies were published (this applies to Google–Scholar which searches for a wider spectrum of papers such as white papers). The diffusion of the methods corresponds to the academic or industrial application of the method. The first search, during which no exclusion criteria were applied, returned a total of 34 documents of which 2 documents were duplicated. After applying the exclusion criteria (a further review round), 15 documents were eventually considered. It is important to mention that the activity during which publications were searched for was checked by two individual authors of this work in order to verify the quality of the place of publication. The quality assessment was then performed separately to verify the information extracted.

3.5 Data Extraction

The goal of this phase is to design data extraction forms with which to accurately record the information obtained from the primary studies. We used a form to store the information extracted from the search results, storing the publication title, the journal or conference/workshop in which the paper was published, the publication date and the main author. After quality assessment, the data synthesis was performed. This was done by collating and summarizing the results of the primary studies, 15 total which are shown in annex 1 (Table 2).

4   Data Analysis

This section presents and analyzes the results obtained after subjecting the primary studies to the extraction and data synthesis activities. The agile methods considered for this work are: SCRUM, Dynamic Systems Development Method (DSDM), Adaptive Software Development (ASD) and Crystal Family. The selected studies provided relevant evidence with which to satisfactorily answer the four RQs, as described below:

4.1 RQ1.- What Agile Approaches Exist Applying Traditional RE Techniques in Their Agile Development Processes?

For eXtreme Programming (XP), Scrum and Crystal methods applying traditional RE techniques in their development processes, the authors use different traditional techniques. In the work presented by [29], the authors use the combination of several techniques in the requirements elicitation process as: interviews, brainstorming, prioritization, analysis, modeling, use case. In [33], the authors propose in the Scrum method some techniques according to the software engineering process as it is, in elicitation the techniques to be used are: use cases, scenarios, interviews; In the analysis phase the proposed techniques integrates the UML diagrams and for the design phase only use cases. For the methodology called Crystal, they suggest interviews, reflection workshops and meetings. The author [16], in his research work, propose other techniques for the Crystal method as use cases implementing UML and brainstorming, for Scrum recommend prototypes, for XP scenarios and for the Dynamic Systems Development Method (DSDM) workshops. In the research presented in, the author contemplates the technique of prototypes in the method Adaptive Software Development (ASD). In [12] the authors include other techniques for the ASD method such as reviews and Joint Application Development (JAD) sessions, for the Crystal and DSDM methods the techniques proposed are documentation, revisions and suggest that observation and social analysis can be used to.

The agile methodologies considered for the elaboration of this paper are: SCRUM, DSDM, Adaptive Software Development (ASD) and Crystal Family, but we find other agile methods that use traditional techniques, such as Agile Unified Process (AUP), Kanban and Lean Software Development [29], these approaches use interviews, brainstorming, prioritization, analysis meetings, modeling, requirements documentation and use cases. In the research carried out by [12], the authors focuses on the Agile Modeling (AM) method, which uses the techniques of modeling and brainstorming, another method that includes in their work is Feature Driven Development (FDD), which includes class diagrams and meetings, for the DSDM method uses JAD sessions and prototypes. In [34], the authors present in their work for the AUP method the modeling in the elicitation phase, in the Iconix method the use cases using UML. Finally, in [35], the authors include in addition to the methods already mentioned the Agile Project Management (APM) with the technique of daily meetings.

4.2   RQ2.- Which RE Techniques Are Commonly Used to Obtain the Users' Needs in Their Agile Development Processes?

As for the requirements engineering techniques applied in agile development methods we find the work of [13] in which the authors describe other non-traditional techniques that use the Scrum method which are: Backlog, Sprint, Sprint planning, Daily Scrum, Sprint Review, for the XP method the use of User Stories. The author [18] mentions in addition that the core practice in Scrum is the use of daily 15-minute team meetings for coordination and integration, face-to-face communication and review meetings In [16], the authors remarks that for the XP method in addition to the user stories he also applies the story cards, list of tasks in paper or chalkboard and visible graphs in a wall. The author [36] establishes tahta before the stories can be written on the cards customers have to think about what they expect the system do to and what functionality is needed.

In the Crystal staging method, standing meetings, methodology tuning technique and user views; for the Scrum method the author also state the effort estimation, burn-down chart, burn-up chart and planning poker. In [12] are proposed other techniques for Crystal method, which contemplates time-boxed, workshops for product.

The following table mentions the techniques of the traditional methods and which are used in the agile methodologies (Table 1):

Table 1. Tradicional techniques in techniques agil methods

RE Techniques in traditional SDP	RE Techniques in ASD
Software requirements e specification	Backlog in Scrum
Interview	In Scrum, Xp, Crystal
Brainstorming	In Scrum, Crystal, points of view in XP
Use cases	In Crystal, story uses in XP
Scenarios	In Scrum, Xp
Meeting	In Xp, Crystal
Prototypes	In Scrum, time-boxed in Crystal and ASD
Priorization	In Scrum, Xp, Crystal, Kanban
Modeling	In Scrum, Xp, Crystal, Kanban
Analysis meetings	In AUP, Kanban, Planning Poker in Scrum
Observation	In Scrum, Xp, ASD, DSDM, Crystal
Social analysis	In Scrum, Xp, ASD, DSDM, Crystal
Documentation	Burn-down and burn-up in Scrum
Reviews	In ASD Reviews Sprint in Scrum

4.3   An Agile Methods Analysis

One of the critical points within software development is requirements satisfaction. It has been shown that most of the errors in software products occur in the RE phase. It should also be considered that within the SE, the requirements are within the early phases of software development process and the cost associated with the correction of an error, once the project is delivered, is significantly higher. Given these reasons, it is necessary that organizations implements software development process ad-hoc to its development team, to do this, is fundamental the adaptation of the RE process according to its team capacity if they wish to make their development process more efficient, i.e., the implementation of CMMI (Capability Maturity Model Integration), which in the first levels requires a documented and formalized RE within the organization [37]. The research should be oriented to the use of new techniques and approaches that strengthen characteristics such as agility in the treatment of requirements, reduction of conflicts between participants, timely recognition of errors or problems in the identification and specification of requirements and the establishment

Table 2. Annexed 1

Article	Publication	Year
A systematic literature review on agile requirements engineering practices and challenges	Computers in Human Behavior	2015
Assumptions underlying agile software development processes	arXiv preprint arXiv:1409.6610	2014
Analysis of requirement engineering processes, tools/techniques and methodologies	International Journal of Information Technology *and Computer Science (IJITCS)*	2013
Metodologías ágiles enfocadas al modelado de requerimientos	Informe Científico Técnico UNPA	2013
A comparative study of agile, component-based, aspect-oriented and mashup software development methods	Tehnicki Vjesnik	2012
Agile software development methodology for medium and large projects	Ágile software development methodology for medium *and large projects*	2011
Complex software project development: agile methods adoption	Journal of Software Maintenance and Evolution: *Research and Practice*	2011
A study of the Agile software development methods, applicability and implications in industry	International Journal of Software Engineering and *its applications*	2011
Management guidelines for scrum agile software development process	Issues in Information Systems	2011
Requirements engineering in agile software development	Journal of emerging technologies in web intelligence	2010
An MDA Approach for Goal-oriented Requirement Analysis in Web Engineering	J. UCS	2010
Las metodologías ágiles como garantía de calidad del software	J. REICIS. Revista Española de Innovación, Calidad *e Ingeniería del Software*	2009
Las Metodologías de Desarrollo ágil como una Oportunidad para la Ingeniería del Software Educativo	Revista Avances en Sistemas e Informática	2008
Factors that Significantly Impact the Implementation of an Agile Software Development Methodology	JSW	2008
Requirements engineering and agile software development	Enabling Technologies: Infrastructure for Collaborative *Enterprises, 2003 WET ICE 2003. Proceedings. Twelfth IEEE International Workshops on*	2003

of controls in its evolution in different phases of the life cycle [38] since, even today, most software projects are considered to fail in one form or another, presenting a series of common symptoms such as:

- Inadequate understanding of the end user's needs.
- Inability to meet changing requirements.
- Modules that can not be coupled to work together.
- Software difficult to maintain or expand.
- Late detection of critical faults.
- Software of low quality.
- Unacceptable software performance.

Next, a set of deficiencies extracted from primary studies are detailed:

1. Not all methodologies can be used in any software development project, this depends on the size of the project, i.e., in the case of very small projects may be enough to use rapid development methodologies such as XP. In projects of much larger scale it will be desirable, on the contrary, to minimize risks by supporting development with project management methodologies that facilitate the handling of aspects such as procurement, third party contracts, risk management, human resources, and In general, aspects that are beyond the scope of simple software development [1].

2. The emphasis that agile methods place on communication can also make it difficult for international teams to work together in an agile way. The transfer of knowledge becomes more difficult when people are not working on the same site or even speaking the same language. In such a case, the use of documentation is necessary, but this often leads to missinterpretation [39].

3. Despite the fact that the use of agile methods offers a number of benefits and has been a widely used adopted by software development teams, agile methods does not offer the same benefits when it comes to medium and large software projects. Some of the reasons for this are the weakness of the documentation, the lack of ignorance to the risk awareness during the development of the software [40].

4. Productivity measured in lines of code also increases if agile methods are used. With regard to product quality, the work presented in [41] indicates that the quality of the product may increase, but it is not conclusive.

5. The main problem for the management of agile methods is the correct quantification and evaluation of the real state of the project. There are not many clear and generalizable conclusions, but we can say that no evidence has been detected against the use of these agile methodologies. Perhaps the most delicate point would be to make the concepts of "software architecture" compatible with that of "agility". The software architecture, defined according to the Rational Unified Process, is defined as the set of decisions about the organization of a software system, the selection of the structural elements and the interfaces of which the system will be composed, along with the behavior that specify those elements [41].

On the other hand, there are a set of benefits of the implementation of agile methods in software development, i.e., it has been found that XP has been more difficult to introduce into complex organizations and that it was more suitable for small groups than for larger projects. The adoption of agile methods is easy in many cases and benefits are found in the collaboration with the client, in the treatment of errors and in some aspects of management and even in estimation. There is also some improvement in the perception of the clients on the effects of communication, although if the contact is very continuous it is perceived tiredness [41].

The success factors with quantitative evidences in the implementation of this type of methods are: (i) the use of a correct strategy of product delivery, (ii) the use of an adequate practice of agile SE techniques, the integration of a group of high qualification work together with a high involvement of the client and an adequate management process. Software architecture is not only concerned with structure and behavior, but also with its use, functionality, performance, reuse, comprehensibility, and economic and technological constraints. Next are listed a set of strengths for the agile methods studied in this review:

- XP. Extreme Programming (XP) is the most popular agile methodology and is based on a series of concepts that include: having the business customer on-site, pair programming, collective code ownership, continuous code integration, small releases, designing test before writing code, standup meetings, refactoring and 40-h work weeks [6].
- SCRUM. Scrum is an iterative, incremental process for developing any product or managing any work. Scrum concentrates on how the team members should function in order to produce the system flexibility in a constantly changing environment [9].
- ASD. The objectives and schedules are set in the initiation phase of the Project. In the collaboration phase, several components are under concurrent development since components are constantly refining the planning cycle is a part of the iterative process. The final phase Reflects on the work that has been done, including project status and client input, and how the process could be improved [39].
- Crystal. Crystal methods focus on security, efficiency and usability (developers should methodology). This method has a number of principles in common, the most important is the delivery of products, comments on improvements and good communication between team members [39]. Focuses on communication in small teams developing software that is not life-critical [11].
- DSDM. There are nine practices that define the ideology and the basis for all activity in DSDM. Some of the underlying principles include active user interaction, frequent deliveries, empowered teams, and testing throughout the cycle. There is an emphasis on high quality and adaptivity towards changing requirements. Like other agile methods, DSDM approaches iterations as short time-boxed cycles of between two and six weeks [9].

5   Conclusion and Future Work

In this SLR, we formulated and applied specific inclusion and exclusion criteria to determine the most relevant studies for our research questions (RQ1 and RQ2 in Sect. 3). The agile methods considered for this work were SCRUM, Dynamic Systems Development Method (DSDM), Adaptive Software Development (ASD) and Crystal Family. Our findings identified 15 works related with ARE, and we conclude that suggest that agile requirements engineering, as a research context, needs additional attention and more empirical results are required to better understand the impact of agile requirements engineering practices e.g. dealing with non-functional requirements and self-organizing teams. Moreover, systematic approaches related to the application of RE techniques in personalized software development methods are not studied in current literature. We suggest, as a future work, that empirical studies should be performed with sufficient rigor to enhance the body of evidence in RE within ASD. In this context, there is a clear need for conducting studies comparing alternative methods combining RE techniques used in agile software development and traditional software development.

In order to address scalability and popularization of the approaches, future research should be invested in tool support and in addressing combined RE traditional adoption strategies. Finally, we conclude our work stating that agile methods assume that it is very hard to elicit all the requirements from the user upfront, at the beginning of a development project. They also assume that such requirements evolve in time as the customer may change its mind or the overall technical and socio-economical environment may evolve. Therefore, software factories are aware that changes are inevitable and they include the management of variability into the development process. Agile methods are fundamented in that (i) requirements are not well known at the beginning of the software development project, (ii) requirements change, always do, and (iii) making changes is not expensive if you have a RE process well-defined.

Acknowledgments. This work has been partially supported by: Universidad Autónoma de Sinaloa (México) through the Programa de Fomento y Apoyo a Proyectos de Investigación (PROFAPI2015/002).

References

1. Bastardo Ordaz, M.A., Giménez, O.: Selección de una metodología para la gerencia de proyectos de desarrollo de software. Master's thesis, Caracas (2006)
2. Livermore, J.A.: Factors that significantly impact the implementation of an agile software development methodology. JSW **3**(4), 31–36 (2008)
3. Cho, J., Huff, R., Olsen, D.: Management guidelines for scrum agile software development process. Issues Inf. Syst. **12**(1), 213–223 (2011)
4. Aguilar, J.A., Garrigós, I., Mazón, J.N., Trujillo, J.: An MDA approach for goal-oriented requirement analysis in web engineering. J. UCS **16**(17), 2475–2494 (2010)

5. Inayat, I., Salim, S.S., Marczak, S., Daneva, M., Shamshirband, S.: A systematic literature review on agile requirements engineering practices and challenges. Comput. Hum. Behav. **51**(Part B), 915–929 (2015)
6. Mishra, D., Mishra, A.: Complex software project development: agile methods adoption. J. Softw. Maint. Evol. Res. Pract. **23**(8), 549–564 (2011)
7. Turk, D., France, R., Rumpe, B.: Assumptions underlying agile software development processes. arXiv preprint arXiv:1409.6610 (2014)
8. Kitchenham, B.: Procedures for performing systematic reviews. Keele, UK, Keele Univ. **33**(2004), 1–26 (2004)
9. Awad, M.: A comparison between agile and traditional software development methodologies. University of Western Australia (2005)
10. Díaz, J.R.: Las metodologías ágiles como garantía de calidad del software. REICIS. Revista Española de Innovación, Calidad e Ingeniería del Software **5**(3), 40–43 (2009)
11. Rao, K.N., Naidu, G.K., Chakka, P.: A study of the agile software development methods, applicability and implications in industry. Int. J. Softw. Eng. Appl. **5**(2), 35–45 (2011)
12. Paetsch, F., Eberlein, A., Maurer, F.: Requirements engineering and agile software development. In: 2003 Proceedings of Twelfth IEEE International Workshops on Enabling Technologies: Infrastructure for Collaborative Enterprises, WET ICE 2003, pp. 308–313. IEEE (2003)
13. Navarro, A., Fernández, J., Morales, J.: Revisión de metodologías ágiles para el desarrollo de software. Prospect **11**(2), 30–39 (2013)
14. Abrahamsson, P., Salo, O., Ronkainen, J., Warsta, J., et al.: Agile software development methods: review and analysis. In: Proceedings of the Conference on the Future of Software Engineering, VTT Finland (2002)
15. Patel, A., Seyfi, A., Taghavi, M., Wills, C., Na, L., Latih, R., Misra, S.: A comparative study of agile, component-based, aspect-oriented and mashup software development methods. Tehnicki Vjesnik **19**(1), 175–189 (2012)
16. Rivadeneira, S., Vilanova, G., Miranda, M., Cruz, D.: El modelado de requerimientos en las metodologías ágiles. In: XV Workshops de Investigadores en Ciencias de la Computación, pp. 383–387 (2013)
17. Stapleton, J.: Dynamic Systems Development Method. Addison Wesley, Boston (1997)
18. De Lucia, A., Qusef, A.: Requirements engineering in agile software development. J. Emerg. Technol. Web Intell. **2**(3), 212–220 (2010)
19. Hull, E., Jackson, K., Dick, J.: Requirements Engineering. Springer Science & Business Media, London (2010)
20. Dieste Tubio, O., López, M., Ramos, F.: Updating a systematic review about selection of software requirements elicitation techniques (2009)
21. Nuseibeh, B., Easterbrook, S.: Requirements engineering: a roadmap. In: Proceedings of the Conference on the Future of Software Engineering, pp. 35–46. ACM (2000)
22. Maiden, N.A., Rugg, G.: Acre: selecting methods for requirements acquisition. Softw. Eng. J. **11**(3), 183–192 (1996)
23. Yu, E.: Modelling Strategic Relationships for Process Reenginering. Ph.D. thesis, University of Toronto, Canada (1995)
24. Bass, L., Bergey, J.K., Clements, P.C., Merson, P.F., Ozkaya, I., Sangwan, R.: A comparison of requirements specification methods from a software architecture perspective (2006)

25. Chrissis, M.B., Konrad, M., Shrum, S.: CMMI for Development: Guidelines for Process Integration and Product Improvement. Pearson Education, Upper Saddle River (2011)
26. Estublier, J.: Software configuration management: a roadmap. In: Proceedings of the Conference on the Future of Software Engineering, pp. 279–289. ACM (2000)
27. urRehman, T., Khan, M.N.A., Riaz, N.: Analysis of requirement engineering processes, tools techniques and methodologies. Int. J. Inf. Technol. Comput. Sci. (IJITCS) **5**(3), 40 (2013)
28. Sommerville, I., Sawyer, P.: Requirements Engineering: A Good Practice Guide. Wiley, New York (1997)
29. Gonz ález, A., Anduquia, D.: type=B.S. thesis, y.: La ingeniería de requisitos en las metodologías ágiles: Requisitos ágiles. Master's thesis
30. Thomas, P.J.: Definición de un Proceso de Elicitación de Objetivos. Ph.D. thesis, Facultad de Informática (2005)
31. Yu, E.: Towards modeling and reasoning support for early-phase requirements engineering. In: RE, pp. 226–235 (1997)
32. Brereton, P., Kitchenham, B.A., Budgen, D., Turner, M., Khalil, M.: Lessons from applying the systematic literature review process within the software engineering domain. J. Syst. Softw. **80**(4), 571–583 (2007)
33. Orjuela, A., Rojas, M.: Las metodologías de desarrollo ágil como una oportunidad para la ingeniería del software educativo. Revista Avances en Sistemas e Informática **5**(2), 159–171 (2008)
34. Figueroa, R., Solis, C., Cabrera, A.: Metodologías ágiles vs metodologías tradicionales. Informe Científico Técnico UNPA **5**(1), 1–29 (2013)
35. Izarraulde, M.: Caracterización de especificación de requerimientos en entornos ágiles: Historias de ususarios. B.S. thesis (2013)
36. Koerner, E., Eberlein, A.: Requirements engineering in agile software development
37. Diéguez, M., Sepúlveda, S., Canullan, D.: Diseño de un documento para la elicitación y especificación de requerimientos: Caso práctico. In: WorkShop International EIG, vol. 11 (2010)
38. Londoño, L.F., Anaya, R., Tabares, M.S.: Análisis de la ingeniería de requisitos orientada por aspectos según la industria del software. Revista EIA **9**, 43–52 (2008)
39. Verdiesen, B.: Agile user experience (2014)
40. Jameel, R.: Agile software development methodology for medium and large projects. IET Softw. **6**, 358–363 (2011)
41. Dolado, J., Rodríguez, D.: Utilidad de los procesos ágiles en el desarrollo de software. Novática. Revista de Asociación de Técnicos de Informática-España **209**, 73–74 (2011)

Workshop on Advances in Remote Sensing for Cultural heritage (RS-CH 2017)

The Geographical Distribution of *nuraghi* in North-Western Sardinia: Analysis and Evaluation of the Influence of Anthropic and Natural Factors

Maurizio Minchilli[✉] and Loredana Francesca Tedeschi

Dipartimento di Architettura, Design e Urbanistica, University of Sassari,
Sassari, Italy
minchilli@uniss.it

Abstract. It is a difficult task to develop an organic and analysis of the geographical disposition of *nuraghi* settlements in Sardinia, due to the high number of sites located the region, which amount to more than 7000 units. A further complication is represented by the fact that many *nuraghi* have been transformed in their purpose and used for different reasons by several generations of inhabitants. This aspect, among the others, makes more difficult the understanding of the causes which pushed to the edification of these monuments in specific locations. By now, it has been accepted that many different distributive factors were at play, which also responded contextual reasons for the establishment of a settlement.

The complexity of this topic would need the adoption of a holistic approach, which takes into account the overlapping historical, anthropological and territorial specificities which promoted the construction of *nuraghi* in different areas of the region. However, in this site, it will be adopted a relatively smaller sample, focusing on two thousands *nuraghi* buildings located in the western area of northern Sardinia. This paper aims at inquiring on the historical-environmental system which promoted their construction, looking more in depth on the matrix of factors which allowed natives' subsistence, such as water reserves, availability of rock and wood for building activities, climate and access to the sea.

Keyword: GIS · Spatial analysis · Archaeology · Geography

1 Purpose of the Research

The striking potential of GIS analyses for archaeological research brought to a broader use of this technology in the is specialised field. Nevertheless, there are regions where this tool is still used only for geographical archiving. This is particularly true for Sardinia, where the use of GIS in archaeology is limited to few instances, mostly related to the analysis of cartographical representations and realisation of specific thematic maps. The implementation of GIS in Cultural Resource Management (CRM)[1]

---

[1] FORTE 2002, pag. 184: "CULTURAL RESOURCE MANAGEMENT = Management of cultural resources in respect to the cultural and economic enhancement of a territory".

© Springer International Publishing AG 2017
O. Gervasi et al. (Eds.): ICCSA 2017, Part V, LNCS 10408, pp. 701–712, 2017.
DOI: 10.1007/978-3-319-62404-4_51

is, however, very important, at a time when several local administrations are showing a growing interest towards Geographic Information Systems especially for the protection of Cultural Resources.

Indeed, those sectors of public administration in charge of the safeguarding of cultural heritage can find this tool very helpful, specifically in regard of the census process, and the cataloguing and monitoring of the heritage. As a matter of fact, GIS is not only an instrument for analysis and research, but can be easily used as a "political" tool, since it provides an important support for the policy-making of regions such as Sardinia, where touristic valorisation is developed in correlation with cultural and landscape itineraries.

This paper aims at the evaluation of parameters that may have influenced the territorial location of approximately two thousand *nuraghi* located in the north-western area of the island (Tedeschi L.F. 2006). The area, of roughly 800.000 ha, shows a mutable morphology, ranging from the northern coastal environment to the hilly mainland, which presents, historically, an intensely developed hydrographical system thanks to the presence of a high number of sources of clean water.

This research aims thus to inquire on the settlement system and motivations that brought to the construction of these structures, focusing on the strategic interplay of territorial location and network of activities that linked the coast to the hinterland, allowing the control and management of the territory and its environmental variables.

2 Data Sources and Data Structure

This research revolves around the analysis of informations gathered from some cartographical layers, both vector and raster, extracted from a wide number of geographic Databases provided by *Regione Autonoma della Sardegna* (*R.A.S.*), Provincial Council of Sassari and Nuoro, and *Soprintendenza ai Beni Archeologici di Sassari e Nuoro*. Another central source of data has been the Regional Landscape Plan (P.P.R. - *Piano Paesaggistico Regionale*), commissioned and formulated by the Provinces of Sassari and Nuoro during the development of their respective *"Territorial Plans for Provincial Coordination"* (*Piani Territoriali di Coordinamento Provinciale - P.T.C.P.*).

The geometrical layer which founds this study is represented by the spatial location of about 1860 *nuraghi* visible on the *P.P.R.*. The Plan has been a central source of geo-referenced data, gathering, albeit in a confused and unordered fashion, some of those databases previously mentioned, both in printed and digital version. *Nuraghi's* spatial locations have been acquired by the P.P.R. from punctual symbology available on IGM (Military Geographic Institute) Sections 1.25.000 created in the 90s. Subsequently, they have been corrected by *AIMA 1997*, *AGEA 2003* and *it 2000* (both 1998 and 2006) orthophotos. Among several georeferenced analyses, the spatial location of mines, swamps, wooded areas, water sources, hydrography, and geolithological and soil maps have been particularly useful for this study.

Finally, it is important to outline how the selection process of cartographical sources have been articulated, used and transformed among different systems for cartographical referencing adopted in Italy and, more specifically, in Sardinia. In this regard, it is also central to make an operational clarification in the wake of the present regional public administration's process of formation and transformation of GeoDB: since January 2007 the regional *Dipartimento del territorio,* and, on its behalf, the Cartographic sector, imposed ETRF89 Cartographic Reference System (schematically defined as *datum WGS'84 - proiezione UTM fuso 32)* as the only tool to use for every ongoing cartographic elaboration. This choice, as a result of the correct application of technical norms suggested by the so-called "GIS National Agreement", is predictably causing diffused problems among users. Indeed, after that the regional Office pushed for a complete transformation of the most important regional geoDatabases, from Gauss-Boaga System to ETRF, those local city councils affected by this transformation have been provided with cartography in GIS structure (*.shp) and high-resolution orthoimages in compressed format (*.ecw). Unfortunately, these changes caused the impossibility for less experienced users of comfortably employ the extensive database currently available. Indeed, those formats require an in-depth knowledge of methodologies and digital environments of GIS elaboration, more easily adapted to the hybrid use of referencing systems.

3 Contents and Editing

The broad availability of data highlighted several problematic aspects of creating a knowledge base in GIS environment:

- Non-homogeneous data in relation to their structure, reference systems and interexchange formats;
- Inability of traditional digital cartography (vector) to provide geoDatabases that would allow an easy reconstruction of topologies;
- Lack of cohesion and coherence among CAD vectors in cartography, causing problems in filtering altimetries or areal, linear and punctual symbols with constant geometric congruence;
- Undeniable errors of georeferencing that can be found in some regional, provincial and local Land Planning zoning.

G.I.S. tools are now widely available on the market and, thanks to the wide diffusion of Open Source procedures, they are commercially less aggressive. In fact, the tendency to set the market on a single standard in format and data-structure has been overcome.

Thanks to the widespread diffusion of open-source data and software procedures, the interexchange of data is now available in a rapid and easy way. Once that the clear separation between vector primitives and alpha-numeric Database has been removed, starting from the structure of *shapes files,* the most recent generation of GIS makes easier to manage only geoDataBases where, on the same record or on the same data structure, there is both the georeferenced description of the features and the description of the attributes. This structure not only makes the management of databases more coherent and compact but also allows a faster and easier building, elaboration and reading of spatial analyses.

4 Definition of the Study Area

At the beginning of our research, it was important to identify the main characteristics of the territory in order to build the perimeter of the study area. Through GIS tools, all the informative layers that define the primary aspects of the territory, namely the geomorphologic map and the distribution of rivers and water sources, have been linked together. These elements represent the dominant environmental aspects that define the selection of a settlement area: due to defence requirements and daily need of supplies, when a perimeter is defined, it usually comprehends both flat and steep areas, reaching also part of the coastline. The perimeter that is obtained is built in vector format through the combination of two elements: (1) the extraction of the whole coast line attached to the area of interest, with a linear structure that comprehends also a simplification through a *step* of 20 mts; (2) the creation of a linear feature related to the internal area, which is defined following the morphologic development of the territory[2] based on the contour lines,. Subsequently, the *study area* feature, obtained through the union of these two linear elements, has been used to formulate some spatial queries based on intersectional algorithms with different informational layers previously defined. These were the basis for the creation of evaluation indexes of those areas and chosen stratifications previously analysed (Fig. 1).

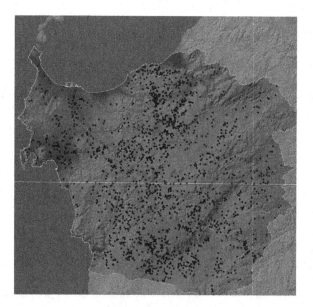

Fig. 1. Localization of *nuraghi* in north-western Sardinia.

---

[2] The choice of how to cu the area has been made after considering whether to do a neat cut of a regular perimeter, for example following the standard cut of medium-scale cartography elements. Actually, it resulted from further analyses that a neat cutting of the area would have represented a limitation for the understanding of the relationship between morphological characteristics and anthropic system.

5 Data Analysis

The organisation of this study can be divided in four main parts, which can be summarised in the following way:

1. Analysis and selection of informative layers;
2. Elaboration and editing of informative layers;
3. Spatial analysis;
4. Evaluation of indexes (Fig. 2).

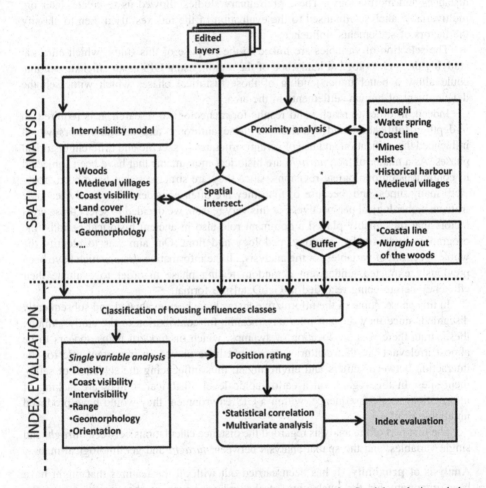

Fig. 2. Third and fourth phase of workflow blocks concerning the Spatial analysis and the
Evaluation of the indexes.

Having already amply discussed the first two phases of this study, which regarded
the selection and editing of informative layers and the enunciation of standard

procedures for Databases' creation, the following section will mainly focus on the formulation of spacial analyses and statistical evaluation of indexes.

Firstly, we created intervisibility maps between the *nuragic* sites, and their spatial intersections with points of attractions such as wooded areas, altimetric zones, and descriptive maps of the soil, slopes and exposition. Moreover, the study of these spatial intersections has been enriched by the analysis of their proximity with the hydrographic network, water sources, mines, historical harbors etc.

In the second and last phase, we set the taxonomy of those factors which influenced the creation of settlement areas through single variable analyses (density, visibility, distances and morphology). These preliminary studies allowed us to create, later on, multivariable analyses finalised to the evaluation of the indexes, used then to classify the factors of settlements' influence.

The selection of variables are linked to the purpose of this study, which aimes at studying the archaeological landscape of the region, using GIS as an efficient tool that could allow a better understanding of those historical phases which witnessed the development of human settlements in the area.

Indeed, in order to reach valid results for archeological research, it is required an in-depth identification and selection of those anthropic and natural factors which influenced the edification and use of certain structures in specific and different historical phases. As a matter of fact, *nuraghi* are historical monuments that have been subjected to continuous chronological revisions, since they are structures that have been 'recycled' many times, and, because of that, they are often considered not easily readable from an archeological perspective. For this very reason, we decided to select those areal factors that presumably played a dominant role also in ancient historical periods: the orography, hydrography, geology, pedology and flora. Our aim was to identify the whole spectrum of variables for the analysis: all the informative strata, which have been previously extracted, underwent a random testing phase in order to evaluate their efficiency before being recorded in GeoDataBase format.

In this phase, some of the informative layers have been evaluated and subsequently discarded, since they did not offer any meaningful contribution to the study. Among these strata there was the location of swamps, which on modern maps appears to be almost irrelevant but that centuries ago might have played an important role for the interaction between settlers and environment, thus influencing the selection of settlement sites. In this regard, on a cartographic level, historical sources are lacking of information; as a consequence, within a GIS environment they would have produced unreliable results.

The first part of the analysis regarded the distance calculations between *nuraghi* and single variables, and the spatial analysis between *nuraghi* and geolithological maps.

Analysis of proximity. It has been carried out with all the features that might have been important for the evaluation of the indexes, such as the positioning of the coastline, the hydrography, the water sources, the *nuraghi*, the woods, in combination with the evaluation of a maximum distance value, represented by a sustainable walking itinerary carrying an average weight load.

Regarding the intervisibility modelling, the study analysed only the frequency of intervisibility between *nuraghi* and between *nuraghi* and the coastal line due to the complexity of creating mutual combinations of few thousands of punctual, linear and areal features. While creating intervisibility models, in addition to the territorial morphology, we decided to set the height of observation point at the top of the buildings (about 12 mts from the ground plane) to simulate a real viewing of the area from the highest point possible.

Subsequently, we classified the distances calculated of each single variable, and, then, the minimum and average distance between the elements contained within a buffer area of 5000 meters-wide radius. In order to identify concentrations of elements in advantageous areas for settlements, two different kind of analysis have been carried out: analyses on GRID for the evaluation of settlement density of *nuraghi*, set up on 100 × 100 mts cells, and the analysis of visibility between different *nuraghi* and between *nuraghi* and the coast line.

With the data collected in this last phase it has been possible to perform a series of statistical evaluation in relation to the relationship between single categories of each variable with *nuraghi* and the correlation between categories of variables and morphological and orientation categories. It was thus created a first definition of some settlement indexes that allowed preliminary observations for a subsequent in-depth analysis and a consistent evaluation of the results (Figs. 3 and 4).

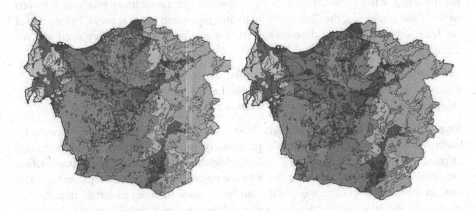

Fig. 3. Distribution of *nuraghi* in relation to lithology. Rhyolites (yellow on the left), Basalt (green on the right). (Color figure online)

6 Evaluation of the Influence Parameters

A first outline of the workflow, in the evaluation of indexes, allowed to make hypothesis on those elements that could have influenced, in a positive or negative way, some of the settlement choices. Among them, the following "relationships" between human activities and environment or surrounding landscape have been identified.

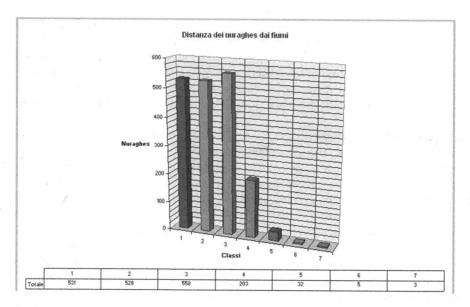

	1	2	3	4	5	6	7
Totale	531	528	558	203	32	5	3

Fig. 4. Statistical analysis of distances from hydrography.

Relationship with water. It has been examined the geometrical relations between *nuraghi* and coastlines, the distance from hydrography and water sources. In this case it has been simulated human dependency from water both as a everyday need and for transport and communication.

Relationship with energy sources. Human dependency only from thermal energy which, at the time, could be provided by wood as a fuel for fire, led us to the choice of analysing the proximity or belonging relation to woods.

Relationship with building materials. Construction techniques amply relied on rocky materials which makes this variable particularly relevant. The territories examined display, indeed, an extraordinary geo-lithological variety. Thus, this examination provided a detailed starting point for a better understanding of this relationship. The lack, in the *nuraghi* geoDatabase of the attribute "stone building material" required the creation of the relationship "geo-lithology/building material", which provided a strong understanding of the technologies available at the time for buildings' construction and transportation of materials (Figs. 5 and 6).

Relationship with climate and morphology of the soil. Our analyses provided the necessary base for the altimetric positioning of the studied elements (a feature that might influence also the relationship with flora and wildlife, in addition to the one with climate), the positioning on flat or sloping land (which can influence transportation or visibility of the surrounding territory), the orientation of lands characterised by strong acclivity (which can influence the location of a settlement in relation to the prevailing winds and sunlight exposition). In this regard, through a multivariate analysis, it was evaluated the correlation between altimetry, acclivity, and sun-exposition

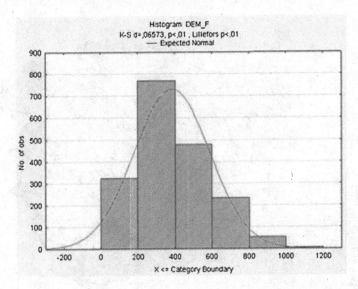

Fig. 5. The statistical distribution in relation to altimetry shows a maximum at about 400 m MSL.

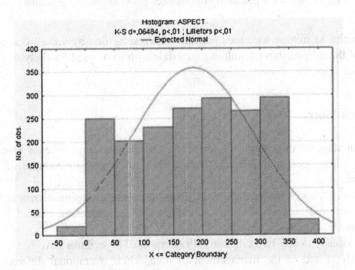

Fig. 6. The distribution of nuraghi does not show any influence in relation to absolute orientation of the land.

characteristics, which provided useful informations on the relationship between inclination and North orientation.

Relationship of proximity and interchange. This analysis, one of the most complex and thus only partially completed, was focused on settlement density but also on distances (minimum, average, and maximum) between the elements studied.

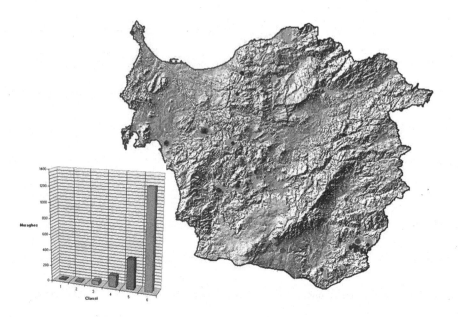

Fig. 7. Statistical evaluation of distances between *nuraghi* and mines.

The proximity to mining locations provided interesting density values that allow the analysis of the relationship of building materials with tools used for daily life, hunting and defence (Fig. 7).

7   Conclusions

In the final stage of this study, we formulated an evaluation of indexes based on set variables, whose potential use has been tested on a statistic sample of *nuraghi* distribution.

The largest part of preparatory work focused on the cleansing of *raw* data, operation that required complex editing and even re-writing processes, needed for further analyses of GeoDataBases on GIS.

As previously stated, two different GIS operational procedures have been used both in the analysis and in the management of data. Their operational differences were positively counterbalanced by some similarities in the user interface. The comparative use of both procedures has been chosen according to the type of analysis performed and speed in terms of data elaboration. This has allowed to identify strengths and weaknesses of both tools, so that only through their synergic use their potentialities could be fully exploited.

This research experience cannot be considered exhaustive in terms of obtained results, requiring further in-depth testings to increase the value of our statistical analysis.

Nevertheless, it clearly shows some relevant aspects: firstly, that the distribution of *nuraghi* is usually planned and mostly depends on their specific function. The *nuraghi* system is developed in a specific natural region, which was functional from a defensive or economic perspective; at the same time, there are also *nuraghi* willingly hidden, or isolated in some wide flat land, which were used for secular or religious needs.

Hence, *nuraghi* were polyfunctional structures, built for different purposes: residential, sacral, economic, and also for passive defense or obstruction. They are often located on low hills, particularly in places nearby natural water sources. One of the primary factors related to their passive defence function is the inter-visibility of the sites, developed through the construction of a tight network that is adapted to different morphological features that the Sardinian territory presents, allowing the control of wider portions of land and, in case of need, helping to anticipate the defence of inner areas. It is also clear how the density of the sites changes depending on the availability of rock and superficial lithic material needed for these megalithic constructions.

This aspect is particularly relevant and represents a great potential for the region, that is more and more interested in not underestimating this attractive sector.

This research was also meant to support and extend knowledge on *nuraghi* civilization: more specifically, it represents the first step of a research which intends to inquire on the historical routes which connect the *nuraghi* system. If it is true that *nuraghi* are some of the most famous landmarks of Sardinia's territory, regarded as typical elements of its landscape, a study on their accessibility in ancient times would allow a new and different assessment of their current reachability; as a consequence, this would open up the possibility of making the most out of key elements of contemporary landscape and Sardinian cultural heritage. The chance to find connections, or rather movement networks, may result in their reacquisition.

The analysis in an informative environment based on geographical data allows to satisfy a wide range of demands: technical, operative, touristic. It also smoothens the complex procedures for management, re-evaluation and use of these sites, working also as a case study that marks the way for many other historical-artistic realities existing on the national territory.

References

1. Amendolea, B. (ed.) Carta Archeologica e pianificazione territoriale: un problema politico e metodologico. Atti dell'incontro di studio, (Roma, 10–12 marzo 1997), Roma (Palombi) (1999)
2. Azzena, G.: L'indagine topografica e la cartografia archeologica. In: AA.VV., Il Mondo dell'archeologia, Roma (Treccani) (2002)
3. Cicilloni, R., Mossa, A., Cabras, M.: Studio dell'insediamento protostorico in un'area della sardegna centro-occidentale tramite strumenti GIS ed analisi multivariate. Archeologia e Calcolatori **26**, 149–168 (2015)
4. Conolly, J., Lake, M.: Geographical Information Systems in Archaelogy. Cambridge University Press, Cambridge (2006)

5. Depalmas, A.: Il Bronzo medio della Sardegna, in La preistoria e la protostoria della Sardegna, Atti della XLIV Riunione Scientifica IIPP (Cagliari-Barumini-Sassari 2009), pp. 123–130. Firenze, Istituto Italiano di Preistoria e Protostoria (2009)
6. Fabrega Álvarez, F., Parcero Oubiña, C.: Proposals for an archaeological analysis of pathways and movement. Archeologia e Calcolatori 18, 121–140 (2007)
7. Francovich, R.: Archeologia medievale e informatica: dieci anni dopo. Archeologia e Calcolatori 10, 45–61 (1999)
8. Francovich, R., Manacorda, D. (eds.): Lo scavo archeologico: dalla diagnosi all'edizione, III ciclo di Lezioni sulla ricerca applicata in Archeologia (Certosa di Pontignano, Siena 1989), Firenze (1990)
9. Francovich, R., Pellicanò, A., Pasquinucci, M. (eds.): La carta archeologica fra ricerca e pianificazione territoriale, Firenze (All'Insegna del Giglio) (2001)
10. Hodder, I., Orton C.R.: Spatial Analysis in Archaeology. Cambridge University Press, Cambridge
11. Hodson, F.R.: Searching for structure within multivariate archaeological data. World Archaeol. 1(1), 90–105 (1969)
12. Ialongo, N.: Sanctuaries and the emergence of elites in Nuragic sardinia during the early Iron Age. J. Mediterr. Archaeol. 26, 2 (2013)
13. Ioannilli, M., Schiavoni Schiavoni, U.M.A.: Fondamenti di Sistemi informativi geografici, Texmat, Roma (2002)
14. Lilliu, G.: "Sardegna nuragica", Il Maestrale – Appunti di Archeologia, Nuoro (2006)
15. Llobera, M., Fábrega-Álvarez, P., Parcero-Oubiña, C.: Order in movement. A GIS approach to accessibility. J. Archaeol. Sci. 38, 843–851 (2011)
16. Lo Schiavo, F., Satta, M.C.: Carta archeologica e pianificazione territoriale: il caso Sardegna. In: AMENDOLEA 1999, pp. 237–247 (1999)
17. Minchilli, M., Tedeschi, L.F.: Le ortofoto digitali ad alta risoluzione: nuove frontiere nelle analisi ambientali e territoriali, Atti del Conv. Naz. ASITA, Bolzano (2006)
18. Navarra, L.: Chiefdoms nella Sardegna Nuragica? Una applicazione della Circumscription theory di Robert L. Carneiro, Origini, Preistoria e Protostoria delle civiltà antiche XXI (1999)
19. Ruestes Bitrià, C.: A multi-technique GIS visibility analysis for studying visual control of an Iron Age landscape. Internet Archaeology 23 (2008). http://dx.doi.org/10.11141/ia.23.4. Last access 8 Feb 2015
20. Trigger, B.G.: Monumental architecture: a thermodynamic explanation of symbolic behaviour. World Archaeol. 22, 2 (1990)
21. Tedeschi, L.F.: Influenza dei fattori antropici e naturali nella distribuzione dei nuraghi nel settore nord-occidentale della Sardegna, analisi e valutazioni in ambiente GIS, Tesi del Master di II livello in "Sistemi Informativi Geografici applicati alla pianificazione e alla progettazione del territorio urbano e rurale". Univ. degli Studi La Sapienza, Roma (2006)
22. Van Leusen, M.: Pattern to Process: Methodological Investigations into the Formation and Interpretation of Spatial Patterns on Archaeological Landscapes. University of Gröningen, Gröningen (2002)
23. Vianello, G.: Centralità della cartografia nei sistemi informativi territoriali. In: Atti del IV convegno internazionale di studi. Pianificazione territoriale e ambiente La Sardegna nel mondo mediterraneo. L'ambiente, l'economia, gli strumenti di conoscenza, 10, a cura di P. Brandis e G. Scanu (Sassari, 15–17 aprile 1993), Bologna (Pàtron), pp. 329–337 (1995)
24. Wheatley, D., Gillings, M.: Spatial Technology and Archaeology. The Archaeological Applications of GIS. Taylor and Francis, New York (2002)

Space Based Monitoring of Archaeological Looting: An Overview in Peruvian Archaeological Areas

Rosa Lasaponara[1](✉) and Nicola Masini[2]

[1] Italian National Research Council, IMAA,
C.da Santa Loja, Tito Scalo, Potenza, Italy
rosa.lasaponara@imaa.cnr.it
[2] Italian National Research Council, IBAM,
C.da Santa Loja, Tito Scalo, Potenza, Italy
n.masini@ibam.cnr.it

Abstract. Illegal excavations represent one of the main risks which affect archaeological heritage throughout the world. Actions oriented to prevent looting can be supported by satellite technologies which can provide reliable information to: (i) detect and quantify looting phenomenon even over large and inaccessible areas, (ii) set up tools to undertake monitoring also for sites not accessible due to war, armed conflicts or other limiting factors. This article is focused on an overview on the methodology developed for the identification of clandestine excavations in Peruvian archaeological areas mainly focusing on two archaeological areas: one near Nasca (Southern Peru) and the second one in Ventarron (Lambayeque, Northern Peru)).

Keywords: Looting · Risk estimation · Satellite images · Peru · Nasca · Lambayeque

1 Introduction

Earth Observation technologies can suitably support the archaeological research [1–14], monitoring and preservation of natural and cultural resources as well as the estimation of risk (see for example urban sprawl, building stability, greenhouse detection in [15–22]) including deliberate destruction and archaeological looting, one of the main risk factors affecting archaeological heritage throughout the world [23–30].

Actions oriented to preventing looting can be supported by aerial (including UAV) and satellite systems. Aerial surveys and the use of UAV can be limited by the extension of the areas under surveillance, whereas the use of satellite can provide reliable information, useful: (i) to quantify the looting phenomenon even if it is at an "industrial scale" over large areas, (ii) to set up a systematic monitoring tool to obtain reliable information also for remote area not accessible due to war or other limiting factors.

Up to now generally a visual inspection of optical satellite pictures has been adopted for the identification and quantification of looting; only pioneering investigations based on automatic identification of illegal excavation of have been recently

© Springer International Publishing AG 2017
O. Gervasi et al. (Eds.): ICCSA 2017, Part V, LNCS 10408, pp. 713–727, 2017.
DOI: 10.1007/978-3-319-62404-4_52

Fig. 1. Location of the investigated sites

conducted by Lasaponara and Masini [24, 26]. This article is focused on an overview on the methodologies developed for the identification of illegal excavation in Peru mainly focusing the archaeological areas of Nasca and Ventarron (Fig. 1).

The methodology adopted for the Peruvian archaeological sites could be suitable applicable to other archaeological areas with similar characteristics being that unfortunately the plundering of archaeological sites is a global problem linked to clandestine market of antiquities. The worldwide extension of this phenomenon made necessary a strong international cooperation to define mitigation strategies. The problem started to be faced globally since 1956, when the General Conference of the United Nations Educational, Scientific and Cultural Organization recommended all the Member States to take "all necessary measures to prevent clandestine excavations and damage to monuments and also to prevent the export of objects thus obtained" [30]. Later, many countries adopted repressive measures and restrictive laws to impose the returning of objects stolen and/or derived from clandestine excavations to their own countries [31].

Today archaeological looting is a pressing issue in the region of middle east where it is a massive phenomena and satellite tools can be the only possible approach to be adopted due the ongoing war conditions.

Fig. 2. Aerial view in Ventarron with the typical looting pattern

2 Looting is an "Ancient" Problem

Peru has an extraordinarily rich archaeological heritage with more than 100,000 archaeological sites, as estimated by the Peruvian government, 12 World Heritage sites listed and other 7 under consideration. Today, only a few percentage (less than 10%) of the Peruvian archaeological sites have been uncovered and, unfortunately, they often do come to public notice because of vandalism actions or looters. Actually, looting in Peru is an "ancient" problem started since the first colonial period (16th-17th century) as the result of trade of pre-Hispanic objects during the Spaniards' "search for gold" [32]. Since the 1960s, Illegal excavation had a strong intensification supplying both national and international markets.

For these reasons, Peru has been one of the first countries of America to adopt a legislation to face looting and protect cultural property. In 1882 the Peruvian state approved a law which prohibited the exportation of archaeological objects without previous governmental authorization and, also, established that all the ancient monuments belonged to the Peruvian Nation [29].

Despite this, in the 20th century illegal excavations increased in all the Peruvian territory. A significant example is the sacking of archaeological sites of Paracas recorded and described by Julio Tello in the 1920s [29].

Cahuachi is another emblematic case of massive looting started from the Colonial Period and extended up to now. The illegal diggings linked to the illicit trade of Nasca pottery in European museums probably started during the 19th century [33]. The phenomenon of looting increases in the 20th century assuming a large-scale dimension and is a pressing issue still today.

3　Satellite Based Monitoring of Looting in Peruvian Archaeological Areas: Methodological Approach

Lasaponara and Masini developed several approaches for the looting extraction, from Very High resolution satellite (VHR) imagery, based on Spatial autocorrelation and classification [25, 26], improved by adding a segmentation step [29], as below detailed.

3.1　Spatial Autocorrelation

Spatial autocorrelation examines changes in homogeneity and measures the strength of the relationship between values of the same variables. In the analysis of satellite image

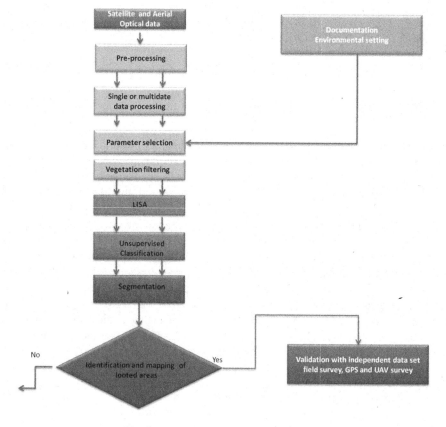

Fig. 3. Flow chart of the data processing

it is a very useful tool since it not only considers the value of the pixel (reflectance, temperature, spectral index), but also the relationships between a pixel and its surrounding in a given window size.

Global measures of spatial autocorrelation provide a single value that indicates the level of spatial autocorrelation within the variable distribution, namely the homogeneity of a given values within the image under investigation.

Local measures of spatial autocorrelation provide a value for each location within the variable distribution and, therefore, they are able to identify discrete spatial patterns that may not otherwise be apparent. The statistics output is an image for each calculated index, which contains a measure of autocorrelation around that pixel.

Global and Local statistics can be calculated using spectral channels, spectral combinations and/or multi- temporal combination as intensity.

For all these cases, the first step is to find the optimal lag distance using global Moran's I. It provides different values of lag distances: the optimal value is the lag that maximizes I and captures the autocorrelation of the image in the best way.

At this point, the local indicators of spatial association should be calculated using the optimal lag distance and the selected contiguity.

Results from this assessment must be interpreted and/or further elaborated (generally using classifications) before interpretation. As a general rule, we can argue that the Getis-Ord Gi index permits the identification of areas characterized by very high or very low values (hot spots) compared to those of neighbouring pixels.

It should be noted that the interpretation of Gi is different from that of Moran's I. In detail the Getis-Ord [34] Gi enables us to distinguish the clustering of high and low values, but does not capture the presence of negative spatial correlation. It permits the identification of areas characterized by very high or very low values (hot spots) compared to those of neighboring pixels.

The Moran's I is able to detect both positive and negative spatial correlations, but clustering of high or low values are not distinguished. In particular, it identifies pixel clustering. It has values that typically range from approximately +1, representing complete positive spatial autocorrelation, to approximately −1, representing complete negative spatial autocorrelation [35].

The Local Geary's C index allows us to identify edges and areas characterized by a high variability between a pixel value and its neighboring pixels [36].

Geostatistical analysis tools are available in several commercial software, such as GIS and image processing (see for example ENVI packages).

3.2   Unsupervised Classification and Segmentation

Unsupervised classification requires limited human intervention in setting up the algorithm parameters. The importance of applying unsupervised classification in archaeological applications is that: (i) it is an automatic process, namely, it usually requires only a minimal amount of initial input compared with a supervised data processing; (ii) classes do not have to be defined a priori; (iii) unknown feature classes may be discovered.

A number of unsupervised classification algorithms are commonly used in remote sensing, including (i) K-means clustering, and (ii) ISODATA (Iterative Self-Organizing

Data Analysis Technique) [37] which are quite similar. In both, the user has only to indicate (i) the number of predefined classes (clusters) and (ii) the number of iterations to be carried out. The only difference is that the K-means assumes that the number of clusters is known a priori whereas the ISODATA algorithm assigns the different number of clusters "dynamically". Both of these algorithms are iterative procedures, based on the following steps: (i) they first assign an arbitrary initial cluster vector, (ii) each pixel is classified to the closest cluster, (iii) new cluster mean vectors are calculated based on all the pixels in one cluster. The second and third steps are iteratively repeated until the "variations" between the iteration is small. These variations can be computed and assessed in several different ways. For example, in the K-means algorithm, the cluster variability is optimized by a least square minimization of the cost functional relating to Eq. 1.

$$MSE = \frac{\sum [x - C(x)]^2}{(N - c)b} \tag{1}$$

where MSE is Mean Squared Error, N is the number of pixels, c indicates the number of clusters, and b is the number of spectral bands, C(x) is the mean value of the cluster that pixel x is assigned to.

Equation 1 clearly shows that the minimization of MSE implies that K-means works best for spherical clusters that have the same variance. This indicates that the K-means algorithm tends to perform better for homogeneous surfaces/objects, as in particular desert areas. The ISODATA algorithm will split a cluster in two, if the cluster's standard deviation exceeds a predefined limit and if the number of pixels is twice the minimum number threshold. ISODATA is considered more flexible compared to the K-means method, but it requires the empirical selection of many more parameters. For this reason, in this study we applied an ISODATA algorithm.

Data output from classification is the input to segmentation step made to obtain meaningful feature class map as well as to improve the interpretation. Each segment is characterized by a set of attributes, which enable the extraction of specific features characterized by: (i) close proximity on the basis of the LISA analysis, (ii) similar spectral characteristics, on the basis of the classification step are grouped together according to the shapes.

4   Satellite Based Monitoring in Ventarron

Ventarron, located in the Lambayeque region in the north coast of Peru, is considered one of the most important archaeological areas in the country. Lambayeque represents an emblematic case for the looting and rescue archaeology in Peru. In this region, as in other part of the country, looting of archaeological areas was a common practice over the century and considered by local people as a work to take pride in so much so distinguished between "looters of finesse" and the "brutal profaners" [33].

Until the early of the 20th century the grave robbers (*huaqueros* in spanish) worked mainly individually, in the subsequent decade they started to work in teams for their own gain or for second parties. The discovery of the Royal Tombs of Sipan in 1989 was made after a "disagreement amongst looters" [38] involved in an illegal excavation. This quarrel caused the intervention of the police and the involvement of a local archaeologist, Walter Alva, to examine the looted objects. As a consequence, archaeological rescue started and the following systematic researchers and excavations of Alva and his wife Susana Menezes enabled the discovery of one of the most richest tombs in South America (Fig. 4).

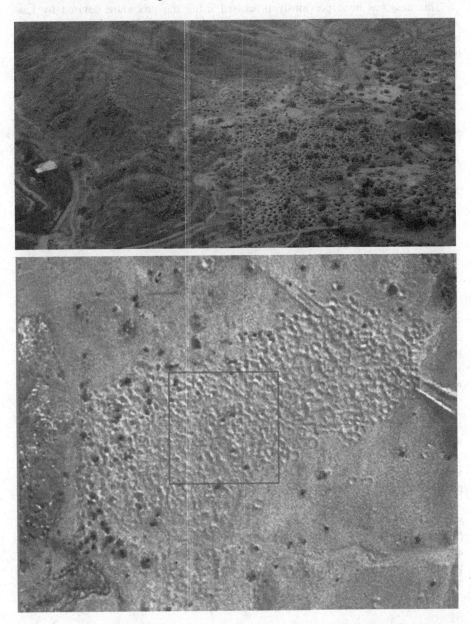

Fig. 4. Typical looting patterns in Lambayeque from aerial view (up courtesy by Ignacio Alva) and from satellite view (bottom).

The site of Ventarron, located at about 20 Kms from Sipán, is an extraordinary case of cultural continuity, covering more than 4000 years. Very close to the village a 4,000-year old temple covering about 2500 square meters started to be excavated in 2007 by Walter Alva, who unearthed probably the oldest wall painting discovered in the Americas.

This area has been previously processed using the procedure devised by Lasaponara et al. 2014 (for additional detail see [26]) by using a time series of panchromatic and multispectral images provided from satellite sensors which provide data Very high spatial resolution. Figures 5 and 6 show the results.

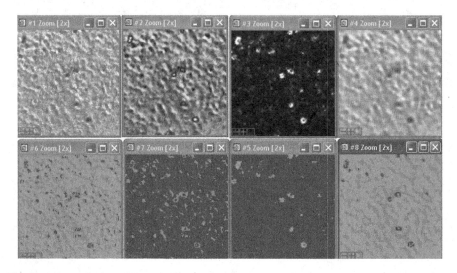

Fig. 5. Subset of selected in Arenal. Upper: red pansharpened band; Medium, from left to right: zoomed detail of red pan-sharpened band, Moran, Geary and Getis applied to red band, respectively; lower, from left to right: Kmeans classification of the zoomed details.

Multi-temporal VHR satellite images acquired for the study area are processed by using both autocorrelation statistics and unsupervised classification to highlight illegal excavation pattern and automatically map these pit spatial clusters. Moreover, as clearly suggested by the significant study area we considered, the looting survey also offers the possibility to investigate already looted areas not previously systematically documented. The reliability of the detection was evaluated by field survey carried out on some test sites selected on mounds and flat areas and some problems were present due to the presence of vegetation. For this reason the methodology was improved and enriched by adding (i) a filter, based on Normalized Difference Vegetation Index, to remove vegetation as preliminary step (before the geospatial analysis) and (ii) the segmentation applied after the classification. Results from this procedure are shown in Fig. 7.

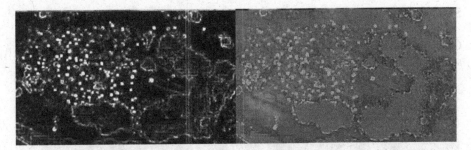

Fig. 6. An additional subset in Arenal some problems are still present due to vegetation cover (see red area in the figure on the right) (Color figure online)

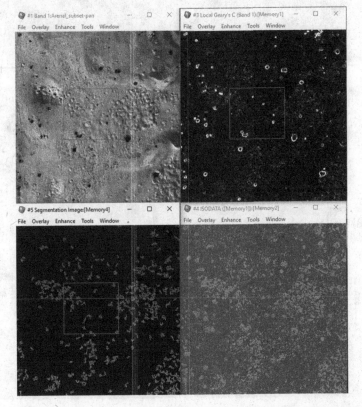

Fig. 7. Arenal in Ventarron. From upper left to bottom left clockwise: panchromatic, Geary result, Isodata of Geary result, Segmentation of Isodata result. Segmentation has been computed considering class 4 (yellow coloured), and assuming as population minimum and number of neighbors the following values: 20 and 4, respectively (Color figure online)

5   Satellite Based Monitoring of Looting in Nasca

Cahuachi (see Fig. 7) is the largest adobe Ceremonial Centre in the World, built in the southern desert of Peru by the Nasca Civilizations (see details [33, 39]).

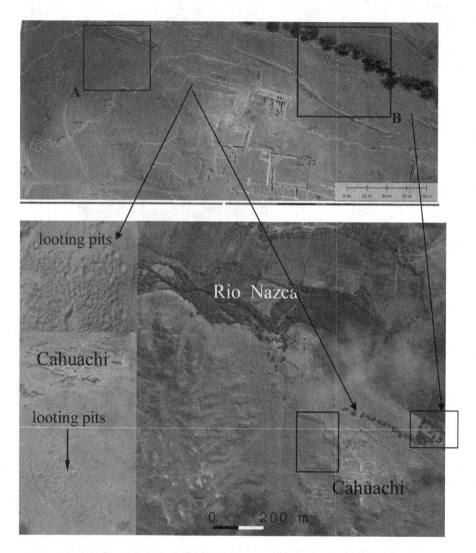

Fig. 8. Archaeological looting: satellite view in Cahuachi (Nasca)

The archaeological evidences are characterized by around forty semi-artificial mounds, spread out on the south bank of the Nasca river (Fig. 8) and facing the Pampa de San Jose, where the majority of the famous geoglyphs (listed in the World Heritage) were etched. [40] The archaeological investigations conducted systematically in the last

30 years also using remote sensing (since the last 10 years) allowed the understanding of the functional and cultural evolution of the site between 400 B.C. – 400 A.D.

Cahuachi is an emblematic case of massively looted sites since the Colonial Period The illegal diggings linked to illicit trade of Nasca pottery in European museums probably started at least since the 19th century [25, 39]. The phenomenon of looting increases in the 20th century assuming a large-scale plundering dimension and still today is a pressing issue (Fig. 9).

Fig. 9. QuickBird satellite images subset acquired in 2002 (upper) and in 2005 (lower). The red squares identify a single pit before the looting (upper left) and after the looting (lower left). On the left panchromatic image of 2002 QuickBird image, on the right RGB composite images (R is Moran'S index, G is Geary's index, B is Getis index) of processed 2002 QuickBird images before (upper right) and after looting, in 2005 (lower right).

Figure 10 shows the results from the procedure (see flow chart in Fig. 3) obtained for the largest sector, located near Estaqueria and characterized by pits with a high variability of diameter size (around 4 to 10 m) and depth.

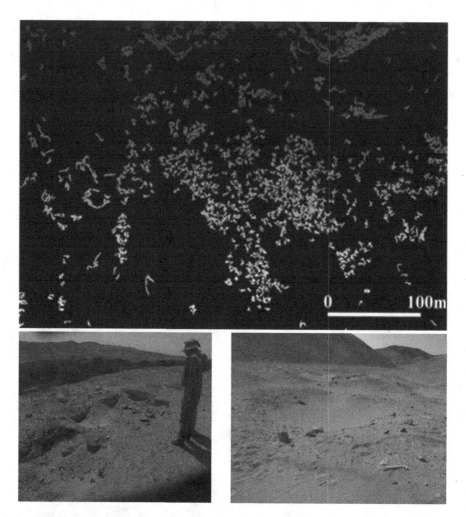

Fig. 10. Up: results from the procedure (see flow chart in Fig. 2) obtained for the largest sector, located near Estaqueria. Bottom; detail of looted areas

The reliability of the detection was evaluated by field survey carried out on some test sites selected on mounds and flat areas characterized by pits with a high variability of diameter size (around 4 to 10 m).

The evaluation has shown that the rate of success was very high for flat areas (higher than 90%).

The comparison between satellite based looting mapping with in situ analysis and UAV survey exhibited a high rate of success at around the 90%. The false detection mainly regards natural features easily recognizable from the optical image such as trees of huarango and geomorphologic signs. As a whole in the area under investigation (with a size of around 2.3 km^2) the portion affected by looting is around 0,18 km^2 close to the 8% of the extension of the total.

6 Conclusion

In this paper we focus on the use of VHR satellite imagery to quantitatively assess looting in Ventarron (Lambayeque, Northern Peru) and Cahuachi (Nasca, Southern Peru) that are very important archaeological sites in Southern America. Multitemporal satellite images acquired for the study area have been processed by using both auto-correlation statistics and unsupervised classification to highlight and extract looting patterns. The mapping of areas affected by looting offered the opportunity to investigate such areas not previously systematically documented.

Illegal excavations represent one of the main risks which affect the archaeological heritage all over the world. They cause a massive loss of artifacts but also, and above all, a loss of the cultural context, which makes the subsequent interpretation of archaeological remains very difficult. Satellite remote sensing offers a suitable chance to quantify and analyze this phenomenon, especially in those countries, where the aerial and on site surveillance is not much effective and time consuming or non practicable due to military or political restrictions as in the middle east area.

References

1. Masini, N., Lasaponara, R.: Sensing the past from space: approaches to site detection. In: Masini, N., Soldovieri, F. (eds.) Sensing the Past. Geoscience and Sensing Technologies for Cultural Heritage, vol. 16, pp. 23–60. Springer, Cham (2016)
2. Agapiou, A., Hadjimitsis, D.G., Sarris, A., Georgopoulos, A., Alexakis, D.D.: Optimum temporal and spectral window for monitoring crop marks over archaeological remains in the mediterranean region. J. Archaeol. Sci. **40**, 1479–1492 (2013)
3. De Laet, V., Paulissen, E., Waelkens, M.: Methods for the extraction of archaeological features from very high-resolution Ikonos-2 remote sensing imagery, Hisar (southwest Turkey). J. Archaeol. Sci. **34**, 830–841 (2007)
4. Chase, A.F., Chase, D.Z., Fisher, C.T., Leisz, S.J., Weishampel, J.F.: Geospatial revolution and remote sensing LiDAR in Mesoamerican archaeology. PNAS **109**(32), 12916–12921 (2013)
5. Evans, D.H., Fletcher, R.J., Pottier, C., Chevance, J.B., Soutif, D., Tan, B.S., Im, S., Ea, D., Tin, T., Kim, S., Cromarty, C., De Greef, S., Hanus, K., Baty, P., Kuszinger, R., Shimoda, I., Boornazian, G.: Uncovering archaeological landscapes at Angkor using lidar. Proc. Natl. Acad. Sci. USA **110**, 12595–12600 (2013)
6. Lasaponara, R., Coluzzi, R., Gizzi, F.T., Masini, N.: On the LiDAR contribution for the archaeological and geomorphological study of a deserted medieval village in Southern Italy. J. Geophys. Eng. **7**, 155–163 (2010)
7. Lasaponara, R., Masini, N., Rizzo, E., Orefici, G.: New discoveries in the Piramide Naranjada in Cahuachi (Peru) using satellite, Ground Probing Radar and magnetic investigations. J. Archaeol. Sci. **9**(38), 2031–2039 (2011)
8. Masini, N., Lasaponara, R., Orefici, G.: Addressing the challenge of detecting archaeological adobe structures in Southern Peru using QuickBird imagery. Journal of Cultural Heritage **10**, e3–e9 (2009)

9. Lasaponara, R., Leucci, G., Masini, N., Persico, R., Scardozzi, G.: Towards an operative use of remote sensing for exploring the past using satellite data: The case study of Hierapolis (Turkey). Remote Sens. Environ. **174**, 148–164 (2016)

10. Tarantino, E., Figorito, B.: Steerable filtering in interactive tracing of archaeological linear features using digital true colour aerial images. International Journal of Digital Earth **7**(11), 870–880 (2014)

11. Traviglia, A., Cottica, D.: Remote Sensing applications and archaeological research in the Northern Lagoon of Venice: the case of the lost settlement of Constanciacus. J. Archaeol. Sci. **38**(9), 2040–2050 (2011)

12. Doneus, M., Verhoeven, G., Atzberger, C., Wess, M., Ruš, M.: New ways to extract archaeological information from hyperspectral pixels. J. Archaeol. Sci. **52**, 84–96 (2014)

13. Menze, B.H., Ur, J.A.: Mapping patterns of long-term settlement in Northern Mesopotamia at a large scale. PNAS **109**(14), E778–E787 (2011). doi:10.1073/pnas.1115472109

14. Chen, F., Masini, N., Yang, R., Milillo, P., Feng, D., Lasaponara, R.: A space view of radar archaeological marks: first applications of COSMO-SkyMed X-band data. Remote Sens. **7**, 24–50 (2014). doi:10.3390/rs70100024

15. Tapete, D., Cigna, F., Masini, N., Lasaponara, R.: Prospection and monitoring of the archaeological heritage of Nasca, Peru, with ENVISAT ASAR. Archaeol. Prospect. **20**(2), 133–147 (2013)

16. Chen, F., Guo, H., Lin, H., Wang, C., Ishwaran, N., Hang, P.: Radar interferometry offers new insights into threats to the Angkor site. Sci. Adv. **3**(3), e1601284 (2017)

17. Lasaponara, R., Masini, N.: Advances in remote sensing for archaeology and cultural heritage management. In: Proceedings of I International EARSeL Workshop on Advances in Remote Sensing for Archaeology and Culturale Heritage Management, Rome, vol. 30 (2008)

18. Nolè, G., Murgante, B., Calamita, G., Lanorte, A., Lasaponara, R.: Evaluation of urban sprawl from space using open source technologies. Ecol. Inform. **26**, 151–161 (2015)

19. Novelli, A., Aguilar, M.A., Nemmaoui, A., Aguilar, F.J., Tarantino, E.: Performance evaluation of object based greenhouse detection from Sentinel-2 MSI and Landsat 8 OLI data: A case study from Almería (Spain). Int. J. Appl. Earth Obs. Geoinf. **52**, 403–411 (2016)

20. Cigna, F., Lasaponara, R., Masini, N., Milillo, P., Tapete, D.: Persistent scatterer interferometry processing of COSMO-SkyMed StripMap HIMAGE time series to depict deformation of the historic centre of Rome, Italy. Remote Sens. **6**(12), 12593–12618 (2014)

21. Lasaponara, R.: Inter-comparison of AVHRR-based fire susceptibility indicators for the Mediterranean ecosystems of Southern Italy. Int. J. Remote Sens. **26**, 853–870 (2005)

22. Chuvieco, E., Congalton, R.G.: Application of remote sensing and geographic information systems to forest fire hazard mapping. Remote Sens. Environ. **29**, 147–159 (1989)

23. Parcak, S.: Archaeological Looting in Egypt: a geospatial view (Case Studies from Saqqara, Lisht, and el Hibeh). Near Eastern Archaeol. **78**(3), 196–203 (2015)

24. Stone, E.C.: Patterns of looting in southern Iraq. Antiquity **82**, 125–138 (2008)

25. Lasaponara, R., Danese, M., Masini, N.: Satellite-Based Monitoring of Archaeological Looting in Peru, In: Lasaponara, R., Masini, N. (eds.) Satellite remote sensing: a new tool for Archaeology, pp. 177-193. Springer, Verlag Berlin Heidelberg (2012). ISBN: 978-90-481-8800-0

26. Lasaponara, R., Leucci, G., Masini, N., Persico, R.: Investigating archaeological looting using satellite images and georadar: the experience in Lambayeque in North Peru. J. Archaeol. Sci. **42**, 216–230 (2014)

27. Casana, J.: Satellite Imagery-based analysis of archaeological looting in Syria. Near Eastern Archaeol. **78**(3), 142–152 (2015)

28. Contreras, D.A.: Huaqueros and remote sensing imagery: assessing looting damage in the Viru Valley, Peru. Antiquity **84**(324), 544–555 (2010)
29. Lasaponara, R., Masini, N.: Combating illegal excavations in Cahuachi: ancient problems and modern technologies. In: Lasaponara, R., Masini, N., Orefici, G. (eds.) The Ancient Nasca World, pp. 605–633. Springer, Cham (2016). doi:10.1007/978-3-319-47052-8_25
30. UNESCO: Recommendation on International Principles Applicable to Archaeological Excavations (1956)
31. UNESCO: Convention on the Means of Prohibiting and Preventing the Illicit Import, Export and Transfer of Ownership of Cultural Property (1970)
32. Proulx, B.B.: Archaeological site looting in global prespective. Nature, scope and frequency. Am. J. Archaeol. **117**, 111–125 (2013)
33. Silverman H., Cahuachi in the Ancient Nasca World. University of Iowa Press (1993)
34. Getis, A., Ord, J.K.: The analysis of spatial association by use of distance statistics. Geograph. Anal. **24**, 189–206 (1994)
35. Moran, P.: The interpretation of statistical maps. J. Roy. Stat. Soc. **10**(2), 243–251 (1948)
36. Geary, R.C.: The contiguity ratio and statistical mapping. Incorporat. Stat. **5**, 115–145 (1954)
37. Ball, G.H., Hall, D.J.: ISODATA, a novel method of data analysis and pattern classification. Technical report, April 1965, prepared for Information Science Branch Office of Naval Research, Contract Nr. 4918, SRI Project 5533 (1965)
38. Alva, W.: The destruction, looting and traffic of the archaeological heritage of Peru. In: Brodie, N.J., Doole, J., Renfrew, C. (eds.) Trade in illicit antiquities: the destruction of the world's archaeological heritage, pp. 89–96. McDonald Institute, Cambridge (2001)
39. Silverman, H.: Cahuachi: non-urban cultural complexity on the south coast of Peru. J. Field Archaeol. **15**, 403–430 (1988)
40. Masini, N., Orefici, G., Lancho Rojas, J.: Nasca geoglyphs: technical aspects and overview of studies and interpretations. In: Lasaponara, R., Masini, N., Orefici, G. (eds.) The Ancient Nasca World, pp. 217–238. Springer, Cham (2016). doi:10.1007/978-3-319-47052-8_11

Low Cost Space Based Monitoring of Forest Fires: An Overview of 2015-2016 Operational Experience of FIRESAT in the Basilicata Region

Rosa Lasaponara[✉], Angelo Aromando, Gianfranco Cardettini,
Gabriele Nole, and Biagio Tucci

Italian National Research Council,
IMAA C.da Santa Loja, Tito Scalo, Potenza, Italy
Rosa.lasaponara@imaa.cnr.it

Abstract. This article is focused on the FIRESAT methodology developed for and funded by the Protezione Civile of the Basilicata Region. The fire monitoring system is based on satellite free of charge data and developed for the dynamic estimation of vegetation fire susceptibility and fire impact in forest and non-forestry ecosystems. The purpose of this fire risk system is the timely (daily) and detailed (from 1 km down to 30 m) monitoring of the vegetation and meteorological conditions which can affect the proneness of vegetation to fire. FIRESAT provides operational monitoring tools for a systematic forest fire management from risk estimation to fire severity mapping, including the estimation of fire damage on hydro-geological risk and vegetation fire resilience.

Keywords: Fire management · Risk estimation · Satellite images · Sentinel · Protezione civile · Basilicata region

1 Introduction

Earth Observation technologies can suitably support the monitoring and preservation of environmental, natural and cultural resources (see for example [1–11]) as well as the estimation of risk (see, for example, urban sprawl, building stability, greenhouse detection [12–15]) including landscape forest fire in the diverse phases of pre fire and post-fire phases ([16–20]) also integrated with ancillary data and statistics on fire occurrence (see for example [21]).

In particular, the management of fire risk is a very complex issue, because it includes a number of diverse parameters related to vegetation characteristics, topographical features, meteorological forecasts, social and human factors, etc. Therefore, It is essential and a very useful to adopt a modeling approach to support fire risk categorization as well as mitigation strategies and fire control.

The development and implementation of a model for predicting fire danger and propagation is a useful tool in the diverse phases of fire management allowing a more rational distribution of means and resources: from fire prevention to risk estimation and mitigation. Furthermore, in addition fire model can be fruitfully used to simulate the

© Springer International Publishing AG 2017
O. Gervasi et al. (Eds.): ICCSA 2017, Part V, LNCS 10408, pp. 728–741, 2017.
DOI: 10.1007/978-3-319-62404-4_53

fire effects and fire propagation to support fire attack and fighting as well as to produce probabilistic maps of damage.

These elements are extremely important for the rationalization and the optimization of the use of the available resources to limit fire damage.

The FIRE-SAT system was developed by Lasaponara and Lanorte at the ARGON Laboratory of CNR-IMAA [25, 27]. The use of FIRESAT system enables the operator in the field to know in real time the fire danger class (of the given areas) and in the speed of fire spreading and the potential severity of fire event. The fire danger classes (low, medium, high, extreme) correspond to different modes of fire attack and intervention (attack with ground teams by manual, attack with ground teams with mechanical means, need for integration with aircraft, or only aircraft, etc.). This means that the fire danger maps provide useful information during the first phase of fire attack that is the most critical and crucial for the extinguishment of fire, and, in turn, for its "management and control" before becoming "uncontrollable".

The forecast of fire spreading and speed is based on the knowledge of one of the main important fire behavior parameters, that is the linear flame intensity, which determines the level of severity of the fire. The linear flame intensity is related to the fire propagation speed, the load and the fuel heating value. Another very important parameter is the length of the flame front that is the length of the perimeter of the fire with active flame. This parameter determines more than others the amount of resources needed for extinction. The proposed system allows fire crews to know the real needs of fire fighting and human resources for switching off the fire taking the fire danger class into account.

FIRESAT is mainly based on MODIS atellite data integrated with meteorological forecast. The features offered by MODIS in terms of free availability, spectral and temporal characteristics, are particularly interesting for the estimation of the proneness of vegetation to fire. The technical characteristics of MODIS are substantial improved compared to those offered by AVHRR and SPOT-VEGETATION, so that today MODIS is considered the main source of information for vegetation and fire monitoring. Additionally, data available from the Sentinel mission (mainly Sentinel 2) will be very useful (and integrated in the next future) in both the pre-fire (danger estimation) and post fire (fire burned area mapping, fire severity) damage assessment. From the operational point of view and the purpose of this paper it is important to consider that these data are available since September 2016 and, therefore, we had preliminary "experiences" based on the effective availability of data. Advanced performance are expended due to the improved spatial and spectral characteristic offered by Sentinel 2 compared to the previously available free of charge data (see Table 1 and Figs. 1 and 2).

Table 1. Short overview on the sensors of the Sentinel satellite missions

Sentinel missions	Number of satellites	Mission
Sentinel-1	2 satellites	Synthetic Aperture Radar (C-band) mission designed to monitor sea ice zones, the Arctic environment, and the risk of land surface motion as well as generate forest, water, and soil mapping
Sentinel-2	2 satellites	Optical mission with a multi-spectral instrument mainly for agricultural applications such as crop monitoring and management, vegetation and forest monitoring (e.g. leaf area index, chlorophyll concentration, carbon mass estimations), monitoring land cover change for environmental monitoring, observation of coastal zones (marine environmental monitoring, coastal zone mapping), inland water monitoring, glacier monitoring, ice extent and snow cover mapping. Burnt area mapping and fire severity estimation
Sentinel-3	3 satellites	Multi-purpose mission with multiple instruments, mainly for sea-surface as well as sea and land ice topography, sea- and land-surface temperature, ocean- and land-surface colour, sea- and inland-water quality and pollution monitoring, land-use change monitoring, forest cover mapping, fire detection, marine and general weather forecasting, snow cover monitoring, measuring Earth's thermal radiation for atmospheric applications, and last but not least for overall environmental and climate monitoring and modeling
Sentinel-4	Will be placed on geostationary Meteosat Third Generation satellites	Monitoring of the composition of the atmosphere for air quality, stratospheric ozone and solar radiation as well as climate monitoring
Sentinel-5	On the polar-orbiting MetOp	Monitoring of the composition of the atmosphere for air quality, stratospheric ozone and solar radiation as well as climate monitoring

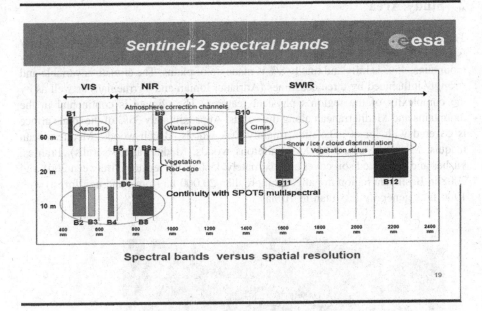

Fig. 1. Sentinel 2 spectral bands (ESA Courtesy)

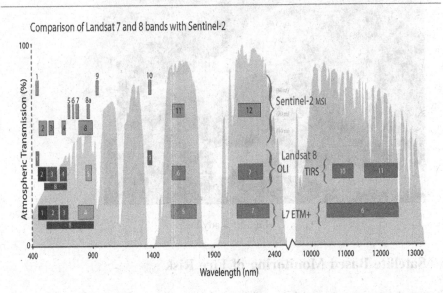

Fig. 2. Comparison of Sentinel 2 and Landsat (7 and 8) TM spectral bands (ESA Courtesy)

2 Study Area

The analysis was performed in Basilicata (9,992 km²) a region in the Southern of Italy (see Fig. 3). It is a mountainous region with around 47% of its area covered by mountains, 45% is hilly and finally 8% is made up of plains. The climate is variable and strongly influenced by three coastlines (Adriatic, Ionian and Tyrrhenian) as well as by the complexity of the region's physical features. The climate is continental in the mountains and Mediterranean along the coasts. Approximately 35% of the total surface is covered with forest vegetation (mainly Oak woods, Beech woods, Mediterranean maquis, Mixed broadleaf and/or coniferous woods, Mediterranean scrubs). Prairies, bushes and cultivated soil cover approximately 45% of the territory. Between 2001 and 2008 in Basilicata region fire affected more than 20.000 ha (forest and non-forest) with 1900 fires generally less than to 10 ha.

Fig. 3. Study area

3 Satellite Based Monitoring of Fire Risk

For the elaboration of fire risk maps it was adopted and significantly reinterpreted the method proposed by Chuvieco and Congalton [18] later revised by [22]. This method has been applied for the first time in Spain and later also used in other territories (Texas, Portugal) and then in the ecosystems of the South Italy [23] due to its flexibility and ease of application. In essence, the algorithm of prediction of fire danger is based on a weighted additive model in which the procedure used is similar to the typical multi-criteria analysis, where we must solve the problem of the determination of a single estimation index from more factors. The objective is achieved by linearly combining the factors used by assigning a weight to each of them. Therefore, each parameter is processed as an information layer in which the factor is classified based on the degree of danger that it poses. The result is a dynamic final map of danger, according to the criteria and the coefficients established by the model. The following paragraphs provide brief details about each parameter both static and dynamic processed to obtain, by subsequent integration, the final map. In particular, the static parameters are not considered variables during "the fire season" and then updated annually, while dynamic ones are variable parameters during the fire season and then updated with a frequency related to its specific temporal dynamics.

From the operational point of view, for the region Basilicata during the period of maximum danger for fires (usually from July to September) fire danger maps are systematically processed daily whereas in other periods the fire danger maps are provided on a weekly or decadal basis (depending on cloud cover). The maps were drawn at the highest MODIS resolution (250 m).

After the pre-processing step, addressed to the georeferencing and cloud masking, the analysis of MODIS data provides parameters useful for the estimation of "fire hazard". In particular, the factors that are taken into account are the following: (i) the type of vegetation in relation to fire (fuel models), (ii) surface area occupied by the vegetation in terms of phytomass and necromass (relative Greenness Index) and (iii) the estimation of change in moisture content of the fuel for both phytomass and necromass (moisture Indices),

Dynamic indices are the expression of those parameters that change during the fire season with physiological and meteorological dynamics (percentage of phytomass and necromass, moisture content, wind, briefly described below).

The Greenness index allows the dynamic discrimination of phytomass from necromass, thus allowing the optimization of fire danger forecasts for both of them. The index is calculated using time series of several years of NDVI (Normalized Difference vegetation Index) that is a widely used indices being that it closely related to vegetation amount and status

The moisture content is definitely one of the most important characteristics of the fuels among those that influence fire behavior. It determines how much fuel is more susceptible to fire and, ultimately, how it is consumed. The moisture absorbs the heat released during combustion, by decreasing the amount of available heat in the fuel preheating stage for the triggering of the fire

The moisture content of phytomass assumes great importance in the estimation of fire hazard especially for the role played in the spread of fire. The moisture content of the necromass assumes greater importance than that of the phytomass especially compared to the danger of fire ignition. This is due to the fact that for necromass, the percentage of water is related exclusively to the weather conditions, whereas. for phytomass the water present inside the plants has more complex dynamics (think about the evapotranspiration phenomenon) also depending on environmental humidity. In the case of experimentation adopted for the Basilicata region we used an innovative model capable of estimating the moisture content of biomass exclusively on the basis of satellite data whereas the moisture content of the necromass is a function of surface temperature and relative humidity at each point. The target place is therefore the determination of the two required parameters (surface temperature and surface relative humidity) using MODIS data.

Static indices are the expression of those parameters that do not change over time or that have relatively long times of change and in any case exceed the value of a single fire season, such as, vegetation factor investigated qualitatively (models/types fuel) and quantitative (fuel load), morphological factor and map of the historic/statistical fire occurrence.

The vegetation fuels are considered a crucial element in the management of fires in particular when other key elements responsible for the fire behavior, for example the slope and the wind, are not significant. The structure and the status of the vegetation complex defines the range of fire behavior and the fire regime. Moreover, a key element in the management and mitigation of fires is the quantification of the spatial full availability of combustible material and its cargo in areas susceptible to fire. This is the reason why the vegetation complexes have been described through stylized types of fuel

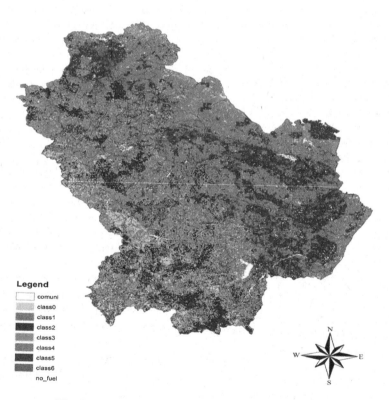

Fig. 4. Map of fire risk as obtained for 16 August 2016

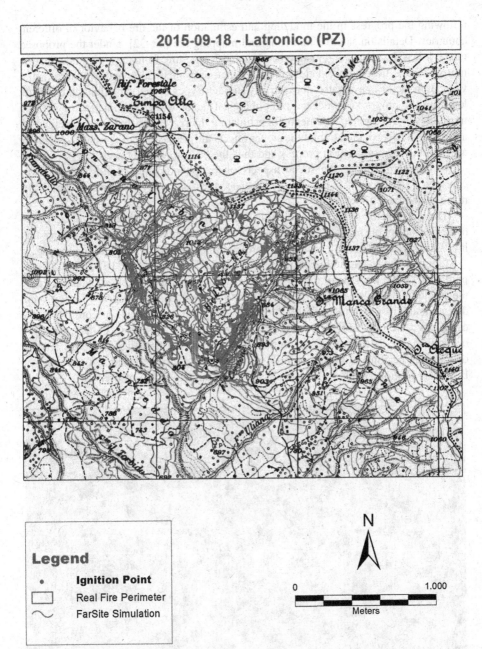

Fig. 5. Map of fire risk as obtained for the Latronico fire (occurred on 18 September 2015) the blue line shows the real expansion of fire and the green area the expansion as simulated by FIRESITE (https://www.firelab.org/project/farsite) an open software developed by the USA forestry service for fire growth simulation modeling (Color figure online)

following the progress in the modeling and estimation of the fire behavior in different countries. Details on satellite modeling and mapping are [22–32]. Under the proposed model it was developed and mapped a static index resulting from the weighted sum of a morphological factor (provided by the combination of inclination and exposure) and a vegetation factor investigated qualitatively (models/types of fuel) and quantitative (fuel load). In the proposed model the morphological factor is the combination of the two most relevant topographic elements for estimating the risk of fire that are the inclination and exposure. The inclination of the slopes affects the pre-heating of the fuel capacity by accelerating the combustion process and thus the diffusion rate of fire.

In order to estimate the social aspects of fire phenomenon in Basilicata, it was considered useful to include a fire occurrence statistical analysis based on the occurrence of the past fire events.

The elaborate maps for the whole Basilicata Region obtained using the model above described are published on the website of the Protezione civile at the following link http://www.protezionecivilebasilicata.it/protcivbas/css/themes/01/images/mappa.jpg.

Figure 4 shows a example of the map of fire risk as obtained for 16 August 2016 as published on the web-site of the Protezione Civile of the Basilicata Region and used by the single municipality to arrange the fire control (field and aerial survey for a prompt detection of fire) and to optimize "management" the fire brigade according to the categorized fire risk level for each area under monitoring. Moreover, in the case of fire occurrence, the exchange of communication between the fire brigade in situ and the operational personnel of the central management of the Protezione Civile of the Basilicata Region enable to monitor in real time the expansion of fire.

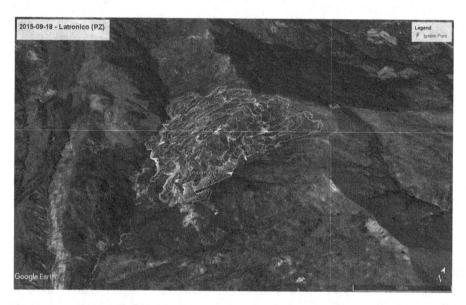

Fig. 6. Map of fire risk as obtained for the Latronico fire occurred on 18 September 2015 overlapped to Google Earth and obtained as in Fig. 4 by FIRESITE (https://www.firelab.org/project/farsite) an open software developed by the USA forestry service for fire growth simulation modeling

The estimation of fire expansion is made using FIRESITE (https://www.firelab.org/project/farsite) an open software developed by the USA forestry service for modeling the simulation of fire growth. Figures 5 and 6 show the results obtained for Latronico fire occurred on 18 September 2015.

4 Satellite Based Monitoring of Burned Areas and Fire Severity

From the methodological point of view burned area mapping and fire severity categorizations are obtained by using supervised and unsupervised classifications applied to single channels or spectral indices suitable/or specifically designed for burned areas mapping. In particular near-Infrared (NIR) and short-wave infrared reflectance (SWIR), Normalized Difference of Vegetation Index (NDVI), Normalized Difference of Infrared Index Burned Area Index (BAI); GEMI, SAVI have been used (for details on each index check Lasaponara [34]. Spectral combinations of different bands is widely used for burned area discrimination since they generally tend to emphasis the spectral changes caused by fire on vegetation. A sensitive analysis was performed by using a simple Separability Index (SI) Eq. 9 (see Kaufman and Remer 1994) specifically applied to burnt area mapping (Lasaponara)

$$SI = |\mu_b - \mu_{nb}|/(\sigma_b + \sigma_{nb}) \tag{1}$$

where μ_b (μ_{nb}) is the mean value of the considered index for burned areas (non burned areas), and σb (σ_{nb}) the standard deviation of the considered index for burned areas (non burned areas). Values of SI higher than 1 show that the index allows for a good separation between burned and unburned areas.

In particular, the BAI (see Eq. 8) appear as one of the most suitable indicator being it is able to account for vegetation deteriorations of pigments and leaf structure caused by fires. This index has been widely used for burned area mapping (see Chuvieco et al. 2002) as a single date or multi-date analysis as a difference between two acquisitions before and after the fire occurrence. In particular, the two date difference is considered particular useful for the estimation of fire severity.

$$BAI = 1 \Big/ \left((\rho cRED - \rho RED)^2 + (\rho cNIR - \rho NIR)^2 \right) \tag{2}$$

where $\rho cRED$ and $\rho cNIR$ are the red and near-infrared reference reflectances. These reference values were defined as 0.1 and 0.06 Outputs from our investigation pointed out that in general the performance is generally dependent on the vegetation types and also on the meteorological conditions (Figs. 7, 8 and 9).

Fig. 7. False colour composition of Sentinel for Maratea Fire occurred on 7 August 2016 the "black area" is related to the fire.

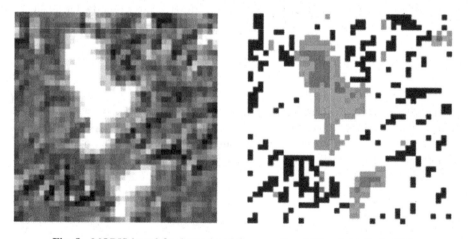

Fig. 8. MODIS based fire burned and fire severity additional details in [34]

Fig. 9. RGB composition of a fire occurred in 2009 in the Ionial coast of the Metapontum Pinus area

5 Conclusion

Remote sensing techniques are the very important tool for supporting risk monitoring and mitigation strategies for natural and man made risk. In particular, Remote sensing techniques for forest fire prevention, assessment and monitoring have been developing since the mid-1980s [20]. These techniques have been employed to address three different temporal fire-effects phases: pre-fire conditions, active fire characteristics and post-fire ecosystem responses [20–23]. Numerous algorithms and approaches have been developed [24–32, 33] for the diverse fire management phases.

This paper provides a short overview of the methods and remotely sensed data used for FIRESAT the operational fire risk system developed by the ARGON laboratory of the CNR-IMAA for the Protezione Civile of the Basilicata Region.

In particular, today a lot of active and passive satellite and aerial sensors provide useful data for the diverse phases of fire risk management from the risk categorization and monitoring to the identification of mitigation strategies. The real challenge is the operational use of these data an and the full exploitation of them.

Improved performance can be achieved in the next future using data from Sentinel missions. Of course data provided by diverse sensors imposes the integration of all the available information (in digital and non digital format) within a GIS environment and the use of suitable software technologies for the management of huge amount of data (big data), as well as the integration, elaboration, exploitation and publication of heterogeneous data sources.

Acknowledgments. The development of FIRESAT system has been funded by Protezione Civile of the Basilicata Region in the framework of collaboration and join experimentation conducted in the Basilicata region

References

1. Masini, N., Lasaponara, R.: Satellite-based recognition of landscape archaeological features related to ancient human transformation. J. Geophys. Eng. **3**(3), 230 (2006)
2. Tapete, D., Cigna, F., Masini, N., Lasaponara, R.: Prospection and monitoring of the archaeological heritage of Nasca, Peru, with ENVISAT ASAR. Archaeol. Prospect. **20**(2), 133–147 (2013)
3. Masini, N., Lasaponara, R., Orefici, G.: Addressing the challenge of detecting archaeological adobe structures in Southern Peru using QuickBird imagery. J. Cult. Herit. **10**, e3–e9 (2009)
4. Lasaponara, R., Nicola, M.: Full-waveform airborne laser scanning for the detection of medieval archaeological microtopographic relief. J. Cult. Herit. **10**, e78–e82 (2009)
5. Lasaponara, R., Masini, N.: Image enhancement, feature extraction and geospatial analysis in an archaeological perspective. In: Lasaponara, R., Masini, N. (eds.) Satellite Remote Sensing. Remote Sensing and Digital Image Processing, vol. 16, pp. 17–63. Springer, Netherlands (2012)
6. Cigna, F., Tapete, D., Lasaponara, R., Masini, N.: Amplitude change detection with ENVISAT ASAR to image the cultural landscape of the Nasca Region. Peru Archaeol. Prospect. **20**(2), 117–131 (2013)
7. Lasaponara, R., Masini, N., Rizzo, E., Orefici, G.: New discoveries in the Piramide Naranjada in Cahuachi (Peru) using satellite, Ground Probing Radar and magnetic investigations. J. Archaeol. Sci. **9**(38), 2031–2039 (2011)
8. Lasaponara, R., et al.: On the LiDAR contribution for the archaeological and geomorphological study of a deserted medieval village in Southern Italy. J. Geophys. Eng. **7**(2), 155 (2010)
9. Lasaponara, R., Masini, N.: Advances in remote sensing for archaeology and cultural heritage management. In: Proceedings of Ist International EARSeL Workshop on Advances in Remote Sensing for Archaeology and Culturale Heritage Management, Rome, vol. 30 (2008)
10. Tarantino, E., Figorito, B.: Steerable filtering in interactive tracing of archaeological linear features using digital true colour aerial images. Int. J. Digital Earth **7**(11), 870–880 (2014)
11. Figorito, B., Tarantino, E.: Semi-automatic detection of linear archaeological traces from orthorectified aerial images. Int. J. Appl. Earth Obs. Geoinf. **26**, 458 (2014)
12. Cigna, F., Lasaponara, R., Masini, N., Milillo, P., Tapete, D.: Persistent scatterer interferometry processing of COSMO-SkyMed StripMap HIMAGE time series to depict deformation of the historic centre of Rome. Italy. Remote Sens. **6**(12), 12593–12618 (2014)
13. Nolè, G., Murgante, B., Calamita, G., Lanorte, A., Lasaponara, R.: Evaluation of urban sprawl from space using open source technologies. Ecol. Inform. **26**, 151–161 (2015)
14. Novelli, A., Aguilar, M.A., Nemmaoui, A., Aguilar, F.J., Tarantino, E.: Performance evaluation of object based greenhouse detection from Sentinel-2 MSI and Landsat 8 OLI data: a case study from Almería (Spain). Int. J. Appl. Earth Obs. Geoinf. **52**, 403–411 (2016)
15. Tarantino, E., Figorito, B.: Extracting buildings from true color stereo aerial images using a decision making strategy. Remote Sens. **3**(8), 1553–1567 (2011)
16. Lasaponara, R.: Inter-comparison of AVHRR-based fire susceptibility indicators for the Mediterranean ecosystems of southern Italy. Int. J. Remote Sens. **26**, 853–870 (2005)
17. Lasaponara, R., Lanorte, A.: On the capability of satellite VHR QuickBird data for fuel type characterization in fragmented landscape. Ecol. Model. **204**(1), 79–84 (2007)
18. Chuvieco, E., Congalton, R.G.: Application of remote sensing and geographic information systems to forest fire hazard mapping. Remote Sens. Environ. **29**, 147–159 (1989)

19. Lanorte, A., Danese, M., Lasaponara, R., Murgante, B.: Multiscale mapping of burn area and severity using multisensor satellite data and spatial autocorrelation analysis. Int. J. Appl. Earth Obs. Geoinf. **20**, 42–51 (2013)

20. Telesca, L., Lasaponara, R.: Pre-and post-fire behavioral trends revealed in satellite NDVI time series. Geophys. Res. Lett. **33** (2006)

21. Tuia, D., Ratle, F., Lasaponara, R., Telesca, L., Kanevski, M.: Scan statistics analysis of forest fire clusters. Commun. Nonlinear Sci. Numer. Simul. **13**(8), 1689–1694 (2008)

22. Lanorte, A., Lasaponara, R.: Fuel type characterization based on coarse resolution MODIS satellite data. iForest–Biogeosci. For. **1**, 60–64 (2008)

23. Lanorte, A., Lasaponara, R.: Fuel type characterization based on coarse resolution MODIS satellite data. Forest@ **4**(2), 235–243 (2007)

24. Lanorte, A., Lasaponara, R.: Uso del telerilevamento per la rappresentazione dei tipi di combustibile. Alberi Territorio **7–8**, 36–40 (2007)

25. Lanorte & Lasaponara Report tecnici 2008, 2009, 2010, 2011, 2012, disponibili presso l'Ufficio di Protezione Civile del Dipartimento Infrastrutture. Opere Pubbliche e Mobilità della Regione Basilicata

26. Lasaponara, R.: Forest Fire Monitoring using NOAA- AVHRR data. Ph.D. Thesis (1998)

27. Lanorte, A., Desantis, F., Aromando, A., Montesano, T., Lasaponara, R.: Monitoraggio satellitare per la previsione del rischio d'incendio Boschivo Sperimentazione pre - operativa in Basilicata, ilmiolibro (2010)

28. Lasaponara, R., Lanorte, A., Pignatti, S.: Characterization and mapping of fuel types for the Mediterranean ecosystems of Pollino national park in the Southern Italy by using Hyperspectral MIVIS data. Earth Interact. **10**(13), 1–11 (2006)

29. Lasaponara, R., Lanorte, A., Pignatti, S.: Multiscale fuel type mapping in fragmented ecosystems: preliminary results from Hyperspectral MIVIS and Multispectral Landsat TM data. Int. J. Remote Sens. **27**, 587–593 (2006)

30. Lasaponara, R., Lanorte, A.: Multispectral fuel type characterization based on remote sensing data and Prometheus model. For. Ecol. Manage. **234S**, S226 (2006)

31. Lasaponara, R., Lanorte, A.: On the capability of satellite VHR QuickBird data for fuel type characterization in fragmented landscape. Ecol. Model. **204**, 79–84 (2007)

32. Lasaponara, R., Lanorte, A.: Remotely sensed characterization of forest fuel types by using satellite ASTER data. Int. J. Appl. Earth Obs. Geoinf. **9**, 225–234 (2007)

Author Index

Printed in the United States
By Bookmasters